The Post-WWI Rise of Turkish Nationalism and Resumption of Genocidal Policies

A Collection of Prime Sources Documenting
the Treatment of Armenians and Greeks in Turkey

Compiled and translated by
Vatche Ghazarian

MAYRENI PUBLISHING
Portsmouth - Rhode Island

This publication was made possible by a generous grant from
The Dolores Zohrab Libmann Fund

Library of Congress Control Number: 2023904576

Title:
The Post-WWI Rise of Turkish Nationalism and Resumption of Genocidal Policies
A Collection of Prime Sources Documenting the Treatment of Armenians and Greeks in Turkey

Subjects:
- Armenian Genocide
- Armenian Question
- Armenian Cilicia
- Allied presence in former Ottoman territories
- French presence in Cilicia and evacuation
- Franco-Turkish Agreement of 1921
- Greek Genocide
- Persecution of Christians and Jews in Turkey
- Kemalism
- Ittihadist and Kemalist convergence

Printed in the United States of America

ISBN 979-8-218-09873-5
Mayreni Publishing, 2023

Dedication

To the victims of massacres and genocides perpetrated by the Ottoman and nationalist Turks;

To the Turks and foreigners who risked their lives to defend the rights and save the lives of Armenians and other subjects of Ottoman-Turkish oppression;

To the humanitarian organizations that extended relief to victims and survivors of Turkish atrocities;

To the fraternity and solidarity of the Armenian and Greek people who shared the same fate and continue their pursuit for justice.

Contents

Բովանդակութիւն

Western Armenian Transliteration Table

Armenian	*English*	*Pronunciation as in*
ա	a	up
բ	p	
գ	k	
դ	t	
ե	e	yet (at the beginning), edge (within words)
զ	z	
է	e’	edge
ը	y	church
թ	t’	tap
ժ	zh	measure
ի	I	it
լ	l	
խ	x	Khmer or sheikh
ծ	dz	adze
կ	g	
հ	h	
ձ	tz	its
ղ	gh	Afghanistan or merci (in French)
ճ	j	
մ	m	
յ	h’	yet
ն	n	
շ	sh	mash
ո	o’	old – (volt at the beginning, at times)
չ	ch	church
պ	b	
ջ	ch’	church
ռ	r’	Arnold
ս	s	
վ	v	
տ	d	
ր	r	
ց	c	its
ւ	w	van
փ	p’	pan
ք	q	
օ	o	
ֆ	f	

Preface

Significant effort has been made in academia in recent years to study events that affected the Christian populations during the transitional period in Turkey's history after the end of World War One in late 1918 and before the Treaty of Lausanne, which, on July 24, 1923, officialized the boundaries of modern Turkey (Türkiye) as the successor of Ottoman Turkey. These populations, who resided for centuries on ancestral lands conquered by the Ottoman Empire, were already decimated through genocide and deportation by the war's end.

Deviating from the pattern of most studies that have based their findings on official documents produced by government officials, diplomats, and missionaries of various countries in languages other than Armenian, the accounts are compiled in this publication in their original language, translated into English.

By presenting these Armenian source materials and their English renditions that speak of what befell the Christians at large and the Armenians in particular in Turkey, the compiler hopes to contribute to subsequent discussions of the period in question and the definition of the true nature of the events.

Premise

The six-hundred-one first-hand accounts of this compilation, derived from letters and telegraphs sent to the Armenian Patriarchate in Constantinople and records of personal visits there, relate to atrocious events unfolding in Turkey from early 1919 through the end of 1922, the four years following the Armistice that signified the end of WWI: A period that would lead to the loss of historically Greek lands in Thrace and Asia Minor and historically Armenian lands in Western Armenia (primarily identified as the six Armenian or Eastern provinces of the Ottoman Empire) and Cilicia.

The perpetrators were nationalist Turks and associated Circassians, Lazes, and Kurds. Their victims were Armenians, Greeks, and other Christians. The authors of these reports were members of the victimized communities whose suffering was witnessed by representatives of the victorious Allied Powers—Great Britain, France, and the United States—and relief workers.

After suffering defeat in the Great War, the Turks were eager to maintain their hold on territories that were under their control for centuries before the war. Contrary to Turkish ambitions, the Allies intended to dismember the former Ottoman Empire by returning parts of it to their rightful owners—Armenians, Greeks, and so on, either through sovereignty or as protectorates. To achieve Turkish objectives, the post-war government professed a conciliatory tone in its dealings with the victorious Powers, promising proper treatment of its Christian subjects. This seeming leniency[1] towards Christians became a motivation underlying the resurgence of clandestinely working intolerant Ittihadist as well as new Kemalist nationalists, who worked together on exciting Muslims against Christians, particularly against Armenians. Some were eager to hold on to appropriated Christian properties, while others were concerned with territorial integrity, commonly disregarding the fact that certain territories belonged to Christians or Kurds.

On the other hand, the Armenians and Greeks were allies of the victorious Powers. They hoped to restore their rights and presence over their historical territories and reestablish dignified lives for their families, even in areas where Turkish authority would remain.

Armenian expectations for justice, peace, and restorations were justified based on the contributions their heroes made to the Allied victory during the war, combined with the promises and assurances given to them by the Allies in specific provisions included in international agreements such as the Mudros Agreement[2] as well as the discussions in the hallways of the League of Nations. Therefore, nurturing aspirations for reunification with their homeland, whether independent or as a protectorate, did not seem unfounded. Specifically, the Armenians native to Cilicia believed that the end of their calamities had arrived: Cilicia had already been placed under French protection, and both the British and the French were encouraging the return of Armenians who had survived deportation to their native cities and towns in the region, assuring them protection.[3]

Meanwhile, in Turkey proper, the Armenians who had survived deportation and were represented by the Armenian Patriarchate in Constantinople as their leading authority used the limited means available to them to tend to the needs of the refugees returning from the tribulations of deportation, to collect the orphans and widows held by Turks and Kurds—whether Islamized or not—and to recover Armenian church and school properties. They worked diligently with the Allied high commissioners to protect the lives of Armenians in areas where the Allies had established control. The prerogative to negotiate the fate of the six Armenian provinces in the east and Cilicia with the Powers was given to the Armenian National Delegation headquartered in Paris.

Realistically, efforts to successfully restore the six provinces to the Armenians were futile from the beginning. The Turks had essentially eradicated Armenians in these provinces by employing mass deportations, forced religious conversions, and killings that later came to be coined as Genocide.

Different was the case of Cilicia. The number of Armenians returning under French protection,[4] combined with armed Armenian legionnaires—albeit under French command—seemed to present a chance for a better life. Even autonomy seemed to be feasible.

However, while united in their war against the Turco-German alliance before the armistice, the Allies were less united after the Bolshevik revolution when Russia parted ways with them. Instead, Britain, France, Italy, and the United States became competitors, each seeking to gain the most, through concessions, from a humbled Turkey. The Turks masterfully applied their centuries-old policy of playing such Powers against one another.

The source materials gathered in this publication are the product of this chaotic and conflicting period in which Armenian aspirations proved to have no chance of realization.

The need for loud shouting voices

Two of the many areas the Armenian authorities focused on in Constantinople after the war included the prosecution of the perpetrators of the deportations and subsequent Genocide and preventing new persecutions against Armenians who had survived and were returning to their native places or other areas presumed safe within Turkey. The prosecution required fact-and-witness-finding efforts to identify the culprits and submit their names to the Ottoman State Special Military Tribunal installed with the support of the Allies. On the other hand, the prevention of new atrocities required the submission of the numerous reports of maltreatment and crimes received from the provinces to the Allies.

For the experienced plights of Armenians to reach the ears of those who could make a difference, a group of concerned Armenians published the *Renaissance*, a French language periodical, on De-

cember 9, 1918. As its founders put it, "it was a reaction of the national will of the Armenians of Turkey ... as soon as the definitive victory of the Allies put an end to the odious regime of oppression of the Great War. They had to cry out their pain, tell the incredible, ask for justice ... expose before the public conscience what was the Armenian ordeal during the dreadful war ... and unmask the authors of the crimes ... hoping to prevent the return of such crimes."[5]

The *Renaissance* started as an independent initiative because the Armenian Patriarch was still in Mosul, where the Turkish government had exiled him, and the Armenian national assembly—disbanded by the same government—still needed to be restored fully. However, despite the moral and financial support the Armenian Patriarchate lent to the periodical, developments made it impossible to save the publication that was "always on the go, valiantly facing all the backlashes of politics that often made the Armenian Cause appear in a dark light. It kept the unalterable hope in the human justice of a martyred race, shouting loud and firm the great truths ... in the face of the shameless oppressor, exposing the press tactics of the Turkish newspapers and pillorying the serious criminals who were trying, with the support of complicit authorities, to ... shirk their responsibilities. It exposed under the heading *Facts and Documents* ... the atrocious crime of the massacre of one million human beings under the pretext of *deportation*."[6]

In February 1919, the British High Commission in Constantinople established an Armenian Greek Section (AGS hereafter). The AGS was made up of British, Greek, and Armenian representatives who met to deal with issues involving Turkish offenders, relief work, repatriation and restitution of property, Islamized Christians and Christians retained by Turks (and Kurds), and Christians detained in Turkish prisons, as explicitly stated during a session on February 26, 1919. However, the prevalent insecurity faced by Christians across Turkey would soon dominate the discussions.[7]

The AGS was met with enthusiasm by the Armenians and Greeks. After all, both nations were Christian, both had suffered massacres and genocide by the Ottoman and nationalist Turks, and both had similar national aspirations for justice, peace, and restoration of rights, properties, and national domains. Moreover, the two nations were allies in their struggle against the Turks. A clear demonstration of their shared history and aspirations transpired on February 24, 1919, when the Ecumenical Patriarch Dorotheos and the Armenian Patriarch Zaven signed a joint memorandum for the Peace Conference in Paris.[8]

Pressured by the immense demands of gathering information and disseminating it in English and French to the high commissioners stationed in Constantinople and needing to fulfill other pressing tasks, the Armenian authorities resolved on August 17, 1919, to establish an Information Bureau. This bureau eventually became the main conduit for gathering and translating the reports discussed during AGS meetings and included in this publication.

In his memoirs, the Armenian Patriarch stated that the Information Bureau "helped the Embassies by providing them with all the information they requested." He went on to say that according to its charter, the Bureau was tasked with gathering ... all kinds of old and new statistics having to do with Armenia or the Armenian Cause; ... incidents and narratives about the persecutions, massacres, and deportations; statistical descriptions about mobile and immobile goods belonging to the Nation or to individuals that have been robbed; in particular, as complete as possible information—including biographical data—on the principal Turkish culprits who were participants in the evil deeds committed during the recent deportations, including documents and testimonies attesting to their criminal acts; and statistical information about Islamized Armenians of both genders and kidnapped orphans," and so on.[9]

The Notebooks

The source materials in this book were copied from their originals in notebooks, and the notebooks were saved thanks to the staff of the Information Bureau.

The only mention of these notebooks is in the Armenian Mixed Council of Constantinople minutes dated September 17, 1919. The minutes referred to them as "Insecurity Notebook[s]" in a section devoted to recording the visit of Reverend Vartan Amirkhanian. This minister had just arrived from Harput to meet with the members of the Council in the hall of the national library of the Armenian Patriarchate. The record in question states: "The Reverend presented with gloomy colors the current situation in Anatolia and the prevailing insecure condition, mentioning in detail numerous incidents that showed the prevalent situation and mentality."[10] (See Reverend Amirkhanian's report under "Insecurity Notebook Number 3," p. 64).

Each notebook carried the stamp of the Information Bureau of the Armenian Patriarchate, along with a handwritten number denoting volume and dates to indicate a chronological scope.

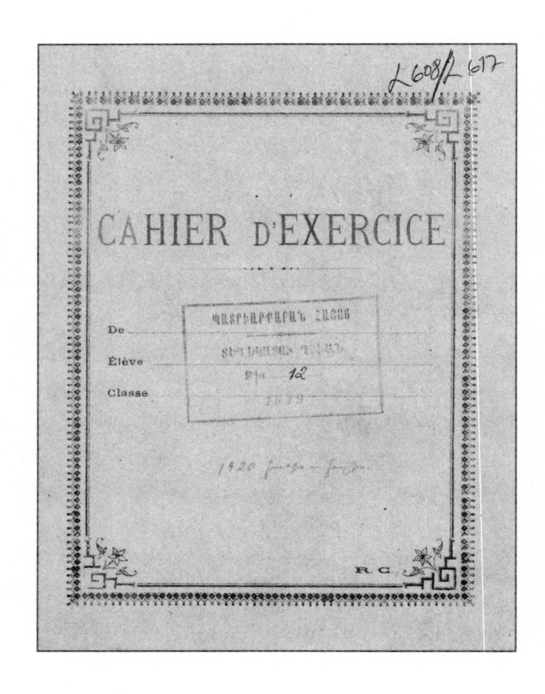

The following list presents the range of numbers assigned to sheets in each notebook. The Armenian character L precedes all:

Notebook 1: L705–715

Notebook 2: L716–725

Notebook 3: L726–737 (Sheets L732–733 are an original stand-alone document entitled "The 'Milli' Movement and its Consequences," separated and included in Notebook [15] as inserts.)

Notebook 4: L738–750 (Sheets L744–745 seemed to have been skipped by mistake. Judging from the content, no text appears missing.)

Notebook 5: L751–760

Notebook 6: L538–547

Notebook 7: L548–567 (Sheets L550–559 are missing. This seems to be a case of misnumbering.)

Notebook 8: L568–577

Notebook 9: L578–587

Notebook 10: L588–597

Notebook 11: L598–607

Notebook 12: L608–617

Notebook 13: L618–627

Notebook 14: L628–637 (Although the cover page of this notebook indicates pages L628–637, it seems that for some reason, pages L638–655 also are attached to them. Sheets L645–646 are missing. The complete original letters numbered L649–654 are interjected as inserts. The impression is that the contents of three separate notebooks have become one, perhaps due to the missing cover and back pages of two notebooks. The continuation of the text on page L655 is found in Notebook [15] as a lone double-faced sheet numbered L656.)

Notebook [15]: L657–666

Notebook [16]: L667–676

Notebook [17]: L677–686

Notebook [18]: L687–696

Notebook [19]: L804–807

In an English document translated from corresponding Armenian texts relating to excerpts from letters mailed to the Armenian Patriarchate in Constantinople on May 27, May 28, and May 23, 1919, from Samsun, Malatya, and Sivas, respectively (see page 8), we find direct evidence that these notebooks constitute a basis for reporting incidents to at least the AGS, if not to other entities. An Armenian handwritten text above the first typewritten English line states: "Weekly report to the Armenian-Greek-English meeting which has been operating for two months."[11]

A comparative examination of the Information Bureau's primary sources revealed that many originals exist, with their versions copied into the notebooks, while others do not. Entries with existing originals are denoted with double asterisks in the Contents. The archives also contain translated versions of some entries in English and French. Those with counterparts in English are indicated with single asterisks in the Contents. They belong primarily to the first and second Notebooks.

Suggesting that many original and translated documents were perhaps lost during the relocation of the archives from Constantinople to Manchester, Marseille, and Jerusalem successively[12] would be speculation short of any supporting evidence. Still, it is not out of the realm of possibility.

Notably, the Notebooks' entries derived from original letters and reports are identical and rarely paraphrased; they are mostly copied with no alteration to the main body of text.

An additional comparison of the entries with the published minutes of the AGS (see annotation 7) revealed that about one-sixth of the six-hundred-one entries are referenced explicitly or plainly during AGS meetings. These are marked with endnotes.

"When a signal is given, you should massacre, sparing no one...."

The reports provide a vivid panoramic picture of the conditions for Armenians and other Christians in Turkey after the armistice.

They demonstrate that there was a central government that was reneging on commitments and promises or failing to enforce:

- Payments for accommodation to Armenian authorities for released orphans and widows

- Exclusion of Armenians from compulsory enlistment
- Disarmament of the Muslim population
- The release of, or compensation for, national and personal properties
- The equal division of the harvest between Turks and returning Armenians
- The recovery of Armenian belongings from the directorates of Abandoned Properties
- The recovery of looted personal properties and livestock from individual Turks
- The return of national estates retained by Turks, except for a few

On the other hand, the government encouraged, be it by action or inaction, the distribution of arms to the Muslim populace. At the same time, Armenians were stripped of any means of self-defense.

The Armenian authorities faced the unsurmountable needs of returning refugees—mostly women and children. Many widows and orphans suffered from malnutrition, leprosy, and other diseases. Surviving adult and non-disabled men were few. Recovered Islamized Armenians were destined to starvation due to the lack of livelihoods and provisions, and tens of thousands of orphans and widows still being retained by Turks and Kurds all needed help. The severe shortage of funds left Islamized girls and women no choice but to return to their captors. The priests of looted churches asked for vessels and vestments; educators sought desks and textbooks.

The Armenians in the interior faced a mixture of bloodless and bloody annihilation:

- Insecurity, lawlessness, chaos
- Hunger, starvation, extreme misery
- Break-ins, lootings of stores, robberies, confiscations, and expropriations
- Abduction, rape, and sale of women
- Threat of jihad (holy war) and massacre, killings, and actual massacres
- Trade prohibitions, leaving them with no livelihood and facing starvation
- Closure of schools and markets
- Involuntary emigration due to threats and boycotts, and fear for life, often leaving all belongings behind
- Persecution of those returning from military service
- Retention of orphans and widows and abduction of those released
- Owners-turned-refugees renting residences and muhacirs enjoying life in Armenian properties
- Dilapidated, torn down, and razed churches, schools, and houses, many filled with human remains
- Stealth demolition of the houses of returning Armenians, leaving them without shelter
- Death threats suffered by those accusing Turkish culprits or providing testimonies before courts
- Torching Armenian houses and shooting residents escaping the fire
- Attempts to eradicate returning Armenians through slander
- Release of criminal elements and perpetrators from prisons to act against Christians
- Fear of starvation during winter with no opportunity to harvest crops
- Vandalized cemeteries and vanished tombstones
- Homeless survivors living among ruins, naked and foodless
- Forced marriages of minor girls with Turks

- Fear of retaliation and execution for returning to Christianity
- Landowners deprived of their crops appropriated by Turks
- Fear of leaving their homes for errands, lest they chanced maltreatment or death
- Refusal to acknowledge rights of inheritance for properties abandoned during deportation
- Refugees left with nothing to eat but grass in the fields

These were not isolated instances. Instead, they were indicative of a pattern. They suggested the existence of centralized directives and coordinated efforts. Of course, the Armenians were mindful that all the bandits were in contact with identical organizations in various cities and acting unanimously (p. 32). The Armenians believed they did not have a chance to overcome the adversities without the protection of the Allies in Turkey and Cilicia or the victories of Greek forces in Asia Minor and Thrace on the west and the Armenian forces on the east. They were also mindful that the presence of Allied forces in coastal areas of the Black Sea and the French in Cilicia would not be a deterrent, mainly when it was observed repetitively that such presence "not only has not been an obstacle to the free activity of the Turks but has been even an encouragement when it was seen that they do not make any effective intervention." (p. 32).

In Cilicia, under the watch of the French "protectors," Armenian men, women, and even children battled the enemy heroically to protect their lives and native lands with improvised ammunition. At the same time, Turkish regular and irregular forces, armed with canons and machine guns, laid months-long sieges around Armenian neighborhoods, destroying them, setting fire to churches and establishments along with Armenians gathered therein, and massacring Christians wherever they were, in villages, towns, cities, or on roads.

Those managing to break through the enemy's military blockade would either freeze to death in harsh winter weather or be "left stranded in the cold and rainy weather: to "wallow in the mud like frogs," as described by a spiritual leader (p. 478).

Contrastingly, the Turks and other Muslim elements enjoyed all that had been created, built, seeded, and owned by victimized Armenians, whether massacred, deported, or survived and returned.

Except for a minority who seemed as upset by the prevailing situation and the brutality of the nationalists as their Christian neighbors, most Turks were determined, as seen in the reports, to keep their booty and privileged status by all means.

The Ittihadists were back, enticing the Turks to finish the incomplete ethnic cleansing of Christians.

Alongside them were the new Kemalist nationalists, as eager as the Ittihadists to do the same and who closely associated themselves with them.

Groups of propagandists roamed the countryside in disguise. They organized secret meetings and incited the Turkish ruling circles and, through them, the Turkish masses to act against the remaining Armenians.

Military officers from various provinces, dressed as civilians, visited parts of Cilicia to lead uprisings.

Muftis were no exception. They, too, gathered the Muslim elements in mosques or squares to excite them against Christians in general and Armenians in particular, often asking audiences if they were ready to slaughter Christians.

Hectic and feverish preparations were underway to form çete bands and arm them and the Muslim population at large with weapons and grenades, replace the security guards of Armenian villages with

Turks, search Armenian homes for arms, and so on. Isolated gangs and bands of robbers, abductors, and killers independently acting in the lawless country were soon brought into the fold of the Milli or Nationalist Movement.

To conclude, the reports contained in this volume demonstrate that the central government, the Ittihadist old guards, the new Kemalist nationalists, and the unbridled çetes, by creating the conditions mentioned above and carrying out the heinous actions enumerated earlier, committed genocide, as stipulated in Articles I and II of the Genocide Convention, and collectively or individually punishable acts under Article III of the same Convention.[13] Furthermore, they erected modern Turkey on the blood and ashes of their Christian citizens, depriving hundreds of thousands of survivors of their historic lands and scattering them anew in foreign lands.

Notes on some translation specifications

The glossary on pages 521 through 528 presents the renditions we have chosen for mostly Turkish and a few other foreign words. Nevertheless, we deemed some clarification to be relevant.

The umbrella organization, established on February 28, 1919, in Constantinople, to care for Armenian orphans, widows, and needy individuals, was named Hah' Azkah'in Xnamadaro'wt'iwn (Հայ Ազգային Խնամատարութիւն)[14]. It has been translated in some sources as trusteeship and, therefore, the body in question, *Armenian National Trusteeship*. However, the word *Xnamadaro'wt'iwn* means the provision of care. Consequently, we chose to adopt the rendition used in the minutes of the AGS as *Armenian National Assistance*.

In rendering Armenian names in the Latin Alphabet, we chose to deviate from traditional transliteration, reserving the letter *u* as it sounds in the word *church* to persons' names containing the corresponding sound. To render the sound *oo,* as in *moon,* we combined the characters *o* and *u,* as they sound in *you*. The combination of the letters *yu* is used for names containing the Armenian diphthong *iw* (իւ) that sounds like *u* in *cute*. The combination of the letters *zh* is used to render the Armenian phoneme ժ (*s* as in *measure*) in proper names.

The Turkish term *çete/çeteci,* used in its transliterated form in the Armenian reports, means *gangster, partisan, brigand, hooligan, bandit, raider, marauder, guerilla, ring member*. Initially, we were inclined to render it as a *brigand* or *irregular* (an armed individual not belonging to or engaged in by regular army forces). Armenians viewed them as brigands and marauders, given their attacks on unarmed people and their participation in wars that cost the Armenians the loss of their native lands. In the end, however, we used the word *çete* for objectivity. Readers can judge whether they were bandits, malefactors, or guerillas. It should be noted that Turkish sources consider at least those who joined the Milli Movement as praiseworthy individuals engaged in partisan or guerilla war.

The word *muhacir* in Turkish means primarily refugee. Armenian refugees were survivors of the Genocide and deportees returning to their native places, or those leaving everything behind and moving to safer places to escape Turkish maltreatment. The *muhacir*s, on the other hand, were Muslim settlers who had been rendered refugees because of the Great War or were brought in by the Turkish authorities from lands near and far to take over Christian lands and properties or to change the demographics of a given area. Therefore, we chose to denote such refugees as *muhacir*s to present the Armenian reports correctly and to distinguish between the wretched Armenian refugees whom the Turkish authorities neglected as opposed to fully protected Muslim refugees.

As for the heads of administrative divisions, *vali*s, *mutasarrıf*s, and *kaimakams*, we have chosen to use the terms *governor-general, district governor,* and *lieutenant governor,* respectively.

Acknowledgment

The compiler wishes to express gratitude to:

His wife, Barbara, who edited the English version of these heartbreaking accounts.

Mr. Sevan Deyirmenjian, a scholar, for assisting with the Turkish texts and specific words.

The Dolores Zohrab Liebmann Fund's decision makers, for supporting this publication.

For further reading

Readers may find the following publications highly illuminating for their direct connection with the period and documents presented here:

Der Yeghiayan, Zaven. *My Patriarchal Memoirs.* Translated by Ared Misirlyan. Edited by Vatche Ghazarian, Waltham, 2002 (pages 175 through 261, specifically).

Yeghiayan, Vartkes, Compiler *British Reports on ethnic cleansing in Anatolia, 1919–1922: The Armenian Greek Section.* Glendale, 2007.

Morris, Benny and Dror Ze'evi. *The Thirty-Year Genocide: Turkey's Destruction of its Christian Minorities 1894–1924.* Cambridge, 2001 (pages 265 through 484, specifically).

Notes:

1 Representing his country during the session of the Council of Ten of the Allied and Associated Powers on June 17, 1919, in Paris and submitting his country's official memorandum, Damat Farid, the Grand Vizier, demonstrated no desire for admission of responsibility or readiness for restitution when he started his speech, saying, "I should not be bold enough to come before this high Assembly if I thought that the Ottoman people had incurred any share of responsibility in the war which has ravaged Europe and Asia with fire and sword." He added that a mass of unfortunate events has made Turkey appear in an unfavorable light and that unjust judgment should not be passed about Turks. Furthermore, he emphasized that his country desires the maintenance of the integrity of the Ottoman Empire (*Papers Relating to the Foreign Relations of the United States, The Paris Peace Conference, 1919,* Volume IV, United States Government Printing Office, Washington, 1943, pp. 509–511). This was a denial of the rights of the original inhabitants for the restoration of territories occupied by the Ottoman Empire. "[President] Wilson commented that he had 'never seen anything more stupid,' while Lloyd George called the delegation and its memorandum 'good jokes' and commented that such a showing was 'the best proof of the political incapacity of the Turks.' Rejecting the concept [that the Turkish people were not responsible for the role they played during the war], the council stated in a written reply that 'a nation must be judged by the Government which rules it.'" (Helmreich, Paul C. *From Paris to Sèvres: The Partition of the Ottoman Empire at the Peace Conference of 1919–1920.* Ohio State University Press, 1974, p. 110).

2 The Mudros Agreement of October 30, 1918, was an armistice signed with Turkey that stipulated the collection and dispatch of all Allied prisoners of war, including Armenian interned persons and prisoners, to Constantinople (Article III) and the demobilization of the Turkish army (Article IV). Furthermore, it gave the Allies the right to occupy any strategic points in the event of any situation arising which threatened the security of the Allies (Article VII), and in case of disorder in the six Armenian vilayets, the Allies' right to occupy any part of them (Article XXIV), (Hurewitz, J. C. *The Middle East and North Africa in World Politics: A Documentary Record.* Vol. 2, 2nd edition, Yale University Press, 1975, pp. 129-130).

[3] "All were intoxicated with the victorious European countries' promises and were self-assuredly counting the days, waiting for the realization of those promises." (Der Yeghiayan, Zaven. *My Patriarchal Memoirs.* Translated by Ared Misirlyan, edited by Vatche Ghazarian, Waltham, 2002, p. 191).

[4] "Upon receiving news of the Armistice, the Armenians dispersed in Mesopotamia and Syria began to return from their places of exile. The Armenians of Cilicia—thanks to Jemal Pasha—had suffered comparatively less. They started returning to Cilicia with the particular encouragement of the French, who at that time ruled that area of Turkey and wanted to use the Armenians as a support." (Der Yeghiayan, *op. cit.*, p. 176). A document prepared by the Armenian National Union of Adana on July 20, 1919, placed the overall number of Christians in Cilicia at 210,000 (150,000 Armenians, 35,000 Greeks, etc.) and non-Christians at 200,000, including Turks, Kurds, Circassians, settlers, Islamized Armenians, and so on (Ghazarian, Vatche, compiler and annotator. *Azkah'in Bado'wirago'wt'ean Ko'rdzo'wne'o'wt'iwny 1915-1915 (Vawerakrer) [The Activities of the Armenian National Delegation 1915–1916 (Documents)].* Beirut, 2017, p. xxix.

[5] From a French report presenting the history, role, and circumstances of the closure of the periodical that had its last issue printed on April 24, 1920. The founding members had initially considered choosing *Truth* as the name of the periodical (Archive of the Information Bureau of the Armenian Patriarchate of Constantinople maintained in Jerusalem [AIBAPIJ, hereafter], Box 6, MD903, Ծ752–776).

[6] Ibid.

[7] Yeghiayan, Vartkes, compiler. *British Reports on ethnic cleansing in Anatolia, 1919–1922: The Armenian Greek Section*. Glendale, 2007, p. xxvii.
This publication encompasses minutes of eighty-five meetings beginning on March 5, 1919, and ending on March 29, 1922, the last session before the dissolution of the section. There are also two minutes of preparatory meetings with the participation of American repatriation officers and without Greek and Armenian participants, dated February 26 and March 4, respectively.
At AIBAPIJ (Box 1, M150-Ջ-Բ-Յ, Բ910–911), we found a copy of a third numberless meeting, dated February 28, 1919, which, unlike the other two sessions, had Mr. Tchakirian as an Armenian participant (*see the entire text in Appendix I*). Tchakirian, or Tchakurian, was a professor of chemistry at the Turkish university in Constantinople and had volunteered to head the orphan collection initiative of the Armenian Patriarchate.
Thanks to copies of minutes kept at AIBAPIJ, we could identify the word missing on page 60 of the *British Reports...* as "feared" and locate the text missing from the minutes of the twenty-sixth meeting on page 100 (see Appendix II for the latter).

[8] See a version of the text in Der Yeghiayan, *op. cit.*, pp. 195–197. See the original text maintained at AIBAPIJ (Box 1, Հ-Ծ-Կ, Հ909–912) in Appendix IV.

[9] Der Yeghiayan, *op. cit.*, pp. 189-190.

[10] Ghazarian, Vatche, compiler and editor. *Hamahawaq adenakro'wt'iwnner T'o'wrqio'h' hah'o'c Azkah'in Eresp'o'xanagan Zho'gho'vi, Hamako'wmar Azkah'in Zho'gho'vi ew Hamazkah'in Xo'rho'wrti (1919–1922) [Corpus of Minutes of the National Representative Assembly, Interdenominational Representative Assembly, and Mixed Council of the Armenians of Turkey (1919-1922)].* Jerusalem, 2021, p. 75.

[11] AIBAPIJ, Box 7, NM101, Դ922. See Appendix IV.

[12] Alarmed with the fall of Smyrna and its destruction by fire by Kemalist forces in September 1922, the Armenian Patriarchate decided to safeguard the archival materials gathered at the Information Bureau in a safe place. Thus, the transfer of these archives to the Armenian church in Manchester between September 27 and early December of 1922. Later, the archives were moved to the Armenian Church in Marseilles and finally to Jerusalem, where they remain at the Armenian convent (Der Yeghiayan, *op. cit.*, p. 189; Ghazarian, *Corpus,* p. xxvii).

[13] *Convention on the Prevention and Punishment of the Crime of Genocide (declared on December 11, 1946, by*

the General Assembly of the United Nations. https://www.un.org/en/genocideprevention/genocide-convention.shtml. Accessed 1 March 2023).

14 See the transliteration table on page xxxix.

Sources of Letters, Reports, and Telegrams

The table below shows the localities where the accounts received by the Armenian Patriarchate originated and their frequency.

There are six hundred and one of them altogether.

To draw attention specifically to the sources of reports related to Cilicia, those provinces are also separately grouped and presented in the third column.

Locality	Count
Adana	40
Afyonkarahisar	7
Aleppo	26
Amasya	2
Ankara	3
Balıkesir	23
Beirut	2
Bilecik	7
Bursa	61
Çanakkale	4
Diyarbakır	7
Düzce	2
Edirne	5
Elazığ	7
Eskişehir	2
Gaziantep	12
Hatay	11
İstanbul	47
İzmir	5
Kahramanmaraş	7
Karaman	1
Kastamonu	2
Kayseri	16
Kilis	2
Kırıkkale	7
Kırşehir	2
Kocaeli	79
Konya	19
Kütahya	3
Larnaca	1
Malatya	10
Mardin	1
Mersin	16
Mosul	1
Niğde	1
Ordu	3
Osmaniye	1
Sakarya	13
Samsun	15
Şanlıurfa	6
Sinop	1
Sivas	13
Tekirdağ	17
Tokat	2
Trabzon	33
Yalova	12
Yerevan	2
Yozgat	32
Zonguldak	10
TOTAL	601

Locality	Count
Adana	40
Aleppo	26
Beirut	2
Gaziantep	12
Hatay	11
İstanbul	2
İzmir	1
Kahramanmaraş	7
Kilis	2
Konya	1
Larnaca	1
Mersin	8
Osmaniye	1
Şanlıurfa	6
Verbal accounts	2
TOTAL	122

The Administrative Divisions of Modern Turkey (Türkiye)

About six hundred sixty-six cities, towns, and villages situated in seventy-two of the eighty-one provinces of modern Turkey are mentioned in the documents. For each province in the map below, we have indicated numerically the number of localities associated with a respective province.

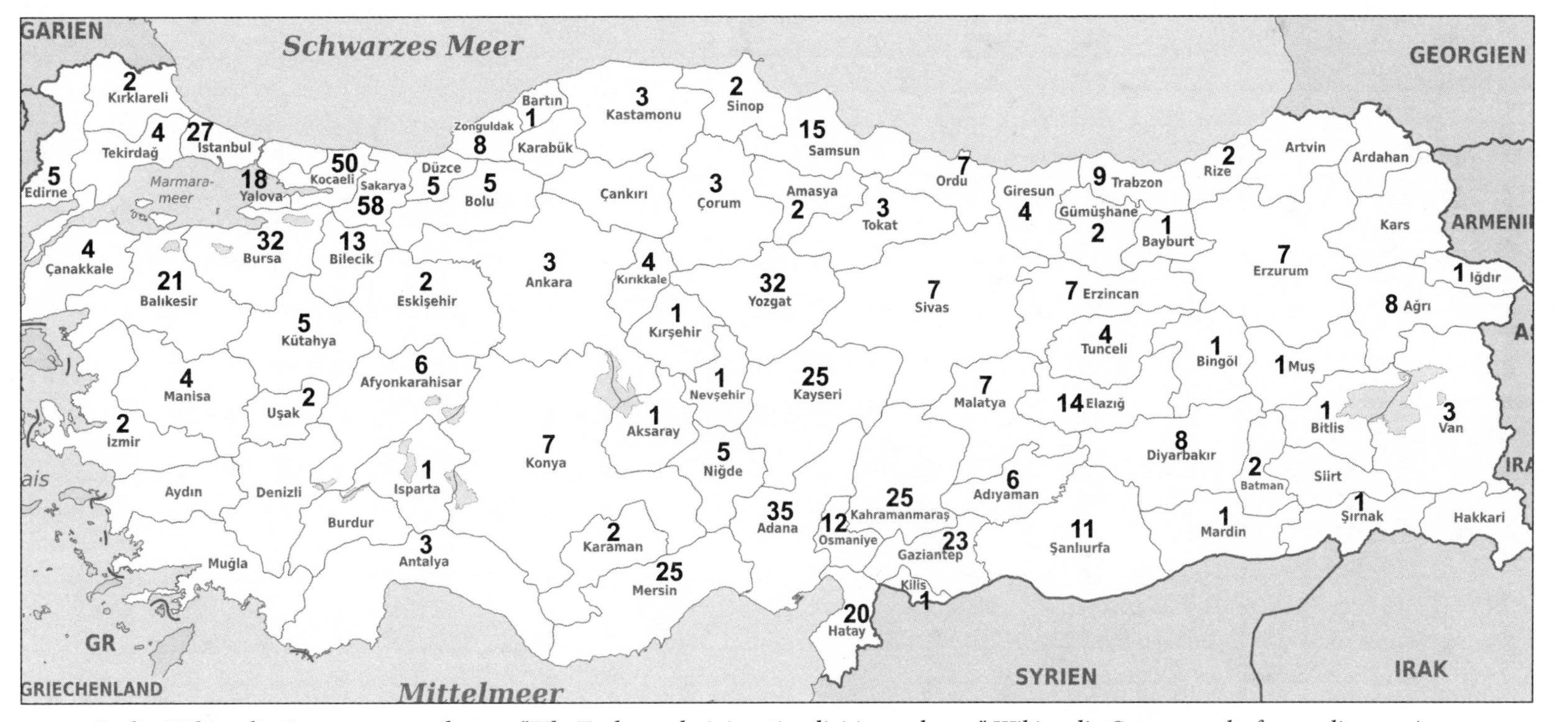

Credit: Wikimedia Commons contributors, "File:Turkey, administrative divisions - de.svg," Wikimedia Commons, the free media repository, https://commons.wikimedia.org/w/index.php?title=File:Turkey,_administrative_divisions_-_de.svg&oldid=695301771 (accessed March 5, 2023).
Note: The numbers on the map are added by the compiler of this book.

The Records
Արձանագրութիւնները

[Insecurity] Notebook Number 1
May–July 1919

Denek Madeni, Keskin—May 7, 1919[1]

Insecurity, anxiety, extreme hunger, and misery.

There are about fifteen hundred widows and orphans and between twenty to twenty-one men who returned from military [service], [and] six to seven Armenian Protestants.

They [local Armenians] raise five thousand [liras] monthly through local means.

Five hundred twelve orphans are gathered in the school.

Harput—April 17, 1919

Misery; need for relief.

Five hundred orphans of both sexes.

Budget up to March 31, 1919: 6,001 liras received.

Malatya—April 17, 1919

Reluctance to hand over orphans; meanwhile, the gendarmes bringing the orphans handed over to Malatya kidnap them on the way.

Two hundred collected orphans; still many remain, but they have not been gathered due to lack of money.

Extreme misery.

Diyarbakır—April 15, 1919

The dilapidated churches have been returned. More than five hundred people, excluding surrounding districts, have been gathered; they include those from Erzurum, Kiğı, etc. The government delivered about fifty orphans but refused to provide them with housing. They are settled in the church.

Due to insecurity, about two hundred somewhat prosperous families are migrating to Aleppo; church vessels and clergy are requested.

St. Giragos [church is] half-ruined, St. Sarkis completely collapsed, and so is the Monastery of the Holy Mother of God in Alipınar [Alipunar]. No help from the government at all; promise only. A list of two hundred orphans is sent [with the letter]; most of them are from Erzurum, Bitlis, and [some from] elsewhere.

Trabzon—April 16, 1919

The cathedral [and the churches of] the Holy Mother of God and St. Hovhannes are entirely ruined; only the four walls remain. The schools and the prelacy also are in decay. The Armenian club only stands.

The number of orphans and deportees: 148; twenty-three Armenians from the villages of Trabzon.

Turks live in houses that belonged to Armenians. Many of those have been destroyed. Some national estates have been returned, others not yet, and some are in ruins.

There is a sum of more than two hundred fifty thousand rubles in a Tbilisi bank, proceeds from the sale of departed Armenians' properties and goods left behind during the Russian occupation.

Keskin Maden—May 10, 1919

Insecurity increases; anarchy; the gangs roam boldly and organize; death threats against those Armenians who accuse them or testify unfavorably in court.

[Անապահովութեան] Տետր Թիւ 1
1919 Մայիս – 1919 Յուլիս

Տէնէք-Մատէն, Քէսկին – 1919 Մայիս 7ին

Անապահովութիւն, տագնապ, ծայրայեղ անօթութիւն ու թշուառութիւն:

1500ի մօտ այրիներ եւ որբեր կան եւ 20–21 այր զինուորութենէ վերադարձած, 6–7 հայ բողոքական անհատներ:

Տեղական միջոցներով 5000 ամսական կը հաւաքեն:

512 որբեր վարժարանին մէջ հաւաքուած են:

Խարբերդ – 1919 Ապրիլ 17

Թշուառութիւն, օգնութեան պէտք:

500 որբ երկսեռ:

Մինչեւ 1919 Մարտ 31ի հաշուեցոյց. ստացուած 6001 ոսկիի հաշիւը:

Մալաթիա – 1919 Ապրիլ 17

Դժկամակութիւն որբեր յանձնելու, տրուած որբերն ալ ճամբուն վրայ Մալաթիա բերող ժանտարմաները կը փախցնեն:

Հաւաքուած որբեր 200 հատ. դեռ շատեր կան բայց դրամի չգոյութեան պատճառաւ չեն հաւաքուիր:

Ծայրայեղ թշուառութիւն:

Տիարպէքիր – 1919 Ապրիլ 15

Խարխուլ եկեղեցիները ետ տրուած. 500էն աւելի բնակչութիւն, բացի շրջակայ գաւառներէն. ասոնց մէջ կան կարնեցի, քղեցի եւլն. կառավարութիւնը 50ի չափ որբեր կը յանձնէ, բայց կը մերժէ բնակութեան տեղ տալ. եկեղեցիին մէջ կը հաստատուին:

Անապահովութեան պատճառաւ 200ի մօտ քիչ շատ բարեկեցիկ ընտանիքներ Հալէպ կը գաղթեն. եկեղեցական անօթ եւ կղեր կը պահանջուի:

Ս. Կիրակոս կիսափուլ, Ս. Սարգիս բոլորովին փլած, նոյնպէս՝ Ալի Փունարի Ս. Աստուածածնայ վանքը. ոչ մի օգնութիւն կառավարութենէն. խոստում միայն: 200 որբի ցանկ մը ղրկուած, մեծագոյն մասը կարնեցի-պիթլիսցի եւլն:

Տրապիզոն – 1919 Ապրիլ 16

Մայր եկեղեցի, Ս. Աստուածածին եւ Ս. Յովհաննէս բոլորովին քայքայուած, միայն չորս պատերը մնացած են: Վարժարանները եւ առաջնորդարան[ը] նոյնպէս քայքայուած: Հայկական քլիւպը միայն կանգուն կը մնայ:

Որբոց եւ տարագրելոց թիւ՝ 148. Տրապիզոնի գիւղերէն եկած 23 հայեր:

Հայոց սեփական տուներ կը բնակին թուրքեր, շատեր ալ քանդուած. իսկ ազգային կալուածներ[էն] ոմանք ետ տրուած, ոմանք դեռ ոչ, եւ կարգ մ'ալ փլած են:

Ռուսական գրաւման ժամանակ, մեկնած հայերու գոյք ու ապրանքներ ծախուելով գոյացած 250,000 րուպլիէ աւելի գումար մը կայ Թիֆլիսի պանքան:

Քէսկին Մատէն – 10 Մայիս 1919

Անապահովութիւնը կ'աւելնայ. անիշխանութիւն. հրոսախումբերը համարձակ կը պտտին ու կը կազմակերպուին. սպառնալիք մահու այն հայերուն դէմ, որ զիրենք կ'ամբաստան[են] եւ կամ

Extreme misery; about fifteen hundred genuinely needy people, including widows and women; cry for help.

Maraş—April 24, 1919

The members of the Ittihadist Assembly of the city who massacred Armenians in Maraş and surrounding cities have not yet been arrested and are keeping three hundred armed Circassian muhacirs. The dispatched judiciary body can do nothing under the influence of influential local Ittihadists.

The leader of the perpetrators of Urfa's massacre, Major Lutfi, commander of the police force, was allowed to escape.

About twelve Armenian refugees wanted to leave Maraş and go to Aleppo to live safely one month after the armistice. Nine of them were killed by Turkish villagers in the place called Türkoğlu [Eloğlu], five to six hours away from Maraş. There is a desire to dispatch Sergeant Süleyman, son of Bayazid, a gendarme who accompanied the Patriarch in exile as a guard, to İstanbul, ostensibly to mediate with the Patriarch to prevent the arrest of the Maraş culprits. This person is a notorious massacrer.

Diyarbakır—April 25, 1919[2]

So far, 130 orphans and women [have been handed over]; the government allocates to them 156 loaves of bread a day, each weighing forty-three drams.[3] Once there is room, the number of orphans and widows will exceed 500.

- Opposition to handing over national estates.
- The Kurds of the villages of Silvan retain many [Armenian] women and orphans.
- In the village of Ğarzan Kolind [Yanarsu, possibly], the chieftain, Hadji Mehmed, has been retaining fifteen hundred Armenians for the past four years. A month ago, an attempt was made to attack and rescue them, but the agha resisted.
- Also, the spiritual leader of local Chaldeans, Mitran Suleiman, has been very helpful to Armenians.
- Insecurity; Şevki, Sıtkı, Salih, and other massacrers, have returned to the city, and sporadic killings are taking place.
- The Ittihadists are at work. Mehmûd Bey, the son of Îbrahîm Pasha of Viranşehir, who was imprisoned for murder, has been released to go to Viranşehir to organize a Kurdish club. There is also a Kurdish club in Diyarbakır, and all the Ittihadist massacrers are enrolled as members.
- An Ittilafist club has also been formed, and peace has been made with the Ittihadists.

Propaganda among Kurds, encouraging armed interference against foreign intervention.

Balıkesir—May 17, 1919[4]

The occupation of İzmir has aggravated the minds. The former police chief, Ittihadist criminal Haşim, is at work threatening. Local Turks are also unhappy and have complained to the government, but it has always been indifferent and tolerant.

Bursa—May 25, 1919

The British soldiers stationed in Bursa have left. The governor-general is also gone.

Extreme levels of insecurity and provocation. Dangerous news reaches Bursa from the locale called Orhangazi. Theft, imprisonment, murder.

դատարանի առջեւ անձնապատ վկայութիւն կուտա[ն]:

Ծայրայեղ թշուառութիւն. իրական կարօտներ 1500ի չափ, բաղկացած այրիներէ ու կիներէ. օգնութեան աղաղակ:

Մարաշ – 24 Ապրիլ 1919

Քաղաքին իթթիհատական ժողովի անդամները՝ Մարաշի ու շրջակայ քաղաքներու հայերուն ջարդարարները, չեն ձերբակալուած դեռ, 300 չէրքէս զինեալ գաղթականներ կը պահեն ու ղրկուած դատական մարմինը ոչինչ չի կրնար ընել տեղւոյն ազդեցիկ իթթիհատականներուն ազդեցութեանը տակ:

Ուրֆայի ջարդարարներուն գլխաւորը՝ ոստիկան զօրաց հրամանատար հազարապետ Լութֆի, թոյլ տուած են որ խոյս տայ:

Զինադադարէն 1 ամիս վերջ 12ի չափ փախստական հայեր Մարաշէն հեռանալով Հալէպ երթալ կ'ուզեն, ապահով ապրելու համար. ասոնցմէ 9ը Մարաշէն 5–6 ժամ հեռու Եւ-օղլու ըսուած տեղը կը սպաննուին թուրք գիւղացիներէն: Պատրիարքի աքսորին ընկերացող պահապան, ոստիկան զինուոր Պայազիտ Զատէ Սիւլէյման չավուշը Պօլիս ղրկուիլ կ'ուզուի, իբր թէ Մարաշի չարագործներուն ձերբակալուիլը արգիլելու համար պատրիարքին միջնորդութեամբը. այս անձը նշանաւոր ջարդարար մըն է:

Տիարպէքիր – 25 Ապրիլ 1919

Մինչեւ հիմա 130 որբ եւ կին. կառավարութիւնը ասոնց համար կուտայ օրական 156 տրամնոց 43 հաց. տեղ գտնուածին պէս որբերու, այրիներու թիւը 500ը պիտի անցնի:

- Ընդդիմութիւն ազգային կալուածները յանձնելու:
- Սըլիվանի գիւղերուն քիւրտերու մօտ բաւական կին եւ որբեր կան:
- Ղարզան Գօլընտ գիւղին մէջ աշիրաթապետ հաճի Մէհմէտի քով 1500 հայեր կան որ 4 տարիէ ի վեր կը պահէ: Ամիս մը առաջ փորձուեր է ատոնց վրայ յարձակիլ ու առնել, բայց աղան ընդդիմացեր է:
- Նոյնպէս տեղւոյն քաղդէացւոց առաջնորդ Միթրան Սիւլէյման հայերու շատ օգտակար եղեր է:
- Անապահովութիւն. ջարդարար Շէվգի, Ստզի, Սալիհ եւլն. նորէն քաղաք վերադարձած են, տեղ տեղ սպանութիւններ տեղի կ'ունենան:
- Իթթիհատականներ գործի վրայ. Վերան Շէհիրի Իպրահիմ փաշայի որդին Մահմուտ պէյ, մարդասպանութեան համար բանտարկուած, ազատ կ'արձակուի երթալ Վերան Շէհիր քրտական քլիւպ կազմելու. Տիարպէքիրի մէջ ալ քրտական քլիւպ կազմուած է եւ բոլոր իթթիհատական ջարդարարները անդամ արձանագրուած են:
- Իթիլաֆի քլիւպ ալ կազմուած եւ իթթիհատականներու հետ հաշտութիւն կնքուած է:

Բրօբականտ քիւրտերու մէջ՝ օտար միջամտութեան զէն ի ձեռին միջամտելու համար:

Պալըքէսէր – 17 Մայիս 1919

Զմիւռնիոյ գրաւումը գրգռած է միտքերը: Իթթիհատական ոճրագործ նախկին ոստիկանապետ Հաշըմ գործի վրայ է եւ սպառնալիքներ կ'ընէ, տեղւոյն թուրքերն ալ գոհ չեն եւ գանգատած են կառավարութեան, բայց նա միշտ անտարբեր ու թոյլատու գտնուած է:

Պրուսա – 25 Մայիս 1919

Պրուսա գտնուած անգլիական զինուորները մեկնած են. վալին ալ մեկներ է:

Ծայր աստիճան անապահովութիւն ու գրգռում: Օրհան Կազի ըսուած տեղէն վտանգաւոր լուրեր կը հասնին Պրուսա: Գողութիւն, բանտարկութիւն, սպանութիւն:

Two young [Armenian] men from Yenisölöz have been imprisoned in Yenişehir by slander. A twenty-seven-year-old wounded young Armenian was brought to Bursa. Schools [are] closed due to the prevailing fear and terror, as are the markets. The rally [*sic*] ended without incident.

Bursa—May 27, 1919
Karnig Effendi Shishmanian, a participant in Bursa's governmental and national affairs and a benefactor exiled to Konya, now lives in Kadıköy. He came from Bursa last night and was very concerned about the local security; he had come specifically for that reason. The Turks are very exasperated and getting ready for a massacre. The Allied troops withdrew from Bursa, which had a terrible effect and made the Turks even more haughty. The dispatch of soldiers is requested, at least temporarily.

Yozgat—May 15, 1919
From the local Political Council: Persons returning and trying to regain the commercial arena are slandered as killers of Turks during deportation and imprisoned. Thus, false witnesses have accused the merchant Ghevont Saraydarian and the machinist Yervant Apkarian. Because of this danger, some returnees are departing the city, leaving their jobs and families behind.

According to the information received, there seems to be an intention to kill such [industrious] Armenians by throwing them in jail.

Harput—May 6, 1919
Governor-General Ali Sait Bey, a staunch Ittihadist and a drunkard, organizes banquets in the homes of notorious criminals and çetes.

The notorious leader of çetes, Kurdish Hadji Kaya Sebati, the murderer of the French citizen Miss Gamault and His Grace [Bishop Sdepan] Israyelian, is a close friend of the governor-general and he left the city and the village for elsewhere on his advice, and, indeed, his arrest warrant came from İstanbul after his departure, and of course, he was not found.

As long as the governor-general stays there, there will be no rest for the Armenians, and none of the Ittihadists will get arrested. Dr. Barton also is aware of the matter.

Bursa—May 25, 1919
Incitement among Turks; grave threats; they are seriously preparing for a massacre; the departure of Allied troops has aggravated the situation further; request for troops. Distribution of weapons through neighborhood representatives.

Balıkesir—May 22, 1919
Inciting the Turks; grave threats; preparation for a massacre; çetes are invited from the villages; former deputy [police] commissioner Haşim plays a significant role by constantly provoking the Turkish mob; the government is indifferent; the removal of Haşim is requested.

Adapazarı—May 23, 1919
The same situation; in particular, an instigation to massacre the Greeks; secret meetings at night. Delegates are dispatched to the surrounding Turkish villages to ready themselves and attack at the first signal. They ask that Armenian newspapers use cautious language.

Մէօլէօզէն զրպարտութեամբ երկու երիտասարդ բանտարկուած են ի Եէնի-Շէհիր: Հայ վիրաւոր 27 տարեկան երիտասարդ մը Պրուսա բերուած: Դպրոցները փակուած, տիրապետող ահ ու սարսափին համար. նոյնպէս՝ շուկաները: Միթինկը կը վերջանայ առանց որեւէ դէպքի:

Պրուսա – 27 Մայիս 1919

Գառնիկ էֆ. Շիշմանեան, Պրուսայի կառավարական ու ազգային գործերու մէջ անդամ ու ձեռնտու, աքսորուած Գոնիա, այժմ Գատը-Գիւղ կը բնակի. Պրուսայէն երէկ իրիկուն եկած է եւ տեղւոյն ապահովութեանը մասին խիստ մտահոգ ու յատկապէս ատոր համար եկած է: Թուրքերը շատ գրգռուած ու ջարդի կը պատրաստուին: Համաձայնական զինուորները քաշուած են Պրուսայէն. եւ ատիկա շատ գէշ ազդեցութիւն գործած ու թուրքերը աւելի խրոխտ ըրած է: Կը խնդրուի զինուոր ղրկել, գէթ առժամեայ կերպով:

Եօզկաթ – 15 Մայիս 1919

Տեղւոյն Քաղաքական Ժողովէն- Վերադարձող եւ նորէն առեւտրական ասպարէզը ձեռք առնելու աշխատող անձերը զրպարտութիւններով կը բանտարկեն որպէս տարագրութեան ժամանակ թուրք սպանող: Այսպէս՝ վաճառական Ղեւոնդ Սարայտարեան եւ մեքենագործ Երուանդ Արզարեան սուտ վկաներով կ՛ամբաստանուին: Այս վտանգին պատճառով, վերադարձողներէն ոմանք գործերնին ու ընտանիքնին ձգած կը մեկնին քաղաքէն:

Առնուած տեղեկութեանց համաձայն, այս կարգի հայերը բանտ նետելով, հոն սպաննել տալու դիտաւորութիւն կայ եղեր:

Խարբերդ – 6 Մայիս 1919

Վալի Ալի Սէյտի պէյ, թունդ իթթիհատական եւ զինով մէկը, կերուխումներ կը սարքէ յայտնի չարագործներու ու չէթէներու տուները:

Նշանաւոր չէթէ րէյիսի, քիւրտ Հաճի Գայա Սէպաթի, սպանիչ փրանսահպատակ Օր. Կամօ-ի եւ Իսրայէլեան Գերապայծառի, մտերիմ բարեկամն է վալիին եւ անոր խորհուրդով քաղաքն ու գիւղը թողելով ուրիշ տեղ կ՛երթայ, եւ արդարեւ իր մեկնելէն վերջ է որ Պոլսէն ձերբակալման հրամանը կուգայ, եւ բնականաբար չի գտնուիր:

Որքան ատեն որ վալին հոն մնայ, հայերուն համար հանգիստ չկայ եւ իթթիհատականներուն եւ ոչ մէկը կը ձերբակալուի: Տոք. Պարթըն ալ տեղեակ է խնդրոյն:

Պրուսա – 25 Մայիս 1919

Թուրքերու մէջ գրգռում. ծանր սպառնալիքներ. լըջօրէն կը պատրաստուին ջարդի. Համաձայնական զինուորներու մեկնիլը կացութիւնը աւելի ծանրացուցած է. զօրքի խնդրանք: Մուխթարներու միջոցաւ զէնքի բաշխում:

Պալըքէսէր – 22 Մայիս 1919

Թուրքերու գրգռում. ծանր սպառնալիքներ. պատրաստութիւն ջարդի. գիւղերէն չէթէներ կը հրաւիրուին. նախկին գոմիսէր մուավինի Հաշիմ մեծ դեր կը կատարէ՝ շարունակ գրգռելով թուրք խուժանը. կառավարութիւնը անտարբեր. Հաշիմի հեռացուիլը կը պահանջուի:

Ատաբազար – 23 Մայիս 1919

Միեւնոյն կացութիւնը. մասնաւորապէս յոյները ջարդելու թելադրանք. գաղտնի գիշերային ժողովներ. շրջակայ թուրք գիւղերը պատուիրակներ ղրկուած են՝ պատրաստ գտնուիլ ու առաջին ազդանշանին յարձակելու. կը խնդրեն որ հայ լրագիրները զգուշաւոր լեզու գործածեն:

Akhisar (Geyve)—May 22, 1919
The same situation; threat of massacre; the Turks are getting organized and are distributing arms.

Alifuatpaşa [Geyvé Station]—May 22, 1919
Serious threat of massacre; [the Armenians there] do not ask for bread and clothes, but for security. If defending them through the Allied troops is not possible, they ask the Patriarchate that the returning two thousand unfortunate Armenians be transported to İzmir free of charge and that they be provisioned there for at least a few weeks until the danger passes.

İstanbul—Hasköy—Üsküdar and Eyüp—[May 1919]
Letters, even from these neighborhoods of İstanbul, have reached the Patriarchate regarding insecurity and asking for help.

Samsun—May 27
More than fifty deportees arrived in Samsun from Sokhumi, impoverished and miserable, primarily natives of Samsun, Çarşamba, Bafra, Tokat, and so on. Lack of means to feed them. Most of them have had their houses demolished, and the Turks are hastily dismantling the homes of new returnees also by night and carrying away the tiles and timber, even in [a place like] Samsun, before everybody's eyes.

- Of the five hundred Armenian houses in the vicinities of Samsun, four hundred have been razed.
- There are two thousand Armenians in Çarşamba, whether they have remained there or have returned, and Muslims hold on to about four to five hundred orphans.
- Complaint about Rami Bey, the head of the Muhacirs Commission in Samsun, who wants to benefit from the travel expenses earmarked for deportees by offering to pay them only half.
- Six to seven hundred orphans within the Samsun diocese have not been collected yet due to a lack of means to care for them; likewise, the Islamized adult girls and [married] women.

Malatya—May 28
Great preparation for resistance. The Kurdish tribal leaders of Arapgir, Maden, Güngörmüş [Pütürge], and the district and rural district are exhibiting great activity, having joined the Turks; they exclaim that it is better to die bravely than to die like this.

- More than four hundred orphans and widows gathered are in great misery and need help.
- [The Turks] of rural districts and villages do not hand over the Armenian orphans; they put them to labor gratis.

Sivas—May 23[5]
A rally on the occasion of İzmir's occupation, fiery speeches, a threat to declare holy war: the adverse effect of the threatening telegram sent by the grand vizier to the Council of Four.

Gürçam [Fatsa] (Samsun)—March 28
This was written to the Greek metropolitan of Samsun to be dispatched to the Patriarchate. Hovhannes Roumian, from the village of Hozagara of Ümit rural district, was not deported somehow and maintained his Armenianness. His house was set on fire by night to kill him. Two family members were burned to death, and several others who ran out of the house were shot dead. He escaped somehow

Աքհիսար (Կէյվէ) – 22 Մայիս 1919

Միեւնոյն կացութիւնը. ջարդի սպառնալիք. թուրքերը կը կազմակերպուին եւ զէնք կը բաժնեն:

Gheyvé Station – 23 Մայիս 1919

Ջարդի լուրջ սպառնալիք. հաց ու զգեստ չեն խնդրեր, այլ՝ ապահովութիւն: Եթէ Համաձայնական զինուորներու միջոցաւ զիրենք պաշտպանելու կարելիութիւն չկայ, Պատրիարքարանի կ'առաջարկեն որ գէթ քանի մը շաբթուան համար վերադարձող 2000 դժբաղդ հայերը ձրիաբար Իզմիր փոխադրուին ու հոն պարենաւորուին, մինչեւ որ վտանգը անցնի:

Պոլիս – Խասգիւղ – Իւսկիւտար եւ Էյուպ – [Մայիս 1919]

Նոյնիսկ Պոլսոյ այս թաղերէն նամակներ հասած են Պատրիարքարան անապահովութեան մասին եւ օգնութիւն կը խնդրեն:

Սամսոն – 27 Մայիս

Սամսոն կը ժամանեն Սօխումէն 50է աւելի տարագիրներ, շատ խեղճ ու թշուառ, մեծ մասամբ սամսոնցի, չարշամպացի, պաւրացի, թոգաթցի եւլն: Միջոցի պակաս զանոնք կերակրելու համար: Ասոնց մեծագոյն մասին տուները քանդուած են եւ թուրքերը նոր վերադարձողներու տուներն ալ փութով կը քանդեն գիշերանց եւ կղմինտր ու փայտերը կը փախցնեն, նոյնիսկ Սամսոնի մէջ, ամէնուն աչքին առջեւ:

- Սամսոնի շուրջը գտնուող 500 հայու տուներէն 400ը փլցուած են:
- Չարշամպայի մէջ մնացած ու վերադարձող 2000 հայ կայ. իսկ իսլամներու մօտը 400–500 որբեր:
- Գանգատ Սամսոնի Մուհաճիր Գոմիսիոնի րէյիս [Իսլամ Գաղթականներու Յանձնաժողովի նախագահ] Րահմի պէյի համար որ տարագիրներու տրուելիք ճանապարհածախսէն օգտուիլ կ'ուզէ՝ կէսը վճարել առաջարկելով:
- Սամսոնի թեմին մէջ գտնուած 6–700 որբերը խնամելու միջոց չգտնուելուն՝ դեռ չեն հաւաքուած, նոյնպէս՝ իսլամացած չափահաս աղջիկ ու կիներ:

Մալաթիա – 28 Մայիս

Դիմադրութեան մեծ պատրաստութիւն: Արապկիրի, Մատէնի, Բէթուրկէի եւ սանճաքի ու գազայի քիւրտ ցեղապետները թուրքերուն միացած մեծ գործունէութիւն կը ցցնեն. կը պոռան թէ՝ այսպէս մեռնելէն քաջաբար մեռնիլը լաւ է:

- 400է աւելի հաւաքուած որբ եւ որբեւայրիներ մեծ թշուառութեան մէջ, օգնութեան կարօտ:
- Գազաներէն ու գիւղերէն հայ որբերը չեն ղրկեր, ձրիապէս կ'աշխատցնեն:

Սեբաստիա – 23 Մայիս

Միթինկ Իզմիրի գրաւման առթիւ, բոցաշունչ ճառեր, ճիհատ հրատարակելու սպառնալիք. Եպարքոսին առ 4երու ղրկած սպառնական հեռագրին գործած վատ ազդեցութիւնը:

Փաթսա (Սամսոն) – 28 Մարտ

Սամսոնի յոյն Մեդրապօլիտին գրուած է պատրիարքարան ղրկուելու համար: Յովհաննէս Րումեան, Իւմիտ Գազարը, Հօզակարա գիւղէն, կերպով մը չէ աքսորուած եւ հայ մնացած է: Չինքը սպաննելու նպատակաւ գիշերանց տունը կ'այրեն: Ընտանիքէն երկուքը կ'այրի եւ դուրս փախչողներէն քանի մը հատն ալ գնդակահար կ'ըլլան: Ինքը կերպով մը կ'ազատի եւ Փաթսա

and came to Gürçam, where he stays with some other unfortunate Armenians. They want assistance and security.

Samsun—May 23
There is a lack of means to care for the six to seven hundred orphans in the Samsun diocese; they want relief from the center [Armenian Patriarchate]. The Americans do not want to cover all the expenses, arguing that they already care for four to five hundred Greeks. The Americans stipulate that the Armenians should provide the facility and the staff, and they will take care of the rest.

• There is a lack of means to collect Islamized women and girls, and those who are collected run away due to a lack of space and [adequate] care.

Malatya—May 25[6]
Satisfaction with District Governor Halil Rami; he endeavors for security.

Yozgat—June 2[7]
Eight to ten out of twenty to twenty-nine people native to İncirli returning to their ruined homes from military service are prosecuted by the government due to slander.

• Lawyer Araboğlu Abdurrahman, the notorious massacrer, has formed a party called "Millet Perveran" [Patriots] and is inciting minds and preparing for a massacre. His removal is requested.

For Yozgat—June 4[8]
From the Armenian Union of Yozgat, formed in İstanbul: Insecurity; above all, efforts to exterminate returning Armenians by all means.

• Thus, Ghevont S[a]raydarian and Yervant Apkarian are accused of killing a Turk near the village of Gelingüllü four and a half years ago.

• Haroutyun Malian, Khacher Khacherian, Nigoghos Nigoghosian (neighborhood representative), Isahag Donigian, and Kerovpé Yosmayan are accused of killing a Turkish emigrant in the locality named Taş Ocak, half an hour away from the city.

• Garabed Chechikian, Arshalouys Tashjian, Khosrof Setragian, Hagop Chekiyan, and Haroutyun Kochakian are accused of killing a Turk five years ago in a forest called Soğuk Oğlu in Yozgat.

An arrest warrant has been issued against all of them.

• Also, two or three months ago, they arrested Hadji Kehya Medzadourian from Sağlık village on charges of killing a gendarme. Even though the military authorities confirmed his military service in the army then, he remains in prison.

• If the situation continues like this, the returning young people also will leave for İstanbul or elsewhere, and finding someone to care for orphans and widows on the spot will not be possible.

Boğazlıyan (telegram)—May 27[9]
Complaint against local attorney general Refik and inquisitor Mustafa for freeing the massacrers of Armenians. To exterminate the returning Armenians, the notables Derviş İbrahim and Kemal are making provocations, sending telegrams, and dispatching the accused Ormancı Hasan, particularly, to the villages to provide false witness against the Armenians.

• Instead of trying the case of the terrible crime committed against the Armenians, the government

կուգայ, ուր կը մնայ ուրիշ կարգ մը խեղճ հայերու հետ. օգնութիւն կ'ուզեն եւ ապահովութիւն:

Սամսոն – 23 Մայիս

Սամսոնի թեմին մէջ գտնուած 6–700 որբերը խնամելու համար միջոց կը պակսի. կեդրոնէն օգնութիւն կ'ուզեն: Ամերիկացիները ամբողջ ծախքը հայթայթել չեն ուզեր, առարկելով թէ 4–500 յոյներ կը խնամեն արդէն: Ամերիկացիները պայման կը դնեն որ հայերը հայթայթեն շէնք եւ պաշտօնէութիւն, մնացածն ալ իրենք կը հոգան:

- Իսլամացած կիներ ու աղջիկներ հաւաքելու միջոցը կը պակսի. հաւաքուածներն ալ կը փախչին՝ տեղի ու խնամքի չգոյութենէն:

Մալաթիա – 25 Մայիս

Մութասարըֆ Խալիլ Րահմի պէյէն գոհունակութիւն: Ապահովութեան մասին կ'աշխատի:

Եոզկաթ – 2 Յունիս

Զինուորական պարտականութիւնը կատարելով իրենց աւերակ տունը վերադարձող ինճիրլիցի 20–29 հոգիէն 8–10 հատը զրպարտուելով կառավարութեան հետապնդումին ենթարկուած են:

- Նշանաւոր ջարդարար փաստաբան Արապ օղլու Ապտիւրրահիման «Միլլէթ Փէրվէրան» [Ազգասէրներ] անունով կուսակցութիւն մը կազմած ու մտքերը կը գրգռէ եւ ջարդի պատրաստութիւն կը տեսնէ: Հեռացումը կը խնդրուի:

Եոզկաթի համար – 4 Յունիս

Պոլսոյ մէջ կազմուած Եոզկաթի Հայ Միութենէն.- Անապահովութիւն. մանաւանդ վերադարձող հայերը որեւէ կերպով բնաջինջ ընելու ջանքեր:

- Այսպէս՝ Ղեւոնդ Սէրայտարեան եւ Երուանդ Արզարեան կ'ամբաստանուին 4 ½ տարի առաջ Կէլին Կիւլիւ գիւղին մօտերը թուրք մը սպաննած ըլլալ:

- Յարութիւն Մալեան, Խաչէր Խաչէրեան, Նիկողոս Նիկողոսեան (մուխթար), Իսահակ Տօնիկեան եւ Քերովբէ Եօսմաեան ամբաստանուած են քաղաքէն ½ ժամ հեռու Թաշ Օճաղի ըսուած տեղը թուրք գաղթական մը սպաննած ըլլալ:

- Կարապետ Չէչիքեան, Արշալոյս Թաշճեան, Խոսրոֆ Սեղրակեան, Յակոբ Չէքիեան եւ Յարութիւն Գոչաքեան կ'ամբաստանուին 5 տարի առաջ Եոզկաթի Սօղուք Օղլու կոչուած անտառին մէջ թուրք մը սպաննած ըլլալ:

Ասոնց բոլորին ալ դէմ ձերբակալման հրամանագիր ելած է:

- Նոյնպէս, 2–3 ամիս առաջ Սաղըր-Գիւղէն կը ձերբակալեն հաճի Քեհեա Մեծատուրեանը ժանտարմա մը սպաննած ըլլալու ամբաստանութեամբ: Հակառակ այդ պահուն դեռ բանակին մէջ զինուորութիւն ընելը զինուորական իշխանութեանց կողմէ հաստատուած ըլլալուն, բանտը կը մնայ:

- Կացութիւնը եթէ այսպէս շարունակուի, վերադարձող երիտասարդներն ալ Պոլիս կամ այլուր պիտի երթան, ու տեղւոյն վրայ որբ ու այրիները հոգացող մարդ գտնել կարելի չպիտի ըլլայ:

Պօղազլեան (հեռագիր) – 27 Մայիս

Գանգատ տեղւոյն ընդհանուր դատախազ Րէֆիքի եւ հարցաքննիչ Մուստաֆայի դէմ, որ հայոց ջարդարարները ազատ կը թողուն: Վերադարձող հայերը բնաջինջ ընելու համար Էշրաֆէն Տէրվիշ Իպրահիմ եւ Քէմալ գրգռումներ կ'ընեն, հեռագիրներ կուտան եւ ամբաստանեալ Օրմանճի Հասան յատկապէս գիւղերը կը ղրկեն, հայոց դէմ սուտ վկաներ հայթայթելու համար:

- Հայոց դէմ գործուած ահագին եղեռնի դատը փոխանակ տեսնելու, կառավարութիւնը

is investigating the accusations against Armenians.

Bursa—June 7
Ittihad's representative İbrahim and the former mayor Muhtar, who are directly responsible for the Mount Adranos [Orhaneli] massacre, are roaming freely and boldly in İstanbul and Bursa, respectively.

• The father of the known Halide Edib Hanum, Edib Bey—a functionary of the Régie of Bursa—constantly comes to İstanbul to meet with the abovementioned İbrahim and others and acts as a mediator for plots in the making.

Keskin (Denek Madeni) —June 5
From the Armenian and Greek neighborhood councils: Insecurity. The local people, ignorant, still have no idea about the current political situation and the brutal defeat of Turkey. As a result of the capture of İzmir, several criminals who were living as fugitives have reappeared and are at work.

• A captain named Kaplan Bey from Beyoba, a fugitive, is now forming a one-hundred-fifty-strong band of çetes, all made up of people with terrible pasts.

• The local government, though aware, observes indifferently.

İzmit—June 9
On Saturday, the 7th of this month, eighteen-year-old Samuel of Arslanbey was found killed ten minutes away from steward Ali's farm, where he was working. The perpetrator has not been found.

• A bullet passed by a man from Arslanbey while working near Bahçecik and missed him.

• It is becoming impossible to work in the fields around here.

Karacabey [Mihaliç] (Bursa)—June 9
Only forty of the [initially] 180 Armenian households have been able to come together.

Reşit Bey, the son of Circassian Ali Bey from a nearby village, is very active and cultivates close ties with the Ittihadists. News has come that by gathering two thousand Circassians, he will declare a Bolshevik regime. The first victims will surely be Christians. The Greeks also have the same anxiety and have informed their Patriarchate.

Balıkesir—June 12
Insecurity has reached a climax; constant threat of massacre. The government has summoned the local Armenian and Greek neighborhood representatives and ordered them to be ready in case soldiers are demanded of them; otherwise, they will be court-martialed.

The people are in despair over insecurity and this suggestion for conscription.

The somewhat wealthy class of returning Armenians has begun to migrate to İzmir and İstanbul, and the poor class, which was starting to make a living, is now engaged, terrified, in selling all that they have, their cottages, and so on—even at prices lower than those at the time of deportation—to depart.

The British military representative of Bandırma has visited Balıkesir but responded to the appeals made by the Armenians that sending soldiers is not possible now.

հայերու դէմ եղած ամբաստանութիւնները կը քննէ:

Պրուսա – 7 Յունիս

Աթրանոս լերան վրայ տեղի ունեցած սպանդին ուղղակի պատասխանատու Իթթիհատի մուրախասս Իպրահիմ ի Պոլիս եւ նախորդ Պէլէտիյէ Րէյիսի Մուխթար ի Պրուսա ազատ համարձակ կը պտտին:

- Ծանօթ Խալիտէ Էտիպ հանըմի հայրը, Պրուսայի Րէճիի պաշտօնեայ Էտիպ պէյ, շարունակ Պոլիս գալով վերոյիշեալ Իպրահիմի եւ ուրիշներու հետ կը տեսնուի եւ դաւեր սարքելու միջնորդ կ'ըլլայ:

Տէնէկ-Մատէն – 5 Յունիս

Հայ եւ յոյն թաղական խորհուրդներու կողմէ.- Անապահովութիւն: Տեղւոյն ժողովուրդը, տգէտ, դեռ գաղափար չունի քաղաքական ներկայ կացութեան եւ Թուրքիոյ չարաչար պարտութեան մասին: Իզմիրի գրաւման հետեւանօք, կարգ մը չարագործներ որ փախստական կ'ապրէին, նորէն երեւան ելած ու գործի վրայ են:

- Պէյ օպացի Գաբլան պէյ անունով հարիւրապետ մը, փախստական, այժմ չէթէյախումբ մը կազմելու վրայ է, 150 հոգինոց, բոլորը սարսափելի անցեալի տէր անձերէ բաղկացած:

- Տեղական կառավարութիւնը թէեւ գիտակ, բայց անտարբեր կը դիտէ:

Իզմիտ – 9 Յունիս

Ասլանպէկցի 18 տարեկան Սամուէլ, ամսուս 7ին, Շաբաթ օրը, սպաննուած կը գտնուի Ալի քեհեայի չիֆլիկէն, ուր կ'աշխատէր, 10 վայրկեան հեռու տեղ մը: Չարագործը չէ գտնուած:

- Ասլանպէկցի մը, Պարտիզակի մօտերը աշխատած պահուն, գնդակ մը քովէն կ'անցնի ու կը վրիպի:

- Այս կողմերը դաշտերը աշխատիլ անկարելի կ'ըլլայկոր:

Գարաճա Պէյ (Պրուսա) – 9 Յունիս

180 տուն հայէն 40 տուն միայն կրցած են հաւաքուիլ:

Շրջակայ գիւղացի չէրքէս Ալի պէյի որդին՝ Րէշիտ պէյ, մեծ գործունէութեան մէջ է եւ իթթիհատականներու հետ սերտ յարաբերութիւն կը մշակէ: Լուր առնուած է որ 2000 չէրքէսներ հաւաքելով պօլշէվիքութիւն պիտի հռչակէ: Առաջին զոհերը քրիստոնեաները պիտի ըլլան անշուշտ: Յոյներն ալ նոյն անձկութեան մէջ՝ իրենց պատրիարքարանը իմացուցած են:

Պալըքէսէր – 12 Յունիս

Անապահովութիւնը ծայր աստիճանի հասած է. շարունակ ջարդի սպառնալիք: Կառավարութիւնը հայ եւ յոյն մուխթարները կանչած եւ պատուիրած է որ զինուոր ուզուած պարագային պատրաստ գտնուելու էք, հակառակ պարագային, պատերազմական ատեան պիտի քաշուիք:

Անապահովութիւնն ու զինուորագրութեան այս առաջարկը ժողովուրդը յուսահատութեան մատնած է:

Վերադարձող հայերու քիչ շատ ունեւոր դասակարգը Իզմիր եւ Պոլիս գաղթել սկսած է, իսկ աղքատիկ դասակարգը, որ սկսած էր օրապահիկ մը հանել, այժմ սարսափահար՝ իր ունեցած չունեցածը, տնակը եւլն. նոյնիսկ գաղթականութեան ատենէն աւելի վար գիներով ծախել ու մեկնիլ [սկսած է]:

Պանտրմայի անգլիական զինուորական ներկայացուցիչը Պալըքէսէր այցելած է, բայց հայերու կողմէ եղած դիմումներուն պատասխանած է թէ այժմ զինուոր ղրկել կարելի չէ:

Adana (from the primate)—April 12, 1919

Of the [Armenian] population of Dörtyol, that numbered eighteen thousand [before deportation], three thousand have now scarcely returned; loss: fifteen thousand people. Armenian homes, vineyards, churches, and schools are entirely destroyed.

• The Kelegian orphanage is standing, and a one-hundred-fifty-person orphanage will be opened with the help of Egyptian Armenians.

• Most of the people of Osmaniye have returned. The churches are destroyed.

• The people of Ceyhan also have had little loss; their church is destroyed.

• Crowdedness and poverty; deportees of the interior provinces cannot return to their homes due to insecurity. The Americans have started organizing relief work. There is an orphanage already with 520 orphans who have received sufficient help from the Americans.

Keskin [Denek Madeni] (from the Armenian and Greek Neighborhood Councils)—June 10

Insecurity; threat of massacre, this time so stern that not a single Christian would be left, and thus both the witnesses of the atrocities would disappear, and the capture of İzmir would be avenged.

• A crowd of çetes, led by former military captain Kaplan Bey of Beyoba, has toured the villages to gather horses and men.

• The villagers have complained to the government, but the acting district governor has not paid attention and, on the contrary, is encouraging [Kaplan Bey].

• The people are migrating to the provinces of Ankara and Eskişehir out of fear.

• The arrest of Kaplan and the deposing of the lieutenant governor is requested.

Gemlik—June 13, 1919

The arrest of perpetrators is requested. Two of them are now in İstanbul. One is Tunali Hilmi, the former lieutenant governor of Gemlik, who currently serves on the Muhacirs Commission; the other is Asım Bey, a former gendarmerie commander in Gemlik, now living around Sultanahmet, in Kabasakal quarter, Akbıyık Street, domicile 36.

Ereğli (Konya)—June 14, 1919

Some of the orphans and widows found in Turkish houses have been taken, and now there are some thirty to forty [more], but the Turks refuse to hand them over. The government has not paid anything for the orphans and widows handed over to the [Armenian] nation.

Request for relief; the church and the school have been destroyed, and the local people cannot repair them; the government has not made any compensation either.

• When the Armenian people of Adapazarı, İzmit, Konya, and so on were deported to Mesopotamia, [while] passing through Ereğli, they could no longer take their property with them, and about eight hundred bales remained there. Local military and civil officials looted most of the property, and a dismal portion was handed over to the Commission of Abandoned Properties. The leading looters of these properties are the current lieutenant governor of Gemlik, Faiz, and his father, who was the chairman of the Commission of Abandoned Properties, and Edhem, a member of that commission and currently the local financial director, also Ereğli's [police] commissioner İzzet, his brothers Şerif and Riza, police Tahsin, Sergeant Major Midhat, and Circassian Ali Çavuş, a gendarme.

Ատանա (Առաջնորդէն) – 12 Ապրիլ 1919

Տէօրթ-Եօլի ժողովուրդը որ 18000 հոգի էին, այժմ հազիւ 3000 վերադարձած են. կորուստ՝ 15000 հոգի: Հայոց տուները, այգիները բոլորովին քանդուած են, ինչպէս եւ եկեղեցիներն ու դպրոցները:

- Քելեկեան որբանոցը կանգուն է եւ եգիպտահայոց օգնութեամբը 150 հոգինոց որբանոց մը պիտի բացուի:
- Օսմանիյէի ժողովուրդը մեծ մասամբ վերադարձած է: Եկեղեցիները քանդուած են:
- Ճիհանի ժողովուրդն ալ քիչ կորուստ ունի. եկեղեցին քանդուած է:
- Խճողում եւ խեղճութիւն. ներքին գաւառներու տարագրեալները իրենց տեղերը չեն կրնար վերադառնալ անապահովութեան պատճառաւ: Ամերիկացիները սկսած են օգնութեան գործը կազմակերպել. որբանոց մը կայ արդէն 520 որբերով որոնց բաւական օգնութիւն ըրած են ամերիկացիները:

Տէնէք Մատէն (Հայ եւ յոյն թաղական խորհուրդներէն) – 10 Յունիս

Անապահովութիւն. ջարդի սպառնալիք եւ այս անգամ այնքան խիստ որ մէկ քրիստոնեայ չմնայ ու այդպէսով թէ՛ չարագործութեանց վկաները անհետանան եւ թէ Զմիւռնիոյ գրաւման վրէժը լուծուի:

- Չէթէի մը բազմութիւնը, որուն պետն է պէյ օպացի, նախորդ զինուորական հարիւրապետ Գաբլան պէյ, գիւղերը պտտած է ձի եւ մարդ հաւաքելու համար:
- Գիւղացիները կառավարութեան զանգատած են, բայց գայմագամը կարեւորութիւն չէ տուած եւ կը քաջալերէ ընդհակառակը:
- Ժողովուրդը վախէն դէպի Գաղատիա կը գաղթէ:
- Կը խնդրուի ձերբակալել տալ Գաբլանը, եւ գայմագամը պաշտօնանկ ընել:

Կէմլեյէկ – 13 Յունիս 1919

Կը խնդրուի չարագործներու ձերբակալումը: Ասոնցմէ երկուքը այժմ Պոլիս կը գտնուին: Մին Կէմլէյիկի նախկին գայմագամ Թունալի Հիլմի, որ այժմ մուհաճիր քոմիսիոնի մէջ կը պաշտօնավարէ. միւսը Կէմլէյիկի նախկին ժանտարմա գոմանտանը Ասըմ պէյ, այժմ կը բնակի Սուլթան Աhմէտի կողմը, Գապասաքալ թաղ, Աք Պըյըք փողոց թիւ 36 տունը:

Էրէյլի (Գոնիա) – 14 Յունիս 1919

Թուրքերու քով գտնուած որբ եւ այրիներէն մաս մը առնուած է. իսկ այժմ 30–40 հատի չափ կան, բայց թուրքերը կը մերժեն յանձնել: Ազգին յանձնուած որբերու, այրիներու համար կառավարութիւնը բան մը չէ վճարած:

Նպաստի խնդրանք - եկեղեցի եւ վարժարան քանդուած են եւ տեղւոյն ժողովուրդը ի վիճակի չէ վերանորոգելու. կառավարութիւնն ալ որեւէ հատուցում չէ ըրած:

- Ատաբազարի, Իզմիթի, Գոնիայի եւայլն հայ ժողովուրդը դէպի Միջագետք աքսորելու ատեն Էրէյլիէն անցնելով իրենց գոյքերը չեն կրցած այլեւս միասին տանիլ եւ 800 հակի չափ հոն մնացած է: Այդ գոյքերը տեղւոյն զինուորական ու քաղաքական պաշտօնեաները մեծ մասամբ կողոպտած եւ շատ չնչին մաս մ'ալ էմլաքը-մէթրուքէի քոմիսիոնին յանձնած են: Սոյն գոյքերը կողոպտողներուն գլխաւորներն են՝ Կէմլէյիկի արդի գայմագամ Ֆաիզ եւ իր հայրը որ լքեալ գոյքերու գոմիսիոնին նախագահն էր, եւ այդ գոմիսիոնի անդամներէն Էտհէմ, այժմ տեղւոյն մէջ մալ-միւտիրի, նոյնպէս՝ Էրէյլիի գոմիսէր Իզզէթ, եղբայրները Շէրիֆ եւ Րիզա, փօլիս Թահսին, ժանտարմըրիի յիսնապետ Միտհատ եւ ժանտարմ Չէրքէզ Ալի չավուշ:

Bursa—June 18, 1919
The notable influential Ittihadists of the village of Karacabey (Mihaliç) who were brought to Bursa and imprisoned are now armed, after their release, and threatening the Armenians by forming bands of çetes.

• Also, as many as two thousand armed Circassians are conducting raids near Bandırma's Manyas district.

• The Ittihadist çetes of Karacabey village are Tahir, Numan, Bayezid, Kurd İsmail, Hasan Pehlivan, and İbrahim.

İstanbul—June 21, 1919
(From Khdrian) Insecurity on the Amasya-Samsun road. Ten or twelve days ago, ten Indian soldiers traveling from Merzifon to Samsun, their British officer, and forty-five Armenian companions carrying about fifty thousand liras and fleeing from Amasya-Marzifon to escape insecurity were robbed six hours away from Samsun by Turkish çetes who also took away the soldiers' weapons.

Urfa—May 23, 1919
(Antranig Sayuyan) Until recently, the person mentioned[10] lived in the village of Samsat in Adıyaman [Hısnımansur] under the patronage of Hacı Şeyh Agha, son of Hasan Agha.

• As a person of knowledge about local events, he ascertains the existence of four to five thousand Armenian orphans who have been placed in the mountains of Malatya and Adıyaman.

• He is offering to gather these orphans in Urfa if help is rendered to him.

Malatya—June 8, 1919
(From Garabed Kulujian)[11] The notorious massacrer, Haşim Beyzade Muhammad, previously a fugitive for some time, has surfaced and is roaming audaciously.

The abovementioned, joining the famous massacrer of Erzurum, Hacı Bedir Ağa, came to Malatya and held consultations with the Kurdish chieftains of Güngörmüş [Pütürge], Atma, Kâhta, Adıyaman [Hısnımansur], and Kesben before leaving.

• The Turks manifestly declare that if foreigners come and occupy this country, they will fight and wipe out all Armenians.

• There are currently two thousand Armenians in Malatya, but if we count the number of those retained by Turks and Kurds, as well as those in the area reaching around Arapgir, there are more than twenty thousand Armenians who are under the threat of death at any time.

• The killer of Bishop Saadetian of Erzurum, throwing him down the mountain, is Hamdi, the son of Hacı Fevzi, a former financial director from the village of Denizli in Keban.

Adana—June 13, 1919
Great want; in addition to many migrants, the Armenian volunteers who have been discharged by the French need help because there is a lack of work.

• In the Cilician region, the French representatives grossly maltreat the Armenians, pursuing a more hypocritical and pro-Turkish policy; help is not being rendered to the Armenians to get their looted goods back.

• As a result of this situation, despite the French occupation of Cilicia, thefts and murders are frequent, and bands of çetes roam the mountains threatening Armenians.

• The collection of arms that the French had initiated has stopped. The Turks somehow aborted

Պրուսա – 18 Յունիս 1919

Գարաճա-պէյ (Միխալըճ) գիւղի երեւելի ազդեցիկ իթթիհատականները որ ասկից առաջ Պրուսա բերուած ու բանտարկուած էին, վերջը ազատ արձակուած ըլլալով, այժմ զինուած եւ չէթէի խումբեր կազմելով հայոց կը սպառնան:

- Պանտըրմայի Մանիաս Գազայի մօտ ալ 2000ի չափ զինեալ չէրքէսներ ապաստակութիւն կ'ընեն:

- Գարաճա-պէյ գիւղի այդ իթթիհատական չէթէներն են՝ Թահիր, Նիւման, Պայազիտ, Քիւրտ Իսմայիլ, Հասան փէհլիվան, Իպրահիմ:

Կ. Պօլիս – 21 Յունիս 1919

(Խտրեանէ) Անապահովութիւն Ամասիա-Սամսոն ճամբան: Ասկէ 10–12 օրեր առաջ Մարսուանէն Սամսոն եկող 10 հնդիկ զինուոր եւ իրենց անգլիացի սպան եւ ասոնց ընկերացող ու Ամասիա-Մարսուանէն անապահովութեան համար փախչող 45 հայեր, որոնց մօտը կը գտնուէր 50000 ոսկիի չափ գումար մը, Սամսոնէն 6 ժամ հեռու կը կողոպտուին թուրք չէթէներու կողմէ, զինուորներուն զէնքերն ալ կ'առնեն:

Ուրֆա – 23 Մայիս 1919

(Անդրանիկ Սայըեան) Ցիշեալը[1] մինչեւ վերջերս Ատիեամանի Սամ[ս]ատ գիւղը կը բնակի եղեր Հասան աղա զատէ հաճի շէյխ աղայի հովանաւորութեան տակ:

- Իբր տեղւոյն իրադարձութեանց տեղեակ, 4–5000 հայ որբերու գոյութիւնը կը հաւաստէ Մալաթիոյ եւ Ատիեամանի լեռներուն մէջ դրուած:

- Կ'առաջարկէ այդ որբերը Ուրֆա հաւաքել, եթէ իրեն օգնող ըլլայ:

Մալաթիա – 8 Յունիս 1919

(Կարապետ Գըլըճեանէ)[2] Նշանաւոր ջարդարար Հաշիմ պէյ զատէ Մուհամմէտ որ ժամանակէ մը ի վեր փախստական էր, այս օրերս մէջտեղ ելած ազատ համարձակ կը պտտի:

Վերոյիշեալը, միանալով Է[ր]զրումի հռչակաւոր ջարդարար Հաճի Պէտիր աղայի հետ, Մալաթիա եկած եւ Բիթիւրկէի, Աթմայի, Քեախթէի, Հիւսնի-Մանսուրի ու Կէսպանի քիւրտ ցեղապետներու հետ խորհրդակցութիւններ ըրած ու ցրուած են:

- Թուրքերը յայտնի կերպով կ'ըսեն թէ՝ եթէ օտարները գան այս երկիրը գրաւեն, պիտի կռուինք եւ հայ մը չպիտի ձգենք:

- Այս պահուս Մալաթիոյ մէջ 2000 հայեր կան, բայց եթէ հաշուենք թուրքերու եւ քիւրտերու քով գտնուածները եւ մինչեւ Արաբկիրի կողմը գտնուողներն ալ, այն ատեն 20000է աւելի հայեր կան որ ժամէ ժամ մահուան սպառնալիքի մէջ կը գտնուին:

- Կարնոյ Առաջնորդ Սաատէթեան Եպիսկոպոսը լեռնէն վար նետելով սպաննողն է Կէպէնի Տենիզլի գիւղէն եւ նախորդ մալ միւտիրի հաճի Փէյզիի տղան՝ Համտին:

Ատանա – 13 Յունիս 1919

Մեծ կարօտութիւն. բազմաթիւ գաղթականներու վրայ աւելցած են ֆրանսացիներու կողմէ արձակուած հայ կամաւորները որոնց օգնել հարկ է, որովհետեւ աշխատութիւն կը պակսի:

- Կիլիկեան շրջանին մէջ ֆրանսական ներկայացուցիչները շատ գէշ կը վարուին հայերու հետ, աւելի երկերեսու ու թրքամոլ քաղաքականութեան մը կը հետեւին. ոչ մէկ օգնութիւն հայերուն՝ իրենց կողոպտուած ապրանքները ետ առնելու մասին:

- Այս կացութեան հետեւանքով, հակառակ Կիլիկիոյ ֆրանսական գրաւման, գողութիւն եւ մարդասպանութիւնները յաճախադէպ են եւ լեռները չէթէներու խումբեր պտտելով հայերու կը սպառնան:

this critical matter.

Gaziantep [Ayntab]—May 15, 1919
About five thousand local Armenians and about three thousand deportees from the surrounding provinces, primarily women and children, are gathered here; extreme misery; barely twenty percent are [entirely] clothed; the rest are all half-naked.

• Because the British occupy the city, deportees are given fourteen piasters or three hundred drams of bread a week per person, most of whom are obliged to live on so little. Great need for help.

Adana—June 17, 1919
Insecurity; formation of bands of çetes; great preparations; the Turkish people are armed, and if the fate of Cilicia is determined unfavorably for the Turks, they will stage a major uprising.

• Numerous [military] officers from İstanbul and other provinces, dressed as civilians, have come to various parts of Cilicia to lead the uprising.

• Many groups of propagandists also roam in disguise and organize secret meetings, inciting and preparing the Turkish ruling circles and, through them, the Turkish masses.

• Assuming it was a serious task, the Armenians surrendered their arms when the French authorities collected weapons in Cilicia. At the same time, a collection of weapons from the Turks was not carried out with the necessary strictness; the Armenians are now left unarmed.

• The French, aware of these events, remain indifferent.

Yozgat—June 19, 1919[12]
Extreme anti-Christian movement. Mustafa Kemal Pasha, commander of the Samsun army and inspector general of the Anatolian provinces, has cabled everywhere, ordering the formation of bands of çetes. According to that order, the municipality of Yozgat enlisted 285 çetes; likewise, in the villages. Besides, recently formed organizations, called Redd-i İlhak [Rejection of Annexation], Millet Perverane Osmaniye [Ottoman Patriots], and Sulh ve Selameti Osmaniye [Ottoman Peace and Salvation], have joined forces with the çetes to raise a vast insurrection and massacre all the Christians, both Armenian and Greek, should Anatolian provinces be given to Armenians.

• Contrary to the decision not to conscript Christians, those born in 1898 in Yozgat have been called to arms.

• Six to seven hundred orphans are near starvation, and a part of the Armenian population of the city is grazing in the fields.

Urfa—May 28, 1919
(From Sarkis Gezourian)[13] The Kurdish chieftains of Samsat and Kâhta have applied for an Armenian-Kurdish reconciliation and agreement, and they want it to happen with British mediation. They [the Armenians] want instruction from İstanbul.

• National and private properties are perpetually under seizure, and the government evidently declines to administer justice.

- Զէնքերու հաւաքումը, որ ֆրանսացիները սկսած էին, դադրեցաւ. թուրքերը կերպով մը վիժեցուցին այդ կարեւոր խնդիրը:

Այնթապ – 15 Մայիս 1919

Տեղացի 5000ի մօտ հայեր հաւաքուած են, իսկ շրջակայ գաւառացի 3000ի մօտ տարագրեալներ, մեծ մասամբ կին եւ մանուկ. ծայր աստիճան թշուառութիւն, հազիւ 20%ը զգեստ ունին, մնացածները՝ բոլորն ալ կիսամերկ:

- Քաղաքը անգլիացւոց կողմէ գրաւուած ըլլալով, տարագիր ժողովրդեան կը տրուի շաբաթական մարդ գլուխ 14 դահեկան կամ 300 տրամ հաց, մեծ մասը այսքան քիչով ապրելու ստիպուած է: Օգնութեան մեծ պէտք:

Ատանա – 17 Յունիս 1919

Անապահովութիւն. չէթէական կազմակերպութիւն. մեծ պատրաստութիւններ. թուրք ժողովուրդը զինուած է եւ Կիլիկիոյ բաղդը թուրքերու աննպաստ կերպով վճռուելու պարագային մեծ ապստամբութիւն մը պիտի հանեն:

- Պոլսէն եւ այլ գաւառներէ բազմաթիւ սիվիլ հագուած սպաներ եկած են Կիլիկիոյ զանազան կողմերը ապստամբութիւնը վարելու համար:

- Նոյնպէս շատ մը բոօբականտիստներու խումբեր ծպտուած կը պտտին եւ գաղտնի գումարումներ կը կազմակերպեն, գրգռելով եւ պատրաստելով թրքական ղեկավար շրջանակները եւ անոնց միջոցաւ թուրք զանգուածը:

- Կիլիկիոյ մէջ ֆրանսական իշխանութեանց կողմէ զէնքերը հաւաքելու պահուն, լուրջ գործ մը ենթադրելով, հայերը յանձնած են իրենց զէնքերը. մինչդեռ թուրքերու զինահաւաքումը պէտք եղած խստութեամբ չէ կատարուած, որով այժմ հայերը անզէն մնացած են:

- Ֆրանսացիները՝ տեղեակ այս իրադարձութեանց, անտարբեր կը մնան:

Եոզկաթ – 19 Յունիս 1919

Ծայր աստիճան հակաքրիստոնէական շարժում: Սամսոնի բանակին հրամանատար եւ Անատոլիի վիլայէթներու ընդհանուր միւֆէթթիշ Մուստաֆա Քէմալ փաշա ամէն կողմ հեռագրով հրաման տուած է չէթէներու խումբեր կազմելու համար: Ըստ այդ հրամանին, Եօզկաթի մէջ քաղաքապետութիւնը 285 չէթէ արձանագրած է. նոյնպէս՝ գիւղերը: Ասոնցմէ զատ, վերջերը կազմակերպուած «Րէտ'տ Իլհաք» [Մերժել կցումը], «Միլլէթ Փէրվէրանէ Օսմանիան» [Օսմանեան Ազգասէրներ] եւ «Սուլհ ու Սէլամէթը Օսմանիյէ» [Օսմանեան Խաղաղութիւն եւ Փրկութիւն] կոչուած կազմակերպութիւնները միացած չէթէներու հետ, Անատօլուի վիլայէթները հայերու տրուելու պարագային, մեծ ապստամբութիւն մը պիտի հանեն եւ բոլոր քրիստոնեաները, հայ թէ յոյն, պիտի ջարդեն:

- Հակառակ քրիստոնեաներէ զինուոր չառնուելու որոշման, Եոզկաթի մէջ 314ի [=1898ի] ծնունդները զէնքի տակ կը կանչուին:

- 6–700 որբերը գրեթէ անօթի են, քաղաքիս հայ բնակչութեան մէկ մասն ալ դաշտերը խոտ կ'արածեն:

Ուրֆա – 28 Մայիս 1919

(Սարգիս Կէզուրեանէ)[3] Սմսաթի եւ Քեախթէի քիւրտ պետերը դիմում կատարած են հայքրտական հաշտութիւն մը եւ համաձայնութիւն մը կատարելու համար եւ կը փափաքին որ Անգլիոյ միջամտութեամբը ըլլայ. Պոլսէն հրահանգ կ'ուզեն:

- Ազգային թէ անհատական ինչքերը եւ կալուածները միշտ գրաւման տակ են եւ կառավարութիւնը որոշ կերպով չ'ուզեր արդարութիւնը գործադրել:

• Complaint against the district governor and especially the director of the office of correspondence. Their removal is requested.

• Complaint about the German Eckart and his friend, Jakob Künzler. The latter is expected here these days; he has sold hundreds of [Armenian] girls. The British authorities here have been indifferent to the complaint against him.

Devrek (Zonguldak)—June 24, 1919

19 men turned Muslim and deceased, buried in the Muslim cemetery
13 women turned Muslim and deceased, buried in the Muslim cemetery
45 Christians deceased
6 hanged by the gallows
1 found hanged in villages
1 stoned to death
2 deceased in prison
2 deceased because of imprisonment (one is the local priest, Father Dimotheos)
2 deceased because of beating
2 deceased after losing their mind
27 deceased or killed during military service
16 vanished during military service
2 captives
3 still bearing arms
1 not-yet-returned alive soldier

Before the war			*After the war*		
house	*family*	*inhabitant*	*house*	*family*	*inhabitant*
95	*109*	*631*	*92*	*101*	*489 (228 male) (261 female)*

• Insecurity; threat of massacre; an arson attempt on the night of June 23, 1919, [by throwing] pieces of cloth dipped in petroleum and burning on the houses of Nshan Minasian, Dikran Keshishian, and Zareh Yeghian. Locals discovered and prevented the fire.

• They ask for a [locally stationed] contingent from the French troops in Zonguldak.

Akhisar (Geyve)—June 7, 1919

Of the 3,670 inhabitants of Kurtbelen, only 300 have returned to date. Out of eight hundred houses, only forty inhabitable houses are now occupied by Turks while the real owners, due to insecurity, are obliged to stay in Akhisar and live in homes rented for three to four liras.

All the villagers' furniture, animals, and other belongings have been looted, and nothing has been returned to date, and the appeals made so far have remained futile.

Should the current situation continue, these villagers will die of cold and starvation in the forthcoming winter, whereas a bit of security and the return of stolen, looted items would save their lives altogether.

Trabzon (from the vicar general)—June 20, 1919

There are 230 orphans (170 girls, 60 boys) gathered in the orphanage from various places. They are cared for by the American Near East Relief and through the revenues of national estates.

- Գանգատ տեղւոյն միւթէսարրըֆին եւ մանաւանդ թահիրիրաթ միւտիրիին դէմ. ասոնց հեռացումը կը պահանջուի:

- Գերմանացի Էքարտի եւ անոր ընկերը Եազուպ Քիւնսլէրի մասին գանգատ: Այս վերջինը հոս պիտի գայ այս օրերս, հարիւրաւոր աղջիկներ ծախեր է: Տեղւոյս անգլիական իշխանութիւնները անհոգ գտնուած են ատոր մասին եղած գանգատին:

Տէօվրէք (Չոնկուլտաք) – 24 Յունիս 1919

19 խլամացած եւ մեռած այր, խլամ գերեզմանատունը թաղուած
13 խլամացած եւ մեռած կին, խլամ գերեզմանատունը թաղուած
45 քրիստոնեայ մեռածներ
6 կախաղան հանուած
1 գիւղերու մէջ կախուած գտնուած
1 քարկոծումով մեռցուած
2 բանտին մէջ մեռած
2 բանտարկութեան հետեւանքով մեռած (մին տեղւոյն Տէր Տիմոթէոս քահանան)
2 ծեծի հետեւանքով մեռած
2 խենդենալով մեռած
27 զինուորութեան մէջ մեռած եւ սպաննուած
16 զինուորութեան մէջ անյայտացած
2 գերի
3 զէնքի տակ տակաւին
1 դեռ չվերադարձած ողջ զինուոր

Պատերազմէն առաջ			*Պատերազմէն վերջ*		
տուն	*ընտանիք*	*բնակիչ*	*տուն*	*ընտանիք*	*բնակիչ*
95	*109*	*631*	*92*	*101*	*489 (228 արու) (261 էգ)*

- Անապահովութիւն. ջարդի սպառնալիք. հրձիգութեան փորձ 1919 Յունիս 23ի գիշերը, Նշան Մինասեանի եւ Տիգրան Քէշիշեանի եւ Չարեհ Եղեանի տուներուն վրայ քարիւղի [մէջ] թաթխուած լաթ[ով] որ վառուած է. տեղացիներու կողմէ գտնուած ու հրդեհին առաջքը առնուեր է:

- Չոնկուլտաք գտնուած ֆրանսական ուժերէն, գէթ ժամանակի մը համար, մնայուն ուժ մը կը խնդրեն:

Ազ-Հիսար (Կէյվէ) – 7 Յունիս 1919

3670 Գուրտպէլէնցիներէն այսօր վերադարձողներն են միայն 300 հոգի: 800ի չափ տուներէն հազիւ 40 տուն մնացած է բնակելի ուր թուրքերը կը բնակին. իսկ բուն բնակիչները անապահովութեան պատճառաւ ստիպուած են Ազ-Հիսար մնալ եւ 3–4 ոսկիով վարձքով տուներու մէջ բնակիլ:

Գիւղացւոց բոլոր կարասիները, կենդանիները եւ ուրիշ ունեցածները կողոպտուած են եւ այսօր բան մը ետ չէ վերադարձուած եւ մինչեւ ցարդ տեղի ունեցած դիմումները ապարդիւն մնացած են:

Եթէ ներկայ կացութիւնը շարունակուի, յառաջիկայ ձմեռ ցուրտէն ու անօթութենէ պիտի մեռնին այս գիւղացիները. մինչդեռ քիչ մը ապահովութիւն եւ գողցուած, կողոպտուած իրերու վերադարձը բոլորովին պիտի փրկէր իրենց կեանքը:

Տրապիզոն (Առաջնորդական Փոխանորդէն) – 20 Յունիս 1919

Որբանոցին մէջ կան 230 որբեր (170 աղջիկ, 60 մանչ) հաւաքուած զանազան վայրերէ: Կը խնամուին Ամերիկեան Նպաստամատոյց մարմնոյն կողմէ եւ ազգային կալուածներու հասոյթով:

• A large number of private estates have not been returned yet, and the Turks live there; appeals remain futile.

• The Turks of Trabzon and the region still have many orphans and Islamized women. The government has the list, but unfortunately, the governor is unwilling and, despite the requests, has not turned over the list or the orphans.

Yozgat—June 23, 1919

According to Mustafa Kemal Pasha's instruction, 285 çetes are enlisted in the city, and fifteen çetes are prepared by the sons of a well-known kahya [steward] İsa from the village of Karahacılı.

• The city's mufti gathered thousands of Turks in the mosque, delivered anti-Christian sermons, and stirred perturbing thoughts.

İstanbul (from Hovhannes Bedigian of Kartsi village)—June 26, 1919

Insecurity and horror of massacre. On Wednesday, the 25th of this month, a thirty-two-year-old man named Ghazaros Nadosian from the village of Kartsi, who had just returned from exile, went to a Turkish village called Denizçalı to sell dry goods. On his return, he was killed near the village, with his head split and one-half of it missing. The killer robbed his victim.

Sugören [Çengiler] (from the Neighborhood Council)—June 27, 2019

On the 25th of this month, gangs attacked the village of Keramet in the rural district of Orhangazi. They entered the mosque and robbed those who were there. The Turks, accusing the Armenians as attackers, besieged Keramet with over twenty gendarmes. They gathered the Armenians and the village headman, beat them, and led them to the district prison.

• Armenian groomers returning to their village from the Sea of Nicaea were beaten and wounded by Turks on the way.

• A young Armenian from the village of Büyük-Yeniköy was transported with his horse to the rural district of Orhangazi in a dying condition.

• Manoug Karakashian, likewise a resident of Büyük-Yeniköy, was beaten by Turks and transported to his house in a half-dead condition.

• Strict boycott against Armenians; Armenians who bring goods to Turkish villages are immediately turned away with threats.

Boğazlıyan—June 28, 1919

Insecurity and threat of massacre.

• Mgrdich Kojayan of Çakmak was killed in a mill.

• Seven Armenian women were raped in the village of Güvençli [possibly Güveçli].

• According to a statistic compiled by local residents, the number of surviving Armenians is 6,150, very few of whom are men, and most of the remaining women are the prisoners of Turks.

Türkmen (Bilecik)—June 28, 1919

On the 17th of this month, robbers entered the Turkish village of Gökçeler near Türkmen. They killed Mustafa, one of the notables of the village, cut off his son's hand, and ransacked their house.

The day after the incident, the intendant of the rural district and the gendarmerie commander came, besieged the village, and arrested Kalousd, Hadji Hayrabed Avedian, Apraham Semerjian, and

- Անհատական մեծ թիւով կալուածներ դեռ ետ չեն տրուած եւ թուրքերը կը բնակին, դիմումները ապարդիւն կը մնան:

- Տրապիզոնի եւ շրջանի թուրքերուն մօտ դեռ շատ որբեր ու խլամացած կիներ կան. ասոնց ցանկը կառավարութեան մօտ կը գտնուի, բայց դժբաղդաբար վալին անբարեացակամ է եւ հակառակ եղած դիմումներու, ոչ ցանկը տուած է, եւ ոչ ալ որբերը:

Եոզկաթ – 23 Յունիս 1919

Մուստաֆա Քէմալ փաշայի հրահանգին համաձայն, քաղաքին մէջ 285 չէթէներ արձանագրուած են, իսկ Գարահաճըլու գիւղէն ծանօթ Էսա քէհեայի տղոց միջոցաւ 15 չէթէներու պատրաստութիւն եղած է:

- Քաղաքին միւֆթին հազարաւոր թուրքեր մզկիթը հաւաքելով հակաքրիստոնէական քարոզներ խօսած ու մտքերը խռոված է:

Կ. Պոլիս (Քարցի գիւղէն Յովհաննէս Պետիկեանէ) – 26 Յունիս 1919

Անապահովութիւն եւ ջարդի սարսափ: Ամսոյս 25ին, չորեքշաբթի օր, Քարցի գիւղէն Ղազարոս Նատոսեան անուն 32 տարեկան անձը, դեռ նոր վերադարձած աքսորէն, մանիֆաթուրա ծախելու համար Տէնիզ-Չայը կոչուած թուրք գիւղը կ'երթայ: Վերադարձին՝ գիւղին մօտ կը սպաննուի՝ գլուխը երկուքի բաժնուած եւ որուն կէսը չկայ: Մարդասպանը իր զոհը կողոպտած է:

Չէնկիլէր (Թաղական Խորհուրդէն) – 27 Յունիս 1919

Ամսոյս 25ին, հրոսախումբեր, Օրխան Ղազի գաւառակին Քէրամէթ գիւղին վրայ յարձակելով՝ մզկիթը կը մտնան եւ հոն գտնուողները կը կողոպտեն: Թուրքերը ամբաստանելով թէ հայերն էին յարձակողները, 20է աւելի ժանտարմաներով Քէրամէթ կը պաշարեն եւ հայերը, գիւղապետը հաւաքելով կը ծեծեն եւ գաւառակի բանտը կ'առաջնորդեն:

- Նիկիոյ ծովէն իրենց գիւղը վերադարձող հայ ձիապաններ ճամբան կը ծեծուին ու կը վիրաւորուին թուրքերու կողմէ:

- Մեծ Նոր Գիւղէն երիտասարդ հայ մը մահամերձ վիճակի մէջ Օրխան Ղազի գաւառակը կը փոխադրուի իր ձիովը:

- Նոյնպէս Մեծ Նոր գիւղացի Մանուկ Գարագաշեան ճամբան թուրքերէն կը ծեծուի ու կիսամեռ վիճակի մէջ իր տունը կը փոխադրուի:

- Խիստ պօյքօթ հայերու դէմ. թուրք գիւղերը ապրանք տանող հայեր անմիջապէս կը վռնտուին սպառնալիքներով:

Պօղազլեան – 28 Յունիս 1919

Անապահովութիւն եւ ջարդի սպառնալիք:

- Չաքմաքցի Մկրտիչ Քօճաեան ջաղացքի մը մէջ կը սպաննուի:

- Կէօվէնչլի գիւղին մէջ 7 հայ կիներ կը բռնաբարուին:

- Ըստ տեղացիներու վիճակագրութեան, վերապրող հայերու թիւն է 6150, որոնցմէ շատ քիչեր այր են, իսկ մնացած կիներու մեծ մասը թուրքերու քով բանտարկուած են:

Թիւրքմէն (Պիլէճիք) – 28 Յունիս 1919

Ամսոյս 17ին Թիւրքմէնի մօտերը գտնուող Կէօքչէլէր թրքաբնակ գիւղը աւազակներ մտնելով, գիւղին երեւելիներէն հաճի Մուստաֆան կը սպաննեն, տղուն ձեռքը կը կտրեն եւ տունն ալ կը թալլեն:

Այս դէպքին հետեւեալ օրը, գաւառակին միւտիրը եւ ժանտարմայի գոմանտանը կուգան գիւղը

Hadji Hagop Kojabashian. They were all taken to prison and beaten, and Kalousd was coerced to produce a so-called confession, confirming that his friends were the murderers, whereas the return of the Turkish bandits was witnessed by oarsmen on the Sakarya River and Turkish residents of the villages of Şahinler and Kasımlar; they are ready to testify and establish the truth.

Despite this fact, the Armenians remain in prison.

Havza (Amasya)—June 5, 1919

Gathering the Turks, the local mufti presents the question of İzmir and asks the people if they are ready to massacre the Christians. Excited, the people answer yes!

Büyük-Yeniköy—July 5, 1919

Insecurity in these Armenian villages so close to İstanbul. On the 3rd of this month, the intendant of the village was sitting with several gendarmes when an Armenian young man passed by riding a horse. The gendarmes immediately attacked him, toppled him off his horse, and fired several rounds of bullets. Fortunately, the bullet(s) missed him.

This incident terrified the people and reminded them of the days of deportation.

Trabzon—July 25, 1919

The American admiral visited Trabzon on June 21. The prefect arranged for the Christian spiritual leaders not to have the opportunity to visit with the admiral and deliver their complaints about the insecurity in the city and its vicinities. Indeed, murders are committed almost daily; immovable and movable properties seized from Armenians have not been returned at all; there are constant threats of a massacre; and [the Turks] do not want to release the Armenian orphans and women in captivity in Turkish harems at any cost.

İzmir—June 30, 1919

On June 12, on the occasion of the capture of Bergama [Pergamon] by the Hellenic Army, Armenian houses and shops were looted by local Turkish bandits; four Armenians were wounded, and a woman and a young man were killed.

İzmit—July 4, 1919

Insecurity; villagers are unable to work in the fields. Complaint against the District Governor Ahmet Bey, who had initially tried to stop the banditry, has now changed his course and, above all, apparently at the instigation of the Turks, has adopted a threatening stance against the Armenians. He has been made to believe that most of the murders and robberies occur in the district at the hands of Armenians.

Unfortunately, he is not an able administrator; otherwise, an honest and fair investigation would have clarified the matter and convinced him that he had formed wrong opinions. His stay in İzmir in these conditions is considered dangerous for the Armenians, and his removal is requested.

• Nvart, the fourteen-year-old daughter of Nshan Minasian, a jeweler from Bahçecik, was abducted by Tosunoğlu Alaeddin of Karamürsel [Karamursal]. She was recovered and temporarily placed in the house of the Armenian neighborhood representative in İzmit. Unfortunately, the impunity of all the crimes committed by the Turks emboldened them so much that when Alaeddin arrived in İzmit the

կը պաշարեն եւ կը ձերբակալեն Գալուստ, Հաճի Աւետեան Հայրապետ, Սէմէրճի Աբրահամ եւ Գօճապաշեան Հաճի Յակոբը: Ասոնք բոլորը բանտ տանելով կը ծեծեն եւ Գալուստէն բռնութեամբ իբր թէ խոստովանութիւններ կ'առնեն եւ մարդասպանները իր ընկերները ըլլալը կը հաստատեն: Մինչդեռ թուրք աւազակներու վերադարձը տեսնուած է Սաքարիա գետին թիավարներէն եւ Շահինլար ու Գասըմլար գիւղերու թուրք բնակիչներէն եւ պատրաստ են վկայելու ու ճշմարտութիւնը հաստատելու:

Այս իրողութեան հակառակ, հայերը բանտը կը մնան:

Հավզա (Ամասիա) – 5 Յունիս 1919

Տեղւոյն միւֆթին թուրքերը հաւաքելով Իզմիրի խնդիրը կը պարզէ եւ ժողովուրդին կը հարցնէ թէ պատրա՞ստ էք քրիստոնեաները ջարդելու: Ժողովուրդը գրգռուած այո՛ կը պատասխանէ:

Մեծ Նոր Գիւղ – 5 Յուլիս 1919

Անապահովութիւն Պօլսոյ այնքան մօտ գտնուող այս հայ գիւղերուն մէջ: Ամսոյս 3ին, գիւղին միւտիրը քանի մը ժանտարմաներով նստած էր, երբ հայ երիտասարդ մը ձիով կ'անցնի: Ժանտարմաները անմիջապէս վրան կը յարձակին, ձիէն վար կ'առնեն ու քանի մը ձեռք զէնք կը պարպեն: Բարեբաղդաբար գնդակը կը վրիպի:

Այս դէպքը ժողովուրդը կը սարսափեցնէ եւ տարագրութեան օրերը կը յիշեցնէ:

Տրապիզոն – 25 Յունիս 1919

Ամերիկեան Ծովակալը այցելած է Տրապիզոն Յունիս 21ին եւ կուսակալը այնպէս մը կարգադրած է որ քրիստոնեայ հոգեւոր պետերը պատեհութիւն չունենան Ծովակալին այցելելու եւ քաղաքին ու շրջակայից մէջ տիրող անապահովութեան մասին գանգատելու: Արդարեւ, գրեթէ ամէն օր սպանութիւններ կը գործուին. հայերէն գրաւուած անշարժ ու շարժուն գոյքերը բնաւ չեն վերադարձուիր. ջարդի սպառնալիքներ կ'ըլլան շարունակ. իսկ թուրք հարեմներու քով՝ գերութեան մատնուած հայ որբերն ու կիները եւ ոչ մէկ գինով չեն ուզեր ազատ թողուլ:

Չմիւռնիա – 30 Յունիս

Յունիս 12ին, հելլէն բանակին կողմէ Պէրկամոնի գրաւման առթիւ, տեղւոյն թուրք աւազակներուն կողմէ հայոց տուներն ու խանութները կը կողոպտուին. 4 հայեր կը վիրաւորուին եւ մէկ կին ու մէկ երիտասարդ ալ կը սպաննուին:

Իզմիթ – 4 Յուլիս

Անապահովութիւն. անկարելիութիւն գիւղացւոց համար դաշտերու մէջ աշխատիլ: Գանգատ տեղւոյն մութասարրըֆ Ահմէտ պէյի դէմ, որ սկիզբները թէեւ ջանքեր մը ըրած է աւազակութիւնը զսպելու համար, բայց հիմա փոխած է իր ընթացքը եւ մանաւանդ կ'երեւի թուրքերու դրդումովը հայերուն հանդէպ սպառնալից դիրք մը բռնած է եւ իրեն այնպէս հաւատացուցած են թէ՝ գաւառին մէջ տեղի ունեցած սպանութիւններուն ու աւազակութիւններուն մէկ մեծ մասը հայերու ձեռքովը տեղի կ'ունենան:

Դժբաղդաբար ինքը վարչագէտ մէկը չէ. ապա թէ ոչ անկեղծ ու արդար քննութեամբ մը խնդիրը պիտի պարզուէր եւ ինքն ալ պիտի համոզուէր որ սխալ գաղափարներ կազմած է: Այս պայմաններուն մէջ իր Իզմիր մնալը հայերուն համար վտանգաւոր կը նկատուի եւ անոր հեռացումը կը պահանջուի:

- Պարտիզակցի ոսկերիչ Նշան Մինասեանի 14 տարեկան Նուվարդ անուն աղջիկը, որ զարամուսալցի Թօսուն օղլու Ալաէտտինի կողմէ առեւանգուած էր, այս անգամ ետ առնուելով Իզմիթի

same day, he took advantage of the neighborhood representative's absence and took the said girl by force to Karamürsel. The local government did not make even the slightest remark.

The government has installed guards in various villages. These days, an instruction has arrived to move the guards of the Armenian villages to the Turkish villages. Accordingly, the long-existing guard of Arslanbey has been relocated to the Turkish village called Çepni.

Karaman—June 28

So far, only six orphans have been handed over and sent to Konya. Although there are many others, they [the Turks] do not want to hand them over, citing various objections. The local government is indifferent and has not provided the slightest financial assistance to these orphans and deportees.

• The Church, the school, and national and private estates have been returned, many dilapidated and unusable, and nothing has been paid yet against the demanded monetary compensation. Kurdish refugees still inhabit the homes of Armenians who have not returned, and many are already in ruins.

• Needless to say, all the real estate of the Armenians has been looted by the local Turks; nothing has been returned.

Malatya—June 22

A Kurdish movement and the establishment of a Kurdish club at the behest of the Ittihadists. Preparations for armed resistance.

• The murder of the head of çetes, Muhammad, son of Haşim Bey, in the village of Eğribük, six hours away from Malatya, at the hands of Taslim, son of İbrahim, a villager from Şeyh Hasan.

• The news of this murder caused great anxiety among the Ittihadist Turks of Malatya. They expressed great sorrow for the disappearance of such a helpful person, so much so that Fazıl Bey, one of the captains of the Pensions Fund, was barely saved from certain death by the gendarmes when the angry Ittihadists attacked him for having publicly expressed his satisfaction over the murder of such a criminal.

The next day, the Ittihadists presented themselves to the governor in large numbers. They threateningly demanded that Fazıl Bey be arrested within twenty-four hours and that the assistant public prosecutor—an official of justice—and the chief of penitentiary be forced to resign immediately because they had not arrested Fazıl Bey.

The governor gave in to this threat and telegraphed İstanbul, and Fazıl Bey's house was searched, but they could not apprehend him because he was hiding elsewhere.

The fact is, however, that Fazıl Bey has written a complete detailed history of the oppression and killings perpetrated on Armenians from Erzurum to Malatya, along with the names of all the actors. He has sent a copy of that report to Aleppo and gave another copy to Dr. Barton. It is for this reason that the Ittihadists want to avenge.

• Fazıl Bey's salvation is requested because he is a helpful and righteous Turk.

• Today, more than two hundred ammunition crates were brought from Silvan to Malatya and placed in the government warehouse.

հայ մուխթարին տունը դրուած էր առժամեայ կերպով: Սակայն դժբաղդաբար, գործուած բոլոր ոճրագործութեանց անպատիժ մնալը թուրքերուն այն աստիճան համարձակութիւն տուած է որ, յիշեալ Ալաէտտին նոյն ցերեկին Իզմիթ գալով, մուխթարին բացակայութենէն օգտուած ու յիշեալ աղջիկը բռնի առած ու Գարամուսալ տարած է եւ տեղական կառավարութիւնը ամենապզտիկ դիտողութիւնը իսկ չէ ըրած:

Զանազան գիւղերու մէջ պահակներ (պէքճի) դրուած են կառավարութեան կողմանէ: Այս օրերս հայ գիւղերու պէքճիները թուրք գիւղերը փոխադրելու հրահանգ եկած է. ըստ այնմ Արսլանպէկի մէջ շատոնց գոյութիւն ունեցող պէքճին մօտակայ Չէփնի կոչուած թուրք գիւղը փոխադրուած է:

Գարաման – 28 Յունիս

Մինչեւ հիմա 6 որբեր միայն յանձնուած են, որոնք Գոնիա ղրկուած են: Թէեւ ուրիշ շատեր կան դեռ, բայց զանազան առարկութիւններով չեն ուզեր յանձնել. տեղական կառավարութիւնը անտարբեր է եւ այս որբերուն ու տարագիրներուն համար ամենափոքրիկ նիւթական օժանդակութիւնը չէ ըրած:

- Եկեղեցի, վարժարան եւ ազգային ու անհատական կալուածներ ետ տրուած են, շատերը քայքայուած ու անգործածելի վիճակի մէջ եւ պահանջուած դրամական հատուցման փոխարէն բան մը չէ վճարուած դեռ: Իսկ չվերադարձող հայերու տուները քիւրտ գաղթականներ կը բնակին դեռ եւ շատերն ալ արդէն քայքայուած են:
- Աւելորդ է ըսել թէ՝ հայերու բոլոր անշարժ գոյքերը տեղացի թուրքերու կողմէ կողոպտուած ըլլալով, որեւէ բան վերադարձուած չէ:

Մալաթիա – 22 Յունիս

Քրտական շարժում եւ քրտական քլիւպի մը հաստատումը՝ իթթիհատականներու թելադրութեամբ: Զինեալ դիմադրութեան պատրաստութիւններ:

- Սպանութիւն Չէթէ Րէիսի Հաշիմ պէյ Զատէ Մուհամմէտի Էյրի-Պիւք գիւղին մէջ, 6 ժամ հեռու Մալաթիայէն, եւ ձեռամբ Շէյխ Հասանի գիւղացիներէն Իպրահիմի որդի Թէսլիմի:
- Այս սպանութեան լուրը մեծ յուզում կը պատճառէ Մալաթիոյ իթթիհատական թուրքերուն մէջ. մեծ վիշտ կը յայտնեն իրենց համար այսպիսի օգտակար մէկու մը անհետանալուն համար, այնքան որ թէքաուտի եիւզ պաշիներէն Ֆատլ պէյ հրապարակաւ այդպիսի ոճրագործի մը սպանութեան համար գոհունակութիւն յայտնած ըլլալուն, իթթիհատական ժողովուրդը կը բարկանայ, անոր վրայ կը յարձակի եւ բոլիս ու ժանտարմա հազիւ կարող կ՚ըլլան ստոյգ մահուանէ մը ազատել զայն:

Հետեւեալ օրը, իթթիհատականները մեծ բազմութեամբ կառավարիչին կը ներկայանան եւ սպառնալից կերպով մը կը պահանջեն որ 24 ժամուան մէջ Ֆատլ պէյը պէտք է ձերբակալել եւ Ատլիյէի պաշտօնեայ մուստայի ումումիի մուավինը եւ ճէզա րէյիսին հրաժարիլ տրուին անմիջապէս, որովհետեւ Ֆատլ պէյը չեն ձերբակալած:

Այս սպառնալիքին վրայ կառավարիչ տեղի կուտայ, Պոլիս կը հեռագրէ եւ Ֆատլ պէյի տունը կը խուզարկուի, բայց կարելի չ՚ըլլար ձերբակալել՝ այլուր պահուըտած ըլլալուն:

Իրողութիւնը այն է, սակայն, որ Ֆատլ պէյ, Կարինէն մինչեւ Մալաթիա հայոց վրայ տեղի ունեցած հարստահարութեանց ու սպանութեանց ամբողջական պատմութիւնը իր մանրամասնութիւններովը գրի առած, ինչպէս նաեւ բոլոր դերակատարներուն անունները նշանակած ու այդ տեղեկագրէն օրինակ մը Հալէպ ղրկած ու օրինակ մ՚ալ Տօք. Պարթըլնի տուած է. եւ ասոր համար է որ իթթիհատականները վրէժ լուծել կ՚ուզեն:

- Ֆատլ պէյի ազատումը կը խնդրուի, որովհետեւ օգտակար ու արդարակորով թուրք մըն է:
- Այսօր Տիգրանակերտէն 200 սնտուկէ աւելի ռազմամթերք Մալաթիա բերուած ու կառավարական տէբօին մէջ դրուած է:

Malatya—June 26

A twenty-three-year-old Armenian, the mill guard, was found brutally killed. The perpetrator has not been arrested yet.

• The Commission of Abandoned Properties, contrary to the order of the governor and appeals, refuses to return the Armenian properties and rents them out on behalf of the government.

Of twenty-three hundred Armenian houses in Malatya, three hundred houses exist today. There are heirs among the Armenians of both Malatya and America, but the government refuses to acknowledge their right to inherit, and thus the unfortunate people are being deprived of the proceeds of their estates and fields.

The government's attention needs to be drawn to this situation. If the damages done to the Armenians are not compensated, at least they should not be deprived of their property; otherwise, everyone will starve to death in the near future.

Emirdağ [Aziziye] (Afyonkarahisar)—July 7

[Emirdağ is] sixteen hours away from Afyon; before the deportation, [there were] sixty-five Armenian households, a church, a school with eighty male and female students, and a teacher with a kindergarten principal.

(Only fifteen families whose members included soldiers or artisans were not exiled; now, forty-five Armenian families and twenty-eight Greek families have returned.)

Insecurity and threat of massacre.

Military lieutenant Arif, the author of the Bergama [Pergamon] affair, constantly incites the Turkish mob against Christians and organizes the çetes.

It has become impossible for Christians to go out. A few days ago, an Armenian returning from Emirdağ to Eskişehir was robbed and brutally tortured.

The Neighborhood Council begs that this letter not be published in newspapers whose writings are considered harmful to the people of the district.

Konya (from the Prelacy)—July 12

Through the individual efforts of Cemal Pasha, commander of the local 12th Division, various bands of çetes are being formed in different parts of Konya and the province. Reports of insecurity and the threat of massacre constantly arrive from nearby rural districts, although no serious incident has occurred.

Prefect Cemal Bey fights against the military authorities and considers forming an irregular army harmful, but the local Ittihadists and the people oppose him and exercise every influence to make him resign. The Armenian and Greek communities demand that the prefect remains in office. Despite his weak and hesitant administrative conduct, at least he is not in for extremism, massacre, and pillage.

Tokat—July 15

Solicitation for help for the orphanage, especially clothes, bedding, medicine, shoes, etc.

• The seized properties and estates have not been returned yet.

• For local security and tranquility, the removal from office and the expulsion of the following is requested:

Accountant Gürcü Ahmed.

Faik, a functionary of the Abandoned Properties [Commission].

The imam of Bilari village, Bekir, and Ğarahasan. They have seized the estates of St. John Chrysostom Monastery.

Մալաթիա – 26 Յունիս

23 տարեկան հայ մը, ջաղացքի պահապան, չարաչար սպաննուած գտնուեր է: Ոճրագործը դեռ չէ ձերբակալուած:

- Էմլաքը մէթրուքէի գոմիսիոնը, հակառակ կառավարիչին հրամանին եւ եղած դիմումներուն, կը մերժէ վերադարձնել հայերու կալուածները եւ կառավարութեան հաշուոյն վարձու կուտայ:

Մալաթիայի 2300 տուն հայերէն 300 տունը գոյութիւն ունի այսօր, եւ թէ՛ Մալաթիայի մէջ եւ թէ Ամերիկա գտնուող հայերէն ժառանգորդներ կան. սակայն կառավարութիւնը կը մերժէ ատոնց ժառանգական իրաւունքը ճանչնալ եւ այդպէսով խեղճ ժողովուրդը կը զրկուի իր սեփական կալուածներու եւ արտերու հասոյթներէն:

Այս մասին կառավարութեան ուշադրութիւնը խնդրել հարկ է: Եթէ հայերուն եղած վնասները չեն փոխարինուիր, գէթ իրենց սեփականութենէն չզրկուին, եթէ ոչ յառաջիկային բոլորն ալ անօթի պիտի մեռնին:

Ազիզիյէ (Աֆիոն-Գարահիսար) – 7 Յուլիս

Աֆիոն-Գարահիսարէն 16 ժամ հեռու. տարագրութենէ առաջ 65 տուն հայ, եկեղեցի մը, վարժարան մը 80 երկսեռ աշակերտներով եւ մէկ ուսուցիչ եւ մանկապարտիզպանուհի:

(Որպէս զինուորի ընտանիք եւ արհեստաւոր չեն աքսորուած 15 տուն միայն. իսկ այժմ վերադարձած են 45 տուն հայ եւ 28 տուն յոյն:)

Անապահովութիւն եւ ջարդի սպառնալիք:

Զինուորական տեղապահ Արիֆ, Պէրկամոնի դէպքին հեղինակը, շարունակ կը գրգռէ թուրք խուժանը քրիստոնէից դէմ եւ չէթէներ կը կազմակերպէ:

Քրիստոնէից համար դուրս ելլելը անկարելի դարձած է. քանի մը օրեր առաջ Ազիզիյէէն Էսկիշէհիր դարձող հայ մը ճամբան կը կողոպտուի եւ չարաչար կը խոշտանգուի:

Թաղական խորհուրդը իր այս գրութիւնը կը խնդրէ լրագիրներու մէջ չհրատարակել, որոնց գրուածքները վնասակար կը նկատեն գաւառի ժողովրդեան համար:

Գոնիա (Առաջնորդարանէն) – 12 Յուլիս

Տեղւոյն 12րդ զօրաբաժնի հրամանատար Ճէմալ փաշայի անհատական ջանքերովը, Գոնիայի եւ նահանգին զանազան կողմերը չէթէական խումբեր կը կազմակերպուին: Շրջակայ գաւառակներէն անապահովութեան տեղեկութիւններ կը հասնին շարունակ եւ ջարդի սպառնալիք, թէեւ որեւէ լուրջ դէպք մը պատահած չէ:

Կուսակալ Ճէմալ պէյ կը պայքարի զինուորական իշխանութեանց դէմ եւ վնասակար կը նկատէ անկանոն բանակի մը կազմութիւնը, բայց տեղւոյն իթթիհատականներն ու ժողովուրդը կը հակառակին եւ ամէն ազդեցութիւն կը բանեցնեն զինքը հրաժարեցնելու համար: Հայ եւ յոյն համայնքը կուսակալին պաշտօնի վրայ մնալը կը պահանջեն. հակառակ իրեն թոյլ ու վարանոտ վարչական ընթացքին, գէթ ծայրայեղութեան ու ջարդ եւ թալանի կուսակից չէ:

Թօգատ – 15 Յուլիս

Որբանոցին համար օգնութեան խնդրանք, մասնաւորապէս հագուստ, անկողնի կազմած, դեղ, կօշիկ եւայլն:

- Գրաւեալ գոյքեր ու կալուածները դեռ չեն վերադարձուած:

- Տեղւոյն ապահովութեան ու հանգստութեանը համար հետեւեալներու հրաժարեցումն ու հեռացումը կը խնդրուի:

Հաշուակալ Կիւրճի Ահմէտ:

Էմվալը մէթրուքէի պաշտօնեայ Ֆայիք:

Պիլէրի գիւղին իմամը՝ Պէքիր, եւ Ղարահասան: Այս վերջինները Ս. Յովհան Ոսկեբերանի

Alınca (Eskişehir district) (from the letter of Protestant minister P. Aprahamian of Çalkara)—June 16

Alınca is a village populated by Armenians. Before the war, it had one hundred twenty houses with more than six hundred inhabitants.

• After the exile [deportation], the government accommodated sixty Turkish families in the village, who took over all the estates and properties in the village, and after demolishing most of the houses, there are now barely fifty houses fit for dwelling.

• There are now about fifty returning Armenian families, but despite their appeals, Eskişehir's Muhacirs Commission has not relocated the Turkish villagers. It is always the Turks who sow and enjoy, and the unfortunate Armenians are doomed to starve to death because they cannot gain ownership of their wealth. The official of the Muhacirs [Commission] tries to persuade the Armenians to live with the Turks and benefit from what they have sown, but the experience of several months has shown that these are false promises and living together is impossible.

The removal of Turkish muhacirs is requested.

Yozgat—July 7, 1919

(From the Armenian and Greek spiritual leaders) According to Mustafa Kemal's telegraphic instruction, bands of çetes were organized under the guise of the National Army and took a threatening stance in Yozgat, Boğazlıyan, Akdağmadeni, and the surrounding villages.

The main organizer and instigator of this movement in Yozgat is the well-known Ittihadist mufti.

By gathering many murderers, whom influential notable Turks join, he incites the Muslim mob by all possible means and, in the mosques, preaches boycotting the Christians.

We have telegraphed the şeyhülislam to remove him (the mufti) from Yozgat. We ask the national authorities also to make the necessary appeals and try to make the aforesaid [mufti] resign.

Samsun—July 12

Miss Mariamanoush Dzarougian, a deportee from Samsun to Malatya, after being forced to live there with a Turk for two years, succeeded in escaping and, on the way to Samsun, in a place called Çğala, was abducted and cruelly raped by a gang of thirty-six people. After the unfortunate girl came to herself, she set out and reached Amasya. There, she complained to the governor, but to no avail. Thence she set forth, and near Havza, again, she encountered bandits who took her to the mountain and cruelly tortured her. Finally, escaping again, she succeeded in reaching Samsun, where although she complained [to the authorities], nobody paid attention.

Samsun—July 17

Absolute lawlessness and perfect insecurity in the province of Sivas and the district of Samsun; regularly occurring robbery, murder, and abduction; and this [is so] not only on the roads but even in the cities, where weapons and grenades are distributed freely and daringly.

It has been seen and clearly confirmed that the bands of çetes are in constant contact with the prominent Ittihadists of the cities. Also, the gendarmes sent to arrest the bandits establish intimacy with them instead of doing their job. To date, not a single villain has been arrested.

վանքին կալուածները գրաւած են:

Ալընճա (Էսկիշէհիրի Մութասարրֆութիւն) (Չալկարայէն բողոքական քարոզիչ Բ. Աբրահամեանի նամակէն) – 16 Յունիս

Ալընճա հայաբնակ գիւղ մըն է որ պատերազմէն առաջ կը պարունակէր 120 տուն 600է աւելի բնակիչներով:

- Աքսորէն յետոյ գիւղին մէջ կառավարութիւնը 60 թուրք ընտանիք կը տեղաւորէ, որոնք գիւղին բոլոր կալուածներուն ու գոյքերուն կը տիրանան եւ տուներուն մեծագոյն մասը փլցնելով, այժմ հազիւ բնակելի 50 տուն կայ:

- Վերադարձող հայերը այժմ 50 ընտանիքի մօտ են, բայց հակառակ իրենց դիմումներուն, Էսկիշէհիրի մուհաճիր քօմիսիոնին թուրք գիւղացիները չէ տեղափոխած եւ միշտ թուրքերն են որ կը ցանեն ու կը վայելեն, եւ խեղճ հայերը իրենց պատկանած այդ հարստութեանց չտիրանալով անօթի մեռնելու դատապարտուած են: Մուհաճիրի պաշտօնեան կը ջանայ համոզել հայերը որ թուրքերուն հետ բնակին եւ ցանուածներէն իրենք ալ օգտուին. բայց քանի մը ամսուան փորձը ցցուցած է որ սուտ խոստումներ են եւ կարելի չէ միասին ապրիլ:

Թուրք գաղթականներուն հեռացումը կը խնդրուի:

Եոզկաթ – 7 Յուլիս 1919

(Հայ եւ յոյն առաջնորդներէն) Մուստաֆա Քէմալի հեռագրական հրահանգին համաձայն, Եոզկաթի, Պօղազլեանի, Աքտաղ-Մատէնի եւ շրջակայ գիւղերու մէջ չէթէական խումբեր կազմակերպուած են ազգային բանակ անուան տակ եւ սպառնական դիրք մը բռնած են:

Եոզկաթի մէջ այս շարժման բուն կազմակերպողն ու դրդողը տեղւոյն վրայ ծանօթ իթթիհատական միւֆթին է:

Մարդասպաններու մեծ թիւ մը խմբելով, որոնց միացած են նաեւ տեղւոյն ազդեցիկ երեւելի թուրքերը, ամէն կարելի միջոցներով կը գրգռէ իսլամ խուժանը եւ մզկիթներու մէջ քրիստոնէից դէմ պօյքօթաժ ընել կը քարոզէ:

Չինք (միւֆթին) Եոզկաթէն հեռացնելու համար Շէյխ-իւլ-իսլամին հեռագրած ենք, կը խնդրենք որ ազգային իշխանութիւններն ալ հարկ եղած դիմումները կատարեն եւ ջանան հրաժարեցնել տալ յիշեալը:

Սամսոն – 12 Յուլիս

Օրիորդ Մարիամանուշ Ծառուկեան, տարագրուած Սամսոնէն ի Մալաթիա եւ հոն բռնի թուրքի մը հետ 2 տարի կենակցելէ վերջ կը յաջողի փախչիլ եւ դէպի Սամսոն գալու ճամբուն վրայ, Զղալա կոչուած տեղը 36 հոգինոց աւազակախումբէ մը կ'առեւանգուի ու չարաչար կը բռնաբարուի: Խեղճ աղջիկը յետոյ սթափելով ճամբայ կ'ելլէ ու կը հասնի Ամասիա: Հոն կառավարիչին կը գանգատի, բայց ոչ մէկ արդիւնք: Անկէ ալ ճամբայ ելլելով Խաւզայի մօտերը նորէն աւազակներու կը պատահի, որ զինքը լեռը կը տանին ու չարաչար կը խոշտանգեն: Վերջապէս կրկին փախչելով կը յաջողի Սամսոն հասնիլ, ուր թէեւ կը գանգատի, բայց կարեւորութիւն տուող չ'ըլլար:

Սամսոն – 17 Յուլիս

Բացարձակ անիշխանութիւն եւ կատարեալ անապահովութիւն Սեբաստիոյ վիլայէթին եւ Սամսոնի սանճաքին մէջ. շարունակ կողոպուտ, սպանութիւն եւ առեւանգում. եւ այս ո՛չ միայն ճամբաները, այլ նոյնիսկ քաղաքներուն մէջ, ուր ազատ ու համարձակ զէնք ու ձեռքի պօմպա կը բաժնուի:

Որոշ կերպով տեսնուած ու հաստատուած է որ չէթէի խումբերը քաղաքներու իթթիհատական երեւելիներուն հետ շարունակական յարաբերութեան մէջ են. նոյնպէս աւազակները ձերբակալելու

Great activity and convening of meetings among the local Turks.

The presence of the Allied forces not only has not been an obstacle to the free activity of the Turks but has been even an encouragement when it was seen that they do not make any effective intervention.

Develi [Everek]—July 10[14]

The Armenians who returned to Develi and Fenese, and those who were already there, began to trade in the market. Unable to tolerate this competition, the new Turkish merchants turned to the local mufti. He preached in the mosques to boycott, specifically, those Armenians who, after conversion to Islam, have now converted back to Christianity. He commanded that trading with such people is forbidden according to sharia [Islamic religious law], and thus he works to create a rift between the two elements.

The removal of this mufti is requested.

The church and the school of Fenese have been destroyed, and the church vessels looted. When it was learned that the looter of these properties was Hacı Ahmet Seyitoğlu of İncesu, his house was searched, a sizable lot of [stolen] property was found, and he was imprisoned. But benefiting from the published general amnesty, he has been released despite still retaining other vessels.

There are still fifteen Islamized [Armenian] people in Develi who are afraid to return to Christianity.

Sivas—July 16[15]

Sisag Chalukian, a native of İzmir and a dentist in Harput with a military assignment, traveled to Sivas to go to Samsun with ten or twelve female deportees. On the way, five hours away from Amasya, in a place called İğne-Pazar, armed çetes attacked and killed him and all his companions on Thursday, July 10, and they set the two carriages belonging to him on fire.

[The primate of Sivas], relaying this news in a letter dated 12 inst. from Samsun, says that before Sisag, at the same place, another caravan of Armenian travelers encountered a band of sixty çetes who asked if there was someone named Sisag among them. When the answer was no, the bandits were satisfied with robbing them only.

Thus, it can be concluded that there was a particular pursuit for Sisag because Sisag, a patriotic and energetic young man, had helped the local Armenian population in Harput and secured the return of many orphans held by the Turks. This proves that all these bandits are in contact with identical organizations in distant cities and act unanimously across.

The primate, writing the letter from Sivas, adds that all these and similar incidents are the results of activities and propaganda in these areas by Mustafa Kemal Pasha and his friend, Rauf Bey, whereby from Amasya to Erzurum the Turkish people are provoked and armed, and they try to exterminate the remaining Christians as well by organizing bands of çetes under the name of National Army.

After completing their propaganda in Sivas, Mustafa Kemal Pasha and Rauf Bey left for Erzurum to attend the Turkish Congress.

The names of Sisag Chalukian's companions:

1. Dalida Boyajian	from Fatsa (Black Sea)
2. Azniv and Hagop Krkalian	same
3. Armenouhi Mnatsaganian	from Adabelan

համար ղրկուած ժանտարմաները ո՛չ միայն իրենց պաշտօնը չեն կատարեր, այլ անոնց հետ մտերմական յարաբերութեան մէջ կը մտնեն: Մինչեւ այսօր ոչ մէկ չարագործ չէ ձերբակալուած:

Մեծ գործունէութիւն եւ ժողովներու գումարում տեղւոյն թուրքերու մէջ:

Համաձայնական ուժերու ներկայութիւնը ոչ միայն արգելք մը չէ եղած թուրքերու ազատ գործունէութեան, այլ նոյնիսկ քաջալերանք մը՝ երբ կը տեսնուի որ անոնք որեւէ գործօն միջամտութիւն չեն ըներ:

Էվերէկ – Յուլիս 10

Էվէրէկ եւ Ֆէնէսէ վերադարձող ու արդէն հոն գտնուող հայերը սկսած են շուկան առեւտուրով զբաղիլ: Թուրք նոր վաճառականները չկրնալով հանդուրժել այս մրցման, տեղւոյն միւֆթիին կը դիմեն որ մզկիթներու մէջ կը քարոզէ պօյքօթաժ ընել մասնաւորապէս այն հայերուն դէմ որ իսլամացած ըլլալով այժմ քրիստոնէական կրօնին վերադարձած են: Այդպիսիներու հետ առեւտուր ընել ըստ Շէրիի արգիլուած ըլլալը կը պատուիրէ եւ այդպիսով երկու տարրերուն մէջ գժտութիւն մը յառաջ բերելու կ'աշխատի:

Այս միւֆթիին հեռացումը կը խնդրուի:

Ֆէնէսէի եկեղեցին ու վարժարանը քանդուած են եւ եկեղեցւոյ անօթները կողոպտուած: Տեղեկութիւն քաղած ըլլալով որ այդ գոյքերը կողոպտողը ինճէսուցի հաճի Մէյիտ Օղլու Ահմէտն է, տունը խուզարկել կը տրուի եւ արդարեւ բաւական քանակութեամբ գոյք կը գտնուի եւ զինք ալ կը բանտարկեն: Բայց հրատարակուած ներման օրէնքէն օգտուելով ազատ արձակուած է, մինչդեռ դեռ քովը պահուած ուրիշ անօթներ ունի:

Էվէրէկի մէջ դեռ 15 իսլամացած անձ կայ որ կը վախնան քրիստոնէութեան վերադառնալու:

Սեբաստիա – 16 Յուլիս

Բնիկ իզմիրցի եւ զինուորական պաշտօնով Խարբերդ գտնուող ատամնաբոյժ Սիսակ Չալըքեան, 10–12 տարագիր կիներու հետ Սեբաստիա կուգայ Սամսոն երթալու համար: Ճամբան, Ամասիայէն 5 ժամ հեռու Իյնէ-Բազար կոչուած տեղը զինեալ չէթէներէ յարձակում կրելով, իր բոլոր ընկերներովը միասին կը սպաննուի 10 Յուլիս, հինգշաբթի օրը, եւ իր սեփական երկու կառքերն ալ կ'այրեն:

[Սեբաստիոյ Առաջնորդը] Սամսոնէն 12 թուական նամակով մը այս լուրը տալով, կ'ըսէ թէ հայ ճամբորդներու ուրիշ կարաւան մը, Սիսակէն առաջ, միեւնոյն տեղը, 60 հոգինոց չէթէներու խումբի մը կը հանդիպի, որ կը հարցնեն թէ իրենց մէջ Սիսակ անունով մէկը կը գտնուի՞: Երբ ոչ պատասխանը կը տրուի, այն ատեն աւազակները կը գոհանան միայն զիրենք կողոպտելով:

Ուրկէ կարելի է հետեւցնել թէ՝ Սիսակի մասին մասնաւոր հետապնդում կար, որովհետեւ Սիսակ՝ ազգասէր ու վառվռուն երիտասարդ մը, Խարբերդ գտնուած ատեն տեղւոյն հայ բնակչութեան օգնած եւ թուրքերու մօտը գտնուող շատ մը որբեր ետ առնել տուած է, ինչ որ կ'ապացուցանէ թէ՝ բոլոր այս աւազակախումբերը հաղորդակցութեան մէջ են հեռաւոր քաղաքներու միեւնոյն կազմակերպութեանց հետ եւ ամէնուրեք համախորհուրդ կը գործեն:

Սեբաստիայէն նամակագիր Առաջնորդը կը յաւելու թէ՝ բոլոր այս եւ ասոր նման դէպքերը արդիւնքն են Մուստաֆա Քէմալ փաշայի եւ ընկերոջը՝ Ռէուֆ պէյի, այս կողմերը կատարած գործունէութեան ու բրօբականտին, որով Ամասիայէն մինչեւ Էրզրում գտնուող թուրք ժողովուրդը գրգռուած ու զինուած է եւ ազգային բանակ անուան տակ չէթէներու խումբեր կազմակերպելով, մնացած քրիստոնեաներն ալ բնաջինջ ընելու կը ջանայ:

Մուստաֆա Քէմալ փաշա եւ Ռէուֆ պէյ Սեբաստիոյ մէջ իրենց բրօբականտը ընելէ վերջ, Էրզրում գացած են թրքական համաժողովին մասնակցելու համար:

Սիսակ Չալըքեանի ընկերացողներու անունները

4. Zepyour Veledian	same
5. Arshalouys (Sisag's maid)	from Maden
6. Hripsimé Papazian	from Erzurum
7. Heranoush Papazian	same
8. Araksi Maloyan	from Hınıs
9. Akabi Jendigian	from Ordu
10. Lousia Lapoyan	from Eleşkirt
11. Veron Hadji Janian	from Amasya
12. Veron's 1½-year-old son Noubar	

All of them [are] women and children; it is assumed that two or three of them were left in Tokat and are alive.

1- Տալիտա Պօյաճեան	փաթսացի (Սեւ ծով)
2- Ազնիւ եւ Յակոբ Գրգալեան	նոյն
3- Արմենուհի Մնացականեան	ատապելանցի
4- Ձեփիւռ Վէլէտեան	նոյն
5- Արշալոյս (Միսակի սպասուհին)	մատէնցի
6- Հռիփսիմէ Փափազեան	կարնեցի
7- Հերանուշ Փափազեան	նոյն
8- Արաքսի Մալօեան	խնուսցի
9- Ազապի Ճէնտիկեան	օրտուցի
10- Լուսիա Լաքօեան	ալաշկերտցի
11- Վերոն հաճի Ճանեան	ամասիացի

12- Վերոնի 1 ½ տարեկան զաւակը՝ Նուպար

Բոլորն ալ կին եւ մանուկներ, կ'ենթադրուի թէ ասոնցմէ 2–3 հատը Թոզաթ մնացած ըլլալով, ողջ մնացած են:

[Insecurity] Notebook Number 2
July–August 1919

Yozgat (from the primate)—July 17, 1919[16]

Local authorities are making reclaiming the Islamized [Armenian] women very difficult.

According to an order from İstanbul, Christian girls under the marriage contract (nuptial), even under the age of twenty, cannot be taken back [by us] and will remain Muslims.

Dictated by this instruction, even ten-year-old girls found in Turkish harems are placed under marriage contracts with just anybody; therefore, demanding [their return] has become impossible.

Sivas—July 20

The propaganda and arrangements carried out here by Mustafa Kemal Pasha and former minister of the marine Rauf Bey are proceeding with the same intensity. All the Turks are arming themselves under the guise of guards, and delegates from everywhere are heading to Erzurum to attend the Turkish Congress.

They [the Turks] do not want to hand over the [Armenian] Islamized girls to us. The governor is very unwilling in this regard. He barely allows us to meet with the forcibly Islamized unfortunate girls for half an hour, provided we meet at the seat of government, which is short of inspiring confidence in them and making them confess their Christianity. They [the Turks] keep everyone under constant threat.

Urfa—July 22

Refugee Armenians are gradually returning, but there is no home to live in, no church to pray at, and no job to earn a living.

The confiscated estates, business books, and so on have not been returned; therefore, nowadays hungry and thirsty Armenian estate owners and merchants wait for justice, which is unfortunately delayed.

Turks keep many Armenian girls and boys in Urfa and the surrounding areas as prisoners. Barely three or four were brought here upon our pleas, but here again, they were kept by the Turks, and they were sent back under terrible duress, forced to insist they are Muslims.

Even the favorable instructions from İstanbul are not implemented here. In particular, the governor, the chief of police, and the director of the correspondence office are very fanatic and full of hatred against Armenians. Their removal from here is desirable.

İstanbul—July 23

The current interior minister Adil Bey is known for his wicked past. At the time of the Adana massacre, he was an adviser to the interior minister. He had telegraphed to Adana, saying to protect the foreigners, which was interpreted on the spot [to mean] that only the Armenians should be massacred.

On his advice, those troops belonging to the Thessaloniki army, who were interned in Gelibolu for their rebelliousness, were dispatched to Adana and carried out the Adana massacre.

At that time, a complaint was lodged against him; as a result, he was promoted to be named adviser to the grand vizier and, more recently, supervisor of the land registry and cadastre office.

[Անապահովութեան] Տետր Թիւ 2
1919 Յուլիս – 1919 Օգոստոս

Եոզկաթ (Առաջնորդէն) – 17 Յուլիս 1919

Իսլամացած կիները ետ առնելու մասին մեծ դժուարութիւններ կը յարուցուին տեղական իշխանութեանց կողմանէ:

Պոլսէն եկած հրամանի մը համաձայն, *նիքեահ*ի (պսակ) տակ գտնուող քրիստոնեայ աղջիկները, նոյնիսկ եթէ 20 տարեկանէն վար ըլլան, ետ չպիտի կրնան առնուիլ [մեր կողմէ] եւ իսլամ պիտի մնան:

Այս հրահանգէն թելադրուած, թուրք հարեմներու քովը գտնուած նոյնիսկ 10 տարեկան աղջիկները նիքեահ կ'ընեն որեւէ մէկուն հետ, որով այլեւս անկարելի եղած է զանոնք պահանջելը:

Սեբաստիա – 20 Յուլիս

Մուստաֆա Քէմալ փաշայի եւ նախորդ ծովային նախարար Րէուֆ պէյի հոս կատարած բրօբականտն ու կազմակերպութիւնները նոյն սաստկութեամբ առաջ կը տարուին: Պահակի անուան տակ կը զինուին բոլոր թուրքերը եւ ամէն կողմէ պատուիրակներ կը մեկնին դէպի Էրզրում թրքական համաժողովին մասնակցելու համար:

Իսլամացած աղջիկները չեն ուզեր մեզ յանձնել. կառավարիչը այս մասին շատ անբարեացակամ է. հազիւ կը թոյլատրէ որ կէս ժամու չափ տեսնուինք բռնի իսլամացած դժբաղդ աղջիկներուն հետ եւ այն ալ կառավարչատան մէջ, ինչ որ բոլորովին անբաւական է անոնց վստահութիւն ներշնչելու եւ քրիստոնեայ ըլլալնին խոստովանցնել տալու համար. շարունակական սպառնալիքի տակ կը պահեն բոլորն ալ:

Ուրֆա – 22 Յուլիս

Գաղթական հայերը հետզհետէ կը վերադառնան, բայց ո՛չ բնակելու տուն կայ, ոչ աղօթելու եկեղեցի եւ ոչ ալ ապրուստ ճարելու աշխատանք:

Գրաւուած կալուածները, առեւտրական տետրակները եւայլն ետ չեն վերադարձուիր, որով կալուածատէր ու վաճառական հայեր այսօր անօթի ու ծարաւ արդարութեան կը սպասեն, որ դժբաղդաբար կը յապաղի:

Ուրֆայի եւ շրջականներու մէջ մեծ թիւով հայ աղջիկներ ու տղաքներ կան թուրքերուն քովը բանտարկուած: Ասոնցմէ հազիւ 3–4 հատ հոս բերուեցաւ մեր դիմումներուն վրայ, բայց հոս դարձեալ թուրքերու մօտը պահուեցան, որով սարսափելի սպառնալիքներու տակ, իսլամ ըլլալնին պնդելով, վերստին ետ դարձուեցան:

Պոլսէն եկած նոյնիսկ նպաստաւոր հրահանգները չեն գործադրուիր հոս: Մասնաւորապէս կառավարիչը, բոլիսի միւտիրը եւ թահրիրաթ միւտիրին շատ կրօնամոլ ու հայատեաց են. ատոնց ասկէ հեռացուիլը փափաքելի է:

Կ. Պոլիս – 23 Յուլիս

Այժմեան ներքին գործոց նախարար Ատիլ պէյ իրեն յոռի անցեալովը ծանօթ է: Ատանայի ջարդի ատեն, ներքին գործոց նախարարի խորհրդական էր եւ Ատանա հեռագրած էր թէ՝ օտարականները պաշտպանեցէք, ինչ որ տեղւոյն վրայ մեկնուեցաւ թէ հայերը միայն ջարդեցէք:

Իր խորհրդովն էր որ Ատանա ղրկուեցան Սէլանիկի բանակին մասը կազմող եւ սակայն ըմբոստ գտնուելով Կէլիպօլի արգելափակուած զօրքերը, որոնք կատարեցին Ատանայի ջարդը:

Նոյն թուականին իրեն դէմ բողոք եղած է, որուն իբր արդիւնք պաշտօնի բարձրացում ունենալով եպարքոսական խորհրդական անուանուած է եւ վերջերս ալ տէֆթերհանէի վերատեսուչ:

İstanbul (Dr. Parounag Vosgian, gathered from a trusted traveler from Amasya)—July 28
As Mustafa Kemal Pasha and his companions were leaving after completing the organization of çetes in Amasya and vicinities, it happened that they forgot a case on the road. An Armenian named Avedis Tabakian found it. Then a Greek showed up, and a dispute arose between them. They were obliged to hand the case over to the government of Amasya.

A few hours later, Mustafa Kemal, noticing the loss of the case, returned, interrogated, and bastinadoed the people he met on the way, and when he arrived in Amasya, he was pleased to see that the case was with the governor.

The case was opened, and the few thousand liras cash were handed over to Mustafa Kemal, but the governor refused to give him some documents, which, upon examination, revealed correspondence with Ittihad's center and instructions and reports about the organization of çetes. The governor announced that the papers would be sent to the central government in İstanbul.

Two days later, when the courier left Amasya to head to Samsun, the çetes confronted [the courier] in a place called Boğaz, located very close to the city, and seized the bundle of documents.

Undoubtedly, this comedy has been accomplished with the complicity of government officials and, perhaps, even the governor.

While about two hundred British troops were on their way to Merzifon, they were pressed to stop when faced by a large band of well-armed çetes in a place called Üçhanlar, fifteen hours away from Samsun. It is said that the çetes allowed the departure of the British troops upon receiving instruction from Samsun.

Kayseri (from the primate)—July 23
Mustafa Kemal Pasha pressures the government to form bands of çetes, arm them, and send them to the provinces of Ankara and Eskişehir.

The local governor and the gendarmerie commander oppose the proposal, but the military presses for its immediate implementation. The matter remains unresolved. The governor seems well-disposed, but unfortunately, he is not influential, and the orders given [by the central government or him, possibly] are not carried out.

The Turks have no intention of returning the Armenian properties, and the government is unable to oblige them. The order from the Ministry of Internal Affairs to divide the harvest in half between the Turks and the returning Armenians has not been implemented yet.

There are currently 770 orphans sheltered in the orphanage. There is a great need for clothes; many orphans only have a shirt and a pair of trousers, and they are barefoot.

Presently, the Armenian population of Kayseri consists of thirty-two hundred people, most of whom are extremely wretched. The prosperous class has migrated to Adana, İstanbul, and Konya over the last three or four months.

İstanbul (from the National Assistance)—August 4
From Ankara's envoy: [There is] an organization of çetes in Keskin under the supervision of a Turkish bey.

Turkish migrants returning to Eastern Anatolia are being armed by the government in the provinces of Ankara and Eskişehir.

Կ. Պոլիս (Տօք. Բարունակ Ոսկեան, քաղուած Ամասիայէն եկող արժանահաւատ ճամբորդէ մը) – 28 Յուլիս

Մուստաֆա Քէմալ փաշա եւ ընկերք, Ամասիոյ եւ շրջակայից մէջ իրենց չէթէական կազմակերպութեան գործը լրացունելէ յետոյ, երբ կը մեկնին, մոռացմամբ ճամբան կը թողուն պայուսակ մը: Աւետիս Թապաքեան անուն հայ մը կը գտնէ զայն, յոյն մը վրայ կը հասնի եւ մէջերնին վէճ ծագելով, կը ստիպուին պայուսակը Ամասիոյ կառավարութեան յանձնել:

Քանի մը ժամ վերջ, Մուստաֆա Քէմալ պայուսակին կորուսիլը նշմարելով, ետ կը վերադառնայ, ճամբան հանդիպած անձերը կը հարցաքննէ ու կը զանակոծէ եւ երբ Ամասիա կը հասնի, գոհութեամբ կը տեսնայ պայուսակին կառավարիչին մօտ ըլլալը:

Պայուսակը կը բացուի, մէջը գտնուած քանի մը հազար հնչուն ոսկիները Մուստաֆա Քէմալի կը յանձնուի, բայց կառավարիչը կը մերժէ իրեն տալ կարգ մը թուղթեր, որոնք քննուելով կը հասկցուի թէ Իթթիհատի կեդրոնի հետ թղթակցութիւններ եւ չէթէական կազմակերպութեան վերաբերեալ հրահանգներ ու տեղեկագիրներ են: Կառավարիչը կը յայտարարէ թէ բոլոր այդ թուղթերը Պոլիս կեդրոնի կառավարութեան պիտի ղրկուին:

Երկու օր յետոյ, երբ Ամասիոյ սուրհանդակը դէպի Սամսոն ճամբայ կ'ելլայ, քաղաքին շատ մօտը *Պօղազ* ըսուած տեղը չէթէներ կը դիմաւորեն ու բռնի կ'առնեն թղթածրարը:

Տարակոյս չկայ թէ կառավարական պաշտօնեաներու եւ նոյնիսկ թերեւս կառավարիչին մեղսակցութեամբ է որ կատարուած է այդ քօմէտին:

200ի մօտ անգլիացի զինուորներ դէպի Մարսուան մեկնելու առթիւ, Սամսոնէն 15 ժամ հեռու, Իւչ-Խանլար կոչուած տեղը, լաւ զինուած չէթէներու ստուարաթիւ խումբի մը հանդիպելով, կանգ առնել կը ստիպուին: Կ'ըսուի թէ՝ Սամսոնէն եկած հրահանգի մը վրայ է որ չէթէները չեն արգիլեր անգլիացի զինուորներու մեկնումը:

Կեսարիա (Առաջնորդէն) – 23 Յուլիս

Մուստաֆա Քէմալ փաշայի կողմէ ճնշում կ'ըլլայ կառավարիչին վրայ, որպէսզի չէթէական խումբեր կազմելով, զանոնք զինէ եւ Գաղատիա ղրկէ:

Տեղւոյն կառավարիչն ու ժանտարմա գոմանտանին կ'ընդդիմանան այս առաջարկի գործադրութեան, իսկ զինուորականները կը ստիպեն որ անմիջապէս գործադրուի. խնդիրը դեռ լուծուած չէ: Կառավարիչը բարեացակամ ըլլալ կը թուի, բայց դժբաղդաբար ազդեցիկ չէ եւ տրուած հրամանները չեն գործադրուիր:

Թուրքերը հայերու գոյքերը վերադարձնելու բնաւ միտում չունին, կառավարութիւնն ալ ստիպելու կարող չէ: Յառաջիկայ հունձքը թուրքերու եւ վերադարձող հայերու մէջ կէս առ կէս բաժնելու մասին ներքին գործոց նախարարութենէն եկած հրամանը չէ գործադրուած դեռ:

Որբանոցին մէջ այժմ 770 որբեր կը պատսպարուին, զգեստի շատ պէտք կայ, որբերէն շատերը միայն շապիկ վարտիկ մը ունին, ոտքերնին ալ բոպիկ է:

Այս պահուս Կեսարիոյ հայ բնակչութիւնը կը բաղկանայ 3200 անձերէ, մեծ մասամբ ծայրայեղ թշուառ: Բարեկեցիկ դասակարգը այս վերջին 3–4 ամիսներու մէջ գաղթած է դէպի Ատանա, Պոլիս եւ Գոնիա:

Պոլիս (Ազգային Խնամատարութենէն) – 4 Օգոստոս

Էնկիւրիի պատուիրակէն.- Քէսկինի մէջ չէթէական կազմակերպութիւն թուրք պէյի մը հսկողութեամբ:

Արեւելեան Անատոլու վերադարձող թուրք գաղթականները Գաղատիոյ մէջ կը զինուին կառավարութեան կողմէ:

Niğde—July 1

The Turks still hold many orphan girls not delivered [to the Armenians].

Out of three hundred fifty houses, there are barely fifteen habitable houses today; the rest are demolished. The church and the school also are destroyed; even the cemetery stones have vanished.

During the deportation, it had been decided to send local Armenians to Aleppo via Elbistan, which meant their extermination due to the journey's length and difficulty. The people, terrified, through a mediator, gave one thousand liras as a bribe to the principal Ittihadists and managed to change the abovementioned decision and travel to Aleppo via Adana.

One part of the population was entirely robbed in Kemerhisar [Kilisehisar], and the other part in Ulukışla by the gendarmes and the police. About fifty families managed to travel by train from Ulukışla by giving two hundred fifty liras as a bribe, but the rest traveled on foot and [the men] mainly were robbed and killed; the children and girls were abducted.

Samsun—July 12

(From the Administrative Council) On July 4, in the village of Şükyan, a village of Çarşamba, the çetes Beşiroğlu İbrahim, Fayiq, Abdullah, Salih, and other companions from the village of Saraçlı abducted a priest's daughter and son.

Two months ago, a woman named Zonag was abducted from the same village. She vanished without any trace.

There have been many such incidents within Samsun's environs. Unfortunately, the government does not exercise force and goodwill to arrest and punish the perpetrators, and the Allied forces intervene indirectly, always through the Turkish government, wherefore practical results cannot be obtained.

Tekirdağ (from the primate)—July 13

Insecurity and impossibility of working in the fields. On July 12, two Armenian coachmen heading from Malkara to Tekirdağ were attacked and looted. One of them, Yesayi, was stabbed with bayonets and seriously wounded by regular soldiers one hour away from the city.

Tremendous activity of çetes. Two days ago, forty-four soldiers fled the local army with their weapons.

Malatya (from Garabed Kulujian)—July 16

The Armenians of Malatya used to comprise twenty-three hundred households or fifteen thousand people. Today, there are five hundred families (two thousand inhabitants). One hundred thirty-five are men, and the rest are women and children.

About twenty Armenian families have been able to earn enough money. Eighty Armenian households can live [by their means], but the rest are totally needy.

There are currently four hundred orphans in the orphanage, in very pitiful condition; there is a need for immediate assistance. One hundred sixty-five orphans were collected and sent to their birthplaces. The Turks still hold more than six thousand orphans. Should the government, especially the Allies, help, they can be collected promptly.

• Governor Bedirhani Halil Ra[h]mi Bey is quite kind to Armenians and wants to be just to the extent the environment allows. The Turkish notables have initiated intrigues to secure his resignation.

• An announcement from Malatya signed as Ali Suzi was publicized containing the following:

Նիկտէ – 1 Յուլիս

Թուրքերու քով կը գտնուին դեռ շատ մը որբուհիներ որոնք վերադարձուած չեն:

350 տուներէն այսօր բնակելի հազիւ 15 տուներ կան, մնացեալները քանդուած են: Կողոպտուած են նոյնպէս եկեղեցի ու վարժարան. գերեզմաննոցին քարերը իսկ անհետացած են:

Տեղահանութեան միջոցին որոշուեր է տեղւոյն հայերը Էլլիսթանի ճամբով Հալէպ ղրկել, ինչ որ բոլորին բնաջնջումը կը նշանակէ ճանապարհին երկարութեանն ու դժուարութեանը պատճառաւ: Ժողովուրդը սարսափահար, միջնորդի մը միջոցաւ 1000 ոսկի կաշառք կուտայ գլխաւոր իթթիհատականներուն եւ կը յաջողի փոխել տալ վերոյիշեալ որոշումը եւ Ատանայի ճամբով Հալէպ մեկնիլ:

Ժողովուրդին մէկ մասը Քիլիսահիսար, միւս մասն ալ Ուլու-Գըշլա բոլորովին կը կողոպտուին ժանտարմներու ու բոլիսներու կողմանէ, 50ի մօտ ընտանիքներ 250 ոսկի կաշառքով կը յաջողին Ուլու-Գըշլայէն երկաթուղիով ճամբորդել, իսկ մնացածները հետիոտն կ'երթան եւ մեծ մասամբ կը կողոպտուին, կը սպաննուին ու մանուկներն ու աղջիկներն ալ կ'առեւանգուին:

Սամսոն – 12 Յուլիս 1919

(Վարչական Ժողովէն) Յուլիս 4ին, Չարշամպայի գիւղերէն Շիւկեանի գիւղին մէջ, քահանայի մը աղջիկը եւ մանչը Սարաճըը գիւղի չէթէներէն Պէշիր Օղլու Իպրահիմ, Ֆայիզ, Ապտուլլահ, Սալիհ եւ ուրիշ ընկերներէ կ'առեւանգուին:

Երկու ամիս առաջ դարձեալ նոյն գիւղէն Զօնակ անուն կին մը առեւանգուած է եւ հետքը կորսուած:

Այս կարգի դէպքերը պակաս չեն Սամսոնի շրջանակին մէջ: Դժբաղդաբար կառավարութիւնը ուժ ու բարի կամք դրած չունի չարագործները ձերբակալել ու պատժելու համար, իսկ Համաձայնական ուժերը ուղղակի չեն միջամտեր, այլ միշտ թուրք կառավարութեան միջոցաւ, որով որեւէ գործնական արդիւնք կարելի չէ ձեռք ձգել:

Ռօտօսդօ (Առաջնորդէն) – 13 Յուլիս

Անապահովութիւն եւ դաշտային աշխատանքի անկարելիութիւն: Յուլիս 12ին Մալկարայէն դէպի Ռօտօսդօ դարձող երկու հայ կառապաններ քաղաքէն 1 ժամ հեռու կանոնաւոր զինուորներու կողմանէ յարձակում կը կրեն, կը կողոպտուին եւ մին ալ` Եսայի, ծանրապէս կը վիրաւորուի սուինի հարուածներով:

Չէթէական մեծ գործունէութիւն: Երկու օր առաջ, տեղւոյն բանակէն 44 զինուոր իրենց զէնքերովը փախած են:

Մալաթիա (Կարապետ Գըլըճեանէ) – 16 Յուլիս

Մալաթիոյ հայութիւնը առաջ 2300 տուն կամ 15000 բնակչութենէ կը բաղկանար. այսօր կայ 500 տուն (2000 բնակիչ): Ասոնցմէ 135ը այր մարդիկ. մնացածը կը բաղկանայ կին եւ տղաքներէ:

Քանի տունի չափ հայեր բաւական դրամ կրցած են շահիլ: 80 տունի մօտ հայեր ալ կրնան ապրիլ, իսկ մնացածները բոլորովին կարօտ են:

Որբանոցին մէջ կան այս պահուս 400 որբեր, շատ արգահատելի վիճակի մէջ. անմիջական օգնութեան պէտք կայ: 165 որբեր ալ հաւաքելով իրենց ծննդավայրերը ղրկուած են: 6000էն աւելի որբեր կան դեռ թուրքերու մօտ: Եթէ կառավարութիւնը, նամանաւանդ Համաձայնութիւնը օգնեն, կարելի է զանոնք շուտով հաւաքել:

- Կառավարիչ Պէտիր Խանի Խալիլ Րա[հ]մի պէյ բաւական բարեացակամ կը գտնուի հայոց հանդէպ եւ միջավայրի ներած սահմանին մէջ կ'ուզէ արդարութիւն գործադրել: Թուրք մեծամեծները սկսած են էնթրիկներ ընել զինքը հրաժարեցնել տալու համար:

- Մալաթիայէն Ալի Սուզի ստորագրութեամբ կոչ մը հրատարակուած է հետեւեալ պարու-

"This place is alleged to be Armenia. Can you imagine the consequences of such an arrangement? The Armenians will kill us, our country and possessions will be seized, and all kinds of atrocities will be committed; therefore, we must arm ourselves beginning now and prepare to resist and die bravely. We are ready to provide weapons if you do not have them."

Boğazlıyan—July 23

The gang of Menteşeli Rıza—the perpetrator of the Armenian massacre—has been released on bail through bribery by gendarmerie commander Nuri Eff[endi]. The Armenian population is now in the mountains. As in the past, the sale of women continues.

Dağkonak [Nerekh] (from the Administrative Council)—July 25

Population: Before the war, twelve hundred Armenian families (five thousand people); now, only thirty families returned. Insecurity and constant persecution and intimidation; looted movable and immovable properties have not been returned, nor have the orphans and Islamized women.

Yozgat—July 28

Five men, three teenagers, and three women, a total of eleven Armenians, after leaving Yozgat to earn a living, have disappeared on the road between Yozgat and Boğazlıyan. According to reliable information obtained, the men were killed, and the women were abducted.

Konya (from the primate) [letter] No. 477—July 30

Ten days before this date, after the disciplinary committee from İstanbul departed Konya, the American Major Furlong and the Englishman captain Mr. Hall, accompanied by a Cretan Turk, Talat Bey, arrived in Konya.

After two days of close contact with the Turks, this commission invited the Armenians on the third day. The Armenian primate, Mr. Antoine Afkerian from the Catholic community, Reverend Hampartsoum Ashjian and Mr. H. Semerjian from the Protestants, and neighborhood council member Mr. Chokkarian represented the Armenian side.

Major Furlong asked what [kind of] political regime they would like regarding Turkey's future.

The visit lasted three hours, and after presenting particularly the history of injustices and atrocities committed during the war, the Armenians declared that they would never want to be under Turkish rule again.

The major tried to convince them that a twenty-year-long American mandate over Turkey would completely change the situation and improve conditions in Turkey; then it would be possible to return Turkey to the Turks with all confidence.

The Armenians remained steadfast and demanded separation.

Major Furlong insisted and even demanded that he be given a written and signed assurance in accordance with his instructions. [The Armenians] refused.

Yozgat (from M. Khalasian, representative of the National Assistance)—July 30

The rural district of Mecidiye, where six Armenian families live in very pitiful conditions, is on the road from Kırşehir to Yozgat.

There are also sixty Armenian families in the village of Saray, four hours away from Yozgat; they are the remnants of 150 Armenian families [living] in a very pitiful and miserable condition.

Four hundred orphans are gathered in Yozgat, all leprous and skeletal. There are about 610 recip-

նակութեամբ. «Հոս Հայաստան պիտի ըլլայ եղեր: Կրնաք երեւակայել այսպիսի կարգադրութեան մը հետեւանքները: Հայերը զմեզ պիտի սպաննեն, մեր երկիրն ու ինչքերը պիտի գրաւուին եւ ամէն տեսակ անգթութիւններ պիտի գործուին, ուստի այժմէն պէտք է զինուինք ու պատրաստուինք դիմադրել եւ քաջաբար մեռնիլ: Եթէ զէնք չունիք, մենք պատրաստ ենք հայթայթելու»:

Պօղազլեան – 23 Յուլիս

Le commandant de gendarmerie Nouri Eff[endi] ayant remis en liberté, moyennant une somme d'argent, la bande de Mentéchéli Riza, auteur du massacre des arméniens, la population arménienne s'est enfin dans les montagnes. On continue comme par le passé la vente des femmes.[4]

Նէրէկ (Վարչական ժողովէն) – 25 Յուլիս

Բնակչութիւն.- Պատերազմէն առաջ 1200 տուն հայ (5000 հոգի). այժմ վերադարձած՝ 30 տուն միայն: Անապահովութիւն եւ շարունակական հալածանք ու սպառնալիք, կողոպտուած շարժուն ու անշարժ գոյքերը չե՛ն վերադարձուած եւ ոչ ալ որբերն ու խլամացած կիները:

Եոզկաթ – 28 Յուլիս

Ապրուստ հայթայթելու համար Եոզղաթէն մեկնող 5 այր, 3 պատանի եւ 3 կին, ընդամէնը 11 հայեր, Եոզկաթի եւ Պօղազլեանի մէջտեղ, ճամբան անհետացած են: Առնուած ստոյգ տեղեկութեանց համաձայն այրերը սպաննուած, իսկ կիներն ալ առեւանգուած են:

Գոնիա (Առաջնորդէն) [նամակ] թիւ 477 – 30 Յուլիս

Պոլսէն մեկնող խռատիչ յանձնաժողովին Գոնիայէն մեկնելէն վերջ, այս թուականէն 10 օր առաջ Գոնիա կը ժամանեն ամերիկացի հազարապետ Փուրլօնկ, անգլիացի հարիւրապետ պր. Հօլ, որոնց կ'ընկերանար կրետացի թուրք մը՝ Թալաթ պէյ:

Այս յանձնաժողովը երկու օր շարունակ թուրքերու հետ սերտ յարաբերութեան մէջ ըլլալէ վերջ, երրորդ օրը իրեն մօտ կը հրաւիրէ հայերը: Հայոց կողմէ կը ներկայանան՝ հայոց Առաջնորդը, կաթոլիկ համայնքաւորութենէն պր. Անթուան Աֆքէրեան, բողոքականներէն պատուելի Համբարձում Աշճեան եւ պր. Ն. Սէմէրճեան եւ թաղական խորհուրդի անդամ պր. Չօքքարեան:

Հազարապետ Փուրլոնկ կը հարցնէ թէ՝ Թուրքիոյ ապագայի մասին քաղաքական ի՞նչ ձեւ կը փափաքին:

Տեսակցութիւնը կը տեւէ 3 ժամ եւ մանաւորապէս պատերազմի միջոցին տեղի ունեցած անիրաւութեանց ու վայրագութեանց պատմականը ընելէ վերջ, հայերը կը յայտարարեն թէ՝ բնաւ չպիտի ուզեն նորէն թուրք տիրապետութեան ենթարկուիլ:

Հազարապետը կը ջանայ համոզել թէ՝ քսան տարուան ամերիկեան mandat մը Թուրքիոյ վրայ կացութիւնը բոլորովին պիտի փոխէր ու Թուրքիոյ վիճակը բարւոքէր, եւ յետոյ ամենայն վստահութեամբ կարելի պիտի ըլլար Թուրքիան նորէն վերադարձնել թուրքերուն:

Հայերը անդրդուելի կը մնան եւ բաժանում կը պահանջեն:

Հազարապետ Փուրլօնկ կը պնդէ եւ կը պահանջէ նոյնիսկ որ իր թելադրութեանց համեմատ գրաւոր ու ստորագրեալ ապահովագիր մը յանձնուի իրեն, ինչ որ կը մերժուի:

Եոզկաթ (Մ. Խալասեանէ, Խնամատարութեան ներկայացուցիչ) – Յուլիս 30

Գըր-Շէհիրէն Եոզկաթ ճամբուն վրայ կայ Մէճիտիյէ գաւառակը, ուր շատ արգահատելի վիճակի մէջ կ'ապրի 6 տուն հայութիւն մը:

Նոյնպէս Եոզկաթէն 4 ժամ հեռու Սէրայ գիւղին մէջ կը գտնուին 60 տուն հայեր. մնացորդը՝ 150 տուն հայութեան մը, շատ արգահատելի ու թշուառ վիճակի մէջ:

Եոզկաթի մէջ հաւաքուած են 400 որբեր, ամէնքն ալ բորոտած ու կմախքացած: 610ի չափ

ients of relief in the city. This region needs help; there is tremendous misery, and the need for help is immediate.

Bandırma (from the primate)—July 31
Organizing the çetes is progressing feverishly; insecurity in all surrounding villages. Secret meetings and great activity among the Turkish element.

Two days ago, a Greek torpedo boat anchored at the port. Immediately, soldiers mounted on horseback were deployed in the surrounding villages, and as a result, the city was filled with a large crowd of armed çetes within a few hours.

At night, a large barge tried to enter the port but was spotted and stopped by the torpedo boat, and its contents—weapons, Mauser rifles, machine guns, and so on—were seized.

Meetings have been convened in Balıkesir, and Ali Riza Bey, lawyer Mehmet, and others have been dispatched as delegates from Bandırma. It has been heard that this assembly decided to rebel against the central government and declare independence.

Weapons continue to be distributed to all Turks.

Nallıhan (from the Neighborhood Council)—July 31
Ittihad's local representative Ramazzade Ahmed, who caused the destruction of the Armenians of Nallıhan [before the armistice], was arrested and sent to Ankara upon the protest of the locals. Although investigations and witnesses proved him to be the culprit, the court did not punish him. He was released on bail as the protégé of Muhittin, the governor-general, and he journeyed to İstanbul to live at Hotel Europe in Sirkeci.

The arrest and trial of the mentioned are requested.

Bursa (from the primate)—August 1
There is always alarming news of insecurity from the vicinities. Yesterday, a search of the Industrial School in Bursa turned up seven hundred Mauser rifles. If the searches continue, a large number of weapons can still be found.

Tütüncü Hakkı, who has been a fugitive for some time and has dramatically harmed the Armenians of Bursa, was arrested upon the primate's request. Konyalı İbrahim, a criminal as dangerous as the one mentioned, is allegedly roaming in İstanbul unhindered. His arrest is requested.

Keskin [Denek Madeni] (from the National Assistance)—August 3[17]
There is absolute insecurity; it is impossible to travel.

- Native[s] Shmavon Boghchelian and Krikor Zeytounjian, while traveling for trade, were robbed by çetes three hours away from the city.
- Twenty-seven armed çetes attacked Ahallı village and stole many cattle.
- On the way to the provinces of Ankara and Eskişehir, seven armed men attacked a coachman named Mikayel. They took the horse of the carriage. The coachman fled and was saved.
- Manasé Baghdadlian, on his way back from the provinces of Ankara and Eskişehir, was chased by the çetes but escaped by taking a different path.
- Armenag Tahmazian was getting ready to go to the provinces of Ankara and Eskişehir to buy goods. A Turkish friend advised him not to travel because the journey of an Armenian would be immediately reported to the çetes by their organizations in the city.
- To prevent Avedis Masoumian from having national activities in this city, they are trying to accuse him of being the killer of two Russian captives.

նպաստաւորեալներ կան քաղաքին մէջ. այս շրջանը օգնութեան կարօտ է, շատ մեծ թշուառութիւն կը տիրէ եւ պէտք կայ անմիջական օգնութեան:

Պանտըրմա (Առաջնորդէն) – 31 Յուլիս

Չէթէական կազմակերպութիւնը առաջ կը տարուի տենդագին. անապահովութիւն բոլոր շրջակայ գիւղերը: Գաղտնի գումարումներ եւ մեծ գործունէութիւն թուրք տարրին մէջ:

Երկու օր առաջ յունական թորփիլանաւ մը կուզայ խարսխել նաւահանգիստը: Անմիջապէս հեծեալ ոստիկան զինուորներ շրջակայ գիւղերը կը ցրուին եւ իբր արդիւնք քանի մը ժամ յետոյ քաղաքը զինեալ չէթէներու բազմութեամբ մը կը լեցուի:

Գիշերը խոշոր մավունա մը նաւահանգիստ մտնել կը փորձէ, բայց թորփիլանաւէն նշմարուելով կ'արգիլուի ու մէջը գտնուած զէնք, մավզէր, գնդացիր եւայլն կը գրաւուին:

Պալըքէսիրի մէջ ժողովներ կը գումարուին, Պանտրմայէն պատուիրակ կը ղրկուին Ալի Րիզա պէյ, փաստաբան Մէհմէտ եւ ուրիշներ: Կը լսուի թէ այս ժողովը որոշեր է կեդրոնի կառավարութեան դէմ ապստամբելով անկախութիւն հռչակել:

Կը շարունակուի զէնք բաժնել բոլոր թուրքերուն:

Նալլու-Խան (Թաղական Խորհուրդէն) – 31 Յուլիս

Իթթիհատի տեղային ներկայացուցիչ Րամէզ Զատէ Ահմէտ, որ Նալլու-Խանի հայութեան փճացման պատճառ եղած էր, տեղացիներու բողոքին վրայ ձերբակալուած ու Էնկիւրի ղրկուած էր: Եղած քննութիւնները եւ վկաները թէեւ ապացուցած էին յիշեալին յանցապարտութիւնը, բայց դատարանը զայն չպատժեց եւ վալի Մուհէտտինի պաշտպանեալը ըլլալուն, երաշխաւորութեամբ ազատ արձակուած ու Պոլիս գալով, Սիրքէճի, Եւրոպա օթէլը կը բնակի:

Յիշեալին ձերբակալումն ու դատուիլը կը խնդրուի:

Պրուսա (Առաջնորդէն) – 1 Օգոստոս

Շրջականերէն անապահովութեան տագնապալի լուրեր կան միշտ: Երէկ անգլիական իշխանութեանց կողմէ Պրուսայի Սէնաիի վարժարանը խուզարկուելով 700ի չափ մավզէր հրացան կը գտնուի: Եթէ խուզարկութիւնները շարունակուին, դեռ շատ քանակութեամբ զէնք գտնել կարելի է:

Պրուսայի հայութեան մեծապէս վնասող Թիւթիւնճի Հազզը, որ ժամանակէ մը ի վեր փախստական էր, կը ձերբակալուի Առաջնորդին դիմումին վրայ: Յիշեալին հաւասար վտանգաւոր ոճրագործ Գոնեալը Իպրահիմ Պօլսոյ մէջ ազատ կը պտտի եղեր. ձերբակալել տրուիլը կը խնդրուի:

Տէնէք-Մատէն (Ազգային Խնամատարութենէն) – 3 Օգոստոս

Բացարձակ անապահովութիւն կայ. անկարելի է ճամբորդելը:

- Տեղացի Շմաւոն Պողչեանեան եւ Գրիգոր Չէյթունճեան, առեւտուրի համար ճամբորդած ատեննին, քաղաքէն 3 ժամ հեռու տեղ մը չէթէներու կողմէ կը կողոպտուին:

- 27 զինեալ չէթէներ Ախալը գիւղին վրայ յարձակելով շատ մը աւար կը գողնան:

- 7 զինեալ չէթէներ Գաղատիոյ ճամբուն վրայ Միքայէլ անուն կառապանի մը վրայ յարձակելով կառքին ձին կ'առնեն, իսկ կառապանը փախչելով կ'ազատի:

- Մանասէ Պաղտատլեան, Գաղատիայէն վերադարձին, չէթէներու կողմէ կը հետապնդուի, բայց կը յաջողի ազատիլ տարբեր ճամբայէ մը երթալով:

- Արմենակ Թահմազեան ապրանք գնելու համար կը պատրաստուի Գաղատիա երթալու: Իրեն բարեկամ թուրք մը խորհուրդ կուտայ իրեն չմեկնիլ, որովհետեւ որեւէ հայու մը ճամբորդութիւնը անմիջապէս իմաց կը տրուի չէթէներուն, քաղաքին մէջ անոնց ունեցած կազմակերպութեանց կողմէ:

- Աւետիս Մասումեանի քաղաքիս մէջ ունեցած ազգային գործունէութեան արգելք ըլլալու

• The headquarters of the band of çetes is a village called Beyoba, where all the groups gather under the command of a bandit leader named Kaplan Bey. The bands raid the surrounding villages.

Complaints from Armenian and Muslim townspeople remain unheard by the governor, who openly encourages these perpetrators.

In this situation, a few local intelligent Armenians, under the constant threat of both çetes from outside and the Turkish armed mob from inside, will be forced to depart and leave the work of relief and caregiving in complete disarray.

Zonguldak (from the Neighborhood Council)—August 4[18]

The Armenian population of Devrek, awestruck by the threatening stance of the local Turkish element, is getting ready to migrate to Zonguldak.

Hagop Tanielian, one of them, was robbed somewhere a quarter of an hour away from Zonguldak. Four or five days after this incident, Roupen Keshishian, a fellow Armenian traveling from Zonguldak to Devrek, was killed en route. Despite the presence of the French gendarmerie in Zonguldak, our complaints have resulted in no practical effect regarding security.

Because of unheard-of insults and ruthless barbarity that the deported Armenians traveling by Seyr-i-Sefain's steamships are subjected to, it is recommended not to send deported Armenians henceforth by the steamships of that Turkish company.

Ezine (Çanakkale [Dardanelles]) (from the priest)—August 13

Barely one hundred of Ezine's four hundred [Armenian] residents have returned. Before the deportation, many returnees had their homes sealed as a deposit in exchange for a loan. The homes were sold during their deportation. Today, the returnees remain on the street unprotected. To remedy such injustice, it is necessary to hastily publish a new law that repeals the law of abandoned properties.

Bursa (from the primate)—August 13[19]

At night, groups of young Turks roam the city and shoot; by day, they are openly enlisted as çetes in the markets.

Ittihadists and criminals exiled under the previous prefect have returned to Bursa and continuously make grave threats against Christians. The situation is becoming dangerous; the Armenians are so frightened that the prosperous class has begun to migrate to İstanbul, and the rest are asking the nation to help them so that they may go to İstanbul or some other safe place for at least a while.

The presence of several Allied soldiers would secure everything and perhaps prevent serious dangers.

Aksaray (Konya) (from the Neighborhood Council)—June 29

Only thirty to forty families are left out of 216 in the city. Of the national estates, only the kindergarten and the girls' school above it have been returned. Half of the Armenian houses are entirely destroyed, and the other half are uninhabitable. As for the claims of refugees from the Commission of Abandoned Properties, Niğde's government has not even responded. The government is unwilling to hand over the orphans and the few Islamized women voluntarily.

համար, կը ջանան զինքը ամբաստանել իբր երկու ռուս գերիներու սպանիչ:

- Չէթէախումբի կեդրոնատեղին Պէյ-Օպա կոչուած գիւղն է, ուր կը հաւաքուին բոլոր խումբերը Գաբլան պէյ կոչուած աւազակապետին հրամանին տակ եւ կ'ասպատակեն շրջակայ գիւղերը:

Հայ եւ իսլամ քաղաքացիներու կողմէ եղած բողոքները անլսելի կը մնան կառավարիչին կողմէ, որ յայտնապէս կը քաջալերէ այդ չարագործները:

Այս կացութեան մէջ, տեղւոյս քանի մը հայ բանիմաց անձերը, արտաքուստ չէթէներու եւ ներքուստ զինեալ թուրք խուժանին շարունակական սպառնալիքին տակ, պիտի ստիպուին հեռանալ եւ բոլորովին անկերպարան վիճակի մը մատնել նպաստի ու խնամատարութեան գործը:

Զօնկուլտաք (Թաղական Խորհուրդէն) – 4 Օգոստոս

Տէվրէկի հայ բնակչութիւնը, տեղւոյն թուրք տարրին բռնած սպառնալից դիրքէն ահաբեկ, հետզհետէ դէպի Զօնկուլտաք գաղթելու վրայ է:

Անոնցմէ Յակոբ Դանիէլեան, Զօնկուլտաքէն ¼ ժամ հեռաւորութեամբ տեղ մը կը կողոպտուի: Այս դէպքէն 4–5 օր վերջ, Զօնկուլտաքէն Տէվրէկ մեկնող Ռուբէն Քէշիշեան ազգայինը ճամբան կը սպաննուի: Հակառակ Զօնկուլտաքի մէջ ֆրանսական ժանտարմըրիի ներկայութեան, մեր բողոքները գործնական արդիւնք մը չունեցան ապահովութեան տեսակէտէն:

Սէյր-Սէֆայինի շոգենաւերով ճամբորդող տարագիր հայերը, շոգենաւին մէջ անլուր անպատուութիւններու եւ անգութ խժդժութիւններու նշաւակ լինելնուն, յետ այսու այդ թուրք ընկերութեան շոգենաւերով տարագիր չղրկուիլը կը յանձնարարուի:

Էգինէ (Տարտանէլ) (քահանայէն) – 13 Օգոստոս

Էգինէի 400 [հայ] բնակիչներէն հազիւ 100ը վերադարձած է: Վերադարձող ժողովուրդէն քանիներ տարագրութենէն առաջ իրենց տուները *խթամէ* ըրած փոխառութեան փոխարէն աւանդ ձգած ըլլալով, իրենց տարագրութեան ատեն ծախուած եւ այսօր վերադարձնուն անպատսպար փողոցը մնացած են: Այս կարգի անիրաւութեանց դարման մը կարենալ տանելու համար, *էմլաքը մէթրուքէ*ի օրէնքը ջնջող նոր օրէնքին փութով հրատարակումը անհրաժեշտ է:

Պրուսա (Առաջնորդէն) – 13 Օգոստոս

Գիշերները խումբ խումբ թուրք երիտասարդներ կը պտտին քաղաքին մէջ եւ հրացանաձգութիւն կ'ընեն. ցերեկները հրապարակաւ շուկաներու մէջ չէթէ կ'արձանագրուին:

Նախորդ կուսակալի օրով աքսորուած իթթիհատականներ ու չարագործներ Պրուսա վերադարձած ու քրիստոնէից դէմ շարունակ ծանր սպառնալիքներ կ'ընեն: Կացութիւնը վտանգաւոր ըլլալ կը սկսի, հայ բնակչութիւնը այնքան ահաբեկած է որ բարեկեցիկ դասակարգը սկսած է Պոլիս գաղթել, իսկ մնացածներն ալ կը խնդրեն որ ազգը օգնէ եւ զէթ ժամանակի մը համար Պոլիս եւ կամ ուրիշ ապահով տեղ մը մեկնին:

Համաձայնական քանի մը զինուորներու ներկայութիւնը ամէն բան պիտի ապահովէ եւ թերեւս ծանր վտանգներու առջեւը պիտի առնէ:

Ագ-Սէրայ (Գոնիա) (Թաղական Խորհուրդէն) – 29 Յունիս

Քաղաքի 216 ընտանիքներէն միայն 30-40 ընտանիք մնացած է: Ազգային կալուածներէն միայն մանկապարտէզը եւ անոր վերնայարկը եղող աղջկանց վարժարանը վերադարձուած է: Հայոց տուներուն կէսը բոլորովին քանդուած են եւ մնացեալներուն ալ կէսը անբնակելի են: Դարձող գաղթականներուն էմվալը մէթրուքէէ պահանջներու մասին Նիկտէի կառավարութենէն նոյնիսկ պատասխան չէ տրուած: Որբերը եւ քանի մը իսլամացած կիները կառավարութիւնը ինքնաբերաբար տալու տրամադիր չէ:

Konya-Aksaray (from the primate of Konya)—August 22

Thirteen abducted female Armenians and orphans remain held by the Turks, despite the primate's official notes and telegrams to Niğde's governor; they remain in the Turks' hands. The governor has not even acquiesced to answer.

Kastamonu (from the primate)—August 2

In the entire diocese, only five percent of the men deported to remote areas have returned alive. The rest [of the parishioners] are in dire need, deprived of their capital and large and small plows.

• Security has been disrupted for a month. There are rumors that a Milli army is being formed and that Turkish çetes are being trained, presumably to oppose the formation of a Pontic government. Moving back and forth from place to place has become dangerous. Sellers in the markets are generally robbed. Murders also happen from time to time. A month ago, an Armenian named Roupen Keshishian, traveling from Zonguldak to Devrek, disappeared. He is said to have been killed.

Merzifon (from the National Assembly)—July 19

A month ago, the dragoman of the American consul in Harput, Haroutyun Begmezian, was attacked by bandits near the village of Uygur in the middle of Amasya-Çengelkayı when he was returning from Harput to Merzifon. They robbed him of all his belongings and left him on the road completely naked. They also robbed his companions—women and children—who, too, were returning from deportation. Haroutyun came to Amasya barefooted. He presented himself to the district governor, who took no action.

In the same way, a score of travelers was robbed on the same road. One of them, an Armenian girl, was brought to the city's outskirts and left in a half-dead state after being raped in every way. Hearing her screams, Armenians took her.

• On July 6, dentist Dr. Sisag Chalukian of İzmir was surrounded by bandits again on [the road to] Uygur. The said person worked in Harput and Malatya after the armistice. He tried to free hundreds of orphans besides girls and women confined in Turkish harems. Apparently, he invited great hatred upon himself because, during all previous robberies, a question became customary: "Are you the dentist?" Finally, they managed to take hold of him when he was coming to Merzifon with two carriages and accompanying two women, four girls, two Armenian coachmen, and two little orphans. The robbers numbered twenty-five people. Their first question was: "Which of you is a dentist?" The robbers drove the two carriages entirely to the mountain. To the complaint made to him, the district governor responded that the incident happened outside his jurisdiction. It has been verified that the dentist, as well as the Armenian coachmen, were killed, and the women are being held by various Turks, such as Kara Osman's nephew İzzet, Paşalıoğlu Mevlut, Cin Hasan, Çatal Zamdan, and Sarı Ömer's sons. It was verified later that they, too, were killed. This crime is premeditated in every aspect.

• The bandits' leader is Nalband İzzetın Kyamil, the former mayor of Amasya and a well-known Ittihadist fugitive whom many have seen in the city with fifty to sixty çetes.

• The Armenians in Amasya and its environs are in a state of panic. The Turks are making threats. There is no opportunity to complain about the crimes being committed. Even a hint people do not make. "Why do you make so much noise for five or ten Armenians, [acting] as if you are saved?" they say.

• Two months ago, Mustafa Kemal Pasha, preoccupied with the [Milli] organization, went to the

Գոնիա-Ազմէրայ (Գոնիայի Առաջնորդէն) – 22 Օգոստոս

13 հատ առեւանգուած հայուհիներ եւ որբեր, որոնք տակաւին թուրքերու մօտ կը գտնուին, հակառակ առաջնորդին Նիյտէի կառավարիչին ուղղած թագրիրներուն եւ հեռագիրներուն, կը մնան դեռ թուրքերու ձեռքը: Կառավարիչը նոյնիսկ պատասխան տալու չէ զիջած:

Գասթէմունի (Առաջնորդէն) 2 Օգոստոս

Բոլոր վիճակին մէջ հեռաւոր վայրեր տարագրուած այրերը միայն 5% համեմատութեամբ ողջ դարձած են եւ մնացեալները կը գտնուին զրկուած իրենց դրամագլուխէն, իրենց արօրէն ու գութանէն, խիստ կարօտ վիճակի մէջ:

- Ապահովութիւնը խանգարուած է ամիսէ մը ի վեր. շշուկներ կան թէ Միլլի բանակ կը կազմուի, թէ թուրք չէթէներ կը պատրաստուին, իբր թէ Պոնտոսի կառավարութեան մը կազմակերպուելուն դէմ դիմադրելու համար: Տեղ տեղ երթեւեկը վտանգաւոր դարձած է. *փաքարճի*ներ առհասարակ կը կողոպտուին. մերթ ընդ մերթ սպանութիւններ ալ կը պատահին: Ասկէ ամիս մը առաջ Զօնկուլ-տաքէն Տէօվրէկ գացող Ռուբէն Քէշիշեան անուն հայ մը անյայտ եղած է: Կ'ըսուի թէ սպաննուած է:

Մարզուան (Ազգային Ժողովէն) – 19 Յուլիս

Մէկ ամիս առաջ Խարբերդի ամերիկեան հիւպատոսին թարգմանը՝ Յարութիւն Պէկմէզեան, Խարբերդէն Մարզուան դարձած ատեն Ամասիա-Չէնկէլի մէջտեղ Ույկուր բռնած գիւղին մօտերը յարձակում կը կրէ աւազակներէ, որոնք բոլոր ունեցածը կը կողոպտեն եւ բոլորովին մերկ կը ձգեն ճամբուն վրայ: Կը կողոպտեն նաեւ իր ընկերուհիները, որոնք եւս տարագրութենէ վերադարձող կիներ եւ մանուկներ էին: Յարութիւն բոկոտն եւ քալելով կուգայ Ամասիա եւ կը ներկայանայ միւթէսարրըֆին, որ ռեւէ ձեռնարկ չ'ըներ:

Միեւնոյն ձեւով տասնեակ մը ճամբորդներ կը կողոպտուին նոյն ճամբուն վրայ: Ասոնց մէջ է հայ աղջիկ մը, որ ամէն կերպ բռնաբարելէ յետոյ կը բերեն քաղաքին եզերքը կիսամեռ վիճակի մէջ կը ձգեն: Իր ճիչերը լսելով հայեր կ'առնեն զինքը:

- Յուլիս 6ին դարձեալ Ույկուրի վրայ իզմիրցի ատամնաբոյժ Տոք. Սիսակ Չալըգեանը կը շրջապատուի աւազակներէ: Յիշեալը զինադադարէն վերջը կը գործէր Խարբերդ եւ Մալաթիա եւ հարիւրաւոր որբեր եւ թուրք հարեմներու մէջ արգելափակուած աղջիկներ եւ կիներ ազատելու աշխատած էր, կ'երեւի թէ բուռն ատելութիւն հրաւիրած էր իր վրայ, վասնզի բոլոր նախորդ կողոպուտներու միջոցին «տիշճի սէն միսին» [Ատամնաբո՞յժ ես] հարցումը սովորական եղած էր: Այս անգամ կը յաջողին զինքը ձեռք անցնել, երբ անիկա Մարզուան կուգար երկու կառքերով եւ հետը ունէր 2 կին, 4 աղջիկ, 2 հայ կառապան եւ 2 փոքրիկ որբեր: Աւազակները 25 հոգի էին: Իրենց առաջին հարցումը կ'ըլլայ «Տիշճի հանկըս[ը] [Ատամնաբոյժը ո՞ր մէկէրնիդ է]»: Աւազակները երկու կառքերը լեռ քշած են ամբողջութեամբ: Միւթասարըֆի եղած բողոքին անիկա պատասխանած է թէ դէպքը իր սահմանէն դուրս տեղի ունեցած է: Ստուգուած է որ ատամնաբոյժը, ինչպէս նաեւ հայ կառապանները, սպաննուած են, իսկ կիները զանազան թուրքերու քով, ինչպէս՝ Գարա Օսմանըն Եկէնի Իզզէթ, Փաշալը Օղլու Մէվլուտ, Ճին Հասան, Չաթալ Զամտան Սարը Էօմէրի տղոց քովը: Յետոյ կը ստուգուի թէ ասոնք ալ սպաննուած են: Այս ոճիրը ամէն կերպով կանխամտածուած է:

- Աւազակներու պարագլուխն է Ամասիոյ երբեմնի թաղապետութեան նախագահ եւ ծանօթ իթթիհատական փախստական Նալպանտ Իզզէթին Քեամիլ, որ զինուած 50–60 չէթէներով քաղաքին մէջ տեսնողներ շատ են:

- Ամասիա եւ շրջակայքը գտնուող հայերը ահուսարսափի մէջ են: Թուրքերը սպառնալիքներ կ'ընեն: Կատարուած ոճիրներուն համար բողոք բառնալու կարելիութիւն չկայ: Նոյնիսկ ակնարկութիւն մը չեն ըներ: «5–10 հայու համար այսքան աղմուկ ինչո՞ւ կ'ընէք, իբր թէ դուք փրկուած էք» կ'ըսեն:

- Ասկէ երկու ամիս առաջ թէշքիլաթով զբաղող Մուսթաֆա Քէմալ փաշան ներսերը գացած է

interior districts to organize. In Merzifon, he was replaced by Mehmet Arif Bey, commander of the Fifth Caucasian Division. This man summoned the local notables blind lawyer Nedim and Topçu Baytar Emin Lutfi to Amasya by a special invitation. They spent the night in the barracks with the chiefs of the çetes and devised plans. His advisers are the leader of çetes deputy Nafiz, gang leader Aksıkalı Kâzım, a fruit-seller officer Sami, Topcoğlu Mustafa Bey, mufti Tevfik Hafız, the director of the office of correspondence Mustafa Bey, the judge, and Sadık, the history teacher of the School of Sultaniye. They have decided that if the foreigners take a single step forward, a score of Armenians there will be annihilated immediately because the Armenians, in the past and the present, have presumably been the cause of foreigners' invasions of Turkey. At the end of this meeting, all the members retired to the house of Şeyh Mevlevi and immediately invited the çetes of the neighborhood, all armed. The Armenians and Greeks, seeing these bold movements of the murderers who had been in hiding after the armistice, are terrorized and ask for help.

• An appeal was made to Allied representative Mr. Geisel and General Controller Captain Solder in Samsun about this situation, the crimes committed, and the robbery. But it did not help at all.

Solder plays with the lives of our remnants with his slothful and licentious lifestyle. Only Mr. Geisel, this kindhearted and daring missionary, did all he could without waiting for instruction from his supreme commander. He threatened the district governor that he would be held accountable if he did not find the perpetrators and return the kidnapped. However, no results were seen. Mr. Geisel also appealed to Captain Solder, who is said to be acting simply as a bribed Turkish functionary. It is suspected that hundreds of reports have been left neglected.

M[amuret]-ul-Aziz (from A. Z. Yeghoyan)—July 28

Barkev Halajian, Zakar Garabedian, Sarkis Kaplakian, and Hagop Yeramian, who were wrongfully sentenced to three years in prison and have eight months left to serve their sentences, remain in prison. Mgrdich Krikorian was sentenced to ten years and still has seven years. They did not benefit from the amnesty.

Keskin [Denek Madeni] (from the Neighborhood Council)—August 10

Kaplan Bey's band of çetes is moving ahead with its marauding in the surrounding villages. It is committing many atrocities, whereby complete anarchy has been generated throughout the region, and the government is powerless and unable to prosecute them. On August 9, the çetes of Kaplan Bey entered the villages of Burhanlı and Şerid Mumlu and after perpetrating tortures, looted a significant number of cattle, horses, jewelry, and other items. Villagers came to the city to complain to the lieutenant governor, but their appeal was fruitless. The lieutenant governor did not even try to take action. Disturbed by this alarming situation, the local Armenians want to leave the city as soon as possible. Migration has become widespread, and they heed no exhortation. Official bodies also are inclined to abandon the organized school, the church, and the orphanage to leave the city. Help is sought regarding this situation.

Adana (from Dr. Kachperouni, plenipotentiary of the National Assistance)—August 24

կազմակերպելու համար: Մարզուանի մէջ զինքը կը փոխանորդէ հինգերորդ կովկասեան զօրաբաժնի հրամատարը, սպայակոյտի տեղակալ Մէհմէտ Արիֆ պէյ: Այս մարդը մասնաւոր հրահանգով Ամասիա կանչած է տեղւոյս երեւելիներէն փաստաբան կոյր Նէտիմ եւ Թօփճու Պայթար Էմին Լութֆին: Ասոնք գիշերները չէթէապետներու հետ կը գումարուին զօրանոցը եւ միշտ խորհուրդ կ'ընեն: Իր խորհրդակիցներն են չէթէի գլուխ մէպուս Նաֆըզը, չէթէ պաշի Ախսխալը Քեազիմը, մրգավաճառ սպայ մը՝ Սամի, թաղապետութեան նախագահ Թօփճիօղլու Մուսթաֆա պէյ, միւֆթի Թէյֆիգ Հաֆըզ, թաիրիրաթ միւտիրի Մուսթաֆա պէյ, դատըն, Մէքթէպի Սուլթանիյէի պատմութեան ուսուցիչ Սատըգ: Ասոնք որոշած են որ եթէ օտարները մէկ քայլ իսկ առաջանան, այն ատեն մէջտեղ գտնուած տասնեակ մը հայերը պէտք է անմիջապէս բնաջնջել, որովհետեւ իբր թէ հայերը անցեալին եւ ներկային մէջ պատճառ եղած են օտարներուն Թուրքիա ասպատակելուն: Այս ժողովը լրանալէ վերջ, բոլոր անդամները քաշուած են Մէվլէվի շէյխին տունը եւ հոն անմիջապէս շրջակայքի չէթէները հրաւիրած են բոլորն ալ զինուած: Հայերը եւ յոյները տեսնելով զինադադարէն յետոյ ծածկուած մարդասպաններու այս համարձակ շարժումները, լեղապատառ եղած են եւ օգնութիւն կը խնդրեն:

- Այս դրութեան եւ գործուած ոճիրներուն եւ կողոպուտին համար դիմում կը կատարուի Համաձայնական ներկայացուցիչ Մր. Կէզըլի եւ Ընդհանուր Գօնթրօլըր Գէբբըն Սօլտրի ի Սամսոն: Սակայն ոեւէ օգուտ չէ ունեցած:

Սօլտըր իր մեղկ ու շուայտ կեանքով կը խաղայ մեր մնացորդին կեանքերուն հետ: Միայն Մր. Կէզըլ, այս բարեսիրտ եւ յանդուգն միսիօնարը, առանց իր վերին հրամանատարին հրահանգին սպասելու ըրած է ինչ որ կրնայ եւ սպառնացած է միւթասարըֆին թէ զինքը պատասխանատու պիտի բռնէ եթէ ոճրագործները չգտնէ եւ առեւանգեալները չվերադարձնէ: Սակայն ոեւէ արդիւնք չտեսնուեցաւ: Մր. Կէզըլը դիմած է նաեւ Գէբբըն Սօլտըրի, որուն համար կ'ըսուի թէ պարզապէս կաշառուած թուրք պաշտօնեայի մը պէս կը գործէ եւ կասկած կայ թէ հարիւրաւոր տեղեկագիրներ աննկատ մնացած են:

Մ[ամուրէթ] իւլ Ազիզ (Ա. Զ. Եղոյեանէ) – 28 Յուլիս

Բանտին մէջ [յ]անիրաւի դատապարտութեամբ բանտարկուած կը մնան Պարգեւ Հալաճեան, Զաքար Կարապետեան, Սարգիս Գափլաքեան եւ Յակոբ Երամեան, որոնք երեքական տարուան դատապարտուած եւ 8 ամիս եւս ունին իրենց պայմանաժամը լրացնելու: Իսկ Մկրտիչ Գրիգորեան դատապարտուած է 10 տարուան եւ դեռ ունի 7 տարի: Ընդհանուր ներումէն ասոնք չեն օգտուած:

Տէնէք Մատեն (Թաղական Խորհուրդէն) – 10 Օգոստոս

Գաբլան պէյի չէթէախումբը շրջակայ գիւղերու վրայ իր ասպատակութիւնները յառաջ կը տանի եւ բազմաթիւ ոճիրներ կը գործադրեն, որով բոլոր շրջանին մէջ առաջ եկած է կատարեալ անիշխանական վիճակ եւ կառավարութիւնը անզօր [է] եւ չի կրնար հետապնդում կատարել: Օգոստոս 9ին Գաբլան պէյի չէթէները Պուրհանլը եւ Շէրիտ Մումլը գիւղերը մտնելով խոշտանգումներ ի գործ դնելէ յետոյ կարեւոր թուով արջառ, ձի, զարդեղէն եւ այլ տեսակ գոյքեր իբր աւար կ'առնեն: Գիւղացիք քաղաք կուգան գայմագամին բողոքելու, սակայն իրենց դիմումը արդիւնք չ'ունենար: Գայմագամը ոեւէ ձեռնարկ ընելու փորձ իսկ չ'ըներ: Տեղւոյն հայերը այս տագնապալի կացութեան առջեւ շփոթած կ'ուզեն ժամ առաջ քաղաքէն հեռանալ: Գաղթը ընդհանուր բնոյթ առած է եւ ոչ մէկ յորդորի կ'անսան: Կազմակերպուած դպրոցը, եկեղեցին ու որբանոցը լքանելով քաղաքէն մեկնելու տրամադրութիւն կայ նաեւ պաշտօնական մարմիններու կողմէ: Օգնութիւն կը խնդրուի այս կացութեան հանդէպ:

Ատանա (Տոքթ. Քաջբերունիէ, Խնամատարութեան լիազօր) – 24 Օգոստոս

Ֆուրնուզի եւ շրջանակներու բնակչութիւնը կեանքի ամենաանհրաժեշտ պէտքերէն զուրկ

The population of Fırnız and its environs is forced to live under trees and rocks, deprived of the most basic necessities of life. Thousands of their animals, goods and chattels, and all their wealth have been seized by the government or looted by their neighbors. Their lives here do not inspire any security. Armed gangs roam around the villages. Recently, three Armenians were killed near Fırnız for no reason, just to satisfy their [the Turks'] usual savagery. To prevent these military men from annihilating the Armenians and to bring a serious and immediate remedy for the safety of life and the return of all the properties seized from the Armenians, Dr. Kachperouni went to Aleppo.

Konya (from the primate)—August 26

During the absence of the prefect, threatening letters signed as "Young Officers" were dropped in the homes of the Greek metropolitan Prokopios and two Greeks. An appeal was made to the Turkish and Allied authorities, and an investigation was requested. There is no result yet.

• On August 10–12, two Turkish military planes made circles over the city and dumped packages wrapped in the shape of telegraph strips, particularly in Christian neighborhoods. The strips were blank, but people feared printed strips would be dropped the next time. The incident was reported to the Allies.

• During the week that ended, a few Turks from known circles arrived in Konya from Afyonkarahisar and, using the prefect's absence, contacted local Turkish circles to persuade them to have Konya support the realization of "Milli movements."

• On August 23, thirty-five Muslims convicted of crimes escaped Karaman's prison. Some of them were killed by guards. An appeal has been made to the prefecture and the British authorities.

• It is understood from reports that arrived from Ereğli, Karaman, Akşehir, and Burdur, which fall within the jurisdiction of the diocese, that the people are in need. The governor has secured fifteen hundred new gendarmes and fifty policemenfor the province from the central government. Three days ago, two hundred fifty Italian troops from Eskikarahisar arrived in Konya and settled in the Armenian neighborhood. About fifteen hundred British and colonial forces came to Eskikarahisar. Karaman, Ereğli, and other inland towns are still without Allied forces.

• Last night, Niğde's district governorate handed over to the prelacy two sisters from Kayseri, Sima and Arshagouhi, whom two Tatar cousins held.

Emirdağ [Aziziye] (from the Neighborhood Council)—August 13

For several days now, all the Turks have been preoccupied with ammunition and organizing bands of çetes: a threatening and dangerous [situation]. Weapons are distributed to the [Turkish] people of the villages to ready them to annihilate the Armenians and to revolt during the occupation of the Eastern Provinces. Due to their predominance, Armenians are terrified, and many are migrating to Adana. Meanwhile, forty-five to fifty families, deprived of livelihood, are in confusion. Villages are the source of livelihood for many, but the unfortunate people, unable to get out of the city, are confined to their houses. Insults against Armenians by Turks are common. Help is requested.

Diyarbakır (from the National Assistance)—July 23

ստիպուած է ծառերու եւ ժայռերու տակ ապրիլ: Ասոնց հազարաւոր կենդանիները, կահ կարասիները, ամբողջ հարստութիւնը գրաւուած են կառավարութենէն կամ կողոպտուած իրենց դրացի գիւղացիներէ: Հոս անոնց կեանքը ոչ մէկ ապահովութիւն չի ներշնչեր: Զինուած աւազակախումբեր գիւղերու շուրջ կը պտտին: Վերջին օրերս, Ֆուրնուզի մօտ, երեք հայեր սպաննուեցան առանց ռեւէ պատճառի, գոհացնելու համար միայն իրենց սովորական վայրագութիւնը: Թոյլ չտալու համար այս զինուորականներու՝ հայերը բնաջնջել եւ ուզելով լուրջ եւ անմիջական դարման մը տանիլ կեանքի ապահովութեան համար եւ վերադարձնել տալու համար հայերու գրաւուած բոլոր ինչքերը, Հալէպ մեկնած է Տոք. Քաջբերունի:

Գոնիա (Առաջնորդէն) – 26 Օգոստոս

Կուսակալին բացակայութեան միջոցին «Երիտասարդ Սպաներ» ստորագրութեամբ սպառնական նամակներ ձգուած են յունաց մետրոբոլիտ Տ. Բրոքբիոսի, ինչպէս նաեւ երկու յոյներու բնակարանները: Դիմում եղած է թուրք եւ Համաձայնական իշխանութեանց մօտ եւ քննութիւն պահանջուած: Դեռ արդիւնք չկայ:

- Օգոստոս 10–12ին քաղաքին վրայ շրջած են թուրք զինուորական երկու օդանաւեր եւ հեռագրի երիզներու ձեւով փաթթուած ծրարներ նետած են մասնաւորաբար քրիստոնեայ թաղերու մէջ: Ձեռք անցուած երիզները պարապ էին, սակայն կը վախցուէր որ յաջորդ անգամ տպագրուած պիտի ձգուէր: Դէպքը Համաձայնականաց հաղորդուեցաւ:

- Վերջացող շաբթու ընթացքին Աֆ[իոն] Գարահիսարէն Գոնիա հասած են ծանօթ շրջանակներու պատկանող կարգ մը թուրքեր եւ օգտուելով կուսակալին տեղէս բացակայութենէն՝ յարաբերութիւն մշակած են տեղացի թուրք շրջանակներու հետ, համոզելու համար որպէսզի Գոնիա եւս սատարէ «Միլլի շարժումներու» իրագործման:

- Օգոստոս 23ին Գարամանի բանտէն ոճիրի ամբաստանութեամբ դատապարտուած 35 իսլամներ փախած են: Ասոնցմէ մէկ քանիները սպաննուած են պահակ ոստիկաններու կողմէ: Կուսակալութեան եւ անգլիական իշխանութեանց դիմում կատարուած է:

- Վիճակին ենթակայ Էրէկլիէ, Գարամանէ, Ագ-Շէհիրէ եւ Պուրտուրէ հասած տեղեկագիրներէ կը հասկցուի թէ ժողովուրդը կը գտնուի կարօտութեան մէջ: Կուսակալը կեդրոնէն ապահոված է նահանգին համար 1500 նոր ոստիկան զինուոր, ինչպէս նաեւ 50 ոստիկան: Գարահիսար գտնուող իտալական 250 զօրք երեք օր առաջ Գոնիա եկած են եւ հաստատուած հայոց թաղին մէջ: Իսկ Գարահիսար եկած են 1500ի մօտ անգլիացի եւ գաղթային զօրք: Գարաման եւ Էրէկլի եւ միւս ներքին քաղաքները տակաւին զուրկ կը մնան Համաձայնական ոյժերէն:

- Նիկտէի միութէսարըֆութեան կողմէ երէկ երեկոյ առաջնորդարան յանձնուեցան երկու թալթար հօրեղբօրորդիներու մօտ գտնուող կեսարացի երկու քոյրեր՝ Սիմա եւ Արշակուհի:

Ազիզիյէ (Թաղական Խորհուրդէն) – 13 Օգոստոս

Քանի մը օրերէ ի վեր թուրք ժողովուրդը ռազմամթերքի եւ չէթէյական կազմակերպութեանց մէջ է, որ սպառնալից եւ վտանգաւոր է: Գիւղերու ժողովրդեան զէնք կը բաժնուի, որպէսզի պատրաստ ըլլան, ի հարկին հայ ժողովուրդը բնաջինջ ընելու եւ Արեւելեան Նահանգաց գրաւումին ժամանակ ապստամբութիւն հանելու համար: Իրենց գերակշռութիւնը մեծ ըլլալով հայոց սարսափը մեծ է եւ շատեր կը գաղթեն Ատանա, իսկ 45–50 ապրուստի միջոցներ[է] զուրկ ընտանիքները շփոթած են: Շատերուն ապրուստի միջոցները գիւղերն են, եւ խեղճերը քաղաքէն դուրս չկրնալով ելլել, տուները փակուած են: Հայոց դէմ թուրքերու կողմէ նախատինքներ սովորական են: Օգնութիւն կը խնդրուի:

Տիարպէքիր (Ազգային Խնամակալութիւն) – 23 Յուլիս

Քաղաքին մէջ դեռ իսլամներու մօտ կան մօտաւորապէս 400–500 որբեր, որոնք իբր սպասաւոր

Muslims in the city still hold about four to five hundred orphans. They are being used as servants. And in the environs, that is, in the villages, they count more than one thousand. The government has taken no steps to return them to the [Armenian] nation. Those taken are cared for with great difficulty due to insufficient means. It is impossible to prepare for the forthcoming winter. There is no medicine either. To date, the [Armenian] nation cares for four hundred ten orphans and widows, feeding them with great difficulty.

Yozgat (from the Political Council)—August 28

Almost three months ago, three men, six women, and four children, altogether thirteen people from Yozgat, arrived in Kayseri to make a living and settled in the Turkish village of Akın, three hours away from the city. The next day, two men (Kevork and Hagop) set out for Kayseri and were killed between the villages of Akın and Alagöz, in a place mentioned as Yozgat İni or Beşik Tepe or Döl Tepesi by Hamdi, son of Şaban of Akın and his friend Palali Mehmet of the village Yazır. They robbed them of three Ottoman gold liras, ten Ottoman lira banknotes, a watch, and two donkeys, then buried their bodies. Two days later, their families discovered the incident and came to Kayseri to appeal to the government and the American Near East Relief in Talas. The government took no action. The remaining eleven Armenians reached Yozgat on August 26 in extreme misery. The governor of Kayseri responded to the appeal of [Armenian] national authorities of Yozgat by refuting the information.

• According to a telegraphic order issued by the prefect of Ankara on May 17, the former governor of Yozgat, Levon Bey, had formed a commission called "Situational Justice Commission" [Equitable Panel], consisting of two Turkish and two Armenian members. Through this commission, the Armenians were able to easily acquire their cattle and other properties held by the Turks. On the third day of his arrival, the new governor abolished the commission and is tearing up the petitions, ordering all applicants to go to court.

Yozgat (from the Political Council)—August 25

The Ministry of Internal Affairs has issued a strict order to prosecute the organizers of the Milli movement and to disperse the organizations, but the local government is turning a blind eye, and the order remains unenforceable. Yozgat, its environs, and all the inner provinces alike are in turmoil, and the Turks are agitated. Decent Turks secretly advise us to appeal to proper entities, and they say that the Ittihadists have seized military power and intend to exterminate the Christians. For the past two weeks, Ittihadist leaders and high-ranking military officers have been visiting in disguise, and they are being hosted by the military authorities, and after accomplishing their plan, they are heading toward Sivas to be ready for the congress scheduled for September 1. Even though the minister of internal affairs strictly ordered their arrest and dispatch, under watch, to the military tribunal in İstanbul, the local government, acting upon the commands of the Ittihadists, is inviting the leaders of the çetes and bandits. They are enlisting çetes with their men, giving them generous salaries. Some of the çetes are being sent to Armenia, while others remain in this city. Governor Levon Bey, whom decent Turks were pleased with, was transferred to Kırşehir by a single telegram from the mufti.

• Ittihadist leaders and fugitives Ceritzade Hüsnü Bey, Divanlızade Hamdi Bey, and Hayrizade Osman Bey, who had been convicted as companions of Lieutenant Governor Kemal—the leading actor in the deportation and massacre of the Armenians of Yozgat and sentenced to death—began to roam freely and daringly, with no one to apprehend them.

կը գործածուին: Իսկ շրջակաները, այսինքն գիւղերը 1000է աւելի կը հաշու[ու]ի: Կառավարութիւնը զանոնք ազգին դարձնելու համար ոեւէ ձեռնարկ չէ ըրած: Առնուածները մեծ դժուարութեամբ կը խնամուին, որովհետեւ միջոցները անբաւական են: Առաջիկայ ձմեռուան պէտքերը հոգալ կարելի չէ: Դեղ ալ չկայ: Մինչեւ հիմա ազգը կը հոգայ 410 որբ եւ այրի, որոնք մեծ դժուարութեամբ կը կերակրուին:

Եօզկատ (Քաղաքական Ժողովէն) – 28 Օգոստոս

Գրեթէ երեք ամիս առաջ եօզկատցի 3 այր, 6 կին, 4 տղայ, ընդամէնը 13 հոգի իրենց ապրուստը հայթայթելու համար տեղ տեղ շրջելով կը հասնին Կեսարիա եւ կ'իջեւանին քաղաքէն 3 ժամ հեռու Ազ-Ին թուրք գիւղը: Հետեւեալ օրը իրենցմէ երկու այր (Գէորգ եւ Յակոբ) Կեսարիա երթալու համար ճամբայ կ'ելլեն, Ազ-Ին ու Ալակէօզ գիւղերուն միջեւ Եօզկատ Ինի կամ Պէշիք Թէփէ եւ կամ Տէօլ Թէփէսի ըսուած տեղը աւազակ ազ-ինցի Շապանի որդի Համտիի եւ ընկերոջ՝ Եազըր գիւղ[ա]ցի Փալալը Մէհէմէտի կողմէ կը սպաննուին: Իրենց վրայ գտնուած երեք օսմ. ոսկի ոսկեղրամը, 10 օսմ. ոսկիի թղթադրամը, ժամացոյցը եւ երկու էշերը կը կողոպտեն եւ անոնց դիակները կը թաղեն: Երկու օր յետոյ եղելութիւնը իրենց ընտանիքները կ'իմանան եւ Կեսարիա գալով կը դիմեն կառավարութեան եւ Թալասի ամերիկեան մարմնոյն: Կառավարութիւնը ոեւէ ձեռնարկ չ'ըներ: Մնացեալ 11-ը օգոստոս 26ին հասան Եօզկատ յետին թշուառութեան մէջ: Եօզկատի ազգային իշխանութեանց կողմէ Կեսարիոյ կառավարիչին եղած դիմումին ալ կառավարիչին կողմէ տեղեկութիւնը հերքուելով պատասխանուած է:

- Էնկիւրիւի կուսակալին 17 Մայիս թուակիր մէկ հեռագրական հրամանին համաձայն, Եօզկատի նախորդ կառավարիչ Լեւոն պէյ կազմած էր «հէյէէթի ատիլէ գոմիսիոնը» անուամբ յանձնաժողով մը, 2 թուրք եւ 2 հայ անդամներէ բաղկացեալ: Այս յանձնաժողովին միջոցաւ հայերը թուրքերու քով իրենց գտած արջառները եւ այլ գոյքերը դիւրաւ կ'առնէին: Նոր կառավարիչը իր ժամանումի երրորդ օրը ջնջեց յիշեալ յանձնաժողովը եւ բոլոր դիմողներուն կը հրամայէ դատարան դիմել եւ աղերսագիրները կը պատռէ:

Եօզկատ (Քաղաքական Ժողով[էն]) – 25 Օգոստոս

Ներքին գործոց նախարարութենէն խիստ հրաման ղրկ[ու]ած է հետապնդելու Միլլի շարժման կազմակերպիչները եւ ցրու[ելու] կազմակերպութիւնները, սակայն տեղական կառավարութիւնը աչք կը գոցէ եւ այս հրամանը անգործադրելի կը մնայ: Ոչ միայն Եօզկատ եւ շրջակայքը, այլ ներքին բոլոր գաւառներու անդորրութիւնը խանգարուած ու թուրքերու միտքերը գրգռուած վիճակ մը ունին: Թուրք պարկեշտ անձեր զաղտնի մեզի խորհուրդ կու տան դիմելու համար ուր որ պէտք է եւ կ'ըսեն թէ իթթիհատականք զինուորական իշխանութիւնը ձեռք առած են եւ մտադիր [են] քրիստոնեաները բնաջնջելու: Երկու շաբաթէ ի վեր իթթիհատական շէֆեր, բարձրաստիճան զինուորական սպաներ ծպտեալ կ'այցելեն ու զինուորական իշխանութեանց կողմէ կը հիւրընկալուին եւ իրենց ծրագիրը կատարելով[5] կ'անցնին Սեբաստիոյ կողմերը, պատրաստ գտնուելու համար Սեպտեմբեր 1-ի գումարուելիք Քօնկրէին: Հակառակ անոր որ ներքին գործոց նախարարը խստիւ հրամայած է ասոնք ձերբակալել եւ ընդ հսկողութեամբ Կ. Պոլիս Պատերազմական Ատեանին ղրկել, տեղական իշխանութիւնը անոնց հրամանով հրոսակապետները եւ աւազակապետները կը հրաւիրէ եւ իրենց մարդերով չէթէ կը գրեն առատ ամսական տալով: Չէթէներէն մէկ մասը Հայաստան կը ղրկուին, մէկ մասն ալ քաղաքս կը մնան: Կառավարիչ Լեւոն պէյ, որմէ գոհ էին պարկեշտ թուրքերը, միւֆթիին մէկ հեռագրով Գըրշէհիր տեղափոխուեցաւ:

- Իթթիհատական շէֆերէն Ճերիտ Զատէ Հիւսնի, Տիվանըը Զատէ Համտի եւ Խայրի Զատէ Օսման պէյերը, որոնք Եոզղատի հայոց տարագրութեան եւ ջարդին իբր գլխաւոր դերակատար եւ մահուան դատապարտեալ գայմագամ Քէմալի ընկերներ դատապարտուած էին եւ ցարդ փախստական էին, այս օրերս ազատ համարձակ շրջիլ սկսան եւ չեն ձերբակալուիր:

Konya (from the vicar general)—August 27
Having obtained a copy of the threatening letters [that had been] dropped at houses against the prefect, the Armenian vicar general and the Armenian Protestant minister presented themselves to the prefect to express their sorrow. The prefect told them that the same night, two copies of the threatening letters, both having the same size, meaning, and writing, had been tossed into his apartment, one of which had a bullet sketched on it. Considering that these threats had been dictated by local military forces, Cemal Bey sent a copy of the threat to the military authorities. According to our investigation, two soldiers were assigned to distribute these threatening letters, intending to create a reactionary movement around the prefect, Cemal Bey.

• Tonight, at ten o'clock, sudden gunfire panicked almost the entire Armenian neighborhood. We found that criminals had escaped from the central prison. The military seems to be behind this case too.

• The Neighborhood Council of Karaman informed us that about thirty-five prisoners have escaped. The prefect confirmed that only ten prisoners escaped, four escapees were killed, and two were seriously injured in quite an intense clash. Again, the complicity of the military authorities is apparent.

Yenipazar [Keller] (from the representative of the National Assistance)—August 11
Five days ago, American[s] Miss Laughridge and Mr. Fowle visited here and were terrified. "It is impossible to make those who have not seen it believe," murmured Mr. Fowle. "In what language should one write to make America believe?" exclaimed Miss Laughridge. Women and children from Yozgat, filled in nine hundred sixty carts, have been murdered here with axes, [along with] two thousand people from Yenipazar [Keller], [ranging in age] from three-month-old breastfeeding children to ninety-three-year-olds. Thousands of people were killed here from Çakmak, Kumkuyu, and Eğlence; altogether, sixteen thousand people. Their bones remain piled up like a mountain. No rifles were used during the massacre, except for the two rifle shots signaling the beginning of the massacre. There are crevices on the skulls; I counted up to sixteen strokes on one skull.

According to a most trustworthy statistic, there were 33,750 Armenians in Boğazlıyan before the massacre; now, only 5,800 Armenians live in twenty Armenian villages and the city. Therefore, 27,950 Armenians were killed with savageries surpassing one another. More than 30,000 people from the Yozgat region were massacred; that is, from the city and forty-five Armenian villages, all in the environs.

Maraş (a telegram from Father Sahag, locum tenens)—September 4
Ten thousand migrants are in a dire situation and need. Armenians want to migrate elsewhere, pressed by misery.

Feneke (Konya) (a telegram from Tovmas Sahagian, Yani Oghlu Savay, and Yani Oghlu Kosti)—September 7
The city was attacked by unknown and armed people, and in addition to looting money and property, they took six Armenians and six Greeks with them. Fifteen days have passed without information on whether those taken away are alive or dead. With this fear, people are leaving their homes to spend the nights in the woods. Pursuing and rescuing these six individuals is what we request.

İslahiye (telegram from the vicar general of Maraş)—September 7
Thirty-three Armenians requested in a telegram dated March 8, 1919, that the trial of the Ittihadists of

Գոնիա (Առաջնորդական Փոխանորդէն) – 27 Օգոստոս

Կուսակալին դէմ տուները ձգուած սպառնագիրներէն օրինակ մը ձեռք անցուած ըլլալով, Հայոց Առաջնորդական Փոխանորդը եւ Հայ Բողոքականաց Պատուելին կուսակալին ներկայանալով ցաւ կը յայտնեն: Կուսակալը կը յայտնէ թէ նոյն գիշերը իր բնակարանն ալ նետուած էր միեւնոյն ծաւալով եւ իմաստով եւ գիրով երկու օրինակ սպառնագիր, որոնցմէ մէկուն վրայ կապար մը ուրուագծուած: Ճէմալ պէյ, նկատելով որ սոյն սպառնալիքները թելադրութիւնն են տեղւոյս զինուորական ոյժերու, պաշտօնագրով մը սպառնագրին մէկ օրինակը ուղղած է զինուորական իշխանութեանց: Մեր կատարած քննութեան համաձայն, երկու զինուորներու պաշտօն տրուած է ցրուել սոյն սպառնագրերը՝ յետաշրջական շարժում մը ստեղծելու փափաքով կուսակալ Ճէմալ պէյի շուրջ:

- Այս գիշեր ժամը 10-ին, յանկարծական հրացանաձգութիւն մը խուճապի մատնեց գրեթէ ամբողջ հայոց թաղը: Ստուգեցինք որ կեդրոնական բանտէն չարագործներ փախուստի ձեռնարկած են: Զինուորականներու մատը կը տեսնուի նաեւ այս գործին մէջ:

- Գարամանի թաղականութիւնը կ'իմացնէ թէ 35ի չափ բանտարկեալներ փախուստ տուած են: Կուսակալ[ը] միայն 10 բանտարկեալ փախուստ տուած ըլլալը եւ բաւական ուժգին ընդհարումի մը միջոցին փախստականներէն չորսին սպաննուած եւ երկուքին ծանրապէս վիրաւորուած ըլլալը կը հաստատէ: Դարձեալ զինուորական իշխանութեանց մեղսակցութիւնը ակներեւ է:

Քէլլէր (Խնամատարութեան Ներկայացուցիչէն) – 11 Օգոստոս

Թուականէս հինգ օր առաջ հոս այցելած են ամերիկացի Միս Լաֆրին եւ Մր. Փաուլ եւ զարհուրած են. «Անկարելի բան է չտեսնողներուն հաւատալ» մրմնջած է Մր. Փաուլ: «Ի՞նչ լեզուով գրելու է որ Ամերիկան հաւատայ» յարած է Միս Լաֆրին: Հոս տապարահար եղած են 960 լեցուն կառք եօզկատցի կին ու մանուկ, 2000 քէլլէրցի՝ երեք ամսուան ծծկերէն իննսունամեայ ծերերը: Հոս կոտորուած են Չագմաքի, Գու[մ]գոյույի, Էյլէնճէի հազարաւորները, ընդամէնը 16,000 հոգի: Ասոնց ոսկորոտին լեռնակուտակ կը մնայ դեռ: Ջարդի միջոցին հրացան չէ գործածուած, բացառութիւն ըլլալով կոտորածը ազդարարող երկու ձեռք հրացանաձգութիւնը: Գանկերուն վրայ կը նշմարուին տապարի փեռեկներ, մինչեւ մէկ գանկին վրայ 16 հարուածներ կրցայ համրել:

Ամենաստոյգ վիճակագրութեան մը համաձայն, Պօղազլեանի մէջ ջարդէն առաջ կար 33,750 հայ, հիմա 5800 հայեր միայն կ'ապրին 20 հայ գիւղերուն եւ քաղաքին մէջ. հետեւաբար 27,950 հայեր զիրար գերազանցող խժդժութեամբ մը սպաննուած են: Եօզկատի շրջանէն՝ այսինքն քաղաքէն եւ 45 հայ գիւղերէն՝ 30,000էն աւելին ջարդուած են, բոլորն ալ շրջավայրին մէջ:

Մարաշ (հեռագիր Առաջնորդական Տեղապահ Սահակ Քահանայէ) – 4 Սեպտեմբեր

10,000 գաղթականներ անձկազին վիճակի մէջ են եւ կարօտ: Հայերը ուրիշ տեղ գաղթել կ'ուզեն թշուառութենէ հարկադրեալ:

Ֆէնէքէ (Գոնիա) (հեռագիր Թովմաս Սահակեանէ, Եանի Օղլու Սավայէ եւ Եանի Օղլու Գօսթիէ) – 7 Սեպտեմբեր

Անծանօթ եւ զինեալ անձերու կողմէ քաղաքին վրայ յարձակում կը գործուի, դրամներ եւ գոյքեր յափշտակուելէ զատ, հայ եւ յոյն 6 հոգի իրենց հետ կը տանին: Տարուածներուն ողջ կամ մեռած ըլլալուն մասին 15 օր է տեղեկութիւն չկայ: Այս երկիւղով ժողովուրդը իրենց տուները ձգելով, գիշերները անտառներու մէջ կ'անցնեն: Կը խնդրուի հետապնդել եւ փրկել այդ վեց անձերը:

Իսլահիյէ (հեռագիր Մարաշի Առաջնորդական Փոխանորդէն) – 7 Սեպտեմբեր

33 հայերու կողմէ 8 Մարտ 1919 թիւ հեռագրով խնդրուած էր [որ] տեղահանութեան եւ ջարդերու եւ հայոց գոյքերու յափշտակութեան մասնակից Մարաշի իթթիհատականներու դատավա-

Maraş, who were involved in deportations, massacres, and the theft of Armenian properties, take place in İstanbul because they lack confidence in the local courts. The trial was requested to be conducted by a neutral and mixed court.

The appeal remained futile; therefore, they continue to apply and demand immediate implementation. The local police have recorded their statement. We ask that the barriers raised against prosecuting these Ittihadist criminals be removed because they are obstacles to the peace of our city and the relations between the people. Please do whatever it takes to punish these Ittihadist criminals.

Diyarbakır (from the Armenian Catholic vicar general)—August 8

The rumor of the formation of the çetes finally finds official confirmation here. Though silently, the Turkish and Kurdish crowds are engaged in a secret and internal feverish organization. The old and the young are arming under the name of "National Protection." According to reliable sources, the weapons are being provided by the government, ostensibly to curb the aggression of foreign nations. Many criminals involved in the Armenian massacre, who were once in hiding, now roam freely and boldly and make threats. The government watches indifferently, and this situation frightens the Armenians. Many are migrating.

Kayseri (from the vicar general)—August 22

Armenians are migrating because of insecurity. The governor lacks goodwill and tramples on justice manifestly. Thus, on July 29, on the occasion of the opening of the church of Efkere and visiting St. Garabed Monastery, the vicar general proposed to the intendant at the request of the local Armenians that twenty-two abducted underage girls be returned [to the Armenians]. The intendant promised and then reneged. Because the girls asked for their freedom, the vicar general reported the matter to the district governor of Kayseri. District Governor Ulvi Bey promised to act and had the twenty-two girls brought to him, but instead of handing them over as he had promised, he raised the issue of "age correction" because the Turkish husbands had brawled. He insisted that the girls were above twenty, although their ages were already checked against the census registers [as being under twenty]. The girls continue to be held by the Turks.

• A telegram from the Ministry of Internal Affairs dated August 19, which the prefect handed to the locum tenens, urged Armenians not to migrate and to trust the state. However, the situation is so uncertain, and the injustices being committed are so apparent that no one dares to deter the migrants from their intention.

• On August 20, a telegram from the ministers of internal affairs and war came to the district governor and the detachment commander, suggesting that squad commanders dispatch the telegrams openly and no longer encrypted. Contrary to this order, the detachment commander of Kayseri again forced the dispatch of an encrypted telegram, indicating that Kayseri's forces have joined Mustafa Kemal's organization.

Afyonkarahisar (from the locum tenens)—September 4

Governor Mahir Bey is a very incapable and feeble old man, and the Ittihadists, taking advantage of his inability, want to cause unrest constantly. All the leaders of Ittihad remain here and are in office, as

րութիւնը տեղի ունենայ Պոլսոյ մէջ, որովհետեւ տեղական դատարաններու վրայ վստահութիւն չունին: Խնդրուած էր որ այդ դատավարութիւնը տեղի ունենայ չէզոք եւ խառն դատարանի մը կողմէ:

Այդ դիմումը հետեւանք ունեցած չըլլալով, շարունակ կը դիմեն եւ օր առաջ գործադրութիւնը կը պահանջեն: Իրենց յայտարարութիւնը տեղւոյս ոստիկանութեան կողմէ արձանագրուած է: [«]Կը խնդրենք որ քաղաքիս անդորրութիւնը եւ ժողովրդոց յարաբերութեան արգելք եղող այս իթթիհատական ոճրագործները դատի ենթարկելու համար յարուցուած արգելքները բառնալով, այդ իթթիհատական ոճրագործները պատժել տալու համար հաճիք գործադրել ինչ որ պէտք է[»]:

Տիարպէքիր (Կաթոլիկ Հայոց Առաջնորդական Փոխանորդէն) – 8 Օգոստոս

Չէթէներու կազմութեան զրոյցը վերջապէս պաշտօնական հաստատութիւն կը գտնէ հոս: Թուրք եւ քիւրտ ամբոխը թէեւ լուռ, բայց գաղտնի եւ ներքին տենդոտ կազմակերպութեան մէջ են. «Մուհաֆազաի Միլլիյէ» [Ազգային Պաշտպանութիւն] անուան տակ մեծն ու պզտիկը կը զինուին: Զէնքերը հաւաստի աղբիւրէ առնուած հաստատ տեղեկութեանց համեմատ՝ կառավարութեան կողմէ կը տրուին, իբր թէ օտար ազգերու ոտնձգութիւնը արգիլելու համար: Հայոց կոտորածին մասնակցող շատ մը ոճրագործներ, որոնք ժամանակ մը ծածկուած էին, հիմա արձակ համարձակ կը շրջին եւ սպառնալիքներ կ'ընեն: Կառավարութիւնը անտարբեր կը դիտէ եւ այս վիճակը ահ ու սարսափի կը մատնէ հայերը: Շատեր կը գաղթեն:

Կեսարիա (Առաջնորդական Փոխանորդէն) – 22 Օգոստոս

Հայերը կը գաղթեն անապահովութեան պատճառով: Կառավարիչը երբեք բարեացակամ չէ եւ յայտնի ոտնակոխ կ'ընէ արդարութիւնը: Այսպէս, Յուլիս 29ին Էֆքէրէի եկեղեցին բանալու եւ Ս. Կարապետի վանքը այցելելու առիթով, տեղւոյն հայոց դիմումին վրայ Առաջնորդական փոխանորդը միւտիրին կ'առաջարկէ 22 առեւանգեալ անչափահաս աղջիկներու վերադարձուիլը: Միւտիրը կը խոստանայ եւ յետոյ կը դրժէ իր խոստումը: Աղջիկները իրենց ազատութիւնը խնդրած ըլլալով, Առաջնորդական Փոխանորդը Կեսարիոյ միւթէսարըֆին կը յայտնէ խնդիրը: Միւթէսարըֆը՝ Ուլվի պէյ, կը խոստանայ եւ 22 աղջիկները բերել կուտայ, բայց փոխանակ 20 տարեկանէն վար եղողները իր խոստումին համաձայն հայոց յանձնելու, թուրք ամուսիններուն պոռչտուքին վրայ «տարիքի սրբագրութեան» («թասհիհի սինն»ի) խնդիր կը հանէ եւ կը պնդէ թէ ասոնք 20էն վեր են, մինչդեռ անոնց տարիքը մարդահամարի տոմարներէն արդէն ստուգուած էր: Աղջիկները թուրքերուն քով կը մնան դեռ:

- Ներքին գործոց նախարարութենէն հասած 19 Օգոստոս թուակիր հեռագիր[ով] մը, որ միւթէսարըֆը Առաջնորդական Տեղապահին յանձնած է, յորդոր կ'ըլլայ խրատներ տալու հայոց որ չգաղթեն եւ վստահին պետութեան: Սակայն կացութիւնը այնքան անստուգութիւն [կը ներկայացնէ] եւ գործուած անարդարութիւնները այնքան բացայայտ են որ ոչ ոք կը համարձակի գաղթողները իրենց դիտաւորութենէն ետ կեցնել:

- Օգոստոս 20ին ներքին եւ պատերազմական նախարարներէ հեռագիր մը կուգայ միւթէսարըֆին եւ փրգա զօմանտանիին, որպէսզի ասկէ յետոյ փրգայի զօմանտանները ծածկագիր հեռագիրներ չփոխանցեն, այլ՝ բաց: Հակառակ այս հրամանին, Կեսարիոյ փրգա զօմանտանին բռնի ուժով դարձեալ ծածկագիր հեռագիր մը տուած է, որմէ կ'երեւի թէ Կեսարիոյ զինուորական ոյժերը Մուսթաֆա Քէմալի կազմակերպութեան միացած են:

Աֆիոն Գարահիսար (Առաջնորդական Տեղապահէն) – 4 Սեպտեմբեր

Կառավարիչ Մահիր պէյ չափազանց անկարող եւ թոյլ ծերունի մըն է եւ իթթիհատականներ օգտուելով իր անկարողութենէն կ'ուզեն շարունակ խլրտումներ հանել: Իթթիհատին բոլոր պարագլուխները հոս կը մնան եւ իրենց պաշտօնի վրայ են, ինչպէս պատժական դատարանի նախագահը՝

is the president of the penal court, Mehmet Rüsdem, and the commander of the gendarmerie, Halit.

• Three weeks ago, four çetes arrived here from Uşak to secretly demand money from Turkish notables and to recruit new ones [çetes]. It has been confirmed that both money and soldiers were given. They have been here daringly for days with the government's knowledge. Their leader is a military lieutenant named Arif from the village of Bayat in Afyonkarahisar. He has committed atrocities unheard of during the war in Syria, and from whom a pregnant woman, a native of Mardin named Mariam, was taken with one child. Upon Arif's orders, a week ago, three or four çetes, armed with grenades and rifles, picked up by daylight three local Turkish merchants who had refused to pay money. After taking their money, they were released and came back.

• On Sunday, sixty-three prisoners escaped from the state prison. Only three were arrested.

• The local Turkish newspaper *Halk Söyle* published a provocative article against Hampartsoumian, an Armenian translator who has been serving in the British forces for about eight months. Its goal was to provoke the mob and turn the nations against each other.

Kırşehir (from the National Assistance branch)—August 20
Due to the prevailing insecurity, many families are about to migrate to Konya, Adana, İstanbul, and İzmir.

Kırşehir (from the National Assistance branch)—September 2
The people are perplexed by the barbaric news of the çetes coming from the inner provinces and the surrounding areas. Signs of enticing the mob are evident. Preparations for migration are seen, and [people] are demolishing their houses and shops to sell the timber to cover travel expenses. Some are abandoning their affairs and leaving.

Antakya (from the National Union)—August 25
The president of the Muhacirs Commission, Maruf (his picture is published in *Tasviri Efkar*, August 4, issue 2802), was the local lieutenant governor four years ago, and he carried out the deportation and the looting and calamities associated with it. As he was leaving, he took two Armenian girls from the people of Musa Dağı, who had taken refuge here at the nunnery of French sisters. He also took all the tools of the photographer Yervant and the watchmaker Arakel. It is surprising and painful that such a person has such an important position.

Diyarbakır (from the Catholic Armenian vicar general)—August 11
The fear of a massacre is becoming more acute day by day. The Turkish and Kurdish crowds proudly announce their plan for crimes in the square and streets. The people are in terror, and ten to fifteen families migrate daily. An immediate solution is requested.

Diyarbakır (from the National Assistance)—August 10
The Kurdish movement is now taking on a different appearance. Although the new prefect officially banned the carrying of weapons in the city, the government distributes weapons to Kurdish villagers under the pretext of self-defense. The Kurdish aghas and begs arm their people with haste; caravans continually carry Russian weapons from Erzurum, which the Turks and the Kurds grab from one

Մէհմէտ Րիւսթէմ եւ ժանտարմայի հրամատար Խալիտ:

- Երեք շաբաթ առաջ Ուշագի կողմէ չորս չէթէներ տեղս հասած են թուրք երեւելիներէ գաղտնի դրամ պահանջելու եւ նորեր արձանագրելու համար: Հաստատուած է որ թէ՛ դրամ եւ թէ զինուոր տրուած է: Ասոնք օրերով արձակ համարձակ են հոս կառավարութեան գիտակցութեամբ: Ասոնց պարագլուխն է Գարահիսարի Պայաթ գիւղէն Արիֆ անունով զինուորական գայմագամ մը, որ պատերազմի ատեն անլուր խժդժութիւններ գործած է Սուրիոյ շրջանակին մէջ, եւ որուն քովէն Մարիամ անուն մարտինցի կին մը առնուած է մէկ զաւակով եւ յղի: Արիֆի հրամանով շաբաթ մը առաջ 3–4 չէթէներ, զինուած ձեռնառումբերով եւ մառթինով, օր ցերեկով վերցուցին երեք տեղացի թուրք վաճառականներ, որոնք չէին ուզած դրամ տալ: Դրամը առնելէ յետոյ ազատ ձգուած եւ վերադարձած են:

- Կիրակի օր պետական բանտէն փախած են 63 բանտարկեալներ, որոնցմէ միայն 3-ը ձերբակալուած են:

- Հոս հրատարակուող «Խալք Սէօլի» թուրք լրագիրը գրգռիչ յօդուած մը կը հրատարակէ անգլիական ուժերու մօտ 8 ամիսէ ի վեր ծառայող հայ թարգման Համբարձումեանի դէմ: Իր նպատակն էր խուժանը գրգռել եւ ազգերը իրարու դէմ հանել:

Գըրշէհիր (Խնամատարութեան մասնաճիւղէն) – 20 Օգոստոս

Տիրող անապահովութեան պատճառով շատ մը ընտանիքներ Գոնիա, Ատանա, Պոլիս, Իզմիր գաղթելու վրայ են:

Գըրշէհիր (Խնամատարութեան մասնաճիւղէն) – 2 Սեպտեմբեր

Ժողովուրդը սահմռկած է ներքին գաւառներէ եւ շրջականերէ հասած չէթէական խժդուժ լուրերէ: Խուժանային գրգռութեան նշաններ կ'երեւին: Գաղթելու պատրաստութիւններ կը տեսնուին եւ իրենց տուները եւ խանութները քանդելով փայտերը կը ծախեն ճամբու ծախք ընելու համար: Կան անանկները որոնք իրենց գործերը երեսի վրայ ձգելով կը հեռանան:

Անտիոք (Ազգային Միութենէն) – 25 Օգոստոս

Մուհաճիր Քօմիսիոնի նախագահ Մարուֆ (պատկերը հրատարակուած է Թասֆիր Էֆքեարի 4 Օգոստոս 2802 թիւին մէջ) չորս տարի առաջ տեղւոյս գայմագամն էր եւ ինք կատարած է տեղահանութիւնը եւ անոր յարակից ալան թալանը եւ զուլումը: Հոսկէ մեկնած ատեն իր հետը տարած է Ճէպէլ-Մուսայի ժողովուրդէն հոս ֆրանսացի քոյրերու քով կուսաստանը ապաստանած երկու հայ աղջիկներ, ինչպէս նաեւ պատկերահան Երուանդի եւ ժամագործ Առաքէլի ամբողջ գործիքները: Այս տեսակ մարդու մը այդ կարեւոր պաշտօնին վրայ գտնուիլը զարմանք ու ցաւ կը պատճառէ:

Տիարպէքիր (Կաթոլիկ Հայոց Առաջնորդական Փոխանորդէն) – 11 Օգոստոս

Կոտորածի երկիւղը օրէ օր աւելի կը շեշտուի: Թուրք եւ քիւրտ ամբոխը հրապարակի եւ փողոցներու մէջ համարձակօրէն իրենց ընելիք ոճիրներուն ծրագիրը պարծանքով կը պարզեն, որով ժողովուրդ ահաբեկութեան մէջ է եւ ամէն օր 10–15 տնուոր կը գաղթեն: Անմիջական դարման կը խնդրուի:

Տիարպէքիր (Խնամակալութենէն) – 10 Օգոստոս

Քրտական շարժումը հիմա տարբեր երեւոյթ կը ստանայ. նորեկ կուսակալը թէեւ քաղաքին մէջ զէնք կրելն արգիլեց պաշտօնապէս, սակայն քիւրտ գիւղացիներու կառավարութեան կողմէ զէնք կը բաժնուի ինքնապաշտպանութեան պատրուակով: Քիւրտ աղաները ու պէկերը իրենց ժողովուրդը կը զինեն փութոյ պնդութեամբ, միշտ կարաւաններ Էրզրումէն ռուսական զէնքեր կը փոխադրեն, որոնք թուրքերու եւ քիւրտերու կողմէ ձեռքէ ձեռք կը խլուին: Քիւրտ աղաները եւ

another. Kurdish aghas and begs hold private meetings. It seems that the appeal of the begs of Silvan to win Hadji Mahmud Agha of Moshkestan over has succeeded. While the American Miss North was visiting the Silvan region of Bsher [with her husband], she was not allowed to go to the villages of Mahmud Agha in Moshkestan, objecting that there were no Armenians there. The ban was imposed by the sergeant major of the police force accompanying them. He had secretly met with Hadji Ma[h]mud Agha and commissioned him not to let the Armenians out and not to give the Armenians an opportunity to meet with Miss North. The government has also instructed the agha to exterminate the Armenians if he wants to merit great honors and rewards. "The Americans are the pioneers," he has said, "of the Armenian-British rule, so it is the duty of every Muslim to oppose it." He assured that the government would assist the Kurdish movement in every way by providing weapons and even artillery. The unfortunate Armenians were pressed not to leave their homes during the days the visiting American woman was there. An Armenian woman who dared to exchange two words with Mr. North in Kurdish was shot dead by a stranger with a rifle a few days later on her way to the spring. Women and men flee from Kurdish villages in Silvan for fear of threats. The Armenian villagers are so frightened that they leave for Aleppo and Urfa, disregarding all advice. The horror is so great that the villagers had secretly sent two Armenians to the city to explain that no appeal should be made for them so that the Kurds would not vent their anger on the villagers. Khatib Beg of Hazro and Sadik Beg of Silvan correspond with Mustafa Kemal Pasha. It is on his instructions that the Kurds are getting organized and armed to exterminate the remaining Armenians and resort to self-defense if Armenian and British soldiers appear on the Kurdish borders. There is a rumor that there will be a draft and that those up to the age of forty-one will be enlisted, in addition to the Armenians who are still under arms; that the Kurds will join the Bolsheviks; and that Mustafa Kemal Pasha has revolted. Delegates from Diyarbakır are preparing to leave for Erzurum to participate in the Committee of Defense for Eastern Vilayets. A few weeks ago, those preparing were the representatives of Itilaf, while today, it is the turn of Ittihad's representatives, Hak[k]ı Bey and Şefki Bey, to prepare. Armenians have already started migrating, and some of the population even wants to relocate the orphanage.

Sometimes he [the prefect] does not want to hand over the Armenian women Muslims hold with an obvious bias. The daughter of an Armenian woman from Kırkpınar [Hretan] village of Eğil town whom the Muslims abducted was not handed over [because of] Muslim witnesses, even though the right to confirm the girl's identity belonged to the mother. The police also contributed to this case.

• To repress the protest of Armenians against the murder of Sekoul Mgrdich, the government imprisoned several Armenians as accused. Later, it acquitted them in the trial.

• The detained Ittihadists were released. Hakkı, the district governor of Muş who annihilated the Armenians of Palu, is sheltered here and walks around free and daringly.

պէկերը մասնաւոր ժողովներ կ'ընեն: Մշքաթանի հաճի Մահմուտ աղան իրենց կողմը շահելու համար Սլիվանի պէկերու դիմումը յաջողած կ'երեւի: Ամերիկացի Միս Նորթ Պշէրի Սլիվան շրջան այցելած ատեն թոյլ չտուին իրեն երթալ Մշքաթանի Մահմուտ աղային գիւղերը, առարկելով թէ հոն հայեր չկան: Այս արգելքը դնողն էր իրեն ընկերացող ոստիկան զօրաց յիսնապետը, որ գաղտնի կերպով կը տեսակցի հաճի Մա[հ]մուտ աղայի հետ եւ կը յանձնարարէ հայերը դուրս չհանել եւ առիթ չտալ հայոց տեսնուելու համար Միս Նորթի հետ: Նոյնպէս կառավարութեան կողմէ պատուիրուած է աղային հայերը կերպով մը բնաջինջ ընել, եթէ կ'ուզէ մեծ պատիւներու եւ վարձատրութեանց արժանանալ: Ամերիկացիներն ռահվիրաներն են, ըսած է, հայ-անգլիական տիրապետութեան, ուստի ընդդիմանալ ամէն իսլամի պարտքն է: Հաւաստած է թէ կառավարութիւնը ամէն օգնութիւն պիտի ընէ քրտական շարժումին զէնք, նոյնիսկ թնդանօթ տրամադրելով: Այցելու ամերիկուհիին հոս գտնուած օրերուն խեղճ հայերը իրենց տուներէն դուրս չելնել ստիպուած են: Հայ կին մը, որ յանդգնած էր երկու բառ փոխանակել Մր. Նորթի հետ, այդ ալ քրտերէն, մի քանի օր վերջը անծանօթի մը կողմէ աղբիւր գացած ատեն հրացանով սպաննուած է: Սլիվանի քիւրտ գիւղերէն կիներ եւ այրեր փախուստ կուտան սպառնալիքներէ վախնալով: Հայ գիւղացիք այնքան ահաբեկած են որ ամէն յորդոր անգոսնելով Հալէպ եւ Ուրֆա կը մեկնին: Սարսափը այնքան մեծ է որ գիւղացիք երկու հայ ծածուկ քաղաք ղրկած էին բացատրելու համար որ իրենց համար ոեւէ դիմում չկատարուի, որ քիւրտերը իրենց զայրոյթը չթափեն գիւղացւոց վրայ: Հազրօյի Խալթիպ պէկն եւ Սլիվանի Սատրզ պէկն Մուսթաֆա Քէմալ փաշային հետ կը թղթակցին: Անոր հրահանգովն է որ քիւրտերը կը կազմակերպուին եւ կը զինուին՝ հայ եւ անգլիացի զինուորներ երբ քրտական սահմաններու վրայ երեւան, մնացորդ հայերը բնաջինջ ընելու եւ ինքնապաշտպանութեան դիմելու համար: Զրոյց կայ թէ զօրակոչ պիտի ըլլայ եւ ցարդ զէնքի տակ պահուած հայերէ զատ մինչեւ 41 տարեկաններն ալ զէնքի տակ պիտի առնուին, թէ քիւրտերը պոլշէվիկներուն պիտի միանան, թէ Մուսթաֆա Քէմալ փաշա ապստամբած է: Տիարպէքիրէն պատուիրակներ մեկնիլ կը պատրաստուին Կարին, Արեւելեան Նահանգներու պաշտպանութեան քօմիթէին մասնակցելու: Քանի մը շաբաթ առաջ պատրաստուողները Իթիլաֆի ներկայացուցիչներն էին, իսկ այսօր Իթթիհատի ներկայացուցիչ Հագի եւ Շէֆգի պէյերը կը պատրաստուին: Հայերը արդէն սկսան գաղթել, եւ ժողովուրդէն մէկ մասը կ'ուզէ նոյնիսկ որբանոցը տեղափոխել:

Իսլամներու քով գտնուած հայուհիները երբեմն ակնյայտ կողմնակալութեամբ չ'ուզեր յանձնել: Ակիլ գիւղաքաղաքին Հըրէտան գիւղէն հայ կնոջ մը աղջիկը, որ իսլամ[ք] առեւանգած էին, հակառակ անոր որ մօրը կը պատկանէր աղջկան ինքնութիւնը ճշդել, իսլամ վկաներով, չյանձնուեցաւ: Ոստիկանութիւնը նոյնիսկ նպաստեց այս գործին:

- Սէգուլ Մկրտիչի սպանութեան համար հայոց բողոք[ը] խեղդելու համար կառավարութիւնը քանի մը հայեր բանտարկեց իբր ամբաստանեալ: Յետոյ դատավարութեան մէջ զանոնք անպարտ արձակեց:

- Ձերբակալեալ իթթ[իհատ]ականները ազատ արձակուեցան: Մուշի միւթասարիֆ Բալուի հայութիւնը բնաջինջ ընող Հազզը հոս ապաստանած է եւ արձակ համարձակ կը շրջի:

[Insecurity] Notebook Number 3
September–October 1919

Harput (information provided by Reverend Vartan Amirkhanian)—September 8

Currently, the movement turning Anadolu [Anatolia] upside down has two aspects: a Turkish, known as Milli, and a Kurdish. The Turkish movement in Harput was embraced after the Erzurum Congress. Mustafa Kemal had wanted a delegate from Harput for this congress, but the governor-general had not allowed [one], just as he had not allowed the representative from Diyarbakır, who was detained in Harput.

On the 5th of September, the Second Congress was convened in Sivas, attended by Mustafa Kemal, who had gone there with a royal entourage, accompanied by numerous officers, carriages, and motorcades.

Before convening the meeting, a telegram was sent to the prefect of Sivas from İstanbul, asking about the purpose of the meeting. The prefect responded that he would assume responsibility and, indeed, he attended the meeting.

The five decisions of the meeting were communicated to the people by notices posted on the walls in Sivas. Those decisions were:

A. They are loyal to His Majesty, the emperor [sultan], recognize him as caliph, and are ready to shed their blood to protect his throne.

B. They do not recognize the present cabinet.

C. They demand the election and convening of the parliament to hand over the country's fate to it.

D. Henceforth, they are ready to fight against any Ottoman land encroachment.

E. They are ready to take back the occupied lands.

In addition to these five decisions, a sixth secret decision was spread by word of mouth, [saying] that if the government did not accept their demands, they would declare independence and sever their relations with İstanbul.

And the Kurdish movement, whose aim appears to be the formation of an independent Kurdistan, is being exploited by the government to repulse or eliminate Armenian demands.

The leading forces of the Kurdish movement are the sons of Ibrahim Pasha [Milli], the chieftain of the Milli tribe in the prefecture of Diyarbakır, and Hacı Bedir Ağa in the Malatya region. The sons of Ibrahim Pasha, surrounded by 300 horsemen, roam from village to village and collect two liras cash per person by force. Those who do not give are imprisoned or intimidated. Since the people of the village of Şabgahan near Lake Hazar [Gölcük] have resisted, they captured and plundered the village. This became an example, and other villages readily gave the amount demanded without objection. The money is appropriated for clothing, food, and weapons.

Aside from these terrifying facts, the weapons openly distributed to Muslims also have an intimidating nature and reveal preparation. The recent haughty behavior of Muslims, the constant threats and insults they dispense against Armenians, and the killings and attacks on girls and women in some places also are significant.

Terrified by this phenomenon, Armenians, especially in Diyarbakır and Harput, began to migrate. The government, in appearance, encourages neither the Milli nor the Kurdish movement but takes no effective measures to curb them.

The people generally believe that the government agrees internally and even encourages their anti-Armenian course in particular.

The center [central government] also appears to be in accord. Several specific cases support this

[Անապահովութեան] Տետր Թիւ 3
1919 Սեպտեմբեր – 1919 Հոկտեմբեր

Խարբերդ (Պատուելի Վարդան Ամիրխանեանի անձամբ բերած տեղեկութիւնները) – 8 Սեպտեմբեր

Այս պահուս Անատոլուն տակնուվրայ ընող շարժումը ունի երկու երես. մին թրքական,- որ Միլլի անունով ծանօթ է,- եւ միւսը՝ քրտական: Թրքական շարժումը Խարբերդի մէջ արձագանգ գտաւ Էրզրումի Քօնկրէէն յետոյ: Մուսթաֆա Քեմալ այս Քօնկրէին համար Խարբերդէն պատուիրակ ուզած էր, սակայն վալին չէր ձգած, նոյնպէս չէր ձգած Տիարպէքիրի պատուիրակը, որ Խարբերդ վար դրուեցաւ:

Իսկ Սեպտեմբեր 5ին Սեբաստիոյ մէջ գումարուեցաւ Բ. Քօնկրէ մը, որուն ներկայ եղաւ Մուսթաֆա Քեմալ, որ արքայական շքախումբով մը եկած է հոն, իբր հետեւորդ ունենալով բազմաթիւ սպաներ, կառքեր եւ օթոմոպիլներ:

Սեբաստիոյ կուսակալին ժողովին գումարումէն առաջ Կ. Պոլիսէն հեռագիր կը տրուի եւ հարցում կ'ըլլայ թէ ի՞նչ է այդ գումարման նպատակը: Կուսակալը կը յայտնէ թէ ինքն պատասխանատուութիւն կը ստանձնէ եւ իրապէս ալ ժողովին ներկայ կ'ըլլայ:

Ժողովին հինգ որոշումները ժողովուրդին կը հաղորդուի[ն] Սեբաստիոյ մէջ պատերուն վրայ փակցուած ծանուցումներով: Այդ որոշումներն էին.

Ա. Վեհափառ կայսեր հաւատարիմ են եւ զինքն կը ճանչնան Խալիֆա եւ անոր աթոռը պաշտպանելու համար իրենց արիւնը թափելու պատրաստ են:

Բ. Ներկայ դահլիճը չեն ճանչնար:

Գ. Երեսփոխանական ժողովին ընտրութիւնը եւ գումարումը կը պահանջեն երկրին ճակատագիրը անոր յանձնելու համար:

Դ. Ասկէ յետոյ օսմանեան երկիրներու վրայ կատարուելիք ոեւէ ոտնձգութեան դէմ պատրաստ են կռուելու:

Ե. Բռնագրաւուած հողերը ետ առնելու պատրաստ են:

Այս հինգ որոշումներէն զատ, բերնէ բերան տարածուած էր նաեւ Զ.րդ գաղտնի որոշում մը, որով եթէ կառավարութիւնը չընդունէր իրենց պահանջները, ինքզինքնին անկախ պիտի հռչակեն եւ պիտի խզեն իրենց յարաբերութիւնները Կ. Պոլսոյ հետ:

Իսկ քրտական շարժումը, որուն նպատակը ըլլալ կ'երեւի անկախ Քիւրտիստանի մը կազմութիւնը, կառավարութեան կողմէ կը շահագործուի հայկական պահանջները վանելու կամ չքացնելու համար:

Քրտական շարժման ղեկավար ուժերն են Տիարպէքիրի կուսակալութեան մէջ Միլլի Աշիրէթի պետ Իպրահիմ փաշայի որդիքը, իսկ Մալաթիոյ սանճաքին մէջ Հաճի Պետիր աղա: Իպրահիմ փաշայի որդիքը շրջապատուած 300 ձիաւորներէ, գիւղէ գիւղ կը շրջին եւ մարդ գլուխ երկու ոսկի հնչուն կը հաւաքեն բռնի: Չտուողները կը բանտարկեն կամ կ'ահաբեկեն: Ծովքի մօտ Շապկահան գիւղին մարդիկը դիմադրած ըլլալով, գիւղը գրաւեցին եւ թալ[լ]եցին եւ ասիկա օրինակ եղաւ եւ ուրիշ գիւղեր անմիջապէս առանց առարկութեան պահանջուած գումարը տուին: Այս դրամներն կը յատկանա[ն] զգեստի, ուտեստի եւ զէնքի:

Այս սարսափ ազդող իրողութիւններէն զատ, ժողովուրդը ահաբեկելու բնոյթ ունի[ն] նաեւ իսլամ ժողովուրդին յայտնապէս բաժնուած զէնքերը, որոնք պատրաստութիւն մը կը մատնեն: Յետոյ նշանակելի [են] իսլամ ժողովուրդին վերջերս առած խրոխտ երեւոյթը եւ շարունակ սպառնալիքներ եւ անարգանքներ տեղալը հայոց եւ տեղ տեղ ալ կատարուած մասնակի սպանութիւնները եւ աղջիկներու ու կիներու վրայ եղած յարձակումները:

Այս երեւոյթէն ահաբեկ, մասնաւորապէս Տիարպէքիրի եւ Խարբերդի մէջ հայերը սկսած են գաղթել: Կառավարութիւնը ըստ երեւոյթին ո՛չ Միլլի եւ ո՛չ ալ քրտական շարժումը կը քաջալերէ,

opinion.

A. The instruction issued by the center to make it difficult for Armenian girls and women to be taken from Muslims was accidentally seen by a Christian. The result of this [instruction] has been witnessed in practice because the lieutenant governor of Harput himself has personally stated that there are still two hundred fifty Armenian boys and girls held by Muslims but that he cannot take and hand them over to the Armenians; let them [Armenians] find and take them.

B. Many [Armenians] from Harput and vicinities in America were sending money by mail to help their relatives. This was a great consolation to the unfortunate. To deprive Armenians of this means of supporting the Armenian reorganization, indubitably by order of the center, the post [ceased] accepting letters [destined] for America, and thus relations were severed, and many Armenians faced hardship.

C. To not return the girls who remained among Muslims [to Armenians], [the Armenian girls] are forced into marriage [to Muslims] as if of their own free will. This certainly is being done upon instructions by the center.

Several other cases confirm the government's persecution of Armenians.

The following provocative statement was posted on the walls in Elazığ [Mezre] on June 6:

"Wake up, an ancient nation, wake up! If you do not wake up, be ashamed; the danger is very close. Delegates for the peace [conference] have been sent to Europe to that awful great court. Kurdistan's death sentence will be announced in a week. Let's wake up before that decision is made. Do you agree to go to church to see the manifold atrocities we committed against the Armenians, [to see] the placement of bells and [hear] their tolling in our mosques, where Muhammad's call to prayer is read, to forget Islam, to abandon prayer? Do you agree to throw our virgin girls into the bosom of Christians and have them make fun of your religion? This cannot be done by words; let the words aside. Let us do our work without delay. Let us liberate the country. Behold, İzmir, which was [taken away] yesterday, is a witness to this. Our fellow believers did not sit there; they worked, they toiled, but because they were late, they failed, and finally, they surrendered their honor to the enemy. The time is now; let us not miss this day; let us not miss this opportunity. Whatever we initiate after the peace [treaty] is signed is useless. The great powers will never efface a peace [treaty] they have signed. If they do not erase it, they have a right because it breaks their dignity. Let us take our arms before the peace is signed. Many forces are helping the self-sacrificing people in arms. Let us not be idle; today is the day. Tomorrow, instead of dying in the hands of Armenians in disgrace, let us die with honor today. Let us liberate the country. Success is from God. God is with us. Long live the country, long live the Muslims, long live Kurdistan, long live the Kurds."

This announcement caused great panic, and the government collected these papers.

Indeed, the consequence was seen when assassination attempts began on a limited scale. Thus, two boys were killed in the village of Akçakiraz [Perçenç]; their bodies could not be found. Later, during these same days, an Assyrian peddler was beheaded on the road to Akçakiraz, for which the Assyrian priest made rigorous appeals. The prefect promised [to look into the murder], but the culprits were not found.

The body of a twelve-year-old boy was found near Harput in the Kayserci valley, stabbed in eighteen places. All [these killings] have gone unpunished; the government never prosecuted the perpetrators.

In Malatya, a young man was torn to pieces in a mill.

The most common incidents in Harput and its environs are beatings of Armenians for no reason [and] attacking Armenian girls. Such incidents happen almost every day.

Thus, Armenians are terrified and fear going [alone] from village to village, and [so] they go in

սակայն ազդու միջոցներ ձեռք չ'առներ զանոնք զսպելու համար:

Ժողովուրդին մէջ առհասարակ սա համոզումը կը տիրէ թէ կառավարութիւնը ներքուստ համամիտ է եւ նոյնիսկ կը քաջալերէ մասնաւորապէս անոնց հակահայ ուղղութիւնը:

Այս ընթացքին կեդրոնն ալ համամիտ կ'երեւի: Մասնաւոր մի քանի դէպքեր այս կարծիքը կը հաստատեն:

Ա. Հայ աղջիկներու եւ կիներու իսլամներու քովէն առնելու գործը դժուարացնելու համար կեդրոնէն տրուած հրահանգը, որ դիպուածով մը քրիստոնեայ մը տեսած է: Աոր արդիւնքն գործնականապէս ալ տեսնուած է, վասնզի Խարբերդի գայմագամը ինք անձնապէս յայտնած է թէ 250 հայ տղայ եւ աղջիկ կան դեռ իսլամներու քով, սակայն ինք չի կրնար առնել եւ յանձնել հայոց. թող անոնք գտնան եւ առնեն:

Բ. Խարբերդի շրջանակէն բազմաթիւ Ամերիկա գտնուողներ իրենց ազգականներուն օգնելու համար դրամ ղրկել սկսած էին բօսթով: Աւիկա մեծ սփոփանք մը կ'ըլլար խեղճերուն: Հայոց վերակազմութեան նպաստող այս միջոցէն ալ զրկելու համար հայերը, անշուշտ կեդրոնին հրամանով, թղթատարութիւնը չառաւ Ամերիկայի համար նամակ եւ ասով ընդհատուեցան յարաբերութիւնները եւ շատ մը հայեր նեղութեան մատնուեցան:

Գ. Իսլամներու քով մնացած աղջիկները չդարձնելու համար անշուշտ կեդրոնէն թելադրուած կ'ամուսնացնեն իբր թէ իրենց ինքնայօժար կամքովը:

Կառավարութեան հայահալած ոգին կը հաստատեն նաեւ ուրիշ մի քանի դէպքեր:

Մեզրէի մէջ Յունիս 6ին պատերուն վրայ փակցուցին հետեւեալ գրգռիչ յայտարարութիւնը.

«Արթնցիր, վաղեմի ազգ, արթնցիր, եթէ չարթննաս՝ այլեւս ամչցիր. վտանգը շատ մօտ է: Հաշտութեան պատուիրակները, Եւրոպա, այդ ահարկու մեծ ատեանին ղրկուեցան: Այլեւս Քիւրտիստանի մահուան վճիռ մէկ շաբաթէն պիտի տրուի: Այդ վճիռը տրուելէն առաջ արթննանք: Հայոց ըրած չարիքներնուս մի քանի պատիկը տեսնալու, Մուհամմէտի էզանը կարդացուած մզկիթներնուս զանգակ դրուելով զարնուելուն, իսլամութիւնը մոռնալով, աղօթքը լքանելով եկեղեցի երթալու համամի՞տ էք: Մեր կոյս աղջիկները քրիստոնեաներու ծոցը նետելու, կրօնքներնիդ ծաղրելի ընելու համաձա՞յն էք: Խօսքով չ'ըլլար, այլեւս խօսքերը մէկ կողմ թողունք: Մեր տեսնալիք գործը օր առաջ տեսնենք: Երկիրը ազատենք: Ահա դեռ երէկ գացող Իզմիրը ասոր վկայ է: Այն տեղ մեր կրօնակիցները չնստեցան, աշխատեցան, տքնեցան, սակայն ուշ մնացած ըլլալով չյաջողեցան, վերջապէս թշնամիին պատիւնին յանձնեցին: Ժամանակը հիմա է, այս օրը չկորսնցնենք, այս առիթը ձեռքէ չփախցնենք: Հաշտութիւնը կնքուելէն յետոյ ինչ որ ձեռնարկենք օգուտ չունի: Մեծ պետութիւնները իրենց ստորագրած մէկ հաշտութիւնը երբեք չպիտի աւրեն: Եթէ չջնջեն՝ իրաւունք ունին, վասնզի իր[ենց] արժանապատուութիւնը կը կոտրէ: Հաշտութիւնը ստորագրուելէն առաջ զէնքերնիս առնենք: Զէնք առնելով մէջտեղ եղող անձնազոհներու օգնող ուժեր շատ կան: Պարապ չկենանք, օրը այսօր է: Վաղը փոխանակ հայոց ձեռքը անպատիւ մեռնելու՝ այսօր պատիւով մեռնինք: Երկիրը ազատենք: Յաջողութիւնը Աստուծմէ է: Աստուած մեզ հետ է: Կեցցէ երկիրը, կեցցեն իսլամները, կեցցէ Քիւրտիստան, կեցցեն քիւրտեր»:

Այս յայտարարութիւնը մեծ խուճապ առաջ բերաւ եւ կառավարութիւնը հաւաքեց այս թուղթերը:

Իրապէս ասոր հետեւանքը տեսնուեցաւ, վասնզի սկսան մասնակի սպանութեան փորձեր: Այսպէս՝ Փէրչէնճ գիւղին մէջ երկու տղայ սպաննուեցան եւ դիակները իսկ չգտնուեցան: Յետոյ նոյն օրերուն Փէրչէնճի ճամբուն վրայ գլխատուեցաւ ասորի փերեզակ մը, որուն համար ասորւոց վարդապետը խիստ դիմումներ ըրաւ: Կուսակալը խոստացաւ, բայց ոճրագործները չգտնուեցան:

Խարբերդի մօտ, Քայսերճի ձորին մէջ 12 տարեկան տղու մը դիակը գտնուեցաւ 18 տեղէ զարնուած: Ասոնք ամէնն ալ անպատիժ մնացին եւ կառավարութիւնը երբեք ոճրագործները չհետապնդեց:

Մալաթիոյ մէջ երիտասարդ մը ջաղացքի մը մէջ կտոր կտոր ըրին:

groups. Due to this situation, the Islamized Armenians dare not declare they are Armenians and remain Muslims. About twenty thousand [Islamized Armenians] are in the Harput prefecture, while today [Christian] Armenians barely number ten thousand.

Now, the Turks are armed against the Armenians and have shown no compassion whatsoever. Last year, they were at least more compassionate and allowed the needy Armenians to collect the particles fallen from the sickle in their fields and provide for themselves. This favor is denied to Armenians this year, so the situation of the Armenians will be very bitter in the forthcoming winter.

Notably, the government facilitates nothing for the residing or refugee Armenians in Harput, whereas it provides food, money, and clothing to Muslim and Kurdish muhacirs originally from the Eastern Provinces who have sought refuge in Harput, with the understanding that they return to their lands. When Armenians apply, the answer they receive is: "There is no money," and ironically, alluding to the American missionaries, they say: "Go to yours, let them help you."

Boğazlıyan (from the Orphan Caring Body)—August 28

On August 26, twenty armed robbers, both local and from the surrounding areas, attacked a house near the town and took out a pretty bride naked. She had been taken away from the Turks eight months earlier and married a young Armenian man. The bride's attempts to resist were all futile; they took her away, dragging her, striking her with whips, and beating her with rifle butts. There was no way to respond to the bride's cries for help. The absent husband had been sent to guard the harvest in a nearby village, and the robbers had placed an armed guard in front of each house in the same neighborhood, with two armed men installed in front of the house of the lieutenant governor residing nearby. This was done to render any attempt for help impossible. Besides, when the girl made a noise, they fired guns in the city to terrorize [the inhabitants]. After the robbers left, the Armenians came out of their hideouts and went to inform the police. The police sergeant answered and sent the Armenians away, saying: "Isn't she Armenian? The one they hanged is a whore, of course. What does it matter?" But given the forceful opposition of Armenians, he was compelled to send two policemen [to investigate]. They exerted no effort and returned, saying: "They are gone." The perpetrators are mainly local government functionaries. The next day it was reported that they were making the bride dance in a cave an hour away. The Armenians again appealed to the lieutenant governor to send two policemen. They returned, saying: "There is no such thing." Angered by the petitions of Armenians, the lieutenant governor summoned Garabed Manougian, a member of the Orphan Caring Body, to the house of a local notable, Seyit Agha, while partying there. "What do you mean, Armenians? Why do you bother me only for a whore? I will show you hostility henceforth. Foreigners already know us; we are despicable in their view already." These statements have terrified intensely the local Armenians, who await death day after day.

On the same day of August 26, at noon, they [the bandits] attacked the house of a poor man from Yenipazar [Keller] living in Ömerli village. They broke his arm, wounded him with the strike of an ax, tore off the little boy's ear with an ax, wounded his wife's head, and trod upon the little child. It is unknown whether the child is dead because the terrorized parents left the boy there, barely saving themselves by fleeing to Boğazlıyan. Such incidents occur almost every day. Facilitations for migration or assistance are requested.

Իսկ Խարբերդ եւ շրջականերու մէջ ամենաստվորական դէպքեր են հայերը ծեծել առանց պատճառի, հայ աղջիկներու վրայ յարձակումներ ընել: Ասանկ դէպքեր գրեթէ ամէն օր կը պատահին:

Այսպէս հայերը սարսափի տակ են եւ գիւղէ գիւղ երթալու կը վախնան եւ խումբերով կ'երթան: Այս կացութեան բերմամբ խլամացած հայերը չեն համարձակիր իրենց հայ ըլլալը յայտնել եւ իսլամ կը մնան դեռ: Խարբերդի կուսակալութեան մէջ անոնց թիւը 20,000ի մօտ է, մինչ հայերը այսօր 10,000 հոգի հազիւ կը հաշուուին:

Թուրքերը հիմա հայերու դէմ զինուած են եւ բնաւ կարեկցութիւն չեն ցոյց տար: Անցեալ տարի գոնէ աւելի զթասիրտ էին եւ կը ձգէին որ հայ կարօտեալներ իրենց արտերուն մէջ հունձքը կատարուած միջոցին մանգաղէն թափուած մասերը հաւաքեն եւ իրենց մաս մը բան ապահովեն: Այս շնորհին այս տարի կը զլանան հայոց, այնպէս որ առաջիկայ ձմեռ հայոց վիճակը շատ դառն պիտի ըլլայ:

Ցետոյ նշանակելի է որ կառավարութիւնը ո՛չ Խարբերդի մէջ գտնուող հայերուն եւ ո՛չ ալ գաղթականներուն ոեւէ դիւրութիւն չ'ընծայեր, մինչ արեւելեան նահանգներէն Խարբերդ ապաստանող իսլամ եւ քիւրտ գաղթականներուն կու տայ ուտեստ, դրամ եւ զգեստ, իրենց երկիրը դարձնելու համար: Հայերը երբ դիմում կ'ընեն իրենց ստացած պատասխանն է. «դրամ չկայ», եւ հեգնօրէն ամերիկացի միսիոնարներուն ակնարկելով «գացէք ձերիններուն, անոնք թող օգնեն ձեզի» կ'ըսեն:

Պօղազլեան (Որբախնամ մարմինէն) – 28 Օգոստոս

Օգոստոս 26ին 20 սպառազէն աւազակներ տեղացի եւ շրջականերէն կը յարձակին գիւղաքաղքին մօտը գտնուող տունի մը վրայ եւ հոն գտնուող գեղանի հարս մը,- որ ութ ամիս առաջ առնուած էր թուրքերուն ձեռքէն եւ ամուսնացած էր հայ երիտասարդի մը հետ,- մերկ վիճակի մէջ դուրս կը հանեն: Հարսին դիմադրութեան ամէն փորձերը անօգուտ կ'ըլլան, քաշկռտելով, խարազանի հարուածներով եւ հրացանի բուներով ծեծելով կը տանին: Հարսին օգնութեան աղաղակներուն պատասխանելու կարելիութիւն չկար: Ամուսինը հունձքի վրայ պահակ ղրկուած էր մօտակայ գիւղ մը եւ բացակայ էր, իսկ նոյն թաղին իւրաքանչիւր տան առջեւ այդ աւազակները դրած էին մէկ մէկ զինեալ պահակ, իսկ այդ տեղւոյն մօտ նստող գայմագամին տան առջեւ ալ երկու զինեալ, որպէսզի օգնութեան ամէն փորձ անկարելի ըլլայ: Ասկէ զատ, աղջիկը երբ աղմուկ կը հանէ, ահաբեկելու համար հրացաններ կը պարպեն քաղաքին մէջ: Աւազակներու երթալէն յետոյ հայերը կ'ելլեն իրենց թաքստոցէն ու կ'երթան իմացնել ոստիկանութեան: Ոստիկանական չաւուշը կը պատասխանէ. «Հայ չէ՞, կախածնին հարկաւ բոզ է. ի՞նչ կարեւորութիւն ունի» ըսելով կը ճամբէ հայերը: Բայց հայոց բուռն ընդդիմութեան վրայ կը ստիպուի ղրկել երկու ոստիկաններ, որոնք «գացեր են» ըսել[ով] կը դառնան, առանց ոեւէ ջանք ընելու: Այս ոճրագործները գլխաւորապէս տեղւոյս կառավարութեան պաշտօնեաներն են: Յաջորդ օրը լուր առնուեցաւ որ ժամ մը հեռուն քարայրի մը մէջ հարսը կը խաղցնեն: Դարձեալ գայմագամին կը դիմեն, որ երկու ոստիկան կը ղրկէ, որոնք «ատանկ բան չկայ» ըսելով կը դառնան: Հայոց դիմումներէն գայմագամը զայրացած տեղւոյն էշրաֆներէն Սէյիտ աղայի տունը խնջոյքի գտնուած պահուն կը կանչէ որբախնամի անդամներէն Կարապետ Մանուկեանը եւ կ'ըսէ. «Ի՞նչ ըսել կ'ուզէք, հայե՛ր, ինչո՞ւ միայն ինծի կը նեղէք կոր բոզի մը համար. այլեւս ձեզի հանդէպ հակառակութիւն պիտի ցոյց տամ: Արդէն օտարները մեզի ճանչցած են, արդէն մեր երեսը սեւ ելած է»: Այս յայտարարութիւնները սաստիկ ահաբեկած են տեղւոյս հայութիւնը, որ օրէ օր մահուան կը սպասէ:

- Միեւնոյն 26 Օգոստոսի օրը կէսօրին Օմարլը գիւղը գտնուող քէլէրցի աղքատ մարդու մը տան վրայ կը յարձակին, թեւը կը կոտրեն, կացինի հարուածով կը վիրաւորեն, պզտիկ տղուն ականջը կը փրցնեն կացինով, կնոջը գլուխը կը վիրաւորեն ու փոքր երեխան ալ ոտնակոխ կ'ընեն: Երեխան մեռած է թէ ոչ անյայտ է, որովհետեւ ծնողքը ահաբեկ տղան հոն ձգելով հազիւ կ'ազատեն ինքզինքնին՝ փախչելով Պօղազլեան: Գրեթէ ամէն օր նման դէպքեր պակաս չեն: Կը խնդրուի այլուր գաղթելու դիւրութիւններ, կամ օգնութիւն:

Yozgat (from the investigator of the provinces of Ankara and Eskişehir)—September 3[20]
Currently, Anadolu [Anatolia] is a theater of conflicts. The power of anarchists carries more weight than that of the government, whose peace-loving stand is obscured. The Turkish vandalism is inflamed by the crescendo of echoes of unrest in the Eastern Provinces. Although the government opposes the movement in appearance, the functionaries go ahead to the point of not disguising their enthusiasm and consensus. This way, the horizon is shrouded with dark clouds; there is a contradictory, conflicting, inimical, and senseless turmoil that terrifies all Christian populations.

Bursa (from the primate)—September 11[21]
There was a Circassian lieutenant governor named Osman Effendi in Karacabey (Mihaliç) who was active and experienced. One of the first tasks of the new prefect was to dismiss him and replace him with one of his followers—an ignorant, fanatic Albanian. It is reported that there has been a clash between Circassians and Albanians in the city, and as many as sixty (60) people have been killed on both sides. The horror of the local Christians can be imagined.

• Tonight, after midnight, at three o'clock, the city woke up to the sound of heavy gunfire. The following morning people realized the reason. A band of eleven çetes besieged the house of a Turk where a wedding was taking place. They robbed the women who were gathered there adorned with their jewelry, and, before leaving, killed a soldier and wounded others who arrived upon the women's screams. None of the robbers was killed or injured. The incident took place in the city near Yeşil.

• Bandits robbed the wife of a Turkish captain returning to Bursa from Karacabey. When the robbers encountered difficulty trying to remove the woman's diamond earrings, they pulled them so hard that they ripped off the woman's ears along with them.

• In Yenişehir, there has been either a clash or a serious incident, but no details have been received yet. It is only confirmed that Halil Pasha and Küçük Talat, who escaped from a prison in İstanbul, are in Yenişehir and that the government does not care to arrest them.

• It has become almost impossible to travel from village to village due to the insecurity in the entire prefecture. Several incidents happen every day. Anarchy is palpable even in the city.

Akdağmadeni (from the investigator of the provinces of Ankara and Eskişehir)—August 28
Recently, the Turks have adopted a new system: through attribution of imaginative crimes, uprisings (which allegedly took place years ago), recruiting false witnesses, and making petitions, they imprison Armenians who dare accuse a Turk, and they bring actions against them for blood or rights; therefore, no Armenian [dares] to complain against a Turk now. Besides, the arrested criminals are already entering the prison from one door and leaving from another. Attorney general Kâzım Effendi and interrogation judge Mustafa play a cynical role in Boğazlıyan. They imprisoned a protesting Armenian and released a Turk accused of crimes after accepting his money. Boğazlıyan's lieutenant governor, Avni Bey, also confessed that this is the case during his visit.

• During a trip from Boğazlıyan to Akdağmadeni, a few hours away from the village of Sarıkaya [Terzili], we were surrounded by a twelve-body-strong notorious gang of thieves who even dared to rob American cars. They wanted to know our identity before attacking us. I already wear a hat, so I pretended to be American and negotiated with the bandits through my interpreter. It would have been

Եօզկատ (Գաղատիոյ քննիչէն) – 3 Սեպտեմբեր

Անատոլուն ներկայիս հակամարտութիւններու թատր մ'է: Անիշխանականներու ոյժը աւելի կը կշռէ քան բուն կառավարութիւնը՝ որուն խաղաղասիրութիւնն ալ ստուերի մէջ է: Արեւելեան նահանգներու խլրտումներու արձագանգը մեծնալով՝ թուրք վանտալութիւնը կը հրա[հ]րուի: Թէպէտեւ կառավարութիւնը երեւութապէս այդ շարժումին հակառակ է՝ բայց պաշտօնէութիւնը իրենց ոգեւորութիւնը եւ համամտութիւնը չծածկելու չափ կը յառաջանան: Այսպէս մթին ամպերով քօղարկուած հորիզոն մը՝ զիրար հակասող, իրարու ընդհարող, անքեւեռ ու խօլական խլրտում մը կայ որ՝ ամբողջ քրիստոնեայ ազգերը սարսափի մէջ կը ձգէ:

Պրուսա (Առաջնորդէն) – 11 Սեպտեմբեր

Գարաճա Պէյ (Մըխալըճ) կը գտնուէր Օսման էֆենտի անուն չէրքէզ գայմագամ մը, որ գործունեայ եւ փորձառու մէկն էր: Նոր կուսակալին առաջին գործերէն մէկը եղաւ զայն պաշտօնանկ ընել եւ տեղը դնել իր արբանեակներէն՝ տգէտ, մոլեռանդ ալպանացի մը: Տեղեկութիւն առնուած է որ քաղաքին մէջ չէրքէզներու եւ ալպանացիներու միջեւ ընդհարում կը պատահի եւ վաթսուն (60) հոգիի չափ երկուստեք սպաննուածներ կան: Կրնայ երեւակայուիլ տեղւոյն քրիստոնեաներու սարսափը:

- Այս գիշեր, կէս գիշերէ վերջը, ժամը 3ին, քաղաքը ընդոստ արթնցաւ բուռն հրացանաձգութեան մը ձայնէն: Հետեւեալ առտուն կը հասկցուի պատճառը: 11 հոգիէ բաղկացեալ չէթէներու խումբ մը թուրքի մը տունը, ուր հարսնիք կը կատարուէր, կը պաշարէ եւ ներկայ արդուզարդերով հաւաքուած կիները կը կողոպտէ: Կանանց վայնասունին վրայ հասնող ոստիկան զինուորներէն մէկը կը սպաննեն եւ մի քանի հատն ալ կը վիրաւորեն եւ յետոյ կը մեկնին: Աւազակներէն սպաննուած կամ վիրաւոր չկայ: Դէպքը պատահած է քաղաքին մէջ, Եէշիլի մօտ:

- Գարաճա Պէյէն Պրուսա վերադարձող թուրք հարիւրապետի մը կինը աւազակները կը կողոպտեն: Երբ կ'ուզեն կնոջ ադամանդ օղերը հանել, դժուարութիւն տեսնելով, այնչափ կը քաշեն որ կնոջ ականջն ալ միասին կը հանեն:

- Եէնիշէհիրի մէջ ալ ընդհարում պատահած է կամ կարեւոր դէպք մը տեղի ունեցած է, սակայն տակաւին մանրամասնութիւններ չեն հասած: Միայն ստուգուած է թէ Խալիլ փաշա եւ Քիւչիւք Թալէադ, որոնք Կ. Պոլսոյ բանտէն խոյս տուած են, Եէնիշէհիր կը գտնուին եւ կառավարութիւնը զանոնք ձերբակալելու բնաւ փոյթ չի տանիր:

- Բոլոր կուսակալութեան մէջ տիրող անապահովութեան պատճառով գիւղէ գիւղ ճամբորդելը գրեթէ անկարելի եղած է: Ամէն օր մի քանի դէպք կը պատահի: Նոյնիսկ քաղաքին մէջ անիշխանութիւնը շօշափելի է:

Ազտաղ Մատէն (Գաղատիոյ քննիչէն) – 28 Օգոստոս

Վերջերս թուրքերը նոր դրութիւն մը որդեգրած են. երեւակայական ոճիրներ, ապստամբութիւններ վերագրելով (որոնք իբր թէ տարիներ առաջ տեղի ունեցած են) սուտ վկաներ ճարելով, հանրագրութիւններ շինելով, բանտարկել կուտան այն հայերը՝ որոնք արեան կամ իրաւունքի դատ բանալով թուրք մը ամբաստանելու համարձակութիւնը ունեցած են, այնպէս որ հիմա ոչ մէկ հայ թուրքի մը դէմ բողոքել [կը համարձակի]: Ձերբակալուած ոճրագործներն ալ արդէն բանտին մէկ դուռէն կը մտնեն միւսէն դուրս կ'ելլեն: Պօղազլեանի մէջ շնական դեր մը կը կատար[են] ընդհանուր դատախազ Քեազիմ էֆենտի եւ հարցաքննիչ դատաւոր Մուստաֆա: Բողոքող հայը կը բանտարկեն ու ոճիրներով ամբաստանեալ թուրքէն գումար մը առնելով ազատ կ'արձակեն: Այս պարագան խոստովանեցաւ նաեւ Պօղազլեանի գայմագամ Ավնի պէյ իր տեսակցութեան ընթացքին:

- Պօղազլըեանէն Ազտաղ-Մատէն ճամբորդած ատեն Թէրզիլի գիւղէն քանի մը ժամ առաջանալէ յետոյ պաշարուեցանք 12 հոգինոց հեծակաւոր աւազակախումբէ մը՝ որոնք նոյնիսկ յանդգնած են կողոպտել ամերիկեան ինքնաշարժները: Նախ քան յարձակում մեր ինքնութիւնը կ'ուզեն

impossible to come out alive had I not been wearing an American hat. A day earlier, I escaped a handful of people similarly. Anarchy is perfect. The power of the minister of internal affairs does not reach here; the gorges have their own prime ministers. The police are worth nothing here.

Edirne (from the vicar general)—13 September

For some time now, secret gatherings have been taking place among the Turkish people almost everywhere in this city and the province. At these gatherings, it was decided to unseat the prefect, Salim Pasha, and the chief of police, Fuad Bey, and they were bold enough to suggest this to the interior minister. The plan remained unimplemented upon the collective telegrams of the Armenian, Greek, and Jewish people. Now, they are holding meetings in a place called Kıyak, far from the city, and passing decisions against Christians. Their leaders are army corps commander Cafer Tayyar Bey, regimental commander of the gendarmerie [and] Lieutenant Governor Rafet Bey, former consul Şükrü Bey, secretary of the consulate in Karaağaç Ahmed Effendi, civil inspector Fahreddin Bey, telegraph director Naim Bey, general prosecutor of the appeals court Ali Fehmi Bey, hospital director Rifat Osman Bey, treasury director Ahmet Bey, census director Ömer Lütfi Effendi, Dr. Hasan Bey, police commissioner Vahap Effendi, mayor Şevket Bey, and lawyer Şerif Bey (president of the Union of Thrace).

Of these, mayor Şevket Bey and lawyer Şeref Bey were summoned to İstanbul by the Ministry of the Interior and are still there, while commissioner Vahap has been fired. A cable has come to the prefecture from the gendarmerie of Kırklareli [Kırkkilise] that if the salaries of the gendarmes are not paid soon, there will be a terrific riot. Today, the British representative left for Keşan, increasing the horror in the city. The gendarmes will certainly obey their leaders. Police chief Fuad Bey dismissed thirty to forty policemen under his command. They turned to the regimental commander of the gendarmerie Rafet Bey, who welcomed and enlisted them as gendarmes. Thus, elements hostile to Christians are getting armed, while the Christians are unarmed.

Bursa (from the primate)—September 15[22]

The Karacabey clash reached a significant proportion. The number of casualties will exceed the previously announced sixty people. The regimental commander who had gone to Karacabey cabled the prefecture for help. Eighty gendarmes and four or five officers were sent from Bursa by carriages. The clashes continue with rage, they say.

Bandırma (from the primate)—September 14

A representative assembly of Muslims had convened in Balıkesir, deliberated the issue of national defense, declared autonomy, and sent telegrams to the [Peace] Conference in Paris announcing that, while respecting the sultan's caliphate, they do not recognize the central government and as such, they have no contact with it; therefore, when the Greek occupying army reaches the borders of the Karasi district, they are prepared and will confront it and will not allow it to enter their borders. The central government presumably is trying to stop this rebellion. It is said that Kemal Paşa, the commander of the gendarmerie traveling to Balıkesir from İstanbul, has succeeded in restraining the unbridled robberies and acts of violence of the çetes, but that there are no practical results in reality. The center assigned two district governors for Balıkesir, but they cabled, saying [they] do not accept it. There has been no district governor since August, and there is anarchy owing to the çetes. The new district gov-

հասկնալ: Արդէն գլխարկ կը կրեմ, ուստի ամերիկացի կը ձեւանամ եւ աւազակներուն հետ կը բանակցիմ թարգմանիս բերնով: Անկարելի էր ողջ դուրս գալ թէ որ ամերիկեան գլխարկ կրած չըլլայի: Օր մը առաջ աւելի սակաւաթիւ մարդոց ձեռքէն ալ նոյն ձեւով ազատած էի: Անիշխանութիւնը կատարեալ է: Ներքին գործոց նախարարին իշխանութիւնը մինչեւ հոս չի հասնիր. կիրճերը իրենց վարչապետներն ունին: Ոստիկանութիւնը ոեւէ արժէք չունի հոս:

Էտիրնէ (Առաջնորդական Փոխանորդէն) – 13 Սեպտեմբեր

Ժամանակէ մը ի վեր քաղաքիս եւ նահանգիս գրեթէ ամէն կողմը թուրք ժողովուրդին մէջ գաղտնագողի հաւաքումներ կ'ըլլան: Այդ հաւաքումներուն մէջ կ'որոշուի կուսակալ Սալիմ բաշան եւ ոստիկանապետ Ֆուատ պէյը պաշտօնանկ ընել եւ նոյնիսկ ներքին գործոց նախարարին կը համարձակին առաջարկել: Հայ, յոյն եւ հրեայ ժողովրդեան հաւաքական հեռագիրներուն վրայ՝ այս ծրագիրը անգործադրելի մնաց: Հիմա քաղաքէն հեռու, Գըեազ ըսուած տեղը երթալով միթինկ կ'ընեն եւ քրիստոնեաներու դէմ որոշումներ կուտան: Իրենց պարագլուխներն են զօլ օրտու զօմանտան Ճաֆէր Թայեար պէյ, ժանտարմա ալայ զօմանտան գայմագամ Րաֆէթ պէյ, երբեմնի հիւպատոս Շիւքրիւ պէյ, Գարաղաճի հիւպատոսարանի քարտուղար Ահմէտ էֆենտի, քաղաքային քննիչ Ֆախրալտին պէյ, հեռագրական տնօրէն Նայիմ պէյ, վերաքննիչ ատեանի ընդհանուր դատախազ Ալի Ֆէհմի պէյ, հիւանդանոցի տնօրէն Րիֆաթ Օսման պէյ, մալ միւտիրի Ահմէտ պէյ, նուֆուզ միւտիրի Էօմէր Լութֆի էֆենտի, Տոքթոր Հասան պէյ, բօլիս քօմիսէր Վահապ էֆենտի, քաղաքապետութեան նախագահ Շէֆգէթ պէյ, փաստաբան Շէրէֆ պէյ (Թրակիոյ Միութեան նախագահ):

Առոնցմէ քաղաքապետութեան նախագահ Շէֆքէթ պէյ եւ փաստաբան Շէրէֆ պէյ ներքին գործոց նախարարութենէն Պոլիս կոչուեցան եւ տակաւին հոն կը մնան, իսկ քօմիսէր Վահապը պաշտօնանկ եղած է: Գըրքիլէսէի ժանտարմայէն հեռագիր եկած է կուսակալութեան թէ եթէ ժանտարմաներու ամսականները մօտ օրէն չվճարուի, մեծ խռովութիւն առաջ պիտի գայ: Այսօր անգլիացի ներկայացուցիչը Քէշան մեկնեցաւ, որով քաղաքին մէջ սարսափը աւելի մեծցաւ: Ժանտարմաները անշուշտ իրենց պետերուն պիտի հնազանդին: Բոլիս միւտիրը Ֆուատ պէյ՝ իր հրամանին տակ գտնուած բոլիսներէն 30–40 հատը պաշտօնանկ կ'ընէ. ասոնք ժանտարմա ալայ զօմանտանին կը դիմեն, Րաֆէթ պէյ գրկաբաց ընդունելով ժանտարմա կ'արձանագրէ եւ այսպէս քրիստոնեաներու հակառակորդ տարրերը կը զինուին, մինչ քրիստոնեայք անզէն են:

Պրուսա (Առաջնորդէն) – 15 Սեպտեմբեր

Գարաճա Պէյի ընդհարումը մեծ համեմատութիւն առած է: Նախապէս ծանուցուած 60 անձի կորուստէն աւելի պիտի ըլլայ կորուստներու թիւը: Ալայ զօմանտանին, որ Գարաճա Պէյ գացած էր, հեռագրած է եւ կուսակալութենէն օգնութիւն կը պահանջէ: Պրուսայէն 80 ոստիկան-զինուոր եւ 4–5 զապիթ կառքերով ղրկուեցան: Ընդհարումները կատաղութեամբ կը շարունակուին կ'ըսեն:

Պանտրմա (Առաջնորդէն) – 14 Սեպտեմբեր

Պալըքէսիրի մէջ իսլամներէ բաղկացեալ ներկայացուցչական ժողով մը գումարուած եւ Ազգային Պաշտպանութեան հարցով զբաղած ըլլալով ինքնօրինութիւն հռչակած եւ ըստ այնմ հեռագրեր ուղղած էին Բարիզի վեհաժողովին՝ յայտարարելով որ յարգելով հանդերձ Սուլթանին խալիֆայութիւնը, չեն ճանչնար կեդրոնի կառավարութիւնը եւ իբր այն չունին անոր հետ ոեւէ կապ, այնպէս որ գրաւման յունական բանակը Գարասիի գաւառի սահմաններուն մօտենալու ատեն պատրաստուած են եւ պիտի դիմակալեն եւ թոյլ չպիտի տան որ իրենց սահմանը մտնեն: Կեդրոնի կառավարութիւնը ջանքեր կ'ընէ իբր թէ այս ըմբոստութեան առջեւը առնելու: Պոլսէն ոստիկան զօրաց հրամանատար Քէմալ փաշա Պալըքէսիր գալով չէթէական սանձարձակ աւազակութիւններուն եւ բռնական արարքներուն կ'ըսուի թէ սանձ դնել յաջողած է, սակայն իրականին մէջ ո՛չ մէկ գործնական արդիւնք: Պալըքէսիրի համար կեդրոնը երկու միւթէսարըֆներ նշանակեց, սակայն

ernor of Balıkesir, Fetin Bey, met with the leaders of the çetes, learned of their plan, and on Sunday, September 7, gathered local Muslim notables and the leaders of the çetes and urged them to end the organization of çetes and to disband all çetes of the National Defense. They asked for an hour to consult, then sent an ultimatum to Fetin Bey, ordering his return to İstanbul the same evening; otherwise, they threatened to deport him to Bandırma the next day in handcuffs and under the watch of çetes. Fetin Bey immediately gave in and left.

The prominent leaders of the çetes or, as they put it, the National Defense, are:

A) Hacım Bey, last year's district governor of Balıkesir, who has recently gone to Afyonkarahisar for organizational work; B) Vehip Bey, the Ittihadist deputy of Balıkesir; [and] C) Keçecizade Hafız Emin Bey, the current head of the municipality.

Urfa (from the National Union)—August 8

The situation of the local Armenians is intolerable regarding misery. The despair of Armenians was boundless when the local British commander Major Brown and his assistant, Adm[inistrative] Commandant Lieutenant John, made pro-Turkish statements and demonstrated an unfavorable attitude toward Armenians. The city is almost in a state of ruin. Only twenty to twenty-five Armenian houses remain inhabitable; the rest are half-ruined and uninhabitable. Ruined houses are full of human skeletons. There are more than nine thousand of them [skeletons]. They [the perished] are not only from Urfa but also from Harput, Erzurum, Sivas, Palu, Şebinkarahisar, and Cilicia. In this city, the Armenian population—mostly women—is economically miserable, owing to the lack of livelihood and the boycott imposed upon Armenians by Muslims. Therefore, Armenians are restrained. The British government provides relief to three to four thousand people, but the subsidies amount to barely forty paras per family, while the American offerings are random and insignificant. Unable to provide daily food, [the Armenian population] has no hope of storing provisions for winter, and the people are vexed by the fear of the forthcoming winter. The vast majority of Armenian movable and immovable properties remain owned by the Turks. The properties seized by the bank and the [Commission of] Abandoned Properties likewise remain entirely held by the Turks. It is harvest time. The Turks reap the harvest and fruits without giving the Armenians a share. The district governor and the director of the office of correspondence raise every obstacle against Armenians pleading to assert their legal rights. The center's instructions remain unenforceable. The government does not support renovating the city, churches, and schools destroyed by Ottoman and German artillery. The British authorities make the wretched women in need of livelihood and a few prematurely aged men repair and clean the city free of charge and without tools, otherwise threatening to cut off the relief. This encourages the Turks to continue their conduct and makes the Armenians suffer even more. No region has so many Armenian [women and orphans] held by Muslims in the city and the surrounding villages. As far as the gates of Siverek, Diyarbakır, and Adıyaman [Hısnımansur]-Harput-Malatya, there are about one hundred thousand of them in this region, and they have not been returned [to Armenians]. The British authorities are very feeble regarding this issue as well. The [Armenian] orphans and girls taken from the homes of the Muslims are returned to the Turks within three days when the Turks insist that they are Muslims, although they are supposed to stay eight days with the Armenians before being returned. The Monastery of St. Sarkis, the National Hotel, and another house have been turned into shelters, but the girls want to return to the Turks because of the lack of financial means. The residents of Urfa find the situation unbearable and want to migrate.

հեռագրով *չենք ընդունիր* կ'ըսեն: Օգոստոսէն ի վեր միւթէսարրըֆ չկայ եւ չէթէներու շնորհիւ անիշխանութիւն կը տիրէ: Պալըքէսիրի նոր միւթէսարրըֆ Ֆէթհին պէյ չէթէներու պետերը տեսաւ, ծրագիրնին հասկցաւ եւ Սեպտեմբեր 7ի Կիրակի օրը հաւաքելով տեղւոյս իսլամ երեւելիները եւ չէթէի վարիչները յորդորներ ըրաւ վերջ տալու չէթէական կազմակերպութեան եւ ցրուել Ազգային Պաշտպանութեան բոլոր չէթէները: Մէկ ժամ միջոց կ'ուզեն խորհրդակցելու համար եւ յետոյ վերջնագիր մը կուտան Ֆէթհին պէյի, հրամայելով որ նոյն իրիկունը իսկ Կ. Պոլիս դառնայ, հակառակ պարագային կը սպառնան հետեւեալ օր ձեռնակապով եւ չէթէներու հսկողութեամբ հեռացնել զինք դէպի Պանտրմա: Ֆէթհին պէյ անմիջապէս տեղի տուաւ եւ մեկնեցաւ:

Պալըքէսիրի չէթէներուն եւ կամ իրենց բացատրութեամբ Ազգային Պաշտպանութեան գլխաւոր վարիչ դէմքերն են՝

Ա. Հանըմ պէյ, անցեալ տարուան Պալըքէսիրի միւթէսարրըֆը, որ վերջին օրերս կազմակերպական գործով Աֆիօն Գարահիսարի կողմերը գացած է: Բ. Վէհիպ պէյ, Պալըքէսիրի իթթիհատական երեսփոխան, Գ. Քէզէճի Զատէ Հաֆըզ Էմին պէյ, թաղապետութեան ներկայ նախագահը:

Ուրֆա (Ազգային Միութենէն) – 8 Օգոստոս

Տեղւոյն հայոց կացութիւնը անտանելի է թշուառութեան տեսակէտով: Հայոց յուսահատութիւնը անսահման եղած է երբ տեղւոյն անգլիացի հրամանատար Major Brown եւ օգնականը՝ Adm. Commandant Leutenant John թրքասէր արտայայտութիւններ ըրած են եւ հայոց աննպաստ վերաբերում ցոյց տուած են: Քաղաքին վիճակը գրեթէ աւերակ է: Հայոց տուներէն միայն 20–25 հատը մնաց[ած] է բնակելի. միւսները կիսաւեր եւ անբնակելի են: Աւերակ տուներու մէջ լեցուն են մարդկային կմախքներ: Ասոնց թիւը 9000-ը կ'անցնի: Ասոնք ոչ միայն ուրֆացի, այլ խարբերդցի, կարնեցի, սեբաստացի, բալուցի, շապին-գարա-հիսարցի եւ կիլիկեցիներ են: Այս քաղաքին մէջ մեծամասնութիւնը կինե֊րէ բաղկացեալ հայ բնակչութիւնը կը գտնուի տնտեսապէս թշուառ կացութեան մէջ, վասնզի զուրկ է ապրուստի միջոցներէ եւ իսլամները *պօյքօթ*ի ենթարկած են հայերը: Որով հայոց ձեռքը ոտքը կապուած է: 3–4000 ժողովուրդին անգլիական կառավարութիւնը նպաստ կուտայ, սակայն ընտանիք գլուխ հազիւ 40 փարայի կուգայ տրուած նպաստը, իսկ ամերիկեան նպաստները պատահական եւ աննշան են: Օրական ուտելիքը հայթայթելու անկարող, ձմեռուան պաշար ամբարելու բնաւ յոյս չունի եւ յառաջիկայ ձմեռուան սոսկումով կը տուայտի ժողովուրդը: Հայոց շարժուն եւ անշարժ կալուածները ստուար մեծամասնութեամբ կը մնան դեռ թուրքերու քով: Պանքայի եւ Էմվալը Մէթրուքէյի գրաւածները ամբողջութեամբ նոյնպէս կը մնան թուրքերու քով: Հունձքի ժամանակ է: Հունձքը եւ պտուղները կը քաղեն թուրքերը՝ առանց հայոց բաժին տալու: Միւթէսարրըֆը եւ թահրիրաթ միւտիրին ամէն դժուարութիւն կը հանեն հայ աղերսարկու ժողովուրդին դէմ իրենց օրինական իրաւունքի տիրանալուն: Կեդրոնի հրահանգները անգործադրելի կը մնան: Օսմանեան եւ գերման թնդանօթներով քարուքանդ եղած քաղաքը, եկեղեցին եւ դպրոցները կառավարութիւնը նորոգելու չի նպաստեր: Անգլիական իշխանութիւնները թշուառ, օրապահիկի կարօտ կիներու եւ վաղահաս ծերացած քանի մը թափառական այրերու նորոգել եւ մաքրել կուտայ քաղաքը ձրի, առանց գործիքի, հակառակ պարագային սպառնալով նպաստը դադրեցնել: Ինչ որ կը քաջալերէ թուրքերը շարունակելու իրենց ընթացքը եւ հայերը դեռ տառապեցնելու: Չկայ շրջանակ մը որ իր մէջը այսչափ բազմաթիւ հայեր ունենայ իսլամներու քովը, քաղաքին մէջ եւ շրջակայ գիւղերը: Մինչեւ Սեւերէկի, Տիարպէքիրի, Ատիեաման-Խարբերդ-Մալաթիոյ դուռները, այս շրջանակին մէջ մօտաւորապէս 100,000 է անոնց թիւը, եւ երբեք չեն դարձուիր: Անգլիական իշխանութիւնք այս մասին ալ շատ թոյլ կը վարուին: 8 օր հայերու քով մնալէ յետոյ իսլամներու տուներէ առնուած որբերը եւ աղջիկները երբ պնդէին իրենց իսլամութեան վրայ՝ անոնց պիտի դարձուէր. սակայն երեք օրէն կը դարձուին: Ս. Սարգիս վանքը, ազգային պանդոկը եւ ուրիշ տուն մը ապաստանարանի վերածուած են, սակայն որովհետեւ նիւթական միջոցներ չկան, աղջիկները թրքաց քով դառնալ կ'ուզեն: Ուրֆացիք անտանելի գտնելով կացութիւնը կ'ուզեն գաղթել:

• Administrative Commandant Mr. John was replaced, and his successor put an end to free labor, promising one thousand British pounds from the British government to partially renovate the ruined houses.

Suşehri [Endires] (from Teotoros Shirinian)—August 30
On August 20, a National Union was formed under the presidency of the Greek priest, and an appeal was made to the government to return the rights of Armenians to them. Under the influence of the local [Turkish] notables, the government facilitates nothing for the Armenians. Likewise, the order to give half of the harvest to the Armenians remained unenforceable. The Turks are once again threatening to massacre the hungry, naked, unfortunate people. Muslim muhacirs are placed in Armenian villages. These muhacirs are destroying the orchards and groves. Altogether 925 people have returned from the township of Suşehri, and they are left thus without sustenance, home, garden, and livelihood.

Sivas (from the primate)—September 4
The news of the relocation of the Erzurum Congress to Sivas has left the local Christian population terrorized. Mustafa Kemal Pasha has already arrived, as have other delegates to the congress. About seventy will gather gradually.

• The missionary of the Swiss Phil-Armenian Association sent two people to Erzincan fifteen days ago, intending to move its orphanage to Erzincan. There, they presented themselves to the district governor and explained their plan, adding that they would also open a hospital next to the orphanage. The governor arrogantly dismissed them, declaring that they did not need an orphanage, a hospital, a doctor, or a cure, that they had everything, and that Armenian orphans could not be allowed to be brought there. This association is also forbidden to enter into relations with the barely fifty to sixty Armenian orphans and widows already in Erzincan. They only managed to understand that the Armenians' lives in Erzincan were unbearable and that they live at the end of the city, under ruins, without food or shelter, threatened and intimidated every hour.

Sivas (from the primate)—September 5
The prefect and the military commander assure that the congress poses no threats to Christians and that every effort will be made to maintain security in the province.

Develi [Everek]-Fenese (from Priest Nerses Nersesian)—September 5
Fearful situation. The Turks wander with arms. The notables and the mob constantly communicate secretively. There is an economic boycott against Armenians. Armenians migrate, horrified by these frightful phenomena. Only the poor, widows, and orphans remain.

Kayseri (from the vicar general)—September 7
A commandant named Jacques came to Kayseri last week as an inspector. This man was invited to a banquet at the summer resort of local massacrers Katipzade Nuh-Hacı and İmamzade Ömer-Lutfi. He took the occasion to promise the release of a few Turkish criminals, natives of Develi, who had massacred Armenians and are imprisoned in Adana, and he cabled Adana to this effect.

• Today, the governor released a copy of a telegram from the Ministry of Internal Affairs with instructions not to attach importance to the Sivas Congress, whose sole purpose is propaganda, and not

- Administrative Commandant Mr. John փոխուեցաւ եւ իր յաջորդը ձրի աշխատցնելու դրութեան վերջ տուաւ եւ անգլիական կառավարութեան կողմէ 1000 անգլիական ոսկի խոստացաւ աւերակ տուները մասամբ նորոգելու համար:

Էնտէրիս (Թէոդորոս Շիրինեանէ) – 30 Օգոստոս

Օգոստոս 20[ին] յոյն քահանային նախագահութեամբ Ազգային Միութիւն մը կը կազմուի եւ կառավարութեան դիմում կը կատարուի հայոց իրաւունքը իրենց դարձնելու համար: Տեղական էշրաֆին ազդեցութեամբ կառավարութիւնը ոչ մէկ դիւրութիւն [կու տայ] հայոց: Հունձքին կէսը հայոց տալու հրամանն ալ անգործադրելի մնացած է: Թուրքերը նորէն սպառնալիք կ'ընեն այս անօթի, մերկ, եւ խեղճ ժողովուրդը ջարդելու: Հայ գիւղերու մէջ իսլամ գաղթականներ զետեղուած են: Այս գաղթականները բոլոր այգիները եւ ծառաստանները կը փճացնեն: Սու-Շէհիր բովանդակ գազայէն ընդամէնը 925 հոգի դարձած են եւ անոնք ալ այսպէս առանց ապրուստի, տունի, այգի[ի] եւ ապրուստի կը մնան:

Սեբաստիա (Առաջնորդէն) – 4 Սեպտեմբեր

Էրզրումի քօնկրէին Սեբաստիա փոխադրելու լուր[ը] տեղւոյն քրիստոնեայ բնակչութիւնը սարսափի մէջ ձգած է: Մուսթաֆա Քէմալ փաշա արդէն եկած է եւ քօնկրէին միւս պատուիրակներն ալ, որոնց թիւը 70 հոգի պիտի ըլլայ, հետզհետէ կը հաւաքուին:

- Զուիցերիական բարեկամ հայերու ընկերակցութեան միսիոնարութիւնը հոս գտնուած իր որբանոցը Երզնկա փոխադրելու մտքով երկու հոգի կը ղրկէ 15 օր առաջ Երզնկա: Հոն կը ներկա[յ]անան միւթէսարըֆին եւ կը պարզեն իրենց ծրագիրը, աւելցնելով թէ որբանոցին յարակից պիտի բանան նաեւ հիւանդանոց մը: Միւթէսարըֆը յոխորտանօք զանոնք ճամբու կը դնէ յայտարարելով որ իրենք ոչ որբանոցի, ոչ հիւանդանոցի եւ ոչ ալ բժիշկի եւ դարմանի կարօտ չեն եւ թէ ամէն բան ունին եւ թէ բնաւ չեն կրնար թոյլատրել որ հայ որբեր բերուին հոն: Այս մարմին[ին] նաեւ արգիլուած է հոս գտնուող հազիւ 50–60 հայ որբ եւ այրիներու հետ յարաբերութեան մտնել: Միայն կրցած են հասկնալ թէ հայերը Երզնկայի մէջ անտանելի կացութեան եւ ամէն ժամ սպառնալիքի եւ ահաբեկումի տակ կ'ապրին, քաղաքին մէկ ծայրը փլատակներու տակ, առանց ուտելիքի, առանց բնակարանի:

Սեբաստիա (Առաջնորդէն) – 5 Սեպտեմբեր

Կուսակալը եւ զինուորական հրամատարը ապահովութիւն կուտան թէ քօնկրէն ոեւէ սպառնալիք չէ քրիստոնեաներու դէմ եւ ապահովութիւնը նահանգին մէջ պահելու համար ամէն հոգ պիտի տարուի:

Էվէրէկ-Ֆէնէսէ (Ներսէս Քահանայ Ներսէսեանէ) – 5 Սեպտեմբեր

Երկիւղալի կացութիւն. թուրքերը զինեալ կը շրջին. էշրաֆը եւ խուժանը շարունակ գաղտնի հաղորդակցութեան մէջ են: Հայերու դէմ տնտեսական *պօյքօթ* կայ: Հայերը այս երկիւղալի երեւոյթներէն սարսափած կը գաղթեն: Աղքատները, այրիները եւ որբերը կը մնան միայն:

Կեսարիա (Առաջնորդական Փոխանորդէն) – 7 Սեպտեմբեր

Անցեալ շաբթու Կեսարիա եկաւ Ժագ անուն զօմանտան մը իբր քննիչ: Ասիկա խնջոյքի հրաւիրուեցաւ տեղւոյս ջարդարարներէն Քեաթիպզատէ Նուհ-Հաճիի եւ Իմամզատէ Էօմէր-Լութֆիի ամարանոցը: Այս առթիւ խոստում կուտայ Ատանայի բանտը գտնուող էվէրէկցի քանի մը հայ ջարդող թուրք ոճրագործները ազատ արձակել տալու եւ այս իմաստով ալ Ատանա հեռագիր կուտայ:

- Կառավարիչը այսօր հաղորդեց ներքին գործոց նախարարութենէն հաղորդուած հեռագրի մը պատճէնը որով կը յանձնարարուի կարեւորութիւն չտալ Սըվազի Քօնկրէին, որուն նպատակը

to be influenced by it.

• The governor opposes the return of the twenty-two Armenian girls left with Muslims in Efkere and raises all kinds of obstacles, although many are under twenty. The girls keep begging for their release.

Trabzon (from the primate)—September 15

There is insecurity. Sporadic threats and assassination attempts. The Turks are armed. Instead of addressing this situation, the government demands the surrender of a scant score of young Armenians who have taken refuge in the mountains for self-defense. The government is ineffective. Ittihad is at work, and all the roads are unsafe. Landless Armenians cannot commute to the villages to make a living. The same situation prevails in Ordu and Giresun. The [Armenian] estates remain confiscated. In the face of the prevailing situation, the Armenians of Trabzon are considering migrating.

Zonguldak (from the Neighborhood Council)—September 22

The insecure situation continues. Recently, Nshan Navasartian and Krikor Nazaretian were robbed by four Lazes belonging to a band of çetes half an hour after leaving the city while they were going to a village for business. Armenians are afraid to travel.

Edirne (from the vicar general)—September 22

The news of Musa Kâzım residing in Edirne has had a devastating effect on the Christian element.

Trabzon (from the primate)—September 22

The political situation is aggravated. To clear the situation, a written request was made to Mr. Lépissier, the delegate of the French high commissioner, and Colonel Crawford, the British military representative.

• An Armenian returning from Romania was detained and sent back with insults.

• There are still Armenians subject to hostile and brutal treatment under military service around Erzurum.

Bursa (from the primate)—September 22

A few days ago, at night, after robbing the house of a man named Münadi Salih, a group of fifteen people took him to a mountain and demanded ransom.

• A few days ago, the mail from İnegöl was sent back forcibly.

• There was intense gunfire tonight; the reason is still unknown.

Bilecik (from the local priest)—September 23

The events around Kütahya, Afyonkarahisar, Sivrihisar, Ankara, and Eskişehir and the Bolshevik movements have caused concerns for the Armenians here. The local Turkish notables, publicly or secretly, threaten the Armenians, saying that the Bolsheviks will come soon and that they must be welcomed. Armed Circassians and Turks roam the city without fear and go to the surrounding villages on horseback. Several coachmen going to Kütahya to bring clay returned this morning because the guards, who were two hours away from the city, had warned them to return. An unknown Turkish officer whose name is kept [secret] has been here since three or four days ago. He goes to Armenian cafés, too, to spy and gather information directly. He has even surveyed the wealth of a few Armenians. He is in contact with the military major and the officers whose count has increased in recent days.

սուկ բրրբականտ է, եւ չտարուիլ:

- Էֆքէրէի մէջ իսլամներու քով մնացած 22 հայ աղջիկներու վերադարձի դէմ կառավարիչը կը հակառակի եւ ամէն դժուարութիւն կը հանէ, անոնցմէ շատերը 20 տարեկանէն վար ըլլալնուն հակառակ: Աղջիկները շարունակ կը թախանձեն զիրենք ազատել:

Տրապիզոն (Առաջնորդէն) – 15 Սեպտեմբեր

Անապահովութիւն կայ: Սպառնալիքներ եւ սպանութեան փորձեր աստ անդ: Թուրքերը զինուած են: Կառավարութիւնը փոխանակ այս վիճակին դարման տանելու, լոկ ինքնապաշտպանութեան համար լեռները ապաստանած հազիւ տասնեակ մը հայ երիտասարդներու անձնատուութիւնը կը պահանջէ: Կառավարութիւնը անազդեցիկ է: Իթթիհատը կը գործէ եւ բոլոր ճամբաները անապահով են: Հողազուրկ հայերը ապրուստ հայթայթելու համար գիւղերը չեն կրնար երթեւեկել: Օրտու եւ Կիրասոն եւս նոյն վիճակը կը տիրէ: Կալուածները կը մնան դեռ բռնագրաւեալ: Տիրող կացութեան առջեւ Տրապիզոնի հայերը գաղթելու վրայ կը մտածեն:

Զօնկուլտաք (Թաղական Խորհուրդէն) – 22 Սեպտեմբեր

Անապահով կացութիւնը կը շարունակէ: Վերջերս գործով դէպի գիւղ գացող Նշան Նաւասարդեան եւ Գրիգոր Նազարէթեան քաղաքէն կէս ժամ անդին կողոպտուած են չորս լազերու կողմէ՝ որոնք մաս կը կազմեն չէթէական խումբի մը: Ճամբորդելու հայերը կը վախնան:

Էտիրնէ (Առաջնորդական Փոխանորդէն) – 22 Սեպտեմբեր

Մուսա Քեազիմի Էտիրնէ բնակելու լուրը քրիստոնեայ տարրին վրայ գէշ ազդած է:

Տրապիզոն (Առաջնորդէն) - 22 Սեպտեմբեր

Քաղաքական կացութիւնը ծանրացած է: Կացութիւնը պարզելու համար գրաւոր խնդրանք եղած է ֆրանսական բարձր զօմիսէրի պատուիրակ պ. Լէբիսիէի եւ բրիտանական զինուորական ներկայացուցիչ Գնդապետ Քրաուֆորտի:

- Ռումանիայէն վերադարձող հայ մը բանտարկուեցաւ եւ նախատինքներով ետ ճամբուեցաւ:

- Կարնոյ կողմերը դեռ զինուորական ծառայութեան տակ հայեր կան, որոնք թշնամական եւ բիրտ վարմունքի առարկայ կ'ըլլան:

Պրուսա (Առաջնորդէն) – 22 Սեպտեմբեր

Քանի մը օր առաջ գիշեր մը 15 հոգինոց աւազակախումբ մը Միւնատի Սալիհ անուն անձի մը տունը կողոպտելէ յետոյ զինքն ալ լեռ կը տանին եւ փրկանք կը պահանջեն:

- Քանի մը օր առաջ Իյնէկէօլի քօստան ետ դառնալու կը ստիպուի:

- Այս գիշեր բուռն հրացանաձգութիւն մը եղաւ, պատճառը դեռ յայտնի չէ:

Պիլէճիկ (տեղւոյն քահանայէն) – 23 Սեպտեմբեր

Քէօթահիայի, Աֆիոն-Գարահիսարի, Սիվրիհիսարի, Էնկիւրի[ի] եւ Էսկի Շէհիր[ի] շրջակայքը տեղի ունեցած դէպքերը եւ պոլշէվիկեան շարժումները հոստեղի հայերը մտահոգութեան մատնած են: Տեղացի թուրք էշրաֆները, հրապարակաւ կամ գաղտնի, հայոց կը սպառնան, կը յայտնեն թէ մօտերս պոլշէվիկները պիտի գան, պէտք է զանոնք սիրով ընդունիլ: Զինուած չէրքէզներ եւ թուրքեր քաղաքին մէջ կը շրջին աներկիւղ եւ ձիով կը մեկնին շրջակայ գիւղերը: Քանի մը կառապաններ, որոնք կաւ բերելու համար Քէօթահիա մեկնած էին, այս առտու դարձան, վասնզի քաղաքէն երկու ժամ հեռու զտնուող պահակներ ազդարարած էին ետ դառնալ: 3–4 օր է հոս կը գտնուի օտարական թուրք սպայ մը, որուն անունը կը պահեն: Ասիկա հայ սրճարաններ ալ կը յաճախէ ուղղակի լրտեսելու եւ տեղեկութիւններ քաղելու մտքով: Նոյնիսկ մի քանի հայոց հարստութեան մասին

Bilecik (from the local priest)—September 24

After the deportation, Albanian muhacirs were placed in the purely Armenian Türkmen village. After the return of the Armenians, the government considered them [the Albanian muhacirs] natives. In addition to assigning them unique houses for their settlement, they want to give them the orchards and lands of those Armenians who have not returned. With this arrangement, Armenians are exposed to great poverty. The grievances remain unheard.

• Today, Bilecik also officially severed its ties with İstanbul, and all local officials declared allegiance to the Bolshevik government. The Ittihadist massacrers have emerged, and they show a threatening stance. The people are terrified and fearful of new disasters.

Adapazarı (from the National Union)—September 29

The Milli organization took over the city government today. They summoned the prominent Armenians and Greeks and told them they had severed ties with the center. A twenty-member council has been formed here. Armenians and Greeks are asked to participate with two members each. The movement seems to have been prepared by the previous lieutenant governor, Sırı Bey. He arrived three weeks ago with someone else to promote it. These twenty people representing the new government are the local members of Ittihad and the main actors in the deportation. Given the threatening tone of the invitation to the Armenians, the Armenians elected two delegates: Dr. Israyelian and lawyer Hayg Fermanian. The [Milli] leaders say this movement is against no one; it only aims to save Anadolu [Anatolia], which they cannot give away after giving Rumeli. The current government being incapable, they [Nationalists] do not recognize it. Regardless, the Turks, seeing the re-establishment of the previous period, have an increased appetite and want to massacre the Christians again. On the night the newly formed government began its work, they ransacked the shop of Nerses Kayayan, a tailor very close to the government office. Nothing remained of merchandise worth 1,500 liras. There are threats to others too.

Harput (from the local priest)—September 1

There is no change in Turkish behavior. Christians are constantly threatened. The terrified people are migrating to İstanbul and Aleppo because everyone here says that in the case of an arrangement unfavorable to the Turks, the Armenians are in danger.

Malatya (from Garabed Kulujian)—September 10

The prefect is here. Hacı Bedir Ağa, his brother, and other Kurdish tribal leaders are gathered here and running continual negotiations with the prefect who massacred the Armenians of Erzurum. The whole city is in fear. The Kurds are fermenting something. The governor, being Kurdish, encourages the Kurdish movement.

Konya (from the vicar general)—September 20

On September 15, Ereğli's government house and postal agency were seized by the organizations of çetes. The prefect sent ten gendarmes, three policemen, and a police chief there.

• The Ittihadists are active in Niğde. Their success in the parliamentary elections is unquestionable.

հարցումներ ըրած է: Ասիկա յարաբերութեան մէջ է զինուորական հազարապետին եւ քանի մը օրէ ի վեր թիւը աւելցած սպաներու հետ:

Պիլէճիկ (տեղւոյն քահանայէն) – 24 Սեպտեմբեր

Թիւրքմէն զուտ հայաբնակ գիւղը տեղահանութենէն յետոյ ալպանացի գաղթականներ զետեղուած էին: Հայերու դարձէն յետոյ կառավարութիւնը զանոնք բնիկ կը նկատէ եւ մասնաւոր տուներ որոշելով բնակեցնել զատ՝ չդարձող հայոց այգիները եւ հողերը անոնց տալ կ'ուզէ: Այս կարգադրութեամբ հայերը կը մատնուին մեծ խեղճութեան: Եղած բողոքները անլսելի կը մնան:

- Այսօր պաշտօնապէս Պիլէճիկ եւս խզեց իր յարաբերութիւնները Կ. Պոլսոյ հետ եւ իրենց հպատակութիւնը յայտնեցին բոլոր տեղւոյս պաշտօնեաները պօլշէվիկ կառավարութեան: Իթթիհատական ջարդարարները երեւան ելած են եւ սպառնական դիրք առած: Ժողովուրդը ահ ու սարսափի մատնուած է եւ նոր աղէտներէ կը վախնայ:

Ատա-բազար (Ազգային Միութենէն) – 29 Սեպտեմբեր

«Թէշքիլաթը Միլլիէն» այսօր ձեռք առաւ քաղաքին կառավարութիւնը: Հայ եւ յոյն երեւելիները կը կոչուին եւ ասոնց կը յայտնուի թէ իրենց յարաբերութիւնները խզած են կեդրոնին հետ: Տեղւոյս մէջ կազմուած է 20 անդամէ բաղկացեալ խորհուրդ մը, որուն մասնակցելու համար երկերկու անդամ ուզուած է հայերէն եւ յոյներէն: Շարժումը պատրաստուած կը թուի նախորդ գայմագամ Սըրրի պէյի կողմէ, որ երեք շաբաթ առաջ ուրիշի մը հետ եկած էր բրոբականտ ընելու: Նոր կառավարութեան կազմը ներկայացնող այս 20 հոգիները Իթթիհատին տեղւոյն անդամները եւ տեղահանութեան գլխաւոր դերակատարներն են: Հայերուս եղած հրաւէրին մէջ սպառնական շեշտ դրուած ըլլալով, հայեր ընտրեցին երկու պատուիրակ՝ բժիշկ Իսրայէլեան եւ փաստաբան Հայկ Ֆէրմանեան: Պարագլուխները կը յայտնեն թէ այս շարժումը ոչ ոքի դէմ է եւ միայն նպատակ ունի փրկել Անատոլուն, զոր չեն կրնար տալ Ռումելին տալէ յետոյ: Արդի կառավարութիւնը անկարող ըլլալով՝ իրենք զայն չեն ճանչնար: Ասով հանդերձ, թուրքերը նախորդ շրջանին վերահաստատութիւնը տեսնալով իրենց ախորժակը սրուած է եւ կ'ուզեն դարձեալ քրիստոնեաները կոտորել: Նոր կազմուած կառավարութեան գործի սկսած օրուան գիշերը կառավարական պաշտօնատան շատ մօտ գտնուող դերձակ[ի] մը՝ Ներսէս Գայայեան, խանութը թալլեցին՝ ոչինչ ձգելով 1500 ոսկիի ապրանքէն: Ուրիշներու ալ սպառնալիքներ պակաս չեն:

Խարբերդ (տեղւոյն քահանայէն) – 1 Սեպտեմբեր

Թրքական վարուելակերպին մէջ ոեւէ փոփոխութիւն չկայ: Շարունակ քրիստոնեաներու կը սպառնան: Ժողովուրդը կը գտնուի սարսափի տակ եւ կը գաղթէ դէպի Պոլիս եւ Հալէպ, որովհետեւ հոս ամէնուն բերանն է թէ եթէ թուրքերուն համար աննպաստ կարգադրութիւն մը ըլլայ, հայերը վտանգի տակ են:

Մալաթիա (Կարապետ Գըլըճեանէ) – 10 Սեպտեմբեր

Կուսակալը հոս է: Հաճի Պէտիր աղա եւ իր եղբայրը եւ ուրիշ քիւրտ ցեղապետներ հոս հաւաքուած են եւ Կարնոյ ջարդարար կուսակալին հետ շարունակ բանակցութեան մէջ [են]: Երկիւղի մէջ [է] ամբողջ քաղաքը: Քիւրտերը խմորումի մը վրայ են: Կառավարիչը քիւրտ ըլլալով կը քաջալերէ քրտական շարժումը:

Գոնիա (Առաջնորդական Փոխանորդէն) – 20 Սեպտեմբեր

Սեպտեմբեր 15ին Էրէյլիի կառավարչատունը եւ թղթատարական վարչութիւնը կը գրաւուին չէթէյական կազմակերպութեանց կողմէ: Կուսակալը հոն կը ղրկէ 10 ոստիկան զինուոր, 3 ոստիկան եւ 1 ոստիկանապետ:

Armenians live under the horror of a massacre. The following people, who had an active role during the deportation, encouraged by their impunity and the establishment of the 11th military detachment, are working feverishly on Ittihad's account and want to spark another massacre. They are Niğde's former mayor Halit, Kerim, İbrahim of Parapara, an official of the [Commission of] Abandoned Properties Avan Ali, former policeman İbrahim, Cemal, son of senior captain Hasan, land registry clerk Rağib, and Sadık Emini Mahmud.

• Upon the news of Ereğli's capture, Prefect Cemal Bey made several statements to the people that anyone who dared to cooperate with the çetes would be arrested and delivered to the military tribunal.

Sivas (from the primate)—September 27

The congress finished its deliberations last week. Some of the members were dispersed, while others are still here. Also present are Mustafa Kemal, Ismail Fazıl Pasha, and Rauf Bey. According to a statement issued by the congress, a representative body has been elected to oversee the affairs of the National Organization and to implement the decisions of the congress. This body will stay in Sivas. They removed Prefect Reşid Pasha, replaced him with Ali Galip Bey, the former prefect of Harput, and severed ties with the center. The Ittihadists have become the masters of the situation here and in the surrounding areas. All the Ittihadist massacrers against whom an arrest warrant had been issued and who had remained fugitives for fear of persecution have surfaced and are roaming freely in the city. Yesterday, one of them, Emir Paşazade Hamit, entered the city leading twenty Circassian horsemen. Those who leave the city are under strict control. Even those who want to go to the villages just an hour away are forced to get a credential from civil and military authorities.

Kütahya (from the vicar general)—October 1

On the night of September 27, the çetes entered the city, and the following day they spread out in the markets and caused much damage. The shops remained closed for two days. The seat of government and the telegraph office are occupied. The officials already knew and waited for the çetes to arrive. The British soldiers stationed at the train station left after the arrival of the çetes. The çetes seized the sizable ammunition stockpile of the British and transported it elsewhere. On September 30, about eight hundred British troops arrived at the station, and a plane or two flew above the city for two days. The frightened çetes left the ammunition crates scattered on the roads and stopped the looting. The number of çetes is increasing day by day. A commission of twenty-five Muslim notables has been set up in the municipality to allocate [shares] and collect the one hundred twenty thousand liras demanded from the city and several surrounding clusters of villages. The city is entirely in the hands of the çetes. They represent a force of six hundred horsemen who may threaten the Christians tomorrow. The British seem to be leaving because they are hastily transporting their ammunition [on] some three hundred wagons. This eventuality terrifies the people.

Aleppo (from Bishop Moushegh)—August 21

General MacAndrew, the British army commander in Aleppo, writes in a secret circular to the Kurds: "The Peace Conference is examining the future of the countries known as Armenia and Kurdistan. It is very clear that the Peace Conference will decide, based on its familiar principles, that nations have the right to adopt their respective governments. The British government assures the Kurds that it will

- Նիկտէի մէջ իթթիհատականները գործունէութիւն ցոյց կուտան: Երեսփոխանական ընտրութեանց մէջ իրենց յաջողութիւնը անկասկած է: Հայերը ջարդի սարսափի տակ են: Տարագրութեան միջոցին գործօն դեր ունեցող հետեւեալ անձերը քաջալերուած իրենց անպատիժ մնալէն եւ քաջալերուած 11րդ փըրգային հաստատուելէն, մեծ եռանդով կ'աշխատին Իթթիհատի հաշույն եւ կ'ուզեն դարձեալ ջարդ առաջ բերել: Ասոնք են՝ Նիկտէի նախկին թաղապետութեան նախագահ Խալիտ, Քերիմ, Բարաքարա Իպրահիմ, Էմվալը Մէթրուքէի պաշտօնեայ Ավան Ալի, նախկին բօլիս Իպրահիմ, Գօլաղասը Հասանի որդի Ճէմալ, Թափու Քեաթիպի Րաղիպ, Սատըգ Էմինի Մահմուտ:

- Էրէյլի[հ] գրաւման լուրին վրայ կուսակալ Ճէմալ պէյ քանի մը յայտարարութիւններ հաղորդեց ժողովրդեան թէ՝ ով որ չէթէներու հետ գործակցելու յանդգնի, պիտի ձերբակալուի եւ պատերազմական ատեան յանձնուի:

Սեբաստիա (Առաջնորդէն) – 27 Սեպտեմբեր

Քօնկրէն անցեալ շաբթու իր աշխատութիւնները վերջացուց. անդամներուն մէկ մասը ցրուեցաւ, իսկ միւս մասն ալ տակաւին հոս կը մնայ: Հոս են նաեւ Մուսթաֆա Քէմալ եւ Իսմայիլ Ֆազըլ փաշաները եւ Րէուֆ պէյ: Քօնկրէին հրատարակած յայտարարութեան համաձայն, Ազգային Կազմակերպութեան գործերուն հսկելու եւ Քօնկրէին որոշումները գործադրելու համար՝ ներկայացուցիչ մարմին մը ընտրուած է: Այս մարմինը պիտի մնայ Սըվազ: Կուսակալ Րէշիտ փաշան պաշտօնանկ ըրին եւ անոր տեղ Խարբերդի նախորդ կուսակալ Ալի Կալիպ պէյը դրին եւ կեդրոնի հետ յարաբերութիւնները խզեցին: Իթթիհատականք հոս եւ շրջականերուն մէջ կացութեան տէր դարձած են: Բոլոր ջարդարար իթթիհատականները որոնց դէմ ձերբակալման հրամանագիր ելած էր եւ որոնք հետապնդումէ վախնալով ցարդ փախստական կը մնային՝ մէջտեղ ելած են եւ ազատ կը շրջին քաղաքին մէջ: Երէկ ասոնցմէ մէկը՝ Էմիր փաշա զատէ Համիտ քանի չափ ձիաւոր չէրքէզներու գլուխը անցած մուտք գործեց քաղաքիս մէջ: Քաղաքէն մեկնողներու վրայ խիստ հսկողութիւն կ'ընեն. նոյնիսկ մէկ ժամ հեռաւորութեամբ գիւղերը երթալ ուզողներ ստիպուած են քաղաքային եւ զինուորական իշխանութիւններէն *վէսիգա* ստանալ:

Քէօթահիա (Առաջնորդական Փոխանորդէն) – 1 Հոկտեմբեր

Սեպտեմբեր 27ի գիշերը չէթէներ քաղաքը մտան եւ հետեւեալ օր շուկաները տարածուելով վնասներ պատճառեցին: Երկու օր խանութները գոց մնացին: Կառավարական պաշտօնատունը եւ հեռագրատունը գրաւուած են: Պաշտօնեաները արդէն գիտէին եւ կը սպասէին անոնց գալուն: Երկաթուղիի կայարանը զտնուող անգլիացի զինուորները չէթէներու գալէն յետոյ մեկնեցան: Իրենց մեծաքանակ ռազմամթերքը չէթէները գրաւեցին եւ այլուր փոխադրեցին: Սեպտեմբեր 30ին 800ի չափ անգլիացի զինուոր եկաւ կայարան եւ երկու օր քաղաքին վրայ 1–2 սաւառնակներ շրջեցան: Չէթէները վախնալով ճամբաներու վրայ աստ անդ ձգեցին ռազմամթերքի սնտուկները եւ թալանը ղադրեցուցին: Չէթէներու թիւը օրէ օր կ'աւելնայ: 25 խլամ երեւելիներէ բաղկացած յանձնաժողով մը կազմուած է թաղապետութեան մէջ քաղաք[է]ն եւ շրջակայ մի քանի գիւղախումբերէ պահանջուած 120 հազար ոսկի բաշխելու եւ գանձելու համար: Քաղաքը կատարելապէս չէթէներու ձեռքն է: 600 ձիաւորներու ոյժ մը կը ներկայացնեն, որոնք կրնան վաղը քրիստոնեաներու սպառնալ: Անգլիացիք կ'երեւայ թէ պիտի մեկնին, վասնզի փութով կը փոխադրեն իբր 300 վակոն հաշուած իրենց ռազմամթերքը: Այս պատահականութիւնը սարսափի կը մատնէ ժողովուրդը:

Հալէպ (Մուշեղ Եպիսկոպոսէն) – 21 Օգոստոս

Հալէպի անգլիական բանակին հրամանատար Ժեներալ Մաք Անտրէուի մէկ գաղտնի շրջաբերականին մէջ ուղղուած քիւրտերուն կը գրէ. «Հաշտութեան Ժողովը Հայաստան եւ Քիւրտիստան անուններով ծանօթ երկիրներուն ապագային քննութեամբ կը զբաղի: Շատ պարզ է, որ Հաշտութեան Ժողովը իր ծանօթ սկզբունքներուն հիման վրայ պիտի որոշէ թէ ազգերը իրաւունք ունին

not ignore the interests of the Kurds in the Peace Conference. Therefore, all the people of Kurdistan must live in peace and tranquility, waiting for the outcome. As for the Armenian massacres ordered by the Turkish government, civilization demands that all officials who issued those orders be severely punished, as will also be punished those responsible for the massacres of Muslims." And then he adds: ". . . It should not be assumed that the British government will pursue a policy of revenge for what the Kurds did during the war; rather, it is ready to grant a general amnesty . . ."

Zonguldak (from the Neighborhood Council)—September 20

The local government is demanding seven thousand kuruş from Armenians through a special official letter as so-called obligatory taxes.

Kayseri (from the vicar general)—September 21

We are under the rule of Mustafa Kemal Pasha and have no ties with İstanbul. Every day, large numbers of Armenians flee in terror, leaving everything behind. The transfer of orphans to Adana is under consideration.

• Nuh Hacı and other local Turkish notables went to Sivas, expressed their obedience and submission to Kemal Pasha, and brought provocative newspapers from there. Meetings are convened in the surrounding villages.

Tokat (from the Administrative Council)—September 26

The following are those who were in the two carriages that accompanied dentist Sisag Chal[uk]ian (a forty-five-year-old man from İstanbul) who left the city and was killed on the road to Amasya with his companions: thirty-year-old Armenouhi from Trabzon; fifty-five-year-old Pampish and her twenty-five-year-old daughter Hranoush from Ordu; twenty-two-year-old Satenig from Ordu; twenty-year-old Veron and her two-year-old child from Amasya; Azniv and Arakel, two sister and brother orphans taken from the American orphanage in Sivas; a girl named Arshalouys, whom he [the dentist] had adopted from Harput. His coachman, forty-five-year-old Garabed of Malatya, was also killed. The two carriages and four horses were taken.

İzmir (from the primate of Konya)—September 26

On September 18, the primate of Konya left İzmir for Antalya [Adalya] by sea and lodged at Mihran Jinivizian's house. Three hours later, he was summoned for questioning, and when he refused, he was placed under the strictest control, deprived of external contacts. He was interrogated later. The primate explained the purpose of his visit and presented the decree of the prefect of Konya. Nevertheless, he was asked to leave Antalya immediately without visiting elsewhere, and he remained under house arrest until the arrival of an order from the Ministry of the Interior to the governor. The primate considered it prudent to return to Konya via İzmir without visiting Burdur, Elmalı, and Isparta.

Büyük Yeniköy (from the Neighborhood Council)—September 27

The American Near East Relief provided fifteen thousand okkas[23] of wheat to the poor in Büyük Yeniköy for the approaching winter. A few carts and horsemen set out yesterday to transport the grain

իրենց մասնաւոր կառավարութիւնները ընդունելու: Բրիտանական կառավարութիւնը կը վստահացնէ քիւրտերը, թէ հաշտութեան ժողովին մէջ անկասկած պիտի չթողու քիւրտերուն շահերը: Ուրեմն Քիւրտիստանի բոլոր ժողովուրդները պէտք է խաղաղ եւ հանդարտ ապրին սպասելով արդիւնքին: Իսկ ինչ որ կը վերաբերի թուրք կառավարութեան հրամանով տեղի ունեցած հայկական ջարդերուն, քաղաքակրթութիւնը կը պահանջէ որ այդ հրամանները հրատարակող բոլոր պաշտօնեաները խիստ կերպով պատժուին, ինչպէս նաեւ պիտի պատժուին խլամներու ջարդերուն պատասխանատուները»: Եւ յետոյ կ'աւելցնէ. «... Թող չկարծուի որ բրիտանական կառավարութիւնը վրէժխնդրական քաղաքականութեան մը պիտի հետեւի քիւրտերուն պատերազմի ընթացքին ըրածին համար, այլ պատրաստ է ընդհանուր ներում շնորհելու...»:

Զօնկուլտաք (Թաղական Խորհուրդէն) – 20 Սեպտեմբեր

Տեղական կառավարութիւնը «Թէքքալիֆը Մէճպուրէ» [Պարտադիր Տուրք] անուան տակ հայերէ կը պահանջէ 7000 ղրուշ գումար մը՝ մասնաւոր պաշտօնագրով:

Կեսարիա (Առաջնորդական Փոխանորդէն) – 21 Սեպտեմբեր

Մուսթաֆա Քէմալ փաշայի տիրապետութեան տակ կը գտնուինք եւ Կ. Պոլսոյ հետ յարաբերութիւն չունինք: Ամէն օր գունդ գունդ հայեր սարսափած կը փախչին ամէն բան լքանելով: Որբերն ալ Ատանա փոխադրել կը խորհուի:

- Նուհ Հաճի եւ ուրիշ թուրք տեղացի երեւելիներ Սվազ գացին եւ հնազանդութիւն եւ հպատակութիւն յայտնեցին Քէմալ փաշայի եւ անկէ գրգռիչ թերթեր բերին: Շրջակայ գիւղերու մէջ ժողովներ կը գումարուին:

Թօզատ (վարչական ժողովէն) – 26 Սեպտեմբեր

Քաղաքէն մեկնող եւ Ամասիոյ ճամբուն վրայ սպաննուող ատամնաբոյժ Սիսակ Չալ[ըք]եանի (45 տարեկան պօլսեցի) ընկերացող երկու կառքերուն մէջ գտնուողները, որոնք նոյնպէս սպաննուած են, հետեւեալներն են: Տրապիզոնցի 30 տարեկան Արմենուհի. օրտուցի 55 տարեկան Բամբիշ եւ աղջիկը Հրանոյշ՝ 25 տարեկան. օրտուցի Սաթենիկ 22 տարեկան. ամասիացի Վերոն 20 տարեկան եւ իր պզտիկը՝ 2 տարեկան. օրտուցի Ազնիւ եւ Առաքէլ երկու քոյր եւ եղբայր որբերը՝ Սեբաստիոյ ամերիկեան որբանոցէն առնուած. Արշալոյս անուն աղջիկ մը, որ Խարբերդէն ինք որդեգիր առած էր: Սպաննուած է նաեւ իր կառապանը՝ մալաթիացի Կարապետ, 45 տարեկան, եւ առնուած են 2 կառքերը եւ 4 ձիերը:

Իզմիր (Գոնիայի Առաջնորդէն) – 26 Սեպտեմբեր

Սեպտեմբեր 18ին Գոնիայի Առաջնորդ[ը] թեմական այցելութեան համար ծովու ճամբով Իզմիրէն Ատալիա կ'երթայ եւ հոն կ'իջեւանի Միհրան Ճինիվիզեանի տունը: Երեք ժամ յետոյ զինքը կը կոչեն հարցաքննութեան եւ երբ ինքը կը մերժէ, զինքը կ'առնեն ամենախիստ հսկողութեան տակ եւ կը զրկեն արտաքին յարաբերութիւններէ: Յետոյ զինքը հարցաքննութեան կ'ենթարկեն: Առաջնորդ[ը] կը բացատրէ իր այցելութեան նպատակը եւ ցոյց կուտայ Գոնիայի կուսակալին հրամանագիրը: Հակառակ ատոնց կը պահանջուի իրմէ շուտով մեկնիլ Ատալիայէն առանց ուրիշ տեղ հանդիպելու, եւ կը մնայ տան մէջ հսկողութեան տակ, մինչ[եւ] որ ներքին գործոց նախարարութենէն հրահանգ կուգայ կառավարիչին: Առաջնորդը խոհեմութիւն կը համարէ առանց Պուտուր, Էլմալը եւ Սպարտա այցելելու Իզմիրի ճամբով դառնալ Գոնիա:

Մեծ Նոր Գիւղ (Թաղական Խորհուրդէն) – 27 Սեպտեմբեր

Ամերիկեան Նպաստամատոյց Մարմնոյն կողմէ 15000 օխա ցորեն յատկացուած էր Մեծ Նոր Գիւղի աղքատներուն համար, առաջիկայ ձմեռուան համար: Կէմլէյիկի մէջ ամբարուած այս ցորենը

stored in Gemlik to the village. They had barely left the village when a quarter of an hour later, in a place called Mira, seven armed Turks waiting in ambush—two masked—besieged them. The bandits robbed the Armenians of their money and clothes and took the seven horses. The travelers came at once to inform the intendant, who, as if unaware of the affair, issued an order to chase [them]. People see this precarious situation as encouraged by the government; therefore, they are terrified and ask for help.

Akhisar (from the Armenia National Union)—October 2

On September 29, Kerovpé, the son of Toros Khashadzian from Kurtbelen, was abducted near the village by a thirty-member gang. They demanded a ransom of two thousand liras, threatening Kerovpé's death otherwise. His father is unable to pay this amount. The boy has not returned as of yet.

• On September 29, Geyve's government severed ties with the center and joined the Milli organization. They demanded the same from the local intendant, who, too, severed [ties] and joined the Milli organization. On October 1, they organized a rally to have the people join them, but the Ittilafists opposed it.

• The people are terrified and want to seek refuge in İstanbul, but they lack financial means.

Samsun (a telegram from the Armenian National Union)—October 2

Large numbers of refugees from interior districts seek refuge in Samsun. Request for help to feed and shelter them.

Bursa (from the vicar general)—October 4

At around four [p.m.] on October 3, the government building was cordoned off by two hundred soldiers, and soldiers armed with bayonets stopped traffic around the headquarters. The next day, in notices distributed to the people, the military authorities announced: "In honor of our martyrs for whom Prefect Mustafa Pasha had used inappropriate language, we caught him and sent him to İstanbul."

Afyonkarahisar (from the Neighborhood Council)—October 4

The Milli movement has terrified local Armenians returning recently from exile. The center of the movement is the village of Yerikmen, half an hour from the city. The çetes come to the city from there every day. These criminals and murderers maltreat the Armenians and ban their trips to villages to earn a living. A few days ago, the çetes kidnapped a man named Haroutyun Yesayan from a place called Güneyköy and moved him around with them for a few days, then took the money he had as ransom and released him. The Allies did not intervene at all, which is a reason for greater despair.

The Milli movement in Afyonkarahisar publishes two newspapers, *Öğüt* (Admonition) and *Halk Sözü* (Folk Word), which contain provocative articles.

• Some Armenians migrate to İzmir and İstanbul, while the poor remain desperate.

Tekirdağ (from the vicar general)—October 7

On September 7, Haroutyun Chapanian, an eighteen-year-old native of Tekirdağ, went to the Galioğlu farm two hours away from the city to deliver a letter. He gave the letter and left. However, he has not

գիւղ փոխադրելու համար երէկ մի քանի կառքեր եւ ձիաւորներ ճամբայ ելած եւ հազիւ գիւղէն քառորդ ժամ մը հեռացած էին երբ *Միրա* ըսուած տեղը պաշարուեցան դարանակալ սպասող եօթը զինեալ թուրքերէ, որոնցմէ երկուքը դիմակ կը կրէին: Աւազակները կը կողոպտեն հայերու դրամները եւ զգեստները եւ 7 ձիերը կ'առնեն: Ճամբորդները կուզան վայրկեանաբար իմացնել *միւտիր*ին, որ իբր թէ գործին անգիտակ՝ հետապնդման հրաման կուտայ: Այս անապահով դրութիւնը կառավարութենէն քաջալերուած կ'երեւայ. ուստի ժողովուրդը մեծ սարսափի մէջ է եւ օգնութիւն կը խնդրէ:

Ագ-Հիսար (Ազգային Միութենէն) – 2 Հոկտեմբեր

Սեպտեմբեր 29ին գուրտպէլէնցի Թորոս Խաչածեանի որդին Քերովբէ 30 հոգիէ բաղկացեալ հրոսախումբի մը կողմէ գիւղին մօտէն կ'առեւանգուի: 2000 ոսկի փրկանք կը պահանջեն, հակառակ պարագային մահ սպառնալով: Հայրը անկարող է վճարելու այս գումարը: Տղան չէ դարձած ցարդ:

- Սեպտեմբեր 29ին Կէյվէի կառավարութիւնը խզեց իր յարաբերութիւնները կեդրոնին հետ եւ յարեցաւ Միլլի կազմակերպութեան: Միեւնոյնը պահանջեցին տեղւոյս միւտիրէն, որ ինքն ալ խզեց եւ յարեցաւ Միլլիին: Հոկտեմբեր 1ին միթինկ մը ընելով ժողովուրդը իրենց միացնել ուզեցին, սակայն իթիլաֆականները դէմ արտայայտուեցան:

- Ժողովուրդը սարսափի մէջ է եւ կ'ուզէ Պոլիս ապաստանիլ, սակայն նիւթական միջոցները կը պակսին:

Սամսոն (հեռագիր Ազգային Միութենէն) – 2 Հոկտեմբեր

Ներքին գաւառներէ մեծ թուով գաղթականներ Սամսոն կ'ապաստանին: Օգնութեան խնդրանք զանոնք կերակրելու եւ պատսպարելու համար:

Պրուսա (Առաջնորդական Փոխանորդէն) – 4 Հոկտեմբեր

Հոկտեմբեր 3ին ժամը 4ի ատեններր կառավարական շէնքը պաշարուեցաւ 200 զինուորներէ եւ սուինաւոր զինուորներու միջոցաւ երթեւեկը կ'արգիլուի պաշտօնատան շուրջը: Հետեւեալ օրը ժողովուրդին կը բաժնուին յայտագիրներ, որոնց մէջ զինուորական իշխանութիւնները կը յայտնեն թէ «կուսակալ Մուստաֆա փաշա մեր *չէհիտ*ներուն համար անպատշաճ լեզու գործածելուն համար, ի յարգանս անոնց զինքը բռնելով Պոլիս ղրկեցինք»:

Աֆ[իոն] Գարահիսար (Թաղական Խորհուրդէն) – 4 Հոկտեմբեր

Միլլի շարժումը սարսափի մատնած է տարագրութենէն նոր դարձող տեղացի հայերը: Շարժումին կեդրոնն է քաղաքէն ½ ժամ հեռու Երիքմէն գիւղը: Չէթէներ քաղաք կուգան անկէ ամէն օր: Ոճրագործ ու մարդասպան այս մարդիկը հայոց հետ գէշ կը վարուին եւ չեն թողուր որ գիւղերը երթան իրենց ապրուստ մը հայթայթելու: Մի քանի օր առաջ Կիւնէյքէօյ ըսուած տեղէն Եսայեան Յարութիւն անուն մէկը չէթէները առեւանգեցին եւ մի քանի օր իրենց հետ պտտցուցին, յետոյ իր քով գտնուած դրամը առնելով իբր փրկանք արձակեցին: Համաձայնականք որեւէ միջամտութիւն չեն ըներ, ինչ որ աւելի մեծ յուսահատութեան պատճառ կ'ըլլայ:

- Միլլի շարժումը Աֆիոն Գարահիսարի մէջ կը հրատարակէ երկու լրագիրներ՝ Էօյիւտ [խրատ] եւ Խալք Սէօզի [հանրային խօսք], որոնք զզուիչ յօդուածներ կը պարունակեն:

- Հայերէն մէկ մասը կը գաղթէ Իզմիր եւ Պոլիս, իսկ աղքատները կը մնան յուսահատ:

Ռոտոսթօ (Առաջնորդական Փոխանորդէն) – 7 Հոկտեմբեր

Բնիկ ռօտոսթօցի 18 տարեկան Յարութիւն Չափանեան անուն պատանին նամակ տանելու համար քաղաքէն երկու ժամ հեռու Կալիօղլու ագարակը կ'երթայ Սեպտեմբեր 7ին եւ նամակը կը

returned, nor has any trace of him been found as of now. He is thought to have been killed.

Urfa (from the delegate of National Assistance, Dr. Mirza Ketenjian)—September 16
At least forty thousand Armenian children remain retained by Muslims in Urfa and its environs. Hired Turkish women bring information daily. Every house has at least one or two [Armenian children], even in the city. There are houses with seven, [even] up to nine Armenian girls and boys. The British authorities appeal to the Ottoman police to take back any orphan they are informed of, but the police often provide means to the kidnappers to take the orphans away.

Konya (from the vicar general)—October 9
Of the Armenians, four to five people are left in Bor now, and those who returned after the armistice—one hundred people—took refuge in Cilicia. The Turks in Bor still retain the following orphans:

With Bayatli Mulla Ali:	a young boy
In Ortaköy:	a bride
With Yazıcı Oğlu Halim:	a girl
With the property manager:	a bride
With Hacı Derviş of Ortaköy:	a young boy
With the assistant public prosecutor:	a girl
In Ciğizlar:	a bride and a girl

The Milli organization has also seized the governments of Niğde and Bor. The governor of Niğde and the lieutenant governor of Bor have been sent to Sivas under surveillance. Terrified Christians are migrating. The Milli organization has launched a fund-raiser and is enlisting the Turks.

Bursa (from the vicar general)—October 10
Migration to İstanbul has begun since the rule of the Milli organization. Yesterday evening, the Milli commander's declaration on the city walls invited all Muslims to attend the midday prayer in the mosques where they [the Millis] would tell them important things.

• The fifteen to twenty Armenian families that had returned to Yenişehir are compelled to participate in municipal elections.

Bursa (from the vicar general)—October 11
Those born in 1898 in Yenisölöz are asked to serve in the army. There has been a complaint.

Üsküdar (from the priest)—October 11
The Turkish villagers of Alemdağı are taking arms provided by the government of Kartal, and the çetes roam the village freely and boldly. The people are terrified.

Bilecik (from the pastor)—October 15[24]
The leaders of Ittihad, Mercimekzade Ahmet, Dedeoğlu Ali, Kadızade Hacı Ahmed, and their followers, returned unpunished from the military tribunal despite grievances and are now getting to work

յանձնէ իր տեղը եւ կը դառնայ: Սակայն ցարդ ոչ եկած եւ ոչ ալ հետքը գտնուած է: Կը կարծուի սպաննուած ըլլալ:

Ուրֆա (Խնամակալութեան պատուիրակ Տոքթ. Միրզա Քէթէնճեանէ) – 16 Սեպտեմբեր

Իսլամներու քով կը գտնուին դեռ Ուրֆայի եւ իր շրջականներու մէջ առնուազն 40,000 հայու զաւակներ: Վարձուած թուրք կիներ ամէն օր տեղեկութիւններ կը բերեն: Քաղաքին մէջ իսկ ամէն տուն առնուազն մէկ-երկու հատ կայ: Տուն կայ ուր 7 հատ, մինչեւ 9 հատ հայ աղջիկներ եւ պզտիկ մանչեր կան: Անգլիական իշխանութիւնները իրենց լուր տրուած իւրաքանչիւր որբին վերստացման համար օսմանեան ոստիկանութեան դիմում կ'ընեն եւ անիկա շատ անգամ առեւանգիչներուն միջոցներ կուտայ որբերը փախցնելու:

Գոնիա (Առաջնորդական Փոխանորդէն) – 9 Հոկտեմբեր

Հիմա Պօրի մէջ 4–5 անձ մնացած է հայերէն եւ զինադադարէն յետոյ դարձողները, որոնք հարիւր հոգի էին, Կիլիկիա ապաստանած են: Պօրի մէջ դեռ թուրքերու քով կը մնան հետեւեալ որբերը՝

Պայաթըլը Մուլլա Ալիի մօտ՝	մանչ մը
Օրթաքէօյի մէջ՝	հարս մը
Եազըճի Օղլու Հալիմի մօտ՝	աղջիկ մը
Մալ միւտիրիի մօտ՝	հարս մը
Օրթաքէօյ հաճի Տէվրիշի մօտ՝	մանչ մը
Մուտտայի ումումի մուավինին մօտ՝	աղջիկ մը
Ճըղըզլարի մէջ	հարս մը եւ աղջիկ մը

Նիյտէի եւ Պօրի կառավարութիւնն ալ Միլլի Թէշքիլաթին գրաւման ենթարկուած է: Նիյտէի կառավարիչը եւ Պօրի գայմագամը ընդ հսկողութեամբ Սեբաստիա ղրկուած են: Քրիստոնեաները սարսափի մէջ են եւ կը գաղթեն: Միլլի Թէշքիլաթը հանգանակութիւն բացած է եւ թուրքերը կը զինուորագրէ:

Պրուսա (Առաջնորդական Փոխանորդէն) – 10 Հոկտեմբեր

Միլլի Թաշքիլաթին տիրապետութենէն ի վեր գաղթը սկսած է դէպի Պոլիս: Երէկ իրիկուն Միլլիի հրամատարին կողմէ *պէյաննամէ* մը փակցուած էր քաղաքին պատերուն վրայ եւ բոլոր իսլամներուն հրաւէր կ'ըլլայ այսօրուան համար կէսօրուան աղօթքի մզկիթները գտնուիլ ուր իրենց կարեւոր ըսելիքներ ունէին:

- Եէնիշէհիրի 15–20 տուն վերադարձող հայերը բռնի հարկադրուած են մասնակցիլ թաղապետական ընտրութեանց:

Պրուսա (Առաջնորդական Փոխանորդէն) – 11 Հոկտեմբեր

Սէօլէօզի 314ի [=1898ի] ծնունդները զինուոր ուզուած են: Բողոք եղած է:

Սկիւտար (քահանայէն) – 11 Հոկտեմբեր

Ալէմ Տաղիի թիւրք գիւղացիները կը զինուին Գարթալի կառավարութեան կողմէ տրուած զէնքերով եւ չէթէներ արձակ համարձակ կը շրջին գիւղին մէջ: Ժողովուրդը ահուսարսափի մատնուած է:

Պիլէճիկ (հոգեւոր հովիւէն) – 15 Հոկտեմբեր

Իթթիհատի պարագլուխները՝ Մերճիմէք զատէ Ահմէտ, Տէտէ-օղլու Ալի, Գատը զատէ հաճի Ահմէտ եւ իրենց արբանեակները, հակառակ բողոքներու պատերազմական ատեանէն անպատիժ

under a new name, terrifying the local Armenians.

Notices were posted in the city, explaining the purpose of the Milli movement. A poisonous language was used in them against Christians. A lawyer called Musa Kâzım delivered a speech in the market square, where after listing the advantages of this new force, he addressed the Armenians, crying out loudly that the Armenians should help this movement financially and morally. Muslims are now engaged in feverish work. After going around everywhere in the market with trumpets and drums while waving the Sancak-ı Şerif [the sacred banner of Muhammad only unfurled in case of a Holy War], at night, they held meetings and exclaimed, "Long live the Ittihad!" all night long. A new election was initiated in the morning. The armed Turks named Sarac and Nazif, who tour the villages and enlist çetes, led the procession. Since their feelings toward the Armenians are well known to the locals, it is easy to comprehend the fear of Armenians. Yetim the Circassian and more than a score of other officers roam the city unofficially and aimlessly, as no soldiers are there in the city. Torumzade İbrahim, Mustafa Bey's son Ali Bey, and the mufti—all agents of Armenocidal policy—are elected as election monitors. Hacı Halit Bey, the enemy of Armenians, plays a significant role in the elections. Robberies have increased around the city, and the Armenians who had returned even to nearby places cannot go to the villages; therefore, they are in danger of being condemned to unemployment and starvation. At night, the city is guarded by başıbozuks [dangerously undisciplined armed men] who are well-known evildoers. A group of Turks, on horseback and armed, march fearlessly in broad daylight, frightening the Armenians. To be good to their supposedly friendly Armenians, someTurks in the city invite them to their homes to avoid imminent danger. The news of Christians being conscripted has caused the men to leave and the elderly, women, and children to remain unprotected. Also, fearing revenge, those [Armenians] who demanded the punishment of the massacrers are leaving because the very massacrers have already come to power.

Bandırma (from the primate)—October 14

Since the Milli movement began in September, particularly after the Islamic Representative Assembly convened in Balıkesir, government functionaries sympathetic to the movement started to allow the çetes to act in an absolutely irresponsible manner and to influence all government affairs, such as interfering in the affairs of [the Commission of] Abandoned Properties, and impose all of their whims.

• Years ago, Hagop Arzoumanian of Balıkesir borrowed five hundred liras from the Orphans' Fund, and after paying in installments, he was left with a debt of sixty-two liras when the deportation began, and Hagop Arzoumanian was sent to Afyonkarahisar. His house was auctioned off for his debt to the Orphans' Fund. When Hagop heard that, he wrote to Balıkesir that he was ready to pay sixty-two liras. However, they ignored [his letter], and the house was sold to Kunduracı Adil, a local çete. After the armistice, Hagop Arzoumanian returned to Balıkesir and settled in his house. Barely four or five days later, Adil succeeded in getting him out of the house using the police, but Hagop managed to obtain an order from the Ministry of the Interior and retake the house. Now that the Milli movement has brought the Ittihadists back into the arena, four armed çetes came a few days ago and are vacating the house under threat.

դարձան եւ այսօր նոր անունով գործի գլուխ կ'անցնին, ահուսարսափ պատճառելով այս տեղի հայերուն:

Քաղաքին մէջ ազդեր փակցուեցան որոնց մէջ բացատրուած էր Միլլի շարժման նպատակը: Քրիստոնէութեան դէմ թունաւոր լեզու մը գործածուած էր: Մուսա Քեազիմ անուն փաստաբան մը, շուկայի հրապարակին վրայ, բանախօսութիւն մը ըրաւ, ուր այս նոր ուժին առաւելութիւնները թուելէ վերջ՝ հայերուն ուղղելով խօսքը, պոռաց թէ՝ պէտք է որ հայերը նիւթապէս թէ բարոյապէս օգնեն այս շարժման: Իսլամները հիմա տենդոտ գործունէութեան մէջ են: Սանճագը Շէրիֆը պարզած, փողերով եւ թմբուկներով շուկային ամէն կողմը պտոյտներ կատարելէ վերջ, գիշերն ալ գումարումներ կ'ընեն ու «կեցցէ Իթթիհատ» աղաղակները տեւեցին մինչեւ լոյս: Առտուն նոր ընտրութեան ձեռնարկուեցաւ: Այս թափորին առջեւէն կ'երթային *Սարաճ* եւ *Նազիֆ* անուն թուրքեր, որոնք զինեալ գիւղերը պտտելով չէթէներ կ'արձանագրեն: Ասոնց հայոց հանդէպ տածած զգացումները տեղացւոց յայտնի ըլլալով, հայոց երկիւղը դիւրին է ըմբռնել: Չէրքէզ Եէթիմ եւ ուրիշ տասնէ աւելի սպաներ կը պտտին քաղաքին մէջ, անպաշտօն եւ աննպատակ, քանի որ զինուոր գոյութիւն չունի քաղաքին մէջ: Թօրում զատէ Իպրահիմ, Մուսթաֆա պէյ զատէ Ալի պէյ եւ միւֆթին,- ամէնքն ալ հայաջինջ քաղաքականութեան գործակալները,- ընտրութեանց հսկող կ'ընտրուին: Հաճի Խալիտ պէյ, հայերու թշնամին, մեծ դեր կը կատարէ ընտրութեանց մէջ: Աւազակութիւնը շատցաւ քաղաքին շրջակայքը, նոյնիսկ մօտ տեղերու մէջ վերադարձող հայերը գիւղերը չեն կրնար երթալ, հետեւաբար անգործութեան եւ անօթութեան դատապարտուելու վտանգին տակ կը մնան: Գիշերները, քաղաքին կը հսկեն պաշը պօզուք զինեալ մարդիկ, որոնք ծանօթ չարագործներ են: Օր ցերեկով կարգ մը թուրքեր ձիաւոր եւ զինեալ՝ կ'երթեւեկեն անվախ, հայերուն վախ պատճառելով: Քաղաքին մէջ կարգ մը թուրքեր, իրենց իբր թէ բարեկամ հայերուն բարիք մը ընելու համար, կը հրաւիրեն իրենց տունը, վերահաս վտանգէն զերծ մնալու համար: Քրիստոնէից զինուորագրութեան լուրը պատճառ եղաւ որ այրերը թողուն երթան եւ ծերերը, կիները եւ տղաքը անպաշտպան մնան: Նոյնպէս վրէժխնդրութենէ վախնալով՝ անոնք որ ջարդարարներու պատժուիլն պահանջած էին, կը մեկնին, քանի որ այդ ջարդարարները արդէն իշխանութեան գլուխ անցած են:

Պանտրմա (Առաջնորդէն) – 14 Հոկտեմբեր

Սեպտեմբերէն ի վեր արդէն Միլլի շարժումը սկսած, մանաւորապէս Պալըքէսիրի մէջ գումարուած իսլամական ներկայացուցչական ժողովէն յետոյ, կառավարական պաշտօնեաները, համակիր այդ շարժումին, թոյլ տալ սկսան որ չէթէները բացարձակ եւ անպատասխանատու կերպով գործեն եւ ազդեցութիւն բանեցնեն կառավարական ամէն գործերու [վրայ], ինչպէս Էմվալը Մէթրուքէի գործերու միջամտեն եւ իրենց ամէն քմահաճոյքները պարտադրեն:

- Տարիներ առաջ պալըքէսիրցի Յակոբ Արզումանեան էյթամի սնտուկէն 500 ոսկի փոխ կ'առնէ եւ մաս առ մաս վճարելով 62 ոսկի պարտքը մնացած էր երբ տեղահանութիւնը կը սկսի եւ Յակոբ Արզումանեան Աֆիոն-Գարահիսար կը ղրկուի: Էյթամի սնտուկին իր ունեցած պարտքին համար իր տունը աճուրդի կը հանուի: Յակոբ լսելով կը գրէ Պալըքէսիր թէ ինքն պատրաստ է 62 ոսկի տալ: Սակայն մտիկ չեն ըներ եւ տունը կը ծախուի տեղւոյն չէթէներէն Գունտրաճը Ատիլ[ի]: Զինադադարէն յետոյ Յակոբ Արզումանեան կը վերադառնայ Պալըքէսիր եւ կը հաստատուի իր տան մէջ: Հազիւ 4–5 օր յետոյ, Ատիլ կը յաջողի ոստիկաններու ձեռքով զինքը տունէն հանել, սակայն Յակոբ կը յաջողի ներքին գործոց նախարարութենէն հրաման բերել տալ եւ տունը առնել նորէն: Հիմա որ Միլլի շարժումը նորէն ասպարէզ հանած է իթթիհատականները, չորս զինեալ չէթէներ քանի մը օր [առաջ] եկան եւ սպառնալիքով տունը կը պարպեն:

[Insecurity] Notebook Number 4
[September]-October 1919

Bandırma (from the primate)—October 14
The principal leaders of the local Milli movement are the following:

1. Hacı Davutoğlu Yahya Sezai Effendi: lieutenant governor of Adapazarı at the time of deportation. On that occasion, he had been appointed district governor to Gümüşhane as a reward for his gangsterlike action of torturing and robbing the local Armenians. Currently, [he resides] in our city without a position, spoiled by the pleasures of the wealth he accumulated. [He is] the leader of the Milli movement.
2. Retired staff liutenant Sabri Bey.
3. Gunner lieutenant Recep Bey.
4. Hacı Haşim Beyoğlu Rıza Bey, member of the Administrative Council.
5. Veli Beyzade Mehmet Effendi, lawyer.
6. Ömer Lütfi Effendi, director of the Public Debt Department and delegate in charge of Ittihad.
7. Mülki Beyzade Mehmed Bey.
8. Servet Bey, mayor.

These are also the prominent figures of the local Ittihad [chapter], and as such, they lead the National Movement.

Malatya (from Garabed Kulujian)—September 12
Major Duville, an Englishman, arrived in Malatya with thirty soldiers, and he was curious to find out how many Armenians were there in Malatya before the armistice. He was shown a very moderate, undercalculated statistic, but the Turkish government refuted that statistic as well, desiring to show still a much smaller number of Armenians. The British commander launched an investigation from Orduzu, where Armenians counted to be fifteen families: seventy people. The investigation confirmed that there were twenty-one families: ninety-six people. Had the investigation continued, the same result would have occurred in many other places, but the Kurdish uprising prevented this investigation.

• The Kurdish uprising started on September 9. The prefect and the governor, both Kurds, the British major with his followers, and the most influential Kurd in the Malatya area, the perpetrator of the massacres of Erzurum Hacı Bedir Ağa of Kâhta, as well as Arpacızade Muhammed Effendi fled toward Kâhta in revolt against the government. On September 10, the Kurdish chieftain Mustafa of Drezhan, Jilbaghzade Mustafa of Atma, Ismayil of Pütürge, Hadji Kaya of İzollu—all Kurdish chieftains—İsmet Effendi of Hekimhan and, of the locals, the executor of halberdiers of Hafız of Tortum, effendis Hadji Khalil Zade Vahab, Karakaş Zade Kadir, and [police] commissioner Fazıl went to Hacı Bedir Ağa to strike an agreement. It seems their initiative was unsuccessful because the next day at noon, all the weapons and ammunition in the government storehouse were distributed to the people, and at night residents carried out vigilance. The nearly fifteen hundred troops in the city went toward Kızlan and Ihdade, while more than two thousand armed civilians went to defend the positions of Banaz and Kündi-Beg.

There are close to six thousand armed Kurds at the disposal of the prefect and Hacı Bedir Ağa. It is said that British troops also will arrive for support.

Mustafa Kemal's troops are in preparation. Hadji Kaya, a fugitive wanted by the military tribunal as the massacrer of Malatya and Harput, has now surfaced and is roaming freely and issuing orders. There is no movement against Armenians for the time being, and the issue has a Turkish and Kurdish nature, but Armenians are afraid of atrocities from both sides. As a result of this movement, the market

[Անապահովութեան] [Տետր Թիւ] 4
[1919 Սեպտեմբեր] – 1919 Հոկ[տեմբեր]

Պանտրմա (Առաջնորդէն) – 14 Հոկտեմբեր

Տեղւոյս Միլլի շարժման գլխաւոր վարիչներն են հետեւեալները՝

1° Հաճի Տավուտ օղլու Եահիա Մէզայի էֆ. տեղահանութեան ատեն Ատաբազարի գայմագամ եւ այդ առիթով տեղւոյս հայութիւնը խոշտանգելու եւ կողոպտելու հրոսակային արարքին ի վարձատրութիւն յետոյ Կիւմիւշխանէյի միւթէսարրֆ կարգուած եւ այժմ անպաշտօն ի քաղաքիս, յղփացած իր դիզած հարստութեան վայելքով, պարագլուխը Միլլի շարժումին:

2° Թէզաիհիւտ էրքեան հարպ գայմագամ Սապրի պէյ.

3° Թօփճը գայմագամ Րէճէպ պէյ.

4° Հաճի Հաշիմ պէյ օղլու Րիզա պէյ, Մէճլիս Իտարէի անդամ.

5° Վէլի պէյ զատէ Մէհմէտ էֆ. փաստաբան.

6° Էօմէր Լութֆի էֆ. Հանրային Պարտուց վարչութեան տնօրէն եւ Իթթիհատի պատասխանատու պատուիրակ.

7° Միւլքի պէյ զատէ Մէհմէտ պէյ.

8° Սերվէթ պէյ թաղապետութեան նախագահ.

Ասոնք Իթթիհատին տեղւոյս կարկառուն դէմքերն ալ են եւ իբր այն կը ղեկավարեն Ազգային Շարժումը:

Մալաթիա (Կար[ապետ] Գըլըճեանէ) – 12 Սեպտեմբեր

Անգլիացի Մաժէօր Տուվիլ 30 զինուորով Մալաթիա կը ժամանէ եւ հետաքրքիր կ'ըլլայ հասկնալու համար թէ զօրաշարժէն առաջ ի՞նչ էր Մալաթիոյ հայոց թիւը: Իրեն ցոյց կու տան վիճակագիր մը շատ չափաւոր եւ նոյնիսկ պակաս գրուած, սակայն թուրք կառավարութիւնը այն վիճակագիրն ալ կը հերքէ եւ շատ աւելի պակաս ցոյց տալ կ'ուզէ հայոց թիւը: Անգլիացի հրամատարը քննութեան կը ձեռնարկէ Օրտուզէն, որուն համար հայերը նշանակած էին 15 տուն եւ 70 անձ: Քննութեամբ կը հաստատուի թէ կար 21 տուն եւ 96 հոգի: Եթէ քննութիւնը շարունակէր, նոյն արդիւնքը առաջ պիտի գար նաեւ ուրիշ շատ տեղերու մէջ, սակայն քրտական ապստամբութիւնը արգելք եղաւ այս քննութեան:

- Քրտական ապստամբութիւնը սկսաւ Սեպտեմբեր 9ին: Կուսակալը, կառավարիչը (որ քիւրտեր են), անգլիական հազարապետը իր հետեւորդներով, եւ Մալաթիոյ շրջանակին ամէն[էն] ազդեցիկ քիւրտը՝ քեաղթեցի Կարնոյ ջարդարար Հաճի Պէտիր աղան, Արբաճի զատէ Մուհամէտ էֆէնտին խոյս տուած են դէպի Քեաղթէ եւ կառավարութենէն ապստամբած են: Սեպտեմբեր 10ին Տրէժանի քիւրտ ցեղապետ Մուսթաֆա, Աթմացի Ճըլպաղզատէ Մուսթաֆա, Բեթիւրկէցի Իսմայիլ, Իզօլուցի Հաճի Գայա – ամէնքն ալ քիւրտ ցեղապետներ – Հաքիմ խանցի Ըսմէթ էֆ. եւ տեղացիներէն կացինաւորներու գործադրիչ թորթումցի Հաֆիզ, Հաճի Խալիլ զատէ Վահապ, Գարագաշ զատէ Գատիր, գոմիսէր Ֆատըլ էֆենտիները կ'երթան Հաճի Պէտիր Աղայի քով համաձայնութեան մը գալու համար: Կ'երեւայ թէ իրենց ձեռնարկը չէ յաջողած, վասնզի յաջորդ օրը կէսօրէն վերջ կառավարական մթերանոցին մէջ գտնուած զէնքը եւ ռազմամթերքը ամբողջութեամբ ժողովուրդին կը բաժնուի եւ գիշերն ալ իւրաքանչիւր թաղի մէջ տեղացիք հսկողութիւն կը կատարեն: Քաղաքին մէջ գտնուած 1500[ի] չափ զօրքերը Գըզլան եւ Իհտատէի կողմը, իսկ զինուած քաղաքացիներէն 2000էն աւելի անձեր Պանազի եւ Քիւնտի-Պէկի դիրքերը պաշտպանելու կ'երթան:

Կուսակալին եւ Հաճի Պէտիր աղայի տրամադրութեան տակ կան 6000ի մօտ զինուած քիւրտեր: Կ'ըսուի թէ անգլիական զօրքեր ալ պիտի հասնին օժանդակութեան:

Մուսթաֆա Քէմալի զօրքերը պատրաստութիւն կը տեսնեն: Հաճի Գայան, որ Պատերազմական Ատեան պահանջուած ըլլալուն համար իբր ջարդարար Մալաթիոյ եւ Խարբերդի փախստա-

is almost closed. The Turks do not dare to open a shop. The two races are armed against each other. A month ago, the Turks, pretending to be Kurds, were joining the Kurdish club and demonstrating fists against the Armenians. Now, the Turks show much more hatred toward the Kurds than the Armenians. No clash between Kurds and Turks has happened yet.

Trabzon (from the primate)—October 4

More than three thousand Turkish ununiformed but fully armed soldiers are scattered in the mountains near Trabzon (near Cevizlik). The military commander of Erzurum leads them. The prefect of Trabzon went to Erzurum to meet with him.

• The British military representative in Trabzon, Captain Crawford, has severed ties with the local government.

• With the Allies' permission, Christians' return to Trabzon continues. Meanwhile, the number of Muslim muhacirs brought here increases daily, even though they are not locals. In response to the primate's remarks, the provincial treasurer—deputy prefect—ascertained that the ban is for Christians and Muslims indiscriminately, but Muslim muhacirs continue to come.

• The insecurity around Trabzon is perfect because even the last Muslim villager is armed and encouraged by the developments. Therefore, crimes are unceasing. On September 10, Sarkis Migilian, a villager from Çimenli [Lazana] in Akçaabat rural district, went to his village to settle his land issue. The next day he had to go down to Akçaabat with the Turkish village headman and wait until September 13. Sarkis and the headman were obliged to spend the night in a coffeehouse owned by a Turk named Elmas. On the night of September 12, a Turk from Akçaabat, Kasap Mevlit, entered the coffeehouse with another Turk armed with pistols and daggers. When Mevlit realized Sarkis was Armenian, he showered him with insults and threw a coffee cup at him. Migilian demanded an explanation, which aggravated Kasap further, causing him to pull out his gun and try to shoot. The headman intervened at that point. Mevlit continued his insults and threats and invited him [Sarkis] outside to settle his account. The headman intervened again. Thereupon, Mevlit and the coffeehouse owner attacked the headman and started slapping him. Taking the opportunity, Sarkis managed to slip out of the coffeehouse, leaving even his shoes there. The two Turks chased him, but he escaped, thanks to the darkness. This incident in Akçaabat coincided with the days the Milli organization took the city under its rule.

• Several Armenians from the villages of Akçaabat, while on their way to make arrangements for their land issues, returned affected by the incident; that is, by the Millis' appearance. Three Armenians—Simon Sourian, fifty-five, from Esentepe [Mayer]; Mgrdich Sourian, thirty-five, from the same village; [and] Haroutyun Kyuvelian, thirty-six, from Haverdia—were insulted and beaten on the way. The old man went to the prelacy with a bloody head. The primate encouraged them to return to their village. They complied with his request and were killed on the way.

• More than a dozen Greeks in Sürmene, transporting goods by steamboat, were brought ashore and slaughtered allegedly by bandits. The perpetrators also set the boat on fire.

• A few days ago, in Akçaabat, some Turks entered Greek houses at night and slaughtered entire households.

կան էր, հիմա երեւան եկած է եւ ազատ կը շրջի եւ հրամաններ կ'արձակէ: Առայժմ հայոց դէմ շարժում չկայ եւ խնդիրը թուրք եւ քիւրտ հանգամանք մը ունի, սակայն հայերը կը վախնան երկու կողմին ալ վայրագութենէն: Այս շարժումին հետեւանօք շուկայ գրեթէ փակուած է: Թուրքերը չեն համարձակիր խանութ բանալ: Երկու ցեղերը իրարու դէմ զինուած են: Ամիս մը առաջ թուրքերը քիւրտ ձեւանալով քիւրտ գիւղին կ'արձանագրուէին եւ հայերու դէմ բռունցք ցոյց կուտային: Հիմա թուրքերը հայերէն շատ աւելի ատելութիւն ցոյց կուտան քիւրտերու նկատմամբ: Դեռ ընդհարում չկայ քիւրտերու եւ թուրքերու միջեւ:

Տրապիզոն (Առաջնորդէն) – 4 Հոկտեմբեր

3000էն աւելի թուրք զինուորներ առանց զինուորական տարազի, բայց կատարելապէս սպառազինուած, ցրուած են Տրապիզոնի մօտակայ լեռներուն մէջ (Ճէվիզլիկի կողմերը), ղեկավարութեամբ Կարինի զինուորական հրամանատարին, որուն հետ տեսակցելու գացած է ի Կարին Տրապիզոնի կուսակալը:

- Տրապիզոնի բրիտանական զինուորական ներկայացուցիչ Գէբթըն Գրաուֆըրտ խզած է իր յարաբերութիւնները տեղական կառավարութեան հետ:

- Համաձայնութեան թոյլտուութեամբ կը շարունակ[ուի] քրիստոնեաներու վերադարձը դէպի Տրապիզոն, մինչ օրէ օր կ'աւելնայ իսլամ գաղթականներու թիւը, որոնք տեղացի չըլլալով հանդերձ, հոս կը բերուին: Առաջնորդին դիտողութեանց ի պատասխան կուսակալի փոխանորդ տէֆթէրտարը կը հաւաստէ թէ արգելքը անխտիր քրիստոնեաներու եւ իսլամներու համար է, սակայն իսլամ գաղթականներ կը շարունակեն գալ:

- Տրապիզոնի շրջակայքը անապահովութիւնը կատարեալ է, վասնզի իսլամ յետին գիւղացին նոյնիսկ զինուած է եւ կը քաջալերուի երեւոյթներէն: Հետեւաբար ոճիրներ անպակաս են: Սեպտեմբեր 10ին Բլաթանայի գաւառակին Լազանա գիւղացի Սարգիս Միկիլեան կ'երթայ իր գիւղը կարգադրելու համար իր հողային խնդիրը: Յաջորդ օրը հարկ կ'ըլլայ թուրք գիւղապետին հետ իջնել Բլաթանա եւ սպասել մինչեւ Սեպտեմբեր 13, ուստի Սարգիս եւ գիւղապետը կը ստիպուին գիշերել Էլմաս անուն թուրքի մը սրճարանը: Սեպտեմբեր 12ի գիշերը, բլաթանացի թուրք մը, Ղասապ Մէվլիտ, ուրիշ թուրքի մը հետ, զինուած ատրճանակներով եւ դաշոյնով, կը մտնեն սրճարան: Մէվլիտ երբ կը հասկնայ Սարգիսի հայ ըլլալը, նախատինքներ կը տեղայ եւ սուրճի գաւաթը անոր կը նետէ: Երբ Միկիլեան բացատրութիւն կը պահանջէ, Ղասապ, աւելի բորբոքած, կը քաշէ ատրճանակը եւ կը փորձէ կրակել՝ երբ գիւղապետը կը միջամտէ: Մէվլիտ կը շարունակէ իր յիշոցները եւ սպառնալիքները եւ կը հրաւիրէ դուրս անոր հաշիւը կարգադրելու համար: Գիւղապետը դարձեալ կը միջամտէ: Ատոր վրայ Մէվլիտ եւ սրճարանապետը կը յարձակին գիւղապետին վրայ եւ կը սկսին ապտակել զայն: Առիթէն օգտուելով Սարգիս կը յաջողի սրճարանէն դուրս սպրդիլ, նոյնիսկ կօշիկները հոն ձգելով: Երկու թուրքերը զինքը կը հետապնդեն, բայց անիկա մութէն օգտուելով կ'ազատի: Բլաթանայի այս միջադէպը կը զուգադիպէր Միլլի կազմակերպութեան քաղաքին տիրապետելու օրերուն:

- Բլաթանայի գիւղերէն կարգ մը հայեր իրենց հողային խնդիրներու համար կարգադրութիւններ ընելու համար իրենց տեղերը գացած ատեն պատահած դէպքէն, այսինքն՝ Միլլիներու երեւան գալէն ազդուած ետ կը դառնան: Երեք հայեր, Սիմոն Սուրեան, մայերցի , 55 տարեկան, Մկրտիչ Սուրեան, նոյն գիւղէն 35 տարեկան, Յարութիւն Գիւվէլեան, հավըրտիացի, 36 տարեկան, ճամբան կը նախատուին եւ կը ծեծուին: Ծերունի[ն] արիւնլուայ գլուխով առաջնորդարան կուգայ: Առաջնորդը կը խրախուսէ զիրենք դառնալ իրենց գիւղը: Անոնք կը համակերպին եւ ճամբան կը սպաննուին:

- Սիւրմէնէի մէջ աւելի քան տասնեակ մը յոյներ, որ շոգեշարժ նաւակով մը ապրանք կը փոխադրէին, ցամաք կը հանուին որպէս թէ աւազակներու կողմէ եւ կը խողխողուին: Նաւն ալ կը վառեն:

Diyarbakır (from the Armenian Catholic vicar general)—September 19
Telegraphic communications are interrupted. Terrified Armenian families are coming here from Harput and leaving for Aleppo in a hurry. The situation is uncertain. The local Armenians also are migrating. On September 15, the American Commission of Inquiry passed through here, staying only two hours in Diyarbakır without contacting Christians.

• A program called [the] Association for the Defense of Rights of Eastern Anadolu [Anatolia], which contains statements that intimidate Christians, was disseminated here in the name of Erzurum's Congress.

• Ihsan Bey, the brother of Zilfi Bey, now locked up in Malta, was sent as a delegate to participate in the Milli Congress of Sivas.

• Ignorant Turks, ostensibly because of a secretive preparation, often threaten the Armenians, saying: "There are a few days left; we will massacre the remaining Armenians as well." These utterances are one of the main reasons Armenians are migrating, fearing mischief.

• Every day, Kurdish and Turkish migrants from Diyarbakır regularly pass through, heading toward Bitlis and Van in large caravans. The government pays for their expenses and provides them with every facility, while the plea of Armenian deportees remains unheard.

Nallıhan (from the Neighborhood Council)—October 2
The Armenians living in the area, some eight hundred people, are in fear and terror because of the crimes committed against Armenians. Twenty to twenty-five days ago, forty-five-year-old Mariam Kasbarian and her son, sixteen-year-old Garabed Kasbarian, and twenty-year-old Haroutyun Parseghian and twenty-year-old Artaki Saghliyan, four people, went to the surrounding Turkish villages for trade and work and disappeared. Suspicious relatives searched for them and found their brutally killed corpses in a canyon between the villages Çiller and Subaşı. As a result of this crime, all Armenians are now confined to their homes because they have no other means of livelihood other than working in the villages. The government already does not compensate them for their abandoned property, which totals seven thousand liras, and if they are deprived of the opportunity also to earn money in this way, not a single Armenian will be able to stock up for winter, wherefore they will perish of hunger.

• An appeal was made to the government for the four Armenians killed. The deputy attorney general, the secretary of the preliminary court, and a man named Fuat, who was expelled from the police force, went to the crime scene along with a few soldiers. After staying there for four or five days, they brought several people and imprisoned them. Fuat accepted a bribe to let the real perpetrators go free. This was confirmed by the local judge, Ahmet Hamdi Effendi, who complained to the proper authorities.

Trabzon (from the locum tenens)—October 7
Migration has begun. Armenians cross to Russia and elsewhere. One hundred sixty people have migrated from Trabzon in a month and a half.

Zonguldak—October 12
Last week, after midnight, Turkish gendarmes entered an inn rented by an Armenian and proposed to take out the customers' horses to accommodate their own. After the innkeeper refused, they started

- Մի քանի օր առաջ Բլաթանայի մէջ կարգ մը թուրքեր գիշերանց կը մտնեն յոյն տուներ եւ կը մորթոտեն ամբողջ տնեցիները:

Տիարպէքիր (Հայ Կաթողիկէ Առաջնորդական Փոխանորդէն) – 19 Սեպտեմբեր

Հեռագրական հաղորդակցութիւնք ընդհատուած են: Խարբերդէն հայ ընտանիքներ աիաբեկ հոս կուգան եւ հապճեպով Հալէպ կը մեկնին: Կացութիւնը անստոյգ է: Այս տեղի հայերն ալ կը գաղթեն: Սեպտեմբեր 15ին ասկէ անցաւ Ամերիկեան Քննիչ Յանձնախումբը, որ միայն երկու ժամ կը մնայ Տիարպէքիր՝ առանց քրիստոնեաներու հետ յարաբերութեան մտնելու:

- Կարնոյ Քօնկրէ անունով հոս ցրուած են «Շարքի Անատօլու Միւտաֆայի Հուգուգ Ճէմիաթի» [Արեւելեան Անատոլիոյ Իրաւունքներու Պաշտպանութեան Միութիւն] անուն յայտագիր մը, որուն մէջ քրիստոնեաները աիաբեկող բացատրութիւններ կան:

- Սեբաստիոյ Միլլի Քօնկրէին մասնակցելու համար իբր պատուիրակ ղրկեցին Իհսան պէկը, որ եղբայրն է հիմա Մալթա արգելափակուած երեսփոխան Չիֆի պէյին:

- Ցէտ թուրքեր կ՚երեւայ թէ գաղտնի տեսնուած պատրաստութեան մը հետեւանօք յաճախ կը սպառնան հայոց ըսելով թէ «քանի մը օր մնաց. մնացած հայերն ալ պիտի ջարդենք»: Այս խօսքերը գլխաւոր պատճառներէն մէկն են որ հայերը կը գաղթեն, չարիքէ մը վախնալով:

- Տիարպէքիրէն շարունակ ամէն օր կանոնաւորապէս քիւրտ եւ թուրք գաղթականներ կ՚անցնին դէպի Պիթլիս եւ Վան, խոշոր կարաւաններով: Կառավարութիւնը կը վճարէ անոնց ծախքերը եւ ամէն դիւրութիւն կուտայ, մինչ հայ տարագրեալներուն դիմումը անլսելի կը մնայ:

Նալլու Խան (Թաղական Խորհուրդէն) – 2 Հոկտեմբեր

Տեղւոյս վերապրող հայերը, իբր 800 հոգի, ահ ու սարսափի մէջ են, վասնզի հայերու դէմ ոճիրներ կը գործուին: Ասկէ 20–25 օր առաջ առեւտուր[ի] եւ աշխատութեան համար շրջակայ թուրք գիւղերը գացող 45 տարեկան Մարիամ Գասպարեան եւ որդին՝ 16 տարեկան Կարապետ Գասպարեան, եւ 20 տարեկան Յարութիւն Բարսեղեան եւ դարձեալ 20 տարեկան Արթաքի Սաղըլեան, չորս հոգի, կ՚անհետանան: Իրենց պարագաները կասկածելով փնտռելու կ՚երթան եւ անոնց խժդժօրէն սպաննուած դիակնին, Չիլէ եւ Սուպաշը գիւղերու միջեւ ձորի մը մէջ կը գտնեն: Այս ոճիրին հետեւանօք հիմա բոլոր հայերը տուները արգելափակուած են, վասնզի ուրիշ ապրուստի միջոց չունին, եթէ ոչ գիւղերու մէջ աշխատելու միջոցը: Կառավարութիւնը արդէն չի վճարեր լքեալ գոյքերու փոխարժէքը՝ 7000 ոսկին, եւ եթէ այսպէս դրամ շահելու միջոցէն ալ զրկուին, ոչ մէկ հայ ձմրան պաշար պիտի կրնայ ճարել, որով անսուաղ պիտի փճանան:

- Սպաննուած չորս հայերուն համար կառավարութեան դիմում եղաւ: Ընդհանուր դատախազի փոխանորդը եւ նախնական դատարանի քարտուղարը, եւ ոստիկանութենէ վտարեալ Ֆուատ անուն մէկը, քանի մը զինուորներով ոճիրին վայրը գացին եւ 4–5 օր մնալէ յետոյ եկան, մի քանի մարդ բերին եւ բանտարկեցին: Բուն ոճրագործները ազատ մնացած են Ֆուատին կաշառք տալով, ինչ որ հաստատելով տեղւոյն դատաւորը՝ Աիմէտ Համտի էֆ., բողոքած է պատկանեալ իշխանութեան:

Տրապիզոն (Առաջնորդական Տեղապահէն) – 7 Հոկտեմբեր

Արտագաղթը սկսած է. հայերը կ՚անցնին Ռուսաստան եւ այլուր: Մէկուկէս ամսուան մէջ Տրապիզոնէն 160 հոգի գաղթած են:

Զօնկուլտաք – 12 Հոկտեմբեր

Անցեալ շաբթու ընթացքին թուրք ժանտարմաներ հայու մը կողմէ վարձուած խան մը կը մտնեն կէս գիշերէն յետոյ եւ կ՚առաջարկեն իրենց ձիերուն տեղ տալ՝ դուրս հանելով յաճախորդներու

beating him. Other Armenians gently intervened to separate the fighters, but the police misinterpreted this intervention and began shouting: "The Armenians are killing us, aren't there any Muslims left? They are not acknowledging [our] government," and so on. Three Armenians were taken to jail by such accusations. They were severely beaten, tortured, and humiliated. Pleas remained useless.

• As has been confirmed, on the night of October 9–10, around eleven o'clock at night, an armed group of more than ten people surrounded one of the houses in the Çaydamar Armenian quarter and asked the landlord's permission to have fun and to drink raki in his house. The landlord rejecting this disgraceful proposal was tortured. One of the rooms in the same house was rented by the [Armenian] Neighborhood Council and inhabited by a young widow, who, feeling the looming danger, managed to escape, taking refuge in a nearby Armenian's house. The armed evildoers besieged the second house and demanded that the woman be handed over to them. Met by another rejection, they abducted her and took her away. No trace of her has been found so far. The woman's cries from the nearby woods were heard for more than half an hour. Neighbors fired warning shots, but the Turkish gendarmes refused to be disturbed, although they were informed [of the abduction] promptly [for them to intercede].

Sugören [Çengiler] (from the Neighborhood Council)—October 13

Onnig Mezbourian, a twenty-eight-year-old educated young man who made a living as a peddler, was killed five days ago in the middle of the road joining Yalova's Kurtköy [Delipazarı] and Paşaköy villages while he was visiting the Laz villages. The investigating body did not find his corpse, although traces of blood and remains of the goods he sold were found at the crime scene, despite the rain pouring for two days. The villagers no longer dare to come out [of their homes] to go even to the nearest places, which means they are in danger of dying of starvation.

Konya (from the vicar general)—October 13[25]

In response to an appeal protesting against the invitation to Armenians to enlist in the Army in Ereğli, the Milli forces stated that a mistake had been made and that Christians would not be enlisted.

• Local newspapers are using provocative language against Christians.

• The district of Bozkır continues to reject joining the government of Mustafa Kemal and resists fiercely.

• Mustafa Kemal's arrival in Konya is anticipated.

Bandırma (from the primate)—October 17

Before and after the Milli movement, it appears that the Allied representatives, by following a policy of counterbalancing and pursuing one another to a noticeable degree, indirectly convinced the Muslim element that they encourage the Milli movement. As soon as a British representative sets foot in a city, village, or any place, suddenly, a French representative or official arrives there, as if caught in a nightmare, and so on, seemingly with a special effort to win over the Turks. Recent articles favorable to Turks in *Le Temps* led the leaders of the Milli movement in Balıkesir to hold [copies of] the newspaper and organize public feasts, celebrations, and demonstrations. The enthusiastic crowd enlivened the Turkish element with the idea of Turkey's territorial integrity through photos showing them [the notables] with French officials and officers.

• The Milli forces want to compel the Christians to participate in the Ottoman parliamentary elec-

ձիերը: Մերժողական պատասխան ստացած ըլլալով, կը սկսին ծեծել պանդոկապետը: Ուրիշ հայեր կը միջամտեն մեղմօրէն՝ կռուողները իրարմէ զատելու համար, սակայն ոստիկանները այս միջամտութեան տարբեր գոյն տալով կը սկսին պոռալ թէ «հայերը մեզի կը սպաննեն, միւսիւլման չէ՞ մնացած միթէ, կառավարութիւն չեն ճանչնար եւայլն» կարգ մը ամբաստանութիւններով հայերէն երեք հոգի բանտ կ՚առաջնորդուին ու չարաչար կը ծեծուին, կը խոշտանգուին եւ կ՚անարգուին: Դիմումները կը մնան անօգուտ:

- Հոկտեմբեր 9–10ի գիշերը զինեալ խումբ մը, որուն տասը հոգիէ աւելի ըլլալը հաստատուած է, կը պաշարէ գիշերուան ժամը 11ին ատեններըը Չայ Տամար հայ թաղին տուներէն մէկը եւ կ՚առաջարկեն տանտիրոջ որպէսզի թոյլ տրուի իրենց զուարճանալ եւ օղի խմել իր տան մէջ: Մերժուած ըլլալով այդ անպատիւ առաջարկը, տանտէրը կը խոշտանգուի: Նոյն տունին սենեակներէն մէկը թաղական խորհուրդին կողմէ վարձուած էր եւ հոն կը բնակէր մանկամարդ այրի կին մը, որ զգալով սպառնացող վտանգը կը յաջողի խոյս տալ եւ ապաստանիլ մօտակայ հայու մը տունը: Զինեալ չարագործները երկրորդ տունը կը պաշարեն եւ կը պահանջեն որ յիշեալ կինը իրենց յանձնուի. մերժումի հանդիպելով՝ բռնի կ՚առեւանգեն զայն եւ կը տանին: Ցարդ ոեւէ հետք չէ գտնուած: Մօտակայ անտառներէն կէս ժամէ աւելի լսուած են կնոջ աղաղակները՝ դրացիները ատրճանակի հարուածներով ազդարարած են վտանգը, թուրք ժանտարմըրին երբեք չէ ուզած անհանգիստ ըլլալ՝ հակառակ որ իրենց լուր տրուած էր ժամանակին:

Չէնկիլէր (Թաղական Խորհուրդէն) – 13 Հոկտեմբեր

Օննիկ Մեզպուրեան, 28 տարեկան ուսեալ երիտասարդը, որ մանրավաճառութեամբ իր ապրուստը կը հանէր, հինգ օր առաջ լազ գիւղերը շրջած պահուն կը սպաննուի Եալօվայի Տէլի Բազար եւ Փաշաքէօյ լազ գիւղերուն իրար միացնող ճամբուն մէջտեղ: Քննութեան համար գացող մարմինը դիակն ալ չէ գտած, թէեւ ոճիրին վայրը արեան հետքերը եւ իր ծախած ապրանքէն մնացորդներ կը մնան հակառակ երկու օրէ ի վեր տեղացող անձրեւին: Գիւղացիք կը վախնան այլեւս դուրս ելլելու եւ ամենէն մօտ տեղերը իսկ երթալու, ինչ որ կը նշանակէ թէ անօթի մեռնելու վտանգին տակ են:

Գոնիա (Առաջնորդական Փոխանորդէն) – 13 Հոկտեմբեր

Էրէյլի[h] մէջ հայերը զինուորագրելու հրաւէրին դէմ բողոքելու համար եղած դիմումին ի պատասխան Միլլի ոյժերու կողմէ պատասխանուած է թէ սխալ մը եղած է եւ քրիստոնեայք չպիտի զինուորագրուին:

- Տեղական թերթեր գրգռիչ լեզու մը կը գործածեն քրիստոնեաներու դէմ:
- Պօզկըրի գաւառը դեռ կը մերժէ յարիլ Մուսթաֆա Քէմալի կառավարութեան եւ բուռն կերպով կը պայքարի:
- Մուսթաֆա Քէմալի Գոնիա ժամանումին կը սպասուի:

Պանտրմա (Առաջնորդէն) – 17 Հոկտեմբեր

Միլլի շարժումէն առաջ եւ յետոյ տեղւոյս եւ շրջակայից մէջ ուշադրութիւն գրաւելու աստիճան Համաձայնական ներկայացուցիչները մին միւսը հակակշռելու եւ հետապնդելու ուղղութեան մը հետեւելով կարծես անուղղակի իմն Միլլի շարժումը քաջալերելու համոզումը տուած են իսլամ տարրին: Հազիւ անգլիական ներկայացուցիչները քաղաք, գիւղ կամ ոեւէ տեղ մը ոտք կը կոխէին,ահա յանկարծ ֆրանսական ներկայացուցիչ կամ պաշտօնեայ վրայ կը հասնէին, կարծես մրձաւանջէ մը բռնուած, եւ այսպէս յաջորդաբար, կարծես թէ մասնաւոր ճիգ մը ընելով շահելու թուրքերը: Վերջերս «Թան»ի թրքաց նպաստաւոր յօդուածները պատճառ եղան որ Միլլի շարժումին գլխաւորները, Պալըքէսիրի մէջ թերթերը ձեռքերնին հրապարակաւ խրախճանութիւններ եւ ցնծութեան տօներ եւ ցոյցեր սարքեն եւ խանդավառ ամբոխը՝ իրեն հետ ունենալով ֆրանսացի պաշտօնեայ եւ սպաներ, լուսանկարուին եւ բարոյալքուած թուրք տարրը ոգեւորուի Թուրքիոյ հողային

tions. In Balikesir, Hulusi Effendi, who belongs to the Milli organization, told a member of the Neighborhood Council that all Christians should take part in the elections; otherwise, they should go to Yerevan.

Aleppo (from R. A. Lambert, representative of the [Near East] Relief)—October 11

The evacuation of Syria having been decided by the British, it was officially announced that all the Armenians living [in the areas] west of the western and southern borderlines of Maraş would be sent to Adana as soon as possible. Implementation of this decision is now underway. Last week, twenty-five hundred Armenians were sent to Adana by train, and another twelve hundred are expected to be sent by train on Monday, October 13. Until November 1, we will have barely fifteen hundred people left in the tents of deportees, all from the territory east of the borderline of Maraş. There are also about one thousand Armenian and non-Armenian deportees in the city who live outside the deportation camp. It is unlikely that they would leave because many of them are employed, particularly after news arrived from Adana that as many as one thousand migrants have remained unprotected.

• Various British officers, some having responsible positions, suggested by hinting or by speaking frankly that there would be a disturbance between Armenians and Arabs after their departure, the nearness of which is now acknowledged officially. Some of them think that with their departure, our relief organization will fail and that the position of the Americans is a bit worrying. However, the Americans feel that they should not follow the British and that their presence will be more necessary after their departure.

• The British governor, who oversees the relief and delivery affairs of the province, said that the boys' station-orphanage of Aleppo should be removed, together with five hundred orphans, and be reestablished farther north. A response came that it could be transferred to Gaziantep [Ayntab] in six days.

• The British consider it impossible to relocate the Armenian orphanage, which contains twenty-one hundred orphans and has an expenditure of twenty-two hundred liras. They will probably stop subsidizing it because [otherwise] they have to care for it too.

Extracted from a letter from Mardin's principal[26]

There is a pretty large demonstration on the night of October 6 against the British vacating the Black Sea ports. These kinds of incidents cause panic among Christians, who have the drive to leave if they can find the means. This outward movement is less in Mardin than in Silvan, which many have already left. Here and in Diyarbakır, we were able to calm the panic through the authorities and inspire confidence that the peace is perfect. We really believe so, but the affair of our liberation will slow down and stop spreading in other directions until political conditions improve. It is evident, of course, that when winter comes, we will have more people to care for than we have now.

• Politically, the Turks are frequently threatening, which is not uncommon now. It seems to me that while there are only threats, it is time for a complete occupation of these parts, which perhaps would save many lives, and that allowing this [situation] to continue like this would be nothing less than foolishness, as few soldiers would be able to stop the propaganda [if intervention takes place now]. We know what happened in Aleppo shortly after May of this year when three hundred people perished, and the Americans there were lucky to have been able to escape. While we have come here

ամբողջութեան գաղափարով:

- Օսմանեան երեսփոխանական ընտրութեանց Միլլի ոյժեր բռնի քրիստոնեաները մասնակցութեան հրաւիրել կ'ուզեն: Պալըքէսիրի մէջ միլլիական Խուլիսի էֆ. թաղական խորհուրդի անդամի մը յայտներ է թէ բոլոր քրիստոնեաները պէտք է մասնակցին ընտրութիւններու, հակառակ պարագային պէտք է Երեւան երթան:

Հալէպ (Ռ. Ա. Լամպէրթ, Reliefի ներկայացուցիչէն) – 11 Հոկտեմբեր

Սուրիոյ պարպումը անգլիացւոց կողմէ որոշուած ըլլալով պաշտօնապէս լուր տրուեցաւ որ բոլոր հայերը, որոնց բնակութիւնը Մարաշի հիւսիսային եւ հարաւային գիծերուն արեւմտակողմի հողամասին մէջ կը գտնուէին, կարելի եղածին չափ շուտ Ատանա պիտի ղրկուէին: Այս որոշումը հիմա կը գործադրուի: Անցեալ շաբթու 2500 հայեր շոգեկառքով Ատանա ղրկուեցան եւ Երկուշաբթի օր 13 Հոկտեմբերին 1200ի եւս ղրկուիլը կը սպասուի: Մինչեւ Նոյեմբեր 1 տարագրելոց տաղաւարներուն մէջ հազիւ 1500 հոգիի մնացորդ մը պիտի ունենանք, որոնց բոլորն ալ Մարաշի գծին արեւելակողմի հողամասէն: Քաղաքին մէջ կան նաեւ 1000[ի] մօտ հայ թէ ոչ-հայ տարագիրներ, որոնք տարագրութեան կայանէն դուրս կ'ապրին, հաւանական չէ որ անոնք մեկնին, որովհետեւ շատերը գործ բռնած են: Մանաւանդ Ատանայէն լուր առնուած է որ հոն ալ 1000ի չափ գաղթականները անպատսպար մնացած են:

- Զանազան անգլիացի սպաներ, որոնցմէ ոմանք պատասխանատու դիրքի մէջ են, ակնարկութիւնով թէ ալ անկեղծ խօսքով սա կարծիքը կը յայտնեն թէ, հայերու եւ արաբներու միջեւ խառնակութիւն մը յառաջ պիտի գայ իրենց մեկնելէն յետոյ, որուն մօտալուտ ըլլալը հիմա պաշտօնապէս ընդունուած է: Անոնցմէ ոմանք այն կարծիքը ունին թէ իրենց մեկնումով մեր խնամատարական կազմակերպութիւնը պիտի վիժի եւ ամերիկացւոց դիրք[ը] քիչ մը մտահոգիչ է: Սակայն ամերիկացիք կը կարծեն թէ իրենք պէտք չէ հետեւին անգլիացւոց եւ անոնց երթալէն յետոյ իրենց ներկայութիւնը աւելի անհրաժեշտ է:

- Անգլիացի կառավարիչը, որ նախանգին խնամատարական եւ առաքման գործերը ստանձնած է, հաղորդեց թէ պէտք է վերցնել Հալէպի մանչերու կայան-որբանոցը, 500 որբերով միասին, եւ տանիլ հաստատել աւելի հիւսիս: Պատասխանուեցաւ թէ վեց օրուան մէջ կարելի է Այնթապ փոխադրել:

- Հայոց որբանոցը, որ 2100 որբեր կը պարունակէ եւ 2200 ոսկեդրամ ծախք ունի, անգլիացիք տեղափոխել անկարելի կը համարեն, սակայն հաւանօրէն պիտի դադրեցնեն իրենց տուած նպաստները, որովհետեւ անիկա ալ հոգալ պէտք պիտի ըլլայ:

Մարտինի տնօրէնին նամակէն քաղուած

Բաւական [մեծ] ցոյց մը կայ Հոկտեմբեր 6ի գիշերը՝ անգլիացիներու Սեւ Ծովու նաւահանգիստները պարպելուն վրայ: Բոլոր այս կարգի դէպքերը պատճառ կ'ըլլան քրիստոնեաներու խուճապին, որոնց միջեւ շարժում մը կայ դուրս երթալու, եթէ կարենան ատոր միջոցները գտնել: Այս դէպի դուրս շարժումը Մարտինի մէջ աւելի քիչ է քան Տիգրանակերտի մէջ, ուրկէ շատերը մեկնած են: Մենք հոս եւ Տիարպէքիրի մէջ կրցինք հանդարտեցնել խուճապը իշխանութեանց միջոցով եւ ամէն տեսակ վստահութիւն ներշնչել թէ անդորրութիւնը կատարեալ է: Մենք իրապէս այդպէս կը հաւատանք, բայց մեր ազատագրման գործը պիտի կաղայ եւ պիտի դադրի ուրիշ ուղղութիւններով տարածուելէ, մինչեւ որ քաղաքական պայմանները բարելաւուին: Բացայայտ է անշուշտ որ, երբ ձմեռը հասնի, աւելի ժողովուրդ պիտի ունենանք հոգալիք քան հիմա:

- Քաղաքականապէս, [թուրքերը] ակռաները շատ կը ցուցնեն եւ այդ բանը հազուագիւտ չէ հիմա: Ինծի այնպէս կուգայ որ մինչ տակաւին միայն այս սպառնալիքները կան, ժամանակն է այս կողմերուն կատարեալ գրաւումին, որ գուցէ շատ մը կեանքեր փրկէ եւ անխելքութենէ քիչ մը պակաս բան մը պիտի ըլլար թողուլ որ այսպէս շարունակուի, քանի որ քանի մը զինուորներ պիտի

to save a loss, it seems that the military authority will preach "restriction." I know that Turkey is in despair, but those who have the freedom to think this way are only a minority; they are those with whom we are supposed to speak as friends, but in reality, they are the [Ittihadist] people who have so far escaped the gallows and who are most afraid of it. They give us presents and tell us that we will be more than their guests because they want Turkey for the Turks and expect us to say the same. They report that they have met twenty times with their committee and have resolved that they will complete the work on the spot before accepting unacceptable conditions. The few, who represent the minority, think the case [of Armenians] will be closed when a single Englishman appears. It may seem strange to say that there has been avoidance from the Americans ever since Harbord's Commission arrived here. This is also the case with Silvan; finding the former sincere support has become difficult. They [the Turks] obviously do not want us to possess anything, and the district governor ignores the non-execution of his orders after putting something in our hands and then taking it back with his signature. Yet he tells us that he wants to help us. He is an apparent adversary, and I think he and other Turks are trying even harder to find something against us. I am firmly convinced that Turkey regrets that it did not complete the work it strove for [the complete annihilation of Armenians].

Konya (from the vicar general)—October 17

Yesterday, Thursday, pre-arranged rallies were held in all the mosques of this city during the noon prayer. The areas around the mosques were guarded by police and troops. The imams of the day invited the Muslims to assess the situation and enlist in the army to liberate İzmir as volunteers, of course. It has been noted that even though it was not a Friday, an unusual number of people were present at these religious-political gatherings. Concerned Armenians of the market closed their shops and took refuge in their houses. It is heard that the case of conscription has not found much sympathy. Nevertheless, the agitation has played its part, and "infidel" is the slogan of the day that Muslims are throwing at Christians' faces.

Adana (from the Armenian National Union)—October 19

The Milli movement has begun throughout Cilicia; hundreds of horsemen in groups [maraud] in the plains of Cilicia. Even the residents of villages an hour or two away from Adana and the husbandmen working in the cotton fields are being massacred these last two days, and the corpses of those martyred in the villages have been brought to the city. The total death toll now stands at sixty-five, and we expect to receive news of new casualties every hour. Although [perpetrators] are being chased, the means are insufficient. The Armenians also formed tracking groups, both cavalry and infantry.

Konya (from the vicar general)—October 23[27]

As a direct result of the recent incidents in Cilicia, twenty, thirty, or forty Turkish volunteering and irregular troops have been mobilized in recent days from various parts of this province. After being armed by the local government, they will leave tomorrow, in irregular groups and under the guise of

կարենային կասեցնել բռնաբարը: Մենք գիտենք թէ ինչ պատահեցաւ Հալէպի մէջ այս տարուան Մայիսէն քիչ վերջ, երբ 300ի չափ կորան եւ այն տեղի ամերիկացին բախտաւոր է եղեր որ կրցաւ ողջ պրծիլ, եւ մինչդեռ մենք կորուստ մը ազատելու համար հոս եկած ենք, այնպէս կ'երեւայ որ բուն զինուորական իշխանութենէն «արգելք» պիտի քաղոզենք: Ես գիտեմ որ Թուրքիան յուսահատութեան մէջ է, բայց անոնք որ մտածելակերպի այս ա[զատ]ութեան մէջ են, միայն փոքրամասնութիւն մը կը կազմեն, որոնք անոնք են, որոնց հետ իբր բարեկամ խօսելու ենք, բայց իրականութեան մէջ ատոնք այն մարդիկն են, որոնք մինչեւ հիմա խոյս տուած են կախա[ղ]անէն եւ որոնք ամենէն աւելի կը վախնան այդ բանէն: Անոնք մեզի նուէրներ կուտան եւ կ'ըսեն մեզի որ մենք իրենց հիւրերէ աւելի պիտի ըլլանք, որովհետեւ անոնք Թուրքիան թուրքին համար կ'ուզեն եւ կ'ակնկալեն որ մենք ալ այնպէս ըսենք: Անոնք կը հաղորդեն որ իր[ենց] քօմիթէն 20 անգամներ ժողով ըրած եւ ընդունած են որ չըլլալիք պայմաններ ընդունելէ առաջ անոնք տեղւոյն վրայ գործը պիտի լմնցնեն: Այն մէկ քանիները, որոնք փոքրամասնութիւնը կը ներկայացնեն, կը կարծեն որ գործը փակուի երբ մէկ հատ անգլիացի երեւայ: Թերեւս տարօրինակ թուի ըսելը թէ Հարպօրթի Յանձնախումբը հոս գտնուելէն ի վեր, ամերիկացիներէն խուսափում մը յառաջ եկած է: Տիգրանակերտի մէջ ալ այսպէս է եւ մենք դժուարութիւն կը քաշենք նախկին անկեղծ աջակցութիւնը ունենալու մէջ: Անոնք ակնյայտնի կերպով չեն ուզեր որ բան մը ունենանք եւ միւթէսարրըֆը իր իսկ տուած հրամաններուն չգործադրուիլը կ'անտեսէ մեր ձեռքին մէջ բան մը դնելով եւ յետոյ զայն ետ կ'առնէ իր իսկ ստորագրութեամբ, բայց մեզի կը յայտարարէ թէ մեզի օգնել կ'ուզէ: Բացայայտ ընդդիմադիր մըն է եւ կարծեմ ան եւ ուրիշ թուրքեր ա՛լ աւելի կը ջանան մեր վրայ բան մը գտնելու համար: Հաստատ կերպով համոզուած եմ որ Թուրքիան կը ցաւի լմնցուցած չըլլալուն համար այն գործը որուն ձգտեցաւ:

Գոնիա (Առաջնորդական Փոխանորդէն) – 17 Հոկտեմբեր

Երէկ, Հինգշաբթի, կանխագոյն պատրաստութեամբ, քաղաքիս բոլոր մզկիթներուն մէջ, կէսօրուան աղօթքի պահուն, տեղի ունեցան միթինկներ: Մզկիթներու շրջակաները ոստիկաններ եւ զօրքեր կը հսկէին: Օրուան աղօթասացները հրաւիրած են իսլամները գնահատել կացութիւնը եւ Իզմիրի ազատագրման համար զինուորագրուիլ, անշուշտ իբր կամաւոր: Նշմարուած է որ, հակառակ Ուրբաթ չըլլալուն, անսովոր բազմութիւն մը ներկայ գտնուած է կրօնական-քաղաքական սոյն հաւաքումներուն: Շուկայի հայերը ազդուած իրենց խանութները փակելով տուն ապաստանած են: Կը լսուի թէ զօրականչի պարագան շատ համակրութիւն չէ գտած: Անով հանդերձ, գրգռութիւնը իր դերը կատարած է եւ «կեավուռ»ը օրուան կարգախօսն է որ իսլամները քրիստոնէից երեսին կը նետեն:

Ատանա (Ազգային Միութենէն) – 19 Հոկտեմբեր

Կիլիկիոյ ամէն կողմը Միլլի շարժումը սկսած է, հարիւրաւոր ձիաւորներ խումբ խումբ Կիլիկիոյ դաշտեր[ը կ'ասպատակեն], նոյնիսկ Ատանայէն 1–2 ժամ հեռաւորութեամբ հայ գիւղերու բնակիչները եւ բամպակի դաշտերուն մէջ աշխատող հայ մշակները կը ջարդուին 2 օրէ ի վեր, եւ քաղաք կը բերուին այն դիակները՝ որոնք գիւղերու մէջ նահատակուած են: Ընդհ. զոհերու թիւը կը հասնի այժմ 65ի եւ ամէն ժամ նոր զոհերու լուրեր առնելու վրայ ենք: Թէեւ հետապնդութիւն կը կատարուի, սակայն միջոցները անբաւական են: Հայերն ալ կազմած են հետապնդիչ խումբեր՝ ձիաւոր եւ հետեւակ:

Գոնիա (Առաջնորդական Փոխանորդէն) – 23 Հոկտեմբեր

Կիլիկիոյ վերջին պատահարներուն իբր անմիջական հետեւանք վերջին օրերս նահանգիս ենթակայ զանազան վայրերէ 20, 30 կամ 40 թուրք կամաւոր եւ անկանոն զօրքեր հաւաքուած են եւ տեղական կառավարութեան կողմէ զինուելէ վերջ, վաղն իսկ պիտի մեկնին, անկանոն խմբակնե-

the gendarmerie, to Kozan [Sis] and then to Adana, crossing the Bıldırcınlık gorges. There are about 300 of them, under the command of a reserve officer, and they want to join larger forces.

Ankara (Halashana)—September 14

• The Armenians of the surrounding cities are fleeing here, hoping to go to İstanbul by rail; however, the railway traffic has stopped. In Keskin [Denek Madeni], the Milli movement has begun to take practical steps, charging Greeks and Armenians large sums of money as a self-defense tax. The tax is assessed at twenty-five to two hundred liras for each family. Armenians used the robberies they suffered as an objection to paying this anonymous tax. Thereupon, the çetes dispersed and threw customers out of Armenian shops. They declared a boycott against the Armenians, and the Armenians closed their shops in terror.

• Many families, neglectful of the great dangers, are leaving terrified and fleeing from Ankara to Eskişehir by land, in the absence of being able to journey by train.

Malatya (from Garabed Kulujian)—September 26

• Armenians continue to go to Urfa and Gaziantep [Ayntab] because we are in a state of intense fear, no matter how much they [the Turks] claim that they have not passed a decision against the Christians in Sivas.

• It is said that the Congress of Sivas appointed the former prefect of Van Haydar Bey as prefect to Mamuretülaziz and the massacrer of Muş Kadri Bey governor to Malatya. Kadri Bey was wanted by the military tribunal in İstanbul, but during his transfer under guard, he and Khalil Effendi, a Kurdish chieftain from the village of Prud in Harput, were taken away from the police by the Kurds. Kadri Bey has not yet arrived in Malatya.

• The imprisoned massacrers and those responsible for the deportation of the Armenians of Malatya and Harput were released and regained their previous offices. The fugitives also have emerged from their hideouts. Upon his release from Erzurum, here came the former chief of police, Hulusi Pasha, now called "Bey," seemingly for having killed thousands of Armenians.

• The Turkish-Kurdish issue is spreading gradually, and many Turks really are dissatisfied, but fearing the followers of Mustafa Kemal, they show themselves in agreement. The previous day, the Kurds tried to demonstrate in connection to Adıyaman [Hısnımansur] but later withdrew to avoid clashes with opposing Kurds.

• The post office has been taken under control, and censorship has been established over correspondence. It is said that telegraphic communications have also been interrupted beyond Sivas.

• There was a telegram from the governor of Sivas to the minister of the interior in the newspaper *İrâde-i Milliye*, in which he said: "I informed you that it is impossible [to isolate] Mustafa Kemal Pasha. Your orders to Ali Galip Bey (prefect of Harput) and Halil Ra[h]mi Bey (governor of Malatya) were superfluous. What did you gain by this? You simply aided the enemy. What did these people do, or could do, except cause a disturbance?"

• Today, Tevfik Bey, lieutenant governor and commander of the gendarmerie, and Hadji Kaya of İzollu went to Yıldızlı [Erzen] to organize a resistance. Hacı Bedir Ağa is also there, as are the Kurdish chieftains of Kâhta, Güngörmüş [Pütürge], and the surrounding areas.

İzmit (from the vicar general)—October 22

Two weeks ago, Hadji Hagop Kalfa's grandson, Kerovpé Hadji Torosian, a resident of Geyve-Eşme,

րով եւ ժանտարմայի երեւոյթին տակ, դէպի Սիս եւ ապա Ատանա, անցնելով Պըլտըրճընկի կիրճերէն: Ասոնք ամէնը 300 անձ են, պահեստի սպայի մը առաջնորդութեան տակ կը գտնուին եւ կ'ուզեն միանալ աւելի ստուար ոյժերու:

Էնկիւրիւ (Խալասխանէ) – 14 Սեպտեմբեր

- Շրջակայ քաղաքներու հայերը փախչելով հոս կը խռնուին երկաթուղիով Կ. Պոլիս երթալու յոյսով, սակայն երկաթուղիի երթեւեկը դադրած է: Քէսկինի մէջ Միլլի շարժումը գործնական քայլեր առնել սկսած է, յունաց եւ հայոց վրայ ահագին գումար մը բեռցնելով իբր *ինքնապաշտպանութեան տուրք*: Տուրքը բաշխուած է 25–200 ոսկի իւրաքանչիւր ընտանիքի վրայ: Հայերը իրենց թալանուած ըլլալը առարկելով մերժեցին վճարել այս անանուն տուրքը: Ասոր վրայ Չէթէները ցրուեցան եւ հայ խանութներէ առուտուր ընող յաճախորդները դուրս նետեցին, հայերու դէմ պօյքօթ հռչակեցին եւ հայերը սարսափահար իրենց խանութները գոցեցին:

- Շատ մը ընտանիքներ թողէնի երթեւեկ չըլլալուն համար ահագին վտանգներ աչք առնելով՝ ցամաք[ի] ճամբով Էնկիւրիէն Էսկիշէհիր կը փախչին, կը հեռանան սարսափով:

Մալաթիա (Կարապետ Գըլըճեանէ) – 26 Սեպտեմբեր

- Հայերը շարունակ Ուրֆա եւ Այնթապ կ'երթան, վասնզի սաստիկ երկիւղի մէջ ենք, որչափ որ Սըվազի Քօնկրէն քրիստոնեաներու դէմ որոշում մը տուած չըլլալը պնդեն:

- Վանի նախորդ կուսակալ Հայտար պէկը կ'ըսուի թէ Սըվազի քօնկրէին կողմէ Մ[ամուրէթ] իւլ Ազիզի կուսակալ կարգուած է, նաեւ Մալաթիոյ կառավարիչ կարգուած է Մուշի ջարդարար Կատրի պէկը, որ պատերազմական ատեանէն Պոլիս ուզուած եւ ընդ հսկողութեամբ տարուած ատենը ճամբան քիւրտերու կողմէ ոստիկաններու ձեռքէն առնուած էր, խարբերդցի Բրուտ գիւղացի քիւրտ ցեղապետ Խալիլ էֆ.ի հետ մէկտեղ: Կատրի պէյը դեռ Մալաթիա չեկաւ:

- Մալաթիոյ եւ Խարբերդի հայ ջարդարարները եւ տեղահանութեան պատասխանատուները, որոնք բանտարկուած կը մնային, ազատ արձակուեցան եւ իրենց նախորդ պաշտօնները ձեռք բերին: Փախստականներն ալ իր[ենց] թաքստոցներէն դուրս ելած են: Էրզրումէն ազատ արձակուե-լով հոս եկաւ նախորդ բոլիս միւտիւրի Խուլուսի էֆէնտին, որ հազարաւոր հայեր սպաննելուն համար կ'երեւի թէ հիմակ «Պէյ» կը կոչուի:

- Թրքօ-քրտական խնդիրը հետզհետէ կը տարածուի եւ շատ թուրքեր իրապէս դժգոհ են, սակայն Մուսթաֆա Քէմալի կուսակիցներուն երկիւղէն ինքզինքնին համամիտ ցոյց կուտան: Անցեալ օր Հիւսնի Մանսուրի վրայ քիւրտերը ցոյց մը ընել փորձած են, սակայն ետ քաշուած են յետոյ ընդդիմադիր քիւրտերու հետ չիյնալու համար:

- Բօսթախանէն քօնթրօլի տակ առնուած է եւ գրաքննութիւն հաստատուած է թղթակցու-թեանց վրայ: Կ'ըսուի թէ հեռագրական հաղորդագրութիւններն ալ Սեբաստիայէն անդին ընդ-հատուած են:

- *Իրադէի Միլլիյէ* թերթին մէջ Սեբաստիոյ կուսակալին մէկ հեռագիրը կար ուղղեալ ներքին գործոց նախարարին, ուր կ'ըսէ թէ ձեզի տեղեկագրած էի թէ Մուսթաֆա Քէմալ փաշա անկարելի է [մեկուսացնել]: Ձեր հրամանները աւելորդ է[ին] Ալի Կալիպ պէկին (Խարբերդի կուսակալ) եւ Խալիլ Րա[հ]մի պէյին (Մալաթիոյ կառավարիչ): Ասով ի՞նչ օգուտ ունեցաք. մինակ թշնամիին հացին իւղ քսեցիք: Այդ մարդիկը ի՞նչ կրցան ընել եւ կրնային բացի խռովութիւն ձգելէ:

- Այսօր կառավարիչի փոխանորդ ժանտարմա զօմանտանի Թէվֆիգ պէյը եւ իզօլուցի ջար-դարար Հաճի Գայեան Արզն զացին դիմադրութիւն կազմակերպելու համար[6]: Հաճի Պէտիր աղա ալ հոն է, նոյնպէս՝ Քեաղթի ու Բեղուրկէի եւ շրջականները գտնուող քիւրտ ցեղապետները հոն են:

Նիկոմիդիա (Առաջնորդական Փոխանորդէն) – 22 Հոկտեմբեր

- Երկու շաբաթ առաջ Կէյվէ-Էշմէի բնակիչներէն Հաճի Յակոբ Գալֆայի թոռը՝ Քերովբէ Հաճի

was taken to a mountain by bandits, and a ransom of two thousand liras was demanded. His body was found beheaded.

• A young collier from Arslanbey was also taken to a mountain two weeks ago, from a hill half an hour away from the village. The Laz robbers demanded one thousand liras for this as well. Probably, he, too, is killed.

• A few days ago, a person named Kurd Mardiros from Ovacık was found murdered in his tobacco field ten minutes away from the village, again by Lazes, most likely.

Konya (from the vicar general)—October 27

• Information received from Ereğli suggests that at noon on October 25, with a notice from the government, people from all elements were called upon to convene in the government square. A group of unarmed soldiers and gendarmes formed a circle led by officers. The flag and a black signboard with the words "İzmir belongs to the Turks, it will remain to the Turks forever" written on it were brought forth, accompanied by the sound of drums and trumpets. Afterward, Hoca Kâzım Effendi took the stage and, speaking about the capture of İzmir and Adana, blamed the primary responsibility on Ottoman Armenians and Greeks. By presenting them as insurgents, they directed insults toward all Christians. He concluded by saying that since the blood of innocent fellow Turks is being shed in İzmir, we must appeal to the Allies and complain to stop it immediately. If our voices remain unheard and useless, we must do the same earnestly to all Christians according to religious provisions. Then schoolchildren read a tragedy about İzmir. A former reserve officer named Suphi gave a speech and said that the Ottoman government could live without guardianship. We do not tolerate dividing our lands at all. Although the Turks are powerless now, they can defend themselves with their teeth and nails. He also read a poem. The mufti concluded the spectacle with a prayer.

• On October 27, soldiers of the National Movement, cavalry and infantry, began touring Konya dressed in national uniforms and carrying arms.

The new prefect, Suphi Bey, took office.

Adana (from the primate)—October 21[28]

[Armenian] refugees arrive daily from Maraş, Kayseri, and Sivas owing to fear of the prevailing situation. The problem of orphans is more serious. We have seven hundred orphans instead of four hundred, and twenty to twenty-five orphans are arriving daily. Within ten days, about three thousand migrants arrived, three hundred of whom are orphans, both male and female. Some of them are housed in villages, while the rest have been placed in newly built camps, but new ones are arriving perpetually; eight thousand people receive bread daily. Approximately twenty-eight to thirty thousand migrants are expected.

• Exactly eight days ago, the çetes attacked the villages near Ceyhan, and we had eight Armenian victims. Two days later, two and a half to three hours away from the city, the village of Şeyhmurat was attacked, and seven or eight people were killed, one of whom was a pregnant woman and another a child; the rest were brave young men. Two other people also [were killed] from nearby villages. The French government took strict measures. Apart from the gendarmerie, it enlisted volunteers and began to chase after the çetes, who crossed over to Tarsus and started killing the Armenians in the villages there, and, behold, we had twelve to fifteen victims there as well. The losses number thirty-five to forty. Çetes, also, were killed in equal numbers, and several were executed by gunfire, and the [severed]

Թորոսեան, աւազակներու կողմէ լեռ տարուած եւ 2000 ոսկի փրկանք պահանջուած էր: Հիմա անոր դիակը գտնուած է գլխատեալ:

- Արսլանպէկցի ածխագործ երիտասարդ մը նոյնպէս երկու շաբաթ առաջ լեռ տարուած է, գիւղէն կէս ժամուան հեռու բլուրէ մը: Լազ աւազակները ասոր համար ալ 1000 ոսկի պահանջած են: Հաւանօրէն աս ալ սպաննուած պիտի ըլլայ:

- Օվաճըգցի Քիւրտ Մարտիրոս անուն անձը, ասկէ քանի մը օրեր առաջ, գիւղէն 10 վայրկեան հեռու իր ծխախոտի արտին մէջ սպաննուած գտնուած է, դարձեալ հաւանօրէն լազերու կողմէ:

Գոնիա (Առաջնորդական Փոխանորդէն) – 27 Հոկտեմբեր

- Էրէյլիէն ստացուած տեղեկութիւններէ կը հասկցուի որ Հոկտեմբեր 25ին կէսօրին կառավարութեան ազդարարութեամբ ամէն տարրէ ժողովուրդին կոչ եղաւ կառավարչատան հրապարակը միթինկ գումարելու: Անգէն զինուոր[նե]րու ու ոստիկան զինուորներու խմբակ մը շրջանակ կազմեց սպաներու ղեկավարութեամբ: Ի ձայն թմբուկի եւ փողոց դրօշակը եւ սեւ թասլէյայի մը վրայ հետեւել խօսքերը գրուած «Իզմիր թուրքին է, յաւիտեան թուրքին պիտի մնայ» մէջտեղ բերին: Յետոյ Հոճա Քեազիմ էֆենտի բեմ ելաւ եւ խօսքը դարձնելով Իզմիրի եւ Ատանայի գրաւման, անոնց բուն պատասխանատուն օսմանցի հայերն ու յոյները ցոյց տուաւ եւ զանոնք իբր ապստամբ ներկայացնելով ընդհանուր քրիստոնէից հասցէին անարգանքներ ուղղեց: Եւ իր խօսքը վերջացուց ըսելով թէ քանի որ Իզմիրի մէջ անմեղ ազգակիցներու արիւն կը թափի, պէտք է անմիջապէս դադրեցնելու համար Համաձայնականներու դիմենք եւ բողոքենք: Եթէ երբեք մեր ձայնը անլսելի եւ ապարդիւն մնայ, ստիպողաբար կրօնքի տրամադրութեան համեմատ պարտաւոր ենք մենք ալ նոյնը գործադրել բոլոր քրիստոնէից: Յետոյ դպրոցականներ կարդացին Իզմիրի վերաբերեալ ողբերգութիւն մը: Նախկին պահեստի սպայ Միւպիի անունով մէկն ալ ատենախօսութիւն մը ըրաւ եւ ըսաւ թէ օսմանեան կառավարութիւնը առանց որեւէ խնամատարութեան կարող է ապրելու. բնաւ չենք հանդուրժեր մեր հողամասերը բաժնելու: Թէեւ թուրքը առայժմ անզօր է, բայց կրնայ ինքզինք պաշտպանել ակռաներով եւ եղունգներով: Կարդաց նաեւ ոտանաւոր մը: Միւֆթին փակեց հանդէսը աղօթքով մը:

- Գոնիայի մէջ 27 Հոկտեմբերին շրջիլ սկսան «Ազգային Շարժում»ի զինուորները ազգային տարազներով եւ զինուած, ձիաւոր եւ հետեւակ:

Նոր կուսակալ Սուպի[հ] պէյ պաշտօնի ձեռնարկեց:

Ատանա (Առաջնորդէն) – 21 Հոկտեմբեր

Մարաշէն, Կեսարիայէն ու Սվազէն ամէն օր գաղթականներ կը հասնին, վախնալով տիրող կացութենէ: Որբերու խնդիրը աւելի ծանր է: 400 որբի տեղ ունինք 700 որբ, եւ ամէն օր 20–25 որբեր կը հասնին: Տասը օրուան մէջ 3000ի մօտ գաղթականներ եկան, որոնց 300ի չափը որբ ու որբուհի են: Մաս մը գիւղերը զետեղուած են, մնացեալներն ալ նոր շինուած *քէմփ*երու մէջ կը զետեղուին, սակայն միշտ նորեր կը հասնին, օրական 8000 անձ հաց կը ստանայ: Մօտաւորապէս 28–30 հազար գաղթականներու կը սպասուի:

- Ճիշդ 8 օր առաջ, Ճիհանի կողմը չէթէները գիւղերու վրայ յարձակեցան եւ 8 հայեր զոհ տուինք: Անկէ 2 օր յետոյ քաղաքէն 2½–3 ժամ հեռու Շէյխ-Մուրատ գիւղին վրայ յարձակեցան եւ սպաննեցին 7–8 անձեր, որոնցմէ մէկը յղի կին մը եւ մին մանկիկ մը, մնացեալները՝ կտրիճ երիտասարդներ: Մօտակայ գիւղերէն ալ երկու ուրիշ մարդ: Ֆրանսական կառավարութիւնը խիստ միջոցներ ձեռք առաւ. ֆրանսական ժանտարմարիէ զատ կամաւորներ արձանագրեց եւ սկսաւ հետապնդել չէթէները, որոնք անցան Տարսոնի հողը եւ հոն սկսան գիւղերու գտնուած հայերը սպաննել եւ ահա 12–15 զոհեր ալ հոն ունեցանք: Կորուստներու թիւը 35–40ի կը հասնի. չէթէներէն ալ նոյնքան սպաննուած են եւ մէկ քանին ալ հրացանի բռնուած, պետի մը գլուխը բերուած է: Չէթէական գործողութիւններու տակ ծածկուած քաղաքական դիտումները աւելի կը յուզեն ժողովուրդը:

head of a leader was brought here. The political intentions behind the çetes' actions disturb the people further.

Bursa (from the vicar general)—October 29

• Two days ago, in Marmaracık, a gendarme shot dead Parounag Shyugyurian—a young Armenian man married to an orphan who had taken refuge in Bursa—for swearing.

• Admiral Bristol visited here yesterday. The Armenian locum tenens presented himself to him and thanked him for the facilitation provided by the American Near East Relief entities. Admiral Bristol recommended "living with wisdom and prudence and not delivering exaggerated news to the center." The locum tenens said, "We have no discontent. Our protest is this: there is silent envy toward our nation's progression and growth in wealth, and that envy is the result of ignorance. Thanks to their education, wild bears brought down from the mountains to the city become tamed and friends with humans; they forget tearing [humans] into pieces and become changed. So long as the Turks do not have education and civility, they remain the same, and our fate remains the fate of the protester."

• A Frenchman visited the prelacy and said: "I came from the French admiral; no one has the right to interfere in your affairs, not even our local commander." It is not clear how much one should believe in his words.

Düzce (from the Neighborhood Council)—October 31[29]

The roads from Bolu to Düzce and from Düzce to Adapazarı have been unsafe for five to six months. So far, twenty-one Armenians have been robbed on the road. During the last month, [the bandits] began to loot bales of goods. These robberies were common up to eight days ago. Turks were also robbed. It has changed now. Four days ago, grocer Minas Agha Nshanian received a threat demanding eight hundred bullets unconditionally. A day later, two hundred liras were demanded from the Greek miller Andriaki. Three days ago, an armed Circassian went to Haroutyun Kalpakjian, a tailor, [for] a dress and promised to pay only half of the actual price, otherwise threatening: "You know [what happens if you refuse]." He forced him to sew the clothes. On the same day, a Circassian went to Krikor Krikorian, a draper, and bought some goods at half the price, also threatening him.

• Four days ago, the government called upon the Armenian neighborhood representative, Hadji Smpad Karaboghosian, and said: "You see that security is disturbed. Lootings take place on the roads every day. Threats are disseminated in the city. You have to choose two watchmen to protect your neighborhood at night, and we will give them state-owned weapons to be able to defend yourselves. If anything happens, we will not be able to defend you, and any appeal you make will remain unheard."

• On the same day, at night, people broke into the weapons storehouse of the gendarmerie headquarters near the government building and took seventeen state-owned weapons and two cases of bullets (twenty-eight hundred pieces). The perpetrators of this theft have not yet been found.

Adana (from the primate)—November 4[30]

Thanks to the effective measures taken by the French authorities, security and calm have been restored. The bandits have dispersed, those caught have been punished by death, and some have died in battle. Their villages have also received exemplary lessons. Help is needed for refugees and orphans.

Պրուսա (Առաջնորդական Փոխանորդէն) – 29 Հոկտեմբեր

- Մարմաճուխի մէջ հայ երիտասարդ մը՝ Բարունակ Ճիւկիւրեան, որ Պրուսա ապաստանած որբուհիի մը հետ ամուսնացած էր, երկու օր առաջ ժանտարմայի մը կողմէ հրազէնով սպաննուած է, վասնզի հայհոյած է:

- Անցեալ օր Ծովակալ Պրիսթոլ հոս այցելեց: Իրեն կը ներկայանայ Հայոց Առաջնորդական Տեղապահը եւ շնորհակալութիւն կը յայտնէ ամերիկեան նպաստամատոյց մարմիններու ընձեռած դիւրութիւններուն համար: Ծովակալ Պրիսթոլ կը յանձնարարէ «իմաստութեամբ եւ խոհեմութեամբ ապրիլ եւ կեդրոն չափազանցուած լուրեր չտալ»: Առաջնորդական Տեղապահը կ'ըսէ թէ «մենք դժգոհութիւն չունինք, մեր բողոքն սա է. մեր ազգին զարգանալուն եւ հարստանալուն հանդէպ խուլ նախանձ մը կայ եւ այդ նախանձն ալ տգիտութեան արդիւնք է: Լեռնէն վայրենի արջեր քաղաք կը բերուին եւ շնորհիւ կրթութեան կ'ընտելանան եւ մարդու ընկեր կ'ըլլան, կը մոռնան յօշոտելը եւ կը փոխուին: Որքան թուրքը կրթութիւն եւ ազնուութիւն չունի, անոնք նոյն կը մնան եւ մեր ճակատագիրը միշտ բողոքողի ճակատագիրը կը մնայ»:

- Ֆրանսացի մը այցելեց առաջնորդարան եւ ըսաւ. «Ես ֆրանսացի ծովակալին կողմէ եկած եմ եւ ոչ մէկը ձեր գործերուն միջամտելու իրաւունք ունի, նոյնիսկ այստեղի մեր հրամատարը»: Յայտնի չէ թէ որքան հաւատ ընծայել պէտք է այս խօսքին:

Տիւզճէ (Թաղական Խորհուրդէն) – 31 Հոկտեմբեր

5–6 ամիսներէ ի վեր՝ Պօլուէն Տիւզճէ եւ Տիւզճէէն Ատըբազար ճամբաները անապահով են: Մինչեւ հիմա 21 հայեր ճամբու վրայ կողոպտուեցան: Վերջին ամիսն ալ ապրանքները հակերով կողոպտել սկսան: Այս կողոպուտները մինչեւ 8 օր առաջ ընդհանուր հանգամանք ունէին եւ թուրքերն ալ կը կողոպտուէին: Հիմա փոխուած է: Չորս օր առաջ նպարավաճառ Մինաս աղա Նշանեանի սպառնագիր մը եկաւ, որով անպայման 800 փամփուշտ կը պահանջեն: Օր մը յետոյ, յոյն ջաղաց[պ]ան Անտրիաքիէն 200 ոսկի կը պահանջեն: երեք օր առաջ զինեալ չէրքէզ մը դերձակ Յարութիւն Գալփաքճեանի կը դիմէ ձեռք մը զգեստ կարելու համար եւ իրական գինին կէսը միայն վճարել կը խոստանայ, հակառակ պարագային «դուն գիտես» ըսելով կը սպառնայ եւ զգեստները կարել կուտայ: Միեւնոյն օրը չէրքէզ մը կը ներկայանայ մանիֆաթուրաճի Գրիգոր Գրիգորեանի՝ սպառնալով կէս գինով մաս մը ապրանք կը գնէ:

- Չորս օր առաջ կառավարութիւնը կը կանչէ հայոց միթարը՝ մահտեսի Սմբատ Գարապօղոսեանը, եւ կ'ըսէ. «Կը տեսնէք որ ապահովութիւնը խանգարուած է. ճամբաները ամէն օր կողոպուտ, քաղաքին մէջ սպառնագիրեր կը ցրուին: Ձեր թաղը պաշտպանելու համար երկու գիշերապահ պէտք է ընտրէք, մենք ալ անոնց ձեռքը մէյ մէկ պետական զէնք կուտանք, այսպէսով զձեզ պաշտպանեցէք: Եթէ երբեք որեւէ դէպք պատահի, մենք չենք կրնար զձեզ պաշտպանել եւ ոեւէ դիմում որ տեղի ունենայ, անլսելի պիտի մնայ»:

- Նոյն օրը կառավարական շէնքին մօտ գտնուած ժանտարմայի պաշտօնատան զէնքերու մթերանոցը գիշերը կը բացուի եւ 17 հատ պետական զէնք եւ երկու սնտուկ փամփուշտ (2800 հատ) կը վերցուի: Այս գողութեան հեղինակները դեռ չեն գտնուած:

Ատանա (Առաջնորդէն) – 4 Նոյեմբեր

Շնորհիւ ֆրանսական իշխանութեանց ձեռք առած ազդու միջոցներուն՝ ապահովութիւնը եւ անդորրութիւնը վերահաստատուած է: Աւազակները ցրուած, ձեռք անցնողը մահուամբ պատժուած եւ ոմանք ալ կռիւի մէջ մեռած են: Իրենց գիւղերն ալ օրինակելի դասեր ստացած են: Օգնութեան պէտք կայ գաղթականներու եւ որբերու համար:

Sivas (from the primate)—October 29[31]

• Ittihadist rule has been re-established. All those who killed Armenians and were hunted after doing so are moving around freely and have resumed their old activities. Among them are the notorious Halis Bey, Emir Paşazade Hamit Bey, [police] commissioner Mahmut, Bacanakzade Edhem, Kütükoğlu Hüseyin, Asker Hamdi, Pazarcı Mehmet, Reverend Father Sahag Odabashian's killer Zaralı Mahir, and others. The previous deputy, Rasim Bey, who was the main organizer of the deportation, upon whose suggestion Prefect Muammer took up a tougher stance toward the Armenians, and who, after the armistice and the closure of the parliament, escaped the police at night from İstanbul, now has gained courage from the prevailing situation and is campaigning again to be elected as deputy. He will likely succeed.

• In recent days, profit tax has been demanded from Armenians, although those returning from deportation were supposed to be exempted. The government also demands rent from those Armenians who returned from deportation to find their homes in ruins and were placed in the houses of Armenians who had not returned. Otherwise, it demands that the houses be vacated. Given this situation, many are considering leaving.

• Three French gendarmes, who had been in Sivas for some time organizing the gendarmerie, were attacked by bandits two hours away from Tokat on their way to İstanbul. After a lengthy fusillade, a companion Circassian gendarme was killed, and the bandits fled.

• It is considered prudent to participate in municipal and parliamentarian elections.

• The government is imposing restrictions against travelers. Guards have been installed around the city, and those who leave are required to have travel documents. For travel documents, an Ottoman official certificate is deemed necessary. This is almost impossible for the deportees to produce, and it takes months to obtain new ones, as their records must be brought from the villages. Even those who have ordinary documents face difficulties. The goal is evident that they [the Turks] do not want to let the Armenians go; instead, they want to keep them under their control. We know for sure that passports are not required in other parts of the province and that non-Armenians travel freely.

Kayseri (from the National Assistance)—November 1[32]

The condition of about fifty Armenian natives of Kayseri sent back [by Turkish authorities] from Niğde has left the people in despair. The government informed the prelacy that "Armenians should not go to Adana henceforth." Now all those who are leaving Kayseri are forbidden under this pretext. Since the Armenians of Kayseri are engaged in trade and commerce only, this will be reason for the people to be condemned to starvation, as they have no other source of income.

Kayseri (from the vicar general)—November 1[33]

After the rule of Mustafa Kemal Pasha's adherents, many began to abandon their possessions and flee because notorious criminals had been released from the prison of Kayseri in the hundreds. Armed and with lavish salaries, they were appointed as çetes and began to wander around. Although the government was reproving, it did not ban those who obtained travel permits. The Greeks also have been migrating, especially recently. On October 25, about forty girls, boys, and women, and four or five men, despite possessing legal passports, were imprisoned in Niğde. They were beaten and then returned to Kayseri under gendarmes' surveillance. On the way, the gendarmes showered them with insults and expressed remorse for not killing these infidels earlier. Some of their property was confiscated by the

Սըվազ (Առաջնորդէն) – 29 Հոկտեմբեր

- Իթթիհատական տիրապետութիւնը վերահաստատուած է: Բոլոր հայասպանները, որոնք կը հետապնդուէին, հիմա ազատ շրջիլ եւ իրենց հին գործունէութեան սկսան: Ի մէջ այլոց հռչակաւոր Խալիս պէյ, Էմիր փաշա զատէ Համիտ պէյ, Գօմիսէր Մահմուտ, Պաճանախ զատէ Էտհէմ, Քիւթիւկ օղլու Հիւսէյին, Ասքէր Համտի, Բազարճը Մէմէտ, Սահակ Վարդապետ Օտապաշեանի սպանիչ Չարալը Մահիր եւայլն: Նախորդ մէպուս Րասիմ պէյ, որ տեղահանութեան գլխաւոր կազմակերպիչն եղաւ, որու թելադրութիւններուն վրայ կուսակալ Մուամմէր աւելի խիստ դիրք բռնած էր հայոց հանդէպ, եւ որ զինադադարէն եւ մէպուսական ժողովին փակումէն յետոյ Կ. Պոլիսէն գիշերանց խոյս տուած էր, հիմա համարձակութիւն առած է տիրող կացութենէն եւ կրկին մէպուս ընտրուելու համար բրոբականտ կ'ընէ եւ հաւանական է որ յաջողի:

- Վերջին օրերս հայերէն սկսան պահանջել *թէմէյթթի*, մինչ տեղահանութենէն դարձողները զերծ պիտի մնային իբր թէ: Նոյնպէս կառավարութիւնը վարձք կը պահանջէ տեղահանութենէն դարձող այն հայերէն, որոնք իրենց տուները փլած գտնելով չդարձող հայերու տուները զետեղուած էին: Հակառակ պարագային, կը պահանջէ տուները պարպել: Այս կացութեան առջեւ շատերը կը խորհին մեկնիլ:

- Երեք ֆրանսացի ժանտարմաներ, որոնք ոստիկան զօրաց կազմակերպութեան համար ժամանակէ մը ի վեր Սըվազ կը գտնուէին, Պոլիս երթալու ատեն Թօզատէն երկու ժամ հեռու յարձակում կը կրեն աւազակներէ եւ բաւական հրացանաձգութենէ վերջ իրենց ընկերացող չէրքէզ ժանտարմա մը կը սպաննուի եւ աւազակները կը փախչին:

- Խոհեմութիւն համարուած է թաղապետական եւ երեսփոխանական ընտրութեանց մասնակցիլ:

- Կառավարութեան կողմէ արգելքներ կը հանուին ճամբորդներու դէմ: Քաղաքին շուրջը պահակներ դրուած են եւ դուրս ելլողներէն *սէյահաթ վարաքասի* կը պահանջուի: *Սէյահաթ վարաքասի* ունենալու համար *թէզքէրէի օսմանիէ*ի պէտքը անհրաժեշտ կը նկատեն, ինչ որ տարագիրներու համար անկարելի [է] ցոյց տալ եւ նորեր ձեռք բերելն ալ ամիսներու կը կարօտի, քանի որ գիւղերէն իրենց արձանագրութիւնները պէտք է բերուի[ն]: Նոյնիսկ կանոնաւոր թուղթեր ունեցողներու ալ դժուարութիւններ կը հանուին: Նպատակնին որոշ է թէ հայերը չեն ուզեր հեռացնել եւ իրենց ձեռքին տակ պահել կ'ուզուի: Որոշ գիտենք թէ նահանգին ուրիշ կողմերը անցագիր չի փնտռուիր եւ բացի հայերէն միւս ազգերը ազատօրէն կ'երթեւեկեն:

Կեսարիա (Խնամատարութենէն) – 1 Նոյեմբեր

Նիյտէէն վերադարձուած 50ի մօտ կեսարացիներու վիճակը յուսահատութեան մատնած է ժողովուրդը: Կառավարութիւնը առաջնորդարանին հաղորդած է թէ «Հայերը ասկէ ետքը Ատանա չպիտի երթան»: Հիմա Կեսարիայէն բոլոր դուրս գացողները այս պատրուակով կ'արգիլուին: Կեսարացիք միայն առեւտուրով եւ վաճառականութեամբ զբաղող մարդիկ ըլլալով, ասիկա պատճառ պիտի ըլլայ որ ժողովուրդը դատապարտուի անօթութեան, քանի որ ուրիշ աղբիւր չունի շահու:

Կեսարիա (Առաջնորդական Փոխանորդէն) – 1 Նոյեմբեր

Մուսթաֆա Քեմալ փաշայի մարդոց տիրապետութենէն յետոյ շատեր իրենց գոյքերը եւ ամէն բան թողլով փախչիլ սկսան, վասնզի յայտնի ոճրագործներ Կեսարիոյ բանտէն արձակուեցան հարիւրներով եւ զինուած եւ ճոխ ամսաթոշակներով չէթէ նշանակուեցան եւ շրջիլ [սկսան] ամէն կողմ: Կառավարութիւնը թէեւ դիտողութիւն կ'ընէր, սակայն *սէյեար վարաքասի* առնողներուն արգելք չէր հաներ: Յոյներն ալ կը գաղթէին մանաւանդ վերջերս: Հոկտեմբեր 25ին, 40ի չափ աղջիկ, տղայ եւ կին եւ 4–5 այր մարդ օրինաւոր անցագիր ունենալով հանդերձ Նիյտէի մէջ կը բանտարկուին, կը ծեծուին եւ ապա ժանտարմաներու հսկողութեամբ կրկին Կեսարիա կը դարձուին: Ճամբան ժանտարմաները լուտանքներ տեղացուցած եւ զզչում յայտնած են թէ ինչո՛ւ կանուխէն

coachmen against their fee. They are in great misery because they have sold everything and now have nothing. The government has responded to a complaint made on October 30 that the interior minister had barred Armenians from traveling to Adana. Surprisingly, Turks and Greeks travel; the ban is only against Armenians. Horror in the face of this situation is common. Echoes of the ban have reached Kayseri's surrounding villages as well as the villages of neighboring Boğazlıyan. They appeal to us daily, and we do not know what they should do or to whom we should turn.

• Upon the appeal of the British Commission, the Ministry of Internal Affairs granted permission to transfer 800 orphans to Adana.

• On September 29, two hundred five orphans from the orphanage, [and] forty-five female orphans from Ereğli, that is, two hundred fifty orphans, were sent to İzmir with Shabouh Nazarian. The rest will be taken to Adana.

• According to information received from the village of Çokradan in Yozgat, the Turkish çetes attacked Çokradan, İğde[li], Fahralı, Konuklar [Ürnac], Menteşe, and other Armenian villages and abducted the women and children, along with their properties, and took them to Boğazlıyan. The lieutenant governor of Boğazlıyan was a silent spectator. Hundreds of Armenian girls, women, and orphans remain in Hamidiye, Burhanköy, Dendil, and the Armenian-populated villages of Boğazlıyan and Sivas.

• The local çetes are sharpening their teeth against Adana and Saimbeyli [Hacın], preparing an attack, and boldly saying that the Armenians have no right to exist.

Bandırma (from the primate)—November 12

When the Armenian primate was returning to Bandırma from a diocesan visit on the 7th of this month, he was attacked by ten armed Turks in a place called Oba Altı between Karacabey [Mihaliç] and Bandırma. There was only an Armenian coachman named Simon Gyulmezian with him. After swearing at and torturing the primate, they started threatening and robbing him while pointing their weapons at him. They seized thirty-seven lira banknotes and seven and a half liras cash. The latter had been entrusted to him [by people] from Mustafakemalpaşa [Kirmasti] to be sent to İstanbul.

Considering this amount insufficient, they coerced him, demanding a gold belt,[34] and then ransacked all the property and the whole carriage, but they found nothing more to take. Eventually, they took the primate's headgear, cowl, watch, and other items. He barely survived.

Trabzon (from the locum tenens)—November 7

The following information was gathered from Asdour Doligian, a pewterer from Kemaliye [Egin].

There are 200 people in Kemaliye, 150–160 of whom are deportees from various places. This number includes orphans, for whom the Armenians had opened an orphanage under their control. The Americans allegedly intend to open a textile factory there.

The person mentioned gave these approximate numbers of Armenians living in the Ağin region.

In Ağin city	200 people
In Lice village	40–50
In Gümüşçeşme [Narver] village	25–30
In Toybelen [Gemürgap/Gamargab]	30
In Apçağa [Abuçeğ]	25–30
In Godushla	20
Total	340–450 people

There is also a small number of Armenians in other villages, mainly near Ovacık [Ova].

այս *քեաֆիր*ներն ալ չեն սպաննած: Ասոնց գոյքերէն մէկ մասը կառապանները վարձի փոխարէն վար դրած են: Ասոնք մեծ թշուառութեան մատնուած են, վասնզի ամէն ինչ ծախած էին եւ հիմա ոչինչ ունին: Կառավարութիւնը իրեն եղած բողոքին 30 Հոկտեմբերին պատասխանեց թէ ներքին գործոց նախարարը արգիլած է հայերուն Ատանա մեկնիլը: Զարմանալի է որ թուրքերը եւ յոյները կ'երթեւեկեն եւ միայն հայերու դէմ է արգելքը: Այս կացութեան առջեւ սարսափը ընդհանուր է: Արգելքին արձագանգը հասած է Կեսարիոյ շրջակայ գիւղերը եւ դրացի Պօղազլեանի գիւղերը: Ամէն օր դիմում կ'ընեն մեզի եւ չենք գիտեր թէ ի՛նչ ընենք եւ որուն դիմենք:

- Անգլիական քոմիսերութեան դիմումին վրայ ներքին գործոց նախարարութենէն արտօնութիւն եկած է որ 800 որբեր Ատանա փոխադրուին:

- Սեպտեմբեր 29ին որբանոցէն 205 որբեր, Էրճյիէն 45 որբուհիներ, այսինքն 250 որբ, Իզմիր ղրկուեցան Շապուհ Նազարեանի հետ: Մնացեալները Ատանա պիտի տարուին:

- Եօզկատի Չորխատան գիւղէն առնուած տեղեկութեան համաձայն, Չորխատան, Իյտէ, Փախրալը, Իւրնէչ, Մէնթէշէ եւ ուրիշ հայ գիւղեր թուրք չէթէները կը կոխեն եւ բռնի կիները, տղաքները եւ ունեցածնին յափշտակելով կը տանին եւ Պօղազլեանի գայմագամը լուռ հանդիսատես կ'ըլլայ: Դեռ հարիւրաւոր հայ աղջիկներ, կիներ, որբեր կը գտնուին Պօղազլեանի եւ Սեբաստիոյ Համիտիյէ եւ Պիւրիհան, Տէնտիլ եւ հայաբնակ գիւղերու մէջ:

- Տեղւոյս չէթէները ակռայ կը սրեն Ատանայի եւ Հաճընի դէմ, եւ յարձակում կը պատրաստեն եւ յայտնի համարձակ կ'ըսեն թէ հայերը գոյութեան իրաւունք չունին:

Պանտրմա (Առաջնորդէն) – 12 Նոյեմբեր

Ամսոյս 7ին թեմական այցելութենէ Պանտրմա վերադարձած ատեն հայոց առաջնորդը Մըխալըճի եւ Պանտրմայի միջեւ Օպա Ալթը ըսուած տեղը տասը զինեալ թուրքերու կողմէ յարձակումի կ'ենթարկուի: Իրեն հետ կը գտնուէր միայն հայ կառապան մը՝ Սիմօն Կիւլմէզեան անունով: Հայհոյանքներէ եւ խոշտանգումներէ յետոյ, սպառնալիքով եւ զէնքերնին իրեն ուղղելով կը սկսին կողոպուտի: Կը յափշտակեն 37 ոսկի թղթադրամ եւ 7½ ոսկի հնչուն դրամ: Վերջինը Քըրմաստըյէ իբր աւանդ իրեն յանձնուած՝ Պոլիս ղրկելու համար:

Այս գումարը անբաւական նկատելով բռնացան վրան, ոսկիի քէմէր պահանջեցին եւ բոլոր գոյքերը եւ ամբողջ կառքը տակնուվրայ ըրին եւ ոչինչ գտան: Ի վերջոյ փակեղը, վեղարը, ժամացոյցը եւ ուրիշ իրեղէններ առին եւ ինքն մազապուր կրցաւ ազատիլ անոնց ձեռքէն:

Տրապիզոն (Առաջնորդական Տեղապահէն) – 7 Նոյեմբեր

Ակնցի կլայեկագործ պ. Աստուր Տոլիկեանէ քաղուած են հետեւեալ տեղեկութիւնները:

Ակնայ մէջ կը գտնուի 200 անձ, որոնցմէ 150–160-ը զանազան վայրերէ տարագիրներ են: Այս թիւին մէջ են նաեւ որբերը՝ որոնց համար բացուած է որբանոց մը հայերու հսկողութեան տակ: Ամերիկացիները մտադիր են եղեր հոն բանալու մանուսայի գործարան մը:

Ակնայ շրջանին մէջ ապրող հայերու թիւի մասին յիշեալը կուտայ մերձաւոր հաշուով հետեւեալ թիւերը:

Ակնայ քաղաքին մէջ	200 անձ
Լիճէ գիւղին մէջ	40–50
Նարվեր գիւղին մէջ	25–30
Կամրկապի մէջ	30
Ապուչէխի մէջ	25–30
Կոտուշլայի մէջ	20
Ընդամէնը	340–450 անձ

Adapazarı (from Dr. Khabadayan and others)—October 30, 1919
The city's deputy governor invited the Frenchman M. Richard Hardi, who stays in the city. He was asked why he lives in a Christian neighborhood, not among Muslims. He was offered [a choice of] either to leave the city or move to the Muslim neighborhood. They threatened to break his legs should he reveal this to anyone, which makes the intent of the offer even more questionable. M. Richard Hardi, a teacher, reported the fact to the French High Commission.

Boğazlıyan (from the Orphan Caring Body)—October 21[35]
The local lieutenant governor, Avni Bey, has been persecuting Armenians for a long time in an unusual manner. On August 22, when the Armenians went to protest against the abduction of a woman named Gülizar from Gemerek, he said with impudence: "O infidels, I will change my position toward you hereafter. The foreigners have already weighed us. I will not be judged again by annihilating you."

Garabed Sarafian and Yeghia Mayisian, members of the Orphan Caring Body, went to the villages to collect orphans. They learned about the propaganda being spread by the lieutenant governor in Turkish villages. He [the governor] was touring everywhere, saying, "Do not give anything to these impudent Armenians; sacrifice one [of them] if you can. If they sue you, you also sue them. Accuse them that they, too, committed crimes during the Armenian massacre. I will arrange everything; I am already in charge; just find two worthy witnesses. In this way, he encouraged all the Turks and stirred them up against Armenians.

• Today, Markar and Krikor Aghas of Uzunlu, neighborhood representatives in their village, are being prosecuted. Markar is a fugitive, and Krikor is a prisoner. The police wanted to arrest Markar's teenage daughter instead of him, but the Armenian neighborhood representative refused to hand her over to them and was tortured with a whip.

• The wife of Kerovpé of Yazıkışla [Gürden] was abducted from him by force and was returned to him after being raped for two hours. Likewise, they abducted the wife of Setrag of Menteşe. Her whereabouts is unknown. The wife of Mihran of Fahralı has been forcibly appropriated by a Turk, and many in similar situations are not heard about in the city.

• An order was issued [from Ankara] for the distribution of the fields; Avni Bey, using his full power, tried to obtain the opposite order and received it. In the end, the prefect of Ankara arrived and faking obedience to his command, Avni promised to go to the villages in person and to take from the Turks what rightfully belonged to Armenians. However, after the prefect left, he and his wife visited the warm mineral springs. He prolonged his stay until all the confiscating Turks reaped the harvest of the Armenians' fields.

• The order of the lieutenant governor's deposition made the Armenians happy and the Turks sad. The Turks petitioned the center and Mustafa Kemal, who reinstated him as lieutenant governor. Under the petition compiled by the Turks, an Armenian named Sarafian also signed because of a threat or fear. (Letters by Sarafian that are kept in the Patriarchate's office protesting against the various actions of Lieutenant Governor Avni indicate that he signed the letter expressing his satisfaction with the lieutenant governor [under pressure].)

About this from the [Patriarchate's] chargé d'affaires. During my continuous daily appeals over several months concerning the cruel treatment of Boğazlıyan's lieutenant governor, Avni Bey, I barely managed his transfer elsewhere. But recently, in conformity with the suggestion of the *Milli organization*, he has been reinstated in Boğazlıyan. This shows that Mustafa Kemal's people control the situation

Կան փոքրաթիւ հայեր նաեւ ուրիշ գիւղերու մէջ, գլխաւորաբար Օվայի կողմերը:

Ատաբազար (Տոք. Խապատայեան եւ այլք) – 30 Հոկտեմբեր 1919

Քաղաքը գտնուող ֆրանսացի Մ. Ռիշարտ Հարտի այսօր կը հրաւիրուի քաղաքին փոխ-կառավարիչին կողմէն եւ իրեն կը հարցուի թէ ինչո՞ւ կը բնակի քրիստոնեաներու թաղը եւ ո՛չ իսլամներու մէջ եւ իրեն առաջարկուած է կամ մեկնիլ քաղաքէս եւ կամ փոխադրուիլ իսլամներու թաղը: Յիշեալին սպառնացած են իրողութիւնը ուրիշի յայտնած պարագային կոտրել իր սրունք-ները, ինչ որ աւելի կասկածելի կը դարձնէ եղած առաջարկին դիտումը: Մ. Ռիշարտ Հարտի, ուսուցիչ, իրողութիւնը տեղեկագրած է ֆրանսական բարձր քոմիսէրութեան:

Պօղազլըեան (Որբախնամ մարմինէն) – 21 Հոկտեմբեր

Տեղւոյս գայմագամ Ավնի պէյ արտասովոր կերպով հայերը կը հալածէ երկար ատենէ ի վեր: Օգոստոս 22ին Կիւլիզար անուն կէմէրէկցի կնոջ առեւանգութեան համար երբ հայերը բողոքելու գացած էին, անիկա անպատկառութեամբ ըսած էր թէ «Կեավուրլա՛ր սիզէ գարշը քիւլահը թէրս կէյինէճէյիմ արթըգ, զաթէն պիզիմ տարամըզը էճանիպ ալմըշտըր. Սիզին իմհանըզլա պէն թէքրար մուհաքէմէյէ ալընաճագ տէյիլիմ»:7

Որբախնամի անդամներէն Կար[ապետ] Սարաֆեան եւ Եղիա Մայիսեան որբեր հաւաքելու համար գիւղերը գացած էին: Ասոնք հասկցած են գայմագամին թուրք գիւղերու մէջ տարածած քարոզութիւնները: Անիկա ամէն տեղ շրջելով ըսած է. «Սա լպիրշ հայերուն ինչք մը մի տաք, հատիկի մը զոհեցէք եթէ կրնաք. եթէ ձեզի համար դատեր բանան, դուք ալ դատ բացէք անոնց մասին զրպարտելով թէ ատոնք ալ ոճիրներ գործած են հայկական ջարդի միջոցին. ես ամէն բան կը կարգադրեմ, արդէն գործը իմ ձեռքս է, միայն թէ երկու արժան վկաներ թող գտնուին. այս կերպով բոլոր թիւրքերը ոգեւորած եւ զինած է հայոց դէմ:

- Այսօր կը հետապնդուին ուզունլուցի Մարգար եւ Գրիգոր աղաները որոնք հայ թաղապետներ են իրենց գիւղը: Մարգարը փախստական է, իսկ Գրիգորը բանտարկուած: Ոստիկանները Մարգարին փոխարէն ուզած են ձերբակալել անոր դեռահաս աղջիկը եւ հայ թաղապետը աղջիկը չուզելով յանձնել ատոնց խարազանով խոշտանգուած է:

- Կիւրտէնցի Քերովբէի կինը իր քովէն բռնի յափշտակած եւ բռնաբարելէ յետոյ երկու ժամ վերջը իր էրկանը յանձնած են: Նոյնպէս մէնթէշէցի Սեդրաքին կինը բռնի տարած են եւ ուր ըլլալը յայտնի չէ: Ֆագրալըցի Միհրանին կինը բռնի իւրացուցած է թուրք մը, եւ դեռ շատեր կան այսպէս, որոնք չեն լուիր քաղաքին մէջ:

- Արտերու բաժանման համար հրաման տրուած էր, բոլոր ոյժովը Ավնի պէյ ջանաց հակառակ հրաման մը ձեռք ձգել եւ ձգեց: Վերջը հոս եկաւ Էնկիւրիի կուսակալը որուն պատուէրին հնազան-դիլ կեղծելով խոստացաւ անձամբ գիւղերը երթալ եւ հայոց իրաւունքը թուրքերէն առնելով դարձնել: Սակայն կուսակալը երթալէն յետոյ իր կնոջը հետ ջերմուկները գնաց եւ հոն այնքան կեցաւ որ բոլոր բռնագրաւող թուրքերը հայոց արտերուն հունձքերը քաղեցին:

- Գայմագամին պաշտօնանկութեան հրամանը հայերը ուրախացուց եւ թուրքերը տխրեցուց: Թուրքերը հանրագրութեամբ դիմում ըրին թէ՛ կեդրոն եւ թէ Մուսթաֆա Քէմալին, որ զինքը վերահաստատեց իր պաշտօնին մէջ: Թուրքերու կազմած հանրագրութեան տակ ի դիմաց հայոց ստորագրած է նաեւ Սարաֆեան անուն հայ մը սպառնալիքով կամ երկիւղով: (Յիշեալ Սարաֆեա-նի գայմագամ Ավնի[ի] զանազան արարքներուն դէմ բողոքող գիրերը պահուած են պատրիարքա-րանի դիւանին մէջ, ինչ որ ցոյց կուտայ թէ ինչպէս ստորագրած է գայմագամին զոհունակութիւն յայտնող գիրը:)

Այս մասին գործակատարութենէն. Պօղազլըեանի գայմագամ Ավնի պէյի յոռի վարմանց համար շարունակ ամէնօրեայ դիմումներուս վրայ հազիւ քանի մը ամիսէն յաջողած էի զինքը փոխադրել տալ այլուր: Բայց վերջերս *Թէշքիլաթը Միլլիէ*ի առաջարկին համաձայն նորէն Պօղազլեանի մէջ

in Anadolu [Anatolia] and that the center submits to his instructions.

Information gathered from Reverend Father Krikor Pehlivanian[36]

(An Armenian Catholic priest, a native of Sivas, deported to Aleppo, where he has remained until now)

There are various orphanages in Aleppo. Reverend Aharon Shirajian has two thousand orphan boys and girls; they are very well cared for. The British army covers the expenses. The American Red Cross orphanage had five hundred orphans. This orphanage was moved to Gaziantep [Ayntab] (a month ago). The French orphanage cared for by the French government was only for Armenians before, but it is mixed currently and has Syrian orphans, too. The number of Armenian orphans is 400. It is administered by Dr. Hartman (an officer):

There are two classes of [Armenian] deportees in Aleppo. Some live in barracks and continue to receive subsidies from the British government. Their number occasionally reached seven to eight thousand. Today, it is two thousand. These, too, will be transferred and settled in Cilicia. The other part consists of those who have been placed in the city and no longer receive subsidies today, while before, the British used to give two kuruş a day to each. There are ten thousand of them. Along with fifteen thousand Armenians native to the city, there are currently twenty-seven thousand Armenians in Aleppo. No French troops entered Aleppo after the withdrawal of the British troops. Many Armenian refugees living in Aleppo today earn their living. The refugees who remain there today belong to the six [Western Armenian] provinces, while migrants from the occupied territories have returned [to their birthplaces]. Their subsidies ceased long ago to force them to return. Most of the refugees are women and children.

In Urfa, Der-Zor, and Mardin districts, the Turks retain at least fifty thousand boys, girls, and women, and there is a lack of means to take them [back].

There are twenty thousand of them in Urfa, Suruç, and the surrounding area. They are originally from [Western] Armenia and are the remnants of the people displaced from the six provinces.

Not many Armenians are left in Syria; therefore, the National Unions of Hama, Homs, and Sham [Damascus] have been abolished. There are barely one to two thousand Armenian women and girls living in obscure villages among the Turks and Arabs.

The refugees who were in Aleppo were transferred to Cilicia on the occasion of the British evacuating Syria, and for this reason, there are challenges for their placement, in particular, in Adana. There was an intention to place the migrants in the villages. For example, it was decided to put three to four thousand people in Şeyhmurat. Then a massacre took place there, and no one went, nor did anyone think of sending people anymore to other villages.

According to information that arrived from Gaziantep, the Turks are armed and waiting for an opportunity [to harm the Armenians]. Turkish officers are seen in the city. An opportunity is awaited, perhaps. This situation causes fear.

Bursa (from the vicar general)—November 16

There are secret deliberations in government circles these days. It is said that just as they had already protested the capture of İzmir, they will now protest the occupation of Urfa, Gaziantep [Ayntab], and Mersin by the French forces.

Adana (from the National Union)—October 30[37]

On October 16, at two o'clock in the afternoon, several women from the village of Şeyhmurat, near

վերահաստատուած է: Ասիկա ցոյց կուտայ թէ Անատոլուի մէջ կացութիւնը Մուսթաֆա Քէմալի մարդոց ձեռքն է եւ կեդրոնը անոր հրահանգներուն կը հնազանդի:

Հայր Գրիգոր Վարդապետ Փէհլիվանեանէ քաղուած տեղեկութիւն

(Հայ Հռոմէական վարդապետ մը, բնիկ սեբաստացի, տարագրեալ ի Հալէպ, ուր մնացած է մինչեւ ցարդ)

Հալէպի մէջ զանազան որբանոցներ կան. Պատուելի Աւարոն Շիրաճեան ունի 2000 որբ եւ որբուհի, որոնք շատ լաւ կը խնամուին: Ծախքը կը հայթայթուի անգլիական բանակէն: Ամերիկեան Կարմիր Խաչի որբանոցը ունէր 500 որբ: Հիմա այս որբանոցը փոխադրուած է Այնթապ (մէկ ամիս առաջ): Ֆրանսական որբանոցը, որ ֆրանսական կառավարութիւնը կը հոգայ, երբեմն զուտ հայոց համար էր, հիմա խառն է եւ ունի նաեւ սուրիացի որբեր: Հայ որբերու թիւն է 400: Զայն կը մատակարարէ Տոք. Հարդման (սպայ):

Հալէպի մէջ գտնուող տարագրեալները երկու դաս են: Մէկ մասը կ'ապրի զօրանոցի մը մէջ եւ դեռ կը ստանայ նպաստ անգլիական կառավարութենէն: Ասոնց թիւ[ը] երբեմն հասաւ մինչեւ 7–8 հազարի: Այսօր 2000ի իջած է: Ասոնք ալ պիտի տարուին Կիլիկիա, հոն տեղաւորուելու համար: Միւս մասը քաղաքին մէջ զետեղեալներն են, որոնց այսօր այլեւս նպաստ չի տրուիր, մինչ ասկէ առաջ անգլիացիք կուտային ամէն մէկուն օրական 2 ղրուշ: Ասոնց թիւը կը հասնի 10,000ի: Քաղաքին բնիկ հայերուն թիւը 15,000 ըլլալով, այսօր Հալէպի մէջ կայ ուրեմն 27,000 հայ: Անգլիացի զօրքերը քաշուելէ յետոյ Հալէպ ֆրանսական զինուոր ալ չէ մտած: Այսօր Հալէպի մէջ ապրող հայ գաղթականներէ շատերը իրենց օրապահիկը կը հայթայթեն: Հոն մնացող գաղթականները այսօր կը պատկանին վեց վիլայէթներու, իսկ գրաւեալ վայրերու գաղթականները դարձած են [իրենց բնօրրանները]: Ասոնց նպաստը վաղուց արդէն դադրած էր, հարկադրելու համար որ դառնան: Գաղթականներու մեծամասնութիւնը կին ու տղայ է:

Ուրֆայի, Տէր-Զօրի եւ Մերտինի սանճագներուն մէջ առնուազն 50,000 տղայ, աղջիկ եւ կին թուրքերու քով [են] եւ զանոնք առնելու միջոցը կը պակսի:

Ուրֆայի, Սուրուճի եւ շրջակայքի մէջ անոնց թիւը 20,000 է: Ասոնք բուն հայաստանցի են եւ վեց նահանգներէն տեղահան եղած ժողովուրդին մնացորդներն են:

Սուրիոյ մէջ հայեր շատ չեն մնացած, այնպէս որ Համայի, Հոմսի եւ Շամի Ազգային Միութիւնները ջնջուած են: Հազիւ 1–2 հազար հայ կին եւ աղջիկ կան թուրքերու եւ արաբներու քով, խուլ գիւղերու մէջ մնացած:

Սուրիոյ անգլիացւոց կողմէ պարպուելուն առթիւ Հալէպ գտնուած գաղթականները Կիլիկիա տեղափոխուած են եւ ասոր համար մասնաւորապէս Ատանայի մէջ զանոնք տեղաւորելու դժուարութիւններ կը քաշուին: Կը մտածուէր գիւղերը զետեղել գաղթականները: Օրինակի համար որոշուած էր Շէյխ-Մուրատ դնել 3–4 հազար հոգի, երբ հոն ջարդ պատահեցաւ եւ միւս գիւղերն ալ ո՛չ մարդ գնաց եւ ո՛չ ալ մարդ ղրկել մտածուեցաւ այլեւս:

Այնթապէն եկած տեղեկութեանց համաձայն թուրքերը զինուած են եւ առիթի կը սպասեն: Թուրք սպաներ կ'երեւան քաղաքին մէջ: Առիթ մը կը սպասուի թերեւս: Այս վիճակը երկիւղ կը պատճառէ:

Պրուսա (Առաջնորդական Փոխանորդէն) – 16 Նոյեմբեր

Կառավարական շրջանակներու մէջ այս օրերս գաղտնի խորհրդածութիւններ կ'ըլլան: Կ'ըսուի թէ ինչպէս Իզմիրի գրաւման [դէմ] բողոքի ցոյցեր ըրած էին, նոյնպէս նաեւ հիմա Ուրֆայի, Այնթապի, Մերսինի ֆրանսական զօրաց կողմէ գրաւման դէմ պիտի բողոքեն:

Ատանա (Ազգային Միութենէն) – 30 Հոկտեմբեր

Հոկտեմբեր 16ին կէսօրէն յետոյ ժամը 2ին քաղաքին մերձակայ Շէյխ Մուրատը գիւղէն քանի

the city, ran into the city and reported that Turkish bandits on horseback attacked the village and shot dead the men of the village. The news of this mass slaughter in front of the gates of Adana and under the nose of the Allied forces deeply moved the Armenians of the city. While [some] representatives of the National Union went to Colonel Brémond to convey the sad news, some of its members, on the other hand, went with Reverend Father Kevork and Dr. Mnatsaganian to Şeyhmurat to investigate the circumstances of the incident and determine the number of victims.

On the same day, in the evening, due to the threats of Turkish shopkeepers in the city's covered market (bedesten), the neighboring Armenian sellers felt obliged to close their shops and leave in a hurry. There was a general panic in the city over this, and there were minor sporadic clashes between Armenians and Turks, with none reaching significant proportions. Only, in a moment of panic, near the exchange market square in the crowded city center, two Turks, who had addressed the Armenians gathered there with threatening and insulting words, were beaten to death with bastinadoes by the extremely agitated crowd. Meanwhile, Zareh Doulkajian, a volunteer of the Armenian Legion, was beaten and wounded by the Turks. He barely escaped from the Turkish mob by resorting to his weapon.

The investigation carried out in Şeyhmurat revealed that on October 16, before noon, around ninety armed Turkish bandits on horseback surrounded the village and shot and killed eight Armenians, including a woman with a baby in her lap. The bodies of three men killed outside the village have been impossible to find as of now. *The bandits searched for the men by name and killed them.* This was proof that the bandits had Turks residing in the city as their guides and accomplices, which was later verified by the confessions of several arrested massacrers. The leading supporter of the bandits was one of the notable Turks in the city, the notorious Turan Ali, who was arrested the next day while returning to the city. He was executed by shooting on October 24 after his involvement was proven.

The bodies of the murdered eight Armenians were brought to the city and buried in the presence of the governor-general, Colonel Brémond.

The day after the incident, at the initiative of the National Union and with the approval of the French authorities, the first detachment of fifty young Armenian volunteers was formed to pursue them. It left the same day to chase the bandits and protect the surrounding Armenian-populated villages from possible attacks. The French authorities gave the volunteers the weapons needed. The commander was a French sub-officer supported by Mr. M. Yepremian from the National Union. A twenty-five-member cavalry pursuit detachment was also formed under the command of an Armenian subofficer of the gendarmerie. These two detachments have been unable to achieve tangible results: the bandits were facilitated in their escape by the Turkish population, mainly, and the Turkish gendarmes who were sent to chase them, in general. An ongoing pursuit in these conditions would have proved dangerous, so they returned. The French appreciated the moderation the Armenian detachments maintained and their magnanimity toward the Turkish villagers, despite their extremely agitated state.

• In addition to the tragic massacre of Şeyhmurat, the following crimes were committed by Turkish bandits in the vicinities of Adana, Ceyhan, and Tarsus during October.

1. On October 14, near Ceyhan, Turkish bandits on horseback attacked Artin Keklikian's farm in a place called Mercin and mercilessly killed the Armenians there, including a woman, two girls, a boy, and two coachmen; six people altogether.

2. On the same day, again in Ceyhan's vicinity, three young men and a woman were attacked by bandits near the village of Küçük Manzer on the road to Akdam and Çifliki Hümayun. All four were killed on the spot.

3. On October 16, Turkish bandits—probably from the gang that attacked Şeyhmurat—killed Giragos in Akdam, Mardiros in Eğriağaç, and Haroutyun in Kamışlı.

մը կիներ հեւիհեւ քաղաք վազելով՝ գուժեցին թէ թուրք հեծեալ հրոսակներ գիւղին վրայ յարձակած եւ գնդակահար սպաննած են գիւղին այր մարդիկը: Ատանայի դռներուն առջեւ եւ Դաշնակից ուժերու քիթին տակ գործուած այս զանգուածային կոտորածին լուրը խորապէս յուզեց քաղաքիս բովանդակ հայութիւնը: Մինչ Ազգային Միութեան կողմէ ներկայացուցիչներ կը դիմեն Գնդ. Պրէմոնի ցաւալի լուրը հաղորդելու, միւս կողմէ իր անդամներէն ոմանք առաջնորդ Գէորգ Վրդ.ի եւ Տոք. Մնացականեանի հետ կը մեկնին Շէյխ Մուրատ քննելու դէպքին պարագաները եւ ճշդելու զոհերու թիւը:

Նոյն օրը, իրիկուան դէմ, քաղաքիս գոց շուկային (պէզկաթէն) թուրք խանութպաններու սպառնալից արտայայտութեանց պատճառաւ, դրացի հայ վաճառորդները կը ստիպուին գոցել իրենց խանութներն ու աճապարանօք մեկնիլ: Ասոր վրայ ընդհանուր խուճապ մը կը սկսի քաղաքին մէջ, եւ տեղ տեղ պզտիկ ընդհարումներ կը պատահին հայերու եւ թուրքերու միջեւ, առանց սակայն մեծ համեմատութեանց հասնելու: Միայն խուճապի պահուն, քաղաքին բազմամարդ կեդրոններէն պօրսայի հրապարակին մօտերը, երկու թուրքեր սպառնալից ու անարգական խօսքեր ուղղած ըլլալով հոն խռնուած հայերու, գերագրգռուած ժողովուրդը այս երկու թուրքերուն վրայ խոյանալով զանահար կը մեռցնէ զանոնք, իսկ Հայ Լեգէոնի կամաւորներէն Զարեհ Տուզլաճեան թուրքերու կողմէ կը ծեծուի եւ կը վիրաւորուի եւ զէնքի դիմելով հազիւ կը պրծի թուրք ամբոխին ձեռքէն:

Շէյխ Մուրատըլըի մէջ կատարուած քննութենէն հասկցուած է որ Հոկտեմբեր 16ին կէսօրէ առաջ 90ի մօտ հեծեալ թուրք զինեալ հրոսակներ գիւղը կը պաշարեն եւ գնդակահար կը սպաննեն 8 հայեր, մին՝ կին գիրկը մանուկով: Իսկ գիւղէն դուրս սպաննուած երեք այր մարդոց դիակները ցարդ անկարելի եղած է գտնել: *Հրոսակները իրենց անուններով փնտռած եւ սպաննած են գիւղին այր մարդիկը*: Ասիկա փաստ մըն էր թէ հրոսակները իրենց առաջնորդ եւ գործակից ունէին քաղաքացի թուրքեր, ինչ որ յետոյ ստուգուած է ձերբակալուած քանի մը ջարդարարներու խոստովանութեամբ: Հրոսակներուն գլխաւոր աջակիցն է եղած քաղաքիս թուրք երեւելիներէն Տուրան Ալի անուն տխրահռչակ անձը, որ դէպքին յաջորդ [օրն] իսկ քաղաք դարձին ձերբակալուեցաւ եւ իր մասնակցութիւնը ապացուցուելով Հոկտ. 24ին հրացանի բռնուեցաւ:

Սպանեալ 8 հայերու դիակները քաղաք բերուեցան եւ թաղուեցան ի ներկայութեան ընդհ. կառավարիչ Գնդ. Պրէմոնի:

Դէպքին յաջորդ օրը ֆրանսական իշխանութեանց հաւանութեամբ եւ Ազգային Միութեան նախաձեռնութեամբ, տեղւոյն հայ երիտասարդներէն կազմուեցաւ կամաւորական առաջին հետապնդիչ խումբը 50 հոգիէ բաղկացեալ, որ նոյն օրը իսկ մեկնեցաւ հրոսակները հետապնդելու եւ շրջականերու հայաբնակ գիւղերը պաշտպանելու համար հաւանական յարձակումներու դէմ: Կամաւորներու հարկ եղած զէնքերը տրուեցան ֆրանսական իշխանութեանց կողմէ: Հրամատարն էր ֆրանսացի ենթասպայ մը, որուն կ՚աջակցէր Ազգային Միութենէն Պ. Մ. Եփրեմեան: Կազմուեցաւ նաեւ 25 հոգինոց հեծեալ հետապնդիչ խումբ մը՝ ոստիկան զօրաց հայ ենթասպայի մը հրամանատարութեամբ: Այս երկու խումբերը չեն կրցած շօշափելի արդիւնքի մը հասնիլ, վասնզի հրոսակախումբերը փախուստի դիւրութիւններ կը գտնէին երկրին թուրք ազգաբնակութենէն մասնաւորապէս եւ հրոսակները հետապնդելու համար ղրկուած թուրք ոստիկան զօրքերու կողմէ ընդհանրապէս: Այս պայմաններու մէջ հետապնդման շարունակութիւնը կրնար վտանգաւոր ըլլալ, ուստի դարձան: Իրենց պահած չափաւորութիւնը եւ թուրք գիւղացւոց նկատմամբ ցոյց տուած վեհանձնութիւնը իրենց գերագրգռուած վիճակին հակառակ գնահատուեցաւ ֆրանսացւոց կողմէ:

- Շէյխ Մուրատըլըի ցաւալի կոտորածէն զատ, Հոկտեմբեր ամսուան ընթացքին, Ատանայի, Ճիհանի եւ Տարսոնի շրջականերուն մէջ թուրք հրոսախումբերու կողմէ գործուած են հետեւեալ ոճիրները:

1° Հոկտեմբեր 14ին հեծեալ թուրք հրոսակներ Ճիհանի շրջականերուն մէջ Մերճին կոչուած վայրը Արթին Քէքլիկեանի ագարակին վրայ յարձակելով անխնայ կը սպաննեն հոն գտնուող հայերը, որոնց մէջ կին մը, երկու աղջիկ, տղայ մը եւ երկու կառապան, ընդամէնը 6 հոգի:

4. On October 16, an Armenian was slaughtered in the area called Yalnızca, near Adana.

5. The following details of the killings by Turkish bandits near Tarsus were verified on October 13. Riding bandits, on October 13, early in the morning, two hours away from the town, attacked the village of Çiçekli [Frengülüs]. After slaughtering an Armenian named Manoug, they looted the houses of the Armenian population in the village and left. On their way, they brutally killed three Armenians in Kavsaran; then they traveled to Kargılı, where they killed four Armenians and another four Armenians in the village of Gökçeler [Gerdan].

This activity, seen in the region of Cilicia, stands for more than being simple cases of robbery: it is a prelude to the so-called Milli movement, which would have indeed infected Cilicia as well because the Allied powers had failed to take radical measures against the savage elements of yesterday and to disarm them; instead, they had allowed suspicious Turkish elements to spread to Cilicia from the neighboring provinces.

Despite the kindness and goodwill shown by the French authorities to remedy the situation caused by the recent tragic events, the restraining measures taken due to the magnitude of the threat are insufficient. Thus, naturally, trusting İbrahim Bey's chasing detachment to pursue the bandits would have been in vain. Only a small number of the bandits would have been captured, as it happened when just a few scores were captured and executed by shooting in Adana, Ceyhan, and Osmaniye. Apart from Duran Ali in Adana, a Turk named Fettah, a bandit leader and one of the perpetrators of the 1909 Adana massacre, was shot on October 25.

• The governor of Adana, Colonel Norman, issued the following decree on October 25. "The representatives of neighborhoods, heads of administrative agencies, and district governors risk their lives if they do not hand over the following to Adana within four days:

A. The weapons of war in their locality and their administration,

B. All the bandits in the region, whether wounded or not."

A day after the massacre of Şeyhmurat, a brief official statement in Turkish was posted on the walls of Adana. It was signed by the governor-general of Cilicia, Colonel Brémond, and Deputy Prefect Esat Bey, stating that the recent bloody events were clearly attributed to bandits. This statement seems to have been an arrangement to calm the irritated minds. In reality, however, that statement despicably reflected the spirit of Turkish deception that [has been] prevalent in this country for years and the fact that the Allies also had become victims to it. This [realization] terribly affected Armenians and other Christian societies. On the 25th of this month, we heard that the deputy of the Turkish prefect was deposed.

Peace is restored now.

2° Նոյն օրը, դարձեալ Ճիհանի շրջակաները, երեք երիտասարդ եւ կին մը, Աղտամի եւ Չիֆլիգը Հիւմայունի ճամբուն վրայ, Քիւչիւք Մանզըր գիւղին մօտ հրոսակներէն յարձակում կրելով չորսն ալ տեղն ի տեղը կը սպաննուին:

3° Հոկտեմբեր 16ին թուրք հրոսակներ,- հաւանաբար Շէյխ Մուրատի վրայ յարձակող հրոսախումբէն,- Աղտամի մէջ կը սպաննեն Կիրակոս, Էյրի Աղաճի մէջ՝ Մարտիրոս եւ Գամըշլի մէջ՝ Յարութիւն անուն երեք հայեր:

4° Հոկտեմբեր 16ին Ատանայի շրջակաները, Եալընըզճա ըսուած վայրին մէջ խողխողուած է հայ մը:

5° Հոկտեմբեր 13ին Տարսոնի մերձականերուն մէջ թուրք հրոսակներու գործած սպանութիւններու մասին ստուգուած են հետեւեալ մանրամասնութիւնները: Հեծեալ հրոսակներ, Հոկտեմբեր 13ին, առտուն կանուխ քաղաքէն 2 ժամ հեռաւորութեամբ Ֆրանկիւլիւ գիւղին վրայ կը յարձակին եւ Մանուկ անուն հայ մը խողխողելէ յետոյ՝ գիւղին հայ բնակչութեան տուները կը թալանեն եւ կը մեկնին: Իրենց ճամբուն վրայ, Գավսարանի մէջ խժդժօրէն կը սպաննեն երեք հայեր, յետոյ կ՚անցնին Գարղըլը՝ ուր կը սպաննեն 4 հայեր, ուրիշ 4 հայեր ալ՝ Կերտան գիւղին մէջ:

Կիլիկիոյ շրջանին մէջ տեսնուած այս շարժումը՝ աւազակային պարզ դէպքեր ըլլալէ աւելի՝ նախաքայլը կը կազմէ «Միլլի» ըսուած շարժումին, որ անշուշտ պիտի վարակէր Կիլիկիա եւս, քանի որ դաշնակից իշխանութիւններ արմատական միջոցներ ձեռք չէին առած երէկի վայրագ տարրերու դէմ, եւ զանոնք զինաթափ չէին ըրած եւ թոյլ տուած էին որ սահմանակից նահանգներէն թուրք կասկածելի տարրեր սպրդին ի Կիլիկիա:

Հակառակ այն բարեացակամութեան ու բարի տրամադրութեանց, զորս ֆրանսական իշխանութիւնները ցոյց տուին վերջին ցաւալի իրադարձութեանց առաջ բերած կացութիւնը դարմանելու համար, սակայն անբաւական են ձեռք առնուած զսպողական միջոցները՝ բաղդատմամբ վտանգի մեծութեան: Այսպէս հրոսախումբերը հետապնդելը Իպրահիմ պէյի հետապնդիչ խումբին վստահիլը բնական է թէ ապարդիւն պիտի մնար եւ բազմաթիւ հրոսակներէն միայն աննշան թիւ մը ձեռք պիտի անցնէր, ինչպէս ալ եղաւ հազիւ քանի մը տասնեակ ձեռք անցնելով եւ գնդակահար ըլլալով Ատանայի, Ճիհանի եւ Օսմանիյէի մէջ: Ատանայի մէջ Տուրան Ալիէն զատ Հոկտեմբեր 25ին հրացանահար եղած է հրոսապետ Ֆեթթահ անուն թուրքը՝ 1909ի Ատանայի կոտորածին դերակատարներէն մին:

- Ատանայի կառավարիչ Գնդ. Նորման հետեւեալ հրամանագիրը հրապարակած է Հոկտեմբեր 25ին: «Մուխթարները, միւտիրները եւ միւթէսարըֆները իրենց գլխով պատասխանատու են չորս օրուան պայմանաժամի մը մէջ Ատանա յանձնելու համար.

Ա. Իրենց տեղւոյն եւ վարչութեան մէջ գտնուող պատերազմական զէնքերը,

Բ. Երկրին մէջ գտնուող բոլոր հրոսակները՝ վիրաւոր կամ ոչ»:

- Շէյխ Մուրատըի կոտորածին յաջորդ օրը, Ատանայի պատերը կը փակցուի թուրքերէն պաշտօնական կարճ յայտարարութիւն մը՝ Կիլիկիոյ ընդհանուր կառավարիչ Գնդապետ Պրեմոնէ եւ կուսակալի փոխանորդ Էսատ պէյէ ստորագրուած, որուն մէջ վերջին օրերս տեղի ունեցած արիւնալի դէպքերը պարզ աւազակաց գործեր ըլլալը կը հաւաստուի: Այս յայտարարութիւնը գրգռուած միտքերը հանդարտեցնելու նպատակով եղած կարգադրութիւն մը ըլլալ կը թուի: Իրականին մէջ սակայն այդ յայտարարութիւնը տգեղօրէն կը ցոլացնէր այս երկրին մէջ տարիներէ ի վեր ի յայտ եկող թրքական խաբէութեան ոգին, որուն Դաշնակիցներուն ալ զոհ երթալը յոռի ազդեցութիւն ըրաւ որքան հայ նոյնքան եւ միւս քրիստոնեայ հասարակութեանց մէջ: Ամսոյս 25ին լսեցինք որ թուրք կուսակալին փոխանորդը պաշտօնանկ եղած է:

Հիմա անդորրութիւնը վերահաստատուած է:

[Insecurity] Notebook Number 5
November 1919–January 1920

Boğazlıyan (from Nouritsa B. Tovmasian, orphanage superintendent)—November 11, 1919[38]
The Turks gradually began to release the women and orphans retained by them. Orphans apply to us every day, and we cannot take them. Countless women wander the streets. There are about two hundred widows, and we can hardly provide bread to a hundred of them.

• When the local lieutenant governor Avni Bey was dismissed, he immediately went to the vicinities and incited the people against Armenians, saying that when [he leaves, they should] attack the Armenians directly, so when the deputy left, they started committing crimes. They removed three brides from Çokradan; three girls from Felahiye [Rumdiğin], aged twelve, fourteen, and sixteen; and two brides from Giniden. They also cut off the Kayseri-Boğazlıyan road and began to rob travelers.

Bursa (from the vicar general)—October 20, 1919[39]
On the night of October 5[40], a thirty-four-member gang attacked the Turkish village named Boyalıca in the İznik district. When one of the robbers entered a coffeehouse, the coffeehouse manager, an Albanian, fearful and suspicious of him, pulled out his pistol, fired, and killed him. Thereupon, the gang opened fire, shooting left and right. Three villagers died, and eleven were severely wounded, three of whom died later.

The robbers cut off the head and penis of their dead friend and took them together.

On October 16, twelve gendarmes from Orhangazi (because the village of Keramet is under its jurisdiction), under the command of a savage and ruthless sergeant named İbrahim, reached the village of Keramet and arrested the following eight young men they met either in coffeehouses or on the street. 1. Hagop Nigoghosian, 2. Krikor Hadji Torosian, 3. Hagop Vartanian, 4. Garabed Vartanian, 5. Hovagim Takvorian, 6. Hadji Mugur Atamian, 7. Garabed Hadji Nigoghosian, 8. Bedros Kevorkian. They took these young men to the Turkish village of Çakırlı, barely a quarter of an hour away from Keramet. There, they severely beat them in a coffeehouse to the point that some fainted and fell, and some had their feet swollen. After a brief pause, they resumed the merciless bastinado. This continued until evening, occasionally pausing for a quarter of an hour.

Late in the evening, five drunk gendarmes returned to Keramet, arrested the following five young men, and took them to Çakırlı: 1. Madat Hagopian, 2. Sdepan Garabedian, 3. Bedros Boghosian (saddler), 4. Hagop Mardirosian, 5. Arakel Hagopian.

That same night, at about nine o'clock, two uninhabited houses on the western edge of the village caught fire simultaneously, and terrible gunfire started so that no one dared leave the house. Fortunately, the wind stopped, and the fire did not reach significant proportions; otherwise, the whole village would have burned to ashes. The detainees were severely tortured that night in Çakırlı, and the morning after, they were tied up to one another and taken to the village of Boyalıca, an hour and a half away. On the road, a gendarme whipped Hagop Nigoghosian in the back and kicked him mercilessly. He was made to run, thus forcing also his friends to run since they were tied to one another. The gendarme hit those unable [to run] with buttstocks and insulted them with swear words. Gendarme number 976 took Bedros Kevorkian's new shoes and Hadji Mgrdich's new fez, while gendarme number 1005 took Arakel Hagopian's new shoes.

After reaching the village of Boyalıca, they began to inflict more horrible torments, and in the coffeehouse, they bastinadoed the Armenians publicly until they fainted and fell. They hit them on their heads, eyes, faces, and elsewhere. One began to vomit blood; another's eye and face swelled. The gendarmes forced the villagers to confess that they had seen Hagop, Krikor, Sdepan, and the rest on the

[Անապահովութեան] Տետր Թիւ 5
1919 Նոյեմբեր – 1920 Յունվար

Պօղազլեան (Նուրիցա Պ. Թովմասեանէ, տեսչուհի որբանոցի) – 11 Նոյեմբեր 1919

Թուրքերը սկսան կամաց կամաց արտաքսել իրենց քով գտնուող կիները եւ որբերը: Ամէն օր որբեր կը դիմեն եւ չենք կրնար առնուլ: Փողոցները թափառող կիները անհամար են: 200ի մօտ այրիներ կան որոնց հարիւրին հազիւ հաց կրնանք տալ:

- Տեղւոյս զայմագամ Ավնի պէյ երբ պաշտօնանկ եղաւ, իսկոյն շրջակայքը գնաց եւ ժողովուրդը գրգռեց ընդդէմ հայոց, ըսելով թէ երբ ես երթամ, իսկոյն յարձակեցէք հայոց վրայ ու երբ տեղակալը գնաց, սկսան ոճիրներու: Չոգրատանէն հանեցին երեք հարսեր, Բումտիկինէն երեք աղջիկներ 12–14–16 տարեկան, Կինիտէնէն նաեւ երկու հարսեր ու ընդհատեցին նաեւ Կեսարիոյ-Պօղազլեանի ճամբան եւ սկսան կողոպտել ճամբորդները:

Պրուսա (Առաջնորդական Փոխանորդէն) – 20 Հոկտեմբեր 1919

Հոկտեմբեր 5ի գիշերը 34 հոգիէ բաղկացեալ աւազակախումբ մը կը յարձակի Իզնիկի գաւառակին Պօեալըճա ըսուած թուրք գիւղին վրայ: Աւազակներէն մէկը երբ սրճարան մը կը մտնէ, սրճարանապետը որ ալպանացի մ'է, անոր երեւոյթէն վախնալով եւ կասկածելով, ատրճանակը կը քաշէ, կրակ կ'ընէ եւ կը մեռցնէ: Ասոր վրայ աւազակախումբը աջ ու ձախ կրակ կը բանայ: Գիւղացիներէն կը մեռնին 3 հոգի եւ 11 հոգի ալ ծանրապէս կը վիրաւորուին, որոնցմէ 3-ը եւս կը մեռնին յետոյ:

Աւազակները իրենց մեռեալ ընկերոջ գլուխը եւ արանդամը կը կտրեն եւ միասին կը տանին:

Հոկտեմբեր 16ին Օրխան Կազիէն (որովհետեւ Քէրէմէթ գիւղը անոր ենթակայ է) 12 ժանտարմաներ Իպրահիմ անուն վայրագ եւ անգութ չավուշի մը հրամանատարութեան տակ Քէրէմէթ գիւղը կը հասնին եւ հոն սրճարաններու մէջ եւ կամ փողոցին մէջ հանդիպած հետեւեալ 8 երիտասարդները կը ձերբակալեն. 1. Յակոբ Նիկողոսեան, 2. Գրիգոր հաճի Թորոսեան, 3. Յակոբ Վարդանեան, 4. Կարապետ Վարդանեան, 5. Յովակիմ Թագւորեան, 6. Հաճի Մկըր Ադամեան, 7. Կարապետ Հաճի Նիկողոսեան, 8. Պետրոս Գէորգեան: Այս երիտասարդները կը տանին Քէրամէթէ հազիւ քառորդ ժամ հեռաւորութիւն ունեցող Չագըրլը ըսուած թուրք գիւղը եւ հոն սրճարանին մէջ սոսկալի կերպով կը ծեծեն այն աստիճան որ շատերը կը նուաղին կ'իյնան եւ շատերուն ոտքերը կ'ուռին: Քիչ մը դադարէ վերջ նորէն կը սկսին անխնայ գանակոծել եւ ասիկա կը շարունակուի մինչեւ իրիկուն, մերթ ընդ մերթ քառորդ ժամուան դադար տալով:

Իրիկուան ուշ ատեն հինգ ժանտարմա, գինով վիճակի մէջ, կրկին Քէրամէթ կը վերադառնան եւ հետեւեալ հինգ երիտասարդները եւս ձերբակալելով Չաքըրլը կը տանին: 1. Մատաթ Յակոբեան, 2. Ստեփան Կարապետեան, 3. Պետրոս Պօղոսեան (սէմէրճի), 4. Յակոբ Մարտիրոսեան, 5. Առաքել Յակոբեան:

Նոյն գիշերը, ժամը 9ին ատենները, գիւղին արեւմտեան ծայրը գտնուող երկու անբնակ տուներէ միաժամանակ հրդեհ կը ծագի եւ սոսկալի հրացանաձգութիւն մը կը սկսի, այնպէս որ ոչ ոք կը համարձակի տունէն դուրս ելլել: Բարեբաղդաբար հովը կը դադրի եւ հրդեհը մեծ համեմատութիւններ չ'առներ, ապա թէ ոչ ամբողջ գիւղը մոխիր կը դառնար: Չագըրլըի մէջ այդ գիշերը սոսկալի տանջանքներ կուտան ձերբակալ[եալ]ներուն եւ հետեւեալ առտուն ամէնն ալ իրարու կապելով, 1½ ժամ հեռու գտնուող Պոքալըճա գիւղը կը տանին: Ճամբան ժանտարմաներէն մէկը Յակոբ Նիկողոսեանին կռնակը կը ծեծէ եւ մտրակով անխնայ հարուածելով կը վազցնէ, իր ընկերներն ալ իրարու կապուած վիճակի մէջ հարկադրելով վազելու, անկարողներուն հրացանի բուներով զարնելով եւ հայհոյանքներով անարգելով: Պետրոս Գէորգեանի նոր կօշիկները եւ Հաճի Մկրտիչի նոր փէսը կ'առնէ թիւ 976 ժանտարման, եւ Առաքել Յակոբեանի նոր կօշիկը թիւ 1005 ժանտարման:

Պօխալըճա գիւղը հասնելէ յետոյ, կը սկսին աւելի սոսկալի տանջանքներ տալ, սրճարանի մէջ

evening of the incident. When the villagers protested, saying that they could not accuse men in vain, they, too, were threatened and then forced to testify that they presumably recognized the eight of them. Behold, an unprecedented interrogation began at that time, never seen before in history. They stripped a handsome, lively young man, Hagop Nigoghosian, bare and said that all the gendarmes would take turns raping his honor in public if he did not confess the truth. The unfortunate man, taken by surprise and gravely embarrassed out of shame and a sense of dignity, was forced to say in despair and bewilderment that, yes, he, too, had been there and that someone else whom they claimed had thrown the bomb indeed had thrown it, and that one of the Armenian men had presumably hosted a bandit in his house and so on.

Another boy named Madat, seventeen or eighteen years old, was beaten so severely and his testicles squeezed so cruelly (later, his testicles dropped off his body) that to evade more torture, he began to name three or four young men, uttering whatever came out of his mouth, and making inaccurate and fabricated statements, some of which were refuted right then. For example, Madat said that some young people were discussing while seated in a coffeehouse at such and such time, whereas some honest Turks and the Turkish manager of the coffeehouse confirmed that they had not come to his coffeehouse that day and dismissed Madat's testimony as false. Nevertheless, based on Madat's testimony, the government insisted that the gang was made up of young Armenian and Greek men from Sugören [Çengiler], Büyük-Yeniköy, Ortaköy, Şahinyurdu [Benli], and Keramet. Therefore, it is feared that [the gendarmes] will also inflict harm upon these villages using this pretext.

The detainees have now been transferred to a prison in İznik. Before placing them there, they were taken around in the city [and] portrayed as well-known, infamous robbers to provoke the mob. The result was seen shortly. Persecutions began in and around Orhangazi and İznik. In İznik and the surrounding areas, it is impossible for Armenians to go out even for trade. Thus, the following incidents happened:

1. Nazaret Yezegielian, a sixty-year-old man from Büyük-Yeniköy, was severely beaten for no reason in İznik.

2. Onnig Dilsizian and Boghosig Torosian from Sugören also were beaten in İznik for no reason.

3. Two gendarmes beat Krikor Mardoyan, Minas Vezirian, and Ghevont Biberian in an olive grove near Sugören, also for no reason.

4. While returning from Orhangazi village, two young Greek women from Elmalı, Velo's daughter Domna and his girlfriend Marika, came across a Dagestani gendarme, Çete Mehmet, who wanted to rape the women. The unfortunate women, screaming and shouting, barely managed to escape from that savage gendarme. They took refuge in Büyük-Yeniköy and, from there, Sugören. These women arrived in Orhangazi a few days later and lodged a complaint against the gendarmerie commander, but it was given no importance.

The hatred against the Armenians of Keramet in nearby Turkish villages seems to have played a significant role in this incident. When the villagers returned decimated after deportation, Boshnaks who had occupied their homes left. Only eighteen of them, all influential people, insisted on remaining and not handing over Armenian houses and olive groves to their rightful owners. An investigation revealed that they had been encouraged by the intendant of Büyük-Yeniköy. These eighteen Boshnaks indeed left after the intendant moved out. Most of them went a quarter of an hour away from Keramet to the Turkish village of Çakırlı, and from there, they continued their hostility toward Armenians. They took back their homes by making them flee through intimidation. Once, they formed a gang and looted the whole village. Another time, they put the two watchmen in prison on pretenses and accusations. The watchmen remain imprisoned in Bursa. Now, using the incident of Boyalıca as a pretext, they put the young men and guards of the entire village in prison and stole approximately ten to twelve

հրապարակաւ *փալախա*յի կ՚ենթարկեն, մինչեւ որ նուաղելով կ՚իյնան: Կը զարնեն անոնց գլխին, աչքին, դէմքին եւայլն, այնպէս որ մէկը կը սկսի արիւն փսխել, ուրիշի մը աչքը եւ դէմքը կ՚ուռի: Ժանտարմաները կը ստիպեն գիւղացիները որպէսզի խոստովանին թէ այդ դէպքին իրիկունը տեսած են Յակոբը, Գրիգորը, Ստեփանը եւայլն, եւ երբ գիւղացիները կը բողոքեն եւ կ՚ըսեն թէ պարապ տեղը զրպարտութիւն չեն կրնար ընել, ահա անոնց ալ կը սպառնան եւ այսպէս բռնի եւ իրենց ցուցմունքին վրայ որպէս թէ 8 հոգի ճանչցնել կուտան: Ահա այդ ատեն ծայր կուտայ պատմութեան մէջ անգամ նմանը չտեսնուած աննախընթաց հարցաքննութիւն մը: Գեղեցիկ եւ կայտառ երիտասարդ մը՝ Յակոբ Նիկողոսեան, բոլորովին կը մերկացնեն եւ կ՚ըսեն թէ բոլոր ժանտարմաները կարգաւ իր պատիւը պիտի բռնաբարեն հրապարակաւ, եթէ ճիշդը չխոստովանի: Խեղճը անակնկալի եկած, ամօթէն եւ արժանապատուութեան զգացումէն գետինը անցած, յուսահատ եւ խելակորոյս կը ստիպուի ըսել թէ այո՛ ինքն ալ կար, թէ ուրիշ մը, որուն համար կը պնդեն թէ պօմպա նետեր է, նետեր է, թէ ուրիշ մը որպէս թէ աւազակախումբը իր տունը հիւրընկալած է եւայլն:

Մատաթ անունով ուրիշ տղայ մը 17–18 տարեկան, այն աստիճան կը ծեծեն եւ ամորձիքները այն աստիճան անգթօրէն կը սեղմեն (վերջը ամորձիքները ինկած է) որ տղան փրկուելու համար տանջանքներէն կը սկսի երեք չորս երիտասարդներու անուններ տալ, բերանին եկածը ըսել, սխալ եւ մտացածին յայտարարութիւններ ընել, որոնցմէ ոմանք նոյն հետայն կը հերքուին. օրինակի համար Մատաթ քանի մը երիտասարդներու համար ըսած է թէ անոնք այնինչ ժամուն այնինչ սրճարանը նստած կը խորհրդակցէին, մինչդեռ թուրք քանի մը բարեխիղճ անձեր եւ թուրք սրճարանապետը կը հաստատեն թէ անոնք այդ օրը իրեն սրճարանը չեն եկած եւ այս կերպով Մատաթին վկայութիւնները կը ջրեն: Սակայն ասով հանդերձ Մատաթին վկայութիւններուն վրայ հիմնուած կառավարութիւնը կը պնդէ թէ աւազակախումբը հայերէ եւ յոյներէ կազմուած է, Չէնկիլէրի, Մեծ Նոր Գիւղի, Միջագիւղի, Պէնլիի եւ Քէրամէթի երիտասարդներէն: Այնպէս որ վախ կայ որ այս պատրուակաւ չարիք հասցնեն նաեւ այս գիւղերուն:

Հիմա ձերբակալ[եալ]ները փոխադրուած են Իզնիկի բանտը, ուր դրուելէ առաջ քաղաքին մէջ կը պտտցուին իբր անուանի եւ նշանաւոր աւազակներ, խուժանը գրգռելու համար: Արդիւնքը շուտով կը տեսնուի, վասնզի հալածանքը սկսած է Օրխան Կազիի եւ Իզնիկի մէջ եւ շրջակայքը: Իզնիկ եւ շրջակայքը հայոց առեւտուրի համար իսկ երթեւեկը կարելի չէ: Այսպէս պատահեցան հետեւեալ դէպքերը.

1° Մեծ Նոր գիւղացի Նազարէթ Եզէկիէլեան անուն 60 տարեկան մարդ մը սոսկալի կը ծեծեն Իզնիկի մէջ առանց պատճառի:

2° Չէնկիլէրցի Օննիկ Տիլսիզեան եւ Պօղոսիկ Թորոսեան նոյնպէս առանց պատճառի Իզնիկի մէջ կը ծեծուին:

3° Չէնկիլէրի մօտ ձիթաստանի մը մէջ երկու ժանտարմաներ կը ծեծեն Գրիգոր Մարտօեանը, Մինաս Վէզիրեանը, Ղեւոնդ Պիպէրեանը, նոյնպէս առանց պատճառի:

4° Էլմալացի երկու յոյն մանկամարդ կիներ՝ Վէլօի աղջիկը Տօմնա եւ իր ընկերուհին՝ Մարիքա, Օրխան Կազիէն գիւղ դարձին, շօսէին վրայ կը հանդիպին տաղեսթանցի ժանտարմա *չէթէ* Մէհմէտի, որ կ՚ուզէ այդ կիներուն պատիւը բռնաբարել. խեղճ կիները պոռալով կանչելով հազիւ կը յաջողին ճողոպրիլ այդ վայրագ ժանտարմային ձեռքէն եւ Մեծ Նոր Գիւղ կ՚ապաստանին, անկէ ալ՝ Չէնկիլէր: Այս կիները մի քանի օր վերջ Օրխան Կազի գալով բողոքեցին ժանտարմա զօմանտանին դէմ, սակայն կարեւորութիւն չտրուեցաւ:

Այս դէպքին մէջ մեծ դեր կատարած ըլլալ կը թուի Քէրամէթի հայոց դէմ շրջակայ թուրք գիւղերու ատելութիւնը: Գիւղացիք տարագրութեան մէջ տասանորդուած երբ դարձան, իրենց տուները գրաւած էին պօշնագներ, որոնք հեռացան: Միայն 18 ազդեցիկները յամառեցան մնալ եւ չյանձնել հայոց տուները եւ ձիթաստանները: Քննութեամբ հասկցուեցաւ թէ անոնք կը քաջալերուէին Մեծ Նոր Գիւղի միւտիր[էն], որուն տեղափոխութենէն յետոյ արդարեւ այդ 18 պօշնագները մեկնեցան: Մեծ մասը անցաւ Քէրամէթէն քառորդ ժամ հեռու Չագըրլը թուրք գիւղը, եւ անկէ

thousand kilos of olives within four or five days because the old men and the women dared not defend their olive groves.

The evidence that the arrest of the young men had been plotted in Çakırlı is that the detainees were taken there instead of Boyalıca, where the incident took place. Besides, the second list whereby they came yesterday to apprehend the five additional men was issued there [in Boyalıca].

There are two [Armenian] sisters from Keramet in Çakırlı who are married to two former Turkish soldiers. One of them, Hacı Osman, has been to Keramet several times with his wife Kadriye (formerly Perpon Yesayan). He wanted to collect olive groves belonging to his wife's father, uncle, mother-in-law, or all [other] relatives. The villagers resisted. They offered to hand over only the olive grove belonging to the father. Hence, the military became very angry and threatening. Hacı Osman played a leading role in preparing this list.

As for the fire, a Turkish woman exclaimed, in the presence of several women in the middle of the day, "We will not let you eat this crop. You will see. We will set this village on fire, and you will all flee terrified." That very evening, the fire started simultaneously from two houses, fifteen or twenty meters apart, and terrible shooting began; the villagers confined themselves to their homes, perplexed. As for the young men, they were absent at the time. A quarter of an hour away, the residents of Çakırlı and the fifteen to twenty gendarmes therein did not come to help. This makes it clear that the fire was not the result of an accident but was a premeditated crime. Therefore, it can be concluded that the young people of Keramet are victims of accusation and remain in prison in vain. In the Armenian-populated villages of Sugören, Ortaköy, Büyük-Yeniköy, Keramet, Yenisölöz, Gürle, and Karsak, which are under the jurisdiction of the Orhangazi district, there can be no peace and security if Abdülrezzak, the local commander of the gendarmes, is not removed from his office and sent away from the prefecture of Bursa as someone who has organized çetes in the past, distributed large quantities of weapons to the Turks, and maintains a close relationship with the bandits and even shares in their booty. Abülrezzak's complicity in these incidents is confirmed by the fact that contrary to the demand of the prelacy in Bursa to bar him from participating in the investigation as unreliable [party], and contrary, therefore, to the prefect's conviction and order to the lieutenant governor to conduct an in-person in Abdülrezzak went to Keramet with him, so the terrified villagers did not express them freely in his presence.

Therefore, a new investigation should be carried out. The previous statements that were extorted by torture should be nullified, and Abdülrezzak should be removed.

• Only three people have been released from İznik prison, one with a swollen eye and one with a swollen leg. It is said that others are to be released, but their release has been delayed because they cannot walk.

Bandırma (from the primate)—November 28

An anti-Milli movement led by Ahmed Anzavur Bey has emerged in and around Balıkesir. The leader of the anti-Milli movement has the reputation of being a kind and pious Turk, and for this, he enjoys the sympathy of the ordinary non-Ittihadist people in and around Balıkesir. The anti-Milli movement

չդադրեցաւ թշնամութիւն ընելէ հայոց, զանոնք ահաբեկելով փախցնելու եւ կրկին տիրանալու համար անոնց տուներուն: Անգամ մը աւազակախումբ կազմեցին եւ ամբողջ գիւղը կողոպտեցին: Ուրիշ անգամ մը սուտ պատրուակներով եւ զրպարտութիւններով երկու պահապանները բանտ դնել տուին, որոնք մինչեւ հիմա Պրուսա բանտարկուած կը մնան: Հիմա ալ Պօխալըճա գիւղին դէպքը պատրուակ բռնելով բանտարկել տուին բոլոր գիւղին երիտասարդները եւ պահապանները եւ 4–5 օրուան ընթացքին մօտաւորապէս 10–12 հազար քիլօ ձիթապտուղը գողցան, որովհետեւ ծեր[եր]ը եւ կիները չէին համարձակեր իրենց ձիթաստանները պաշտպանել:

Երիտասարդներու ձերբակալման դաւը Չագըրլըի մէջ կազմուած ըլլալուն ապացոյցը ձերբակալ[ուած]ներուն հոն տարուիլն [է] փոխանակ Պօխալըճա տարուելու, քանի որ դէպքը հոն պատահած էր: Ցետոյ հոն է որ կը տրուի երկրորդ ցուցակը որով կուզան բռնել երէկուան հինգ երիտասարդներ[ը] եւս:

Չագըրլըի մէջ կը գտնուին քէրէմէթցի երկու քոյրեր, որոնք ամուսնացած են երկու թուրք նախկին զինուորականներու հետ: Անոնցմէ մէկը, Հաճի Օսման, քանիցս Քէրամէթ եկած է իր կնոջ Գատրիէյի (նախկին անունով Փերփոն Եսայեան) հետ եւ այդ կնոջ հօրը, հօրեղբօրը, մօրեղբօրը կամ բոլոր պարագաներուն ձիթաստանները հաւաքել կ'ուզէ: Գիւղացիք կ'ընդդիմանան եւ կ'ուզեն միայն իրենց հօր ունեցած ձիթաստանը յանձնել, որմէ զինուորականը սաստիկ կը զայրանայ եւ կը սպառնայ: Հաճի Օսման այս ցանկին պատրաստութեան մէջ մեծ դեր կատարած է:

Գալով հրդեհին, արդէն ցորեկին թուրք կին մը քանի մը կիներու ներկայութեան կը պոռայ, կ'ըսէ թէ «այս բերքը ձեզի պիտի չկերցնենք: Կը տեսնէք դուք: Այս գիւղը կրակի պիտի տանք եւ ամէնքդ ալ լեղապատառ պիտի փախչիք»: Այդ իրիկունն իսկ հրդեհը միաժամանակ կը ծագի երկու տարբեր տուներէ, որոնք իրարմէ 15–20 մէթր հեռաւորութիւն ունին եւ կը սկսի սոսկալի հրացանաձգութիւն, գիւղացիք սահմռկած տուները կը կծկուին: Երիտասարդներն ալ հոն չէին որպէսզի դուրս ելլէին: Քառորդ ժամ հեռու Չագըրլըի բնակիչները եւ հոն գտնուող 15–20 ժանտարմաներն ալ օգնութեան չեն հասնիր: Ասկէ պարզ է հետեւցնել թէ այս հրդեհը արկածի արդիւնք չէր, այլ կանխամտածուած ոճիր մը: Ասկէ կ'երեւի թէ Քէրէմէթի երիտասարդները զրպարտութեան զոհ են եւ ի զուր բանտը կը մնան: Օրխան Կազի գաւառակին ենթակայ Չէնկիլէր, Օրթաքէօյ, Մեծ-Նոր-Գիւղ, Քէրամէթ, Սէօլէօզ, Կիւրլէ եւ Գարսագ հայաբնակ գիւղերուն մէջ անդորրութիւն եւ ապահովութիւն չի կրնար հաստատուիլ, եթէ տեղւոյն ժանտարմա զօմանտանի Ապտիւլըէզագ չհանուի իր պաշտօնէն եւ չհեռացուի Պրուսայի կուսակալութենէն, որովհետեւ անիկա երբեմն չէթէներ կազմակերպած է, մեծաքանակ զէնք բաժնած է թուրքերուն եւ աւազակներու հետ սերտ յարաբերութիւն եւ մտերմութիւն ունի եւ նոյնիսկ բաժնեկից է անոնց գողօնին: Ապտիւլըէզագի այս դէպքերուն մէջ մեղսակցութիւնը կը հաստատուի անով որ, հակառակ Պրուսայի առաջնորդարանին պահանջին, որ անիկա իբր ոչ վստահելի չմասնակցի քննութեան եւ հակառակ կուսակալին համոզուած եւ ըստ այնմ զայմագամին անձամբ քննութիւն կատարելու հրամայած ըլլալուն, նոյնիսկ զայմագամին ազդարարութեան հակառակ, Ապտիւլըէզագ միասին Քէրամէթ կ'երթայ, եւ գիւղացիք ի տես իրեն սարսափահար ազատօրէն չեն արտայայտուիր:

Արդ, հարկ է որ նոր քննութիւն մը կատարուի չէզոք համարելով նախորդ տանջանքներով կորզուած յայտարարութիւնները, եւ Ապտիւլըէզագը այնտեղէն հեռացնելով:

- Իզնիկի բանտէն արձակուած են երեք հոգի միայն, մէկուն աչքը ուռած, մէկուն՝ ոտքը: Կ'ըսուի թէ ուրիշներ ալ կան արձակուելիք, սակայն քալելու անկարող ըլլալով՝ անոնց արձակումը յետաձգուած է:

Պանտրմա (Առաջնորդէն) – 28 Նոյեմբեր

Պալըքէսիրի եւ շրջակայից մէջ առաջ եկած է հակամիլլի շարժում մը զոր կը վարէ Ահմէտ Անզիւար պէյ: Հակամիլլի շարժման ղեկավարը բարի եւ կրօնասէր թուրքի մը համբաւը ունի եւ ասոր համար Պալըքէսիրի եւ շրջակայից մէջ ոչ-իթթիհատական հասարակ ժողովուրդին համակ-

sprang up in the vicinities of Balıkesir in the center of the commune called Susuzurluk or Susurluk, where Ahmed Bey occupied the government seat. After making a speech, he released the soldiers, expelled the functionaries, and took the work into his hands.

• Two days ago, the anti-Milli force reached the district of Gönen six hours away from Bandırma. They ousted the lieutenant governor and functionaries, seized the telegraph office, and let people loot the shops of one or two wealthy leading Ittihadists while assuring the people, especially the Christians, that their business is with the Milli force only and that there is no need to worry at all.

• The Milli horror has become especially noticeable in Balıkesir. The unfortunate people are forced to confine themselves to the city. Free activities, free movements, and free works are prohibited in public and private affairs. The unfortunate people are barred from going out at night, singing, and walking around with a hat. They are obliged to pay what they owe to the Turks and not to demand what the Turks owe them, not to report to the newspapers, and not to communicate with Allied representatives. This is the Milli Ittihadist mentality and their requirements for Balıkesir and the region. The situation in Balıkesir and the region is worrisome because mysterious Milli forces have a threatening appearance. The local *İzmire Doğru* newspaper has begun to follow a direction reminiscent of the Ittihadist mentality. In the fourth issue of the newspaper, provocative news against the Armenians was published, [titled] *Armenian Atrocities in Adana,* and *From Pozantı,* and *Pozantı's Mosque and the Words of the Scripture,* the primary intent being the insinuation that the Armenians kill Turks, loot mosques, and desecrate Islamic sanctities.

Eskişehir (from Priest Antreas Baronian of Çalkara)—November 16[41]

On November 6, Mehmet Bey of Söğüt [and] the bandit leader of Hisarcık [Asarcık], Bolu'nun İbrahim, stormed Çalkara with their six followers. Shortly afterward, Turks from the nearby villages besieged the village. Searches immediately began inside, at which time they looted Krikor Akbeyekian's twenty-eight-and-a-half Ottoman liras and new clothes, five liras cash from Hagop Karaoghlanian, and oil and items from some other houses. At the request of the gendarmes of the guard house, the search was limited, but eight to ten detainees were severely tortured because, presumably, they had not confessed to the accusations against them. The abovementioned Krikor and Hagop were brutally beaten, and after attempts to cut their flesh to pieces, they were sent half-dead to prison, without having committed any crime, like the other detainees. When the local priest (Father Antreas Baronian) demanded from Bolu'nun İbrahim the property worth twenty-five liras in his possession, they [the bandits] approached him after consulting with each other angrily and began whipping and pushing him, trying to take him to the government headquarters, [while] demanding his son as a robber. That he would have been killed under the beating was doubtless, but fortunately, the corporal of the guardhouse somehow managed to snatch the priest from the bandits. While beating, torturing, and looting, the robbers kept shouting, "We have the right to act independently and to ruin this village, to turn it into ashes. May your friendly Englishmen save you from us if they can." Terrified by these threats and cruelty, the priest took a gendarme with him and fled to Eskişehir, where he presented himself, with the Armenian Catholic priest, Reverend Father Sdepan Kalpakjian, to the local British deputy commander, who told them of his inability to make any arrangements until the commander was back.

The Armenians of Çalkara are gradually migrating to Eskişehir and thinking of moving thence to Cilicia to find security.

Hagop Guragoudian, a native of Çalkara, and Varteres Hadji Yezegielian had gone to work in the villages. On their way back, while they were bringing a cow and one hundred liras with them in ex-

րութիւնը կը վայելէ: Հակամիլլիներու շարժումը ծնունդ առաւ Պալըքէսիրի շրջակայքը Սուսըրլըգ կամ Սուսուրլըգ կոչուած նահիյէի կեդրոնը, ուր Ահմէտ պէյ ատենախօսութեամբ մը գրաւած է կառավարական շէնքը, զինուորները արձակած, պաշտօնեաները վռնտած եւ գործի ձեռնարկած:

- Երկու օր առաջ հակամիլլի ուժը Պանտրմայէն 6 ժամ հեռու Կէօնէն գաւառակը հասած, գայմագամը եւ պաշտօնեաները վտարած, հեռագրատունը ձեռք առած եւ մէկ երկու իթթիհատական ջոջ հարուստներու վաճառատուները թալանի տուած է ժողովուրդին եւ մանաւանդ քրիստոնեաներու ապահովութիւն տալով թէ իրենց գործը միմիայն Միլլի ուժին հետ է եւ թէ տեղի չկայ բնաւ մտահոգուելու:

- Միլլի սարսափը մասնաւորապէս Պալըքէսիրի մէջ զգալի դարձած է: Խեղճ ժողովուրդը ստիպուած է քաղաքին մէջ արգելափակուիլ: Արգիլուած է ազատ գործ, ազատ պտոյտ, ազատ աշխատանք, թէ՛ ազգային եւ թէ անհատական գործերու մէջ: Խեղճերը ստիպուած են գիշերները դուրս չելլել, երգ չկանչել, գլխարկով չպտտիլ, թուրքերուն պարտքերնին վճարել եւ պահանջնին չուզել, թերթերուն լուր չհաղորդել, Համաձայնական ներկայացուցիչներու հետ չյարաբերուիլ. ահա իթթիհատական Միլլի մտայնութիւնը եւ պահանջները Պալըքէսիրի ու շրջանին համար: Պալըքէսիրի եւ շրջանին մէջ կացութիւնը մտահոգիչ է, վասնզի միլլիական մութ ոյժեր սպառնական երեւոյթ ունին: Հոս հրատարակուած *Իզմիրէ Տօղրու* լրագիրը իթթիհատական մտայնութիւն բուրող ուղղութեան մը հետեւիլ սկսած է: Այդ լրագրին 4րդ թիւին [մէջ] կային հայերու դէմ գրգռիչ լուրեր, *Առանատան էրմէնի վահշէթի* [Հայկական վայրագութիւն յԱտանա] եւ *Պօզանթիտէ* [Բիւզանդիէն] եւ *Պօզանթի ճամիի շէրիֆի վէզէհքէյի սա՛ատէմ* [Բիւզանդիի մզկիթը եւ Ս. Գրոց խօսքերը], որոնց բուն դիտումն էր հասկցնել թէ հայերը թուրքեր կը սպաննեն, մզկիթներ կը յափշտակեն եւ իսլամական նուիրականութիւնները կը պղծեն:

Էսկիշէհիր (Չալկարայի Տէր Անդրէաս քահանայ Պարոնեանէ) – 16 Նոյեմբեր

Նոյեմբեր 6ին սէօյիւտցի Մէհմէտ պէյ, սարըճզցի աւազակապետ Պէօլի[ն]ին Իպրահիմ իրենց վեց հետեւորդներով Չալկարա կը խուժեն: Քիչ յետոյ շրջակայ գիւղերու թուրքերը գիւղը կը պաշարեն: Ներսը իսկոյն սկսան խուզարկութիւններու: Այս պահուն կողոպտեցին Գրիգոր Ագպըյըգեանի 28½ օսմանեան ոսկին եւ նոր հագուստները, Յակոբ Գարաօղլանեանէ 5 ոսկի հնչուն դրամ, եւ կարգ մը ուրիշ տուներէ իւղ եւ իրեր: Պահականոցի ժանտարմաներու խնդրանքին վրայ խուզարկութիւնը սահմանափակուեցաւ, սակայն ձերբակալուած 8–10 հոգիները չարաչար խոշտանգուեցան, վասնզի իրենց վրայ եղած զրպարտութիւնները չեն խոստովաներ եղեր: Վերոյիշեալ Գրիգորը եւ Յակոբը չարաչար ծեծելէ եւ միսերնին կտոր կտոր փետտելու փորձեր ընելէ վերջ կիսամեռ վիճակի մէջ բանտ առաջնորդուեցան առանց ոեւէ յանցանք ունենալու, ինչպէս միւս ձերբակալեալները: Երբ տեղւոյն քահանան (Տէր Անդրէաս քահանայ Պարոնեան) Պէօլի[ն]ին Իպրահիմէ իր քովը գտնուած 25 ոսկինոց գոյքերը կը պահանջէ, իրարու հետ խորհրդակցելէ յետոյ զայրացած, անոր կը մօտենան եւ կը սկսին խարազանել եւ հրմշտկելով կառավարութեան պաշտօնատունը տանելու փորձ ընել, իբրեւ աւազակ քահանային Էսկիշէհիր բնակող զաւակը պահանջելով: Իր ծեծի տակ սպաննուիլը անտարակուսելի էր, սակայն բարեբաղդաբար պահականոցին տասնապետը յաջողեցաւ կերպով մը խլել քահանան անոնց ձեռքէն: Ծեծերը, խոշտանգումները եւ կողոպուտները գործադրած ատեն աւազակները շարունակ պոռալով կ'ըսէին թէ «մենք անկախ գործելու եւ այս գիւղը փճացնելու, մոխիր դարձնելու իրաւունք ունինք: Թող եթէ կրնան ձեր բարեկամ անգլիացիները ազատեն ձեզ մեր ձեռքէն»: Այս սպառնալիքներէն եւ կատարուած անգթութիւններէն սարսափած, հետը ժանտարմա մը առնելով Էսկիշէհիր փախուստ կուտայ քահանան եւ հոն գտնուող հայ կաթոլիկ Տէր Ստեփան Վարդապետ Գալփաքճեանի հետ կը ներկայանայ տեղւոյն անգլիացի փոխ-հրամատարին, որ մինչեւ հրամատարին գալը ոեւէ կարգադրութիւն ընելու վիճակին մէջ չըլլալը կը յայտնէ:

Չալկարայի հայերը հետզհետէ կը գաղթեն Էսկիշէհիր, ուրկէ կը մտածեն անցնիլ Կիլիկիա,

change for their work, they met the same çetes and, on the pretext that the cow had been stolen, they were arrested, beaten terribly, and taken to Söğüt to be presented to the lieutenant governor. After reviewing [the matter], the lieutenant governor was convinced that slander had occurred and released the Armenians. He reprimanded the çetes, but the one hundred liras that the çetes had taken were not returned and remained with them.

Sivas (from the primate)—November 18[42]

During the past month, Karasarlı Köl Hello, Orun Bayram, Aşir, and Erzurumlu Mehmet have been raiding the area of Sivas and Kangal with their gangs of thieves. During this period and on various dates, they raided eleven mills, the tenants of which were Armenians. They robbed the millers in broad daylight and transported wheat and barley belonging exclusively to the Armenians to their dens in the village known as Karasar. They even took the miller Iknadios Shirvanian to the mountain, threatening to kill him and demanding a ransom of one hundred liras. They set him free after he paid a thirty-lira bail. Let me not forget to add that the same mill has been attacked twice or more previously by them [the gang members], demanding that a ransom [be ready] for their next visit. Being robbed of everything and, therefore, unable to satisfy the robbers during their [next] visit, the millers were forced to close the mills and return to Sivas, losing their only livelihood. It is reported that the bandit leader, Köl Hello, was killed while gendarmes were pursuing the gang during a skirmish.

Bandırma (from the primate)—November 28

The elections for the Ottoman parliament are over. The voters were the Ittihadists and representatives of the Milli forces. The Armenians of Bandırma, Edincik, Ermeni-Köy, Gündoğdu [Mihaliç]-Karacabey, and Mustafakemalpaşa [Kirmasti] have absolutely abstained. In Balıkesir, Milli forces, under threat and pressure, succeeded in setting up a constituency for Armenians and Greeks, provided a ballot box, and forced the election of one Armenian and one Greek as second voters under the supervision of a committee of Armenian and Greek priests and members of the two nations. A few scores of fearful Armenians and Greeks took part and, as instructed by the Millis, cast their votes in favor of the Armenian Tavit Asadourian, a member of the administrative council, and the Greek doctor Socrates. In anticipation of coercion, Armenian voters were instructed [by Armenian authorities] not to give in to pressure if they were forced to vote for an Armenian; nevertheless, they were so frightened that they dropped the ballots they were given in the ballot box producing this result.

Kozan [Sis] (from the National Union)—November 10

On November 4, an Armenian officer and four Armenian gendarmes traveling from Kozan to Saimbeyli [Hacın] were killed on the way by gangs. Knowing in advance that the officer and the soldiers were on their way to Saimbeyli, the robbers waited in ambush somewhere near Fekke, and when these travelers were inside the perimeter of their trap, all fired at once and killed them along with their horses. Only the Turks are allowed to interrogate and pursue a person. Government circles are engaged in silent and secretive activities. They are working hard both to cover up this issue and to come up with other machinations.

ապահովութիւն գտնալու համար:

- Չալկարայի բնիկներէն Յակոբ Կըրակուտեան, Վարդերես Հաճի Եզէկիէլեան, որ գիւղերը աշխատիլ գացած էին եւ իրենց վերադարձին կով մը եւ 100 ոսկի դրամ աշխատանքի փոխարէն առած միասին կը բերէին, կը հանդիպին նոյն չէթէներուն եւ պատրուակելով թէ կովը գողցուած է, կը ձերբակալեն եւ սուսկալի ծեծերով Սէօյիւտ կը տանին եւ գայմագամին կը ներկայացնեն: Գայմագամը քննելով զրպարտութիւն ըլլալու կը համոզուի եւ հայերը կ'արձակէ չէթէները յանդիմանելով, սակայն 100 ոսկին որ չէթէները առած էին չի դարձուիր եւ անոնց քով կը մնայ:

Սեբաստիա (Առաջնորդէն) – 18 Նոյեմբեր

Վերջին ամսուան ընթացքին Գարասարլը Քէօլ Խէլլօ, Օրուն Պայրամ, Աշիր, Էրզրումլու Մէհմէտ իրենց աւազակախումբերով կ'ասպատակեն Սըվազ եւ Գանկալ գազաներու շրջանը: Ասոնք սոյն ժամանակամիջոցին մէջ եւ այլեւայլ թուականներով կոխած են տասնըմէկ ջրաղացներ, որոնց վարձակալները հայեր են, եւ օր ցերեկով կողոպտած են ջաղացպանները եւ բացառապէս հայերու պատկանող ցորեն եւ գարիները սայլերով փոխադրած են իրենց որջերը, Գարասար անունով ծանօթ գիւղը: Նոյնիսկ ջաղացպան Իգնատիոս Շիրվանեանը լեռը տարած եւ հարիւր ոսկեդրամ լիրա փրկանք պահանջած եւ 30 լիրայի երաշխաւոր առնելով օձիքը թող տուած են, սպաննելու սպառնալիքով: Չմոռնամ աւելցնելու որ միեւնոյն ջաղացքը երկու եւ աւելի անգամներ ասոնց յարձակումին ենթարկուած եւ դրամական փրկանք պահանջուած է իրենց յաջորդ այցելութեան համար: Ջաղացպանները ամէն ինչ կողոպուտի տալով՝ որովհետեւ ի վիճակի չեն անոնց վերջին այցելութեան զիրենք գոհացնել, ստիպուած են ջրաղացները փակելով վերադառնալ Սեբաստիա, զրկուելով իրենց ապրուստի միակ միջոցէն: Կը լսուի թէ աւազակապետ Քէօ[լ] Խէլլօ զիրենք հետապնդող ժանտարմաներու կողմէ սպաննուած է ընդհարումի մը պահուն:

Պանտրմա (Առաջնորդէն) – 28 Նոյեմբեր

Օսմանեան երեսփոխանական ժողովոյ ընտրութիւնները աւարտեցան: Ընտրողները իթթիհատականներ եւ Միլլի ոյժերու ներկայացուցիչներն են: Պանտրմայի, Էտինճիգի, Հայ-Գիւղի, Միխալըճ-Գարաճապէյի եւ Քերմասթիի հայերը բացարձակապէս ձեռնպահ մնացած են: Պալըքէսիրի մէջ Միլլի ուժերը սպառնալիքով եւ ճնշումով յաջողեր են հայերու եւ յոյներու համար ընտրական շրջանակ մը որոշել, քուէտուփ տրամադրել եւ հայ ու յոյն քահանաներէն եւ երկու ազգերու *մէճլիս խուարէ*ի անդամներէն բաղկացեալ յանձնախումբի մը հսկողութեան տակ՝ պարտադրել մէկ հայ եւ մէկ յոյն *միւնթէխիպը սանի* ընտրել: Քանի մը տասնեակ հայ եւ յոյն առ ահի մասնակցեր եւ Միլլիին ցուցմունքին վրայ քուէնին տուեր են *մէճլիս խուարէ*ի անդամ Դաւիթ Ասատուրեանի (հայ բողոքական) եւ Տոք. Սոկրատի (յոյն): Նախատեսելով ճնշումի պարագան թէեւ [ազգային մարմինները] հրահանգ տուած էին ընտրութեան մասնակցիլ հարկադրուած ատեն հայու քուէ չտալ, սակայն այնքան վախցած են որ իրենց ձեռք տրուած թուղթերը քուէտուփ նետած են եւ այս արդիւնքը առաջ եկած է:

Սիս (Ազգային Միութենէն) – 10 Նոյեմբեր

Նոյեմբեր 4ին Սիսէն դէպի Հաճըն ուղեւորող հայ սպայ մը եւ չորս հայ ոստիկան-զինուորներ ճամբան սպաննուեցան հրոսախումբերու կողմէ: Յիշեալ սպային եւ զինուորներուն դէպի Հաճըն մեկնիլը նախապէս իմացած ըլլալով, աւազակները Վահկայի մօտ տեղ մը դարանակալ կը լինին եւ երբ սոյն ճամբորդները իրենց լարած ծուղակին սահմանին մէջ կը մտնեն, ամէնքը մէկէն ասոնց վրայ կրակ ընելով իրենց ձիերով մէկտեղ դիտապաստ կ'ընեն: Հարցաքննութիւնները եւ հետապնդումները թուրքերու միայն արտօնուած են: Կառավարական շրջանակները լուռ եւ գաղտնի գործունէութեան մէջ են, թէ՛ այս խնդիրը ծածկելու եւ թէ ուրիշ մեքենայութիւններ հնարելու մասին ոգի ի բռին կ'աշխատին:

Bursa (from the vicar general)—December 3, 1919

The prelacy sent a priest to the parts of the prefecture where the olives grow just to oversee the harvest based on the agreement reached [between the local government and the Armenians]. The priest reports daily that the wretched Armenians who returned from deportation are prosecuted severely for taxes, contrary to the government's order. Tolls and income taxes are demanded from them, and they [the Turks] would take even their shirts off their backs if they could. The governor pretends to listen to the diocesan complaints, but we do not see the result.

Yenice (from Priest Atanas Ayvazian)—November 28

On November 27, on the day of the İnegöl Bazaar, in the presence of a large crowd in the square of the local Ishak Paşa Mosque, a Turkish personality directed in his speech, among other things, insults and derogatory expressions toward the Armenian nation, trying to stir the Turkish public up against the Armenians with emotional rhetoric. This man is thought to be a Turk named Nuhad Bey, who came from around Eskişehir.

Kayseri (from the vicar general)—November 29[43]

The travel ban is still in place, as is the insecurity of the roads and the agitated state of the Turks. Unbeknownst to the prelacy, the government has elected an Armenian to the administrative council. The Armenians were absolutely unaware of his election. Turkish *muhacirs* are demolishing the homes and properties of absent Armenians despite protests.

• Fifteen days ago, we appealed to the government after the church vessels in Tomarza were looted by Turkish soldiers. There was no result. The same [government] did not give this year's harvest to the poor people of Tomarza, who suffer in misery.

• The government's tax collectors came to the prelacy this week demanding the current year's taxes for ecclesiastical estates and Armenian homes, despite the arrangement that the misplaced would be exempt from the tax.

• Insecurity continues in Boğazlıyan. Instigated by Lieutenant Governor Avni, the Turks of Babayağmur attacked the Armenians of Karahalil and stole money, property, and other things. They abducted three Armenian women from the same village. They raped them and took them from village to village. The savage Turks still hold thousands of [Armenian] orphans and women.

Edirne (from the vicar general)—November 24

Although Armenians and Greeks did not participate in the parliamentary elections, the prefect offered the Greek metropolitan and the Armenian vicar general the opportunity to sign the election report at the administrative council meeting. Both refused. Finally, they signed a separate document on the prefect's insistence: "We decline to sign the report because our people did not participate in this election."

Emirdağ [Aziziye] (from the National Assistance branch)—November 27

The local Turks and Turks in the surrounding areas still retain many orphan girls and boys. Exposed to intolerable conditions, orphans come [to us] every day. Their numbers increase daily. It has now reached seventy. In a few days, their numbers could likely double and triple.

The Armenian survivors living here consist of forty families, all poor and needy.

Պրուսա (Առաջնորդական Փոխանորդէն) – 3 Դեկտեմբեր 1919

Առաջնորդարանի կողմանէ քահանայ մը ղրկուած է կուսակալութեան այն կողմերը, ուր ձիթապտուղ կը հասնի, պարզապէս հսկելու համար գոյացած համաձայնութեան հիման վրայ հունձքը քաղելու համար: Ցիշեալ քահանան ամէն օր կը տեղեկագրէ թէ տարագրութենէ դարձած թշուառ հայերը հակառակ կառավարական հրամանին խստիւ կը հետապնդուին տուրքի համար: Անոնցմէ կը պահանջուի ճանապարհի եւ թէմէթթիւի տուրք եւ եթէ կարելի ըլլայ անոնց կռնակի շապիկը իսկ պիտի առնեն: Կուսակալը առաջնորդարանի բողոքներուն լսել կը ձեւացնէ, բայց արդիւնքը չենք տեսներ:

Եէնիճէ (Աթանաս քահանայ Այվազեանէ) – 28 Նոյեմբեր

27 Նոյեմբերին Իյնէկէօլի բազարի օրը տեղւոյն Իսիազ փաշա կոչուած մզկիթին հրապարակը ստուար բազմութեան մը ներկայութեան՝ թուրք անձնաւորութիւն մը բանախօսելով ի միջի այլոց հայ ազգին հասցէին կարգ մը նախատական եւ վիրաւորիչ խօսքեր ուղղելէ յետոյ, յուզուած շեշտերով ջանացած է թուրք հասարակութիւնը գրգռել հայոց դէմ: Կը կարծուի թէ այս մարդը Էսկիշէհիրի կողմերէն եկող Նուհատ պէյ անուն թուրքն է:

Կեսարիա (Առաջնորդական Փոխանորդէն) – 29 Նոյեմբեր

Ճամբորդութեան արգելքը դեռ կը շարունակէ, ինչպէս նաեւ ճամբաներու անապահովութիւնը եւ թուրքերու գրգռուած վիճակը: Առանց առաջնորդարանին գիտութեան կառավարութիւնն իր կողմէն *մէճլիսի իտարէ*ի անդամ ընտրած է հայ մը, որուն ընտրութեան հայերը բացարձակ անգիտակ են: Թուրք *մուհաճիր*ներ կը քանդեն հակառակ եղած բողոքներու բացակայ հայերու տուները եւ կալուածները:

- 15 օր առաջ Թոմարզայի եկեղեցիին անօթները թուրք զինուորներու կողմէ կողոպտուած ըլլալով կառավարութեան դիմեցինք: Ուէ հետեւանք չունեցաւ: Նոյն[ը] ներկայ տարուան հունձքը չտուաւ աղքատ թոմարզացիներուն, որոնք թշուառութեան մէջ կը տուայտին:
- Այս շաբթու կառավարական հարկահաւաքները առաջնորդարան գալով, ներկայ տարուան համար եկեղեցական կալուածներէն ինչպէս նաեւ հայոց տուներէն տուրք կը պահանջեն, հակառակ այն կարգադրութեան թէ տեղահան եղողները տուրքէ զերծ պիտի մնային:
- Պօղազլեանի մէջ անապահովութիւնը կը շարունակէ: Գայմագամ Ավնիի թելադրութիւններով Պապա-Եաղմուրի թուրքերը յարձակած են գարա-հալիլցի հայերուն վրայ եւ գողցած են դրամ, գոյք եւ ուրիշ բաներ: Երեք հայ կիներ նոյն գիւղէն առեւանգած եւ բռնաբարած ու գիւղէ գիւղ տարած են: 1000աւոր որբեր ու կիներ դեռ կը մնան վայրագ թուրքերուն քով:

Էտիրնէ (Առաջնորդական Փոխանորդէն) – 24 Նոյեմբեր

Հակառակ անոր որ հայերը եւ յոյները երեսփոխանական ընտրութեանց չէին մասնակցած էտարէի ժողովին մէջ կուսակալը առաջարկած է յունաց մեթրոպոլիտին եւ հայոց առաջնորդական փոխանորդին ստորագրել ընտրութեան տեղեկագիրը: Երկուքն ալ կը մերժեն: Վերջապէս կուսակալին պնդումներուն վրայ կը ստորագրեն առանձին գիր մը, ուր կը յայտնէին թէ «մեր ժողովուրդը այս ընտրութեան մասնակցած չըլլալով, տեղեկագիրը ստորագրելէ կը հրաժարինք»:

Ազիզիյէ (Խնամատարութեան Մասնաճիւղէն) – 27 Նոյեմբեր

Տեղւոյն եւ շրջակայից թուրք ժողովրդեան մօտ կը գտնուին տակաւին բազմաթիւ որբ եւ որբուհիներ, որոնք անտանելի դրութեան ենթարկուած ըլլալով, ամէն օր կը դիմեն եւ օրէ օր կ'աւելնայ որբերու թիւը, որ հիմա 70ի հասած է: Հաւանական է որ քիչ օրէն ասոնց թիւը կրկնապատկուի եւ եռապատկուի:

Տեղւոյս վերապրող հայութիւնը 40 ընտանիքէ կը բաղկանայ, ամէնքն աղքատ ու կարօտ:

Sinop (Kuyluş) (from the Neighborhood Council)—December 1, 1919
The local Armenians are in a miserable situation. They have been in a state of severe anguish and suffering for two months. The Turks want to exterminate all Armenians. A few incidents give some idea as to the situation that prevails here.

1. Fifty days ago, a thirty-year-old local, Hagop Kasoumian of Göldağı, was killed by bandits. Although the government pretended to pursue the perpetrators, the results were not seen. Armenians know who the bandits are, but they did not report them to the government out of fear.

2. A month ago, [the bandits] raided the houses of two residents from the village of Kuyluş, Nahabed Geozian and Haroutyun Geozian, intending to take their daughters-in-law to the mountains to entertain them. The unfortunate terrorized families, forced to flee to the Muslim beys, were dispersed thus and subjected to a miserable situation. The perpetrator of this crime is also known, but they are afraid to report it to the government.

3. On November 25, Diran Geozian, a barely twenty-five-year-old brave and patriotic young man involved in national affairs, was killed while heading to Sinop from Kuyluş. The young man's enemies being known were reported to the government. He was the sole support of his family and relatives, who are now in a state of misery, and the entire Armenian population, who loved him and were helped by him, is deeply saddened by this incident.

Konya (from the vicar general)—December 2, 1919
After the fall of Cemal Bey, the people of Bozkır showed fierce opposition to the Milli organization and dared to approach Konya's gates with regular forces. On this occasion, Major Arif, a bandit leader who raided Afyonkarahisar, arrived in Konya a month ago by way of land with five hundred armed cavalrymen to quell the Bozkır uprising. Indeed, three days ago, Major Arif and his five hundred cavalries entered Konya victoriously after the capture of Bozkır by the Millis. On Friday, November 28, in front of the government building, in an upright position on the back of his horse and surrounded by his supporters, Arif delivered a speech praising his bravery and inviting the audience to join him and organize, with the same ideal, an invasion on İzmir, saying that they will easily expel the Greeks from İzmir like a prickle of ordure. The next day, Saturday, these Milli horsemen, who had been active for four years during the war, crossed the government square. Arif's group remains in Konya because the Allies did not provide him with a wagon. It is very likely that they will return to Eskikarahisar on foot.

Armenians arriving in Konya today from Bozkır say that Arif's horsemen committed unspeakable looting everywhere they went without sparing Muslims or Christians. They plundered numerous villages, robbing houses and shops in broad daylight and pillaging the shops owned by Christians by force, while the people, struck by fear, could not resist. For a month now, all kinds of property stolen from Bozkır has been sold in Konya's market. The pharmacy of pharmacist Karekin Effendi was also robbed in Bozkır by Milli bandits, and the unfortunate man was forced to come to Konya.

Prefect Suphi Bey, who had left for Bozkır on the orders of the Interior Ministry, returned today. It is said that he resigned on the pretext that his tour of duty had ended and asked for permission to leave for İstanbul.

• Since the [formation of the] Milli organization, the publication of a Turkish newspaper named [*Öğüt*] was launched in Konya. It produces the most provocative articles against Armenians and especially Greeks. Recently, [the newspaper] having taken its audacity to an extreme, the Armenian vicar general complained to the British authorities and Hurşid Pasha. After cessation of a week, the newspaper's publication resumed this time with even more provocative allusions.

Մինոպ (Գույլուճ) (Թաղական Խորհուրդէն) – 1 Դեկտեմբեր 1919

Տեղւոյս հայերը թշուառ վիճակի մէջ [են]: Երկու ամիսէ ի վեր ծանր տագնապի եւ չարչարանքներու մէջ են: Թուրքերը կ'ուզեն բոլոր հայերը բնաջինջ ընել: Մի քանի դէպքեր որոշ գաղափար մը կուտա[ն] թէ ինչ կացութիւն կը տիրէ հոս:

1° 50 օր առաջ տեղւոյս բնակիչներէն կէօլտաղցի Յակոբ Գասըմեան 30 տարեկան երիտասարդը աւազակներու կողմէ սպաննուեցաւ: Կառավարութիւնը թէեւ հետապնդել կեղծեց, սակայն արդիւնքը չտեսնուեցաւ: Հայերը գիտեն թէ որոնք են աւազակները, սակայն իրենց վախէն չկրցան կառավարութեան տեղեկացնել:

2° Մէկ ամիս առաջ տեղւոյս բնակիչներէն Գույլուճ գիւղի Նահապետ Կէօզեանի եւ Յարութիւն Կէօզեանի հարսերը, սարերը խաղցնելու գաղափարով, յիշեալներուն տուները կը կոխեն եւ խեղճերը վախցնելով ընտանեօք ստիպեալ տաճկաց պէյերուն քով փախչելով ցիրուցան եւ թշուառ վիճակի ենթարկուեցան: Այս ոճիրն ալ կատարողը ծանօթ է, սակայն կը վախնան տեղեկագրել կառավարութեան:

3° Նոյեմբեր 25ին Տիրան Կէօզեան անուն քաջ, ազգասէր եւ ազգային գործերու աշխատող երիտասարդը, հազիւ 25 տարեկան, Գույլուճէն Մինոպ եկած ատեն սպաննուեցաւ: Երիտասարդին թշնամիները ծանօթ ըլլալով կառավարութեան հաղորդուած է: Յիշեալին ընտանիքը եւ ազգականները,- որոնց նեցուկը ինքն էր,- հիմա թշուառ վիճակի ենթարկուած [են] եւ բոլոր հայ բնակչութիւնը, որուն սիրելի եւ օգտակար եղած էր ինք, խիստ զգացուած են այս դէպքէն:

Գոնիա (Առաջնորդական Փոխանորդէն) – 2 Դեկտեմբեր 1919

Ճէմալ պէյի անկումէն յետոյ պոզկըրցիք ցոյց տուած էին կատաղի ընդդիմութիւն մը Միլլի կազմակերպութեան եւ համարձակած էին կանոնաւոր ուժերով մօտենալ Գոնիայի դռներուն: Այս առթիւ Աֆիոն Գարահիսարի մէջ ապաստանող Միլլի հրոսապետ հազարապետ Արիֆ զինեալ 500 ձիաւորներու գլուխ անցած ցամաքի ճամբով Գոնիա հասած էր ամիս մը առաջ, նուաճելու համար Պոզկըրի ապստամբութիւնը: Արդարեւ, երեք օր առաջ, հազարապետ Արիֆ իր 500 ձիաւորներով յաղթական մուտք գործեց Գոնիա, Միլլիի կողմէ գրաւելէ ետք Պոզկըրը: Նոյեմբեր 28ին, Ուրբաթ օրը, կառավարական շէնքին առջեւ Արիֆ իր ձիուն կռնակին վրայ կանգուն եւ շրջապատուած իր համակիրներէն, ճառ մը խօսեցաւ դրուատիքն ընելով իր քաջագործութիւններուն եւ հրաւիրեց ներկաները միանալ իրեն եւ նոյն գաղափարով կազմակերպել արշաւանք մը Իզմիրի վրայ, ըսելով որ աղբիւսի շիւղի մը նման դիւրաւ պիտի վտարեն հելլէնները Իզմիրէն: Յաջորդ օրը, շաբաթ, կառավարչատան հրապարակէն անցան այս Միլլի ձիաւորները, որոնք չորս տարիէ ի վեր, պատերազմի ընթացքին, գործի վրայ էին: Արիֆի սոյն խումբը տակաւին կը մնայ Գոնիա, որովհետեւ Համաձայնականք վակոն չեն տրամադրեր իրեն եւ շատ հաւանական է որ հետի դառնան Գարահիսար:

Պոզկըրէն այսօր Գոնիա հասնող հայերը կը պատմեն թէ Արիֆի ձիաւորները անլուր աւարառութիւններ գործած են ամէն ուր մտած են, առանց խնայելու իսլամի եւ քրիստոնեայի, աւարի տուած են խիստ բազմաթիւ գիւղեր, օր ցերեկով թալանած են տուներ եւ խանութներ, եւ բռնի աւարի տուած են նաեւ քրիստոնեաներու խանութները եւ խեղճ ժողովուրդը լեղապատառ չէ կրցած դիմադրել: Արդէն ամիսէ մը ի վեր Գոնիայի շուկային մէջ կը ծախուին Պոզկըրէն թալանուած ամէն տեսակ գոյքեր: Պոզկըրի մէջ թալանուած է նաեւ Միլլի հրոսակներու կողմէ դեղագործ Գարեգին էֆէնտիի դեղարանը եւ խեղճը ստիպուած է Գոնիա գալ:

Կուսակալ Սուպհի պէյ, որ ներքին գործոց նախարարութեան հրահանգով Պոզկըր մեկնած էր, այսօր վերադարձաւ: Կ'ըսուի թէ իր պաշտօնին դադրած ըլլալը առարկելով Պոլիս մեկնելու հրաման ուզած է:

- Միլլի կազմակերպութենէն ի վեր Գոնիայի մէջ հրատարակուիլ սկսած է թուրքերէն [Էօյիւտ] անուն թերթ մը, որ հայոց ու մանաւանդ յունաց դէմ ամենագրգռիչ հրատարակութիւններ կ'ընէ:

• Four [days] ago, the local municipality sent an official written invitation to the prelacy to be present and to seal the ballot box of second-tier voters. The Armenian primate did not go, but the Greeks were present and sealed it officially.

Aleppo (from Dr. Ketenjian)—November 10

The British forces withdrew from Maraş-Gaziantep [Ayntab] and Urfa and were replaced by French forces. The French, unlike the British, do not want to remain in a spectator role, so they are organizing the police, the gendarmerie, the control, and so on. The French forces are preparing to advance to Silvan. The Armenians suffered during the British occupation since they could not approach them because few among them knew the language. The translators and scribes [serving the British] were usually Syriacs who did not behave honestly. And now, there is a need for functionaries who know French; if not Syriacs again, Arabs will come forward, and perhaps again, they will misinform and mislead the French deliberately.

• In recent days, the Armenians of Urfa have experienced a second deportation sparked by the news of the withdrawal of British forces. Terror and panic have taken hold. At a meager price, all have sold the little supplies, properties, and furnishings they had acquired with a thousand hardships and sacrifices to leave the city, and some have left. Shortly afterward, French troops arrived, and now the situation is said to be comforting.

Aleppo (from Vahan Kavafian)—December 2

Traffic from Diyarbakır has been difficult for some time already, and recently it has been banned altogether so that even the 150–200 women and girls in the Mardin station cannot come.

• It has been heard that last week, again, some Armenians were arrested and imprisoned in Diyarbakır and Siverek.

Aleppo (from Dr. Kachperouni)—December 2

According to information received from Maraş, the French ordered recently the Turkish flag to be brought down from the fortress of the same city. Upon the district governor's rejection of this directive, they [the French] brought it down. Last Friday, a Turkish mob stormed the fort, despite the presence of sixty to seventy French soldiers guarding it. They raised the Turkish flag again, chanted prayers of blessing, rallied, and directed blasphemies at the French and Armenians. To prevent this act by the Turkish mob, the French seem to have felt powerless, so the French governor Captain André immediately left Maraş with his family. As a result of this unrest, the market remained closed for several days. Armenians were terrified. A French functionary was beaten by the Turks, imprisoned for a whole day, and three (3) Algerian soldiers were killed. Peculiar lootings and murders are unending around Maraş.

Boğazlıyan (from Sarafian)—December 6

The çetes led by Rıza and Gayıp said during the last Ramadan, "Now it is Ramadan; to do good, it is necessary to slaughter Armenians, kidnap women." They attacked the village of Menteşe and kidnaped Arshag Chopourian's eighteen-year-old wife, Lousaper; Setrag Chopourian's wife, Chichek, fifteen or

Վերջերս իր յանդգնութիւնը ծայրայեղութեան տարած ըլլալով հայոց Առաջնորդական Փոխանորդը բողոքեց անգլիական իշխանութեանց եւ Խուրշիտ փաշայի մօտ: Արդարեւ շաբթուան մը դադարէ վերջ թերթը սկսաւ հրատարակուիլ, այս անգամ աւելի գրգռիչ ակնարկութիւններով:

- Չորս [օր] առաջ տեղւոյս թաղապետութենէն պաշտօնական գրաւոր հրաւէր մը հասաւ առաջնորդարանը ներկայ ըլլալու եւ կնքելու համար Բ. կարգի ընտրողներուն քուէտուփը: Հայոց առաջնորդը չգնաց, սակայն յոյները ներկայ գտնուած եւ պաշտօնապէս կնքած են:

Հալէպ (Տոք. Քէթէնճեանէ) – 10 Նոյեմբեր

Անգլիական ուժերը քաշուած են Մարաշ-Այնթապէն եւ Ուրֆայէն եւ անոնց տեղը անցած են ֆրանսական ուժեր: Ֆրանսացիք անգլ[ի]ացւոց պէս հանդիսատեսի դերին մէջ չեն ուզեր մնալ եւ կը կազմակերպեն ոստիկանութիւն, ժանտարմըրի, քօնթրօլ եւայլն: Ֆրանսական ուժերը կը պատրաստուին առաջանալ մինչեւ Տիգրանակերտ: Հայերը տուժեցին անգլիական գրաւման ատեն անոնց չկարենալով մօտենալ, վասնզի լեզուն գիտցող շատ քիչ էր: Սովորաբար ասորիներ էին իրենց թարգմանը եւ գրագիրը, որոնք ուղղամիտ կերպով չէին վարուեր: Հիմա ալ ֆրանսերէն գիտցող պաշտօնեաներու պէտք կայ, եթէ ոչ նորէն ասորիներ, արաբներ պիտի անցնին գործի գլուխ եւ գուցէ դարձեալ դիտումնաւոր տեղեկութիւններ տան եւ շփոթեցնեն ֆրանսացիները:

- Վերջին օրերը Ուրֆայի հայութիւնը ապրած է երկրորդ տարագրութիւն մը անգլիական ուժերու քաշուելու լուրին վրայ, սարսափը եւ խուճապը տիրած է, ամէն մարդ հազար դժուարութիւններով եւ զոհողութիւններ[ով] ձեռք բերած քիչ մը պաշարը, գոյքը, կարասին շատ չնչին գիներով ձեռքէ հանած է հեռանալու համար քաղաքէն եւ մաս մըն ալ հեռացած է: Քիչ յետոյ հասած են ֆրանսական զինուորներ եւ հիմա կացութիւնը մխիթարական է կ'ըսուի:

Հալէպ (Վահան Գավաֆեանէ) – 2 Դեկտեմբեր

Արդէն ժամանակէ մը ի վեր Տիարպէքիրէն հոս երթեւեկութիւնը դժուարացած էր եւ վերջերս բոլորովին արգիլուեցաւ, այնպէս որ Մարտինի կայարանին մէջ գտնուող 150–200 կնիկ աղջիկները իսկ չեն կրնար գալ:

- Կը լսուի թէ անցեալ շաբաթ կարգ մը հայեր դարձեալ ձերբակալուած եւ բանտարկուած են Տիարպէքիրի եւ Սեւերէկի մէջ:

Հալէպ (Տոք. Քաջբերունիէ) – 2 Դեկտեմբեր

Մարաշէն ստացուած տեղեկութեանց համաձայն, Մարաշ գտնուող ֆրանսացիք վերջերս նոյն քաղաքի բերդին վրայէն թրքական դրօշը իջեցնել հրամայած են: Միութէսարըֆին մերժման վրայ, իրենք իջեցուցեր են: Անցեալ Ուրբաթ օր, թուրք խուժանը զինեալ կը յարձակի բերդին վրայ, հակառակ 60–70 բերդապահ ֆրանսացի զինուորներու ներկայութեան, կրկին կը պարզէ թրքական դրօշը, զոհունակութեան աղօթքներ կը կարդացուին եւ ցոյցեր ըլլալով հայհոյանքներ կ'արձակուին ֆրանսացիներու եւ հայերու հասցէին: Թուրք խուժանին այս արարքը արգիլելու համար ֆրանսացիք կ'երեւի թէ անզօր զգալով ինքզինքնին, ֆրանսական կառավարիչ քափիթէն Անտրէն ընտանեօք անմիջապէս մեկնած է Մարաշէն: Իբրեւ արդիւնք այս խառնակութեան, շուկան քանի մը օր փակ մնացած է, հայերը երկիւղի ենթարկուած են եւ ֆրանսացի պաշտօնեայ մը թուրքերէն ծեծուած է, ամբողջ օր մը բանտարկուած է եւ երեք (3) ալճէրիացի զինուոր ալ սպաննուած է: Մարաշի շրջակայքը մասնակի կողոպուտ եւ սպանութիւն անպակաս են:

Պօղազլըեան (Սարաֆեանէ) – 6 Դեկտեմբեր

Րիզայի եւ Ղայիպի չէթէները վերջին Րամազանին «հիմա Րամազան է սէվապ գործելու համար անհրաժեշտ է հայ ջարդել, կին առեւանգել» կ'ըսեն եւ կը յարձակին Մէնթէշէ գիւղին վրայ եւ կ'առեւանգեն Արշակ Չօփուրեանի կինը՝ Լուսաբերը, 18 տարեկան, Սեդրակ Չօփուրեանի կինը՝

sixteen years old; [and] Garabed Yeleyenian's wife Ilimon, fifteen to sixteen years old. Only the last of them found an opportunity to escape. When the prefect visited Boğazlıyan, he interrogated an Armenian named Soghomon from Menteşe, who was in prison owing to Lieutenant Governor Avni's slander because he had protested against these actions. Soghomon explained the situation at length and asked for help. In the presence of Avni Bey, it was verified that the women were taken by the çetes of Rıza and Gayıp to the mountains. While Soghomon was in prison, Lieutenant Governor Avni was threatening the people of Menteşe that they should send a cable [to central authorities saying] that Rıza was an imam and that they were in peace.

Rıza and Gayıp are notorious criminals and have massacred thousands of Armenians. Gathering nineteen Armenian boys aged thirteen to fifteen, he [Rıza or Gayıp] said: "You are well versed in gymnastics." He lined them up and killed seventeen boys with one bullet. The other two were killed with an ax.

And now they are saying: "Beautiful Armenian women should not be infidels; they are worthy of Islam." They are being forced into marriage with young Turks. All appeals are useless.

Trabzon (from the locum tenens)—December 7

A few days ago, ten people from Erzincan came from Batumi to Trabzon in a Russian steamboat. The police, by order of the prefect, forbade them to go ashore. The unfortunate people stayed on the sea for two or three days, almost starving, resulting in a woman falling ill. Only after three days was the prelacy notified about the fact, and the locum tenens hurried to write a personal letter to the prefect asking for their transfer ashore. The prefect rejected the request, considering their documents irregular. The next day, the people of Erzincan residing in Trabzon turned to the French consul, who promised to settle the matter. They [the petitioners] showed the [consul] the appeal to the governor-general and the answer they had received. The consul approached the prefect. The prefect told the consul, "The locum tenens considers himself very important; that steamboat would have gone long ago, but I know who prevented it to finally [manage to] get the people out." Then he voiced his suspicion that they may be revolutionaries.

• Three or four weeks ago, a policeman in disguise asked an Armenian telegraph official, not knowing he was Armenian, "Which clergymen are subject to the Armenian prelacy?" When the official asked why he did not go directly to the prelacy for information, the policeman answered: "It must be kept secret."

Balıkesir (from V. Zeytountsian)—December 11

Local Armenians are interested in the issue of freedom of migration. Although there is no immediate need yet, since the day newcomer elements began to enter the ranks of local Milli leaders, the course of the Turkish people gradually turned more dangerous against Christian societies, especially against the Armenians. The dominant newspaper of the Millis is just pouring poison. There is an apparent boycott against Christians. Therefore, the people want to know if they can collectively migrate to Bandırma or İzmir without any restrictions.

Sivas (from the primate)—November 28

The inspector of Anadolu [Anatolia], Feyzi Pasha, arrived in Sivas a few days ago and invited the Armenian primate to meet him on November 27. At the end of an ordinary conversation, he asked what he thought about the city's security, the people's condition, and whether he has a complaint about any issue. The primate responded that the security issue belongs to the government, that the situation of the people is deplorable in terms of livelihood in and around Sivas, and that terror surrounds the vil-

Չիչէք, 15–16 տարեկան, Կարապետ Եէլէյէնեանի կինը՝ Իլիմօն, 15–16 տարեկան: Ասոնցմէ միայն վերջինը առիթը գտնելով կը փախչի: Կուսակալը երբ կ'այցելէ Պօղազլեան, հարցաքննեց Սողոմոն անուն մէնթէշէցի հայը, որ բողոքած էր այս արարքներուն դէմ եւ ասոր համար գայմագամ Ավնիի գրպարտութեամբ բանտը կը գտնուէր: Սողոմոն երկարօրէն պարզեց կացութիւնը եւ օգնութիւն խնդրեց: Ավնի պէյի ներկայութեան ստուգուեցաւ թէ Րիզայի եւ Ղա[յ]իպի չէթէները լեռ տարած են այդ կիները: Սողոմոնի բանտը գտնուած ատեն գայմագամ Ավնի կը սպառնար մէնթէշէցիներուն որ հեռագրով յայտարարեն թէ Րիզան իմամ է եւ իրենք հանգիստ են:

Րիզա եւ Ղայիպ երեւելի ոճրագործներ են եւ հազարաւոր հայեր ջարդած: 13–15 տարեկան 19 հայ տղաք ժողովուելով «դուք մարմնամարզ լաւ գիտէք» կ'ըսէ եւ կը շարէ կարգով ու մէկ փամփուշտով 17 տղաքը կը սպաննէ: Մնացորդ երկու հատն ալ կացինով կը սպաննեն:

Հիմա ալ «գեղանի հայ կիները կեավուր ըլլալու չեն, *տիկը խալամի* արժանի են» կ'ըսեն եւ բռնի թուրք երիտասարդներու *նիքեահ* կ'ընեն: Ամէն դիմում ապարդիւն կը մնայ:

Տրապիզոն (Առաջնորդական Տեղապահէն) – 7 Դեկտեմբեր

Քանի մը օր առաջ ռուսական շոգեմակոյկով մը Պաթումէն Տրապիզոն կուգան 10 երզնկացիներ: Ոստիկանութիւնը, կուսակալին հրամանով, կ'արգիլ[է] անոնց ցամաք ելլելը: Խեղճերը 2–3 օր կը մնան ծովին վրայ, գրեթէ անօթի, որուն հետեւանքով կին մը կը հիւանդանայ: Երեք օրէն վերջ միայն առաջնորդարան կ'իմացնեն իրողութիւնը եւ Առաջնորդական Տեղապահը կը փութայ կուսակալին գրել անձնական նամակ մը, որով կը խնդրէր անոնց ցամաք հանուիլը: Կուսակալը անոնց թուղթերը անկանոն նկատելով կը մերժէ: Յաջորդ օրը Տրապիզոն գտնուող երզնկացիները կը դիմեն ֆրանսական հիւպատոսին, որ կը խոստանայ խնդիրը կարգադրել: Վալիին եղած դիմումը եւ ստացուած պատասխանը ցոյց կու տան: Հիւպատոս[ը] կուսակալին կը դիմէ: Կուսակալ[ը] հիւպատոսին կ'ըսէ թէ «Առաջնորդական Տեղապահը շատ բարձր դիրք մը կու տայ ինքզինքին. այդ շոգեմակոյկը շատոնց մեկնած պիտի ըլլար, բայց ես գիտեմ թէ ո՛վ կեցնել տուաւ զայն, որպէսզի մարդիկը վերջապէս դուրս հանել տայ»: Յետոյ անոնց *քօմիթէճի* ըլլալուն կասկածը կը յայտնէ:

- Ասկէ 3–4 շաբաթ առաջ ծպտուած ոստիկան մը հեռագրական հայ պաշտօնեայի մը, առանց գիտնալու անոր հայ ըլլալը, կը հարցնէ թէ «որ եկեղեցականները ենթակայ են հայոց առաջնորդարանին»: Երբ պաշտօնեան կ'ըսէ թէ ինչո՞ւ ուղղակի առաջնորդարան չ'երթար առնել այդ տեղեկութիւնը, ոստիկանը կը պատասխանէ. «Անկէ գաղտնի պէտք է մնայ»:

Պալըքէսիր (Վ. Չէյթունցեանէ) – 11 Դեկտեմբեր

Տեղւոյս հայերը կը հետաքրքրուին գաղթելու ազատութեան հարցով: Թէեւէտ առայժմ անմիջական պէտք մը չկայ, միայն թէ այն օրէն ի վեր որ Միլլիի տեղական վարիչներուն մէջ սկսան մտնել եկուոր տարրեր, քրիստոնեայ հասարակութիւններու, մանաւանդ հայոց դէմ թուրք ժողովուրդին ընթացքը հետզհետէ սկսաւ աւելի վտանգաւոր դառնալ: Միլլիճիներու տիրական լրագիրը ուղղակի թոյն կը թափէ: Քրիստոնեաներու դէմ յայտնի պօյքօթ կայ: Ուստի ժողովուրդը կ'ուզէ հասկնալ թէ կրնա՞յ դէպի Պանտրմա կամ դէպի Իզմիր խմբովին գաղթել առանց արգելքի:

Սեբաստիա (Առաջնորդէն) – 28 Նոյեմբեր

Անատոլուի քննիչ Ֆէյզի փաշա քանի մը օր առաջ Սեբաստիա հասնելով նոյեմբեր 27ին հայոց առաջնորդը իր մօտը կը հրաւիրէ. սովորական խօսակցութենէ վերջ կը հարցնէ թէ քաղաքին ապահովութեան մասին ինչ կարծիք ունի, թէ ժողովուրդը ի՞նչ վիճակի մէջ է եւ թէ ոեւէ խնդրոյ մը մասին բողոք մը ունի՞: Առաջնորդը կը պատասխանէ թէ ապահովութեան խնդիրը կառավարութեան կը պատկանի, թէ ժողովուրդին վիճակը ցաւալի է ապրուստի տեսակէտով Սեբաստիոյ եւ

lages along with hunger. As for complaint [the primate said], he should contact the prefect for better information because there are so many reasons for complaining, and he has complained so much in writing and orally that he is embarrassed to repeat it.

Feyzi Pasha asked what kind of a person the prefect is and if he listens to the complaints and gives satisfaction. The primate replied that the prefect Pasha is a very good man, he listens attentively and reads the complaints, and demonstrates goodwill in providing satisfaction, but in reality, no satisfaction is given. He is sure that the prefect wants to eliminate the reasons for complaints and, therefore, he issues orders [accordingly], but nobody executes them. The subordinate staff lacks goodwill. Feyzi Pasha asked: "Can you explain what kind of problems your complaints are about?" The primate responded that the order from the Ministry of the Interior regarding the revenues of the fields was never implemented; that is, the actual owner of a field was not receiving even a tiny part of half of the income. Appeals, pleas, and complaints were meaningless. Villagers demanding their rights received only the threat of beating and death. The primate added that there is no need to be surprised because the primate himself, before the eyes of the prefect, has not been able to use the proceeds of the monastery's fields because the sowers are the local notables, who either ignored the government order, or the government wanted witnesses to know who sowed how much, but the primate could not find a witness for the sole reason that Turks do not testify and Armenians are afraid to testify.

The second reason for the protest is demolishing Armenian houses in the villages. To this day, the Turks destroy [them], and when we protest, they blame the Armenians. Third, in many villages, the Armenians have not become [yet] the owners of their fields; the Turks sow them by force, and when an owner wants to prohibit usage, they threaten or say: "Go and confirm through official government documents that the land is yours."

The hungry and naked people have neither the time nor the means to go to the city for weeks to seek trial. Therefore, he [the primate] considers it unnecessary to give the list of those occupiers to both the prefect and Feyzi Pasha since he is sure that apart from not executing the order issued from here, the unfortunate villagers will be tortured for complaining.

Another reason for the protest is the women and girls that the Turks hold. The primate has so far demanded only those who have secretly sent news and begged to be released. The government does everything in its power not to deliver them to the Armenians. First, it presents a record that they have accepted Islam, and then they [the Turks] take the woman or girl in question under strict surveillance to prevent her escape. For this reason, the primate stated that he has decided to demand no longer [that the women and girls be released] not to aggravate their position. Those having some courage and opportunity run away and come, while those under strict control remain under the rule of tyrants, which does not bring honor to the ruling government at all.

Finally, the primate described the extreme misery and poverty of the Armenian people in the city and villages and insinuated that every day they come to the city in groups and head to the prelacy. [The prelacy has] not a single rag with which to cover them, not a cloth to have them put on, and especially the most vital one, no ability to offer even a piece of bread.

Feyzi Pasha was curious to understand if the government was helping the poor. The primate replied, never, although he has repeatedly spoken to the prefect about help and has seen no results.

Kastamonu (from the locum tenens)—December 21

An hour away from Zonguldak, Laz çetes kidnapped an Armenian called Garabed Avedikian from the

շրջակայից մէջ, իսկ գիւղերը անօթութեան հետ սարսափին ալ շրջապատած է: Գալով բողոքին՝ աւելի լաւ տեղեկութիւն առնելու համար պարտի դիմել կուսակալին, որովհետեւ այնքան բողոքի պատճառներ կան եւ այնքան բողոքած է գրաւոր եւ բերանացի, որ կրկնելու համար ինքն կ'ամչնայ:

Փէյզի փաշա հարցում կ'ուղ[ղ]է թէ կուսակալը ի՞նչպէս մարդ է եւ թէ բողոքները կը լսէ եւ գոհացում կուտա՞յ: Առաջնորդը կը պատասխանէ թէ կուսակալ փաշան շատ լաւ մարդ է, ամենայն ուշադրութեամբ մտիկ կ'ընէ եւ կը կարդայ բողոքները եւ գոհացում տալու բարեացակամութիւն ցոյց կուտայ, բայց իրականին մէջ գոհացում տրուած չէ. վստահ է որ կուսակալը չ'ուզեր բողոքի պատճառներ տալ եւ հրամաններ կուտայ, բայց գործադրող չկայ: Ստորադաս պաշտօնէութիւնը բարեացակամութիւն չունի: Փէյզի բաշա կը հարցնէ թէ կրնա՞ք բացատրել թէ ի՞նչ տեսակ խնդիրներու մասին են ձեր բողոքները: Առաջնորդը ի պատասխան կ'ըսէ թէ ներքին գործոց նախարարութենէն արտերու հասոյթներու մասին եկած հրամանը չգործադրուեցաւ երբեք. այսինքն ոչ թէ հասոյթին կէսը, այլեւ փոքր մաս մը անգամ չկրցաւ ստանալ արտին բուն տէրը: Դիմում, աղաչանք, բողոք նշանակութիւն չունեցան. իրաւունքը պահանջող գիւղացին ծեծելու, սպաննելու սպառնալիքը միայն կը ստանար: Առաջնորդը կը յարէ թէ պէտք չկայ զարմանալու, զի ինքն՝ առաջնորդը իսկ, կուսակալին աչքին առջեւ չէ կրցած վանքին արտերուն հասոյթէն օգտուիլ, որովհետեւ ցանողները տեղւոյն երեւելիները ըլլալով՝ կառավարութեան հրամանը առ ոչինչ համարեցին եւ կամ կառավարութիւնը վկայ ուզեց թէ ո՞վ որքան արտ ցանած է եւ առաջնորդը չկրցաւ վկայ գտնել, սա միակ պատճառով որ թուրքը վկայութիւն չէր ըներ, հայն ալ վկայելու կը վախնար:

Բողոքի երկրորդ պատճառն է գիւղերու մէջ հայոց տուները քակուիլը. մինչեւ այսօր թուրքերը կը քանդեն, երբ բողոքենք՝ հայերուն վրայ կը նետեն: Երրորդ, շատ գիւղերու մէջ հայերը իրենց արտերուն տէրը չեն եղած, թուրքերը բռնի կը ցանեն եւ երբ տէրը արգելք ըլլալ ուզէ՝ կը սպառնան եւ կամ գնա՛, արտը քուկդ ըլլալը կառավարութեան պաշտօնագրով հաստատէ կ'ըսեն:

Անօթի եւ մերկ ժողովուրդը շաբաթներով քաղաք երթալու, դատավարութեան ետեւէ ըլլալու ո՛չ ժամանակ եւ ոչ ալ միջոց ունի. հետեւաբար, այդ գրաւողներուն ցանկը ինչպէս կուսակալին, նոյնպէս Փէյզի փաշային տալ աւելորդ կը համարէ [Առաջնորդը][8], յայտնելով թէ ինքն վստահ է որ ասկէ տրուած հրամանը չգործադրուելէ զատ, խեղճ գիւղացին պիտի խոշտանգուի բողոքած ըլլալուն համար:

Բողոքի մէկ ուրիշ պատճառ մըն է թուրքերուն քով գտնուած կիներն ու աղջիկները: Առաջնորդը մինչեւ հիմա պահանջած է այսպիսիներն միայն [անոնք] որոնք գաղտնի լուր ղրկած եւ աղաչած են որ զիրքն ազատեն: Կառավարութիւնը ամէն միջոց ի գործ կը դնէ զանոնք հայոց չյանձնելու համար, նախ մահմետականութիւնը ընդունած ըլլալուն համար *մազպաթա* կը ներկայացնէ եւ ապա խնդրոյ առարկայ կինը կամ աղջիկը խիստ հսկողութեան տակ կ'առնեն, որպէսզի խոյս չտայ: Այդ պատճառաւ առաջնորդը կը յայտնէ թէ որոշած է ասկէ յետոյ զանոնք ա՛լ չպահանջել, անոնց դիրքը չծանրացնելու համար: Քիչ շատ քաջութիւն եւ առիթ ունեցողը կը փախչի կուգայ, իսկ խստութեան ներքեւ եղողները կը մնան բռնաւորներու իշխանութեան տակ, ինչ որ բնաւ պատիւ չի բերեր տիրող կառավարութեան:

Վերջապէս առաջնորդը կը բացատրէ քաղաքին եւ գիւղերուն մէջ հայ ժողովրդեան ծայրայեղ թշուառութիւնը ու աղքատութիւնը եւ կը հասկցնէ որ ամէն օր խմբովին քաղաք կուգան եւ առաջնորդարան կ'իյնան. ո՛չ վրանին ծածկելու ջուլ մը կայ, ո՛չ հազցնելիք լաթ եւ մանաւանդ ամենէն կենսականը՝ պատառ մը հաց տալու վիճակ[ի] մէջ չէ:

Փէյզի փաշա հետաքրքրիր կ'ըլլայ հասկնալու թէ կառավարութիւնը չի՞ նպաստեր աղքատներուն: Առաջնորդը կը պատասխանէ թէ երբեք, հակառակ անոր որ ինք քանիցս խօսած է կուսակալին օգնութեան մը համար եւ արդիւնք չէ տեսած:

Գասթէմունի (Առաջնորդական Տեղապահէն) – 21 Դեկտեմբեր

Չօնկուլտաքէն մէկ ժամ հեռու Քէլիմլի կոչուած գիւղէն Կարապետ Աւետիքեան անուն

village of Kilimli and released him after receiving a ransom of 800 liras. Greek friends raised the money because he is a simple shopkeeper and does not have that much money.

- Last week, on the road from the village to the city, çetes killed a thirty-five-year-old Armenian named Diran, a villager near Sinop and a father of a family and children. He was wounded in three places.
- There are a lot of Laz bandits in the vicinity of İnebolu who were prosecuted by the government a couple of weeks ago; some perished, and the rest were arrested.

Büyük-Yeniköy (from the Neighborhood Council)—December 27

The situation of Armenians in this area is very dangerous and delicate. Turkish çetes from the surrounding districts are waiting, armed and ready. There were new clashes in Kartsi with the gendarmes, two of whom were killed and two fell wounded. The people are in a very precarious situation. There is no possibility of going to work and laboring. The government is demanding forty to fifty young villagers; handing them over would have meant killing them. Turkish villagers are armed with state weapons.

Kartsi (from the Neighborhood Council)—December 29

Early in the morning of December 26, more than 120 gendarmes and residents of nearby Turkish villages besieged the village of Kartsi. They were accompanied by Aslan, a notorious Dagestani criminal, who committed all kinds of crimes and atrocities during deportation.

The commander of the gendarmerie in Yalova entered the village with several gendarmes and besieged Onnig Baronian's house. Onnig was not home; he had gone to the nearby villages. Using as a pretext the weapon found on Hovhannes Manougian (a miller), who by chance happened to be in his house, they surrounded the house and gave him five minutes to surrender; otherwise, they threatened to burn the house down. And because they attacked with weapons and terrorized those in the house, especially Baronian's children, the mob completely robbed them and dumped the half-dead surrendering Hovhannes in one of the corners of the coffeehouse. They then raided the house of Hovagim Kinosian and killed his brother, Takvor Kinosian, piercing his body with bullets. Afterward, they shot dead a young man named Hagop Manougian, who had returned from deportation a few days ago. For a moment, they tried to set fire to Kinosian's house, and taking an okka[44] of petroleum, they forced the individuals named Hovhannes Vartanian and Antranig Kechejian to torch that house. Two people were killed, eight were injured, and five are missing. It is not known what happened [to them].

The mob looted all the houses in the village, and the terrified people were unable to resist.

Sugören [Çengiler] (from the Neighborhood Council)—December 30, 1919

A state of siege has been declared in and around Bursa over the endless atrocities and robberies that have taken place. Since December 24, in Orhangazi, Yalova, and Gemlik, gendarmerie commanders are patrolling the Armenian villages of Orhangazi and Yalova with their followers. More than one hundred armed men came from Büyük-Yeniköy to arrest an Armenian and surrounded that young man's house. The young man escaped at night under the cover of darkness. Consequently, they arrested five to ten people, sent them to prison, and sent a cable to Bursa, whence the gendarmerie major immediately rushed to the scene to investigate. Those hundred gendarmes came from Büyük-Yeniköy to Su-

ազգայինը լազ Չէթէններու կողմէ առեւանգուած է եւ 800 ոսկի փրկանք առնելէ յետոյ թողած են: Այս դրամը յոյն բարեկամներու միջոցաւ հանգանակուած է, վասնզի ինքն պարզ խանութպան մըն է եւ այդքան դրամ չունի:

- Սինօպի մօտակայ գիւղացի 35 տարեկան Տիրան անուն հայը ընտանիքի եւ զաւակներու հայր, անցեալ շաբթու գիւղէն քաղաք իջած ատեն ճամբան նոյնպէս Չէթէններու կողմէ կը սպաննուի երեք տեղ վիրաւորուելով:

- Ինէպօլու[ի] շրջակայքը կան բաւական թուով լազ հրոսակներ, որոնք մէկ երկու շաբաթ առաջ կառավարութեան կողմանէ հետապնդուելով փճացեր են մի քանիի սպանութեամբ եւ մնացողները ձերբակալուելով:

Մեծ-Նոր-Գիւղ (Թաղական Խորհուրդէն) – 27 Դեկտեմբեր

Այս շրջանի հայոց վիճակը խիստ վտանգաւոր է եւ փափուկ: Շրջակայ գաւառներու թուրք չէթէները զինեալ եւ պատրաստ կը սպասեն: Քարցի[ի] մէջ նոր բաղխումներ եղեր են ժանտարմաներու հետ, որոնցմէ երկուք[ը] սպաննուած եւ երկուքը վիրաւոր ինկեր են: Ժողովուրդը ծայր աստիճան անապահով վիճակի մէջ է: Գործի եւ աշխատելու երթալու կարելիութիւն չկայ: Կառավարութիւնը կը պահանջէ 40–50 գիւղացի երիտասարդներ, որոնք յանձնել զանոնք սպաննել պիտի նշանակէր: Թուրք գիւղացիք զինուած են պետական զէնքերով:

Քարցի (Թաղական Խորհուրդէն) – 29 Դեկտեմբեր

26 Դեկտեմբերի առտուն կանուխ, Քարցի գիւղը կը պաշարուի 120է աւելի ժանտարմաներէ եւ շրջակայ թուրք գիւղերու բնակիչներէն: Իրենց հետ էր նաեւ նշանաւոր ոճրագործ տաղեսթանցի Ասլան, որ տարագրութեան միջոցին ամէն ոճիր եւ վայրագութիւն գործած էր:

Եալովայի ժանտարմայի զօմանտանը մի քանի ժանտարմով կը մտնէ գիւղ եւ կը պաշարէ Պարոնեան Օննիկի տունը: Օննիկ շրջակայ գիւղերը գացած ըլլալով, տունը չէր: Իր տունը դիպուածով գտնուող Յովհաննէս Մանուկեանի (ջաղացպան) վրայ գտնուած զէնքը պատրուակ ընելով տունը կը շրջապատեն եւ հինգ վայրկեան միջոց կուտան անձնատուր ըլլալու, հակառակ պարագային սպառնալով տունը այրել: Եւ որովհետեւ զէնքով յարձակում կ'ընեն եւ ահուդողի կը մատնեն տան մէջ գտնուողները, բայց մանաւանդ Պարոնեանի զաւակները, խուժանը բոլորովին կը կողոպտէ եւ անձնատուր եղող կիսամեռ Յովհաննէսը սրճարանին մէկ անկիւնը կը նետէ: Յետոյ կը յարձակին Գինոսեան Յովակիմի տունին վրայ եւ եղբ[օ]րը՝ Թագւոր Գինոսեանի մարմինը գնդակներով ծակ ծակ ընելով կը սպաննեն: Յետոյ գնդակահար կը սպաննեն տարագրութենէ քանի մը օր առաջ դարձող Յակոբ Մանուկեան անուն երիտասարդը: Պահ մը կը փորձեն կրակի տալ Գինոսեանի տունը եւ օխա մը քարիւղ առնելով, Յովհաննէս Վարդանեան եւ Անդրանիկ Քէչէճեան անուն անձերը բռնի կը տանին որ անոնք կրակի տան այդ տունը: Երկու հոգի սպաննուած է, ութ հոգի վիրաւորուած, եւ հինգ անձ ալ անհետացած է եւ չի գիտցուիր թէ ինչ եղած է:

Խուժանը կը թալլէ գիւղի բոլոր տուները եւ սարսափա[հա]ր ժողովուրդը ոչ մէկ ձայն կրնայ հանել:

Չէնկիլէր (Թաղական Խորհուրդէն) – 30 Դեկտեմբեր 1919

Պրուսայի կուսակալութեան եւ շրջակայից մէջ պաշարման վիճակ կը յայտարարուի պատահած անծայր ոճիրներու եւ աւազակութիւններու պատճառով: Դեկտեմբեր 24էն ի վեր Օրհան Ղազի, Եալովա եւ Կէմլէյիկ ժանտարմա զօմանտանները իրենց հետեւորդներով կը շրջին Օրհան Ղազի եւ Եալովա հայ գիւղերը: Մեծ-Նոր-Գիւղէն հայ մը ձերբակալելու համար 100է աւելի զինեալ ուժով կուգան եւ այդ երիտասարդին բնակած տունը կը պաշարեն: Երիտասարդը գիշերը մութէն օգտուելով կը փախչի: Անոր վրայ ժողովուրդէն 5–10 անձ կը ձերբակալեն եւ բանտ կը դրկեն եւ կը հեռագրեն Պրուսա, ուրկէ ժանտարմայի հազարապետը անմիջապէս կը փութայ դէպքին վայրը եւ

gören with large demonstrations. The terrified people offered them food, drink, and respect to prevent an incident. TThey left on the morning of the following day. News came from Kartsi that the one hundred gendarmes went and besieged the coffeehouse and started shooting the people. Two Armenians were killed in the clash, one of whom was an inexperienced sixteen-year-old boy, and the other, seeing his younger friend killed, resorted to his shotgun and opened fire on the police. Well-known çetes and bandits from Dagestan were part of these forces. One of them is dead, and two are wounded. Upon this incident, the firing resumed, and the young Armenian shooter resorted to self-defense again with his weapon, but he suffered wounds and fell to the ground dead. After that, they arrested several local youths and took them to Yalova. On the way, they also arrested three Armenian hunters from the village of Kilic, [allegedly] as aides to the people of Kartsi. The intendant of Büyük-Yeniköy is responsible for these incidents. Instead of peacefully settling the matter, a cable was sent to Orhangazi [by him] and thence to Bursa that armed Armenians from the surrounding villages, particularly from Sugören, attacked our troops, opened fire, took the fugitive Armenians, and left. That's why an investigator came from Bursa.

All the villages are besieged. Workers cannot go to work. Only with the guarantee of the headman were the villagers released.

• On December 29, in the village, the major demanded the extradition of five young men, but they were not here. He left threatening.

İstanbul (from the chargé d'affaires [of the Armenian Patriarchate])—January 2 [1920]

The last time a cable was sent from the Ministry of the Interior to the district governor of İzmit upon the appeal for the murder of Kerovpé of Geyve-Eşme, a collier from Arslanbey, and Mardiros of Ovacık. The district governor responded that the killers of Kerovpé are İlyas Oğlu Ahmet, Topal Oğlu Ahmet, and Haşim, villagers from Dağınıksu in Bahçecik, and Hasan, a villager from Kazandere, and that these and the killers of the collier and Mardiros have not been found, although prosecutions continue and the case has been transferred to the judiciary.

Now, behold, even the district governor of İzmit is pointing out the criminals, but the criminals have not been found, and [the case] has been transferred to the judiciary, while when it comes to the Armenians, instead of looking for the perpetrators and bringing them to justice by lawfully apprehending them, they besiege the villages, dispatch çetes, kill, damage houses, and so on.

Bandırma (from the primate)—December 26

The Milli [Organization] was operating irresponsibly in a private building across from Balıkesir's seat of government. And now, in a similar fashion, it began to show activity settled in a building across from the seat of government in Bandırma. By raising the price of bread sold in the city from seventeen and a half to twenty kuruş, it collects two and a half kuruş [per loaf] from the bakers each on account of the Milli movement. Furthermore, they [the Millis] capriciously force tributes for goods and animals exported to İstanbul and elsewhere.

Turkish soldiers returning from captivity in Egypt and the surroundings are detained here on the spot by the executive body of the same Milli movement, and then they are sent to the İzmir front after changing their clothes, despite the explicit terms of the armistice.

The Englishman, Mr. Mace, tasked to supervise the implementation of the terms of the armistice, watches this reality indifferently.

հոն քննութիւն կը կատարէ: Մեծ-Նոր-Գիւղէն այդ հարիւր ժանտարմաները մեծ ցոյցերով Չէնկիլէր կուգան: Լեղապատառ ժողովուրդը դէպքի մը տեղի չտալու համար անոնց ուտելիք, խմելիք եւ յարգանք կ'ընծայէ: Հետեւեալ օրը առտուն անոնք կը մեկնին: Քարցիէն արձագանգ կը հասնի ուր գացած էին այդ հարիւր ժանտարմաները եւ հոն կը պաշարեն եւ սրճարանին մէջ գտնուողներու վրայ կրակ ընել կը սկսին: Այս բախումին մէջ կը սպաննուին երկու հայ, որոնցմէ մին 16 տարեկան անփորձ տղեկ մը, իսկ միւսը տեսնելով իր փոքր ընկերոջ սպաննուիլը, զէնքի կը դիմէ ու կրակ կը բանայ ոստիկաններու վրայ: Այս ուժերուն կը միանային տաղեսթանցի հանրածանօթ չէթէներ ու աւազակներ. ասոնցմէ 1 մեռած եւ 2 վիրաւոր կը մնան: Այս դէպքին վրայ կը սկսի կրակը եւ ահա նորէն կրակող հայ երիտասարդը իր զէնքով ինքնապաշտպանութեան կը դիմէ, սակայն վիրաւորուելով կը փռուի գետին անկենդան: Ասկէ յետոյ տեղւոյն երիտասարդներէն քանի մը անձեր ձերբակալուելով կը տարուին Եալովա: Ճամբան կը ձերբակալեն նաեւ Գըլճ գիւղացի որսորդ 3 հայեր եւս իբր Քարեցիներու օժանդակ: Այս դէպքերուն պատասխանատուն է Մեծ-Նոր-Գիւղի միւտիրը, որ փոխանակ գործը խաղաղօրէն կարգադրելու, Օրխան Ղազի եւ այնտեղէն ալ կը հեռագրեն Պրուսա թէ շրջակայ գիւղերու հայեր, ի մասնաւորի չէնկիլէրցիք, զինեալ վիճակի մէջ մեր զօրքերու վրայ յարձակեցան եւ կրակ բանալով փախստական հայերը առնելով հեռացան: Ասոր համար էր որ Պրուսայէն քննիչ եկաւ:

Բոլոր գիւղերը կը պաշարուին: Գործաւորները գործի չեն կրնար երթալ. միայն գիւղապետին երաշխաւորութեամբ գիւղացիք կ'արձակուէին:

- 29 Դեկտեմբերին գիւղին մէջ հազարապետը հինգ երիտասարդներու յանձնումը կը պահանջէ, սակայն անոնք հոս չէին: Սպառնալիքներ ընելով մեկնեցաւ:

Կ. Պոլիս (գործակատարութենէն) – 2 Յունուար [1920]

Վերջին անգամ կէյվէ-էջմեցի Քերովբէի եւ արսլան-պէկցի ածխագործի մը եւ օվաճըգցի Մարտիրոսի սպանութեան մասին եղած դիմումին վրայ ներքին գործոց նախարարութենէն հեռագրուած է Նիկոմիդիոյ մութասարըֆին: Միւթասարըֆը պատասխանած է թէ Քերովբէի սպանիչներն են Պարտիզակի Տաղընըք Սու գիւղացի Իլիաս օղլու Ահմէտ եւ Թօփալ օղլու Ահմէտ եւ Հաշիմ եւ Գազան Տէրէ գիւղացի Հասան, թէ ասոնք եւ թէ ածխագործին եւ Մարտիրոսի սպանիչները չեն գտնուած, թէեւ հետապնդումները կը շարունակուին եւ գործը ատլիյէ յանձնուած է:

Արդ, ահաւասիկ Իզմիտի մութասարըֆը իսկ կը մատնանշէ ոճրագործները, բայց ոճրագործները չեն գտած ու ատլիյէին կը յանձնեն, մինչդեռ երբ խնդիրը հայերու մասին է, փոխանակ բուն ոճրագործները փնտռելու եւ ըստ օրինի ձերբակալելով արդարութեան յանձնելու, գիւղերը կը պաշարեն, չէթէներ կը ղրկեն, սպանութիւններ կը կատարեն, տուներ կը վնասեն եւայլն եւայլն:

Պանտրմա (Առաջնորդէն) – 26 Դեկտեմբեր

Պալըքէսիր կառավար[չ]ատան դէմ մասնաւոր շէնքի մը մէջ հաստատուած՝ անպատասխանատու կերպով կը գործէր Միլլին: Հիմա ալ Պանտրմայի մէջ նոյն ձեւով կառավարչատան դէմ շէնքի մը մէջ հաստատուած՝ սկսաւ գործունէութիւն ցոյց տալ: Քաղաքին մէջ 17½ ղրուշի ծախուած հացերը 20 ղրուշի բարձրացնելով 2½ական ղրուշը փռապաններէն կը գանձէ ի հաշիւ Միլլի շարժումին, ասկէ զատ Պոլիս եւ այլուր արտածուած բոլոր ապրանքներէն եւ կենդանիներէն կամայական տուրքեր կը պահանջեն բռնի ոյժով:

Եգիպտոսէն եւ շրջակայքէն գերութենէ դարձող թուրք զինուորները հոս տեղւոյս մէջ նոյն Միլլի շարժումին գործադիր մարմնոյն կողմէ վար կը դրուին եւ հագուստնին փոխելով կը ղրկեն Իզմիրի ռազմաճակատը, հակառակ զինադադարի բացորոշ պայմաններուն:

Զինադադարի պայմաններուն գործադրութեան հսկելու պաշտօնն ունեցող անգլիացի Մ. Մայս այս իրողութիւնը անտարբերութեամբ կը դիտէ:

Samsun (extracted from a letter addressed to Setrak Elbekian)—January 10, 1920

In Merzifon, the government has become Milli, or rather, Ittihadist again: primarily, the name has been changed, and partly the individuals. In the last two [to] three months, they have completed the work of arming the villages. And now, they are openly arming the able-bodied men in the city. Anyone who wants to be armed gets a Mauser and a horse. There is no monthly salary, but they promise to give it in the future. Hence, it is understood that they have a plan for an upcoming robbery. The Turks have understood the meaning of this word, and those who at the beginning were not interested in arming themselves have begun arming themselves in recent weeks. Now there are few weapons and ammunition left in the depots; all have been put in the hands of the Turkish mob. The number of Turkish officers has also increased significantly around here. In the fields across from Merzifon College, the çetes receive training as an army. This is said secretively: "The land will be given to strangers. Even if the sultan commands you, you should not heed. Mustafa Kemal and his friends of the Milli Congress are the masters of the country. If they say strike, you must strike."

Beyoğlu [Pera] (Th. Rizo, engineer-geometrician)—December 25

The Armenian church in Konya was demolished from April 7 through September 20, 1917, by eighty-five convicts sentenced by the Turkish government under the command of Prefect Muhammet and Bekir Sami, the geometrician of the general directorate of foundations. All the old Armenian sculptures that covered the walls were demolished and smashed by the prefect and his associates and used to repair the avenue that ends in front of the prefect's office. In this way, the most beautiful and enduring religious and historical monument of Lycaonia became a victim of the Turkish administration.

Aleppo (from Sister Ellen, Superior of [. . .] Nuns)—January 12

Schoolwork in Maraş had a good start, but the political situation [now] prevents its continuation. It [the sisterhood] is forced to close the schools, often under Turkish terror. The killings continue unabated despite the presence of French forces, with twenty-five Armenians brutally killed in the vicinity of the city over the past month, while others have been arrested and imprisoned unjustly.

Konya (from the vicar general)—January 12

During the noon prayer on Thursday, Muslim women conducted a large rally in the Şerafettin mosque of the government house, demanding the return of Adana and İzmir [to Turkey]. Delegates presented themselves to the local Allied officers and made a written request.

Yesterday, Sunday afternoon, a large rally was held on Alâeddin Hill for the same purpose.

In recent days, a marked nervousness has been noticed among government officials toward Armenians, for obvious reasons, of course, but the prefect is maintaining his previous approach.

Bilecik (from the Neighborhood Council)—January 14

Ittihad rules here under the name of the National Movement, and the policy of persecuting Armenians continues. They do not return the stolen property; the perpetrators have received acquittal from the military tribunal of Bursa. The election of former criminals as deputies already shows the Turkish men-

Սամսոն (Սեդրաք Էլպէքեանի ուղղուած նամակէ մը քաղուած) – 10 Յունվար 1920

Մարզուանի մէջ, կառավարութիւնը միլլիական, աւելի ճիշդը խօսելով նորէն իթթիհատականի վերածուած է. անունը գլխաւորապէս փոխուած է եւ մասամբ ալ անձերը: Վերջին 2–3 ամսուան մէջ գիւղերը զինելու գործը լրացուցին: Հիմա ալ քաղաքին մէջ զէնք բռնելու կարող արուները բացէիբաց կը զինեն: Զինուիլ ուզողը Մավզէր մը ու ձի մը կը ստանայ. ամսական չկայ, բայց յառաջիկային տալ կը խոստանան: Ասկէ կը հասկցուի թէ առաջիկային թալանի ծրագիր մը ունին: Թուրքերը հասկցած են այս խօսքին նշանակութիւնը եւ նախ զինուելու սիրտ չունեցողներն ալ զինուիլ սկսան վերջին շաբաթներս: Հիմա տէփօները զէնք եւ ռազմամթերք քիչ մնացած է. բոլորը թուրք խուժանին ձեռքը դրուած է: Թուրք սպաներն ալ չափազանց շատցան այս կողմերը: «Մարզուան Գոլէճ»ի դէմի արտերուն մէջ չէթաները զօրքի պէս կը մարզեն կոր: Ըսուածն ալ գաղտնի սա է. «Երկիրը օտարներուն պիտի յանձնուի. դուք Սուլթանն ալ հրաման տայ՝ մտիկ չպիտի ընէք: Մուսթաֆա Քէմալը ու Միլլի Գօնկրէի իր ընկերներն են երկրին տէրերը. անոնք եթէ զարկէք ըսեն, պէտք է զարնէք»:

Բերա (Th. Rizo, ճարտարագէտ-երկրաչափ) – 25 Դեկտեմբեր

Գոնիայի հայ եկեղեցին քանդուած է 7 Ապրիլ-20 Սեպտեմբեր 1917ին թուրք կառավարութեան կողմէ 85 դատապարտեալ բանտարկեալներու կողմէ, կուսակալ Մու[հա]մէտի եւ էվգաֆի երկրաչափ Պէքիր Սամիի հրամանին տակ: Հին հայկական բոլոր քանդակները, որոնք կը ծածկէին պատերը, կուսակալին եւ իր գործակիցներուն կողմէ քանդուեցան եւ փշրուեցան եւ գործածուեցան նորոգելու այն պողոտան, որ կը վերջանայ կուսակալին պաշտօնատան առջեւ: Այս կերպով Լիկաօնիոյ ամէնէն գեղեցիկ եւ հաստատուն կրօնական եւ պատմական յիշատակարանը եղաւ մէկ զոհը թրքական վարչութեան:

Հալէպ (Քոյր Էլէնէ, մեծաւոր <...> Խ. քոյրերու) – 12 Յունվար

Մարաշ դպրոցական գործը գեղեցիկ սկզբնաւորութիւն մը ունեցաւ, բայց քաղաքական կացութիւնը թոյլ չի տար շարունակելու իր ընթացքը: Յաճախ կը ստիպուին փակել դպրոցները թրքական պատճառած սարսափին տակ: Հակառակ ֆրանսական ոյժերու ներկայութեան սպանութիւնները կը կրկնուին շարունակ, այնպէս որ վերջին ամսուան ընթացքին 25 հայեր քաղաքին շրջակայքը սպաննուեցան վայրագօրէն եւ ուրիշներ ձերբակալուեցան եւ բանտարկուեցան անարդարօրէն:

Գոնիա (Առաջնորդական Փոխանորդէն) – 12 Յունվար

Հինգշաբթի կէսօրուան աղօթքի պահուն, կառավարչատան Շէրէֆէտտին մզկիթին մէջ իսլամ կիներու կողմէ սարքուած մեծ միթինկ մը տեղի ունեցաւ, ուր պահանջուեցաւ Ատանայի եւ Իզմիրի վերադարձը: Պատգամաւորուհիներ ներկայացան տեղւոյս Համաձայնական սպաներուն եւ գրաւոր խնդրանք մատուցին:

Երէկ, Կիրակի, կէսօրին Ալաէտտինի բլուրին վրայ տեղի ունեցաւ կրկին մեծ միթինկ մը, միեւնոյն նպատակաւ:

Վերջին օրերու մէջ կառավարական պաշտօնեաներու վրայ յայտնի ջղագրգռութիւն մը կը նշմարուի հայոց հանդէպ, ծանօթ պատճառներով անշուշտ, սակայն կուսակալը կը պահէ իր նախորդ ուղղութիւնը:

Պիլէճիկ (Թաղական Խորհուրդէն) – 14 Յունվար

Ազգային Շարժում անուան տակ Իթթիհատը կ'իշխէ հոս եւ հայահալած քաղաքականութիւնը կը շարունակուի: Կողոպտուած ինչքերը չեն դարձներ. չարագործները՝ Պրուսայի պատերազմական ատեանէն անպարտութեան վճիռ առած դարձած են: Նախկին չարագործներուն մէկուս

tality. Mehmet Bey, the former deputy of İnegöl, and Mercimekzade Ahmet Bey, a well-known Ittihadist from Bilecik, were elected deputies again. The district governor is also their man; therefore, the old situation continues here. Under the pretext of self-defense against bandits, Muslim villagers and city inhabitants are getting arms . . .

ընտրուիլն արդէն ցոյց կուտայ թուրք մտայնութիւնը: Նախկին մէպուս իյնէկէօլցի Մէհմէտ պէյ եւ յայտնի իթթիհատական պիլէճիկցի Մէրճիմէք զատէ Աhմէտ պէյ դարձեալ մէպուս ընտրուեցան: Միւթէսարրըֆն ալ անոնց մարդն է, որով հին վիճակը հոս կը շարունակէ: Աւազակներու դէմ ինքնապաշտպանութեան պատրուակով գիւղացի իսլամները եւ քաղաքացիները կը զինուին ...

[Insecurity] Notebook Number 6
January–February 1920

. . . from the government. Massacring and harming are mentioned everywhere, and fear and horror are common.

İzmit (from the vicar general)—January 16, 1920[45]

Last week was a period of new crimes and robberies. Four or five days ago, the journey of people from Ovacık was interrupted near Başiskele, and all the men and women coming to İzmit were detained by Lazes waiting in ambush. Some had injuries on their face, others on their fingers, and after all their money was looted, they ran, thanks to the gunshots of two Armenians left outside the besieged circle.

• The morning of the following day, we heard that an Armenian woman singing at the city's seafront casino had been shot dead by an eighteen- or twenty-year-old boy for rejecting his indecent solicitation. The perpetrator was arrested immediately, but by the very time of the victim's burial, he had been released in broad daylight. After all, the perpetrator's father is a wealthy Ittihadist, and the victim is an Armenian . . .

• This morning, a telegram from Bahçecik reported that the Lazes organized by the Millis had entered by night the house of gunstock maker Garabed from Camidüzü [Kilisedüzü/Zhamavayr] in Ovacık. They had inflicted severe injury upon Garabed and killed his elder and two-year-old daughters before leaving.

Bursa (from the vicar general)—January 17

A few days ago, a gang attacked the village of Marmaracık in the district of Yenişehir. They robbed all the residents, especially our fellow Armenians, who comprise barely twenty-five to thirty families. Responding to a request made to him, the prefect said that the lieutenant governor of Yenişehir had telegraphed that six of the robbers had been arrested. Only one had not been caught, and no one had been injured or killed in the village.

İstanbul (from Mgrdich Mazloumian, a pharmacist from Hasköy)—January 23[46]

(1919) On October 18, a traveler, who had remained in Van as a pharmacist since August 1918, arrived from Van in İstanbul by way of Erzurum. He gave the following information on the condition of Van and the major cities of Armenia.

There are now four to five hundred Armenians in Van, of whom only thirty-five are men; the rest are women and children.

These Armenians are the last remnants of a segment of the Armenian population of Van that numbered twenty-five hundred and that in August–September 1918, when the [rest of] Armenians retreated [to Eastern Armenia], sought refuge on the two Sea of Van islands. They stayed there for two or three months and did not surrender to the Turks. Lacking a boat at hand, the Turks were unable to invade the islands and had to satisfy themselves by shelling from afar. Eventually, out of hunger, they were forced to surrender to Ali İhsan Pasha, the commander of the 4th Army Corps. He accepted their offer of surrender, then handed over the arrangement to civic authorities and went to Khoy [in Iran].

A commission consisting of Deputy Prefect İsmail Bey, accountant Vasıf Effendi, and others took the people from the island to the land, registered them, and confiscated all the money found on them while pretending to write the amounts. After the Armenians' transfer to the city, an epidemic ensued, and ostensibly to prevent it, fifteen to twenty days later, after running medical examinations, they [the

[Անապահովութեան] Տետր Թիւ 6
1920 Յունվար – 1920 Փետրվար

... կառավարութեան կողմէ: Ամէնուրեք ջարդելու, վնասելու խօսքեր կ'ըլլան եւ ահ ու սարսափը ընդհանուր է:

Նիկոմիդիա (Առաջնորդական Փոխանորդէն) – 16 Յունվար 1920

Անցնող շաբաթը նոր ոճիրներու, աւազակութեանց շրջան մը եղաւ: 4–5 օր առաջ օվաճըգ-ցիներու ճամբան կը բռնեն Պաշ Իսկէլէի մօտը եւ Նիկոմիդիա եկող բոլոր այրերն ու կիները դարանակալ եւ զինեալ լազերու կողմէ վար կը դրուին, ոմանց երեսները, ոմանց ձեռքի մատներն կը վիրաւորուին եւ իրենց ունեցած բոլոր դրամը կողոպտելէ վերջ, շնորհիւ պաշարուած շրջանակէն դուրս մնացած երկու հայերու արձակած զէնքերուն, կը փախչին:

- Յաջորդ առաւօտ լսեցինք որ քաղաքիս թաղապետական ծովեզրեայ գազինօն երգող հայ կին մը գնդակահար սպաննուեր է 18–20 տարեկան տղու մը կողմէ, կնոջ իր ըրած մէկ անբարոյ դիմումը մերժուած ըլլալուն համար: Ոճրագործը իսկոյն կը ձերբակալուի, սակայն զոհին թաղում կա-տարուած պահուն իսկ օր ցերեկով ազատ կ'արձակեն, վասնզի ոճրագործին հայրը մեծահարուստ իթթիհատական մըն է եւ սպաննուածը՝ հայ մը...:

- Այս առաւօտ Պարտիզակէն հեռագիր մը կը հաղորդէ թէ Օվաճըգի վրայ գտնուած Ժամա-վայրէն (Քիլիսէ Տիզի) ցուլնտագճի Կարապետի տունը Միլլիին կազմակերպած լազերը գիշերանց կը մտնեն, ծանրապէս կը վիրաւորեն Կարապետը եւ մեծ աղջիկը եւ երկու տարեկան փոքրիկ աղջիկը սպաննելով կը հեռանան:

Պրուսա (Առաջնորդական Փոխանորդէն) – 17 Յունվար

Եէնի Շէհիրի գաւառակին վերաբերող Մարմաճըգ անուն գիւղին վրայ մէկ քանի օր առաջ աւազակախումբ մը կը յարձակի եւ կը կողոպտէ բոլոր բնակիչները, մասնաւորապէս մերինները, որոնք հազիւ 25–30 տունէ կը բաղկանան: Կուսակալին եղած դիմումի մը ի պատասխան անիկա հաղորդեց թէ Եէնի-Շէհիրի գայմագամը հեռագրած է թէ աւազակներէն 6 (վեց) հոգի ձերբա-կալուած են եւ միայն մէկը չէ բռնուած, թէ ուէ վիրաւոր կամ սպաննեալ չկայ գիւղին մէջ:

Կ. Պոլիս (Մկրտիչ Մազլումեանէ, խազգիւղցի դեղագործ) – 23 Յունվար

(1919) 18 Հոկտեմբերին Վանէն ճամբայ ելլալով Էրզրումի ուղեգիծով Կ. Պոլիս հասած ճամբորդ մը, որ 1918 Օգոստոսէն սկսեալ Վան մնացած է իբր դեղագործ, հետեւեալ տեղեկութիւն-ները կուտայ Վանայ եւ Հայաստանի գլխաւոր քաղաքներու վիճակին վրայ:

Վանայ մէջ հիմա կը գտնուին 4–5 հարիւր հոգի հայ, որոնցմէ միայն 35ի չափը այր, մնաց-եալները կին ու տղայ:

Այս հայեր[ը] վերջին մնացորդներն են Վանայ հայ ազգաբնակչութեան այն հատուածին, որ 2500 հոգիի չափ էր եւ որ 1918 Օգոստոս-Սեպտեմբերի ատենները երբ հայերը նահանջեցին, ապաստանեցան Վանայ Ծովուն երկու կղզիները եւ հոն մնացին 2–3 ամիս եւ անձնատուր չեղան թուրքերուն, որոնք նաւ չունենալով առձեռն չկրցան այս կղզիները արշաւել եւ հեռուէն ռմբակոծելով բաւականացան: Ի վերջոյ անօթութենէ հարկադրուեցան անձնատուր [ըլլալ] Ալի Իհսան փաշայի, որ Դ. Գօլ Օրտուի հրամանատարն էր: Անիկա անձնատուութեան առաջարկը ընդունեց եւ կարգադրութիւնը քաղաքային իշխանութեան յանձնելով ինքն անցաւ Խոյ գնաց:

Կուսակալի փոխանորդ Իսմայիլ պէյէ եւ Մուհասըպէճի Վասըֆ էֆէնտիէ եւ ուրիշներէ բաղկացեալ յանձնաժողով մը ժողովուրդը կղզիէն ցամաք փոխադրեց եւ զանոնք արձանագրեց եւ անոնց վրայ գտնուած բոլոր դրամը գրաւեց, իբր թէ արձնագրելով: Իրենց քաղաք փոխադրութենէն յետոյ առաջ եկաւ համաճարակ մը, որուն առաջքն առնելու համար իբր թէ 15–20 օր յետոյ այդ

authorities] began to disperse these Armenians to the nearby villages of Van. After this dispersal, some of them, those of military age, were enlisted. The rest were forced to work as laborers. They moved government property in exchange for one kilo of bread daily under the whip of gendarmes.

After the Armenians had suffered in this situation for a month and a half, all the people were deported and taken to Diyarbakır, with many losses on the way.

When the people had almost approached Diyarbakır, they made them stop for three or four days, then brought them back to Van and settled them there. The armistice took place in those days, and Haydar Bey was appointed prefect of Van. By the end of this back-and-forth journey, barely four to five hundred people were left out of twenty-five hundred.

During the first months of the armistice, that is, from November to March, the people remained in poor condition. In March, Haydar Bey began to give the people eleven kilos of wheat a month. This arrangement lasted until his dismissal (August 15). The next prefect, Mithat Bey, terminated the allowance, and they [the authorities] began to provoke the Turks against the Armenians again. After the departure of the Armenians, the Turks had already begun to return to the city, but occasionally there was talk that Van is left to [the Republic of] Armenia, leading the Turks to prepare to abandon the city and leave. The Kurds also wanted to migrate; therefore, they wanted to refrain from engaging in agricultural work. Contrary to the prefect's assurances, the Kurds did not sow.

However, when it was seen that there was no movement, the migration plan was abandoned, and [the Turks and Kurds] remained in Van. The Turks became even more excited when the Milli movement was launched and found reception also in Van. The Turks of Van and some Kurds follow the Milli movement. The majority of Kurds are opposed to Millis and are in a state of turmoil.

Simko formed an independent government on the border with Persia with an army of twenty-five thousand men. Other tribal leaders have similar plans. Kurdish tribal leaders even convened a large meeting in Van under the government's watchful eye.

Sometime after the armistice, the Armenians demanded that the money they had handed over to the deputy prefect, İsmail Bey, be returned. It was then revealed that the records had been made unscrupulously and that five hundred manat had been written down next to the name of a person who had given five thousand manats. There is no trace of seized furniture, nor was any recorded. Church property and vessels also have vanished. Only a part of the church property of Akdamar [Ağtamar] remains in the government house, and fourteen to fifteen pieces of very precious antiquities were sent to the museum in İstanbul.

With the price of an okka of bread in Van [at] twenty-five piasters in silver coins—banknotes are not accepted—one can imagine how much poverty there is. Now that the Americans do not allow the flour to enter that area, the price of bread probably has risen even more since there is no harvest. Famine is inevitable, and the lives of four to five hundred Armenians are in danger.

Most of the houses in Van are destroyed. In Bağlar [Aykesdan], [undamaged] houses can be counted on fingers. Despite all the government's support, the number of Turks gathered in Van does not exceed three to four thousand people, which demonstrates that not only is Armenia empty of Armenians but also of Turks.

The same phenomenon is also seen in Erzurum, Doğubayazıt, Dikili [Karakilise], and Pasinler [Hasankale], where the Turks number as follows.

There are 7,000–8,000 Turks and a few Armenians in Erzurum.

There are 800–1,000 Turks in Doğubayazıt.

There are 800–[9]00 Turks and not a single Armenian in Dikili.

There are 2,500–3,000 Turks and not a single Armenian in Pasinler.

There are 1,000–1,500 Turks and not a single Armenian in Bayburt.

հայերը բժշկական քննութենէ անցնելէ յետոյ սկսան ցրուել Վանայ շրջակայ գիւղերը: Այս ցրուումն ընելէ յետոյ անոնցմէ մէկ մասը,- անոնք որ զինուորական տարիքի մէջ էին,- զինուոր առին: Մնացեալները հարկադրուած էին ծառայական աշխատութեամբ եւ օրական մէկ քիլօ հացի փոխարէն կառավարական գոյքերու փոխադրութեան գործերով զբաղիլ *ժանտարմ*ներու խարազանին տակ:

Ամիսուկէս ալ այս վիճակին մէջ հայերը տառապելէն յետոյ, բոլոր ժողովուրդը տեղահան ըրին եւ Տիարպէքիր տարին, ճամբան բազմաթիւ կորուստներ տալով:

Ժողովուրդը հազիւ թէ Տիարպէքիրի մօտեցած էր, հոն կանգ առնել տուին եւ 3–4 օր մնալէ յետոյ դարձեալ ետ բերին եւ Վան հաստատուեցան: Այդ օրերուն զինադադարը եղաւ եւ Հայտար պէյ կուսակալ կարգուեցաւ Վանայ: Այս երթեւեկէն վերջ 2500 հոգիէն հազիւ 400–500 հոգի մնացած էր:

Զինադադարին առաջին ամիսները, այսինքն Նոյեմբերէն Մարտ, ժողովուրդը մնաց խեղճ վիճակի մէջ: Մարտին Հայտար պէյ սկսաւ ժողովուրդին ամսական մարդ գլուխ 11 քիլօ ցորեն տալ: Այս կարգադրութիւնը տեւեց մինչեւ Հայտար պէյի պաշտօնանկութիւնը (Օգոստոս 15): Յաջորդ կուսակալը՝ Միդհատ պէյ, նպաստը դադրեցուց եւ հայոց դէմ դարձեալ թուրքերը գրգռել սկսաւ: Հայոց հեռանալէն յետոյ թուրքերը արդէն սկսած էին դառնալ քաղաք, սակայն երբեմն զրոյց կ'ըլլար թէ Վան թողուած [է] Հայաստանի եւ թուրքերը կը պատրաստուէին թողուլ քաղաքը եւ մեկնիլ: Նոյնպէս քիւրտերը կ'ուզէին գաղթել եւ ասոր համար երբեք չէին ուզեր երկրագործական աշխատութեանց ձեռնարկել: Կուսակալին բոլոր հաւաստիքներուն հակառակ՝ քիւրտերը սերմնացան չըրին:

Սակայն երբ տեսնուեցաւ որ ռեւէ շարժում չկայ, գաղթելու ծրագիրը մէկ կողմ ձգուեցաւ եւ մնացին Վան: Թուրքերը ա՛լ աւելի ոգեւորուեցան երբ Միլլի շարժումը սկսաւ եւ Վան ալ արձագանգ գտաւ: Միլլի շարժումին կը հետեւին Վանի թուրքերը եւ քիւրտերէն մաս մը, մինչ քիւրտերու մեծագոյն մասը հակառակ է Միլլիին եւ խլրտած վիճակ մը ունի:

Սըմկօն Պարսկաստանի սահմանին վրայ կազմած է անկախ իշխանութիւն մը 25,000 հոգինոց բանակով մը: Միւս ցեղապետներն ալ նման ծրագիրներ ունին: Նոյնիսկ քիւրտ ցեղապետները խոշոր գումարում մը ըրին Վանայ մէջ, կառավարութեան աչքին տակ:

Զինադադարէն քաւական յետոյ հայերը պահանջեցին իրենց յանձնած դրամները կուսակալ[ի] փոխանորդ Իսմայիլ պէյէն: Այն ատեն երեւան եկաւ թէ արձանագրութիւնները կատարուած էին անբարեխիղճ եղանակով մը եւ 5000 մանէթ տուողին անունին դէմ 500 մանէթ յանձնած նշանակուած էր: Իսկ գրաւուած կարասիները երբեք մէջտեղ չկայ, ոչ ալ նշանակուած է: Եկեղեցական գոյքերը եւ անօթները նոյնպէս անյայտացած են: Աղթամարի եկեղեցական գոյքերէն միայն մէկ մասը դեռ կը մնայ կառավարական պաշտօնատունը, իսկ 14–15 կտոր շատ թանկագին հնութիւններ Կ. Պոլսոյ *միւզէ*ն ղրկուած են:

Վանայ մէջ հացի օխան 25 ղրուշ արծաթ դրամ ըլլալով,- թղթադրամ հոն չ'անցնիր,- կրնայ երեւակայուիլ թէ ինչ մեծ խեղճութիւն կը տիրէ հոն: Հիմա որ դէպի այդ շրջանակը ալիւրի ներածումը թոյլ չեն տար ամերիկացիք, հաւանօրէն աւելի բարձրացած պիտի ըլլայ հացին գինը, քանի բերք ալ չկայ: Սովը անխուսափելի է եւ 4–5 հարիւր հայերու կեանքն ալ վտանգի տակ:

Վանի տուները մեծ մասամբ փճացած են: Այգեստանի մէջ մասի վրայ կը համրուին տուները: Հակառակ կառավարութեան ամէն օժանդակութեան, Վանայ մէջ հաւաքուած թուրքերու համագումարը 3–4 հազար հոգիէն աւելի չէ, ինչ որ ցոյց կուտայ թէ Հայաստան ոչ միայն հայերէ, այլ նաեւ թուրքերէ դատարկուած է:

Նոյն երեւոյթը կը տեսնուի նաեւ Կարնոյ, Պայազիտի, Գարաքիլիսէի, Հասանգալէի մէջ, որոնց մէջ գտնուող թուրքերու թիւը հետեւեալն է:

Կարնոյ մէջ կայ 7–8 հազար թուրք եւ քանի մը հայ

Պայազիտի մէջ կայ 800–1000 թուրք եւ ոչ մէկ հայ

Գարաքիլիսէի մէջ կայ 8–[9] հարիւր թուրք եւ ոչ մէկ հայ

There are 2,000 Turks and not a single Armenian in Gümüşhane.

Some of the Armenians from these places have managed to cross to the Caucasus, where they remain. At the same time, the Turks, escaping from the Russian armies, fell victim to poverty in Anadolu [Anatolia] and thus were decimated.

The center of the 15th Army Corps and one of the main stations of the Milli movement is in Erzurum. It was there that the first [Milli] Congress was convened, in which Enver Pasha also took part. He stayed in Erzurum for three or four days on occasion.

The situation in Erzurum is no better than in Van. There is a real famine there as well. Banknotes are accepted. Bread costs fifty-four piasters in banknotes, but prices must have risen there, too, by now.

There is an extraordinary strictness in Erzurum. Christians cannot live there or cross through. The current traveler was also jailed for seven days in the prison of the military tribunal. His life would have been at risk for sure had the former prefect of Van, Haydar Bey, not been there by accident and not interceded for his release.

Erzurum is one of the centers of the Milli [organization]. After the armistice, British officers came to seize the Turkish army's ammunition and concentrated all the weapons and ammunition of their army there, but as they were piling the ammunition on wagons to take it to the Caucasus, the Turks attacked and took the weapons. They are in the hands of the Milli army today. In Erzurum and in other cities of [Western] Armenia, there are no Allied forces today. No British or American missionaries or functionaries in charge of provisions have been allowed to enter. Two American missionaries reached Van with great difficulty, but they barely managed to stay for two or three days. The Turks would have killed them, but the government managed to free them with great difficulty, and they left Van with police protection.

The Milli [organization] works here in an unruly and tyrannical way. The government in İstanbul abolished the military service of Christians, and all Christian soldiers in the army were released. However, the nearly four hundred fifty soldiers who were released from the Caucasian front, all born in 1898–1894, have been detained by order of Mustafa Kemal Pasha and put to work between Erzurum and Pasinler in the coal mines that were set to operate by the Russians.

About two hundred fifty are Armenians; the rests are Greeks and Jews. These unfortunate people have been subjected to horrific, forced labor for over a year.

İstanbul (from the Patriarch)—January 24

The Millis work freely and boldly in the province of Bursa. They arm the people and also collect money from them. Weapons, even machine guns, are transported there from İstanbul. The Millis decided to collect one million liras from the province of Bursa. After determining the amount each village should pay, the amount is first demanded by a notice. If it is not paid on time, the çetes plunder the village. They decided to take ten thousand liras a month from manufacturer Osman Effendi and obtained a commitment for that amount from him. The *Ertuğrul* newspaper of Bursa writes openly about these [events]. For this reason, many people flee from Bursa to İstanbul.

Düzce (from Hadji Smpad Karaboghosian, headman of İcadiye's Neighborhood Council)—January 25[47]

Arif Bey, the son of Abaza Hasan Bey, a villager from Darıyeri in Düzce, has been trading with bond-

Հասանքալէի մէջ կայ 2500–3000 թուրք եւ ոչ մէկ հայ
Պայպուրտի մէջ կայ 1000–1500 թուրք եւ ոչ մէկ հայ
Կիւմիւշխանէի մէջ կայ 2000 թուրք եւ ոչ մէկ հայ

Այս տեղերու հայերը կրցած են մասամբ անցնիլ Կովկաս, ուր կը մնան դեռ, մինչ թուրքերը ռուսական բանակներու առջեւէն խոյս տալով Անատոլուի մէջ խեղճութեան զոհ գացած են եւ այսպէս չնչին թիւերու վերածուած են:

Կարնոյ մէջ է 15րդ Գօլ Օրտուի կեդրոնը եւ Միլլի շարժման գլխաւոր կայաններէն մէկը: Հոն էր որ գումարուեցաւ առաջին Քօնկրէն, որուն մասնակցած է նաեւ Էնվէր փաշա, որ 3–4 օր այդ առթիւ Էրզրում մնացած է:

Էրզրումի մէջ ալ դրութիւնը աւելի լաւ չէ քան Վան: Հոն ալ իրապէս սով կը տիրէ: Հոն թղթադրամը կ'անցնի եւ հացին օխան 54 դրուշ է թղթադրամ, սակայն հոն ալ հիմա պէտք է բարձրացած ըլլայ:

Էրզրումի մէջ կը տիրէ արտասովոր խստութիւն: Քրիստոնեաներու բնակութիւնը կամ անկէ անցնիլը կարելի չէ: Պատերազմական ատեանի բանտը 7 օր բանտարկած են նաեւ ներկայ ճամբորդը, որ ապահովաբար իր կեանքը վրայ պիտի տար եթէ դիպուածով Վանայ նախորդ կուսակալ Հայտար պէյ հոն չգտնուէր եւ ինքն չբարեխօսէր անոր արձակման համար:

Կարին կը կազմէ Միլլիին կեդրոններէն մէկը: Զինադադարէն յետոյ թուրք բանակին ռազմամթերքը գրաւելու համար անգլիացի սպաներ հոն կուգան եւ հոն կը կեդրոնացնեն բանակին բոլոր զէնքերը ու ռազմամթերքը, որ վակոն դնելով դէպի Կովկաս տանելու վրայ էին երբ թուրքերը յարձակեցան եւ այդ զէնքերը իրենք առին: Անոնք այսօր Միլլի բանակին ձեռքն են: Կարինի, ինչպէս նաեւ Հայաստանի միւս քաղաքներուն մէջ, այսօր Համաձայնական ոյժ գոյութիւն չունի: Հոն անգլիացի եւ ամերիկացի միսիոնարներ կամ պարենաւորման պաշտօնեաներ ալ չեն կրցած մտնել: Երկու ամերիկացի միսիոնար մեծ դժուարութեամբ հասած են Վան, ուր հազիւ կրցած են մնալ 2–3 օր: Թուրքերը պիտի սպաննէին զանոնք, կառավարութիւնը մեծ դժուարութեամբ կրցաւ ազատել եւ ոստիկանական պաշտպանութեամբ անոնք Վանէն մեկնեցան:

Միլլին հոս կը գործէ սանձարձակ եւ բռնակալ եղանակով մը: Հակառակ անոր որ Կ. Պոլսոյ մէջ կառավարութիւնը քրիստոնէից զինուորագրութիւնը ջնջեց եւ բանակին մէջ գտնուող բոլոր քրիստոնեայ զինուորները արձակուեցան, Մուսթաֆա Քէմալ փաշայի հրամանով կովկասեան ճակատէն արձակուած 450ի չափ զինուորներ, ամէնքն ալ 314–310ի [=1898–1894ի] ծնունդ, վար դրուած են եւ Կարնոյ եւ Հասանքալէի միջեւ գտնուած եւ ռուսերու կողմէ շահագործուիլ սկսած հանքածուխի հորերուն մէջ կ'աշխատցուին:

Ասոնցմէ 250ի չափը հայ են, մնացեալը՝ յոյն եւ հրեայ: Տարիէ աւելի է որ այդ խեղճերը հող տարապարհակ այս զարհուրելի աշխատանքին ենթարկուած են:

Կ. Պոլիս (Պատրիարքէն) – 24 Յունվար

Միլլիները արձակ համարձակ կը գործեն Պրուսայի նահանգին մէջ եւ կը զինեն ժողովուրդը, անոնցմէ դրամ եւս հաւաքելով: Պոլիսէն հոն զէնք կը փոխադրուի, նոյնիսկ՝ միթրայլէօզ: Միլլիները մէկ միլիոն ոսկի որոշած են Պուրսայի նահանգին համար: Իւրաքանչիւր գիւղին գումարը որոշուելէն յետոյ, նախ ազդարարագրով մը կը պահանջուի այդ գումարը եւ երբ չտրուի իր ժամանակին մէջ, չէթէները կ'երթան եւ գիւղը կը կողոպտեն: Փայրիքաթոռ Օսման էֆէնտիէն ամսական 10,000 ոսկի առնելու որոշում տուած են եւ խօսք առած են: Պրուսայի *Էրթուղրուլ* թերթը բացէ ի բաց կը գրէ ասոնք: Շատեր այս պատճառով Պրուսայէն Պոլիս կը փախչին:

Տիւզճէ (Իճատիյէ թաղի մուխթար Հաճի Սմբատ Գարապօղոսեանէ) – 25 Յունվար

Հինէն ի վեր *ճարիյէ* առնել ծախելը բան գործ ըրող Տիւզճէի Տարը Եէրի գիւղացի Ապազա Հասան պէյի որդի Արիֆ պէյ մէկ շաբաթ առաջ Նիկոմիդիայէն երկու հայ աղջիկ փախցնելով հոս

maids for a long time. He kidnapped two Armenian girls from İzmit a week ago and then returned to the village after staying overnight in Arif Agha's hotel here. The [Armenians] immediately appealed to the lieutenant governor, demanding [that] the two girls be transferred to the Armenian orphanage. At the time of the interrogation, Arif Bey said that these girls were the children of Captain Abdül Bey, a member of the Permanent Court Martial of İzmit, and that he has brought them because they were orphaned after their mother's death. But according to confidential information provided by some of the villagers of Darıyeri, it is clear from the Armenian brands found on the young girls' clothes (likely the initials of their names) that the girls are Armenian. Even the girls declared, "We went to Damascus when we were little, and this time we came to Adana from Damascus. We embroidered the Armenian brands on our clothes," and so on, which leaves no doubt that they are Armenian. Especially in this harsh winter, it would not be natural for anyone to hand a child to a stranger if the child was his or her own. Therefore, there is no doubt that they were Armenian. Consequently, Arif Bey was lying. To not close the case after a simple investigation, they demanded that the seven- or eight-year-old girls be brought to İstanbul after stamping their arms at the department. The matter has been telegraphed to the grand vizier, the Ministries of Interior and Foreign Affairs, and the Senate.

Maraş (from Dr. Kachperouni)—January 3

Armenians tumble here in misfortune. The local conditions have become hellish. Two weeks ago, Dr. Kachperouni, the inspector of the National Assistance, while returning from a meeting with the Americans and French, barely escaped certain death with his servant [while traveling] on a public avenue.

Four days ago, three young men from Maraş went to the orchard three minutes away from the city to collect firewood. Two of them, Manoug and Bedros Davakian, were killed by bullets. Meanwhile, the brother of the second man, Hovsep Davakian, was killed on the Maraş-İslahiye road two weeks ago. The third young man, although his arm was smashed, managed to escape and reached the city. He reported that his friend's killer is the son of Çuhadar Zade—a notable of Maraş—and this was his twenty-fifth crime. After receiving the testimony, the Turkish [police] commissioner complained privately that it was a pity that they had not made him [the surviving Armenian] vanish. The injured young man is now in the hospital; his life is in danger.

• Three days ago, the çetes attacked the Armenian neighborhood at night. We heard, with our ears, the whistling of hundreds of bullets along our street.

• Two days ago, two young men from Çamlıbel [Alabaş] and six from Süleymanlı [Zaytun] were leaving Maraş for Süleymanlı. All were brutally killed a mile away from the Üngüt Bridge near a Turkish house called Güzlüsi (where a Turkish guard stands). Today, a French officer and his soldiers found four of the missing bodies. The other corpses are thought to have been dumped in the water.

• A Turk was killed in the market yesterday morning. He physically resembled an Armenian whom the Turks had decided to kill. Mistakenly, the Turk was killed instead of the Armenian.

• A few days ago, six Armenians arrived here from Yenicekale; they were attacked by çetes on the way. Fortunately, being noticed by a policeman, the çetes were forced to retreat.

• Today, we received news from the village of Kişifli, located four hours southwest of Maraş, that neighboring Kurdish villagers have attacked the village and wounded a young man in the leg. The villagers managed to defend themselves, thanks to their only weapon.

• In these conditions, the thirteen hundred Armenians living in the surrounding villages are wholly desperate and intend to take refuge in the city.

Արիֆ աղայի օթէլն մէկ գիշեր մնալէն յետոյ ետ գիւղը գացած է: Անմիջապէս գայմագամին դիմելով անոնց հայ որբանոցը ղրկուիլն կը պահանջեն: Քննութեան պահուն Արիֆ պէյ կ'ըսէ որ այս աղջիկներն Իզմիտի Տիվանը Հարպի տայիմի անդամ հարիւրապետ Ատիլ պէյի զաւակներն են, որոնց մայրը մեռած եւ որբ մնացած ըլլալով՝ բերած է: Բայց Տարը Եէրի գիւղացւոց ոմանց տուած գաղտնի տեղեկութեան համաձայն, տղոց լաթերուն վրայի հայերէն *մարզա*ներէն (որք իրենց անուանց սկզբնատառերն պէտք է ըլլան) անոնց հայ ըլլալը հասկցուած է: Նոյնիսկ աղջիկները յայտարարած են թէ «պզտիկ եղած ատեննիս Շամ գացինք եւ այս անգամ Շամէն Ատանայի ճամբով եկանք: Լաթերնուս վրայ հայ մարզաները մենք բանեցանք եւայլն», ինչ որ տարակոյս չէր ձգեր անոնց հայ ըլլալուն: Մանաւանդ այս խիստ ձմրան ոեւէ մէկը իր զաւակը բնական չէր որ օտար ձեռքերու յանձնէր եթէ իրր եղած ըլլար: Ուստի տարակոյս չկայ որ հայ էին: Հետեւաբար, Արիֆ պէյ կը ստէր, եւ որպէսզի հոս պարզ քննութեամբ մը գործը չգոցեն, 7–8 տարեկան այդ աղջիկներուն թեւերն խտարէի մէջ կնքուելով Պոլիս բերուիլը կը պահանջեն: Խնդիրը եպարքոսին, ներքին եւ արտաքին գործոց նախարարութեանց եւ ծերակոյտին ալ հեռագրուած է:

Մարաշ (Տոքթ. Քաչբերունիէն) – 3 Յունուար

Հայերը հոս դժբաղդութեան մէջ կը տապլտկին. տեղւոյս պայմանները դժոխային դարձած են. երկու շաբաթ առաջ Խնամատարութեան քննիչ Տոքթ. Քաջներունի ամերիկացիներու եւ գաղիացիներու հետ տեսակցութենէ մը վերադարձին, հանրային պողոտայի մը վրայ մազապուր կ'ազատի ստոյգ մահէ մը իր ծառային հետ:

4 օր առաջ մարաշցի երեք երիտասարդներ քաղաքէն 3 վայրկեան հեռաւորութեամբ այգեստան կ'երթան վառելիք հաւաքելու համար: Երկուքը՝ Մանուկ եւ Պետրոս Տավաքեաններ, կը սպաննուին *տըմտըմ* գնդակներով: Երկրորդին եղայրը՝ Յովսէփ Տավաքեանն ալ Մարաշ-Խպահիէ ճամբուն վրայ սպաննուած է երկու շաբաթ առաջ: Երրորդ երիտասարդը, թէեւ թեւը ջախջախուած, սակայն կը յաջողի փախչիլ եւ հասնիլ քաղաք, եւ կը յայտնէ [որ] իր ընկերներուն սպանիչը Մարաշի էշրաֆներէն Զուլխատար զատէի տղան է, որուն քանըհինգերորդ ոճիրն է այս: Թուրք գոմիսէրը վկայութիւնը ստանալէ ետքը մեկուսի կը տրտնջայ թէ ինչպէս եղեր է որ այս մէկն ալ չեն անհետացուցած: Վիրաւոր երիտասարդը այժմ հիւանդանոցն է եւ կեանքը վտանգի տակ:

- Երեք օր առաջ Չէթէները գիշերը յարձակեցան հայկական թաղին վրայ. մեր փողոցին քովէն սուրացող հարիւրաւոր գնդակներու սուլումը մեր ականջովը լսեցինք:

- Երկու օր առաջ Մարաշէն Զէյթուն մեկնող երկու ալապաշցի եւ վեց զէյթունցի երիտասարդներ ամէնքն ալ խժդժօրէն կը սպաննուին Իւնկիւտի կամուրջէն (ուր թրքական պահակ մը կը կենայ) մղոն մը անդին Քիւզլիւսի կոչուած թուրք տանը քովիկը: Անհետացած դիակներէն չորս հատը այսօր գտնուեցան փրանսական սպայի մը եւ զինուորներուն միջոցաւ. կը կարծուի թէ միւս դիակները ջուրը ձգուած են:

- Երէկ առտու շուկային մէջ սպաննուեցաւ թուրք մը, որ ֆիզիքապէս խիստ կը նմանի եղեր հայու մը, զոր թուրքերը որոշած էին սպաննել: Զուգադիպութեամբ մը թուրքը հայուն տեղը զոհուած է:

- Քանի մը օր առաջ Եէնիճէ Քալէէն տեղս ժամանեցին 6 հայեր, որոնք ճամբան յարձակում կրած էին չէթէներէ: Բարեբաղդաբար ոստիկանէն նշմարուած ըլլալով չէթէները ստիպուած են թողուլ եւ քաշուիլ:

- Այսօր Մարաշէն 4 ժամ հարաւ-արեւմուտք Գիշիֆլի գիւղէն լուր առինք որ դրացի քիւրտ գիւղացիներ նոյն գիւղին վրայ յարձակած եւ երիտասարդ մը ոտքէն վիրաւորած են: Գիւղացիք շնորհիւ իրենց միակ զէնքին կրցած են ինքնապաշտպանուիլ:

- Այս պայմաններուն մէջ, շրջակայ գիւղերը ապրող 1300 հայերը բոլորովին յուսահատ՝ մտադիր են քաղաք ապաստանիլ:

Adana (from Dr. Kachperouni)—January 15

On January 6, three hundred French soldiers (on their way to meet a detachment of Senegalese traveling to Maraş) were making their way from Maraş to İslahiye carrying cannons and machine guns when they were caught in gunfire that came from the villages of Ceceli or Tecili. The French responded to the gunfire with shelling. After two days of fighting, the soldiers returned to Maraş without joining the Senegalese. As a result of these battles, Ceceli and other small villages were burned. The large village known as Türkoğlu [Eloğlu] was pillaged. A couple of other villages were shelled from afar, and four and a half hours to the south of Maraş, in the direction of Türkoğlu, the Armenian men, only seven people, of the village Kale [Camustil] (mixed Armenian [and] Turkish [population]), were brutally killed by Turkish villagers led by the sergeant of the gendarmerie. The terrorized women and children of the village took refuge in Maraş at night. In this region, all Armenian villages are waiting for their turn [to be attacked], completely defenseless. During the last month, it has been impossible for an Armenian villager coming to the city for work to return home [alive]. Maraş is full of such unfortunate people. All travelers to and from the city, without racial or other discrimination, are screened by gendarmes to see if they are circumcised. Behold a new and practical method for passports discovered by the Maraş government. Woe to the traveler who lacks a proper passport!

• A reliable source from Gaziantep [Ayntab] informs us that the telegraph wires between Gaziantep and Maraş have been cut.

• A car going from Gaziantep to Maraş, in which there was a driver and three passengers, two men and one woman, all four of them American, disappeared without any trace. No one knows how the car was stopped an hour from the city. The car was left on the road, crushed.

Boğazlıyan (from the National Assistance)—January 10

The prevailing horror continues. The Turks of Boğazlıyan and the surrounding area have enlisted as çetes during the rule of the current deputy acting governor, Besim. Rumors of massacres [to be perpetrated] have increased. The Turks intimidate the people with slander. Several cases [mentioned below] prove the psychology of Turks.

• Mullah Veli of Kürkçü takes the belongings of the [Armenian] people of Kürkçü and leaves, saying, "You will be massacred in a few days; give the possessions you have taken [back] from us [beforehand]."

• On December 28, at half past one at night, Manoug Der Sarkisian, orphanage administrator, and Vramshabouh were arrested and imprisoned by the police, saying, "They were urinating on the road, we have arrested them."

• Hapet of Çat has been in jail for twenty-six days due to slander.

• Sara Sarkisian, a fifteen- or sixteen-year-old girl from Çokradan, took refuge at the house of a Turkish woman named Hacca. On the night of December 23, Kel-Bekir, Kör-Seit, Haci Aliş of Siluk Agha, Mitosın Oğlu Memet, Cemal, Nasir, and Mustafa from Çokradan stormed the house and took the girl to the mountains. Now she is in the orphanage.

• On the night of November 30, Kel Selam (of Karalık) and his friends stormed the house of Hovsep of Felahiye [Rumdiğin] and kidnapped a fourteen-year-old girl named Mariam. Hovsep appealed to the government several times but in vain.

• Also, Anna, the daughter of Zadig of Fahralı, was taken to the mountain by Hassan Ali-i Abdullah, Çöküyan Ali, Molla Memet, and friends.

There are many instances like these, for which appeals have been made to the government, but

Ատանա (Տոքթ. Քաչբերունիէն) – 15 Յունուար

Յունուար 6ին Մարաշէն Իսլահիէ ճամբայ ելած 300 զաղիացի զինուորներ իրենց հետ ունենալով թնդանօթներ եւ գնդացիրներ (ասոնք դիմաւորելու կ'երթային դէպի Մարաշ զալիք վաշտ մը սենեկալցիներուն) ճամբան Ճէճէլի կամ Թէճիլի ըսուած գիւղէն կրակ կը բացուի եւ անոր կը յաջորդէ ֆրանսացիներուն կողմէ թնդանօթաձգութիւն մը: Երկու օրուան կռիւէ վերջը, զինուորները Մարաշ կը վերադառնան առանց սենեկալցիներուն միանալու: Այս կռիւներուն արդիւնքը՝ Ճէճէլին եւ ուրիշ փոքրիկ գիւղեր կ'այրին, Էլ Օղլու ըսուած մեծ գիւղը աւարի կը տրուի, ուրիշ մէկ երկու գիւղեր հեռուէն կը ռմբակոծուին, իսկ Մարաշ[էն] 4½ ժամ դէպի հարաւ, Էլ Օղլուի ուղղութեան վրայ, Ճամըսղըլ գիւղի (հայ թուրք խառն) հայ այր մարդիկ, ընդամէնը 7 հոգի, խժդժօրէն կը սպաննուին թուրք գիւղացիներուն միջոցաւ, որ ղեկավարուած եւ առաջնորդուած էին ժանտարմա Չավուշի կողմէ: Գիւղին կիները եւ մանուկները գիշերով Մարաշ ապաստանեցան ահ ու սարսափի մէջ: Այս շրջանին բոլոր հայ գիւղերը բոլորովին անպաշտպան իրենց կարգին կը սպասեն: Վերջին մէկ ամսուան մէջ ոեւէ գործով քաղաք եկող հայ գիւղացին կարելի չէ որ իր տունը վերադառնայ: Մարաշ լեցուած է այս կարգի խեղճերով: Բոլոր ճամբորդները քաղաքէն ներս կամ դուրս, առանց ցեղի եւայլնի խտրութեան, քննութեան կ'ենթարկուին ժանտարմաներու կողմէ, ստուգելու համար թէ թլփատուած է կամ ոչ. ահա նոր եւ բրայթիք մեթոտ մը passportի համար, զոր Մարաշի կառավարութիւնը գտած է: Վայ այն ճամբորդին որ պատշաճ passportէն զուրկ է:

- Այնթապէն վստահելի աղբիւրէ կը տեղեկացնեն թէ Այնթապի եւ Մարաշի միջեւ հեռագրական թելերը կտրած են:

- Այնթապէն դէպի Մարաշ գացող օթօմոպիլ մը, որուն մէջ կը գտնուէին մէկ շօֆֆէր եւ երեք ճամբորդներ, երկուքը այր մարդ եւ մէկը կին, չորսն ալ ամերիկացի, քաղաքէն 1 ժամ հեռանալէ վերջը չի գիտցուիր ինչ կերպով օթօմօպիլը կը կեցուի, շօֆֆէրը եւ ճամբորդները կ'անհետացնեն առանց հետք մը ձգելու, իսկ օթօմօպիլը ճամբուն վրայ կը ձգուի ջախջախուած:

Պօղազլեան (Ազգային Խնամատարութենէն) – 10 Յունվար

Տիրող ահուսարսափը կը շարունակէ: Ներկայ փոխ-գայմագամ Պէսիմի օրով Պօղազլեանի եւ շրջականներու թուրքերը *չէթէ* արձանագրուեցան եւ ջարդի շշուկները շատցած են: Թուրքերը զրպարտութիւններով կ'ահաբեկեն ժողովուրդը: Քանի մը դէպքեր կ'ապացուցանեն թրքաց հոգեբանութիւնը:

- Քիւրքճի Մուլլա Վելի քիւրքճիներուն ունեցածը կ'առնէ ու կ'երթայ, ըսելով թէ «մի քանի օրէն պիտի ջարդուիք, տուէք մեզմէ առած ինչքերը»:

- Դեկտեմբեր 28ին իրիկունը ժամը 1½ին որբանոցին մատակարար Մանուկ Տէր Սարգիսեանը եւ Վռամշապուհը ոստիկանները կը ձերբակալեն եւ կը բանտարկեն «ճամբան կը շռէին կոր, ձերբակալեցինք» ըսելով:

- Չաթցի Յաբէթը 26 օրէ ի վեր բանտն է զրպարտութիւններով:

- Բնիկ չորգատանցի Սառա Սարգիսեան 15–16 տարեկան դեռատի աղջիկ մը կ'ապաստանի թուրք Հաճճա անուն կնկան մը տունը: Դեկտեմբեր 23ին գիշերը չորգատանցի Քէլ-Պէքիր, Քէօր-Մէյտ, Սիլուզ աղանըն Հաճի Ալիշ, Միթօըն օղլու Մէմէտ, Ճէմալ, Նասիր, Մուսթաֆա զինեալ կը կոխեն կը հանեն աղջիկը լեռ: Հիմա որբանոց կը գտնուի:

- Նոյեմբեր 30ին գիշերանց կը կոխէ րումտիկինցի Յովսէփին տունը Քէլ Սելամ (զարալըզցի) ընկերներով եւ 14 տարեկան Մարիամ անուն աղջիկը կ'առեւանգէ: Յովսէփ դիմեց քանի մը անգամ կառավարութեան բայց ի զուր:

- Նոյնպէս փակրալըցի Զատիկի աղջիկը՝ Աննան, լեռ հանած են Հասան Ալիի Ապտուլլահ, Չէօքիւեան Ալի, Մուլլա Մէմէտ իրենց ընկերներովը:

Ասոնց նման բազմաթիւ իրողութիւններ կան, որոնց համար կառավարութեան դիմումներ կ'ըլլա[ն] բայց ապարդիւն կը մնա[ն], որովհետեւ բոլոր գիւղերու կեձռոտ խնդիրները գայմագամը

they result in nothing because the lieutenant governor refers the complicated problems of villages to the head of Çayıralan [Akdağ] commune Münir Bey, whom he has appointed police after [Münir Bey] spent his days and nights banqueting with notorious fugitive criminals. It is these fugitives who torture the Armenian remnants.

Trabzon (from the locum tenens)—January 12
The nearness of the days of [signing the] Turkish Peace [Treaty] has again provoked a movement among the Turks. The Turks are caught up in the dream of resistance. The military force is gradually concentrating in the city. A plan to move to Azerbaijan also seems to be under development [should adverse developments occur]. There are proponents of peaceful conformity. The capture of Trabzon is necessary to enervate some ambitions. Although resistance preparations may not be taken seriously, they can ultimately have unpleasant consequences.

Keramet (from the Neighborhood Council)—January 14
A young man named Bedros Boghosian (twenty years old) from Keramet went to Orhangazi on business. On his way back, he disappeared with his horse on the border of the Turkish villages of Ereğli and Çakırlı. The incident happened on January 12. Bedros's arrival at Çakırlı's border was witnessed by his tired pedestrian companion, Krikor Janigian, a relative of his, who was sitting at Ereğli's cemetery for a moment to rest.

After the incident was reported to the headmen of Çakırlı and Ereğli, a search was conducted in the mountain and the plain, but no trace [of Bedros] could be found. The incident has also been reported to the government. The commander of the gendarmerie has promised to pursue it.

• Recently, the same thing happened to an Armenian named Isgender from Büyük-Yeniköy. His body has been impossible to find.

Bursa (from the vicar general)—January 19
On the 12th of this month, at half past one at night, the following ill-famed bandits entered Marmaracık: Emin of Burcun, Deli Ahmet from the village of Tere, Mustafa Pehlivan of Telcık and his two sons, Halil İbrahim and Nuri, and several others. They first beat the Turkish and Armenian headmen severely. The Armenian headman, Kapriel Moutafian, is slightly injured in the leg. Krikor Garmirian and Hayrabed Nazarian were also slightly injured and are receiving medical treatment. They took from the Armenians 155 Ottoman liras cash, [five of them one denomination], two hundred banknotes, and the weapons they had for self-defense.

Trabzon (from the locum tenens)—January 22
A Turkish rally was held on January 19. Five speakers, one of whom was drunk, referred to the talks about the capture of İstanbul, calling the Europeans "traitors," targeting particularly the prime minister of England. Speaking about Eastern Anadolu [Anatolia], they said: "They will allegedly hand it over to the hand-painted kerchief makers [i.e. Armenians]." There was no widespread enthusiasm. The rally was dispersed peacefully, thanks to French and British representatives who threatened to hold the prefect responsible for any inconvenience.

Tekirdağ (from the Armenian vicar general and Greek metropolitan)—January 28
Until now, the Milli organization had been preparing secretly, but now they are organizing openly in this city, and Milli troops are being sent to Malkara, Çorlu, and the villages. The enlisted put dark blue

հէվալէ կ'ընէ Ազատաղ նահիյէի միւտիր Մունիր պէյին, որ գիշեր ցերեկ երեւելի փախստական ոճրագործներու հետ կերուխումէ յետոյ իբր ոստիկան պաշտօնի կանչած է: Արդէն հայոց մնացորդներուն չարչարանք տուողները փախստականներն են:

Տրապիզոն (Առաջնորդական Տեղապահէն) – 12 Յունվար

Թրքական հաշտութեան օրերուն մօտաւորութիւնը դարձեալ թուրքերուն մէջ առաջ բերած է շարժում: Թուրքերը դիմադրելու երազներով կը տարուին: Չինուորական ոյժը հետզհետէ կը կեդրոնանայ քաղաքին մէջ: Հակառակ պարագային դէպի Ատրպէյճան քաշուելու ծրագիր մըն ալ կ'երեւի թէ կը մշակուի: Հանդարտ համակերպելու կողմնակիցներ կան: Տրապիզոնի գրաւումը անհրաժեշտ է ջլատելու համար կարգ մը յաւակնութիւններ: Թէեւ դիմադրութեան պատրաստութիւնները կարելի չէ նկատել լրջօրէն մտահոգիչ, բայց վերջապէս անոնք կրնան ունենալ անախորժ հետեւանքներ:

Քէրէմէթ (Թաղական Խորհուրդէն) – 14 Յունվար

Քէրէմէթէն Պետրոս Պօղոսեան անուն երիտասարդը (20 տարեկան) գործով Օրխան-Ղազի գացած ըլլալով՝ վերադարձին Իւրէյ[իլ] եւ Չաքրըլը անուն թուրք գիւղերու սահմանին վրայ ձիով միասին կ'անյայտանայ: Դէպքը պատահած է 12 Յունվարին: Պետրոսի մինչեւ Չաքրըլըի սահմանը հասնելուն ականատես եղած է իր ուղեկից Գրիգոր Ճանիկեան ազգականը, որ հետիոտն ըլլալուն համար քիչ մը յոգնութիւն առնել ուզելով պահ մը կը նստի Իւրէյ[իլ]ի գերեզմանատունը:

Դէպքը լուր տալով Չաքրըլը եւ Իւրէյ[իլ]ի մուխթարներուն, լեռ դաշտ փնտռտուք կը կատարուի, բայց կարելի չ'ըլլար գտնել ոչ մէկ հետք: Դէպքը տեղեկագրուած է նաեւ կառավարութեան: Ժանտարմա-զօմանտանին խոստացած է հետապնդել:

- Վերջերս Մեծ-Նոր-Գիւղի Իսկէնտէր անուն հայուն ալ միեւնոյնը պատահեցաւ: Ասոր ալ դիակը անկարելի եղաւ գտնել:

Պրուսա (Առաջնորդական Փոխանորդէն) – 19 Յունվար

Ամսոյս 12ին, իրիկուան ժամը 1½ին (ը[ստ] թ[ըրքաց]) Մարմարճըգ կը մտնեն հետեւեալ չարահամբաւ աւազակները: Էմին Պուրճու[ն]ցի, Տէլի Ահմէտ Թէրէ գիւղէն, Մուսթաֆա Փէհլիվան եւ երկու զաւակները՝ Խալիլ Իպրահիմ եւ Նուրի՝ Թէլճուգցի եւ ուրիշ քանի մը հոգիներ: Ասոնք նախ սաստիկ կը ծեծեն թուրք եւ հայ մըխթարները, եւ հայ մըխթարը՝ Գաբրիէլ Մուլթաֆեան, ոտքէն թեթեւակի վիրաւորուած է: Նոյնպէս թեթեւապէս վիրաւորուած են Գրիգոր Կարմիրեան եւ Հայրապետ Նազարեան, որոնք կը դարմանուին: Հայերէն առած են 155 հնչուն օսմանեան ոսկի, 5 հատ հինգը մէկնոց, 200 թուղթ դրամ եւ ինքնապաշտպանութեան համար իրենց ունեցած զէնքերը:

Տրապիզոն (Առաջնորդական Տեղապահէն) – 22 Յունվար

Յունվար 19ին տեղի ունեցաւ թրքական միթինկ մը: Հինգ ճառախօսներ, որոնցմէ մէկը զինով, անդրադարձան Պոլսոյ գրաւման զրոյցներու շուրջ, «խային» անուանելով եւրոպացիները եւ իրենց սլաքները ուղղելով մասնաւորապէս Անգլիոյ վարչապետին: Անատոլուի արեւելեան մասին վրայ խօսելով ըսեր են «ան ալ *եազմաճը*ներուն պիտի յանձնենք եղեր»: Ժողովրդային խանդավառութիւն չկար: Միթինկը ցրուած է խաղաղօրէն, շնորհիւ ֆրանսացի եւ անգլիացի ներկայացուցիչներու՝ որոնք սպառնացեր են կուսակալին՝ զինքը ճանչնալ պատասխանատու ոեւէ անպատեհութեան:

Ռոտոսթօ (Հայոց Առաջնորդական Փոխանորդէն եւ Յունաց Մետրապոլիտէն) – 28 Յունուար

Հոս մինչեւ ցարդ «Միլլի Թէշքիլաթը» գաղտնի կը պատրաստուէր, բայց հիմա բացէ ի բաց

caps on their heads, and with their weapons over their shoulders, they cross the square during the day. They enlist twenty-three to thirty-year-old Muslims in the army to prepare them to act on the first order. The wealthy [Turks] of Tekirdağ and the surrounding area donate money. These forces are getting prepared, supposedly, to defend the homeland.

The Armenian and Greek religious leaders appealed to the British representative, who promised to report the situation.

İzmit (from the vicar general)—January 23

The new Turkish horrors are becoming official. The headman of Akmeşe, the son of Kürçü Osman Bey, setting aside all government work, visits the Turkish villages of his area in person and freely and boldly urges all the villagers to sell some of their cattle or sheep and to buy weapons to protect the rest of their sheep.

Seeing this zeal to arm, the villagers of Mecidiye [Khach] came to İzmit in terror to understand the reasons behind this official propaganda under the pretext of protecting the sheep.

The behavior of a government functionary who oversees the management of a cluster of villages is nothing but a purposeful duty assigned by a senior official. It is truly a cause for concern.

The villagers want to move to both a safe and Armenian-populated place, considering the most recent crime in Camidüzü [Kilisedüzü/Zhamavayr], in which Garabed Koundakjian also suffered wounds.

Akmeşe (from the directorate of the Agricultural College)—February 3, 1920

The Milli movement started around Akmeşe, too, and there is insecurity in those areas. The Milli Hüsnü, followed by the Milli Bedri, came from İzmit to the nearby villages, Kandıra and Adalı, where through advocacy, they armed the Muslim people and are collecting money.

Adana (from the National Union and Mihran Damadian)—January 31

The atmosphere in Cilicia was dark for several months, but it has been even darker since January 1. The Turks of Maraş raised the first alarm. The Turkish mob gathered together and formed into bands of çetes, attacked unarmed Armenian villages. They massacred them, looted them, and abducted them. A regular war has been going on around Maraş for a month. Now it is not the Turkish mob; it is the regular [Turkish] soldiers who are waging war against the French and Armenian soldiers under the command of Turkish officers. There is no exact information from Maraş; it is said that the city is on fire. We do not know the extent of our loss; only this is certain that close to eighteen hundred people of Dönüklü [Fındıcak], Dereköy, and the surrounding villages have been massacred, and the houses have been demolished. The news we received today is even more disturbing: Süleymanlı [Zeytun], Fırnız, and the surrounding Armenian villages were besieged by the Turks for twenty-five days. Three days ago, the whole population was massacred, plundered, and the towns and villages were destroyed. The whole of mountainous Cilicia is in fear and horror. The unarmed people are constantly crying for help. They do not want to die with their hands folded like timid rabbits. They are ready to fight, and they demand weapons. And we, having no means to satisfy this just demand of the people, turned to the local French authorities, which satisfied us with evasive answers. These appeals have met with negative results for months. Not wanting to take responsibility for this challenging situation, in agreement

քաղաքիս մէջ [կը] կազմակերպուին եւ Միլլի զօրքերը կը ղրկուին Մալկարա, Չօրլու եւ գիւղերը: Արձանագրուողները մութ կապոյտ գտակ մը կը դնեն գլուխնին եւ զէնքը ուսին ցերեկով կ'անցնին հրապարակէն: 23–30 տարեկան խլամները զօրք կ'առնեն, որպէսզի առաջին հրամանին պատրաստ ըլլան գործելու: Ռօտոսթօյի եւ շրջականներու հարուստներն ալ դրամով կ'օգնեն: Այս ոյժերը կը պատրաստուին իբր թէ հայրենիքը պաշտպանելու համար:

Հայ եւ յոյն հոգեւոր պետերը դիմում կատարեցին անգլիական ներկայացուցիչին, որ խոստացաւ տեղեկագրել կացութիւնը:

Նիկոմիդիա (Առաջնորդական Փոխանորդէն) – 23 Յունվար

Թրքական նոր սարսափները պաշտօնական հանգամանք կ'առնեն: Արմաշու միւտիր, Կիւրճի Օսման պէյի որդին, մէկ կողմ ձգած կառավարական ամէն գործ, իր շրջանակի թուրք գիւղերը կը պտտի անձամբ եւ ազատ համարձակ կը յորդորէ բոլոր գիւղացիները ծախել իրենց արջառ կամ ոչխարներէն մէկ մասը եւ անպայման զէնքեր գնել, անոնցմով մնացած ոչխարները պահելու նպատակով:

Խաչ-գիւղացիք զինուելու այս եռանդը տեսնելով, ահ ու սարսափի մատնուած կուգան Նիկոմիդիա, հասկնալու համար ոչխար պահպանելու պատրուակին տակ եղած պաշտօնական այս բրօպականտին պատճառները:

Գիւղախումբի մը վարչութիւնը ձեռք առած կառավարական պաշտօնեայի մը ընթացքը ուրիշ բան չէ եթէ ոչ նպատակաւոր դեր մը, յանձնուած աւելի բարձր պաշտօնեայի մը կողմէ, եւ իսկապէս մտահոգութիւն պատճառող:

Գիւղացիք կ'ուզեն ապահով եւ հայաշատ տեղ մը փոխադրուիլ, աչքի առաջ ունենալով Ժամավայրի շատ նոր եղերական դէպք[ը], որուն զոհ գնաց նաեւ վիրաւոր Կարապետ Գունտաքճեան:

Արմաշ (Գիւղատնտեսական Վարժարանի տնօրէնութենէն) – 3 Փետրուար 1920

Արմաշի շրջակայքն ալ ծայր տալ սկսած է Միլլի շարժումը եւ անապահովութիւն կը տիրէ այդ կողմերը: Նիկոմիդիայէն նախ Հիւսնի եւ ապա Պէտրի անունով միլլիճիներ եկած եւ շրջակայ գիւղերը՝ Գանտրա եւ Ատալի բրօբականտ ընելով խլամ ժողովուրդը զինած են եւ դրամ կը հաւաքեն:

Ատանա (Ազգային Միութենէն եւ Միհրան Տամատեանէ) – 31 Յունուար

Մի քանի ամիսներէ ի վեր կիլիկեան մթնոլորտը մթագնած էր, սակայն Յունուար 1էն ի վեր ա՛լ աւելի խաւարած է: Մարա՛շի թրքութիւնն է որ առաջին ահազանգը կը հնչեցնէ: Թուրք խուժանը ի մի հաւաքուած, խումբ խումբ Չէթէներ կազմած կը յարձակին անզէն հայ գիւղերու վրայ, կը ջարդեն, կը կողոպտեն եւ կ'առեւանգեն: Մարաշի շուրջը ամիսէ մը ի վեր կանոնաւոր պատերազմը կը շարունակէ. այժմ թուրք խուժանը չէ, կանոնաւոր զինուորն է, թուրք սպաներու հրամատարութեանը տակ պատերազմ կը մղեն ֆրանսական եւ հայկական զինուորներու դէմ: Մարաշէն ստոյգ տեղեկութիւն մը չկայ, կ'ըսեն թէ քաղաքը բոցերուն մէջ է: Չենք գիտեր թէ որքան կորուստ ունինք, միայն սա ստոյգ է թէ՝ *Ֆընտըճագ, Տէրէքէօյ* եւ շրջակայ գիւղերու 1800ի մօտ բնակչութիւնը ջարդուած եւ բնակարանները քարուքանդ եղած [են]. այսօրուան մեր ստացած լուրերը աւելի վրդովեցուցիչ են, *Զէյթուն, Ֆոնուզ* եւ շրջակայ հայ գիւղերը 25 օրէ ի վեր պաշարուած էին թուրքերու կողմէ. 3 օր առաջ ամբողջ բնակչութիւնը ջարդուած, թալլուած եւ քաղաք ու գիւղերն ալ քարուքանդ եղած են: Ամբողջ լեռնային Կիլիկիան ահ ու սարսափի մէջ է. անզէն ժողովուրդը շարունակ օգնութեան աղաղակ կը բարձրացնէ, չեն ուզեր երկչոտ ճագարներու նման ձեռքերը ծալլած մեռնիլ. պատրաստ է կռուիլ եւ զէնք կը պահանջէ մենէ. իսկ մենք չունենալով միջոցներ ժողովուրդի այս արդար պահանջին գոհացում տալու, դիմեցինք տեղական ֆրանսական իշխանութեան՝ որը խուսափողական պատասխաններով զմեզ գոհացուց: Այս դիմումները ամիսներէ ի վեր եղած են միշտ ժխտական արդիւնքով: Այս ծանր կացութեան հանդէպ չուզելով պատասխանատուութիւնը

with Mr. M[ihran] Damadian, the plenipotentiary representative of the [Armenian National] Delegation, the National Union convened an extraordinary meeting, which was attended by Catholicos Sahag, the primate of Adana, the Armenian Catholic prelate, and the minister of the Armenian Protestants, as well as political parties and local dignitaries. There, after scrupulously examining the situation, they concluded that if the French did not meet our demands, all the authorities would resign and hand over the reins of the country to the people, [although] continuing to stay with them and leading them in an unofficial capacity. A lengthy telegram was sent to General Gouraud in Beirut for this purpose.

Thousands of extremely agitated people assembled in Adana called upon Mr. Damadian and the members of the National Union with demands that they immediately provide them with weapons so that they could avenge their slaughtered brothers and protect the rest. It was decided to wait for the outcome of the appeal to General Gouraud [before taking further action].

Kayseri (from the vicar general)—January 18

Mustafa Kemal Pasha came to Kayseri with his followers and visited the Armenian orphanage. He told the orphans not to be afraid, that there is no danger for them, and that protecting the homeland is his lone task. After touring the orphanage for five minutes, he left.

• The Turkish newspaper *Adanaya Doğru*, published in Kayseri, described recently imaginary atrocities committed by Armenians against Turks in Adana. During the same days, a Turkish hoca in the mosque spoke ill of Christians in general and Armenians in particular. The Armenian locum tenens protested to the district governor against this newspaper and the hoca mentioned above, saying that a dangerous effect can come forth in the current situation [by doing so]. Some of the Turks also having made remarks—whether with ill or goodwill, it is not known—the newspaper was impeded shortly after [the appeal], and the hoca was sent away.

The current situation here is far from enviable, although it is still calm. The local authorities show themselves as obliging toward appeals but give no satisfaction at all in practice.

Kayseri (from the vicar general)—January 20

Garabed Effendi Markarian, an assistant inspector at Sivas prefecture, is undoubtedly an honest man as attested by those who know him. While passing through Kayseri on his way to his office, he had a meeting in a hotel with Turkish soldiers and passed the following information to the prelacy confidentially: "A Turkish captain, thinking that I am a Muslim, whispered to me in the presence of other servicemen, 'We are arming [groups of] thirty people each and sending them toward Adana to loot and kill Armenians with such dexterity that those bands of çetes will seem to be Armenians who are robbing and killing each other. We have succeeded in this endeavor.'" The same person asserted that Milli forces always take up positions in small places, in the corner of a cluster of villages, away from the eyes of the Armenians. This time he saw with his own eyes their military training. The Turkish captain added that they are pretty strong in the Kayseri district.

Bursa (from the vicar general)—February 6

The Millis show great activity: gatherings night and day, arming the çetes, threatening here and there. The newspaper *Ertuğrul*, in particular, showers the Armenians and the French with poison and fire,

ստանձնել, համաձայն Պատուիրակութեան Լիազօր Ներկայացուցիչ Պ. Մ. Տամատեանի հետ, արտակարգ ժողով մը կը գումարէ Ազգային Միութիւնը, որուն ներկայ կ'ըլլան Սահակ Կաթողիկոսը, Ատանայի Առաջնորդը, Հայ Կաթոլիկ առաջնորդը եւ Հայ Բողոքականներու հովիւը, նաեւ քաղաքական կուսակցութիւնները եւ տեղւոյս մեծամեծները, հոն կացութիւնը մանրամասնօրէն քննելէ յետոյ, սա եզրակացութեան կուգան որ եթէ ֆրանսացիք մեր պահանջներուն գոհացում չտան, ամբողջ իշխանութիւնները հրաժարին եւ ժողովրդեան յանձնեն երկրին ղեկը, միշտ մնալով ժողովրդեան հետ եւ առաջնորդելով զայն անպաշտօն կերպով: Այս նպատակով ընդարձակ հեռագիր մը կ'ուղղուի Ժեներալ Կուրօյի ի Պէյրութ:

Ատանայի ժողովուրդը չափազանց յուզուած, համախմբուած հազարներով, կը կոչէ Պ. Տամատեանը եւ Ազգային Միութեան անդամները եւ կը պահանջէ անմիջապէս իրենց զէնք տրամադրել, որպէսզի երթան իրենց խողխողուած եղբայրներու վրէժը լուծելու եւ մնացեալները պաշտպանելու: Զօրավար Կուրօյի եղած դիմումին հետեւանքին սպասել որոշուեցաւ:

Կեսարիա (Առաջնորդական Փոխանորդէն) – 18 Յունվար

Մուսթաֆա Քէմալ փաշա իրեն հետեւորդներով Կեսարիա եկաւ եւ այցելեց հայոց որբանոցը եւ որբերուն յայտարարեց թէ չվախնան, իրենց համար վտանգ չկայ, միայն իր գործն է հայրենիքին պաշտպանութիւնը: 5 վայրկեան որբանոցը աչքէ անցնելէ յետոյ մեկնած է:

- Վերջերս Կեսարիոյ մէջ հրատարակուող «Ատանայա Տօղրու» թուրք թերթը կը նկարագրէր Ատանայի մէջ հայոց կողմէ թուրքերու դէմ գործադրուած երեւակայական խժդժութիւններ: Միեւնոյն օրերուն թուրք հօճա մը մզկիթին մէջ քրիստոնեաներու դէմ ընդհանրապէս եւ հայերու դէմ մասնաւորապէս չարախօսութիւններ կ'ընէր: Միւթէսարըֆին հայոց Առաջնորդական Տեղապահը բողոքեց թէ՛ այս թերթին եւ թէ յիշուած հոճային դէմ, յայտնելով որ ներկայ կացութեան մէջ կրնայ վտանգաւոր ազդեցութիւն յառաջ բերել: Թուրքերէն ոմանք ալ դիտողութիւն ըրած ըլլալով,- նենգամտութեամբ թէ բարեմտութեամբ, ասիկա յայտնի չէ,- քիչ յետոյ թերթը խափանուեցաւ եւ հօճան ճամբուեցաւ:

Տեղւոյս կացութիւնը նախանձելի ըլլալէ հեռու է [թէեւ] առայժմ հանդարտ: Տեղական իշխանութիւններն ինքզինքնին հաճոյակատար ցոյց կուտան հանդէպ դիմումներու, սակայն ոչ մէկ գոհացում կուտան գործնականին մէջ:

Կեսարիա (Առաջնորդական Փոխանորդէն) – 20 Յունվար

Կարապետ էֆէնտի Մարգարեան, Սեբաստիոյ կուսակալութեան օգնական քննիչ, որ իր պաշտօնատեղին երթալու առթիւ Կեսարիայէն կ'անցնէր եւ որուն պարկեշտութիւնը ամէն տարակոյսէ վեր ըլլալը կը հաւաստեն զինքը ճանչցողները, պանդոկին մէջ թուրք զինուորականներու հետ տեսնուած է, հետեւեալ տեղեկութիւնները մտերմօրէն հաղորդած է հայոց առաջնորդարան. «Թուրք հարիւրապետ մը զիս իսլամ կարծելով, ուրիշ զինուորականներու ներկայութեան ականջս ի վեր յայտնեց թէ 30ական հոգի կը զինենք եւ Ատանայի կողմերը հայ կոտորելու եւ սպաննելու կը ղրկենք այնպիսի ճարտարութիւնով մը, որ իբր թէ այդ չէթէի խումբերը հայ եղած ըլլան ու զիրար կոտորած եւ սպաննած ըլլան: Մեր այս ձեռնարկին մէջ յաջողած ենք»: Նոյն անձը հաւաստեց թէ Միլլի ուժը միշտ դիրք կը բռնէ պզտիկ վայրերու մէջ, հայերու աչքէն հեռու նահիյէներու մէկ անկիւնը, ինչպէս որ այս անգամ ինքն իր աչքովը տեսած է անոնց զինուորական պատրաստութիւնները: Թուրք հարիւրապետը աւելցուցած է թէ՝ Կեսարիոյ սանճագին մէջ բաւական ոյժ մը կը ներկայացնեն:

Պրուսա (Առաջնորդական Փոխանորդէն) – 6 Փետրուար

Միլլին մեծ գործունէութիւն ցոյց կուտայ. գիշեր ցորեկ հաւաքոյթ, չէթէներու սպառազինում, ասդին անդին սպառնալիք: Մասնաւորապէս *Էրթողրուլ* թերթը թոյն եւ կրակ կը թափէ հայոց եւ

inciting the minds [of Turkish readers]. There is a boycott against Armenians and Greeks. It was written in that newspaper yesterday that Bandırma had been captured by the British. Anger and excitement have reached an extreme; there is great fear that an incident will happen; the Armenians are very cautious.

Samsun (telegram from the primate)—February 7
The resignation of Hamit Bey from governorship is a threat to local security. The people are fearful and want to see him reinstated.

Yerevan (from Yeprem Demirjian)—February 10
Residents of Armenian villages near the village of Abana near Şebinkarahisar say that this village of 540 people, never deported, was besieged by the Beys called Çeçenzade and nearby Turks and villagers. They [the Armenians] were massacred entirely, their bodies dumped in ditches. The entire Armenian quarter is destroyed and turned into ruins. Out of the 540 [Armenian] people of Abana, only 35 live now, and that is because they are in İstanbul.

Yerevan (from Vahan H. Mouradian of Eleşkirt)—January 26
The exodus of Eleşkirt to Yerevan via Iğdır took place on December 11, 1914. They could hardly enter Iğdır in the snowy winter weather in thirteen days because they encountered many frozen corpses at every step. Some survived, thanks to Russian-Kazakh troops.

Those killed before the migration were:
67 prominent people native of Eleşkirt from the district of Toprakkale
8 girls and a bride were taken from the inhabitants of the district of Toprakkale
150 men from Başak village
32 women from Başak village
41 girls and a bride from Başak [Zidikan] village
199 people from Mollasüleyman village killed in the district of Toprakkale
37 teenagers ages fifteen to seventeen from the same village in the district of Toprakkale
69 brides and girls were taken from the village of Mollasüleyman
24 men from Tezeren [Amad] village
7 women and a girl from Tezeren village
22 people from Yücekapı [Khastur]
12 men from Üçoymak [Khoshian]
8 brides and women from Üçoymak
11 people from Akbulgur [Yeritsu] and Kayabey villages

Armenians suffered 657 casualties in the district of Toprakkale alone, except in Dikili [Karakilise] and Doğubayazıt. In addition to these victims of Turkish barbarism, three-fourths of the Turkish-Armenian migrants in and around Yerevan perished due to famine and cold, thus leaving [alive only] about ten percent of the total population.

Bilecik (from the Neighborhood Council)—February 10
The activities of the Millis are increasing day by day. A detachment of troops (Albanian, Circassian, and Turkish) came to Bilecik from Bursa these days. They are all elderly people, armed from head to toe.

Chests full of ammunition and bombs were brought to Bilecik also. Most soldiers do not have

ֆրանսացւոց հասցէին, մտքերը կը գրգռէ: Հայոց եւ յունաց դէմ պօյքօթ կայ: Երէկի այդ թերթին մէջ գրուած էր թէ Պանտրմա գրաւուած է անգլիացւոց կողմէ: Զայրոյթը եւ յուզումը ծայր աստիճանի հասած է. շատ կը վախցուի որ դէպք մը կը պատահի. հայերը շատ զգոյշ են:

Սամսոն (Առաջնորդէն հեռագիր) – 7 Փետրուար

Համիտ պէյի կառավարիչութենէն հրաժարիլը սպառնալիք մըն է տեղւոյս ապահովութեան համար: Ժողովուրդը վախի մէջ է եւ կը փափաքի զինքը վերահաստատուած տեսնել:

Երեւան (Եփրեմ Տէմիրճեանէ) – 10 Փետրուար

Շապին-Գարահիսարի մօտակայ Ապանայ գիւղի մերձակայ հայ գիւղերու բնակիչները կը պատմեն թէ այս 540 անձ պարունակող գիւղը, առանց տեղահան ըլլալու չէչէն-զատէ բռուած պէյերու եւ շրջակայ ու գիւղացի թուրքերու կողմէ պաշարուելով ամբողջովին ջարդուած են եւ փոսեր լեցուած են եւ ամբողջ հայոց թաղը քանդուած եւ աւերակի վերածուած է: Ապանայի 540 անձ բնակչութենէն հիմա միայն 35 հոգի կ'ապրի, անոնք ալ Կ. Պոլիս գտնուելնուն համար:

Երեւան (ալաշկերտցի Վահան Յ. Մուրատեանէ) – 26 Յունվար

1914 Դեկտեմբեր 11ին տեղի ունեցաւ Ալաշկերտի գաղթը դէպի Երեւան Իգտիրի գծով: 13 օրուայ մէջ հազիւ կրցան մտնել Իգտիր, ձիւն ձմեռ եղանակի մէջ, որով ամէն քայլափոխին կը հանդիպէին սառած դիակներու, որոնց թիւը շատ մեծ էր: Ռուս ղազախ զինուորներու շնորհիւ մէկ մասը ազատեցաւ:

Գաղթէն առաջ սպաննուած են

67 նշանաւոր անձեր Ալաշկերտի բնիկ Թօփրագգալէ գաւառի բնակիչներէն

8 աղջիկ եւ հարս տարուեցաւ Թօփրագգալէ գաւառի բնակիչներէն

150 այր Զիտկան գիւղէն

32 կին Զիտկան գիւղէն

41 աղջիկ եւ հարս Զիտկան գիւղէն

199 անձ Մօլլասլէման գիւղէն սպաննուեցան Թօփրագգալէ գաւառին մէջ

37 15–17 տարեկան պատանիներ նոյն գիւղէն Թօփրագգալէ գաւառին մէջ

69 հարս եւ աղջիկ տարուեցան Մօլլասլէման գիւղէն

24 այր Ամատ գիւղէն

7 կին եւ աղջիկ Ամատ գիւղէն

22 անձ Խաստուրէն

12 այր Խօշեանէն

8 հարս եւ կին Խօշեանէն

11 անձ Երիցու եւ Գայաբէկ գիւղերէն

657 զոհ եւ կորուստ ունեցած են հայերը միմիայն Թօփրագգալէ գաւառին մէջ, բացի Գարաքիլիսայի եւ Պայազիտի շրջանակէն: Թրքական բարբարոսութեան այս զոհերէն զատ հոս Երեւանի մէջ եւ շրջակայքը գտնուող թրքահայ գաղթականներէն ¾-ը սովէն եւ ցուրտէն կոտորուեցան, որով ընդհանուր բնակչութեան գրեթէ տասը առ հարիւրը մնացած է:

Պիլէճիկ (Թաղական Խորհուրդէն) – 10 Փետրուար

Միլլիճիներու գործունէութիւնը օրըստօրէ կ'աւելնայ: Պրուսայէն Պիլէճիկ եկաւ այս օրերս ջոկատ մը զօրք (ալպանացի, չէրքէզ եւ թուրք), ամէնքն ալ տարիքոտ մարդիկ, զինուած իրենց ոտքէն մինչեւ գլուխ:

Նոյնպէս Պիլէճիկ բերուեցան սնտուկներով լեցուն ռազմամթերք եւ պօմպաներ: Զինուորնե-

uniforms, and the leaders are elderly officers. They are increasing their numbers daily by enlisting Turkish and Circassian youths from the surrounding villages, particularly, by distributing weapons. Thus Turkish villagers carry guns on their shoulders when they travel to or from their villages.

• The case of the release of an Armenian female orphan from the home of a Turkish court examiner failed due to the government's unwillingness.

• We are in a difficult situation. Yesterday's massacrers are roaming freely and boldly, and the great monster Mercimekzade Ahmet was elected deputy from Bilecik, and although he was afraid to go to İstanbul, he sows the seeds of evil all around. Urgent help is needed; otherwise, there is danger.

Kayseri (from the vicar general)—February 4[48]

About fifteen hundred of the thirty-five hundred abandoned Armenian homes have been dismantled. The rest are being dismantled before the eyes of the government and with its permission, every day, one or two a day, and sold by the [department of] State Property. Contrary to the denial of the minister of the interior, the looting of the church in Tomarza by Turkish soldiers is an absolute fact. The vicar general examined the issue in person. In addition, the local intendant confirmed the vicar general's suspicions confidentially and pointed at the captain as responsible. He then promised to examine the issue in more detail and to inform the vicar general confidentially. But now, perhaps because of a warning he has received, he is using a different language. Attributing theft to the neighborhood council by the government is a Turkish trick. The previous intendant had closed the church days before the robbery, filled the yard with soldiers, and barred Armenians from entering. After the theft, he called the Armenians and rebuked them for leaving the church open. The thieving captain left for Kayseri on vacation during the same period to sell the booty, most probably.

• [The Turks] are using extreme violence to collect taxes in the surrounding villages, Develi [Everek], and Tomarza.

• Excited by the frequent rallies in and around Kayseri, as well as in Develi, the notables and lieutenant governor of Develi have contemplated a newly devised way to defame the Armenian vicar general and the neighborhood council of the Armenian church of Develi with a dangerous charge. They have announced that we have made political formations to instigate the local Armenians against the government and the Turkish people, whereas the vicar general and the neighborhood council, aware of this mentality and with foresight, had informed the lieutenant governor and other officials and Turkish notables in advance about all affairs related to the church, school, and [other] national functions. The vicar general had even introduced the chairmen of the neighborhood councils of Develi and Fenese as representatives of the people to the lieutenant governor and the notables, asking them to satisfy their appeals. This particularity made them very happy, and the vicar general, while he was there, had also been honored by the Turks. Twenty to twenty-five days after his return to Kayseri, this new charge is now being brought to light to discredit the prelacy in Kayseri and the people in Develi and to raise new problems. The primary purpose of these slanders seems to be inciting hatred against the Armenians and to [justify] carrying out new massacres and robberies. The author of these machinations is the lieutenant governor of Develi, who, during the Armenian deportation, tortured and robbed the Armenians of Bünyan Hamit and inflicted unprecedented mischief upon them. This Laz monster still keeps an Armenian girl and uses her sisters brutally in his house. He is also utterly unworthy of his position intellect-wise.

On January 7, the lieutenant governor summoned the two chairmen to his office, and in the presence of Hacı Seyitzade Osman Effendi, Abdullah Bey, the commander of the gendarmerie, and Hacı

բուն մեծ մասն համազգեստ չունի եւ պարագլուխները ծեր սպաներ են: Օրէ օր իրենց թիւը կ'աւելցնեն մօտակայ գիւղերու թուրք եւ չէրքէզ երիտասարդները արձանագրելով եւ մասնաւորապէս անոնց զէնք բաժնելով, այնպէս որ թուրք գիւղացիները իրենց գիւղերը երթալ գալու ատեն հրացանները ուսերնին կը կրեն:

- Թուրք դատական քննիչի մը տունը գտնուող հայ որբուհիին ազատագրման գործն ալ ձախողեցաւ կառավարութեան անբարեացակամութեամբ:

- Դժուարին կացութեան մը մէջ կը գտնուինք: Երէկուան ջարդարարները ազատ համարձակ կը շրջին եւ մեծ ճիւաղը «Մէրճիմէզզատէ Ահմէտ», երեսփոխան ընտրուած է Պիլէճիկէն եւ թէեւ Պոլիս երթալու կը վախնայ, բայց հոս ամէն կողմ չարութեան սերմ կը ցանէ: Շուտափոյթ օգնութեան պէտք կայ, եթէ ոչ՝ վտանգ կայ:

Կեսարիա (Առաջնորդական Փոխանորդէն) – 4 Փետրուար

Անտէր հայերու 3500ի մօտ տուներէն 1500 տունը քակուած է: Մնացածներն ալ կառավարութեան աչքին առջեւ եւ անոր արտօնութեամբ ամէն օր մաս-մաս,- օրական մէկ-երկու հատ,- կը քակուին եւ Էմվալը Էմիրիյէի կողմէ կը ծախուին: Հակառակ ներքին գործերու նախարարին հերքումին, բացարձակ իրողութիւն մըն է Թոմարզայի եկեղեցիին կողոպտուած ըլլալը թուրք զինուորներու կողմէ: Առաջնորդական փոխանորդը անձնապէս քննած է խնդիրը: Ասկէ զատ, տեղւոյն միւտիրը Առաջնորդական Փոխանորդին խորհրդաբար հաստատած է Առաջնորդական Փոխանորդին կասկածները եւ հարիւրապետը պատասխանատու ցոյց տուած է: Յետոյ խոստացած է ինքն ալ աւելի մանրամասն քննել խնդիրը եւ մտերմաբար Առաջնորդական Փոխանորդին լուր տալ: Բայց հիմա թերեւս իրեն եղած ազդարարութեան մը վրայ, տարբեր լեզու կը գործածէ: Կառավարութեան կողմէ գողութիւնը թաղական խորհուրդին վերագրուիլը թրքական դարձուածք մը[ն է]: Եկեղեցին՝ գողութենէն օրեր առաջ, նախորդ միւտիրը փակած եւ բակը զինուոր լեցուցած եւ հայերը ներս մտնելէ արգիլած էր: Գողութիւնը կատարուելէ յետոյ, կը կոչէ հայերը, կը յանդիմանէ թէ ինչո՞ւ եկեղեցին բաց ձգած են, մինչ գող հարիւրապետը այդ օրերուն իսկ արձակուրդով Կեսարիա գացած էր, ապահովաբար գողօնները ծախելու համար:

- Տուրքի համար շրջակայ գիւղերը, Էվէրէկ եւ Թօմարզա, ծայր աստիճան բռնութիւն կը բանեցնեն:

- Վերջերս Կեսարիոյ եւ շրջակայից, ինչպէս նաեւ Էվէրէկի մէջ յաճախակի տեղի ունեցող միթինկներէն խանդավառուած, Էվէրէկի էշրաֆը եւ գայմագամը նորահնար միջոց մը խորհեր են հայոց Առաջնորդական Փոխանորդը եւ Էվէրէկի հայ եկեղեցի[ի]ն թաղական խորհուրդը վտանգաւոր ամբաստանութեամբ մը մրոտելու, յայտարարելով որ քաղաքական կազմակերպութիւններ կատարեր ենք, տեղւոյն հայերը կառավարութեան եւ թուրք ժողովուրդին դէմ հանելու համար: Մինչդեռ Առաջնորդական Փոխանորդը եւ թաղական խորհուրդը եկեղեցական, դպրոցական, ազգային բոլոր գործերը գայմագամին եւ միւս պաշտօնատարներուն եւ թուրք գլխաւորներուն կանխահոգ մտածութեամբ մը յայտնած էին, անոնց մտայնութեան ծանօթ ըլլալով: Առաջնորդական Փոխանորդը նոյնիսկ Էվէրէկի եւ Ֆէնէսէի թաղական խորհուրդներու ատենապետներն իբր ներկայացուցիչ ժողովուրդին ներկայացուցած էր գայմագամին եւ էշրաֆին, խնդրելով որ անոնց դիմումներուն գոհացում տան: Այս պարագան զիրենք մեծապէս ուրախացուցած էր եւ Առաջնորդական Փոխանորդը հոն գտնուած ատեն թուրք[երու] կողմէ ալ պատիւներ գտած էր: Իր Կեսարիա դարձէն 20–25 օր յետոյ, հիմա այս նոր ամբաստանութիւնը երեւան կը հանեն՝ Առաջնորդարանը Կեսարիոյ մէջ իսկ ժողովուրդը Էվէրէկի մէջ վարկաբեկելու եւ նոր խնդիրներ յարուցանելու համար: Այս չարախօսութեանց բուն նպատակը ըլլալ կը թուի հայերու դէմ գրգռութիւն յարուցանել եւ նոր ջարդ ու կողոպուտ գործադրել: Այս մեքենայութեանց հեղինակն է Էվէրէկի գայմագամը, որ տարագրութեան միջոցին Պիւնեան-Համիտի հայերը խոշտանգած, զանոնք կողոպտած եւ անօրինակ չարիքներ հասցուցած է: Ազգով լազ այս հրէշը դեռ հիմա կը

İbrahim, a notable of Eskicamiikebir [Develi], announced that the purpose of the visit of the primate and his followers to Develi [Everek] was focused on political-organizational issues and that, indeed, as a result, a [political] committee called "Goyichmoch" (??) [*sic*] has been organized by Armenians here. [He made] many other statements. The chairmen of the neighborhood councils insinuated the absurdity and fancifulness of the statements and tried in vain to say that nothing but a neighborhood council was formed. Then the audience was asked if they had any news from this supposed committee. Abdullah Bey and Hacı İbrahim Effendi simply said, "we heard" and nothing more, but Hacı Seyitzade, the president of the Muslim Union, made ruder and harsher statements than those made by the lieutenant governor. He also referenced a series of things past. These words terrified the peaceful population. Despite this, on January 23, the chairmen of the neighborhood councils again turned to the governor, who replied that the prelacy should assure him and the Muslim Union of Develi in separate letters sent through the district governor of Kayseri that the visit of the primate to Eskicamiikebir had not served any hidden purpose apart from forming a neighborhood council.

Consequently, the neighborhood council appealed to the vicar general, who, when [he] presented himself to the district governor, [the latter] considered those words [uttered by the aforementioned Turks] insignificant and did not write the required documents.

Sivas (from the primate)—February 6[49]

During the past two weeks, the local political situation has turned delicate. The latest issue of the *İrâde-i Milliye* newspaper clearly shows that the events in Maraş and the surrounding areas have greatly influenced the minds of leading local circles. Thus, provocative publications against Armenians are being made through the same newspaper and by secret flyers.

In the past week, within a few days, two Armenian homes and the headquarters of the Oriental Carpet Company have been searched by the government on the pretext of looking for tobacco or stolen goods; however, they are actually searching for weapons possessed by Armenians. When the primate turned to the governor about this, the governor answered that these are issues related to theft and tobacco and that they are insignificant. He said his house also could be searched for cigarettes and so on. It is to be noted that the director of the Régie stated in writing that he has no knowledge of a search for tobacco.

Also, Armenians who take to the streets at night are interrogated and even searched. The other day, a gun was fired at an Armenian for refusing to comply with the "Stop" warning.

• Recently, letters sent to Armenians by hand are being opened and translated on the pretext that they suspect Armenians are communicating with Maraş.

• Some Turks cautioned their Armenian acquaintances and expressed fears of a massacre. Despite this, the governor wants to inspire confidence in general and says that he suspects neither the Armenians nor the Turks of Sivas. He absolutely denies that any tragic incident has happened.

There is no specific incident or event, but the people feel threatened and terrified by the phenomena.

պահէ հայ աղջիկ մը եւ անոր քոյրերը առած վայրագօրէն կը գործածէ իր տան մէջ: Իմացականապէս ալ իր պաշտօնին բոլորովին անարժան մէկն է:

Այս գայմագամը Յունվար 7ին իր քովը կը կանչէ երկու ատենապետները իր պաշտօնատեղին, եւ ի ներկայութեան Հաճի Սէյիտ Զատէ Օսման էֆէնտիի, Ժանտարմա Գոմանտանի Ապտուլլահ պէյի եւ Տէվէլլուի էշրաֆներէն Հաճի Իպրահիմ էֆէնտիի, կը յայտարարէ թէ Կեսարիոյ Առաջնորդին եւ իր հետեւորդներուն Էվէրէկ այցելութեան նպատակը քաղաքական կազմակերպական խնդիրներու շուրջ կը դառնար եւ արդարեւ իրր արդիւնք «Կօյիգմօզ» (??) անուամբ զօմիթէ մը կազմուած է hոս այժմ հայերու կողմէ եւ այլ շատ մը յայտարարութիւններ՝ որոնց բոլորովին անհիմն եւ մտացածին ըլլալը թաղական խորհուրդի ատենապետները կը զգացնեն եւ ի զուր կը ջանան ըսել թէ կազմուածը լոկ թաղական խորհուրդ մըն էր: Յետոյ կը hարցնեն ներկաներուն թէ լուր ունի՞ն այս կարծեցեալ քօմիթէէն: Ապտուլլահ պէյ եւ Հաճի Իպրահիմ էֆէնտի «լսեցինք»ով միայն շատացան, իսկ Հաճի Սէյիտ Զատէն, որ Ճէմիյէթը Իսլամիյէի նախագահն է, գայմագամէն աւելի բրտօրէն ու ծանր յայտարարութիւններով եւ անցեալի շարք մը մէջբերումներով կ'արտայայտուի: Այս խօսքերը ահ ու սարսափ կ'ազդեն խաղաղ բնակչութեան: Ասով հանդերձ, թաղական խորհուրդներու ատենապետները Յունվար 23ին կրկին կը դիմեն գայմագամին որ կը պատասխանէ թէ Առաջնորդարանը պէտք է հաւաստիացնէ Կեսարիոյ միւթեսարըֆին միջոցաւ [իրեն] եւ Էվէրէկի Ճէմիյէթը Իսլամիյէին ուղղեալ մէյմէկ գրութեամբ թէ՝ Առաջնորդին Տէվէլու այցելութիւնը միմիայն թաղական խորհուրդի կազմակերպութենէն դուրս ուէ յետին նպատակի չէ ծառայած:

Ասոր վրայ թաղական խորհուրդը կը դիմէ Առաջնորդական Փոխանորդին, որ երբ միւթեսարըֆին կը ներկայանայ, այդ խօսքերը կարեւորութենէ զուրկ կը համարէ, բայց պահանջուած թուղթերը չի գրեր:

Սըվազ (Առաջնորդէն) – 6 Փետրուար

Վերջին երկու շաբաթներու միջոցին տեղւոյս քաղաքական կացութիւնը փափուկ հանգամանք մը առաւ: Հոստեղի «Իրատէի Միլլիյէ» թերթին վերջին թիւին մէջ յայտնի կ'երեւայ թէ Մարաշի մէջ եւ շրջակաները տեղի ունեցած դէպքերը մեծապէս ազդած են տեղւոյս վարիչ շրջանակներու մտքին վրայ եւ այսպէս հայերու դէմ գրգռիչ հրատարակութիւններ կ'ըլլան նոյն թերթին եւ գաղտնի թռուցիկներու միջոցաւ:

Անցեալ շաբթու մէջ մէկ քանի օրուան մէջ երկու հայ տուներ եւ Օռհանթալ Քարբէթի ընկերութեան կեդրոնատեղին խուզարկուեցան կառավարութեան կողմէ, ծխախոտ փնտռելու կամ գողութեան պատրուակներով, մինչդեռ իրականին մէջ հայերու քով զէնք կը փնտռեն: Երբ այս մասին Առաջնորդը կուսակալին կը դիմէ, պատասխան կը ստանայ թէ գողութեան եւ ծխախոտի խնդիրներ են, թէ կարեւորութենէ զուրկ են, եւ թէ իր տունն ալ կրնան ծխախոտի համար խուզարկութիւն կատարել եւայլն: Դիտելի է որ ծխախոտի համար խուզարկութիւն կատարուելէն *Րէժի Միւտիրին* գրաւոր կերպով կը յայտարարէ թէ տեղեկութիւն չունի:

Նոյնպէս գիշեր ատեն փողոց ելնող հայեր կը հարցաքննուին եւ նոյնիսկ վրայ գլուխնին կը խուզարկուի: Անցեալ օր հայու մը վրայ զէնք բացուած է՝ «Կեցիր» ազդարարութեան չհամակերպելուն համար:

- Վերջին օրերս ձեռքէ ղրկուած հայերու նամակներ կը բացուին եւ կը թարգմանուին, պատրուակելով թէ Մարաշի հետ հայոց հաղորդակցութեան մասին կը կասկածին:

- Կարգ մը թուրքեր իրենց ծանօթ հայերը կը զգուշացնեն եւ ջարդի երկիւղ կը յայտնեն: Հակառակ ասոնց, կուսակալը ընդհանուր կերպով վստահութիւն ներշնչել կ'ուզէ եւ կ'ըսէ թէ Սեբաստիոյ ո՛չ հայերէն եւ ո՛չ ալ թուրքերէն կը կասկածի եւ բացարձակապէս կը մերժէ ուէ ցաւալի դէպքի պատահումը:

Որոշ դէպք մը եւ պարագայ մը չկայ, սակայն երեւոյթները սպառնալից են եւ ժողովուրդին համար ահաբեկիչ:

Gemlik (from the primate of Bursa)—February 8

There is an Armenian community of fifty families here, mostly gathered from the surrounding villages. They have a school with twenty-five male and female students and a monthly budget of thirty liras. There are now 100–120 people in the nearby village of Şahinyurdu [Benli]. They came together during the deportation and heroically took refuge in the mountains. After the armistice, they managed to reorganize around Hovhannes Aleksanian, who, taking advantage of the general amnesty, had returned to the village. Şahinyurdu, in the past, had seven thousand Armenian residents or about seven hundred households. Today, it is a nest of ruins. Thirty elderly people were left in the village at the time of the deportation, ostensibly being pitied, but after the villagers had gone, the archpriest of the village, Father Krikor Tavitian, a disabled eighty-five-year-old man, was taken, dumped in the bushes, and burned alive along with thirty companions. Hovhannes Aleksanian dug a grave with his sword in the mountain and assembled their bones there. Elsewhere, a father and son were buried alive, tied back-to-back. There are still exposed and unburied piles of bones in the mountains, among which children's bones can also be seen. Among the murdered, there were also vacationing soldiers killed by order of the local military major, who is still in office.

• In Gemlik, a prominent Turk visited the Armenian primate and told him that there was a strong Milli organization here as well. He [the Turk] complained that they are harassing and demanding large sums of money. He said that a fifteen-member Milli force, composed of people sentenced to death and hard work, had already left for Orhangazi to collect money. So far, there is no direct movement against the Armenians, but horror and panic hang over the Armenians like the sword of Damocles.

Maraş (telegram)—February 15

(Signed: Abdalian Nshan; Minas; Chorbadjian Hovhannes; Abdullah Verdian; Shahanian Nigoghos; Halatian Shukri; archpriest of the Latin church, Baljian; Shamlian Asadour, member of the neighborhood council; Chorbadjian Garabed; Aghazarian Sarkis)

So far, we have lived amicably with our Turkish and Muslim compatriots, and there has been no discriminatory incident between us. But with the provocation of a few propagandists sent to our country by the French a few months ago, under the pretext that the lives of the Christian people were insecure after the retreat of the British army, the need for another force [replacing the British] was pointed out. In this way, the French captured the city at the end of December, and from the first days onward, they organized incidents that disrupted the city's security. The French staged demonstrations through people whom the propagandists had appeased, punished those committed to Turkish friendship, set fire to the city on January 21 to massacre the Muslims, and after a twenty-two-day war to capture the city, they shelled and destroyed three-quarters of the city and then fled. All the complaints against Muslims had absolutely no purpose other than to incite hatred between the two [Muslim and Christian] elements. Nevertheless, we are informing you that after the withdrawal of the French, our Muslim compatriots again have offered their old friendship and honored us.

Maraş (telegram)—February 15

(Signed: Ohannes Mouradian; Priest . . . Kebadian; Dr. Avedis, Khoren; Avedis, Armenian Catholic representative; Bedros Der Hagopian; Hagop Kulujian; Khachadour Kalpakjian, [Apostolic] Armenian representative; Dajad Dakesian; Dr. Souabian)

1. The French forcibly occupied several houses and churches.

Կէմլէյիկ (Պրուսայի Առաջնորդէն) – 8 Փետրուար

Հոս կը գտնուի 50 տունով հայ գաղութ մը, մեծ մասամբ շրջակայ գիւղերէ հաւաքուած: Ունին վարժարան մը 25 երկսեռ ուսանողներով, ամսական 30 ոսկի պիւտճէով: Մերձակայ Պէնլի գիւղը այժմ կան 100–120 հոգի, որոնք հաւաքուելով տարագրութեան միջոցին դիւցազնաբար լեռ ապաստանած եւ յետոյ զինադադարէն յետոյ ընդհանուր ներումէն օգտուելով գիւղ դարձած Յովհաննէս Ալեքսանեանի շուրջը, կրցած են վերակազմուիլ: Պէնլի երբեմն ունէր 7000 բնակիչ հայ, իբր 700 տուն: Այսօր աւերակներու բոյն մըն է: Տարագրութեան ատեն երեսունի չափ ծերեր գիւղը թողուցած են իբր թէ արգահատելով ու գիւղացիին մեկնելէն յետոյ գիւղին աւագերէց Տէր Գրիգոր քահանայ Դաւիթեանը, 85-ամեայ անդամալոյծ ծերունին, տարած մացառներու մէջ ձգած ու ողջ ողջ այրած են իր 30 ընկերներուն հետ: Յովհաննէս Ալեքսանեան, իր սուրովը գերեզման փորած ու անոնց ոսկերոտիքը ամփոփած է լերան մէջ: Ուրիշ տեղ մը հայր եւ որդի կռնակ կռնակի կապած՝ ողջ ողջ թաղած են: Դեռ անպատսպար եւ անթաղ կը մնան լեռները ոսկորի կոյտեր, որոնց մէջ կը նշմարուին մանուկներու ոսկորներ ալ: Հոն սպաննուածներուն մէջ են նաեւ օդափոխութեան եկած զինուորները, որոնք սպաննուած են տեղւոյս զինուորական հազարապետին հրամանով, որ դեռ իր պաշտօնը կը պահէ:

- Կեմլեյէկի մէջ թուրք երեւելի մը հայոց Առաջնորդ[ին] այցելեց եւ յայտնեց թէ Միլլի ուժեղ կազմակերպութիւն մը կայ հոս եւս, եւ գանգատ յայտնեց թէ կը նեղեն ու մեծագումար դրամներ կը պահանջեն: Յայտնեց միանգամայն թէ մահուան ու թիապարտութեան դատապարտուածներէ կազմուած 15 հոգինոց Միլլի ոյժ մը այսօր իսկ Օրխան-Կազի մեկնած են՝ գանձումի նպատակով: Առ այժմ հայութեան դէմ ուղղակի շարժում մը չկայ, բայց արհաւիրքն ու սարսափը Դամոկլեան սուրի մը պէս կախուած է հայոց գլխուն:

Մարաշ (հեռագիր) – 15 Փետրուար

(Ստորագրեալ՝ Ապտալեան Նշան, Մինաս, Չորպաճեան Յովհաննէս, Ապտուլլահ Վերտեան, Շահանեան Նիկողոս, Հալաթեան Շիւքրի, Լատին Եկեղեցւոյ աւագերէց Պալճեան, Շամլեան Ասատուր թաղական, Չորպաճեան կարապետ, Աղազարեան Խաչէր, Գազազեան Սարգիս)

Հակառակ որ մինչեւ ցարդ մեր թուրք եւ իսլամ հայրենակիցներուն հետ բարեկամութեամբ ապրած եւ մեր միջեւ խռովութեան ոեւէ դէպք պատահած չէ, քանի մը ամիս առաջ ֆրանսացիներու կողմէ մեր երկիրը ղրկուած քանի մը բռոպականթիսթներու գրգռութեամբ, իբր թէ քրիստոնեայ ժողովուրդին կեանքը անապահով ըլլալուն համար, անգլիական գրաւման բանակին քաշուելէն վերջ, ուրիշ ուժի մը գոյութեան պէտքը ցոյց տուին: Այս կերպով Դեկտեմբերի վերջերը քաղաքը գրաւեցին եւ առաջին օրերէն սկսեալ քաղաքին ապահովութիւնը խանգարող դէպքեր կազմակերպեցին: Ֆրանսացիք բռօբականթիսթներու կողմէ սիրաշահուած անձերու կողմէ ցոյցեր կազմակերպեցին, թուրքերու բարեկամութեան յանձնառու եղողները պատժեցին եւ Յունուար 21ին իսլամները ջարդելու համար քաղաքը կրակի տուին եւ քաղաքը գրաւելու համար 22 օրուան պատերազմէ վերջ քաղաքին երեք քառորդը թնդանօթի բռնելով քանդելէ յետոյ փախան: Իսլամներու հանդէպ յայտնուած բոլոր գանգատները բացարձակապէս ուրիշ նպատակ չունէին, եթէ ոչ երկու տարրերու մէջ ատելութիւն առաջ բերել: Այսուհանդերձ ֆրանսացիներուն քաշուելէն յետոյ, մեր իսլամ հայրենակիցները դարձեալ իրենց վաղեմի բարեկամութիւնը ընծայեցին եւ մեզի պատուեցին, ինչ որ ձեզի կ'մացնենք:

Մարաշ (հեռագիր) – 15 Փետրուար

(Ստորագրեալ՝ Օհաննէս Մուրատեան, ... քահանայ Քէպապեան, Տքթ. Աւետիս, Խորէն, Հայ Կաթոլիկ ներկայացուցիչ՝ Աւետիս, Պետրոս Տէր Յակոբեան, Յակոբ Գըլըճեան, [Առաքելական] Հայոց ներկայացուցիչ՝ Խաչատուր Գալբաքճեան, Տաճատ Տաքեսեան, Տոքթ. Սուապեան)

1- Ֆրանսացիներ բռնութեամբ քանի մը տուներ եւ եկեղեցիներ գրաւեցին:

2. They forcibly armed the Armenian youth and incited them against the Turks.

3. By finding out those who were friends with the Turks, they threatened, imprisoned, and took some away with them.

4. By setting the city on fire, they caused the deaths of thousands of Armenians, then they got lost.

5. Having the desire to live together with our Turkish compatriots, as we have done for centuries in our homeland, we curse the Armenians whom inciters and foreign money bought.

6. Be informed that after the withdrawal of the French, there has been no violation of life, property, and honor, nor any massacre and that our lives are in a completely safe state.

2- Հայ երիտասարդները բռնի զինեցին եւ թուրքերու դէմ զրգռեցին:

3- Թուրքերու բարեկամները հասկնալով սպառնալիք ըրին, բանտարկեցին եւ մէկ մասն ալ մէկտեղ տարին:

4- Քաղաքը կրակի տալով հազարաւոր հայոց մահուան պատճառ եղան եւ կորսուեցան գացին:

5- Դարերէ ի վեր եղածին պէս մեր հայրենիքին մէջ թուրք հայրենակիցներու հետ մէկտեղ ապրելու ցանկութիւնը ունենալով զրգռիչներու եւ օտար դրամով գնուած հայերը կ'անիծենք:

6- Փրանսացիներու քաշուելէն յետոյ, կեանքի, ինչքի եւ պատիւի ոեւէ բռնաբարութիւն եւ ոեւէ ջարդ պատահած չըլլալը եւ մեր կեանքը բոլորովին ապահով վիճակի մէջ գտնուիլը կ'իմացնենք:

[Insecurity] Notebook Number 7
February–March 1920

Samsun (from the primate)—February 2

A large rally was held in Samsun on February 1 in the presence of armed çetes. Fiery speeches were made, advocating taking back İzmir, keeping İstanbul, and not giving an inch of land to anyone else. The people were invited to arm themselves and be ready to shed their last drop of blood. During the rally, it was said, among others: "The Christians, whom we have so far kept and safeguarded as beloved subjects entrusted to us, unfortunately, are snakes that we kept warm in our bosom, and now they want to bite us from everywhere. Be ready to crush the heads of those snakes as soon as we give the order." These words have had a very disturbing effect on the Armenians, who think about ways for self-defense. These issues have been reported to the local Anglo-French representatives. The Armenians also submitted a reprimand to the district governor, who assured the people not to be afraid.

Kilis (from the National Union)—December 30, 1919

The Armenians of Kilis, more than one thousand families, upon their return from deportation naked, hungry, and languished, saw that most of their houses had been demolished, their gardens and trees uprooted, and the threshing floors occupied. Of the returning Armenians who had survived slaughter and starvation, most are orphans and widows. When the British army captured Kilis, all the Armenians who were sympathetic to the Allies had high hopes. The British provided good financial aid, opened an orphanage [for the orphans] and a shelter for the widows, distributed relief to the poor, and collected the women and girls driven from distant cities to Der-Zor. They even began registering the ruined houses, supposedly to restore them to their original condition. It was also said that there would be compensation for the damages. A committee made up of Armenian and Turkish members was formed. All the legal actions taken in connection with the deportation were declared null upon an order from İstanbul, and most of the Armenians' real estate and those portions of movable property that could be recovered were returned partially. These measures provided some comfort, although not completely satisfactory because the perpetrators were still present.

But when the British withdrew, the situation worsened. All the subsidies provided to orphanages, schools, the poor, and migrants were discontinued. Then, French troops arrived to occupy the city, and after many requests, only some dismal help was given to the school. The work to compensate the Armenians for damages and losses and [to] return the seized property to the rightful owners ceased, even though the French commander had promised to take the committee under his leadership and continue the work and protect Armenian rights. Indeed, a new committee was called upon, but the lieutenant governor presented an order from the ministry [of interior] dated December 2, stating, "The committee is not a legitimate assembly . . . it can only do something through the willingness of both sides . . . when a Turk declines to give back a property he holds, the committee cannot enforce its decision," and so on. This order contradicted the previous instructions and was a clear expression of anti-Armenian policy. The Armenian members of the committee told the French commander: "We did not expect anything good from the same government that deported and massacred us. Do you have the authority to pursue justice?" To the extent we have understood his words, the French commander appears to be more inclined to follow the instructions of the Sublime Porte.

Given this reality, the Armenians of Kilis want to know with great interest: (a) Is the negligence of Armenians' rights by France a consequence of the French commander's personal policy and preferences, or has the French state, for reasons unknown to us, decided to persecute the Armenians and

[Անապահովութեան] Տետր Թիւ 7
1920 Փետրուար – 1920 Մարտ

Սամսոն (Առաջնորդէն) – 2 Փետրուար

Փետրուար 1ին մեծ միթինկ կը կատարուի Սամսոնի մէջ, զինեալ չէթէներու ներկայութեան: Բոցավառ ճառեր կը խօսուին Իզմիրը ետ առնելու, Պոլիսը պահելու եւ թիզ մըն հող ուրիշին չտալու համար: Ժողովուրդը կը հրաւիրուի զինուիլ եւ պատրաստ գտնուիլ մինչեւ իր վերջին արեան կաթիլը թափելու: Միթինկին մէջ կ'ըսուի ի մէջ այլոց. «քրիստոնեաները զորոնք ցարդ իբր մեր սիրելի աւանդները պահեցինք պահպանեցինք, դժբաղդաբար օձեր են եղեր որ մեր ծոցին մէջ տաքցուցեր ենք եւ որոնք հիմա ամէն կողմէ մեզ խայթել կ'ուզեն: Պատրաստ գտնուեցէք որ երբ հրաման ընենք, անմիջապէս ջախջախէք այդ օձերուն գլուխները»: Այս խօսքերը մեծապէս կը յուզեն հայերը, որոնք կը խորհին ինքնապաշտպանութեան միջոցներու վրայ: Այս խնդիրները հաղորդուած են տեղւոյն անգլեւֆրանսական ներկայացուցիչներուն: Մութասարըֆին ալ հայոց կողմէ դիտողութիւն կ'ըլլայ այս մասին եւ որ կ'ապահովցնէ թէ ժողովուրդը թող չվախնայ:

Քիլիս (Ազգային Միութենէն) – 30 Դեկտեմբեր 1919

Քիլիսի 1000 տունէ աւելի հայութիւնը տարագրութենէ դարձին, մերկ, անօթի, ծիւրած վիճակի մէջ, իր տուները մեծ մասամբ հիմէն քանդուած, պարտէզները, ծառերը արմատախիլ եղած եւ կալւ-ըը գրաւուած տեսաւ: Վերադարձող հայերը, որոնք ջարդէ եւ սովէ ազատուած էին, մեծ մասամբ որբերէ եւ այրիներէ կը բաղկանան: Երբ անգլիական բանակը Քիլիսը գրաւեց, բոլոր հայերը որոնք Համաձայնութեան համակիր եղած են, մեծ յոյսեր ունեցան: Անգլիացիք դրամական լաւ օժանդա-կութիւններ ցոյց տուին, որբանոց եւ այրիանոց բացին, աղքատներուն նպաստ բաժնեցին, հեռաւոր քաղաքներէ դէպի Տէր-Զօր քշուած կիները եւ աղջիկները ժողվեցին: Նոյնիսկ սկսան աւերակ տուները գրել որպէս թէ ասոնք իրենց առաջուան վիճակին մէջ դնելու համար: Նոյնպէս ըսուեցաւ թէ վնասուց հատուցում պիտի ըլլար: Կազմուեցաւ հայ եւ թուրք անդամներէ կազմուած մասնա-խումբ մը եւ Պոլսէն տրուած հրահանգի մը վրայ տարագրութեան առթիւ կատարուած բոլոր օրինական գործողութիւնները չեղեալ նկատուեցան եւ հայերուն անշարժ կալուածներէն մեծ մասն եւ շարժուն գոյքերէն անոնք որ կրնային գտնուիլ մասամբ վերադարձուեցան: Ասոնք քիչ շատ մխիթարական երեւոյթներ էին եթէ կատարեալ գոհացում մը չէր, քանի որ ոճրագործները դեռ մէջտեղն էին:

Սակայն երբ անգլիացիք քաշուեցան, կացութիւնը ծանրացաւ. որբանոցի, դպրոցի, աղքատ-ներու, գաղթականներու տրուած բոլոր նպաստները դադրեցան: Յետոյ ֆրանսական զինուորներ եկան գրաւել քաղաքը եւ շատ մը դիմումներէ յետոյ միայն դպրոցին պզտիկ օգնութիւն մը կ'ըլլայ: Իսկ հայոց վնասներուն եւ կորուստներուն դարման տալու, գրաւումները իրենց օրինաւոր տէրե-րուն դարձնելու գործը կասած է, հակառակ անոր որ ֆրանսացի հրամատարը խոստացած էր մասնախումբը իր նախագահութեան տակ առնել եւ գործը շարունակել, իրաւունքը պահպանել: Արդարեւ նոր մասնախումբ մըն ալ կոչուեցաւ, սակայն Դեկտեմբեր 2 թուակիր եկած հրահանգ մը՝ նախարարութենէն, գայմագամը կը ներկայացնէ ուր կ'ըսուի թէ «էնճիւմէնը օրինական ժողով մը չէ ... ան միմիայն երկու կողմերը յօժար[ե]ցնելով կրնայ գործ մը ընել ... թուրքը երբ իր ձեռքը եղած կալուածը դարձնել չուզէ՝ էնճիւմէնը չի կրնար իր որոշումը գործադրել եւայլն»: Այս հրահանգը կը հակասէր առջի հրահանգներուն եւ հակահայ քաղաքականութեան բացորոշ մէկ արտայայտու-թիւնն էր: Մասնախումբին հայ անդամները ըսին ֆրանսացի հրամատարին թէ «մենք զմեզ տարագրող, ջարդող այս կառավարութենէն արդէն բարիք չէինք սպասեր: Դուք արդարութիւնը հետապնդելու իրաւասութիւն ունի՞ք»: Ֆրանսացի հրամատարը՝ որչափ կը հասկցուի իր խօսքերէն, աւելի տրամադրութիւն ցոյց կու տայ Բ. Դրան հրահանգները գործադրել:

Այս իրողութեան առջեւ, Քիլիսի հայութիւնը մեծ հետաքրքրութեամբ կ'ուզէ իմանալ թէ՝ Ա.

encourage the persecutors? (b) What is the motive behind these contradictory instructions given by the Ottoman government? (c) Where and to whom should we turn for help because of the prevailing complete insecurity, especially in the vicinity of this city, where several Armenians have been killed?

Aleppo (from the Prelacy)—February 2

The Armenians settled in and around Aleppo, and parts of Cilicia are in critical condition due to the activities of Turkish çetes. After hardly being able to engage in peaceful and creative work during a short period of rest, they are now living under the threat of massacre. Murder cases, frequently occurring recently, show us that we are on the eve of a massacre. Maraş and all its environs, from Gaziantep [Ayntab], Urfa, Kilis, and Aleppo to İskenderun, echo violent killings, in which the Turkish actors seem to have stepped up their activities to influence the impending decision on their fate. In Maraş, the Turks gathered in mosques, think of ways to organize the massacre better. The entire male population in Kale [Camustil] has been massacred, Armenian travelers on the road are disappearing, and killings continue daily in Gaziantep. The communication between Maraş and Gaziantep has been severed completely, [and] the horror is growing daily. The French army is insufficient and weak.

News has been received of killings and robberies between İskenderun and Aleppo by two- to three-hundred-strong Turkish çetes. In broad daylight, threats and killings in Gaziantep's market have terrorized Kilis and its environs. The French guard troops of Bi[r]ecik have fled under the threat of the Arabs, and Turkish gendarmes have gathered the Armenians in the church while waiting for an order from the[ir] highest authority. This news was received three days ago, but it is thought that the situation is still going on. The Baghdad railway has been cut off by the Arabs beyond the Jarablus station, pushing back the French force. Many French officers are missing or have been killed in battle.

Aleppo (from the National Union)—February 2

The agitation of Milli çetes is growing day by day both in Cilicia of the Plains and especially in Mountainous Cilicia. According to Mustafa Kemal's plan, the strike is aimed at the very existence of Armenians. The government is arming the Turks everywhere, [there is] enmity against the Armenians everywhere, and terrible news is coming from Maraş and its environs, Gaziantep [Ayntab], Kilis, and İskenderun. In mid-January alone, 105 Armenians were killed in those areas. And in Maraş, the night-watch mercilessly kill the Armenians they meet. There is absolute insecurity in the city. Hundreds of armed Turks gather in the mosques in Armenian neighborhoods every night. The men of Kale [Camustil] village, an hour away from Maraş, have been wiped out. Eight passengers from Süleymanlı [Zeytun] were killed on the Ceyhan bridge in broad daylight. French soldiers discovered their corpses. Leaving the city has become entirely impossible, while at the same time, the free movement of the massacrers has become a reason for the entire Armenian population to close their shops and confine themselves to their homes, forgoing earnings, which is a bloodless terror for the Armenians who have recently returned from deportation. People arriving from Gaziantep testify that the Turks are arming themselves quickly. Fifteen [Armenian] people have been killed and wounded. The same horrible situation prevails in Kilis, where there are dead people.

Արդեօ՞ք հայերու իրաւունքներուն Ֆրանսայի կողմէ անտեսումը հետեւանք է Քիլիսի ֆրանսացի հրամատարին անձնական քաղաքականութեան եւ նախասիրութեանց, թէ ֆրանսական պետութիւնը մեզի անծանօթ պատճառներով ինքն ալ որոշած է հայերը հալածել, եւ հալածողները քաջալերել: Բ. Օսմանեան կառավարութեան կողմէ տրուած այս հակասական հրահանգներուն մէջ ի՞նչ շարժառիթ կայ: Գ. Տիրող կատարեալ անապահովութեան համար, մասնաւորապէս քաղաքիս շրջակայքը, ուր ճամբու վրայ մի քանի հայեր սպաննուեցան, ո՞ւր եւ որո՞ւ դիմէ:

Հալէպ (Առաջնորդարանէն) – 2 Փետրուար

Հալէպ[ի] շրջանակին եւ Կիլիկիոյ մէկ մասին մէջ հաստատուած հայերը ճգնաժամային վիճակի մէջ են, շնորհիւ թուրք չէթէներու գործունէութեան: Կարճ հանգստութեան մը մէջ հազիւ թէ խաղաղ եւ ստեղծագործ աշխատանքի սկսած, հիմա կոտորածի սպառնալիքի մը տակ կը գտնուին: Սպանութեան դէպքեր, որոնք վերջերս յաճախ կը պատահին, ջարդի մը նախօրեակին մէջ գտնուիլնիս ցոյց կուտան: Մարաշ իր բոլոր շրջականներով, Այնթապ, Ուրֆա, Քիլիս եւ Հալէպէն մինչեւ Իսկէնտէրուն արձագանգ կուտան խժդուժ սպանութիւններու, որոնց դերակատար թուրքերը կարծես ազդելու համար իրենց ճակատագրին մօտալուտ որոշման վրայ, մեծ թափ տուած են իրենց գործունէութեան: Մարաշի մէջ թուրքերը մզկիթներու մէջ հաւաքուած կը մտածեն ջարդը լաւ կազմակերպելու միջոցներու վրայ: Ճամըսթըլի մէջ ամբողջ այր բնակչութիւնը կը ջարդեն, ճամբու վրայ պատահած հայ ճամբորդները կ'անհետացնեն, Այնթապի մէջ ամէն օր սպանութիւնները կը շարունակուին: Մարաշի եւ Այնթապի միջեւ յարաբերութիւնները բոլորովին խզուած են, սարսափը օրէ օր կը մեծնայ: Ֆրանսական բանակը անբաւական է եւ տկար:

Լուր առնուեցաւ թէ 200–300 հոգիէ բաղկացեալ թուրք չէթէներու կողմէ Իսկէնտէրունի եւ Հալէպի միջեւ սպանութիւններ եւ կողոպուտներ գործուած են: Այնթապի շուկային մէջ օր ցերեկով գործուած սպառնալիքները եւ սպանութիւնները սարսափ ազդած են Քիլիսի եւ շրջակայից մէջ: Դի[ը]էճիկի ֆրանսական պահակ զօրքերը արաբներու կողմէն սպառնալիքի ենթարկուելով փախած են եւ հայերը եկեղեցիին մէջ հաւաքելով թուրք ժանտարման հրամանի կը սպասէ բարձրագոյն իշխանութենէն: Այս լուրը երեք օր առաջ առնուած է, սակայն կը կարծուի թէ տակաւին վիճակը կը շարունակուի: Պաղտատի երկաթուղին կտրուած է արաբներու կողմէն Ճարապլուսի կայարանէն անդին, ֆրանսական ոյժը ետ մղուելով: Շատ մը ֆրանսացի սպաներ անյայտացած են կամ կռիւի մէջ սպաննուած:

Հալէպ (Ազգային Միութենէն) – 2 Փետրուար

Միլլի-չէթայական խմորումը օր աւուր կը մեծնայ թէ՛ դաշտային եւ թէ մանաւանդ լեռնային Կիլիկիոյ մէջ: Հարուածը ուղղուած է հայոց գոյութեան, Մուսթաֆա Քէմալի ծրագրով: Ամէն կողմ թուրքերը կը զինուին կառավարութեան կողմէ, ամէն տեղ թշնամանք հայոց դէմ, եւ սոսկալի լուրեր կը հասնին Մարաշի ու շրջականներու, Այնթապի, Քիլիսի եւ Ալէքսանտրէթի կողմերէն: Միայն յունվարի կէսին 105 հայեր սպաննուած են այդ կողմերը: Իսկ Մարաշի մէջ գիշերապահ ոստիկաններ անխնայ կերպով կը սպաննեն հանդիպող հայը. քաղաքին մէջ բացարձակ անապահովութիւն կը տիրէ. հայ թաղերու մզկիթներուն մէջ ամէն գիշեր կը հաւաքուին հարիւրաւոր զինուած թուրքեր: Մարաշէն 1½ ժամ հեռու Ճամըսթալ գիւղի այրերը ջնջուած են: Ճիհանի կամուրջին վրայ սպաննուած են օր ցերեկով 8 զէյթունցի ճամբորդներ, որոնց դիակները ֆրանսական զինուորներու կողմէ երեւան հանուած են եւ քաղաքէն դուրս ելնել բոլորովին անկարելի դարձած է եւ միեւնոյն ատեն ջարդարարներու ազատօրէն շրջիլը պատճառ դարձած է որ ամբողջ հայ ազգաբնակութիւնը՝ փակած իր խանութները՝ տուներու մէջ պահուած մնայ առանց շահու, ինչ որ տարագրութենէ նոր դարձող հայերուն համար սպիտակ տէրօր մըն է: Այնթապէն հասնողներ կը վկայեն թէ թուրքերը փութով կը զինուին: 15 հոգի սպաննուած եւ վիրաւորուած են: Նոյն ահաւոր կացութիւնը նաեւ Քիլիսի մէջ, ուր մեռեալներ կան դարձեալ:

Twice, more than ten Armenian coachmen have been killed on the road to İskenderun. [Traveling] Turks are always left free. Communication with Urfa has come to a complete halt. The railway line is cut off beyond the Jarablus bridge, and the situation is similar for the Armenians of Birecik. The two hundred thousand Armenians living in this region are in grave danger judging by these phenomena because the French forces, in particular, are insufficient.

Aleppo (from the plenipotentiary of the National Assistance, Dr. Kachperouni)—February 2
It has been impossible to receive official information from the Maraş region since January 20. Even the French have no means of communication. They have been able to understand this much only: By the end of January 20, three or four neighborhoods in Maraş have been burned, partly by the Turks and partly by French artillery. There are thousands of human casualties. In the last eight to ten days, ten to fifteen murders have been committed by the Turks in the Amik [Amuq] plain and three more in the area of Hasanbeyli. One to two miles of the railway line between Jarablus and Karapınar (Urfa Station) is shattered. Communications with Urfa have been severed. The French soldiers are allegedly pursuing the criminals. The Armenians of Birecik are locked in a church, and the Turks have installed guards. The fifteen to twenty Frenchmen who were there have taken refuge in Jarablus, and they do not know what happened to the rest of the people of Dönüklü [Fındıcak] or to the population of neighboring Dereköy and Kişifli (about fifteen hundred) who had been left completely defenseless.

In Gaziantep [Ayntab], Armenians are terrified and cannot leave their homes. Fourteen Armenians have been killed in the last week. The telegraph and telephone lines between Gaziantep and Qatma have been cut.

The Turks and the Arabs are said to have agreed to a treaty of twenty-one articles, the contents of which remain unknown.

It has been heard that three Americans were killed between Kilis and Gaziantep.

Tekirdağ (from the vicar general)—February 26
According to information received from Malkara, the Milli organization is organized effectively and now operating openly. Nearby villagers move around with their weapons on their shoulders because they have received them from the government. Almost a month and a half ago, guns were transported to Malkara overnight in a jam-packed automobile and distributed to the villagers. As many as 150 volunteer Circassians have been dispersed to organize Turkish villages. Six of them roam the city as watchmen at night.

On the day of the Mardi gras, the houses of three Armenians were searched for weapons, but nothing was found. Naturally, this has disturbed the people, especially since after the Balkan War, those çetes who had burned and looted Malkara and killed the Armenians there are again heading the same offices.

Notices have been posted on the walls of Malkara (a copy was enclosed [in the letter received]) to provoke the Turks.

• The situation is almost the same in Tekirdağ. The organization is perfect. The locals and the villagers are armed. Every day secret meetings are held, all with the purpose of massacring and plundering. We are living in critical moments. Armenians are exercising prudence.

• Two days ago, four drunken Turks traveled to the quarter called Kurnal in a carriage and started swearing at the Armenians, flashing their weapons, and so on, to provoke agitation and start acting. However, young Armenians acted prudently, took the weapons from their hands, and did not let anything happen.

Ալէքսանտրէթի ճամբուն վրայ երկու անգամ սպաննուեցան 10էն աւելի հայ կառապաններ, թուրքերը միշտ ազատ ձգուելով: Դէպի Ուրֆա հաղորդակցութիւնը բոլորովին դադրած է: Կտրուած է երկաթուղիի գիծը Ճարապլուսի կամուրջէն անդին եւ նոյն[ն է] դրութիւնը Պիրէճիկի հայութեան համար: 200,000 հայեր որոնք այս շրջանին մէջ կ'ապրին լրջօրէն վտանգի տակ են այս երեւոյթներէն դատելով, քանի որ մանաւանդ ֆրանսական ոյժերը անբաւական են:

Հալէպ (Ազգային Խնամատարութեան լիազօր Տոքթ. Քաջբերունիէ) – 2 Փետրուար

20 Յունվարէն սկսեալ Մարաշի շրջանէն ոչ մի պաշտօնական տեղեկութիւն կարելի եղած է ստանալ: Մինչեւ անգամ ֆրանսացիք ոեւէ յարաբերութեան միջոց չունին. միայն այսչափը կրցած են հասկնալ թէ Յունվար 20էն վերջ Մարաշի 3–4 թաղերը այրուած են մէկ մասը թուրքերու եւ մաս մըն ալ ֆրանսական թնդանօթներու միջոցաւ. մարդկային կորուստներու թիւը 1000ներու կը հասնի: Վերջին 8–10 օրուան միջոցին Ամուգի դաշտին մէջ 10–15 սպանութիւններ պատահեցան թուրքերու կողմէն. 3 հատ ալ Հասան-Պէյլիի շրջակաները: Ճարապլուսի եւ Գարաբունարի (Ուրֆայի Սթասիօնը) միջեւ երկաթուղիի գիծը խորտակուած է 1–2 մղոն երկարութեամբ: Ուրֆայի հետ յարաբերութիւնները խզուած են: Իբր թէ ֆրանսական զինուորները կը հետապնդեն չարագործները: Պիրէճիկի հայերը բանտարկուած են եկեղեցիի մէջ ու պահակներ դրուած են թուրքերու կողմէ, եւ գտնուող 15–20 ֆրանս[ացիները] Ճարապլուս ապաստանած են եւ չեն գիտեր թէ ինչ եղած են մնացեալ ֆնտճազգիներ եւ իրենց դրացի Տէրէքէօյի եւ Քիշիֆլիի բնակչութիւնը (մօտ 1500 հոգի), որոնք բոլորովին անպաշտպան մնացած էին:

Այնթապի մէջ հայերը սարսափի մէջ են եւ տուներէն դուրս չեն կրնար ելլել եւ վերջին շաբթուան ընթացքին 14 հայեր սպաննուած են. Այնթապի եւ Գաթմայի միջեւ հեռագրի եւ թէլէֆօնի թելերը կտրուած են:

Կ'ըսուի թէ թուրքերը եւ արաբները համաձայնած են 21 յօդուածներէ բաղկացեալ պայմանագրութեամբ մը, որուն պարունակութիւնը անծանօթ կը մնայ:

Լուեցաւ թէ Քիլիսի եւ Այնթապի միջեւ 3 ամերիկացիներ սպաննուած են:

Ռօտոսթօ (Առաջնորդական Փոխանորդէն) – 26 Փետրուար

Մալկարայէն առնուած տեղեկութեանց համաձայն, *Միլլի Թէշքիլաթը* զօրաւոր կերպով կազմակերպուած է եւ հիմա յայտնապէս կը գործէ: Շրջակայ գիւղացիները զէնքերը ուսերնին կը շրջին, քանի որ կառավարութիւնը տուած է: Գրեթէ մէկուկէս ամիս առաջ օթօմօպիլով լեցուն զէնք գիշերանց Մալկարա տարած եւ գիւղացիներուն բաժնած են: 150ի չափ կամաւոր Չէրքէզներ թուրք գիւղեր ցրուած են կազմակերպելու համար: Ասոնցմէ վեց հատ քաղաքին մէջ իբր գիշերապահ կը պտտին:

Բարեկենդանի օրը երեք հայերու տուն կը խուզարկուի զէնքի համար. սակայն չեն գտած: Բնական է որ ասիկա ժողովուրդը յուզած է, մանաւանդ որ Պալքանեան պատերազմէն յետոյ չէթէ ըլլալով Մալկարան այրած, թալանած, հայերը սպաննողները կրկին նոյն պաշտօնին գլուխն են:

Մալկարայի պատերու վրայ փակցուած են ազդեր (օրինակը ներփակ էր), որով թուրքերը գրգռելու ձեռնարկ կ'ըլլայ:

- Ռօտոսթոյի մէջ ալ գրեթէ կացութիւնը նոյնն է. կազմակերպութիւնը կատարեալ է. տեղացին եւ գիւղացին զինուած [են]. ամէն օր գաղտնի ժողովներ՝ որոնց ամէնուն ալ նպատակը ջարդել, թալանել է: Ճգնաժամային վայրկեաններ կ'ապրինք: Հայերը խոհեմութեամբ կը վարուին:

- Երկու օր առաջ 4 թուրք զինով վիճակի մէջ Գունեալ ըսուած թաղը կ'երթան կառքով եւ կը սկսին հայհոյութիւններով հայոց հասցէին լուտանքներ արձակել, զէնք ցոյց տալ եւայլն, որպէսզի գրգռութիւն առաջ գայ եւ գործի սկսին: Սակայն հայ երիտասարդներ խոհեմութեամբ կը վարուին, զէնքերը անոնց ձեռքէն կ'առնեն եւ դէպքի տեղի չեն տար:

Tekirdağ (from the vicar general)—February 27

The Milli organization is gaining momentum in these areas, and sad news is coming daily from Greek villages around Malkara. The notables of the Armenian and Greek society convened today and decided to send a delegation of two Armenians and two Greeks to İstanbul to present the alarming situation.

Adana (from M[ihran] Damadian)—February 27

There were two panicky situations in Adana during the past five days, on Tuesday and Wednesday (February 24 and 25). The first took place at eight o'clock in the morning on the occasion of a Greek gunning down another Greek in the market because of a love affair. People thought the "incident" had begun. The matter was clarified shortly after. The next day there was a greater panic. The French troops were conducting a defensive operation outside the city at night. On that occasion, traffic from and into the city was banned until a particular hour late in the morning. The people panicked, assuming that the city was under attack. People closed their shops and locked themselves at home. Around noon, the top administrator of the city, Mr. Brémond, the governor, the representative of the [Armenian] National Delegation, the primate, the spiritual leader of the Armenian Catholics, the Armenian Protestant minister, and the members of the [Armenian] National Union, accompanied by Turkish, Arab, and Greek dignitaries and ulemas [learned Muslims] formed a procession and toured the city from one end to the other, pleading for people to open their shops. However, three-quarters of the shops remained closed until evening. Tonight, an ultimatum made by the French authority was announced to the public; it demanded the surrender of a large number of weapons by March 5.

According to this document, eight thousand of the twenty thousand Armenians of Maraş are there [in Adana]. Two thousand have fled. Ten thousand people, then, have been massacred in the city, aside from residents of the surrounding Armenian villages, who count one or two thousand people.

• The news from the provinces is far from comforting. Saimbeyli [Hacın] and Kozan [Sis] are well protected. Although amassed [Turkish] people and commotions surround them, and frequent killings occur on the roads, we think the danger in these parts is not imminent. The Armenians of Kadirli have taken refuge in Kozan. Mersin and Tarsus are peaceful. Dörtyol, likewise. The areas around Bahçe and Düziçi, so turbulent previously, are calm for now. The area near Andırın has become a nest of çetes. Between Belen and İslahiye, Kurt Dağı, that is, Ekbez and all the environs up to Osmaniye, indications of large-scale movements and preparations by the çetes have been observed.

Adana (from M[ihran] Damadian)—February 20

The French suddenly and secretly fled from Maraş on February 11 without any serious, fundamental reason. The Armenians, who had lost ten thousand people until then, were caught by indescribable panic. The first group of escapees, more than twenty-five hundred people, managed to follow the retreating French troops. Of a second group of two thousand people, barely twenty-five or thirty escaped Turkish bullets. Somehow this group of escapees continued its journey to Belpınar. Thence, because of the snow and the horrible snowstorm and the cold, many froze and were buried on the road. Barely eighteen hundred people reached İslahiye, arriving in inexplicable wretchedness. Nobody knows what happened to the remaining six to eight thousand Armenians in Maraş.

• Gaziantep [Ayntab] and Kilis, where there are thirty-two thousand Armenians, are in danger. The Aleppo line from Qatma to Rajo has been destroyed by the çetes, whereby French communications with the region have almost been severed. Colonel Flye-Sainte-Marie is in Gaziantep, with a part of the legion and with little force. It is said that events have already begun, and the çetes have besieged

Ռօտոսթօ (Առաջնորդական Փոխանորդէն) – 27 Փետրուար

Միլլի Թէշքիլաթը այս կողմերը սկսած է զօրանալ եւ ամէն օր Մալկարայի շրջակայ յունական գիւղերէ տխուր լուրեր կ'առնուին: Հայ եւ յոյն հասարակութեան երեւելիները գումարուելով այսօր որոշեցին Կ. Պոլիս ղրկել երկու հայերէ եւ երկու յոյներէ բաղկացեալ պատուիրակութիւն մը, կացութեան տագնապալի հանգամանքը ներկայացնելու համար:

Ատանա (Մ[իհրան] Տամատեան է) – 27 Փետրուար

Անցեալ հինգ օրերու միջոցին երկու անգամ խուճապ պատահեցաւ Ատանայի մէջ, երեքշաբթի եւ չորեքշաբթի օրերը (24 եւ 25 Փետրուար): Առաջին[ը] առտուն ժամը 8ին շուկային մէջ յոյնի մը սիրային պատճառով ուրիշ յոյնի մը գնդակահար սպաննելուն առթիւ տեղի ունեցաւ՝ կարծուելով որ «դէպքը» սկսած է: Քիչ վերջը խնդիրը լուսաբանուեցաւ: Յաջորդ օրը աւելի մեծ խուճապ պատահեցաւ: Ֆրանսացի զինուորները քաղաքին դուրսը պաշտպանողականի փորձ մը կը կատարէին գիշերով: Այդ առթիւ քաղաքէն դուրս եւ դուրսէն քաղաք երթեւեկը արգիլուեցաւ մինչեւ առտուան յառաջացած մէկ ժամը: Ժողովուրդը ենթադրելով որ քաղաքին վրայ յարձակում կ'ըլլայ, խուճապի կը մատնուի: Խանութները գոցեցին եւ տուները փակուեցան: Կէսօրին մօտ, քաղաքին վերին վարիչ Մ. Պրէմօն, վալին, Ազգային Պատուիրակութեան ներկայացուցիչը, Առաջնորդը, Հայ Կաթողիկէներու Գերապայծառը, Հայ Բողոքականաց Հովիւը, Ազգային Միութեան անդամները, ընկերացած թուրք, արաբ եւ յոյն երեւելիներու եւ *հլէմա*ներու, քաղաքին մէկ ծայրէն միւսը թափօրով պտըտեցան, ջանալով խանութները բանալ տալ: ¾ը խանութներուն մինչեւ իրիկուն փակ մնաց: Այսօր երեկոյին հանրութեան հաղորդուեցաւ ֆրանսական իշխանութեան պահանջագիրը, որով մեծ քանակութեամբ զէնքերու յանձնուիլը կը պահանջէր մինչեւ Մարտ 5:

Այս վաւերագիրին համաձայն, Մարաշի 20,000 հայերէն 8000-ը հոն են, 2000 ալ փախուստ տուած, ուրեմն 10000 հոգի քաղաքին մէջ ջարդուած են, բացի շրջակայ հայ գիւղերու բնակիչներէն, որոնց թիւը մէկ երկու հազարի կը հասնի:

- Գաւառներէ եկած լուրերը մխիթարական ըլլալէ հեռու են: Հաճըն եւ Սիս ըստ բաւականին պաշտպանութեան տակ կը գտնուին, թէեւ անոնց շուրջն ալ համախմբումներ եւ խլրտումներ կան, ինչպէս նաեւ ճամբաներու վրայ յաճախադէպ սպանութիւններ, բայց կը կարծենք թէ անմիջական չէ այս կողմերու վտանգը: Կարս-Բազարի հայերը Սիս ապաստանած են: Մերսին եւ Տարսոն խաղաղ են: Չօք-Մարզուան՝ նոյնպէս: Պաղչէի եւ Խասանիի կողմերը որ ասկէ առաջ այնքան խլրտումներ եղան՝ առ այժմ հանդարտ կ'երեւան: Անտէրունի կողմը չէթէներու բոյն դարձած է: Պէյլանի եւ Իսլահիէի միջեւ Քիւրտ Տաղը՝ Էքպէզ եւ բոլոր շրջակաները մինչեւ Օսմանիյէ, չէթական ընդարձակ շարժումներու նախանշաններ եւ պատրաստութիւններ կը նշմարուին:

Ատանա (Մ[իհրան] Տամատեան է) – 20 Փետրուար

Մարաշէն ֆրանսացիք առանց ոեւէ լուրջ, հիմնական պատճառի՝ Փետրուար 11ին յանկարծական եւ զաղտնի կերպով խոյս տուին. մինչեւ այդ, 10000ի չափ կորուստ ունեցող հայութիւնը կը մատնուի աննկարագրելի խուճապի: Առաջին փախչողներու խումբ մը, 2500է աւելի, կը յաջողի հետեւիլ նահանջող ֆրանսական զօրքերուն: 2000է բաղկացած երկրորդ խումբէ մը հազիւ 25–30ը կ'ազատուին թուրքերու գնդակներէն: Փախչողներու այս խումբը մինչեւ Պէլ Բունար աղէկ գէշ ճամբան կրնայ շարունակել. անկէ անդին տեղացած ձիւնին եւ ահռելի բուքին ու ցուրտին երեսէն, շատեր կը սառին, ճամբան կը թաղուին եւ հազիւ 1800 մարդ կը հասնի Իսլահիյէ անբացատրելի խեղճութեան մէջ: Ի՞նչ եղած են մնացած 6–8000 հայերը Մարաշի մէջ, ո՛չ ոք գիտէ:

- Այնթապ եւ Քիլիս, ուր կայ 32,000 հայութիւն, վտանգի տակ են: Հալէպի գիծը Գաթմայէն մինչեւ Ռաճօ՝ չէթէներու կողմէ քանդուած է, որով այս շրջանի հետ ֆրանսացւոց յարաբերութիւնները գրեթէ կտրուած են: Այնթապ կը գտնուի Col. Flye Ste Marie, լէգէոնի մէկ մասով եւ քիչ ուժով եւ կ'ըսուի թէ արդէն դէպքերը ծայր տուած են ու քաղաքը պաշարուած է չէթէներէ: Դիւրին է գուշակել

the city. It is easy to predict that it will not be difficult for the Turks to turn Gaziantep into a second Maraş. The fate of Kilis is dependent on Gaziantep already.

• A dangerous situation has been created in Adana. The Armenians are waiting for an attack by the Turks, and the Turks are waiting for an attack by the Armenians. A spark is enough to ignite a fire. We are in a very delicate situation. The French also have serious fears of an uprising, be it from the çetes from within or outside. They are preparing to defend the city. There is a tendency to migrate, especially among the Greeks.

Aleppo (from the vicar general)—February 9

The dangerous situation of the region under French occupation continues. The Aleppo-Damascus and Aleppo-Adana railway is in terrible danger. There is general unrest among all Turks. The Christians of Aleppo, especially the Armenians, are terrified. There are still about seven thousand [Armenian] refugees in this city and two thousand orphans with no possibility to transport them to Adana.

For four days now, mail censorship has become much more complicated. The Armenians of this area are in danger of extinction. The French authorities do not listen to the Armenian complaints and requests.

• The local government is demanding troops from Christian communities. With Sharif Faisal's order, upon the appeal of the Catholicos of Cilicia to Prince Faisal, the prince decided to make an exception for refugees and to conscript the locals, which is a disaster for the Armenians.

Bursa (from the vicar general)—February 25

The Bursan newspaper *Ertuğrul* and new publications appearing daily use provocative and poisonous language against Armenians to arm the mob against Armenians.

A fierce boycott has begun against Christians, and all the bloodthirsty beasts who committed all sorts of crimes and were fugitives for a while, have reappeared today as Milli organizers and roam the markets in armed bands, terrifying their victims of the past. Yesterday, a former [police] commissioner named Çerkes Tevfik, who, together with Mehmetcik, was notorious for beating and torturing [people] and who had killed prominent Bursans in Orhaneli [Adranos], haughtily walked past the market, armed from head to toe.

• The distribution of weapons to Turks is being carried out with great enthusiasm. Fundraising is conducted almost openly. It is no longer a secret.

Bursa (from the vicar general)—March 1

Machine guns have been placed in the highest positions in the city. Milli bands of çetes walk around with arms.

Tekirdağ (Delegate)—March 1, 1920

All government offices are engaged only in the distribution of weapons. The daily feverish activity of some influential Turkish çetes is very significant. There is a rumor among the Turks that they will regain their former status in a few days, that everything will be free for them, that they will get rich, and so on. The entire Greek and Armenian Christian population has begun to think seriously. It is said that French soldiers will come in a day or two if it is not too late for them to arrive: the danger is at the point of being fermented and may explode in a few days.

որ դժուար չ'ըլլար թուրքերուն Այնթապը երկրորդ Մարաշի վերածել: Քիլիսի բաղդը արդէն կախուած է Այնթապէն:

- Ատանայի մէջ վտանգաւոր վիճակ մը ստեղծուած է: Հայերը՝ թուրքերու կողմէ յարձակումի մը կը սպասեն, իսկ թուրքերը՝ հայերու: Կայծ մը բաւական է հրդեհը բոցավառելու համար: Խիստ փափուկ վիճակի մէջ ենք: Ֆրանսացիք ալ լուրջ վախեր ունին ներսէն եւ դուրսէն չէթէական ապստամբութենէ մը, եւ պատրաստութիւններ կը տեսնեն քաղաքը պաշտպանելու: Գաղթելու տրամադրութիւն մը կայ, մանաւանդ յունաց քով:

Հալէպ (Առաջնորդական Փոխանորդէն) – 9 Փետրուար

Ֆրանսական գրաւման տակ գտնուող շրջանակին վտանգաւոր վիճակը կը շարունակէ: Հալէպ-Դամասկոս եւ Հալէպ-Ատանա երկաթուղին սոսկալի վտանգի տակ է. ընդհանուր խլրտում կայ ամբողջ թրքաց մէջ. Հալէպի քրիստոնեայ բնակչութիւնը, մանաւանդ հայերը սարսափի մատնուած են: Քաղաքիս մէջ 7000ի մօտ տակաւին գաղթական կայ եւ 2000 որբ, որոնք Ատանա փոխադրելու կարելիութիւն չկայ:

Չորս օրէ ի վեր թղթատարական գրաքննութիւնք մեծապէս դժուարացած են: Այս շրջանակի հայութիւնը բնաջնջման վտանգի տակ է: Ֆրանսական իշխանութիւնք չեն լսեր հայոց բողոքները եւ խնդրանքները:

- Տեղական կառավարութեան կողմէ քրիստոնեայ հասարակութիւններէն զօրք կը պահանջուի: Շէրիֆ Ֆայսալի հրամանաւ Կիլիկիոյ Կաթողիկոսը առ Ն. Բարձրութիւն Էմիր Ֆէյսալ կատարած դիմումին վրայ, Էմիրը գաղթականները բացառութիւն ընելով տեղացիները զէնքի տակ առնելու որոշում տուած է, ինչ որ հայոց համար աղէտ մըն է:

Պրուսա (Առաջնորդական Փոխանորդէն) – 25 Փետրուար

Պրուսա հրատարակուող «Էրթող[ր]ուլ» լրագիրը եւ ամէն օր նոր նոր հրատարակութիւնները գրգռալից եւ թունաւոր լեզու մը կը գործածեն հայոց դէմ, խուժանը հայոց դէմ զինելու համար:

Խիստ պօյքօթ մը սկսուած է քրիստոնեաներու [դէմ[9]] եւ բոլոր արիւնա[ր]բու գազանները, որոնք ամէն ոճիր ըրած էին եւ երբեմն փախստական կը մնային, այսօր իբր Միլլիի կազմակերպիչներ երեւան ելած են եւ շուկաները զինեալ խումբերով կը շրջին, ահ ու սարսափի մատնելով իրենց երբեմնի զոհերը: Երէկ Չէրքէզ Թէվֆիգ կոչուած երբեմնի քօմիսէրը, որ Մէհմէտճէի հետ ծեծով եւ խոշտանգութեամբ նշանաւոր եղած է եւ Աթրանոսի մէջ սպաննած էր Պրուսայի երեւելիները, յոտից ցգլուխ զինուած յոխորտ կերպով շուկայէն կ'անցնի:

- Թուրքերու զէնքի բաշխումը մեծ ոգեւորութեամբ առաջ կը տարուի: Դրամահաւաքութիւնը գրեթէ հրապարակով կը կատարուի եւ այլեւս գաղտնիք մը չէ:

Պրուսա (Առաջնորդական Փոխանորդէն) – 1 Մարտ

Քաղաքին ամէնէն բարձր դիրքերուն վրայ *միթրալյէօզ*ներ զետեղուած են: Միլլի չէթէախումբեր զինուած կը շրջին:

Ռօտոսթօ (Պատուիրակէ) – 1 Մարտ 1920

Բոլոր կառավարական պաշտօնատուները միայն եւ միայն զէնք բաժնելու գործով զբաղած են: Կարգ մը ազդեցիկ թուրքերու չէթէականներու ամէնօրեայ տենդոտ գործունէութիւնը նշանակալից է շատ. թուրքերու մէջ շշուկ կայ թէ՝ մէկ քանի օրէն դարձեալ իրենց նախկին դիրքին պիտի տիրանան, ամէն բան իրենց ձրի պիտի ըլլայ, պիտի հարստանան եւայլն: Յոյն եւ հայ ամբողջ քրիստոնեայ բնակչութիւնը սկսած է խորիհլ լրջօրէն: Կ'ըսուի թէ մէկ երկու օրէն ֆրանսական զինուոր պիտի գայ, եթէ ուշ չըլլայ սակայն անոնց գալը, զի վտանգը խմորուելու վրայ է եւ գուցէ քիչ օրէն պայթի:

Kartal (from Priest Hmayag Bakhtiarian)—March 5

From February 25 to date, the Millis have been holding secret, closed-door meetings every night in Kartal; sometimes in the municipality, sometimes at the mayor's residence, and sometimes in the mosque. During assembly, gendarmes guard the door. It has been observed that a meeting has also been convened during daylight. During the meeting, a particular person went to the telegraph office, negotiated through cable, and returned to the meeting hall with new instructions.

During the days of these meetings, particularly on March 1, ammunition in carts and Mauser rifles wrapped in blankets on horses were taken to the village of Yakacık. And on March 4, a specially dispatched trusted woman saw in mayor Ethem Kaptan's residence more than ten Mausers that are still there today. In response to the lady's surprise about the weapons, she was assured that the weapons would be used against the British.

As to agitating the crowd, on March 2, a Turkish grocer named Hüsnü told a Greek baker in an Armenian coffeehouse: "Go, go, earn money to send to Greece! All of you (present were ten to twelve Armenians) will see in eight or ten days . . ."

When weapons were being transported, grocer Yorgi's son, Yanko, asked one of his Turkish clients why the weapons were being transported. The Turk answered: "Milli forces will come in a few days; these weapons will be used against them; be assured."

It must be noted that Kartal's district governorship officially and the Turkish people collectively have joined Mustafa Kemal.

Because of these phenomena, Christians are terrified, field cultivation has stopped, and people remain confined to their homes.

The Greeks are as agitated as we are. We think the danger is preventable by stationing a few hundred soldiers from the British garrison of Bostancık in Kartal.

Kayseri (from the Armenian vicar general, the Armenian Catholic prelate, and the Armenian Protestant minister)—February 18

After Develi [Everek], [the Turks] raised a problem of fictitious Armenian çetes accusing the Armenians of Yeşilyurt [Mancusun]. It was prevented after a series of robberies [conducted by bandits]. It is obvious that the existence of Armenians disturbs the Turks, who doubt they will be held accountable one day. Therefore, they are trying to eradicate the Armenians to take over their pathetic houses, household goods, and fields.

• Milli forces have delivered to the central administration in Kayseri extremely provocative statements written in large letters on its door. Therein, it is announced allegedly that massacres and plunders are being carried out against Turks in Armenia. Allegedly, Turkish children and women are being slaughtered mercilessly in Zangezur. Allegedly, in Süleymanlı [Zeytun] and Fırnız, the Armenians have risen and are inflicting horrific harm upon the Turks; likewise, the Armenians of Maraş and Saimbeyli [Hacın] have allegedly forced the Turks to roam the mountains naked and hungry. In Armenia, too, Muslim subjects allegedly did not obey the ruling government, and Halil Bey saved them from assured massacres and atrocities. It is stated at the same time that the people who can read should understand the sufferings of the Turks well and be prepared accordingly, materially, morally, and physically. Needless to say, these statements greatly impressed the Turks, and the immediate result appeared as a boycott. Even Turkish merchants renting Armenian national estates do not want to renew lease agreements. Apart from the Turkish people, Turkish government officials have taken a stern look. It is feared that a storm could break during a fit of agitation, and everything could be stained with blood.

• It is written from Develi that there is a terrible boycott against Christians, particularly against

Գարթալ (Հմայեակ քահանայ Պախթիարեանէ) – 5 Մարտ

Փետրուար 25էն սկսեալ մինչեւ այսօր Գարթալի մէջ Միլլիականներ ամէն գիշեր, երբեմն պէլէտիյէի շէնքին, երբեմն պէլէտիէի րէյիսին բնակարանին եւ երբեմն ալ մզկիթին մէջ գաղտնի եւ դռնփակ ժողովներ կը գումարեն: Ժողովի ատեն դուռը ժանտարմաներով կը պահպանուի: Դիտուած է որ ցերեկ ատեն եւս ժողով գումարած են: Ժողովի միջոցին հեռագրատուն գացած եւ հեռագրով բանակցած եւ նոր հրահանգներ ստանալով ժողովատեղի դարձած է մասնաւոր անձ մը:

Այս ժողովներու օրերուն, մասնաւորապէս Մարտ 1ին, կառքով ռազմամթերք իսկ ձիով պաթանիէներու մէջ փաթթուած Մավզէրներ տարուած են Եազաճըգ գիւղը: Իսկ Մարտ 4ին յատկապէս ղրկուած վստահելի կին մը պէլէտիէ րէիսին՝ Էտհէմ Գափտանի տունը տեսած է 10էն աւելի Մավզէրներ, որոնք դեռ այսօր հոն կը մնան: Երբ տիկինը զարմանք կը յայտնէ զէնքերուն համար, կ'ապահովցնեն զինքը թէ ատոնք անգլիացիներու դէմ պիտի գործածուին:

Գալով ամբոխային գրգռութեանց, Մարտ 2ին Պագգալ Հիւսնի անուն թուրք մը հայ սրճարանի մէջ գտնուող յոյն հացագործի մը սապէս արտայայտուեցաւ. «Գնա, գնա, դրամ վաստկէ որ Յունաստան ղրկես. դուք ամէնքդ ալ (ներկաները 10–12 հայեր են) 8–10 օրէն կը տեսնէք...»:

Զէնքերու փոխադրութեան առթիւ պագգալ Եօրկիի տղան՝ Եանքօ, իր յաճախորդներէն թուրքի մը երբ կը հարցնէ այդ զէնքերու փոխադրութեանց պատճառը, թուրքը սապէս կը պատասխանէ. «Մէկ քանի օրէն Միլլի ուժեր պիտի գան, այդ զէնքերը անոնց դէմ պիտի գործածուին. դուք ապահով եղէք»:

Դիտելի է որ Գարթալի գայմագամութիւնը պաշտօնապէս եւ թուրք ժողովուրդը հաւաքապէս միացած են Մուսթաֆա Քէմալի:

Այս երեւոյթներէն քրիստոնեա[յ]ք ահ ու սարսափի մատնուած են, դաշտի աշխատանքները դադրած են եւ տուները փակուած կը մնան:

Յոյներ ալ մեզի պէս յուզման մէջ են: Եթէ Պօսթանճըգի մէջ անգլիական զինուորական կայանէն մէկ քանի հարիւր զինուոր Գարթալ դրուի, կը կարծենք թէ վտանգին առաջքը կ'առնուի:

Կեսարիա (Հայ Առաջնորդական Փոխանորդէն, Հայ Կաթողիկէ Առաջնորդէն, Հայ Բողոքական հովիւէն) – 18 Փետրուար

Էվէրէկէն յետոյ Մանճուսունի հայոց դէմ ալ երեւակայական հայ չէթէներու խնդիր մը հանած են, որուն առջեւը առնուած է կարգ մը թալանումներէ ետք: Յայտնապէս կ'երեւի թէ հայու գոյութիւնը անհանգիստ կ'ընէ թուրքերը, որոնք կը կասկածին թէ օր մը հաշիւ պիտի պահանջուի իրենցմէ: Ասոր համար կը ջանան ջնջել հայերը, անոնց կտոր բրդուճ տուներուն, կարասիներուն եւ արտերուն տիրանալու համար:

- Միլլի ուժերու կողմէ Կեսարիոյ Հիյէթը Մէրքէզիէյի հասած են գերազգիռ յայտարարութիւններ, որոնք դրան վրայ խոշոր գիրերով գրած են: Անոնց մէջ կը ծանուցուի թէ որպէս թէ Հայաստանի մէջ թուրքերուն դէմ ջարդեր [եւ] թալաններ կը գործուին: Զանգեզուրի մէջ անխնայ կը մորթոտեն թուրք մանուկներ, կիներ: Իբր թէ Զէյթուն, Ֆրնուզ ոտքի ելած զարհուրելի աւերներ կը գործեն եղեր թուրքերուն [դէմ], նոյնպէս Մարաշի, Հաճընի հայերը թուրքերը բռնադատեր են եղեր որ մերկ ու անօթի լեռները [դեգ]երին: Նոյնպէս Հայաստանի մէջ որպէս թէ իսլամ հպատակները տիրող կառավարութեան չեն հնազանդեր եւ Խալիլ պէյ զանոնք ազատեր է ստոյգ ջարդերէ ու զուլումներէ: Յայտարա[ր]ուած է միեւնոյն ատեն, որ, ընթերցող ժողովուրդը լաւ ըմբռնելով թուրքերուն կրած տառապանքները, ըստ այնմ պատրաստուի, նիւթապէս, բարոյապէս եւ ֆիզիքապէս: Աւելորդ է ըսել թէ՝ այս յայտարարութիւնները մեծապէս ազդած են թուրքերուն, որուն արդիւնքը անմիջապէս երեւան եկած է պօյքօթի մը խնդրով: Նոյնիսկ ազգային կալուածները վարձքով նստող թուրք վաճառականները չեն ուզեր վարձքերու պայմանագիրերը նորոգել: Թուրք ժողովուրդէն զատ թուրք կառավարական պաշտօնեաներն ալ դէմքերնին դաժանցուցած են եւ կը վախցուի որ անոնց գերագրգռութեան մէկ նոպային, յանկարծ փոթորիկ մը փրթի եւ ամէն ինչ արիւնով ներկուի:

Armenians. They are even prohibiting Armenians from purchasing necessities. In this way, the boycott, on the one hand, and persecution and horror, on the other hand, have terrorized our unfortunate fragments.

İstanbul (various testimonies relayed by Tekirdağ Compatriotic Union)—March 5[50]

On Sunday, February 29, a Milli leader arrived in Tekirdağ and presented himself to the governor. On March 1, about twenty Millis came and went to the seat of government with that leader. The people, particularly the people of Armatoka, joined these forces and began roaming the city together. Meetings are held in mosques every other day, and the people are incited. Weapons are distributed to all Turks secretly. On March 2, the [Christian] people were not allowed to go to the field because they wanted to hide that weapons were being distributed to the [Muslim] people from the barracks that day. According to the testimony of the Turks, weapons were distributed to all the [Muslim] villagers on that day.

The Turks have taken a threatening position against the Armenians. Upon their return from their meetings, they want to throw themselves at the people like angry dogs, but they restrain themselves because, according to the circulating rumors, the decided time has not arrived yet. All the boatmen are armed. The organizers of this agitation and arms distribution are the current deputy of Tekirdağ Rahi Bey, who has recently gone to Tekirdağ; his father, Adil Bey; the former head of census Kazım; Hasan Bey, Kanlı Hilmi; lawyer Hilmi; Fuat Bey; İbrahim Bey; Kimallar Hasan; Kesedar Ali; Şakir Effendi Haci Mehmet; registrar Hüseyin Effendi; Fuat Bey; İbrahim Bey; the harbor master; teachers of the high school; all the notables; Bezaz Haci Muhittin; Refik Bey; Testereci Riza; Ahmet Effendi, son of Karamehmet. Government personnel are also their accomplices and supporters.

• On March 2, gendarmerie commander Nazim Bey of Malkara came from Tekirdağ to İstanbul. He said in the steamer: "Big events will happen in less than ten days, and the government will not say anything."

İstanbul (from the Armenian and Greek neighborhood councils of Yenikapı Langa)—March 5

An honorable Greek resident of the Yenikapı quarter has learned that preparations are underway for a massacre of Christians. A Turkish officer, in particular, encouraged the four soldiers who were with him, saying that when a signal is given, you should massacre, sparing no one, so that we become a majority in İstanbul and be able to arrange everything by our hands.

İstanbul (from Khachig Der Tavitian, a traveler from Bilecik)—March 5[51]

On the night of March 1, one hundred cavalrymen belonging to the Milli forces arrived in Bilecik. The next day they began an armed tour of the city. Both Armenians and Turks were asked to contribute money that day. Armenians, in particular, were subjected to violence when they tried not to give money. They said that if we give, we do well. They added that they are brothers with Armenians and would take their revenge on the Greeks, whom they no longer consider brothers. Thus, three to four hundred liras were collected from the Armenians. The people are extremely horrified. The Turks have chosen a very troubling position toward Christians; weapons are being distributed to the Turks every day, and Turkish villagers are being forced to enlist as soldiers in the Milli forces. On the day of fund-raising, the Armenians and the director of the Ottoman Bank appealed to the local governor. The fund-raising campaign was stopped in the evening, and at night a meeting was held in the municipality at which the Turks opposing the Millis protested about what had happened. Thereupon, the money col-

- Էվէրէկէն կը գրուի թէ սարսափելի պօյքօթ մը կայ քրիստոնեաներու դէմ, մանաւանդ հայերուն դէմ: Նոյնիսկ կենսական պէտքերնին գնել չեն տար: Այս կերպով պօյքօթը մէկ կողմէն, հալածանքը եւ սարսափը միւս կողմէն ահաբեկած է մեր դժբաղդ քեկորները:

Կ. Պոլիս (Ռօտոսթօյի Հայրենակցականէն հաղորդուած զանազան վկայութիւններ) – 5 Մարտ

Կիրակի օրը՝ Փետրուար 29ը, Միլլի պետ մը Ռօտոսթօ հասնելով կառավարիչին կը ներկայանայ: Մարտ 1ին 20ի չափ Միլլիճիներ կուգան եւ այդ պետին հետ կառավարչատուն կ'երթան: Ժողովուրդը, մանաւանդ արմաթոքցիները, այս դժերուն միանալով քաղաքին մէջ շրջիլ սկսած են: Երկու օրը անգամ մը ժողով կը գումարուի մզկիթներու մէջ եւ ժողովուրդը կը գրգռեն: Բոլոր թուրքերուն գաղտնի զէնք կը բաժնուի: Մարտ 2ին ժողովուրդը արգիլեցին դաշտը ելլալ, վասնզի այն օրը զօրանոցներէն ժողովուրդին զէնք բաժնուիլը գաղտնի պահել կ'ուզէին: Այդ օրը բոլոր գիւղացիներուն ալ զէնք բաժնուեր է, ըստ թուրքերու վկայութեան:

Թուրքերը սպառնական դիրք առած են հայոց դէմ: Իրենց գումարումներէն դարձին կատղած շուներու նման ժողովուրդին վրայ կ'ուզեն նետուիլ, բայց շրջած զրոյցներուն նայելով որոշուած ժամանակը հասած չըլլալով, ինքզինքնին կը զսպեն: Բոլոր նաւավարները զինուած են: Այս գրգռութեան եւ զէնքի բաժանման գործին կազմակերպիչներն են Ռօտոսթօյի այժմեայ մէպուս Րահի պէյ, որ Ռօտոսթօ գացած է վերջին օրերս, իր հայրը՝ Ատիլ պէյ, նախորդ Թահրիրաթ միւտիրին՝ Քեազիմ, Հասան պէյ, Գանըը Հիլմի, փաստաբան Հիլմի, Ֆուատ պէյ, Իպրահիմ պէյ, Գիմալլար Հասան, Քէսէտար Ալի, Շաքիր էֆէնտի Հաճի Մէհմէտ, նփուս մէմուրը Հիւսէյին էֆէնտի, Ֆուատ պէյ, Իպրահիմ պէյ, Լիման Րէյիս, խոատիի դասատուները, բոլոր էշրաֆը, պէզազ հաճի Մուէտտին, Րէֆիք պէյ, Թէսթէրէճի Րիզա, Գարայ Մէհմէտի որդի Ահմէտ էֆէնտի: Կառավարական կազմն ալ ասոնց մեղսակից է եւ քաջալերող:

- Մարտ 2ին Ռօտոսթօյէն Կ. Պոլիս եկած է ծովու ճամբով ժանտարմայի զօմանտան մալկաբացի Նազըմ պէյ: Շոգենաւին մէջ ըսած է թէ «տասը օր չեղած մեծ դէպքեր պիտի պատահին եւ կառավարութիւնն ալ բան մը չպիտի ըսէ»:

Կ. Պոլիս (հայ եւ յոյն թաղական խորհուրդէն Եէնի-Գաբու Լանկայէն) – 5 Մարտ

Եէնի-Գաբու թաղին բնակիչներէն պատուաւոր յոյն մը տեղեկացած է որ քրիստոնեաներու ջարդի մը կազմակերպութիւնները կը կատարուին: Մասնաւորապէս թուրք սպայ մը իր քով գտնուող չորս զինուորները խրախուսած է ըսելով որ երբ որ նշան տրուի, ոչ մէկուն չխնայելով պէտք է ջարդէք, որ Պոլսոյ մէջ մեծամասնութիւն կազմելով ամէն գործ կարգադրած պիտի ըլլանք մեր ձեռքով:

Կ. Պօլիս (Պիլէճիկէ եկող ճամբորդէ մը՝ Խաչիկ Տէր Դաւիթեան) – 5 Մարտ

Մարտ 1ին գիշերը Միլլի ուժերու պատկանող 100 ձիաւոր Պիլէճիկ եկան եւ հետեւեալ օրը սկսան զինեալ շրջիլ քաղաքին մէջ: Այդ օրը թէ՛ հայերէն եւ թէ թուրքերէն դրամ ժողովուիլ սկսան: Մասնաւորապէս հայոց վրայ բռնութիւն կը բանեցնեն, եթէ դրամ չտալու փորձ մը ընեն: «Եթէ տաք, աղէկ կ'ընէք, կ'ըսեն. մենք հայերուն հետ եղբայր ենք. մենք մեր վրէժը յոյներէն պիտի առնենք եւ մենք անոնց եղբայրութիւնը տետրակէն աւրեցինք»: Այսպէսով հայերէն 3–400 ոսկիի չափ դրամ ժողովուեցին: Ժողովուրդը վերջին աստիճան սարսափի մէջ է: Թուրքերը քրիստոնէից հանդէպ շատ գէշ ընթացք մը բռնած են, ամէն օր թուրքերուն զէնք կը բաժնուի եւ գիւղացի թուրքերը բռնի կերպով Միլլի ուժերու զինուոր կ'արձանագրուին: Դրամ հաւաքած օրերնին թէ՛ հայոց եւ թէ Օսմանեան Պանքայի տնօրէնին կողմէ դիմում եղած է տեղւոյն կառավարիչին: Իրիկուան դէմ դրամ հաւաքելու գործողութիւնը դադրեցուցին, իսկ գիշերը պէլէտիյէի մէջ ժողով կ'ընեն եւ Միլլիի հակառակորդ թուրքերը այս եղածներուն վրայ կը բողոքեն: Ասոր վրայ Մարտ 3ին հաւաքած

lected on March 3 was returned [to each contributor]. However, the Millis continue to wander around in the city, especially in the Armenian villages, with weapons. Wretched Armenians think of migrating elsewhere.

Maraş (a telegram from the Armenian primate, the Armenian Catholic prelate, and the Protestant minister)—March 5

Thousands of Armenians were killed because of the latest incident. Immediately after the retreat of the French, we were taken under protection, thanks to the Ottoman government. Our district governor Bey works very hard to ensure peace. Only, since the potentiality of the return of the French endangers our lives, we ask in the name of humanity to eliminate the potentiality mentioned through immediate political initiatives.[52]

İstanbul (Takvim 3793)—March 6

Official refutation: Recently, some rumors have been circulating about the massacre of Armenians in Anadolu [Anatolia] again, and these rumors were published and repeated by the newspaper "Journal d'Orient" through Armenian newspapers.

There have been incidents between Turks and Armenians in the vicinity of Maraş, and there has been no attack anywhere in Anadolu [Anatolia] except for the unprovoked fight caused by the Armenians to harm the lives of the Muslim population and violate their honor. This news, when the fate of the Ottoman state is in question, is announced to have been done with the hidden motive of creating a current damaging to the sublime government before the public opinion of Europe and the Peace Conference.

İstanbul (from the National Assistance)—March 6

Pharmacist Simon Tyoutelian, dispatched especially to İstanbul from Akmeşe, reports that the distribution of weapons and bombs in Uzunlar, Alandağı, Pirahmet, Ketenciler, and other Circassian and Turkish villages has been proceeding for some time and that the attitude of Turkish villagers in the Akmeşe area has begun to be threatening to the point of causing concern.

Üsküdar (petition with many signatures)—March 8[53]

The lives of the Armenians of Üsküdar are in danger. The number of unfamiliar Turkish people rises daily in Armenian neighborhoods. Gatherings of crowds take place in the vicinities of Çamlıca. Two days ago, çetes [with some] Turkish soldiers came to the Armenian village of Alemdağı and demanded an illegal duty. Although the villagers told them that they were legally exempt from duties as new returnees from deportation and that they did not want to pay, the soldiers made threats. Unidentified armed Turks threatened Christians in the taverns and coffeehouses of Yenimahalle in Üsküdar.

Former Ittihadists get together at the guard house of the firehouse in Selamsız and hold secret meetings.

The number of soldiers in the barrack [of Selamsız] has also doubled recently. The residents of the quarter have also noticed the existence of ammunition in that barrack. From that depot weapons and ammunition are transported to the Turkish quarters at night. Thus, on Wednesday, February 25, at half past eleven at night, the special cart of the barrack for fire hoses was used two or three times to transport cases of grenades to quarters populated by Turks. Three days later, that is, on Saturday, Feb-

դրամնին մէկիկ մէկիկ կը դարձնեն, բայց իրենք դարձեալ զէնքով քաղաքին մէջ, մանաւանդ հայոց գիւղերը շարունակ կը պտտին: Խեղճ հայերը կը մտածեն այլուր գաղթել:

Մարաշ (հեռագիր Հայ Առաջնորդէն, Հայ Կաթողիկէ Առաջնորդէն, Բողոքական հովիւէն) – 5 Մարտ

Վերջին դէպքին հետեւանքով հազարաւոր հայեր զոհ եղան: Ֆրանսացիներու նահանջէն անմիջապէս յետոյ Օսմանեան կառավարութեանը շնորհիւ պաշտպանութեան տակ առնուեցանք: Մեր միութէնաբրրֆ պէկը անդորրութեան ապահովութեանը չափազանց կ'աշխատի: Միայն ֆրանսացիներու վերադարձի հաւանականութիւնը մեր կեանքը վտանգի ենթարկելու պատճառ ըլլալուն՝ յիշեալ հաւանականութեան բարձումը,- քաղաքական անմիջական ձեռնարկներու գործադրութեամբ,- յանուն մարդկութեան կը խնդրենք:[10]

Պօլիս (Թագվիմ 3793) – 6 Մարտ

Թէրզիպի ըէսմի.- Անատօլուտա երմէնիլէրին եէնիտէն զաթլը ամմա մարուզ գալտըգլարընա տայիր սօն զէմանլարտա պիր թագըմ շայիա տէվրան իյլէմիշ վէ պու շայիա երմէնի ճէրաիտի իլէ ժուռնալ տ'օրիան ղազէթասը նէշր ու թէքրար իթմիշ տիր:

Մարաշ ճիվարնտա թիւրքլէր իլէ երմէնիլէր արասընտա հատիս օլուպ պիլա սէպէպ էհալիի իսլամիյէնին հայաթլարընա գաստ վէ ըրզլարընա թէճավիւզ իլէ երմէնիլէրին սէպէպիյէթ վերտիքլէրի միւսատիմաթտան դայրը Անատօլունըն հիչ պիր թարաֆնտա երմէնիլէրէ գարշու հիչ պիր թէաբ-րուզ վուգու պուլմամըշ օլտուղը վէ պու շայիանըն տէվլէթը Օսմանիէնին մուզատտէրաթը մէվզուի պահս օլտուղը պիր սրատա կէրէք Էվրոփա էֆքեարը ումումիէսինտէ կէրէք սուլհ զօնֆէրանսը մէհաֆիլինտէ հիւքիւմէթը սէնիյէ ալիյհինէ պիր ճէրեան թէվլիտ իթմէք կիպի մազսէտը պէտխահանէ իլէ նէշր իտիլմէքտէ պուլանտըղը պէյան վէ իլան օլունուր:[11]

Կ. Պոլիս (Ազգային Խնամատարութենէն) – 6 Մարտ

Արմաշէն յատկապէս Կ. Պոլիս ղրկուած դեղագործ Սիմոն Թիւթէլեան կը հաղորդէ թէ Արմաշու շրջակաները գտնուած Ուզունլար, Ալանտաղ, Փիր-Ահմէտ, Քէթէնճիլէր եւ ուրիշ չէրքէզ ու թուրք գիւղերու մէջ ժամանակէ մը ի վեր զէնքի եւ պօմպաներու բաշխման ձեռնարկուած է եւ թէ Արմաշի շրջականերու մահմետական գիւղացիներուն ընթացքը սկսած է մտահոգութիւն պատճառելու աստիճան սպառնական ըլլալ:

Սկիւտար (բազմաթիւ ստորագրութեամբ հանրագիր) – 8 Մարտ

Սկիւտարի հայոց կեանքը վտանգի տակ է: Հայ թաղերու մէջ թուրք անծանօթ դէմքեր կ'աւել-նան օրէ օր: Չամլըճայի շրջակայքը ամբոխային հաւաքումներ տեղի կ'ունենան: Ալէմտաղի հայ գիւղը երկու օր առաջ շարք մը թուրք զինուորներով չէթէներ եկած եւ ապօրինի տուրք պահանջած են, թէեւ գիւղացիք իբր տարագրութենէ վերադարձող ըստ օրինի պարտքէ զերծ ըլլալնին յայտնած են, վճարել չեն ուզած, բայց անոնք ալ սպառնալիքներ ըրած են: Սկիւտար Եէնի-Մահալլէի զինե-տուններու եւ սրճարաններու մէջ զինուած անծանօթ թուրքեր հոն գտնուող քրիստոնեաներուն սպառնացած են:

Նախկին իթթիհատականներ Սէլամսըզի էթֆայիէյի պահականոցը կը հաւաքուին եւ գաղտնի ժողովներ կ'ընեն:

Նաեւ սոյն զօրանոցին զինուորներուն թիւը վերջերս կրկնապատկուած է: Նաեւ այդ զօրա-նոցին մէջ ռազմամթերքի գոյութիւնը նշմարուած է թաղեցիներու կողմէ: Այդ տեղէն գիշերանց զէնք ու ռազմանիւթ կը փոխադրուի դէպի թուրք թաղերը: Այսպէս՝ Փետրուար 25 Չորեքշաբթի իրիկուան ժամը 11½ին զօրանոցին հրդեհի խողովակներու յատուկ կառքը երկու երեք անգամ

ruary 28, around two o'clock, a horrible and mighty explosion terrified the people.

• On Saturday, March 6, at half past three or four in the afternoon, near Bağlarbaşı's Kısıklı, four unarmed men wearing uniforms of British soldiers were spotted running, accompanied by a young civilian, toward the house of Mithat Bey. They approached a parked cart. Two thirty- to forty-year-old Turkish villagers were accompanying the cart. The civilian wore the Armenian tricolor on his lapel and spoke English to the soldiers. One of them approached the horses, grabbed the reins, [and] turned the cart in the opposite direction, and they all left together. As the cart turned around, the young man following them saw a row of Mauser rifles when the wind lifted a tent piece covering the cargo.

• There has been and still is frequent transportation of ammunition. The students of the friars' [school] in Yenimahalle witnessed this and informed their principal.

Boğazlıyan (telegram No. 312, signature: Anna from the village Fahralı, Sara from İğdeli village, Eva's daughter from the village of Felahiye [Rumdiğin])—March 8

There is adversity between all people, which is forbidden by religion and commandments. Could it be that people continue to attack our honor [presuming that] religious commandments do not apply to Armenians? [We ask this question] because we cannot free our honor from the inquisitor Hasan Effendi and the other criminals; since they consider every Muslim's threat to the Armenian honor a charity, they even hide our letters of protest. This does not conform with anything. We ask for our protection in the name of humanity and freedom of conscience.

İstanbul (from Priest Tavit Tbirian, delegate of the people of Adapazarı)—March 8

The Armenians, who had just returned to Adapazarı after being wanderers, began to migrate, terrified. The mob has surrounded the city. The right wing of the başıbozuks [dangerously uncontrollable people] extends to Eşme (on Lake Sapanca), and the left wing reaches Hamidiye [Gazelli], Adapazarı. There is no government in the vicinities.

Saimbeyli [Hacın] (a telegram from Diran Terzian)—March 4

"Most effective appeals and assistance [are needed; otherwise,] we will perish." This telegram shows that Saimbeyli's situation is far from being peaceful, and an attack by Milli forces is feared.

Saimbeyli [Hacın] (a telegram received yesterday, March 9, from Dr. Terzian)

"We are pleading for the last time. The danger is terrible. Do all you can. We will be massacred. Help!"

Sugören [Çengiler] (from the Neighborhood Council)—March 6

The Turkish element of the villages in the prefecture of Orhangazi is at work again. Recently, the organizers of the Milli [movement] have been sent from village to village to collect money and enlist soldiers. The Tatar muhacirs of the village of Reşadiye are being enlisted voluntarily for twenty to thirty liras a month, doubling the strength of the Millis. The former prefect of Bursa went to this village and delivered an encouraging speech to the Milli organization and volunteers. A meeting was convened by night at the headquarters of the sub-governorship, and weapons were distributed the next day. The sheikh of Reşadiye, Şerafeddin Effendi, was present at that meeting, whence he left for the center of

ձեռնառումբեր սնտուկներով թրքաբնակ թաղեր փոխադրելու գործածուած է, երեք օր վերջ ալ, այսինքն Շաբաթ 28 Փետրուար ժամը 2ին միջոցները աւռելի եւ շատ ուժեղ պայթում մը ժողովուրդը ահ ու սարսափի մատնած է:

- Պաղլար Պաշի Խըսխըլի մօտերը Շաբաթ օրը, մարտ 6ին ժամը 3½-4ին նշմարուած են չորս (4) անգլիական զինուորի տարազով անզէն մարդիկ, որոնք Միտհատ պէյի տան կողմը կը վազէին ընկերակցութեամբ սիվիլ երիտասարդի մը: Ասոնք կը մօտենան բեռնակառքի մը, որ կեցած էր: Այդ կառքին կ'ընկերանային երկու թուրք գիւղացիի տարազով 30–40 տարեկան մարդիկ: Սի[վ]իլ պարոնը իր լամբակին վրայ կը կրէր հայկական եռագոյնով քօքարտ մը եւ անգլերէն կը խօսէր զինուորներուն հետ: Ասոնցմէ մէկը ձիերուն մօտենալով սանձէն կը բռնէ ու կառքը հակառակ ուղղութեամբ դարձնելով ամէնքն միասին կը հեռանան: Հետապնդող երիտասարդը կառքին շրջան բրած միջոցին, բեռներուն ծածկոց եղող վրանի կտորներէն մին հովէն բարձրանալով որոշ կը տեսնէ Մավզէրներու շարք մը:

- Ռազմամթերքի յանձնախակի փոխադրութիւն եղած է եւ կ'ըլլայ դեռ: Եէնի-Մահալլէ փըրներու աշակերտները ականատես եղած են ու տեղեկացուցած են իրենց տնօրէնին:

Պօղազլեան (թիւ 312 հեռագիր, ստորագրութիւնը.- Ֆախրալը գիւղացի Աննա, Իկտէլի գիւղէն Սարա, Բումտիքէն գիւղէն Եւայի աղջիկ Ֆիլոր) – 8 մարտ

Ամէն մարդու մէջ հակառակութիւն կայ, ինչ որ կրօնքով եւ օրէնքով արգիլեալ է: Արդեօք հայերը կրօնական օրէնքէն բաժին չունի՞ն որ դեռ մեր պատուին կը յարձակին: Վասնզի հարցաքննիչ (միւսթանթիք) Հասան էֆէնտի[ի]ն ու միւս ոճրագործներու ձեռքէն մեր պատիւը չենք կրնար ազատել, որովհետեւ ամէն խլամի հայուն պատւոյն սպառնալիքը բարեգործութիւն (սէվապ) համարելով՝ մեր բողոքագրերը նոյնիսկ կը ծածկուին. սա ոչ մէկ բանի համաձայն է. մեր պաշտպանութիւնը յանուն մարդկութեան եւ խղճի ազատութեան կը խնդրենք:

Կ. Պոլիս (Դաւիթ քահանայ Դպիրեանէ, Ատաբազարցւոց պատուիրակ) – 8 Մարտ

Ատաբազարի աստանդական վիճակէ դեռ նոր դարձած հայութիւնը սարսափի մանուած՝ սկսած է գաղթել: Խուժանը շրջապատած է քաղաքը. պաշը պօզուքներու աջ թեւը կ'երկարի մինչեւ Էշմէ (Սապանճա Լճին վրայ), իսկ ձախ թեւը կը հասնի Ղազէլլէր, Ատաբազար: Շրջաններու մէջ կառավարութիւն չկայ:

Հաճըն (Տիրան Թերզեանէ հեռագիր) – 4 Մարտ

«Ամէնաազդու դիմումներ եւ օգնութիւն. պիտի փչանանք»: Այս հեռագիրը ցոյց կուտայ թէ Հաճընի վիճակն ալ խաղաղ ըլլալէ հեռու է եւ Միլլի ուժերու կողմէ յարձակումէ կը վա[խ]ցուի:

Հաճըն (երէկ 9 Մարտին ստացուած հեռագիր մը Տոք. Թերզեանէ)

«Վերջին անգամ կը պաղատինք, ահաւոր է վտանգը, ըրէք ինչ որ կրնաք, պիտի ջարդուինք. օգնութիւն»:

Չէնկիլէր (Թաղական Խորհուրդէն) – 6 Մարտ

Օրխանը Ղազի գայմագամութեան գիւղերուն մէջ թուրք տարրը կրկին գործի գլուխ անցած է: Վերջերս Միլլիի կազմակերպիչները գիւղէ գիւղ դրկելով դրամ կը հաւաքեն ու զինուոր կ'արձանագրեն: Բէշատիյէ գիւղի թաթար գաղթականները կամաւոր կ'արձանագրուին Միլլի ուժը կրկնապատկելու համար, ամսական 20–30 ոսկիով: Պրուսայի նախորդ կուսակալը այս գիւղը երթալով խրախուսական ճառ մը խօսած է Միլլիի կազմակերպութեան եւ կամաւորներու համար: Գայմագամութեան կեդրոնը գիշերանց ժողով գումարուած է եւ յաջորդ օրն ալ զէնքերու բաշխում կատարուած է: Բէշատիյէի Շէխը՝ Շէրէֆէլէտտին էֆէնտի, ներկայ եղած է այդ ժողովին, ուրկէ

the prefecture.

So far, the relations between Reşadiye and Sugören have been good, thanks to Sheikh Şerafeddin Effendi's promise. Now the situation seems to be disturbed. No one comes to Sugören for trade. The people are terrified. They dare not leave the village for trade and cultivation.

Bursa (from the vicar general)—March 8

The Armenians of the city have started migrating. Some left last week, and another group will leave this week. Only the poor class remains here. The çetes' numbers have significantly increased. They roam the city freely. Local newspapers furiously speak out against Armenians. Therefore, the [Armenian] people feel endangered. The trial of the perpetrators of the deportation and the crimes of Beyce [Adranos] ended in their favor, and they have been released.

Tekirdağ (from the vicar general)—March 8

On the 5th of this month, on Friday, the British battleship *Ramillies* and a torpedo [boat] visited the city under the command of Captain John Lux. On Saturday morning, British troops conducted a military parade in the city and toured all the quarters. Acting like wolves a few days before, the Turks became lambs given the giant battleship and the glorious parade.

On the same day, at half past two in the afternoon, the Greek metropolitan and the Armenian vicar general visited the battleship on a special steamboat as the English representative Mr. Scott arranged. Also present were the mayor Halis Bey, the president of the Muslim Society Hilmi Effendi, and two Jewish representatives. First, the Greek and Armenian spiritual leaders presented themselves to the admiral and explained the local situation. After listening carefully to their words, he replied: "We have come to demonstrate that we arrive when there is a need." The hearing lasted half an hour. The Protestant preacher acted as a translator. After the Christian representatives, the admiral received the Turkish and Jewish representatives briefly, standing.

Arslanbey (from the Neighborhood Council)—March 8

The Turks of the surrounding villages are arming themselves, intending to act at the right moment. The attitude of the Turks toward us has become threatening recently. Especially during the last eight or ten days, they are preparing on a larger scale by taking advantage of the presence of about fifteen hundred soldiers gathered at a state factory near Arslanbey. Since its inception, never before have so many soldiers been assembled in this factory.

İzmit (from the vicar general)—March 8

For a month now, the heads of Akmeşe and Hendek communes have been visiting Turkish villages in person. They are coercing the Turkish people into selling some of their sheep [and] their real or movable possessions and buying weapons with the funds. They threaten to punish those who are unresponsive. This reality has become so clear that no one can hide it.

• The headman of Bahçecik has publicly instructed the local Turks to withdraw from there and join the Turkish villagers because, he said, preparation is being made to attack this village. Rejecting the headman's offer, the Turks immediately informed the local Armenians, expressing their disagreement [with the headman].

վերջը մեկնած է կուսակալութեան կեդրոնը:

Մինչեւ հիմա Րէշատիյէի եւ Չէնկիլէրի միջեւ շնորհիւ Շէխ Շէրէֆէլէտտին էֆէնտիի խոստումին, յարաբերութիւնները լաւ էին. հիմա վիճակը խախտած կը թուի: Ոչ մէկը կուզայ Չէնկիլէր առեւտուրի համար: Ժողովուրդը ահ ու սարսափի մատնուած է, առեւտուրի եւ մշակութեան համար գիւղէն դուրս ելթալու չի համարձակիր:

Պրուսա (Առաջնորդական Փոխանորդէն) – 8 Մարտ

Քաղաքին հայութիւնը գաղթել սկսած է: Մէկ մասը գնաց անցեալ շաբթու, այս շաբթու ալ պիտի մեկնի ուրիշ խումբ մը: Միայն աղքատ դասակարգը կը մնայ հոս: Չէթէները խիստ շատցած են եւ քաղաքին մէջ ազատօրէն կը շրջին: Տեղական թերթերն ալ հայոց դէմ բուռն կերպով կ'արտայայտուին: Այնպէս որ ժողովուրդը վտանգուած կ'զգայ ինքզինքը: Տարագրութեան եւ Ատրանօզի ոճրագործներուն դատավարութիւնը վերջացաւ ի նպաստ անոնց եւ ոճրագործները ազատ արձակուեցան:

Ռոտոսթօ (Առաջնորդական Փոխանորդէն) – 8 Մարտ

Ամսոյս 5ին, Ուրբաթ օր, քաղաքս այցելեցին Քաբիթէն Ճօն Լիւքսի հրամատարութեամբ Ռամիլիս անգլիական զրահաւորը եւ թօրփիտօ մը. Շաբաթ առաւօտ քաղաքիս մէջ զօրանցք մը կատարեցին անգլիական զօրքերը եւ ամբողջ թաղերը պտտեցան: Ի տես հսկայ զրա[հա]ւորին եւ փառաւոր զօրանցքին, մի քանի օր առաջ գայլ կտրած թուրքերը գառնուկ դարձեր էին:

Նոյն օրը ժամը 2½ին անգլիական ներկայացուցիչ Մ. Սքօթի միջոցաւ մասնաւոր շոգեմակոյկով յունաց մեղրապօլիտը եւ հայոց Առաջնորդական Փոխանորդը զրա[հա]ւոր կ'այցելեն: Ներկայ էր նաեւ քաղաքապետութեան նախագահը՝ Խալիս պէյ եւ Ճէմիյէթը Իսլամիյէի նախագահ Հիլմի էֆէնտի եւ երկու հրեայ ներկայացուցիչ: Նախ ներկայացան յունաց եւ հայոց առաջնորդը Ծովակալին եւ բացատրեցին տեղւոյն կացութիւնը: Ուշադրութեամբ այս խօսքերը մտիկ ընելէ յետոյ պատասխանեց թէ «Մենք եկանք ցոյց տալու թէ ի պահանջել հարկին կը հասնինք»: Ունկնդրութիւնը տեւեց կէս ժամ: Թարգմանի պաշտօնը կը կատարէր բողոքականաց քարոզիչը: Քրիստոնեայ ներկայացուցիչներէ յետոյ ընդունեց թուրք եւ հրեայ ներկայացուցիչները ոտքի վրայ կարճ միջոց մը:

Արսլանպէկ (Թաղական Խորհուրդէն) – 8 Մարտ

Շրջակայ գիւղերու թուրք բնակչութիւնը կը զինուի յարմար րոպէին գործելու մտադրութեամբ: Թուրքերու վարմունքը հանդէպ մեզի սպառնական դարձած է վերջերս: Մանաւանդ վերջին 8–10 օրուան ընթացքին անոնք աւելի լայն գետնի վրայ պատրաստութիւններ կը տեսնեն օգտուելով Արսլանպէկի մերձակայ պետական գործարանին մէջ համախմբուած մօտ 1500 զինուորներու ներկայութենէն: Այս գործարանին մէջ իր հիմնարկութենէն մինչեւ հիմա ոչ մէկ պարագայի այդքան զինուոր համախմբուած էր:

Նիկոմիդիա (Առաջնորդական Փոխանորդէն) – 8 Մարտ

Արմաշի եւ Խանտէկի նահիյէ միւտիրներն ամիսէ մը ի վեր իրենց շրջանակի թուրք գիւղերն անձամբ պտտելով կը ստիպեն թուրք ժողովուրդը ծախել իրենց ոչխարներուն մէկ մասը, ունեցած անշարժ կամ շարժուն ստացուածքը եւ անոնցմով զէնք գնել անպատճառ, անսաստողներն պատժոյ ենթարկել սպառնալով: Այս ճշմարտութիւնը այնքան պարզ բան մը դարձած է որ, ո՛չ ոք չի կրնար ծածկել:

- Պարտիզակի միւտիրը հրապարակաւ թելադրած է նոյն վայրը բնակող թուրքեր[ու]ն որ քաշուին անկէ եւ թուրք գիւղացիներուն միանան, վասնզի, ըսած է, պատրաստութիւն կայ այս գիւղին վրայ յարձակ[ելու]: Թուրքերը մերժելով հանդերձ միւտիրի առաջարկն, անմիջապէս

• The same thing happened in a threatening way to four or five Turkish families living in Ovacık. Although they wanted to leave, they were stopped by the Armenians, and again one of them sincerely confessed to a local Armenian honorable man that this was the case. He urged the Armenian to at least move to a safe place to escape [the potential attack on the village].

• Weapons and machine guns have been transported overnight from the Turkish barracks across İzmit cemetery to unknown locations in the city for a week now. Turkish villagers also come to the military headquarters at night and leave the city before dawn, taking uniforms and weapons with them. Armenians have seen all of this. It has become widespread for Turks to announce on appropriate occasions in villages or towns: "We shall inflict calamities upon you in a short time!"

• Every day, five or six families from Adapazarı and the surrounding area abandon their homes, shops, and businesses to come to this city to take refuge in terror. As if it were a safe place. Most of them go to İstanbul.

Büyük-Yeniköy (from the Neighborhood Council)—March 10

Organizing Milli forces has become an accomplished reality in recent days. Armed groups wander from village to village. Today, three armed men, believed to be from Dagestan, for no reason, organized a shooting exercise on an Armenian villager from Sugören [Çengiler] while he was crossing the road. The young man died without even suspecting anything. Weapons are being transported during broad daylight to nearby Turkish villages under the eye of the Armenian population of Sugören. The people are very excited. Migration to İstanbul has begun because they lack the means of self-defense.

Akmeşe (from the director of the Agricultural College and the Neighborhood Council of Akmeşe and EskiMecidiye [Khaskal])—March 9[54]

The recent events in Cilicia, and in particular the blatant activities of the Milli forces in Adapazarı and other cities, the distribution of large numbers of weapons to all the villages in the vicinities, and the dangerous general activities of the Milli organization are cause for excitement and concern, particularly considering the responsibility [we have] for the lives of two hundred orphans. If it is impossible to arrange for the dispatch of Allied soldiers, at least [arrange] for the provision of weapons so we can protect ourselves.

Boğazlıyan (from Soghomon of Menteşe addressed to the Armenian Patriarchate)—March 13

Since the government headman of Misa quarter and the town, Münip, and the interrogating police effendis have taken massacrers under their auspices, the massacre has begun again. The Armenian families of Menteşe, as they were migrating to the city driven by the horror they saw, were killed together with their animals. This has been terrible. No Armenian can go anywhere. If our fate is left to the Turks after this, very good; if not, we ask with bitter tears that this suffering end.

Boğazlıyan (from Mgrdich, Garabed and Krikor)—March 13

The lack of intervention in the vicious attacks on our lands by the Turks of our village is an obstacle to our preparations to live there; they do not even let [us be] among workers. Those disturbing the local calm are the leaders of the çetes, Sheikh Ali and Mustafa Şakir. With their armed comrades and violent persecutions, they say: "Infidels! You will depart soon . . ."

տեղեկացուցած են տեղւոյն հայերուն, յայտնելով իրենց տարակարծիք ըլլալը:

- Սպառնական ձեւով նոյն բանը եղած է նաեւ Օվաճըգ բնակող 4-5 տնուոր թուրքերու ալ, որոնք թէեւ ուզած են մեկնիլ, բայց հայերու կողմէ արգիլուած են, ու դարձեալ անոնցմէ թուրք մը անկեղծօրէն խոստովանած է այս պարագան տեղւոյն հայերէն պատուաւոր մէկու մը, թէ խնդիրը այսպէս է եւ հարկ է որ ինքը գոնէ ապահով վայր մը փոխադրուի, ազատելու համար:

- Նիկոմիդիոյ գերեզմանատան դէմի թուրք զօրանոցէն գիշերանց զէնքեր ու գնդացիր կը փոխադրուի շաբաթէ մը ի վեր քաղաքին մէջ դէպի անծանօթ վայրեր. թուրք գիւղացիներ նոյնպէս կու գան զինուորական պաշտօնատուն գիշերանց եւ զգեստ ու զէնքեր առած արշալոյսէն առաջ կ'իջնեն քաղաքէն. ասոնք բոլորն ալ տեսնուած են հայոց կողմէ: Իսկ շատ սովորական դարձած է թուրքերու կողմէ գիւղերու կամ քաղաքներու մէջ պատեհ առիթներով յայտարարել թէ «քիչ ժամանակէն ի՜նչ ձիւներ պիտի բերենք ձեր գլխուն»:

- Ատաբազարի եւ շրջակայից մէջ օրական հինգ-վեց ընտանիքներ, ձգած իրենց տունը, խանութը, գործը, քաղաքս կու գան ապաստանիլ աիաբեկ, իբր թէ ապահով վայր մը ըլլար հոս, եւ մեծագոյն մաս մըն ալ Պոլիս կ'երթան:

Մեծ-Նոր-Գիւղ (Թաղական Խորհուրդէն) – 10 Մարտ

Վերջին օրերս Միլլի ուժերու կազմակերպութեան գործը կատարուած իրողութիւն մըն է: Զինուած վիճակի մէջ խումբեր գիւղէ գիւղ կը թափառին: Այսօր երեք զինուած մարդիկ, որոնք Տաղեսթանցի ըլլալ կը կարծուին, առանց պատճառի ճամբէն անցած ատենը չէնկիլէրցի հայ գիւղացիի մը վրայ նշանառութեան փորձ կը կատարեն: Երիտասարդը նոյնիսկ առանց բանէ մը կասկածելու կը մեռնի: Շրջակայ թուրք գիւղերը օր ցերեկով զէնք կը փոխադրուի Չէնկիլէրի հայ բնակչութեան աչքին տակ: Ժողովուրդը սաստիկ յուզուած է: Դէպի Կ. Պոլիս գաղթականութիւնը սկսած է, վասնզի ինքնապաշտպանութեան միջոցներէ զուրկ են:

Արմաշ (Երկրագործական Վարժարանի տնօրէնէն եւ Արմաշի եւ Խասկալի թաղական խորհուրդէն) – 9 Մարտ

Վերջերս Կիլիկիոյ մէջ պատահած դէպքերը եւ մասնաւորապէս Ատապազար եւ այլ քաղաքներու մէջ Միլլի ուժերու հրապարակային գործունէութիւնը, շրջակայ բոլոր գիւղացիներուն մեծ քանակութեամբ զէնքեր բաժնուիլը եւ Միլլի Թէշքիլաթի վտանգաւոր ընդհանուր գործունէութիւնը յուզում եւ մտատանջութիւն կը պատճառէ՝ մասնաւորապէս [նկատի ունենալով] 200 որբերու կեանքին պատասխանատուութիւնը: Եթէ կարելիութիւն չկայ համա[ձա]յնական զինուորներ ղրկել տալու, գոնէ մեզի զէնք տրամադրուի ինքզինքնիս պաշտպանելու համար:

Պօղազլեան (մէնթէշէցի Սողոմոնէ, ուղղած հայոց պատրիարքարանին) – 13 Մարտ

Կառավարութեան Միսաթաղի եւ գիւղաքաղաքի միւտիրը Միւնի[ր] եւ միւսթանթիք էֆէնտիներուն եւս ջարդարարները իրենց հովանաւորութեան ներքեւ առնելուն՝ դարձեալ կոտորածը սկսաւ. իրենց տեսած սարսափէն դէպի քաղաք գաղթող մէնթէշէցի հայ ընտանիքներ կենդանիներով մէկտեղ սպաննուած են եւ դա սոսկալի լինելուն ոեւէ մէկ հայ մէկ կողմ չի կրնար երթալ. ասկէ վերջն ալ մեր ճակատագիրը թուրքերուն յանձնուած է եթէ՝ շատ լաւ, եթէ ոչ կը խնդրենք որ սա տառապանքները,- աղի արցունքներով,- վերջանան:

Պօղազլեան (Մկրտիչէ, Կարապետէ եւ Գրիգորէ) – 13 Մարտ

Մեր գիւղի թուրքերուն ծայր աստիճան յարձակումները մեր հողերուն [վրայ] չմիջամտելով այնտեղ ապրուելնուս համար մեր պատրաստութիւններուն արգելք կը լինին. գործաւորներու մէջ նոյնիսկ չեն ձգեր: Տեղւոյն անդորրութիւնը [խանգարողները] չէթէապետ շէյխ Ալի եւ Մուսթաֆա Շաքիրն են: Ցիշեալները ընկերներով, զինեալ, բռնի հետապնդումներով այսպէս կ'ըսեն. «Կեա-

Here is [one example of] a crime: Mustafa and his friends made an Armenian woman disappear forcibly. The current perpetrator is under the caring protection of the government. If our death is not handed over to the Turks and the hardships we have already seen have been enough, we ask, with teary eyes, for an edict granting us protection.

Adana (telegram from the primate of Saimbeyli [Hacın])

We continue the war in Çardak Deresi. Rush to help. They have reached Cıtrak, that is, half an hour from Saimbeyli; help!

Adana (from the primate, school principal, [and] Armenian Protestant minister of Saimbeyli [Hacın])—March 10

Agitated by the retreat of the French troops in Maraş and the massacre of twenty thousand Armenians, the primate traveled to Kozan [Sis] to calm the Armenians of Saimbeyli. On the road between Kozan and Saimbeyli, at the place called Hordum, he was attacked by Turkish çetes. He reached Kozan after a battle that lasted five hours. There, he heard about the murder of Armenians half an hour away from the city. Staying a few days, he set off and reached Adana. The next day, telegrams arrived from Saimbeyli, reporting that Şarköy had been massacred and captured by the çetes of Tufanbeyli [Mağara] and Rum communes and that Saimbeyli had been besieged. They were asking for help. These telegrams have continued [to arrive] every day since March 5. Every day the primate addressed the French Governor-General Mr. Brémond and requested, in particular, the dispatch of troops to Saimbeyli. After consulting with General Dufieux, Mr. Brémond replied that France could not send troops to Saimbeyli. Thereupon, the formation of a group of four hundred people from Saimbeyli residing in Adana was proposed to reach out to Saimbeyli. This offer was accepted, but when an appeal was made today (March 10) to arm the group and provide food and ammunition, they [the French] gave vague and ambiguous answers. An appeal will be made again tomorrow, hoping that in the end, they will not allow Saimbeyli to share the fate of Maraş.

For now, there is a great fear that the Armenian-populated villages around Bağarası [Feke], which were under siege, are ruined. Gaziantep [Ayntab] has been under siege for fifty days. Cilicia is infested with bands of çetes, and blood smells everywhere. If they [the French] do not come to the rescue, all the Armenians of Cilicia will perish.

Adana (from M[ihran] Damadian)—March 5

The situation has not improved, although thousands of French troops are coming to Cilicia. The çetes are acting unhindered. Recently, the deputy police commissioner of the Adana, Mr. Yesayi Bzdigian, felt obliged to resign from his post due to the French security chief's harsh treatment of him and the unbecoming encroachment of his function. Mr. Bzdigian's predecessor, Vahan Bedrosian, was also forced to resign over jurisdiction issues. This issue is directly related to the most current and alarming case of public safety. The resignations have caused excitement. When Mr. Brémond suggested that the Armenians name a new candidate, they replied, "in the current circumstances, we do not have a candidate."

Adana (from M[ihran] Damadian)—March 10

Now, the attack has been directed at Saimbeyli [Hacın]. The danger may not be immediate, but the situation is grave because not only is Saimbeyli under siege, but also, as it appears from a document au-

վուռնե՛ր, մօտ ժամանակէն պիտի երթաք...»:

Ահաւասիկ ոճրագործութիւն մը. Մուսթաֆա ընկերներով բռնի հայ կին մը անյայտացուցին. ներկայ ոճրագործը կառավարութեան գուրգուրալի պաշտպանութեան ներքեւ է: Եթէ մեր մահը թուրքերուն չէ յանձնուած եւ մեր տեսած նեղութիւնները բաւական են այլեւս, մեր պաշտպանութեան շնորհուիլը արցունքոտ աչքերով կը խնդրենք փէրման[ով]:

Ատանա (Հաճընի Առաջնորդէն հեռագիր)

«Զարտակ Տէրէսի պատերազմը կը շարունակենք. օգնութեան փութացէք: Ծթրազ հասան, այսինքն Հաճընէն կէս ժամ հեռու. օգնութիւն»:

Ատանա (Հաճընի Առաջնորդէն, վարժարանի տնօրէնէն, հայ բողոքականաց հովիւէն) – 10 Մարտ

Մարաշի ֆրանսական զօրքերու նահանջէն եւ 20,000 հայերու կոտորածէն յուզուած, Հաճընի հայերը հանդարտեցնելու համար Առաջնորդը դէպի Սիս ճամբայ կ'ելլէ: Ճամբան Սիսի եւ Հաճընի միջեւ Հօրտում ըսուած տեղը թուրք չէթէճիներու յարձակման կ'ենթարկուի եւ 5 ժամ շարունակ կռուելէ յետոյ կը հասնի Սիս: Հոն քաղաքէն կէս ժամ հեռու հայոց սպանութեան դէպքեր լսուած ըլլալով, մի քանի օր կենալէ յետոյ ճամբայ կ'ելլեն կը հասնին Ատանա: Հետեւեալ օրը իսկ Հաճընէն կուգան հեռագիրներ, որոնք կը հաղորդեն Ծարը ջարդուած ըլլալը եւ Մաղարայի եւ Ռում նահիյէի չէթէներու կողմէ գրաւուած եւ Հաճընը պաշարուած ըլլալը, եւ օգնութիւն կը խնդրէին: Մարտ 5էն սկսեալ այս հեռագիրները ամէն օր կը շարունակուին: Առաջնորդը ամէն օր կը դիմէ ֆրանսացի ընդհանուր վարիչ Մ. Պրէմոնին եւ կը խնդրէ մասնաւորապէս զինուորական ոյժերու առաքումը դէպի Հաճըն: Մ. Պրէմօն Զօրավար Տիւֆիւէօյի հետ խորհրդակցելէ յետոյ, պատասխանեց թէ Ֆրանսա Հաճըն զօրք չի կրնար ղրկել: Աօր վրայ կ'առաջարկուի Ատանա բնակող 400 հաճընցիներէն խումբ մը կազմել եւ օգնութեան հասնիլ Հաճընի: Այս առաջարկը ընդունուեցաւ, սակայն երբ այսօր (10 Մարտ) դիմում եղաւ յիշեալ խումբը զինելու եւ պարէն եւ ռազմամթերք տալու, անորոշ եւ երկդիմի պատասխաններ տուին: Վաղը նորէն դիմում պիտի կատարուի, յուսալով որ ի վերջոյ չպիտի թողուն որ Հաճըն եւս վիճակակից ըլլայ Մարաշի:

Առ այժմ մեծ երկիւղ կայ որ Վահկայի շրջակայ հայաբնակ գիւղերը, որոնք պաշարուած էին, փճացած են: Այնթապ 50 օրէ ի վեր պաշարման մէջ է: Ամբողջ Կիլիկիա չէթէական խումբերով լեցուած, ամէն տեղ արիւն կը հոսի: Եթէ օգնութեան չհասնին, ամբողջ Կիլիկիոյ հայութիւնը պիտի փճանայ:

Ատանա (Մ[իհրան] Տամատեան) – 5 Մարտ

Կացութիւնը չէ բարւոքած, հակառակ անոր որ հազարներով ֆրանսական զօրք կուգայ Կիլիկիա: Չէթէները սանձարձակ կը գործեն: Վերջին օրերս ոստիկանութեան Ատանայի փոխտնօրէն Պ. Եսայի Պզտիկեան ստիպուեցաւ իր պաշտօնէն հրաժարական տալ ֆրանսացի ապահովութեան պետին կոշտ վարմունքին եւ իր պաշտօնին կիրարկութեանը մէջ անտեղի ոտնձգութիւններ ընելուն համար: Պ. Պզտիկեանի նախորդը՝ Վահան Պետրոսեան, նոյնպէս իրաւասութեան խնդիրներով ստիպուած էր հրաժարիլ: Այս խնդիրը,- որ հանրային ապահովութեան ամէնէն այժմէական եւ տագնապալի հարցին հետ անմիջական կապ ունի,- մտքերը յուզեց: Պ. Պրէմօն երբ նոր թեկնածու մը ներկայացնելու առաջարկ ըրաւ հայոց, անոնք պատասխանեցին թէ «ներկայ հանգամանքներուն մէջ մենք թեկնածու չունինք»:

Ատանա (Մ[իհրան] Տամատեան) – 10 Մարտ

Հիմա ալ յարձակումը ուղղուած է Հաճընի վրայ: Վտանգը թերեւս անմիջական չէ, բայց կացութիւնը ծանր է, զի ո՛չ միայն Հաճըն պաշարուելու վրայ է, այլեւ, ինչպէս կ'երեւի Col. Brémondի

thored by Colonel Brémond, the French do not see the need to defend Saimbeyli and are not prepared to send troops there. Thoughts of organizing an Armenian resistance with the help of the French are being considered. Also, around Amanos, on land evacuated by the French, where the Turkish çetes abound now, the Armenians are thinking of ways to defend themselves.

On March 8, at the first news of the attack on Saimbeyli, Mr. Damadian appealed to General Dufieux in Adana in a letter informing him of the situation. On the second morning, the primate of Saimbeyli, Bishop Bedros Sarajian, with the Protestant Garabed Khachadourian, and the director of the schools, Mr. Shmavon, went to Brémond to ask again for weapons, food, and so on, and their protection. Brémond made promises. But it is noteworthy that the French do not want to defend Saimbeyli, [viewing it] "as an insignificant route."

• The people in Adana held a rally yesterday. They protested and called on the French authorities to help.

• Today all the shops are closed and, despite the pressure exerted by the French government, they did not open. They will probably stay closed like this for a few days.

• There is no news about Süleymanlı [Zeytun]. Colonel Brémond reports that a Circassian agha named İbrahim Bey allegedly transported the Süleymanlı people collectively to Göksun [Kokison] and took them under his protection. We are doubtful about the accuracy of the news.

• Colonel Brémond said that he had received a telegram from General Gouraud informing him that if there were Armenians in Cilicia who wanted to migrate to the Caucasus, they would be given the necessary facilities and provided with a steamboat. The answer was: "No Armenian is leaving Cilicia, except perhaps those Armenians who would like to enlist in the Armenian army." The colonel replied that he did not refer to them [fighters] but to those who would like to move with their families. But he also agreed that there were no such departers and answered [Gouraud's] question negatively. Also, "to have one less chance for panic," he wished this news would not be spread.

• There are persistent rumors that new international troops (British, Italian, and French) will come to these parts in the near future.

• Catholicos Sahag will leave for Paris tomorrow, or very soon, to ask European cabinets for protection for his disaster-stricken flock.

Ordu (from the Neighborhood Council)—March 7

There has been anxiety among the Armenians of this city for four or five days. The anxiety is based on whispers and statements made by irresponsible people. Recently, *sealed envelopes* prophesying a repetition of the events of 1915 were distributed to the Turkish headmen of the villages. Many are preparing to migrate, despite the misery that awaits them again.

Tekirdağ (from the vicar general)—March 12

As a result of Biga's alarming condition, Armenians began migrating to Tekirdağ. An official statement on March 7 banned the migration, making the horror of local Armenians more incredible.

մէկ պաշտօնագրէն, ֆրանսացիք Հաճընի եւս պաշտպանութեան պէտք չեն տեսնար եւ հոն զօրք ղրկելու տրամադիր չեն: Կը մտածուի հայկական դիմադրութիւն մը կազմակերպել ֆրանսական օգնութեամբ: Նոյնպէս Ամանոսի կողմը (Հասան Պէյլի) ֆրանսացիներու կողմէ պարպուած հողամասին վրայ, ուր այժմ թուրք չէթէները կը վխտան, հայերը ինքզինքնին պաշտպանելու միջոցներու վրայ կը խորհին:

Մարտ 8ին, Հաճընի վրայ յարձակման առաջին լուրին իսկ, Ատանայի մէջ Մ. Տամատեան կը դիմէ Général Dufieuxին, նամակ մը կը գրէ եւ կացութիւնը կը տեղեկացնէ: Երկրորդ առաւօտուն Հաճընի Առաջնորդ Սարաճեան Պետրոս Եպիսկոպոսի, Բողոքական Կարապետ Խաչատուրեանի եւ վարժարաններու տնօրէն Պ. Ճմաւոն[ի] հետ Մ. Պրէմօնի կը ներկայանայ դարձեալ զէնք, մթերք եւայլն եւ իրենց պաշտպանութիւնը խնդրելու համար: Խոստումներ ըրաւ: Բայց ուշագրաւ է որ չեն ուզեր Հաճընը պաշտպանել «իբրեւ երկրորդական ճամբայ մը»:

- Երէկ Ատանայի մէջ յուզուած ժողովուրդը միթինկ մը կազմեց եւ բողոքի ու օգնութեան կոչեր ըրաւ ֆրանսական իշխանութեանց:

- Այսօր բոլոր խանութները փակ են եւ հակառակ ֆրանսական իշխանութեան ստիպումին՝ չբացուեցան. խիստ հաւանօրէն մէկ քանի օր այսպէս փակ պիտի մնան:

- Զէյթունի մասին լուր չկայ: Col. Brémond կը յայտնէ թէ իբր թէ Իպրահիմ պէյ անունով չէրքէզ աղա մը զէյթունցիները խմբովին փոխադրած է Կոկիսոն (Կէօքսուն) եւ իր պաշտպանութեան տակ առած: Լուրին ստուգութեան մասին կը տարակուսինք:

- Գնդ. Պրէմօն յայտնած է թէ Զօրավար Կուրօյէ հեռագիր ստացած է, որով կը յայտնուի թէ, եթէ Կիլիկիոյ մէջ հայեր կան որոնք կ'ուզեն Կովկաս գաղթել, անոնց պէտք եղած դիւրութիւնները պիտի տրուին, շոգենաւ պիտի տրամադրուի: Պատասխանուած է թէ Կիլիկիայէն մեկնող հայեր չկան, բացի թերեւս այն հայերէն, որոնք պիտի ուզէին զինուորագրուիլ հայկական բանակին համար: Գնդապետը կը պատասխանէ թէ խօսքը անոնց համար չէ, այլ անոնց համար, որոնք պիտի ուզէին ընտանեօք փոխադրուիլ: Բայց ինքն ալ համամիտ գտնուեցաւ որ այդպիսի մեկնողներ չեն գտնուիր ու այդ հարցումին պատասխանեց բացասական կերպով, նաեւ «խուճապի առիթ մը պակաս ըլլալու համար», փափաքեցաւ որ այս լուրը չտարածայնուէր:

- Ցամաք զրոյցներ կը շրջին որ մօտ օրէն միջազգային (անգլիական, իտալական եւ ֆրանսական) նոր զօրքեր պիտի գան այս կողմերը:

- Տ. Սահակ Կաթողիկոս վաղը կամ խիստ մօտ օրէն կը մեկնի Բարիզ, իր աղէտեալ հօտին պաշտպանութիւնը խնդրելու համար եւրոպական դահլիճներէն:

Օրտու (Թաղական Խորհուրդէն) – 7 Մարտ

4–5 օրէ ի վեր վրդովում կայ քաղաքիս հայ ժողովուրդին մէջ: Վրդովումը հիմնուած է շշուկնե-րու եւ անպատասխանատու մարդոց յայտարարութեանց վրայ: Վերջերս գիւղերու թուրք մխթար-ներուն ցրուած [են] *զոց պահարաններ*, որոնք 1915ի դէպքերուն կրկնութիւնը նախատեսել կուտան: Շատերը կը պատրաստուին գաղթել, նորէն թշուառութեան մատնուիլ աչք առնելով:

Ռօտոսթօ (Առաջնորդական Փոխանորդէն) – 12 Մարտ

Պիղայի վիճակին տագնապալից ըլլալուն հետեւանօք հայերը Ռօտոսթօ գաղթել սկսած են: Մարտ 7ին պաշտօնական յայտարարութիւն մը արգիլած է գաղթը, որով տեղացի հայոց սարսափը աւելի մեծ եղած է:

[Insecurity] Notebook Number 8
March 1920

Bahçecik (from the National Union)—March 6

Bahçecik [which housed] ten thousand [Armenians before the armistice] was able to gather no more than fifteen hundred [Armenian] people after the armistice and engaged in constructive work. And in these months, it suffered casualties again, on the way to work or in neighboring villages, yet again they endured. Now, the surrounding forces of darkness from Bahçecik to Arslanbey are so dense, prepared, and connected that they are ready to attack upon a single trigger and annihilate the last fragments of the Armenians.

An example of this was seen a few days ago when, based on a false tale born of local Turks, two hundred armed Muslim Lazes living behind St. Minas Hill approached Bahçecik. Muslim shopkeepers clearly confirmed this [fact] with their mouths in a meeting. The Lazes, before this [approach], had invited the Georgians living to the west of Bahçecik to cooperate with them, but when the Georgians were late, due to a misunderstanding about the time of the attack, [the Lazes] decided to go back, leaving [the execution of] their plan for another time.

On the other hand, the Milli people are making preparations far from the eyes of the Allies. They relentlessly transport ammunition in sacks to the Muslim villages around Bahçecik and already started a boycott against consumers. The mysterious trips of the headman, too, are no lesser cause for suspicion and fear. The atmosphere is threatening, and an attack will be inevitable if help does not arrive.

İstanbul—Balat (from the Orphan Caring Body)—March 15

At three o'clock on Friday evening, February 13, and around seven o'clock on Saturday evening, March 14, two strangers attempted to enter the orphanage in Balat through the outer wall. Two guards noticed them, [at which point] their attempt failed, and they fled.

Bandırma (from the primate)—March 15

The movements of the Millis in the region of Balıkesir and Bandırma, like elsewhere, have the characteristics of attaining increasingly threatening proportions.

The local and surrounding Milli forces are made up of local and muhacir Turks, most of them from Thessaloniki and Rumeli. It is thought that the native elements, comparatively, do not have unforgiving and hidden intentions toward the Armenians. Meanwhile, the people from Thessaloniki have treated Armenians with an irreconcilable attitude, and as the newspaper *İzmire Doğru*, published by the Millis, spells out openly, they await the moment that they can implement a crafted Turkish plan to turn the [remaining] fragments of Armenians prey to the rage of çetes and the mob that follows them.

Unfortunately, Armenians living here and in the surrounding areas are deprived of the necessary means of self-defense, so somewhat well-to-do families are compelled to move to İstanbul. The middle and poor classes do not have the financial means to move to İstanbul. The prevailing horror is naturally explained by the fact that no Allied force is here.

• A few days ago, the son of Veli Beyzade Ömer, known for his anti-Christian feelings and deeds in the area, along with twenty-five to thirty of his companions, threatened the Armenians. They terrorized them with knives and cudgels in hand, saying: "We demand blood for blood. You were saved from Aleppo['s massacre][55], but you will not escape our swords."

• All Turks are armed here, so Christians are in constant danger. Armenians exercise great caution to avoid trouble and potential clashes.

[Անապահովութեան] Տետր Թիւ 8
1920 Մարտ

Պարտիզակ (Ազգային Միութենէն) – 6 Մարտ

10,000նոց Պարտիզակը, զինադադարէն ետք, հազիւ 1500 հոգի կրցաւ հաւաքել իր մէջ եւ սկսաւ իր շինարար աշխատանքին: Եւ այս ամիսներուն դարձեալ զոհեր ունեցաւ, աշխատանքի ճամբուն վրայ կամ դրացի գիւղերու մէջ, եւ դարձեալ համբերեցին: Հիմա, Պարտիզակէն մինչեւ Ասլանպէկ շրջապատող մութ ուժերը՝ այն աստիճան լեցուած, պատրաստուած, շղթայուած են, որ մէկ նշանի մը զսպանակէ մղուած պիտի թափին եւ պիտի բնաջնջեն վերջին բեկորները հայոց:

Օրինակը տեսնուեցաւ քանի մը օր առաջ, երբ տեղացի թուրքերէ ծնունդ առած սուտ զրոյցի մը վրայ, Ս. Մինասի բլուրին կռնակը բնակող խլամ լազերէն 200 հոգի, զինուած, Պարտիզակի կը մօտենան, ինչ որ խլամ խանութպաններ ժողովի մը մէջ որոշապէս կը հաստատեն իրենց բերնով: Լազերը, անկէ առաջ, Պարտիզակի արեւմտակողմի կիւրճիներուն՝ իրենց հետ համագործակցելու համար՝ հրաւէր ղրկած ըլլալով, երբ յարձակման ժամի մասին սխալ հասկացողութեամբ անոնք ուշ կը մնան, կ'որոշեն ետ դառնալ, ուրիշ ատենի թողլով իրենց ծրագիրը:

Միւս կողմէ, Միլլիճիները Համաձայնականներու աչքէն հեռու պատրաստութիւններ կը տեսնեն, շարունակ պարկերով ռազմանիւթ կը փոխադրեն Պարտիզակի շրջակայ խլամ գիւղերը ու պօյքօթ մըն ալ արդէն սկսած են գործադրել սպառող ժողովուրդին դէմ: Միւտիրին խորհրդաւոր պտոյտներն ալ ոչ նուազ կասկած եւ վախ կը պատճառեն: Մթնոլորտը սպառնալից է եւ եթէ օգնութիւն չհասնի, յարձակումը անխուսափելի պիտի ըլլայ:

Կ. Պոլիս – Պալաթ (Որբախնամ մարմնէն) – 15 Մարտ

Փետրուար 13ի Ուրբաթ գիշերը ժամը 3ին եւ Մարտ 14ի Շաբաթ գիշերը ժամը 7ի ատենները, երկու անծանօթներ Պալաթի որբանոցին արտաքին պատէն ներս մտնելու փորձ ըրած ատեննին, երկու պահապաններէն նշմարուած ըլլալով՝ չէ յաջողած իրենց փորձը եւ փախուստ տուած են:

Պանտրմա (Առաջնորդէն) – 15 Մարտ

Պալըքեսիրի եւ Պանտրմայի շրջանին մէջ Միլլիներու շարժումները, ինչպէս ուրիշ տեղեր, հետզհետէ սպառնալից համեմատութիւններ առնելու բնութիւնն ունին:

Տեղւոյս եւ շրջակայից Միլլի ուժերը բաղկացած են տեղացիներէ եւ գաղթական թուրքերէ, մեծագոյն մասը Սելանիկէն եւ Ռումելիէն: Բնիկ տարրը համեմատաբար հայերու հանդէպ աններող եւ յետին միտքեր չունին կը կարծուի, մինչ սելանիկցիները անհաշտ տրամադրութիւններով վերաբերուած են հայոց հանդէպ եւ ինչպէս *Իզմիրէ Սօղու* Պալըքէսիրի մէջ Միլլիներու կողմէ հրատարակուած թերթը բացորոշ կերպով կ'արտայայտուի, մշակուած թրքական ծրագրի մը գործադրելու րոպէն կը հետապնդեն հայութեան խլեակները չէթէներու եւ անոնց հետեւող խուժանին կրից զոհ ընելու համար:

Տեղւոյս եւ շրջակայից հայերը դժբաղդաբար զուրկ են ինքնապաշտպանութեան անհրաժեշտ միջոցներէն եւ այս պատճառով քիչ շատ բարեկեցիկ ընտանիքները ստիպուած Պոլիս կ'երթան, իսկ միջակ եւ աղքատիկ դասակարգը Պոլիս անցնելու համար նիւթական միջոցները չունի: Հոս ոչ մէկ Դաշնակից ուժ գոյութիւն ունի, որով բնական է բացատրել տիրող սարսափը:

- Քանի մը օր առաջ տեղւոյս մէջ հակաքրիստոնեայ զգացումներով եւ գործերովը ծանօթ Վէլի պէյ Չատէ Էօմէրի տղան 25–30 ընկերներով ձեռքերնին դանակներ եւ սօփաներ հայերու թաղը շրջած «արիւնի տեղ արիւն կը պահանջենք. Հալէպէն ազատեցաք բայց մեր սուրերէն չէք ազատիր» ըսելով սպառնալիքներ ըրած եւ հայերը ահ ու սարսափի մատնած են:

- Բոլոր թուրքերը հոս զինուած են, այնպէս որ քրիստոնեայք ամէն վայրկեան վտանգի տակ

Konya (from the primate)—March 11, 1920

The train from İstanbul did not arrive in Konya yesterday morning, and thereby grave news began circulating among all classes, which became a cause for serious concern. In the evening, we learned that all the British forces of Afyonkarahisar had received an instant order to evacuate the city and leave for İstanbul immediately. All the local French forces were already gone a week ago. The local British commander told some of his Armenian acquaintances to leave as soon as the British departed.

It has also been reported that the entire Allied force of Eskişehir, too, has been instructed to leave. Thinking that the grave situation in Cilicia has triggered the withdrawal of the Allied forces, information was requested by cable immediately from Adana, whence very disturbing news arrived about Saimbeyli [Hacın], Gaziantep [Ayntab], and Urfa particularly. Cries for help had reached Adana from these places, and [it has been learned] that Colonel Brémond had informed [the Armenians] that he could not send reinforcements to those places.

While people were confused by this troubling news, a very long and urgent telegram from the British High Commission of İstanbul reached the British command of the Konya station. Accordingly, all the Italian forces, which had opened a school in this city two days ago, were ordered to leave within three days, that is, by March 14. It was impossible not to be alarmed by this dreadful news. A wireless telegram from Rome notified the local Italian commander of his and all his troops' departure.

This morning, the Armenian primate visited the Latin monks and Miss Cushman to find out if they had received any news from İstanbul. The answer was no. He then visited the Italian commander, who announced that he would be regrettably leaving without knowing the reason at all and being unaware of the sudden change in the situation. Some Armenians are considering leaving for İstanbul with the Allied forces.

In the afternoon, the Armenian primate and the Protestant minister visited Prefect Suphi Bey, who said he was absolutely unaware of the departure of the Allied forces from Anadolu [Anatolia]. He immediately requested information by telegram from the Interior Ministry and received a response, stating: "There is nothing, do not be alarmed." The prefect urged them not to lose tempers or fear that anything could happen in Konya and [gave] other assurances, adding that it would have been indeed very good if the Italians had not left here . . .

Given this alarming situation, all are confused and do not know what to do.

• Numerous Turks wounded during the recent Greco-Turkish engagements have arrived in Afyonkarahisar.

Konya (postscript to the previous letter)—March 12, Friday

This morning, the following official message was communicated from Kayseri to Konya.

"Compelled by urgency and due to necessary and imperative reasons, we would like to send about two hundred orphans to your local American orphanage, confident of your immediate efforts." Signature: Priest Serovpé. The primate turned immediately to Miss Cushman and asked her to grant this request. Today, a telegram was sent to Kayseri instructing that the orphans be shipped immediately, considering their bad situation.

• Because of the new situation, Miss Cushman is going to İstanbul today.

են: Հայերը ամէն զգուշութիւն կ'ընեն խռովութեան եւ հաւանական ընդհարումներու տեղի չտալու համար:

Գոնիա (Առաջնորդէն) – 11 Մարտ 1920

Պոլսոյ կառավարումը երէկ առաւօտ Գոնիա հասած չըլլալով ծանրակշիռ լուրեր սկսան շրջիլ ամէն դասակարգի մէջ, որով լուրջ մտահոգութիւն մը սկսաւ ծայր տալ: Երեկոյեան տեղեկացանք թէ Աֆիոն-Գարահիսարի անգլիական բոլոր ուժերը վայրկենական հրաման ստացած են իսկոյն պարպելու քաղաքը եւ Պոլիս մեկնելու համար: Արդէն շաբաթ մը առաջ տեղւոյն ֆրանսական բոլոր ուժերը հեռացած էին: Տեղւոյն անգլիացի հրամատարը հաղորդած է կարգ մը ծանօթ հայերու, որպէսզի իրենց մեկնումին հետ անոնք ալ հեռանան:

Հաղորդուեցաւ նաեւ թէ Էսկի-Շէհիրի Համաձայնական բովանդակ ոյժը նոյնպէս հրահանգ ստացած է մեկնելու: Խորհելով որ Կիլիկիոյ մէջ ծագած ծանր կացութեան հետեւանօք է որ Համաձայնական ոյժերը կը հեռանան, իսկոյն հեռագրով տեղեկութիւն ուզուեցաւ Ատանայէն ուրկէ կը ստացուին չափազանց վրդովիչ լուրեր, մասնաւորապէս Հաճընի, Այնթապի եւ Ուրֆայի մասին, ուրկէ օգնութեան աղաղակներ հասած են Ատանա եւ թէ՝ Գնդապետ Պրէմօն հաղորդած է թէ չի կրնար օգնական ուժեր ղրկել սոյն վայրերը:

Երբ այս վրդովեալի լուրերու առջեւ շփոթած էր ժողովուրդը, հասաւ Կ. Պոլսոյ անգլիական վերին քոմիսէրութեան խիստ երկար եւ շատ ստիպողական հեռագիրը Գոնիայի կայարանի անգլիական հրամանատարութեան, որով մինչեւ երեք օր, այսինքն ցՄարտ 14, անպայման տեղէս պէտք է մեկնին իտալական բոլոր ուժերը, որոնք տակաւին երկու օր առաջ վարժարան բացած էին քաղաքիս մէջ: Այս շանթահարիչ լուրին առջեւ անկարելի էր չտագնապիլ: Հռոմէն հասած անթել հեռագիր մը կը զեկուցանէ տեղւոյս իտալական հրամանատարին իր եւ բոլոր զօրքերուն մեկնումը:

Այս առտու հայոց առաջնորդը այցելեց լատին վարդապետներուն եւ Միս Գուշմանի, հասկնալու համար թէ Պոլիսէն լուր մը ունի՞ն արդեօք: Պատասխանը ժխտական եղաւ: Յետոյ այցելեց իտալական հրամատարին, որ հաղորդեց թէ ցաւով պիտի բաժնուի եւ սակայն երբեք չեն գիտեր պատճառը եւ անծանօթ կը մնան կացութեան մէջ ստեղծուած անակնկալ փոփոխութեան առջեւ: Հայերէն ոմանք կը մտածեն Համաձայնական ուժերու հետ Կ. Պոլիս մեկնիլ:

Հայոց Առաջնորդը եւ Բողոքականաց հովիւը կէսօրէ յետոյ կը ներկայանան կուսակալ Սուպհի պէյի, որ հաղորդեց թէ բացարձակապէս կ'անգիտանայ Համաձայնական ոյժերու Անատոլուէ մեկնումին եւ անմիջապէս հեռագրով տեղեկութիւն ուզեց ներքին գործոց նախարարութենէն, որմէ սա պատասխանը եկաւ. «Ոչինչ չկայ, մի՛ տագնապիք»: Կուսակալը կը յանձնարարէ չկորսնցնել պաղարիւնութիւնը եւ երկիւղ չունենալ թէ Գոնիայի մէջ ոեւէ դէպք կրնայ պատահիլ եւ այլ հաւաստիքներ, աւելցնելով որ անշուշտ շատ լաւ կ'ըլլար եթէ իտալացիք չմեկնէին ասկէ...:

Այս տագնապալի կացութեան առջեւ ամէն մարդ շփոթած է եւ չի գիտեր ի՛նչ ընելը:

- Աֆիոն Գարահիսար հասած են բազմաթիւ թուրք վիրաւորներ յունա-թուրք վերջին ընդհարումներէն:

Գոնիա (Յետ Գրութեան նախորդ նամակին) – 12 Մարտ, Ուրբաթ

Այս առաւօտ Կեսարիայէն Գոնիայի առաջնորդարան հաղորդուած է հետեւեալ պաշտօնագիրը.

«Անյետաձգելի հարկէ ստիպուած եւ անհրաժեշտ ու հրամայական պատճառներու բերումով իբր 200 որբեր կը փափաքինք ղրկել տեղւոյդ Ամերիկեան որբանոցը, վստահ ձեր կատարելիք անմիջական ջանքերուն». ստորագրութիւն՝ Սերովբէ քահանայ: Առաջնորդը իսկոյն դիմեց Միս Գուշմանի եւ աղերսեց իրեն զոհացում տալ սոյն խնդրանքին: Այսօր հեռագրուեցաւ Կեսարիա անմիջապէս ճամբայ հանելու այդ որբերը, նկատի առնելով անոնց վատ դրութիւնը:

- Նոր կացութեան բերումով այսօր Միս Գուշման Պոլիս կ'երթայ:

Boğazlıyan (No. 347, Garabed, Krikor, Yeghia, and Soghomon)—March 15
The Turks are fully armed, [and] intending to act upon the intensity of [their hatred] against Armenians, massacres have begun in Armenian villages everywhere. The first criminals of Menteşe were found; the [traces of] others are lost. Since no Turk had been punished for past atrocities, [since] the perpetrators of the crimes are under the government's protection, [and since] the government's influence is in alignment with that of the criminals', it is impossible to seek Armenian rights. The twenty-three Armenian villages are surrounded by terror. Although new assassinations are being carried out in every village with the knowledge of the government, [this type of] activity [endorsed by the government] does not justify any Turk, and our appeals are met with disbelief. Listen to our latest cries. The Turks will bring an end to us, the last remnants. In the name of conscience, we ask for the dispatch of fair investigators capable of investigating the killers and treating our protection fairly.

Boğazlıyan (No. 343, Canlı Hovhannes, Setrag)—March 14
We cannot leave our village to head anywhere. The Circassians say: "You will be massacred again soon." They destroy our homes and use weapons against us. The state of our siege is terrible. We cannot even report the situation to the government. Have the Turks created the Armenians to [have the right to] threaten our lives at any time? The sensational calamities befalling us remain unheard by the government. What should we do? To whom should we appeal? Is it possible to send our telegrams directly to God because we cannot see justice and help among his believers? An edict [please].

Boğazlıyan (No. 329, Toros, Setrag, Misak, Diran, Sarafian Garabed, Catlı Garabed, Soghomon of Menteşe)—March 13
Happiness relating to the world and peace to nature, your eminence is a source of justice. Forlorn tribes, hungry and thirsty for the exercise of law, still languish with suffering and look with great expectation to the life-giving bounties of the world, hoping for satiation from the nourishment that gushes from your fountain.

Hear the cries of the Armenians deprived of the world's happiness and justice! We recognize the Holy Scripture and God, but our priests have been killed [and] our churches have been destroyed and turned into hospitals. Under the burden of all kinds of slander, our men have been wiped out. As the security of their honor and tranquility became too distant, the Armenians in the villages were subjected to the tribulation of times past. No Armenian can go anywhere. Two Armenians disappeared while traveling between Menteşe and the city. When we appeal to the government, they say, "You are lying," and ignore us. Along with our pain, we are facing conscription. Therefore, we ask countries that let other nations dwell in their lands, saying: "Do you also afflict your own subjects with such distress?" Is it the same as internationalism and world civilization when Muslims convert Armenians as they wish [or] torture them?

Has the fate of the more than two thousand Greeks who came as exiles all the way to Boğazlıyan from Trabzon, Samsun, and Bafra, and the sixty thousand Armenians who came from all over, as well as the local Armenians, been left to local Turks? When the list of Lieutenant Governor Kemal and his accomplices was sent by mail, only Kemal was sentenced for the massacres perpetrated by the efforts and participation of local notables. When the others took possession of the honor and wealth of the Armenians without punishment, as if their crimes were not enough [before the armistice], they [again] killed Armenians [based on] conspiratorial documents sent to the Turkish villages beforehand. Also, to kill the surviving Armenians with torment and hunger in the jails through slanders, the Turks set

Պօղազլեան (թիւ 347, Կարապետ, Գրիգոր, Եղիա եւ Սողոմոն) – 15 Մարտ

Թուրքերը ամբողջութեամբ զինուած են, իրենց [ատելութեան] սաստկութիւնը հայերու հանդէպ ի գործ դնելու մտադրութեամբ ամէն կողմ հայ գիւղերու մէջ ջարդը սկսաւ: Այն առաջին մէնթէշէցի ոճրագործները ձերբակալուեցան. միւսները կորուստ են: Անցեալ ոճրագործութիւններէն ոչ մի թուրք պատիժ չկրելուն պէս, ոճրագործութեան հեղինակներն կառավարութեան պաշտպանութեան ներքեւ գտնուելուն՝ կառավարութեան ազդեցութիւնը ոճրագործներու համամիտ ըլլալուն՝ հայ իրաւունքներուն փնտռուիլը անկարելի է: Քանիերեք գիւղերու հայոց շրջապատը սոսկումով շրջապատուած է: Նոր սպանութիւնք ամէն գիւղի մէջ ծանօթ կառավարութեան տեղեկութիւնովը կատարուելով հանդերձ, միեւնոյն գործունէութիւնը ուէ թուրք չի մեղմացներ եւ մեր դիմումներուն ալ չի հաւատացուիր: Սա մեր վերջին աղաղակներուն լսեցէք. դոյզն մնացորդներուս ալ վերջը պիտի բերեն: Մեր բողոքը լսուելու համար սպաննողներուն քննութեան կարող, մեր պաշտպանութեանը արդար[ութեամբ վերաբերող] քննիչներ ղրկուիլը կը խնդրուի խղճի անունով:

Պօղազլեան (թիւ 343, Չանլը Յովհաննէս, Սեդրակ) – 14 Մարտ

Մեր գիւղէն ուէ տեղ չենք կրնար ելնել: Չէրքէզները «այսօր վաղը դարձեալ պիտի ջարդուիք» ըսելով մեր տուները կը քանդեն եւ մեզի [դէմ] զէնք կը գործածեն: Մեր ենթարկուած պաշարման վիճակը սոսկալի է. կացութիւնը կառավարութեան նոյնիսկ յայտնելու չենք կրնար ելնել: Արդեօք հայերուն Արարիչը թուրքե՞րն են, որ ուզած ատեննին մեր կենաց պիտի սպառնան: Մեր զգայացունց աղէտները կառավարութեան կողմէ անլսելի կը մնան. ի՞նչ ընենք, որո՞ւ դիմենք. արդեօք կարելի՞ է որ մեր հեռագիրները շիտակէ շիտակ Աստծոյ քաշենք, վասնզի իր հաւատացեալներու մէջ արդարութիւն եւ օգնութիւն չենք կրնար տեսնել. փէրման [*sic*]:

Պօղազլեան (թիւ 329, Թորոս, Սեդրակ, Միսաք, Տիրան, Սարաֆեան Կարապետ, Չաթլը Կարապետ, Մէնթէշէցի Սողոմոն) – 13 Մարտ

Երջանկութիւնը աշխարհի եւ խաղաղութիւնը բնութեան վերաբերելով՝ Ձեր բարձրութիւնն ալ արդարութեան աղբիւր է: Իրաւունքի գործադրութեանը անօթցած եւ ծարաւցած դեռ տառապանքով հիւծող անոք ցեղեր Ձեր աղբիւրէն վազող սնունդէն կշտանալով, կենսապարգեւ աշխարհի բարեաց չորս աչքերով կը հային:

Աշխարհի երջանկութիւնովը եւ արդարութենէն զրկուած հայոց աղաղակները լսեցէ՛ք. Ս. Գիրքը եւ Աստուածը կը ճանչնանք, բայց մեր քահանաները սպաննուած, մեր եկեղեցիները քանդուած եւ հիւանդանոցի վերածուած է: Ամէն կարգի զրպարտութեանց բեռին տակ արու մարդիկը ջնջուեցան: Իրենց պատուին ապահովութիւնը եւ հանգիստը չափազանց հեռու ըլլալուն պէս, գիւղերու մէջ գտնուած հայերը անցեալի փորձանքին մատնուեցան: Ոչ մէկ հայ տեղ մը չի կրնար երթալ, որովհետեւ Մէնթէշէի եւ քաղաքին միջեւ երկու հայեր ճամբորդութեան պահուն անհետացուցին: Կառավարութեան երբ կը դիմենք՝ սուտ կը խօսիք ըսելով, կարեւորութիւն չի տրուիր: Այս մեր ցաւերուն հետ մէկտեղ ալ զօրք պահանջուելու վրայ ենք: Հետեւաբար իրենց հողին վրայ զանազան ազգեր բնակեցնող երկիրներուն կը հարցնենք թէ «դուք եւս ձեր հպատակներուն այսպիսի նեղութիւններ կուտա՞ք»: Իսլամներուն հայերը իրենց ուզած զոյնին դարձնելը, տանջանքներու ենթարկելը, միջազգայնութեան եւ աշխարհի քաղաքակրթութեան համեմա՞տ է:

Տրապիզոնի, Սամսոնի, Պաֆրայի կողմերէն իբր աքսոր մինչեւ Պօղազլեան եկող 2000է աւելի յոյն եւ ամէն կողմէ եկող 60,000 հայերուն եւ հոս գտնուող -տեղական- հայոց ճակատագիրը այստեղի թուրքերո՞ւն յանձնուած է, որ զայմազամ Քէմալի եւ արբանեակներուն ցանկը փոստայով երբ ղրկուեցաւ՝ տեղական երեւելիներուն ջանքերով եւ մասնակցութեամբ ջարդերուն փոխարէն միայն Քէմալ սպաննուեցաւ: Միւսները երբ առանց պատժուելու հայոց պատուին ու հարստութեան տիրացան, իբր թէ քիչ եկած իրենց ոճրագործութիւնները առաջուց թուրք գիւղերը ղրկուած դաւադրութեան թուղթերով հայերը մեռուցին ու ողջ մնացողներն ալ շինծու զրպարտութիւններով

up a Slander Committee, and the perpetrator Ormanci Hüseyin Effendi was dispatched to the villages to produce affidavits with the seal of the headmen and the imams to launch lawsuits against many absentees. The plaintiff is a criminal; the witnesses also are criminals. They are Muslim, and the government also is Muslim, whereas we, the unfortunate, are Armenians. It is as if the Armenians intimidated the Turks and took their money when they resisted as they were dragged away to be killed with an ax. For this reason, influential local notables have complained to the government, which [consequently] is imprisoning them [the Armenians], saying: "You did not die [submissively] with your hands tied." Whether that [former] policy [of annihilating Armenians] has not ended or our destiny is left to the [perpetrators] again, we do not know.

If protecting our rights as God's servants and Christians has been initiated [at all], at least deliver us by pointing us where to go. We entreat you in the name of conscience with tears in our eyes.

Boğazlıyan (No. 2136, Hovsep of Fahralı, Hovsep of Felahiye [Rumdiğin], Mihran of Fahralı, Haroutyun of Çuferdan)—March 16

[The Turks] took our families forcibly to the mountain and subjected them to their will, [but] our appeals to the government remained fruitless. The violators seem not to be satisfied with the troubles they have inflicted. Now they want to harm us more and even use weapons, so we have to flee from village to village.

Considering these intolerable situations as adverse to the government's honor, we ask for your protection and solicitude to preserve our integrity and existence in the name of humanity.

Boğazlıyan (from Vicar General G. Sarafian)—January 31

Today, Diran and Misak of Çatköy and Toros of Konuklar [Ürnac] were brought to our city in handcuffs. To escape the massacres, these people had taken refuge in the mountains. The sultan eventually pardoned them, and they surrendered to the government. After five months of free movement, they went to Adana unhindered and then set out for Çatköy. On the way, near Kayseri, they were imprisoned for about three months, and [local Turkish] people were invited to launch a lawsuit against them. Nobody applied. Hence, they were taken to Hamidiye, where they stayed for fifteen days, but no one showed up as a plaintiff. Now they [the Turks] have brought them to Boğazlıyan and want to sentence them unconditionally.

İstanbul (from the Patriarchate)—March 15

The priest Manoug of Büyük-Yeniköy in Yalova and two locals—Father Hovhannes, the local priest from Silivri, and Father Dajad, the local priest from Ovacık, had come as delegates to explain the insecurity in their area. The villagers of Büyük-Yeniköy and Ovacık want to move their wives and children to a safe place.

İstanbul (from the Patriarchate)—March 16

Four delegates from Afyonkarahisar came and reported that because of the withdrawal of the Allied soldiers and officials, the people are in a state of great fear, almost panic. If the Allied authorities hold local government officials, religious and secular leaders, and notables responsible for disturbances and incidents, the ordinary people will never dare to harm the Armenians or Christians.

բանտերու մէջ նեղութենէ եւ անօթութենէ մեռցնելու համար, Չրպարտութեան Յանձնաժողով մը կազմեցին եւ ոճրագործ Օրմանճի Հիւսէյին էֆէնտիին պաշտօնով գիւղերը ղրկուեցաւ որ մուխթարներուն եւ իմամներուն կնիքովը շատերուն ալ առանց ներկայութեանը հաստատագիր կազմելով դատ բացին: Դատ բացողը ոճրագործ, վկաներն ալ ոճրագործ. իրենք իսլամ, կառավարութիւնն ալ իսլամ, մինչ մենք դժբաղդներս հայեր ենք: Իբր թէ կացինով սպաննուելու տարուած ատեն դիմադրող հայերը թուրքերը վախցուցեր եւ դրամնին կ'առնեն եղեր ու այս պատճառաւ տեղական մեծամեծները իրենց ազդեցութեամբ բողոքեր են կառավարութեան որ «դուք ձեռքերնիդ կապուած չմեռաք» ըսելով կը բանտարկէ: Արդեօք այդ քաղաքականութիւնը չէ՞ վերջացած, թէ ոչ դարձեալ մեր ճակատագիրը անոնց ձգուած է, չենք գիտեր:

Եթէ իբր Աստուծոյ ծառաները եւ քրիստոնեաներ մեր իրաւունքը պաշտպանելու ձեռնարկուած է, գոնէ գնալիք տեղ մը ցուցունելով ազատեցէք: Արտասուալի աչքերով յանուն խղճի կը հայցենք:

Պօղազլեան (թիւ 2136, փախրա[ըը]ցի Յովսէփ, բումթիքէնցի Յովսէփ, փախրա[ըը]ցի Միհրան, չուֆէրտանցի Յարութիւն) – 16 Մարտ

Մեր ընտանիքները բռնի լեռը [տանելով] եւ իրենց կամքին ներքեւ առնելով, կառավարութեան մեր դիմումները անպտուղ մնացին: Բռնաբարողները կարծես գոհ չեղած իրենց [տուած] նեղութիւններէն, հիմա ալ վնասել եւ նոյնիսկ զէնք գործածել կ'ուզեն, որով գիւղէ գիւղ փախչելու ստիպուած ենք:

Սա անհանդուրժելի կացութիւնք կառավարութեան պատւոյն հակառակ տեսնուելով, մեր պատւոյն եւ գոյութեանը պահպանման համար ձեր պաշտպանութիւնը եւ հոգածութիւնը կը խնդրենք յանուն մարդասիրութեան:

Պօղազլեան (Առաջնորդական փոխանորդ Կ. Սարաֆեանէ) – 31 Յունվար

Այսօր քաղաքս բերին ձերբակալուած չաթցի Տիրան, Միսաք եւ իւրնէճցի Թորոս: Այս անձերը ջարդերէն ազատելու համար լեռները ապաստանած էին եւ ի վերջոյ կայսերական ներման արժանացած եւ կառավարութեան յանձնուած էին: Հինգ ամիս ազատ պտտելէ յետոյ, Ատանա գացին առանց արգելքի եւ յետոյ կը վերադառնան Չաթ: Ճամբան Կեսարիոյ մէջ զիրենք կը բանտարկեն երեք ամիսի մօտ, եւ հրաւէր կ'ընեն որ անոնց դէմ դատ ունեցողը թող դիմէ: Ոչ ոք կը դիմէ: Ասկէ կը փոխադրեն Համիտիյէ, ուր կը մնան 15 օր եւ ոչ ոք դատախազ կ'ըլլայ: Հիմա բերած են Պօղազլեան եւ կ'ուզեն անպատճառ դատապարտել:

Կ. Պոլիս (Պատրիարքարանէն) – 15 Մարտ

Եալովայի Մեծ-Նոր-Գիւղէն Տէր Մանուկ քահանայ եւ 2 տեղացիներ, Սիլիվրիէն տեղւոյն Տէր Յովհաննէս քահանան եւ Օվաճըգէն տեղւոյն Տէր Տաճատ քահանան պատուիրակ եկած էին իրենց շրջանակներու մէջ տիրող անապահովութիւնը բացատրելու համար: Մեծ-նոր-գիւղացիք եւ օվաճըգցիք իրենց կիները եւ տղաքը ապահով վայր տեղափոխել կը փափաքին:

Կ. Պոլիս (Պատրիարքարանէն) – 16 Մարտ

Աֆիոն Գարահիսարէն չորս պատգամաւորներ կը ներկայանան եւ կը հաղորդեն թէ Համաձայնական զինուորներու եւ պաշտօնեաներու քաշուելովը ժողովուրդը մեծ երկիւղի եւ գրեթէ խուճապի մատնուած է: Համաձայնական իշխանութեանց կողմէ եթէ տեղւոյն կառավարական պաշտօնեաները եւ կրօնական եւ աշխարհիկ պետերն ու երեւելիները պատասխանատու նկատուին խռովութեանց եւ դէպքերու, հասարակ ժողովուրդը բնաւ չպիտի համարձակի հայոց կամ քրիստոնէից չարիք հասցնել:

İstanbul (from the Patriarchate; the priest has another letter with the same meaning dated March 17)—March 17

The pastor of Beykoz, Father Samuel, and three villagers report that çetes have shown up in the vicinities of Beykoz, and the people are terrified.

• Two locals from Lüleburgaz also report that the people are in great fear because the Greek soldiers have withdrawn.

Ordu (from Father Kevork Sahagian)—February 27

During the Armenian deportation in 1915, [the Turks] gathered the residents of Akpınar [Mahmat] village of Mesudiye and herded them into the Armenian church, deceiving them that they would soon journey. But they kept them not for one or two days but for a week. They brought them out every day, and after beating them to death, they crammed those who remained into the church again. Later, after robbing the villagers of everything, they also killed them. These [acts] were done by Salih, the imam of the village Derinçay [Kotanı] in Ordu; his brother Emin; Boduroğlu Şevket, one of the elders of the village of Topçam [Gebeme]; Köloğlu Niyazi from the same village; and a man named Hasan from the same village, who had killed by his own hands all the family members of Priest Kevork Sahagian and who now lives in his house.

These massacrers are now in the same village. Therefore, the villagers that survived miraculously, including Priest Kevork Sahagian, cannot return to the village, nor can they appeal to the government for their effects and estates.

Priest Kevork Sahagian was tortured. They made cuts and holes in his face, and then they would have killed him had he not escaped.

İstanbul (petition signed by Armenian and Greek prisoners of the Central Prison)—March 10

Because of the massacres in the interior, there is hatred against Christian prisoners by Turkish prisoners who wait for an opportunity to massacre them as well. [The Christian] prisoners ask for the security of life rather than a release from prison. They would like the two to three hundred Armenian and Greek prisoners to be transferred to another prison if possible.

Mersin (from the National Union)—March 8

Danger looms over all the Armenians of Cilicia after the events in Maraş. The activities of the çetes launched from around Silifke are expanding daily, and the rings of fire are getting tighter and tighter. They have surrounded Mersin from a distance barely five hours away. Milli bandits have been crossing the border since March 1. As of now, they have captured Arslanköy [Efrenk], Gözlü, Alata, Fındıkpınarı, and Değirmençay [Erçel]. The latter is only five hours away from Mersin. The people are terrified. In the village of Karaburun, near Arslanköy, four Greek families were raped and abducted by bandits, and nine Lebanese Maronites who were working near the village were brutally killed, including a nine-month-old boy who was placed on a rock, shot dead, and then used as a target for the çetes. The child's body was transported to the city; it was punctured entirely with bullets. Another fourteen Greek workers in the area were arrested by çetes and tied up, but their fate remains unclear.

From February 16 to the beginning of March, about seven to eight thousand French troops landed in Mersin; barely twenty-five hundred remain here; the rest have been sent to the Silifke frontier.

All Turkish gendarmes who were sent to act against the bandits have voluntarily turned themselves into captives and joined them. The entire Turkish peasantry, well-prepared and armed, supports the çetes by all possible means.

Կ. Պոլիս (Պատրիարքարանէն. նոյնիմաստ գիր մըն ալ քահանան ունի 17 Մարտ թուով) – 17 Մարտ

Պէյքօզի հոգեւոր հովիւ Տէր Սամուէլ քահանայ եւ երեք գիւղացիք կը յայտնեն թէ չէթէներ երեւցած են Պէյքօզի շրջակայքը եւ ժողովուրդը ահ ու դողի մատնուած է:

- Լիւլէ-Պուրկազէն ալ երկու տեղացիք կը հաղորդեն թէ յունական զինուորները քաշուած ըլլալով՝ ժողովուրդը մեծ երկիւղի մատնուած է:

Օրտու (Տէր Գէորգ քահանայ Սահակեան) – 27 Փետրուար

1915ի հայկական տարագրութեան միջոցին Մեսուտիյէի Մահմատ գիւղիս բնակիչները այսօր վաղը ճամբայ հանելու համար խաբելով ժողվեցին եւ հայոց եկեղեցին լեցուցին: Բայց ոչ թէ մէկ երկու օր, այլ շաբաթ մը պահեցին, ամէն օր դուրս հանել եւ մեռցնելու աստիճան ծեծելէ վերջ կրկին կը լեցնէին եկեղեցին: Ասկէ վերջ գիւղացիին ամբողջ ունեցածները կողոպուտի տալէ յետոյ իրենք ալ մեռցուցին: Ասոնք կատար[եցի]ն Օրտուի Քօթան գիւղին իմամը Սալիհ, եղբայրը Էմին, Կէպէմէ գիւղին մեծերէն Պօտուր օղլու Շէվքէտ, նոյն գիւղէն Քէօլ օղլու Նիազի, նոյն գիւղէն Թիմ Հասան անունով մէկը, որ Տէր Գէորգ քահանայ Սահակեանի ընտանիքին բոլոր անդամները իր ձեռքով մեռցուցած է եւ հիմա անոր տունը կը բնակի:

Այս ջարդարարները հիմա կը զտնուին նոյն գիւղը, որով հրաշքով ազատող գիւղացիք, ընդ որս նաեւ Տէր Գէորգ քահանայ Սահակեան, չեն կրնար գիւղ երթալ եւ ոչ ալ կառավարութեան դիմում ընել իրենց գոյքերուն եւ կալուածներուն համար:

Տէր Գէորգ քահանայ Սահակեան անձնապէս չարչարանքներու ենթարկուած, երեսները կտրտած եւ ծակծկած են, եւ յետոյ պիտի մեռցնէին եթէ փախած չըլլար:

Կ. Պոլիս (կեդրոնական բանտի հայ եւ յոյն բանտարկեալներէն ստորագրեալ հանրագրութիւն) – 10 Մարտ

Թուրք բանտարկեալներու կողմէ քրիստոնեայ բանտարկեալներու դէմ ատելութիւն կայ գաւառի ջարդերուն հետեւանօք, եւ առիթ կը սպասեն որ զանոնք ալ ջարդեն: Բանտարկեալները կը խնդրեն կեանքի ապահովութիւն եւ ոչ թէ բանտէն արձակում: Եթէ կարելիութիւն կայ, կ՚ուզեն որ 2–3 հարիւր հայ եւ յոյն բանտարկեալները ուրիշ բանտ փոխադրուին:

Մերսին (Ազգային Միութենէն) – 8 Մարտ

Մարաշի դէպքերէն յետոյ վտանգ կը սպառնայ բոլոր Կիլիկիոյ հայութեան: Սելեւկիոյ կողմէ սկսած չէթէական գործունէութիւնները օրէ օր կ՚ընդարձակուին, կրակի օղակները երթալով աւելի կը սեղմուին ու շրջապատած են Մերսինը հազիւ 5 ժամ հեռուէն: Միլլի հրոսակները սահմանէն ներս խուժելով Մարտ 1-էն մինչեւ հիմա գրաւեցին Էֆրէ[ն]կ, Կէօզլիւ, Ալաթթա, Ֆընտըզ Բունար եւ Էրչէլ: Այս վերջինը Մերսինէն 5 ժամ հեռու է միայն: Ժողովուրդը սարսափի մատնուած է: Էֆրէնկի մօտերը Գարապուրուն ըսուած գիւղին մէջ 4 յոյն ընտանիքներ հրոսակներու կողմէ կը բռնաբարուին եւ կ՚առեւանգուին եւ այդ գիւղի մօտերը գործով պարապող 9 լիբանանցի մարօնի-ներ խժդուժօրէն կը սպաննուին, որոնց մէջէն 9 ամսուայ երախայ մը քարին վրայ դրուելով հրացա-նազարկ կ՚ըլլայ ու իբր նշանառութեան տախտակ կը ծառայէ չէթէներու: Դիակը քաղաք փոխադ-րեցին, որ ամբողջութեամբ գնդակներու տակ ծակ ծակ եղած էր: Այդ շրջանին մէջ դարձեալ 14 յոյն աշխատաւորներ չէթէներու կողմէ ձերբակալուելով կը կապուին, բայց իրենց վճռուած բախտը տակաւին անորոշ է:

Փետրուար 16էն մինչեւ Մարտի սկիզբը 7–8 հազարի մօտ ֆրանսացի զինուորներ ցամաք ելան Մերսին, հազիւ 2500-ը հոս կը մնայ, մնացեալը Սելեւկեան սահմանագլուխ ղրկուեցան:

Հրոսակներու դէմ ղրկուած բոլոր թուրք ժանտարմաները կամովին գերի ինկած, միացած են

The unarmed and defenseless Armenians have been almost abandoned and left to their fate. If they [the Allies] do not come to the rescue, the Armenians of Cilicia are doomed.

Bilecik—March 15

The Turks are creating new organizations. The Armenians, after hearing from several Turkish individuals about the distribution of weapons to the young people of the village, the preparation for a massacre against Armenians, [and] especially the election of Mercimekzade Ahmet as deputy, are terrified and live under the threat of massacre. The people want to migrate.

İstanbul (from Khachig Der Tavitian of Bilecik)—March 18

Hayrabed Kevorkian and Kalousd Zournajian from the Türkmen village of Bilecik have been jailed for a crime. Their trial took place on March 13. Their plaintiffs—the wife and son of Hacı Mustafa of Gökçeler—were incited to accuse these Armenians of being criminals because the two Armenians had left property worth fifteen- to twenty-thousand liras with Hacı Mustafa, and when they returned, they demanded the property or its value in cash from him. Mustafa dismissed them, and the Armenians turned to the government. The crime was committed at that same time. Mustafa's wife and son seized the opportunity to have these Armenians imprisoned as criminals. The observable circumstance in the trial was that the accusations of the woman and the son did not match at all and contradicted each other. It is also surprising that the daughter-in-law of the murdered person was heard as a witness, which is illegal because she could appear as a plaintiff. The court is clearly biased.

Seven or eight people were brought as witnesses, all of whom testified in favor of the defendants. The witnesses testified that two days before the crime, five armed men and a pedestrian came to the waterfront of Tuzaklı in the middle of the night and shouted to the boatman that they were gendarmes and that they must cross the water that night to go to Türkmen. They crossed to the other shore with a boat. Early morning of the crime, these five people returned to the shore, this time armed, three of them on horseback. [The witnesses] saw that one of the horses belonged to the murdered Hacı Mustafa. Also, on the night of the crime, many gunshots were fired in Gökçeler, so when the villagers of [a village] called Çengeller, located a quarter of an hour away, went to help, on the way they came across the criminals, four of whom were pedestrians, and one of whom rode Hacı Mustafa's horse. They recognized even the possessions on the horse. The criminals tied up two of these villagers and took them somewhere for an hour under the pretext of showing them the way [to Mustafa's house]. The perpetrators called a young man and forced him to show them Hacı Mustafa's house on the night they went to Gökçeler. None of the witnesses had seen the defendants among the perpetrators. The perpetrators went to the village school on the night of their departure from Gökçeler and had an extended visit with the hoca who was there. Although the whereabouts of the hoca is unknown now, during the initial interrogation, these two Armenians were presented to him and confirmed by him that they were not among the perpetrators. During the arrest of the accused Kalousd Zournajian, bloodstains were noticed on him, and they wanted to use this as evidence, but [the garment, possibly] was sent to İstanbul to be examined, and it was confirmed that the stains were not traces of human blood. Despite all these facts, the court was in the mood for a conviction; the defendants demanded that their witnesses be heard to prove that they had been in their village on the night of the crime. The trial has been adjourned until April 10.

As far as can be judged from the phenomena, the court will yield to Turkish public opinion and inevitably condemn these two innocent Armenians to satisfy the Muslim element.

անոնց: Ամբողջ թուրք գիւղացիութիւնը կազմ ու պատրաստ, զինուած, կարելի բոլոր միջոցներով կ'օժանդակէ չէթէներուն:

Անզէն ու անպաշտպան հայութիւնը գրեթէ լքուած եւ թողուած է իր բախտին: Եթէ օգնութեան չհասնին, Կիլիկիոյ հայութիւնը փչանալու դատապարտուած է:

Պիլէճիկ – 15 Մարտ

Թուրքերը նորանոր կազմակերպութիւններ կ'ընեն: Գիւղացի երիտասարդներուն զէնք բաժնուիլը ու մի քանի թուրք անհատներէ հայերու հանդէպ ջարդի մը պատրաստուիլը լսելով՝ սա մանաւանդ Մէրճիմէք զատէ Աhմէտի երեսփոխան ընտրուիլը [հայութեան] սոսկում պատճառած է եւ ջարդի սպառնալիքի տակ կը գտնուի: Ժողովուրդը գաղթել կը փափաքի:

Կ. Պոլիս (Խաչիկ Տէր Դաւիթեանէ, պիլէճիկցի) – 18 Մարտ

Պիլէճիկի Թիւրքմէն գիւղէն Հայրապետ Գէորգեան եւ Գալուստ Զուրնաճեան անձերը ոճրագործութեան մը առթիւ բանտարկուած են: Ասոնց դատավարութիւնը Մարտ 13ին տեղի ունեցաւ: Յիշեալ[ներու]ն դատախազները են սպանեալին կէօքճէլէրցի Հաճի Մուսթաֆա[յ]ի կինը ու տղան, որոնք դրդուած իբրեւ ոճրագործ կ'ամբաստանեն այս հայերը, որովհետեւ այս հայերը յիշեալ Հաճի Մուսթաֆայի քով 15–20 հազար ոսկի արժողութեամբ գոյքեր ձգած են եւ երբ կը վերադառնան, այդ գոյքերը կամ փոխարժէքը կը պահանջեն իրմէ: Մուսթաֆա կը վռնտէ եւ հայերը կառավարութեան կը դիմեն: Ճիշդ այս պահուն ոճիրը կը գործուի: Մուսթաֆայի կինը ու տղան առիթը ներկայացած համարելով, իբրեւ ոճրագործ այս հայերը բանտարկել կուտան: Դատավարութեան մէջ դիտելի պարագան սա էր որ կնոջը եւ տղուն ամբաստանութիւնները երբեք զիրար չէին բռներ եւ իրար կը հակասէին: Նոյնպէս զարմանալի է որ սպանեալին հարսը իբր վկայ կը լսուի, ինչ որ ապօրէն է, քանի որ անիկա իբր դատախազ կրնայ ներկայանալ: Դատարանը յայտնի կերպով կողմնակալութիւն կ'ընէ:

7–8 անձեր իբր վկայ բերուած էին, ամէնքն ալ ամբաստանեալներուն նպաստաւոր վկայութիւն տուին: Վկաները հաստատեցին թէ ոճիրէն երկու օր առաջ Դուզագլըի ջուրին եզերքը 5 հոգի զինեալ եւ հետիոտն կուգան կէս գիշերին եւ նաւավարին կը պոռան ըսելով թէ իրենք ժանտարմա են, անպատճառ այս գիշեր ջուրէն անցնելով Թիւրքմէն երթալնին պէտք է եւ նաւակով ջուրին միւս եզերքը կ'անցնին: Իսկ ոճիրին առտուն կանուխ այս հինգ հոգին դարձեալ ջուրին եզերքը կուգան, այս անգամ զինեալ, երեքը ձիաւոր: Ձիերէն մին սպանեալ Հաճի Մուսթաֆայի ձին ըլլալը տեսած են: Դարձեալ ոճիրին գիշերը Կէօքճէլէրի մէջ շատ մը զէնք պարպուելով քառորդ ժամ հեռաւորութեամբ Չէնկէլէր ըսուած թիւրք գիւղացիները օգնութեան կ'երթան. ճամբան ոճրագործներուն կը պատահին, որոնց չորսը հետիոտն իսկ մէկն ալ Հաճի Մուսթաֆայի ձին հեծած, այնպէս որ նոյնիսկ ձիուն վրայի գոյքերն անգամ կը ճանչնան: Ոճրագործները այս գիւղացիներէն երկուքը կապելով ճամբայ ցոյց տալու պատրուակով ժամի մը չափ տեղ կը տանին: Ոճրագործները Կէօքճէլէր գացած գիշերնին երիտասարդ մը կանչելով բռնի Հաճի Մուսթաֆային տունը ցոյց տալ կուտան: Վկաներէն ոչ մէկը ամբաստանեալները ոճրագործներուն մէջ տեսած էր: Ոճրագործները Կէօքճէլէրէն գացած գիշերնին գիւղին դպրոցը կ'երթան եւ հոն գտնուող *Հօճա*յին հետ երկարօրէն կը տեսնուին: Թէպէտեւ հիմա այս *հօճա*յին ուր ըլլալը անյայտ է, բայց նախնական հարցաքննութեանց մէջ այս երկու հայերը անոր ցոյց տուած են եւ անոնց՝ ոճրագործներուն մէջ չըլլալը հաստատած է: Ամբաստանեալ Գալուստ Զուրնաճեանի ձերբակալման ատեն վրան արեան բիծեր կը նշմարեն եւ ասիկա իբր փաստ կ'ուզեն գործածել, սակայն քննելու համար Կ. Պոլիս կը ղրկուի եւ կը հաստատուի թէ անոնք մարդու արեան հետքեր չեն: Հակառակ այս բոլոր փաստերուն, դատարանին տրամադրութիւնը դէպի դատապարտութիւն ըլլալով, ամբաստանեալները պահանջեցին որ լսուին իրենց վկաները, որոնք պիտի հաստատեն ոճիրին գիշերը իրենց գիւղը ըլլալը: Դատը յետաձգուեցաւ Ապրիլ 10ին:

İstanbul (from the Patriarchate)—March 22

It is reported from Alemdağı that armed Turks are moving around in the area. There are now nine Armenian households in Ermeniköy (Upper Village) and twenty-one Armenian households in Sultançiftliği (Lower Village), all poor and defenseless.

Boğazlıyan (from Hapet of Çatköy)—March 8

Five people are still in prison. Their offense is that they had taken refuge in the mountain. They have been put through torture and held in prison for five months without reason. Slander has been fabricated as if they have made threats to the Turks.

• The Circassians, who have been placed in Armenian houses, continue to demolish them and exercise armed threats [against Armenians].

Boğazlıyan (from the National Assistance)—March 8

The Turks, who massacred the Armenians with inexplicable brutality in 1915–1918 and who went unpunished, started imprisoning prominent Armenians based on slander. Boğazlıyan's assassin was not Kemal the monster alone; he had followers who, too, looted, butchered with axes, abducted brides and girls, and led thousands of young Armenians to the slaughterhouse with their hands tied to one another. They have now found a device to put the Armenian remnants in a situation that would prevent them from demanding the return of their goods, houses, and places and suing the perpetrators. They are fabricating slanders with false witnesses, accusing many Armenians of extorting money from Turks. Previously, they had already imprisoned five Armenians from Çatköy, and now they are getting ready to imprison fourteen more Armenians from the twenty-three Armenian villages [of Boğazlıyan].

• Only two people of the thirty-five-member family of Hayg Ka[h]ramanian, who was serving the army in Baghdad, had survived, one of whom was his wife Tshkho, who is with a Circassian named Ali Kehya of Kasaba, allegedly having married him. Despite an appeal to the government to have Tshkho return to her legal husband Hayg Ka[h]ramanian, they have not handed her over for a month because Ali Kehya is one of those witnesses whom Boğazlıyan's influential notable Cemal Bey—the destroyer of the twenty-three Armenian villages of Boğazlıyan—has recruited to slander Armenians. There are hundreds like her, whose husbands are alive, but to please the local notables, Judge Hasan Hüseyin rejects the applicants relying on the new law, saying: "Those who are pregnant with a Turk shall not be given," or "Tashihi sin" [age correction].

Bursa (from Priest Iknadios)—March 21

Insecurity continues in Bursa; the Milli forces continue to act as before. Even if an order has been given from the center [central government], there is no change here. They constantly go around armed. Therefore, people still live in moments of fear and terror. The local Turkish newspapers also continue their provocative publications.

Trabzon (from the vicar general)—March 11

The political situation in Trabzon is seriously worrying. Governor Hamit Bey and the Allied representatives assure people that there is no danger, but it is not possible to believe the prefect's words because

Որքան կարելի է դատել երեւոյթներէն, դատարանը թուրք հանրային կարծիքին առջեւ տեղի տալով եւ խլամ տարրը գոհացնելու համար պիտի դատապարտէ անպատճառ այս երկու անմեղ հայերը:

Կ. Պոլիս (Պատրիարքարանէն) – 22 Մարտ

Ալէմտաղիէն կը տեղեկացնեն թէ զինեալ թուրքերը կը շրջին այդ կողմերը: Հայ Գիւղի մէջ (Վերին Գիւղ) հիմա կայ 9 տուն հայ, իսկ Սուլթան Չիֆլիկի մէջ (Վարի Գիւղ) 21 տուն հայ, ամէնքն ալ աղքատիկ եւ անպաշտպան:

Պօղազլեան (չաթցի Յաբէթէն) – 8 Մարտ

Հինգ հոգի տակաւին բանտը կը մնան, որոնց յանցանքը լեռը ապաստանած ըլլալն է: Ասոնք կ'ենթարկուին չարչարանքներու եւ հինգ ամիս է որ բանտը կը մնան առանց պատճառի: Շինծու զրպարտութիւններ կը յօրինուին, իբր թէ ասոնք սպառնալիքներ ըրած են թուրքերու:

- Չէրքէզները, որ հայոց տուները դրուած են, շարունակ կը քանդեն, զինեալ սպառնալիքներ կը գործադրեն:

Պօղազլեան (Ազգային Խնամատարութենէն) – 8 Մարտ

Թուրքերը, որ 1915–1918 տարիները անբացատրելի վայրագութեամբ ջարդած են հայերը եւ անպատիժ մնացած, սկսած են զրպարտութիւններով երեւելի հայերը բանտարկել: Պօղազլեանի ջարդարարը մի[ն]ակ հրէշ Քէմալը չէր, այլ ունէր նաեւ իր արբանեակները, որոնք կողոպտեցին, կացիններով մորթեցին, հարսեր եւ աղջիկներ առեւանգեցին, հայ հազարաւոր երիտասարդներ թեւ թեւի կապած դէպի սպանդանոց առաջնորդեցին: Ասոնք հիմա հնարք մը գտած են հայ մնացորդները դնելու այնպիսի վիճակի մը մէջ, որ անիկա չպահանջէ իր ապրանքը, տունը, տեղը եւ ոճրագործներու դէմ դատ չբանայ: Ասոնք զրպարտութիւններ կը ստեղծեն սուտ վկաներով, որով կ'ամբաստանեն շատ մը հայեր որ իբր թէ սպառնալիքով թուրքերէ դրամներ կորզած են: Ասկէ առաջ արդէն բանտարկած էին 5 չաթցի հայեր, հիմա ալ կը պատրաստ[ուին] 23 հայ գիւղերէն 14 հայեր եւս բանտարկելու:

- Պաղտատի մէջ զինուորութիւն ընող Հայկ Գա[հ]րամանեանի 35 հոգինոց ընտանիքէն փրկուած էին միայն երկու անձ, որոնցմէ մէկը իր կինը՝ Դշխոյ, որ կը գտնուի Գասապայէն Ալի Քէհեա կոչուած չէրքէզին քով, իբր թէ անոր ամուսնացած: Հակառակ անոր որ կառավարութեան դիմում եղած է Դշխոյն դարձնելու համար իր օրինաւոր ամուսնոյն՝ Հայկ Գա[հ]րամանեանի, ամիսէ մը ի վեր չեն յանձներ, վասնզի Պօղազլեանի 23 հայ գիւղերը փճացնող գիւղացի ազդեցիկ էշրաֆէն Ճէմալ պէյի հայերը զրպարտելու համար ասկէ անկէ ճարած վկաներէն մէկը այդ Ալի Քէհեան է: Ասոր նման հարիւրաւորներ կան, որոնց ամուսինները ողջ են, սակայն տեղացի էշրաֆին խաթեր համար դատաւոր Հասան Հիւսէյնը նոր օրէնքով կը մերժէ դիմողները, ըսելով թէ «թուրքէն յղի եղողը չպիտի տրուի» կամ «թա[սհիհ]ի սին» կ'ըսեն:

Պրուսա (Տէր Իգնատիոս քահանայէն) – 21 Մարտ

Պրուսայի մէջ կը շարունակէ անապահովութիւնը, Միլլի ուժերը տակաւին իրենց նախկին գործունէութիւնը կը շարունակեն: Կեդրոնէն եթէ հրահանգ ալ տրուած է, հոս փոփոխութիւն չկայ: Շարունակ զինեալ կը շրջին, որով ժողովուրդը դեռ կ'ապրի ահ ու սարսափի վայրկեաններ: Հոս հրապարակուող թուրք թերթերն ալ կը շարունակեն իրենց գրգռիչ հրատարակութիւնները:

Տրապիզոն (Առաջնորդական Փոխանորդէն) – 11 Մարտ

Տրապիզոնի քաղաքական կացութիւնը լրջօրէն մտահոգիչ է: Կուսակալ Համիտ պէյ եւ Համաձայնական ներկայացուցիչներ կ'ապահովցնեն թէ վտանգ չկայ, սակայն կարելի չէ կուսակալին

those who want to cause a massacre do not recognize the government's authority. And the Allied representatives take seriously the official assurances, which may even be deliberately false.

The Armenians have been completely deprived of self-defense, while the Turks are completely well-armed.

İstanbul (from Priest Kalousd Boghosian upon his return from Çatalca)—March 24[56]

The Greek metropolitan Bishop Joakim and headman Kavriel Effendi in Çatalca reported that Cafer Tayyar Pasha has terrified all the Armenian and Greek people in the province of Edirne, as well as Çatalca. A couple of days ago, Major Hamdi Bey visited Çatalca with four followers as a delegate of Cafer Tayyar. Calling upon prominent Turks, Greeks, and the headmen, he announced that Edirne has completely severed its ties with İstanbul. He then issued a conscription order and instructed that a list of all potential servicemen be compiled. The Greeks absolutely rejected it, saying, "We have no soldiers, and we do not want a war." Major Hamdi Bey left. The Turks are all armed, while the Christians are absolutely unarmed and unprepared. In Çatalca, the commander of the gendarmerie Captain Mehmet Bey, alimony clerk Murad Bey, the leader of the Millis Hacı Hamdi Bey, and Fahri Bey, who resigned from the police, are terrorizing the people as Millis. Recently, the latter, intoxicated, shouted in the square one morning: "Let the Muslims join me, and the infidels come out against us. We will kill them all by the sword." It seems that the Turks did not like this very much either, so they had him arrested by the police. The people, Armenians and Greeks together, are asking for help.

Mersin (from Reverend Father Mampré [Sirounian])—March 15[57]

According to the news received from Maraş, if immediate help does not reach the victims of the disaster, who are primarily women and children, they, too, will be doomed to die. The [Milli] movement extends to all parts of Cilicia. After Maraş, it is the turn of Saimbeyli [Hacın]. On the eleventh of this month, fighting broke out in Doğanbeyli [Rumlu], north of Saimbeyli. Yesterday, the Catholicos of Cilicia announced that the çetes were now an hour away from Saimbeyli and that the city was in danger. And today, according to information received from the National Union of Adana, the Armenians of Saimbeyli were instructed to retreat and take refuge in Kozan [Sis]. The primate of Saimbeyli, Bishop Bedros Sarajian, is currently in Adana working to bring useful forces to his flock.

The overall situation in Cilicia is unfavorable. The movement of çetes is expanding and gaining momentum. The movement is led by Turkish officers. The troops are made up of regular soldiers with plenty of ammunition and food. The long and orderly struggle in Maraş has convinced sensible people that it is the result of serious preparation. Experienced forces are leading the movement.

Horror and fear are common. News of new destructions and murders reaches us every day. Armenian villages are being destroyed, Armenian properties are being looted, and the Armenians' honor is being violated. Behold the life of the Armenians of Cilicia! Murders and looting are frequent, especially in areas lacking French forces. Kozan, Dörtyol, Adana, Tarsus, and Mersin[58] are calm and peaceful for now, but the looming danger is and will remain there forever. Adana and Mersin are well protected militarily, but Kozan, Dörtyol, and Tarsus remain defenseless. Recently, a large number of French forces arrived in Mersin. There is no shortage of warships.

An American armored cruiser arrived in Mersin yesterday morning, and it left in the evening. The situation changes every moment. The explosion of a bomb in Adana on Saturday, March 15, left people in a state of panic. The Armenians of Cilicia are on edge. The slightest explosion of a weapon, or an in-

խօսքին հաւատ ընծայել, վասնզի անոնք որ կ'ուզեն ջարդ առաջ բերել, կառավարութեան հեղինակութիւնը չեն ճանչնար: Իսկ Համաձայնական ներկայացուցիչները կշիռ կուտան պաշտօնական հաւաստումներու, որոնք կրնան նոյնիսկ գիտակցութեամբ սուտ ըսուած ըլլալ:

Հայերը բոլորովին զուրկ են ինքնապաշտպանութենէ, իսկ թուրքերը ամբողջութեամբ լաւ զինուած են:

Կ. Պոլիս (Տէր Գալուստ քահանայ Պօղոսեանէ, Չաթալճայէն դարձին) – 24 Մարտ

Չաթալճայի մէջ յունաց Մեթրոպոլիտ Տէր Յովակիմ Եպիսկոպոս եւ Միխթար Գավռիէլ էֆէնտի հաղորդած են թէ Ճաֆէր Թայեար փաշա ահ ու սարսափի մատնած է Էտիրնէի կուսակալութեան մէջ գտնուող բոլոր հայ եւ յոյն ժողովուրդը, ինչպէս Չաթալճայի: Մէկ երկու օր առաջ Ճաֆէր Թայեարի կողմէ Չաթալճա պատուիրակ եկած էր հազարապետ Համտի պէյ չորս հետեւորդներով, եւ թուրք եւ յոյն երեւելիները, մուխթարները կոչելով անոնց յայտարարած է թէ Էտիրնէն Կ. Պոլիսէն բոլորովին անջատուած է: Յետոյ զօրակոչի հրաման տուած է եւ բոլոր զինուորցուներու ցուցակը կազմելու հրահանգ տուած է: Յոյները բացարձակապէս մերժած են ըսելով որ «ոչ զինուորցու ունինք եւ ոչ ալ պատերազմ կ'ուզենք»: Հազարապետ Համտի պէյ մեկնած է: Թուրքերը ամէնն ալ զինուած են, իսկ քրիստոնեայք բացարձակապէս անզէն ու անպատրաստ են: Չաթալճայի մէջ իբր Միլլիճի ժողովուրդը սարսափահար կ'ընեն ժանտարմա-զօմանտանը հարիւրապետ Մէհմէտ պէյ, Նաֆաա Քեաթիպի Մուրատ պէյ, Միլլիճիներու շէֆ Հաճի Համտի պէյ, ոստիկանութենէ հրաժարեալ Ֆահրի պէյ: Այս վերջինը անցեալները առտու մը զինով վիճակի մէջ հրապարակին վրայ կեցած կը պոռար թէ միւսլիմմաները թող ինծի միանան եւ կեավուրներն ալ մեր դէմ ելլան, ամէնքն ալ մէկ սուրէ կ'անցնենք: Այս բանը կ'երեւի թէ թուրքերուն ալ շատ հաճոյ չ'երեւար, ուստի ոստիկանութեան միջոցաւ ձերբակալել կուտան: Ժողովուրդը՝ հայ եւ յոյն միասին, օգնութիւն կը խնդրեն:

Մերսին (Մամբրէ Վարդապետ [Սիրունեանէ]) – 15 Մարտ

Մարաշէն ստացուած լուրերուն նայելով՝ եթէ անմիջական օգնութիւն չհասնի աղէտէն վիրաւորեալ դժբաղդներուն, որոնք մեծ մասամբ կիներ ու մանուկներ են, անոնք ալ դատապարտուած պիտի ըլլան մեռնելու: [Միլլի] Շարժումը կը ծաւալի Կիլիկիոյ ամէն վայրերուն մէջ ալ: Մարաշէն վերջ կարգը Հաճընինն է: Ամսոյս 11ին սկսած են կռիւները Հաճընէն հիւսիս գտնուող Ռումլուի մէջ: Երէկ Կիլիկիոյ Կաթողիկոսը հաղորդեց թէ չէթաները այժմ մէկ ժամ հեռու կը գտնուին Հաճընէն եւ քաղաքը վտանգի մէջ է: Իսկ այսօր Ատանայի Ազգ. Միութենէն առնուած տեղեկութեան մը համաձայն, հրահանգ տրուած է Հաճնոյ հայերուն որպէսզի նահանջեն եւ ապաստանին Սիս: Հաճնոյն առաջնորդը՝ Պետրոս Եպս. Սարաճեան, այժմ Ատանա կը գտնուի եւ կ'աշխատի օգտակար ոյժեր հասցնել իր հօտին:

Կիլիկիոյ ընդհանուր կացութիւնը աննպաստ է: Չէթէական շարժումը կը ծաւալի ամէն կողմ եւ կը զօրանայ: Շարժումը կը վարեն թուրք սպաներ եւ բանակները կազմուած են կանոնաւոր զինուորներէ, որոնք ունին առատ ռազմամթերք եւ ուտելիք: Մարաշի երկարատեւ ու կանոնաւոր պայքարը համոզել կուտայ խելահաս անձնաւորութիւնները թէ ան արդիւնքն էր լուրջ պատրաստութեան մը: Շարժումը կը վարեն փորձառու ոյժեր:

Սարսափը եւ երկիւղը ընդհանուր է, ամէն օր նոր աւերումներու եւ սպանութեանց լուրեր կը հասնին մեզի: Հայ գիւղեր կը փճացուին, հայուն ինչքը աւարի կը տրուի եւ հայուն պատիւը կը բռնաբարուի. ահա Կիլիկիոյ հայութեան կեանքը: Սպանութիւնները եւ թալանները յաճախադէպ են մանաւանդ այն տեղերը, ուր ֆրանսական ոյժեր կը պակսին: Սիս, Տէօրթ-Եօլ, Ատանա, Տարսոն ու Սիս[12] առ այժմ հանդարտ եւ խաղաղ են, սակայն սպառնացող վտանգը կայ եւ կը մնայ յաւիտեան: Ատանա[ն] ու Մերսինը զինուորապէս լաւ պաշտպանուած են, սակայն Սիս, Տէօրթ-Եօլ եւ Տարսոն անպաշտպան կը մնան: Այս օրերս ֆրանսական ստուար ոյժեր եկան Մերսին: Պատերազմական նաւերն ալ պակաս չեն:

cident in the square, causes much public unrest.

• No news can be received about Gaziantep [Ayntab]. The French authorities communicate with the city by plane, which proves the alarming situation there.

• Although Mersin's Turks sometimes show a fang, they dare not move because the French are stronger militarily here. However, if the situation continues like this and the çetes do not encounter resistance, the fight will soon likely move to Mersin, the last refuge of the Armenians. Many from Adana have already sought refuge in Mersin as a haven.

• One recent night, a warning to the Turks of Mersin, written with poisonous and fanatical spirit, was posted by the Turks near the city hall entrance on March 16. The signature on the statement was significant: "Mersin's Socialist Representative and Commander of National Forces." Thus, a connection between the Bolsheviks and the Milli movement is seen.

Biga (from Priest Nerses Maloumian)—March 21

Biga has been in turmoil for three months, with Milli leaders twice being bitterly defeated by the solidarity of more than fifty thousand villagers. On March 13, the Millis again besieged the city with great readiness for the third time, with all military personnel, cannons, machine guns, a large amount of ammunition, twelve hundred to fifteen hundred soldiers, and a part of the cavalry. A fierce battle was fought for five whole days. The townspeople were cut from external communication. The villagers fought to the death and defeated the Millis. The Millis left Biga, and the villagers chased them for quite a distance. Here the government has been dissolved, and the villagers keep order. The market has been closed for a long time, and the artisanal class is in a desperate state owing to the deprivation of livelihood. Of the eighty Armenian families in Biga, thirty-five families from the prosperous class left in fear before the Milli forces arrived. The rest are preparing to leave for fear that the Millis will return again, and that this time it will be impossible to escape the impending danger.

Tekirdağ (from the vicar general)—March 28

A few weeks ago, the city passed grave crises, as the military commander of Edirne, Cafer Tayyar Bey, ordered mobilization, armed the villagers, and enticed the Turkish mob to harass the Christians. The Millis were walking around the city armed. A catastrophe would have been very likely if District Governor Feruhan Bey and Division Commandant Salahettin Bey had not objected to Cafer Tayyar's instructions. During those same days, an English armored cruiser arrived. The ship's commander told the division commandant and the deputy district governor that if a Christian's nose bled, he would burn the whole city. He also urged the Greek metropolitan and the Armenian vicar general to instruct the people to gather at a specific place in the event of an incident. The presence of the armored cruiser frightened the Turkish people for fifteen days, but today the armored cruiser left for İstanbul, leaving us here alone. The British representative and District Governor Feruhan Bey also have gone to İstanbul. Meanwhile, Division Commandant Salahettin Bey has been dismissed, and the Milli Cemil Bey [has replaced him]. Therefore, no one able to counterbalance the Milli forces is left here, and the Millis resumed their work, and Cafer Tayyar's instructions have begun to be issued plentifully. Our communi-

Երէկ առտու ամերիկեան զրահաւոր մը Մերսին եկաւ եւ իրիկունը մեկնեցաւ: Ամէն վայրկեան կացութիւնը կը փոխուի: Ատանայի մէջ պայթումի մը հետեւանօք, որ Մարտ 15ի Շաբաթ օրը պատահած է, ժողովուրդը խուճապի մատնուած է: Կիլիկիոյ հայութիւնը զսպանակի վրայ կը գտնուի: Ամենափոքրիկ զէնքի պայթում մը, կամ հրապարակի վրայ տեղի ունեցող միջադէպ մը պատճառ կը դառնայ ժողովրդային մեծ յուզումի մը:

- Այնթապի մասին ոչ մէկ լուր կարելի է առնել: Ֆրանսական իշխանութիւնը օդանաւով կը հաղորդակցի քաղաքին հետ, ինչ որ կ'ապացուցանէ հոն տիրող տագնապալի կացութիւնը:

- Մերսինի թրքութիւնն ալ թէեւ երբեմն ժանիք ցոյց կու տայ, բայց չի համարձակիր ոեւէ շարժում ընել, վասնզի ֆրանսացիներ հոս աւելի ուժով են զինուորապէս: Սակայն կացութիւնը եթէ այսպէս շարունակուի եւ չէթէները ոեւէ ուժ չգտնեն իրենց առջեւ, կռիւը հաւանական է որ ի մօտոյ փոխադրուի նաեւ Մերսին, որ վերջին ապաստարանն է հայութեան: Ատանայէն շատեր Մերսին կ'ապաստանին արդէն իբր ապահով վայր:

- Թունալից եւ մոլեռանդ ոգիով գրուած ազդարարութիւն մը ուղղուած Մերսինի թուրքերուն՝ վերջերս գիշերանց թուրքերը փակցուցած էին քաղաքապետարանին դրան մօտ, 16 Մարտ թուականով: Նշանակելի էր յայտարարութեան տակ դրուած ստորագրութիւնը, որ էր «*Մերսին ւսօսիալիսթ միւմէսսիլի վէ գուվվէի միլլիյէ գօմանտանը*»[13]: Պոլշէվիքութեան եւ Միլլիճիներուն միջեւ կապ մը կ'երեւայ այս կերպով:

Պիղա (Տէր Ներսէս քահանայ Մալումեանէ) – 21 Մարտ

Պիղայի անդորրութիւնը երեք ամիսէ ի վեր խիստ տագնապալից եղած է, երկու անգամ Միլլի պետեր չարաչար պարտուած էին 50000է աւելի գիւղացւոց համերաշխութեան շնորհիւ: Երրորդ անգամ ըլլալով Մարտ 13ին Միլլիճիները դարձեալ մեծ պատրաստութեամբ, զինուորական բոլոր կազմով, թնդանօթով, մեթրայէօզով եւ մեծաքանակ ռազմամթերքով, 1200–1500 զինուորով եւ մաս մը հեծելազօրքով քաղաքը պաշարեցին: Ամբողջ 5 օր կատաղի կռիւ մղուեցաւ: Քաղաքացիք արտաքին յարաբերութենէ զրկուած էին: Գիւղացիք մահու եւ կենաց պայքար մղեցին եւ Միլլիճիներուն յաղթեցին: Միլլիճիները հեռացան Պիղայէն եւ գիւղացիք բաւական տեղ հալածեցին զանոնք: Հոս կառավարութիւնը լուծուած է եւ գիւղացիք կը պահեն կարգը: Երկար ատենէ ի վեր շուկան փակ է, արհեստաւոր դասակարգը օրապահիկէ զրկուած յուսահատ վիճակ մը ունի: Պիղայի 80 տուն հայերէն 35 ընտանիք բարեկեցիկ դասէն, վախէն հեռացած էր Միլլի ուժերու գալէն առաջ: Մնացեալներն ալ կը պատրաստուին մեկնելու այն վախով թէ Միլլին նորէն պիտի վերադառնայ եւ այս անգամ այլեւս անկարելի պիտի ըլլայ վերահաս վտանգէն ազատիլ:

Ռօտոսթօ (Առաջնորդական Փոխանորդէն) – 28 Մարտ

Ասկէ մի քանի շաբաթ առաջ ծանր տագնապներ անցուց քաղաքը, վասնզի Էտիրնէի զինուորական հրամատար Ճաֆէր Թայեար պէյ հրահանգ կուտար զօրահաւաքութեան, գիւղացիները կը զինէր, քրիստոնեաները նեղելու կը պարտադրէր թուրք խուժանը գրգռելով: Միլլիճիները զինեալ կը շրջէին քաղաքին մէջ: Աղէտ մը պատահիլը շատ հաւանական էր, եթէ միւթասարրֆ Ֆէրուղան պէյ եւ ֆըրգա քօմանտանի Սալահէտտին պէյ չընդդիմանային գործադրելու Ճաֆէր Թայեարի հրահանգները: Նոյն օրերը հասաւ նաեւ անգլիական զրահաւոր մը, որուն հրամատարը ֆըրքա քօմանտանիին եւ միւթասարրըֆի փոխանորդին յայտնեց թէ՝ եթէ քրիստոնէի մը քիթը արիւնի, ամբողջ քաղաքը կ'այրեմ: Նոյնպէս յունաց Մեթրոպոլիտին եւ հայոց Առաջնորդական Փոխանորդին յանձնարարեց որ ժողովուրդը հրահանգեն որոշեալ տեղ մը հաւաքուելու դէպքի մը պատահականութեան: Զրահաւորին ներկայութիւնը ահ ու սարսափի մատնած էր թուրք ժողովուրդը 15 օրի չափ, սակայն այսօր անակնկալ կերպով զրահաւորը Կ. Պոլիս գնաց, հոս մեզ առանձին ձգելով: Անգլիացի ներկայացուցիչն ալ, կառավարիչ Ֆէրուղան պէյն ալ Կ. Պոլիս գացած են եւ ֆըրքա քօմանտանի Սալահէտտին պէյ պաշտօնէ ելած եւ Միլլիճի Ճէմիլ պէյ [զինք փոխարինած է]: Որով

cations with İstanbul and the vicinities have been severed because the Millis are censoring the post in Çorlu. Travelers from Malkara have confirmed that the horror continues there.

Bandırma (from the primate)—March 31

Two days ago, a statement was posted on the municipal buildings and the Grand Mosque of the bazaar in Bandırma by the "Corps of Milli Forces," under which there was a remarkable note by the district governor of Balıkesir.

The meaning of that statement is this: "This notice is compelled by the need to inform the populations in the villages that the capture of İstanbul by the British, the arrest of a large number of valuable members of the National Assembly, and their expulsion to unknown places, the placement of cannons and machine guns on both ends of the bridge of our capital, as well as the installment of foreign armed soldiers on the bridges, the interruption of our travel within Anadolu [Anatolia] and the allowance to travel only with an English passport and only by issuing it to those whom they want, is intolerable.

"Corps of Milli Forces"

"This notice [must be] sent to the villages also and hung in places deemed appropriate to notify everyone of the abovementioned notice.

"District Governor of the Kaza"

After the occupation of İstanbul by the Allied army, a state of war was declared by the commander of the 14th Army Corps, Yusuf Izzet, for Balıkesir, Bandırma, and the region, and accordingly, announcements were posted everywhere.

Letters and newspapers from İstanbul are indiscriminately censored, just as they were during the war, and those who have been censored are stamped "Inspected by Bandırma's censorship." Letters are required to be delivered to the post unsealed.

Karaağaç (from Simon Armen, correspondent of *Yergir* [Armenian weekly])—March 21

Influenced by the occupation of İstanbul, it appears that in accordance with an order from the center, the commander of the first Turkish military detachment in Edirne, Cafer Tayyar Bey, declared the prefecture of Edirne autonomous and independent on the morning of the 17th of March. This proclamation was announced to the people through particular statements signed by Cafer Tayyar. Cafer Tayyar stated that "our beloved capital, İstanbul, was attacked by British troops brutally. The British took over the official places, the telegraph office, the post office, etc. They expelled the Turkish functionaries and placed their appointees in charge. The government was overthrown, and various arrests were made. Of course, the Anatolian Milli national forces will fulfill their patriotic responsibilities to save the Turkish and Islamic nations and the capital of the Ottoman Caliphate from the current situation. As we wait for their activities, and until a credible government in the capital comes to power, we will declare the prefecture of Edirne, the most beloved of our homeland, independent and autonomous. By taking this initiative and informing the people indiscriminately, we invite our fellow officers and military personnel to remain in charge of their posts and to oversee the implementation of the orders given by the new independent government. In the same way, all the elements of the people considered our dear compatriots must be preoccupied with their daily affairs. Troublemakers and suspects will be arrested immediately and sent to a military tribunal. A state of war has been declared, and everyone must obey the government's order.

Միլլի ույժերը հակակշռող ոչ ոք մնաց աստ եւ Միլլիճիները կրկին սկսան գործի եւ Ճաֆէր Թայեարի հրահանգները տեղալ սկսան: Կ. Պոլիսի եւ շրջակայ վայրերու հետ մեր յարաբերութիւնները խզուած են, զի Չօրլուի մէջ միլլիճիները բօսթա կը քննեն: Մալկարայէն եկած ճամբորդներ կը հաստատեն թէ հոն սարսափը կը շարունակէ:

Պանտրմա (Առաջնորդէն) – 31 Մարտ

Երկու օր առաջ Պանտրմայի թաղապետական շէնքին եւ շուկայի մեծ մզկիթին վրայ յայտարարութիւն մը փակցուած էր «Գուվվէի Միլլիէ Հէյէթ»ի կողմէն, որուն ներքեւը Պալըքէսիրի միւթէսարըֆին մէկ ուշագրաւ *շէրհ*ը կար:

Այդ յայտարարութեան իմաստը սա էր թէ «Կ. Պոլսոյ անգլիացւոց կողմէ գրաւումը, Ազգային Ժողովի արժէքաւոր անդամներէն մէկ մեծ մասին ձերբակալուելով՝ անծանօթ վայրեր տարուիլը, մեր մայրաքաղաքին կամուրջին երկու ծայրերը թնդանօթներ դրուիլը, պաշտօնական տեղերու եւ պաշտօնատուններու ամէն կողմը թնդանօթի եւ միթրաեօզ դրուիլը, ինչպէս նաեւ անոնց վրայ զինեալ օտար զինուորներ զետեղուիլը, մեր Անատոլուին ներսը երթեւեկի ընդհատուիլը եւ միայն անգլիական անցագիրով եւ ան ալ միայն իրենց ուզած անձերուն տրուելով ճամբորդութիւն կատարելը անհանդուրժելի կէտեր ըլլալը մինչեւ գիւղերու բնակչութեան տեղեկա[ցնե]լու պէտքը այս ծանուցման հարկադրած է»

Գուվվէի Միլլիէ Հէյէթի:

«Վերոյիշեալ ծանուցումը ամէնուն ծանուցանելու համար գիւղերը նաեւ ղրկուելով հարկ տեսնուած տեղերը կախել»

Գազէսի Միւթէսարըֆը

Դաշնակից բանակին կողմէ Պոլսոյ գրաւումէն վերջ Պալըքէսիրի, Պանտրմայի եւ շրջանին համար Ժ.Դ. Գօլ Օրտուի հրամանատար Եուսուֆ Իզզէթի կողմէ պատերազմական վիճակ յայտարարուեցաւ եւ ըստ այսմ ալ յայտարարութիւններ փակցուեցան ամէնուրեք:

Պոլսէն եկած նամակներ թէ լրագիրներ անխտիր գրաքննութեան կ'ենթարկուին ճիշդ պատերազմի շրջանին եղածին նման եւ գրաքննուածները «*Պանտրմա սանսիւրինէ մուայէնէ օլունմըշ տըր*»[14] կնիքով մը կը կնքեն եւ նամակները կը պարտադրեն բաց յանձնել բօսթան:

Գարա[ա]ղաճ (Սիմօն Արմէնէ, *Երկիր*ի թղթակից) – 21 Մարտ

Պոլսոյ գրաւումէն ազդուելով, կ'երեւի կեդրոնէն եկած հրամանի մը համեմատ Էտիրնէի մէջ գտնուող առաջին թուրք զօրամասի հրամատար Ճաֆէր Թայեար պէյ Էտիրնէի կուսակալութիւնը ինքնավար եւ անկախ հռչակեց, Մարտ 17ի առտուն: Այս հռչակումը մասնաւոր յայտարարութիւններով -զոր Ճաֆէր Թայեար ստորագրութիւնը կը կրէր- ժողովուրդին ծանուցուեցաւ: Այդ ծանուցումին մէջ Ճաֆէր Թայեար կը յայտնէ թէ «մեր սիրեցեալ մայրաքաղաքը՝ Պոլիս, անգլիական զօրաց կողմէ բռնի յարձակում կրեց: Անգլիացիք կռուով գրաւեցին պաշտօնական վայրերը, հեռագրատունը, փօստը եւայլն, եւ մէջի թուրք պաշտօնէութիւնները արտաքսելով իրենց կողմէ նշանակեալ անձեր գործի գլուխ բերին: Կառավարութիւնը իջեցուցին եւ զանազան ձերբակալութիւններ ըրին: Անշուշտ Անատոլուի Միլլի ազգային ույժերը իրենց հայրենասիրական պարտականութիւնները պիտի կատարեն ներկայ վիճակէն փրկելու համար թուրք եւ իսլամ ազգը եւ Օսմանեան խալիֆայութեան մայրաքաղաքը: Մենք սպասելով անոնց գործունէութեան, մինչեւ որ մայրաքաղաքին մէջ վստահելի եւ ազգին ուժերուն կռթնած կառավարութիւն մը գործի գլուխ գայ, մենք մեր հայրենիքին ամենասիրելի Էտիրնէի կուսակալութիւնը անկախ եւ ինքնավար կը հռչակենք: Մեր սոյն ձեռնարկը ընելով եւ հաղորդելով բոլոր ժողովրդեան անխտիր, կը հրաւիրեմք մեր պաշտօնակից սպայ եւ զինուոր անհատները իրենց պաշտօնին գլուխը գտնուիլ եւ հսկել նոր անկախ կառավարութեան տալիք հրամաններու գործադրութեան: Նմանապէս բոլոր ժողովրդական տարրերը որոնք մեր սիրելի հայրենակիցները կը նկատուին, պարտին իրենց առօրեայ

"March 17, [1]920

"Commander of the First Army Corps, Cafer Tayyar"

The people were surprised. The shops were partly closed and [then] reopened. Cafer Tayyar immediately declared himself dictator and ordered a meeting of all the elements. Turkish, Armenian, Greek, and Jewish invitees, as well as religious leaders, attended the meeting. There, Cafer Tayyar Bey presented the new situation of the country. He asked every religious leader to urge his people to remain calm and to do their jobs. He stated that no one's nose would bleed and that every effort would be made to maintain order, peace, and so on.

Cafer Tayyar wants to play in Rumeli the role Mustafa Kemal plays in Anadolu [Anatolia]. He issues numerous commands left and right.

He started to form an army by issuing a draft. It is said that the seventeen- to forty-year-olds have been called to arms and that groups are being sent to barracks hourly to be armed and trained. The staff and the majority of the Turkish people, who are entirely Ittihadist and want to participate in the movements of the Milli forces, cooperate with and share Cafer Tayyar's views and are in contact with the representatives of Mustafa Kemal and İstanbul. Yesterday, Cafer Tayyar seized all the money from the Agricultural Bank. He also wanted to seize the money from the Islamic Milli Bank, but the mufti did not allow it, objecting that the money belonged to the people and not the government. However, there is a great fear that the stringency will gradually increase and individual riches also will be touched. No one dares comment, fearing the severity of the state of siege. Although people are preoccupied with their affairs, they are always in a state of anxiety and horror. All Turks are armed, while Christians are unarmed. Many have moved to Karaağaç and taken refuge there, but they do not feel safe here either because the Allied forces are very scanty here.

The traffic from Edirne to Karaağaç has been blocked by the Turks, and it is said that passports will not be issued for İstanbul either.

Weapons are being transported without hindrance and with daring from Edirne to Kırklareli [Kırkkilise], Babaeski, Tekirdağ, Malkara, and throughout the prefecture.

Cafer Tayyar has openly stated to the French commandant of Karaağaç that he will oppose any occupation and that such a move should not be attempted. With this, you can imagine how alarming the situation is here for the Armenian and Greek people.

Censorship has been in place in Edirne since March 17, and newspapers from İstanbul have been detained since then. Letters are opened, inspected, and deletions are made before being handed over to their owners.

Mersin (from Reverend Father Mampré [Sirounian])—March 23[59]

Eight days ago, the primate of Saimbeyli [Hacın], Bishop Bedros Sarajian, came to Mersin to bring aid to his heroic people. Two hours away from Saimbeyli, the fight continues with fierce intensity. Armenians resist the enemy by their own means. Governor Mr. Brémond replied to the appeal of the National Union in Adana regarding sending military aid to Saimbeyli, saying, "We cannot send any military force to Saimbeyli. We can only give you some ammunition and secure the line of retreat for your fellow Armenians at the last minute."

In addition, the governor of Adana, Mr. Brémond, added: "Not now, but in the future as well, we

գործերով պարապիլ: Անդորրութիւնը խանգարել փորձողներ եւ կասկածելիներ անմիջապէս ձերբակալուելով պատերազմական ատեան պիտի ղրկուին: Պատերազմական վիճակ հրատարակուած է եւ ամէն ոք պէտք է հնազանդի կառավարութեան հրամանին:

17 Մարտ [1]920

Առաջին Գօլ-Օրտուի հրամատար Ճաֆէր Թայեար

Ժողովուրդը անակնկալի եկաւ: Խանութները մասամբ գոցուած էին եւ բացուեցան: Անմիջապէս Ճաֆէր Թայեար տիկտատոր հռչակեց ինքզինքը եւ հրամայեց բոլոր տարրերէն ժողով մը կազմել: Թուրք, հայ, յոյն եւ հրեայ ազգէն հրաւիրեալներ, ինչպէս եւ հոգեւոր պետերը ներկայ գտնուեցան սոյն ժողովին: Հոն Ճաֆէր Թայեար պէյ երկրին նոր գոյավիճակը պարզեց, խնդրեց որ ամէն հոգեւոր պետ իր ժողովուրդը հանդարտութեան եւ իր գործերով զբաղիլ յորդորէ. յայտնեց որ ոչ ոքի քիթը չպիտի արիւնի եւ ամէն միջոց պիտի գործադրուի կարգը ու խաղաղութիւնը պահպանելու համար, եւայլն:

Ճաֆէր Թայեար Ռումէլիի մէջ կ'ուզէ կատարել այն դերը, ինչ որ Մուսթաֆա Քէմալ կը կատարէ Անատոլուի մէջ: Աջ ու ձախ հրամաններ կը տեղայ:

Զօրակոչ հրատարակելով սկսաւ բանակ կազմել. 17–40 տարեկաններ կոչուած են կ'ըսուի եւ ամէն ժամ խումբ-խումբ կը ղրկուին զօրանոցները՝ զինուելու եւ մարզուելու: Ճաֆէր Թայեարի գործակից եւ համամիտ են սպայակոյտը եւ թուրք ժողովրդեան մեծ մասը, որոնք ամբողջովին իթթիհատական են եւ Միլլի ուժերու շարժումներուն կ'ուզեն մասնակցիլ, յարաբերութեան մէջ ըլլալով Մուսթաֆա Քէմալի եւ Պօլսի ներկայացուցիչներուն հետ: Երէկ Ճաֆէր Թայեար երկրագործական պանքայի բոլոր դրամները գրաւեց, նմանապէս ուզեց խլամ Միլլի պանքային դրամներն ալ գրաւել, բայց միւֆթին չթոյլատրեց, առարկելով թէ այդ դրամները ժողովրդեան կը պատկանին եւ ո՛չ կառավարութեան: Սակայն մեծ վախ կայ որ հետզհետէ խստութիւնները շատնան եւ անհատական հարստութիւններու ալ ձեռք զարնուի: Ոչ ոք դիտողութիւն ընել կը համարձակի, պաշարման վիճակին խստութիւններէն ահաբեկ: Թէեւ ժողովուրդը իր գործերով կը զբաղի, սակայն միշտ յուզման եւ սարսափի մէջ են: Բոլոր թուրքերը զինուած են, մինչ քրիստոնեայք զէնք չունին: Շատերը Գարա Աղաճ փոխադրուեցան եւ ապաստանեցան, սակայն հոս եւս ապահով չեն զգար ինքզինքնին, որովհետեւ Համաձայնական շատ քիչ ոյժ կը գտնուի հոս:

Էտիրնէէն Գարա Աղաճ երթեւեկը արգիլուեցաւ թուրքերու կողմէ եւ կ'ըսուի թէ Պօլսոյ համար եւս անցագիր չպիտի տրուի:

- Արձակ համարձակ զէնք կը փոխադրուի Էտիրնէէն դէպի Գըրք Քիլիսէ, Պապա Էսկի, Ռօտոսթօ, Մալկարա եւ բոլոր կուսակալութեան շրջանին մէջ:

Ճաֆէր Թայեար բացէիբաց յայտարարած է Գարա[ա]ղաճի ֆրանսական զօմանտանին թէ պիտի ընդդիմանայ ռեւէ գրաւումի դէմ, եւ պէտք չէ փորձել այդպիսի շարժում մը: Ա՛լ կրնաք երեւակայել թէ ինչքան տագնապալից է դրութիւնը հոս եւ վիճակը հայ եւ յոյն ժողովրդեան:

Մարտ 17էն ի վեր գրաքննութիւն հաստատուած է Էտիրնէի մէջ եւ Պոլիսէն եկած թերթերը ամբողջութեամբ վար կը դրուին անկէ ի վեր: Նամակները կը բացուին, կը քննուին եւ կը ջնջուին եւ այդպէս կը յանձնուին իրենց տէրերուն:

Մերսին (Մամբրէ Վարդապետ [Միրունեան]է) – 23 Մարտ

Անկէ 8 օր առաջ Հաճընի Առաջնորդ Պետրոս Եպիսկոպոս Սարաճեան Մերսին եկած էր օգնութիւն հասցնելու համար իր հերոս ժողովուրդին: Հաճընէն 2 ժամ հեռաւորութեան վրայ կռիւը կը շարունակուի կատաղի սաստկութեամբ: Հայերը իրենց անձնական միջոցներով է որ կը չափուին թշնամիին հետ: Հաճնոյ համար զինուորական օգնութիւն ղրկուելու մասին Ատանայի Ազգային Միութեան դիմումին՝ կառավարիչ Մ. Պրէմօն պատասխանած է թէ «զինուորական ոչ մէկ ոյժ կրնանք ղրկել Հաճըն. միայն կրնանք որոշ չափով ռազմամթերք տալ ձեզի եւ վերջին պահուն ապահովել ձերիններուն նահանջի գիծը»:

will not be able to send troops to Saimbeyli, and we advise that the women and children who are there be transferred to Kozan [Sis] now because the situation there is more peaceful than elsewhere. We will work to secure their lives during the retreat. Armenian fighters should endeavor to ensure that neither guns nor ammunition belonging to the French government remain in the hands of the Turks."

Indeed, the French government provided enough ammunition to be sent to Saimbeyli and to arm, particularly, a large number of young Armenians who were rushing from Adana, Mersin, and other places to aid their brothers and sisters in Saimbeyli. A day before Bishop Bedros arrived in Adana, it had already dispatched sufficient ammunition and young forces to Saimbeyli.

The primate of Saimbeyli holds great faith in his people and great hope that the people of Saimbeyli will be able to endure for a long time and even win if auxiliary forces and ammunition is sent to him [there].

• There is no specific information from Gaziantep [Ayntab]; it is impossible to communicate with the Armenians there because Turkish çetes besiege the city.

• Adana and the environs, Tarsus, and Mersin are still peaceful, but horror always reigns over the Armenians.

The ambiguous stance of the French government puts Armenians in a predicament. The Armenians of Cilicia will not know despair; instead, they will resist bravely and die like heroes. To counter the bands of çetes, Armenian groups are now being formed with feverish haste; they will act on the path of their activity according to the Mosaic Law. All political parties are united. Everyone is preparing to face the threatening danger. There is quiet activity everywhere. However, the ambiguous stance of the French government discourages weak souls. The policy of winning the Turks over is evident everywhere. This situation spoils those scoundrels who boost their destructive activities. All the Turks of Cilicia are ready and waiting for the signal to start their work. Turkish gendarmes serving in the French government, who have been sent, thoughtlessly, against the çetes, side with them with their weapons. The government was watching this particularity undisturbed and only recently began to disarm the Turkish gendarmes and replace them with Armenians.

Kozan [Sis] (from a volunteer?)—March 19

The volunteers left Adana for Saimbeyli [Hacın], provided that they could operate freely and independently, but as soon as they reached Kozan, the French governor announced that they were under the command of the French commander and could not operate without his knowledge. The position of the French is very ambiguous. Despite their assurances, not a single French soldier has gone to Feke to open the road. Enemy forces are an hour away from Kozan. The French troops do not take even a step outside the fortress of Kozan. The Armenians are waiting here confidently.

• Four days ago, they wanted to send forty thousand bullets, 150 bombs, twenty-four rifles, and ninety-five French soldiers accompanied by local and Saimbeyli civilians to help Saimbeyli. The leader of the ninety-five-member Armenian group explained that the road was dangerous. The French governor assured them they would be accompanied and followed by French soldiers. Ninety-five people took the abovementioned ammunition and set off, but not a single French soldier accompanied the Armenians. Eight hours away from Kozan, they were attacked by numerous çetes in Akçalıuşağı. Upon receiving the news of the battle, the French governor took the weapons of the Armenians away, imprisoned the volunteers with their leaders, released the imprisoned Turkish mob, and released the

Անկէ զատ, Ատանայի կառավարիչը՝ պ. Պրէմօն, աւելցուցած է թէ «ոչ թէ այժմ, այլեւ ապագային ալ չպիտի կրնանք զինուորական ոյժ ղրկել Հաճըն եւ խորհուրդ կուտանք որպէսզի հոն գտնուող կիները եւ տղայք այժմէն իսկ փոխադրուին Սիս, վասնզի հոն աւելի խաղաղ է կացութիւնը քան այլուր: Մենք պիտի աշխատինք ապահովել անոնց կեանքը նահանջի ժամանակ: Հայ կռուողները աշխատելու են որպէսզի ֆրանսական կառավարութեան պատկանող ոչ հրացան եւ ոչ ալ ռազմամթերք մնայ թուրքերուն ձեռքը»:

Իրապէս ֆրանսական կառավարութիւնը բաւականաչափ ռազմամթերք տուաւ ղրկուելու համար Հաճըն եւ մանաւանդ զինելու համար Ատանայէն, Մերսինէն եւ զանազան վայրերէ իրենց հաճընցի եղբարց եւ քոյրերուն օգնութեան փութացող ստուար թուով երիտասարդ հայերուն, եւ Պետրոս Եպիսկոպոս Մերսին գալէն օր մը առաջ արդէն բաւականաչափ ռազմամթերք եւ երիտասարդ ոյժեր փութացուցած էր Հաճըն:

Հաճընի Առաջնորդը մեծ հաւատք ունի իր ժողովուրդին վրայ, եւ մեծ յոյս՝ թէ հաճընցիք պիտի կարենան երկար տոկալ եւ նոյնիսկ յաղթանակել՝ եթէ օգնական ոյժ եւ ռազմամթերք ղրկուի իրեն:

- Այնթապէն որոշ տեղեկութիւններ չկան, հոն գտնուող հայութեան հետ հաղորդակցութեան մտնել անկարելի է, վասնզի քաղաքը պաշարուած է թուրք չէթաներու կողմէ:

- Ատանա եւ շրջակաները, Տարսոն եւ Մերսին առայժմ խաղաղ են, բայց միշտ սարսափն է որ կը տիրէ հայոց վրայ:

Ֆրանսական կառավարութեան երկդիմի ընթացքը անել կացութեան մը մէջ կը դնէ հայերը: Կիլիկիոյ հայութիւնը յուսահատիլ չպիտի գիտնայ, այլ՝ քաջի պէս դիմադրել եւ հերոսի պէս մեռնիլ: Չէթայական խումբերուն հակազդելու համար այժմ տենդոտ փութկոտութեամբ կը կազմուին նաեւ հայ խումբեր, որոնք մովսիսական օրէնքով պիտի շարժին իրենց գործունէութեան ճամբուն վրայ: Բոլոր կուսակցութիւնները միացած են: Ամէն ոք կը պատրաստուի դիմագրաւել սպառնացող վտանգը, անաղմուկ գործունէութիւն կը տիրէ ամէնուրեք. միայն ֆրանսական կառավարութեան երկդիմի ընթացքն է որ կը յուսահատեցնէ տկար հոգիները: Թուրքերը սիրաշահելու քաղաքականութիւնը յայտնի կը տեսնուի ամէնուրեք: Այս պարագան կը շփացնէ այդ սրիկաները, որոնք իրենց քանդիչ գործունէութեան աւելի թափ եւ ոյժ կուտան: Կիլիկիոյ բոլոր թուրքերը կազմ եւ պատրաստ կը սպասեն ազդանշանին՝ սկսելու համար իրենց գործին: Ֆրանսական կառավարութեան ծառայող թուրք ժանտարմաները, որոնք կը ղրկուին անխորհուրդ կերպով չէթէներու դէմ, իրենց զէնքերով կ՚անցնին անոնց կողմը: Այս պարագան անվրդով կը դիտէր կառավարութիւնը, որ միայն վերջերս սկսաւ զինաթափ ընել թուրք ժանտարմաները եւ անոնց տեղ հայեր առնել:

Սիս (կամաւորէ՛ մը) – 19 Մարտ

Ատանայէն կամաւորները մեկնած էին դէպի Հաճըն ազատ եւ անկախ գործելու պայմանով, բայց Սիս հասնելնուն պէս ֆրանսացի կառավարիչը հաղորդեց թէ ֆրանսացի հրամանատարին հրամանին տակ են եւ առանց անոր գիտակցութեան չպիտի կրնան գործել: Այս ֆրանսացւոց դիրքը խիստ երկբայական է: Ֆէքքէ մէկ հատ ֆրանսացի զինուոր անգամ գացած չէ ճամբայ բանալու համար, հակառակ իրենց ըրած հաւաստումներուն: Թշնամի ոյժերը Սիսէն մէկ ժամ հեռաւորութեան վրայ կը գտնուին: Ֆրանսացի զինուորները Սիսի բերդէն քայլ մը անգամ դուրս չեն ելլեր: Հայերը ինքնավստահ կը սպասեն հոս:

- Հաճնոյ օգնութեան համար չորս օր առաջ 40000 փամփուշտ, 150 պօմպա, 24 հրացան եւ 95 տեղացի ու հաճընցի սիվիլներու ընկերակցութեամբ ֆրանսացի զինուոր ղրկել ուզեցին: 95 հոգինոց հայ խումբին պետը ճամբան վտանգաւոր ըլլալը պարզեց: Ֆրանսացի կառավարիչը հաւաստեց թէ իրենց պիտի ընկերանան եւ հետեւին ֆրանսացի զինուորներ: 95 հոգի վերոյիշեալ ռազմամթերքը առնելով ճամբայ ինկան, սակայն ոչ մէկ ֆրանսացի զինուոր ընկերացաւ հայոց: Սիսէն 8 ժամ հեռու Աղչալ-Ուշաղիի մէջ յարձակման ենթարկուեցան բազմաթիւ չէթէներու կողմէ: Կռիւի լուրն ստանալուն պէս ֆրանսացի կառավարիչը հայերուն զէնքերը առաւ, կամաւորները

criminal [police] commissioner Hamdi from prison and reinstated him as head police commissioner. We heard a few hours after these incidents that the volunteers were surrounded. An appeal was made to the French governor, who replied, "These cases are insignificant, and the volunteers would escape and travel at night." The next day, barely three people arrived and reported that the other volunteers had been besieged in the village of Ayıcık, two hours away from Kozan, and that they asked for help. The governor said. "I can do nothing, and I cannot send any force." A second appeal was made asking for help and permission to send the Armenians. The French governor promised to send French troops, but they returned after wandering around the city for about ten minutes. Thereupon, the relatives of the besieged Armenians rushed to the rescue and got into a fierce battle. The sound of gunfire could be heard from the city at noon. At that time, ten to fifteen Armenian gendarmes were sent to repel the mob. At the last moment, ten French soldiers were also sent, who simply made a stroll. The besieged could not be saved, and we do not know what happened to them.

The governor of Kozan has reported that Saimbeyli has surrendered, but this is not certain. The siege of Saimbeyli extends to dozens of chains from Kozan to Saimbeyli. The Armenian armed forces of Kozan do not trust leaving because they have no ammunition and are subject to French command. If they were given the privilege to act freely, along with some reinforcement, the Armenians would be able to reach out to the besieged Armenians of Saimbeyli.

• Telegrams have been placed under the control of the governor of Kozan.

իրենց պետովը բանտարկեց, բանտարկեալ թուրք խուժանը արձակեց եւ ոճրագործ քօմիսէր Համտին բանտէն հանելով նորէն սէր քօմիսէր ըրաւ: Այս դէպքերէն քանի մը ժամ յետոյ, կամաւորներուն պաշարուած ըլլալը լուեցաւ: Ասոր վրայ ֆրանսացի կառավարիչին դիմում եղաւ եւ պատասխան առնուեցաւ թէ «այս դէպքերը կարեւորութենէ զուրկ են եւ թէ կամաւորները գիշերը փախչելով կուգան»: Հետեւեալ օրը հազիւ երեք հոգի եկան, որ Սիսէն 2 ժամ հեռու Այէճըզ գիւղը միւս կամաւորներու պաշարուած ըլլալը եւ օգնութիւն ուզելը յայտնեցին: Կառավարիչը ըսաւ. «Բան մը չեմ կրնար ընել եւ ոչ ալ ոյժ կրնամ ղրկել»: Երկրորդ անգամ կրկին դիմում ըրին օգնութիւն խնդրելու եւ հայերն ղրկելու թոյլտուութեան հրաման առնելու համար: Ֆրանսացի կառավարիչը խոստացաւ ֆրանսացի զինուորներ ղրկել, սակայն ասոնք քաղաքին շուրջը 10 վայրկեան պտտելով վերադարձան: Ասոր վրայ պաշարուած հայոց պարագաները օգնութեան փութացին եւ սաստիկ կռիւի բռնուեցան: Կէսօրին հրացանաձգութեան ձայնը քաղաքէն կը լուէր: Այն ատեն 10–15 հայ ժանտարմա ղրկուեցան, որոնք խուժանը վանեցին: Վերջին պահուն ղրկուեցաւ նաեւ 10 ֆրանսացի զինուոր, որոնք միայն պտոյտ մը ըրին: Պաշարուածները չկրցան ազատիլ եւ չենք գիտեր թէ ի՞նչ եղած են:

Սիսի կառավարիչը կը հաղորդէ թէ Հաճըն անձնատուր եղած է, սակայն ստոյգ չէ: Հաճընի պաշարումը Սիսէն մինչեւ Հաճըն տասնեակ շղթաներու կը հասնի: Սիսի հայոց զինեալ մասը չի վստահիր դուրս ելլալու, զի ռազմամթերք չունի եւ ֆրանսական հրամատարութեան հրամանին ենթարկուած է: Ազատ գործելու արտօնութիւն եթէ ունենան եւ օգնական ոյժ հասնի, կրնան հայերը օգնութեան հասնիլ Հաճընի պաշարուած հայերուն:

- Սսոյ կառավարիչին քօնթրօլին ենթարկուած է հեռագիրը:

[Insecurity] Notebook Number 9
April 1920

İstanbul (Verbal information provided by the Armenian courier of the American Red Cross)—April 1

On the Aleppo-Adana-Mersin road, it was seen that the French troops in Syria and Cilicia do not inspire any respect or fear in the Arabs and Turks; therefore, the influence of the French authority extends today only over Beirut and Zahle. To protect Beirut, eight or ten tanks have been moved ashore.

• Mustafa Kemal is thought to have made a pact with the Arabs to drive the French, the common enemy, out of the country. Turkish çetes allegedly roam Aleppo freely and boldly. Pan-Islamic ideas are prevalent in Cilicia and Syria. Some want to credit England behind these collaborations because it is said that while the British troops were withdrawing from Cilicia and Syria, they announced to Armenian, Arab, and Turkish dignitaries: "We will be back shortly."

• The Armenians of Syria are also alarmed by the tendency of the Arabs toward Pan-Islamism.

• The situation in Cilicia is not safe. The Turks are armed and ready to attack the French and the Armenians at the first opportunity. Although reinforcements arrived, one cannot rely on these soldiers, most of whom are Muslim Algerian pro-Turkish soldiers who do not want to die on foreign soil and for the interests of others. The Algerians killed about one hundred Armenians while fleeing Maraş, but they, too, unaccustomed to the cold climate, suffered heavy casualties. French officers transported their immodest mistresses in carriages during the retreat. Meanwhile, the wounded were dying on the road due to a lack of transportation.

• There are twelve hundred French soldiers in Gaziantep [Ayntab], but the city is almost besieged [by Turks], or, more accurately, traveling is not safe. One can only communicate with the city by plane.

• The siege of Saimbeyli [Hacın] is getting stricter daily. After many appeals by the Armenians of Adana, the French authorities finally kindly allowed the Armenian legionnaires to rush to help [their compatriots in Saimbeyli]. Weapons were given to some of them in Adana, while others were instructed to receive their firearms in Kozan [Sis]. The [French] authority in Kozan not only declined to give weapons to them but also prevented them from leaving for Saimbeyli. After emphatic appeals [to the French authorities] in Adana, the Armenian volunteers finally left with their arms. Information is lacking about their role and their fate.

• Two of the three missionaries of Saimbeyli managed to escape from [Saimbeyli turned to] hell to Adana. There is only one left in Saimbeyli. The two missionaries appealed to Adana's prefect for the orphanage's relocation. The Turkish official stated that the orphanage would not be harmed, only that the orphans should huddle in the back of the building to avoid being injured by the bullets fired.

• The Americans have sent many important telegrams from Cyprus to America, stating that their lives and the lives of Armenians were in danger and asking for help.

• The whole population of Syria and Cilicia, even the Nestorians, are extremely dissatisfied with the French.

[Անապահովութեան] Տետր Թիւ 9
1920 Ապրիլ

Կ. Պոլիս (Ամերիկեան Կարմիր Խաչի հայազգի թղթատարին բերանացի տեղեկութիւնները) – 1 Ապրիլ

Հալէպ-Ատանա-Մերսին ճամբուն վրայ տեսնուած է որ Սուրիոյ եւ Կիլիկիոյ մէջ ֆրանսացի զինուորները ոչ մէկ պատկառանք, ոչ մէկ երկիւղ չեն ներշնչեր արաբներուն եւ թուրքերուն, այնպէս որ ֆրանսական իշխանութեան ազդեցութիւնը կը տարածուի այսօր մի միայն Պէյրութի եւ Սաիլէի վրայ: Պէյրութը պաշտպանելու համար 8–10 թանքեր հանուած են ցամաք:

- Մուսթաֆա Քէմալ կը կարծուի թէ արաբներուն հետ դաշնադրութիւն կնքած է, հասարակաց թշնամին՝ ֆրանսացիները երկրէն վտարելու համար: Թուրք չէթէներ յայտնի համարձակ կը պտտին եղեր Հալէպի մէջ: Համիսլամական գաղափարներ տարածուած են Կիլիկիոյ եւ Սուրիոյ մէջ: Այս գործակցութեանց մէջ ոմանք կ'ուզեն տեսնել Անգլիոյ մատը, վասնզի կ'ըսուի թէ Կիլիկիայէն եւ Սուրիայէն անգլիացի զինուորները քաշուած ատեն հայ, արաբ, թուրք երեւելիներու յայտարարած են «քիչ ժամանակէն պիտի վերադառնանք»:

- Սուրիոյ հայերն ալ տագնապի մէջ են արաբներու դէպի համիսլամութիւն ցոյց տուած հակումին պատճառով:

- Կիլիկիոյ մէջ կացութիւնը ապահով չէ: Թուրքերը զինուած են եւ պատրաստ յարձակելու առաջին առթիւ ֆրանսացւոց եւ հայոց վրայ: Օգնական ոյժեր թէեւ եկան, սակայն կարելի չէ վստահիլ այդ զինուորներուն, որոնց մեծ մասը կը բաղկանայ թուրքերու կուսակից իսլամ ալճերիացի զինուորներէ, որոնք չեն ուզեր մեռնիլ օտար հողի վրայ եւ ուրիշին շահերուն համար: Մարաշէն հայերը փախուստ տուած միջոցին ալճերիացիները սպաննած են 100ի մօտ հայեր, բայց իրենք ալ ցուրտ կլիմայի անվարժ՝ շատ կորուստ ունեցած են: Ֆրանսացի սպաներ նահանջի միջոցին կառքերով փոխադրած են իրենց տարփածու անպարկեշտ կիները, մինչ անդին վիրաւորներ, փոխադրութեան միջոցներու չգոյութեան պատճառով, ճամբուն վրայ կը մեռնէին:

- Այնթապի մէջ 1200 ֆրանսացի զինուոր կը գտնուի, բայց քաղաքը գրեթէ պաշարուած է, կամ աւելի ճիշդ ճամբորդելու ապահովութիւն չկայ: Քաղաքին հետ կարելի է հաղորդակցիլ միայն օդանաւով:

- Հաճընի պաշարումը օրըստօրէ կը խստանայ: Ատանայի հայութ[եան] քանիցս կատարած դիմումին վրայ ֆրանսական իշխանութիւնը կը հաճի թոյլատրել հայ լէգէոնականները օգնութեան փութալ: Մէկ մասին զէնք կը տրուի Ատանայէն, միւս մասին կը յանձնարարուի Սիսի մէջ ընդունիլ իրենց հրազէնները: Սսոյ իշխանութիւնը ոչ միայն այս վերջիններուն չ'ուզեր զէնք տալ, այլ կ'արգիլէ անոնց մեկնումը դէպի Հաճըն: Ատանայի մէջ կատարուած ազդու դիմումներու վրայ վերջապէս հայ կամաւորները կը մեկնին զինուած: Ասոնց կատարած դերին եւ իրենց վիճակուած ճակատագրին վերաբերմամբ տեղեկութիւններ կը պակսին:

- Հաճընի երեք միսիոնարներէն երկուքը յաջողած են դժոխքէն խոյս տալ դէպի Ատանա: Մէկը միայն կը մնայ Հաճըն: Ատանայի կուսակալին մօտ դիմումներ կը կատարեն երկու միսիոնարները որբանոցի փոխադրութեան համար: Թուրք պաշտօնեան կը յայտարարէ թէ որբանոցին վնաս չի հասնիր, միայն թէ շէնքին ետեւի մասին մէջ որբերը թող կծկտին արձակուած գնդակներէն չվնասուելու համար:

- Ամերիկացիք Կիպրոսէն շատ կարեւոր հեռագիրներ տեղացուցած են Ամերիկա. յայտնած են թէ իրենց եւ հայերու կեանքը վտանգի տակ է եւ խնդրած են օգնութիւն:

- Սուրիոյ եւ Կիլիկիոյ ամբողջ բնակչութիւնը, նոյնիսկ նեստորականները, վերջին ծայր դժգոհ են ֆրանսացիներէն:

Büyük-Yeniköy—April 2

Eight or nine days ago, the headman of this village and Priest Manoug went together to Orhangazi for business and presented themselves to the lieutenant governor. The lieutenant governor, as good news, reported that he sent the former deputy governor, Baytar—an Ittihadist—and the former functionary of the Islamic spiritual court, Devriş Effendi, to Eskişehir. However, on March 31, these two beasts arrived in Orhangazi from Bursa to attend the wedding of a prominent Turk. They arrived with fifty to sixty Milli cavalrymen and the band of the notorious İbo. When a young man from Büyük-Yeniköy saw this, he came and relayed the news. The headman went to the township center again and confirmed, personally, that the said men and the armed forces were really moving around freely. On April 1, the Millis left, but İbo's band remained. According to reports, the prefect of Bursa sent a delegate to İbo, summoned him, and advised him to join the Milli movement and to serve the Millis. Indeed, the fact that İbo has a good relationship with the Millis raises doubts. The people are terrified when they see this friendship and the return of Baytar and Devriş to their former den. This horror increased when the village intendant and the commandant of the sentry station of the village called the headman and told him that they had news from the center that a platoon command would be established in the village as one had been established in Karsak, while the township would have a company command, adding that people should not migrate being suspicious of this arrangement. These arrangements, which mean the siege of all Armenian villages of the township, naturally could not have been heard by the people without indignation, especially when there was an attempt to convey it so cautiously. It will be impossible to keep people here if this decision is implemented.

Sugören [Çengiler]—April 3

On the day of the occupation of İstanbul, the Millis disappeared in the prefecture of Orhangazi, but a few days later, they appeared with more forces and are now settling also in Armenian villages, such as Büyük-Yeniköy and Karsak. They might settle possibly in Sugören as well.

Bursa (from the vicar general)—April 2

A few days ago, a statement by Mustafa Kemal was posted on the walls in some places in Bursa. Excessive censorship has been established on letters. It is said that preparation is underway to accept Anzavur Bey as a liberator and to persecute the Millis. Milli newspapers continue to publish violent articles.

Adana (through the Prelacy of İzmir)—March 26

Mountainous Cilicia is in immediate danger. Bahçe, Düziçi [Haruniye], and Hasanbeyli, which form the Amanos line, were attacked by Turkish çetes made up of regular Turkish soldiers. Hasanbeyli has been besieged on all sides. The Armenians rose in self-defense and are strongly resisting. The war on the other fronts also continues with intensity. French-Armenian forces are fighting near Bahçe and Düziçi. The enemy will enter Cilicia from the plain on that side if this line breaks.

Saimbeyli [Hacın] has been completely besieged. The people were fighting like lions. There has been no news since the seventh of this month. Only the Armenians are fighting on this front.

Kozan [Sis] has been surrounded on three sides. The news of clashes is expected from one moment to another.

1,500 Armenians, besieged in the French monastery, are fighting bravely in Akbez.

The monastery in Işıklı [Şeyxli] was torched, and the Latin priest Phelipon died inside.

Turks and fellahs besiege the 2,200 Armenian survivors from the pre-deportation nine-thousand-

Մեծ-Նոր-Գիւղ – 2 Ապրիլ

8–9 օր առաջ գիւղիս գիւղապետը եւ Մանուկ քահանայ միասին գործով Օրխանը Խազի կ'երթան եւ գայմագամին կը ներկայանան: Գայմագամը իբր աւետիս կը յայտնէ թէ նախկին փոխ կառավարիչ Պայթարը,- որ իթթիհատական մըն էր- եւ Շէրիի դատարանին նախկին պաշտօնեայ Տէվրիշ էֆէնտին Էսկիշէհիր ղրկած է: Սակայն Մարտ 31ին այդ երկու գազանները Պրուսայի կողմէն 50–60 ձիաւոր Միլլիճի չէթէներու հետ, ինչպէս նաեւ համբաւաւոր Հիպօյի խումբով Օրխանը Խազի կուգան իբր թէ երեւելի թուրքի մը հարսնիքին ներկայ ըլլալու համար: Մեծ-նոր-գիւղցի երիտասարդ մը երբ այս կը տեսնայ, կուգայ լուր կուտայ եւ գիւղապետը կրկին կ'երթայ գազային կեդրոնը եւ անձամբ կը ստուգէ թէ իրապէս յիշեալները եւ զինեալ ոյժեր ազատ համարձակ կը շրջագային: Ապրիլ 1ին Միլլիճիները կը մեկնին, իսկ Հիպօյի խումբը կը մնայ: Առնուած տեղեկութեանց համաձայն, Պրուսայի կուսակալը Հիպօյին պատգամաւոր ղրկած եւ իր քով կոչելով յորդորած է Միլլի շարժման միանալու եւ անոնց ծառայելու: Արդարեւ, Հիպօյին Միլլիճիներու հետ լաւ վերաբերում ունենալը կասկածներ կուտայ: Ժողովուրդը տեսնելով այս բարեկամութիւնը եւ Պայթարին եւ Տէվրիշին իրենց նախկին որջը վերադառնալը, ահ ու սարսափի մատնուած է: Այս սարսափը շատ աւելի մեծ եղաւ երբ գիւղին միւտիրը եւ գարագօլ զօմանտանին գիւղապետը կը կոչեն եւ կ'ըսեն որ կեդրոնէն լուր ունին թէ այս գիւղը *թագըմ զօմանտանութիւն* պիտի հաստատուի ինչպէս Գարսաքի մէջ, իսկ գազան պիտի ըլլայ *պէօլիւք զօմանտանի*, եւ կ'աւելցնի թէ այս կարգադրութիւններէն ժողովուրդը կասկածելով գաղթի չդիմէ: Այս կարգադրութիւնները, որոնք գազային ամբողջ հայ գիւղերը պաշարման ենթարկել կը նշանակէր, բնական է թէ առանց վրդովման չէր կրնար լսուիլ ժողովուրդէն, երբ մանաւանդ զայն այսպէս զգուշութեամբ հաղորդելու փորձ կ'ըլլայ: Ժողովուրդը անկարելի է հոս պահել, եթէ այս որոշումը գործադրուի:

Չէնկիլէր – 3 Ապրիլ

Կ. Պոլսոյ գրաւման օրը Օրխանը Ղազի գայմագամութեան մէջ Միլլիճիները անհետացան, սակայն մի քանի օր յետոյ աւելի ոյժերով երեւան եկան եւ սկսած են հիմա հայ գիւղերու մէջ ալ հաստատուիլ, ինչպէս՝ Մեծ-Նոր-Գիւղ եւ Գարսաք: Հաւանական է որ Չէնկիլէր ալ հաստատուին:

Պրուսա (Առաջնորդական Փոխանորդէն) – 2 Ապրիլ

Մի քանի օր առաջ Մուսթաֆա Քէմալի մէկ յայտարարութիւնը Պրուսայի մէջ տեղ տեղ պատերու վրայ կը փակցնեն: Չափազանց գրաքննութիւն մը հաստատուած է նամակներու վրայ: Շրջականերու մէջ կ'ըսուի թէ պատրաստութիւն կայ Ազնաւուր պէյը ընդունելու իբր ազատ[ար]ար եւ հալածելու Միլլիճիները: Միլլիական թերթերը կը շարունակեն բուռն յօդուածներ հրատարակել:

Ատանա (Զմիւռնիոյ առաջնորդարանին միջոցաւ) – 26 Մարտ

Լեռնային Կիլիկիան անմիջական վտանգի տակ է. Պաղչէ, Հարունիյէ եւ Հասան Պէյլի, որ Ամանոսի գիծը կը կազմեն, յարձակման ենթարկուած են թուրք չէթէներու կողմէ, որ կանոնաւոր թուրք զինուորներէ կը բաղկանան: Հասան Պէյլին պաշարուած է ամէն կողմէ, հայութիւնը հոդ ինքնապաշտպանութեան դիմած՝ զօրաւոր կերպով կը դիմադրէ: Միւս ճակատներուն վրայ եւս պատերազմը իր բոլոր սաստկութեամբը կը շարունակէ: Պաղչէի եւ Հարունիյէի կողմը ֆրանսահայ ոյժերը կը կռուին. եթէ այս գիծը խզուի, թշնամին այդ կողմէն դաշտային Կիլիկիա իջած պիտի ըլլայ:

Հաճըն բոլորովին պաշարուած է, ժողովուրդը առիւծներու պէս կը կռուէր: Ամսոյս 7էն ի վեր երբեք լուր չկայ: Այս ճակատին վրայ միայն հայերը կը կռուին:

Սիսը երեք կողմէ պաշարուած է. վայրկեանէ վայրկեան ընդհարումներու լուրերուն կը սպասուի:

Էքպէզ՝ հոն 1500 հայեր ֆրանսական վանքին մէջ պաշարուած կը կռուին քաջաբար:

Շէյխլիի վանքը այրած են՝ լատին ապունա Ֆիլիպուն եկեղեցականն ալ մէջը մեռած է:

strong community of Kessab.

There has been no news from Urfa and Mardin since February 17.

The situation in Birecik, Gaziantep [Ayntab], and Kilis is uncertain, and the guarding French troops are not strong enough to withstand the situation.

Significant çeteci forces are attacking from Silifke's side, as well as from Çamalan, located between Pozantı and Tarsus.

The enemy has launched a general offensive. In many places, telegraph lines and, in some areas, railway lines have been destroyed. The situation is grave, but the Armenians are focusing without despair on organizing self-defense to the extent of their means.

Refugees are coming to Adana. Tomorrow, the female population is expected [to arrive] from Kozan and the surrounding areas, excluding the warrior women.

Samsun (from the primate) March 26[60]

Unfortunately, fear prevails here and in the surrounding areas. The government of Anadolu [Anatolia] has declared seferberlik [mobilization] from those parts, and almost all the people are ready and prepared to depart. It is not yet clear whether Christians will also enlist in the army. The able are fleeing here breathlessly, but it is unknown how long the roads will remain open. The Milli government has set up a new military tribunal to deal with the disobedient, employing extreme measures. They have appropriated all sources of state revenue and allocated them to the military. Rumor has it that an exceptional tax will be allegedly imposed. They have ordered the selection of new deputies for the parliament to be convened in Ankara. Identical orders came here too. The local notables convened a meeting and gave a negative answer. They consider that joining that government would be detrimental to their personal interests and the country. I do not know what means of resistance the opposition will have if the Milli government sends a force here large enough to subjugate this place as well to its will. The situation is still uncertain and depends on Mustafa Kemal's decision.

• The representative of the British Commissionership of Samsun went to Amasya. Mustafa Kemal took him under his control and detained him as a hostage. It has been heard many times that he is dead, but this news has not been confirmed. The audacity and contempt shown by the Millis against the Allied forces can be deduced from this.

• A large number of refugees from the inner provinces have arrived in miserable conditions. The district governor has assured the people that Mustafa Kemal cannot extend his influence to Samsun, but there is no [genuine] assurance in this regard.

Trabzon (from the locum tenens)—March 17[61]

Pressed by the current situation in Trabzon and its surroundings, the relocation of about four hundred orphans from Trabzon, Ordu, and Giresun to İstanbul has been suggested to save them from a possible massacre.

Adana—March 31

The situation in Cilicia is as follows.

We have no communication with Saimbeyli [Hacın]. Only the plane sometimes visits. [The pilot] has found the city calm; the çetes are still in a waiting position; it is thought that they are avoiding a

Քէսապի մէջ տարագրութենէ առաջ 9000 հոգիէ բաղկացեալ գաղութէն վերապրող 2200 հայութիւնը պաշարուած է թուրքերէ եւ ֆէլլահներէ:

Ուրֆայէն եւ Մարտինէն Փետրուար 17էն ի վեր ոչ մի լուր կայ:

Պիրէճիկի, Այնթապի եւ Քիլիսի վիճակը անստոյգ է եւ անոնց ֆրանսական պահակազօրքերը բաւական չեն կացութեան դիմագրաւելու:

Սելեւկիոյ կողմէ, ինչպէս նաեւ Պօզանթի եւ Տարսոնի միջեւ գտնուող Չամ Ալանէն չէթէական կարեւոր ոյժեր յարձակում մը գործեն:

Թշնամին ընդհանուր յարձակողականի սկսած է, շատ տեղ հեռագրաթելերը եւ տեղ տեղ ալ երկաթուղիի գիծերը քանդուած են: Կացութիւնը խիստ ծանր է, սակայն հայերը առանց յուսահատելու միջոցներուն ներած չափով ինքնապաշտպանութեան կազմակերպութիւններուն ոյժ կուտան:

Ատանա կուզան գաղթականներ: Վաղը կը սպասուի Սիսի եւ շրջակայից իգական սեռը, բացի ռազմիկներէն:

Սամսոն (Առաջնորդէն) 26 Մարտ

Դժբաղդաբար այս միջոցիս հոս ալ մթնոլորտը իրենց շրջականներով ահ ու դողի մէջ են: Անատոլուի կառավարութիւնը այդ կողմերէ սէֆերպէրլիք յայտարարե[ր է] եւ բոլոր ժողովուրդը գրեթէ կազմ եւ պատրաստ է. առ այժմ որոշ չէ թէ քրիստոնեայք ալ պիտի զինուորագրուի՞ն: Կարողութիւն ունեցողները շնչահատ հոս կը փախչին, բայց յայտնի չէ ճամբաները մինչեւ երբ բաց պիտի մնան: Միլլի կառավարութիւնը նոր պատերազմական ատեան ստեղծած է, որոնք անհնազանդներու հանդէպ ծայրայեղ խստութիւններու պիտի դիմեն եղեր: Բոլոր պետական հասոյթի աղբիւրները իւրացուցեր եւ բացարձակապէս զինուորականութեան յատկացուցեր են: Չրոյց կայ որ բացառիկ տուրք մըն ալ պիտի հաստատուի եղեր: Հրահանգ տուեր են Էնկիւրիւ գումարուելիք մէպուսա[րա]նին համար նոր մէպուսներ ընտրել: Ճիշդ նման հրամաններ ալ հոս եկան. տեղւոյս էշրաֆը ժողովներ գումարեց եւ մերժողական պատասխան տուաւ, այդ կառավարութեան հետ միանալը իրենց անձնական շահերուն եւ երկրին վնասակար նկատելով: Չեմ գիտեր որ եթէ Միլլի կառավարութիւնը բաւական ուժ ղրկէ հոս, այս տեղն ալ իր կամքին հպատակեցնելու համար, այս տեղի ընդդիմադիրները դիմադրութեան ինչ միջոցներ պիտի ունենան: Առ այժմ կացութիւնը անորոշ է եւ Մուսթաֆա Քէմալի տալիք որոշումին կապուած:

- Անգլիական քօմիսէրութեան Սամսոնի ներկայացուցիչը Ամասիա գացած էր: Մուսթաֆա Քէմալ զայն հսկողութեան տակ կ'առնէ եւ վար կը դնէ իբր պատանդ: Քանիցս լսուեցաւ թէ մեռած է, բայց այս լուրը չէ հաստատուած: Ասկէ կարելի է հետեւցնել Համաձայնական ոյժերու դէմ Միլլիներու յանդգնութիւնը եւ ցոյց տուած արհամարհանքը:

- Ներքին գաւառներէ մեծ թուով գաղթականներ եկած են խղճալի վիճակի մէջ: Միւթէսարըֆը կը հաւաստէ թէ Մուսթաֆա Քէմալ չի կրնար իր ազդեցութիւն[ը] տարածել մինչեւ Սամսոն, սակայն ռեւէ հաւաստիք չկայ այս մասին:

Տրապիզոն (Առաջնորդական Տեղապահէն) – 17 Մարտ

Տրապիզոնի եւ շրջակայից ներկայ կացութեան առջեւ կ'առաջարկուի Կ. Պոլիս տեղափոխել Տրապիզոնի, Օրտուի եւ Կիրասոնի 400ի մօտ որբերը, հաւանական կոտորածէ մը փրկելու համար զանոնք:

Ատանա- 31 Մարտ

Կիլիկիոյ կացութիւնը հետեւեալն է:

Հաճընի հետ հաղորդակցութիւն չունինք: Միայն օդանաւը երբեմն կ'այցելէ: Քաղաքը հանդարտ զգած է, չէթէները առ այժմ սպառողական դիրք մ'ունին, կը կարծուի թէ բախումէ կը

clash. Our fellow Armenians are well-armed, and the plane sometimes delivers bullets there.

Kozan [Sis] is besieged at a distance of five kilometers; we keep in touch by crossing the çetes' siege line when needed. Tomorrow, a group of two hundred volunteers will head to Kozan after joining a group of two hundred people already in Misis. There are four hundred [volunteers] in Kozan; therefore, the eight hundred who will unite in Kozan will join forces to march against the çetes of Saimbeyli.

Hasanbeyli is besieged. The Armenians are fighting heroically, inflicting a significant loss on the enemy, but despite this, the enemy is growing larger day by day. We are obliged to send Armenian forces.

The clash around Bahçe has begun vehemently.

In Düziçi [Haruniye], the çetes have burned all the houses. Only the orphanage, the Protestant church, and one house remain standing. The war between the Franco-Armenian forces and the Turks has been going on for twenty-one days. The enemy is estimated at two to three thousand; the Armenians have been obliged to evacuate the village. I think they have retreated tonight.

İslahiye is calm now. There are enough forces there.

The spirit of the people is high. Although the çetes are inching closer, the Armenians have vowed to die with honor. Hunger enervates our strength the most.

We have no news from Kessab, Kilis, and Urfa.

Mersin (from Greeks who took refuge in Mersin from Silifke [petition ratified by the Greek metropolitan of Mersin])—March 15

Mustafa Kemal's followers have been in Silifke for two months, and the entire Muslim population and government officials have joined them. Seeing the situation deteriorate daily, the local Greeks were obliged to take refuge in Mersin, leaving their families and jobs behind. After reaching Mersin, until February 20, they managed to secretly correspond with their families, who reported that they were in danger. However, there has been no news from Silifke, Olukbaşı [Alakilise], Mut, Ahairpazar, Aydıncık [Kilindire], Arkarası, Bahçe, and Çınlık since that date. More than ten thousand Greeks living in these places have been out of communication for more than ten days and are in obvious danger. It is not even known if they are alive. The village of Kırobası [Mara] is in the same situation; it has been without communication for more than forty days. According to what the travelers arriving from Karaman said, more than 150 regular soldiers, under the guise of çetes, carry weapons and ammunition to Mut and the various parts of Silifke, where their commanders are located. In the French-occupied Mersin region, more than two hundred brutal killings by insurgents—or, more accurately, by local Turks—have taken place in the last ten days. When this is the case here, it is undoubtedly easy to deduce what the situation of the Christians left under the Turkish administration in Silifke is like. Bringing their dangerous situation to the attention of the Christian world and asking for help is pleaded.

Bandırma (from the primate)—April 7

On April 3, the imperial prince who was in Bandırma, the judge, the mufti, the head of the officer corps, the prince's bodyguard, and Hafız Effendi, a member of the municipality, visited Ahmet Anzavur in Gönen as delegates and pleaded with him to avoid clashes and potential unwanted incidents.

The anti-Milli leader stated that his aim was only to implement the following four conditions.

1. Immediate dispersal of the Milli forces that hurt national interests.
2. Protection of the sultan's rights as caliph.

խուսափին: Մերինները լաւ զինուած են եւ օդանաւը երբեմն փամփուշտ կը տանի:

Միս հինգ քիլոմէթր հեռաւորութեամբ պաշարուած է, հաղորդակցութիւնը կը պահենք ի հարկին չէթէներու պաշարման գիծը կտրելով: Վաղը Միս կը մեկնի 200 հոգիէ բաղկացեալ կամաւորներու խումբ մը, որ արդէն Միսիս գտնուող 200 հոգինոց խումբին միանալով Միս պիտի երթան: Սոյն մէջ կը գտնուի 400 հոգի, հետեւաբար Միս համախմբուող 800 հոգին միանալով պիտի քալեն Հաճնոյ չէթէներուն դէմ:

Հասան Պէյլի պաշարուած է: Հայութիւնը հերոսաբար կը կռուի թշնամւոյն տալով ահռելի կորուստ, սակայն հակառակ ատոր, թշնամին կը ստուարանայ օր ըստ օրէ: Հայոց ույժ ղրկելու պարտաւորուած ենք:

*Պաղճէ*ի շուրջը ընդհարումը սկսած է սաստկօրէն:

*Հարունիէ*ի մէջ չէթէները այրած են բոլոր տուները, միայն կանգուն կը մնան որբանոցը, բողոքականաց եկեղեցին եւ ուրիշ տուն մը: 21 օրէ ի վեր պատերազմը կը շարունակուէր ֆրանքո-հայկական ույժերու եւ թուրքերուն միջեւ: Թշնամին 2000–3000 կը հաշուուի, հայերը պարտաւորուած են գիւղը պարպել: Կարծեմ այս գիշեր քաշուած են:

*Իսլահիյէ*ն այժմ հանդարտ է: Հոն բաւականաչափ ույժ կայ:

Ժողովուրդին հոգեկան վիճակը բարձր է: Թէեւ չէթէները հետզհետէ կը մօտենան, սակայն հայութիւնը ուխտած է պատուով մեռնիլ: Սովը ամէնէն աւելի կը ջլատէ մեր ույժերը:

Քեսապէն, Քիլիսէն եւ Ուրֆայէն լուր չունինք:

Մերսին (Սէլէֆքէէն Մերսին ապաստանող յոյներէ [հանրագիր վաւերացեալ Մերսինի հելլէն հասարակապետէն]) – 15 Մարտ

Մուսթաֆա Քեմալի արբանեակները երկու ամիսէ ի վեր Սելեֆքէ մտած են եւ ամբողջ իսլամ բնակչութիւնը եւ կառավարական պաշտօնէութիւնը իրենց յարած են: Տեսնելով որ կացութիւնը օրէ օր կը վատթարանայ, ստիպուեցան տեղւոյն յոյները Մերսին ապաստանիլ, իրենց բաղդին ձգելով թէ՛ իրենց ընտանիքները եւ թէ՛ իրենց գործերը: Մերսին հասնելէ յետոյ, մինչեւ Փետրուար 20, յաջողած են գաղտնի թղթակցիլ իրենց ընտանիքներուն հետ, որոնք կը յայտնէին թէ կը գտնուէին վտանգի մէջ: Սակայն այդ թուականէն ի վեր ոեւէ լուր չկայ Սելեֆքէէն, Աղաքիլիսէէն, Մութէն, Ահայիրբազարէն, Քելինտիրէն, Արքարաշէն, Պաղչէէն եւ Ճինլիքէն: Այս տեղերը ապրող 10,000է աւելի յոյները տասը օրէ աւելի է որ հաղորդակցութենէ զրկուած եւ ակներեւ վտանգի մը տակ կը գտնուին, եւ նոյնիսկ յայտնի չէ թէ ողջ ե՞ն: Մարա անուն գիւղն ալ նոյն վիճակին մատնուած է եւ 40 օրէ աւելի է զրկուած է հաղորդակցութենէ: Գարամանէն եկած եւ ճամբորդներուն ըսածին նայելով, ամէն օր 150է աւելի կանոնաւոր զինուորներ չէթէ անուան տակ զէնք եւ զինամթերք կը տանին Մութ եւ Սելեւկիոյ զանազան կողմերը, ուր կը գտնուին իրենց հրամատարները: Ֆրանսական զրաւման տակ գտնուող Մերսինի շրջանակին մէջ, 10 օրէ ի վեր, 200է աւելի վայրագ սպանութիւններ տեղի ունեցան ըմբոստներու կամ աւելի ճիշդ է ըսել տեղացի թուրքերու կողմէ: Երբ հոս այսպէս է, անշուշտ դիւրին է մակաբերել թէ Սելեֆքիոյ թրքական վարչութեան տակ մնացած քրիստոնեաներուն վիճակը ի՞նչ է: Կը խնդրուի քրիստոնեայ աշխարհին ուշադրութեան ներկայացնել անոնց վտանգաւոր կացութիւնը եւ օգնութիւն խնդրել:

Պանտրմա (Առաջնորդէն) – 7 Ապրիլ

Ապրիլ 3ին Պանտրմա գտնուող կայսերազուն իշխանը, հաքիմը, միւֆթին, սպայակոյտի պետը, իշխանին թիկնապահը եւ թաղապետութեան անդամներէն Հաֆըզ էֆէնտին, իբրեւ պատգամաւոր Կէօնէն Ահմէտ Ազնաւուրի մօտ երթալով խնդրեր էին որ տեղի չտրուի բաղխումներու եւ հաւանական անհաճոյ դէպքերու:

Հակամիլլի ղեկավարը յայտարարեր է որ կէտ նպատակի ունի միայն հետեւեալ չորս պայմաններու գործադրութիւնը:

3. Freedom of religion for Muslims, Christians, and Jews, and the security of their lives, property, and honor.

4. In the event of attempting resistance, Bandırma's capture by force would follow the capture of Edincik, and he would annul the arbitrary duties imposed by the Millis on the people and oversee in person the reestablishment of order.

In this regard, he fully assured the delegation about the comfort and well-being of all classes of the local people.

The next day, the delegates returned here in the evening. The same night, the commander of the 14th Army, Yusuf İzzet Pasha, his followers, and many Milli soldiers rushed from the city out to Bursa in carriages. On the morning of April 5, others also threw themselves on a train in panic and left for Balıkesir.

On the same day, Şevki Bey, the lieutenant governor of Bandırma, summoned the religious leaders and prominent figures of the Muslim and Christian societies to the seat of government. He explained the situation to the attendees, and it was decided unanimously that if Ahmet Anzavur came to Bandırma, resistance should not be attempted and that he should be met with a welcoming reception.

Later, to calm the people down, he posted a message directed to the people on the city walls.

• On April 6, the censorship of newspapers and letters that Commander of the 14th Army Yusuf İzzet Pasha had sanctioned was revoked.

Bandırma (from the primate)—April 9

Today, the lieutenant governor (Şevki Bey of Amasya) sent a message to the Armenian primate that Ahmet Anzavur Bey would arrive in an hour with his followers and, apart from not attempting any resistance, he should be met with good reception. Therefore, he recommends inspiring assurance to Armenians to prevent any fear and panic.

Indeed, the Millis have evacuated Gönen, Bandırma, and Mihaliç (Karacabey), but Balıkesir is preparing to form a fierce opposition as the center of local and regional Milli forces.

According to the latest news, the Millis are very busy in Balıkesir; no one is allowed to leave Balıkesir, and those who go there are strictly inspected, their property is searched, and they are subjected to difficulties for insignificant reasons.

The mentality of Balıkesir's Millis suggests future extreme actions by force, especially since Balıkesir's District Governor İzzet Bey lacks the competency of the current lieutenant governor and is a toy in the palm of the Millis, as the notes placed under Mustafa Kemal's announcements clearly indicate.

Bandırma (from the primate)—April 11

On April 9, at five o'clock, Ahmet Anzavur Bey entered Bandırma with his followers. The government and the people gave him an enthusiastic reception. Upon the government's invitation, the Armenian vicar general Father Vosgi and the metropolitan vicar general of the Greeks Papa Nicola were at the reception.

Ahmet Anzavur gave separate speeches explaining his plan to the people in the square of the government building and the dignitaries waiting for the reception. The impression is good.

By order of Ahmet Anzavur, a body has been set up here tasked with temporarily overseeing local

1° Ազգայնաս Միլլի ուժերու անմիջական ցրուումը:

2° Սուլթանին խալիֆայական իրաւունքներուն պաշտպանութիւնը:

3° Իսլամներու, քրիստոնէից եւ հրէից կրօնի ազատութիւնը եւ անոնց կեանքին, ինչքին եւ պատւոյն ապահովութիւնը:

4° Դիմադրութիւն մը փորձուելու պարագային, Էտհէմիկը գրաւելէ յետոյ Պանտրման գրաւել բռնի ոյժով եւ ջնջել Միլլիի կողմէ ժողովրդեան վրայ դրուած կամայական տուրքերը եւ հոն անձամբ հսկել կարգ ու կանոնին վերահաստատումին:

Այս առթիւ կատարելապէս ապահովցուցեր է պատգամաւորութիւնը տեղւոյն ամէն դասակարգի ժողովրդեան հանգստութեան եւ բարօրութեան մասին:

Հետեւեալ օրը իրիկուան դէմ տեղս վերադարձան պատգամաւորները: Նոյն գիշերը Ժ.Դ. զօրաբանակի հրամանատար Եուսուֆ Իզզէթ փաշա, իր հետեւորդները եւ շատ մը Միլլի զինուորականներ կառքերով աճապարանօք հեռացած են քաղաքէս դէպի Պրուսա: Մէկ մաս մըն ալ Ապրիլ 5ին առտուն հեւ ի հեւ եւ խուճապով շոգեկառք նետուած եւ Պալըքէսիր մեկնած են:

Պանտրմայի գայմագամ Շէվգը պէյ նոյն օրը իսլամ եւ քրիստոնեայ հասարակութեանց հոգեւոր պետերը եւ երեւելիները կառավարատուն հրաւիրած եւ իրերուն վիճակը պարզելով ներկաներու միաձայն հաւանութեամբ որոշուած է որ եթէ Ահմէտ Ազնաւուր Պանտրմա գայ՝ ոեւէ դիմադրութիւն չփորձուի եւ լաւ ընդունելութիւն մը ըլլայ:

Յետոյ ժողովուրդը հանդարտեցնելու համար, ժողովուրդին ուղ[ղ]եալ յայտարարութիւն մը փակցուցած է քաղաքին պատերուն վրայ:

- Ժ.Դ. զօրաբանակի հրամանատար Եուսուֆ Իզզէթ փաշայի կողմէ հաստատուած թերթերու եւ նամակներու գրաքննութիւնը ջնջուած է Ապրիլ 6ին:

Պանտրմա (Առաջնորդէն) – 9 Ապրիլ

Այսօր գայմագամը (ամասիացի Շէֆգը պէյ) լուր կը ղրկէ հայոց առաջնորդին թէ մէկ ժամէն Ահմէտ Անզաւուր պէյ իր հետեւորդներով տեղս պիտի հասնի եւ դիմադրութեան ոեւէ փորձ չըլլալէ զատ, լաւ ընդունելութիւն մըն ալ պիտի ըլլայ, որով երկիւղի եւ խուճապի առիթ չտրուելու համար կը յանձնարարէր ապահովութիւն ներշնչել հայոց:

Արդարեւ, Կէօնէն, Պանտրմա եւ Միխալըճ (Գարաճա-պէյ) այժմ պարպուած [են] Միլլիներէ, սակայն Պալըքէսիր կը պատրաստուի բուռն ընդդիմութիւն մ'ընելու իբր կեդրոն տեղւոյս եւ շրջանի Միլլի ուժերու:

Վերջին լուրերու համաձայն, Պալըքէսիրի մէջ միլլիականք մեծ գործունէութեան մէջ են, ոչ ոքի թոյլ կուտան Պալըքէսիրէն դուրս ելլելու եւ հոն գացողները խիստ քննութեան կ'ենթարկուին եւ իրենց գոյքերը կը խուզարկուին եւ ոչինչ պատճառներով դժուարութեանց կ'ենթարկուին:

Պալըքէսիրի Միլլիներու մտայնութիւնը ենթադրել կուտայ թէ ծայրայեղութիւններու տեղի պիտի տրուի բռնական միջոցներով, մանաւանդ որ Պալըքէսիրի միւթէսարըֆը՝ Իզզէթ պէյ, տեղւոյս գայմագամին վարողութիւնը չունի եւ խաղալիկ մըն է Միլլիներու ափին մէջ, ինչպէս որ Մուսթաֆա Քէմալի յայտարարութիւններուն ի ստորեւ տրուած *Շէ[րի]*երը բացայայտ կը ցուցնեն:

Պանտրմա (Առաջնորդէն) – 11 Ապրիլ

Ապրիլ 9ին ժամը 5ին Ահմէտ Ազնաւուր պէյ իր հետեւորդներով մտաւ Պանտրմա: Կառավարութիւն եւ ժողովուրդ խանդավառ ընդունելութիւն մը ըրին: Կառավարութեան հրաւէրով հայոց Առաջնորդական Փոխանորդ Տ. Ոսկի քահանայ եւ յունաց Մետրապոլիտի Փոխանորդ Փափա Նիկօլա ընդունելութեան ներկայ եղան:

Ահմէտ Ազնաւուր թէ՛ կառավարութեան շէնքին հրապարակը՝ ժողովուրդին, եւ թէ կառավարատան մէջ ընդունելութեան համար սպասող պաշտօնական անձերուն զատ զատ բանախօսութիւններ ըրած է, իր ծրագիրը բացատրած է: Տպաւորութիւնը լաւ է:

security. It is chaired by the lieutenant governor and consists of Turkish, Greek, and Armenian members.

A delegation has been elected, consisting of two Turks, one Greek, and one Armenian. They will travel to İstanbul after joining the delegates of Erdek, Gönen, and Mihaliç (Karacabey) to express gratitude for being liberated from the dictatorship of the Milli forces.

On April 10, Ahmet Anzavur left Bandırma for Mustafakemalpaşa [Kirmasti] to march against Balıkesir by way of Susurluk.

Assurances have been obtained that no attempt at resistance will be made in Mustafakemalpaşa and Susurluk, but there is a fear that resistance will be met in Balıkesir, considered the citadel of the Millis.

Adana (from the National Union)—April 4[62]

The situation has not in any way improved. The Milli çetes' operation spread from the Amanos Mountains to the entire highlands of Toros Dağlari. Therefore, the whole region of Cilicia has been taken in the tight grip of the çetes' siege. The French military's hard work to remove the bands of çetes with fierce fighting has not hindered the çetes from reaching as far as Adana's northern and northwestern borders.

Saimbeyli [Hacın], Kozan [Sis], Hasanbeyli, and Bahçe remain in the same state of siege.

Pressed by this situation, the National Union of Adana has tried to make necessary and appropriate arrangements with its own resources to rush to the aid of the local Armenians in distress. So far, more than six volunteer groups have been sent to help Armenian-populated centers to prevent danger and keep the people's morale high.

Adana (from Zabel Yesayan, Delegate of the Joint [Armenian] Delegation of Paris)—April 4[63]

The situation in Cilicia is very grave. The enemy force is estimated at forty thousand, and they hold the strongest positions. Saimbeyli [Hacın] and Süleymanlı [Zeytun] remain under siege. A ten-thousand-strong enemy force is in front of Kozan [Sis]; the Amanos Mountain line is entirely in battle. Düziçi [Haruniye] was set on fire and abandoned. Hasanbeyli and Bahçe are at war, and the unarmed Christian inhabitants of those places have retreated to Adana, but Adana itself is in danger. An enemy force of fourteen thousand is threatening the city, and it is expected to attack at any time, especially since there is great suspicion about the Muslims in the city. The French have made serious preparations. The Armenians also are doing their best, especially since the French government is providing the necessary weapons and ammunition.

Fifteen hundred orphans will be relocated with the support of the French government. Should this happen, there is also a desire to relocate the defenseless people.

Kayseri (from the locum tenens)—February 22

Despite the failure of the plot by the local government to persecute alleged Armenian political organizations and Armenian çetes in Develi [Everek] and Yeşilyurt [Mancusun], this innovative method [of attributing political agendas and guerilla activities to Armenians] continues under the influence of Milli extremely provocative statements. In the prevailing situation, the Armenian Catholic prelate Bishop Andon Bahabanian turned to the new governor and demanded security of life for the Armenians. The governor replied that he cannot prevent the provocative statements cabled by the Millis

Ահմէտ Ազնաւուրի հրահանգով հոս կազմուած է մարմին մը գայմագամին նախագահութեամբ եւ թուրք, յոյն եւ հայ անդամներով, որ պաշտօն ունի առժամապէս հսկել տեղւոյս ապահովութեան:

Պատգամաւորութիւն մը ընտրուած է երկու թուրքէ, մէկ յոյնէ եւ մէկ հայէ բաղկացած, որը Էրտէկի, Կէօնէնի, Միխալըճի (Գարաճապէյ) պատգամաւորութեանց միացած Պոլիս պիտի մեկնի Միլլի ուժերու բռնապետութենէն ազատուած ըլլալնուն շնորհակալութիւն յայտնելու համար:

Ահմէտ Ազնաւուր Ապրիլ 10ին Պանտրմայէն մեկնեցաւ դէպի Քերմասթի, ուրկէ Սուսուրլըղի ճամբով պիտի քալէ Պալըքէսիրի վրայ:

Քերմասթի[ի] եւ Սուսուրլըղի մէջ դիմադրութեան փորձ չըլլալու մասին հաւաստիքներ ձեռք բերուած են, միայն կը վախցուի Պալըքէսիրէն, որը Միլլիներու միջնաբերդը կը համարուի:

Ատանա (Ազգային Միութենէն) – 4 Ապրիլ

Կացութիւնը ոչ մէկ կերպով բարելաւուած է: Միլլի ասպատակներու գործունէութիւնը Ամանոսի լեռնավայրէն տարածուած է նաեւ Տաւրոսի բովանդակ լեռնամարզերուն մէջ, այնպէս որ ամբողջ Կիլիկիոյ շրջանը չէթէական պաշարումի սեղմ գիծի մը մէջ առնուած է: Ֆրանսական զինուորական ույժեր թէեւ տեղ տեղ կ'աշխատին բուռն կռիւներով հեռացնել չէթէական խումբերը, բայց սակայն արգելք մը չէ որ չէթէները մինչեւ Ատանայի հիւսիսային եւ հիւսիս արեւմտեան սահմանները չհասնին:

Հաճըն, Սիս, Հասանպէյլի եւ Պաղչէ կը մնան դեռ պաշարման նոյն վիճակին մէջ:

Իրաց այս կացութեան առջեւ, Ատանայի Ազգային Միութիւնը աշխատած է իր սեփական միջոցներով պարտ ու պատշաճը տնօրինել՝ տեղւոյն աղէտեալ հայութեան օգնութեան փութալու համար: Մինչեւ հիմա հայաշատ կեդրոններու օգնութիւն ղրկուած է վեցէ աւելի կամաւորական խումբեր, թէ՛ վտանգին առաջքը առնելու եւ թէ ժողովուրդին հոգեկան վիճակը բարձր բռնելու համար:

Ատանա (Զապէլ Եսայեանէ՝ պատուիրակ Բարիզի Միացեալ Պատուիրակութեան) – 4 Ապրիլ

Կացութիւնը Կիլիկիոյ մէջ շատ ծանր է: Թշնամի ուժը կը համարուի 40,000 եւ բռնած է ամենէն ամուր դիրքերը: Հաճըն եւ Զէյթուն պաշարուած կը մնան: Սիսի առջեւ կայ 10,000նոց թշնամի ուժ, Ամանոս լերանց գիծը ամբողջովին կռիւի մէջ է. Հարունիյէն հրդեհուած եւ լքուած է: Հասան-Պէյլի եւ Պահչէ կռիւի մէջ են եւ այդ վայրերուն անզէն քրիստոնեայ բնակիչները քաշուած են դէպի Ատանա, բայց Ատանան ինքը վտանգի մէջ է. 14,000նոց թշնամի ուժ մը կը սպառնայ քաղաքին, օրը օրին եւ ժամը ժամին յարձակման կը սպասուի, մանաւանդ որ մեծ կասկած կայ քաղաքին մէջ եղած մահմետականներուն վրայ: Ֆրանսացիք լուրջ պատրաստութիւններ տեսած են. հայերն ալ իրենց կարելին կ'ընեն, մանաւանդ որ ֆրանսական կառավարութիւնը կու տայ հարկ եղած զէնքը եւ ռազմամթերքը:

1500 որբերը ֆրանսական կառավարութեան օժանդակութեամբ այլուր պիտի փոխադրուին: Փափաք կայ վերջին պարագային փոխադրել նաեւ անպաշտպան ժողովուրդը:

Կեսարիա (Առաջնորդական Տեղապահէն) – 22 Փետրուար

Էվէրէկի եւ Մանճուսունի մէջ կարծեցեալ հայ քաղաքական կազմակերպութիւնները ու հայ չէթէները հետապնդ[ելու հնարքը] տեղական կառավարութենէն, անհետեւանք մնալով հանդերձ, այս նորահնար մեթոտը կը շարունակուի դեռ, Միլլիի գերագրգռող յայտարարութիւններուն ազդեցութեան տակ: Տիրող կացութեան մէջ, Հայ-Կաթոլիկ Առաջնորդ Անտօն Եպիսկոպոս Պահապանեան նոր կառավարիչին դիմելով հայոց կեանքին ապահովութիւն կը պահանջէ: Կառավարիչը կը պատասխանէ թէ ինքը Միլլիի կողմէ եկած ծածկագիր հեռագիրներով Հիյէթը Մէրքէզիյէյի դրան

through coded telegrams and posted on the doore of the central committee. However, he has established strict censorship on the local newspapers *Erciyes* and *Kayseri,* and scandalous writings involving the [Muslim and Christian] elements will not appear. He added that the prominent [Turkish] merchant class of Kayseri has two thoughts: one wants to sincerely live well with the Armenians, and the other, if not frankly, at least because it is bored [with the current situation], wants to live a good life. Then there is another class, the Millis. They are harsh and suspect the Armenians. They want the Armenian homes to be searched based on suspicions that the Armenians of Kayseri are keeping harmful people. The governor said: "Pressure has been mounted on us many times to search [homes]. If it happens again, we will have to allow some Armenian homes to be searched." He also said: "If the restless Turkish fraction demonstrates against the Armenians, the Armenians should be careful and withdraw. Accordingly, you need to warn the people through exhortation."

• There have been demonstrations of joy in Kayseri over the news that İstanbul has been left to the Turks. On this occasion, the governor regarded the security of the lives of Christians as necessary in his speech.

Develi [Everek] (from the Neighborhood Council)—March 11

The situation of Armenians in and around our place is extremely alarming. Five days ago, four Armenians were brutally killed in Gömedi. One of the unfortunate victims fell to the ground after being missed by a bullet, pretending to be dead. Half an hour later, he sought refuge in the guardhouse near the village of Fırakdın, terrified. [Later,] on the way, he came across the same bandits, who slaughtered him brutally on the spot. Three people, too, were killed the next day in Satı and Çataloluk, for seven. It has been three weeks since a terrible boycott against Armenians and Greeks occurred there. Armenians have closed their shops and confined themselves to their houses. There are rumors of a massacre. The government is an indifferent spectator. The Turkish people are arming themselves. The National Defense [Organization] is trying to persuade Armenians not to be afraid, but the killing of the seven unfortunate victims is unconvincing, as the Armenians consider this a sign of a general massacre. Three days ago, the Turks took the majority of Armenians and Greeks to the barracks under the pretext of collecting soldiers' uniforms. They beat them terribly and stripped them naked from head to toe while insulting and threatening them. Complaints remain unheard.

Kayseri (from the vicar general)—March 17

The Turks' fury against the Armenians in Kayseri has no limits. Tonight, four hundred armed çetes are leaving for Cilicia. They are gnashing their teeth for Cilicia. They plan to attack Saimbeyli [Hacın]. Statements calling for a boycott against the Armenians have been posted on the doors of mosques and the main buildings. The district governor found one of these, showed it to the headquarters' intendant, and gave strict orders demanding the arrest of the authors. The newly arrived district governor is trying to bring the Turks and Armenians closer, but because there are two governments here, too, the governor's goodwill is not enough to remove the danger. Every day people come from the surrounding villages to ask for a remedy for the insecurity of life. Today, twenty-five to thirty carriages of Armenians left for Ereğli to go to Adana.

• Outside Kayseri, near Bezirhane, which belongs to the jurisdiction of Develi [Everek] township, the governor provided information to the locum tenens about the four Armenians who had been killed a few days ago. The governor assured him that he would do whatever was necessary. He also recommended that the Armenian locum tenens write to Develi to find out whether the crime was the work of çetes, who had come from Adana, or the people from Develi. On the same day [the primate

վրայ փակցուած գրգռիչ յայտարարութիւնները չի կրնար արգիլել, միայն տեղական «Էրճիաս» եւ «Գայսէրի» թերթերուն վրայ խիստ գրաքննութիւն մը հաստատած է եւ տարրերու միջեւ գայթակղեցի գրուածքներ պիտի չերեւին: Աւելցուցած է թէ՝ Կեսարիոյ բարձր վաճառական դասը երկու մտայնութիւն ունի. մէկը հայերուն հետ լաւ ապրիլ կ'ուզէ անկեղծօրէն, միւսն ալ եթէ ոչ անկեղծօրէն, գոնէ ձանձրացած ըլլալով կ'ուզէ աղէկ ապրիլ, իսկ ուրիշ դասակարգ մըն ալ կայ,- որոնք են Միլլիները,- որ հայերուն դէմ խիստ է եւ կասկածոտ, եւ կ'ուզէ որ հայոց տուները խուզարկութիւն կատարուի, կը կասկածի որ Կեսարիոյ հայերը վնասակար մարդիկ պահած են: Կառավարիչը յայտնած է թէ «մեզի քանի անգամ կ'ըլլայ կը ստիպեն որ խուզարկութիւն կատարենք: Եթէ կրկնուի, ստիպուած պիտի ըլլանք արտօնել որ քանի մը հայ տուներ խուզարկուին»: Նոյնպէս ըսած է որ «եթէ թուրք անհանդարտ մասը հայերուն դէմ ցոյց ընէ, հայերը պէտք է զգուշանան եւ քաշուին: Ըստ այսմ, պէտք է ժողովուրդը զգուշացնելու համար յորդորներ տար ժողովուրդին»:

- Կ. Պոլսոյ թուրքերու թողուելու լուրին վրայ ուրախութեան ցոյցեր եղած են Կեսարիոյ մէջ: Կառավարիչը այդ առթիւ քրիստոնէից կեանքին ապահովութիւնը անհրաժեշտ համարած է իր ճառին մէջ:

Էվէրէկ (Թաղական Խորհուրդէն) – 11 Մարտ

Տեղւոյս եւ շրջակայ հայոց կացութիւնը չափազանց տագնապալի է: Հինգ օր առաջ Կէօմէտիի մէջ 4 հայեր խժդժօրէն սպաննուած են: Դժբաղդ զոհերէն մին գնդակի վիրպումով գետին կ'իյնայ ինքզինքն մեռած ձեւացնելով: Կէս ժամ վերջ՝ սարսափահար կ'ապաստանի Փըրագտըն գիւղի մօտ պահականոց: Ճամբան կը հանդիպի նոյն աւազակներուն, որոնք տեղնի տեղով խժդժօրէն կը մորթոտեն զայն: 3 հոգի ալ հետեւեալ օրը Սադըյի եւ Չաթալ-Օլուգի մէջ կը սպաննեն, ընդամէնը 7 հոգի: Երեք շաբաթ է որ հայոց եւ յունաց դէմ սոսկալի *պօյքօթ* մը կայ: Հայերը խանութները փակած եւ տուները փակուած են: Զարդի շշուկներ շրջան կ'ընեն: Կառավարութիւնը անտարբեր հանդիսատես մըն է: Թուրք ժողովուրդը կը զինուի: Միւտաֆայի Միլլիյէն կը ջանայ համոզել հայերը թէ չվախնան, [բայց] եօթը դժբաղդ զոհերուն սպանութիւնը անհամոզելի կ'ընէ զանոնք, վասնզի այդ դէպքը նախանշանը կը համարեն ընդհանուր ջարդի մը: Երեք օրէ ի վեր հայերու եւ յոյներու մեծամասնութիւնը զրչլա տարին, զինուորի հագուստ հաւաքելու պատրուակին տակ, սոսկալի ծեծեցին եւ ոտքէն մինչեւ գլուխը մերկացնելով մերկ դուրս ձգեցին նախատական եւ սպառնալից բառերով: Բողոքները անլսելի կը մնան:

Կեսարիա (Առաջնորդական Փոխանորդէն) – 17 Մարտ

Կեսարիոյ մէջ թուրքերուն կատաղութիւնը հայոց հանդէպ չափ ու սահման չունի: Այս իրիկուն 400 զինեալ ձիաւոր չէթէներ դէպի Կիլիկիա կը մեկնին: Ակռայ կը կրճտեն Կիլիկիոյ համար: Ծրագիր[ն]ին է Հաճընի վրայ խուժել: Հայերուն դէմ պօյքօթի յայտարարութիւններ փակցուցած են մզկիթներուն դուռները եւ գլխաւոր շէնքերու վրայ, որոնցմէ մէկուն հանդիպելով միւթէսարրըֆը առած եւ մէրքէզ մէմուրիին ցոյց տուած եւ խիստ հրամաններ տուած եւ պահանջած է ձերբակալել անոնց հեղինակները: Միւթէսարրըֆը, որ նոր եկած է, թուրքերուն եւ հայերուն միջեւ մերձեցում յառաջ [բերելու] ջանքեր կ'ընէ, սակայն որովհետեւ հոս ալ երկու կառավարութիւն կայ, ուստի կառավարիչին բարեացակամութիւնը բաւական չէ վտանգը հեռացնել[ու համար]: Ամէն օր շրջակայ գիւղերէ կուգան կեանքի անապահովութեան համար դարման խնդրելու: Այսօր 25–30 կառք հայեր Էրէյլի մեկնեցան՝ Ատանա երթալու համար:

- Կեսարիայէն դուրս, Էվէրէկի գազային վերաբերեալ Պէզիր Խանի մօտերը, քանի մը օր առաջ սպաննուած 4 հայերուն մասին կառավարիչը տեղեկութիւն տուաւ Առաջնորդական Փոխանորդին եւ հաւաստեց թէ ի՛նչ որ պէտք է պիտի ընէ: Ցանձնարարեց նաեւ որ հայոց Առաջնորդական Փոխանորդը գրէ Էվէրէկ հասկնալու համար թէ ոճիրը Ատանայէն եկած չէթէներո՞ւ գործն է, թէ

met the governor], information reached the prelacy that three people had also been killed in Satı and Çataloluk. Two days later, the governor again informed [the primate] that besides the [aforementioned] four murdered Armenians, four Armenians had been taken away, and all traces of them had been lost. Seeing the horrors being experienced by the Armenians, the governor described his pursuit in a message and urged calm. But the malice of the lieutenant governor of Develi, combined with his known friendship with the Millis, leaves little hope that the perpetrators will be found.

(The governor secretly came to the prelacy and expressed his pain over the victims and the primate's situation.)

• News has arrived that two Armenians have been killed around Boğazlıyan. There have been atrocities against Armenians perpetrated in those parts. Bad news is coming from the villages of Sivas close to Kayseri, especially from Gemerek, where Armenians are not allowed to leave the village. At the same time, Turkish çetes threaten to take the Armenians along into service to them. Threats, beatings, robberies, and looting are usual for these victims. Consequently, the Armenian villagers of Gemerek and its environs are starving.

Trabzon (from the vicar general)—April 3

Political calmness ostensibly continues in Trabzon. Internal machinations are perpetual. The delay in occupation may be catastrophic. Mustafa Kemal has issued arrest warrants for British representatives everywhere. Amasya's representative has already been arrested and probably taken to Sivas. It is rumored that General [Colonel] Rawlinson, who is in Erzurum, has also been arrested. They dare not arrest the representatives of the coastal cities.

After Mr. Crawford, the British military representative of Trabzon, left for İstanbul due to illness, Mr. Popplewell, who was staying as his deputy, was urgently summoned along with all of his followers by a telegram from İstanbul. Needless to say, this has left a shocking impression.

Now that the authorities and the bodies in charge are leaving, driven by precaution or fear, the Armenians have been left confused, thinking about what they can do since they are a handful of people without any means of self-defense.

Trabzon (from the vicar general)—April 4[64]

It has been heard, from a reliable source, that a new Milli Congress will be convened in Erzurum upon the invitation of Mustafa Kemal. A delegate has been requested from Trabzon too. The prefect has refused to send one. Upon this refusal, the Millis have demanded the prefect's resignation, but he does not want to give in. If he were to give in, the situation would be graver.

Topal Osman, the notorious leading brigand of Giresun, traveled to Trabzon to attend the Erzurum Congress; he seemed restrained by the warnings of Prefect Hamit Bey. According to reliable information received, Topal [Osman], who hates the Greeks, had recently attempted to establish a Greek-Turkish fraternity with a mysterious transfiguration. In a meeting convened for this purpose, sweet words were exchanged.

• Telegraphic communications with İstanbul have absolutely ceased. All communications between the center and the provinces have been severed. Kemal is the absolute ruler.

• The Millis are trying to get a new weapon; it does not matter that they do not have the gift to use it. It is the weapon of *Bolshevism* that now astonishingly preoccupies the minds of the Turkish masses. They think that *Bolshevism* and robbery are identical.

տէվէլուցիներու: Նոյն օրը տեղեկութիւն կը հասնի Առաջնորդարան թէ Սաղույի եւ Չաթալ Օլուգի մէջ սպաննուած են նաեւ 3 հոգի: Երկու օր յետոյ դարձեալ կառավարիչը կը տեղեկացնէ թէ սպաննուած 4 հայերուն հետ 4 հայեր ալ միասին տարած են, որոնց հետքը կորսուած է: Կառավարիչը հայոց սարսափը տեսնելով *թէզքէրէ*ով մը իր հետապնդութիւնները կը նկարագրէ եւ հանդարտութեան յորդոր կ'ընէ: Սակայն Էվէրէկի գայմագամին չարամտութիւնը եւ Միլլիին բարեկամ ըլլալը ծանօթ ըլլալով, յոյս չկայ որ ոճրագործները գտնուին:

(Կառավարիչը գաղտնի Առաջնորդարան գալով սպանեալներուն եւ իր կացութեան մասին ցաւ յայտնած է)

- Պօղազլըեանի կողմն ալ երկու հայեր սպաննուած ըլլալու լուրը կը հասնի: Այդ կողմերը խժդժութիւններ կը կատարուին հայերու դէմ: Նոյնպէս գէշ լուրեր կը հասնին Սեբաստիոյ՝ Կեսարիոյ մօտաւոր գիւղերէն, մանաւանդ Կէմէրէկէն, ուր արգիլուած է հայոց գիւղէն դուրս ելլալ: Միեւնոյն ատեն թուրք չէթէներ կը սպառնան միասին տանիլ զիրենք ծառայելու համար իրենց: Սպառնալիք, ծեծ, կողոպուտ եւ թալան սովորական են այդ դժբաղդներուն համար: Հետեւաբար Կէմէրէկի եւ անոր մօտաւոր հայ գիւղացիները անօթի են:

Տրապիզոն (Առաջնորդական Փոխանորդէն) – 3 Ապրիլ

Տրապիզոնի քաղաքական մակերեւոյթին խաղաղութիւնը կը շարունակէ: Ներքին մեքենայութիւններ անպակաս են: Գրաւումի յապաղումը կրնայ աղէտաբեր ըլլալ: Մուսթաֆա Քէմալը անգլիացի ներկայացուցիչները ձերբակալելու հրամաններ արձակած է ամէն կողմ: Ամասիայի ներկայացուցիչը ձերբակալուած է արդէն եւ հաւանաբար տարուած Սեբաստիա: Զրոյց կը շրջի թէ ձերբակալուած է նաեւ Կարին գտնուող Զօրավար [Գնդապետ] Ռոլինսընը: Չեն համարձակիր ձերբակալելու ծովեզերեայ քաղաքներու ներկայացուցիչները:

Տրապիզոնի անգլիական զինուորական ներկայացուցիչ Պ. Գրաւֆըրտի հիւանդութեան պատճառով Պոլիս մեկնելէն վերջ՝ իբր փոխանորդ մնացող տեղակալ պ. Բօբըլուէլի (Popplewell) ալ Պոլիսէն հեռագրով եւ ստիպողաբար եւ իր ամբողջ հետեւորդներով կանչուիլը աւելորդ է ըսել թէ ցնցող տպաւորութիւն գործած է:

Հայ[եր]ը շփոթած մնացած են մտածելով թէ երբ իշխանութեան եւ կացութեան տէր մարմինները նախազգուշութեան համար կամ վախնալով այսպէս կը մեկնին, իրենք որ ինքնապաշտպանութեան ամէն միջոցներէ զուրկ ափ մը մարդ են, ի՞նչ ընելու են:

Տրապիզոն (Առաջնորդական Փոխանորդէն) – 4 Ապրիլ

Լսուած է՝ հաւաստի աղբիւրէ՝ թէ Մուսթաֆա Քէմալի հրաւէրով Միլլիական նոր համաժողով պիտի գումարուի Կարնոյ մէջ: Պատգամաւոր ուզուած է նաեւ Տրապիզոնէն: Կուսակալը մերժած է ղրկել: Այս մերժումին վրայ Միլլիճիները կուսակալին հրաժարումը պահանջած են, սակայն ան չ'ուզեր տեղի տալ: Եթէ տեղի տայ, կացութիւնը պիտի ծանրանայ:

- Կարնոյ Համաժողովին մասնակցելու համար Տրապիզոն եկած է Կիրասոնի համբաւաւոր աւազակապետ Թօփալ Օսման, որ կուսակալ Համիտ պէյի խիստ ազդարարութիւններուն վրայ զսպուած կը թուէր: Առնուած ստոյգ տեղեկութեանց համաձայն, այդ յունատեաց թօփալը վերջերս, խորհրդաւոր գունափոխութեամբ մը, յոյն եւ թուրք եղբայրակցութիւն մը հիմնելու փորձ է ըրեր: Այս նպատակով հրաւիրուած ժողովի մը մէջ անոյշ խօսքեր փոխանակուեր են:

- Հեռագրական հաղորդակցութիւնները բացարձակապէս դադրած են Պոլսոյ հետ: Կեդրոնին եւ գաւառին միջեւ ամէն կապ խզուած է: Քէմալ միահեծան կը տիրէ:

- Միլլիականութիւնը կը ջանայ ձեռք բերել նոր զէնք մը, հոգ չէ թէ զայն գործածելու շնորհքը չունենայ: Այդ զէնքն է *պոլշէվիզմ*ը, որ զարմանալիօրէն կը զբաղեցնէ այժմ թուրք ամբոխին միտքը, որուն մէջ սա գաղափարը տեղ գտած է թէ *պոլշէվիզմ* եւ կողոպուտ նոյն բանն են:

Adana (from M[ihran] Damadian)—April 4

The local situation always maintains the same grave and dangerous character. The whole population is in a state of alarm, and it seems that the circle is gradually contracting around Cilicia. The çetes appear and act even near Adana, Tarsus, and Mersin, although not yet in large numbers. The French have begun to show vigor, and the Armenians have started to show organized resistance, both of which have paid off. Today, in one form or another (legionnaires, gendarmes, militias, volunteers, and armed resistance groups that have been formed in the attacked areas), five to six thousand armed Armenians are fighting as best as they can.

İzmit (from Hayrabed Sakayan, a refugee from Geyve)—April 16

On the second day of Easter (April 12), at midnight, two hundred cavalry and armed Millis entered Eşme. Shortly afterward, five hundred foot soldiers arrived with four machine guns. Then these forces left Eşme. In the morning, the sound of gunfire was heard around Ortaköy. The Millis demanded five hundred rifles with bullets, bombs, two machine guns, and sixty young men from Ortaköy. The villagers said that they did not have any. Lieutenant Governor Hamdi Bey, who was with the Millis, gave them an hour [to comply], saying: "If you do not deliver, I will burn the village." An hour later, the attack began, and Turkish mobs from nearby villages joined [the attackers]. On Tuesday night, Ortaköy was ablaze. The fire could be seen from Kurtbelen's [Geyve's] elevation. Ten hours later, the smoke billowing from Ortaköy could be seen again from Keltepe.

On April 14, the British and Greek representatives were informed of the incident.

Ortaköy had a population of 4,500, of which barely one-tenth may have survived because the mob besieged the village beside the Millis. The residents of Ortaköy are all Greeks; there were only six Armenian families. After deportation, the rest [of the survivors] had come to Eşme. Five of those six families had arrived in Eşme for Easter, and only one Armenian family and eight brave [Armenian] men were present in Ortaköy.

Given what the Milli leaders said, all surrounding Armenian villages are in danger.

Immediate assistance is requested.

Mersin (from a personal letter)—April 11[65]

The state of insecurity continues in Cilicia. We do not know what will become of us an hour later. The çetes have arrived at Adana's door. Saimbeyli [Hacın] is besieged, as is Kozan [Sis]. There is no news from Pozantı, Halkırı, Beymelek, or even Dorak stations. It is understood that all Christians in the area have been annihilated. The French soldiers have also been besieged around Pozantı. The situation is very grave. The Dorak-Pozantı railway from Yenice station has stopped. The road is completely destroyed. A train from Yenice can move perhaps no more than five to eight kilometers toward Pozantı.

Some people are going to Cyprus because the situation in Adana is perilous. A person can go crazy. Controlling these çetes would be very easy, but there is no one to take action. Panic reigns in Adana. The people are in fear.

The few hundred Armenians traveling by way of Misis to help Kozan were attacked by Turkish çetes on the outskirts of Tumlu Kale (three hours away from Misis). Seventy of them were besieged. Adana also will be surrounded in a few more days, and self-defense will be ineffective.

The group of 180 [volunteers] going from Misis to Kozan was recalled before it reached Kozan, and their provisions and ammunition were taken away. Consequently, half turned back, and the other half were besieged in Tumlu Kale without supplies and ammunition.

Three to four thousand French soldiers broke the siege of Gaziantep [Ayntab]. They evacuated

Ատանա (Մ[իհրան] Տամատեան) – 4 Ապրիլ

Տեղական կացութիւնը միշտ կը պահէ նոյն ծանրակշիռ եւ վտանգալից հանգամանքը: Ամբողջ ազգաբնակութիւնը տագնապի մէջ է եւ կարծես օղակը երթալով կը նեղնայ Կիլիկիոյ չորս բոլորտիքը: Նոյնիսկ Ատանայի, Տարսոնի եւ Մերսինի մօտերը չէթէներ կ'երեւին եւ կը գործեն, թէեւ առ այժմ ո՛չ ստուար թուով: Ֆրանսացիք սկսան կորով ցոյց տալ, իսկ հայերը՝ սկսան կազմակերպուած դիմադրութիւն ցոյց տալ, ինչ որ իր արդիւնքը տուաւ: Այսօր այս կամ այն ձեւով (լէգէոնական, ոստիկան զինուոր, միլիս, կամաւոր, չէթէ, յարձակման ենթարկուած տեղերու մէջ կազմուած դիմադրող զինեալ խումբեր) 5–6000 զինեալ հայ կայ, որ կը մաքառին ըստ կարելւոյն:

Նիկոմիդիա (Կէյվէէն փախստական Հայրապետ Սագաեան) – 16 Ապրիլ

Զատկի Բ. օրը (12 Ապրիլ) կէս գիշերին 200 հեծեալ եւ զինեալ Միլլիճիներ Էշմէ կը մտնեն: Քիչ յետոյ 500 հետեւակ զինեալներ եկան, իրենց հետ ունենալով չորս մեթրայեօզ: Յետոյ այս ուժերը հեռացան Էշմէէն: Առտուան մօտ Օրթաքէօյի կողմերը լսելի եղաւ զէնքի ձայներ, որոնք երկար կը շարունակուէին: Միլլիճիները Օրթագիւղէն կը պահանջեն 500 հրացան փամփուշտներով, պոմպա եւ երկու մեթրայեօզ եւ 60 երիտասարդ: Գիւղացիք կը յայտնեն թէ չունին: Գայմագամ Համտի պէյ, որ հետերնին էր, մէկ ժամ միջոց տուաւ. «Եթէ չյանձնէք, գիւղը պիտի վառեմ» ըսելով: Մէկ ժամ յետոյ յարձակումը սկսաւ եւ շրջապատի գիւղերու թուրք խուժանն ալ միացաւ: Գշ. գիշեր Գուրտ-պէլէնի բարձունքէն կը տեսնուէր թէ Օրթագիւղ հրդեհի մէջ էր: Տասը ժամ յետոյ Քէլ Թէփէէն դարձեալ Օրթագիւղի մխալը կը տեսնուէր:

Ապրիլ 14ին անգլիացի ներկայացուցիչին եւ յոյն ներկայացուցիչին տեղեկացուցին եղելու-թիւնը:

Օրթագիւղ ունի 4500 բնակիչ, որուն 1/10րդը հազիւ կրնայ ազատած ըլլալ, զի Միլլիճիներէն զատ խուժանն ալ պաշարած էր: Օրթագիւղի բնակիչները բոլորն ալ յոյն են, միայն 6 ընտանիք հայ կար: Աքսորէն յետոյ մնացեալն Էշմէ եկած էր: Այդ 6 ընտանիքէն հինգն ալ Զատկի առիթով Էշմէ եկած էր եւ 1 հայ ընտանիք եւ 8 կտրի[ճ] կար հոն:

Միլլիճիներու պետերու ըսածին նայելով, շրջակայ հայ գիւղերուն բոլորն ալ վտանգի մէջ են:

Անմիջական օգնութիւն կը խնդրուի:

Մերսին (անհատական նամակէ մը) – 11 Ապրիլ

Անապահով վիճակը կը շարունակէ Կիլիկիոյ մէջ: Մէկ ժամ վերջը ի՞նչ ըլլալնիս չենք գիտեր: Չէթէները մինչեւ Ատանայի դուռը եկած են: Հաճըն պաշարուած է, Սիս նմանապէս: Բիւզանթի, Հալկըրը, Պէյէմէլէկ, նոյնիսկ Տօրագ կայարաններէն երբեք լուր չկայ: Հոդ տեղերը գտնուող բոլոր քրիստոնեաները փչացած ըլլալը հասկցուած [է]: Բիւզանթիի կողմերը գտնուող ֆրանսական զինուորները նաեւ պաշարուած են. կացութիւնը խիստ գէշ է: Եէնիճէի կայարանէն Տօրագ եւ Բիւզանթի երկաթուղին դադրած է: Ճամբան բոլորովին քանդուած է: Եէնիճէ[է]ն թերեւս մինչեւ 5–8 քիլոմէթր դէպի Բիւզանդի կառախումբ կրնայ երթալ:

Ժողովուրդէն մաս մը Կիպրոս կ'երթայ, վասնզի Ատանայի կացութիւնը խիստ վտանգաւոր է: Մարդ կը խելացնորի: Այս չէթէները զսպել շատ դիւրին է, սակայն գործադրող չկայ: Ատանայի մէջ խուճապ կայ: Ժողովուրդը երկիւղի մէջ է:

Սիսի օգնութեան Միսիս[ի] ճամբով գացող մի քանի հարիւր հայերը Թումլու Գալայի կողմերը (Միսիսէն 3 ժամ հեռու) թուրք չէթէներու յարձակման ենթարկուած են եւ 70 հոգի պաշարուած է իրենցմէ: Ատանա եւս քանի մը օրէն պիտի պաշարուի եւ ինքնապաշտպանութիւնը անզօր պիտի ըլլայ:

Միսիսէն Սիս գացող 180 հոգինոց խումբը Սիս չհասած ետ կանչուած է, պարէնը եւ ռազմա-մթերքը առնուած է: Ասոր վրայ կէսը ետ դարձած եւ միւս կէսը Թումլու Գալայի մէջ պաշարուած է

the five hundred Armenian volunteer soldiers and replaced them with French soldiers. A few days later, the three to four thousand soldiers left. Now the shops are closed again.

It has been reported at the last minute that the Mersin-Adana line has been cut off. There is no telegraph or railway. Gaziantep, too, is said to have shared the fate of Maraş.

Yenisölöz [Sölöz] (from the Neighborhood Council)—April 19

Prominent people from the Greek village of Pambucak Dervent in the district of İznik have written a letter to the Yenisölöz Armenian Neighborhood Council urging them to help in the face of impending danger because the people of İznik and Yenişehir have advised them to protect themselves well, for the Milli forces that plundered and pillaged Ortaköy of Geyve will attack their village within three or four days. The unfortunate villagers are terrified and are appealing for help everywhere. They sent messengers to İzmit and Gemlik. Yenisölöz also is close to a similar situation. We, too, are waiting for an attack by the Millis.

Tekirdağ (from the locum tenens)—April 19

On April 15, Governor Feruhan Bey arrived here. Even though Cafer Tayyar Bey had ordered his arrest, he was able to land, thanks to the precautionary measures taken by Greeks and Armenians, and he was able to go home without incident.

During the visit of the Greek metropolitan and the Armenian locum tenens, Feruhan Bey stated that he came not as a governor but an envoy. He came to relay the orders and instructions of the Ministry of War to Cafer Tayyar and to invite him to obey, and he is waiting for a response. However, on the same day, he escaped on a Greek steamer to İstanbul.

The Millis hold the power in their hand in Tekirdağ. There is almost no government. Cafer Tayyar commands, and his deputy, lieutenant commander of detachment Cemil Bey, manages the city, which is still peaceful, but its future remains very uncertain and dubious.

• Not a single Allied representative remained here.

Kilis (from the Armenian National Union)—April 4

Like everywhere else, the Turks of the city are perfectly armed, waiting for convenient opportunities to attack the Armenians. A boycott reigns; Armenians are constantly forced to pay double the price for everything. The Armenians of Kilis are generally carpenters, gardeners, and workers. They are in danger of dying of starvation without work. It is impossible to venture farther than half an hour from the city. It is impossible to pass through Turkish neighborhoods. The people are left in need of relief in this situation. So far, more than one thousand beneficiaries are being fed just to the extent of avoiding hunger. The French command is providing considerable assistance to those in need, but it is far from sufficient. The hungry are increasing in number daily. After the arrival of the French forces here, the political insecurity eased a bit comparatively, but the financial distress doubled as the Turkish people persist in their adversity due to a lack of immediate [restraining] action.

In the absence of the American Red Cross or similar aid organizations in Kilis, the people are forced to make a living from what they have. In the Armenian quarter, families flocked on top of each other because [Armenian] residents from neighborhoods next to Turkish neighborhoods deserted

առանց պաշարի եւ ռազմամթերքի:

Այնթապի մէջ պաշարումը 3000–4000 ֆրանսացի զինուորները գացած խզած են եւ հոն գտնուող 500 կամաւոր հայ զինուորները դուրս հանած են եւ անոնց տեղը ֆրանսական զինուոր ձգած են եւ մէկ քանի օր յետոյ մեկնած են 3000–4000 զինուորը: Հիմա խանութները փակ են դարձեալ:

Վերջին պահուն լուր առնուած է որ Մերսին-Ատանա գիծը խզուած է: Հեռագիր եւ երկաթուղի չկայ: Այնթապ եւս Մարաշի բաղդին վիճակակից եղած է կ'ըսուի:

Սէօյէօզ (Թաղական Խորհուրդէն) – 19 Ապրիլ

Նիկիոյ գաւառին Փամ[պ]ուճազ Տէրվէնթ անուն յոյն գիւղին երեւելիները նամակով մը կը դիմեն Սէօյէօզի հայոց թաղական խորհուրդին, որով կոչ կ'ընեն իրենց օգնելու գալիք վտանգին դէմ, որովհետեւ թէ՛ Նիկիոյ եւ թէ Եէնիշէհիրի բնիկներէն իրենց խորհուրդ տրուած է որ ինքզինքնին աղէկ պաշտպանեն, զի 3–4 օրէն Կէյվէ Միջագիւղը թալանի եւ աւարի տուող Միլլի ոյժը իրենց գիւղին վրայ պիտի քալէ: Խեղճ գիւղացին ահ ու սարսափի մատնուած է եւ ամէն կողմ օգնութեան կոչ կ'ընէ: Նիկոմիդիա եւ Կէմլէյիկ մասնաւոր մարդ ղրկած են: Այս վիճակին Սէօյէօզ եւս ենթարկուելու վիճակի մէջ է եւ մենք եւս կը սպասենք Միլլիներու կողմէ յարձակման մը:

Ռօտոսթօ (Առաջնորդական Տեղապահէն) – 19 Ապրիլ

15 Ապրիլին հոս հասաւ կառավարիչ Ֆէրուղան պէյ: Հակառակ անոր որ Ճաֆէր Թայեար պէյ անոր ձերբակալումը հրամայած էր, յունաց եւ հայոց ձեռք առած նախազգուշական միջոցներով կրցաւ ցամաք ելլել եւ կրցաւ իր տունը երթալ առանց միջադէպի:

Յունաց Մեթրապոլիտին եւ հայոց Առաջնորդական Տեղապահին այցելութեան միջոցին Ֆէրուղան պէյ կը յայտնէ թէ ոչ թէ իբր կառավարիչ այլ իբր բանագնաց եկած է. պատերազմական նախարարութեան հրամանները եւ հրահանգները Ճավէր Թայեարին հաղորդելու եւ ի կարգ հրաւիրելու պաշտօնով եկած է եւ պատասխան կը սպասէ: Սակայն նոյն օրը յունական շոգենաւով խոյս տուաւ Կ. Պոլիս:

Ռօտոսթոյի մէջ իշխանութիւնը առ այժմ Միլլիներու ձեռքն է. կառավարութիւն չկայ գրեթէ: Ճաֆէր Թայեար կը հրամայէ, իր փոխանորդը՝ Ֆըրգա զօմանտան վէքիլի Ճէմիլ պէյ սոսկալի Միլլիճի մը, կը կառավարէ քաղաքը, որ առ այժմ հանդարտ է, սակայն ապագան՝ շատ անստոյգ եւ կասկածելի:

- Համաձայնական ոեւէ ներկայացուցիչ չմնաց հոս:

Քիլիս (Հայ Ազգային Միութենէն) – 4 Ապրիլ

Քաղաքիս թուրքերը ինչպէս ամէն տեղ՝ նոյնպէս հոս կատարելապէս զինուած կը սպասեն յարմար առիթներու, որպէսզի յարձակին հայերուն վրայ: Պօյքօթը կը տիրապետէ, հայերը միշտ ստիպուած են ամէն ինչ կրկին արժէքով ծախու առնել: Քիլիսի հայերը առ հասարակ կառապաններ, այգեպաններ եւ բանուորներ են, եւ բոլորովին գործէ դադրած անօթի մեռնելու վտանգին տակ կը գտնուին: Քաղաքէն ½ ժամ հեռանալ անհնարին է, ինչպէս անկարելի է թուրք թաղերու մէջէն անցնիլ: Այս կացութեան մէջ նպաստի կարօտ մնացած է ժողովուրդը: Առ այժմ նպաստ ստացողներու թիւը 1000-ը կ'անցնի, որոնք միայն անօթի չմնալու չափ կը կերակրուին: Ֆրանսական հրամանատարութիւնը բաւական օժանդակութիւն կ'ընձեռնէ կարօտեալներուն, սակայն բաւականաչափ ըլլալէ շատ հեռու է: Անօթիներու թիւը օր ըստ օրէ կը ստուարանայ: Ֆրանսական ուժերու հոս ժամանումէն վերջ քաղաքական անապահովութիւնը բաղդատմամբ նախկինին քիչ մը թեթեւցաւ, սակայն նիւթական անձկութիւնը կրկնապատկուեցաւ, քանզի անմիջական գործունէութիւն չըլլալուն՝ թուրք ժողովուրդը կը յամառի իր հակառակութիւնը շարունակելու:

Քիլիսի մէջ Ամերիկեան Կարմիր Խաչի կամ նմանօրինակ օգնութեան կազմակերպութիւն

their homes and resettled in the Armenian-populated neighborhoods.

Murders and robberies are commonplace. If the situation remains uncurbed, catastrophe will be inevitable.

Gaziantep [Ayntab] (from catholicosal vicar Priest Nerses Tavoukjian and the National Union)—April 7

GAZIANTEP BIMONTHLY SITUATION: Gaziantep has been under siege by Turkish çetes for three months, and no Armenian can leave the city. If only the city had been besieged from the outside, it would have certainly been less intolerable. But, unfortunately, the Armenians in the city, some fifteen thousand people, are in a state of siege, huddled and piled on top of each other under very unfavorable circumstances. Only some men, more often women, go to the market to trade if the boycott allows. Now, the joblessness during these three months has subjected the people, who were barely sustaining themselves, anew to extreme misery. Today, six thousand of the fifteen thousand people are relief recipients. About two thousand people receive relief from the French. The American Near East Relief also provides for some of them. However, the need is so great that it is impossible to combat [the need]. There is much fear that those who survived the massacre will now succumb to hunger.

The political situation in Gaziantep is even more appalling. Dissatisfaction among the Turks began on the day they heard that the British were leaving and the French were replacing them. The British were still here when the Milli movement began, and weapons were distributed to the people. After the arrival of the French, despite their efforts to flatter the Turks, the Turks always showed them opposition and hatred. On his arrival, General Quérette announced to the people that these areas were under the control of victorious France. The wrath of the Turks grew over this, and violent acts broke out everywhere.

From that day on, it became impossible for Armenians to leave the city, and the boycott began to intensify, fueled with hatred.

The Turks expressed their dissatisfaction and anger against the French occupation of Gaziantep on the anniversary of the establishment of the Ottoman State (January 10).

On that day, the Turkish people organized a big demonstration and formed a huge procession. A large crowd of twenty thousand passed through all the neighborhoods of the city, waving Turkish flags before the eyes of the French authorities without any hindrance.

Shortly afterward, communication between Maraş and Gaziantep was cut off, and echoes of the Maraş incident reached Gaziantep.

The excited Turks tried to come up [with an excuse for] an incident in Gaziantep, too. And they found that excuse. On the evening of January 22, an Algerian soldier killed a young Turkish man near the municipality inn. The next day, the Turks closed all the shops. That demonstration greatly excited the Turkish mentality. From January 22 through 31, the Turks started to look at the Armenians with aversion and frighten the Armenians in the market. As a result, the Armenians also started not going to the market. They began to move their families to the upper neighborhoods and cluster there.

The Turkish government began searching the homes of Armenians under the pretext of looking for weapons and imprisoning Armenians based on accusations.

On January 31, in connection with a fight a French soldier of Tunisian origin had with a grocer, all the Turkish shopkeepers closed their shops, called the people to arms, and began to afflict the Armenians. The Armenians panicked. Many were beaten. Seven people were injured, and one person was killed that day. The next day, a policeman in the market wanted to take the Mauser gun from a

բնաւ գոյութիւն չունենալուն՝ ժողովուրդը ստիպուած է իր սեփական ունեցածովը իր ապրուստը ճարել: Հայոց թաղին մէջ ընտանիք ընտանիքի վրայ խռնուած է, վասնզի թուրք թաղերու դրացի բնակիչները իրենց տուները լքանելով հայաշատ թաղերը եկած են:

Սպանութիւններ եւ կողոպուտներ բնական դարձած են եւ եթէ դարման չտարուի այս վիճակին, աղէտը անխուսափելի պիտի ըլլայ:

Այնթապ (Կաթողիկոսական Փոխանորդ Ներսէս քահանայ Թավուզճեանէ եւ Ազգային Միութենէն) – 7 Ապրիլ

ԱՅՆԹԱՊԻ ԵՐԿԱՄՍԵԱՅ ԿԱՑՈՒԹԻՒՆԸ.- Այնթապ երեք ամիսէ ի վեր պաշարուած է թուրք չէթէներու կողմէ եւ ոչ մէկ հայ դուրս չի կրնար ելլել քաղաքէն: Եթէ միայն քաղաքը դուրսէն պաշարուած ըլլար՝ նուազ անտանելի պիտի ըլլար անշուշտ. բայց դժբաղդաբար քաղաքին մէջն ալ հայերը՝ իբր 15 հազար ժողովուրդ, քանի մը թաղերու մէջ շատ աննպաստ պարագաներու տակ խռնուած եւ իրարու վրայ դիզուած, պաշարուած վիճակ մ'ունին: Ստիպողական պէտքերու համար միայն ոմանք եւ շատ անգամ կիներ շուկայ կ'իջնեն եւ առեւտուր կ'ընեն, եթէ պօյքօթը թոյլատու ըլլայ: Արդ, այս երեք ամսուան անգործութիւնը հազիւ ինքզինքը ապրեցնող ժողովուրդը անգամ մը եւս մատնեց ծայր աստիճան թշուառութեան եւ այսօր 15 հազար ժողովրդեան 6 հազարը նպաստընկալ է արդէն: 2000ի մօտ մարդոց ֆրանսացիք նպաստ կու տան: Ամերիկեան Նպաստամատոյց մարմինն ալ անոնց մէկ մասը կը հոգայ: Սակայն պէտքը այնքան մեծ է որ կարելի չէ մաքառիլ, շատ կը վախցուի որ ջարդին դիմագրաւողները անօթութեան չկարենան տոկալ:

Այնթապի քաղաքական կացութիւնը աւելի եւս արհաւրալից է: Անգլիացիներուն երթալ[ը] եւ անոնց տեղը գաղղիացիներուն գալը լսուած օրէն սկսելով թուրքերուն մէջ դժգոհութիւնը սկսաւ: Դեռ անգլիացիները հոս էին երբ Միլլի շարժումը սկսաւ եւ ժողովուրդին զէնք բաժնուեցաւ: Գաղղիացիներուն հոս ժամանումէն ետքը հակառակ թուրքերը սիրաշահելու համար իրենց ըրած ջանքերուն, թուրքերը միշտ հակառակութիւն ու ատելութիւն ցոյց տուին: Ժեներալ Քէրէթ իր ժամանած ատեն յայտարարութեամբ մը ժողովուրդին հաղորդեց թէ Ֆրանսայի յաղթութեամբ պսակուած զէնքին ներքեւ [են] այս կողմերը: Ասոր վրայ թուրքերու ցասումը մեծ եղաւ եւ ամէն կողմ պոռթկալ սկսաւ:

Այն օրէն ի վեր հայոց համար անկարելի եղաւ քաղաքէն դուրս ելլել եւ պօյքօթը սկսաւ հետզհետէ սաստկանալ ատելութեան հետ:

Թուրքերը ֆրանսական գրաւման դէմ իրենց դժգոհութիւն եւ ցասումը արտայայտեցին Օսմանեան պետութեան հաստատման տարեդարձին (10 Յունուար) առթիւ Այնթապի մէջ:

Այդ օրը թուրք ժողովուրդը մեծ ցոյց մը ընելով 20000ի ահագին բազմութեամբ մը հսկայ թափօր մը կազմեց եւ թուրք դրօշներով քաղաքիս բոլոր թաղերէն անցան ֆրանսական իշխանութեանց աչքին առջեւ, առանց ոեւէ արգելքի:

Քիչ յետոյ խզուեցաւ Մարաշի եւ Այնթապի հաղորդակցութիւնը եւ Մարաշի դէպքին արձագանգները հասան Այնթապ:

Թուրքերը գրգռուած աշխատեցան Այնթապի մէջ ալ դէպք մը հանել: Եւ այդ պատրուակը գտան: Յունուար 22ին իրիկուան մօտ Պէյլէտիէ Խանի մօտը ալճերիացի զինուոր մը թուրք երիտասարդ մը սպաննեց: Հետեւեալ օրը թուրքերը բոլոր խանութները գոցեցին: Այն ցոյցը թուրք մտայնութիւնը գրգռեց մեծ չափով: Յունուար 22–31 թուրքերը գրգռուած սկսան հայերուն խեթիւ նայիլ եւ շուկայի մէջ հայերը խրտչեցնել, հետեւաբար հայերն ալ սկսան շուկայ չիջնել եւ տուները վերի թաղերը փոխադրել եւ ամփոփուիլ:

Թուրք կառավարութիւնն ալ սկսաւ հայերուն տուները խուզարկել, զէնք փնտռելու պատրուակին տակ, եւ հայերը զրպարտութեամբ բանտարկել:

Յունուար 31ին Թունուզ[ց]ի գաղղիական զինուորի մը պազզալի մը հետ ունեցած կռիւին առթիւ բոլոր թուրք խանութպանները խանութները կը գոցեն, ի զէն կը հրաւիրեն ժողովուրդը եւ

Turkish villager, but the Turk resisted. A general panic ensued, and two Armenians were injured. While these events were taking place, the French government and the local [Armenian] National Union, anticipating the forthcoming danger, wanted to prevent it, so they appealed to the Turkish government and the Muslim Union to avoid more catastrophic consequences.

Consequently, the Turkish government responded in writing and posted the response on the walls. The statement read: "We mourned the murder [of the Turkish victim killed by the Algerian] and closed our shops." The Turkish officials began to try to deceive the Armenians using various means. However, the Armenians were not fooled and did not open their shops because news of new murders was arriving from the surrounding areas every day.

The appeal of the Armenians to the Turkish government in this regard was futile. When the Armenians turned to the French, they replied: "We cannot act according to your wishes. We cannot interfere in the affairs between you and the Turks. Live well with the Turks." The French colonel even rebuked the Armenians, saying they generalize casual incidents and disturb the city.

He advised the Armenians to go to the market and do their business without attaching importance to such casual incidents.

The Armenians were keen on making peace with the Turks, but the latter were committing increasingly furious killings. Consequently, contrary to the colonel's order, the Armenians left the markets altogether. Those [Armenians living] in the lower neighborhoods retreated to the Armenian neighborhoods, just as the Turks living in Armenian neighborhoods left the Armenian neighborhoods, placing Turkish çetes in their homes.

The Turkish government is providing weapons to ordinary people pretending they are policemen while also setting up new military guardhouses around the Armenian neighborhood by selecting points that actually mean the siege of Armenian neighborhoods. With this arrangement, in case of any potential massacre, they aimed to thwart any self-defense measures the Armenians would resort to. Because of the closure of the shops, prices have increased daily, and life has become more hardened. Besides, the cold has inflicted terrible harm, causing diseases.

The Turks are waging a fierce boycott against the Armenians and making their situation completely intolerable. Nevertheless, the Armenians agreed to try to show solidarity with the Turks on the colonel's instruction. To this end, several Armenians, Turks, and members of the Muslim Union were selected as members of an "Accord Committee," aiming at establishing solidarity between Armenians and Muslims. This initiative was useless, and the killings continued periodically.

By becoming increasingly aware of the events in Maraş, the Turks became more agitated and more inclined to try such an event in Gaziantep. In the face of this threatening situation, the colonel continues to oblige the Armenians to approach the Turks and live in solidarity. He even threatens to turn his back on the Armenians altogether. The Turkish fury collapsed for an instant when news of the bombing of Maraş was heard. The Turks are trying to live in peace. They are even talking about and convening meetings to raise money for Maraş, but they are failing to attain positive results. Meanwhile, these crimes and isolated killings continue.

Thus, those killed during the two-month siege of Gaziantep were:

Eight to eleven millers native of Sason in village mills;

Four people native of Sekili [Orul], somewhere an hour and a half away from the city;

Three people in the city (one on the day of the January 31 incident; the other two were killed in Turkish neighborhoods a few weeks later);

Two artisans going to work in the villages of Maraş toward İslahiye;

Two people were killed while coming from Aleppo or Adana on the road to Kilis;

Nine people were injured in connection with the January 31 incident and the next day.

կը սկսին հայերը խոշտանգել: Հայերը խուճապի կը մատնուին, շատեր կը ծեծուին, եօթը հոգի կը վիրաւորուին եւ մէկ հոգի կը սպաննուի այդ օրը. հետեւեալ օրը շուկայի մէջ ոստիկան մը թուրք գիւղացիի մը ձեռքէն Մավզէրը առնել կ'ուզէ եւ թուրքը կ'ընդդիմանայ: Ասկէ առաջ կու գայ ընդհանուր խուճապ եւ երկու հայ կը վիրաւորուի: Մինչ այս դէպքերը կը կատարուէին, ֆրանսական կառավարութիւնը եւ տեղւոյն Ազգային Միութիւնը, նախատեսելով ապագայ վտանգը, առաջքը առնել ուզեցին եւ դիմեցին թուրք կառավարութեան եւ «Ճէմիէթի Իսլամիէ»ին որպէսզի աւելի աղիտալի հետեւանքներու տեղի չտրուի:

Ասոր վրայ թուրք կառավարութիւնը հետեւեալ իմաստով պատասխանեց գրաւորապէս, նոյնպէս յայտարարութեան ձեւով պատերը փակցուց. «Մենք կատարուած սպանութեան վրայ սուգ բռնելով մեր խանութները գոցեցինք» եւ պէս պէս միջոցներով սկսան հայերը խաբելու աշխատիլ. սակայն հայերը չխաբուեցան եւ իրենց խանութները չբացին, վասնզի ամէն օր նոր սպանութեանց լուրեր կը հասնէին շրջականերէն:

Այս առթիւ հայերուն թուրք կառավարութեան մօտ ըրած դիմումը ապարդիւն մնաց: Հայերը երբ ճարահատ ֆրանսացիներուն դիմեցին, անոնք պատասխանեցին թէ «մենք ձեր փափաքին համեմատ չենք կրնար գործել. ձեր եւ թուրքերուն միջեւ եղած գործերուն չենք կրնար միջամտել. թուրքերուն հետ լաւ ապրեցէք»: Նոյնիսկ ֆրանսացի զօրօնէլը կը յանդիմանէ հայերը ըսելով թէ հասարակ դէպքերուն ընդհանուր երեւոյթ կու տան եւ քաղաքը կը վրդովեն:

Անիկա խորհուրդ կու տայ որ հայերը շուկայ երթան եւ իրենց գործերով զբաղին, եւ ասանկ հասարակ դէպքերու կարեւորութիւն չտան:

Հայերը կ'ուզէին հաշտ ապրիլ թուրքերուն հետ, սակայն այս վերջինները հետզհետէ աւելի կատղած սպանութիւններ կը կատարէին: Հետեւաբար հայերը հակառակ զօրօնէլին հրահանգին, շուկաներէն բոլորովին կը հեռանան եւ վարի թաղերը գտնուողները կը քաշուին հայ թաղերու մէջ կը հաւաքուին, ինչպէս հայ թաղեր բնակող թուրքերն ալ հայոց թաղերէն կը մեկնին եւ իրենց տուներուն մէջ թուրք չէթէներ կը բնակեցնեն:

Թուրք կառավարութիւնը ոստիկանի անունի տակ հասարակ մարդոց զէնք կու տայ եւ հայ թաղին շուրջը զինուորական նոր պահականոցներ կը հաստատէ, ընտրելով այնպիսի կէտեր, որ իրականին մէջ հայկական թաղերու պաշարումը կը նշանակէ: Այս կարգադրութեամբ ռեւէ պատահական ջարդի պարագային նպատակ ունէին ջլատել հայերու կողմէ կատարուելիք ինքնապաշտպանութեան ռեւէ ձեռնարկ: Խանութներուն գոց մնալուն պատճառով սղութիւնը օրըստօրէ մեծ համեմատութիւն առաւ եւ կեանքը դժուարացաւ. ցուրտը միւս կողմէն ահաւոր վնասներ հասցուց տեղի տալով հիւանդութիւններու:

Թուրքերը հայոց դէմ կատաղի պօյքօթ մը կ'ընեն եւ բոլորովին անհանդուրժելի կը դարձնեն իրենց վիճակը: Ասով հանդերձ հայերը կը համաձայնին զօրօնէլի հրահանգին վրայ համերաշխութեան փորձ մը ընել թուրքերու մօտ: Այս նպատակով հայերէ, թուրքերէ եւ Ճէմիէթի Իսլամիէէն քանի մը անձեր կ'ընտրուին իբր «իմթիզաճ գօմիսիօն»ի անդամ, որուն նպատակն պիտի ըլլար հայոց եւ իսլամաց միջեւ համերաշխութեան կապեր հաստատել: Այս ձեռնարկն օգուտ մը չունեցաւ եւ առանց արգելքի սպանութիւնները պարբերաբար շարունակուեցան:

Թուրքերը հետզհետէ աւելի իրազեկ դառնալով Մարաշի դէպքերուն, աւելի կը գրգռուին եւ աւելի տրամադիր կը դառնան նման դէպք մըն ալ Այնթապի մէջ փորձել: Այս սպառնալից կացութեան առջեւ զօրօնէլը միշտ կը ստիպէ հայերուն որ թուրքերուն մօտ երթան եւ համերաշխաբար ապրին, նոյնիսկ կը սպառնայ հայոցմէ բոլորովին երես դարձնել: Թրքական կատաղութիւնը պահ մը տեղի կու տայ երբ Մարաշու ռմբակոծումը կը լսուի: Թուրքերը անդորրութեամբ ապրելու ջանքեր կ'ընեն: Նոյնիսկ Մարաշի համար հանգանակութիւն ընելու խօսքեր եւ ժողովներ կ'ընեն, բայց չեն յաջողիր արդիւնքի մը հասնիլ: Մինչ այս ոճիրները եւ մասնակի սպանութիւնները կը շարունակուին:

Այսպէս Այնթապի երկամսեայ պաշարման միջոցին սպաննուեցան՝

[Armenians] are instructed to consider all these ordinary incidents and to be patient, bearing in mind the danger of a massacre. The çetes spared not even foreigners.

Two Americans and two drivers were killed on the road to Kilis on February 2. The çetes became so audacious that they looted the relief funds exceeding two thousand liras sent for Maraş by American charitable institutions . . .

8–11 հոգի սասունցի ջաղացպաններ գիւղերու ջաղացքներու մէջ:

4 հոգի օրուլցիներ քաղաքէն 1½ ժամ հեռու տեղ մը:

3 հոգի քաղաքին մէջ (մէկը Յունուար 31ի դէպքին օրը, միւս երկուքը քանի մը շաբաթ յետոյ թուրք թաղերու մէջ կը սպաննուին):

2 հոգի Իսլահիէի կողմը Մարաշու գիւղերը գործելու գացող արհեստաւորներ:

2 հոգի Հալէպէն կամ Ատանայէն գալու պահուն Քիլիսի ճամբուն վրայ սպաննուածներ:

9 հոգի Յունուար 31ի դէպքին առթիւ եւ միւս օրը վիրաւորեալներ:

Ասոնք ամէնը կը յանձնարարուի հասարակ դէպքեր նկատել եւ ընդհանուր ջարդի վտանգը ի նկատ ունենալով համբերել: Չէթէները չէին խնայեր նոյնիսկ օտարներուն:

Քիլիսի ճամբուն վրայ երկու ամերիկացիներ եւ երկու *շոֆէօր*ներ կը սպաննեն Փետրուար 2ին: Չէթէները յանդգնութիւնը այնքան առաջ կը տանին որ ամերիկեան ...

[Insecurity Notebook] Number 10
April–May 1920

. . . , and they dared to block the road to Kilis altogether and even prevent the delivery of supplies and ammunition to the French troops. Consequently, the Turks of the city became absolutely haughty and dared the colonel to leave Gaziantep. Learning this news, the Armenians' fear increased. Night and day, they are vexed by the horror of massacre and plunder. Finally, after a long wait, on March 27, some twenty-five hundred French soldiers brought victuals for the French troops from Qatma to Gaziantep.

General de Lamothe made the following statement (posted on the walls) during this period: "We did not come to capture the Turkish government. It will maintain its former composition. We only came to punish the çetes and those who support the çete movement." This statement, however, had no effect.

Instead of sobering, the Turks grew even more enraged; they quit their occupations, formed gangs, and engaged in preparations to attack the French troops.

The French always encouraged the Armenians and urged them not to be afraid. They assured their strength was enough to restrain the Turks. But the Armenians feared they would already suffer and be massacred before the French could restrain them. Unfortunately, the French did not keep their even insufficient force there. On March 31, the force that had arrived from Qatma, and some of the French forces that had already been there [in Gaziantep], withdrew to Qatma (including the Armenian Legion's soldiers and seventy-five-millimeter cannons), which had been similarly brought [to Gaziantep] with the convoy.

With Colonel Flye-Sainte-Marie's permission, about sixty-five Armenians set out with the military convoy, and some crossed into Aleppo.

The convoy was attacked by çetes at a distance of forty-five minutes outside the city near Karataş but escaped under cover of seventy-five-millimeter cannon shells. Up to that point, the French forces had suffered six wounded people and six dead horses. After walking for two more hours, they approached Zeytinli [Ulumasere], where the çetes started firing again. There, too, the cannons forced the çetes to retreat, striking them with deafening blows.

After another two hours of walking, they reached Beşgöz, where they spent the night. The çetes suddenly opened fire at night, but the cannon dispersed them again.

The following morning, April 1, the convoy set out and reached Kazıklı after light skirmishes on the road [between the çetes] and the vanguards.

They arrived in Kilis on April 2 without incident. On the morning of April 2, a plane departed for Gaziantep on the orders of General de Lamothe. There was no information about it for two days. Upon the plane's return, we learned that fighting was going on in Gaziantep.

The çetes had even hit the plane with a few bullets, but the areas hit posed no danger.

Therefore, it can be concluded that, most likely, the Turks attacked the Armenians, encouraged by the withdrawal of the French soldiers. It is not known what position the French took in the fighting. The military force in Gaziantep consisted of nine hundred men, mostly natives of Senegal and Algeria, along with a small group of French. Most of the Armenians in Gaziantep were returnees from the deportation and lacked weapons and other means of self-defense.

The French troops are not in the city; instead, they are on the west side, stationed in the American college built fifteen minutes away. There is no guardhouse or garrison in the city. The convoy left Kilis on April 5 after leaving part of the French troops there. That same day they reached Qatma, where the soldiers remain under the command of Colonel Normand.

[Անապահովութեան Տետր] Թիւ 10
1920 Ապրիլ – Մայիս

... բարեգործական հաստատութիւններուն կողմէ Մարաշի համար ղրկուած նպաստը, որ 2000 լիրայէն աւելի էր, կը կողոպտեն, եւ կը յանդգնին Քիլիսի ճամբան բոլորովին գոցել եւ նոյնիսկ ֆրանսական զինուորներուն պիտոյք եւ ռազմամթերք բերուելուն արգելք ըլլալ: Ասոր վրայ քաղաքին թուրքերը բոլորովին ամբարտաւան դարձան եւ համարձակեցան զօրօնէլին առաջարկել որ Այնթապէն հեռանայ: Այս լուրը իմանալով հայերու վախի երկիւղը կ'աւելնայ եւ գիշեր ցերեկ ջարդի եւ թալանի ու սարսափի ներքեւ կը տուայտին: Վերջապէս երկար սպասումէ ետքը Մարտ 27ին իբր 2500 ֆրանսական զինուոր Գաթմայէն Այնթապ կը բերեն ֆրանսական զօրաց համար ուտեստեղէն:

Ժեներալ տը լա Մոթ հետեւեալ յայտարարութիւնը ըրաւ (պատերուն փակցնելով) այս միջոցին: «Մենք թուրք կառավարութիւնը գրաւելու նպատակաւ չենք եկած. անիկա իր նախկին կազմը պիտի պահպանէ. մենք միայն չէթէները եւ չէթէճիութեան ուժ տուողները պատժելու եկանք»: Այս յայտարարութիւնը սակայն ռեւէ ազդեցութիւն չունեցաւ:

Թուրքերը փոխանակ զգաստանալու, առաւել եւս կը կատղին, բանը գործը կը թողուն եւ հրոսախումբեր կը կազմեն, ֆրանսական զօրաց վրայ յարձակելու պատրաստութիւններ կ'ընեն:

Ֆրանսացիք միշտ կը քաջալերէին հայերը եւ կը յորդորէին որ չվախնան. կը հաւաստէին թէ իրենց ուժը բաւական է թուրքը զսպելու. սակայն հայերը կը վախնային որ մինչեւ ասոնց զսպելը իրենք արդէն կրնան կոտորուիլ եւ վնասուիլ: Ֆրանսացիք դժբաղդաբար նոյնիսկ իրենց այս անբաւական ոյժը հոն չպահեցին: Մարտ 31ին Գաթմայէն հասած ուժը եւ հոն նախապէս գտնուող ֆրանսական ուժերէն մաս մը քաշեցին Գաթմա (մէջը հաշուելով Հայկական Լեգէոնի զինուորները եւ 75նոց թնդանօթները), որոնք նմանապէս convoi-ին հետ բերուած էին:

Col. Fly Ste. Marie-ի թոյլտուութեամբ 65ի մօտ հայեր ճամբայ ելան զինուորական convoi-ին հետ, որոնց մէկ մասը Հալէպ անցաւ:

Convoi-ն քաղաքէն ¾ ժամ դուրս Քարաթաշի մօտերը չէթէներէն յարձակում կրեց, սակայն 75նոց թնդանօթի հարուածներուն տակ փախուստ տուին: Մինչ այդ ֆրանսական ուժերը 6 մարդ վիրաւոր եւ 6 ձի սպաննուած կորուստ ունէին: Երկու ժամ եւս քալելով կը հասնին Ուլու-Մահսերէի մօտերը, ուր չէթէները կրկին հրացանաձգութեան կը սկսին եւ հոն ալ թնդանօթները խլացուցիչ հարուածներով զանոնք ստիպեցին նահանջ տալ:

Երկու ժամ եւս քալելէ յետոյ կը հասնին Պէշ-Կէօզ, ուր կը գիշերեն: Գիշերը յանկարծ չէթէները կրակ կը բանան, սակայն նորէն թնդանօթը զիրենք կը ցրուէ:

Հետեւեալ առաւօտ, Ապրիլ 1ին, convoi-ն ճամբայ կ'ելլէ եւ կը հասնի Գազըգլը, ճամբան թեթեւ ընդհարումներ տեղի կ'ունենան առաջապահներու հետ:

Ապրիլ 2-ին կը հասնին Քիլիս առանց միջադէպի: Ապրիլ 2ին առտուն օդանաւ մը ճամբայ կ'ելլէ Ժեներալ տը լա Մոթի հրամանաւ երթալու Այնթապ, որու մասին տեղեկութիւն չկայ երկու օրէ ի վեր: Օդանաւը վերադարձին կ'իմացնէ թէ Այնթապի մէջ կռիւ կայ:

Չէթէներ նոյնիսկ օդանաւին հանդիպցուցած էին մի քանի փամփուշտ, որոնք անվնաս տեղերու հանդիպած էին:

Ասկէ կարելի է հետեւցնել թէ թուրքերը ֆրանսական զինուորին քաշուելէն քաջալերուած հաւանական է յարձակած են հայոց վրայ: Չի գիտցուիր թէ ֆրանսացիք ինչ դիրք բռնած են: Այնթապի մէջ մնացող զինուորական ոյժը կը բաղկանար 900 հոգիէ, մեծ մասամբ սենեկալցի եւ ալճերիացի եւ փոքր մաս մը ֆրանսացի: Այնթապի հայոց մեծամասնութիւնը տարագրութենէ դարձած ըլլալով զէնքէ եւ ուրիշ ինքնապաշտպանութեան միջոցներէ զուրկ կը գտնուէր:

Ֆրանսական զօրքն ալ քաղաքին մէջ չէ, այլ՝ արեւմտեան կողմը ¼ ժամ հեռու կառուցուած Ամերիկեան Գոլէճին մէջ զետեղուած են եւ քաղաքին մէջ ռեւէ պահականոց եւ կայան չկայ: Convoi-ն Քիլիսէն մեկնած է Ապրիլ 5ին հոն ձգելէ յետոյ մաս մը ֆրանսական զօրք եւ նոյն օրը հասած է

Aleppo (from the Armenian National Union)—March 25

According to information received from Maraş, the number of survivors in Maraş is ten thousand, of whom there are almost no men. It has been heard that only thirty [Armenian] men live there and that they are confined by the new district governor, Irfan Bey, to protect them against falling into the hands of the çetes. During the incident, the sixty-seven girls in the shelter who had been recovered from the Islamic harems were abducted by çetes. They were returned after they served the men's animal passions for some time. Now they are with the Americans. The ten thousand survivors are in a very precarious situation; there is no housing because all the houses of the Armenians have been burned down, and they are crammed in several churches. Also, there is a lack of means to supply them with provisions since money cannot be sent due to the insecurity of the roads. The means of the Americans in Maraş are also minimal. They, too, cannot transfer money. And thus, those who survived are now doomed to die of starvation and disease. Communicable diseases have already begun to wreak havoc.

• Gaziantep [Ayntab] is also in a terrible situation. Ali Kılıç entered the city with fifteen hundred çetes while the French are still present. Armenians have closed their stores and have been living in terror for forty days. What is most horrifying is that Ali Kılıç has suggested that the considerable number of Armenians who are not natives of Gaziantep (migrants) should leave the city and that the local Armenians should hand over their weapons to the Turkish government. Ali Kılıç, the perpetrator of the massacres of Maraş, is the leader of the çetes.

In this terrible situation, Armenians and all Christians, in general, are subjected to a boycott. The Turks do not want to sell anything to the Armenians and demand a very high price when they do sell something. A liter (two and a half okkas) of flour is sold to the Turks for twelve and a half kuruş and to Christians for sixty kuruş.

In Gaziantep, the Armenians have retired to the churches, and the French forces are on a hill outside the city. The followers of Ali Kılıç are armed and have machine guns. They are becoming increasingly threatening. The Turkish leaders support them in every way possible. They raise money, consider the rapid arming of the people as a duty dictated by the government, and receive weapons and ammunition from everywhere.

• The Armenians of Birecik have now been delivered after going through hard times. Four or five days ago, they began to open their stores. The French dominate the city. The Armenians suffered no losses there because they supported the Turkish government. Although the surrounding areas are insecure, Basravi Bey has an agreement with the French.

• There is no news about Urfa. There are ten thousand Armenians out there; nobody knows what they are doing.

İzmit (from the vicar general)—April 15

Refugee Armenian coachmen report that Adapazarı has barely rested for a day or two thanks to a group of Circassian and Abaza anti-Millis who came to the rescue. But eventually, they gave in to the Millis, who surpass them in numbers and strength, and took refuge in the mountains, again exposing the local Christians to terror.

• Two Armenians and one young Greek man escaping the fire arrived in İzmit on April 14 and reported that on April 12, the Millis besieged the Ortaköy village of Geyve. They demanded weapons and youngsters and shelled the entire village, where more than seven hundred Catholic Armenian and four or five [Apostolic] Armenian households lived.

Գաթմա, ուր զինուորները կը մնան Col. Normand-ի հրամանին տակ:

Հալէպ (Հայ Ազգային Միութենէն) – 25 Մարտ

Մարաշէն առնուած տեղեկութեանց համաձայն, Մարաշի մէջ վերապրողներուն թիւը 10000 է, որոնց մէջ այրեր գրեթէ չկան: Լսուած է թէ միայն 30 հոգի կ'ապրին, որոնք բանտարկուած են նոր միւթէսարրֆ Ըրֆան պէյի կողմէ, չէթէներուն ձեռքը չիյնալու համար: Դէպքի միջոցին պատսպարանի մէջ գտնուող իսլամ հարեմներէ առնուած 67 աղջիկները չէթէներու կողմէ կ'առեւանգուին եւ բաւական ժամանակ անոնց անասնական կիրքերուն ծառայելէ յետոյ կը վերադարձուին: Հիմա կը գտնուին ամերիկացիներուն քով: Վերապրող 10000 հոգին շատ արգահատելի վիճակի մէջ կը գտնուին, բնակարան չկայ, որովհետեւ այրուած են հայերու բոլոր տուները, եւ այս խառնամբոխ բազմութիւնը կուտակուած է մէկ քանի եկեղեցիներու մէջ: Միջոցներն ալ կը պակսին զանոնք պարենաւորելու, որովհետեւ դրամ չէ կարելի ղրկել ճամբաներու անապահովութեան պատճառով: Մարաշ գտնուող ամերիկացիներու միջոցներն ալ շատ սուղ են, անոնք ալ չեն կրնար դրամ փոխադրել: Եւ այսպէս վերապրողները սովէ եւ հիւանդութենէ մեռնելու դատապարտուած են: Տարափոխիկ հիւանդութիւնները արդէն աւեր գործել սկսած են:

- Այնթապ եւս ահաւոր կացութեան մէջ է: Ալի Գըլըճ 1500 չէթէներով քաղաք մտած է ֆրանսացիներու ներկայութեան: Հայերը խանութնին փակած 40 օրէ ի վեր սարսափի տակ կը մնան եւ ինչ որ սարսափելի է, Ալի Գըլըճ առաջարկած է որ այնթապցի չեղոք հայերը (գաղթականներ), որոնք պատկառելի թիւ կը կազմեն, հեռանան քաղաքէն եւ տեղացի հայերն ալ իրենց զէնքերը յանձնեն թուրք կառավարութեան: Ալի Գըլըճ Մարաշի նախճիրները գործող չէթէյապետն է:

Այս ահաւոր կացութեան մէջ հայերը եւ ընդհանրապէս բոլոր քրիստոնեաները պօյքօթի ենթարկուած են. թուրքերը ո՛չ մէկ բան կ'ուզեն ծախել հայերուն եւ ծախելու ատեն ալ շատ բարձր գին կը պահանջեն: Ալիւրին լիտրը (2½ օխա) թուրքերուն կը տրուի 12½ դրուշի, իսկ քրիստոնեաներուն՝ 60 դրուշի:

Այնթապի մէջ հայերը առանձնացած են եկեղեցիներու մէջ, իսկ ֆրանսական ոյժերը քաղաքէն դուրս բլուրի մը վրայ են: Ալի Գըլըճի մարդիկը զինուած են եւ ունին զնդացիրներ. ասոնք հետզհետէ սպառնալից կը դառնան: Թուրք շէֆերը ամէն կերպով կ'աջակցին ասոնց, դրամ կը հանգանակեն, արագ զինուիլը պարտականութիւն կը նկատեն թելադրուած կառավարութենէն եւ զէնք ու ռազմամթերք ամէն կողմէ կը հասնի իրենց:

- Պիրէճիկի հայերը նեղ օրեր անցնելէ յետոյ այժմ ազատած են. 4–5 օրէ ի վեր խանութնին բանալ սկսած են: Ֆրանսացիք տէր են քաղաքին: Հոն հայերը կորուստ չեն ունեցած, վասնզի թրքական կառավարութեան աջակցութիւն ցոյց տուած են: Շրջակաները անապահով են թէեւ, սակայն Պասրավի պէյը ֆրանսացիներուն հետ համաձայնած է:

- Ուրֆայի մասին ոեւէ լուր չկայ: 10000 հայ կան հոն որ չի գիտցուիր թէ ի՞նչ կ'ընեն:

Նիկոմիդիա (Առաջնորդական Փոխանորդէն) – 15 Ապրիլ

Փախստական հայ կառապաններ լուր կը բերեն թէ Ատաբազար հազիւ մէկ երկու օր հանգիստ ունեցած է շնորհիւ օգնութեան հասնող կարգ մը Չէրքէզ ու Ապազայ հականիլլիճիներու, որոնք սակայն ի վերջոյ տեղի տուած են թուով եւ ուժով գերազանց Միլլիճիներու ու լեռը ապաստանած են, կրկին սարսափի մատնելով տեղւոյն քրիստոնեաները:

- Կրակէն ազատուած երկու հայ եւ մէկ յոյն երիտասարդ 14 Ապրիլին Նիկոմիդիա գալով պատմեցին թէ Ապրիլ 12ին Միլլիճիները պաշարելով Կէյվէ-Օրթագիւղը, զէնքերը եւ երիտասարդները ուզած են եւ թնդանօթի բռնած են ամբողջ գիւղը, ուր կը բնակին 700է աւելի հայ-հոռոմ եւ 4–5 տուն հայ:

• The entire gendarmerie, after exiting the fence upon an arrangement by the British authorities of İzmit, set up a tent camp in a field ten minutes away from Arslanbey. With their weapons and machine guns, they are terrorizing the unfortunate villagers whose women and children, all of them, following the suit of [the women and children of] Ovacık and Bahçecik, are arriving in İzmit in carriages, on horses, and foot, group after group, in an extremely pitiful state, reminiscent of the cruel and horrible days of exile.

The wretched have delivered their entire provisions gathered for the forthcoming winter and their wealth to the earth, remaining now entirely destitute and in want. The city is congested. There is no housing. From Bahçecik, Miss Newnham came to İzmit with her orphans. The national school has been placed at their disposal, and the male and female students, augmented with the children of villagers, have been transferred to the church. Miss Newnham provides valuable services to migrant women, especially lactating and pregnant women, by offering them condensed milk, cocoa, and legumes. There is no communication beyond İzmit.

Bursa (from the locum tenens)—April 18
The migration to İstanbul continues. Ali Fuat Pasha, the deputy commander of the National Forces, who is barely thirty to thirty-five years old, came to Bursa yesterday. He met with the Armenian primate and made reassuring promises.

İstanbul (from five female delegates from Adapazarı)—April 26
Besieged and captured by the Millis, Adapazarı is engulfed in fear. The terrified people are considering leaving the city, but very few have managed to reach İzmit with only impossible difficulties. The delegation has requested that a safe means of transportation to İzmit be found with the aid of the Allied authorities. There is misery because they have abandoned all efforts to work and occupation. They are preoccupied only with saving their lives.

Bandırma—April 26
On April 19, at six o'clock, Milli forces reached the city and captured Bandırma and its environs. Lieutenant Governor Şevki Bey, originally from Amasya, is disposed very well toward Armenians and endeavors to inspire security. İsmail Hakkı Bey, the local Discipline and Education commander of the Milli forces, visited the prelacy and assured that the Armenians would not be harmed. The English representative Mr. Koki departed Bandırma. According to an order issued by Mustafa Kemal Pasha, all correspondence will be conducted in Turkish locally and in the region. Censorship has been reestablished, and since relations with İstanbul have been severed, a motorboat that arrived yesterday morning was sent back with its passengers. Mail is not allowed in or out.

Adana (from Garabed Nalbandian)—April 17
Everyone is ready to leave. It is still impossible to get out of the city. There has been no information received from Kozan [Sis] for twenty days. According to reports, the çetes have occupied the Kozan bridge and deprived the people of water. The çetes have turned the settlements of the nearby Turkish muhacirs from Kırıt near the bridge into a bulwark. There has been no exact information from Saimbeyli [Hacın] as there is no traffic. According to a rumor, the çetes are far from Saimbeyli. It has been heard that the war continues along with the siege. According to the information received by plane seven or eight days ago, there is calm in Saimbeyli. The number of çetes gathered around Kozan is estimated at seven thousand, but we do not know how accurate that is. The day before, three thousand

- Նիկոմիդիայէն անգլիական իշխանութեան կարգադրութեամբ իրենց զէնքերովը ցանկապատէն դուրս հանուած ամբողջ ոստիկան զօրաց կազմը, Արսլանպէկի տասն վայրկեան մնացած դաշտավայրի մը մէջ վրան դրած է եւ իրենց զէնքերովը եւ միթրալիօզներովը ահ ու սարսափ կ'ազդեն խեղճ գիւղացիներուն, որոնց բոլոր կիները ու զաւակները Օվաճըգի եւ Պարտիզակի օրինակին հետեւելով գունդագունդ Նիկոմիդիա կուգան կառքերով, ձիերով եւ հետիոտն, աքսորի չարաշուք ու զարհուրելի օրերը յիշեցնող վերջին ծայր արգահատելի վիճակով:

Խեղճերն յառաջիկայ ձմրան իրենց բովանդակ պաշարն ու հարստութիւնը յանձնած են հողին, մնալով այժմ բոլորովին ձեռնունայն ու կարօտ: Քաղաքն ալ խճողուած է. բնակարան չկայ: Պարտիզակէն Միս Նիւնիըմ Նիկոմիդիա եկած է իր որբերով, որոնց տրամադրուած է ազգային վարժարանը, իսկ երկսեռ ուսանողութիւնը՝ աճած գիւղացւոց զաւակներով, եկեղեցի փոխադրուած են: Միս Նիւնիըմ եկող գաղթական կիներու, մանաւանդ ծծմայր ու յղի կանանց, գնահատելի ծառայութիւն կը մատուցանէ՝ տալով խտացած կաթ, քաքաօ, ընդեղէններ: Նիկոմիդիայէն անդին հաղորդակցութիւն չկայ:

Պրուսա (Առաջնորդական Տեղապահէն) – 18 Ապրիլ

Դէպի Պոլիս գաղթը կը շարունակէ: Երէկ Պրուսա եկաւ Ալի Ֆուատ փաշա, Ազգային Ույժերու պետին փոխանորդը, հազիւ 30–35 տարու: Հայոց Առաջնորդին հետ տեսնուած է եւ վստահեցուցիչ խոստումներ ըրած է:

Կ. Պոլիս (ատաբազարցի 5 կին պատուիրակներէ) – 26 Ապրիլ

Ատաբազար մեծ երկիւղի մէջ է, Միլլիճիներէն պաշարուած եւ գրաւուած ըլլալով: Ժողովուրդը ահաբեկած կը խորհի հեռանալ քաղաքէն եւ շատ քիչեր միայն անհնարին դժուարութիւններով ինքզինքնին կը նետեն Նիկոմիդիա: Պատուիրակութիւնը կը խնդրէ որ Նիկոմիդիա փոխադրուելու ապահով միջոց մը գտնուի, Համաձայնական իշխանութեանց միջոցաւ: Թշուառութիւն կայ, վասնզի ամէն գործ եւ զբաղում լքած միայն կեանքի փրկութեան մտազբաղումն ունին:

Պանտրմա – 26 Ապրիլ

Ապրիլ 19 ժամը 6ին Միլլի ուժերը քաղաքս հասնելով Պանտրման եւ շրջակայքը գրաւեցին: Գայմագամ ամասիացի Շէվքը պէյ հայերու հանդէպ լաւագոյն տրամադրութիւններ ունի եւ կ'աշխատի ապահովութիւն ներշնչել: Միլլի ուժին տեղւոյս միւրէթթէպիյէ եւ թէէտիպիյէ զօմանտան Իսմայիլ Հագգը պէյ ալ Առաջնորդարան այցելելով վստահութիւն տուաւ թէ հայերու վնաս չպիտի հասնի: Անգլիացի ներկայացուցիչ Մստր Գօզի Պանտրմայէն մեկնեցաւ: Մուսթաֆա Քէմալ փաշայի կողմէ տրուած հրամանի մը համաձայն բոլոր թղթակցութիւնները թուրքերէն պիտի կատարուին տեղւոյս եւ շրջանիս մէջ: Գրաքննութիւնը վերահաստատուած է եւ Պոլսոյ հետ յարաբերութիւնները խզուած ըլլալով՝ երէկ առաւօտ ժամանող *մօթէօր* նաւ մը ճամբորդներով միասին ետ դարձուեցաւ: Ոչ թղթաբերը կ'ընդունուի եւ ոչ թղթատար կ'արտօնուի առ այժմ:

Ատանա (Կարապետ Նալպանտեանէ) – 17 Ապրիլ

Ամէն ոք մեկնելու պատրաստ է: Առ այժմ քաղաքէն դուրս ելլել անհնար է: 20 օրէ ի վեր Սիսէն ոեւէ տեղեկութիւն չկայ: Առնուած լուրերու համեմատ, Սիսի կամուրջը գրաւած են չէթէները եւ ժողովուրդը ջուրէ զրկած են: Կամուրջին շրջակայ կիրիտցի թուրք գաղթականներու բնակավայրերը իրենց *հիթիհքամ* ըրած են չէթէները: Երթեւեկ չըլլալով Հաճընէն ստոյգ տեղեկութիւն չկայ: Չրոյցի մը համաձայն, չէթէները Հաճընէն հեռու կը գտնուին եղեր: Նմանապէս կը լսուի թէ պաշարումը տեւելով հանդերձ, պատերազմը կը շարունակուի: 7–8 օր առաջ օդանաւով առնուած տեղեկութեան համաձայն, Հաճընի մէջ հանդարտութիւն կայ: Սիսի շրջակայքը հաւաքուած չէթէները 7000 հոգի են կ'ըսուի, սակայն որքան ճիշդ ըլլալը չենք գիտեր: Առջի օր 3000 ֆրանսական

French troops were transferred to Kozan. If they stay there, Kozan Armenians will be naturally saved from danger. But if they return, there will be great panic in Adana, and the Christians will migrate entirely.

Today (April 17), we heard that the French soldiers have entered Kozan. There was no fighting on the road, and the villagers calmly retreated to their places. Thus, the çetes vacated the arena because in this area, the çetes get their strength from the villagers, who gently put their weapons down in front of a force [the French].

After leaving two martyrs behind, the remaining forty-five Armenians besieged in Tumlu arrived alive in Adana by night.

• In Adana, a notice calling for the solidarity of Muslim and Christian peoples is in the making. With this proclamation, the two peoples have been invited to do their work peacefully during this harvest season. It also explains the continuing harmfulness of the current situation and urges them to obey the decision to be made by the [Peace] Conference and to be approved by the government. It warns that those who oppose the decision will be punished.

Some Armenians did not want to sign this petition. Quite noisy meetings ensued, and it is thought that the Armenians will not sign it.

Balıkesir (from the correspondent of *Yergir*)—April 25

On April 10, the Millis of Balıkesir convened a large meeting at the Sultaniye School. They invited the governor and several dignitaries to attend it. The president of the Milli [organization], Vasıf Bey of İzmir, warned the participants at the meeting that should anyone go against its decisions, they would cut off the dissenter's ears and nose.

The decision at the meeting was to deport the Armenians and Greeks and send them to Sındırkı. As many as eighty participants have signed the resolution under threat. The governor and three local elders, preferring to die, opposed this decision, and therefore the execution of this decision was postponed for a while. The Millis speak publicly, saying that if they see [even] a slight defeat, they will not leave a single Christian alive after looting the city; they will massacre them. Looting and violence have started already. A few days ago, when the Efe [leader of çetes] Sarı and his five-hundred-strong force reached the station in Balıkesir, they ransacked Mihran Arabian's brewery, and the damage amounted to three thousand liras. Later, several houses were forcibly evacuated in the city, and çetes were brought to collect beds and so on from the houses for the efes. Although the government wants to curb all of this, it lacks power. Most government functionaries sympathize with the Millis and favor spreading fake news to provoke the people against Christians. By order of Mustafa Kemal, the duty of steering Karasi and its environs, including the government, has been given to the local detachment commander Kâzım. They have issued an edict to hang three or four local Ittilafists. Not satisfied by forcing the rest of the Muslims into enlistment and collecting money from the unfortunate people, now in their assembly hall, the Millis have begun to prepare the list of Armenians and Greeks who, according to the register, were born between 1884 and 1894, and assign quotas to the rest of the people to be paid as homeland protection levy.

Trabzon[66] (from the locum tenens)—April 21

The nationalists of the city elected five people, led by Prefect Hamit Bey, to participate in the Turkish

զինուորներ Սիս փոխադրուեցան: Եթէ հոն մնան, բնական է Սիսի հայերը վտանգէ կ'ազատին: Իսկ եթէ վերադառնան՝ Ատանայի մէջ մեծ խուճապ առաջ պիտի գայ եւ քրիստոնեաները ամբողջովին պիտի գաղթեն:

Այսօր (Ապրիլ 17) լուր առինք որ ֆրանսական զինուորները Սիս մտած են: Ճամբան ռեւէ ընդհարում չէ պատահած եւ գիւղացիք հանդարտօրէն իրենց տեղերը քաշուած են: Այս կերպով չէթէները քաշուած են հրապարակէն, զի այս շրջանին մէջ չէթէճիները իրենց ուժը կը ստանան գիւղացիներէ, որոնք ուժին առջեւ կամաց մը զէնքը վար կը դնեն:

Թումլուի մէջ պաշարուած հայերը երկու նահատակ տալով մնացեալ 45 հոգին ողջամբ եւ գիշերանց Ատանա ժամանեցին:

- Ատանայի մէջ խլամ եւ քրիստոնեայ ժողովուրդը համերաշխութեան հրաւիրող ծանուցագիր մը պատրաստուելու վրայ է: Այս յայտարարութեամբ երկու ժողովուրդները կը հրաւիրուին խաղաղութեամբ այս հունձքին եղանակին իրենց գործերովը զբաղիլ: Նոյնպէս կը բացատրուի ներկայ կացութեան շարունակութեան երկուստեք վնասակար ըլլալը եւ յորդոր կ'ըլլայ հնազանդիլ Վեհաժողովին տալիք եւ կառավարութենէն հաստատուելիք որոշման եւ կ'ազդարարուի թէ պիտի պատժուի այն որ հակառակ կը շարժի:

Այս հանրագրութ[իւնը] մաս մը հայեր չեն ուզած ստորագրել, որուն վրայ բաւական աղմկալի ժողովներ տեղի ունեցան եւ կը կարծուի թէ հայերը չստորագրեն:

Պալըքէսիր («Երկիր»ի թղթակիցէն) – 25 Ապրիլ

Ապրիլ 10ին Պալըքէսիրի Միլլիճիներն «Սուլթանիյէ» դպրոցին մէջ մեծ ժողով մը գումարելով կառավարիչը եւ մի քանի երեւելիները կոչած են ներկայ գտնուելու: Միլլիի նախագահը՝ Իզմիրի Վասըֆ պէյ, ազդարարած է ժողովի անդամներուն որ՝ եթէ երբեք մեր որոշումներուն հակառակ գտնուող ըլլայ, ականջները եւ քիթը պիտի կտրենք:

Ժողովին որոշումն եղած է հայերը եւ յոյները տեղահան ընել եւ Սընտըրկը ղրկել: 80ի չափ անդամներ՝ սպառնալիքի տակ, ստորագրած են որոշմնագիրը: Իսկ կառավարիչը եւ տեղացի երեք ծերունիներ մահը նախընտրելով հակառակ գտնուած են այս որոշումին եւ այս պատճառով յետաձգուած է ժամանակի մը համար այս որոշումին գործադրութիւնը: Միլլիճիները հրապարակաւ կը խօսին ըսելով թէ՝ եթէ պզտիկ պարտութիւն մը տեսնանք, նախ քաղաքը թալանել վերջ՝ մէկ հատ քրիստոնեայ չպիտի թողունք, պիտի ջարդենք: Հիմակուընէ սկսած են թալան եւ բռնութիւն. քանի մը օր առաջ Սառը Էֆէն իր 500 ոյժերով Պալըքէսիրի կայարանը հասած ատեն, հոն գտնուող Միհրան Արապեանի գարեջրատունը թալլած են եւ վնասը 3000 ոսկիի կը հասնի: Յետոյ քաղաքին մէջ ալ քանի մը տուներ բռնի ոյժով պարպել տալէ վերջ չէթէներ տարած են եւ տուներէն անկողին եւայլն ժողովուած են էֆէներուն համար: Կառավարութիւնը թէպէտեւ կ'ուզէ այս ամէնը զսպել, սակայն ոյժը կը պակսի եւ արդէն կառավարութեան պաշտօնեաներն մեծ մասամբ Միլլիի համակիր են, որ չըլլայ որ սուտ լուր չտարածայնեն ժողովուրդը քրիստոնեաներու դէմ գրգռելու: Գարասիի եւ շրջականերու ղեկավարման պաշտօնը Մուսթաֆա Քէմալի հրամանով տեղւոյս ֆըրքա զօման-տանի Քեազիմ պէյի յանձնուած է՝ կառավարութիւն ալ մէջը ըլլալով: Տեղացի իթ[ի]լաֆականներէն կախաղան բարձրացնելու համար 3–4 հոգիներուն իրենց կողմէ ֆէրման հանած են: Քեազիմ պէյը՝ տեղւոյս զինուորական հրամատար ճանչցուած է բարձրագոյն հրամանաւ: Մնացած տաճիկները զինուորագրել եւ բռնի կերպով խեղճ ժողովուրդէն դրամ հաւաքելէն չգոհանալով, հիմակ ալ սկսած են իրենց ժողովատեղիին մէջ ըստ արձանագրութեան տոմարի հայերու եւ յոյներու 300էն 310ի [= 1884-էն 1894-ի] ծնունդներու ցանկը պատրաստել եւ մնացածներուն ալ որոշ գումարներ յատկացնել իբր հայրենիքի պաշտպանութեան տուրք:

Տրապիզոն (Առաջնորդական Տեղապահէն) – 21 Ապրիլ

Էնկիւրիւի թրքական գոնկրէին մասնակցելու համար քաղաքիս ազգայնականները իրենց

Congress of Ankara. It is assumed that in this way, the Millis wanted to remove the prefect who did not blindly serve them. The prefect guessed this and aborted their plan.

The sultan's decree and the religious fatwa arrived here but were not publicized. On the contrary, the local Turkish newspapers—the extremist *Istikbal* and the moderate *Ikbal*—continue their provocative publications against the English, whose captive they consider the sultan to be.

Istikbal issued the fatwa yesterday, attaching the "Anatolian Fatwa." This release aimed at disturbing minds and inciting Islamic fanaticism.

The Millis are very interested in the Bolshevik movement. Telegrams report Bolsheviks' successes daily. Local newspapers report these successes with pleasure. In this movement, they see Turkey's last refuge. "We are all already Bolsheviks," the prefect once said to the Armenian prelate laughingly. The Turks have placed high expectations on [the occurrence of] disagreements among the Allies.

Trabzon—April 21

This Sunday, April 18, two British dreadnoughts and one torpedo boat anchored in front of Trabzon, thus bringing the number of battleships guarding the area to four. After delivering a warning to the prefect, a parade of naval troops took place a day later near Boztepe, a mountain south of the city. After blowing up and destroying several large but useless artillery pieces placed there by the Russians, they retired to their ships in the evening. The dreadnoughts left with their commanders that night to return to İstanbul after passing by Giresun and Samsun. This visit of the armored cruisers caused, for a moment, fear and abandonment among the Turks in general and the Millis in particular. Many left the city; others went into hiding. In contrast, Christians were encouraged. But the departure [of the vessels], after an insignificant demonstration of force, had the opposite effect. The Turks became bolder and began to despise the British insolently. In its coverage, *Istikbal* has attributed a series of [allegedly unbecoming] actions to the British soldiers.

• A half an hour away toward the southwestern part of Trabzon, on a hill of the village called Özsoğuksu [Soğuksu], cannons were placed by the Millis. The British, surprisingly, did not destroy these [functional cannons]; they only destroyed the unusable cannons.

Trabzon (from the locum tenens)—April 23

To stir up adversity between the Allies, the Millis pretend to see enemies in the British and friends in the French. A week ago, a French military commander landed here. He mocked the visit of the British armored cruisers. As for Armenia, he made the following remarks: 1. Do you think that present-day Armenia will expand further? 2. Are there enough Armenians to be able to rule an integral Armenia? 3. It is necessary to settle the issues of Armenia and Turkey with an arbitration.

The absence of a British representative is more encouraging for the Turks.

• The information reported by *Sabah* [newspaper] that the fatwa of İstanbul was read here as well and that people pledged obedience to the sultan is absolutely false. On the contrary, the Turk who brought a large package of fatwas with him was arrested and sent to prison.

կողմէ ներկայացուցիչ էին ընտրեր հինգ անձեր՝ որոնց գլուխը կը գտնուէր կուսակալ Համիտ պէյ: Կ'ենթադրուի թէ Միլլիականք այս կերպով [կ'ուզեն] հեռացնել կուսակալը, որ կուրօրէն չի ծառայեր իրենց: Կուսակալը կռահած է այս պարագան եւ վիժեցուցած է անոնց ծրագիրը:

Սուլթանին *իրատէ*ն եւ կրօնական *ֆէթվա*ն հոս հասան, սակայն հրապարակ չելան: Ընդհակառակը, տեղական թուրք թերթերը՝ ծայրայեղական *Իսթիգլալ* եւ չափաւոր «*Իզլալ*», կը շարունակեն իրենց գրգռիչ հրատարակութիւնները անգլիացիներուն դէմ՝ որոնց գերին կը նկատեն Սուլթանը:

Իսթիգլալ երէկ հրատարակեց *ֆէթվա*ն, անոր կցելով «*Անատօլուի Ֆէթվա*»ն: Այս հրատարակութիւնը նկատի ունէր պղտ[որ]ել միտքերը եւ գրգռել խլամ մոլեռանդութիւնը:

Միլլիութիւնը շատ կը հետաքրքրուի լրջօրէն պոլշեվիկեան շարժումով: Հեռագիրները օրը օրին կը հաղորդեն պոլշեվիկեան յաջողութիւնները: Տեղական թերթերը այդ յաջողութիւնները գոհունակութեամբ կը հաղորդեն: Այս շարժման մէջ կը փնտռեն Թուրքիոյ վերջին ապաւէնը: «Արդէն ամէնքս ալ պոլշեվիկ ենք» կ'ըսէ անգամ մը կուսակալը ծիծաղելով հայոց Առաջնորդին: Թուրքերը մեծ յոյս դրած են նաեւ Համաձայնական պետութեանց անհամաձայնութեան վրայ:

Տրապիզոն – 21 Ապրիլ

Այս Կիրակի՝ 18 Ապրիլ, Տրապիզոնի առջեւ խարսխեցին երկու տրէթնօթներ եւ մէկ թօրբէթօ անգլիական: Պահակ զրահաւորին հետ անոնք եղան չորս: Կուսակալին եղած ազդարարութենէ մը վերջ, յաջորդ օր ծովային զինուորներու կողմէ տեղի ունեցաւ զօրանցք մը դէպի Պոզթէբէ՝ քաղաքին հարաւակողմի լեռը: Հոն ռուսերու կողմէ զետեղուած քանի մը խոշոր բայց անգործածելի թնդանօթները պայթեցնելէ եւ ոչնչացնելէ վերջ՝ իրիկունը քաշուեցան իրենց նաւերը: Տրէթնօթները իրենց առաջնորդներով գիշերանց մեկնեցան՝ Կիրասոն եւ Սամսոն հանդիպելով Պոլիս վերադառնալու նպատակով: Մարտանաւերու այս այցելութիւնը վայրկեան մը վախ եւ լքում պատճառեց թուրքերուն ընդհանրապէս եւ Միլլիականներուն մասնաւորապէս: Շատեր հեռացան քաղաքէն, ուրիշներ ծակամուտ եղան: Ասոր հակառակ, քրիստոնեայք սրտապնդուեցան: Բայց անոնց մեկնումը՝ աննշան ցոյցէ մը վերջ՝ տուաւ հակառակ արդիւնք եւ թուրքերը դարձան աւելի յանդուգն, լրբութեամբ արհամարհել սկսան անգլիացիները: *Իսթիգլալ* նկարագրականի մը մէջ անգլիացի զինուորներուն կը վերագրէ կարգ մը արարքներ:

- Տրապիզոնի հարաւ-արեւմտեան կողմը, կէս ժամ հեռաւորութիւն ունեցող Սովուգ-Սու կոչուած գիւղին բարձունքին վրայ զետեղուած են Միլլիներու կողմէ թնդանօթներ, որոնք զարմանալի է որ անգլիացիք չփճացուցին եւ միայն անգործածելի թնդանօթները քանդեցին:

Տրապիզոն (Առաջնորդական Տեղապահէն) – 23 Ապրիլ

Միլլիականները հակառակութիւններ ստեղծելու համար Դաշնակիցներու միջեւ այնպէս կը կեղծեն թէ անգլիացւոց մէջ թշնամիներ եւ ֆրանսացւոց մէջ բարեկամներ կը տեսնեն: Շաբաթ մը առաջ ցամաք ելաւ ֆրանսացի զինուորական հրամանատար մը, որ հեգնանքով անդրադարձաւ անգլիական զրահաւորներու այցելութեան: Իսկ Հայաստանի մասին անիկա ըրաւ հետեւեալ նկատողութիւնները.- 1. Կը կարծէ՞ք որ ներկայ Հայաստանը աւելի ընդարձակուի. 2. Հայերը բաւական թիւ ունի՞ն՝ կարենալ տիրելու համար ամբողջական Հայաստանի: 3. Հարկ է իրաւախոհութեամբ կարգադրել Հայաստանի եւ Թուրքիոյ խնդիրները:

Անգլիացի ներկայացուցիչ մը գոյութիւն չունենալը աւելի քաջալերական է թրքաց համար:

- «Սապահ»ի տուած տեղեկութիւնը թէ Պոլսոյ ֆէթվան այստեղ ալ կարդացուեր եւ ժողովուրդը կայսեր հնազանդութիւն խոստացեր է բացարձակապէս սուտ է: Ընդհակառակը, ֆէթվաներու խոշոր ծրար մը իր հետ բերող թուրքը ձերբակալուեր եւ բանտ առաջնորդուեր է:

Amanos (from a volunteer's letter)—April 23
In Amanos, the Armenian volunteers—serving in the trenches of Dörtyol and Hasanbeyli—have no bread. Bread, flour, and bullets are vital necessities for Amanos. We are under urgency. We ask the Patriarchate and political parties to appeal to pro-Armenian and philanthropic individuals for donations on behalf of the volunteers of Amanos and the National Unions. We undertake the repayment of the funds given in the form of an internal loan within two years. The people of Amanos are determined not to be massacred and to defeat their attacking executioners. Not to be defeated, they need flour and ammunition, which can be arranged with money. Armenians, by their means, can secure their right to live, at least in Amanos, if they have money for flour and ammunition.

Mersin (from Reverend Father Mampré Sirounian)—April 23[67]
According to information delivered by the French plane, there is peace in Saimbeyli [Hacın]. The battle is taking place three hours away from the city, and the Armenians are resisting with perfect courage. There has been no information from Saimbeyli and Kozan [Sis] since April 1. The Armenian remnants of Maraş will die of starvation. There is no news from Süleymanlı [Zeytun] at all. There is fighting in Gaziantep [Ayntab]. Refugees from Kilis and Gaziantep have come to Adana.

• Four days ago, the çetes succeeded in destroying the bridge between Tarsus and Yenice and capturing the railway line. Thus, Adana has been separated from Tarsus. The French are trying to repair the destroyed bridge, but the çetes, sheltered behind the best positions, are keeping the area under constant fire and forcing the French to leave. At the last moment, we learned that the first station on the Mersin-Tarsus line had also been captured and that the three cities of Adana, Tarsus, and Mersin were disconnected.

• Düziçi [Haruniye], Bahçe, and other places have been completely destroyed. With very few casualties, a fraction of Armenians arrived in Adana and another fraction in Mersin.

• The çetes have also appeared around Mersin. There have been battles between them and the French forces.

İstanbul (information taken from a Kurdish pilot officer named Reshid)—May 5
Most of the volunteers sent against the Milli forces are Kurds, and the rest are Anatolians or discharged Turkish soldiers, who generally enlist in the army to flee to their native places. They boldly declare this to be the case. The Turks from İstanbul do not move from where they are. If the Kurdish people do not support Mustafa Kemal and the government, a great effort to establish peace in Turkey will not be needed. The Kurds of Tunceli [Dersim] and Kazazan, the Kizilbash in general, refrain in a way.

• The Kurdish Progress Committee [members], beginning with Abdulkadir, all of them are after personal interests. They lack an organization in the region to give the necessary instructions to the Kurdish nation.

• Three weeks ago, the government sent three police battalions to Bandırma-Balıkesir. The police killed their commanders and joined Mustafa Kemal's çetes.

• Yesterday, government troops managed to capture more than a hundred Kemalist çetes, whose uniforms and weapons were allegedly Italian. The Italians are said to be helping Mustafa Kemal against the Greeks.

• Government troops will either flee or join the Kemalists; therefore, Ferid Pasha's restraining measures will probably be ineffective.

Ամանոս (կամաւորի մը նամակէն) – 23 Ապրիլ

Ամանոսը՝ Տէօրդ-Եօլ եւ Հասան-Պէյլիի խրամներուն մէջ հայ կամաւորները՝ հաց չունին: Հաց, ալիւր եւ փամփուշտ Ամանոսի համար կենսական անհրաժեշտութիւններ են: Ստիպողականութեան տակ ենք: Կը խնդրուի պատրիարքարանէն, քաղաքական կուսակցութիւններէն, հայասէր եւ մարդասէր անհատներու դիմում կատարել Ամանոսի կամաւորներուն եւ Ազգային Միութիւններու անունով, դրամ հասցնելու համար: Ներքին փոխառութեան ձեւին տակ տրուած դրամը յանձն կ'առնենք երկու տարիէն վերադարձնելու: Ամանոսցիք վճռած են չկոտորուիլ այլ յաղթել յարձակող դահիճներու: Չյաղթուելու համար ալիւրի եւ ռազմամթերքի պէտք ունին, ինչ որ դրամով կրնայ ճարուիլ: Հայերը իրենց սեփական միջոցներով կարող են ապահովել իրենց ապրելու իրաւունքը՝ գէթ Ամանոսի մէջ, եթէ դրամ ունենան ալիւր եւ ռազմամթերքի համար:

Մերսին (Մամբրէ Վարդապետ Սիրունեանէ) – 23 Ապրիլ

Ֆրանսական օդանաւով առնուած տեղեկութեանց համաձայն, Հաճընի մէջ խաղաղութիւն կը տիրէ: Կռիւը տեղի կ'ունենայ քաղաքէն երեք ժամ հեռու եւ հայերը կը դիմադրեն կատարեալ արիութեամբ: Ապրիլ 1էն ի վեր ոչ մէկ տեղեկութիւն կա[ր] Հաճընէն եւ Սիսէն: Մարաշի հայոց մնացորդները անօթութենէ պիտի մեռնին: Զէյթունէն բնաւ լուր չկայ: Այնթապի մէջ կռիւ կայ: Քիլիսէն եւ Այնթապէն գաղթականներ եկած են Ատանա:

- Չէթէները չորս օր առաջ յաջողեցան խորտակել Տարսոնի եւ Եէնիճէի միջեւ գտնուած կամուրջը եւ բռնել երկաթուղիի գիծը: Այսպէս Ատանան բաժնեցին Տարսոնէն: Ֆրանսացիք կը ջանան նորոգել քանդուած կամուրջը, սակայն չէթէները ապաստանած լաւագոյն դիրքերու ետին, շարունակ կրակի տակ կը պահեն այդ վայրը եւ կը ստիպեն ֆրանսացիները հեռանալ անկէ: Վերջին պահուն կ'իմանանք թէ Մերսինէն Տարսոն գիծին առաջին կայարանը եւս գրաւած են եւ Ատանա, Տարսոն եւ Մերսին երեք քաղաքները իրարմէ բաժնած են:

- Հարունիէ, Պաղճէ եւ ուրիշ վայրեր հիմնայատակ կործանած են: Հայերը շատ քիչ զոհեր տալով հասան մաս մը Ատանա մաս մըն ալ Մերսին:

- Չէթէները Մերսինի շուրջն ալ երեւցած են եւ կռիւներ եղած [են] անոնց եւ ֆրանսական զօրաց մէջ:

Կ. Պոլիս (օդանաւորդ քուրտ Րէշիտ անուն սպայէ մը քաղուած տեղեկութիւն) – 5 Մայիս

Միլլի ուժերու դէմ ղրկուած կամաւորներու մեծագոյն մասը քուրտ են, իսկ մնացեալ մասը անատոլցիներ կամ արձակուած թուրք զինուորներ, որոնք առհասարակ կը զինուորագրուին իրենց հայրենիքը փախչելու նպատակով եւ այս պարագան համարձակ կը յայտարարեն: Պոլսեցի թուրքերը տեղերնէն չեն շարժիր: Եթէ քիւրտ ցեղը թէ՛ Մուսթաֆա Քէմալի եւ թէ՛ կառավարութեան չօժանդակէ, Թուրքիոյ մէջ խաղաղութիւն հաստատելու համար մեծ ճիգի պէտք չկայ: Տէրսիմի եւ Գազազանի քուրտերը, ընդհանրապէս զըզըլպաշները, կերպով մը ձեռնպահ կը մնան:

- Քիւրտ Թէալի Քոմիթէն՝ Ապտ-իւլ Գատէրէն սկսեալ, ամէնքն ալ անձնական շահեր կը հետապնդեն: Գաւառի մէջ կազմակերպութիւն չունին՝ ի հարկին քուրտ ազգին պէտք եղած հրահանգները տալու համար:

- Երեք շաբաթ առաջ կառավարութեան կողմէ երեք վաշտի մօտ ոստիկաններ ղրկուած էին Պանտրմա-Պալըքէսիր: Ոստիկանները կը սպաննեն իրենց հրամատարները եւ կը միանան Մուսթաֆա Քէմալի չէթէներուն:

- Անցեալ օր կառավարութեան զինուորները կը յաջողին բռնել հարիւրէ աւելի քեմալական չէթէներ, որոնց տարազը եւ զէնքերը իտալական են եղեր: Իտալացիները կ'ըսուի թէ ի հեճուկս յոյներու կ'օգնեն Մուսթաֆա Քէմալի:

- Կառավարական զինուորները կա՛մ պիտի փախչին, կա՛մ քէմալականներուն պիտի միանան, որով Ֆէրիտ փաշայի զսպողական ձեռնարկները հաւանական չէ որ արդիւնաւորուին:

Bursa (from the vicar general)—May 6

Traffic has stopped; therefore, there is no news even from İstanbul. Life in the city is almost monotonous, and Armenians live in fear and suspicion, even though the new prefect, Hazım Bey, assures them that no harm will come to the Armenians.

Urfa (from Dr. Mirza Ketenjian)—April 20[68]

The Armenians of Urfa are still alive and well. We remained under siege for precisely three months. Currently, we are living desperately in a semi-uncertain state. On January 17, a joint Kurdish, Arab, and Turkish movement began against the French. The city was besieged on all sides. Meanwhile, panic and horror broke out in the city. The Armenians and the Turks took up arms, and the campaign began. The Armenian quarter was besieged on all sides, all passages sealed. Positions and barricades were erected at every passage, and the Turks took the Armenian quarter under an iron siege. The fighting began on February 3 and lasted for two months, night and day. The Turks attacked with artillery and machine guns from all sides, but the French remained in their defensive positions and waited for auxiliary forces, which could not reach Urfa. Before the war, the Turks tried hard to engage the Armenians, but the Armenians declared neutrality and remained neutral. Some Armenian fighters stationed on the hill behind the Armenian neighborhood thwarted all the Turkish attacks. The Turks needed to pass through the Armenian neighborhood, but the Armenians refused to allow them passage. The Turks wrote, threatened, and fired to no avail. The Armenians refused to be trampled. The only weakness the Armenians had was the shortage of victuals. Thousands of orphans and the poor had been hungry for food even before the fighting began, and there was no money or food. The Turks gave not a single bite of food. But the Armenians took care of them [the orphans and needy] and kept them alive by making the neighborhood's victuals available to all. They opened a public kitchen. They ate whatever was edible: grass, barley, millet, cotton seed; all the horses, donkeys, and dogs were slaughtered, and regular food was prepared. The Armenians endured and resisted, but the expected help did not come. The stock of the French forces was exhausted, and they were forced to accept the Turkish condition, that is, to withdraw from the city, taking their weapons and equipment with them. This was one of the Turks' hellish plans. They could not defeat (nor would have defeated) the French without a plot as long as they maintained their positions. The French barely numbered five hundred. They had no artillery or car and never made any offensive attempts. They always remained on the defensive, waiting for their forces, which did not come. Finally, they had to withdraw from the city. However, their grave had already been prepared [treacherously] in a valley four to five hours away from the city. As soon as the Turks obtained the promise that the French would leave the city, they built new trenches and positions and secretly placed two to three thousand people there. The French left with the promise and belief that they had struck an honorable accord and that the Turks would not attack them. When they reached the site set for the treachery, all of them were immediately annihilated by a sudden fire; only 134 Algerians were saved and brought to the city. Here is the reality and the fact.

The Turks, for now, pretend to be kind to the Armenians. They seem entirely forgiving of what happened. So much forgetfulness and kindness are very questionable. Although the Armenians have not had fights with them, except for a few clashes, the Armenian neutrality has cost them dearly. On the other hand, they [the Turks] are aware of the Armenians' direct support of the [French]. They know that the French survived on the back hill of the Armenian neighborhood thanks to the Armenians and their support. They know that the Armenian volunteers helped the French. They know that the Armenians made bombs and dynamite. They know that the Armenians built a cannon and a catapult to use against them. They know that some people were the direct organizers of all these events and were in direct contact with the French. Knowing all this, there is a mystery behind their being so for-

Պրուսա (Առաջնորդական փոխանորդէն) – 6 Մայիս

Երթեւեկը դադրած է, որով լուր չկայ նոյնիսկ Կ. Պոլիսէն: Քաղաքին կեանքը գրեթէ միօրինակ կ'ընթանայ եւ վախի ու կասկածի մէջ կ'ապրին հայերը, հակառակ անոր որ նոր կուսակալ Հազըմ պէյ ապահովութիւն կուտայ հայոց վնաս չհասնելուն:

Ուրֆա (Տոք. Միրզա Քէթէնճեանէ) – 20 Ապրիլ

Մինչեւ այս ժամս Ուրֆայի հայութիւնը ողջ եւ առողջ է: Ճիշդ երեք ամիս պաշարման տակ մնացինք եւ այսօր կէս մը անստոյգ վիճակի մը մէջ յուսահատական օրեր կ'ապրինք: Յունվար 17ին սկսաւ քրտական, արաբական եւ թրքական միացեալ շարժումը ֆրանսացիներուն դէմ: Քաղաքը պաշարուեցաւ ամէն կողմէ: Նոյն ատեն քաղաքին մէջ խուճապը եւ սարսափը սկսաւ: Հայերը եւ թուրքերը դիմեցին զէնքի, զօրաշարժը սկսաւ: Հայ թաղը պաշարուեցաւ ամէն կողմէ, բոլոր անցքերը գոցուեցան: Ամէն անցքի վրայ դիրքեր եւ պատնէշներ կանգնեցան եւ թուրքեր իրենք ալ հայ թաղը պաշարման երկաթէ օղակի տակ առին: Փետրուար 3ին սկսան կռիւները, տեւեցին գիշերներ եւ ցերեկներ ամբողջ երկու ամիս: Թուրքերը թնդանօթով եւ միթրայէօզներով ամէն կողմէ յարձակում տուին, բայց ֆրանսացիք իրենց դիրքերուն վրայ մնացին պաշտպանողական եւ սպասեցին օգնական ուժերու, որոնք չկրցան հասնիլ: Թուրքերը դեռ կռիւը չսկսած շատ աշխատեցան հայերը իրենց կապել, բայց հայերը յայտարարեցին չէզոքութիւն եւ մնացին չէզոք: Հայ կռուողներու մէկ մասը հայ թաղին կռնակի բլուրին վրայ դիրք բռնած, թուրքերու բոլոր յարձակումները անյաջողութեան կը մատնէր: Թուրքերը պէտք ունէին հայ թաղէն անցնելու, բայց հայերը մերժեցին անցք տալ: Թուրքերը գրեցին, սպառնացան, կրակեցին, բայց անօգուտ: Հայերը չթողուցին որ կոխկրտուին: Հայոց միակ տկարութիւնը ուտեստի խնդիրն էր: Արդէն հազարներով որբեր եւ աղքատներ օրական հացի կը կարօտէին, դրամ չկար, ուտելիք չկար: Թուրքերը մէկ պատառ ուտելիք չէին տար: Բայց հայերը [հոգ] տարին, ապրեցուցին, թաղին ուտեստը եւ պաշարը հասարակաց դարձուցին, հասարակաց խոհանոց բացին: Կերան ինչ որ կարելի էր ուտել,- խոտ, գարի, կորեկ, բամպակի կուտ, բոլոր ձիերը, էշերը, շուները մորթեցին եւ կանոնաւոր կերակուր շինեցին: Հայերը դիմացան եւ դիմադրեցին, սակայն սպասուած օգնութիւնը չեկաւ, ֆրանսական ուժերու պաշարը լմնցաւ եւ ստիպուեցան ընդունիլ թրքական պայմանը. այսինքն իրենց զէնքերով եւ կազմածներով քաշուիլ քաղաքէն: Թրքական դժոխային ծրագիրներէն մին էր այս. չկրցան եւ չպիտի կրնային յաղթել ֆրանսացիներուն առանց դաւի, քանի իրենց տեղերն էին: Ֆրանսացիք հազիւ 500 հոգի էին, թնդանօթ չունէին, օթոմոպիլ չունէին, որեւէ յարձակողական փորձ չըրին, միշտ մնացին պաշտպանողականի վրայ, սպասելով իրենց ուժերուն, որոնք չեկան եւ ի վերջոյ պարտաւորուեցան քաղաքը ձգելու: Սակայն քաղաքէն 4–5 ժամ հեռու ձորի մը մէջ արդէն իրենց գերեզմանը պատրաստուած էր: Թուրքերը ֆրանսացիներու քաղաքը թողնելու խոստումը առնելնուն պէս նոր խրամներ եւ դիրքեր շինեցին եւ 2–3000 հոգի գաղտնի տեղաւորեցին: Ֆրանսացիք մեկնեցան այն խոստումով եւ հաւատքով որ պատուաւոր դաշինք կապած են եւ թուրքերը իրենց վրայ ոեւէ յարձակում չպիտի գործեն: Երբ կը հասնին դաւադրուած վայրը, յանկարծական կրակի տակ անմիջապէս կ'ոչնչանան բոլորն ալ, միայն 134 ալճերիացիներ կ'ազատին եւ կը բերուին քաղաք: Ահաւասիկ իրականութիւնը եւ եղելութիւնը:

Թուրքերը առ այժմ հայերու հետ լաւ վերաբերում ցոյց տալ կը ձեւացնեն, բոլորովին անյիշաչար կը թուին եղածին եւ անցած դարձածին մասին: Այսքան մոռացում եւ բարեացակամութիւն շատ կասկածելի է: Հայերը թէեւ իրենց հետ ուղղակի կռիւներ չունեցան բացի քանի մը ընդհարումներէ, սակայն հայոց չէզոքութիւնը իրենց սուղի նստաւ, միւս կողմէ հայոց ուղղակի աջակցութեան մասին ալ ծանօթութիւն ունին: Գիտեն թէ հայ թաղի կռնակի բլուրի վրայի ֆրանսացիք հայոց միջոցաւ եւ աջակցութեամբ կրցան դիմանալ: Գիտեն թէ հայ կամաւորները օժանդակեցին ֆրանսացիներուն: Գիտեն թէ հայերը պոմպա, տինամիտ շինեցին: Գիտեն թէ հայերը թնդանօթ մը եւ քարաձիգ մեքենայ մը շինեցին՝ իրենց դէմ գործածելու համար: Գիտեն թէ կարգ մը անձեր

giving and silent that we cannot solve it. The city is desperate, especially since the departure of the French; the spirit of self-defense is enervated. The misery and hunger are causing fear. How will two to three thousand homeless poor women and orphans live under this suffering? Help is indispensable.

Gaziantep [Ayntab] (Priest Nerses Tavoukjian, catholicosal vicar)—April 20[69]

On April 1, the French forces that had arrived in Gaziantep on March 28 marched on Kilis just before dawn. They took some of the pre-existing troops and the heavy artillery that had become a thorn in the Turks' side. The news of both the departure of the French and the Armenians shot in the center of the market was heard in the morning simultaneously. Shortly afterward, the sound of Mauser guns was heard on both sides of the city, on the hills. This was a signal. The Turkish çetes attacked the Armenian neighborhoods not as a plundering mob but as warrior soldiers who had built barricades with the help of *privates* and, of course, fortified their backs. The Armenians, who were waiting for this attack, had turned the windows that overlooked the big streets into positions. They had prepared many barricades to open them instantly. They immediately took those positions [once the attack began]. As soon as the people heard the news of the riot, they started blocking the entrances of the streets with stones, and two hours later, all measures of self-defense had been taken. The Armenians continued to defend themselves against the Turkish attack. The Turks simultaneously attacked the Armenians from all sides, and they had incomparably more weapons than the Armenians. The grenades they had made were the only advantage the Armenians had, which saved them from uninterrupted attacks for two days and nights. Today marks the nineteenth day that the Armenians have been besieged. The Armenians fought for sixteen days with heroic courage and valor and with a discipline befitting Armenians. On the fourth day of the war, the Turks realized that the Armenian positions were invincible. After that, as if in a regular battle, they would terrorize the Armenians with light attacks during the daytime followed by two- to three-hour-long constant attacks at night, but fortunately, they were always repulsed. During these sixteen days, the first two days being an exception, in the other fourteen days, they carried out three fiercest attacks on all fronts, and once, on the night of April 8, they opened fire on the French army as well. The American hospital and the orphanages were constantly under fire during the fighting. On the first day, a French soldier, after fleeing from the street, took refuge in the Latin church north of the city and stayed there. This soldier defended the church all day until he ran out of bullets. The Armenians helped this soldier with their limited bullets. The French colonel, with whom the Armenians were in contact, ordered the Armenians to get the soldier out of there, evacuate the people, and vacate the monastery. There was a real challenge in doing this because an open space between the monastery and the Armenian positions was exposed to Turkish gunfire, and if that place was vacated, the Turks would occupy it and [consequently] threaten the northern Armenian front. Despite this, the Armenians attempted. They dug a hole in the wall of an Armenian house and a hole in the opposite wall of the monastery. They entered the monastery despite the opposition of Padre Amadeo, a monk in the monastery. Then the Armenians built barricades connecting the holes from both sides. In this way, they saved both the [people stranded in the] monastery and the Frenchman. When this news reached the colonel on the second day, and he was informed that his troops could be safely transported to the monastery, he sent twenty-five soldiers to protect it as a place belonging to foreigners. Also, in the first four or five days, the Armenians built a trench from the hospital to the college. They worked under Turkish fire all night with thousands of workers, and the French colonel sent twenty-five soldiers to protect the Americans in the hospital. And when the Armenians came into contact with the French in this way, the officers came to the Armenian quarter and appreciated the Ar-

ուղղակի կազմակերպիչը եղան այս բոլոր ձեռնարկներուն եւ ֆրանսացւոց հետ ուղղակի յարաբերութեան մէջ էին: Այս բոլորը գիտնալով այնքան ներող եւ լուռ ըլլալը զաղտնիք մը ունի, որ չենք կրնար լուծել: Քաղաքը յուսահատ է, մանաւանդ ֆրանսացւոց մեկնումէն վերջ ինքնապաշտպանութեան ոգին ջլատուած է. թշուառութիւնը եւ անօթութիւնը սարսափ կ'ազդեն: 2–3000 անտէր աղքատ կիներ, որբեր այս տառապանքին տակ ինչպէ՞ս պիտի ապրին: Օգնութիւնը անհրաժեշտ է:

Այնթապ (Տէր Ներսէս քահանայ Թավուզճեանէ, Կաթողիկոսական Փոխանորդ) – 20 Ապրիլ

Մարտ 28ին Այնթապ հասնող ֆրանսական ոյժերը Ապրիլ 1ին առտուն արեւածագէն առաջ մեկնեցան դէպի Քիլիս, իր[ենց] հետ տանելով նախապէս գտնուող ոյժերէն մէկ մասը եւ մինչեւ այն ժամանակ թուրքերուն աչքին փուշ դարձած ծանր թնդանօթները: Առտուն լուեցաւ ֆրանսացւոց մեկնումը եւ միեւնոյն ատեն շուկայի կեդրոնին մէջ հայերու զարնուիլը: Քիչ յետոյ քաղաքին երկու կողմէն, բլուրներու վրայէն Մավզէրի ձայներ լուեցան: Ասիկա ազդանշան եղաւ: Թուրք չէթէներ հայ թաղերու վրայ եկան ոչ թէ իբր թալանող խուժան, այլ իբր պատերազմիկ զինուոր, պատնէշներ շինելով, անշուշտ *մասնաւորներու* միջոցաւ եւ իրենց կռնակը ամրացնելով: Հայերը որ կը սպասէին այս յարձակումին, մեծ փողոցներու վրայ նայող պատուհանները դիրք շինած էին եւ շատ մը պատեր անմիջապէս բանալու համար պատրաստած էին, անմիջապէս այդ դիրքերը բռնեցին: Ժողովուրդը խռովութեան լուրը առնելուն պէս սկսաւ փողոցներու բերանները քարով գոցել եւ երկու ժամ յետոյ արդէն ինքնապաշտպանութեան բոլոր միջոցները ձեռք առնուած էին: Թրքական յարձակման դէմ հայերը շարունակեցին ինքզինքին պաշտպանել: Թուրքերը ամէն կողմէ միանգամայն յարձակեցան հայոց վրայ եւ իրենց զէնքերը անհամեմատ առատ է[ին] քան հայերու զէնքերը: Միակ առաւելութիւնը սա էր որ հայերը պատրաստած ունէին ձեռնառումբեր, որոնք երկու օր գիշեր ցերեկ անընդհատ շարունակուող յարձակումէն փրկեցին հայերը: Այսօր 19 օր է որ պաշարուած են հայերը: 16 օր շարունակ պատերազմեցան հայերը հերոսական քաջութեամբ եւ հայուն արժանավայել կրթութեամբ: Կռիւին 4րդ օրը արդէն թուրքերը հասկցան թէ հայոց դիրքերը անառիկ են: Ասկէ յետոյ իբր կանոնաւոր պատերազմ ցորեկները թեթեւ եւ գիշերները 2–3 ժամ շարունակ յարձակումով կ'ահաբեկէին հայերը, բայց բարեբաղդաբար միշտ ետ մղուելով: Այս 16 օրուան մէջ, առաջին երկու օրը բացառութիւն համարելով, միւս 14 օրերուն մէջ երեք անգամ ամենաասատիկ յարձակում ըրին բոլոր ճակատներէն եւ անգամ մը 8 Ապրիլի գիշերը՝ ֆրանսական բանակին վրայ եւս կրակ բացին: Կռիւի միջոցներուն Ամերիկեան Հիւանդանոցին եւ որբանոցներուն վրայ անընդհատ կրակ կը տեղացնէին: Առաջին օրը, քաղաքին հիւսիսային կողմը գտնուող լատինաց եկեղեցիին մէջ գաղղիացի զինուոր մը մնացած էր, փողոցէն փախչելով հոն ապաստանած ըլլալով: Այս զինուորը ամբողջ օրը եկեղեցին կը պաշտպանէ, սակայն փամփուշտները կը սպառին: Հայերը իրենց համրուած փամփուշտներով այս զինուորին օգնեցին: Ֆրանսացի գնդապետը, որուն հետ հայերը յարաբերութեան մէջ էին, հրահանգ տուաւ որ զինուորը այնտեղէն հայերը ազատեն եւ հոն գտնուող մարդիկը հանուին եւ վանքը պարպուի: Ասիկա ընելու համար իրական դժուարութիւն մը կար, որովհետեւ վանքի եւ հայոց դիրքերուն միջեւ բացաստան մը կար որ թրքական կրակին տակ էր, եւ եթէ այդ տեղը պարպուէր՝ թուրքերը պիտի գրաւէին այն տեղը եւ պիտի սպառնային հայոց հիւսիսային ճակատին: Հայերը ասով հանդերձ փորձ մը ըրին: Վանքի պատին դիմացը հայու մը տունէն ծակ մը բացին, դիմացի պատը եւս ծակեցին եւ հակառակ վանքը գտնուող Բատրէ Ամատեօ անուն կրօնաւորի մը ընդդիմութեան, ներս մտան, երկու ծակերը իրարու հետ միացնող երկու կողմէն պատնէշներ շինեցին եւ վանքն ու ֆրանսացին ազատեցին: Երբ երկրորդ օրը այս լուրը հաղորդեցին գնդապետին եւ իմացուցին թէ իր զինուորները ապահով կերպով կրնայ փոխադրել վանք, 25 զինուոր ղրկեց հոն, իբր օտարահպատակ տեղ մը զայն պաշտպանելու: Նոյնպէս առաջին 4–5 օրերուն մէջ հայերը Հիւանդանոցէն մինչեւ Գոլէժ թուրքերու կրակին տակ գիշերները մինչեւ լոյս հազարաւոր բանուորներով աշխատելով խրամ մը շինեցին եւ

menians' work. The colonel then began to assist by providing some bullets now and then and encouraging them.

On the sixteenth day, a French force came from the east, and a [second] force arrived from Kilis. For three days, the Armenians took a deep breath as French troops surrounded the city and periodically fought the çetes on the hills for three days. The çetes in front of the Armenian barricades still maintain their positions and fire sometimes. The commander of the troops from the east is Colonel Normand. He has 2,500 soldiers. Coming from the west is Colonel de la Breg, who has one thousand soldiers. Today, also General de Lamothe flew in with a plane. He corresponded with the district governor all day and left in the evening. The force from Kilis will leave at half past eight o'clock tonight because it is said that its only function was to bring supplies. The general advised the Armenians—the Armenian spiritual leaders and the members of the National Union—to stay strong behind their barricades, to defend themselves in the case of an attack, use bullets sparingly, and save food, assuring them that they would be delivered in the near future. He also praised the Armenians' courage, vigilance, and organizational spirit and promised to pass on his favorable impressions to General Gouraud. He also said that by this act [of aggression], the Turks have lost their case and that the Armenians have gained the right to live under French protection.

From the words of the general, it is understood that the current situation will continue. While we realized that, with all estimates done, our means of sustenance would last barely twenty days, even though in nineteen days, by order of the Central Body for Provisions that was formed by the Armenians, the victuals of all people had been combined and equal portions of food were being delivered to everybody. Food was sold to those who could pay and given free of charge to those who could not.

A population of more than fifteen thousand, primarily women and children, naturally cannot withstand famine, so Armenians need immediate help.

Sugören [Çengiler] (from the Neighborhood Council and the priest)—May 8

On May 6, two hundred armed çetes from Bursa arrived at Orhangazi and captured the local government building. This band of çetes was accompanied by mounted police, led by special officers, to steer the group. The çetes in carriages got down in front of the government building and started shooting on both sides. Fortunately, there was no loss of life. The residents were terrified. The government building was officially occupied by Milli forces, who met no resistance. Traffic has stopped, and everyone needs a passport to go from village to village.

Sending any product, wheat, barley, oats, and so on, to İstanbul by way of Yalova is prohibited. Special guards have been deployed on Yalova's roads, called Soğucak, Reşadiye, and Üst Bez, to prevent the passage of cargo. This immobility will lead to famine.

The well-known Ibo Agha from Yalova and the sheikh of Reşadiye village, the rich Alaeddin Bey of Orhangazi, were urgently summoned to Bursa. They went to Bursa yesterday. We do not know for what purpose. So far, there is no movement against Armenians, but we are unsure about tomorrow. There are already signs in this regard. A young man named Hagop Salian, arriving today in Sugören from Orhangazi, was caught. He was told: "There are deserters from military service in your village; we will come and search for them," and so on. This young man came to Sugören with a credential.

ֆրանսացի գնդապետը հիւանդանոցը գտնուող ամերիկացիները պաշտպանելու համար 25 զինուոր ղրկեց: Եւ երբ այս կերպով յարաբերութեան մտան հայերը ֆրանսացւոց հետ, սպաները եկան հայոց թաղը եւ գնահատեցին հայոց գործը: Գնդապետը ատկէ յետոյ սկսաւ օգնել քիչ քիչ փամփուշտ տալով եւ քաջալերելով:

Տասնըվեցերորդ օրը ֆրանսական ույժ մը արեւելքէն եւ ույժ մը Քիլիսի կողմէն եկան: Երեք օրէ ի վեր հայերը քիչ մը շունչ առին, որովհետեւ ֆրանսական զինուորները քաղաքը շրջապատեցին եւ երեք օրէ ի վեր բլուրներու վրայ պարբերաբար կը կռուին չէթէներու հետ: Հայ պատնէշներուն դիմացը գտնուող չէթէները տակաւին իրենց տեղերը կը մնան եւ երբեմն կրակ կ'ընեն:

Արեւելքէն եկող զինուորական ույժերու հրամատարն է Գնդապետ Նորման եւ ունի 2,500 զինուոր: Արեւմուտքէն եկողն է Գնդապետ տը լա Պրէկ եւ ունի 1000 զինուոր: Այսօր եկաւ օդանաւով նաեւ Ժէնէրալ տը լա Մօ[թ] եւ առտուընէ մինչեւ իրիկուն թղթակցեցաւ միւթեսարըֆին հետ եւ իրիկուան մօտ գնաց: Այս գիշեր ժամը 8½ին պիտի մեկնի Քիլիսէն եկող ույժը, վասնզի անիկա միայն պարէն բերելու պաշտօն ունի կ'ըսուի: Զօրավար[ը] հայերուն խորհուրդ տուած է, հայոց հոգեւոր պետին եւ Ազգային Միութեան անդամներուն, որ իրենց պատնէշներուն ետեւը ամուր մնան եւ երբ յարձակում ըլլայ՝ ինքզինքնին պաշտպանեն, փամփուշտները խնայողութեամբ գործածեն եւ կերակուրի խնայողութիւն ընեն եւ ապահով ըլլան որ մօտ օրէն պիտի ազատուին: Դրուատեց նաեւ հայոց արիութիւնը, արթնամտութիւնը, կազմակերպական ոգին եւ խոստացաւ իր առած նպաստաւոր տեղեկութիւնները հաղորդել Զօրավար Կուրօին: Նոյնպէս ըսաւ թէ թուրքերը իրենց այս արարքով կորսնցուցին իրենց դատը եւ հայերը ֆրանսական հովանաւորութեան տակ ապրելու իրաւունքը ձեռք բերին:

Զօրավարին խօսքերէն այնպէս կը հասկցուի թէ տակաւին արդի վիճակը դեռ պիտի շարունակուի, մինչ ամէն հաշիւ ընելով տեսանք որ հազիւ 20 օրուան ապրելու միջոցներ ունինք, հակառակ անոր որ 19 օրուան մէջ հայոց կողմէ կազմուած պարէնաւորման կեդրոնական մարմնին կարգադրութեամբ բոլոր ժողովուրդին ուտեստեղէնը ի մի հաւաքուած եւ ամէնուն հաւասար քանակութեամբ սնունդ տրուած է, կարողներուն՝ դրամով եւ չունեցողին ձրի տալով:

15 հազարէ աւելի ժողովուրդ մը մեծ մասամբ կիներէ եւ տղաքներէ բաղկացեալ, բնական է չի կրնար անօթութեան տոկալ, հետեւաբար անմիջական օգնութեան կը կարօտին հայերը:

Չէնկիլէր (Թաղական Խորհուրդէն եւ քահանայէն) – 8 Մայիս

6 Մայիսին Պրուսայէն 200 զինեալ չէթէներ Օրխան Ղազի գալով տեղւոյն կառավարչատունը գրաւեցին: Այս չէթէներու խումբին կ'ընկերանային հեծեալ ոստիկաններ, որոնց գլուխը կը գտնուէ[ին] մասնաւոր սպաներ՝ խումբը վարելու համար: Չէթէները, որ կառքերով էին, իջան կառավարչատան առջեւ եւ հրացաններ պարպել սկսան երկու կողմին: Բարեբաղդաբար անձի կորուստ չկայ: Բնակիչները սարսափի մատնուեցան: Կառավարչատունը պաշտօնապէս Միլլի ուժերու կողմէ գրաւուած է առանց դիմադրութեան: Երթեւեկութիւնը դադրած է եւ ամէն մարդ գիւղէ գիւղ իսկ երթալու համար պարտաւոր է անցագիր ստանալ:

Եալովայի ճամբով ոեւէ ապրանք, ցորեն, գարի, վարսակ եւայլն Կ. Պոլիս ղրկելը արգիլուեցաւ: Մասնաւոր պահապաններ դրուած են Եալովայի Սովուճագ, Րէշատիյէ եւ Վէրի Պէգ կոչուած ճամբաները եւ բեռ անցնելու թոյլ չեն տար: Այս անշարժութիւնը սով պիտի առաջ բերէ:

Եալովայէն հանրածանօթ Իպօ աղա եւ Րէշատիյէ գիւղի շէյխը Օրխան Ղազիէն մեծահարուստ Ալայէտտին պէյ ստիպողաբար Պրուսա կանչուած են եւ երէկ գացին Պրուսա, չենք գիտեր ի՞նչ նպատակով: Առ այժմ հայոց դէմ շարժում չկայ, սակայն վաղուան համար ապահով չենք: Այս մասին ալ նշաններ կան արդէն: Այսօր Օրխան Ղազիէն Չէնկիլէր ժամանող Յակոբ Սալեան անուն երիտասարդը բռնելով ըսած են «Ձեր գիւղը զինուոր[ութեն]է փախստականներ կան, պիտի գանք եւ խուզարկութիւն պիտի ընենք» եւայլն: Այս երիտասարդը *վէսիքա*յով մը եկած է Չէնկիլէր:

Adana (from Garabed Nalbandian)—May 2

The situation in Cilicia continues to be alarming. Communication between Kozan [Sis] and Adana is accomplished through a plane only. According to information received, provisions in the besieged city decreases daily. Prices are rising, and some necessary supplies have been completely consumed. Therefore, people are asking for help. The French sent three to four thousand troops to Kozan and are sending supplies. There is no news from Saimbeyli [Hacın] and no contact. Being in a much more unfavorable position, finding [in Saimbeyli] as many resources as in Kozan is impossible. Besides, the population of Saimbeyli is larger than that of Kozan, for there are more than eight to ten thousand people there. When Kozan, within a month, ended up in such an alarming situation regarding food and supplies, it is natural that the people of mountainous and rocky Saimbeyli, who receive help from nowhere, are at a graver juncture since Saimbeyli was besieged long before Kozan. In all likelihood, the people of Saimbeyli have nothing to eat. Perhaps starving is doing what the enemy wanted to do with their failed attacks until now. If it is impossible to deliver food immediately, those ten thousand Armenians will starve to death unmistakably. An appeal has been made to the French authorities in Adana, and efforts are being made [to alleviate the situation]. If there is any possibility on your part to save the Armenians of Saimbeyli from this predicament, do it; otherwise, the Armenians of Saimbeyli will inevitably share the fate of the Armenians of Maraş.

Samsun (from the Administrative Council)—April 30

The Armenians of Samsun are going through an alarming period. A week ago, several British battleships arrived, and a few hundred soldiers disembarked. They conducted a military parade in the city. Around that time, army commander Selâhattin Bey had come with his followers, but they fled to Kavak (twelve hours inland from Samsun) when the British battleships arrived. Two days later, when the battleships left, the runaways returned to the city, and they persuaded, forced, and threatened the governor, the people, and all the servicemen to join the Millis. First, these people showed signs of hesitation, then joined the Millis, and now they are obeying their orders. Censorship is established now. Two days ago, the police besieged the house of Hagop Entrigian, a blacksmith living in the Armenian neighborhood. They searched it and found about fifteen bombs left open in the cellar. Hagop remained perplexed. At the same time, they also searched the house and store of Vahan Ohanian, a local merchant, but found nothing and released him, detaining only Hagop. According to British representative Captain Tidrick's information, this search was carried out because of an Armenian letter by an Armenian named Hadji Bey from the mountains of Çarşamba, addressed to Ohanian, in which he talks about money exchanged between them, as well as bullets and Hagop's bombs. Presumably, the letter ended up in the hands of the police, who searched and found the bombs. The fact is that the letter is fabricated, and the affair is a plot by the Milli people. There are many reasons to suspect an Armenian who owes a debt to Ohanian and feels animosity with Entrigian, and therefore he wrote the letter on behalf of the police. This plot also aims to discredit Armenians in general and incite new hatred. For this reason, local Armenians are demanding an impartial investigation and want the trial to be moved to İstanbul for examination in an environment free of local Millis.

• Communication with the center is severed. Telegrams were cut off from İstanbul after its capture. The people are in fear and ready to migrate if there is no mitigation to the situation.

Ատանա (Կարապետ Նալպանտեանէ) – 2 Մայիս

Կիլիկիոյ մէջ կացութիւնը կը շարունակէ տագնապալի ըլլալ: Սիս եւ Ատանայի միջեւ միայն օդանաւով հաղորդակցութիւն կը կատարուի: Ստացուած տեղեկութեանց համաձայն, պաշարուած քաղաքին մէջ պաշարը օրէ օր կը պակսի, զիները տարապայման կը բարձրանան եւ կարգ մը անհրաժեշտ պիտոյքներ բոլորովին սպառած են: Հետեւաբար ժողովուրդը օգնութիւն կը խնդրէ: Ֆրանսացիք 3–4 հազար զինուոր ղրկեցին Սիս եւ պաշար կը ղրկեն: Հաճընէն բնաւ լուր չէ ստացուած եւ յարաբերութիւն ալ չկայ: Հաճըն գտնուելով անհամեմատ կերպով աւելի աննպաստ դիրքի մը մէջ, Սիսի չափ ալ պաշար գտնել կարելի չէ: Ցետոյ Հաճընի բնակչութիւնը թիւով աւելի շատ է քան Սիսի, վասնզի հոն կայ 8–10 հազարէ աւելի բնակչութիւն մը: Սիս երբ մէկ ամսուան մէջ ուտեստի եւ պաշարի կողմէ այսպէս տագնապի կ'ենթարկուի, բնական է որ լեռնային ու քարոտ դիրք ունեցող Հաճընի ժողովուրդը, որ ոչ մէկ տեղէն օգնութիւն կը ստանայ, աւելի մեծ տագնապի մէջ է, քանի որ Հաճըն Սիսէն շատ առաջ պաշարուած է: Ամէն հաւանական հաշիւ ցոյց կուտայ թէ Հաճընի մէջ ժողովուրդը ոչինչ ունի ուտելիք եւ սովը գուցէ կ'ընէ այն ինչ որ թշնամին իր յարձակումներով կ'ուզէր ընել եւ չկրցաւ մինչեւ հիմա: Եթէ անմիջապէս ուտելիք հասցնել կարելի չըլլայ այդ 10 հազար հայերու սովամահ ըլլալը անվրէպ է: Ատանայի մէջ ֆրանսական իշխանութեան դիմում կատարուած է եւ ջանքեր կ'ըլլան. եթէ ձեր կողմէ ոեւէ հնարաւորութիւն կայ, այս նեղ կացութենէն Հաճընի հայերը փրկելու, ըրէք, եթէ ոչ հաճընցիք ալ Մարաշի հայոց վիճակին բաղդակից պիտի ըլլան անխուսափելի կերպով:

Սամսոն (վարչական խորհուրդէն) – 30 Ապրիլ

Սամսոնի հայերը տագնապալի շրջան մը կ'անցնեն: Շաբաթ մը առաջ անգլիական քանի մը զրահաւորներ եկան եւ քանի մը 100 զինուոր ցամաք հանելով քաղաքին մէջ զինուորական անցք մը կատարեցին: Նոյն օրերը Սըվազէն հոս եկած էր Քօլ օրտու քօմանտանը Սէլահէտտին պէյ, իր հետեւորդներով, որ անգլիական զրահաւորները գալուն փախան Գավար (Սամսոնէն 12 ժամ հեռու դէպի ներս): Երկու օր վերջը, երբ զրահաւորները մեկնեցան, փախստականները դարձեալ քաղաք եկան, եւ հոս կը համոզեն, կը ստիպեն, կը սպառնան կառավարիչին, ժողովուրդին եւ բոլոր զինուորականներուն որ միանան Միլլիճիութեան: Նախ վարանելու ձեւեր առին, յետոյ միացան եւ կը հպատակին անոնց հրամանին: Հիմա գրաքննութիւն հաստատուած է: Երկու օր առաջ, ոստիկաններ կը պաշարեն հայոց թաղը [բնակող] երկաթագործ Յակոբ Էնթրիկեանի տունը եւ խուզարկելով հոն կը գտնան 15ի չափ պօմպաներ, դրուած մառանին մէջ բացը: Յակոբ ափիբերան կը մնայ: Նոյն պահուն կը խուզարկեն նաեւ տեղւոյս վաճառականներէն պ. Վահան Օհանեանի տունը եւ խանութը, բան մը չեն գտնար եւ զայն ազատ կ'արձակեն, բանտարկելով միայն Յակոբը: Անգլիացի ներկայացուցիչ Քաբիթէն Թէտրիկի տեղեկութեանց համաձայն այս խուզարկութիւնը կատարուած է Չարշամպայի լեռներէն Հաճի Պէյ անուն հայու մը հայերէն մէկ նամակէն, ուղղեալ Օհանեանի, որով իրարու ղրկուած դրամի, փամփուշտի եւ Յակոբին պօմպաներուն մասին կը խօսի եւ իբր թէ այդ նամակը ոստիկանութեան ձեռքը կ'անցնի եւ կը խուզարկեն եւ կը գտնան պօմպաները: Իրողութիւնը սա է որ նամակը շինծու է եւ գործն ալ՝ դարբնուած դաւ մը Միլլիճիներու կողմէ, եւ շատ պատճառներ կան կասկածելու հայու մը վրայ, որ պարտք ունի Օհանեանի եւ հակառակութիւն՝ Էնթրիկեանի եւ հետեւաբար ան է որ գրած է այդ նամակը ի հաշիւ ոստիկանութեան: Այդ դաւը նպատակ ունի նաեւ հայերը առ հասարակ վարկաբեկելու եւ նոր ատելութիւններ գրգռելու համար: Ասոր համար այս տեղի հայերը կը պահանջեն անաչառ քննութիւն մը եւ կ'ուզեն որ դատը Կ. Պոլիս փոխադրուի՝ տեղացի Միլլիներէ զերծ միջավայրի մը մէջ քննուելու համար:

- Կեդրոնին հետ յարաբերութիւնները խզուած են: Հեռագիրները կտրուած են Պոլսոյ հետ, Պոլսոյ գրաւումէն յետոյ: Ժողովուրդը երկիւղի մէջ է եւ պատրաստ գաղթելու՝ եթէ կացութեան մէջ ոեւէ մեղմացում չտեսնուի:

Edirne (from the vicar general)—May 11

On the morning of May 10, the religious leaders of all communities were invited to a meeting by Prefect Ali Riza Bey. At the set time, the prefect read a telegram from the prime minister conveying his imperial greetings to the people and urging all communities to live in solidarity and with love for one another, to avoid unpleasant consequences, and especially to keep the city of Edirne inseparable from the government's authority as before. In this regard, the prime minister was pointing out the essentiality for people to be engaged in their jobs and not interfere in the political practices of the government because the government is making every effort to save the homeland from imminent danger.

After reading this telegram, as usual, mufti Hilmi Effendi read a prayer for the emperor's longevity, and the people left.

Today, a record was composed and sent to the emperor in the same sense.

Büyük-Yeniköy—May 18

Millis have been in charge in the Yalova region for a week. They besieged Büyük-Yeniköy and wanted several young men, including lame Vatche, whom the villagers were forced to hand over along with several other young men. They also recruited brave young men from Sugören [Çengiler] and Ortaköy and enlisted them as volunteers.

Although the Millis always say that Armenians will never be harmed, the people do not value or trust these words.

The travel credential requirement is strictly enforced; therefore, not everyone can travel.

Konya (from the vicar general)—March 22

(A delayed report covering ten days of events from March 12 to March 22.)

Many Armenians are leaving for İstanbul, and so is Miss Cushman. The Italian and British troops are preparing to leave. The Italians will leave in the evening. On March 15, news arrived that the railway would no longer function. A complete panic ensued, and the Armenians rushed to the station to leave. Prefect Suphi Bey advised the Armenian vicar general to have the travelers return to their places, assuring him that there was no danger. The Milli newspaper *Öğüt* is published again in green color. Armenians have been given forty-eight hours to give back the houses they recovered to the confiscators. To provoke the crowd, there also arrived a rumor that the prelacy here has appealed to the Patriarchate to bring in a new Allied force. Fortunately, the mob has not been encouraged by Çelebi Effendi.

On March 17, it was reported that the train heading to Adana had been miraculously halted. The passengers were rescued ten kilometers from Ulukışla, as the Millis had destroyed the fifteen-meter-long Iron Bridge of Çiftehan.

On March 18, the small remnants of all the Allied military forces departed, and it was reported that İstanbul is occupied. A prisoners' revolt disturbed the city the same day, but peace was soon restored.

Էտիրնէ (Առաջնորդական Փոխանորդէն) – 11 Մայիս

Մայիս 10ին առաւօտուն կուսակալ Ալի Րիզա Պէյի կողմէն յատուկ հրաւիրագիրերով կուսակալին քով հրաւիրուած էին բոլոր ազգերու կրօնապետները: Որոշեալ ժամուն կուսակալը կարդաց վարչապետին մէկ հեռագիրը, որով կայսերական բարեւները կը հաղորդուէր ժողովրդեան եւ յետոյ յորդոր կ'ըլլայ բոլոր ազգաց համերաշխութեամբ իրարու հետ սիրով ապրիլ եւ տեղի չտալ անհաճոյ հետեւանքներու, մանաւանդ Էտիրնէ քաղաքին ըստ առաջնոյն կառավարութեան իշխանութենէն անբաժան պահելու մասին: Այս առթիւ վարչապետը կը մատնանշէր սա էական կէտը թէ ժողովուրդը պէտք է իր գործերովը զբաղի եւ չմիջամտէ կառավարութեան քաղաքական գործելակերպին, որովհետեւ կառավարութիւնը այդ մասին ամէն ջանք ի գործ դնելով հայրենիքը մօտալուտ վտանգէ մը ազատել կ'աշխատի:

Այս հեռագրին ընթերցումէն յետոյ ըստ սովորութեան միւֆթի Հիլմի էֆէնտիի կողմէ կայսեր արեւշատութեան համար աղօթք կարդացուեցաւ եւ ժողովուրդը մեկնեցաւ:

Այսօր նոյն իմաստով *մազպաթա* մը շինուեցաւ եւ կայսեր ղրկուեցաւ:

Մեծ-Նոր-Գիւղ – 18 Մայիս

Միլլիները շաբաթէ մը ի վեր Եալովայի շրջանին մէջ կացութեան տէր են: Անոնք Մեծ-Նոր-Գիւղը պաշարելով քանի մը երիտասարդներ ուզեցին, ի մէջ այլոց թօփալ Վաչէն, որը գիւղացիք ստիպուեցան յանձնել ուրիշ քանի մը երիտասարդներու հետ: Նոյնպէս Չէնկիլէրէն եւ Միջագիւղէն ալ քաջի անուն հանող երիտասարդներ ալ առին եւ զանոնք արձանագրեցին իբր կամաւոր իրենց շարքերուն մէջ:

Թէեւ Միլլի մարդիկը միշտ կը յայտնեն թէ հայոց երբեք վնաս չպիտի հասնի, սակայն ժողովուրդը այս խօսքերուն արժէք չի տար եւ չի վստահիր:

Ճամբորդութեան համար վէսիգայի դրութիւնը խստօրէն կը գործադրուի, այնպէս որ ամէն ոք չի կրնար ճամբորդել:

Գոնիա (Առաջնորդական փոխանորդէն) – 22 Մարտ

(Մարտ 12էն մինչեւ 22 Մարտ տասնօրեայ դէպքերու յապաղած տեղեկագիր մը:)

Բազմաթիւ հայեր կը մեկնին դէպի Կ. Պոլիս, ինչպէս նաեւ Միս Գուշման: Իտ[ալ]ական եւ անգլիական զօրքերը մեկնելու պատրաստութիւն կը տեսնեն եւ իտալացիք կը մեկնին երեկոյին: Մարտ 15ին լուր կը հասնի թէ երկաթուղին պիտի դադրի երթեւեկելէ: Անոր վրայ կատարեալ խուճապ մը առաջ կուգայ եւ հայերը կը փութան կայարան մեկնելու համար: Կուսակալ Սուպհի պէյ հայոց Առաջնորդական Փոխանորդը կը թելադրէ ճամբորդները վերադարձնել իրենց տեղերը, վստահեցնելով թէ ոեւէ վտանգ չկայ: Միլլիական «Էօյիւտ» թերթը կը հրատարակուի վերստին կանանչ գոյնով: Հայոց 48 ժամ միջոց կը տրուի իրենց վերստացած տուները վերադարձնել բռնագրաւողներուն: Հոս զրոյց կը հասնի նաեւ թէ Առաջնորդարանէն դիմում կատար[ու]ած [է] պատրիարքարան Համաձայնական նոր ուժ բերել տալու համար, ասով ամբոխը գրգռելու համար: Բարեբաղդաբար խուժանը չքաջալերուեցաւ Չէլէպի էֆէնտիէն:

Մարտ 17ին լուր առնուեցաւ որ Ատանա մեկնող կառաշարը Ուլու-Գըշլայէն 10 քիլոմեթր դէպի առաջ հրաշքով կարելի եղած է կեցնել եւ ճամբորդները փրկել, վասնզի Չիֆթէ Խանի 15 մեթր երկաթեայ կամուրջը քանդուած է Միլլիներու կողմէ:

Մարտ 18ին բոլոր Համաձայնական զինուորական ուժերու փոքր մնացորդները կը մեկնին եւ լուր կը հասնի թէ Կ. Պոլիս գրաւուած է: Նոյն օրը բանտարկեալներու կողմէ յարուցուած ըմբոստութեան մը պատճառով քաղաքը կը վրդովուի, սակայն շուտով կարելի կ'ըլլայ խաղաղութիւնը վերահաստատել:

Mosul (from Priest Krikor Der Hagopian)—February 23

It has been a year since the British entered Mosul. So far, it has not been possible to collect a single orphan from the surrounding areas, even nearby villages. The commitment to collect orphans has been expressed many times, along with the readiness to face any danger and eventuality, but the British consider it dangerous and prohibit it. Father Krikor Der Hagopian will most likely be dispatched soon to collect orphans in the vicinities of Tal Afar.

Bursa (from the vicar general)—May 10[70]

The situation in Bursa remains as it was, with the exception that the issue of traveling has become increasingly difficult for Christians and Jews alike because, according to an order issued this week, applicants appealing to the police chief for a credential were told that Christians and Jews absolutely cannot have a credential, while in their presence credentials were given to all Muslims. The primate immediately appealed to the prefect, who promised to issue credentials, provided that he personally inspected the travelers. After this promise, two or three people presented themselves and were actually given credentials; however, they were not granted permission for a voyage at sea, only to travel by land.

Tekirdağ (from the vicar general)—May 21[71]

The more the news indicates that Thrace will be[long to] Greece, the more the wrath of the Turks intensifies. The strictness started today. No pass is being issued for İstanbul. The farmers' oxen have been seized for the needs of the army. The officers are sending their families to İstanbul: preparation is probably underway for resistance. This is understood, given the traffic ban, the seizure of animals, and the mobilization of troops. The people are as frightened again in a seaside town like Tekirdağ as they are in the more inland districts: Malkara and Çorlu.

Մուսուլ (Տէր Գրիգոր քահանայ Տէր Յակոբեանէ) – 23 Փետրուար

Մէկ տարի է որ անգլիացիք մտան Մուսուլ: Մինչեւ հիմա ոչ մէկ որբ կարելի եղաւ շրջականերէն հաւաքել, նոյնիսկ մերձակայ գիւղերէն: Քանի անգամներ յանձնառութիւն յայտնուած է ամէն վտանգի ու պատասխանատուութեան առջեւ պատրաստ ըլլալու պայմանով որբերը հաւաքել, սակայն անգլիացիք վտանգաւոր կը համարեն եւ չեն թողուր: Հաւանական է որ Տէր Գրիգոր քահանայ Տէր Յակոբեան մօտերս ղրկուի Թալաֆարի կողմերը որբեր հաւաքելու համար:

Պրուսա (Առաջնորդական Փոխանորդէն) – 10 Մայիս

Պրուսայի կացութիւնը ըստ առաջնոյն կը շարունակէ, միայն թէ ճամբորդներու երթեւեկութեան խնդիրը հետզհետէ ծանր հանգամանք առնել սկսած է՝ հանդէպ քրիստոնէից եւ հրէից, քանի որ այս շաբթու տրուած հրամանի մը համաձայն, վէսիգա առնելու համար *Բօլիս Միւտիրի*յին դիմողներուն բացարձակ կերպով ըսուած է թէ քրիստոնեաներու եւ հրեաներու կարելի չէ *վէսիգա* տրուիլ, ու իրենց ներկայութեանը իսլամներու բոլորին ալ տրուած է: Ասոր վրայ անմիջապէս կուսակալին դիմում կ'ընէ Առաջնորդը եւ ասիկա կը խոստանայ վէսիգաներ տալ, պայմանով որ ինքն անձամբ ստուգէ ճամբորդողները: 2–3 հոգի այս խոստումէն յետոյ կը ներկայանան եւ իրապէս անոնց կը տրուին *վէսիգա*ներ, առանց նաւարկութեան հրամանի, միայն ցամաքի վրայ ճամբորդելու պայմանով:

Ռօտոսթօ (Առաջնորդական Փոխանորդէն) – 21 Մայիս

Որքան Թրակիան Յունաստան ըլլալու լուրերը կը հաստատուին, նոյնքան թուրքերու զայրացումը կը սաստկանայ: Այսօրուընէ սկսաւ խստութիւնը. Պոլսոյ համար անցագիր չի տրուիր. բանակին պէտքերուն համար երկրագործներու եզները կը գրաւուին. սպաները իրենց ընտանիքները Պօլիս կը ղրկեն. դիմադրելու պատրաստութիւն կը տեսնուի հաւանօրէն, ինչպէս կը հասկցուի երթեւեկի արգելքէն, կենդանիներու գրաւումէն, զօրահաւաքութենէն: Ժողովուրդը կրկին սարսափի մատնուած է, որքան Ռոտոսթոյի պէս ծովեզերեայ քաղաքի մը մէջ, նոյնքան եւ աւելին ներքին գաւառներու մէջ՝ Մալկարա եւ Չորլու:

[Insecurity] Notebook Number 11
April–June 1920

Dörtyol (from the National Union)—April 16[72]

To join their families who had been relocated to Adana, fourteen people native of Akbez set out toward Toprakkale on April 12 in two Armenian coachmen's carriages. With half an hour left to Erzin, twenty-seven armed Turks attacked the carriages around the village of Başlamış. Two Armenians fled: one of them was killed, and the other, who sheltered in the bushes, managed to take refuge in the city the next day. He reported that the other fourteen Armenians had been tied with a rope and taken farther away, and then sixteen gunshots were heard. The incident has been reported to the authorities, but contrary to assurances that the perpetrators would be prosecuted, neither the perpetrators nor any traces of the missing Armenians have been found.

Yesterday (April 15), of the sixty French soldiers in the barracks, about forty (Senegalese) allegedly rebelled against their French commander and entered the Armenian quarters of the village of Özerli with their weapons, where they beat several Armenians and wanted to perform immoral acts on women. The people panicked and took refuge in the city. The local French commander and the barracks commander went to the site. They managed to restrain the soldiers and take them to the barracks. Precisely two hours after this incident, eight or ten of these Senegalese soldiers, this time armed only with their bayonets, went to threaten the girls' school for the same purpose. Another panic in the city erupted, and the markets were closed instantly. The French managed once again to prevent the bloodshed with incredible difficulty. The French authorities responded to the appeal to avoid such incidents—which have happened before as well—saying that measures will be taken.

• The siege around Dörtyol is getting tighter. Along with the abovementioned cases of internal insecurity, hunger has also left people anxious. The Turks of the nearby villages have retreated and are concentrated in their mountainous areas and Turkish-populated places; therefore, nothing associated with food enters Dörtyol.

It is impossible for an Armenian to leave the city because he will be killed immediately. The French government had not been assisting the needy locals already, and now half of the migrants also are deprived under a new order. It is said that the benefits that have been cut from them would be, allegedly, given to those Armenians who are forced to migrate to Adana from Akbez, Düziçi [Haruniye], and elsewhere.

Now, unless help for local Armenians arrives before the new harvest, they will starve to death.

İstanbul (from Siroun Serovpé Adalian)—May 25[73]

On May 10, Siroun S. Adalian, an Armenian native of Sugören [Çengiler], traveled from Sugören to İstanbul to see her mother. As soon as she set foot on land, she was stripped naked and searched, looking for instructions or letters sent from İstanbul. The villages of Sugören, İznik, Büyük-Yeniköy, Yeni-sölöz, and their vicinities have been entirely surrounded by çetes. Eight days ago, Yeghishé Dobroyan and Khachig Dobroyan of Sugören, along with two other young Armenians, went to İznik to bring flour. Because of the financial documents they were carrying, they were thrown into the lake and suffocated, as has been testified by the villagers of İznik. For this reason, no one dares to leave the villages and transport wheat, which puts the people at risk of starvation once their wheat is consumed within

[Անապահովութեան] Տեառ Թիւ 11
1920 Ապրիլ – Յունիս

Տէօրթ-Եօլ (Ազգային Միութենէն) – 16 Ապրիլ

Իրենց Ատանա փոխադրուած ընտանիքներուն միանալու համար Տէօրթ-Եօլ գտնուող 14 էքպէզցիներ երկու հայ կառապաններու կառքերով Ապրիլ 12ին դէպի Թօփրագ Գալէ ճամբայ կ'ելլեն: Էրզինի ½ ժամ մնացած՝ Պաշլամըշլը գիւղին միջեւ 27 զինեալ թուրքեր կը յարձակին կառքերուն վրայ: Երկու հայեր փախուստի կը դիմեն, որոնցմէ մէկը կը սպաննուի, իսկ միւսը թուփերուն մէջ պահուըտելով կը յաջողի հետեւեալ օրը ապաստանիլ քաղաք, եւ կը պատմէ թէ մնացեալ 14 հայերը չուանով մը կապելէ վերջ կը տանին աւելի առաջ եւ յետոյ կը լսուի հրացանի 16 հարուած: Եղելութիւնը հաղորդուած է իշխանութեանց, սակայն հակառակ տրուած հաւաստիքներուն թէ ոճրագործները կը հետապնդուին, ո՛չ ոճրագործները գտնուած են եւ ոչ ալ անհետացած հայոց հետքը գտնուած է:

- Երէկ (Ապրիլ 15) զօրանոցի մէջ գտնուող ֆրանսական 60 զինուորներէն մօտաւորապէս 40 հատը (սենեկալցի) իբր թէ ընդվզելով իրենց ֆրանսացի հրամանատարին դէմ, իրենց սեփական զէնքերով կը մտնեն Էօզէրլի գիւղի հայ թաղերը, ուր քանի մը հայեր ծեծելէ վերջ կիներու վրայ անբարոյական արարքներ գործել կ'ուզեն: Ժողովուրդը խուճապի մատնուած քաղաք ապաստանեցաւ: Տեղւոյս ֆրանսացի կառավարիչը եւ զօրանոցի հրամատարը դէպքին վայրը երթալով յաջողեցան զսպել եւ զօրանոց տանիլ զինուորները: Այս դէպքէն ճիշդ 2 ժամ վերջ, այս սենեկալցի զինուորներէն 8–10 հատը, այս անգամ անզէն միայն իրենց սուիններով, միեւնոյն նպատակով կ'երթան սպառնալ աղջկանց վարժարանին: Նորէն տեղի ունեցաւ մեծ խուճապ մը քաղաքիս մէջ, շուկաները գոցուեցան անմիջապէս: Ֆրանսացիք այս անգամ ալ մեծ դժուարութեամբ կրցան առաջքն առնել արիւնահեղութեան: Ֆրանսական իշխանութեանց մօտ նման դէպքերու,- որոնք առաջին անգամ չէ որ կը պատահին,- կրկնութեան տեղի չտրուելու համար եղած դիմումին պատասխանուած է թէ միջոցներ ձեռք պիտի առնուին:

- Տէօրթ-Եօլի շուրջը գոյութիւն ունեցող պաշարումը աւելի կը սեղմուի: Ներքին անապահովութեան վերոյիշեալ դէպքերուն հետ անօթութիւնն ալ մտատանջութեան մէջ ձգած է ժողովուրդը: Մօտակայ գիւղերու թուրքերը քաշուելով կեդրոնացած են իրենց լեռնային վայրերը եւ թրքաշատ տեղերը, որով ուտեստի վերաբերեալ ոեւէ բան մը չի մտներ Տէօրթ-Եօլ:

Քաղաքէն դուրս ելլել անկարելի է հայու մը համար, որովհետեւ անմիջապէս կը սպաննուի: Ֆրանսական կառավարութիւնը տեղացի կարօտեալներուն արդէն նպաստ չէր տար, այժմ գաղթականներուն ալ կէսը զրկուեցաւ նոր կարգադրութեան մը համաձայն: Կ'ըսուի թէ անոնցմէ կտրուած նպաստը պիտի տրուի եղեր Էքպէզէն, Հարունիյէէն եւ ուրիշ զանազան տեղերէ Ատանա գաղթել տրուող հայերուն:

Արդ, եթէ մինչեւ նոր հունձք օգնութիւն մը չըլլայ տեղւոյս հայութեան, սովամահ պիտի մեռնին:

Կ. Պոլիս (Միրուն Սերովբէ Ատալեանէ) – 25 Մայիս

Միրուն Ս. Ատալեան, բնիկ չէնկիլէրցի հայը, Մայիս 10ին Կ. Պոլիսէն Չէնկիլէր կ'երթայ իր մայրը տեսնալու համար: Հազիւ թէ ցամաք ոտք կոխած, զինքը մերկացնելով վրան կը խուզարկեն եւ իր վրայ կը փնտռեն Կ. Պոլիսէն բերուած հրահանգ կամ նամակ: Գիւղերէն Չէնկիլէր, Իզնիկի Մեծ-Նոր-Գիւղը, Սէօլէօզ եւ շրջակաները ամբողջութեամբ չէթէներու կողմէ պաշարուած են: Անկէ 8 օր առաջ չէնկիլէրցի Եղիշէ Տօպրօեան եւ Խաչիկ Տօպրօեան, ուրիշ երկու հայ երիտասարդներու հետ, Իզնիկ գացած էին ալիւր բերելու: Ասոնց վրայէն հաշուեթուղթեր գտնուած ըլլալով, անոնք լիճը նետուած և խեղդամահ եղած են, ինչպէս կը վկայեն Իզնիկի գիւղացիները: Այս պատճառով ոչ ոք կը համարձակի գիւղերէն դուրս ելլել եւ ցորեն փոխադրել, որով ժողովուրդը մէկ քանի օր

a few more days.

• On May 22, the villages were instructed to have the priest and officials go to Orhangazi, where the governor-general of Bursa also had just arrived. The governor-general, who was there with many military men, said in his speech that if any Armenian or Turkish person declined to give his life, property, and existence to the Milli [movement], he would be killed. Hinting at the Armenians, he said that no matter their feelings, their sympathy for the British would not save them because they are subjects of the Turkish government, which can do whatever it wants if the Armenians refuse to join them [the Millis]. Unfortunately, contrary to the assurances and appeals made, the governor-general's words have been put into action. Millis are seizing mules, horses, and oxen from the villages, demanding money, and asking for soldiers. Given these conditions, one can imagine the degree of Armenians' disquietness.

Gaziantep [Ayntab] (from the National Union)—April 28

On April 16, important French auxiliary forces arrived in Gaziantep under the command of Colonel Normand and Colonel Debieuvre. In this circumstance, the Armenians breathed a sigh of relief, thinking that they had finally escaped the nightmare of annihilation, but unfortunately, they were disappointed again. The French laid siege to the city, and after partially bombing some Turkish houses lightly, acting upon the assumption that çetes were sheltered there, they again took up the position of a spectator, and the Turks, encouraged by this, prepared for a longer resistance. General de Lamothe also flew to Gaziantep and promised to help the Armenians with provisions, but he refused to give them weapons, saying that they had no extra weapons to spare.

On April 28, a significant portion of the French forces withdrew, again exposing the Armenians to despair. Now, the Armenians of Gaziantep, after a month of desperate fighting, are where they started at the beginning of the incident, even though a large number of French forces came and went. Now, the provisions the Armenians have will barely suffice for fifteen days to [be able to] continue the struggle. Provisions were received from Kilis twice within a month, but they are barely enough for four or five days. Henceforth, we very much doubt that we will be able to get help from outside. Help is needed to avoid starvation.

Tekirdağ (from the locum tenens)—May 26

The situation in Tekirdağ and the surrounding areas has become extremely dangerous. Cafer Tayyar Bey has started acting like a dictator. A few days ago, the Turks held a meeting and decided to give neither money nor troops, but today they are terrified because Cafer Tayyar has ordered their arrest and severe punishment. The mobilization started today. The city is almost deserted. Everyone is terrified. Cafer Tayyar Bey is now in Malkara; some say he will come to Tekirdağ and collect money from Christians and Jews. There is also a rumor that he will disperse the Christians to villages three hours away from the city. If the Greeks begin their occupation from the sea during the siege, he intends to burn the whole city. Again,he warns with a command that anyone who disobeys his order or makes a remark or complaint about him will be sentenced to death. The people are going through very difficult times. Dangerous days appear. If an armored cruiser is sent, at least it may be possible to save the city of Tekirdağ from imminent danger.

Adana (from the delegates of Saimbeyli [Hacın]: Principal of the school Shmavon Posdoyan and Reverend H. Khachadourian)—April 30

Looking at the information received indirectly, Saimbeyli is now under direct fire from the enemy and

բաւելու իր ցորենին սպառումէն վերջ անօթութեան ենթարկուելու վտանգին պիտի մատնուի:

- Մայիս 22ին գիւղերը հրահանգ եկած էր, որպէսզի քահանան եւ պաշտօնական անձեր Օրխան Ղազի երթան, ուր ժամանած էր նաեւ Պրուսայի վալին: Հոն շատ մը զինուորականներու հետ գտնուող վալին ճառ մը խօսելով, ըսաւ թէ եթէ հայ կամ թուրք ոեւէ մէկը իր կեանքը, ինչքը եւ գոյութիւնը չտրամադրէ Միլլիին, այդպիսիները պիտի սպաննուին: Հայերու ակնարկելով ըսած է թէ ինչ որ ալ ըլլան իրենց զգացումները, չեն կրնար փրկուիլ անգլիացիներուն համակրութիւնով եւ ենթակայ են թրքական իշխանութեան, որ ուզածը պիտի ընէ, եթէ հայերը չմիանան իրենց: Դժբաղդաբար հակառակ տրուած հաւաստիքներու եւ դիմումներու՝ խօսքէն գործի անցուած է: Գիւղերէն ջորի, ձի, եզ կը գրաւեն, դրամ կը պահանջեն, զինուոր կ'ուզեն: Այս պայմաններուն մէջ կրնայ երեւակայուիլ թէ հայերը որ աստիճան տագնապի մատնուած են:

Այնթապ (Ազգային Միութենէն) – 28 Ապրիլ

Ապրիլ 16ին Այնթապ ժամանեցին ֆրանսական կարեւոր օգնական ուժեր Գօլոնէլ Նորմանի եւ Գօլոնէլ տը Պիէօվրի հրամանատարութեամբ: Հայերը այս պարագային քիչ մը ազատ շունչ առին, կարծելով թէ բնաջնջումի մղձաւանջէն վերջապէս ազատած են, բայց դժբաղդաբար կրկին յուսախաբ եղան: Ֆրանսացիք պաշարելով քաղաքը եւ թեթեւօրէն մասնակի ռմբակոծելով թրքական կարգ մը տուներ,- ուր չէթէներ ապաստանած կ'ենթադրէին,- նորէն հանդիսատեսի դիրք առին եւ թուրքերը ասկէ քաջալերուած պատրաստուեցան աւելի երկար դիմադրութեան մը համար: Զօրավար Տըլամօթն եւս օդանաւով Այնթապ եկաւ եւ հայոց խոստացաւ իրենց պարենաւորման նպաստել, սակայն զէնք տալ զլացաւ, պատասխանելով թէ աւելորդ զէնք չունին:

28 Ապրիլին, ֆրանսական ուժերէն կարեւոր մաս մը քաշուեցաւ, կրկին յուսահատութեան մատնելով հայերը: Հիմա Այնթապի հայերը մէկ ամսուան յուսահատ կռիւէ մը յետոյ կը գտնուին հոն՝ ուրկէ մեկնած էին դէպքին սկիզբը, հակառակ անոր որ ֆրանսական մեծ ուժեր եկան ու գացին: Հայոց իրենց ունեցած պարէնին մեծ մասը [*sic*] եւ հիմա հազիւ 15 օրուան պաշար ունին շարունակելու համար պայքարը: Մէկ ամսուան միջոցին Քիլիսէն երկու անգամ պաշար ստացուած է, սակայն ասիկա հազիւ 4–5 օրուան կը բաւէ: Ասկէ յետոյ շատ կը կասկածինք թէ պիտի կարենանք դուրսէն օգնութիւն ստանալ: Օգնութիւն մը անհրաժեշտ է անօթութենէ չմեռնելու համար:

Ռօտոսթօ (Առաջնորդական Տեղապահէն) – 26 Մայիս

Ռօտոսթոյի եւ շրջակայից վիճակը խիստ վտանգալից եղած է: Ճաֆէր Թայեար պէյ սկսած է իբր թիկնապահ գործել: Մի քանի օր առաջ թուրքերը ժողով մը ըրին եւ որոշեցին ոչ դրամ եւ ոչ ալ զօրք տալ, սակայն այսօր սարսափած են, վասնզի Ճաֆէր Թայեար անոնց ձերբակալման հրաման եւ խիստ պատիժի ենթարկուելու հրահանգ տուած է: Այսօր զօրահաւաքութեան սկսան: Քաղաքը գրեթէ ամայացած է: Ամէն ոք ահ ու սարսափի մատնուած է: Ճաֆէր Թայեար պէյ այժմ Մալկարա կը գտնուի, ոմանք կ'ըսեն թէ Ռօտոսթօ պիտի գայ եւ քրիստոնեաներէն եւ հրեաներէն դրամ պիտի հաւաքէ: Տարաձայնութիւն մըն ալ կայ թէ քրիստոնեայ ժողովուրդը քաղաքէն երեք ժամ դուրս գիւղերը պիտի ցրուէ: Եթէ գրաւման ժամանակ յոյները ծովու կողմէն գրաւման սկսին, ամբողջ քաղաքը այրելու մտադրութիւնը յայտնած է եւ կրկին հրամանով կ'ազդարարէ որ ամէն ոք որ իր հրամանին չանսայ եւ իր մասին դիտողութիւն մը կամ բողոք մը ընէ, մահուան պիտի դատապարտուի: Ժողովուրդը շատ ծանր վայրկեաններ կ'անցնէ: Վտանգի օրեր կ'երեւան: Եթէ զրահաւոր մը ղրկուի, թերեւս կարելի ըլլայ ազատել գէթ Ռօտոսթօ քաղաքը վերահաս վտանգէ:

Ատանա (Հաճընի պատուիրակներէն. տնօրէն վարժարանաց՝ Շմաւոն Փոստոյեան, Վերապատուելի Յ. Խաչատուրեան) – 30 Ապրիլ

Կողմնակի միջոցներով ստացած տեղեկութիւններու նայելով, Հաճընը այլեւս թշնամիին

the siege line has become very tight. The enemy is barely fifteen minutes away from all sides. There is no fear if the bullets don't run out. Probably they [the Armenians] have narrowed their sphere of self-defense to save bullets. No matter what, their ammunition must be near running out by now. They had 170,000 rounds of ammunition for a total of nine thousand rifles, of which the French government had provided only 145,000.

Bandırma (from the primate)—June 1

Since April 19, the city and its environs have been under the control and governance of Milli forces. Initially, postal communications with İstanbul were severed, and travel by steamship was strictly forbidden. About ten days ago, after they allowed the export of goods to İstanbul, the steamers resumed their traffic, but without the transportation of passengers. A few days ago, passenger traffic resumed, but the price of steamer tickets doubled to benefit the Milli organization. The same price hike has occurred for all goods and animals exported and imported. There have been three incidents involving Armenians since the capture of Bandırma and the region by Milli forces.

A. On Thursday, April 22, Haroutyun Jingeozian of Bandırma (a blacksmith) bought eight or ten kilos of gunpowder to sell for a profit from a Turkish soldier. He kept it in his shop near the hearth. The following morning, a spark ignited the gunpowder. It caused an explosion that shook the market and its surroundings. Haroutyun Jingeozian suffered injuries to his face and hands and was taken home. He is still under treatment by doctors. The lieutenant governor, government functionaries, and Milli representatives immediately rushed to the explosion scene to give instructions about containing the fire, and Armenian firefighters were able to extinguish the blaze. Fortunately, it has been possible to persuade [the authorities] to avoid the attribution of political color to the case, and thus the issue is closed.

B. At the time of the arrival of Milli forces in Bandırma, the Commandership of Discipline and Education, first, through town criers and then through notices sent to the Armenian and Greek prelacies, warned the Muslim and Christian peoples to 1. Not hide in their houses the followers of Anzavur Ahmed Bey, and if there are [already followers] in hiding, to inform the police commander; 2. Immediately deliver the weapons and property found or handed over to private individuals by Anzavur Ahmed Bey and his followers; 3. Within three days, hand over to the same commandership weapons and ammunition if private individuals have any.

On Saturday, May 1, one of the followers of Anzavur Ahmed Bey, who had been hiding in the house of a Greek, revealed during an interrogation after he was captured that he had sold all his weapons on April 19 to Krikor H. Terlemezian, after which Krikor was arrested along with the Greek who was hiding the Turk.

After the interrogation, it was decided to take the Armenian and the Greek to Balıkesir to give them the punishment they deserved, but by employing every possible measure, the Armenian was successfully saved, while the Greek was taken to Balıkesir the next day, where he was sentenced to death. All the weapons belonging to the Turk found with Krikor H. Terlemezian were handed over to the government.

C. About fifteen days ago, a young man named Mgrdich Baghdasar Badeyan, a native of Balıkesir, was working in a mill three hours away from Balıkesir. A few armed Turks approached him and demanded a large sum of money, which he could not afford to pay, so they left him with serious injuries. The unfortunate young man died of his wounds the following day. The murderers escaped and have not been arrested yet.

կրակին ուղղակի ազդեցութեան տակ է եւ պաշարման գիծը չափազանց նեղցած է: Ամէն կողմէն 15 վայրկեան հազիւ հեռաւորութիւն ունի թշնամին: Եթէ փամփուշտնին չսպառի, երկիւղ չկայ: Հաւանօրէն փամփուշտի խնայողութեան համար նեղցուցած են ինքնապաշտպանութեան շրջանակը: Ինչ որ ալ ըլլայ, ռազմամթերքնին այլեւս սպառելու մօտ պէտք է եղած ըլլայ: Իրենց ունեցածը ընդամէնը 9000 հրացանի վրայ 170,000 փամփուշտ էր, որուն 145,000ը միայն ֆրանսական կառավարութիւնը տուած է:

Պանտրմա (Առաջնորդէն) – 1 Յունիս

Ապրիլ 19էն ի վեր քաղաքս եւ իր շրջանը Միլլի ուժերու իշխանութեան տակ գտնուելով կը կառավարուի նոյն ուժերու կողմէ: Նախ Պոլսոյ հետ թղթատարական յարաբերութիւնները խզուած եւ շոգենաւի երթեւեկը արգիլուած էր բացարձակապէս: Թուականէս 10 օր առաջ քաղաքէս Պոլիս ապրանքի արտածութիւնը թոյլատրուելով շոգենաւերը կ'երթեւեկէին առանց ճամբորդ տանիլ բերելու: Քանի մը օր առաջ ճամբորդներու երթեւեկութիւնն ալ արտօնուեցաւ շոգենաւի տոմսակներու գինը կրկնապատկուելով՝ ի նպաստ Միլլի կազմակերպութեան: Միեւնոյն յաւելումը՝ արտածուած եւ ներածուած ամէն ապրանքի եւ կենդանիի համար: Միլլի ուժերու Պանտրմա եւ շրջանը գրաւելէն ի վեր երեք դէպքեր պատահած [են] հայոց վերաբերեալ:

Ա. Պանտրմացի Յարութիւն Ճինկէօզեան (դարբին) Ապրիլ 22 հինգշաբթի օր թուրք զինուորէ մը 8–10 քիլոյի չափ վառօդ կը գնէ ծախելով շահ մը ձեռք բերելու նպատակով եւ կը պահէ իր խանութին մէջ, օճախին մօտ: Հետեւեալ առաւօտ կրակի կայծէ մը վառօդը կրակ կ'առնէ եւ շուկան ու շրջակայքը դղրդելու աստիճան պայթում մը առաջ կը բերէ: Յարութիւն Ճինկէօզեան դէմքէն եւ ձեռքերէն վիրաւորուելով տուն կը փոխադրուի, ուր ցայսօր կը դարմանուի բժիշկներու կողմէ: Գայմագամը, կառավարական պաշտօնեաները եւ Միլլի ներկայացուցիչները անմիջապէս պայթումի վայրը փութալով յառաջ եկած հրդեհներ[ուն] առաջքը առնուելու հրահանգներ տուին եւ հայ ջրհանկիրները յաջողեցան հրդեհը մարել: Բարեբաղդաբար կարելի եղած է համոզել որ գործին [չտրուի] քաղաքական գոյն եւ այսպէսով խնդիրը փակուեցաւ:

Բ.- Միլլի ուժը Պանտրմա հասնելու ատեն նախապէս մունետիկներու միջոցով եւ յետոյ հայոց եւ յունաց Առաջնորդարանները *միւրէթթէպիյէ եւ թէէտիպիյէ գօմանտան*ութեան կողմէ ղրկուած զեկուցագրերով ազդարարուեցաւ իսլամ եւ քրիստոնեայ ժողովուրդին որպէսզի 1. Ա[նզ]աւուր Ահմէտ պէյի հետեւորդները տուներու մէջ չպահեն եւ եթէ կան պահուըտածներ, իմացնեն *ինզըպաթ գօմանտան*ին: 2. Անզաւուր Ահմէտ պէյի եւ հետեւորդներուն կողմէ մասնաւորներու մօտ գտնուած կամ յանձնուած զէնքերը եւ գոյքերը յանձնել անմիջապէս: 3. Պատերազմական զէնքեր եւ իրեղէններ, եթէ կան մասնաւորներու մօտ, յանձնել նոյն *գօմանտան*ութեան երեք օրուան մէջ:

Մայիս 1 շաբաթ օր Անզաւուր Ահմէտ պէյի հետեւորդներէն մէկը -յոյնի մը տուն պահուած- ձերբակալուելով հարցաքննուելու ատեն իր բոլոր զէնքերը Ապրիլ 19ին տեղւոյս ազգայիններէն սեղանաւոր Գրիգոր Հ. Թէրլէմէզեանի ծախած ըլլալը կը յայտնէ, որուն վրայ յիշեալը կը ձերբա-կալուի թուրքը պահող յոյնին հետ:

Հարցաքննութենէ վերջ՝ հայը եւ յոյնը Պալըքէսիր տանելու եւ հոն արժանի պատիժը տրուելու որոշումին վրայ ամէն հնարաւոր միջոց ի գործ դնելով կարելի եղած է ազատել հայը, մինչ յոյնը հետեւեալ օրը տարուած է Պալըքէսիր, ուր մահուամբ պատժուած է: Գրիգոր Հ. Թէրլէմէզեանի մօտ գտնուած թուրքին բոլոր զէնքերը յանձնուեցան կառավարութեան:

Գ.- Թուականէս մօտաւորապէս 15 օր առաջ բնիկ պալըքէսիրցի Մկրտիչ Պաղտասար Պատէ-եան անուն երիտասարդը Պալըքէսիրէն 3 ժամ հեռու ջաղացքի մէջ աշխատելու ատեն քանի մը թուրքեր զէն ի ձեռին կը ներկայանան եւ մահու սպառնալիքով մեծկակ գումար մը կը պահանջեն իրմէ, որը չկրնալով տալ, ծանրապէս վիրաւորելով կը հեռանան: Խեղճ երիտասարդը ստացած վէր-քերէն կը մեռնի յաջորդ օրն իսկ, իսկ մարդասպանները խոյս կու տան եւ ցարդ չեն ձերբակալուած:

Bandırma (from the primate)—June 2

Until recently, Milli forces in Bandırma and the region only recruited Muslims, but according to reports from Balıkesir and Mihaliç (Karacabey) received in recent days, there are plans to recruit soldiers from the local Christian element as well.

Karnig Divriglian of Balıkesir went to the Milli headquarters, as usual, to obtain a credential to travel with last Sunday's mail carrier from Balıkesir to Bandırma and thence to İstanbul. He was told that he could not travel anywhere outside Balıkesir because he is of military service age.

About ten days ago, the Milli military authorities in Karacabey invited the Greek and Armenian priests and neighborhood representatives to their headquarters and demanded the list of those born in 1898. There were seventeen Greeks and no Armenians of that age. The Greeks of the designated age were drafted and sent to Bursa to serve in the military. Considering these partial cases of conscription as a sign of a future general call for conscription, the Armenian youth of military age living here and in the surrounding areas have been leaving for İstanbul since yesterday. The conscription of Christians has not yet begun in Bandırma.

Trabzon (from the vicar general)—May 28

The political situation here and in the environs is stable. The Turkish treaty made an unpleasant impression on the Turks; some are astonished, and others are furious. The general opinion is that the treaty is unacceptable, but they do not feel they are able to fight. Desertions have already begun among the soldiers in Erzurum. Conscription notices remained almost ignored and have even led to rebellion. Military authorities arrested two doctors who did not want to obey the order to join the army. They had even spoken harshly about the stupidity of the Kemalists.

The prefect, though a Milli, is a farsighted, strong, and influential leader. He is extremely cunning, and so far, he has managed to maintain a seeming calm. The only troublesome circumstance is that the prefect has no influence over the military. He is gaining time by lulling the military.

Mr. Lépissier, the French representative, also agrees.

He said to the Armenian locum tenens: "Yes, there is calm so far in appearance, but maybe this is purposeful. They will probably say tomorrow, 'We have made every effort to maintain peace, but we were unable to suppress the outburst of hurt feelings against our death sentence.'"

Indeed, Mr. Lépissier seems concerned and pessimistically observes the events in the Caucasus.

• Three days ago, a young Armenian man, a native of Trabzon, came here from Harput to inform us that the political situation in Harput is similar to that of Trabzon for now. There has been no initiative for mobilization there either. The same situation prevails in Kemaliye [Egin].

Adana (from the Compatriotic Union of Saimbeyli [Hacın])—May 15

Saimbeyli has been besieged for nine weeks. There is no hope of salvation because all attempts have been in vain. The alarming situation is especially frightening when one thinks about the lack of provision.

Mersin (from the National Union)—June 7[74]

On May 30, in Beirut, General Gouraud, the high commissioner of Syria and Cilicia, and Mustafa

Պանտրմա (Առաջնորդէն) – 2 Յունիս

Պանտրմայի եւ շրջանի Միլլի ուժերը մինչեւ վերջին օրերս կը զինուորագրէին միայն իսլամնե-րը, սակայն քանի մը օրէ ի վեր Պալըքէսիրէ եւ Միխալըճէ (Գարաճա Պէյ) առնուած լուրերու համաձայն, տեղւոյն քրիստոնեայ տարրէն ալ զինուոր առնելու ձեռնարկեր են:

Վերջին Կիրակիի թղթաբերով Պալըքէսիրէ Պանտըրմա եւ անկէ Պոլիս երթալու համար վէսիգա առնելու նպատակաւ պալըքէսիրցի Գառնիկ Տիվրիկլեան Միլլի պաշտօնատունը կը դիմէ ըստ սովորութեան, որուն պատասխան կը տրուի թէ՝ զինուորական տարիքի մէջ ըլլալուն չի կրնար Պալըքէսիրէն այլուր ճամբորդել:

Միխալըճի Միլլի զինուորական իշխանութիւնը շուրջ 10 օր առաջ ինչպէս յունաց նոյնպէս եւ հայոց քահանան եւ մխթարը պաշտօնատուն հրաւիրելով 314ի [=1898ի] ծնունդներու ցուցակը կը պահանջէ. յոյներէն 17 անձ կը գտնուի, իսկ հայերէն նոյն տարիքը ունեցող ոչ ոք: Որոշուած տարիքն ունեցող յոյները զինուորագրուելով կը ղրկուին Պրուսա, զինուորական ծառայութեան ենթար-կուելու համար: Զօրակոչի այս մասնակի դէպքերը յառաջիկայի համար ընդհանուր զօրակոչի յայտարարութեան նախանշաններ համարելով, տեղւոյս եւ շրջակայից զինուորական տարիքի մէջ գտնուող հայ երիտասարդութիւնը երէկուընէ սկսեալ կը մեկնի քաղաքէս դէպի Կ. Պոլիս: Պանտրմայի մէջ դեռ չէ սկսած քրիստոնէից զինուորագրութիւնը:

Տրապիզոն (Առաջնորդական Փոխանորդէն) – 28 Մայիս

Քաղաքական կացութիւնը այստեղ եւ շրջակայքը՝ կայուն է: Թրքական դաշնագիրը անախորժ տպաւորութիւն ըրած է թրքաց վրայ, որոնցմէ ոմանք ապշութեան եւ ուրիշներ կատաղութեան մատնուած են: Ընդհանուր կարծիքը սա է թէ դաշնագիրը անընդունելի է, սակայն կռուելու կարո-ղութիւն չեն զգար իրենց մէջ: Դասալքութիւնը արդէն ծայր տալ սկսած է Էրզրում գտնուող զինուոր-ներու մէջ: Զօրակոչը գրեթէ անլսելի մնաց եւ նոյնիսկ ըմբոստացումի տեղի տուաւ: Զինուորական իշխանութիւնը ձերբակալեց երկու բժիշկներ՝ որոնք չէին ուզեր հնազանդիլ բանակին մէջ մտնելու հրամանին: Անոնք ծանր խօսքեր ըրած էին նոյնիսկ Քեմալականներու յիմարութիւններու հասցէին:

Կուսակալը, թէեւ Միլլիական, բայց հեռատես, կորովի եւ ազդեցիկ ղեկավար մըն է, չափազանց խորամանկ, եւ առ այժմ կը յաջողի պահել առերեւոյթ հանդարտութիւն մը: Միակ մտահոգիչ պարագան կուսակալին զինուորական ոյժերու վրայ ոեւէ ազդեցութիւն չունենալն է: Անիկա զինուորականները օրօրելով ժամանակ կը շահի:

Պ. Լէբիսիէ՝ ֆրանսացի ներկայացուցիչը եւս այս կարծիքը ունի: Անիկա հայոց Առաջնորդա-կան Տեղապահին ըսաւ.- Այո՛, առերեւոյթ անդորրութիւն մը կայ առ այժմ. բայց գուցէ այդ նպատակաւոր է: Անոնք հաւանաբար վաղը ըսեն. «Մենք ամէն ջանք թափեցինք խաղաղութիւնը պահպանելու. բայց մեր մահավճիռին դէմ անկարող եղանք զսպելու վիրաւորուած զգացումներու պոռթկումը»:

Իսկապէս պ. Լէբիսիէ մտահոգ կ'երեւայ եւ յոռետեսութեամբ կը դիտէ կովկասեան դէպքերը:

- Երեք օր առաջ Խարբերդէն հոս եկաւ տրապիզոնցի հայ երիտասարդ մը, որ տեղեկացուց թէ Խարբերդի մէջ ալ քաղաքական կացութիւնը Տրապիզոնի նման է առ այժմ: Հոն ալ ձեռնարկ չէ եղած զօրահաւաքութեան: Ակնայ մէջ ալ նոյն կացութիւնը կը տիրէ:

Ատանա (Հաճընի Հայրենակցական Միութենէն) – 15 Մայիս

Ինը շաբաթ է որ պաշարուած [է] Հաճըն եւ ոչ մէկ յոյս չկայ փրկութեան, որովհետեւ ամէն փորձ ապարդիւն եղած է: Տագնապը մասնաւորապէս ահարկու է երբ մտածուի պաշարի չգոյութեան վրայ:

Մերսին (Ազգային Միութենէն) – 7 Յունիս

Մայիս 30ին Պէյրութի մէջ Սուրիոյ եւ Կիլիկիոյ ընդհանուր քոմիսէր Զօր. Կուրօյի եւ Մուսթա-

Kemal signed a cease-fire between the French military authorities and the Turkish forces. It stipulates the cessation of hostilities and animosities on both sides, the exchange of prisoners, and the withdrawal of French troops from Gaziantep [Ayntab], Kozan [Sis], and Pozantı. This official document secured for Turkish farmers the harvest of new crops.

Colonel Brémond and General Dufieux initially opposed this agreement. The following events occurred in the Cilician region a few days after the decided date. They show the familiar deceptive Turkish policy.

Milli forces took more than forty-eight Armenians from Adana's orchards prisoner, and there has been no news from them since. Quite many Armenians and Greeks were taken from the orchards of Tarsus and Armenian farms. Cows were driven from the outskirts of Mersin and taken away. The Karataş township was attacked, and the local Greek fellah and Armenian residents were robbed and killed. The remnants took refuge in Mersin by way of the sea fraught with a thousand and one dangers. The Mersin-Adana railway is being demolished daily, and traffic has become challenging. In Osmaniye, the çetes are re-emerging with greater vigor. In short, many more incidents have taken place during the twenty-day cease-fire by the çetes, who make up the regular Turkish military and have military equipment, cannons, machine guns, weapons, and explosives.

The Turks in Adana, Tarsus, and Mersin post new notices daily. The Turks of Mersin flee the city every day. Sadık Pasha, a member of the previous parliament, has also left Tarsus with his followers. As for the prefect of Adana and four other notables, they have been brought here. Suspecting they might flee, the French authorities took them under surveillance to an armored cruiser anchored in front of Mersin. The çetes enter Adana unhindered and negotiate with Mr. Brémond with an almost threatening stance toward him. Seeing this, the Turkish people are encouraged and have again taken a dominant role throughout Cilicia. This has demoralized the Armenians, and mass migration has begun to Cyprus, İzmir, İstanbul, and America. More than a thousand Armenians leave every week.

This demoralization was greatly facilitated by the official statement made by the French government that "very soon the French forces will leave Mersin, Tarsus, and Adana to the Turks, and will keep control only beyond the Seyhan River." This statement outraged the Armenians in general. They are confused by this new development, which leaves them defenseless.

From Gaziantep, five thousand women and children went to Beirut on foot to be transported from there to an unknown location. [People in] Samandağı [Suedia] and Kessab have been eating grass for a long time and are helpless. The entire population of Kozan left their homes and nests and came to Misis in a state of extreme poverty and deprivation, shelterless and starved. There is no news from Saimbeyli [Hacın]. At the last minute, we learned that the American orphanage and hospital on the outskirts of the city were attacked by çetes, and that mature Armenian female orphans were taken [by the çetes] to Kayseri and elsewhere. Only American missionaries are spared. Armenians are starving to death in Saimbeyli.

The Pozantı line is occupied by Milli forces. It is routinely used to transport weapons and ammunition up to Dorak.

As for Amanos, a new situation has emerged there. According to news spread in Mersin, Armenian autonomy, under a French mandate, has been created under General Serop Roupinian, and Dörtyol might join it soon. The commander issued Mustafa Kemal an ultimatum on Saturday with the following content: "After the withdrawal of French forces, if the Armenian massacres are not stopped, all the responsibility will remain on you." He delivered a notice to Colonel Brémond in the following sense: "In the name of God, the French government and the nation, and my people, please inform me forty-eight hours in advance should you [decide to] leave the city of Adana and hand it over to Mustafa Kemal."

փա Քէմալի միջեւ կնքուեցաւ զինադադար մը, ընդմէջ ֆրանսական զինուորական իշխանութեան եւ թրքական ոյժերու, որով երկու կողմերէն ալ հակառակութիւնները եւ թշնամութիւնները պիտի դադրեցուին, գերիներու փոխանակութիւն պիտի կատարուի եւ Այնթապէն, Սիսէն եւ Պօզանթիէն ֆրանսական ոյժերը պիտի քաշուին Մերսին Ատանա գծին վրայ. սոյն պաշտօնագիրը կ'ապահովէր թուրք հողագործներու նոր բերքին հաւաքումը:

Այս համաձայնագրին սկ[զբ]մամբ հակառակ կը գտնուին Գնդ. Պրեմոն եւ Զօր. Տիւֆիէյօն: Որոշուած թուականէն քանի մը օր վերջ տեղի կ'ունենան կիլիկեան շրջանի մէջ հետեւեալ դէպքերը, որոնք ցոյց կու տան թրքական ծանօթ խաբեպատիր քաղաքականութիւնը:

Ատանայի այգիներէն 48է աւելի հայեր գերի կը տարուին Միլլի ոյժերու կողմէն, եւ անոնցմէ ոեւէ լուր չկայ: Տարսոնի այգիներէն եւ հայոց ագարակներէն բաւական թուով հայեր եւ յոյներ կը վերցուին եւ կը տարուին: Մերսինի քաղաքի եզերքէն կովեր կը քշուին եւ կը տարուին: Գարաթաշ նահիյէին վրայ կը յարձակին եւ տեղւոյն յոյն, ֆէլլահ, հայ բնակիչները կը թալլուին, կը սպաննուին եւ մնացեալը ծովի ճամբով Մերսին կ'ապաստանին հազար եւ մէկ վտանգներով: Մերսին-Ատանա երկաթուղին ամէն օր կը քանդուի եւ երթեւեկութիւնը կը դժուարանայ: Օսմանիյէի մէջ չէթէները վերստին երեւան կու գան աւելի մեծ թափով: Վերջապէս դեռ բազմաթիւ դէպքեր, որոնք 20օրեայ զինադադարի մէջ տեղի ունեցան չէթէներու կողմէ, որոնք թրքական կանոնաւոր զինուորութիւնը կը կազմեն եւ ունին պատերազմական գործիներ, թնդանօթ, գնդացիր, զէնքեր ու պայթուցիկ:

Նորանոր ազդարարութիւններ կը փակցուին ամէն օր թուրքերու կողմէ Ատանայի, Տարսոնի եւ Մերսինի մէջ: Մերսինի թուրքերը ամէն օր քաղաքէն դուրս կը փախին: Տարսոնէն իր արբանեակներով հեռացաւ նախորդ խորհրդարանի անդամ Սատըգ փաշա եւս: Իսկ Ատանայի կուսակալը եւ երեւելիներէն 4 հոգիներ հոս բերուելով, ֆրանսական իշխանութեան կողմէ կասկածելով որ փախին, հսկողութեան տակ փոխադրեցին Մերսին[ի] առջեւ խարսխած զրահանաւին մէջ: Չէթէները անարգել Ատանայի մէջ կը մտնան եւ կը բանակցին Մ. Պրէմոնի հետ, զրեթէ սպառնական դիրք բռնելով անոր հանդէպ: Թուրք ժողովուրդը ասիկա տեսնելով քաջալերուած է եւ դարձեալ տիրական դեր մը առած է ամբողջ Կիլիկիոյ մէջ: Ասիկա բարոյալքում առաջ բերաւ հայոց մէջ եւ զանգուածային գաղթը սկսաւ դէպի Կիպրոս, Իզմիր, Կ. Պոլիս եւ Ամերիկա: Ամէն շաբաթ հազարէ աւելի հայեր կը հեռանան:

Այս բարոյալքման մեծապէս նպաստեց ֆրանսական իշխանութեան այն պաշտօնական յայտարարութիւնը թէ «շատ մօտերս ֆրանսական ոյժեր թուրքերուն պիտի լքեն Մերսին, Տարսոն եւ Ատանան, եւ պիտի տիրանան միայն Սիհուն գետէն անդին»: Այս յայտարարութիւնը վրդովում առաջ բերած է հայոց վրայ առհասարակ, որոնք շփոթած են այս նոր կացութեան հանդէպ, որ զիրենք կը թողու անպաշտպան:

Այնթապէն 5000 կին ու մանուկ հետիոտն կ'երթան Պէյրութ, անկէ փոխադրուելու համար անծանօթ վայր մը: Սուետիա եւ Քէսապ խուռն կ'ուտեն շատոնց ի վեր եւ ձգուած են անօգնական վիճակի մէջ: Սիսի ամբողջ բնակչութիւնը լքելով իրենց տունը եւ բոյնը եկան յետին չքաւորութեան եւ զրկանքներու մէջ ի Միսիս, անպատսպար, անօթի վիճակի մէջ: Հաճընէն ոեւէ լուր չկայ: Վերջին ժամուն կ'իմանանք որ քաղաքէն քիչ մը դուրս գտնուող ամերիկեան որբանոցը եւ հիւանդանոցը չէթէներու յարձակման ենթարկուած է եւ հասուն որբ հայ աղջիկներ վերցուած եւ տարուած են Կեսարիա եւ այլուր. միայն ամերիկեան միսիոնարներու խնայուած է: Հայերը սովէն կը կոտորուին Հաճընի մէջ:

Պօզանթի գիծը գրաւուած է Միլլի ոյժերէն եւ մինչեւ Տօրազ կանոնաւորապէս կը բանեցնեն փոխադրելով զէնք ու ռազմամթերք:

Գալով Ամանոսի, հոն նոր վիճակ մը կը ստեղծուի: Զօր. Սեռոբ Ռուբինեանի ղեկավարութեամբ կը ստեղծուի Հայկական Ինքնավարութիւն մը Ֆրանսայի մանտային տակ,- ինչպէս Մերսինի մէջ կը խօսուի,- որուն թերեւս մօտերս միանայ Տէօրթեօլ եւս: Յիշեալ զօրավարը շաբթուս ընթացքին վերջնագիր մը տուած է Մուսթաֆա Քէմալին հետեւեալ պարունակութեամբ. «Ֆրանսական

Given these circumstances, it is easy to conclude that the Armenians of Cilicia are in danger of a general massacre if the Allies do not delay the affair of evacuating Cilicia.

Kozan [Sis] (from Zakaria Djerejian, landowner-merchant)—May 26[75]

(Private letter): We are under siege half an hour away. We are in a war and experiencing casualties. There are cannons installed on all sides of the fortress, and the enemy is unable to approach the city thanks to this. The enemy has a numerical superiority, and an attack on Kozan is likely after they increase their numbers. There is hope that the French artillery and machine guns and the young Armenian fighters can save Kozan, whose population is particularly troubled by famine. An okka of oil is 2,500 kuruş. The price of a bucket of wheat (22 okkas) is 1,500 kuruş, and the [sack of] barley is 500 kuruş if it could be found.

As for Saimbeyli [Hacın], there has been no information since March 20. We have given up all hope. Today, Karabeyoğlu Mehmet Bey of Kadirli [Kars Pazarı] approached the battle line and amicably asked for Chakalian Arakel of Kadirli. Arakel took permission from Mr. Taillardat and went to the battle line with a guard. Their meeting took place between two trenches and lasted about a quarter of an hour. Arakel inquired about Saimbeyli and was told that Saimbeyli was still safe and calm on that day at that hour. There are five thousand çetes stationed against Saimbeyli. They have attacked two or three times but have not been able to succeed. A day or two ago, Sehşoğlu Hasan Effendi of Kozan went to Saimbeyli because he wants to launch an attack with great force. Since Arakel is certain that Mehmet Bey does not lie, it follows that Saimbeyli is still enduring.

He also inquired about Feke and the environs. Mehmet Bey replied that he had heard that Feke and its vicinities were conquered, but he did not know what happened [to the people]. Since the fall of those places had been expected, it is likely that the news was accurate and that many people had been killed.

• Five days ago, a man named Sachian Asdour was sent to Saimbeyli as a messenger. He had chosen to proceed on foot at night through the mountains. It is thought that he has arrived in Saimbeyli. He will return.

• In eight or ten days, soldiers will come from Adana to bring ammunition. There is a tendency to move with them from Kozan to Adana because our provisions are almost used up. The Armenians are in distress.

Mersin (from Hrand Moroukian)—June 7[76]

A cease-fire has been signed between the French and the Turks, according to which Pozantı, Kozan [Sis], Gaziantep [Ayntab], and Saimbeyli [Hacın] are to be entirely evacuated by the French during the cease-fire. However, after a second negotiation, the French decided to withdraw their troops completely [also] from Mersin-Tarsus-Adana, provided that they keep only a controlling entity in those areas and that free negotiations take place between the çetes and the local Turkish government during the twenty-day cease-fire. In addition to these basic stipulations, there are other conditions, including the exchange of prisoners. In the wake of this cease-fire, some çetes, police, and so on have begun to travel freely to Mersin, Tarsus, and Adana. Speeches, rallies, and programs come to light daily as if it were a mobilization time.

ոյժերու քաշուելէն վերջ եթէ Հայկական կոտորածները չդադրեցուին, բոլոր պատասխանատուութիւնը ձեր վրայ կը մնայ»: Իսկ Գնդ. Պրեմոնին կու տայ հետեւեալ իմաստով ծանուցագիր մը. «Աստուծոյ, ֆրանսական իշխանութեան եւ ազգին եւ իմ ժողովուրդին անունով կը խնդրուի, այն պարագային երբ դուք Ատանա քաղաքը կը պարպէք Մուսթաֆա Քէմալին յանձնելու համար, 48 ժամ առաջ ինծ հաղորդեցէք»:

Այս պայմաններուն մէջ դիւրին է եզրակացնել թէ ընդհանուր ջարդի մը վտանգին տակ կը գտնուին Կիլիկիոյ հայերը, եթէ Համաձայնականք Կիլիկիան պարպելու գործը չյապաղեցնեն:

Սիս (Զաքարիա Ճէրէճեանէ՝ կալուածատէր-վաճառական) – 26 Մայիս

(Մասնաւոր նամակ).- Կէս ժամ հեռաւորութեամբ պաշարման մէջ ենք եւ պատերազմի մէջ եւ անձի կորուստներ ալ կ'ունենանք: Բերդին չորս կողմէ թնդանօթներ լարուած են եւ շնորհիւ ասոր է որ թշնամին չի կրնար մօտենալ քաղաքին: Թշնամին ունի թուական գերազանցութիւն եւ հաւանական է որ աւելի իրենց թիւը շատցնելով յարձակին Սիսի վրայ: Ֆրանսական թնդանօթները եւ գնդացիրները եւ հայ կռուող երիտասարդները կը յուսացուի որ փրկեն Սիսը, որուն բնակչութիւնը կը նեղուի մասնաւորապէս սովէն: Իւղին քաշը 2500 դրուշ, ցորենին *քէիլէկը* (22 օխան) 1500 դրուշ, գարին՝ 500 դրուշ կը ծախուի, ան ալ չկայ:

Գալով Հաճընի, 20 Մարտէն ի վեր ոչ մէկ տեղեկութիւն: Ամէն յոյս կտրած էինք: Այսօր Կարս-Պազարէն Ղարայ պէյին օղլու Մէհմէտ պէյ կռուի շարքը գալով կարս-պազարցի Չաքալեան Առաքելը բարեկամաբար կ'ուզէ: Առաքել Մ. Թայեարտայէն հրաման առնելով հսկողի մը հետ կռիւի գիծ եկաւ. երկու խրամներուն մէջտեղը քառորդ ժամ մը տեսնուեցան: Առաքել Հաճընի մասին տեղեկութիւն կը հարցնէ եւ պատասխան կը ստանայ թէ այսօր այս ժամուս դեռ Հաճըն փրկուած եւ հանգիստ է: Հաճըն[ի] դէմ 5000 չէթէ կայ, 2–3 անգամ յարձակում ըրած են սակայն չեն կրցած բան մը ընել: Մէկ երկու օր առաջ սիսցի Սեհշ օղլու Հասան էֆ. գնաց եւ մեծ ուժով յարձակում մը կ'ուզէ կազմակերպել Հաճընի վրայ: Առաքել՝ որովհետեւ վստահ է Մէհմէտ պէյի սուտ չխօսելուն, ասկէ կը հետեւցնի թէ Հաճըն դեռ կը դիմանայ:

Ֆէքէի եւ շրջակայից մասին ալ տեղեկութիւն հարցուցած է եւ Մէհմէտ պէյ պատասխանած է թէ Ֆէքէ եւ շրջակայքը նուաճուած ըլլալը լսած է, սակայն չի գիտեր թէ ինչ եղած են: Որովհետեւ այն տեղերու անկումը կ'ակնկալուէր, ուստի հաւանական է որ տրուած լուրը ճիշդ ըլլայ եւ շատ զոհուած ըլլան:

- Թուականէս 5 օր առաջ Սաչեան Աստուր անուն մէկը Հաճըն դրկուեցաւ իբր թղթատար: Հետի, գիշերները լեռներէն պիտի երթայ: Կը կարծուի թէ Հաճըն հասած է: Պիտի վերադառնայ:

- 8–10 օրէն Ատանայէն ռազմամթերք բերող զինուոր պիտի գայ, կը մտածուի Սիսէն անոնց հետ Ատանա փոխադրուիլ, քանի որ պաշարը կը սպառի: Հայերը նեղ դրութեան մէջ են:

Մերսին (Հրանտ Մօրուքեանէ) – 7 Յունիս

Ֆրանսացւոց եւ թրքաց միջեւ զինադադար կնքուած է, որուն համաձայն այդ զինադադարի պահուն Պօզանթի, Սիս, Այնթապ, Հաճըն ամբողջութեամբ ֆրանսացւոց կողմէ պիտի պարպուէր, բայց յետոյ երկրորդ բանակցութեան մը հետեւանօք ֆրանսացիք Մերսին-Թարսուս-Ատանայէն եւս ամբողջովին զինուորները քաշել որոշ[եցին], պայմանով որ միայն Controle-ի մարմին մը մնայ եւ այդ 20 օրուան զինադադարի պահուն չէթէներու եւ տեղական թուրք կառավարութեան միջեւ ազատօրէն բանակցութիւն պիտի ըլլայ: Այս հիմնական տրամադրութիւններէն զատ, գերիներու փոխանակութեան եւ այլ պայմաններ կան: Այս զինադադարի տրամադրութեանց համաձայն չէթէներէն մաս մը, ոստիկաններ եւայլն, ազատօրէն Մերսին, Տարսոն եւ Ատանա երթալ գալու սկսան: Ամէն օր ճառեր, միթինկներ, ծրագիրներ կը պարզուին, կարծես թէ զօրաշարժի ատեն ըլլայ:

On the other hand, during this period, the Armenians of Adana have been making all kinds of preparations, provided that their military corps, the staff, and everything else was regular. In Hasanbeyli, located between Adana and İslahiye, some twenty-five hundred to three thousand Armenian volunteers have retreated to the Amanos Mountains. They have proclaimed sovereignty designated as the *Armenian Independence of Amanos*. The Armenian volunteers in İslahiye, in addition to those who arrived when Kozan was evacuated, have joined together, combining their provisions and supplies. With some other young Armenians gathered there from outside, they formed a six-to-seven-thousand-strong force. This force is prone to increase day by day, hour by hour. There are also all the French officers of the Legion d'Orient with them, detained as captives. On June 4, they issued an ultimatum to Milli's command acting in Cilicia, sending a copy to General Dufieux and the Turkish prefect of Adana.

The memo stipulated "the withdrawal of Milli forces within forty-eight hours from the entire Cilician region and handing over both mountainous Cilicia and Cilicia of the plains to the Armenian Independence of Amanos, including Mersin, Tarsus, and Adana. Otherwise, in villages encountered, the people, starting with the children, will be massacred mercilessly . . ."

Only the memo given to General Dufieux is slightly different, and it states: "The withdrawal of French troops from Cilicia has been announced, but we cannot hand over Cilicia to the çetes. Because you are going to withdraw, withdraw! We will occupy [the region] with our own forces. We want the controling entity to remain under the supervision of the Americans and foreign powers," and so on.

The people are completely confused in the face of this situation. Seven to eight thousand Armenians came to Adana from Gaziantep [and] Kozan and, in part, from Saimbeyli. Tarsus is almost void of Armenians. Some of the Armenians of Adana came to Mersin, while most of them went to Cyprus. This situation cannot last long. It will end within twenty-five to thirty days because both sides are armed. Apart from Pozantı, the district of Adana—Misis, Dörtyol, Hasanbeyli, Ceyhan—is entirely in the hands of the Armenians. It is as if the French have no power. The natives of Adana were concerned about the outside, but now the outside is secured. Those who are leaving Adana are those who did not join that "organization."

Even when we were leaving Adana, it was said that part of the forces that were defending Saimbeyli and Gaziantep for some time would go to Adana and another part to Hasanbeyli (Amanos Mountains).

• The organization [declaring independence] takes sixty percent of the people's money under the guise of internal borrowing. There is a very urgent need for officers and flour.

• The Armenians of Kozan are placed in the Turkish district of Adana, and the Turks have been driven out of the city toward İncirli.

İstanbul (from Mrs. Bonapartian of Adapazarı)—June 22[77]

The Millis have stringently demanded fifteen hundred liras from the Armenians, twenty-five hundred from the Greeks, and one thousand from the Jews. All the horses and weapons were collected from the Christians, but the horses and weapons taken from the Turks were returned by vouchers. They [the Millis] took three hundred pairs of shoes from Hagop Anoushian. They confiscated forty to fifty pairs from [all other] shoemakers. The houses of Armenians are being searched at night on the suspicion that they are keeping Circassians. There are 120 orphans in the orphanage run by the American Miss Mary Kinney. They [the Millis] wanted the orphanage but then occupied the Dzoullouyans' house across the street. The soldiers that are housed there dine in the garden of the orphanage. They arrested the Englishman Mr. Muffett and sent him with a coachman to an unknown location. The Millis allegedly brought four to five thousand soldiers, and it is said that about two thousand more will arrive.

Այս միջոցիս միւս կողմէն Ատանայի հայերը ամէն տեսակ պատրաստութիւններ [կ'ընեն], զինուորական մարմին, սպայակոյտ եւ այլ ամէն բան կանոնաւոր ըլլալու պայմանաւ: Ատանայի եւ Իսլահիյէի միջեւ Հասան Պէյլիի մէջ գտնուող 2500–3000ի չափ հայ կամաւորները Ամանոսի լեռները քաշուելով *Ամանոսի Հայկական Անկախութիւն* անունով իշխանութիւն մը հռչակեցին, եւ ասոր Իսլահիյէ գտնուող հայ կամաւորները եւ Միսի պարպումով եկող հայ կամաւորները իրենց զէնքերով եւ պարէններով եւ պաշարով միացան եւ դուրսէն կարգ մը հայ երիտասարդներ հաւաքուելով 6–7000 անձի չափ ուժ մը երեւան բերին եւ այս ուժը օրէ օր, ժամէ ժամ աւելնալու վրայ է: Ասոնց հետ Legion d'Orientի բոլոր ֆրանսացի սպաները հիմա իրենց քով իբր գերի վար դրուած են: Ասոնք Յունիս 4ին վերջնագիր մը տուին Կիլիկիոյ մէջ գործող Միլլիին հրամանատարութեան, օրինակն ալ հաղորդելով Զօր. Տիւֆիէօյի եւ Ատանայի թուրք կուսակալին:

Այդ նօթային իմաստը սա էր. «Կը պահանջուէր 48 ժամուան միջոցին բոլոր Կիլիկիոյ շրջանակէն Միլլի ուժերուն քաշուիլը եւ թէ՛ լեռնային եւ թէ՛ դաշտային Կիլիկիոյ, Մերսին, Տարսոն եւ Ատանա եւս մէջը ըլլալով, Ամանոսի Հայկական Անկախութեան յանձնուիլը: Հակառակ պարագային հանդիպած գիւղերը, ժողովուրդը տղաքներէն սկսեալ անխնայ պիտի կոտորուին...»:

Միայն Զօր. Տիւֆիյօյի տրուած նօթան քիչ մը տարբեր է, եւ սապէս է. «Կիլիկիայէն ֆրանսացւոց զինուորական ուժերուն քաշուիլը յայտարարուած է, ուստի մենք Կիլիկիան չենք կրնար չէթէներուն յանձնել: Քանի որ դուք պիտի քաշուիք, քաշուեցէք, մեր ուժերով կը գրաւենք, ամերիկացւոց եւ օտար պետութեանց հսկողութեան տակ Controle-ի մարմինին պահպանուիլը կ'ուզենք եւայլն»:

Այս կացութեան առջեւ ժողովուրդը բոլորովին շփոթած է: Այնթապէն, Միսէն եւ մաս մըն ալ Հաճընի կողմէն 7–8 հազար հայեր Ատանա եկան: Տարսոն գրեթէ հայերէ պարպուած է. Ատանայի հայոց մէկ մասը Մերսին եկաւ եւ մեծ մասը գնաց Կիպրոս: Այս վիճակը չի կրնար երկար տեւել, 25–30 օրէն եզրակացութեան մը կու գայ, վասնզի երկու կողմերն ալ սպառազէն են: Վասնզի Բիւզանդիէն զատ Ատանայի շրջանակը՝ Միսիս, Տէօրթեօլ, Հասան Պէյլի, Ճիհան ամբողջովին հայոց ձեռքն է, կարծես թէ ֆրանսացիք երբեք ուժ չունին: Ատանայի բնիկները դուրսը կը մտածէին, հիմա դուրսը ապահովուեցաւ: Ատանայէն մեկնողները այդ «կազմակերպութենէն» դուրս մնացողներն են:

Նոյնիսկ մեր Ատանայէն մեկնած ատեն կ'ըսուէր թէ ժամանակէ մը ի վեր Հաճընը եւ Այնթապը պաշտպանող ուժերէն մէկ մասը Ատանա եւ միւս մասը Հասան Պէյլի (Ամանոս լեռները) պիտի երթար:

- Կազմակերպութիւնը կ'առնէ ներքին փոխառութեան անունին տակ ժողովուրդին դրամին 60%-ը: Սպայի եւ ալիւրի պէտք կայ խիստ ստիպողաբար եւ դրամ կ'ուզուի:

- Միսի հայերը զետեղուած են Ատանայի թրքաց թաղը եւ թուրքերը դուրս հանուած են քաղաքէն դէպի Ինճիրլիի կողմերը:

Կ. Պոլիս (Ատաբազարէն Տիկ. Պօնափարթեանէ) – 22 Յունիս

Միլլիճիները հայերէն ուզած են 1500, յոյներէն 2500, հրեաներէն 1000 ոսկի խստիւ: Բոլոր ձիերը եւ զէնքերը հաւաքած են քրիստոնեաներէն, իսկ թուրքերէն առնելէն յետոյ վէսիքայով վերադարձուած են: 300 զոյգ կօշիկ առին Յակոբ Անուշեանէն. նոյնպէս բոլոր կօշկակարներէն՝ 40–50ով: Հայերուն տուները գիշերով խուզարկուած են չէրքէզներ պահելու կասկածով: Միս Մէյրի Քենի ամերիկուհիին որբանոցը կայ 120 որբուհի: Որբանոցը ուզած են, բայց յետոյ դիմացը գտնուած Ծուլլուեաններու տունը գրաւած են եւ հոն տեղաւորած են զինուորները որ կը ճաշեն որբանոցին պարտէզը: Անգլիացի Մր. Մաֆէթը բռնելով կառապանով ղրկեցին անծանօթ տեղ մը: 4–5000ի չափ զինուոր բերած են եղեր Միլլիները եւ կ'ըսուէր թէ 2000ի չափ եւս պիտի հասնին: 4–5 հազար զինուոր ալ Տիւզճէի կողմը եւ միւսը Նիկոմիդիոյ կողմերը ղրկած են: Նիկոմիդիոյ տէփօէն առնուած զէնքերը եւ ռազմամթերքը ի սկզբան կարծելով թէ անգլիացիք հոն պիտի գան, ցրուեցին Գանտրա

Four to five thousand troops were sent to Düzce and others to İzmit. The weapons and ammunition taken from İzmit's storage were initially dispersed in Kandıra and the surrounding villages, thinking that the British would come there, but later they had them brought from Kandıra and sent to İzmit. Each family in the villages has several weapons. Their plan was, when the attack on İzmit began, to capture Gebze on the other hand and strike the English from behind. That is why the population was armed in advance.

Since in the villages of İncirli the Greeks joined forces with the Circassians beforehand, the Millis had sent soldiers to collect their arms; however, because they had turned in few [weapons], it is said that the Greeks, all of them, will be deported from the villages.

A military man gathered the crowd in İncirli and delivered a speech, saying: "Whoever speaks out against the Millis will be hanged, his house will be burned, his family will be exiled." Then, speaking against the British, he invited the people to enlist to fight against the British, to drive them out of İzmit and İstanbul. He pointed out that the Armenians and the Greeks have been kinder toward the Circassians than the Millis and concluded by saying: "Down with the British, the Greeks, and Armenians!" An enlistment was also conducted to send [the enlisted] against İzmit. [The military man added:] "The sultan is on our side, but the British have installed guards by his door and forced him to sign the decree. All of the servicemen are with us, as well as the people of İstanbul. Whoever keeps a Circassian in his house will be hanged."

The crowd said that the Greeks in İzmir are inflicting all kinds of mischief upon Muslims, while the Armenians, jointly with the French, are burning the mosques in Adana and advancing in this direction.

The same announcement was made in Adapazarı.

Three Greeks were killed in the village of Kestanepınar, near İncirli. One cannot go to the villages of Adapazarı. An Armenian returning from the villages was killed. Credential is required from those who come from the villages; otherwise, they will be detained or turned back.

An announcement was posted in İncirli stating that if the British did not leave İstanbul and the Greeks did not leave İzmir, all Christians would be massacred.

İpsiz Recep, the pirate whose base is İnsiz Ada, came to İncirli and took other Lazes with him to Ereğli.

Kozan [Sis] (from catholicosal locum tenens Bishop Yeghishé Garoyan)—May 24

We have been besieged by the Kemalists for two months. After the Maraş incident, the Kemalists marched toward Kozan. The Armenians of Kadirli [Kars Pazarı], six hours away, took refuge in Kozan in a state of panic, even abandoning their provisions at home. A few days later, seeing a threat from Develi, forty-five people from Karaköy left their families and children and took refuge here. Upon their arrival, communications from these two areas at once ceased. It was possible to communicate with Adana for a while, but at the beginning of March, that road, too, was closed, and we have been besieged from all sides within an hour's distance since.

There are French guards in Kozan, and about four hundred Armenian volunteers came from Adana, so there is enough protection, but we do not have exact information on the number of besiegers. Saimbeyli [Hacın] is also under siege and is said to be regularly bombarded by cannons. Their surrender soon is probable, or perhaps it has happened already, as the besieging forces assure us by shouting from afar. Then the force besieging Saimbeyli will undoubtedly come upon us, and we do not know what the end will be.

Forty days ago, a three-thousand-strong force from Adana arrived in the city with cannons and machine guns to supply the local French army. The troops then returned to Adana after leaving the

եւ շրջակայ գիւղերը, բայց յետոյ Գանտրայէն բերել տալով ղրկեցին դէպի Նիկոմիդիա: Գիւղերու իւրաքանչիւր ընտանիք քանի մը զէնք ունի: Իրենց ծրագիրն էր, երբ Նիկոմիդիոյ վրայ յարձակումը սկսի, միւս կողմէն Կէյվէէն զրաւել եւ անգլիացիները կռնակէն զարնել: Ատոր համար կանխաւ զինած էին բնակչութիւնը:

Ինճիրլիի գիւղերուն մէջ կանխաւ յոյները չէրքէզներուն հետ միացած ըլլալով Միլլիականները զինուոր ղրկած էին որպէսզի անոնց զէնքերը հաւաքեն, բայց որովհետեւ անոնք շատ քիչ բան յանձնած էին, կ'ըսուէր թէ բոլոր յոյները գիւղերէն տեղահան պիտի ընեն:

Ինճիրլիի մէջ զինուորական մը ժողովուրդը հաւաքելով ճառ մը խօսեցաւ եւ ըսաւ թէ «ով որ Միլլիներուն հակառակ խօսի կախաղան պիտի հանուի, տունը պիտի այրուի, իր ընտանիքը պիտի աքսորուի»: Յետոյ անգլիացիներուն դէմ խօսելով ժողովուրդը հրաւիրեց որ զինուոր գրուին անգլիացւոց դէմ կռուելու համար, որ Նիկոմիդիայէն եւ Պոլիսէն հանեն զանոնք. յիշեց թէ հայերն եւ յոյները չէրքէզներուն աւելի սիրալիր վերաբերում ունեցան քան մեզի եւ վերջացուց անկցին անգլիացիք, անկցին յոյները եւ հայերը ըսելով: Զինուորագրութիւն եղաւ Նիկոմիդիոյ դէմ ղրկելու համար եւս: Սուլթանը մեր կողմէն է, բայց անգլիացին անոր դրան առջեւ պահակ կեցուցած է եւ բռնութեան տակ ստորագրել տուած է իրատէն: Զինուորականներէն ամէնքն ալ մեզի կողմնակից են, ինչպէս նաեւ Պոլսոյ ժողովուրդը: Ով որ չէրքէզ պահէ իր տան մէջ, պիտի կախուի:

Ամբոխը ըսաւ թէ Իզմիրի մէջ յոյները իսլամներուն ամէն տեսակ գէշութիւն կ'ընեն, իսկ հայերը Ատանայի մէջ ֆրանսացւոց միացած մզկիթներ կ'այրեն եւ կը յառաջանան դէպի այս կողմ:

Նոյնը յայտարարած են նաեւ Ատաբազար:

Ինճիրլիի շրջականերէն Քէսթէնէ-Բունար գիւղին մէջ երեք յոյն սպաննած են: Ատաբազարի գիւղերը երթալ կարելի չէ: Հայ մը, որ գիւղերէն դարձած է, սպաննուած է: Գիւղերէն եկողներէ վէսիքա կը պահանջուի, ապա թէ ոչ կը բանտարկեն կամ ետ կը դարձնեն:

Ինճիրլիի մէջ յայտարարութիւն մը փակցուած էր թէ, եթէ անգլիացիք Պոլիսէն եւ յոյները Իզմիրէն չելլեն, բոլոր քրիստոնեաները պիտի ջարդուին:

Իփսիզ Ռէճէպ, ծովահէնը, որուն կայանն է Ինսիզ Ատա, Ինճիրլի եկաւ եւ իրեն հետ ուրիշ լազեր առնելով գնաց Էրէյլի:

Սիս (Կաթողիկոսական Տեղապահ Եղիշէ Եպիսկոպոս Կարոեանէ) – 24 Մայիս

Երկու ամիսէ ի վեր պաշարուած ենք Քէմալիսթներու կողմէն: Մարաշի դէպքէն յետոյ Քէմալիսթները կը քալեն Սսոյ կողմը: Կարս-Բազարի,- որ 6 ժամ հեռու է,- հայերը Սիս կ'ապաստանին խուճապով, նոյնիսկ իրենց պարէնները թողլով տուներու մէջ: Քանի մը օր վերջ ալ Էվէրէկի կողմէն սպառնալիք տեսնելով Գարաքէօյէն 45 հոգի իրենց ընտանիք եւ զաւակները ձգելով նոյնպէս հոս ապաստանեցան: Ասոնց հասնելէն վերջ այդ երկու կողմերու հաղորդակցութիւնները անմիջապէս դադրեցան: Ատանայի հետ ժամանակ մը կարելի եղաւ հաղորդակցիլ, սակայն Մարտի սկիզբները այդ ճամբան ալ գոցուեցաւ եւ անկէ ի վեր ժամու մը հեռաւորութեամբ շուրջանակի պաշարուած ենք:

Սսոյ մէջ ֆրանսացի պահակ զինուոր կայ, Ատանայէն ալ 400ի մօտ հայ կամաւորներ եկան, հետեւաբար պաշտպանութեան բաւական միջոց կայ, սակայն պաշարողներու թիւին վրայ ստոյգ տեղեկութիւն չունինք: Հաճըն նոյնպէս պաշարուած է եւ թնդանօթներով կանոնաւորապէս կը ռմբակոծուի կ'ըսեն: Հաւանական է որ մօտերս անձնատուր ըլլայ կամ թէ արդէն եղաւ, ինչպէս որ կը հաւաստեն մեզ պաշարող ոյժերը հեռուանց բարձրաղաղակ կանչելով: Այն ատեն Հաճընը պաշարող ոյժը մեր վրայ պիտի գայ անտարակոյս եւ վախճանը չենք գիտեր թէ ինչ պիտի ըլլայ:

40 օր առաջ տեղւոյս ֆրանսական զօրքը պարենաւորելու համար Ատանայէն 3000 հոգինոց

provisions they had brought. The city's military governor pressed some people to go to Adana with the same soldiers; no one agreed because of the snow and winter. Now, living has become more expensive, with the price of wheat rising to twelve Ottoman paper liras and meat, oil, soap, sugar, and similar supplies having dried up altogether. There is talk of a forthcoming convoy and the military governor intends to send noncombatants to Adana by force. It is equally dangerous to stay or go. In short, the situation is unbearable. Once every eight or ten days, an airplane flies above us. It delivers and receives letters sometimes, and then it leaves. This is the only consolation we receive from the outside.

• Yesterday, we were able to arrange a meeting in a neutral zone with a Turk, a native of Kadirli, besieging Kozan. From him, we learned that Saimbeyli had not surrendered yet, but said it cannot resist much longer.

Trabzon (from the vicar general)—June 9[78]

It is rumored that conscription will be announced in Trabzon for Muslims and Christians indiscriminately after Bairam [the Muslim festival]. It has been heard that riots and even terrorist acts have already started around Giresun and Ordu. The Greek villagers of Giresun are subjected to the atrocities of the chief brigand Topal Osman. It is said that the metropolitan of Niksar, Bishop Polycarpos, was arrested and sent to Ankara. In fact, the absence of a battleship in the port has had an encouraging effect on the Turks here, and similar things will likely happen here.

Üsküdar (from Priest Moushegh Gopetsie of Alemdağı)—June 29[79]

The people of the Armenian village of Alemdağı were uprooted [during World War I], their household goods were looted, and they were driven to Mosul-Der-Zor. Barely three people of those forty-five Armenian households were back [after the armistice]. Today, they are displaced again, fleeing to Üsküdar. The residents of Ermeniköy and Sultançiftliği (upper and lower villages) have abandoned their house goods, fields, and wheat and left; the police have entered the houses and are selling the house goods. The villagers are deprived of enjoying the results of their work. The villagers have only been able to save their cattle and are asking for means to reap the harvest. There are 166 fugitives.

Gaziantep [Ayntab] (from Priest Nerses Tavoukjian, catholicosal vicar)—June 1

It has been two months since Gaziantep was besieged. Fifteen thousand people perpetually eat from what they have, and today we have barely a month's worth of food if we eat only one hundred drams [of food] (daily) per person, which means that if Gaziantep does not get enough food, the people will starve to death. The people of Gaziantep have become accustomed to being among flames and swords and living under fire, but the fear of starvation has begun to torment their minds.

The people of Gaziantep have been facing an unforeseen situation for five days and have been worried for fifteen days. Two weeks ago, the colonel, summoning the National Union, urged the departure of a part or half of the people from Gaziantep, as there is a shortage of provisions. This news had a terrible effect on the people, and a gradual demoralization ensued because the people were concluding that France would forsake Gaziantep. Finally, an agreement was reached with the colonel that the orphans, the deportees in Gaziantep, and the people of Gaziantep who wanted to go should be sent.

Tuesday night, May 25, three thousand Armenians set out under the watch of French troops, in a condition more deplorable than during the Turkish deportations. Each person was allowed to take only a blanket [and] food sufficient for a few days and was obliged to travel on foot. The impression was very depressing, especially when the Turks fired three cannons at the people gathered near the

ոյժ մը թնդանօթով եւ գնդացիրներով քաղաքս ժամանեց եւ բերած պարէնը ձգելով դարձաւ: Քաղաքիս զինուորական կառավարիչը ստիպեց որ ժողովուրդին մէկ մասը նոյն զինուորներուն հետ Ատանա երթայ. ոչ ոք համակերպեցաւ՝ ձիւն ձմեռ ըլլալուն: Հիմա ապրուստը սղեց, ցորենին գինը 12 օսմանեան թուղթ ոսկիի բարձրանալով, միս, իւղ, օճառ, շաքար եւ նմանօրինակ պարէն-ները բոլորովին սպառելով: Մօտերս նոր *զօնվոյ* մըն ալ գալու խօսք կայ եւ զինուորական կառա-վարիչը մտադրութիւն կը յայտնէ ոչ պատերազմիկները բռնութեամբ Ատանա ուղարկելու. մնալն ալ վտանգաւոր է, երթալն ալ: Վերջապէս կացութիւնը անտանելի է. 8–10 օրը անգամ մը օդանաւ մը կը սաւառնի վրանիս, երբեմն նամակ կ'առնէ կուտայ եւ կը մեկնի. դրսէն մեզի հասած միակ մխիթարութիւնն այս է:

- Երէկ Սիսը պաշարող կարս[-բազար]եցի թուրքի մը հետ կարելի եղաւ տեսութիւն մը կարգադրել չէզոք գօտիի մէջ. ասկէ իմացանք թէ Հաճըն տակաւին անձնատուր եղած չէ, սակայն երկար չի կրնար դիմանալ ըսած է:

Տրապիզոն (Առաջնորդական Փոխանորդէն) – 9 Յունիս

Զրոյց կը շրջի թէ Տրապիզոնի մէջ պայրամէն վերջ պիտի յայտարարուի զօրակոչ իսլամներու եւ քրիստոնեաներու համար անխտիր: Կը լսուի թէ Կիրասոնի եւ Օրտուի կողմերը սկսած են արդէն խլրտումներ եւ նոյնիսկ ահաբեկիչ գործողութիւններ: Կիրասոնի յոյն գիւղացիութիւնը մատնուած է աւազակապետ Թօփալ Օսմանի խժդժութիւններուն: Կ'ըսուի թէ Նիքսարի Մետրապոլիտը՝ Տ. Պօլիկարպոս, ձերբակալուած Էնկիւրիւ ղրկուած է: Նաւահանգիստին մէջ մարտանաւ մը չըլլալը հոս թուրքերը կը քաջալերէ եւ հաւանական է որ հոս ալ պատահին այս տեսակ դէպքեր:

Սկիւտար (Ալէմ Տաղիի Տ. Մուշեղ քահանայ Կոբեցիէ) – 29 Յունիս

Ալէմ Տաղիի Հայ Գիւղի ժողովուրդը տեղահանուած եւ իր կարասիները կողոպտուած էին եւ իրենք Մուսուլ-Տէր-Զօր քշուած էին: Այդ 45 տնուոր հայերէն հազիւ երեք անձ վերադարձած էր: Այսօր կրկին տեղահան եղած են փախուստ տալով դէպի Սկիւտար: Հայ Գիւղի եւ Սուլթան Չիֆլիկի (վերի եւ վարի գիւղերը) բնակիչները իրենց կարասիները եւ արտերը ու ցորենները լքելով մեկնած են, եւ ոստիկանութիւնը տուները մտնելով կարասիները կը ծախէ: Գիւղացիք զրկուած են իրենց աշխատութեան արդիւնքը վայելելէ: Գիւղացիք միայն իրենց տաւարները կրցած են ազատել եւ կը խնդրեն որ իրենց միջոցներ տրուին հունձքը քաղելու: Փախստականները 166 անձ են:

Այնթապ (Կաթողիկոսական Փոխանորդ Ներսէս քահանայ Թավուզճեանէ) – 1 Յունիս

Երկու ամիս եղաւ որ Այնթապ պաշարուած է: 15 հազար ժողովուրդ միշտ կ'ուտէ ունեցածէն եւ այսօր մարդ գլուխ 100 տրամ (օրական) միայն ուտելով հազիւ ունինք մէկ ամսուան պարէն, որով եթէ Այնթապ պարէն չհասնի՝ ժողովուրդը անօթութենէ պիտի մեռնի: Այնթապի ժողովուրդը վարժուեցաւ հուրի եւ սուրի մէջ մնալու եւ կրակի տակ ապրելու, բայց անօթութեան երկիւղը հիմնակուրնէ սկսած է տանջել միտքերը:

Հինգ օրէ ի վեր անակնկալի մը առջեւ է Այնթապի ժողովուրդը եւ 15 օրէ ի վեր մտատանջ: Երկու շաբաթ առաջ քօլօնէլը Ազգային Միութիւնը կանչելով յորդորեց որ ժողովուրդին մէկ մասը կամ կէսը Այնթապէն հեռանայ, քանի որ պարենաւորումի դժուարութիւն կայ: Այս լուրը շատ գէշ ազդեց ժողովուրդին վրայ եւ կամաց կամաց բարոյալքում մը սկսաւ, որովհետեւ ժողովուրդը ասկէ կը հետեւցնէր թէ Ֆրանսա պիտի լքէր Այնթապը: Վերջապէս քօլօնէլին հետ համաձայնութիւն մը գոյացաւ որ որբերը եւ Այնթապ գտնուող տարագիրները եւ երթալ ուզող այնթապցիները ղրկուին:

Մայիս 25 Բշ. գիշեր 3000 հայեր ճամբայ ելան ֆրանսական զինուորներու հսկողութեան տակ, թրքական տարագրութենէն աւելի գէշ վիճակի մէջ, որովհետեւ ամէն մէկ անձ միայն արտօնուած էր առնել իրեն հետ ծածկոց մը եւ քանի մը օրուան ուտելիք եւ պարտաւորուած էր հետիոտն երթալ: Տպաւորութիւնը շատ գէշ էր, մանաւանդ երբ իրիկուան մօտ ֆրանսական բանակի մօտ հա-

French army in the evening. Fortunately, the cannonballs fell far afield and did not explode. After [the first caravan] had left, the colonel ordered a second caravan to be made ready; he considered the number of those who had left to be few. This time the people wanted to go all at once since they were being forced to go in increments. When General de Lamothe came to Gaziantep, he made the same recommendation, except that he focused on a slightly less number and after making peace with keeping at most eight thousand people in Gaziantep. The next day, the colonel reported that a cease-fire had been signed between General Gouraud and Mustafa Kemal, the primary condition of which was allegedly spreading Turkish rule again over the Armenian neighborhoods of Gaziantep. This news shocked the Armenians of Gaziantep. The next day, General de Lamothe returned to Gaziantep. The day before, the colonel had called upon the district governor of the Turks to talk about the cease-fire, but he did not come, replying that if the colonel wanted to consult about the evacuation of Gaziantep, he should go to them. When the general arrived, on the same day the district governor and Orfan Bey, the functionary appointed by Kemal Pasha, arrived at staff headquarters, they consulted for three hours and failed to agree because the Turks insisted that Kemal Pasha had instructed them that the French would evacuate Gaziantep. Meanwhile, the general said that he had received an order from Gouraud to withdraw his troops from their two or three positions in the city of Gaziantep and to sit with his troops in the college. Then, the two [negotiators] requested new instructions and departed after deciding to sign the local conditions of a cease-fire in Kilis. The Turkish delegates went to Kilis today. The colonel has been telling us for two days that the Armenian quarters would be handed over to the Turks on June 8 and that they would rule. The Armenians are objecting, arguing that as soon as the Turks enter, even if they do not massacre all the Armenians, they would find them guilty and rebellious and otherwise condemn and hang them. He was convinced and suggested that the notables and activists retreat and leave immediately. We did not accept this, considering his suggestions both impossible and disgraceful for ourselves. We have been arguing over this issue for two days. He insists that we dismantle the positions and give in to the Turkish government on June 8, as if it could not harm the Armenians. Finally, this morning we offered to migrate completely. He said there was no means of transportation but promised to provide eighty to one hundred carriages.

Eleven to twelve thousand people cannot be transported in eighty carriages. All the wealth of Gaziantep will remain with the Turks. We even wanted to gather our property in the church and give him the key; he declined to accept, arguing that he cannot put anybody inside and watch over them. The Armenians had not been willing to leave to begin with, and their offer was only a show, but it did not help. Today, around noon, all the people aged twenty and above assembled at the church and were informed about the situation. Some people delivered speeches. The deliberations lasted for two hours, and there was a large crowd in the First Protestant Church. We held a referendum. In a very orderly manner, the absolute majority of the people, almost unanimously—because there were only two opposing votes against thousands of raised hands—decided to stay in Gaziantep. They voted to fight without any help against the Turks, not to dismantle the barricades, and to die on the barricades. We announced this decision to the colonel, who was stunned because he had always said that resisting the cease-fire law would mean acting against the French and that they could never help us. On June 7, the Turks will probably suggest that the Armenians dismantle the positions, otherwise threatening to attack us with guns and cannons. Armenians will get ready to enter a disproportionate war.

Aleppo (from the vicar general Father Haroutyun)—June 9

According to information received today from Gaziantep [Ayntab], the situation has not changed because the disputed points of several articles of the agreements to be signed between the French military

ւաքուած էր ժողովուրդը, թուրքերը երեք թնդանօթ կ՚արձակեն ամբոխին վրայ, որոնք բարեբաղդաբար հեռուն ինկան եւ չպայթեցան: Ասոնք երթալէ յետոյ քօլօնէլը հրամայեց երկրորդ կարաւանի մը պատրաստութիւնը տեսնել՝ մեկնողներուն թիւը քիչ համարելով: Այս անգամ ժողովուրդը ուզեց բոլորովին երթալ, քանի որ մաս մաս պիտի երթար: Երբ Ժէնէրալ տը լա Մօթ Այնթապ եկաւ, միեւնոյն յանձնարարութիւնը ըրաւ սա տարբերութեամբ միայն որ թիւը քիչ մը նուազ ցոյց տուաւ եւ Այնթապի մէջ առ առաւելն 8000 հոգի մնալուն հաւանեցաւ: Յաջորդ օրը քօլօնէլը հաղորդեց թէ Ժէնէրալ Կուրօյի եւ Մուսթաֆա Քէմալի միջեւ զինադադար մը կնքուած է, որուն հիմնական պայմանն է եղեր Այնթապի հայոց թաղերուն վրայ դարձեալ թուրք իշխանութեանց տարածուիլը: Այս լուրը շանթահարեց Այնթապի հայերը: Հետեւեալ օրը կրկին Այնթապ եկաւ Ժէնէրալ տը լա Մոթ: Օր մը առաջ քօլօնէլը թուրքերուն միւթէսարըֆը կանչեց որ զինադադարի վրայ խօսի, չեկաւ եւ պատասխան ղրկեց թէ եթէ Այնթապը պարպելու մասին կ՚ուզէ խորհրդակցիլ, քօլօնէլը իրենց քովը պէտք է որ երթայ: Երբ Ժէնէրալը հասաւ, նոյն օրը միւթէսարըֆ[ը] եւ Քէմալ փաշայի կողմէ կարգուած պաշտօնեան՝ Էօրֆան պէյ, եկան սպայակոյտ, երեք ժամ խորհրդակցեցան, եւ չկրցան համաձայնիլ, որովհետեւ թուրքերը պնդեցին որ իրենք հրահանգ առած են Քէմալ փաշայէն թէ ֆրանսացիք պիտի պարպեն Այնթապը. Ժէնէրալն ալ ըսաւ թէ ինքը Կուրօյէն հրաման առած է Այնթապ քաղաքին մէջէն իր երկու երեք տեղ գտնուող զինուորները քաշել եւ իր բանակով նստիլ Գոլէճին մէջ: Ետքը երկուքն ալ նոր հրահանգ ուզելէ յետոյ Քիլիսի մէջ զինադադարի տեղական պայմանները կնքելու որոշումով բաժնուեցան իրարմէ: Այսօր թուրք պատուիրակներ գացին Քիլիս: Քօլօնէլը երկու օրէ ի վեր կը հաղորդէ մեզի թէ հայ թաղերը պիտի յանձնուին Յունիս 8ին թուրքերուն եւ անոնք պիտի կառավարեն: Հայերը կ՚ընդդիմանան առարկելով թէ եթէ թուրքերը անգամ մը ներս մտնեն՝ բոլոր հայերը եթէ չջարդեն իսկ, յանցաւոր ու ապստամբ կը նկատեն, այլեւայլ կերպով կը դատապարտեն ու կախաղան կը հանեն: Ասոր համոզուեցաւ եւ առաջարկեց որ երեւելիներ եւ գործի վրայ գտնուողներ քաշուին երթան հիմակուընէ: Մենք ասիկա թէ՛ անկարելի եւ թէ՛ անպատուաբեր նկատելով մեր անձին համար, չընդունեցինք: Երկու օրէ ի վեր կը վիճաբանինք այս խնդրոյն վրայ: Ինքը կը պնդէ որ Յունիս 8ին դիրքերը քակելու ենք եւ թուրք իշխանութեան տեղի տալու ենք, իբր թէ այն հայոց վնաս մը չի կրնար հասցնել եղեր: Վերջապէս այսօր առտուն առաջարկեցինք ամբողջովին գաղթել: Փոխադրութեան միջոց չկայ ըսաւ ու հազիւ 80–100 կառք տրամադրել խոստացաւ:

11–12 հազար ժողովուրդ 80 կառքով կարելի չէ փոխադրել: Այնթապի հարստութեան բոլորը պիտի մնայ թուրքին, նոյնիսկ մեր գոյքերը եկեղեցի հաւաքելով բանալին իրեն յանձնել ուզեցինք, չկրցաւ ընդունիլ, որովհետեւ ես ներսը մարդ չեմ կրնար դնել ու չեմ կրնար հսկել ըսաւ: Հայերը արդէն երթալ չեն ուզեր եւ միայն ցոյց մըն էր որ կ՚ընէին, բայց օգուտ չըրաւ: Այսօր կէսօրուան մօտ 20 տարեկանէ վեր բոլոր մարդիկը հաւաքուեցան եկեղեցի, կացութեան տեղեկացան, ժողովուրդէն խօսողներ եղան, երկու ժամ տեւեց խորհրդակցութիւնը, բողոքականաց առաջին եկեղեցիին մէջ խուռն բազմութիւն կար: *Րեֆերանտօմ* մը ըրինք, բայց շատ կանոնաւոր, բոլոր ժողովուրդը բացարձակ մեծամասնութեամբ, գրեթէ միաձայնութեամբ, որովհետեւ միայն երկու հակառակ քուէ կար հազարաւոր բարձրացեալ ձեռքերու դէմ, ժողովուրդը որոշեց Այնթապ մնալ, անօգնական կռուիլ թուրքին դէմ, պատնէշները չքակել եւ պատնէշին վրայ մեռնիլ: Այս որոշումը հաղորդեցինք քօլօնէլին, որ ապշահար մնաց, վասնզի միշտ կ՚ըսէր թէ եթէ զինադադարի օրէնքին դէմ կռուիք մեզի հակառակ ըրած կ՚ըլլաք եւ մենք երբեք չենք կրնար օգնել ձեզ: Յունիս 7ին թուրքերը հաւանօրէն պիտի առաջարկեն հայոց քակել դիրքերը, հակառակ պարագային սպառնալով յարձակիլ մեր վրայ հրացանով եւ թնդանօթով: Հայերը պիտի պատրաստուին մտնել անհաւասար կռիւի մը:

Հալէպ (Առաջնորդական Փոխանորդ Տէր Յարութիւն [Եսայեանէ]) – 9 Յունիս

Այսօր Այնթապէն առնուած տեղեկութեանց համաձայն կացութիւնը չէ փոխուած հոն ֆրանսական զինուորական իշխանութեանց եւ Քէմալիստներու միջեւ կնքելի պայմանագրու-

authorities and the Kemalists have not been finally resolved yet. Nevertheless, the danger exists and remains with the same or greater intensity. The Armenians of Aleppo have been very disturbed for a week now because they do not have the means to financially support their fellow Armenians from Gaziantep.

• We learn from official and personal letters from Maraş that the Armenians' situation there is indescribable. Although no official massacre has occurred, fear and horror have exhausted the Armenians. "The Armenians have been decimated to one-third in five months." In these prevailing circumstances, what will be the condition of the people who want to be brought out of that cursed place and who have accepted starvation to death in the mountains and plains?

Dörtyol (from the National Union)—June 4

After a months-long systematic siege, Dörtyol has been under attack for two weeks day and night, by thousands of besieging Turkish bandits. The Armenians have secured the task of self-defense thanks to weapons the French government allocated to Armenian self-defense and weapons the Armenians owned. Although the enemy has besieged Dörtyol on all sides, the Armenians have always managed to keep the sea route under their control, whence they sometimes communicate with İskenderun and Mersin by boats. The people who have barely returned from [the forced] migration have long since exhausted their provisions and supplies. Besieged by the enemy, they are in a desperate situation with victuals that will barely last fifteen days. Without help, Dörtyol will be destroyed.

Aleppo (from Dr. Ketenjian)—May 9

During the surrender of the French forces in Urfa and their assassination by means of ambush, the advance of new French forces was taking place at the train station fifty kilometers from Urfa. Although the Turks were filled with intense animosity against the Armenians, as long as there was a fear of French advance, they were naturally unable to oppress the Armenians and remained silent. Armed young Armenians are waiting in the neighborhood. Women and children are going to the market now, but the horror is always there.

The financial and economic situation is pathetic. It was already very tight when, during the siege, the means of those who had some were taken away; many lived eating grass along with the meat of animals. Now they are completely abandoned. During the events in Urfa, the Armenians were economically wiped out completely. Several houses had been left intact; they, too, are destroyed. But there has been little loss of life so far. We have had seven or eight dead and thirteen wounded during the entire fighting.

Gaziantep [Ayntab] (from Priest Nerses N. Tavoukjian, catholicosal vicar)—June 12[80]

On June 8, Tuesday morning, the French colonel in Gaziantep invited the National Union and announced that the French could no longer have relations with the Armenians. Second, Armenian neighborhoods would be occupied by the Turkish government this afternoon. Third, the western part of the city under French occupation, such as the Turkish hospital in the southwestern part of the American hospital, will be handed over to the Turks, and Turkish soldiers will be stationed there. Fourth, the Armenians should go to the Turks an hour before noon today to settle their affairs with them alone. After hearing these instructions as the result of strict and seemingly irreversible order, the impression with which the Armenians departed the colonel cannot be narrated. One can imagine how the responsible body of a people who fought heroically and made every sacrifice for seventy days, always being victorious, felt when the colonel while giving this order, announced that the hostility should not re-

թեանց մի քանի յօդուածներու վիճելի կէտերը տակաւին վերջնապէս չլուծուելուն պատճառով: Այսու հանդերձ, վտանգը նոյնութեամբ կամ աւելի ահռելի սպառնալիքով կայ եւ կը մնայ: Շաբաթէ մը ի վեր Հալէպի հայերը խիստ յուզուած են, վասնզի միջոցներ ալ չունին գէթ նիւթապէս նպաստելու իրենց այնթապցի ազգակիցներուն:

- Մարաշէն հասած պաշտօնական եւ անհատական նամակներէն կը տեղեկանանք որ այդ տեղի հայոց կացութիւնը աննկարագրելի է, թէպէտեւ պաշտօնապէս ջարդ չկայ, սակայն ահ ու սարսափը հալումաշ ըրած է հայութիւնը. «5 ամիսէ ի վեր հայութեան 1/3-ը մնացած է»: Այդ անիծեալ վայրէն դուրս հանուիլ [ուզող] եւ լեռներու, դաշտերու մէջ սովամահ լինելու յանձնառու ժողովրդեան մը վիճակը ի՞նչ պիտի ըլլայ արդեօք տիրող այս պայմաններուն մէջ:

Տէօրթ-Եօլ (Ազգային Միութենէն) – 4 Յունիս

Ամիսներ տեւող սիսթէմաթիք պաշարումէ մը վերջ, երկու շաբաթ է որ գիշեր ցերեկ յարձակման ենթակայ է Տէօրթ-Եօլ շրջապատող հազարաւոր թուրք հրոսակներու կողմէ: Ֆրանսական կառավարութեան հայոց ինքնապաշտպանութեան յատկացուցած զէնքերուն շնորհիւ եւ իրենց ունեցածով ապահոված են ինքնապաշտպանութեան գործը: Թէպէտեւ թշնամին ամէն կողմէ Տէօրթ-Եօլ պաշարած է, սակայն ծովու ճամբան հայերը յաջողած են պահել միշտ իրենց ձեռքը, ուրկէ կը հաղորդակցին երբեմն մակոյկներու միջոցաւ Ալէքսանտրէթի եւ Մերսինի հետ: Գաղթէ հազիւ դարձած ժողովուրդը արդէն շատոնց սպառած է իր ունեցած պարէնն ու պաշարը եւ այսօր պաշարուած թշնամիէն՝ հազիւ 15 օրուան պարէնով կը գտնուի յուսահատական դրութեան մէջ: Առանց օգնութեան Տէօրթ-Եօլ պիտի փճանայ:

Հալէպ (Տոքթոր Քէթէնճեանէ) – 9 Մայիս

Ուրֆայի ֆրանսական զօրաց անձնատուութեան եւ դարանակալ սպանութեան միջոցին Ուրֆայէն 50 քիլոմէթր անդին շոգեկառքի կայարանը ֆրանսական նոր ոյժերու յառաջացումը տեղի կ'ունենար: Թուրքերը թէպէտեւ հայերու դէմ շատ լարուած, բայց քանի ֆրանսական յառաջացման վախը կար, բնական է չպիտի կրնային հայերը նեղել ու մնացին լուռ: Հայ երիտասարդութիւնը զէնք ի ձեռին կը սպասէ թաղին մէջ, կիներ եւ մանուկներ այլեւս շուկայ կ'իջնեն, բայց սարսափը միշտ գոյութիւն ունի:

Նիւթական, տնտեսական վիճակը արգահատելի է: Արդէն շատ նեղն էր, պաշարման շրջանին քիչ թէ շատ ունեցողինն ալ ձեռքէ առնուեցաւ, անասուններու միսին հետ խոտով ապրողներ շատ եղան: Այժմ բոլորովին լքեալ վիճակ մը ունին: Ուրֆայի դէպքերու միջոցին նիւթապէս հայութիւնը ամբողջովին փճացաւ. մի քանի ողջ տուներ կային՝ ոչնչացան: Բայց ցարդ անձի կորուստ քիչ կայ. ամբողջ կռիւներու ընթացքին ունեցանք 7–8 մեռեալ եւ 13 վիրաւոր:

Այնթապ (Կաթողիկոսական Փոխանորդ Ներսէս քահանայ Ն. Թավուզճեանէ) – 12 Յունիս

Յունիս 8 Գշ. առտուն Այնթապի ֆրանսացի քօլօնէլը Ազգային Միութիւնը հրաւիրելով կը յայտարարէ թէ այլեւս ֆրանսացիք հայերուն հետ ոեւէ յարաբերութեան մէջ չեն կրնար գտնուիլ: Երկրորդ՝ այսօր կէսօրին հայ թաղերը թուրք կառավարութեան կողմէ պիտի գրաւուին: Երրորդ՝ քաղաքիս արեւմտեան կողմը ֆրանսացւոց գրաւման տակ գտնուող, զոր օրինակ, Ամերիկեան հիւանդանոցին հարաւային արեւմտեան կողմի թուրք հիւանդանոցը թուրքերուն պիտի յանձնուի եւ հոն թուրք զինուորներ պիտի դրուին: Չորրորդ՝ հայերը այսօր կէսօրէն ժամ մը առաջ պիտի երթան թուրքերու քով իրենց գործերը պիտի կարգադրեն թուրքերուն հետ առանձինն: Այս հրահանգը կտրուկ եւ իբր անդառնալի հրամանի մը արդիւնք լսելէ ետքը ինչ տպաւորութեամբ հայերը մեկնեցան քօլօնէլին քովէն կարելի չէ պատմել: Կարելի է երեւակայել թէ 70 օր հերոսաբար եւ ամէն զոհողութիւն յանձն առնելով կռուող եւ միշտ յաղթող հանդիսացող ժողովուրդի մը պատասխանատու

sume because the result would be dangerous and the Armenians would be left on their own. After leaving the colonel, the National Union gathered the public at large, explained the situation, formed a responsible body with broader representation, and began communicating with the Turks. Around the evening of June 9, the Turkish hospital was handed over to the Turks, and the following night the Armenians handed over the Akyol mosque: one of their strategic positions. The Armenian streets will be opened today, and all the avenues, tomorrow. The Turkish government has announced martial law.

Late last night, upon the terms given to the Armenian delegates, it [the government] posted a statement on the walls stating that no Armenian would be persecuted or punished in any way for past events. The Armenians could keep their weapons, and a series of exhortations [were given] to the people to live in peace with each other and so on.

It was learned that as of yesterday, the government of Gaziantep was officially under the administration of Mustafa Kemal. The delegates of the National Union sent a telegram yesterday on behalf of the Armenian people to Kemal Pasha, saying that the Armenians of Gaziantep accept his rule and promise to live and cooperate sincerely with their Muslim compatriots.

At the same time, the Armenian people are constantly worried, afraid, and unsure about the Turks. Many people want to leave Gaziantep at any cost, even naked and on foot, but there are no means. The current situation is unbearable.

Aleppo (from Priest Haroutyun Yesayan)—June 16

To alleviate the situation of the Armenians in Gaziantep [Ayntab], we dispatched two representatives to Beirut, where they appealed in writing to General Gouraud. General Gouraud replied that "he could not disrespect the agreement signed with Mustafa Kemal. Armenians have to conform." To a second appeal, he answered through his adviser that

a) not a single Armenian would be arrested or imprisoned by the Turkish authorities; Armenians would not turn in their weapons;

b) the lives of Armenians would be secured absolutely, and if there is ever any encroachment on Armenians by the Turks, they [the French] will practically defend them; [and]

c) they will provide Armenians' livelihood.

He promised to cable these instructions to Gaziantep for implementation immediately, and indeed he did so.

Two weeks ago, those in Gaziantep who were old, wretched, handicapped, and incapable of fighting began to leave Gaziantep with their families—about thirty-five hundred people—at the request of the American Red Cross or the decision of the French authorities, pressed by food shortages. The transfer of those sheltered in the American orphanage in Gaziantep to Beirut (there are about three thousand) began three weeks ago. The Red Cross is bringing to Beirut those ready to go from Gaziantep to America at their own expense.

Aleppo (from the locum tenens)—June 24

The situation in Maraş is extremely dangerous and deplorable. They plead through official letters to end the situation, or better yet, for a collective relocation. The misery is horrible, as functionaries of the American Red Cross have testified. Recently, Dr. Lambert (consul) returned from Maraş. He considers it impossible for the Armenians of Maraş to live there in this condition.

մարմինը ինչ կը զգայ, քօլօնէլը երբ կը յայտարարէր այս հրահանգը տուած ատեն թէ թշնամութիւնը վերսկսելու չէ, որովհետեւ արդիւնքը վտանգաւոր կ'ըլլայ եւ հայերը իրենք իրենց գլխուն կը մնան եւայլն: Ազգ. Միութիւնը քօլօնէլէն բաժնուելէն յետոյ ընդհանուր ժողովուրդը համախմբելով կացութիւնը պարզեց եւ աւելի ընդարձակ շրջանակէ պատասխանատու մարմին մը կազեց եւ սկսաւ թուրքերու հետ յարաբերութեան մտնել: Յունիս 9 իրիկուան մօտ թուրք հիւանդանոցը յանձնուեցաւ թուրքերուն, հետեւեալ գիշերը հայերը իրենց դիրքերէն կարեւոր մէկ տեղը, Ազէօլի մզկիթը յանձնեցին: Հայոց փողոցները այսօր պիտի բացուին եւ վաղը՝ բոլոր պողոտաները: Թուրք կառավարութիւնը խարբէի էօրֆիէ յայտարարած է:

Առջի իրիկուն ուշ ատեն հայ պատուիրակներուն տրուած պայմաններուն վրայ, յայտարարութիւն փակցուց պատերը, որով կը յայտարարէ թէ անցած դէպքերուն համար ոչ մէկ հայ ոչ մէկ կերպով չպիտի հետապնդուի եւ չպիտի պատժուի կառավարութեան կողմէ: Հայոց զէնքերը իրենց քովը պիտի մնան, եւ կարգ մը յորդորներ ժողովրդեան որ իրարու հետ հաշտ պիտի ապրին եւայլն:

Այնթապի կառավարութիւնը երէկ իմացուեցաւ որ պաշտօնապէս ենթակայ եղած է Մուսթաֆա Քէմալի վարչութեան եւ երէկ Ազգային Միութեան պատուիրակները հայ ազգին կողմէ հեռագիր մը ուղղեցին Քէմալ փաշային թէ Այնթապի հայերը կ'ընդունին իր իշխանութիւնը եւ կը խոստանան խալամ հայրենակիցներուն հետ ապրիլ եւ գործակցիլ անկեղծօրէն:

Հայ ժողովուրդը ասով հանդերձ միշտ մտատանջ է, երկիւղի մէջ եւ անվստահ թուրքերու նկատմամբ: Շատեր կը փափաքին մեկնիլ Այնթապէն ամէն գնով, նոյնիսկ մերկ եւ հետիոտն, բայց միջոց չկայ: Ներկայ կացութիւնը անտանելի է:

Հալէպ (Յարութիւն քահանայ Եսայեանէ) – 16 Յունիս

Այնթապի հայութեան կացութիւնը մեղմացնելու համար երկու ներկայացուցիչ ղրկեցինք Պէյրութ ուր Ժէնէրալ Կուրօյին դիմած են գրաւոր: Զօր. Կուրօ պատասխանած է թէ «ինք չի կրնար յարգել Մուսթաֆա Քէմալի հետ կնքած պայմանագրութիւնը. հայերը պէտք է որ համակերպին»: Երկրորդ դիմումի մը իր խորհրդականին միջոցաւ պատասխանած է թէ

Ա. Հայերէն ոչ մէկը թուրք իշխանութեանց կողմէ չպիտի ձերբակալուի կամ բանտարկուի, հայերը զէնքերնին չպիտի յանձնեն:

Բ. Բացարձակապէս հայոց կեանքը պիտի ապահովուի եւ եթէ երբեք թուրքերուն կողմէ հայոց վրայ ոտնձգութիւն ըլլայ, իրենք գործնականապէս պիտի պաշտպանեն:

Գ. Հայոց ապրուստը պիտի ապահովեն:

Այս հրահանգները կը խոստանայ անմիջապէս հեռագրել Այնթապ առ ի գործադրութիւն, եւ իրապէս ալ կը հեռագրէ:

Երկու շաբաթէ ի վեր Այնթապի հայերէն անոնք որ ծեր, թշուառ, անկարող ու կռուելու անընդունակ էին, իրենց ընտանիքով 3500ի մօտ Այնթապէն հեռացած էին Ամերիկեան Կարմիր Խաչի դիմումով կամ ֆրանսական իշխանութեանց որոշումով, քանզի պարէնի դժուարութիւնը ստիպած է այդ կարգադրութեան: Իսկ Այնթապի Ամերիկեան Որբանոցին պատսպարեալները կը փոխադրուին ի Պէյրութ (3000ի չափ են) երեք շաբաթէ ի վեր: Այնթապէն իրենց ծախքով Ամերիկա երթալու պատրաստուածները Կարմիր Խաչը մինչեւ Պէյրութ կը ղրկէ:

Հալէպ (Առաջնորդական Տեղապահէն) – 24 Յունիս

Մարաշի վիճակը վերջին ծայր վտանգաւոր եւ խեղճ է: Պաշտօնական նամակներով կը թախանձեն այդ կացութեան վերջ տալու կամ լաւ եւս է ըսել հաւաքաբար այլուր փոխադրութեան համար: Թշուառութիւնը ահռելի է, ինչպէս կը վկայեն Ամերիկեան Կարմիր Խաչի պաշտօնեաները: Այս օրերս Տոքթոր Լէմպըրթ (հիւպատոս) Մարաշէն դարձաւ: Անիկա անկարելի կը նկատէ որ Մարաշի հայութիւնը այս վիճակով կարենայ հոն ապրիլ:

[Insecurity] Notebook Number 12
June–July 1920

Trabzon (from the locum tenens)—June 21[81]

Governor Hamit Bey is leaving after being summoned from Ankara. It is said that the goal of the "Great National Assembly" is to establish military dictatorship everywhere. The Christian population is concerned because of the lack of any means of protection. The implementation of conscription will be a complete disaster. Deportation and massacre can also occur without urgent and immediate measures or at least the presence of an armored cruiser in the port.

- The situation in and around Ordu and Giresun is grave. Bloody incidents abound.

Trabzon (from the Administrative Council)—June 29

Both Muslim and non-Muslim elements are strictly banned from traveling. The mobilization has already begun for Muslims. No one has responded yet, except for a few bandits who are already soldiers ready to massacre and plunder left and right regardless. Local Turkish newspapers continue provocative publications. A rally was held in Akçaabat, where speakers, speaking in highly provocative tones, praised conscription as the only means of salvation for Muslims. The areas near Sürmene and Rize have not responded to the call to arms. Presently, the number of deserters is high among those conscripted. The armed mob, however, is ready to massacre and loot, despite conscription. People want to migrate, but there is no way. The security of the people requires the presence of an armored cruiser in the port.

Azadlı (from Priest Hovhannes Der Sdepanian)—July 13

Some monstrous people, armed with weapons and knives, having taken refuge in nearby bushes in the vicinities of the village of Azadlı (near Yeşilköy [San Stefano]), have attacked and robbed the villagers several times. The abovementioned robbers told some victims: "We want to catch and kill the Armenian priest of the village, in particular, as well as several other Armenians and Greeks, whose names they mentioned. If we fail to catch these people on the road, we will come to the village, enter their houses, take them out to the mountain, and massacre them there."

The village is terrified because they [the villagers] lack the means for self-defense.

İzmit (from the primate)—July 16

Boghos Papazian, an Armenian from the Ortaköy village of Geyve, fled to İzmit and related that a month and a half ago, İppasıcıoğlu Ali, a Turkish villager from Epçeler in Geyve, allegedly said: "If İstanbul is not left to us, we will annihilate the Christians." From Friday, July 9, until Sunday, the Millis have massacred Armenians and Greeks: 1,000 Catholic Armenian families in Ortaköy of Geyve, 150 Apostolic Armenian families in Eşme, 350 Catholic Armenian families in Saraçlıüstü, 200 Catholic Armenian families in Burhaniye, 100 mixed Armenian and Greek families in Köprü of Geyve, and the 200 Apostolic Armenian families of Kıncılar. All were massacred.

There is a fear that Arslanbey, Ovacık, Bahçecik, Greek Yeniköy, Karay, and Tüsı, all besieged since yesterday, will also be burned and [the people] massacred, as they have threatened to do.

It is not known what has happened to the Christian population of Adapazarı. Likewise, no news has been received from the surrounding villages of Ferizli, Tamlik, Upper İstiklal [Papazköy], Revend

[Անապահովութեան] Տետր Թիւ 12
1920 Յունիս - Յուլիս

Տրապիզոն (Առաջնորդական Տեղապահէն) – 21 Յունիս

Կուսակալ Համիտ պէյ կը հեռանայ Էնկիւրիէն կանչուած ըլլալով: «Ազգային Մեծ Ժողով»ին նպատակն է կ'ըսուի զինուորական տիկտատորութիւն հաստատել ամէն կողմ: Քրիստոնեայ բնակչութիւնը մտահոգ է զուրկ ըլլալով պաշտպանութեան ամէն միջոցներէ: Զօրակոչի գործադրութիւնը կատարեալ աղէտ մը պիտի ըլլայ: Տեղահանութիւն եւ ջարդ ալ կրնայ պատահիլ եթէ ստիպողական եւ անմիջական ձեռնարկներ չըլլան կամ գոնէ զրահաւոր մը չսպասէ նաւահանգիստի մէջ:

- Օրտուի եւ Կիրասոնի մէջ եւ շրջակայքը կացութիւնը ծանր է: Արիւնալի դէպքեր անպակաս են:

Տրապիզոն (Վարչական Խորհուրդէն) – 29 Յունիս

Երթեւեկութիւնը՝ իսլամ եւ ոչ-իսլամ տարրերու, բացարձակապէս արգիլուած է: Արդէն սկսած է զօրահաւաքը առայժմ իսլամներուն համար, որուն ոչ ոք պատասխանած է ցարդ, բացի մի քանի աւազակներէ, որոնք առանց անոր ալ արդէն զինուոր են աջ ու ձախ կոտորելու եւ կողոպտելու պատրաստ: Տեղական թուրք թերթերը կը շարունակեն իրենց գրգռիչ հրատարակութիւնները: Բլաթանայի մէջ միթինկ մը կազմակերպուած է, ուր խօսողները՝ վերին աստիճան գրգռիչ թօնով, փառաբանած են զօրակոչը իբրեւ միակ փրկարար միջոցը իսլամութեան: Սիւրմէնէի եւ Րիզէի կողմերը չեն պատասխանած զինակոչին: Իսկ առայժմ հաւաքուածներուն մէջ ալ դասալիքներու թիւը շատ է: Զինուած ամբոխը թէեւ հակառակ զինուորագրութեան պատրաստ է կոտորելու եւ կողոպտելու: Ժողովուրդը գաղթել կ'ուզէ բայց միջոց չկայ: Ժողովուրդին ապահովութեան համար անհրաժեշտ է զրահաւորի մը գոյութիւնը նաւահանգիստին մէջ:

Ազատլը (Տ. Յովհաննէս քահանայ Տէր Ստեփանեանէ) – 13 Յուլիս

Ազատլը գիւղին (Այ-Սթէֆանոյի մօտ) շրջակաները այս օրերս կարգ մը այլանդակ մարդիկ՝ զէնքերով ու դանակներով զինուած՝ գիւղին մօտ մացառներու մէջ ապաստանելով, քանի մը անգամներ գիւղացիներու վրայ յարձակած եւ զանոնք կողոպտած են: Յիշեալ աւազակները այս կողոպտուողներէն մէկ քանիներուն ըսած են թէ՝ մենք մասնաւորապէս գիւղի հայ քահանան, նաեւ ուրիշ քանի մը հայ եւ յոյն անձերու անունները տալով, անոնք բռնել եւ սպաննել կ'ուզենք: Եթէ այս մարդիկը ճամբան չկարողանանք բռնել, գիւղ պիտի գանք եւ իրենց տուները մտնելով զիրենք լեռը պիտի հանենք եւ հոն պիտի ջարդենք, ըսած են:

Ահ ու սարսափի մէջ է գիւղը, զի ինքնապաշտպանութեան միջոցներէ զուրկ են:

Նիկոմիդիա (Առաջնորդէն) – 16 Յուլիս

Կէյվէյի օրթագիւղցի հայ մը՝ Պօղոս Փափազեան, փախ[չ]ելով կուգայ Նիկոմիդիա եւ կը պատմէ թէ ամիսուկէս առաջ Կէյվէյի Էպճէլէր թուրք գիւղացի Իպպասիճի օղլու Ալի կ'ըսէ եղեր թէ երբ Պոլիսը մեզի չյանձնուն՝ քրիստոնեաները պիտի բնաջնջենք: Յուլիս 9 Ուրբաթ օրէն սկսեալ մինչեւ Կիրակի օրը հայերը եւ յոյները ջարդած են Միլլիճիները.- Կէյվէ Միջագիւղի 1000 տուն հայ-հոռոմները, Էշմէի 150 տուն հայերը, Սարաճըը Իւսթիւ[հ] 350 տուն հայ-հոռոմները, Պիւրհանիյէի 200 տուն հայ-հոռոմները, Կէյվէի Կամուրջի 100 տուն հայ եւ յոյն խառն բնակչութիւնը, Գրնճըլարի 200 տուն հայերը բոլորն ալ ջարդեր են:

Երկիւղ կայ որ Արսլանպէկ, Օվաճըզ, Պարտիզակ, յոյն Եէնի Քէօյ, Գարայ, Թիւսիէ, որոնք պաշարուած են երէկուընէ ի վեր, նոյնպէս այրուին եւ ջարդուին, ինչպէս կը սպառնան:

Չի գիտցուիր թէ Ատաբազարի քրիստոնեայ բնակչութիւնը ինչ եղած է: Նոյնպէս լուր չկայ շրջակայ Ֆէրիզլի, Թամլըզ, Վերին Փափազ, Րէվէնտ եւ Գանթարի, Ալմալու գիւղերէն: Կը լսուի թէ

and Kantar, and Elmalı. It has been heard that the Armenians of Upper Fındıklı and the Greeks of the village of Fulacık in Yalova have already been massacred, and the villages have been burned.

Trabzon (from the Administrative Council)—July 7[82]

Traffic is strictly forbidden. The Armenian refugees, working for the Americans for a small daily wage, have been dismissed. It is not known why. As a result, poverty has intensified. Two days ago, Topal Osman Agha, the famous chief bandit of Giresun, came to Trabzon with about twenty comrades. On the evening he arrived, he beat, in public, the inspector of Regie who had just come from Harput and saddler Züftü. Both are now in prison for not supporting the desired movement. The Armenians' condition continues to become more dangerous and uncertain day by day. Rumors of deportation and massacre circulate constantly. The number of spies and secret police has increased, like the unique situation prevailing during the Hamidian period.[83] The prelacy and prominent Armenians are under strict surveillance. Although [it is] mysterious and silent, we feel surrounded by a monstrous element led by a high authority and organized by a local anti-Armenian group. There is no accountability whatsoever. People are motivated to rob and seize the opportunity at all costs.

Unemployed Armenian migrants want to leave but have no permission [to leave]. The slaughterers of old are in control of the situation. They walk around the city armed and threatening.

The Turkish crowd is secretly and feverishly preparing. The military encourages and guides them. The arrival of an armored cruiser can only prevent the explosion of a catastrophe.

The Millis have succeeded in removing the Greek Red Cross hospital staff. Giving in to threatening orders, they [the staff] closed the hospital today and left. A few days ago, the government appealed to local neighborhood representatives and demanded weapons.

• Today, three hundred people have been invited to get together in a Turkish club, where they will hold closed-door deliberations about their course.

M[amuret] ul Aziz (from the primate)—June 17

This place is ruined materially and morally. The situation is so sad that it is impossible to imagine from the outside. There is nothing that does not reveal a despairing scene of destruction; misfortunes surpassing each other appear at every step; curtains open on new moral depravities every moment, all resulting from the people and events that surround them.

According to an order issued by the central government after the armistice, the [local] government, based on the testimony of two people, began to give permanent title deeds for Armenian properties to close or distant relatives of Armenian owners. This procedure provided an opportunity for some abuse. Those who were quick and managed to arrange two witnesses took the ownership of a house, garden, and fields. They started pursuing the issue in court a little later when the real heirs appeared. In this case, though, only those who were able to produce influential advocates could gain the right to their properties. Many times the actual owners have been deprived of their rights.

Sivas (from the primate)—June 30[84]

Until now, it was forbidden for men to travel, while women and children were allowed to travel with incredible difficulty. Nowadays, however, according to an order from the central government in Ankara, Armenians are entirely barred from leaving the city, whether they are locals or outsiders. Many people from Harput, Malatya, Devrek, and other places come here en route to their destinations or

Վերին Փընտըզլըի հայ-հոռոմները եւ Եալովայի Փուլանըզ գիւղի յոյները արդէն ջարդած եւ գիւղերը այրած են:

Տրապիզոն (Վարչական Խորհուրդէն) – 7 Յուլիս

Երթեւեկութիւնը բացարձակապէս արգիլուած է: Հայ գաղթականները՝ որոնք չնչին օրավարձով կ'աշխատէին ամերիկացիներու մօտ՝ արձակուած են, չի գիտցուիր ինչո՞ւ: Ասոր հետեւանքով կարօտութիւնը ծանրացաւ: Երկու օր առաջ Տրապիզոն եկաւ Կիրասոնի յայտնի հրոսապետ Թօփալ Օսման աղան՝ իր քանի չափ ընկերներով: Եկած իրիկուն հրապարակով ծեծեց Խարբերդէն նոր եկող Րէժիի միւֆէթթիշը եւ թամբագործ Չիւփտին, որոնք համախոհ չըլլալով փափաքուած շարժումին՝ բանտարկուած են: Հայոց վիճակը օրէ օր կը դառնայ վտանգաւոր եւ անստոյգ: Տեղահանութեան եւ կոտորածի մասին յամառ լուրեր կը շրջին: Համիտեան շրջանի յատուկ դրութեամբ լրտեսներու եւ գաղտնի ոստիկաններու թիւը աւելցած է: Առաջնորդարանը եւ յայտնի հայ անձեր լուրջ հսկողութեան տակ են: Թէեւ խորհրդաւոր եւ լուռ, բայց կը զգանք որ մեր շուրջը կը դառնայ հրէշային զգացումներով տարուած տարր մը ղեկավարուած վերին իշխանութենէ եւ կազմակերպուած տեղական հակահայ խմբակի կողմանէ: Ոեւէ պատասխանատուութիւն գոյութիւն չունի եւ անձեր կան որոնք թալանելու եւ ամէն զնով առիթը օգտագործելու նպատակով տարուած են:

Հայ գաղթականներ, անգործ, կ'ուզեն մեկնիլ, սակայն հրաման չկայ: Հին ջարդարարները կացութեան տէրն են եւ զինուած կը շրջին քաղաքին մէջ սպառնալով:

Գաղտնի եւ տենդոտ պատրաստութեան մէջ է թուրք ամբոխը: Չինուորականները կը քաջալերեն եւ կը ղեկավարեն զայն: Աղէտի մը պայթումը միայն կրնայ արգիլուիլ զրահաւորի մը գալով:

Միլլին յաջողեցաւ Յունական Կարմիր Խաչի հիւանդանոցի պաշտօնէութիւնը հեռացնել: Այսօր հիւանդանոցը փակեցին եւ մեկնեցան սպառնական հրամաններու առջեւ տեղի տալով: Քանի մը օր առաջ կառավարութենէն դիմում եղած է տեղական մըխթարներուն եւ զէնք է պահանջուած:

- Այսօր 300 անձերու հրաւէր մը եղած է թուրք գլիւպ հաւաքուելու համար, ուր դռնփակ խորհրդակցութիւններ տեղի պիտի ունենա[ն] իրենց ընթացքին մասին:

Մ[ամուրէթ] իւլ Ազիզ (Առաջնորդէն) – 17 Յունիս

Տեղւոյս նիւթական եւ բարոյական վիճակը քայքայուած է: Այնքան տխուր է կացութիւնը որ դուրսէն երեւակայել կարելի չէ: Չկայ բան մը, որ աւերումի յուսահատ[ե]ցնող տեսարան չպարզէ, ամէն քայլափոխի զիրար գերազանցող թշուառութիւններ երեւան կուգան, ամէն վայրկեան բարոյական այլանդակութիւններու նոր վարագոյրներ կը բացուին, ամէնքն ալ արդիւնք՝ զիրենք շրջապատող դէմքերու եւ դէպքերու:

Կառավարութիւնը, զինադադարէն յետոյ, կեդրոնէն տրուած հրամանին համաձայն՝ հայերու կալուածները երկու անձերու վկայութեամբ սեփականատիրոջ մերձաւոր կամ հեռաւոր մէկ ազգականին տուած է *զաիմ հէօճէթի*ով եւ ասիկա կարգ մը զեղծումներու առիթ եղած է. ով որ ճարպիկ գտնուած է եւ կրցած է երկու վկայ յարմարցնել՝ տէր դարձած է տան, այգիի եւ արտերու. քիչ վերջը բուն ժառանգը երեւան ելած եւ սկսած է դատական եղանակով հետեւապնդել խնդիրը. այս պարագային ալ ազդեցիկ պաշտպան մը ունեցողը միայն կրցած է իրաւունք շահիլ եւ շատ անգամ պատահած է, որ բուն իրաւատէրը զրկուած է իր իրաւունքէն:

Սեբաստիա (Առաջնորդէն) – 30 Յունիս

Մինչեւ ցարդ այր մարդոց համար տեղէս մեկնիլ արգիլուած ըլլալով՝ կիները եւ փոքրները հազար դժուարութեամբ կ'արտօնուէին ճամբորդելու, սակայն այս օրերս Էնգարէի կեդրոնական կառավարութենէն եկած հրահանգի մը համեմատ՝ հայերուն ի սպառ արգիլուած է քաղաքէս դուրս ելնել, ըլլան տեղացի, ըլլան դուրսեցի: Խարբերդէն, Մալաթիայէն, Տիվրիկէն եւ այլ տեղերէ շատեր

İstanbul, but now they are not allowed to leave, and they, too, weigh on us, as if the needs of our people were not enough. There were already orphans and widows in the city who wanted to go to their guardians in İstanbul or their birthplaces—Samsun, Giresun, Trabzon, and their vicinities. We were waiting to send them after the winter to lighten the local burden, but as the summer barely arrived, the obstacles and the difficulties also arrived. In addition to the government ban on travelers, there are also road insecurities. Under these circumstances, we would have preferred to keep everyone in their place and not allow them to leave, but since the villagers already could not benefit from their fields, and even the prospect of enjoying the results of the seeds that we distributed does not exist because of the current turmoil and confusion, the hope to see the misery of the people alleviated partially exists no more. In short, the financial situation here and in the surrounding areas has remained unchanged throughout the year. Otherwise, aside from waiting for relief, the people would have been able to keep the orphanage and the shelter functioning presently with their means.

Judging from the current situation, the place's future is dark and gloomy. The people see themselves as hostages, which can be considered a fair assessment, as Armenians are not allowed to leave. Those who did manage to reach Samsun were detained there.

One of the things that left an unbecoming impression on the people was the gradual departure of the American Near East Relief from various places because of [the state of] security and fear. Some of their personnel have been expelled by local authorities or the çetes.

Clashes between Turks are frequent in some parts of the province. The prefect and the government assure [us] that there is no danger to the Armenians, claiming that Armenians were not harmed during the recent tragic incident in Zile.

However, these promises are not enough to assure the people.

• There has been information about Saimbeyli [Hacın] that it has been besieged by Turkish and Circassian çetes and is in danger of extinction. The American Near East Relief, which may have partially supported their livelihood, has been expelled from the vicinity of Saimbeyli, and even their building was set on fire; therefore, one can imagine the alarming and dangerous situation of thousands of Armenians in Saimbeyli. In the face of imminent danger, the Armenian primate of Sivas has appealed to the prefect and asked for means to reach an agreement between the Armenian and Turkish elements in Saimbeyli since the headquarters and governing body of the [Milli] organization are there. The prefect has expressed regret that both sides are locked in a tense situation to crush and annihilate each other and that he wishes to see an agreement between the two elements. He has suggested that either the primate goes to Saimbeyli in person with a functionary appointed by them or that he send a capable person on his behalf. The primate is reluctant to act on his own.

• A few days ago, the government issued enlistment orders for Muslims born in 1884–1893 to quell the disturbances in various parts of the province of Sivas, which began with an anti-Milli appearance and have now attained the characteristics of sheer robbery.

Gaziantep [Ayntab] (from Priest Nerses Tavoukjian, catholicosal vicar)—June 15[85]

The food could only last for eight to ten days. Realizing that in fifteen to twenty days, they would surrender due to starvation, the Armenians authorized the assembly they had elected to act at its discretion. When the assembly was convened, as a first step, it was decided to hand over the two [military] positions and enter into negotiations with the Turks with the following conditions: a) to not open any

կուզան հոս՝ իրենց տեղերը կամ Պոլիս երթալու համար, բայց թոյլ չեն տրուիր մեկնելու եւ այդպիսիներն ալ կը ծանրանան մեր վրայ, իբր թէ չքաւէին մերինները: Արդէն քաղաքիս մէջ ալ կան որբեր եւ այրիներ որոնք իրենց պաշտպաններուն Պոլիս եւ կամ իրենց ծննդավայրերը՝ Սամսոն, Կիրասոն, Տրապիզոն եւ այդ շրջակաները երթալ կ'ուզեն եւ կը սպասուէր ձմեռը ելնելէն յետոյ ղրկել զիրենք, որպէսզի տեղւոյս բեռը քիչ մը թեթեւնար, սակայն հազիւ ամառը հասաւ եւ ահա արգելքն ու դժուարութիւններն ալ վրայ հասան: Ճամբորդներու համար կառավարական արգելքէն զատ ճանապարհի անապահովութիւններն ալ կան. այս պարագաներու տակ աւելի լաւ պիտի համարէինք ամէն մարդ պահել իր կեցած տեղը եւ թոյլ չտալ մեկնելու, սակայն գիւղացիք արդէն չկրցան օգտուիլ իրենց արտերէն եւ նոյնիսկ մեր կողմէն բաժնուած սերմնցուներու արդիւնքն վայելելու հաւանականութիւնը չկայ ներկայ խառնակ եւ շփոթ կացութեան պատճառով, որով՝ ժողովրդեան թշուառութիւնը մասամբ դարմանուած տեսնելու յոյսն ալ չմնաց: Վերջապէս տեղւոյս եւ շրջակայից նիւթական վիճակը մէկ տարւոյ շրջանին մէջ անփոփոխ մնաց. եթէ ոչ ժողովուրդը այսօր նպաստի չսպասելէ զատ որբանոցն ու պատսպարանն ալ իր միջոցներով պահելու վիճակին մէջ պիտի գտնուէր:

Ներկայ կացութենէն հետեւցնելով տեղւոյս ապագան մութ ու մռայլ է եւ ժողովուրդը ինքզինքը իբր պատանդ վար դրուած կը նկատէ, ինչ որ արդարացի կրնայ համարուիլ, քանի որ հայերուն արգիլուած է հեռանալ ասկէ: Անոնք որ յաջողած էին մինչեւ Սամսոն հասնիլ՝ հոն վար դրուած են:

Ժողովրդեան վրայ յոռի տպաւորութիւն գործող մէկ պարագան ալ Ամերիկեան Նպաստամատոյց Մարմնոյն մաս առ մաս ասկէ անկէ մեկնիլն է ապահովութեան եւ երկիւղի պատճառով. ոմանց ալ պարզապէս արտաքսումը տեղական իշխանութեանց կամ *չէթէ*ներու կողմէ:

Նահանգիս շրջակաները տեղ տեղ անպակաս են ընդհարումներ թուրքերու մէջ: Կուսակալը եւ կառավարութիւնը ապահովութիւն կուտան թէ հայոց համար վտանգ չկայ, ինչպէս որ վերջերս Զիլէի մէջ պատահած ցաւալի դէպքէն արդարեւ հայերը չեն վնասուած ըստ յայտարարութեան կուսակալին:

Այս խոստումները սակայն բաւարար չեն ժողովուրդը ապահովելու:

- Հաճընի մասին հոս տեղեկութիւն կայ թէ պաշարուած է թուրք եւ չէրքէզ *չէթէ*ներու կողմէ եւ կը գտնուի բնաջնջման վտանգին տակ: Ամերիկեան Նպաստամատոյցը որ թերեւս մասամբ կրնար անոնց ապրուստին նպաստել, այսօր արտաքսուած [է] Հաճընի շրջակայքէն, նոյնիսկ շէնքերնին ալ այրուած, հետեւաբար կարելի է երեւակայել Հաճընի մէջ գտնուող հազարաւոր հայերու տագնապալի եւ վտանգաւոր վիճակը: Անմիջական վտանգի առջեւ Սեբաստիոյ հայոց Առաջնորդը կը դիմէ կուսակալին եւ Հաճընի հայ եւ թուրք տարրերու միջեւ համաձայնութիւն գոյացնելու միջոցներ [կը խնդրէ], քանի որ *Թէշքիլաթ*ին կեդրոնը եւ վարիչ մարմինը հոս է: Կուսակալը ցաւ կը յայտնէ թէ երկու կողմն ալ իրարու հակառակորդ եւ զիրար ջարդելու, բնաջինջ ընելու համար լարուած վիճակի մէջ են եւ ինքն ալ փափաքող է երկու տարրին մէջ համաձայնութիւն գոյացած տեսնելու եւ առաջարկեց որ իրենց կողմէն նշանակուած պաշտօնէի մը հետ կամ առաջնորդը անձամբ երթայ Հաճըն եւ կամ կարող անձնաւորութիւն մը ղրկէ իր կողմէ: Առաջնորդը վարանած է ինքնագլուխ գործելու:

- Սեբաստիոյ նահանգին այլեւայլ կողմերը տիրող խռովութիւնները զսպելու համար՝ որ հակամիլլի երեւոյթով սկսա[ն] եւ այժմ պարզ աւազակութեան հանգամանք ստացած [են]՝ կառավարութիւնը քանի մը օրէ ի վեր 300–309ի ծնունդ խլամները զէնքի տակ կոչեց:

Այնթապ (Կաթողիկոսական Փոխանորդ Ներսէս քահանայ Թավուքճեանէ) – 15 Յունիս

8–10 օրուան ուտելիք միայն մնացած էր, ուստի նկատելով որ 15–20 օրէն անօթութեան հետեւանօք անձնատուր պիտի ըլլան հայերը, իրենց ընտրած ժողովին լիազօրութիւն տուին իր յարմար դատած եղանակով գործելու: Ժողովը գումարուեցաւ եւ իբր առաջին նախաքայլ որոշեց երկու դիրքերը յանձնել եւ բանակցութեան մտնել թուրքերու հետ սա պայմաններով. Ա. հայոց

of the Armenian positions and keep the situation intact until the end of the deliberations; b) [to] obtain a promise for provisions; [and] c) [to] invite a commission made up of Arabs and Americans from Aleppo to mediate the reconciliation formally. But if they only accepted the first of these three conditions, we would hand over the two positions; otherwise, hostilities would resume. The Turks accepted the first condition precisely as it was; for the second, they said people could go to the market and furnish food; for the third, they said that this would very much delay [reconciliation], and therefore the Turks suggested that both sides be satisfied with [the mediation of] Dr. Shepard. Consequently, that day around the evening, the two positions were handed over to the Turks, who were supposed to station 20 to 30 people in each, but instead placed 160 people in both. The next day, the Armenians presented these proposals:

a) As a result of the situation that has arisen for some time, no Armenian should be persecuted or punished in any way; b) the weapons of Armenians should not be seized; c) there should be no boycott [against Armenians]; d) those who want to leave the city should be free [to do so]; [and] e) new guardhouses should not be installed in addition to the old ones in Armenian neighborhoods.

They accepted almost all the conditions but offered nothing in writing. Simply, the government officially issued a statement in which the first suggestion of the Armenians was kept intact; for the second, it was said that the Armenians should leave their weapons at home and walk around unarmed; for the third, the Turks said that it [the boycott] was already prohibited by law and cannot take place; as for the fourth, they said that anyone who wanted to leave should come, get a credential, and leave; for the fifth, they said that they did not intend to establish guardhouses. The matter of dismantling the positions was left to June 13, Sunday. On June 10, a telegram was dispatched to Mustafa Kemal for allegiance.

On June 9, the Turks occupied the Akyol mosque with a pretext; on June 12, they occupied the Kalanlı guardhouse with the Armenians' knowledge, and on the 13th, all the streets were opened.

On June 11, people started going to the market and buying flour and so on. On Sunday, June 13, the commander of the Milli forces, his aide Celal Kadri, and the district governor came to the First Church, and while all the people were there, they spoke about the necessity of fraternity, expressing trust in Mustafa Kemal's newly formed government, and cooperating as compatriots against the enemy. As a piece of cable news, the district governor announced there that the Allied powers had withdrawn their decision on Turkey from the sultan and entered into direct communication with Kemal Pasha. He also said that the Germans had declared war on France, so the French were forced to withdraw from here, and so on.

Today, June 15, the Turks have captured the Kazanlı guardhouse up to the end of Paşa Sokağı. They also captured the winery near the Topbashians' mill; Ishkhan's house, which was an important position for the Armenians; the Çınarcı mosque; and the house of Agha Nigoghos. The French vacated the Latin monastery. They [the Turks] occupied the Akyol mosque. They placed soldiers in the Armenian National Hotel and occupied the hotel of draper Ahmed and the Turkish hospital. In this way, the Armenians are besieged on all sides. Today, despite their promise, they placed twenty soldiers in Ali Bey's house as guards after three days of circumnavigation.

Today, the Armenians categorically decided that if the Turks made any new encroachment tomorrow or the next day, they would oppose it, but if there were no reason [for opposing], we would live in peace and quiet.

Relations between the Armenians and the French have been severed since June 8.

By opening the positions, the Armenians have not incurred any loss yet. Cessation of the fighting benefited the Armenians because they understood the conditions of the Turks in Gaziantep and the composition and strength of the newly formed government and the Milli troops of Gaziantep. Gazi-

դիրքերէն ոչ մէկը չքանալ եւ կացութիւնը անխախտ պահել մինչեւ խորհրդակցութեան վերջը: Բ. պարենաւորման համար խոստում առնել, Գ. Հալէպէն արաբներէ եւ ամերիկացիներէ կազմուած յանձնախումբ մը հրաւիրել հաշտութեան պաշտօնապէս միջնորդելու համար: Բայց այս երեք պայմաններէն եթէ միայն առաջինն ալ ընդունուէր, պիտի յանձնէինք երկու դիրքերը, իսկ եթէ չընդունուէր՝ այն ատեն պիտի սկսուէր թշնամութեան: Թուրքերը առաջին պայմանը ընդունեցին ճիշդ եղածին պէս, Բ.ին համար ըսին որ ուզողը թող շուկայ իջնայ եւ պարէն հայթայթէ. Գ.ին համար ըսին թէ ասիկա շատ կ'ուշացնէ, հետեւաբար Տոքթ. Շեփըր[տ]ով թող գոհանայ երկու կողմն ալ: Արդ, այն օրը իրիկուան մօտ երկու դիրքերը յանձնուեցան թուրքերուն, որոնք իւրաքանչիւրին մէջ 20–30 մարդ պիտի դնէին, բայց երկուքին մէջ 160 մարդ տեղաւորեցին: Հետեւեալ օրը հայերը սա առաջարկները ներկայացուցին:

Ա. Ժամանակէ մը ի վեր յառաջ եկած վիճակին իբր արդիւնք դէպքերու համար որեւէ հայ ոչ մէկ կերպով չպիտի հետապնդուի եւ չպիտի պատժուի: Բ. Հայոց զէնքերը չպիտի գրաւուին: Գ. *Պօյքոթ* չպիտի ըլլայ: Դ. Քաղաքէն մեկնիլ ուզողները ազատ պիտի ըլլան: Ե. Հին պահականոցներու վրայ հայ թաղերու մէջ նորեր չպիտի հաստատուին:

Այս պայմանները ամէնն ալ գրեթէ ընդունեցին, բայց գրաւոր բան մը չտուին: Միայն կառավարութիւնը պաշտօնապէս յայտարարութիւն հրապարակեց, որուն մէջ հայոց առաջին առաջարկը նոյնութեամբ պահուած էր, Բ.ին համար ըսուած էր թէ հայերը իրենց զէնքերը տունը պիտի թողուն եւ անզէն պիտի պտտին, Գ.ին համար թուրքերը ըսին թէ արդէն օրէնքով արգիլուած է եւ չի կրնար ըլլալ, Դ.ին համար ալ ըսին թէ մեկնիլ ուզողը թող գայ *վէսիքա* առնէ երթայ, Ե.ին համար ըսին թէ պահականոց հաստատելու միտք չունին: Եւ դիրքերը բանալու խնդիրը թողուեցաւ Յունիս 13 Կիրակի օրուան: Յունիս 10ին Մուսթաֆա Քէմալի հեռագիր մը քաշուեցաւ հաւատարմութեան:

Թուրքերը Յունիս 9ին գրաւեցին պատրուակով մը Ազէօլի մզկիթը, Յունիս 12ին գրաւեցին Գալանըլըյի պահականոցը հայոց գիտութեամբ եւ 13ին բացուեցան բոլոր փողոցները:

Ժողովուրդը Յունիս 11ին սկսաւ շուկայ իջնել եւ առնել ալիւր եւայլն: Յունիս 13 Կիրակի օրը Գուվվէյի Միլլիյէ[ի] գոմանտանը եւ անոր *եաւէրը*՝ Ճելալ Գատրի եւ միութեասրրըֆը առաջին աղօթարանը եկան եւ բոլոր ժողովուրդը հոն ըլլալով խօսեցան եղբայրակցութեան, նորակազմ կառավարութեան՝ Մուսթաֆա Քէմալ փաշայի վստահութիւն յայտնելու եւ թշնամիին դէմ իբր հայրենակից գործակցելու պէտքերուն վրայ: Հոն իբր հեռագրական լուր [միութեասրրըֆը- Վ.Դ.] յայտարարեց թէ դաշնակից պետութիւնք Թուրքիոյ մասին իրենց որոշմնագիրը սուլթանէն առին եւ Քէմալ փաշային հետ յարաբերութեան մէջ մտան: Ըսաւ նաեւ գերմանները ֆրանսայի դէմ պատերազմ յայտարարած են, ֆրանսացին ասկէ քաշուիլ ստիպուած է եւայլն:

Այսօր, Յունիս 15, թուրքերը գրաւած են Գազանըլը պահականոցը մինչեւ Փաշա Սոգաղըի ծայրը. գրաւեցին նաեւ Թօփպաշեաններու ջաղացքին քովի զինետունը, Իշխանի տունը, որ հայոց կարեւոր մէկ դիրքն էր, Չինարչի ճամին եւ Նիկողոս աղայի տունը իրենց ձեռքն է. լատինաց վանքը ֆրանսացիներէն պարպուեցաւ. Ազէօլի մզկիթը գրաւեցին: Հայոց ազգային օթէլը զինուոր դրին, պէզազ Աhմէտի օթէլը գրաւեցին, թուրք հիւանդանոցը գրաւուած է: Այս կերպով հայերը պաշարուած են ամէն կողմէ: Այսօր հակառակ իրենց խոստումին Ալի պէյին տունը դրին 20 զինուոր իբր պահակ 3 օրուան քաշքշուքէ ետքը:

Այսօր հայերը վճռապէս որոշեցին որ եթէ վաղը կամ միւս օրը թուրքերը նոր ոտնձգութիւն ընեն՝ ընդդիմանան, իսկ եթէ պատճառ չտրուի, ապրինք հաշտ ու լուռ:

Յունիս 8էն ի վեր ֆրանսացիներու հետ հայոց յարաբերութիւնները խզուած են:

Դիրքերը բանալով հայերը կորուստ մը չեն ըրած դեռ: Այս կռիւի դադարը հայոց համար սա օգուտը ունեցաւ թէ հասկցան թէ ի՞նչ է Այնթապի թուրքերուն վիճակը եւ Այնթապի նորակազմ կառավարութեան եւ Միլլի զինուորներու կազմը եւ ուժը: Այնթապ կը գտնուի հիմա Միլլիներու տիրապետութեան տակ. հարուստները թալլուած եւ ցրուած են, եւ երբեք ուժ չեն ներկայացներ. միջին դասակարգը գոհ չէ Միլլիներէն բայց ձայն չի կրնար բարձրացնել. զինուորական կազմակեր-

antep is now under the rule of the Millis. The wealthy [Turks] have been robbed and are scattered; they have no power. The middle class is unsatisfied with the Millis but cannot complain openly. The military organization is loose and weak. The soldiers always desert and scatter. If the çetes increase in number, many people are afraid that there will be looting in Gaziantep. Now they have begun to turn the çetes into the legitimate military. There is no single powerful organization. Ordinary people harbor ill feelings against Armenians, but the officers assure us that there is no bad intention against Armenians and cannot be. Wheat, flour, and oil are scarce. Armenians buy little, hardly as much as they need daily. An Armenian can never sell anything; there is a strict boycott. Armenian artisans cannot work because Turks are forbidden to bring business to Armenians and nobody can object.

Armenians suspect that Armenian neighborhoods will be occupied from within and outside, that the weapons of Armenians will be confiscated, and that Armenians will be evicted from their neighborhoods and scattered in other neighborhoods. But Armenians will oppose this.

It is said that the Turkish soldiers are now sitting in Sam. Some say that they have gone toward İslahiye, perhaps to fight against the Armenians of Amanos. If the French withdraw from Gaziantep, we will be absolutely constrained in terms of provisions. If they stay, perhaps something can be provided through Kilis.

İzmit (from the primate)—July 19

Although it is impossible to get accurate information, it is thought that as of July 8, the [following] were massacred and burned:

1. Catholic Armenians' Ortaköy of Geyve, more than one thousand families
2. Greeks and Armenians in Saraçlıüstü
3. Sazlı, Catholic Armenians
4. Burhaniye, 500 Catholic Armenian families
5. Eşme, Apostolic Armenians, all of them
6. Köprü, Apostolic Armenians, all of them
7. Kıncılar Apostolic Armenians, all of them
8. Ferizli, Apostolic Armenians, all of them
9. Temlik, Apostolic Armenians, all of them
10. Asmalı, Apostolic Armenians, all of them
11. Dağköy, Catholic Armenians
12. Lower Fındıklı
13. Upper Fındıklı—Revend
14. İstiklal [Papazköy]
15. Kantar
16. Fulacık, Greek village
17. Kızderbent, Greek village

Villagers from Bahçecik, Aragez, Ovacık, and Arslanbey, who took refuge in İzmit, petitioned Mr. Lister for weapons to protect their village and their children and wives.

• Two eyewitnesses gave the following details about the massacre committed by the Turkish mob and Kafir Ali's gang in the Geyve region.

On July 8, a town crier was sent out, and the Turkish headmen were invited to the local agency for the following Friday. In the evening, the headmen reported that a deliberation during the meeting decided to establish a Turkish-Armenian fraternity so that the people could be carefree. The following morning, the lieutenant governor of Geyve, accompanied by a group of gendarmes and native Turkish notables, arrived at Geyve's station and announced: "Within two hours, all the Armenians and Greeks

պութիւնը թոյլ եւ տկար է. զինուորները միշտ կը փախչին եւ կը ցրուին. չէթէները եթէ շատնան կը վախնան որ թալան ըլլայ Այնթապի մէջ: Հիմա սկսած են չէթէական դրութիւնը օրինաւոր զինուորութեան վերածել: Ոչ մէկ ուժով կազմակերպութիւն չկայ. հասարակ ժողովուրդին մէջ ոխակալութիւն կայ հայոց դէմ, բայց սպաները կը վստահեցնեն թէ հայերուն դէմ գէշ միտք չկայ եւ չի կրնար ըլլալ. ցորեն, ալիւր եւ իւղ շատ չկայ. հայերը կ'առնեն բայց քիչ եւ առօրեայ պէտքին չափ հազիւ: Հայը երբեք բան մը չի կրնար ծախել, սաստիկ *պօյքոթ* կայ. հայ արհեստաւորները չեն կրնար գործել, վասնզի գործ բերող թուրքը կ'արգիլուի եւ կարելի չէ ձայն հանել:

Հայերը կը կասկածին թէ հայ թաղերը պիտի գրաւուին ներսէն եւ դուրսէն, հայոց զէնքերը պիտի առնեն եւ հայերը պիտի հանեն իրենց թաղերէն՝ փոխադրելով եւ ցրուելով ուրիշ թաղերու մէջ: Սակայն այս բանին հայերը պիտի հակառակին:

Թուրք զինուորները հիմա Սամ կը նստին կ'ըսուի. ըսողներ ալ կան թէ Իսլահիյէի կողմերը գացած են, թերեւս Ամանոսի հայոց դէմ ճակատելու: Եթէ ֆրանսացիք քաշուին Այնթապէն, պաշարի տեսակէտով պիտի նեղուինք բացարձակապէս, զի անոնց մնալուն պարագային թերեւս Քիլիսի ճամբով բան մը հայթայթել կարելի ըլլայ:

Նիկոմիդիա (Առաջնորդէն) – 19 Յուլիս

Թէեւ ճշգրիտ տեղեկութիւններ առնելու կարելիութիւն չկայ, սակայն 8 Յուլիսէն սկսեալ կը կարծուի թէ ջարդուած եւ այրուած են.

1 Հայ-հոռոմներու՝ Կէյվէ-Օրթաքէօյը 1000 տունէ աւելի
2 Յոյն եւ հայ, Սարաճըլը-Իւստիւ
3 Սազլը, հայ-հոռոմ
4 Պուրհանիյէ հայ-հոռոմ 500 տուն
5 Էշմէ բոլորն ալ զուտ հայ
6 Կամուրջ բոլորն ալ զուտ հայ
7 Գընճըլար բոլորն ալ զուտ հայ
8 Փէրիզլի բոլորն ալ զուտ հայ
9 Թամլըգ բոլորն ալ զուտ հայ
10 Ազմալը բոլորն ալ զուտ հայ
11 Տաղ-Գիւղ հայ-հոռոմ
12 Ստորին Ֆընտըգլը
13 Վերին Ֆընտըգլը – Րէվէնտ
14 Փափազ
15 Գանթար
16 Ֆօլաճըգ յոյն գիւղն
17 Գըզտէվրէնտ յոյն գիւղը

Իզմիթի ապաստանող պարտիզակցի, արակէզցի, օվաճըզցի եւ արսլանպէկցի գիւղացիներ հանրագրութեամբ մը դիմեցին Մըսթըր Լիսթէրի, խնդրելով որ իրենց զէնք տրուի իրենց գիւղը եւ զաւակները ու կիները պաշտպանելու համար:

- Երկու ականատեսներ տուած են հետեւեալ մանրամասնութիւնները Կէյվէի շրջանին մէջ թուրք խուժանին եւ *Կեավուր Ալի* հրոսախումբին կողմէ գործադրուած ջարդին մասին:

Յուլիս 8ին Կէյվէյի մէջ մունետիկ կը հանեն եւ կը հրաւիրեն թուրք մուխթարները հետեւեալ Ուրբաթ օրուան համար տեղւոյն պաշտօնատունը: Իրիկունը մուխթարները կը յայտնեն թէ ժողովին մէջ խորհրդակցութիւն կատարելով որոշուած է թուրք եւ հայ եղբայրակցութիւն մը կազմել, ուստի ժողովուրդը կրնայ անհոգ ըլլալ: Հետեւեալ առտուն,Կէյվէի գայմագամը խումբ մը

living around the station, numbering about four hundred, must gather in the nearby Armenian village of Eşme. Disobeyers will be executed by gunshot."

At the news of this announcement, the people left everything in horror and began to rush to the village of Eşme, crossing the bridge over the Sakarya River under a torrent of bullets.

A group of women, using the chaos, tried to sneak into the mountains of Kıncılar village. They were spotted and mercilessly killed immediately by Kafir Ali's çetes.

That same Saturday evening, after the Armenians and Greeks gathered in Eşme, the commander of Geyve's gendarmerie, leading the local armed mob, came to Eşme and announced: "You should not go out. I have placed guards everywhere. We will take care of your safety . . ." He left with his bandits for Ortaköy, an hour away.

Before dawn on Sunday, the more than two thousand Greek population of Ortaköy and a few scores of Armenians were brought to Eşme. They were driven like a flock and placed in the homes of more than twelve hundred local Armenian and Greek residents.

An hour later, the armed mob stormed the houses, and sixteen people, making up two families in one house, were killed with bombs thrown at them by the mob.

Under the influence of this horror, they began to gather all the men from the houses one by one. They tied their hands to each other and took them to a place fifteen minutes away, under the watch of the armed mob; then, they formed dense circles in the form of a ring and began showering bullets. The people in the center of the circle, who had been wounded but had not yet died, were killed with bayonets. After carrying out this massacre, the Turks returned to Eşme, gathered the remaining women and children, and took them to a place called Çay Boğazı. Heartbreaking cries could be heard in the distance, but we could not find the details of the massacre. In the evening, the mob returned from Eşme and started looting.

After Eşme, a mob of hundreds of men and women returned to Ortaköy and, after looting, set fire to all the buildings.

Kıncılar was besieged on Monday and set on fire. Most of the residents were burned, and the escapees were shot.

The villages of Saraçlı, Burhaniye, Sazlı, and Küp near the Greek village of Ortaköy were also burned down like Kıncılar. The inhabitants fell prey, some to flames, others to bayonets and bullets.

The Armenian population of Akhisar was also driven out of the city and killed. Since Akhisar has Turkish inhabitants also, the buildings were not burned down.

Armenian and Greek businessmen and several employees who were in Geyve, numbering ninety-two, were tied to one another in prison at night and taken near Sakarya, where ninety people were killed. Two hid among the corpses and survived.

Bursa (from the primate)—July 22

Very sad news is coming from the surrounding areas through letters and arriving escapees. The Millis have taken the priests and notable Armenians of Cerrah and Yenice to the mountains and sent them away to an unknown destination. It is unknown what happened [to them]. No Armenians are left in Yenisölöz, Gürle, and Karsak; they have fled to Gemlik and the mountains, abandoning their homes and everything.

A letter dated July 17 [and] received from Yenisölöz indicates that the commander of Gök Bayrak Battalion's First Company of the Milli forces came and settled in the village of Turkish Sölöz, an hour

ժանտարմաներով եւ ընկերակցութեամբ բնիկ թուրք երեւելիներու, Կէյվէի կայարանը գալով ծանոյց՝ թէ «կայարանի շուրջ բնակող բոլոր հայերն ու յոյները,- որոնք 400 հոգիի չափ էին,- երկու ժամուան մէջ պարտաւոր են մօտակայ հայաբնակ Էշմէ գիւղը հաւաքուիլ: Անսաստողները վայրկեանապէս հրացանի պիտի բռնուին»:

Ի լուր այս յայտարարութեան, ժողովուրդը սարսափահար ամէն ինչ թողած, գնդակներու տեղատարափին տակ Սաքարիա գետին կամուրջէն անցնելով հանդիպակաց Էշմէ գիւղը սկսաւ խուժել:

Իսկ կարգ մը կիներ, որոնք խառնաշփոթութենէն օգտուելով գաղտագողի փորձած էին Գնճըլար գիւղի լեռներու ճամբան բռնել, Կեավուր Ալիի չէթէներուն կողմէն նշմարուելով նոյնհետայն խժդժօրէն սպաննուեցան:

Նոյն Շաբաթ իրիկունը հայերը եւ յոյները Էշմէ հաւաքուելէն վերջ, Կէյվէյի ժանտարմա զօմանտանին տեղացի զինեալ խուժանին գլուխը անցած Էշմէ եկաւ եւ յայտարարեց թէ «դուրս պիտի չելնէք, ամէն կողմ պահապաններ կարգած եմ, ձեր ապահովութեան հոգ պիտի տանին»... եւ ինքը հրոսակներու հետ ժամ մը հեռուն գտնուող Օրթագիւղ գնաց:

Կիրակի արշալոյսէն առաջ 2000է աւելի օրթագիւղի յոյն բնակչութիւնը եւ մի քանի տասնեակ հայեր հօտի նման քշելով Էշմէ բերին եւ դրին հոն գտնուող 1200էն աւելի հայ եւ յոյն բնակիչներուն տուները:

Ժամ մը վերջ զինեալ խուժանը սկսաւ տուներուն վրայ յարձակիլ եւ տուն մը ուր 16 հոգիէ բաղկացեալ երկու ընտանիք հաւաքուած էին, խուժանին կողմէ նետուած պօմպաներով սպաննուեցան:

Այս սարսափի ազդեցութեան տակ, տուներու մէջ գտնուած բոլոր այր մարդիկը մի առ մի հաւաքելով սկսան ձեռք ձեռքի կապել եւ զինեալ խուժանի հսկողութեան տակ գիւղէն քառորդ մը հեռի տարուեցան, ապա օղակի ձեւով խիտ առ խիտ շրջանակ կազմել տուին ու սկսան գնդակներու տեղատարափին: Շրջանակին կեդրոնը գտնուած անձերը, որոնք վիրաւորուած եւ դեռ մեռած չէին, սուիններով սպաննեցին: Այս սպանդը կատարելէ յետոյ, կրկին վերադարձան Էշմէ եւ մնացած կիները ու երախաները հաւաքելով Չայ Պօղազը կոչուած վայրը տարին: Հեռուէն աղեկտուր վայնասունները կը լսէին, սակայն նախճիրին պարագաները չկրցինք մանրամասնօրէն իմանալ: Իրիկուան խուժանը վերադարձաւ Էշմէ եւ սկսաւ թալանին:

Էշմէէն յետոյ հարիւրաւոր այր եւ կին մարդիկներէ կազմուած խուժանը կրկին դիմեց Օրթագիւղ եւ թալանելէ յետոյ կրակի տուաւ բոլոր շէնքերը:

Գնճըլար Երկուշաբթի պաշարուեցաւ եւ կրակի տրուեցաւ. բնակիչներու մեծ մասը այրած է եւ փախչողները գնդակահար եղած են:

Օրթագիւղի մերձաւոր յունաբնակ Սարաճըլը, Պուրհանիյէ, Սազլը եւ Քիւփ գիւղերն ալ Գնճըլարի նման այրած եւ բնակիչները ոմանք բոցերու ոմանք ալ սուինի եւ գնդակներու ճարակ եղան:

Ագ-Հիսարի հայ բնակչութիւն[ն] ալ քաղաքէն դուրս հանուելով սպաննուած է: Ագ-Հիսար թուրք բնակիչ ալ ունենալով՝ շէնքերը չ[են] այրուած:

Կէյվէ գտնուող հայ եւ յոյն առեւտրականներ ու մի քանի պաշտօնեաներ, որոնք 92 հոգի էին, գիշերը բանտին մէջ մէկզմէկու կապուելով Սաքարիայի մօտ կը տանին եւ հոն 90 հոգի կը սպաննեն: Երկու հոգին դիակներու մէջ պահուելով կ'ազատուին:

Պրուսա (Առաջնորդէն) – 22 Յուլիս

Շրջականերէն շատ տխուր լուրեր կը հասնին գիրերով եւ փախուստով եկողներէ: Միլլիճիներն Ճերահի եւ Ենիճէի քահանաները եւ երեւելի ազգայինները լեռները տարած եւ անծանօթ ճանապարհով հեռացուցած են: Չի գիտցուիր թէ ի՞նչ եղած են: Սէօլէօզ, Կիւռլէ, Գարսաք հայ մնացած չէ. Կէմլէյիկ եւ լեռները փախած են, տուն տեղ ամէն բան ձգած:

17 Յուլիս թուականով Սէօլէօզէ ստացուած նամակէ մը կը հասկցուի թէ գիւղէն մէկ ժամ հեռաւորութեամբ թուրք Սէօլէօզ գիւղը Գուվվէյի Միլլիյէի կէօք պայրագ դապուրի պիրինճի պէօլիւկ զօմանտանը իր զինուորներով եկած նստած է, գրեթէ 70–80 հոգիով, եւ գիւղին մուխթարին գիր մը

away from the village [Yenisölöz], with his almost seventy to eighty soldiers, and sent a note to the village headman. We have also been informed that a camp has been established in the place called Gölyaka [Arapgazi], and three to four thousand Kemalist forces are expected to arrive.

The çetes have occupied the garrison of Karsak. On July 20, three hundred people—elderly, women, and children—took refuge in Gemlik, and others are expected. Orhangazi's lieutenant governor went to Karsak's police station and prevented [their arrival in Gemlik] and scattered the people in the plain in Gürle and Karsak.

İzmit (from the primate)—July 22

According to information received, the villages of Geyve (204), Geyve's Eşme (300), Kıncılar-Köprü (226), Ferizli (159), Temlik (54), Yeniköy of Temlik (3), Fındıklı, (5), [and] Almalı (70)—all in all, 1,021 Armenians—have been wholly massacred. It is also said that the Armenians of Akhisar were massacred, too.

All the Catholic Armenians of Geyve's Ortaköy (one thousand families), Saraçlıüstü or Havdi (three hundred families), Burhaniye (two hundred families), Sazlı, Osmaneli [Lefke], Fındıklı, Kantar, Revend, Küplü, and Fulacık have also been massacred.

Bundles of silk, household goods, dresses, copper pots and pans, cash and paper money, sheep, oxen, horses, buffaloes, donkeys, mules, pigs, chickens, and all kinds of goods and chattels have been taken to Ankara.

İzmit (from the primate)—July 24

A native of Geyve-Eşme, Antranig Arabian, escaped by chance from the slaughter of Geyve. He arrived in İzmit on July 23 and related that on July 10, Saturday, commander of the gendarmerie Esat Bey, company commander Ihsan Effendi, Sergeant Edhem, registrar Hafız Fuat, forest intendant Inla Bey, mayor Antakyalı Ali Effendi, chief of Milli forces Bekir Effendi, Regie intendant Sefer Bey, the land registry intendant, the director of the Agricultural Bank, intendant of public council Major Şükrü Effendi, branch chief, and the lieutenant governor of Geyve exhorted the people and assured them that they would protect the people by all means against incidents and attacks by the çetes and the government. Then they deceitfully transported the Armenian and Greek people to the village of Eşme of Geyve-Ortaköy, located between Geyve and Ortaköy, claiming it was a haven.

They placed these people—mixed men and women, old and young—in four local houses and installed soldiers as guards in front of the houses.

The next day, on Sunday (July 11), they separated the men, tied them up to each other, took them to the gorge called Karaçay, and massacred them with axes, swords, bullets, and so on.

Separating also the women on the same day, they brutally killed them and dumped their bodies in the Karaçay gorge.

On the 12th of July, the Catholic Armenians of Saraçlıüstü or Havdi and Burhaniye were also taken to the Karaçay gorge and, like the Apostolic Armenians, were all killed. To make the corpses tossed in the Karaçay gorge disappear, they burned them with petroleum for three days.

Those who escaped to the mountains were chased and brutally killed.

On Sunday, July 11, they herded the Catholic Armenians of Geyve-Ortaköy, 7,300 people, young and old, men and women, into the Armenian church and set it on fire, immolating 7,300 innocent people.

On July 12, they set the Armenian population of Kıncılar and the village of Kıncılar on fire. Not a single person was saved.

On the same day, they mercilessly massacred also the Armenian population of Akhisar, dumped

ուղղած է: Նոյնպէս կը տեղեկանանք որ *Արապղագի* ըսուած վայրը բանակատեղի հաստատուած եւ Քէմալականներէն 3–4 հազար ուժերու ժամանման կը սպասուի:

Գարսագի պահականոցը չէթէները գրաւած են: Յուլիսի 20ին 300 անձեր, ծեր, կին, տղայ, Կէմլէյիկ ապաստանեցան եւ ուրիշներու ալ կը սպասուէր: Օրխան Ղազիի գայմագամը Գարսագի զարագօլը իջնալով արգիլած է եւ ժողովուրդը դաշտին մէջ Կիւրլէ, Գարսագ տարտղնած է:

Նիկոմիդիա (Առաջնորդէն) – 22 Յուլիս

Առնուած տեղեկութեանց համաձայն, Կէյվէ Միջագիւղի (204), Կէյվէ Էշմէի (300), Գընճըլար-Կամուրջի (226), Ֆէրիզլի[ի] (159), Թամլըգի (54), Նոր-Գիւղ Թամլըգի (3), Ֆընտըգլըի (5) եւ Ալմալուի (70) համագումար 1021 անձ հայերը ամբողջովին ջարդուած են: Նոյնպէս կ'ըսուի թէ Ագիհսարի հայերն ալ ջարդուած են:

Նոյնպէս ջարդուած են Կէյվէ-Օրթագիւղի (1000 տուն), Սարաճըլը Իւստիւ կամ Հաւտի (300 տուն), Պուրհանիյէ[ի] (200 տուն), Սազլըի, Լէֆքէի, Ֆընտըգլըներու, Գանթարի, Բէվէնտի, Քիւփլիի, Ֆուլաճըխի հայ-հոռոմները ամբողջովին:

Մետաքսի կապոցներ, կարասիներ, զգեստներ եւ պղնձեղէն, եւ ինչուն եւ թուղթ դրամներ, ոչխարներ, եզներ, ձիեր, գոմէշներ, էշ, ջորի, խոզ, հաւ եւ տունի ամէն տեսակ կահ կարասի Էնկիւրիւ կը տանին:

Նիկոմիդիա (Առաջնորդէն) – 24 Յուլիս

Բնիկ Կէյվէ-Էջմեցի Անդրանիկ Արապեան Կէյվէի կոտորածէն դիպուածաւ ազատուած Յուլիս 23ին Նիկոմիդիա գալով պատմած է թէ Յուլիս 10 Շաբաթ օր ժանտարմա քոմանտանը Էսատ պէյ, պէօլիւկ քոմանտանը Իհսան էֆէնտի, Էթհէմ Չավուշ, Նուֆուզ Մէմուրի Հաֆըզ Ֆուատ, Օրման Մէմուրի Ինլա պէյ, պէլէտիյէի րէյիս Անթաքեալը Ալի էֆէնտի, Գուվվէթի Միլլիյէ րէյիզի Պէքիր էֆէնտի, Րէժի մէմուրը Սէֆէր պէյ, Թափու մէմուրու, Զըրաաթ Պանքայ միւտիւրիւ, տույունը ումումիյէ մէմուրու Շիւքրի էֆէնտի, Շիւպէ րէիզի պինպաշը եւ Կէյվէյու գայմագամը ժողովուրդը կը յորդորեն եւ կ'ապահովցնեն որ չէթէական եւ կառավարական դէպքերէ եւ յարձակումներէ ամէն գնով պիտի պաշտպանեն բոլոր ժողովուրդը, եւ իբր ապահով վայր խաբեբայութեամբ հայ եւ յոյն ժողովուրդը կը փոխադրեն Կէյվէ Օրթագիւղի Էշմէ գիւղը, որ կը գտնուի Կէյվէյի եւ Օրթագիւղի միջեւ:

Այս ժողովուրդը խառն այր եւ կին, մեծ եւ փոքր, տեղւոյն չորս տուներուն մէջ կը տեղաւորեն եւ զինուորներ ալ պահակ կը կեցնեն տուներուն առջեւ:

Հետեւեալ օրը Կիրակի (Յուլիս 11) այրերը զատելով իրար կը կապեն եւ Գարայ-Չայ ըսուած կիրճը կը տանին եւ կը ջարդեն տապարով, սուրով, գնդակով եւայլն:

Նոյն օրը կիներն ալ զատելով, զանոնք ալ չարաչար կը սպաննեն եւ կը լեցնեն Գարայ-Չայի պօղազը:

Յուլիս 12 օրն ալ Սարաճըլը Իւսթիւ կամ Հաւտիի եւ Պուրհանիյէի հայ-հոռոմներն ալ կը տարուին յիշեալ Գարայ-Չայ պօղազը եւ հայոց նման անոնք ալ ամբողջովին կը սպաննուին: Գարայ-Չայ պօղազը խռնուած այս դիակները անհետացնելու համար երեք օր շարունակ բեթրոլով կը վառեն:

Իսկ անոնք որ լեռները խոյս տուած էին, կը հետապնդուին եւ չարաչար կը սպաննուին:

Յուլիս 11ի Կիրակի օր Կէյվէ-Միջագիւղի հայ-հոռոմները 7300 հոգի, մեծ-պզտիկ, այր եւ կին Միջագիւղի հայոց եկեղեցին կը լեցնեն եւ կազով կ'այրեն եկեղեցին եւ հոն 7300 անմեղներ կ'ողջակիզուին:

Յուլիս 12ին Գընճըլարի հայ բնակչութիւնն եւ Գընճըլար գիւղը կրակով կը վառեն առանց մէկ

their bodies in wells, and burned the corpses that were left out.

On July 15, they changed their decision to distribute the innocent little children—girls and boys collected from various places—to Muslim Georgians. Instead, they took them all to the gardens near Geyve and filled the wells after massacring them.

İzmit (from the primate)—July 25

Four or five days ago, the Laz intendant, who had deported [in 1915 the Armenians of] Akmeşe, sent news to Akmeşe that he would come with five hundred people and slaughter the entire population and burn the village, allegedly because the people of Akmeşe had wanted the Greek soldiers to enter Akmeşe. The population of Akmeşe is terrified.

About two hours from İznik, three Greeks from the Greek-Laz population of the village of Karpuz-Hünkârçiftliği —1. Socrat Khristo Khoraloglu, 2. Yorgi Costantin Papazoglu, [and] 3. Nicoli Yani Kalayjioglu—who, driven by fear, quite long ago traveled from their village to Arslanbey to take shelter, related that during the burning of the Greek village of Fulacık with its church, two hours away from İznik, the Greek village of Derbent [Pambucak] (250–300 families) resisted the Millis for fifteen days, but when their strength faded, eighty armed people fled and the Millis entered the village. They gathered the people in the church, burned it, and then immolated the bodies with bombs and cannons. One of the two priests in the village was burned among the people; the other, Papa Nicola, fled.

After the Millis committed and finished this monstrosity, they took girls, brides, and women with them and departed rejoicing.

Aleppo (from vicar general Father Haroutyun Yesayan) June 30

The letter of the catholicosal locum tenens Father Nerses of Gaziantep [Ayntab], dated June 22, presents a very sad and dangerous situation. It is believed that the government will collect the weapons. The Armenians have decided not to hand over their weapons. There is also a rumor that Armenians will be moved to Turkish neighborhoods. On June 20, an announcement was posted in the city stating that anyone interacting with the French would be punished severely. In short, the danger is inevitable. The agreement between Mustafa Kemal and the French has been dissolved.

Maraş is in a severely alarming situation.

A letter from the National Union of Urfa, dated June 27, expresses from beginning to end its satisfaction with their fraternal agreement with the Milli forces and for the security [that prevails]. On the contrary, however, the American Red Cross staff reported that the letter was written due to the horror suffered in a terrible situation.

Aleppo: the entry of nonresident Armenians to Aleppo has been strictly forbidden for a month. Emigrant and refugee Armenians face great difficulties. The reason [for this restriction] remains unknown to us.

As for the situation of Gümüşgün [Ehneş], according to eyewitness accounts, in the first half of March 1920, police arrived from Halfeti to transport the people of Gümüşgün to Halfeti. Three weeks later, they brought them back to Gümüşgün under watch. From Erenköy [Kâhtin], Molla Hasanoğlu Helel, his brother's sons, Himo's sons, Abaş's son, and İbrahim's son; from Çardaklı, Mustafa Agha, his brother Ahmet, and his son and followers; from Kamışlı, Kuro, Keloninoğlu Mustafa, and Sheikho; from Habibli, Sefer and son, Müslim, Oso's son, Lazo; from Cağıt, Alloz, Hami Mısdık, and Müskıarüklı Ali Bey came on April 2 and the next day, April 3, on Saturday, they killed two people, a man named Vruo and a woman named Mariam, and they began to steal oxen and cattle. At the same time, the

մարդ ազատելու:

Նոյն օրը, Ագ-Հիսարի հայ բնակչութիւնն եւս անխնայ կը կոտորեն եւ ջրհորներու մէջ կը լեցնեն եւ դուրսը մնացած դիակներն ալ կը վառեն:

Յուլիս 15ին ալ զանազան տեղերէ հաւաքուած մանր անմեղ տղաքը, աղջիկ ու մանչ իսլամ կիւրճիներու բաժնելու որոշումնին փոխեցին եւ ամէնքն ալ Կէյվէի մօտ պօստաններ կը տանին եւ ջարդելէ յետոյ հորերը կը լեցնեն:

Նիկոմիդիա (Առաջնորդէն) – 25 Յուլիս

Արմաշը տարագրող լազ միւտիւրը 4–5 օր առաջ լուր ղրկեր է Արմաշ թէ 500 հոգիով պիտի գամ եւ բոլոր բնակչութիւնը պիտի ջարդեմ եւ գիւղը պիտի այրեմ, վասնզի արմաշցիք յոյն զինուորին Արմաշ մտնելուն կը փափաքին եղեր: Արմաշի բնակչութիւնը սարսափի մատնուած է:

- Իզնիկի 2 ժամ մօտ Գարփուզ-հունքար գիւղի յոյն-լազ բնակչութենէն երեք յոյներ՝ 1. Սոկրատ Խրիսթօ Խօրալ Օղլու, 2. Եորկի Կոստանդինի Փափազ օղլու, 3. Նիքօլի Եանի Գալայճի օղլու, որոնք վախով իրենց գիւղէն Արսլանպէկ եկած ապաստանած են բաւական ժամանակ առաջ, կը պատմեն թէ յոյն Ֆուլաճըգ գիւղը եկեղեցիով այրուած ժամանակներուն Իզնիկէն 2 ժամ հեռու Բամբուճագ յոյն գիւղն (250–300 տուն) 15 օր Միլլիճիներու դէմ կը դնէ ու երբ կը տկարանայ, 80 հոգիներ զէն ի ձեռին կը փախչին, Միլլիճիներն գիւղ կը մտնեն, ժողովուրդը կը ժողովեն եկեղեցին կը լեցնեն եւ պօմպաներով, թնդանօթներով ժողովուրդը մէջը կ՚այրեն եւ կ՚ողջակիզեն: Գիւղին երկու քահանաներէն մէկը ասոնց մէջ կ՚այրի, միւսը՝ Փափայ Նիքօլա, փախեր է:

Միլլիճիները երբ այս հրէշութիւնը ըրեր լմնցուցեր են, աղջիկներ, հարսներ ու կնիկներ հետերնին առած, ուրախ զուարթ կ՚երթան:

Հալէպ (Առաջնորդական Փոխանորդ Յարութիւն քահանայ Եսայեանէ) 30 Յունիս

Այնթապի Կաթողիկոսական Փոխանորդ Տէր Ներսէս քահանայի 22 Յունիս թուականով նամակը շատ տխուր եւ վտանգալի կը ներկայացնէ վիճակը: Կը կարծուի թէ կառավարութիւնը զէնքերը պիտի հաւաքէ: Հայերը որոշած են չյանձնել իր[ենց] զէնքերը: Նոյնպէս հայերը թուրք թաղերը փոխադրելու շշուկ մը կը շրջի: Յունիս 20ին ազդ մը փակցուած է քաղաքին մէջ թէ ով որ ֆրանսացւոց հետ յարաբերութիւն ընէ՝ խստիւ պիտի պատժուի: Վերջապէս վտանգը անխուսափելի է: Մուսթաֆա Քէմալի եւ ֆրանսացւոց համաձայնութիւնը լուծուած է:

Մարաշ կը գտնուի ծանր տագնապի մէջ:

Ուրֆայի Ազգային Միութեան 27 Յունիս թուակիր նամակ մը ծայրէ ծայր գոհունակութիւն կը յայտնէ Միլլի ուժերու հետ իրենց եղբայրակցական համաձայնութեան եւ ապահովութեան համար: Սակայն ընդհակառակը, սոսկալի կացութեան մէջ սարսափի հետեւանքով գրուած ըլլալը Ամերիկեան Կարմիր Խաչի պաշտօնեաները տեղեկացուցած են:

Հալէպ՝ դուրսէն հայու մը [Հալէպ] մտնելը խստիւ արգիլուած է ամիսէ մը ի վեր: Պանդուխտ եւ գաղթական հայերը մեծ դժուարութիւններ կը կրեն: Պատճառը մեզի անծանօթ կը մնայ:

Գալով Էհնէշի կացութեան, ականատեսներէն առնուած տեղեկութեանց համաձայն, [1]920 Մարտի առաջին կիսուն Խէլֆէթիյէն ոստիկաններ գալով Էհնէշի ժողովուրդը կը փոխադրեն Խէլֆէթի: Երեք շաբաթ վերջ դարձեալ ընդ հսկողութեամբ Էհնէշ կը բերեն: Ապրիլ 2ին Գահտինէն՝ Մունլա Հասան օղլու Խէլէլ, եղբօր տղաքը, Հիմոյի տղաքը, Ապաշ[ի]ն տղաքը եւ Իպրահիմի տղան, Չարտագլոյէն՝ Մուսթաֆա աղա, եղբայրը Աhմէտ, տղան եւ իր մարդիկը, Գամըշլոյէն՝ Կուրօ, Քէօնըն-օղլու Մուսթաֆա, Հիւսէյնի տղան՝ Շէյխօ, Հապիպլիյէն՝ Սէֆէր եւ տղաքը, Միւսլիմ, Օսօյի տղան, Լազօ, Ճաղըտ[էն] Ալլօզ, Համի, Մըստըզ եւ Մուսկիարիւքլիւ Ալի պէյ: Անոնք կու գան եւ հետեւեալ օրը՝ Ապրիլ 3 Շաբաթ օրը երկու հոգի, Վրուօ անուն էրիկ եւ Մարիամ անուն կին մարդիկը կը մեռցնեն եւ կ՚սկսին եզներ, տաւարներ թալլել առնել: Նոյն պահուն Էհնէշ գտնուող

police in Gümüşgün prevented a general massacre. In the afternoon, the lieutenant governor of Halfeti (from Kilis), an officer named Salah Effendi, came with about twenty policemen and gathered all the villagers in the house of Keyvan Agha. They separated six of them (the families of Girbish and Khacher Agha) and took them to Erenköy on the pretext that they had six hundred liras, which they must give to the police. The lieutenant governor himself took them [to Erenköy].

Two of those policemen who remained in the village evicted the people—old and young—from the village, ostensibly with the promise of taking them to Halfeti, but instead, they took them to Kamışlı. First, they herded them into caves. At sunset, they took them out, tied them all, and made them sit. First, they cut the little children into pieces; then they took the men to the bank of the Euphrates, where they killed them by inflicting various tortures: shooting, slaying, smashing heads on stones, and cutting them into pieces while they were still alive. Then they put the women on the sandy bank of the Euphrates and set them on fire, burning them to death.

On Saturday, while heading from Gümüşgün to Kamışlı, some managed to escape and take refuge in the homes of Sheikh and Ali, Feyzullah's sons. They were detained there. After spending Saturday night there, on Sunday night, they were all taken out and driven to the bank of the Euphrates near Tellikaya, where they were killed with tortures unheard of. All thirty-two of them were killed. One hid in the house of Feyzullah's son and escaped at night after finding the door open. Another jumped into the Euphrates to save himself, and thirty people were martyred there. The massacrers are Feyzullah's son, Sheikh Müslim, the paternal uncle's son Ali, his son, his brother Zeki, Hami Mısdık of Cağıt, his brother Bozo and others, and Hacı Baba's son (from Birecik). The narrator of all this is Hagop, the son of Karageozian Khacho, the man who ran away from Feyzullah's house. The other escapee is Boyajian Haroutyun (Father Hagop's brother). He fell into the water after being hit and survived. Karageozian Haroutyun's wife also fell into the water and survived. The number of people killed is 764. It is said that three more women fled and went to the Turkish village of Salkım [Khıyam]. The people of Halfeti have promised one hundred liras for each corpse of a native Armenian from Gümüşgün, and the lieutenant governor himself promised to give ten liras for each murderer of an Armenian personally.

Had it been left to the lieutenant governor of Halfeti, Saylakkaya [Cibin] also would have shared the fate of Gümüşgün, but Köklülı Hacı Agha went to Saylakkaya with four hundred followers and saved all [the remaining] Armenians from an inevitable massacre.

There are now sixty-four people from Gümüşgün in Birecik, twenty-three in Gaziantep, and four in Kilis.

İzmit (from the primate, two letters with the same date)—July 26

Today, three escapees from Akmeşe arrived in İzmit and reported that the villages Akmeşe, EskiMecidiye [Khaskal], and Mecidiye [Khach] are besieged by Milli çetes for three days. There are close to 2,000 Armenians there.

- It was reported from Adapazarı, indirectly, that the Millis have removed two wagons full of Armenians from the city.

İzmit (a telegram from the primate)—July 27

Akmeşe and its environs are besieged by six hundred Millis. The situation is grave.

There is fear of a massacre. Petition the British authorities to permit the local British authorities to take action.

İzmit (from the primate)—July 28

Only two of the seven escapees from the massacre in Geyve and its environs reached İzmit. The men

ոստիկաններ կ'արգիլեն ընդհանուր ջարդը: Կէսօրէն ետքը Խէլֆէթէյի գայմագամը (քիլիսցի), քովը Սէլահ էֆէնտի անուն սպայ մը եւ 20ի չափ ոստիկաններով կու գայ բոլոր գիւղացիները կը հաւաքեն Քէյվան աղայի տունը եւ անոնց մէջէն վեց հոգի կը զատեն (Կըրպըշի եւ Խաչեր աղայի ընտանիքը) եւ իբր թէ անոնց քով 600 լիրա կան թող տան եւ ազատուին ըսելով Գահտին կը տանին: Տանողը նոյն ինքն գայմագամը կ'ըլլայ:

Գիւղը մնացող ոստիկաններէն երկու հոգի ժողովուրդը մեծ ու պզտիկ գիւղէն կը հանեն իբր թէ Խալֆէթի տանելու խոստումով եւ Գամըշլը կը տանին: Նախ այրերու մէջ կը թիմեն եւ արեւամուտին կը հանեն ամէնն ալ կը կապեն ու կը նստեցնեն: Նախ պզտիկ երախաները կը յօշոտեն, ետքը էրիկ մարդիկը Եփրատի եզերքը կը տանին եւ հոն այլեւայլ չարչարանքով կը մեռցնեն, հրացանազարկ կ'ընեն, կը մորթեն եւ գլուխը քարին վրայ կը ճզմեն, ողջ ողջ կը յօշոտեն եւ վերջը կիները Եփրատի եզերքը աւազներուն վրայ դնելով կրակ կուտան եւ կ'այրեն:

Շաբաթ օրը Էնէշէն Գանէշլը [Գամըշլը] երթալու պահուն ոմանք կը յաջողին փախչիլ եւ ապաստանիլ Փէյզուլլահի տղուն՝ Շէյխի եւ Ալիի տուները: Ասոնք կը բանտարկուին հոն եւ Շաբաթ գիշերը հոն անցնելէ յետոյ Կիրակի գիշերը բոլորն ալ կը հանեն ու կը տանին Եփրատի եզերքը Թէլլի Գայայի մօտ եւ հոն անլուր չարչարանքներով կը սպաննեն ամէնը, որոնք 32 հոգի են եղեր: Մէկը Փէյզուլլահի տղուն տունը կը պահուի կը մնայ եւ գիշերը դուռը բաց գտնելով կը փախչի կ'ազատի. ուրիշ մը Եփրատ նետուելով ինքզինքը կ'ազատէ, իսկ 30 հոգի հոն կը մարտիրոսանան: Ջարդարարները են Փէյզուլլահի տղան, Շէյխ Միւսլիմ, հօրեղբօրորդին Ալի, տղան, եղբայրը Զէքի, Ճաղըտլը Համի Մըստըզ, եղբայրը Պօզօ եւայլն եւ Հաճի Պապայի տղան (պիրէճիկցի): Այս բոլորը պատմողն է Փէյզուլլահի տունէն փախչող Գարակէօզեան Խաչոյի տղան՝ Յակոբ: Միւս փախչողն է Պօյաճեան (Տէր Յակոբ քահանայի եղբայրը) Յարութիւն, որ զարնուելէն ետքը ջուրը ինկած եւ ազատուած է: Գարակէօզեան Յարութիւնի կինն ալ ջուրը ինկած եւ ազատուած է: Սպաննուողներուն թիւը 764 է: Երեք կին եւս փախած եւ Խըլյամ թուրք գիւղը գացած են կ'ըսուի: Խէլէֆէթէյի մարդիկը իւրաքանչիւր ազատուող էնէշցիի դիակը բերողին հարիւր լիրա խոստացեր են եւ գայմագամը իւրաքանչիւր հայ մեռցնողին անձնականէն ըլլալու պայմանով տասը լիրա տալ խոստացեր է:

Թէեւ Խէլֆէթիյի գայմագամին մնար Ճիպինն ալ Էնէշի բախտին պիտի արժանանայ եղեր, բայց Կէօկլիւլի հաճի աղան 400 հոգիով Ճիպին գացած եւ բոլոր հայերը փրկած է ստոյգ ջարդէ մը:

Հիմա էնէշցիներէն Պիրէճիկ կը գտնուին 64 հոգի, Այնթապ 23 հոգի, իսկ Քիլիս 4 հոգի:

Նիկոմիդիա (Առաջնորդէն, կրկին նամակներ նոյն թուականով) – 26 Յուլիս

Այսօր Արմաշէն փախստական երեք անձեր Նիկոմիդիա գալով կը հաղորդեն թէ Արմաշ, Խասկալ եւ Խաչ (Մէճիտիէ) գիւղերը, որոնց մէջ մերձաւորապէս 2000 հայ կան երեք օր է պաշարուած են Միլլի չէթէներէն:

- Ատաբազարէն անուղղակի կերպով լուր առնուեցաւ թէ քաղաքէն երկու վակոն լեցուն հայեր հեռացուցած են Միլլիճիք:

Նիկոմիդիա (Առաջնորդէն, հեռագիր) – 27 Յուլիս

Արմաշ եւ շրջակայքը պաշարուած են 600 Միլլիականներու կողմէ: Կացութիւնը ծանր է:

Ջարդէ մը կը վախցուի: Դիմեցէք անգլիական իշխանութեանց որ արտօնեն տեղական անգլիական իշխանութիւնները միջոցներ ձեռք առնելու:

Նիկոմիդիա (Առաջնորդէն) 28 Յուլիս

Կէյվէի եւ շրջականներու կոտորածէն փախստական եօթը անձեր 10–15 օր անօթի ծարաւ,

spent ten to fifteen days hungry and thirsty, crossing mountains, valleys, fields, and bushes, and lost five companions on the road. According to their information, all the mountain roads are occupied by the Millis, who make every effort not to let anyone escape. İzmit's military authorities sent food for one week to Bahçecik's volunteer watchmen five or six days ago.

• Twenty-five Akmeşe residents, along with the commitment to add twenty-five more people, asked the British to arm them so they could defend their village. They have not received an answer yet.

• The British authorities have permitted people to move freely by sea and land in the territories they occupied.

İzmit (from the primate)—July 28

Today, stealthily, ten men from Akmeşe arrived in İzmit. Their journey took four days. On Sunday, six hundred Millis surrounded Akmeşe. The Millis came from Adapazarı and Şevketiye [Saçmalı] and allegedly declared that their numbers would increase to one thousand.

Akmeşe is expected to be ruined at any moment by them. The ten men from Akmeşe have also presented themselves to the English commander of İzmit.

Zonguldak (from the Neighborhood Council)—July 11

Due to the relatively secure situation here, the Armenians who numbered 120 families in Zonguldak since the armistice, now count as 200 families.

Here, too, the Milli movement has begun, despite the presence of French troops. Hundreds of Lazes working in the mines have enlisted as çetes and have been armed with state weapons. A persistent rumor immediately followed that Zonguldak would be attacked, Christians would be massacred, and French soldiers would be dumped into the sea. There are genuinely provocative sermons being delivered in nearby cities: In Devrek, the mufti Sheikh Hacı Abdullah, who was Devrek's delegate to the Ankara Congress, spoke in the mosque upon his return from Ankara. On the night of June 10–11, the Muslim population of the city, 40 to 50 families, left for the mainland, and the migration continued the next day. The Christians grew more doubtful and, in turn, began to flee to İstanbul. A week later, the government banned the migration of Christians. So far, 180–200 Armenian and Greek families have migrated from here, and 15 Armenian families from Devrek have come to Zonguldak.

French troops have begun digging trenches and placing cannons on the hills. This situation continues. There has been no attack yet, but leaving the city is impossible. To give an idea about the situation, it may be enough to recount the following incident on July 3. Muslim muhacirs, natives of Ordu in İstanbul, were sent by the government to Zonguldak by sea to be dispatched back to their homeland by sea. Aghavni, the wife of Haroutyun Kojabuyukian of Bolu, joined these thirty-five to forty migrants in Bolu to come to Zonguldak to visit her husband, along with her seventeen-year-old daughter named Yebraksé and two sons, Ghazar, fifteen years old, and Krikor, twelve years old; four people altogether. They arrived safely at the place called Kokaksu, half an hour from Zonguldak. There, the notorious bandit eighteen-year-old Hacı Hasanoğlu Çakıcı Halil, from the village of Keşap in Ordu, who has been in the city for many years, attacked the caravan of migrants. He let the Muslims go free with great respect. They abducted the Armenian woman with her daughter, Yebraksé, and took them to a mountain. Four hours later, they released the mother, demanding a ransom of seven hundred liras. "Go and appeal to Zonguldak's priest; let him find seven hundred liras for you. Bring them to me, and I will release your daughter." In addition, another threatening letter was sent to the priest Yeremia Mirijanian.

The Turkish government managed to keep the whole area under siege for fifty hours. They arrested the bandits and handed over the girl intact as a virgin.

լեռներ, ձորեր, դաշտեր ու թուփեր անցնելէ վերջը 5 ընկերները ճամբան կորսնցնելով միայն երկու հոգի կը հասնին Նիկոմիդիա: Ասոնց տուած տեղեկութեանց համաձայն լեռնային բոլոր ճամբաները բռնած են Միլլիճիները եւ ամէն ջանք կ'ընեն ոչ ոք չփախցնելու համար: Նիկոմիդիոյ զինուորական իշխանութիւնները 5–6 օր առաջ մէկ շաբթուան սնունդ ղրկեցին Պարտիզակի պահապանաց կամաւորներուն:

- 25 արմաշցիներ ի հարկին 25 հոգի եւս աւելցնելու յանձնառութեամբ խնդրած են անգլիացիներէն որ զիրենք զինեն, պաշտպանելու համար իրենց գիւղը: Դեռ պատասխան չեն ստացած:

- Անգլիական իշխանութիւնները իրենց գրաւման տակ գտնուած վայրերու մէջ ծովու եւ ցամաքի ճամբով երթեւեկութիւնները ազատօրէն կատարելու հրաման տուած են:

Նիկոմիդիա (Առաջնորդէն) – 28 Յուլիս

Այսօր Նիկոմիդիա ժամանեցին զաղտագողի ճամբաներէ՝ Արմաշէն 10 այր մարդիկ: Իրենց ճամբան տեւած է 4 օր: Կիրակի 600 Միլլիճիներ պաշարած են Արմաշը: Միլլիճիները եկած են Ատաբազարէն եւ Սաչմալըէն, եւ կը յայտարարեն եղեր թէ 1000էն աւելի պիտի ըլլան:

Վայրկեանէ վայրկեան կը սպասուի որ Արմաշը փճացնեն: Տասը արմաշցիները Նիկոմիդիոյ անգլիական հրամանատարին ալ ներկայացան:

Զօնկուլտագ (Թաղական Խորհուրդէն) – 11 Յուլիս

Տեղւոյս համեմատաբար ապահով դրութեան հետեւանօք Զօնկուլտաքի հայոց թիւը, որ 120 տուն էր զինադադարէն ի վեր, բարձրացած է 200 տունի:

Հոս եւս սկսաւ Միլլի շարժումը հակառակ ֆրանսական զինուորներու ներկայութեան: Հանքերու մէջ աշխատող հարիւրաւոր լազեր չէթէ արձանագրուեցան եւ զինուեցան պետական զէնքերով, որուն անմիջապէս յաջորդեց յամառ զրոյց մը թէ Զօնկուլտաքի վրայ պիտի յարձակին, պիտի ջարդեն քրիստոնեաները եւ ծով պիտի թափեն ֆրանսացի զինուորները: Իրաւապէս մօտակայ քաղաքներու մէջ գրգռիչ քարոզներ կը խօսուին. այսպէս՝ ի Տէվրէկ միւֆթի շէյխ Հաճի Ապտուլլահ, որ Էնկիւրիի ժողովին մէջ Տէվրէկի պատգամաւորն էր, Էնկիւրիէն դառնալով մզկիթին մէջ կը խօսի: 10–11 Յունիսին գիշերը քաղաքին իսլամ բնակիչները՝ 40–50 ընտանիք, մեկնեցան դէպի ցամաքակողմ եւ յաջորդ օրն եւս շարունակուեցաւ գաղթը: Քրիստոնեայք աւելի կասկածիլ սկսան, եւ անոնք ալ իրենց կարգին սկսան փախչիլ դէպի Պոլիս: Շաբաթ մը յետոյ կառավարութիւնը արգելք դրաւ քրիստոնէից գաղթին: Մինչեւ հիմա 180–200 ընտանիք հայ եւ յոյն գաղթած են ասկէ եւ Տէվրէկէն 15 հայ ընտանիք Զօնկուլտաք եկած են:

Ֆրանսական զինուորները սկսան խրամներ պատրաստել եւ բլուրներու վրայ թնդանօթներ զետեղել: Այս վիճակը կը շարունակէ: Դեռ յարձակում չէ եղած, սակայն քաղաքէն դուրս ելլել կարելի չէ: Գաղափար մը տալու համար տիրող կացութեան վրայ, կը բաւէ պատմել 3 Յուլիսին պատահած հետեւեալ դէպքը:- Պոլիս գտնուող օրտուցի իսլամ գաղթականները կառավարութեան կողմէ կը ղրկուին Զօնկուլտաք [անկէ] ծովու ճամբով, [հոսկէ] ծովով իրենց հայրենիքը ղրկուելու համար: Պոլսէն այս 35–40 գաղթականներուն կը միանայ Զօնկուլտաք իր էրկան քով գալու համար պօլուցի Քօճապըյըգեան Յարութիւնի կինը՝ Աղաւնի, իր 17 տարեկան Եպրաքսէ անուն աղջկան, 15 տարեկան Ղազար եւ 12 տարեկան Գրիգոր անուն զաւակներով, ընդամէնը 4 հոգի. անվնաս կուգան մինչեւ Զօնկուլտաքէ կէս ժամ հեռու Քօքաք Սու ըսուած տեղը. հոն նշանաւոր աւազակը՝ Օրտուի Քէշապ գիւղէն երկար տարիներէ ի վեր քաղաքս գտնուող 18 տարեկան Հաճը Հասան օղլու Չագըճը Խալիլ, կը յարձակի գաղթականներու կարաւանին վրայ, իսլամները մեծ յարգանքով ազատ կը թողու: Հայ կինը իր աղջկան՝ Եպրաքսէին հետ առեւանգելով լեռ կը տանին եւ 4 ժամ վերջը ազատ կ'արձակեն մայրը՝ 700 ոսկի փրկանք պահանջելով. «Գնա՛ Զօնկուլտաք քահանային դիմէ, քեզի համար զտնէ 700 ոսկի, բեր ինձ եւ աղջիկդ ազատ արձակեմ»: Բաց աստի սպառնագիր մը եւս ղրկուած է Տէր Երեմիա քահանայ Միրիճանեանի:

The bandits were delivered to the Milli forces and sent to Çaycuma to be sent thence to the military tribunal in Bolu.

• Yesterday, about one thousand new troops arrived in Zonguldak.

İstanbul (statement by Murad Agha)—July 30

Murad Agha from Akhisar of Armenian descent—a notable local merchant—who had converted to Islam to save his life as a result of a crime committed forty years ago, had always been detested by the Turks because he kept some Armenians in his home during the massacre in Akhisar in 1895. This time, coming to the Patriarchate for the latest events, he related the following personally:

On July 10, Saturday night, when everyone was asleep, at five o'clock in the morning (Turkish time), a town crier announced that all those who had weapons must surrender them to the government within an hour and that no one should go out without a lantern. The Turks went to the government's door to hand over their weapons, and so did Murad Agha's son. They were instructed to return home with their weapons and never to protect the Armenians, otherwise threatening them with death. During this time, the Millis besieged the Armenian houses and took the Armenians from their homes to the government office, where they said: "You will go into exile." First, they took all the men—tied in pairs—to the brink of the well of Yeghisé, a native of Kıncılar, and killed them with knives and dumped them in the well. Two young men, Hovhannes Lafjian and house painter Kapriel Der Kaprielian, spontaneously threw themselves into the well to not be killed with a knife.

On Sunday morning, they collected the rest of the population, women, and children, and crammed them in the silkworm nursery of Nalband Gabig Boghos. They also took Murad Agha's eighty-year-old mother, Noyemzar, who had remained a Christian in his house, and two Greek women from Osmaneli [Lefke], silkworm breeders Fotintza and Elanko, to that silkworm nursery. On Monday night, all were taken to the threshold of the same well and killed, thus leaving the local Armenian population, about 350 people, slaughtered by the brink of that well. Only two little girls survived. One was a servant to the intendant, and the other was a wounded eight-year-old little one who shouted when she was being thrown in the well that she has twelve and a half kuruş and would accept Islam. They pitied her on this [statement], removed her from the already full well, and gave her to a gypsy to keep.

In addition, a porter named Bedros, a native of [Western] Armenia, was the only other Armenian of Akhisar to survive. He hid in the station and fled to Geyve's station by night.

Akhisar had no Greek population; only two Akhisar station employees were Greek. They were also captured, taken to the same well, and killed as the Armenians. The çetes then came to Murad's house and demanded Minju Boghos's wife. When they saw she was not there, they took Murad Agha to kill him and demanded five thousand liras for his release.

They took the key to Murad Agha's chest and seized nine thousand liras, [and] then they set him free, and he took the opportunity to escape. The Millis stormed his house, looted the goods and chattels, and threatened to kill his wife and sons, demanding Murad Agha. Because Murad had fled, they killed one of his sons, Hidayet, and were about to kill his youngest son, Salim, when locals testified that he was separated from his family and did not live with his father, so he was released. Murad's wealth of about twenty thousand [liras] was looted. Five beautiful women, whom the Millis took with them, are also thought to have survived the general massacre. Only two of them are known: Tolian Souren's wife and house painter Kerovpé Der Kaprielian's wife. The other three have not been identified. Murad Agha, who had escaped from Akhisar by way of the mountains, managed to reach Bahçecik in ten days and thence came to İstanbul via İzmit. After the massacre, muhacirs were placed in the Armenians' houses. The main organizers of Akhisar's slaughter were: Mufti Zade Rüştü Effendi, his

Թուրք կառավարութիւնը յաջողեցաւ 50 ժամ պաշարման մէջ պահելով ամբողջ [շրջանը] ձերբակալել աւազակները եւ աղջիկը կոյս վիճակի մէջ յանձնել:

Աւազակները Միլլի ուժերու յանձնուեցան եւ ղրկուեցան Չայ Ճումա'ա, հոնկէ Պոլու, պատերազմական ատեան ղրկուելու համար:

- Երէկ 1000ի չափ նոր զօրք եկաւ Զօնկուլտաք:

Կ. Պոլիս (յայտարարութիւն Մուրատ աղայի) – 30 Յուլիս

Ազ-հիսարցի Մուրատ աղա, տեղւոյն երեւելիներէն, վաճառական, ծագումով հայ եւ ասկէ 40 տարի առաջ իսլամացած ոճիրի մը հետեւանօք իր կեանքը փրկելու համար, 1895ին Ազ-Հիսարի մէջ պատահած ջարդին ատեն կարգ մը հայեր իր տունը պահած ըլլալուն՝ միշտ թուրքերու կողմէ գէշ աչքով դիտուած է. այս անգամ վերջին դէպքերու համար պատրիարքարան գալով անձամբ հետեւեալը պատմեց:-

Յուլիս 10 Շաբաթ օրուան գիշերը ամէն մարդու բնացած ատեն, թրքական ժամը 5ին մունետիկ ելաւ թէ բոլոր զէնք ունեցողները մէկ ժամուան մէջ պէտք է կառավարութեան յանձնեն եւ առանց լապտերի ոչ ոք դուրս չելլէ: Թուրքերը իրենց զէնքերը յանձնելու համար կառավարութեան դուռը կ'երթան,- ինչպէս նաեւ Մուրատ աղայի տղան,- եւ հոն հրահանգ կը ստանան իրենց զէնքերով տուն դառնալու եւ հայերը երբեք չպաշտպանելու, հակառակ պարագային մահ սպառնալով: Այս միջոցին հայոց տուները կը պաշարեն Միլլիճիները եւ հայերը իրենց տուներէն առնելով կառավարական պաշտօնատուն կը տանին, ուր կ'ըսեն թէ «աքսոր պիտի երթաք»: Նախ բոլոր այր բնակիչները երկ-երկու կապուած կը տանին զընճըլարցի Եղիսէի հորին գլուխը եւ դանակով կը սպաննեն ու հորը կը նետեն: Երկու երիտասարդներ՝ Լաֆճիեան Յովհաննէս եւ Պօյաճի Տ. Գաբրիէլեան Գաբրիէլ ինքնաբերաբար իրենք հորը կը նետուին, դանակով չսպաննուելու համար:

Կիրակի առտուն մնացեալ բնակչութիւնը՝ կին, տղայ հաւաքելով Նալպանտ Կապիկ Պօղոսի շերամատունը կը լեցնեն: Մուրատ աղայի տունը գտնուող 80ամեայ իր մայրը՝ Նոյեմզար, որ քրիստոնեայ մնացած էր եւ երկու շերամապահ լէֆքէցի յոյն կիները՝ Ֆօթինցա եւ Էլանքօ եւս կը տարուին այդ շերամատունը եւ Բշ. լուսնալու գիշերը նոյն հորին գլուխը կը տանին ամէնն ալ կը սպաննեն, այնպէս որ տեղւոյն հայ բնակչութիւնը՝ մերձաւորապէս 350 հոգի, հոն այդ հորին գլուխը կը մորթուին: Կ'ազատուին միայն երկու փոքր աղջիկներ, մէկը միւտիւրին քով ծառայ, միւսը՝ 8 տարեկան փոքրիկ մը՝ վիրաւորուած հորը նետուած ատեն կը պոռայ թէ 12½ ղրուշ ունի կուտայ եւ իսլամութիւնը կ'ընդունի: Ասոր վրայ կը մեղքնան եւ արդէն լեցուած հորէն կը հանեն եւ գնչուի մը կուտան պահելու:

Բացի ասկէ Ազ-Հիսարի հայ բնակչութենէն կ'ազատի հայաստանցի Պետրոս անուն բեռնակիր մը, կայարան պահուելով եւ անկէ Կէյվէի կայարանը փախչելով գիշերը:

Ազ-Հիսար յոյն բնակչութիւն չունէր, այլ միայն Ազ-Հիսարի կայարանի պաշտօնեաներէն երկուքն յոյն էին: Ասոնք ալ կը բռնեն եւ նոյն հորը տանելով կը սպաննեն հայոց պէս: Չէթէները յետոյ կուգան Մուրատի տունը եւ Մինճը Պօղոսի կինը կը պահանջեն եւ երբ կը տեսն[են] որ հոն չէ, Մուրատ աղան սպաննելու համար կը տանին եւ 5000 ոսկի կը պահանջեն ազատ ձգելու համար:

Մուրատ աղայէ սնտուկին բանալին առնելով կը գրաւեն 9000 ոսկի դրամը: Չինքը կը թողուն ազատ, ուրկէ օգտուելով խոյս կուտայ: Միլլիները կը յարձակին իր տան վրայ եւ կահ կարասին կը կողոպտեն եւ կնոջ ու տղաքներուն ալ մահուան սպառնալիք կ'ընեն եւ Մուրատ աղան կը պահանջեն: Որովհետեւ Մուրատ փախած էր, իր մէկ տղան՝ Հիտայէթը կը սպաննեն, իսկ պզտիկ տղան՝ Սալիմն ալ պիտի սպաննէին, երբ տեղացիներ վկայեցին թէ տունէն զատուած է եւ հօրը հետ չի բնակիր, որով ազատ ձգուեցաւ: Մուրատի մօտաւորապէս 20000ի մօտ հարստութիւնը կողոպտուած է: Ընդհանուր կոտորածէն ազատուած ըլլալ կը կարծուին նաեւ հինգ գեղեցիկ կիներ ալ, որոնք Միլլիճիները իրենց հետ տարած են. ասոնցմէ միայն երկուքը ճանչցուած են եւ են՝ Թօլեան Սուրէնի կինը, Պօյաճի Տ. Գաբրիէլեան Քերովբէի կինը. իսկ երեքը չի գիտցուիր թէ ո՞վ են: Մուրատ

brother Hamız Rıza, Mahmut Agha Zade Mustafa Bey, Regie intendant Huseyin, real estate clerk Edhem Effendi, muhacir Rasim Bey, muhacir Idris, Topal Mustafaoğlu Hakkı, retired major Ziya Bey, Mustafa Çapal from Katırız village, Orman Odalıkcısı Ali Effendi, Duralıoğlu Zade Hafız Rıza and his brother mayor Hakkı Effendi, Bushnak Mehmet Effendi, Aksarlı Safet, Huseyin Pehlivan, Çömlek Zade Halil İbrahim Mekeclı, Evrerlı Çerkez İbrahim, Mağdamı İbrahim, Emin Usta Mahtumı Mehemed Çavush, former telegrapher muhacir Mehmet and his brother Muhettin (Taraklı's intendant), and the new telegrapher Ata Effendi.

The commander of Akhisar's gendarmerie squad Arif Çavush, collector Ali Effendi, draper Süleyman, Asım Mahtumı Hafız, Fayit Hasan, Ustası Hafız Ahmet Effendi, Manisalı Hafız Ahmet Effendi.

İzmit (from the primate)—July 30

This morning, Souren Garabed Altounian, one of the sixty-five young Armenians guarding Arslanbey, stealthily came to the prelacy with weapons of protection and said that six to seven hundred Millis made up of natives of Çepni, Serindere, Turks from nearby Fındıklı, Çınardere, Kızın Elinde, and Hazan-Dere have surrounded Arslanbey from four sides. The resistance of some of the watchmen has weakened because they lack ammunition and a capable chief.

Six of those resisting [the Millis] have fallen dead, two of whom were Mgrdich Misak Zhamgochian from Arslanbey and Donig from Ovacık.

The Millis wanted to set fire to the village, but British ships shelled the village, and the Millis fled. As many as seventy to eighty Armenians still there fled and set out for İzmit. Greek troops turned them back from Çuhahane. Several families from İzmit also went to the village, encouraged by the presence of Greek soldiers.

İzmit (from the primate)—July 30

There is a rumor that the English are going to Hendek via Akmeşe. Migrants from Akmeşe and Arslanbey are complaining.

աղա, որ խոյս տուած էր Ագ-Հիսարէն լեռնային ճամբով, 10 օրէն Պարտիզակ կրցած է հասնիլ եւ անկէ Նիկոմիդիոյ ճամբով Պոլիս եկած է: Ջարդէն յետոյ հայոց տուները մուհաճիրները կը գետեղուին: Ագ-Հիսարի ջարդի գլխաւոր կազմակերպողներն են Միւֆթի զատէ Րիւշտի էֆէնտի, եղբայրը Համըզ Րիզա, Մահմուտ աղա զատէ Մուսթաֆա պէյ, Րէժի Մէմուրի Հիւսէյին, Էմլագ Քեաթիպի Էտհէմ էֆէնտի, մուհաճիր Րասիմ պէյ, մուհաճիր Իտրիս, Թօփալ Մուսթաֆա օղլու Հազզը, Թագավիտ Պին Պաշը Ջիա պէյ, Գաթըրըզ գիւղէն Մուսթաֆա Չափալ, Օրման Օտաըղճըսը Ալի էֆէնտի, Տուրալը օղլու զատէ Հաֆըզ Րիզա եւ եղբայրը՝ Պէլէտիէ Րէիսի Հազզը էֆէնտի, Պօշնագ Մէհմէտ էֆէնտի, Ագսարըլը Սաֆէտ, Հիւսէին Փէհլիվան, Չէօմլէք զատէ Խալիլ Իպրահիմ Մէքէճլի, Էվրէյլի Չէրքէզ Իպրահիմ, Մաղտամի Իպրահիմ, Էմին ուստա մախտումը Մէհմէտ Չավուշ, Սապըզ Թէլէկրաֆճի Մէհաճիր Մէհմէտ եւ եղբայրը՝ Մուհէտտին (Թարագլըի միւտիր) եւ նոր թէլէկրաֆճի Աթա էֆէնտի:

Ագ-Հիսար ժանտարմա թագըմ քօմանտանը Արիֆ Չավուշ, Թահսիլտար Ալի էֆէնտի, Մանիֆաթուրաճի Սիւլէյման, Ասըմ Մախթումը Հաֆըզ, Փահտ Հասան, ուստասը Հաֆըզ Ահմէտ էֆէնտի, Մանիսալը Հաֆըզ Ահմէտ էֆէնտի:

Նիկոմիդիա (Առաջնորդէն) – 30 Յուլիս

Այսօր առաւօտուն Արսլանպէկի պահապան 65 հայ երիտասարդներէն մէկը՝ Սուրէն Կար[ապետ] Ալթունեան, փախստեայ եւ պահպանութեան զէնքերով առաջնորդարան եկաւ եւ ըսաւ թէ 6–700 Միլլիճիներ չէփնիցիներ, սէրին տէրէցիներ, գիւղին մօտակայ թուրք ֆընտըգլըցիներ, Չընար Տէրէի, Կիզին Եւանտիի, Խազան Տէրէի թուրքերէն բաղկացեալ, Արսլանպէկը չորս կողմէն կը պաշարեն: Պահապաններէն մէկ մասին դիմադրութիւնը կը տկարանայ, վասնզի ռազմամթերք չունէին եւ կարող պետ մը կը պակսէր:

Դիմադրողներէն վեց հոգիներ կ'իյնան դի[տ]ապաստ, որոնցմէ երկուքն են արսլանպէկցի Մկրտիչ Միսաք Ժամկոչեան, միւսն՝ օվաճըգցի Տօնիկ:

Միլլիները կ'ուզեն գիւղը կրակի տալ: Անգլիական նաւեր թնդանօթի կը բռնեն եւ Միլլիճիները կը փախ[չ]ին եւ տակաւին 70–80ի չափ հայեր, որ հոն կը գտնուին, կը փախչին եւ Իզմիթ գալու համար ճամբայ կ'իյնան: Յոյն զօրքեր Չուխախանէէն ետ կը դառնան: Նիկոմիդիայէն ալ քանի մը տնուոր գիւղ կ'երթան քաջալերուելով յոյն զինուորներու ներկայութենէն:

Նիկոմիդիա (Առաջնորդէն) – 30 Յուլիս

Չրոյց կայ թէ անգլիացիք Արմաշու ճամբով Հէնտէք կ'երթան: Արմաշցի եւ արսլանպէկցի գաղթականներ աղմուկ կը հանեն:

[Insecurity] Notebook Number 13
July–September 1920

Bursa (from the primate)—July 29

This morning, many hungry, thirsty, and naked migrants from Yenice and Cerrah arrived in Bursa. Among them were the priest Athanasius of Yenice and the prominent Armenians of the two villages of Yenice and Cerrah, who had been taken to İnegöl and miraculously survived.

Thirteen Greek villages around Bursa were also attacked, and many Greeks were killed. The five to six thousand rescued people were brought to a nearby village, all suffering extreme misery.

There have been no murders in Armenian villages so far, but it is feared that they will happen.

On July 27, there was a fierce battle between the locals in İnegöl and the Milli çetes. Significant losses were suffered on both sides. The bandit leader İzzet Pasha and Muhamet were killed, and the village was set on fire. The fifteen Armenian houses were not damaged.

Gemlik (from the Neighborhood Council)—July 29

Yesterday, the çetes sent word to Yenisölöz that they should be given weapons, money, and soldiers; otherwise, they would attack the village with a force of one to two thousand people. The villagers immediately engaged in self-defense. They decided to send the aged, women, and children of the village first to Gemlik. The same Milli horror has spread to Gürle and Karsak, so today, five to six hundred people from these three villages took refuge here, and thousands are expected tomorrow.

The problem of these migrants' livelihood is very grave, and their poverty is extreme.

Refugees from Gürle arrived in Gemlik today. They report that the Kemalists besieged their village and shot dead the defenseless women and children whose passionate voices rose to the skies.

The Armenians of Karsak have taken refuge in Gemlik also. The çetes looted their houses through the village Turks.

Gemlik (from Manoug Semerjian from Yenisölöz)—July 29

Today at noon, a group of two hundred fierce çetes exterminated the Armenians of Gürle with swords and fire. Some Armenians were able to take refuge in Gemlik and the rest in the mountains. A survivor from the massacre related the horrible details.

Although Yenisölöz was given an ultimatum, and horses and weapons were demanded, the young men of the village, having sent all the women and children to Gemlik, decided to resist with the scarce means they had.

İzmit (from the primate)—July 30

On July 29, the people of Arslanbey and the priest, Father Parsegh Parseghian, definitively abandoned their village and the sowing of wheat, corn, and tobacco, as well as all the goods and chattels and the houses they had. They came to İzmit almost naked. Hungry and thirsty, death also awaits them here.

The situation of four villages in Pazarköy, four in Yalova, two in Karamürsel [Karamursal], and the Greeks [who live there] is frightful. Although they are fleeing from the Millis, the lieutenant governor and the intendant are not allowing them to cross to İstanbul, so that they—that is, the Turks who have joined the Millis—can slaughter those unfortunate people mercilessly.

• Yesterday, a declaration by the commander Wilson of the Allied forces announced [the follow-

[Անապահովութեան] Տետր Թիւ 13
1920 Յուլիս – 1920 Սեպտեմբեր

Պրուսա (Առաջնորդէն) – 29 Յուլիս

Այս առտու բազմաթիւ ենիճէցի եւ ճերահցի գաղթականներ Պրուսա հասան անօթի, ծարաւ եւ մերկ: Ասոնց մէջ էր Ենիճէի Տէր Աթանաս քահանան եւ Ենիճէի եւ Ճերահի երկու գիւղերու հայ երեւելիները, որոնք Ի[ն]նէկէօլ տարուած էին եւ հրաշքով փրկուած են:

Պրուսայի շրջակայ 13 յունաբնակ գիւղեր ալ կողոպտուած եւ շատ մը յոյներ սպաննուած են: 5–6 հազար անձ, որոնք ազատած են, մօտակայ գիւղ մը բերած են յետին ծայր թշուառութեան մէջ:

Մինչեւ ցարդ հայ գիւղերու մէջ սպանութիւն չէ պատահած, սակայն կը վախցուի որ պատահի:

Յուլիս 27ին Իյնէկէօլի մէջ տեղացւոց եւ Միլլիի չէթէներու մէջ ուժգին կռիւ մը եղած է: Երկու կողմէ մեծ կորուստ կայ: Աւազակապետ Իզէթ փաշա եւ Մուհամէտ սպաննուած են, գիւղը այրած է, հայոց 15 տուներուն ռեւէ վնաս չէ հասած:

Կէմլէյիկ (Թաղական Խորհուրդէն) – 29 Յուլիս

Երէկ չէթէները Սէօյէօզ լուր ղրկած են որ իրենց զէնք, դրամ եւ զինուոր տրուի, հակառակ պարագային 1–2000 հոգինոց ուժով մը պիտի յարձակին գիւղին վրայ: Գիւղացիք իսկոյն ինքնապաշտպանութեան կը դիմեն եւ կ'որոշեն նախ գիւղին ծերերը, կիները եւ տղաքը Կէմլէյիկ ղրկել: Նոյնպէս նոյն Միլլիական սարսափը կը տարածուի Կիւրլէի եւ Գարսագի մէջ ալ, այնպէս որ այսօր 5–600 անձեր այս երեք գիւղերէն ապաստանեցան հոս եւ կը սպասուի վաղը հազարաւորներու:

Այս գաղթականներու ապրուստի խնդիրը շատ ծանր կը կշռէ եւ չքաւորութիւնը ծա[յ]ր աստիճան է:

Այսօր Կիւրլէէ Կէմլէյիկ հասան փախստական կիւրլէցիներ, որոնք կը պատմեն որ Քէմալականներ իրենց գիւղը պաշարելով հրացանի բռնած են գիւղին մէջ գտնուող անպաշտպան կիները եւ տղաքներ, որոնց աղիողորմ ձայները երկինք բարձրացած են:

Գարսաքի հայերն ալ Կէմլէյիկ ապաստանած են եւ չէթէները թալանի տուած են անոնց տուները գիւղացի թուրքերու ձեռքով:

Կէմլէյիկ (սէօյէզցի Մանուկ Սէմէրճեանէ) – 29 Յուլիս

Այսօր կէսօրին 200 հոգինոց կատաղի չէթէներու խումբ մը սրով ու հուրով բնաջինջ ըրած է Կիւռլէի հայութիւնը, որոնցմէ մէկ մասը Կէմլէյիկ, իսկ մնացածը լեռները ապաստանած են: Ջարդէն ազատած մէկը կը պատմէ սոսկալի մանրամասնութիւններ:

Սէօյէօզի ալ վերջնագիր տուած ու ձիերն ու զէնքերը պահանջած են թէեւ, սակայն գիւղին երիտասարդութիւնը Կէմլէյիկ ղրկած ըլլալով ամբողջ կիները ու մանուկները, որոշած է դիմադրել իր տկար միջոցներով:

Նիկոմիդիա (Առաջնորդէն) – 30 Յուլիս

29 Յուլիսին վերջնապէս արսլանպէկցիները եւ քահանան՝ Տէր Բարսեղ Բարսեղեան, ձգեցին իրենց գիւղը եւ ցորենի եւ եգիպտացորենի ցանքն ու թիւթիւնը, ինչպէս նաեւ ամէն կահ կարասի, տուն տեղ, Նիկոմիդիա եկան, զրեթէ մերկ: Անօթի եւ [ծ]արաւ՝ հոս ալ իրենց մահ կը սպասէ:

Բազարի չորս, Եալովայի չորս եւ Գարամուսալի 2 գիւղերուն եւ յոյներուն վիճակը երկիւղալի է: Ասոնք թէեւ կը փախ[չ]ին Միլլիճիներէն, սակայն գայմագամ, միւտիր չեն թողուր որ Պոլիս անցնին, որ[պէսզի] իրենք՝ Միլլիճիներու հետ միացած թուրքերն, անխնայ ջարդեն այդ խեղճերը:

- Երէկ Նիկոմիդիոյ ամէն կողմերը Դաշնակից զօրաց հրամանատար Ուիլսընի կողմէ յայտարարութիւն մը կը յայտարարէ թէ

Ա. Պատերազմական զէնքերը պահողները, գործածողները եւ տունը եւ վրան պահողները,

ing] throughout İzmit:

A. Those who keep weapons, those who use them, and those who keep them at home or carry them,

B. those who fire at the Allied forces, [and]

C. those who own the homes wherefrom Allied forces are fired upon,

if they fail to prove that [these actions happened] unbeknown to them, they will be sentenced to death or severe punishment.

İzmit (from the primate)—July 31

It is said that yesterday's massacre in Arslanbey caused the loss of seventy to eighty Armenians. So far, thirty-five deceased people have been verified by name: they were guarding Arslanbey. Fifteen of them are from Ovacık, sixteen from Arslanbey, two from Mecidiye [Khach], one from İzmit, and one from Camidüzü [Kilisedüzü/Zhamavayr] village. The number of Millis attacking Arslanbey was more than fifteen hundred. They suffered 150 casualties.

• The British clashed [with the Millis] in the place called Çıbaklı, on the Akmeşe road, and lost twelve people. They were caught by surprise because the Millis came out of the woods suddenly and attacked them.

It is heard that hundreds of Turks, Lazes, Georgians, and Albanians who are imprisoned in İzmit will be tried and punished.

• It is said that in the Arslanbey massacre of yesterday, the Millis appeared dressed in Greek uniforms and that the Armenians had been trapped and killed by that deception.

Allegedly, those Greek uniforms had been made in Adapazarı weeks ago.

Bursa (from the primate)—July 31

About 135 migrants from Yenice and Cerrah came to Bursa. It was reported that the Millis have withdrawn from Yenice and Cerrah. The villagers will slowly go [back] to their places.

• Three weeks ago, Miss Allen traveled from here to Ankara, Konya, Afyonkarahisar, and Eskişehir on behalf of the American Near East Relief and returned. Miss Allen confirms that quarterly food has been secured for the orphanages in these places and that the situation in those places is calm. Etem Bey immediately even hanged a Milli for raping an Armenian girl.

Samsun (from Chairman of the National Board, [numbered] 7920)—July 19

Anti-Christian rallies are taking place after Milli's rule. No letter or newspaper has arrived except for the Turks for two months now. Travel to İstanbul is banned for Christians. Many women and children from Sivas, Harput, and other places (there is no permission for men at all) have come here to go to İstanbul and America, but they have remained here because they are not allowed [to leave]. Yesterday, the governor ordered them to return to their places, and under this pretext, the police registered the names of all Armenians. The people have closed their shops out of fear and taken refuge in their houses, thinking that there would be new deportation, but in the end, upon the intervention of a couple of prominent Turks, the governor has attributed what happened to a misunderstanding. The people have been partially assured after this.

The local British representative has already left. It is said that the French consul will also leave. Only the American consul remains.

The formation of çete Turks has reached significant proportions. A special organization and commission have been formed to increase the number of çetes. They spend big money.

Բ. Դաշնակից զօրաց վրայ զէնք պարպողները,

Գ. Դաշնակից զօրաց վրայ զէնք պարպուող տան տէրերը,

եթէ չկարենան ապացուցանել թէ իրենց գիտութեամբ չէ, մահուան պիտի դատապարտուին կամ ծանր պատիժի պիտի ենթարկուին:

Նիկոմիդիա (Առաջնորդէն) – 31 Յուլիս

Երէկի Արսլանպէկի կոտորածէն կ'ըսուի որ 70–80[ի] չափ կորուստ տուած են հայերը: Առայժմ որոշ անուններով ստուգուած են 35 մեռեալներ, որոնք Արսլանպէկի պահապաններն էին: Ասոնցմէ 15-ը օվաճըգցի, 16-ը արսլանպէկցի, 2-ը Խաչ-գիւղացի, 1-ը նիկոմիդիացի, 1-ը Ժամավայր գիւղէն [են]: Արսլանպէկի վրայ յարձակող Միլլիճիներու թիւը 1500էն աւելի էր եւ 150 հոգի կորուստ տուած են:

- Անգլիացիք Արմաշու ճամբուն վրայ Չպուգլու ըսուած տեղը ընդհարում կ'ունենան եւ անգլիացիք 12 անձ կը կորսնցնեն, որովհետեւ անակնկալի կուգան, վասնզի Միլլիճիները անտառէն դուրս գալով յանկարծ կը յարձակին:

- Կը լսուի թէ Նիկոմիդիոյ մէջ բանտարկուած հարիւրի չափ զանազան թուրքեր, լազեր, կիւրճիներ եւ ալպանացիներ պիտի դատուին եւ պատժուին:

- Արսլանպէկի երէկի կոտորածին կ'ըսուի թէ Միլլիճիները յունական տարազով երեւցած են եւ այդ խաբեբայութեամբ հայերն թակարդը ինկած ու սպաննուած են:

Այդ յունական տարազները շաբաթներ առաջ Ատաբազար պատրաստած են եղեր:

Պրուսա (Առաջնորդէն) – 31 Յուլիս

Ենիճէէն եւ Ճէրրահէն մօտ 135 գաղթականներ Պրուսա եկած են: Լուր առնուեցաւ թէ Ենիճէէն եւ Ճէրրահէէն Միլլիճիները քաշուած են: Գիւղացիք ալ կամաց կամաց իրենց տեղերը պիտի երթան:

- Ամերիկեան նպաստամատոյցի մարմնոյն կողմէ Միս Ալէն ասկէ երեք շաբաթ առաջ մեկնելով ասկէ Էնկիւրիւ, Գոնիա, Աֆիոն Գարահիսար, Էսկի Շէհիր այցելած է եւ դարձած է: Միս Ալէն կը հաւաստէ թէ այս տեղերու որբանոցներուն եռամսեայ սնունդ ապահովուած է եւ այդ տեղերու մէջ կացութիւնը հանդարտ է: Նոյնիսկ Միլլիճի մը հայ աղջիկ մը բռնաբարած ըլլալուն համար Էթէմ պէյ զայն անմիջապէս կախած է:

Սամսոն (Ազգային Վարչութեան ատենապետէն, 7920 [թուահամարով]) – 19 Յուլիս

Միլլի տիրապետութենէն յետոյ քրիստոնէից դէմ գրգռիչ միթինկներ տեղի կ'ունենան: Երկու ամիս է բացի թուրքերէն ոչ նամակ եւ ոչ լրագիր կուգայ: Քրիստոնէից դէպի Կ. Պոլիս ճամբորդութիւնը արգիլուած է: Սեբաստիայէն, Խարբերդէն եւ ուրիշ տեղերէ շատ մը կիներ եւ տղաքներ (այրերու բնաւ հրաման չկայ) հոս եկած են Կ. Պոլիս եւ Ամերիկա երթալու համար, սակայն հոս մնացած են, վասնզի չեն թողուր: Կառավարիչը անցեալ օր հրաման ըրաւ որ ասոնք իրենց տեղերը դառնան եւ այս պատրուակով ոստիկաններ բոլոր հայոց անունները ցուցակագրեցին: Ժողովուրդը վախէն խանութները գոցեց եւ տուները ապաստանեցաւ՝ կարծելով թէ նոր տարագրութիւն մը պիտի ըլլայ, բայց ի վերջոյ մէկ երկու թուրք երեւելիներու միջամտութեան վրայ, կառավարիչը թիւրիմացութեան մը վերագրեց եղածը: Ժողովուրդն ասոր վրայ մասամբ ապահովուեցաւ:

Տեղւոյս անգլիացի ներկայացուցիչը արդէն մեկնած է: Կ'ըսուի թէ ֆրանսական հիւպատոսն ալ պիտի մեկնի: Միայն կը մնայ ամերիկեան հիւպատոսը:

Թիւրքերու չէթէական կազմութիւնը մեծ համեմատութիւն առած է: Մասնաւոր *Թէշքիլաթ* եւ քօմիսիոն կազմուած է չէթէներու թիւը աւելցնելու համար: Խոշոր դրամներ կը ծախսեն:

To exterminate the nearly two hundred Armenians who took refuge in the mountains of Çarşamba for several years, all Turkish çetes were sent to attack them. [Regular] troops also will be sent these days. Absolutely, the goal is to annihilate them first so they may slaughter Samsun's [remaining] Armenians comfortably. It is necessary to take [preventive] measures; otherwise, all Armenians will be massacred.

• Mustafa Kemal's forces in Yozgat and Zile are said to have massacred Armenians and looted the shops. There are no details yet. A similar incident took place in Çarşamba a few days ago.

İzmit (from the primate)—August 2[86]

Barely fifteen to twenty families are left in Bahçecik, and they do not want to move to İzmit.

Today, the deputy of the British commander, the deputy district governor, and the vicars of the Greek and Armenian spiritual leaders convened a meeting. In this meeting, the deputy district governor suggested that the fifteen hundred people from Bahçecik sheltered in İzmit be returned to Bahçecik where they could make peace with the Turks and live safely, reaping their wheat, tobacco, and corn. The Armenian vicar general replied that the primate was so moved by the massacres in Geyve and Arslanbey that he prefers that the people of Bahçecik stay here and starve to death.

• Yesterday, a functionary representing a British information officer came to the prelacy and offered to find and send someone to the Turkish village of Kumlar, located between Arslanbey and the imperial haircloth factory, because, allegedly, Armenians were attacking the Turks. The primate expressed astonishment and said he could not find anyone [fitting the claim] but was ready to write a letter to those supposed Armenians instructing them not to do such things. The British official repeated his instruction. It has been reported that the [British] commander drove there yesterday and was attacked. Fifty Greek soldiers belonging to the factory were with him. They resisted but failed to defeat the Millis. He ordered the Greeks to withdraw, and he retreated to İzmit.

Behold! The Turkish officials and notables of İzmit want to present these Millis as Armenians. They always slander the Armenians in front of the British. The Turkish government and notables are in contact with the Millis, and the uniforms of the Greek troops here, too, have been made by the Turks.

İzmit (from the primate)—August 2

Seven people injured during the Arslanbey massacre have been transferred to İstanbul.

İzmit (from the primate)—August 3

Yesterday, about three thousand soldiers were sent to the haircloth factory. There is a rumor that Greek troops also will come from Bursa.

The British, the Turkish government, and Turkish notables insist on the return of the [Armenians] of Bahçecik to their village; otherwise, they are threatening to terminate benefits to migrants coming to İzmit. The people of Bahçecik refuse to go because the Millis attack with great force, and often the English withdraw not to suffer losses.

İzmit (from the primate)—August 4

Yesterday, Greek and British troops burned the village named Çepni, which is half an hour from Arslanbey and where 610 Turkish Laz families live. Also, they burned the villages of İflabiye and Şevketiye

Մի քանի տարիներէ ի վեր Չարշամպայի լեռները ապաստանող 200ի չափ հայեր ոչնչացնելու նպատակով, բոլոր թուրք չէթէները ասոնց վրայ ղրկուած են: Այս օրերս զինուոր ալ պիտի ղրկուի: Բացարձակ է որ նպատակնին է նախ ասոնք ոչնչացնել, որպէսզի կարելի ըլլայ Սամսոն հայերը ի հարկին հանգիստ ջարդել: Միջոցներ ձեռք առնել անհրաժեշտ է, եթէ ոչ բոլոր հայերը պիտի ջարդուին:

- Եօզղատի եւ Զիլէի մէջ Մուսթաֆա Քէմալի ուժերը հայերը ջարդած եւ խանութները կողոպտած են կ'ըսուի: Մանրամասնութիւններ չկան դեռ: Նմանօրինակ դէպք մըն ալ քանի մը օր առաջ Չարշամպայի մէջ տեղի ունեցած է:

Նիկոմիդիա (Առաջնորդէն) – 2 Օգոստոս

Պարտիզակ 15–20 տուն հազիւ մնաց[ած] են եւ անոնք ալ չեն ուզեր անցնիլ Նիկոմիդիա:

Այսօր անգլիացի հրամանատարի փոխանորդը, միութասարըֆի փոխանորդը, յունաց եւ հայոց առաջնորդներու փոխանորդները ժողով ըրին: Այս ժողովին մէջ միութասարըֆի փոխանորդը առաջարկած է որ պարտիզակցի 1500 հոգի Նիկոմիդիա ապաստանողները դառնան Պարտիզակ եւ հաշտուին թուրքերուն հետ եւ ապահով ապրին, իրենց ցորենը, ծխախոտը, եգիպտացորենը քաղեն: Հայոց առաջնորդի փոխանորդը պատասխանած է թէ Առաջնորդը Կէյվէի եւ Արսլանպէկի ջարդերէն այնքան յուզուած եւ զգացուած է, որ կը նախընտրէ որ պարտիզակցիք հոս մնան եւ անօթի մեռնին:

- Երէկ անգլիացի տեղեկատու պաշտօնեան ներկայացնող պաշտօնեան կուգայ առաջնորդարան եւ կ'առաջարկէ մարդ գտնել եւ ղրկե[լ] դէպի թուրք Ղումլար գիւղը՝ Արսլանպէկի եւ կայսերական չուխայի գործարանին միջեւ, վասնզի հոն իբր թէ հայեր կան, որոնք թուրքերուն վրայ յարձակում կ'ընեն: Առաջնորդը զարմանք կը յայտնէ եւ կը յայտնէ թէ մարդ չի կրնար գտնել, եւ կ'ըսէ թէ պատրաստ է նամակ գրելու այդ կարծեցեալ հայերուն, որ այս տեսակ բաներ չընեն: Անգլիացի պաշտօնատարը կը կրկնէ իր հրամանը: Կ'ըսուի թէ հրամանատարը օթոմոպիլով երէկ ցորեկ հոն գացեր եւ յարձակումի ենթարկուեր է: Գործարանին յոյն զօրքերէն յիսուն հոգի հետը ըլլալով դիմադրեր եւ չեն յաջողեր յաղթել Միլլիճիներուն: Յոյներուն կը հրամայէ նահանջել եւ ինքն ալ դէպի Նիկոմիդիա ետ կը քաշուի:

Նիկոմիդիոյ թուրք պաշտօնեաները եւ երեւելիները ահա այս Միլլիները կ'ուզեն իբր հայ ցոյց տալ: Ասոնք արդէն միշտ հայերը կը զրպարտեն անգլիացւոց առջեւ: Թուրք կառավարութիւնը եւ երեւելիները յարաբերութեան մէջ են Միլլիճիներուն հետ եւ յունական զօրքերու զգեստները հոս ալ պատրաստուած են թուրքերու միջոցաւ:

Նիկոմիդիա (Առաջնորդէն) – 2 Օգոստոս

Արսլանպէկի կոտորածին վիրաւորուած եօթը անձեր Կ. Պոլիս փոխադրուեցան:

Նիկոմիդիա (Առաջնորդէն) – 3 Օգոստոս

Երէկ 3000ի չափ զինուոր ղրկուեցաւ դէպի չուխայի գործարանը: Զրոյց կայ որ հելլէն զինուոր ալ պիտի գայ Պրուսայի կողմերէն:

Անգլիացիք, ինչպէս նաեւ թուրք կառավարութիւնը եւ թուրք երեւելիները կը պնդեն որ պարտիզակցիները իրենց գիւղը վերադառնան, հակառակ պարագային սպառնալով Իզմիթ եկող գաղթականներու նպաստը դադրեցնել: Պարտիզակցիք չեն ուզեր երթալ, վասնզի Միլլիճիները մեծ ուժերով կը յարձակին եւ յաճախ անգլիացիք կորուստ չտալու համար ետ կը քաշուին:

Նիկոմիդիա (Առաջնորդէն) – 4 Օգոստոս

Երէկ յոյն եւ անգլիացի զինուորները այրեր են Արսլանպէկէն կէս ժամ հեռու Չէփնի անուն 610 տնուոր թուրք լազերու գիւղը: Նոյնպէս Իֆլապիյէ 40–50 եւ Ճէֆքէթիյէ 100 տունի մօտ լազերու

[Saçmalı], populated respectively by forty to fifty and close to 100 Laz families, because these villages were Milli stations. There is a rumor that the village called Seydi Dere, which consists of forty families and extends from the edge of Sapanca to the edge of Karamürsel [Karamursal], has also been burned as it is a suitable hideout for the Millis since each house is a half or a quarter of an hour apart from another.

The Millis also took the rest of those who had remained in Arslanbey, Döngöl, Ovacık, Sapanca, Dağköy, and Bahçecik to use them for road construction in faraway places so that their atrocities would go unnoticed.

• Seven of the thirty-five people believed to have been martyred in Arslanbey have managed to survive and come to İzmit.

Üsküdar (from Priest Hmayag Exerjian)—July 28

Hayg Kahramanian was killed in the latest incident in Alemdağı. He was shot dead by five Turks from Alemdağı, three of whom are apprehended. They are called İdris, Ayincihlı Mustafa, and Cemal. The other two, Aşır and Arab Hacı, are being chased after.

The Turks buried Hayg three weeks ago in the forest of Sultançiftliği (the so-called Lower Village) without the presence of a priest. At the time of his murder, Hayg had twenty-one Ottoman lira banknotes on him. His wife and five children remain without a protector.

Cabinetmaker Hovagim Leventian, one of the members of the Alemdağı Neighborhood Council, is nowhere to be seen. It is rumored that he was killed in the church room. It is not known where he was buried.

Maraş (from the Armenian locum tenens Very Reverend Father Khachadour Der Ghazarian, Armenian Catholic prelate Archbishop Avedis Arpiarian, Armenian Evangelical minister Reverend A. H. Haroutyunian) . . .

It is impossible to describe all the horribly frightful tribulations that the surviving Armenians of Maraş have gone through. All breathing Armenians have returned from the threshold of the grave. The explanation "breathing Armenians" is the most accurate term to describe surviving Armenians. They do not live; life does not exist; they only breathe. We are leading an organic, not a rational, life.

The incident, which began on January 21 of this year and seemingly ended on February 12, cost the lives of more than twelve thousand people to the Armenians of Maraş and its environs. In Maraş itself, nine thousand people were massacred, along with all the Armenians in the surrounding villages, without exception. These numbered more than three thousand. The mode and method of extermination remain unknown to us.

After the French forces abandoned the city and withdrew, members of the American Near East Relief Committee and the Missionaries of the [American] Board made every effort to save the lives of Armenians; we owe our lives to them primarily. Meanwhile, it was a straightforward task for the mob and the bandits to end the lives of the Armenians with one blow and in a very short time, as they were crammed into the four main centers, that is, the St. Savior [Church] of Catholic Armenians, the Latin church, the orphanage called Beit Shalom, and the buildings of American institutions.

To get an idea of the living conditions of thousands of Armenians piled on top of each other in these four buildings, one has to live that life; otherwise, one cannot imagine it. This life has been a mixture of constant horrors, starvation to death, nightmares, filth, and even lying on dry decks. This harsh prison of crowdedness has lasted for weeks. Hence, we hardly dare to walk around the city, and we visit each other only during the day.

After the Armenian exodus, the Americans kindly thought of feeding a little and protecting the

գիւղերն այրած են, վասնզի այս գիւղերը Միլլիճիներու կայաններ էին: Չրոյց կայ որ Սէյտի Տէրէ ըսուած գիւղն որ 40 տունէ կը բաղկանայ, Սապանճայի գլուխէն մինչեւ Գարամուսալի գլուխը տարածուած, որովհետեւ ամէն տուն կէս կամ քառորդ ժամ իրարմէ հեռու են, նոյնպէս այրուած է իբր յարմար թաքստոց Միլլիներու:

Նոյնպէս Արսլանպէկի, Տէօնկէօլի, Օվաճըգի, Սապանճայի, Տաղ գիւղի եւ Պարտիզակի մէջ մնացածները Միլլիճիները ճամբու շինութեան գործածելու համար վակոններով հեռու տեղեր կը տանին, որ իրենց վայրագութիւնները դուրսը արձագանգ չգտն[են]:

- Արսլանպէկի մէջ նախատակուած կարծուած 35 անձերէն 7-ը կրցած են ողջ ազատիլ եւ Իզմիթ գալ:

Սկիւտար (Հմայեակ քահանայ Էքսէրճեանէ) – 28 Յուլիս

Ալէմտաղիի վերջին դէպքի միջոցին սպաննուած է Հայկ Գահրամանեան, որ հրացանազարկ եղած է ամլէմտաղցի հինգ թուրքերէ, որոնց երեքը ձերբակալուած են եւ կը կոչուին Խտրիս, Այընճըխլը Մուսթաֆա, Ճէմալ, իսկ մնացեալ երկուքը՝ Աշըր, Արապ Հաճի կը հետապնդուին:

Հայկը թուրքերը կը թաղեն Սուլթան Չիֆլիքի (վարի գիւղ ըսուածը) անտառին մէջ առանց քահանայի ներկայութեան երեք շաբաթ առաջ: Հայկ սպաննուած ատեն վրան 21 լիրա օսմանեան թղթադրամ ունի եղեր: Կինը եւ 5 զաւակները կը մնան անպաշտպան:

Ալէմտաղիի թաղական խորհրդոյ անդամներէն մասաճի Յովակիմ Լէվէնթեան ալ մէջտեղ չկայ եւ կը զր[ու]ցուի թէ եկեղեցիի սենեկին մէջ սպաննած են եւ ո՞ւր թաղուած ըլլալը յայտնի չէ:

Մարաշ (Հայոց Առաջնորդական Տեղապահ Խաչատուր Ծ. Վրդ. Տէր Ղազարեանէ, Հայ Կաթողիկէ Առաջնորդ Աւետիս Արքեպ. Արփիարեանէ, Հայ Աւետարանականաց հովիւ Վեր. Ա. Յ. Յարութիւնեանէ) ...

Անկարելի է նկարագրել այն բոլոր զարհուրելիօրէն սոսկառիթ փորձանքներն, որոնց մէջ[էն] անցաւ Մարաշի վերապրող հայութիւնը: Բոլոր շնչող հայերը գերեզմանի սեմէն ետ դարձած են: *Շնչող հայեր* բացատրութիւնը է՛ն ճիշտն է զոր կարելի է գործածել վերապրող հայերը որակելու համար: Չեն ապրիր, կեանքը գոյութիւն չունի, միայն կը շնչեն: Գործարանային՝ ոչ թէ բանաւոր կեանքն է զոր կը վարենք:

Ներկայ տարւոյ Յունվար 21ին սկսող եւ երեւոյթապէս Փետրուար 12ին վերջացող դէպքը Մարաշի եւ շրջակայ հայութեան աւելի քան 12,000 հոգի արժեց: Բուն Մարաշի մէջ 9000 անձ կոտորեցին եւ շրջակայ գիւղերու ամբողջ հայութիւնը առանց բացառութեան, որ աւելի քան 3000 էր, որոց բնաջնջման ձեւն ու եղանակը անծանօթ կը մնայ մեզ:

Ֆրանսական ոյժերու քաղաքը լքելով քաշուելէն վերջ Ամերիկեան Մերձաւոր Արեւելքի Օգնութեան Կոմիտէի անդամներն եւ Պօրտի միսիոնարք միանալով ամէն ջանք ի գործ դրին հայոց կեանքը փրկելու համար. ամենամեծ չափով անոնց կը պարտինք մեր կեանքը: Մինչ շատ դիւրին գործ մըն էր խուժանին ու հրոսակներուն համար մէկ հարուածով ու շատ կարճ ատենուան մէջ վերջացնել կեանքն հայերու, որոնք խճողուած մնացած էին չորս գլխաւոր կեդրոններու մէջ, այն է՝ հայ-հռովմէականներու Ս. Փրկիչ, Լատիններու եկեղեցւոյն, Պէյթ-Շալըմ ըսուած որբանոցին եւ ամերիկեան հաստատութեանց շէնքերուն մէջ:

Հազարաւոր հայերու այս չորս շէնքերուն մէջ իրարու վրայ դիզուած կեանքի պայմաններուն մասին գաղափար մը կազմելու համար մարդ պէտք է այն կեանքն ապրի, այլապէս երեւակայել կարելի չէ: Այս կեանքը տեւական սարսափներու, անօթութենէ մահուան դատապարտութեան, մղձաւանջի, աղտուկեղտի եւ նոյնիսկ չոր տախտակամածներու վրայ պառկելու, խճողումի ամենախիստ բանտարկութեան խառնուրդ մը եղած է եւ շաբաթներ տեւած է: Ասկէ վերջ հազիւ համարձա-

people who needed help from others since they had been deprived of their homes—eighty percent of which were burned and most of the rest destroyed—and their property, all of which was looted. They were, therefore, left unsheltered, homeless, naked, and starving, and their lives were in constant danger.

There are now ten thousand Armenians here, including sixteen hundred orphans sheltered in an orphanage; there are thirty-five hundred widows and orphans in the city whom Americans partly support. Only a tiny fraction of the remaining five thousand manage to make ends meet, and the rest, deprived of all opportunities to work, live a life of horror, not knowing what awaits them. Squeezed in an iron circle, they have no security to go to the surrounding orchards, at least as workers and cultivators.

We are deprived of all kinds of contacts. We cannot correspond, travel, or read newspapers.

If this situation continues, the rest of the people will starve to death in the forthcoming winter.

İzmit (from the primate)—August 7

Last night, ten to fifteen young Armenians from Adapazarı and sixty to seventy Catholic Armenians from Geyve-Ortaköy, old and young, fled to İzmit via Akmeşe. While fleeing from Adapazarı, one of them, a Catholic Armenian bride, gave birth to a son in Akmeşe.

On Friday, in broad daylight, suddenly, it was heard in Adapazarı that about four hundred Millis entered the city. The Millis daringly shouted that they have come to Adapazarı again and will shed the last drop of their blood and resist surrendering this city to the British alive. It was also heard that nearly two hundred more Millis arrived in Namert Köprü (which is also Beşköprü) near Adapazarı. They have allegedly installed cannons and prepared trenches on Ereğli's elevation.

The Armenian and Greek inhabitants of Adapazarı rushed out of the city with horror and uproar. Perhaps having heard that the British were around Sarmanlı, they headed there.

Allegedly, those who escaped from Adapazarı and arrived in Akmeşe first numbered seven or eight people.

By a surprising coincidence, ten British soldiers and an officer arrived in Akmeşe on the same day.

The people of Akmeşe asked for help and voiced fear about the Millis' possible return to Akmeşe.

The English officer answered: "Inform us in İzmit. We are there." They advised the use of telephones that the Millis had left during their escape to communicate with İzmit.

• So far, [altogether] eighty to ninety Catholic and Apostolic Armenians from Adapazarı, and others from Akmeşe, have come to İzmit, twenty of whom are natives of Akmeşe. Allegedly, many people will set out from Akmeşe this morning.

Sivas (from the primate)—June 11

Several Armenians, natives of Sivas in İstanbul, allegedly are pursuing and accusing a few massacrer Turks in Sivas, which is leaving a bad impression on the local element.

կութիւն ունինք քաղաքին մէջ շրջիլ եւ զիրար այցելել ցորեկ ատեն միայն:

Ամերիկացիք հայոց դուրս ելլելէն յետոյ ազնիւ գաղափարն ունեցան դոյզն ինչ կերակրելու եւ պաշտպանելու ժողովուրդը, որ ուրիշին օգնութեան կարօտ մնացած է, զրկուած ըլլալով իր տուներէն, որոնք 80% այրած եւ մնացեալներուն մեծ մասն ալ փլած են, եւ իր գոյքերէն՝ որոնց բոլորն ալ կողոպտուած են եւ հետեւաբար կը մնան անպատսպար անտուն, մերկ ու անօթի եւ իրենց կեանքը միշտ վտանգի տակ:

Հիմա հոս կան 10,000 հայեր, որոնց[մէ] 1600 որբեր՝ որբանոց պատսպարուած, 3500 այրիներ եւ որբեր քաղաքին մէջ, որոնք մասամբ ամերիկացիներէն կը նպաստաւորուին, մնացեալ 5000էն աննշան մաս մը միայն կը յաջողի գէշ աղէկ ճարել իր օրապահիկը, իսկ մնացեալը՝ զրկուած աշխատութեան ամէն պատեհութիւններէն՝ սարսափի կեանք մը կը քաշէ առանց գիտնալու թէ ի՞նչ կը սպասէ իրեն: Երկաթէ շրջանակի մը մէջ սեղմուած, գոնէ իբր բանուոր եւ մշակ շրջակայ այգիներն երթալու ապահովութիւն չկայ:

Ամէն տեսակ յարաբերութենէ զրկուած ենք. ո՛չ կրնանք թղթակցիլ, ո՛չ ճամբորդել եւ ոչ ալ լրագիր կարդալ:

Եթէ այս վիճակը շարունակէ, անօթութենէ պիտի կոտորուի ժողովուրդի միւս մասը յառաջիկայ ձմեռ:

Նիկոմիդիա (Առաջնորդէն) – 7 Օգոստոս

Երէկ իրիկուն Արմաշի ճամբով Ատաբազարցի 10–15 հայ երիտասարդներ եւ Կէյվէ Միջագիւղի հայ-հոռոմներէն 60–70 հոգի, մեծ պզտիկ փախստական, Նիկոմիդիա եկան: Իրենց մէջէն հայ-հոռոմ հարս մըն ալ փախած ատեն Ատաբազարէն Արմաշ զաւակ մըն ալ կը ծնի:

Ուրբաթ օրը ցորեկին, յանկարծ լուր կ՚ելնէ Ատաբազար թէ 400ի չափ Միլլիճի մտած են քաղաք: Միլլիճիները համարձակ կը պոռան թէ ահա կրկին եկանք Ատաբազար եւ մինչեւ մեր արեան վերջին կաթիլը պիտի թափենք ու դիմադրենք որ այս քաղաքն անգլիացիներուն ողջ չյանձնենք:

Նոյնպէս լուեր է որ Ատաբազարի մօտիկ Նամէրտ Քէօփրիւն,- որ է Պէշ Քէօփրիւ,- ալ 200ի մօտ Միլլիճի եկած է: Էրէկլէյի բարձունքին վրայ ալ թնդանօթներ զետեղեր ու խրամներ պատրաստեր են եղեր:

Ատաբազար հայ եւ յոյն բնակիչները սարսափելի ահ ու դողով ու վայնասունով քաղաքէն դուրս խուժած եւ թերեւս լսած ըլլալով որ անգլիացիները Սարմանլըի կողմերը կը գտնուին դէպի հոն դիմած ըլլան:

Ատաբազարէ Արմաշ առաջին անգամ փախչելով հասնողները 7–8 հոգիներ են եղեր:

Զարմանալի զուգադիպութեամբ մը նոյն օրն նաեւ Արմաշ կը հասնին 10 անգլիացի զինուոր եւ մէկ սպայ:

Արմաշցիք օգնութիւն կը խնդրեն եւ երկիւղ կը յայտնեն թէ մի գուցէ Միլլիճիք դարձեալ Արմաշ գան:

Անգլիացի սպան կը պատասխանէ թէ «Նիկոմիդիա մեզի լուր տուէք. մենք հոն ենք» ու կը յանձնարարեն որ Միլլիճիներու՝ իրենց փախուստի ատեն թողած թէլէֆոնները զետեղեն եւ անով հաղորդակցին Նիկոմիդիոյ հետ:

- Մինչեւ հիմա Ատաբազարէն հայ-հոռոմ եւ հայ ու Արմաշէն 80–90 հոգի Նիկոմիդիա եկած են, որոնց 20-ը արմաշցի: Արմաշէն շատեր այս առաւօտ ճամբայ պիտի ելնեն եղեր:

Սեբաստիա (Առաջնորդէն) – 11 Յունիս

Պոլիս գտնուող սեբաստացի մի քանի հայերու [կողմէ] քանի մը Սեբաստիոյ ջարդարար թուրքերու մասին հետապնդումներ եւ ամբաստանութիւններ կ՚ըլլան եղեր, ինչ որ յոռի տպաւորութիւններ կը պատճառէ տեղւոյս տարրին վրայ:

Trabzon (from the locum tenens Reverend Father Karekin)—August 4

The primate of Trabzon arrived on July 23. His chattels, primarily books, were searched but were returned to him intact in two days. Men's travel abroad and to İstanbul is prohibited. A local militia has been formed of only Turks. Friday has been set as a training day. All the Turks are armed from head to toe.

Bolshevik propagandists have come but failed. The decision to sign the [Peace] Treaty and the occupation of Thrace have horrified and bewildered the Turks, who continue to be provoked artificially. They are still threatening and giving false hope to the people who rapidly yield before the powerful.

The siege is becoming increasingly oppressive and despairing, and, unfortunately, this coincides with the abstention of the American Near East Relief.

Trabzon (from the primate)—August 5

It is rumored that the Turkish government in İstanbul will send a restraining commission and troops to these areas. The travel ban has become stricter for Christians. Even women are not allowed to travel. The pass of a tuberculosis patient was obtained with incredible difficulty. Therefore, they [Armenians] are frightened.

There has been no shortage of bloody incidents in the villages. An Armenian was killed in Şanlı [Şana] two weeks ago. The number of Greek victims is higher. The situation in Ordu and Giresun, and probably also in Samsun, is worse.

It is harvest time, but no one dares to go to the villages. It will be an irreparable disaster for the surviving villagers if the ravishers [again sollely] enjoy this year's harvest.

Adana (from Very Reverend Father Kevork Aslanian, primate)—July 18[87]

The Turks of Adana, almost all of them, went with their families to the çetes, of course, at the urging or coercion of those mentioned. Some left or were sent all the way to Konyat thence. This departure is attributed to a massacre allegedly committed by Armenians. This kind of activity has never happened. On the contrary, in five or six months, more than ten thousand Armenians have been massacred atrociously by çetes in Cilicia. Entire villages have been destroyed, and a general desolation prevails in villages, towns, and cities [once] populated by Armenians. The number of Armenians abducted, killed, and robbed by the çetes in areas very close to Adana has surpassed one thousand, and just ten days ago, at the edge of one of the city's neighborhoods, sixteen people were killed and eleven taken away. These fabrications of the Turkish çetes and Millis [regarding an alleged massacre by Armenians] are deliberate, and they want to exonerate their savage atrocity by doing so. Had the French government not been here, Adana would have been a river of blood. Adana's distress is too much: all the orchards are destroyed, as are all the crops of the plain. Adana, which feeds many cities, has fifteen days of bread remaining today. The French government and we are making great efforts to obtain part of the remaining harvest, and young people, defying death, are running here and there for a handful of wheat. Going as far as ten minutes away from the city means certain death, but the stomach needs compel the unfortunate [youngsters] to go to the orchard for some food, [and] many do not return alive.

Our condition is becoming unbearable in terms of lifestyle. Although the French government makes great efforts and sacrifices to transport some food from the plain by employing a special column and making sacrifices, many challenges remain. Hunger is waiting for us with its sharpened teeth; mothers are abandoning their children here and there on the street and leaving; ten thousand, twenty thousand, and more women and children cry for bread and clothes every day. The French government

Տրապիզոն (Առաջնորդական Տեղապահ Գարեգին Վարդապետ) – 4 Օգոստոս

Յուլիս 23ին հասաւ Տրապիզոնի Առաջնորդը: Գոյքերը,- մեծ մասամբ գիրքեր,- խուզարկու-թեան ենթարկուեցան, բայց երկու օրէն ամբողջութեամբ դարձուեցան: Արգիլուած է այրերու ճամբորդութիւնը օտար սահման, ինչպէս եւ Պոլիս: Կազմուեր է տեղական միլիս զուտ թուրքերէ, մարզանքի օր սահմանելով Ուրբաթը: Ամբողջ թուրքերը զինուած են ոտից ցգլուխ:

Պոլշէվիկ բրոբականտիստներ եկած են, սակայն չեն կրցած յաջողութիւն գտնել: Դաշնագրի ստորագրումը որոշուիլը եւ Թրակիոյ գրաւումը սահմռկած եւ շուարեցուցած են թուրքերը, որ արուեստական կերպով կը հրահրուին դեռ: Դեռ շարունակ կը սպառնան եւ սուտ լուրերով կը յուսադրեն ժողովուրդը, որ շուտով տեղի կուտայ զօրաւորին առջեւ:

Պաշարման վիճակը աւելի եւս կը դառնայ ճնշող եւ յուսահատական եւ դժբաղդաբար ասոր կը զուգադիպի Ամերիկեան Նպաստամատոյցին ձեռնպահութիւնը:

Տրապիզոն (Առաջնորդէն) – 5 Օգոստոս

Զրոյց կը շրջի թէ Պոլսոյ թուրք կառավարութիւնը զսպիչ յանձնախումբ եւ զինուոր պիտի ուղարկէ այս կողմերը: Ճամբորդելու արգելքը քրիստոնեաներու համար աւելի խստացած է: Նոյնիսկ կիներու չեն թոյլատրեր: Թոքախտաւորի մը անցագիրը մեծ դժուարութիւններով կարելի եղաւ ձեռք բերել: Ասոր համար երկիւղի մէջ են:

Արիւնոտ միջադէպեր անպակաս են գիւղերու մէջ: Երկու շաբաթ առաջ Շանայի մէջ հայ մը սպաննուած է: Յոյն զոհերու թիւը աւելի շատ է: Օրտուի եւ Կիրասոնի, հաւանաբար նաեւ Սամսոնի շրջաններուն մէջ կացութիւնը աւելի ծանրակշիռ է:

Հունձքի ժամանակ է, բայց ոչ ոք կը համարձակի գիւղերը երթալ: Վերապրող գիւղացիներուն համար անդարմանելի աղէտ մը պիտի ըլլայ՝ եթէ այս տարուան հունձքերն ալ վայելեն յափշտա-կիչները:

Ատանա (Առաջնորդ Գէորգ Ծ. Վրդ. Ասլանեան) – 18 Յուլիս

Ատանայի թուրքերը գրեթէ բոլորն ալ իրենց ընտանիքներով մեկնեցան չէթէներուն մօտ, անշուշտ յիշեալներուն դրդմամբը կամ ստիպումովը եւ չէթէներուն քովէն ալ մինչեւ Գոնիա մեկնողներ կամ ղրկուողներ կան. այս մեկնումը կը վերագրեն ջարդի մը, որ իբր թէ հայերը ըրած են: Այս տեսակ գործ բնաւ տեղի ունեցած չէ: Ընդհակառակը, 5–6 ամսուան ընթացքին Կիլիկիայի մէջ չէթէներու կողմէ 10,000է աւելի հայեր սպաննուած են խժդժօրէն, բոլոր գիւղեր քար ու քանդ եղած, ընդհանուր ամայութիւն է որ կը տիրէ հայաբնակ գիւղերուն, աւաններուն եւ քաղաքներուն մէջ, իսկ Ատանայի շատ մօտերը 1000-ը կ'անցնի չէթէներուն կողմէ առեւանգուած, սպաննուած ու խողխողուած [հայերու թիւը] եւ դեռ 10 օր առաջ քաղաքի մէկ թաղի ծայրին 16 հոգիներ սպան-նուեցան եւ 11 հոգի տարուեցան: Թուրք չէթէներու եւ Միլլիներու այս ստայօդ լուրերը դիտումնա-ւոր են եւ ասով կ'ուզեն իրենց վայրենի խուժդուժ արարքը չքմեղացնել: Եթէ ֆրանսական կառավա-րութիւնը հոս չլինէր, Ատանան ալ արդէն արեան գետ մը պիտի լինէր: Ատանայի նեղութիւնը շատ շատ է. բոլոր այգիները փճացան, բոլոր դաշտի հունձքը նմանապէս: Շատ մը քաղաքներ կերակրող Ատանան այսօր 15 օրուան հաց ունի. թէ՛ ֆրանսական կառավարութիւնը եւ թէ՛ մենք զօրաւոր ջանքեր ու ճիգեր կ'ընենք մնացած հունձքերէն մաս մը ձեռք անցնել եւ մահը աչք առած երիտասարդներ հոս ու հոն կը վազեն բուռ մը ցորենի համար եւ քաղաքէս 10 վայրկեան հեռու գնալ ստոյգ մահ մըն է եւ ստամոքսի պէտքը շատ անգամ կը ստիպէ որ խեղճերը այգի երթան քիչ մը ուտելիք ճարելու ու շատեր ողջ չեն դառնար:

Վիճակնիս ապրելակերպի կողմանէ անտանելի կը դառնայ: Թէեւ ֆրանսական կառավարու-թիւնը զօրաւոր ճիգեր եւ զոհողութիւններ կ'ընէ դաշտէն մաս մը ուտելիք փոխադրելու եւ մասնա-ւոր զօրախումբով եւ զոհողութիւններով, բայց դժուարութիւնները բազմատեսակ են: Սովը իր սրած ատամներով ակնդէտ կը սպասէ մեր գլխին, մայրեր իրենց մանուկները հոս ու հոն փողոցի գլուխը

is indeed distributing bread to twelve to fourteen thousand people a day, but what is the use when today, about one hundred thousand Armenians are huddled here? When there is this great misery in this summer season here, what will [their condition] be a little later? Our condition will be terrible if flour, rice, oil, and other foods are not delivered. The need for help is still very much necessary. There has been no news from Saimbeyli [Hacın] yet.

Tarsus (addressed to Sergeant-Major Mgrdich Takejian)—July 30

Tarsus had been under siege for five weeks and could not communicate with Mersin or Adana. Along with this, Armenian volunteers, partly with the support of French troops, attacked the rebel villages three times. After burning three villages successfully, they returned with a very light loss (one dead and three wounded). Yesterday, five thousand French troops launched an attack from Adana and reached Tarsus. The çetes suffered four hundred dead, eight hundred wounded, and three hundred captives.

Bursa (from the primate)—August 11[88]

The priest Atanas of Yenice, who had gone to Gemlik, reported that there had not been any significant danger in the villages yet, but there is always fear. There are approximately twelve to fifteen hundred refugee villagers from the villages of Yenisölöz, Gürle, Karsak, and Orhangazi in Gemlik. They are hungry, thirsty, and extremely miserable. Bad or good, everybody has been given an abode there, and the Hellenic authorities will provide bread.

• Turks from Söl (neighbors to the Armenian Sölöz [Yenisölöz]) went to the Armenian prelacy to ask the Armenian prelate for housing. Mecitoğlu Cemal was leading them like a bear wounded by a bullet in the heart, like an expiring tiger. Their whole village was burned with petroleum; four or five villagers and one hundred fifty to two hundred Millis were killed. The rest of the Turkish villagers came to the Armenians of Yenisölöz and Gemlik. The Millis made the Turkish women and young girls of Pazarköy dance naked, and then they raped and killed them.

İzmit (from the primate)—August 10

For two days now, the Circassians have been waging war against the Millis on the side of the so-called Yanık in Büyük Derbent. Yesterday, the Circassians wanted ammunition and received it from İzmit, while the British fought at the mouth of the Black Sea at the place called Çahna.

It was heard yesterday that the Greek village of Geke in Karamürsel [Karamursal], which is at the edge of Kefne İskele, has been besieged and burned by the Millis. We do not know what happened to the inhabitants, who comprise two to three hundred families.

There is also news that the Greek seaside village of Zonca (six to seven hundred families) is under siege by the Millis.

Greek troops were sent to the Greek village of Kepe of Karamürsel from Çuhahane, and [other] troops were sent by way of sea to Karamürsel.

İzmit (from the primate)—August 10

Between Bahçecik and Ovacık, there is a village called Döngöl. It has eighty to one hundred houses, above which there is a place of pilgrimage named after St. Sarkis. There is also a place of pilgrimage called Manishag on Mount Bahçecik, where migrants from Trabzon have been living over the last thirty to forty years. Later, some moved to St. Sarkis and formed a village there. This village was burning yesterday, as it was seen from İzmit. It is said that the area's Muslim Lazes burned the village.

կը թողուն եւ կ'երթան, օրական 10000 ու 20000 ու աւելի կիներ, փոքրիկներ հաց ու զգեստ կը պոռան. ֆրանսական կառավարութիւնը իրաւ է թէ օրական 12–14 հազար անձերու հաց կը բաշխէ, բայց ի՞նչ օգուտ, երբ այսօր 100000ի մօտ հայութիւն մը հոս խռնուեր է եւ երբ ամրան այս եղանակին այս խոշոր թշուառութիւնը [կայ], քիչ մը վերջը ի՞նչ պիտի ըլլայ: Եթէ ալիւր, բրինձ, իւղ եւ այլ ուտելիքներ չհասցուի՝ կացութիւննիս սոսկալի է: Օգնութեան պէտքը տակաւին շատ անհրաժեշտ է: Հաճընէն դեռ լուր չկայ:

Տարսոն (Յիսնապետ Մկրտիչ Թագըճեանի ուղղուած) – 30 Յուլիս

Հինգ շաբաթէ ի վեր Տարսոն պաշարուած էր եւ ոչ Մերսինի ոչ ալ Ատանայի հետ ոեւէ հաղորդակցութիւն չէր կրնար ունենալ: Ասով հանդերձ հայ կամաւորներ՝ մաս մը ֆրանսացի զինուորներու աջակցութեամբ, երեք անգամներ յարձակում գործեցին ապստամբ գիւղերու վրայ եւ երեք գիւղ այրելէ յետոյ յաջողութեամբ, շատ թեթեւ կորուստով (մէկ մեռեալ երեք վիրաւոր) կը վերադառնան: Երէկ ալ 5000 ֆրանսացի զինուորներ Ատանայէն յարձակումի սկսելով Տարսոն հասան: Չէթէները կորուստ ունեցան 400 մեռեալ, 800 վիրաւոր եւ 300 գերի:

Պրուսա (Առաջնորդէն) – 11 Օգոստոս

Ենիճէի Տ. Աթանաս քահանան Կէմլէյիկ գացած ըլլալով, կը տեղեկագրէ թէ գիւղերը ոեւէ աչքառու վտանգ ցարդ չէ պատահած, սակայն միշտ վախ կայ: Կէմլէյիկի մէջ մօտաւորապէս 1200–1500 գիւղացի գաղթականներ կան սէօյէօզցի, կիւռլէցի, գարսաքցի եւ Օրխանխազի գիւղերէ, անօթի, ծարաւ եւ վերջին ծայր թշուառ: Հոն գէշ աղէկ ամէնուն ալ բնակարան տրուած է եւ հաց պիտի տրուի հելլէն իշխանութեանց կողմէ:

- Թուրք սէօյցիներ (հայ Սէօյէօզի դրացի) հայոց Առաջնորդարան եկան հայոց Առաջնորդէն տուն ուզելու համար: Սրտէն գնդակով վիրաւորուած արջի, օրհասական վագրի պէս իրենց գլուխն անցած էր Մէճիտ օղլու Ճէմալ: Քարիւղով ամբողջ գիւղն այրած են, 4–5 գիւղացի սպաննած են եւ 150–200 Միլլիճի սպաննուած են: Մնացած ողջ թուրք գիւղացիք հայ սէօյէօզցւոց քով եւ Կէմլէյիկ եկած են: Միլլիճիները Բազար-գիւղի թուրք գիւղացի կիները, մանկամարդ աղջիկները նախ մերկ խաղցուցած են եւ վերջը բռնաբարած եւ սպաննած:

Նիկոմիդիա (Առաջնորդէն) – 10 Օգոստոս

Երկու օր է որ մեծ Տէվրէտ, Եանըխ ըսուած կողմը չէրքէզները կը պատերազմին Միլլիճիներու դէմ: Երէկ չէրքէզները ռազմամթերք կ'ուզեն եւ կը ստանան Նիկոմիդիայէն, իսկ անգլիացիք կը պատերազմին Սեւ Ծովու բերանը Չախնայ ըսուած տեղը:

Երէկ լսուեցաւ որ Գարամուսալի յունաց Կէքէ գիւղն որ Կէֆնէ Իսկէլէին գլուխն է Միլլիճիներն պաշարեր են եւ գիւղն այրեր են. չենք գիտեր թէ ինչ եղած [են] բնակիչները որ 2–3 հարիւր տուն են:

Նոյնպէս լուր կայ թէ ծովեզերեայ յոյն Զօնճայ գիւղն ալ (6–700 տունենոց) Միլլիճիներն պաշարած են:

Գարամուսալի Կէփէ յոյն գիւղն Չուխախանէէն յոյն զօրք ղրկուած է եւ ծովի ճամբով ալ Գարամուսալ զինուոր ղրկուած է:

Նիկոմիդիա (Առաջնորդէն) – 10 Օգոստոս

Պարտիզակի եւ Օվաճըգի մէջտեղը Տէօնկէլ անունով գիւղ մը կայ 80–100 տունով, որուն վերեւը կայ Ս. Սարգիս անուն ուխտատեղի մը, իսկ Պարտիզակի լեռն ալ կայ Մանիշակ անուն ուխտատեղի մը, ուր Տրապիզոնէ բերուած գաղթականներ կը բնակէին 30–40 տարիէ ի վեր: Ասոնցմէ մէկ մասը յետոյ տեղափոխուած էր Ս. Սարգիս եւ հոն գիւղ մը կազմած էր: Երէկ այս գիւղը կ'այրէր, ինչպէս Նիկոմիդիայէն կ'երեւէր: Կ'ըսուի թէ այդ կողմեր գտնուող իսլամ լազերը այրած

İzmit (from the primate)—August 10
The Millis have burned the Greek village of Fulacık of Karamürsel [Karamursal]. The escapees took refuge in İzmit via Karamürsel because they were suffering persecution from the Turks in Karamürsel.

The Greek soldiers will go to the besieged village of Karatepe after going to Karamürsel first.

İzmit (from the primate)—August 11
The British commander is looking for a young Armenian who knows the roads of Akmeşe. The primate introduced [one].

İzmit (from the primate)—August 15
Yesterday, after forty Greek soldiers were suddenly attacked by the sons of Aziz from Gaz village, located between Ovacık and Karadere villages, six wounded Greek soldiers were brought to İzmit.

İzmit (from the primate)—August 16
The Millis again besieged Akmeşe and clashed with the Armenians who were about to leave Akmeşe for İzmit. The sound of the guns has terrified the entire population of Akmeşe.

İzmit (from the primate)—August 16
According to the information received, in addition to the clash around Akmeşe, fighting has also started in the village. Since the Millis were few, they asked for help from Adapazarı. The Armenians appealed to the British military authorities in İzmit to send the necessary support the British colonel promised five days earlier.

İzmit (from the primate)—August 17
As of yesterday evening, we had more than five hundred people coming from Akmeşe and a few from EskiMecidiye [Khaskal] and Gaz. Some people came from Adapazarı. They are all forced to live outside, in the churchyard, and the open air, in extreme misery.

The British did not send any troops to Akmeşe.

İzmit (from the primate)—August 18
The people are in great misery. The help expected from the British has not yet arrived, while Greek troops are leaving for Bursa.

İzmit (from the primate)—August 21
The British have posted an announcement in İzmit asking everyone to hand over their weapons, but the Turkish houses have not been searched, although there were four to five weapons in each house. Under the command of a British major, the Greek army marched, guided by two Turkish Lazes, on the Laz villages above Bahçecik to collect weapons. At first, they sent news [to] Hampartsoum, the headman of Bahçecik, asking him to collect the existing weapons using locals and to bring and hand them over to the authorities.

Headman Hampartsoum undertook the task and went to the Laz villages on August 19, but he

են այդ գիւղը:

Նիկոմիդիա (Առաջնորդէն) – 10 Օգոստոս

Գարամուսալի Փօլաճըգ յոյն գիւղը այրած են Միլլիճիք: Բնակիչներէն փախչողները Գարամուսալի ճամբով Նիկոմիդիա ապաստանած են, Գարամուսալի մէջ թուրքերէն նեղութիւն կրելով:

Յոյն զինուորները Գարայ Թէփէ պաշարուած գիւղը պիտի երթան, նախ Գարամուսալ երթալէ յետոյ:

Նիկոմիդիա (Առաջնորդէն) – 11 Օգոստոս

Անգլիացի հրամանատարը Արմաշի ճամբաներուն գիտակ հայ երիտասարդ մը կ'ուզէ: Առաջնորդը կը ներկայացնէ:

Նիկոմիդիա (Առաջնորդէն) – 15 Օգոստոս

Երէկ երբ Օվաճըգի եւ Գարատէրէ գիւղերուն միջեւ յոյն 40 զինուորներ յանկարծական յարձակման առարկայ կ'ըլլան Ղազ գիւղի Ազիզին տղոցը կողմէն, 6 վիրաւոր յոյն զինուոր կը բերուին Նիկոմիդիա:

Նիկոմիդիա (Առաջնորդէն) – 16 Օգոստոս

Արմաշ Միլլիճիներէ դարձեալ պաշարուած է եւ Արմաշէն Նիկոմիդիա գալու ելլող հայերու հետ Միլլիճիներ ընդհարում ունեցած են: Հրացանի ձայնէն բոլոր Արմաշ սարսափի մատնուած է:

Նիկոմիդիա (Առաջնորդէն) – 16 Օգոստոս

Առնուած տեղեկութեանց համա[ձայն] Արմաշի շուրջը պատահած ընդհարումէն զատ գիւղին մէջ ալ կռիւը սկսած է: Միլլիճիները քիչ ըլլալով Ատաբազարէն օգնութիւն ուզած են, հայերն ալ Նիկոմիդիա անգլիացի զինուորական իշխանութեան դիմած են, որպէսզի ինչպէս 5 օր առաջ անգլիացի գնդապետը խոստացած էր, հարկ եղած օգնութիւնը ղրկուէր:

Նիկոմիդիա (Առաջնորդէն) – 17 Օգոստոս

Արմաշէն մինչեւ երէկ իրիկուն 500 հոգիէն աւելի եկաւ, քիչ մըն ալ Խասկալէն ու Խաչէն: Ատաբազարէն ալ եկողներ կան. ամէնքն ալ բացը, ժամուն բակը եւ բացօդեայ ապրելու հարկադրուած՝ յետին թշուառութեան մէջ:

Անգլիացիք ոեւէ զինուորական առաքում չեն ըներ դէպի Արմաշ:

Նիկոմիդիա (Առաջնորդէն) – 18 Օգոստոս

Ժողովուրդը մեծ թշուառութեան մէջ է: Անգլիացւոց կողմէ ակնկալուած օգնութիւնը դեռ չէ հասած: Յոյն զօրքերն ալ Պրուսա կը մեկնին:

Նիկոմիդիա (Առաջնորդէն) – 21 Օգոստոս

Անգլիացիք Նիկոմիդիոյ մէջ յայտարարութիւն մը փակցուցին որպէսզի ամէն մարդ զէնքերը յանձնէ, սակայն թրքաց տուները խուզարկութիւն չըրին, մինչ 4–5 ձեռք կը գտնուի ամէն տուն: Յոյն զօրքեր անգլիացի հազարապետի մը հրամանատարութեամբ Պարտիզակի վրայի լազի գիւղերը կ'երթան լազի գիւղերէն զէնք ժողվելու երկու թուրք լազերու առաջնորդութեամբ: Առաջին անգամ լուր կը ղրկեն Պարտիզակի միխթար Համբարձում[ին] որ գտնուած զէնքերը հաւաքեն տեղացի[ներ]ով եւ իրենց բերեն յանձնեն:

Միխթար Համբարձում յանձն կ'առնու այս պաշտօնը եւ կը մեկնի Օգոստոս 19ին լազ գիւղերը,

has not yet returned.

On August 20, Greek soldiers advanced through the upper fields of Bahçecik, guided by two Lazes, because they were not familiar with the road. While they were crossing through a narrow passage of a valley, they were surrounded by Lazes waiting in ambush. The Lazes shot at them. The Greek soldiers wanted to fire back, but the British major forbade them to open fire. At that very moment, he was shot in the forehead and died. It was then that the Greek soldiers started firing, but due to the tight position, they retreated irregularly, suffering the death of six or seven soldiers and several injured casualties.

Zonguldak (from Priest Yeremia Merjanian)—August 19

On August 14–15, the Kemalists attacked the Armenian neighborhood of Bolu. The entire neighborhood—about 180 families: 580 individuals—was burned down. According to the information provided by Karekin Somuonjian and Soukias Hayrabedian, who survived the massacre, it is believed that about 150–200 people escaped and were saved.

• Nine hours away from Zonguldak, in the town of Devrek, on the day of the Bolu incident, a mufti gave a speech in the local market and pointed the Armenians out as the cause of all misfortunes. Twenty to thirty widowed families live in Bolu. The local government prohibits their departure from the city.

İzmit (from the primate)—August 20

According to a compiled statistic, until August 20, [the following] have fled to İzmit from the horror of the Millis:

from Arslanbey	228 households	919 people
from Ovacık	191 households	512 people
from Bahçecik	401 households	1,467 people
from Adapazarı	21 households	105 people
from Dağköy	39 households	130 people
from Kurtbelen	6 households	13 people
from Kıncılar	8 households	10 people
from Çakar village	55 households	205 people
from Camidüzü [Kilisedüzü]	27 households	111 people
from Akmeşe	170 households	608 people
from EskiMecidiye [Khaskal]	8 households	30 people
from Gaz village	23 households	147 people
Subtotal	1,177	4,257 people
From different places		24 people
from Döngöl	23 households	72 people
[Total]	1,200	4,353

All need compassion and suffer, almost helpless and hungry.

[The surveyor] also managed to check, with accuracy, that the victims of the villages massacred by the Millis recently are:

Ortaköy of Geyve	55 families	110 males	94 females	204 people
Eşme of Geyve	104 families	146 males	154 females	300 people
Kıncılar-Köprü	71 families	118 males	108 females	226 people

Excluded from this count are the Armenians of Solsar and the losses of Kıncılar and Eşme of Ortaköy, which have not been verified. However, it appears from the massacres that occurred in these

բայց մինչեւ ցարդ չէ դարձած:

Օգոստոս 20ին յոյն զինուորներ կը յառաջանան Պարտիզակի վերի արտերու ճամբով, երկու լազերու առաջնորդութեամբ, զի ճամբան չեն գիտեր ու կիրճի մը նեղ անցքէ մը անցնելու միջոցին՝ դարանակալ լազերէ կը պաշարուին: Լազերը իրենց վրայ զէնք կը պարպեն: Յոյն զինուորները կ'ուզեն զէնքով փոխադարձել, սակայն անգլիացի հազարապետը կ'արգիլէ կրակ բանալ: Ճիշդ այդ վայրկեանին ճակատէն հարուած մը ընդունելով կ'իյնայ կը մեռնի: Այն ատեն յոյն զինուորները կրակելու կը սկսին, սակայն նեղը ինկած ըլլալով անկանոն կը նահանջեն 6–7 զինուոր զոհ տալով եւ քանի մըն ալ վիրաւոր ունենալով:

Չօնկուլտաք (Երեմիա քահանայ Մերճանեանէ) – 19 Օգոստոս

Օգոստոս 14/15 օրերը Պոլուի հայոց թաղին վրայ Քէմալականներու կողմէ յարձակում տեղի կ'ունենայ, ամբողջ թաղը հրոյ ճարակ կ'ըլլայ, մօտաւորապէս 180 տուն եւ 580 անձի մօտիկ թաղ մը: Ջարդէն ազատող Գարեգին Սօմունճեան[ի] եւ Սուքիաս Հայրապետեանի տուած տեղեկութեան համաձայն, կը հասկցուի թէ 150–200 անձի չափ փախչողներ կան, որոնք ազատուած են:

- Չօնկուլտաքէն 9 ժամ հեռու Տէվրէկ գիւղաքաղաքին մէջ Պօլու[ի] դէպքին օրը՝ տեղւոյն միւֆթին շուկայի մէջ ճառ մը կը խօսի եւ բոլոր թշուառութեանց պատճառը հայերը կը ցուցնէ: Հոն կը գտնուին 20–30 տուն որբեւայրի ընտանիքներ, որոնց քաղաքէն դուրս ելլելը կ'արգիլէ տեղական կառավարութիւնը:

Նիկոմիդիա (Առաջնորդէն) – 20 Օգոստոս

Կազմուած վիճակագրութեան մը համաձայն, մինչեւ 20 Օգոստոս, Միլլիներու սարսափէն Նիկոմիդիա ապաստանած են.

Արսլանպէկէն	228 տնուոր	919 անձ
Օվաճըգէն	191 տնուոր	512 անձ
Պարտիզակէն	401 տնուոր	1467 անձ
Ատաբազարէն	21 տնուոր	105 անձ
Տաղ-Գիւղէն	39 տնուոր	130 անձ
Գուրտպէլէն[էն]	6 տնուոր	13 անձ
Գընճըլար[էն]	8 տնուոր	10 անձ
Չաքար գիւղ[էն]	55 տնուոր	205 անձ
Ժամավայր[էն]	27 տնուոր	111 անձ
Արմաշ[էն]	170 տնուոր	608 անձ
Խասկալ[էն]	8 տնուոր	30 անձ
Խաչ գիւղ[էն]	23 տնուոր	147 անձ
Փոխադրեալ	1177	4257 անձ
Զանազան տեղերէ	.....	24 անձ
Տէօնկէօլէ	23 տնուոր	72 անձ
[Գումար]	1200	4353

Ասոնք ամէնն ալ գթութեան կարօտ վիճակի մէջ են եւ գրեթէ անպատսպար ու անօթի կը տուայտին:

Նոյնպէս կրցած է ճշտագոյն կերպով ստուգել թէ վերջին անգամ Միլլիճիներէ ջարդուած գիւղերու զոհերն են.

Օրթաքէօյ=Միջագիւղ Կէյվէյու	55 տուն	110 արու	94 էգ	204 անձ
Էշմէ Կէյվէյու	104 տուն	146 արու	154 էգ	300 անձ
Գընճըլար-Կամուրջ	71 տուն	118 արու	108 էգ	226 անձ

Այս հաշիւէն դուրս [են] Սօլսարի հայերը եւ Գընճըլարի եւ Օրթաքէօյի Էշմէի կորուստները,

places that very few people survived.

Zonguldak (from correspondence in *Jagadamard* [Armenian daily])—August 20[89]

As a result of the capture of Düzce by the Circassians, the Milli forces in the nearby town of Bolu—barely a few scores of soldiers and government functionaries—fled. On the 10th of this month, immediately after the Millis' escape, forty to fifty Circassian horsemen entered and captured the city. Bolu's Muslim and Christian populations welcomed the newcomers, considering them their leaders. But their joy was short-lived. On Saturday, August 14, five to six hundred Kemalist horsemen entered Bolu. The Circassians fled because they did not have enough forces. Without wasting time, the çetes besieged the Armenian neighborhood and began looting and massacring the men, claiming they had helped the Circassians. Then they gathered all the women, boys, and girls in the Armenian church, which they set on fire, burning everybody inside alive. Then they set fire to the Armenian neighborhood, now reduced to ashes.

A mere ten to fifteen people of approximately seven hundred Bolu Armenians survived this horrific massacre. Some of them managed to reach Zonguldak. It is from them that we have gotten this information.

A few days ago, Abdullah Şükrü, the mufti of the town of Devrek, located ten hours away from Zonguldak, with a sword in hand, delivered a sermon in the square to the Muslim community. He advocated massacring and slaughtering the Armenians, calling them desecrators of the Islamic holy religion. The city mentioned, as well as the nearby village of Çaycuma, are now in danger.

The Kemalists have also recently begun to show considerable activity in Zonguldak. The prices of imported goods have increased from five to one hundred percent compared to previous prices. Many traders, unable to pay that much, are leaving their goods at customs. Three liras are being demanded per ton of exported coal, so the export of coal has been at a halt for three or four days.

• The following was heard from another source:

Upon entering the city, the Millis occupied the hills called Hisar, and the soldiers stormed the Armenian neighborhood and, under the pretext of looking for Circassians, evicted the residents one by one and gathered the men in the church. They killed anyone trying to escape. Then they entered the houses of the wealthy and demanded large sums of money from the women. First, the soldiers dispersed into the houses and feasted until morning, violating the honor of women and girls. In the morning, they began to mercilessly slaughter the women and the men confined to the church. Then, they picked up the corpses dumped in the streets in the carriages of Süleyman, Mustafa, and Kadri and transported the bodies to the house of Agha Garabed Merzifanlian, where they burned them. When the men, women, and children hiding in their houses emerged, desperate because of starvation, the Millis shot them dead one by one.

After the massacre, the perpetrators, with the participation of local Turks, looted the victims' valuables and transported them to their homes by cart. Armenian and Greek shops in the market were also raided. Excluding thirteen people, who arrived in İstanbul from Zonguldak (Sarkis Terzian, Haroutyun Kalpakjian, Hagop Kalpakjian, Karekin Somounjian, Soukias Hayrabedian, Sdepan Garabedian, Sdepan Navasartian, Kevork Giragosian, Haroutyun Garabedian, and Garabed Cherkezian), the almost six hundred Armenians and eighty Greeks of Bolu have all been slaughtered and burned.

The Millis broke into the Ottoman Bank's safe and stole the money.

որոնք չեն կրցած ճշտուիլ, թէեւ այս տեղերու կոտորածէն կ'երեւի թէ շատ քիչ մարդ ազատած է:

Զօնկուլտազ (*Ճակատամարտի* թղթակցութիւն) – 20 Օգոստոս

Չէրքէզներու կողմէ Տիւզճէի գրաւման հետեւանքով մօտակայ Պօլու քաղաքին մէջ գտնուող Միլլիական ուժերը, հազիւ քանի մը տասնեակ զինուոր եւ կառավարական պաշտօնեաներ, կը փախչին: Ամսոյս 10ին, անոնց փախուստէն անմիջապէս յետոյ, 40–50 ձիաւոր չէրքէզներ քաղաք կը մտնեն եւ կը գրաւեն զայն: Պօլուցի իսլամ եւ քրիստոնեայ բնակչութիւնը մեծ ընդունելութիւն կ'ընէ նորեկներուն, զանոնք իրենց առաջնորդը նկատելով: Բայց իրենց ուրախութիւնը կարճ կ'ըլլայ: Օգոստոս 14ին, Շաբաթ օր, 5–600 ձիաւոր Քէմալականներ Պօլու կը մտնեն: Չէրքէզները մեծ ուժ մը չունենալնուն համար փախուստ կուտան: Առանց ժամանակ կորսնցնելու, չէթէները կը պաշարեն հայոց թաղը եւ առարկելով թէ անոնք չէրքէզներուն օգնած են, կը սկսին կողոպուտի եւ կը ջարդեն այրերը: Յետոյ բոլոր կին, տղայ եւ աղջիկ կը հաւաքեն հայոց եկեղեցին, զոր կրակի կուտան ողջ ողջ այրելով բոլոր մէջը գտնուողները: Յետոյ կրակի կուտան հայոց թաղը, որ այժմ ամբողջ մոխիրի վերածուած է:

Մօտաւորապէս 700 պօլուցի հայերէն հազիւ 10–15 հոգի կրցած են ճողոպրիլ այս սոսկալի կոտորածէն: Անոնցմէ մէկ քանիները կրցած են հասնիլ Զօնկուլտաք, որոնցմէ կը քաղենք այս տեղեկութիւնները:

Քանի մը օր առաջ, Զօնկուլտաքէն 10 ժամ հեռու գտնուող Տէվրէք քաղաքի միւֆթին՝ Ապտուլլահ Շիւքրի, հրապարակի վրայ սուր ի ձեռին քարոզ մը կը կարդայ իսլամ հասարակութեան, ջարդելու եւ կոտորելու հայերը, զանոնք նկատելով իսլամական սուրբ կրօնքը պղծողներ: Յիշեալ քաղաքը, ինչպէս նաեւ մօտը գտնուող Չայ-Ճումա կոչուող գիւղը, այժմ վտանգի տակ են:

Քէմալականները Զօնկուլտաքի մէջ ալ բաւական մեծ գործունէութիւն մը ցոյց տալ սկսած են վերջերս: Ներածուած ապրանքներու վրայ 100ին 5էն մինչեւ 100ին 100 բարձրացում մը տեղի ունեցած է նախորդ սակագինին վրայ՝ այնպէս որ շատ մը վաճառականներ չկրնալով այդքան մեծ գումարներ վճարել, իրենց եկած ապրանքները մաքսատունը կը թողուն: Արտածուած հանքածուխին մէկ թօնին համար 3 ոսկի կը պահանջուի, այնպէս որ հանքածուխին արտածումն ալ 3–4 օրէ ի վեր կասած է:

- Ուրիշ աղբիւրէ մը հետեւեալը լսուած է.

Միլլիճիները քաղաքը մտնելով Հիսար ըսուած բլուրները կը գրաւեն եւ զինուորներ հայ թաղը կը խուժեն եւ չէրքէզներ փնտռելու պատրուակին տակ, մէկիկ մէկիկ տուներէն կը հանեն բնակիչները եւ եկեղեցին կը հաւաքեն այրերը: Փախչողները կը սպաննեն: Յետոյ հարուստներուն տուները մտնելով մեծաքանակ գումարներ կը պահանջեն կիներէն: Նախ զինուորները տուները ցրուելով մինչեւ առաւօտ կերուխում կ'ընեն եւ կիներու եւ աղջիկներու պատիւը բռնաբարելով ժամանակ կ'անցնեն: Առտուն կը սկսին անխնայ կերպով ջարդել կիները եւ եկեղեցին բանտարկուած այրերը: Յետոյ կառապան Սիւլէյմանի, Մուսթաֆայի եւ Գատրիի կառքերով կը հաւաքեն փողոցները նետուած դիակները եւ Մէրզիֆանլեան Կարապետ աղայի տունը փոխադրելով կ'այրեն: Տուներու մէջ պահու[ը]տած այրերը, կիները եւ տղաքները երբ անսուաղութենէ յուսահատած դուրս կ'ելլեն, Միլլիճիները հրացանով մէկիկ մէկիկ կը սպաննեն զանոնք:

Կոտորածէն վերջ, ոճրագործները տեղացի թուրքերու մասնակցութեամբ կը կողոպտեն թանկարժէք առարկաները եւ կառքով իրենց տուները կը փոխադրեն: Շուկայի հայ եւ յոյն խանութներն ալ աւարի տուած են: Բացի 13 անձէ, որոնք Զօնկուլտաքէն Կ. Պոլիս եկած են (Սարգիս Թերզեան, Յարութիւն Գալփաքճեան, Յակոբ Գալփաքճեան, Գարեգին Սօմունճեան, Սուքիաս Հայրապետեան, Ստեփան Կարապետեան, Ստեփան Նաւասարդեան, Գէորգ Կիրակոսեան, Յարութիւն Կարապետեան եւ Կարապետ Չէրքէզլեան), Պօլուի 600ի չափ հայերը եւ 80ի չափ յոյները բոլորն ալ ջարդուած եւ այրուած են:

Միլլիճիները Օսմանեան Պանքայի դրամարկղը կոտրելով յափշտակած են մէջի դրամները:

İstanbul (from Priest Vartan Bedrosian of Sungurlu)—August 26[90]

On the night of July 12, the group of Milli Çakir Efe arrived in Sungurlu from Yozgat and besieged the city. Twenty Millis surrounded Father Vartan Bedrosian's house and invited him to come out. The priest refused. Then they broke down the door of the house, caught the priest, and took him to the gallows in front of the lieutenant governor's office. Before reaching there, one of the influential local people, Circassian Zakaria Bey, arrived, saying that the gang leader [Çakir] wanted to see the priest. They then took him to the house of Ipranosian's agent, Hacı Sıtkı, where local Turks mediated and interceded. Çakir Efe granted the priest his life as a result. Çakir Efe left for Ankara with his men the next day.

The gang of Küçük Ethem Bey arrived the following day, and the local notables had to intercede and rescue the priest again.

On July 18, the lieutenant governor summoned the priest. When the priest went there, he saw with the governor another çete named Niazi Bey, [in front of] whom also the priest had been accused. After listening to the priest, Niazi Bey ordered him to leave [the town]. The priest agreed and asked for a passport. He was dispatched to Samsun under the watch of two gendarmes. While leaving, the priest asked for his people to be spared, and the lieutenant governor and Hacı Sıtkı swore not to harm the Armenians.

Armenians were not harmed in the surrounding cities, too, until July 18.

There are now 220 Armenian households and sixty Greek households in Sungurlu. There are 10 Armenian families in Alaca and 20 Armenian families in Çorum.

• Once information about the Yozgat incident had been received in Sungurlu, the Armenians sent an Armenian, in disguise, to Yozgat. A Turk accompanied him. That Armenian brought back the following information.

In early July, Galib and Celal Bey of Yozgat's Çapanoğlus, dissatisfied with the oppression being exercised by the Millis, set fire to the local Milli headquarters and took control of the city.

Learning this, Mustafa Kemal sent his çetes to Yozgat. They defeated the Çapanoğlus and entered the city. They attacked the Armenians and Greeks and plundered their wealth. Houses that kept their doors closed were burned down, like the houses of the Greek Khederoglu and others.

During this disturbance, twenty-four Armenians were killed, and five women were injured. Fifty-five Greeks were also killed.

All Christians were robbed.

Among those killed was the priest Garabed Ohanian, who fell victim to an Armenian-turned-Turk, Bedros Kasbarian. He reported that the priest knew where three thousand liras cash belonging to the Armenian community were being kept.

Father Garabed Ohanian was killed despite handing the money over.

After this massacre, the Armenians of Yozgat retired to their homes and did not come out.

On the other hand, it was heard that the Çapanoğlus, gathering forces from Tunceli [Dersim], had arrived in Tokat after burning and destroying Zile and intended to attack Yozgat.

İzmit (from the primate)—August 24

The village of EskiMecidiye [Khaskal] (near Akmeşe) is in fear because the Millis have approached the village. It is said that no one is left in Akmeşe. The village of Sarıdoğan, populated by Greeks and

Կ. Պոլիս (Սունկուրլուի Տ. Վարդան քահանայ Պետրոսեանէ) – 26 Օգոստոս

Յուլիս 12ի գիշերը Եօզկատէն Սունկուրլու կուգայ Միլլիճի Չաքըր էֆէի խումբը, կը պաշարէ քաղաքը: Միլլիճիներէն 20 հոգի ալ Տ. Վարդան քահանայ Պետրոսեանի տունը կը պաշարեն եւ կը հրաւիրեն որ վար գայ: Քահանան կը մերժէ: Այն ատեն տան դուռը կոտրելով կը մտնեն եւ քահանան բռնելով կը տանին դէմի գայմագամին պաշտօնատան առջեւ գտնուող կախաղանին տակ: Հոն չհասած, տեղացի ազդեցիկներէն Զաքարիա պէյ անուն չէրքէզ մը կուգայ եւ կ'ըսէ թէ չէթէպաշին քահանան տեսնել կ'ուզէ: Այն ատեն կը տանին Իբրանոսեանի գործակատար Հաճի Սըւզըի տունը, ուր տեղացի թուրքեր կը միջնորդեն եւ կը բարեխօսեն: Չաքըր էֆէ ասոր վրայ քահանային կեանքը կը շնորհէ: Չաքըր էֆէ յաջորդ օրը կը մեկնի դէպի Էնկիւրիւ իր մարդերով:

Յաջորդ օրը կուգայ Քիւչիւք Էտէհմ պէյի չէթէախումբը, որուն նոյնպէս կը բարեխօսեն տեղացի էշրաֆները եւ դարձեալ քահանան կը փրկուի:

Յուլիս 18ին գայմագամը քահանան կը կանչէ: Քահանան երբ հոն կ'երթայ, կը տեսնայ անոր քովը Նիազի պէյ անուն ուրիշ չէթէ մը, որուն դարձեալ քահանան ամբաստանած էին: Նիազի պէյ քահանան լսելէ յետոյ հրաման կ'ընէ որ մեկնի: Քահանան կը համակերպի եւ անցագիր կ'ուզէ: Երկու ժանտարմայի հսկողութեան տակ Սամսոն կը ղրկուի: Քահանան մեկնած ատեն երբ կը խնդրէ իր ժողովուրդին խնայել, գայմագամը եւ Հաճի Սըւզը երդումով կը խոստանան հայոց ոեւէ վնաս չհասցնել:

Շրջակայ քաղաքներուն մէջ ալ հայոց մինչեւ Յուլիս 18 ոեւէ վնաս հասած չէր:

Սունկուրլուի մէջ կան հիմա 220 տուն հայ եւ 60 տուն յոյն. Ալաճայի մէջ՝ 10 տուն հայ եւ Չորումի մէջ՝ 20 տուն հայ:

- Եօզկատի դէպքի մասին երբ տեղեկութիւն առնուեցաւ Սունկուրլուի մէջ, հայերը ծպտուած հայ մը ղրկեցին Եօզկատ, թուրքի մը ընկերակցութեամբ: Այդ հայը բերած է հետեւեալ տեղեկութիւնները:

Յուլիսի սկիզբները Միլլիճիներու հարստահարութիւններէն դժգոհ Եօզկատի Չափան օղլուներէն Կալիպ եւ Ճէլալ պէյ տեղւոյն Միլլի կառավար[չատունը] կը վառեն եւ քաղաքին վարչութիւնը իրենց ձեռքը կ'առնեն:

Մուսթաֆա Քէմալ իմանալով իր չէթէները կը ղրկէ Եօզկատի վրայ: Ասոնք կը յաղթեն Չափանօղլուի մարդոց եւ կը մտնեն քաղաք, կը յարձակին հայոց եւ յունաց վրայ եւ կը թալանեն անոնց հարստութիւնները:

Այն տուները որոնք իրենց դուռները չէին բանար, կ'այրուէին, ինչպէս յոյն Խտըր օղլուի եւայլն տուները:

Այս խառնակութեան ատեն կը սպաննուին 24 հայ եւ կը վիրաւորուին 5 կին, եւ 55 յոյն կը սպաննուին:

Բոլոր քրիստոնեաները կը թալանուին:

Սպաննուածներուն մէջ է նաեւ Տ. Կարապետ քահանայ Օհանեան, որ զոհ կ'ըլլայ թրքացած հայու մը՝ Պետրոս Գասպարեանի մէկ տեղեկատուութեան, թէ անիկա գիտէ ազգին 3000 ոսկի դրամին պահուած տեղը:

Տ. Կարապետ քահանայ Օհանեան թէեւ դրամ կը յանձնէ, սակայն դարձեալ զինքը կը սպաննեն:

Այս ջարդէն յետոյ Եօզկատի հայերը իրենց տուները փակուած են եւ դուրս չեն ելլեր:

Միւս կողմէ լսուեցաւ որ Չափանօղլուները Տէրսիմ[ի] կողմերէն ուժ հաւաքելով Թօզատ եկած են Զիլէն այրելէ եւ փչցնելէ յետոյ եւ մտադրած են Եօզկատի վրայ գալու:

Նիկոմիդիա (Առաջնորդէն) – 24 Օգոստոս

Խասկալ գիւղը (Արմաշի մօտ) երկիւղի մէջ է, վասնզի Միլլիճիները գիւղին մօտերը եկած են: Կ'ըսուի թէ Արմաշ մարդ չէ մնացած: Յունաբնակ Սարը Տօղան գիւղը, որ Ատաբազարի բարձուն-

located on the hill of Adapazarı, is surrounded by Millis.

İzmit (from the primate)—August 22
The Armenians of Akmeşe are fleeing. On this day, twenty carriages arrived, about one hundred people. It is said that the rest will come incrementally. Those who arrived here from Akmeşe say that gang leaders Bedri and Demir sent word through a man that they plan to massacre and burn Akmeşe, EskiMecidiye [Khaskal], and Mecidiye [Khach] villages at the first opportunity.

• An armored cruiser (from the Seim) went to Bahçecik's wharf. It bombarded the surrounding areas yesterday, at night, and today.

İzmit (from the primate)—August 27
A British officer and a soldier in Akmeşe went to the nearby occupied villages. A bullet in a mountain killed the officer. The Greek soldiers protected Bahçecik by holding positions around it. It is said that Greek soldiers from Bursa are coming to Bahçecik by way of İzmit to join those in Bahçecik or to besiege Bahçecik's Lazes from both sides.

• British officials intend to relocate the three to four thousand Greeks who have taken refuge in this city to the Muslim villages on Çuhahane's side. As for the four to five thousand Armenians, the British want to relocate them to Derince to avoid causing an epidemic stemming from crowding ten thousand people here. But wouldn't it be better to secure the surrounding villages so that everybody could go to their own villages, reap the fruits of their fields or orchards, and not starve to death in winter? Otherwise, they will starve to death. We think that a great sacrifice would not be needed to accomplish this.

İzmit (from the primate)—August 28
There are still 250–300 people in Akmeşe because the British are still there. The Armenians of EskiMecidiye [Khaskal] are procrastinating and not leaving. Only fifty-three people from EskiMecidiye have come to İzmit so far.

The village of Mecidiye [Khach] is no longer inhabited. So far, twenty-three families (147 people) have come from there.

Now, there are 311 people left in Akmeşe
37 people in Mecidiye village
422 people in EskiMecidiye
• There was a clash in Bahçecik, and two officers—a Greek and an Englishman—were killed.

İzmit (from the primate)—August 30
The people in Sugören [Çengiler] are still in good condition. The Millis left the Orhangazi (Pazar[köy]-Yeniköy) area and took refuge in İznik. Thus, the protection of the surrounding villages and the four villages of Yalova and the two villages of Yalakdere and Avcıköy [Merdigöz] in Karamürsel [Karamursal] is ensured, except that the British handed over the defense of these villages to a Georgian named Ibo. In recent days he has been arrested and transported to Gemlik. The villagers fear that Ibo's arrest will anger his followers, that the security of Armenians will be disrupted, and that massacres will take place in the ten Armenian villages of Orhangazi, Yalova, and Karamürsel.

İzmit (from the primate)—September 1
Upon the retreat of the British troops from Akmeşe's vicinities, the villagers of EskiMecidiye [Khaskal]

քին վրայ է, Միլլիճիներէն պաշարուած է:

Նիկոմիդիա (Առաջնորդէն) – 22 Օգոստոս

Արմաշի հայերը կը փախչին: Այս օր եկան 20 կառք, իբր 100 հոգի: Կ'ըսուի թէ մնացեալներն ալ մաս մաս պիտի գան: Արմաշէն հոս հասնողները կ'ըսեն թէ Պետրի եւ Տէմիր չէթէ պաշիները մարդու մը միջոցաւ լուր ղրկեր են որ առաջին առթիւ Արմաշը, Խասկալը ու Խաչ գիւղն պիտի ջարդեն եւ կրակեն:

- Երէկ եւ գիշեր[ը] եւ այսօր Պարտիզակի նաւամատոյցը (Սէյմէն) զրահաւոր մը գացած է եւ շրջակայքը կը ռմբակոծէ:

Նիկոմիդիա (Առաջնորդէն) – 27 Օգոստոս

Արմաշ գտնուող անգլիացի սպայ մը եւ զինուոր մը շուրջը գրաւուած գիւղերը կ'երթան: Լերան մը մէջ սպան գնդակով մը կը սպաննուի: Յոյն զինուորներ Պարտիզակը կը պահեն, շուրջի դիրքերը բռնելով: Կ'ըսուի որ Պրուսայէն յոյն զինուորներ Նիկոմիդիոյ ճամբով դէպի Պարտիզակ կուգա[ն] Պարտիզակ գտնուողներուն միանալու կամ երկու կողմով պաշարելու Պարտիզակի լազերը:

- Անգլիացի պաշտօնատարներ մտադիր են քաղաքս ապաստանող յոյները, որոնք 3–4 հազար հոգի են, Չուխախանէի կողմերը գտնուած տաճիկ գիւղերը տեղաւորել, իսկ 4–5 հազար հայերը Տէրինճէ, սա պատճառով որ հոս 10000 հոգիներու խճողումը համաճարակի առիթ չտայ: Սակայն աւելի լաւ չէ՞ որ շրջակայ գիւղերը ապահովուին եւ ամէն մարդ իր գիւղերը երթայ եւ իր արտին, այգիին բերքերը քաղէ եւ ձմեռը անօթի չմեռնի. հակառակ պարագային, անօթի պիտի մեռնի: Ասոր համար կը կարծենք թէ շատ մեծ զոհողութիւն մը ընելու պէտք չկայ:

Նիկոմիդիա (Առաջնորդէն) – 28 Օգոստոս

Արմաշ տակաւին 250–300 հոգի կայ, վասնզի անգլիացիք դեռ կը մնան: Խասկալցիք կը դանդաղին եւ չեն մեկնիր: Խասկալէն միայն 53 հոգի Նիկոմիդիա եկած են ցարդ:

Խաչ գիւղը այլեւս մարդ չէ մնացած: Մինչեւ ցարդ այդ տեղէն եկած են 23 տուն (147 հոգի):

Հիմա Արմաշ կը մնան 311 հոգի

Խաչ գիւղ 37 հոգի

Խասկալ 422 հոգի

- Պարտիզակի մէջ ընդհարում մը եղած է եւ երկու սպայ՝ մին յոյն եւ միւսը անգլիացի, մեռած են:

Նիկոմիդիա (Առաջնորդէն) – 30 Օգոստոս

Չէնկիլէրի մէջ ժողովուրդը առայժմ լաւ վիճակ ունի: Օրհանը Ղազի (Փազար Եէնի Քէօյ) շրջանէն դուրս ելած են Միլլիճիները եւ Իզնիք ապաստանած են: Այսպէսով շրջակայ գիւղերու եւ Եալովայի չորս գիւղերու եւ Գարամուսալի երկու գիւղերու, Եալազտէրէի եւ Մերտիկէօզի պաշտպանութիւնը ապահովուած է. միայն թէ անգլիացիք այս գիւղերուն պաշտպանութիւնը Իպօ անուն կիւրճիի մը յանձնած [են] եղեր, սակայն վերջին օրերս զայն ալ ձերբակալեր ու Կէմլէյիկ փոխադրեր են: Հիմա կը վախնան գիւղացիք որ Իպօյի ձերբակալութիւնը իր մարդիկը զայրացնէ եւ հայերու ապահովութիւնը խանգարուի եւ ջարդեր տեղի ունենա[ն] Օրհանը Խազի, Եալովայի եւ Գարամուսալի 10 հայ գիւղերուն մէջ:

Նիկոմիդիա (Առաջնորդէն) – 1 Սեպտեմբեր

Արմաշու շրջակայքը գտնուող անգլիացի զինուորներու ետ քաշուելուն վրայ այս խասկալցի

and Akmeşe came to İzmit in fifteen carriages. There is no shelter. The refugees have been left on the street.

İzmit (from the primate)—August 30

A while ago, the British troops went to the areas near Kandıra and distributed more than one hundred weapons to local Turks to arm them against the Millis. After a while, the British came again and besieged Kandıra when the Millis had already entered Kandıra without any resistance. On the day of Bairam [Muslim festival], when the Turks, unaware that they were under siege, were leaving the mosque, one of the Milli commanders ordered that every soldier fires five shots in celebration of Bairam. At that very moment, the British entered the city and surprised the Millis. Ten to thirteen people were wounded, as many were killed, and ten to thirteen were taken as prisoners. Despite numbering barely thirty to thirty-five people, the Millis collected twenty-two thousand liras from Kandıra and its environs. Also wounded was a leader of the çetes who was sent to İstanbul. The British set fire to Kaylançık, Salmanlı, and three other Turkish villages. When the Millis entered Kandıra, they forcibly took from the people the weapons previously distributed by the British.

• A threat to Armenians in Adapazarı had been issued that if the Armenian bandits did not stop acting, they would be slaughtered. Since Armenians have only been engaged in self-defense without committing acts of revenge, it is clear that this threat is more of an excuse [for perpetrating a massacre].

İzmit (from the primate)—September 1

It is said that the Millis are massacring Greeks around İznik. A young Greek refugee from that area brought this news.

• Ibo and with twenty-five people were taken to Gemlik, saying he [Ibo] is hostile to the Greeks. If the Millis learn this and be confident that Ibo's seven to eight hundred followers do not have a leader, the Millis will likely annihilate Keramet, Büyük-Yeniköy, Sugören [Çengiler], [and] the Armenian villages Kartsi, Kılıc, Şakşak and Çakır of Yalova, and Yalakdere and Avcıköy [Merdigöz].

İzmit (from the primate)—September 1

Today, two Armenian [escapees] and one Greek escapee from Düzce arrived in İzmit after seven days of travel. They say Bolu's Armenian neighborhood was burned, and some Armenians were killed while others took refuge in the mountains. The Circassians and the Abazas were also massacred. Hendek and the village of Ermeniköy, too, were burned, and the residents were partially slaughtered. If those sheltered in the mountains manage to escape the persecution of the Millis, they will surely die of starvation.

İzmit (from the primate)—September 2

A band of twenty-seven Laz çetes and seventeen gendarmes entered Ferizli. They threatened [the occupants] with death and looted the houses. Four prominent families fled to Mount Fındıklı on August 23, where the [attackers of] the three Greek villages of Fındıklı—Kantar, Revend, and İstiklal [Papazköy]—shot five to six people in each house and set the houses on fire with the people inside. All three villages are annihilated. The bandits drove away four thousand sheep and appropriated jewelry, oxen, and buffaloes.

• It is heard that Ermeniköy, one of the Armenian Laz villages near Hendek, has also been burned down during the events of Bolu, Düzce, and Hendek. The newly ordained local priest (ordained on September 21, 1919), Father Hovhannes, was beheaded.

եւ արմաշցի գիւղացիք 15 սայլերով Նիկոմիդիա եկան: Պատսպարան չկայ: Գաղթականները փողոց մնացած են:

Նիկոմիդիա (Առաջնորդէն) – 30 Օգոստոս

Գանտըրայի կողմերը երբեմն անգլիացի զօրքեր գացած եւ 100էն աւելի զէնք բաժնած էին տեղւոյն թուրքերուն՝ Միլլիճիներուն դէմ զինուելու համար: Ժամանակ անցնելէ յետոյ, կրկին կուգան անգլիացիք եւ կը պաշարեն Գանտ[ը]րան, երբ Միլլիճիներ արդէն Գանտ[ը]րա մտած էին առանց ոեւէ դիմադրութեան հանդիպելու: Պայրամի օրը՝ թուրքերը առանց գիտնալու թէ պաշարման մէջ են, մզկիթէն դուրս ելած ատեն Միլլի պետերէն մին հրաման կ'ընէ [որ] ի պատիւ գուրպան պայրամի ամէն զինուոր հինգ անգամ հրացան արձակէ: Ճիշտ այդ պահուն անգլիացիք քաղաք կը մտնեն եւ Միլլիճիները յանկարծակիի կը բերեն: 10–13 հոգի կը վիրաւորուի, նոյնքան կը սպաննուին, 10–13 հոգի գերի կը բռնուին: Միլլիճիները հազիւ 30–35 հոգիէ բաղկացեալ ըլլալնուն հակառակ, Գանտ[ը]րայէն եւ շրջականերէն 22,000 ոսկի ժողված են: Վիրաւորուած է նաեւ չէթէապետ մը, որ Պոլիս ղրկուած է: Անգլիացիք կրակի տուած են նաեւ Խայլանճըխ, Սալմանլը եւ ուրիշ երեք թուրք գիւղեր: Միլլիճիները Գանտ[ըրա] երբ մտած են, ժողովուրդէն բռնի առած են անգլիացւոց նախապէս բաժնած զէնքերը:

- Ատաբազարի հայոց սպառնալիք եղած է որ եթէ հայ հրոսակները չդադրին գործելէ, իրենք պիտի ջարդուին: Հայերը սոսկ ինքնապաշտպանութեամբ զբաղած եւ վրէժխնդրական արարքներ գործած չըլլալով, յայտնի է թէ այս սպառնալիքը աւելի պատրուակ մըն է:

Նիկոմիդիա (Առաջնորդէն) – 1 Սեպտեմբեր

Իզնիկի կողմերը Միլլիները յոյները կը ջարդեն կ'ըսուի: Այդ կողմեր[էն] փախստական յոյն երիտասարդ մը այս լուրը բերած է:

- Իպօն 25 հոգիով Կէմլէյիկ տարուած է իբր յունաց հակառակորդ: Ասիկա եթէ Միլլիները իմանան եւ ապահով ըլլան թէ իր 7–8 հարիւր մարդիկը անգլուխ են, հաւանական է որ Քէրէմէթը, Մեծ-Նոր-Գիւղն, Չէնկիլէրը, Եալովայի Քարձի, Գըլըճ եւ Շագ-Շագ ու Չագար հայ գիւղերը եւ Եալագտէրէն եւ Մերտիկէօզն բնաջինջ ընեն:

Նիկոմիդիա (Առաջնորդէն) – 1 Սեպտեմբեր

Այսօր, երկու հայ եւ մէկ յոյն Տիւզճէէն փախստական 7 օրէն Նիկոմիդիա կուգան: Ասոնք կը պատմեն թէ Պօլուի հայ թաղը այրած են եւ հայերէն մէկ մասը սպաննուած, միւս մասն ալ լեռները ապաստանած են: Կը ջարդեն նաեւ չէրքէզները եւ ապազաները: Այրած են նաեւ Խանտէկն ու Հայոց գիւղն եւ բնակիչները մասամբ ջարդած: Լեռները ապաստանողները եթէ Միլլիճիներու հետապնդութենէն ազատին, ապահովաբար անօթութենէ պիտի մեռնին:

Նիկոմիդիա (Առաջնորդէն) – 2 Սեպտեմբեր

27 լազերէ բաղկացեալ չէթէ[ախումբ] մը եւ 17 ժանտարմա Փէրիզլի կը մտնեն եւ տուները կը թալլեն մահու սպառնալիքով: Չորս երեւելի տուներ կը փախչին Օգոստոս 23ին Փընտըգլըի լեռը, ուր [յարձակողները] երեք փընտըզլըներն՝ Գանթար, Րէվէնտ, Փափազ գիւղերն յոյն, ամէն տուն 5–6 հոգի, կը զարնեն եւ տունը կրակի կուտան մէջիններով: Այս երեք գիւղերն ալ կը բնաջնջուին: 4000 ոչխար կը տանին եւ զարդոսկիներ, եզներ, գոմէշները կ'առնեն:

- Կը լսուի թէ Խանտէկի մօտ հայ լազերու գիւղերէն Հայոց գիւղը նաեւ այրուած է Պօլուի, Տիւզճէի եւ Խանտէկի դէպքերու միջոցին եւ տեղւոյն նորընծայ քահանան՝ (ձեռնադրուած 1919 սեպտեմբեր 8/21[ին]) Տ. Յովհաննէս, գլխատուած է:

İzmit (from the primate)—September 4

The British have begun moving troops and Circassians and Abaza auxiliaries toward Adapazarı.

The Greek troops have also launched an operation with the support of local Christians. Around Bahçecik, clashes have already begun between Greek soldiers and Lazes. The Greeks suffered twelve wounded and one dead.

Armored cruisers from the coast of Bahçecik are supporting the ground movements.

Refugees native to Bahçecik, fleeing İzmit to Bahçecik, returned to İzmit after hearing gunshots.

Նիկոմիդիա (Առաջնորդէն) – 4 Սեպտեմբեր

Ատաբազարի ուղղութեամբ անգլիացին զօրք եւ չէրքէզ ու ապազա օժանդակներ շարժել սկսաւ:

Նոյնպէս յոյն զինուորները սկսած են գործողութեան տեղացի քրիստոնեաներու օժանդակութեամբ: Պարտիզակի կողմը արդէն ընդհարումները սկսած են յոյն զինուորներու եւ լազերու միջեւ: Յոյները 12 վիրաւոր եւ մէկ մեռեալ ունեցած են:

Պարտիզակի ծովեզերքէն զրահաւորներ կ'օժանդակեն ցամաքային շարժումներուն:

Նիկոմիդիայէն Պարտիզակ գացող պարտիզակցի փախստականներ վերադարձան դարձեալ Նիկոմիդիա զէնքի ձայն առնելով:

[Insecurity] Notebook Number 14
September–October 1920

Trabzon (from the locum tenens)—August 18

Upon a strict order from Ankara, the French vice-consul, Mr. Lépissier, will leave tomorrow. Although the Turkish people oppose this arrangement, the military authorities do not listen to anyone. [News of] Mr. Lépissier's departure has had a terrible effect on Christians, particularly on Armenians. The anxiety is complete. A threatening and dangerous situation has been created. A rather persistent rumor goes around that the Armenian primate and some prominent Armenians will be exiled to Erzurum. Although the chief financial officer and the chief secretary deny this and find it impossible, one cannot be assured, as there is complete anarchy in Trabzon.

It is known that going to Erzurum means going to death, so feasible help has been requested.

The Armenian-Catholic priest is leaving with Mr. Lépissier. The Armenian primate could have followed his lead, but he does not want to be separated from his people.

With the departure of Mr. Lépissier, Trabzon will be under siege. The French post office is already closed.

Trabzon (from the locum tenens)—August 30[91]

On August 27, a French hydroplane flew over Trabzon. It scattered leaflets in Turkish, warning the Muslims against trusting the Bolsheviks, pointing to their hostile and destructive attitude toward Islamic Azerbaijan.

• The Kemalist force has lost its charm recently and is causing even disgust among the Turkish majority. Most Turks are waiting impatiently, more than we are, for the government in İstanbul or the Allies to act without delay.

• Mr. Lépissier is visiting the Black Sea coastal areas with an armored cruiser. He is gathering French subjects to take them to İstanbul. Needless to say, the Christian population is deeply troubled by this.

İzmit (from the primate)—September 9

The priest Sdepanos Derderian arrived in İzmit yesterday from Akmeşe. He had escaped from Düzce with four or five people and reached Adapazarı after enduring significant hardship upon hearing that the Millis would slaughter the Abazas and the Armenians of Düzce.

This priest relates that a month ago, the male Armenians of Bolu and twelve Greek families were crammed [by the Turks] into the Armenian church and burned by bombs, while the Armenian women and girls of Bolu were driven to the mountains near Ilıca.

In Düzce, it was heard that the Millis massacred the Armenians who were in Devrek-Hamidiye five to ten days before the Bolu incident. A Greek priest from Bartın was brought to Bolu five to ten days before the incident and hanged. Bartın was also burned. As many as sixty Armenian families are thought to have been slaughtered. There are as many as two hundred Greek families in Ereğli on the Black Sea, and six or seven people have been massacred there. Twelve people were brought and hanged in Düzce two months ago. Also, a month and a half or two months ago, two laypeople and a priest from Karay Yavuz village of Ereğli were taken to Bolu by the Millis. The priest was hanged, but what happened to the two laypeople is unknown.

This time, when the Millis entered Düzce, four to five hundred Armenians, naked, barefoot, and

[Անապահովութեան] Տետր Թիւ 14
1920 Օգոստոս – 1921 Ապրիլ

Տրապիզոն (Առաջնորդական Տեղապահէն) – 18 Օգոստոս

Էնկիւրիւէն եկած խիստ հրամանի մը վրայ ֆրանսացի փոխ-հիւպատոս պ. Լէբիսիէ վաղը կը մեկնի: Թէեւ թուրք ժողովուրդը հակառակ է այս կարգադրութեան, բայց զինուորական իշխանութիւնը ոչ ոքի մտիկ կ'ընէ: Պ. Լէբիսիէի մեկնումը շատ գէշ ազդած է քրիստոնեաներու եւ մասնաւորապէս հայոց վրայ: Ցուցումը կատարեալ է: Սպառնալից եւ վտանգաւոր կացութիւն մը ստեղծուած է: Բաւական յաման զրոյց մը կը շրջի բերնէ բերան թէ հայ Առաջնորդը քանի մը ծանօթ հայերու հետ պիտի աքսորեն Կարին: *Տէֆտէրտարը* եւ *մէքթուպճին* թէեւ կը հերքեն եւ անկարելի կը նկատեն այդ բանը, բայց կարելի չէ վստահիլ, քանի որ կատարեալ անիշխանութիւն կայ Տրապիզոնի մէջ:

Յայտնի է թէ դէպի Կարին երթալ մահուան երթալ կը նշանակէ, ուստի կը խնդրուի որ կարելի օգնութիւնը ըլլայ:

Հայ-կաթոլիկ վարդապետ[ը] կը մեկնի պ. Լէբիսիէի հետ: Հայոց Առաջնորդը կրնայ նոյն օրինակին հետեւիլ, սակայն չ'ուզեր բաժնուիլ իր ժողովուրդէն:

Պ. Լէբիսիէի հեռացումով Տրապիզոն պաշարուած վիճակ մը պիտի ունենայ: Ֆրանսական բօսթան արդէն փակուած է:

Տրապիզոն (Առաջնորդական Տեղապահէն) – 30 Օգոստոս

Օգոստոս 27ին Տրապիզոնի վրայ սաւառնեցաւ ֆրանսական ջրօդանաւ մը՝ ցրուելով թրքերէն թռուցիկներ, որով կը զգուշացնէին խլամութիւնը վստահելէ պօլշէվիկներու վրայ՝ մատնանշելով անոնց թշնամական եւ կործանարար վերաբերմունքը իսլամ Ատրպէյճանի հանդէպ:

- Քէմալական ոյժը այս վերջերս մանաւանդ կորսնցուցեր է իր հմայքը եւ նոյնիսկ զզուանք կը պատճառէ թուրք մեծամասնութեան: Եւ թուրք մեծամասնութիւնը մեզմէ աւելի անհամբեր կը սպասէ որ Պոլսոյ կառավարութիւնը կամ Համաձայնութիւն[ը] առանց դանդաղելու ձեռնարկեն գործողութեան:

- Պ. Լէբիսիէ Սեւ Ծովու ծովեզերքները կը հանդիպի զրահաւորով եւ ֆրանսական հպատակները հաւաքելով Կ. Պոլիս կը տանի: Աւելորդ է ըսել թէ ո՛ր աստիճան յուզումի կը մատնէ այս բանը քրիստոնեայ բնակչութիւնը:

Նիկոմիդիա (Առաջնորդէն) – 9 Սեպտեմբեր

Տ. Ստեփաննոս քահանայ Տէրտէրեան երէկ Արմաշէն Նիկոմիդիա եկաւ: Անիկա Տիւզճէէն 4–5 հարիւր հոգիներով փախած էր եւ մեծ նեղութիւններով հասած էր Ատաբազար, երբ լուր առած էր թէ Տիւզճէի ապազաները եւ հայերը Միլլիճիներու կողմէ պիտի ջարդուին:

Այս քահանան կը պատմէ թէ ամիս մը առաջ Պօլուի արու հայերը եւ 12 տուն յոյները հայոց եկեղեցին կը լեցնեն եւ պօմպաներով կ'այրեն, իսկ Պօլուի հայ կիները ու աղջիկները Ըլըճայի կողմերը լեռները կը քշեն:

Տիւզճէ կը լսուի որ Պօլուի դէպքէն 5–10 օր առաջ Տէվրէկ-Համիտիյէ գտնուող հայերը ջարդեր են Միլլիճիները: Պարթընէն յոյն քահանայ մը Պօլու կը բերեն դէպքէն 5–10 օր առաջ ու կը կախեն: Պարթըն ալ այրեր են: 60 տունի չափ հայերն ալ ջարդուած են կը կարծուի: Սեւ Ծովու Էրէյլին 200 տունի չափ յոյն կայ եւ 6–7 հոգի ալ հոն կոտորուած են: 12 հոգի ալ Տիւզճէ բերեր կախեր են երկու ամիս առաջ: Նոյնպէս Էրէյլիի Խարայ Եավուզ գիւղէն 1½–2 ամիս առաջ երկու աշխարհական եւ մէկ քահանայ Պօլու կը տանին Միլլիճիները եւ քահանան կը կախեն, սակայն երկու աշխարհականները չի գիտցուիր թէ ինչ եղած են:

Այս անգամ երբ Միլլիճիները Տիւզճէ կը մտնեն, հայերը մերկ, բոպիկ եւ առանց բան մը առնելու 4–500 հայ կը փախչին դէպի Հէնտէք, իսկ 20–21 հոգիներ, տեղայոյն երեւելիներէն, հոն կը մնան յոյս

without taking anything, fled to Hendek. Twenty or twenty-one local notables remained there, trusting their friendly Turks, but all were massacred.

The Millis killed the draper Minas, a native of Adapazarı who had settled in Düzce, in the Bıçkıcılar village populated by Abazas. It was heard that the newly ordained priest Hovhannes had been slaughtered after the Millis cut his legs. The priest Sdepannos says that an Abaza told him that he had kept the priest to prevent his killing. Düzce's Abazas asked for help from the British commander of İzmit but did not receive an answer, so they begged the Armenians to appeal, and the Armenians cabled an appeal. The response received urged them to resist for a few days until they arrived.

It was after this appeal that the Bolu massacre took place, and then [the Millis] came to Düzce, and when they entered there for the first time—that is, before the people fled—they found a copy of this telegram in the telegraph office and took the authors away.

The priest Sdepannos has informed us that the Millis entered Adapazarı the day before. The Abazas and Circassians also entered Adapazarı from this side. It is not known what is going on there.

The priest Sdepannos says that Karnig, the eighteen- to twenty-year-old son of Hagop Kyurdian from Bolu, was caught by the Millis in the coastal city of Alablı located between Akçakoca [Akçaşehir] and Ereğli while fleeing from Düzce to İstanbul. He was accompanied by a man named Khachig from Eskişehir and two brothers from Nallıhan, one of whom was Düzce's teacher, along with his wife. Altogether five people were slaughtered and thrown into the sea.

Karnig, Khachig, and the teacher were robbed of two hundred liras cash and seven hundred Ottoman banknotes by the Milli Miskin Recep, who then slaughtered them.

Hagop Portoukalian of Bolu, who was residing in Düzce, was pulled out of the car in Şile while fleeing to İstanbul. The four thousand liras in banknotes he was carrying were taken.

İzmit (from the primate)—September 9

The fear of the Millis prevailed in Adapazarı, and the people of Adapazarı and Düzce fled to Akmeşe. They heard in Akmeşe that the Millis had entered Adapazarı and demanded ten thousand liras from the local government. A month ago, they had already taken six thousand liras from the Greeks because they had not been deportees and four thousand liras from Armenians.

İzmit (from the primate)—September 10

Hagop Santourjian and Haroutyun Dyundenian, two teenagers who survived the Bolu massacre, relate that the Millis, with the contribution of Turkish citizens, Turkish women, and the hocas of Aktaş, entered Bolu on August 14. On the same day, they thoroughly looted the houses of all the Christians, and then at night, they took the beautiful women, brides, and girls toward Ilıca. On Sunday, August 15, they put the men in the local stone-made Holy Mother of God church and the wooden St. Garabed church. Then they burned the churches with dynamite at eleven o'clock at night while they took those left outside to the high school and slaughtered them.

Trabzon (from the locum tenens)—September 2

The Kemalist rule continues. The military establishment, relying on some criminals, constitutes the single Milli force. Muslims also are dissatisfied with Kemal and look forward to foreign intervention. A rift between the Bolsheviks and the Kemalists of Trabzon has finally arisen. Muslims cannot reconcile themselves with Bolshevik ideas. Bolshevik defeats also have had an impact on this rift.

դնելով իրենց բարեկամ թուրքերու վրայ, սակայն ամէնքն ալ կը ջարդուին:

Ատաբազարցի եւ Տիւզճէ հաստատուած մանրավաճառ Մինաս՝ Պըչկընըլար ապազայ գիւղին մէջ Միլլիճիք կը սպաննեն: Հէնտէքի հայոց գիւղի նորընծայ Տ. Յովհաննէս քահանային համար լսուած էր թէ մորթուած էր, երկու ոտքերը կտրելէ վերջ: Տ. Ստեփաննոս քահանայ կ'ըսէ թէ ապազայ մը ըսած է իրեն թէ ինքն պահած է որ չսպաննեն: Տիւզճէի ապազաները Նիկոմիդիոյ անգլիացի հրամանատարէն օգնութիւն կը խնդրեն եւ պատասխան չեն ստանար, ուստի հայոց կ'աղաչեն որ իրենք դիմում ընեն եւ թելով կը դիմեն: Պատասխան կը ստանան որ առ այժմ իրենք քանի մը օր դիմադրեն մինչեւ որ իրենք հասնին:

Այս դիմումէն յետոյ է որ Պոլուի ջարդը կը պատահի եւ յետոյ Տիւզճէ կուգան եւ երբ հոն կը մտնեն առաջին անգամ,- այսինքն ժողովուրդին փախչելէն առաջ,- հեռագրատունէն այս հեռագրին օրինակը կը գտնեն եւ գրողները կ'առնեն կը տանին:

Տ. Ստեփաննոս քահանայ կը տեղեկացնէ թէ օր մը առաջ Ատաբազար մտած են Միլլիճիները: Ապազաները եւ չէրքէզներն ալ այս կողմէն Ատաբազար մտած են: Չի գիտցուիր թէ ինչ կ'ըլլայ հիմակ հոն:

Տ. Ստեփաննոս քահանայ կ'ըսէ որ պօլուցի Քիւրտեան Յակոբի 18–20 տարեկան զաւակը՝ Գառնիկ, Տիւզճէէն Պոլիս փախած ատեն, Ազճէ-Շէհիրի եւ Էրէյլիի մէջտեղ Ալապլը ծովեզերեայ գիւղին մէջ կը բռնուի Միլլիճիներէն: Իրեն հետ էին նաեւ Խաչիկ անուն էսկիշէհիրցի մը եւ նալլըխանցի երկու եղբայրներ որոնցմէ մին Տիւզճէի վարժապետը եւ իր կինը, ընդամէնը հինգ հոգի, որոնք ամէնն ալ կը ջարդեն եւ ծովը կը նետեն:

Գառնիկի, Խաչիկի եւ վարժապետին 200 հնչուն եւ 700 օսմ.թղթադրամը կողոպտած է զանոնք ջարդող Միլլիճին, որ է Միսկին Րէճէպ:

Պօլուցի Յակոբ Փորթուգալեան, որ Տիւզճէ հաստատուած էր, Պոլիս փախած ատեն ի Շիլէ մօթէօրէն դուրս կը հանեն ու վրայի դրամը՝ 4000 թղթադրամը կ'առնեն:

Նիկոմիդիա (Առաջնորդէն) – 9 Սեպտեմբեր

Ատաբազարի մէջ Միլլիճիներու վախը կը տիրէ եւ ատաբազարցիք եւ տիւզճէցիները Արմաշ կը փախչին եւ Արմաշ կը լսեն որ Միլլիճիները Ատաբազար կը մտնեն եւ տեղւոյն կառավարութենէն 10,000 ոսկի կը պահանջեն, մինչդեռ ամիս մը առաջ յոյներէն 6000 ոսկի կ'առնեն, տարագիր եղած չըլլալնուն [համար], 4000 ալ՝ հայերէն:

Նիկոմիդիա (Առաջնորդէն) – 10 Սեպտեմբեր

Պօլու[ի] ջարդէն ճողոպրած երկու պատանիներ՝ Յակոբ Սանթուրճեան եւ Յարութիւն Տիւնտէնեան, կը պատմեն թէ Օգոստոս 14ին Պօլու կը մտնեն Միլլիճիները, որոնց կը գործակցին Պօլուի թուրք քաղաքացիները, թուրք կնիկները, Ագ Թաշի հոճաները: Նոյն օրը ասոնք նախ բոլոր քրիստոնէից տուները ամբողջովին կը կողոպտեն, իսկ նոյն գիշերն ալ կին, հարս, աղջիկ գեղեցիկները Ըլըճայի կողմը կը տանին, իսկ Օգոստոս 15ին Կիրակի օրը տեղւոյն Ս. Աստուածածին քարաշէն եւ Ս. Կարապետ փայտաշէն եկեղեցին կը լեցնեն այրերը եւ իրիկուան ժամը 11ին տինամիթ պօմպայով կը վառեն եկեղեցիները եւ դուրսը մնացածներն ալ խատտի վարժարան կը տանին կը մորթեն:

Տրապիզոն (Առաջնորդական Տեղապահէն) – 2 Սեպտեմբեր

Կը շարունակէ Քէմալական տիրապետութիւնը: Զինուորականութիւնը յենած կարգ մը ոճրագործներու վրայ, կը կազմէ Միլլիական միակ ոյժը: Իսլամներն ալ դժգոհ են Քէմալէն եւ անհամբեր կը սպասեն օտար միջամտութեան: Պոլշէվիկներու եւ Տրապիզոնի Քէմալականներու միջեւ խզում առաջ եկաւ վերջապէս: Իսլամները չկրցան հաշտուիլ պոլշէվիկ գաղափարներու հետ: Պոլշէվիկ պարտութիւններն ալ իրենց ազդեցութիւնը ունեցան այս խզումին մէջ:

İzmit (from the primate)—September 10

The British are cultivating friendship with the Turks here and treating the Armenians as savages and slaves. They took a 1,261-square-cubit silkworm nursery, measuring 18 cubits wide with a 40-cubits-long floor above, which had been turned into a school for boys and girls. Barely ten to fifteen Englishmen are in this building. First, they made it into an orphanage, [and] now the orphans have been transferred to İstanbul. Since the building is empty [and] no orphans will come, the building should be returned [to the Armenians].

After the building was taken away from the Armenians, the Armenians turned the coffeehouse—one of the school's estates and a source of income—into a school. Under the pretext that it was unhealthy and cluttered, the British forced the evacuation of this national school also within two hours. Immediately after clearing it, the English moved in and did not even pity the boys left on the streets or show them a [substitute] place.

In addition, they continue to evacuate Armenians' homes and settle in them without paying any rent.

There are large Turkish mansions. They place one Turkish woman in each of them and refuse to let anyone [else] in under the pretext of *namahrem* [unrelatedness].

Would it not be better if those large buildings were vacated?

• There are now more than 400 Greeks besides Armenians in Derince receiving half a bread a day from their prelacy. The Armenians number 179 people from fifty families from Akmeşe, plus nineteen families (72 people) from Arslanbey, a total of 251 people. They receive from the Americans one okka of bread and, every other day, beans. The Americans promised to provide for the Armenians. Armenians remain uncared for presently.

İzmit (from the primate)—September 15

Dr. Gabaydayan and Hovhannes Der Boghosian from Adapazarı arrived in İzmit yesterday and, accompanied by Greek and Circassian delegates from Adapazarı, presented themselves to the British commander and asked for British protection for Adapazarı.

Residents, one after another, are leaving everything behind and fleeing from their city of Adapazarı to Akmeşe and thence to İzmit.

Although it has been said before that the British had entered Adapazarı, now it is confirmed that only three or four officers have entered the city to buy ten to twenty thousand okkas of potatoes. The local people were deceived into thinking that the British had liberated them, which made them very happy, but when they saw the British departure, they fell into great despair. Therefore, those who can, run away naked and barefoot. There is great hardship because no shelter can be found in İzmit.

Trabzon (from the locum tenens)—September 8

Resistance preparations are underway. The Bolshevik movement failed.

• Conscription in Erzurum is strict. The newly enlisted are being sent to the Armenian border.

• Giresun's condition is extremely worrying. Topal Osman acts as a plague in that region.

Bursa (from Haroutyun Jeverganian's [*sic*] private letter sent from Kütahya to Mr. Sarkis Garabedian)—September 14

It is understood from a letter dated September 10 from Kütahya that forty-four Armenians, twenty-

Նիկոմիդիա (Առաջնորդէն) – 10 Սեպտեմբեր

Անգլիացիք հոս թուրքերու հետ բարեկամութիւն կը մշակեն եւ հայերը վայրենի, ստրուկ[ի] տեղ կը դնեն: 1261 կանգուն քառակուսիի վրայ շերամատուն մը առին, վրան ալ 18 կանգուն լայնքով եւ 40 կանգուն երկայնքով յարկ մը, որ երկսեռ վարժարանի վերածուած էր: Այս շէնքին մէջ կան հազիւ 10–15 անգլիացի: Նախ որբանոց ըրած էին, հիմա որբերն փոխադրուած են Պոլիս: Քանի որ շէնքը պարպուած է, որբերը չպիտի գան, շէնքը պէտք է վերադարձուի:

Հայոց ձեռքէն այս շէնքը առնուելէն յետոյ, հայերը դպրոցին կալուածներէն եւ հասոյթի աղբիւրներէն մէկը եղող սրճարանը դպրոցի վերածեցին: Անգլիացիք անառողջապահիկ եւ խճողուած ըլլալը պատրուակ ընելով ազգային այս վարժարանն ալ երկու ժամուան մէջ պարպել տուին: Սակայն անմիջապէս մաքրելով անգլիացիք ներս մտան եւ գոնէ խղճմտանք չըրին փողոցը մնացող տղոց տեղ մը ցոյց տալու:

Ասկէ զատ շարունակ հայերու տուները կը պարպեն եւ իրենք կը նստին, առանց ոեւէ վարձք վճարելու:

Թուրքերու խոշոր ապարանքներ կան, մէջը մէկ թուրք կին կը դնեն եւ *համէհրամ*ը պատրուակ ընելով ներս մարդ չեն առներ:

Աւելի լաւ չէ՞ր ըլլար որ այդ խոշոր շէնքերը պարպուէին:

- Տէրինճէի մէջ հիմա կան հայերէ զատ 400 հոգի ալ յոյն, որոնք իրենց մետրապոլիտարանէն կը ստանան օրական կէս հաց: Իսկ հայերն 179 հոգի են, 50 տուն Արմաշէն եւ 19 տուն՝ 72 հոգի Արսլանպէկէն, ընդամէնը 251 հոգի, ամերիկացիներէն կը ստանա[ն] մէկ օխա հաց եւ օրընդմէջ լուբիա: Ամերիկացիք խոստացած են հայերը պարենաւորել: Հայերը առայժմ կը մնան անխնամ:

Նիկոմիդիա (Առաջնորդէն) – 15 Սեպտեմբեր

Ատաբազարէն Տոքթոր Գապայյտայեան եւ Յովհաննէս Տ. Պօղոսեան երէկ հասան Նիկոմիդիա եւ Ատաբազարէն եկող յոյն եւ չէրքէզ պատուիրակներու հետ անգլիացի հրամատարին ներկայացան եւ խնդրեցին անգլիացւոց պաշտպանութիւնը Ատաբազարի համար:

Ատաբազարցի[ք] իրենց քաղաքէն Արմաշ եւ անկէ Նիկոմիդիա կը փախ[չ]ին հետզհետէ իրենց ամէն ինչքերը լքանելով:

Թէեւ ասկէ առաջ ըսուեցաւ որ անգլիացիք Ատաբազար մտած են, սակայն հիմա կը հաստատուի որ միայն 3–4 սպաներ քաղաք մտած են 10–20 հազար օխա բաթաթէս գնելու համար: Տեղացի ժողովուրդը խաբուելով կարծած է թէ անգլիացիք զիրենք ազատած են, ուստի մեծապէս ուրախացած են, բայց երբ անոնց մեկնիլը տեսած են, մեծ յուսահատութեան մատնուած են: Ուստի կրցողը մերկ ու բոպիկ կը փախչի: Նիկոմիդիոյ մէջ պատսպարուելու տեղ չըլլալուն՝ մեծ նեղութիւն կայ:

Տրապիզոն (Առաջնորդական Տեղապահէն) – 8 Սեպտեմբեր

Դիմադրական պատրաստութիւններ կը տեսնուին: Պոլշէվիկ շարժումը անյաջողութեան մատնուեցաւ:

- Կարնոյ մէջ զինուորագրութիւնը խիստ է: Նորագիրները կը ղրկուին հայկական սահմանագլուխ:

- Կիրասոնի կացութիւնը չափազանց մտահոգիչ է: Թօփալ Օսման իբր պատուհասը այդ շրջանին կը գործէ:

Պրուսա (Յարութիւն Ճէվէրկանեանի մասնաւոր նամակէն՝ ուղարկուած Քէօթահիայէն առ Տիար Սարգիս Կարապետեան) – 14 Սեպտեմբեր

Քէօթահիայէն առնուած 10 Սեպտեմբեր թուակիր նամակէն կը հասկցուի որ Չորեքշաբթի

five Greeks, and twenty-three Catholics, altogether ninety-two people, all wealthy, were rounded up and sent to Eskişehir by train on Friday night. Shamkoulian, Ghongianos, Apraham, Setrag, Chyouryougdishian, Sijidian, and Onnig are in that category. The bank director, Maksoud Effendi, and others were also taken away. For now, we think they went to Eskişehir, but it has been written: "We also hear that they were taken to Ankara."

The director of the Ipranosian store, Ardashes, and Sallabashian were also [among them]. They immediately appealed to the command in Bursa.

Bursa (from the primate)—September 18[92]

During the week, young Armenian refugees from Kütahya and Tavşanlı came here by way of the mountains, saying that on September 10, ninety-two local Armenians and Greeks were taken [by Millis] to Eskişehir and that no one knows what they did [to them]. Then they forced [the residents] to open the shops. Once opened, they robbed them. It has been learned by hearsay that the Greek inhabitants of Küplü, located close to Bilecik, three hundred families, have been annihilated; we do not know about the acts committed in Bilecik.

Upon this, the Armenian primate of Bursa, the prelate of Armenian Catholics, and the locum tenens of the Greek metropolitan have appealed in writing to the Greek high commander Dimitro Yuvan, who, having already been informed in advance, promised to immediately send Mr. Venizelos a cable asking to be allowed to put a categoric end to those unspeakable barbarities of Anadolu [Anatolia].

On September 16, Major Stesveri [*sic*], the British high controller of the Hellenic Army, visited the prelacy in Bursa. The situation was explained to him as well. He also made promises. Today, a second appeal was made to him. He is consulting with the Hellenic commander.

Bursa (Haroutyun Chezerganian's [*sic*] private letter addressed to Sarkis Garabedian)—September 15

On the night of September 10, at three o'clock, forty-four Armenians, twenty-three Armenian Catholics, and twenty-five Greeks, a total of ninety-two people, were sent by train from Kütahya to Eskişehir. Today, Srab Agha's Garabed and five others came from Tavşanlı to Bursa and related that after taking these ninety-two people away on Thursday night, on Friday, town criers were put to work and people were forced to open the shops. After looting the open shops, they apprehended all the Armenian and Greek males under fifteen and sent them toward Yenikent [Stanos]. The three priests also were taken with the people.

The coffers of Ipranosian and others were also taken, as were the men found during a search of the homes on Friday night.

A woman from Tavşanlı had one child in Kütahya and another in Tavşanlı. When the one in Kütahya, a fifteen-year-old, was taken away, the woman, intending to put at least her other [son] to flight dressed as a Turkish woman, escaped to Tavşanlı on Saturday and reported the incident. With the help of the people of Tavşanlı, five to eight young Armenians came to Bursa today.

İzmit (from the primate)—September 16

Hoping that the Turks would keep them, a few Armenians stayed in Düzce. Two of them, Yervant and Mihrtad, the sons of glassmaker Nigoghos Agha of İstanbul, took shelter in a Turk's home, but when a town crier announced that those sheltering Armenians would be hanged, the Turk helped the two flee his house. He hid them in a corn barn where they were caught and killed, as verified by the wife of one of the murdered men who managed to escape and come to İzmit.

գիշեր Քէօթահիայի մէջ բոլորը հարուստ ըլլալու պայմանաւ 44 հայ, 25 յոյն եւ 23 կաթոլիկ, ընդամէնը 92 հոգի հաւաքելով, Ուրբաթ օր երկաթուղիով ղրկած են Էսկիշէհիր: Այդ կարգին կը գտնուին Շամգուլեան, Ղօնկիանոս, Աբրահամ, Սեդրակ, Չիւրիւկտիշեան, Սիճիտեան, Օննիկ: Պանքայի տնօրէն Մազլում էֆէնտին եւ ուրիշներ ալ տարեր են. առայժմ Էսկիշէհիր գնացին կը կարծենք, սակայն «դէպի Էնկիւրիւ տանելնին եւս կը լսենք» գրուած է:

Իբրանոսեան վաճառատան տնօրէնը՝ Արտաշէս եւ Սալլապաշեան ալ կա[ն] եղեր. անմիջապէս Պրուսայի հրամանատարութեան դիմում կ'ընեն:

Պրուսա (Առաջնորդէն) – 18 Սեպտեմբեր

Շաբթուան ընթացքին լեռնային ճամբով փախստական հայ երիտասարդներ Քէօթահիայէն ու Թաւշանլըյէն հոս եկած են, կը պատմեն թէ Սեպտեմբեր 10ին տեղւոյն գլխաւորներէն 92 հոգի հայ եւ յոյն դէպի Էսկիշէհիր ճամբայ հանած են եւ ոչ ոք գիտէ թէ ինչ ըրած են: Ցետոյ ստիպած են խանութները բանալու եւ բացումէն յետոյ թալլած են: Դարձեալ ի լրոյ կ'իմացուի թէ Պիլէճիկի մօտ գտնուող Քիւրլիւյի յոյն բնակչութիւնը՝ 300 տուն, բնաջինջ ըրած են, չենք գիտեր թէ Պիլէճիկի մէջ ինչե՛ր չեն ըրած:

Ասոր վրայ Պրուսայի հայոց Առաջնորդը, հայ կաթոլիկներու Առաջնորդը եւ յունաց Մեթրոպոլիտի փոխանորդը գրաւոր կերպով կը դիմեն հելլէն բարձր հրամանատար Տիմիթրօ Եուվանիի, որ նախապէս արդէն տեղեկացած ըլլալով, կը խոստանայ անմիջապէս հեռագրել պ. Վենիզելոսի որպէսզի վերջնականապէս հրամայուի Անատոլուի այդ անլուր բարբարոսութեանց վերջ տրուելու համար:

Սեպտեմբեր 16ին Պրուսա Առաջնորդարան կ'այցելէ անգլիացի Մէճըր Բսթէսվէրի, որ հելլէն բանակին վերին քօնթրօլէօռն է: Ասոր եւս կը բացատրուի իրաց կացութիւնը: Ան ալ խոստումներ կ'ընէ: Այսօր կրկին իրեն դիմում եղաւ: Հելլէն հրամանատարին հետ կը խորհրդակցին:

Պրուսա (մասնաւոր նամակ Յարութիւն Չըզըրկանեանի ուղղուած առ Սարգիս Կարապետեան) – 15 Սեպտեմբեր

Սեպտեմբեր 10ին գիշերը ժամը 3ին 44 հայ, 23 հայ-կաթոլիկ եւ 25 յոյն՝ ընդամէնը 92 հոգի՝ հարուստներէն երկաթուղիով Քէօթահիայէն Էսկիշէհիր ղրկուած էին: Այսօր Թավշանլուէն Սրապ աղային Կարապետը եւ հինգ հոգի եկան Պրուսա եւ կը պատմեն թէ Հինգշաբթի գիշերը այս 92 հոգին տանելէ վերջ, Ուրբաթ օրը մունետիկ պտտցնելով ստիպողաբար բանալ կուտան խանութները: Բացուած խանութները աւարի տալէ յետոյ, մինչեւ 15 տարեկան հայ եւ յոյն որչափ այր մարդ որ ձեռք կ'անցնեն կը ղրկեն Սթանոսի կողմը: Ժողովուրդին հետ կը տանին նաեւ երեք քահանաները:

Իբրանոսեանի եւ ուրիշներու դրամարկղներն ալ տարուած են, ինչպէս նաեւ Ուրբաթ գիշեր տուները խուզարկելով գտնուած արու մարդիկը:

Թավշանլուցի կին մը, որուն մէկ զաւակը Քէօթահիա եւ միւսը Թավշանլու կը գտնուի եղեր, Քէօթահիայինը -15 տարեկան- երբ կը տանին, գոնէ միւսը փախցնելու մտօք թուրք կնոջ տարազով Շաբաթ օր Թավշանլու կը փախչի եւ եղելութիւնը կը պարզէ այնտեղ: Թավշանլուի ժողովրդեան միջոցաւ հայ երիտասարդներէն 5–8 հոգի այսօր Պրուսա եկան:

Նիկոմիդիա (Առաջնորդէն) – 16 Սեպտեմբեր

Տիզճէի մէջ յոյս ընելով թէ թուրքերը զիրենք կը պահեն մնացող քանի մը հայեր կ'ըլլան: Ասոնցմէ երկուքը ՝ Երուանդ եւ Միհրդատ՝ որդիք կ. պոլսեցի Ճամճի Նիկողոս աղայի, թուրքի մը քով կ'ապաստանին, սակայն երբ մունետիկ կ'ելլայ թէ հայերը պահողները կախաղան պիտի ելլան՝ թուրքը տունէն կը փախցնէ այս երկուքը եւ եգիպտացորենի ամբարի մը մէջ կը պահէ, ուր ձեռք անցնելով կը սպաննուին, ինչպէս կը հաւաստէ սպաննուողներէն մէկուն կինը, որ կրցած է փախչիլ

• It was reported that Father Hovhannes, the newly ordained priest of the Armenian village of Hendek, had been killed. However, now, they claim that he has been saved. Although he was taken to be killed, he somehow escaped, changed his attire, and reached Adapazarı.

• The houses of Armenians in Hendek were looted completely when the inhabitants went to the mountains. Six people were killed. The bodies of four of them have been found; the [whereabouts of the other] two [bodies] is unknown.

Kütahya (from a merchant's letter)—September 6

"No goods have been left in the store and no money in the pockets. If only our dry soul survives, we will praise God. God knows the troubles we have suffered."

Bursa—September 13

Yesterday, Garabed Der Garabedian arrived here and reported the following:

"On Thursday, September 9, from half past one at night (Turkey time) until morning, whoever's name was written, and whoever was sought, ninety-two Greeks and Armenians, were arrested and sent as hostages to Eskişehir. Their location is unknown.

"On the morning of Friday, September 10, a town crier was sent with orders for everyone to open their shops. After that, the shops were looted hours later, and the shopkeepers were arrested. On Saturday night, September 14, all night long, the houses were searched, and all the men over the age of fifteen, including three priests, two of whom were Armenian-Catholic and one Apostolic Armenian, were rounded up and taken away.

"Hagop Karabajakian, who worked at the faience workshop, was taken away on a stretcher because he could not walk due to his weak body.

"Carpets were collected by cart in the Greek neighborhood. The Greek neighborhood is now under siege. The Greek army is a few hours away from Kütahya but did not attack to rescue them, arguing that they had no permission to attack."

A telegram from Kütahya to Bursa sent on Sunday, September 12, states, in ciphers, that great mischiefs and mishaps occurred on Sunday.

• According to information received in Bursa from fugitive travelers fleeing from Bilecik to Bursa through the mountains on September 17, the Armenians of Bilecik were deported (probably to Ankara), while the people of Küplü, a Greek village near Bilecik, were all put to the sword.

Trabzon (from the locum tenens)—September 16[93]

Giresun's lame [Topal] Osman arrived in Trabzon on September 12 with a group of about six hundred bandits. An editorial published in the Trabzon-based *Ikbal* newspaper (no. 601) praised the band. Supposedly, they will go to Oltu's front, but they are still here. They roam the city freely and without weapons. No disturbance has happened so far, perhaps because a British cruiser is guarding these shores, and two armored cruisers are in front of Atina [Pazar].

İzmit (from the primate)—September 22

The Greeks of Osmaneli [Lefke], Küplü, Aşağıköy, and Vezirhan are said to have been massacred. There is also a rumor that the Armenians of Bilecik and Nallıhan have also been massacred.

ու գալ Նիկոմիդիա:

- Հէնտէքի հայոց գիւղի նորընծայ Տ. Յովհաննէս քահանայի համար ըսուած էր թէ սպաննուած է: Հիմա կը հաւաստեն թէ ազատած է: Թէեւ տարուած է սպաննուելու, սակայն կերպով մը խոյս տուեր եւ տարազափոխ ըլլալով ինքզինք Ատաբազար նետեր է:

- Հէնտէքի հայոց տուները ամբողջ կողոպտուած են, երբ բնակիչները լեռները ելած էին: Վեց հոգի ալ սպաննուած են: Ասոնցմէ չորսին մարմինը գտնուած է, իսկ երկուքինը անյայտ է:

Քէօթահիա (վաճառականի մը նամակէն) – 6 Սեպտեմբեր

«Խանութի մէջ ապրանք եւ գրպաններու մէջ դրամ չմնաց, միայն եթէ չոր հոգինիս ողջ մնայ, փառք պիտի տանք, քաշած նեղութիւննիս Աստուած գիտէ»:

Պրուսա – 13 Սեպտեմբեր

Երէկ Կարապետ Տէր Կարապետեան հասաւ հոս ու հաղորդեց հետեւեալները.

«Սեպտեմբեր 9, Հինգշաբթի իրիկուն ժամը 1½էն (ըստ թրքաց) մինչեւ առտու գրածնին եւ ուզածնին՝ 92 հոգի՝ բռնած են եւ իբրեւ պատանդ Էսկիշէհիր խաւրած են, յոյն եւ հայ: Ո՞ւր ըլլալնին յայտնի չէ:

Ուրբաթ 10 Սեպտեմբերի առտուն մունետիկ ելած է որ ամէն մարդ խանութները բանայ: Ետքէն քանի մը ժամ վերջը, խանութները կողոպտած են եւ խանութպանները ձերբակալուած են:

Շաբաթ 14 Սեպտեմբերի գիշերը մինչեւ առտու տուները խուզարկելով 15 տարեկանէն վեր եղող բոլոր այր մարդիկը ժողված տարած են, նաեւ երեք քահանաները, որոնց երկուքը հայ-կաթոլիկ եւ մէկը հայ:

Չինիի ([faïences]) գործատունը բանող Յակոբ Գարապաճագեանը կազմուածքը տկար ըլլալուն քալել չկարենալով զայն ալ պատգարակով տարած են:

Յունաց թաղին մէջ կառքերով գորգեր ժողված տարած են. այժմ յունաց թաղը պաշարման վիճակի մէջ է: Յունական բանակը Քէօթահիայէն մէկ քանի ժամ հեռու է եւ յարձակում չ՚ըներ օգնութեան փութալու՝ առարկելով թէ հրաման չունինք յարձակում ընելու:

Կիրակի 12 Սեպտեմբերին Քէօթահիայէն Պրուսա քաշուած հեռագիր մը ծածուկ բառերով կ՚իմացնէ որ Կիրակի օր մեծ չարիք եւ դժբաղդութիւններ պատահած են:[»]

- Սեպտեմբեր 17ին Պրուսա եկած տեղեկութեանց համաձայն, որոնք քաղուած են Պիլէճիկէն լերանց մէջէն փախչելով Պրուսա ապաստանող ճամբորդներէն, Պիլէճիկի հայերը տեղահան ըրած են (հաւանաբար դէպի Էնկիւրիւ), իսկ Քիւփլիւ, որ յունական գիւղ մըն է Պիլէճիկի մօտ, ամբողջ սրէ անցուցած են:

Տրապիզոն (Առաջնորդական Տեղապահէն) – 16 Սեպտեմբեր

Կիրասոնի կաղ Օսմանը Սեպտեմբեր 12ին Տրապիզոն եկաւ՝ մօտ 600 աւազակներո[ւ] խումբով: Տրապիզոն հրատարակուող «Իզպալ» թերթին մէջ (թիւ 601) խմբագրականով մը ներբող մը [յոյս տեսաւ] այդ յելուզակախումբին համար: Ասոնք իբր թէ պիտի երթան Օլթիի ճակատը, սակայն առայժմ հոս կը մնան: Քաղաքին մէջ ասոնք կը շրջին ազատ եւ առանց զէնքի: Առայժմ անկարգութիւն մը չէ պատահած հաւանօրէն անոր համար որ անգլիական յածանաւ մը այս եզերքները կը շրջի իբր պահակ եւ Աթինայի առջեւ երկու զրահաւորներ կան:

Նիկոմիդիա (Առաջնորդէն) – 22 Սեպտեմբեր

Լէֆքէի, Քիւփլիւի, Աշաղը Քէօյի, Վէզիր Խանի յոյները ջարդուած են կ՚ըսուի. նոյնպէս զրոյց կայ թէ Պիլէճիկի եւ Նալլը Խանի հայերն ալ ջարդուած են:

Bursa (from the primate)—September 22

The Armenians of Tavşanlı took refuge in Bursa, where they were given shelter and bread.

The Armenians of Marmaracık have returned to their homes and resettled there. Four Armenians from Marmaracık were killed, and the leader of the killers, Hüseyin, was arrested by the Greeks and sent to Gemlik.

İzmit (from the primate)—September 27

When the train arriving from İzmit to Arifiye left for Adapazarı, the Millis fired at it from inside the gardens. The Millis numbered fifty to sixty. The train was empty. Only the windows were damaged, and one woman and one man were injured, but the panic in Adapazarı was tremendous, and most Armenians ran to take the train to İzmit. Some others, having heard that there would be no more rail traffic, fled to Akmeşe, while Georgian and Circassian forces from Adapazarı went to Arifiye to attack the Millis, and, indeed, they succeeded in making them flee. Three or four Millis died. The rest took the corpses with them. Some Georgian and Circassian forces voluntarily traveled to Sapanca to protect the Armenians of Adapazarı, who were crammed in wagons. The Armenians of Adapazarı arrived in İzmit this evening and remain unsheltered.

Bursa (from the primate)—September 27

A few days ago, the priest Nerses of Cerrah, along with 60 people plus 70 people from Yenice, altogether 130 Armenians and Greeks, were taken away by the Millis. The Greek forces chased them and entered İnegöl but then retreated to their previous positions. The people taken away are said to have been sent toward Ankara.

Trabzon (from the vicar general)—September 23

On September 22, two French hydroplanes flew over Trabzon. They dropped leaflets in Turkish, similar to those dropped by a French hydroplane that flew on August 27. These leaflets warn Muslims against Bolshevism, although there is no fear of Bolshevism here. The entire Muslim population, except some responsible military men and notorious criminals, is absolutely opposed to Bolshevism. They eagerly await a new arrangement, finding, like Christians, the hesitation and delay of the Allies inexplicable. An open reception awaits them. No serious resistance is possible.

• The five-hundred-member gang of Topal Osman from Giresun set out yesterday with a grand ceremony. All demonstrations of enthusiasm were pretended, and the people ridiculed them. The group is heading to Oltu, the Armenian front. It is doubtful that this regiment of eighteen- to twenty-two-year-old brigands, especially given the approaching winter and the bad conditions in which they find themselves, will be willing to continue their way.

• It is rumored here that in ten to fifteen days, the government in İstanbul will send troops to Trabzon and Samsun.

İzmit (from the primate)—September 28

Kızderbent, a Greek village of six to seven hundred families in Karamürsel's jurisdiction, has been besieged by the Millis for five days but continues to resist. The people of Kızderbent sought help through a Turk, but the Turkish messenger brought the news five days later [from the date he left]. It is said

Պրուսա (Առաջնորդէն) – 22 Սեպտեմբեր

Թավշանլուի հայերը Պրուսա կ'ապաստանին ուր իրենց ապաստան եւ հաց կը տրուի:

Մարմարճըգի հայերը իրենց տեղերը դարձած են եւ հոն վերահաստատուած: Մարմարճըգի հայերէն 4 հայ սպաննուած էր եւ սպաննողներուն պարագլուխը՝ Հիւսէյին, հելլէնները ձերբակալելով Կէմլէյիկ ղրկած են:

Նիկոմիդիա (Առաջնորդէն) – 27 Սեպտեմբեր

Նիկոմիդիայէն Արիֆիյէ հասնող կառախումբը երբ դէպի Ատաբազար կը մեկնի, Միլլիճիները պարտէզներու մէջէն կառախումբին վրայ զէնք կը պարպեն: Միլլիճիներուն թիւն էր 50–60: Կառախումբը պարապ էր եւ միայն ապակիները վնասուած են եւ մէկ կին ու մէկ այր վիրաւորուած [են], սակայն Ատաբազարի մէջ խուճապը մեծ կ'ըլլայ եւ հայերուն մեծ մասը կայարան կը վազեն շոգեկառքով Նիկոմիդիա անցնելու համար: Ուրիշ մէկ մասն ալ լսելով որ այլեւս շոգեկառք չպիտի բանի, մազապուր կը փախչին դէպի Արմաշ, իսկ Ատաբազարէն կիւրճի, չէրքէզ ուժեր Արիֆիյէ կը դիմեն Միլլիճիներու վրայ յարձակելու համար եւ արդարեւ կը յաջողին անոնք փախուստի մատնել: Միլլիճիներէն կը մեռնին երեք-չորս մարդ, սակայն անոնք դիակները հետ[երնին] կը տանին: Կիւրճի եւ չէրքէզ ուժեր[էն] մաս մը ինքնաբերաբար վակոններով մինչեւ Սապանճա կուգան, վակոններու մէջ իրարու վրայ խռնուած Ատաբազարի հայերը պաշտպանելու համար: Ատաբազարի հայերը այսօր իրիկուն հասան Նիկոմիդիա եւ անպատսպար կը մնան:

Պրուսա (Առաջնորդէն) – 27 Սեպտեմբեր

Քանի մը օր առաջ Ճէրահի Տ. Ներսէս քահանան 60 անձով եւ Եէնիճէէն ալ 70 անձ, ընդամէնը 130 հայ եւ յոյն, Միլլիճիները առած տարած են: Հելլէն ուժերը զանոնք հալածած են եւ Ինէկէօլ մտած են, սակայն յետոյ դարձեալ քաշուած են իրենց նախորդ դիրքերը: Այս տարուածները Էնկիւրիւի կողմերը ղրկուած են կ'ըսուի:

Տրապիզոն (Առաջնորդական Փոխանորդէն) – 23 Սեպտեմբեր

Սեպտեմբեր 22ին Տրապիզոնի վրայ սաւառնեցան երկու ֆրանսական ջրօղանաւեր, թափելով թրքերէն թռուցիկներ, նոյն եւ նման այն թռուցիկներուն զոր[ս] Օգոստոս 27ին սաւառնող ֆրանսական ջրօղանաւ մը ձգեր էր: Այս թռուցիկները իսլամները [կը] զգուշացնեն պոլշէվիկութենէ, մինչ հոս ոչ մէկ երկիւղ չկայ պոլշէվիկութեան: Ամբողջ իսլամութիւնը,- բացի կարգ մը պատասխանատու զինուորականներէ եւ յայտնի ոճրագործներէ,- բացարձակապէս հակառակ է պոլշէվիկութեան եւ անհամբեր կը սպասէ նոր կարգադրութեան՝ քրիստոնեաներու հետ անբացատրելի գտնելով Համաձայնականներու վարանումը ու յապաղումը: Գրկաբաց ընդունելութիւն մը կը սպասէ անոնց եւ երբեք հաւանական չէ լուրջ դիմադրութիւն մը:

- Կիրասոնի Թօփալ Օսմանի 500 հոգինոց աւազակախումբը երէկ ճամբայ ելաւ մեծ հանդիսութեամբ: Բոլոր խանդավառութիւնները բռնազբօսիկ են եւ ժողովուրդին հեգնանքին նշաւակ: Խումբը կ'երթայ դէպի Օլթի, հայկական ճակատը: Կասկածելի է որ այս 18էն 22 տարեկան յելուզակներէ բաղկացեալ գունդը, նկատի առնելով մանաւանդ մօտալուտ ձմեռը եւ այն վատ պայմանները, որոնց մէջ կը գտնուին, ուզեն շարունակել իրենց ճամբան:

- Զրոյց կը շրջի հոս թէ 10–15 օրէն Պոլսոյ կառավարութիւնն Տրապիզոն եւ Սամսոն զինուոր պիտի ղրկէ:

Նիկոմիդիա (Առաջնորդէն) – 28 Սեպտեմբեր

Գարայ-Մուրսալի ենթակայ Գըզտէվրէնտ [Գըզտէրպէնտ] անուն յոյն գիւղ մը, 6–700 տուն, հինգ օրէ ի վեր պաշարուած է Միլլիճիներէ եւ կը դիմադրէ: Գըզտէվրէնտցիք [Գըզտէրպէնտցիք] թուրքի մը միջոցաւ օգնութիւն կ'ուզեն, բայց թղթաբեր թուրքը հինգ օր վերջը լուրը կը բերէ:

that there are Greek soldiers in Keramet or Greek soldiers will be sent from İzmit. If this news is not confirmed, along with Kızderbent, the Armenian villages of Avcıköy [Merdigöz] and Yalakdere will also be massacred and destroyed, as they are only two hours away from Kızderbent.

It is said that the Millis demanded one hundred fifty to two hundred weapons from the people of Kızderbent. Those weapons were allegedly given [to the people] by the Greek soldiers.

Bursa (from the locum tenens)—September 29[94]

It is heard that the Millis have taken the beautiful girls and women aged fifteen and above to unknown places from the two villages of Yenice and Cerrah.

Several young escapees came here from Bilecik by mountain road and said that the Millis had perpetrated everything in Bilecik: robbery, violence, crime, and so on. These young people, accompanied by the priest Sarkis of Marmaracık, presented themselves to the commander of the Hellenic forces, General Dimitro Yuvan, and told him about the incident.

After looting shops, beating the people on the pretext that they possessed weapons, and kidnapping beautiful girls and women, the Armenian and Greek peoples of the villages of Bilecik have been completely displaced and driven to unknown places.

İzmit (from the primate)—September 29

Some of the Geyve massacre survivors have been aided and abetted by Muslim Georgians in this area, as confirmed by those who survived and came to İzmit, thanks to them. They related that the Millis found and ruthlessly slaughtered more than thirty old and young people who had taken shelter in the mountains, to the point of disgusting even Muslims with their brutality.

It is being said that there are still mostly Greeks and a small number of Armenians, altogether about one hundred fugitives, who are being protected and kept by the Georgians.

İzmit (from the primate)—October 2[95]

The Muslim villages around Avcıköy [Merdigöz] have joined the Millis and sent word to Avcıköy and Yalakdere that the people will be massacred and the Armenian villages will be burned. On the morning of September 30, the Millis burned, using cannons, Kızderbent [Kızdevrent], the village of seven hundred Greek families, located an hour and a half or two away. It is not yet clear whether the population managed to escape or was massacred.

Two Greeks and one Armenian were sent from Avcıköy to bring information, but all three have not returned. Taking shelter in Keramet can be ruled out for them because it has been burned. Consequently, if the Greeks of Kızderbent could not escape to the mountains, they may have been completely slaughtered.

The fire in Keramet was visible in Avcıköy. Avcıköy has one hundred households, with five hundred people, while Yalakdere has seventy households, with about two hundred fifty people. They have all gone down to Karamürsel [Karamursal] to escape to İstanbul.

Some of them came to İzmit by steamer today. Two hundred guns were fired at the steamer from the three-hundred-family Turkish village of Karamürsel-Ereğli. Fortunately, no harm was done.

There are rumors that Ortaköy and Büyük-Yeniköy of Orhangazi [Pazarköy] have been set to fire. The Armenian village of Kılıc in Yalova is under siege.

İzmit—October 5

When the people of Avcıköy [Merdigöz] and Yalakdere fled to Karamürsel [Karamursal] and İstanbul

Կ'ըսուի թէ Քէրէմէթ յոյն զինուոր[ներ] կան եւ կամ Նիկոմիդիայէ յոյն զինուորներ պիտի ղրկուին: Եթէ այս լուրը չհաստատուի, Գըզտէվրէնտի [Գըզտէրպէնտի] հետ Մերտիկէօզ եւ Եալազտէրէ հայ գիւղերն ալ պիտի կոտորուին ու քանդուին, վասնզի Գըզտէվրէնտէն [Գըզտէրպէնտէն] հազիւ 2 ժամ հեռու կը գտնուին:

Միլլիճիները զըզտէվրէնտցիներէն [Գըզտէրպէնտցիներէն] 150–200 զէնք կը պահանջեն, կ'ըսուի: Այդ զէնքերը իբր թէ յոյն զինուորները տուած են եղեր:

Պրուսա (Առաջնորդական Տեղապահէն) – 29 Սեպտեմբեր

Կը լսուի թէ Եէնիճէի եւ Ճերահի երկու գիւղերուն 15էն վեր գեղանի աղջիկները եւ կիները Միլլիճիք անծանօթ տեղեր տարած են:

Լեռնային ճանապարհով փախստական քանի մը երիտասարդներ Պիլէճիկէն հոս եկան եւ պատմեցին թէ Պիլէճիկի մէջ ամէն ինչ գործած են Միլլիճիք՝ կողոպուտ, բռնութիւն, ոճիր եւայլն: Այս երիտասարդները ընկերակցութեամբ Մարմարճըզի Տ. Սարգիս քահանային հելլէն զօրաց հրամանատար Զօր. Տիմիթրօ Եուվանի ներկայացան եւ եղելութիւնը պատմեցին:

Պիլէճիկի շրջակայ գիւղերու հայ եւ յոյն ժողովուրդը ամբողջութեամբ տեղահան ըրած են եւ անծանօթ վայրեր տարած են, նախ խանութները կողոպտելէ, զէնքը պատրուակ ընելով ծեծելէ եւ գեղեցիկ աղջիկները եւ կիները առեւանգելէ յետոյ:

Նիկոմիդիա (Առաջնորդէն) – 29 Սեպտեմբեր

Կէյվէ[ի] ջարդերէն ազատողներէն ոմանք այս շրջանակին մէջ իսլամ կիւրճիներու կողմէ օգնութիւն գտած եւ պատսպարուած են, ինչպէս անոնց շնորհիւ ազատելով Նիկոմիդիա եկողներէ կը հաստատուի: Անոնք կը պատմեն թէ Միլլիճիները լեռները ապաստանողներէն 30էն աւելի մեծ, պզտիկ գտած ու անխնայ ջարդած են՝ իսլամներու իսկ զզուանք առթելու չափ վայրագութեամբ:

Դեռ կան, կ'ըսուի, մեծ մասամբ յոյն եւ փոքր մաս մը հայ, ընդամէնը 100ի չափ փախստականներ, որոնք կիւրճիները կը պաշտպանեն ու կը պահեն:

Նիկոմիդիա (Առաջնորդէն) – 2 Հոկտեմբեր

Մերտիկէօզի շրջակայ իսլամ գիւղերը Միլլիճիներու յարելով Մերտիկէօզ եւ Եալազտէրէ լուր կը ղրկեն թէ հայ գիւղերը պիտի ջարդենք եւ պիտի այրենք: 1½–2 ժամ հեռու գտնուած Գըզ-Տէվրէնտ [Գըզտէրպէնտ] 700 տուն յոյն գիւղն ալ Սեպտեմբերի 30ի առտուն Միլլիճիները թնդանօթով կ'այրեն: Դեռ չէ կրցած հասկցուիլ թէ բնակչութիւնը կրցա՞ծ է փախ[չ]իլ թէ ջարդուած է:

Մերտիկէօզէն երկու յոյն եւ մէկ հայ կը ղրկուին տեղեկութիւն բերելու, բայց երեքն ալ չեն դառնար այլեւս: Քէրէմէթ ալ ապաստանած չեն կրնար ըլլալ, վասնզի ան ալ այրած է: Հետեւաբար Գըզ-Տէրպէնտի յոյները լեռները եթէ չեն կրցած փախչիլ, ամբողջ ջարդուած են:

Քէրէմէթի հրդեհը Մերտիկէօզէ տեսնուած է: Մերտիկէօզ ունի 100 տնուոր՝ 500 հոգի, իսկ Եալազտէրէ 70 տուն՝ 250ի [չափ] ժողովուրդ: Անոնք սարսափահար կ'իջնեն Գարամուսալ՝ Պոլիս փախ[չ]ելու համար:

Անոնցմէ մէկ մասը շոգենաւով այսօր Նիկոմիդիա եկաւ: Շոգենաւին վրայ 200 ձեռք զէնք կը պարպուի 300 տնուոր թուրք Գարամուսալ-Էրէյլիի գիւղէն: Բարեբաղդաբար վնաս մը չէ պատահած:

Զրոյց կայ թէ Պազարու Օրթաքէօյ եւ Մեծ-Նոր-Գիւղն ալ կը հրդեհեն: Եալովայի Գըլըճ հայ գիւղը պաշարուած է:

Նիկոմիդիա– 5 Հոկտեմբեր

Գըզ Տէվրէնտ յոյն գիւղին Միլլիճիներէն այրուելուն վրայ մերտիկէօզցիք եւ եալազտէրէցիք երբ

after the Greek village of Kızderbent was set on fire by the Millis, the lieutenant governor of Karamürsel urged them not to move out or flee, saying: "Have no fear, I will send forces, do not be afraid, do not take the household goods," and he sent six gendarmes for the Millis to come and surrender to them. The primate appealed to İzmit's lieutenant governor to send a telegram to the lieutenant governor of Karamürsel asking him to let the people flee the village with their belongings and take refuge in İstanbul. However, İzmit's lieutenant governor, İbrahim Hakkı Bey, refused to send the telegram, explaining [that] Karamürsel's lieutenant governor is Milli and that communication between İzmit and Karamürsel has been severed for quite some time and that there are no telegrams.

- Credible people coming to İzmit from Yalova say that at the time of the burning of Kızderbent, the people of Kızderbent fought against the Millis for eight to ten hours. Ten or twelve of them were slaughtered, and forty to fifty Millis were killed. The people of Kızderbent, all of them, have taken refuge in the Turkish villages in the mountains and have been saved.
- In Keramet, out of 150 Armenian families, only 17 families are left now. [The rest of the] Armenians have fled.

In retaliation, in the Turkish villages of Bayındır [Kokarca] 50 houses, in Selimiye [Ayvalıca] 40 to 50 houses, in Yürükler 40 to 50 houses, in Ormuzdere 30 to 40 houses, and in Çakırlı 200 houses of Muslim muhacirs and Turks have been thoroughly looted and burned [by Greeks]. The areas near Orhangazi [Pazarköy] and Yalova are now under Greek rule. The Greek authority captured İzmit two hours before noon on October 2.

İzmit (from the primate)—October 5

According to information received from Bolu, 120–130 young and old male people were massacred and burned. There are about 20 to 25 murdered women, some of whom were burned in their homes. The remaining women, 350–400, are alive and engaged in sewing all day for the Millis, each receiving a loaf of bread daily. One of the women sent a letter by way of Zonguldak, asking if there is a way to free them from Bolu because they want to escape. The women are afraid. Urban Turks and Millis do not let them leave. About 25 to 30 of the men of Bolu fled to Zonguldak and İstanbul and survived. Barely fifteen to twenty men are left in Bolu. Some of the women from Bolu are obtaining credentials by saying they would like to go to Turkish villages to make their living. They are also sending horse drivers from Zonguldak to take women to Zonguldak at a high cost secretly, but if the Millis and the urban Turks learn that they are fleeing in this way, they fear their lives will be in danger.

Aleppo (from the National Union)—September 18[96]

General Gouraud, the high commander of the Eastern Army, arrived in Aleppo on September 12 and left two days later. After his departure, the director of the French Immigration and Armenian Assistance, Captain Vidal, invited the entire body of the National Union and the spiritual leaders of the three Armenian denominations to an urgent meeting where he made the following statements on behalf of the general.

"Due to very grave issues, I have invited you here. Due to the provisions of the Peace Treaty, the French army will evacuate Cilicia and hand it over to the Turks. There are now thirteen thousand deported Armenians and six thousand Armenian orphans there, whom the general cannot leave prey to Turks' revenge after his army's withdrawal; therefore, he will move them out of Cilicia. He will bring the orphans and four thousand refugees to Aleppo. Four thousand refugees will be resettled in Dörtyol and surrounding villages (with the latest arrangement, Dörtyol is part of the İskenderun district, and the entire region has been annexed to the Aleppo province, which is autonomous and completely in-

որ կը փախչին ի Գարամուսալ եւ ի Պոլիս, Գարամուսալի գայմագամը կը ստիպէ որ չելլեն, չփախչին, վասնզի վախ չկայ, ես ոյժ պիտի ղրկեմ, մի՛ վախնաք եւ կարասինները մի՛ տանիք կ'ըսէ ու վեց ժանտարմաներ է ղրկած որ Միլլիճիները գան անոնց թէսլիմ ըլլան: Առաջնորդը Նիկոմիդիոյ միւթէսարրըֆին կը դիմէ հեռագիր քաշելու համար Գարամուսալի գայմագամին, որ արգելք չնէ ու թողու որ բոլոր ժողովուրդն ալ գոյքերով փախչի գիւղէն ու Պոլիս ապաստանի: Սակայն Նիկոմիդիոյ միւթէսարրըֆը՝ Իպրահիմ Հազզը պէյ, չ'ուզեր քաշել այդ հեռագիրը, ըսելով [թէ] Գարամուսալի գայմագամը Միլլիճի է եւ բաւական ժամանակ կ'ընէ որ հաղորդակցութիւնը ընդմէջ Նիկոմիդիոյ եւ Գարամուսալի խզուած է ու հեռագիր ալ չկայ:

- Եալօվայէն Նիկոմիդիա եկող արժանահաւատ անձեր կ'ըսեն թէ Գըզ Տէրվէնտի [Գըզտէրպէնտի] կրակին, գըզտէվրէնտցիք [Գըզտէրպէնտցիք] 8–10 ժամ Միլլիճիներուն դէմ կռուած են: Իրենցմէ 10–12 հոգի ջարդուած են, իսկ Միլլիճիներուն կողմէ սպաննուած են 40–50 հոգիներ: Գըզտէվրէնտցիք [Գըզտէրպէնտցիք] ամբողջ լեռներն թուրք գիւղեր ապաստանած եւ ազատած են:

- Քէրէմէթ, ուր 150 տուն հայ կար, հիմա միայն 17 տուն մնացած է: Հայք փախած են:

Ի վրէժ Գօզարճայ 50 տուն, Այվալճայ 40–50 տուն, Էօրիւկլեր՝ 40–50 տուն, Որմուզտէրէ 30–40 տուն, Չագըլը 200 տուն մի[ւհ]աճիրներու եւ թուրքի գիւղեր ամբողջապէս թալանուած ու այրուած են: Այժմ յոյն իշխանութեան տակ են Պազարու կողմը, ինչպէս նաեւ Եալովայի կողմը: Իսկ յոյն իշխանութիւնն Հոկտեմբեր 2ին կէսօրէն երկու ժամ առաջ Նիկոմիդիան կը գրաւէ:

Նիկոմիդիա (Առաջնորդէն) – 5 Հոկտեմբեր

Պօլսէն առնուած տեղեկութեանց համաձայն այր մարդիկ, մեծ-պզտիկ 120–130 հոգի ջարդուած, այրուած են. կին մարդոցմէ սպաննուած կան 20–25 հոգիի չափ, որոնցմէ ոմանք տան մէջ այրուած: Մնացած կին մարդիկ, 350–400 հոգի, ողջ մնացած են եւ օրական մէյ մէկ հացով մինչեւ իրիկուն Միլլիճիներու կար կը կարեն: Զօնկուլտաքի ճամբով գիր ղրկեր է կնիկներէն մին որ զիրենք Պօլսէն ազատելու ճարը նային, վասնզի փախչիլ կ'ուզեն. կին մարդիկ կը վախնան. քաղաքացի թուրքերը ու Միլլիճիները չեն թողուր: Պօլուցի այր մարդոցմէ 25–30 հոգիի չափ ազատած են փախչելով Զօնկուլտաք եւ Կ. Պոլիս: Պօլուի մէջ 15–20 հոգիի չափ հազիւ այր մարդ կամ արու մնացած է: Պօլուի կիներէն ոմանք *չէմիքա* կ'առնեն, թուրք գիւղերն երթանք հաց ճարենք ըսելով: Զօնկուլտաքէն ալ ձիապան կը ղրկեն ու սուղ գնով տաճիկ գիւղէն գաղտուկ Զօնկուլտաք կ'իջեցնեն, բայց եթէ Միլլիճիք եւ քաղաքացի թուրքերը իմանան թէ այսպէս կը փախչին, կը վախնան որ իրենց ալ կեանքն կը վտանգուի:

Հալէպ (Ազգային Միութենէն) – 18 Սեպտեմբեր

Արեւելքի բանակի վերին հրամանատար Զօր. Կուրօ Սեպտեմբեր 12ին Հալէպ հասաւ եւ երկու օր յետոյ մեկնեցաւ: Իր մեկնումէն յետոյ ֆրանսական ներգաղթի եւ Հայկական Խնամատարութեան տնօրէն Capitaine Vidal Ազգային Միութեան ամբողջ կազմը եւ երեք յարանուանութիւններու պետերը ստիպողական կերպով իր քով հրաւիրեց եւ յանուն Զօրավարին ըրաւ հետեւեալ յայտարարութիւնները:

«Շատ ծանրակշիռ խնդիրներու պատճառով ձեզ իմ քովս հրաւիրեցի. Հաշտութեան Դաշնագրի տրամադրութեանց պատճառներով ֆրանսական բանակը Կիլիկիան պիտի պարպէ եւ յանձնէ զայն թուրքերուն. հոն այժմ կան 13,000 տարագիր հայ եւ 6000 հայ որբ, զորս Զօրավարը չի կրնար թուրքերուն վրէժխնդրութեան զոհ ընել իր բանակին քաշուելէն յետոյ, ուստի եւ զանոնք ալ պիտի հանէ Կիլիկիայէն եւ որբերն ու 4000 գաղթականներ Հալէպ պիտի բերուին. 4000 գաղթական Տէօրթեօլի եւ շրջակայ գիւղերուն մէջ պիտի տեղաւորուին (վերջին կարգադրութեամբ Տէօրթեօլ Ալէքսանտրէթի Գազային մաս կը կազմէ, իսկ այս ամբողջ շրջանը միացած է Հալէպի վիլայէթին,

dependent of Damascus). The rest will be settled in Beirut. I have been entrusted with caring for all of them as the high official of work in this area. Those migrants who can work will find work in my workshops, and I will care in shelters for those who cannot work.

"As for the orphans, I will have separate orphanages for them. I will place all the orphans in my orphanages along with the orphans of the Armenian orphanage of Aleppo. I will hand over only the physically disabled and the ill (lame, blind, etc.) to the orphanage director, Reverend Shirajian, and I will lend him the necessary relief. The orphans, whether boys or girls, will be educated in French education and spirit. The principals and teachers will be French clergy and nuns from France, and the education and the orphans' upbringing will be purely French. By doing this, we will succeed in raising an educated generation that will be very useful for Greater Armenia to be formed in the future. With deep respect for their religion and faith, we will educate and bring them up."

Those present did not respond immediately to these grave statements. Instead, they asked the captain to make these statements in writing.

It is clear from this decision made by the French government that the people who had been gathered from the deserts and who migrated to Cilicia will once again be deported and taken to a foreign land. The survivors who had migrated from Syria to Cilicia, driven by the pressure of British and French forces, will once again be returned to Syria and settled there.

Mersin (from the [Armenian] National Union)—September 21

The French authorities in Adana proposed that more than fourteen thousand uprooted refugees from Kozan [Sis], Bahçe, Saimbeyli [Hacın], and other Armenian-populated places, who had taken refuge in Adana, leave for İstanbul, İzmir, America, Dörtyol, and İskenderun at the expense of the French authorities. Enrollments to this effect in the hands of special functionaries needed to be completed by September 14. Subsidy for bread for those refusing to leave was supposed to cease as of that date. Although the offer was not binding, it contained specific intentions that threaten to put Armenians back in a state of being vagabonds open to new suffering.

Knowing that this unenviable situation awaited them, almost all the Armenians rejected this offer, stating that they would rather die in Cilicia than migrate elsewhere.

It is said that the Turks, who are away from the city and had fled to the çetes, offered this condition to the French authorities to return to the city, arguing that they fear the Armenian presence and feel intimidated. General Gouraud had planned this decision in advance, but its execution was reserved for this date.

Saimbeyli's military campaign has not yet been organized, although feverish work is in process for its success.

It appears that the French authorities will bring the Armenians of Osmaniye also to Adana because of the dangers around there. This presents a new disaster for the Armenians. In an important battle in Osmaniye, the Armenians are fighting side by side valiantly with the French forces, but considerable enemy forces are pressing the French to abandon Osmaniye, especially since Amanos had already been vacated of Armenians.

The movement of çetes in Adana is somewhat weak, and the people have begun to do some work. In the Üreğli plain, it is the Armenian forces that continue to facilitate the essential task of provisioning

որ ինքնավար է եւ անկախ բոլորովին Դամասկոսէն): Մնացածներն ալ Պէյրութ պիտի հաստատուին: Ասոնց բոլորին հոգատարութիւնը ինծ յանձնուած է իբրեւ այս շրջանի աշխատանքի վերին պաշտօնեայ: Գաղթականներէն անոնք որ կրնան աշխատիլ, անոնց գործ պիտի հայթայթեն իմ աշխատանոցներուս մէջ, իսկ աշխատանքի անընդունակ եղողները պատսպարաններու մէջ պիտի խնամեմ:

Գալով որբերուն, անոնց համար առանձին որբանոցներ պիտի ունենամ, Հալէպի մէջ գտնուած Հայկական Որբանոցի որբերն ալ բոլորը պիտի տեղաւորեմ իմ որբանոցներուն մէջ. միայն մարմնական թերութիւն ունեցողները ու վատառողջները (կաղ, կոյր եւայլն) պիտի յանձնեմ որբանոցի տնօրէն Վերապատուելի Ճիրաճեանին եւ հարկ եղած նպաստը պիտի տամ անոր: Իսկ որբերը, ըլլան մանչ կամ աղջիկ, պիտի կրթուին ֆրանսական կրթութեամբ եւ ոգիով, տնօրէնները եւ ուսուցիչները պիտի ըլլան Ֆրանսայէն գալիք ֆրանսացի père-եր եւ soeur-եր եւ կրթութիւնը, դաստիարակութիւնը պիտի ըլլայ զուտ ֆրանսական ու այս միջոցով պիտի յաջողինք հասցնել կրթուած սերունդ մը, որ ապագային կազմուելիք Մեծ Հայաստանին համար պիտի ըլլայ շատ օգտակար: Խորին յարգանք տածելով դէպի անոնց կրօնքն ու հաւատքը, մենք պիտի կրթենք ու դաստիարակենք զիրենք»:

Այս ծանրակշիռ յայտարարութեանց ներկաները անմիջապէս չեն պատասխաներ ու կը խնդրեն որ գրաւոր կերպով ընէ Capitaine-ը այդ յայտարարութիւնները:

Ֆրանսական կառավարութեան այս որոշումէն կը հասկցուի թէ անապատներէն հաւաքուած եւ Կիլիկիա ներգաղթող ժողովուրդն է որ անգամ մը եւս տեղահան պիտի ըլլայ եւ պիտի տարուի օտար հողամաս մը: Այդ վերապրողները որոնք անգլիական եւ ֆրանսական ուժերու ստիպումին տակ Սուրիայէն ներգաղթած էին դէպի Կիլիկիա, անգամ մըն ալ Սուրիա կը դարձուին եւ հոն կը հաստատուին:

Մերսին (Ազգային Միութենէն) – 21 Սեպտեմբեր

Ատանայի ֆրանսական իշխանութեանց կողմէն հոն ապաստանած 14000է աւելի սսեցի, պաղչէցի, հաճընցի եւ այլ հայաբնակ վայրերէ բռնահան գաղթականներուն առաջարկուեցաւ Ատանայէն հեռանալ Կ. Պոլիս, Իզմիր, Ամերիկա, Տէօրթեօլ, Իսկէնտէրուն ֆրանսական իշխանութեանց ծախքով: Այս մասին արձանագրութիւնք պիտի լինէին մինչեւ 14 Սեպտեմբեր մասնաւոր պաշտօնեաներու ձեռքով: Մեկնիլ չուզողներուն հացի նպաստը պիտի դադրի այդ թուականէն սկսեալ: Առաջարկը թէեւ պարտաւորիչ չէ, սակայն իր մէջ կը պարունակէ որոշ նպատակներ, որոնք կը սպառնան հայեր կրկին մատնելու թափառիկ վիճակի եւ նոր տառապանքներու:

Հայերը գիտնալով այս աննախանձելի վիճակը որ իրենց կը սպասէ, գրեթէ ամբողջութեամբ մերժած են այս առաջարկը եւ յայտնած են թէ կը նախընտրեն մեռնիլ Կիլիկիոյ մէջ քան այլուր գաղթել:

Կ'ըսուի թէ թուրքերը, որոնք քաղաքէն դուրս կը գտնուին եւ չէթէներու քով փախած էին, քաղաք դառնալու համար ֆրանսական իշխանութեանց պայման դրած են այսպիսի առաջարկութիւն մը, քանի որ հայուն ներկայութենէն կը վախնան ու կը խրտչին: Այս որոշումը նախապէս ծրագրուած էր Զօր. Կուրօյի կողմէն, սակայն գործադրութիւնը վերապահուած էր այս թուականին:

Հաճընի զինուորական արշաւը տակաւին չէ կրցած կազմակերպուիլ, թէեւ ոգի [ի] բոլին կ'աշխատուի ատոր յաջողութեան համար:

Օսմանիյէի հայութիւնն ալ,- այդ կողմի վտանգուելէն,- կ'երեւի թէ ֆրանսական իշխանութիւնք Ատանա պիտի բերեն, ինչ որ նոր աղէտ մըն է հայութեան համար: Օսմանիյէ մղուող կարեւոր ճակատամարտի մը մէջ հայերը ֆրանսական ուժերու հետ կողք կողքի կը կռուին քաջաբար, սակայն թշնամի կարեւոր ուժեր կը ստիպեն որ ֆրանսացիք Օսմանիյէն լքեն, երբ մանաւանդ Ամանոս պարպուած է նախապէս հայերէ:

Ատանայի մէջ չէթէական շարժումը մասամբ թոյլ է եւ ժողովուրդը քիչ մը սկսած է զբաղիլ իր

the city and monitoring the security of the road between Adana and Karataş. Cotton and sesame remain untouched in all the fields, and husbandry cannot continue. This is primarily due to the lack of security, livestock, working arms, and other means: a situation that ultimately endangers the state of the region and exposes it to future famine.

Mersin, Tarsus, and Adana remain besieged, facing the horror of çetes, and in a state of broken trade; therefore, all Armenians and other Christians living [in the area] live in poverty, when we consider the exorbitant prices.

A 250-member Armenian military force has been formed in Mersin by French order.

On September 18, General Gouraud officially gave the following order to Mersin's French governor: "Immediately take steps to establish a Turkish government and appoint the necessary Turkish officials in office ad hoc."

The one hundred thousand surviving Armenians in the plain of Cilicia, and the entire Christian element, have thus been exposed to a critical situation leading to adversity with catastrophic consequences beyond the scope of these tight lines.

On the other hand, it has been learned that the view of the French government is to respect the signature it placed under the Turkish Treaty, completely separating the issue of the re-establishment of a Turkish government from the Milli movement, by which the Armenians of Cilicia—whom the Millis are threatening, this time with special warnings made just a little while ago, "to completely annihilate the remaining Armenians and seal the Cilician issue forever"—will live under the attacks of the çetes on the one hand and the pressure of a Turkish government on the other.

Mersin (from Dr. Ourfallian)—September 27

To support the besieged Armenians of Saimbeyli [Hacın], a purely Armenian detachment of five hundred was formed with the knowledge and assistance of the French government, and they were provided with ammunition, machine guns, weapons, and so on. The Armenians spent seventy thousand liras for the group's leadership and handed it over to officers named Armaghanian and Kevork Chavush. They were in a village called Akarca on their way to Saimbeyli. However, on the night of September 22, suddenly, they were surrounded by 2,200 French soldiers with eight cannons, tanks, machine guns, and more. The Armenian forces, bewildered by this surprise, demanded to know why. When they were shown the French government's order to disarm them, the Armenian officers responded: "One soldier alone would have sufficed for the French government to have this order carried out because we were going to liberate Saimbeyli under the French flag and with the ammunition and weapons provided by the French government. Since the French government wants to disarm us, we would be ready to hand over everything to them according to their order, but it would have been better to have brought a representative from the [Armenian] National Union who dispatched us," and they surrendered to the French officers without any slight action. The French officers' first task was to take them as captives to Karataş. They arrived there extremely weary. They were immediately placed in a steamer and arrived in Mersin. (Although the captured soldiers—cavalry and infantry—numbered 500, many took refuge in Adana, fleeing (unarmed), bringing the total number of the rest to precisely 202). They arrived in Mersin on the morning of September 25 at seven o'clock after suffering significant deprivation and insults from the steamer's Algerian guards. After waiting for six hours in barges in front of Mersin like

գործով, Իւրէյլիի դաշտին մէջ հայ ոյժերն են որ կը շարունակեն քաղաքին պարենաւորման կենսական գործը դիւրացնել ինչպէս նաեւ Ատանա-Գարաթաշ ճամբուն ապահովութեան հսկել: Բոլոր դաշտերուն մէջ բամպակն ու կնճիթը կը մնան անքաղ եւ հողագործական աշխատութիւնք կարելի չեն ըլլար շարունակուիլ, նախ առ ի չգոյէ ապահովութեան, լծկան անասուններու, աշխատող բազուկներու եւ այլ միջոցներու. կացութիւն մը, որ ի սպառ կը վտանգէ [երկրին] վիճակը՝ մատնելով զայն ապագայ սովի:

Մերսին-Տարսոն-Ատանա կը մնան միշտ պաշարուած եւ չէթէական սարսափի դէմ եւ կազմալուծեալ առեւտրական վիճակի մը մէջ, այնպէս որ ապրող բոլոր հայութիւնն ու քրիստոնեայ ուրիշ ազգերը, երբ նկատի առնենք կեանքի տարապայման սղութիւնն ալ՝ մատնուած են յետին չքաւորութեան:

Մերսինի մէջ ֆրանսական հրամանով կազմուած է 250 հոգիէ բաղկացեալ հայ զինուորական ոյժ:

Սեպտեմբեր 18ին Զօր. Կուրօ Մերսինի ֆրանսական կառավարիչին պաշտօնապէս տուաւ հետեւեալ հրամանը. «Անմիջապէս միջոցներ ձեռք առէք հաստատելու համար թրքական կառավարութիւն եւ առ այդ պէտք եղած թուրք պաշտօնեաները զետեղեցէք իրենց պաշտօնին վրայ»:

Կիլիկիոյ հողին վրայ վերապրող 100,000 հայութիւնը, ընդ որս համայն քրիստոնեայ տարրը, կը դրուին այս կերպով քրիթիք կացութեան մը առջեւ որմէ յառաջ գալիք անպատեհութեանց իսկապէս որքան աղէտաբեր ըլլալը աւելորդ է պարզել այս անձուկ տողերուն մէջ:

Միւս կողմէն կ'իմացուի թէ ֆրանսական կառավարութեան տեսակէտը եղած է յարգել իր դրած ստորագրութիւնը թուրք դաշնագրին տակ, Միլլիական շարժումէն բոլորովին անջատելով թրքական կառավարութեան մը վերահաստատութեան հարցը, որով մէկ կողմէ չէթէական յարձակումներու իսկ միւս կողմէ հաստատուած թուրք կառավարութեան մը ճնշումին տակ պիտի ապրի Կիլիկիոյ հայութիւնը, որուն դեռ քիչ առաջ Միլլիականները մասնաւոր ազդարարութիւններով կը սպառնային այս անգամ «կատարելապէս բնաջնջել մնացեալ հայութիւնը եւ կիլիկեան հարցը փակել ընդմիշտ»:

Մերսին (տրքթ. Ուրֆալլեանէ) – 27 Սեպտեմբեր

Հաճնոյ պաշարեալ հայութեան օժանդակելու համար 500 հոգիէ բաղկացեալ զուտ հայ խումբ մը կազմուած էր ֆրանսական կառավարութեան գիտակցութեամբ եւ օգնութեամբ, ատոնց տրամադրուելով ռազմանիւթ, միթրայէօզ, զէնք եւայլն: Խումբին ղեկավարութեան համար հայերը ծախսած էին 70 հազար ոսկի եւ յանձնած Արմաղանեան եւ Գէորգ Չավուշ անուն սպաներուն: Ատոնք կը գտնուէին Ախարճա անուն գիւղ մը, ատկից ուղեւորելու համար դէպի Հաճըն: Սակայն 22 Սեպտեմբերի գիշերը յանկարծ ատոնք կը շրջապատուին 2200 ֆրանսացի զինուորներէ, որոնք ունէին 8 թնդանօթ, թանք, միթրայէօզ եւայլն: Հայ ուժերը այլայլմէ եղած այս անակնկալին առջեւ, կ'ուզեն իմանալ պատճառը: Երբ ատոնք ցոյց կուտան զինաթափելու համար ֆրանսական կառավարութեան հրամանը, հայ սպաները կը պատասխանեն. «Մէկ զինուոր իսկ բաւական էր ֆրանսական կառավարութեան գործադրել տալու համար այս հրամանը, քանի որ ֆրանսական դրօշի տակ եւ ֆրանսական կառավարութեան [կողմէ] տրամադրուած ռազմանիւթերով եւ զէնքերով կ'երթայինք[ք] ազատելու համար Հաճընը. քանի որ ֆրանսական կառավարութիւնը կ'ուզէ [մեզ] զինաթափել, պատրաստ էինք իրենց յանձնել ամէն ինչ իրենց հրամանին [համաձայն], սակայն աւելի լաւ կ'ըլլար մեզ ղրկող Ազգային Միութենէն ներկայացուցիչ մը բերել», եւ առանց ոեւէ պզտիկ շարժումի կը յանձնուին ֆրանսական սպաներուն: Ֆրանսական սպաներու առաջին գործը կ'ըլլայ գերի վարել զանոնք դէպի Գարա-Թաշ: Ցետին յոգնութիւններով կը հասնին հոն եւ անմիջապէս շոգենաւ մը դրուելով կը հասնին Մերսին: Բռնուած զինուորներուն թիւը ձիաւոր եւ հետեւակ թէեւ 500 էր, սակայն մեծ մասը Ատանա ապաստանած են փախչելով (առանց զէնքի), այնպէս որ ճիշդ 202ի կը յանգէր մնացողներուն թիւը: Ատոնք Մերսին կը հասնին 25 Սեպտեմբերին առտուն ժամը

animals, they were taken out at one o'clock and sent straight to prison, despite the French governor's assurance to the national authorities that if they stayed away from unbecoming movements and threats against the captain on the steamer, they would be placed in a quiet place prepared for them. However, they were sent to prison upon the captain's report, whereas it is understood that it was the Armenian volunteers who were insulted by the Algerian soldiers and not the other way around.

While this was happening in Akarca, other unpleasant and unexpected events were taking place in Adana.

The successor of Brémond hosted a reception to which all religious leaders and national representatives, except the National Union, were invited. Monsignor Keklikian revolted against this unjust act and brought to their attention that "the only official body was the National Union, and that that only body of the Armenian nation should have been invited to this banquet." They answered that they did not recognize such a body. The official presentation to the colonel took place at the same gathering, and the members of the National Union were invited to the government house around evening. When they arrived there, a sentencing decision was read to them in this sense: "Noting that the Armenian body called the National Union is trying to organize an Armenia here, it has been decided to expel the members of the same union from Cilicia's borders." The unfortunate [men] had to comply with this bitter decision. On the same day, they were sent via a truck to Karataş and thence directly to İskenderun via the steamboat *August* to be dispatched from there to places of their choice. The members of the National Union are Dr. Mnatsaganian (chairman), S. Gebenlian (secretary), F. Khanzadian (secretary), G. Ashukian (treasurer), Dr. Salipian (public relations), and Aram Mndigian (lawyer), all of whom were arrested, while M. Boyajian fled. They were joined by S. Shahen (a Hunchak activist who arrived a few months ago) and Shishmanian, an American-Armenian commander of the gendarmerie (by order of the French authorities).

In addition to these two tragic events, the pre-planned relocation of the migrants took place and was executed immediately: two hundred wretched people native of Sivas and Erzurum were taken to Karataş and from Karataş to Mersin (on September 25), where they disembarked in extreme misery and were placed in tents. They will be sent to Yerevan by the first steamer via İstanbul. Gradually, natives of Van [and] Muş and locals would come to be dispatched to Yerevan, and the fourteen thousand migrants from other places would soon be deported to İstanbul, İzmir, America, Egypt, Beirut, İskenderun, Yerevan, Dörtyol, and Aleppo, according to their choices. Thus, the migrants receiving relief from the French government, approximately twenty to twenty-five thousand, would be deported from Adana, Tarsus, and Mersin.

These three major blows have incredibly depressed all Armenians and demoralized them. Everyone is terrified of these unexpected happenings carried out by the French government.

People are speculating about large conspiracies associated with the five hundred Armenian volunteers, as well as the issue of the National Union. We shall write, with reservations, what has been heard and spoken so far. For the volunteer movement of Saimbeyli, it has been said that allegedly they would join the forces of Mustafa Kemal to attack the French forces; as for the National Union, we have already written about the condemnation and what the French government says. Regarding the case of the refugees, the Turks imposed a condition on the French that non-native refugees must be expelled from cities since they did not trust them, and so on. Thereby, all three operations were carried out simultaneously.

On the other hand, some say that the primate and Demirkapoulian, Yeretsian, and Zhamgochian (Hunchaks) have played a very grim role in all these painful events. We write this with reservation. The future will be the judge.

The French government allegedly had one other view: it considered the Armenians as an opposing

7ին, շոգենաւին ալճերիացի պահակներէն խոշոր զրկանք ու նախատինքներու ենթարկուելով: Մերսինի առջեւ 6 ժամ մավունաններուն մէջ անասուններու նման սպասելով ժամը 1ին կը հանուին դուրս եւ կ'առաջնորդուին ուղղակի բանտ, թէեւ ֆրանսացի կառավարիչը վստահացուցած է Ազգային իշխանութիւնները թէ՝ եթէ ատոնք շոգենաւի մէջ նաւապետին դէմ անհաճոյ շարժումներ եւ սպառնալիք չընէին, պատրաստել տրուած հանգիստ տեղ մը պիտի դրուէին, սակայն նաւապետին *քաբորթ*ին վրայ ատոնք առաջնորդուած էին բանտ, մինչդեռ կը հասկցուի թէ ալճերիացի զինուորներու կողմէ նախատուած են հայ կամաւորներն եւ ոչ թէ հակառակը:

Երբ սա բանը Ախարճայի մէջ տեղի կ'ունենար, անդին Ատանայի մէջ ուրիշ անախորժ եւ անակնկալ դէպքեր տեղի կ'ունենային:

Brémond-ի յաջորդը ընդունելութիւն մը կը սարքէ որուն կը հրաւիրուին բոլոր կրօնական պետերն եւ ազգային ներկայացուցիչներ, բացի Ազգային Միութենէն: Այս անիրաւ աքթին դէմ Գերապայծառ Քէքլիկեան Եպիսկոպոս կը ծառանայ եւ կը զգացնէ իրենց թէ «պաշտօնական միակ մարմինը Ազգային Միութիւնն էր, եւ պէտք էր որ հայ ազգին այդ միակ մարմինը հրաւիրուէր այս հաւաքոյթին». սակայն անոնք կը պատասխանեն որ այդպիսի մարմին մը չէին ճանչնար: Colonel-ին պաշտօնական ներկայացումը կը կատարուի նոյն հաւաքոյթին մէջ եւ երեկոյեան մօտ Ազգային Ժողովոյ անդամներ կառավարատուն կը հրաւիրուին: Երբ անոնք կը հասնին հոն, իրենց կը կարդացուի դատապարտութեան որոշում մը սա իմաստով. «Նկատելով որ Ազգային Միութիւն ըսուած հայ մարմինը հոս Հայաստան մը կազմակերպելու կը ձգտի, որոշուած է նոյն միութեան անդամները արտահանել կիլիկեան սահմանէն դուրս»: Խեղճերուն ուրիշ բան չի մնար եթէ [ոչ] համակերպիլ այս դառն որոշման: Այդ օրն իսկ բեռի օթօմօպիլով մը ճամբայ կը դրուին դէպի Գարաթաշ եւ անկից Օկիւսթ շոգենաւով կը ղրկուին ուղղակի Իսկէնտէրուն, ուրկից պիտի ղրկուին իբր թէ իրենց ընտրած տեղերը: Ազգային Միութեան անդամներն են (ձերբակալուած) Տր. Մնացականեան (ատենապետ), Ս. Կէպէնլեան (ատենադպիր), Փ. Խանզատեան (ատենադպիր), Կ. Աշըգեան (գանձապետ), Տր. Սալիբեան (յարաբերական պաշտօնեայ), Արամ Մնտիկեան (փաստաբան), Մ. Պօյաճեան (փախած է), իսկ ասոնց կը միանան դարձեալ Ս. Շահէն (հնչակեան գործիչ, որ քանի մը ամիս առաջ եկած էր), ինչպէս նաեւ քաղաքապահ զինուորներու հրամատար (ֆրանսական իշխանութեանց հրամանով) ամերիկահայ Շիշմանեան:

Այս երկու ցաւառիթ դէպքերէն զատ տեղի կ'ունենայ նոյնպէս նախապէս ծրագրուած գաղթականաց տեղափոխումի գործողութիւնը եւ այս միջոցին անմիջապէս գործադրութեան կը դրուի. 200 հատ սեբաստացի եւ կարնեցի խեղճեր Գարաթաշ կը բերուին եւ Գարաթաշէն Մերսին (25 Սեպտեմբերին) յետին թշուառութեան մէջ եւ քաղաք կը հանուին եւ կը տեղաւորուին վրաններու տակ, առաջին շոգենաւով Պօլսոյ ճամբով Երեւան ղրկուելու համար: Հետզհետէ վանեցի, մշեցի եւ տեղացիներ պիտի զան ու ղրկուին Երեւան, իսկ ուրիշ վայրերու թուով 14,000 գաղթականները պիտի արտահանուին քիչ ժամանակի մէջ Պոլիս, Իզմիր, Ամերիկա, Եգիպտոս, Պէյրութ, Իսկէնտէրուն, Երեւան, Տէօրթ-Եօլ, Հալէպ, ըստ իրենց ընտրութեան, այնպէս որ Ատանայէն, Տարսոնէն, Մերսինէն պիտի արտաքսուին այն գաղթականները, որոնք նպաստ կը ստանան ֆրանսական կառավարութենէն, վեր վար թուով 20–25 հազար:

Այս երեք խոշոր հարուածները մեծապէս ընկճած են բովանդակ հայութիւնը եւ զանոնք բարոյալքած: Սարսափի տակ է ամէն ոք այս անակնկալ պատահարներու առջեւ որ տեղի կ'ունենա[ն] ֆրանսական կառավարութեան ձեռքով:

Կ'ենթադրուի թէ 500 հայ կամաւորներու համար ինչպէս նաեւ Ազգային Միութեան խնդրոյն շուրջ խոշոր դաւադրութիւններ երեւան ելած են, յորոց առայժմ վերապահութեամբ պիտի գրենք լռւածը եւ խօսուածը: Հաճնոյն կամաւորական շարժումին համար ըսած են եղեր թէ անոնք Մ[ուսթաֆա] Քէմալի զօրքերուն հետ միանալով պիտի յարձակին ֆրանսական ոյժերու վրայ, իսկ Ազգային Միութեան դատապարտութեան մասին գրեցինք արդէն թէ ինչ կ'ըսէ ֆրանսական կառավարութիւնը, իսկ գաղթականներուն պարագան, թուրքերու կողմէ պայման պարտադրուած

element to implementing the decision of the [Treaty of] Sèvres.

This sums up the general situation in Cilicia.

Mr. Damadian was informed of his exodus abroad after a few days [from the rest of the National Union members], but he replied that they can remove only his body with a bayonet; he will leave only when those sent him called him back.

The only and foremost reason for these troubles is the Catholicos of Cilicia. He sits in Beirut and often in Lebanon [*sic*] to secure his comfort. We have learned from the last dispatch that he has left for Damascus.

Last Hour (with reservation)—The National Union of Adana has been reorganized upon the primate's indication, but we do not know who they are or whether the French have accepted them.

After disarming the Armenian soldiers, the French government issued a decree [for the Turks], saying: "We disarmed the Armenian soldiers; you can come to the city safely." They sent thirty to forty automobiles to the Turks in Kurttepe; however, the Turks killed all the drivers and seized the automobiles. Triggered by this, the force that disarmed the Armenians attacked the çetes, who suffered more than one thousand casualties. Thereupon, according to the latest news, the French wanted a five-hundred-strong Armenian force, in response to which the Armenians said that their disarmed force should be returned, along with the exiled members of the National Union. The outcome of this exchange is unknown to us.

İstanbul (Patriarchate)—October 15

Yesterday, 666 Armenian migrants were evacuated from a steamer from Cilicia to İstanbul. Unbeknownst to them, the national authorities were unprepared to shelter and feed them. These unfortunate people, primarily women and children, were abandoned on the wharf of İstanbul under adverse weather. They had no choice but to go to the Armenian Church of Galata and enter the Central School. Lecturing at the school has ceased.

These migrants were brought from Adana by the French government against their will. They were forcibly transferred to Karataş, whence they were taken to Mersin and then sent by an Italian steamer to İstanbul.

It is said that this first group, which others will follow it, consists of 838 people, some of whom were evacuated in İzmir.

They are natives of various places and recently disarmed Armenian legionnaires.

The following illustrates where they are from and how many of them disembarked in İzmir and İstanbul.

	disembarked in İzmir	disembarked in İstanbul	total
from Erzurum	-	175	175
from Muş	22	180	202
From Sivas	-	233	233
Various	-	20	20
Legionnaire (volunteer)	150	58	208
[Total]	172	666	838

է ֆրանսացիներուն վրայ որ քաղաքացի չեղող գաղթականներ պէտք է անպայման հեռացուին քաղաքներէն, ատոնց վրայ վստահութիւն չունինք եւայլն, որով կատարուած են միաժամանակ այս երեք գործողութիւններն ալ:

Միւս կողմէ ըսողներ կան թէ Առաջնորդը եւ Տէմիրգաբուլեան, Երէցեան, Ժամկոչեան (հնչակեաններ) շատ տխուր դեր կատարած են այս ամէն ցաւալի դէպքերուն մէջ: Վերապահութեամբ կը գրենք ասոնք: Ապագան պիտի պարզորոշէ այս ամէնը:

Ֆրանսական կառավարութեան մի այլ տեսակէտն է եղեր [թէ] Սէվրի որոշման գործադրութեան իբր հակառակող տարր կը նկատէ եղեր հայերը:

Այս է կիլիկեան ընդհանուր վիճակը:

Պ. Տամատեանին հաղորդուած է իր արտասահման ելքը քանի մը օր վերջ, սակայն յիշեալը պատասխանած է որ իր դիակը միայն կրնան հանել սուինով. ինք միայն կը մեկնի այն ատեն, երբ զինք ղրկողներ ետ կանչեն զինքը:

Միակ եւ գլխաւոր պատճառը այս դժբաղդութեանց Կիլիկիոյ Կաթողիկոսն է: Յիշեալը իր հանգստութիւնը ապահովելու համար նստած է Պէյրութ եւ յաճախ Լիբանան [*sic*]: Վերջին թղթաբերով կ'իմանանք որ Դամասկոս մեկնած է: .....

Վերջին ժամ (վերապահութեամբ) — Ատանայի Ազգային Միութիւնը վերակազմուած է Առաջնորդի ցուցմունքով, սակայն չենք գիտեր թէ որոնք են եւ թէ ընդունուա՞ծ է ֆրանսացիներէն:

Հայ զինուորները զինաթափելէն վերջ ֆրանսական կառավարութիւնը հրամանագիր մը կը հրատարակէ, որով կ'ըսէ. «Հայ զինուորները զինաթափեցի[նք], քաղաք կրնաք գալ ապահով» եւ թուրքերուն 30/40 օթօմօպիլ կը ղրկեն Գուրտ Թէփէ, սակայն թուրքերը բոլոր շօֆէօռները կը սպաննեն եւ օթօմօպիլները կը գրաւեն: Ասոր վրայ հայերը զինաթափող ոյժը կը յարձակի չէթէներուն վրայ, որ 1000էն աւելի կորուստ կուտան: Ֆրանսացիք, ըստ վերջին լուրերու, ասոր վրայ 500 հայ ուժ կ'ուզեն, որուն ի պատասխան հայերը կ'ըսեն թէ՝ պէտք է որ մեր զինաթափուած ուժը վերադարձուի, ինչպէս նաեւ աքսորուած Ազգային Միութեան անդամները: Չենք գիտեր թէ վերջը ուր մնաց:

Կ. Պոլիս (Պատրիարքարան) – 15 Հոկտեմբեր

Երէկ Կիլիկիայէն Կ. Պոլիս եկող շոգենաւէ մը դուրս հանուեցան 666 հայ գաղթականներ: Ասոնց ժամանումը իմաց տրուած չըլլալով, ազգային իշխանութիւնները չէին կրցած ոեւէ պատրաստութիւն տեսնել զանոնք պատսպարելու եւ կերակրելու համար: Աննպաստ օդով Կ. Պոլսոյ քարափը ձգուած այս խեղճերը, որոնց ստուար մասը կին եւ տղայ, ճարահատ Ղալաթիոյ հայոց եկեղեցին դիմած եւ Կեդրոնական Վարժարան մտած են: Դպրոցին դասախօսութիւնները դադրած են:

Այս գաղթականները բերուած են Ատանայէն ֆրանսական կառավարութեան միջոցաւ եւ հակառակ իրենց կամքին, բռնի տեղափոխուելով Գարաթաշ, ուրկէ նախ Մերսին տարուած են եւ յետոյ իտալական շոգենաւով մը դէպի Կ. Պոլիս ճամբայ հանուած են:

Այս առջին խումբը, որուն պիտի յաջորդեն կ'ըսուի ուրիշներ, 838 անձէ կը բաղկանայ, որոնցմէ մէկ մասը Իզմիր դուրս ելած է:

Ասոնք զանազան տեղերու բնիկներ եւ վերջերս զինաթափ եղած հայ լէգէոնականներ են:

Հետեւեալ պատկերը ցոյց կուտան անոնց ուրտեղերէն ըլլալը եւ անոնց Իզմիր եւ Կ. Պոլիս ելող հատուածները:

	Իզմիր ելլող	Կ. Պոլիս եկող	Գումար
Կարնեցի	-	175	175
Մշեցի	22	180	202
Սեբաստացի	-	233	233
Զանազան	-	20	20
Լէգէոնական (կամաւոր)	150	58	208
[Գումար]	172	666	838

Of the 666 people arriving in İstanbul, 180 from Muş and 40 volunteers; that is, 220 people will be taken to Yerevan, and 438 people will remain in İstanbul.

Now, apart from the legionnaires in İstanbul, the other 608 migrants have the following breakdown:

	male	female	child	total
from Erzurum	20	125	30	175
From Sivas	30	133	70	233
from Muş	80	90	10	180
Various	-	20	-	20
[Total]	130	368	110	608

The national authorities are confused and do not know how to take care of the needs and wants of these migrants.

Trabzon (from the locum tenens)—October 7

On October 1, Hamit Bey, the prefect of this city, returned from Adjara and resumed his post. This return brought joy to the people, but it was very short-lived because today, we hear that he has been appointed prefect to Erzurum and will leave in a few days. The Armenian locum tenens rushed to express his anguish. Hamit Bey said: "I was already obliged to go to Erzurum for eight or ten days for a critical task. There might be new administrative arrangements in the near future. Erzurum and Trabzon will unify, and I will be the governor-general of these two prefectures. When I go to Erzurum, I will leave a deputy here."

• The Kurds of Tunceli [Dersim] are disturbing the area around Erzincan and Kemah. A few days ago, they attacked Kemah for plunder.

Bursa (from the locum tenens)—October 7

The Armenian refugees from Cerrah and Yenice came to Bursa and took refuge. The Greek authority provides daily bread for these wretched people.

M[amuret] ul Aziz (from Bishop Kyud, primate)—August 9

No letters have been received from İstanbul since March. Recently, the issue of the conscription of Armenians-turned-Muslim surfaced, and appeals to the local military authorities remained futile.

As Nihat Pasha, commander of the Mesopotamian front, was passing through M[amuret] ul Aziz on his way to Diyarbakır, the Armenian primate, using the opportunity, turned to him and asked for an arrangement regarding the matter because Nihat Bey was named to his position with very vast authority. He promised to do whatever he could after arriving at his destination and reviewing the orders.

İzmit (from the primate)—October 11

On October 8, it was reported in Adapazarı that Beşköprü and Namert Köprü [bridges], located as close as half an hour away from the city, had been cut off by the Milli. Armenian, Greek, Circassian, and Abaza volunteers went against them. The lieutenant governor of Adapazarı also went to the battlefield only to return shortly after in despair. He summoned the Armenian and Greek priests and recommended that the Christians flee the city to Akmeşe and İzmit. He insinuated that he, too, would flee to Akmeşe. In the afternoon, the priests announced the news to the people, who fled naked and

Կ. Պոլիս հասնող 666 անձերէն՝ 180 մուշեցիները եւ 40 կամաւորները, այսինքն՝ 220 անձերը պիտի տարուին Երեւան, իսկ 438 անձ պիտի մնան Կ. Պոլիս:

Հիմա Կ. Պոլիս գտնուող լէգէոնականներէն զատ միւս գաղթականները, որոնք 608 հոգի են, ունին հետեւեալ բաժանումը:

	այր	կին	տղայ	գումար
Կարնեցի	20	125	30	175
Սեբաստացի	30	133	70	233
Մշեցի	80	90	10	180
Զանազան	-	20	-	20
[Գումար]	130	368	110	608

Ազգային իշխանութիւնները շփոթած են եւ չեն գիտեր թէ ինչպէս հոգան այս գաղթականներուն պէտքերը եւ կարօտութիւնները:

Տրապիզոն (Առաջնորդական Տեղապահէն) – 7 Հոկտեմբեր

Հոկտեմբեր 1ին Աջարայէն վերադարձաւ քաղաքիս կուսակալ Համիտ պէյ եւ վերստանձնեց իր պաշտօնը: Այս վերադարձը ուրախութիւն պատճառեց ժողովուրդին, սակայն շատ կարճ տեւեց այդ ուրախութիւնը, վասնզի այսօր կը լսենք թէ անիկա կուսակալ կարգուած է Կարինի եւ պիտի մեկնի քանի մը օրէն: Հայոց Առաջնորդական Տեղապահը կը փութայ իր մօտ ցաւ յայտնելու համար: Համիտ պէյ կ՚ըսէ թէ «Շատ կարեւոր գործով մը արդէն պարտաւորուած էի 8–10 օրուան համար երթալ Կարին: Հաւանաբար մօտ ատենէն վարչական նոր կարգադրութիւններ պիտի ըլլան, Կարին եւ Տրապիզոն պիտի միանան եւ ինքս պիտի ըլլամ այս երկու կուսակալութեանց վալին: Երբ մեկնիմ Կարին՝ ինքս փոխանորդ մը պիտի թողում հոս»:

- Տերսիմի քիւրտերը անհանգիստ կ՚ընեն Երզնկայի շրջակայքը ու Քէմախը: Քէմախի վրայ քանի մը օրեր առաջ յարձակում մը գործեր են աւարառութեան նպատակով:

Պրուսա (Առաջնորդական Տեղապահէն) – 7 Հոկտեմբեր

Ճէրահցի եւ եէնիճեցի հայ գաղթականներ Պրուսա եկան եւ պատսպարուեցան: Հելլէնական իշխանութիւնը այս թշուառներուն ամէն օր հաց կուտայ:

Մ[ամուրէթ] իւլ Ազիզ (Առաջնորդ Գիւտ Եպիսկոպոսէն) – 9 Օգոստոս

Մարտէն ի վեր Կ. Պոլիսէն նամակ չէ առնուած: Վերջին օրերս իսլամութիւնը ընդունող հայերու զինուորագրութեան խնդիր մը երեւան եկաւ մէջտեղ եւ տեղական զինուորական իշխանութեանց մօտ կատարուած դիմումները անհետեւանք մնացին:

Միջագետքի ճակատին (*Ճէզիրէ Ճէպհէսի*) հրամանատար Նիհատ փաշա Մ[ամուրէթ] իւլ Ազիզէն անցնելով Տիարպէքիր երթալու պատեհութենէն օգտուելով՝ անոր կը դիմէ հայոց Առաջնորդը եւ այս մասին կարգադրութիւն մը կը խնդրէ, վասնզի Նիհատ պէյ շատ ընդարձակ իրաւասութիւններով այդ պաշտօնին կոչուած էր: Կը խոստանայ տեղը հասնելէն յետոյ եկած հրամանները աչքէ անցնելէ յետոյ կարելին ընել:

Նիկոմիդիա (Առաջնորդէն) – 11 Հոկտեմբեր

Հոկտեմբեր 8ին Ատաբազարի մէջ լուր կ՚ելլէ թէ քաղաքին կէս ժամ մօտ գտնուող Պէշ Քէօփրիւ եւ Նամերտ Քէօփրիւ կտրուած է Միլլիճիներէն: Հայ, յոյն, չէրքէզ եւ ապազա կամաւորներ անոնց դէմ կ՚երթան: Ատաբազար[ի] գայմագամն ալ կռիւի վայրը կ՚երթայ ու քիչ վերջը կը դառնայ յուսահատ ու հայ եւ յոյն քահանաները կը կանչէ եւ կը յանձնարարէ որ քրիստոնեաները փախչին քաղաքէն դէպի Արմաշ եւ Նիկոմիդիա, ու ինքն ալ որպէս թէ Արմաշ պիտի փախչի: Քահանաները կէսօրէն վերջ կը հաղորդեն այս լուրը ժողովուրդին որ բոկոտն ու մերկ կը փախչի դէպի Օսման պէյի

barefooted to Osman Bey's farm on the road to Akmeşe. Until midnight, Armenians and Greeks gradually gathered there in the rain. Their number reached five hundred. In the middle of the night, they heard that the Millis had entered Adapazarı and that their position at the farm was in danger. Therefore, they decided to go to Akmeşe soon, but because it was raining, they hesitated. Four armed men showed up and demanded weapons from those gathered there. They argued that they had taken nothing [with them]. Thereupon, the armed men demanded that the men present themselves since they did not have weapons. They robbed the first person who presented himself of his two hundred liras. A commotion ensued in the farm building. The four armed men threatened those who were making noise. In short, five hundred liras were collected and given to these four armed men. Then the militants sent the Greek priest up to collect money from the women. The women gave him everything they had not to be killed, but the four men found the sum insufficient and threatened to burn down the building with them inside. Again, an uproar ensued over this, and the robbers fled.

Early in the morning, the people, young and old, men and women, set out toward Alandüzü, which is in the hands of the Hellenic forces. They all arrived there drenched and tired. It is from there that they will gradually go to Akmeşe. From there, the Hellenic authorities are sending the people to İzmit in carts driven by oxen. Yesterday, they arrived in İzmit in perfect misery. Neither the Turkish government nor the British and Greek military authorities will care for them. Only one hundred twenty of the one thousand Armenian houses are left, with thousands living in them. One hundred to one hundred twenty tents have been requested but not given.

- The railway between Adapazarı and İzmit ceased functioning on October 10.
- It is said that the Hellenic Command has decided to send local Armenians and Greeks to Adapazarı to fight against the Millis.

Beirut (from Priest Nerses Tavoukjian, president of the Armenian National Union of Gaziantep [Ayntab] and catholicosal vicar)—October 2

When the war between Armenians and Turks in Gaziantep ceased and peace was established, we had food for only eight days. The Armenian reconciliation with the Turks lasted fifty days. During these fifty days, the Turks provided Armenians food with coupons and with such consideration that we saved nothing. On August 11, when the French occupation army came and laid siege to the city, the Armenians had food for barely ten to fifteen days. Although they immediately began to exercise frugality and satisfy themselves by giving the poor only one hundred drams of bread daily, two weeks later, the entire population—the haves and have-nots—became needy for bread because from the day the French besieged the city, our relations with the Turks had been cut and trade between Turks and Armenians became impossible. Vegetables, oil, meat, and so on ran out from the first day. Two weeks later, flour and wheat also began to end.

The French authority and the administration of the Red Cross remained the only basis of hope for the Armenians, and it must be admitted that without their partial assistance, the Armenians of Gaziantep would have died of starvation after a heroic struggle against the Kemalists.

Unfortunately, to benefit from the relief of the French and the Red Cross, the Armenians of Gaziantep needed some means of transportation—something they lacked. The Armenians of Gaziantep are obliged to buy food from Aleppo and bring it to the city in a two-day-long trip in the company of a French convoy, once every eight or ten days. To give one hundred dram of provision per person daily, we need twenty-five hundred okkas provisions daily. One hundred fifty camels are required to transport that amount. To date, we have been able to provide carts, horses, donkeys, and camels equivalent to only seventy or eighty camels altogether, which covers only half of the need.

If the Armenians of Gaziantep have been able to live on so little food until today, it is only thanks

Չիֆթլիկ, որ Արմաշի ճամբուն վրայ է: Մինչեւ կէս գիշերուան մօտ հայեր եւ յոյներ հետզհետէ հոն կը համախմբուին, անձրեւին տակ: Ասոնց թիւը կը հասնի 500ի: Կէս գիշերին լուր կ'առնեն թէ Միլլիճիները Ատաբազար մտած են եւ իրենց դիրքը վտանգուած է, ուստի կ'որոշեն շուտով Արմաշ երթալ, սակայն որովհետեւ անձրեւ կուգար, կը վարանէին: Ահա վրայ կուագն չորս զինեալ մարդիկ եւ կը պահանջեն հոն հաւաքուածներէն զէնքերը: Անոնք կ'առարկեն թէ ոչինչ առած են: Ասոր վրայ կը պահանջեն որ այր մարդիկը ներկա[յ]անան քանի որ զէնք չունին: Եւ առաջին ներկայացողը կը կողոպտեն, վրան գտնուած 200 ոսկի դրամը կ'առնեն: Ասոր վրայ ազարակի շէնքին մէջ վայնասուն կը փրթի: Զինեալ չորս մարդ[իկ]ը կը սպառնան աղմուկ հանողներուն: Վերջապէս 500 ոսկի հաւաքելով կը տրուի այս չորս զինեալ մարդոց: Ասոր վրայ այս զինեալները վեր կը ղրկեն յոյն քահանան որ կիներէն դրամ հաւաքէ: Կիները իրենց բոլոր ունեցածը կուտան որ չսպաննուին, սակայն այդ չորս մարդիկը այս գումարը քիչ կը գտնան եւ կը սպառնան շէնքը այրելով զիրենք մէջը վառել: Ասոր վրայ կրկին վայնասուն մը կը սկսի եւ այդ աւազակները կը փախչին:

Առաւօտուն կանուխ ժողովուրդը քալելով, մեծ ու պզտիկ, այր ու կին ճամբայ կ'ելլեն դէպի Ալան Տիւզ, որ հելլէն զօրաց ձեռքն է, եւ հոն կը հասնին ամէնքն ալ թրջած ու յոգնած: Անկէ է որ հետզհետէ կ'երթան Արմաշ, ուրկէ հելլէն իշխանութիւնները եգան կառքերով Նիկոմիդիա կը ղրկեն ժողովուրդը: Երէկ ասոնք հասան Նիկոմիդիա կատարեալ թշուառութեան մէջ: Ոչ թուրք կառավարութիւնը եւ ոչ ալ անգլիական եւ հելլէն զինուորական իշխանութիւնները ասոնց խնամք կը տանի[ն]: Հայոց 1000 տուներէն միայն 120-ը մնացած է, ան ալ լեցուն է հազարներով: 100–120 վրան ուզուած է, սակայն չէ տրուած:

- Ատաբազարի եւ Նիկոմիդիոյ միջեւ երկաթուղին դադրած է բանելէ Հոկտեմբեր 10-էն ի վեր:

- Կ'ըսուի թէ հելլէն հրամատարութիւնը տեղացի հայերը եւ յոյները Միլլիներու դէմ կռուելու համար Ատաբազար ղրկելու որոշում տուած է:

Պէյրութ (Ներսէս քահանայ Թավուզճեանէն՝ Այնթապի Հայ Ազգային Միութեան նախագահ եւ Կաթողիկոսական Փոխանորդ) – 2 Հոկտեմբեր

Երբ Այնթապի մէջ թուրքաց հետ հայոց կռիւը դադրեցաւ եւ հաշտութիւն գոյացաւ, ութ օրուան համար ուտելիք ունէինք միայն: 50 օր տեւեց թրքաց հետ հայոց հաշտ յարաբերութիւնը: Այս 50 օրուան մէջ թուրքերը հայոց պարէնը *վէսիքա*յով տուին եւ այն հաշուով՝ որ բան մը չկարենանք աւելցնել: Օգոստոս 11ին երբ ֆրանսական զրահման բանակը եկաւ եւ քաղաքը պաշարեց, հազիւ 10–15 օրուան համար ուտելիք ունէին հայերը, որոնք թէեւ անմիջապէս խնայողութեան սկսան եւ աղքատներուն օրական 100 տրամ հաց միայն տալով բաւականացան, սակայն երկու շաբաթ ետքը, բոլոր ժողովուրդը,- ունեւոր եւ չունեւոր,- ամէնն ալ հացակարօտ եղան, որովհետեւ ֆրանսացւոց քաղաքը պաշարած օրէն իսկ մեր յարաբերութիւնը թուրքին հետ խզուեցաւ եւ առեւտուրը անկարելի եղաւ թուրքերու եւ հայոց մէջ: Բանջարեղէն, իւղ, մեղրէն եւայլն առաջին օրէն հատան ու երկու շաբաթ յետոյ, ալիւրն ու ցորենն ալ արդէն սկսած էին հատնիլ:

Հայոց միակ յոյսը ֆրանսական իշխանութեան եւ Կարմիր Խաչի տնօրէնութեան վրայ էր եւ պէտք է խոստովանիլ թէ՝ եթէ անոնց մասնակի օգնութիւնները չըլլային, Այնթապի հայութիւն[ը] քէմալական չէթէներու դէմ դիւցազնօրէն մաքառելէ յետոյ սովէն պիտի մեռնէր:

Դժբաղդաբար թէ՛ ֆրանսացիներու եւ թէ՛ Կարմիր Խաչի նպաստէն օգտուելու համար Այնթապի հայերը պէտք ունին փոխադրութեան միջոցներու - ինչ որ կը պակսէր: Այնթապի հայերը ստիպուած են պարէնը Հալէպէն գնելու եւ ֆրանսական *զօնվուայ*ի ընկերանալով երկու օրուան ճամբայէ քաղաք բերելու – 8–10 օրը անգամ մը: Մարդ գլուխ օրական 100 տրամ պարէն տալու համար օրական 2500 օխա պարէնի պէտք կայ, որու փոխադրութեան համար 150 ուղտ անհրաժեշտ է, մինչդեռ մինչեւ այսօր կառք, ձի, էշ եւ ուղտ ըլլալով ընդամէնը 70–80 ուղտի համազօր ուժ մը հազիւ կրցանք հայթայթել, ինչ որ պէտքին հազիւ կէսը կը լրացնէ:

Եթէ Այնթապի հայերը մինչեւ այսօր կրցան այդքան քիչ պարէնով ապրիլ՝ միայն եւ միայն

to the local grapes that they can harvest from the orchards without hindrance. Unfortunately, the grapes will be entirely gone in a few days.

Those who render relief to the Armenians of Gaziantep want them to provide the means of transportation themselves. The Armenians of Gaziantep have not been working for nine months, and they live spending what they have. The wealthy have given all they have to help their compatriots. A thousand gold liras have been raised locally for the poor. However, all of this is insufficient because the needs are tremendous, and eight thousand of the ten thousand Armenians in Gaziantep take their bread from the communal bakery.

For this purpose, Priest Nerses Tavoukjian—catholicosal locum tenens and president of the National Union—was sent to Beirut to appeal to the French authorities and the American Near East Relief for an arrangement for the forthcoming winter.

Promises have been made to him about food, but no means of transportation have been provided, whereby the necessity to provide for that need persists. Renting transportation is impossible due to local conditions, so the Armenians of Gaziantep are confused.

• The French occupation army is doing its best to capture the city and establish peace by annihilating the Turkish nationalists. Intense bombardment on Turkish neighborhoods and çetes fortified behind stone walls or under earthen forts continues daily. Considering the weakening of the Turks in the last forty to fifty days, it is hoped that they will surrender soon. On the other hand, there are reasons to believe that the Turkish resistance may continue for several more months, or even if they surrender, that Armenians will have to buy their food from Aleppo for some time, at least this winter.

İzmit (from the primate)—October 27[97]

Today, fifteen families came from Karamürsel [Karamursal] as fugitives. They want to go to İstanbul. They relate that twenty-five Greek soldiers were going to the Turkish villages around Karamürsel to collect weapons. As they were passing by a mosque, they saw a crowd in the courtyard and wanted to approach. [When they did,] those gathered in the mosque courtyard opened fire on the Greek soldiers, killing some of them. The attack intensified. Shortly after, two armored cruisers from Karamürsel's shore, one British and the other Greek, shelled and destroyed the Turkish villages around there while the Greeks and Turks were still fighting. Greek casualties number fifteen to twenty wounded and dead. The Turks escaped, and the Greeks chased them.

After entering Karamürsel, the Greek authorities began arresting all Muslim men.

Trabzon (from the locum tenens)—October 2198

Yesterday, the government seized and sealed the store of the Ipranosian brothers' branch in Trabzon as the property of Ibranoszade Ahmet, with whose death, according to sharia law, the government inherits it. The order came from Ankara.

• Turkish-Bolshevik relations have become extremely elastic in Trabzon. "Bolshevism is vandalism, we cannot be Bolsheviks, but we try to benefit from them politically," said Hamit Bey upon his return from Ankara. It is not improbable that the Bolsheviks think the same of the Turks. What both sides are doing in this way is a rope dance.

• There is a rumor in Trabzon that a ground for reconciliation is being prepared between the center and Kemal and that it could yield a result.

• Giresun's notorious gang leader Topal Osman's soldiers, who were sent against Armenia, have

տեղական խաղողին շնորհիւ է, զոր այգիներէն կրնային քաղել անարգել: Դժբաղդաբար այն ալ քանի մը օրէն բոլորովին կը հատնի:

Այնթապի հայոց նպաստ տուողները կ'ուզեն որ փոխադրութեան միջոցը իրենք հայթայթեն: Այնթապի հայերը ինը ամիս է որ գործելէ եւ աշխատել[է] դադրած են եւ իրենց ունեցածը ծախսելով կ'ապրին: Հարուստները իրենց հայրենակիցներուն օգնելու համար իրենց ունեցածը տուած են եւ տեղային հանգանակութեամբ հազար լիրա ոսկեդրամ հաւաքուած է աղքատներու համար: Սակայն ասոնք ամէնը անբաւական են, վասնզի պէտքերը մեծ են եւ 10000 Այնթապի հայերէն 8000ը հաւաքակաց փուռէն կ'առնէ իր հացը:

Այս նպատակով դիմում կատարելու համար ֆրանսական իշխանութեանց եւ ամերիկեան Նպաստամատոյցին մօտ Պէյրութ ղրկուած է Կաթողիկոսական Փոխանորդ եւ Ազգային Միութեան նախագահ Ներսէս քահանայ Թավուգճեանը, որ յառաջիկայ ձմեռուան համար կարգադրութիւն մը ըլլայ:

Իրեն խոստումներ եղած [են] պարէնի մասին, սակայն փոխադրութեան միջոցներ չ[են] տրուած, որով այդ անհրաժեշտ պէտքը կը մնայ հայթայթել: Վարձքով փոխադրել անկարելի է տեղական պայմաններու բերմամբ, ուստի Այնթապի հայերը շփոթած են:

- Ֆրանսական գրաւման բանակը իր կարելին կ'ընէ թուրք ազգայնականները բնաջնջելով քաղաքը գրաւելու եւ անդորրութիւնը հաստատելու: Թուրք թաղերու վրայ, քարէ պատնէշներու ետին կամ հողէ ամրոցներու ներքեւ ամրացած *չէթէ*ներու վրայ սաստիկ ռմբակոծում կայ եւ կը շարունակէ ամէն օր: Նկատի ունենալով 40–50 օրէ ի վեր թուրքերու կրած տկարացումը, յոյս կայ որ ի մօտոյ անձնատուր ըլլան: Միւս կողմէ պատճառներ կան ենթադրելու որ թրքաց ընդդիմութիւնը քանի մը ամիս եւս կրնայ շարունակուիլ, կամ՝ անձնատուր ըլլան իսկ, հայերը դեռ ատեն մը՝ գէթ այս ձմեռ՝ իրենց պարէնը Հալէպէն գնելու ստիպուած պիտի ըլլան:

Նիկոմիդիա (Առաջնորդէն) – 27 Հոկտեմբեր

Գարամուսալէն 15 տնուոր եկան այսօր իբր փախստական: Ասոնք կ'ուզեն Կ. Պոլիս անցնիլ: Ասոնք կը պատմեն թէ 25 հոգի յոյն զինուորներ Գարամուսալի շուրջ գտնուած թուրք գիւղերը կ'երթան զէնք հաւաքելու: Մզկիթի մը քովէն կ'անցնին, բազմութիւն մը կը տեսնեն բակը եւ կ'ուզեն մօտենալ: Մզկիթի բակը հաւաքուողները կրակ կ'ընեն յունաց վրայ եւ կը սպաննեն յոյն զինուորներ: Յարձակումը կը սաստկանայ: Քիչ վերջը Գարամուսալի ծովեզերքէն երկու զրահաւորներ, մին անգլիական եւ միւսը յունական, այդ կողմեր գտնուած թուրք գիւղերը թնդանօթի կը բռնեն եւ կը քանդեն, մինչ յոյները եւ թուրքերը իրարու հետ դեռ կը կռուէին: Յունաց կորուստն է 15–20 վիրաւոր եւ մեռեալ: Թուրքերը խոյս կուտան եւ յոյները զանոնք կը հետապնդեն:

Յոյն իշխանութիւնները Գարամուսալ մտնելէ յետոյ ձերբակալել սկսան բոլոր իսլամ այր մարդիկը:

Տրապիզոն (Առաջնորդական Տեղապահէն) – 21 Հոկտեմբեր

Կառավարութիւնը երէկ գրաւեց ու կնքեց Իբրանոսեան եղբարց Տրապիզոնի մասնաճիւղի վաճառատունը, որպէս սեփականութիւն Իպրանոս զատէ Ահմէտի, որուն մահուամբ ըստ Շէրիի օրինաց, ժառանգութեան տէր կը դառնայ ինք՝ կառավարութիւնը: Հրամանը Էնկիւրիւէն եկած է:

- Թրքօ-պօլշէվիկեան յարաբերութիւնները Տրապիզոնի մէջ չափազանց առաձգական են դարձեր: Համիտ պէյ, Էնկիւրիւէն դարձին ըսած էր թէ «պոլշէվիզմը վանտալութիւն է, մենք չենք կրնար ըլլալ պոլշէվիկ, բայց կը ջանանք քաղաքականապէս օգտուիլ անոնցմէ»: Անհաւանական չէ որ պոլշէվիկներն ալ նոյն կերպով կը խորհին թուրքերու մասին: Լարախաղացութիւն մըն է այս կերպով երկու կողմին ալ ըրածը:

- Տրապիզոնի մէջ զրոյց կը շրջի թէ կեդրոնի եւ Քէմալի միջեւ հաշտութեան մը գետին կը մշակուի եւ հաւանաբար արդիւնաւորուի:

escaped and dispersed without exception.

Mersin (from the National Union)—October 25[99]

Two Armenians, native of Saimbeyli [Hacın], narrowly escaped and arrived in Adana three days ago. They delivered the sad and shocking news that the Armenians of Saimbeyli, who had been fighting heroically since March 13, 1920, were massacred entirely on October 15.

The three [*sic*] daring people from Saimbeyli came to Adana after a torturous seventeen-day trip. They related that the people of Saimbeyli, [after consuming] all the horses, mules, cats, and dogs [in Saimbeyli], stormed the village of Doganbeyli [Rumlu], a village five hours away populated by Turks and Circassians. It seems they did not succeed, and that attack was another catastrophe for the unfortunate [Armenians]. Other Armenian newcomers who fled from the incident to Adana reported that the enemy, attacking in great numbers and with the help of many cannons, began to wipe out the city's population and burn it. One hundred Armenians took refuge in the mountains, and the rest of the people surrendered.

There were the 216 orphans of the Armenian General Benevolent Union in the city, forty-two orphans of Mr. Ibo (Englishman), and sixty-eight orphans of Curdet (American). Mr. and Mrs. Yesayi Garabedian serve as doctors at the Benevolent Union's hospital, and Mr. and Mrs. H. Papazian as pharmacists. Dr. Diran Terzian serves as the neighborhood doctor.

Adana—October 23

Refugees from Saimbeyli [Hacın] started arriving today because Saimbeyli has fallen. Saimbeyli underwent a great attack. The Turks entered the city, set it on fire, and the massacre began. Those who were able to escape escaped. The escapees were caught in a fight in Tapan-Oğlu. Some of them managed to cross through.

Women, children, and men roam the mountains, plains, valleys, and roads, crossing through hostile çetes and heading to Adana.

Mersin—October 25

Mersin's French forces have been working feverishly for four to five days. The regiment that came to Tarsus caught many çetes and hanged several leaders. The French seized two cannons that the çetes were using to destroy the city. The same regiment also cleared the çetes on the Mersin-Tarsus line. Insurgents are surrendering themselves with their weapons in these areas daily. The Adana-Mersin line will start operating in ten days. The çetes have suffered a great defeat around Pozantı. French forces are expected to enter Pozantı on October 28.

The British want to close the Lord Mayor's workshop in Adana. Thousands of workers were making their living there.

There is a large influx of migrants here.

Mersin—October 30

New details are arriving about the fall of Saimbeyli [Hacın]. After the success in Doganbeyli [Rumlu], the extremely excited Turks attacked Saimbeyli on October 15 with three [one hundred fifty millimiters] cannons. After smashing the resistance by Armenians from the houses of the Ezians, they dominated the city, set fire everywhere, and massacred. They spared no Armenian or American establishment; they burned them all. They burned the stone-built school, which had been turned into a hospital, with the patients alive inside. They captured Chalian and all the prominent people. After cramming

- Կիրասոնի յայտնի հրոսապետ Թօփալ Օսմանի զինուորները, որոնք Հայաստանի վրայ ղրկուած էին, առանց բացառութեան փախուստ տուած եւ ցրուած են:

Մերսին (Ազգային Միութենէն) – 25 Հոկտեմբեր

Հաճնոյ հայութենէն մազապուր ազատելով երեք օր առաջ Ատանա ժամանող երկու հայեր ցաւալի ու ցնցող լուր մը կը հաւցնեն որ 13 Մարտ 1920էն ի վեր հերոսաբար պայքարող Հաճնոյ հայութիւնը ամբողջապէս ջարդուած [է] Հոկտեմբեր 15ին:

Երեք կտրիճ հաճընցիները 17 օրուան տաժանելի ուղեւորութենէն վերջ Ատանա եկած էին. կը պատմեն թէ Հաճընի ժողովուրդը բոլոր ձի, ջորի, կառու, շուն կերած էին խոյանալով դէպի Րումլու գիւղը, որ 5 ժամ հեռու թուրք եւ չէրքէզաբնակ գիւղ մըն է, սակայն կ'երեւի թէ չեն յաջողած եւ այդ խոյանքը աւելի աղիտաբեր եղած է խեղճերուն համար: Ուրիշ նորեկ հայեր դէպքէն խոյս տալով կը հասնին Ատանա եւ կը պատմեն թէ թշնամին թնդանօթներու օգնութեամբ եւ մեծ թուով յարձակելով, սկսած է քաղաքի բնակչութիւնը ջնջել եւ քաղաքը այրել: Հայերէն 100 հոգի լեռները ապաստանած են, իսկ մնացեալ ժողովուրդը յանձնուած է:

Քաղաքին մէջ կը գտնուէ[ին] Հ. Բ. Ը. Միութեան 216 որբերը, 42 Մսթր Իպօի (անգլիացի), 68 Քրտէթի (ամերիկացի): Բարեգործականի հիւանդանոցին մէջ իբր բժիշկ կը ծառայեն Տէր եւ Տիկին Եսայի Կարապետեան, դեղագործ տէր եւ տիկին Հ. Բաբազեան եւ իբր թաղական բժիշկ Տիրան Թերզեան:

Ատանա – 23 Հոկտեմբեր

Այսօր սկսան հասնիլ Հաճընի փախստականները, որովհետեւ Հաճըն ինկած է: Հաճըն մեծ յարձակումի մը ենթարկուած է, թուրքերը քաղաք մտած են, կրակի տուած են զայն, կոտորածը սկսած է: Ժողովուրդէն ով որ կրցած է փախած է. փախստականները կռուի բռնուած են Թափան-Օղլու. մաս մը յաջողած է անցնիլ:

Լեռ, դաշտ, ձոր, ճամբան ցիրուցան կը թափառին կիներ, երախաներ, այրեր, որոնք թշնամի չէթէներու մէջէն կը դիմեն դէպի Ատանա:

Մերսին – 25 Հոկտեմբեր

4–5 օրէ ի վեր Մերսինի ֆրանսական ուժերը տենդոտ կը գործեն: Տարսոնի եկած գունդը շատ մը չէթէներ բռնեց եւ մի քանի շէֆեր կախեց: Ֆրանսացիք ձեռք անցուցին երկու թնդանօթ, որով չէթէները աւեր կը գործէին քաղաքին: Նոյն գունդը մաքրեց նոյնպէս Մերսին-Տարսոն գծին չէթէները: Ամէն օր ապստամբներ կը յանձնուին իրենց զէնքերով այս կողմերը: Ատանա-Մերսին գիծը 10 օրէն կը սկսի բանիլ: Պօզանթիի կողմը չէթէները խոշոր պարտութեան մատնուեցան: 28 Հոկտեմբերին Պօզանթի կը կարծուի թէ պիտի մտնեն ֆրանսական ուժերը:

Ատանա գտնուող Լո[ր]ս Մայօրս գործանոցը անգլիացիները փակել կ'ուզեն: Հոն հազարաւոր գործաւորներ կը ճարէին իրենց հացը:

Հոս գաղթականներու մեծ խռնում կայ:

Մերսին – 30 Հոկտեմբեր

Հաճընի անկման մասին նոր մանրամասնութիւններ կը հասնին: Րումլուի յաջողութենէն վերջ թուրքերը գերազրգռուած երեք հատ 10½նոց թնդանօթներով եկան յարձակիլ Հոկտեմբեր 15ին Հաճընի վրայ եւ Էզեաններու տուներէն եղած հայ դիմադրութիւնը խորտակելով տիրած են քաղաքին, ամէն կողմ կրակ եւ ջարդ տուած են, հաստատութիւն մը չէ մնացած թէ՛ ամերիկեան եւ թէ հայկական, ամբողջ այրած են: Քարաշէն դպրոցը, որ հիւանդանոցի վերածուած էր, մէջի հիւանդներով այրած են ողջ ողջ: Չալեան եւ բոլոր երեւելիները բռնած եւ վանք լեցունելէ վերջ գերի

them in the church, they took them as captives to the country's interior. Several prominent people, who were wounded in the war, ended their lives with poison to avoid captivity by the enemy. On October 14 and 15, the enemy mercilessly massacred people wherever they found them. Finally, facing this unbearable situation, a group of four hundred people climbed the mountain, forsaking the city to its destiny. Commander Jebeji[an] and neighborhood doctor Diran Terzian ended their lives with poison. Aram Gaydzag and his companions broke through the siege and reached Gökçeyol [Tlan], three hours north of Kozan [Sis].

When the news reached Adana, the extremely excited people gathered in defiance of the state of siege, attacked the primate, and wounded him. The primate was taken to the French military hospital. The people attacked the members of the National Union, locked the doors [of the union center], took the key, and went and shut the church. Black veils were placed everywhere. The crowd gradually grew larger despite the governmental guards. Political party clubs and all other places were covered with black. The tremendous mourning was unprecedented. No tolling of the bells was heard, and no Sunday church services were held. All institutions and markets were closed as if mourning in general grief.

The presence of newly arrived escapees on Monday put Adana in a more agitated and troubled state. At eight o'clock in the morning, they assembled in the church and started tolling the bells. A large crowd began to gather in the yard and outside [its perimeter]. The demonstrators headed to Damadian's apartment to press him to go to the government to explain the situation and seek a solution for those who have taken refuge in Gökçeyol. Damadian arrived in a carriage and invited the people to calm down, reminding them of the state of siege. But the people insisted on their word. The religious leaders and Damadian decided to send a delegation to the governor's headquarters again since the response the previous delegation had received had been unsatisfactory and insufficient.

The new delegation made a fresh appeal, but unfortunately, from the point of view of the French government and the Armenian nation, it was deemed inappropriate to send Armenian auxiliary forces. They only promised to send a plane to Gökçeyol to examine the positions, [undertaking also] to send others again after its return. Indeed, the plane was sent.

The people still live in hours of turmoil, with commotion and crying everywhere.

• We learned from a private letter from Adana at the last moment that 450 escapees made it safely to Ceyhan, a safe place. They will be transported thence to Adana by train.

Zonguldak (from the Neighborhood Council)—November 1

There was no exact information yet about the massacre of Armenians that took place in Bolu on August 14, 1920, but now it has been possible to get precise and detailed information from the surviving Armenian women who arrived in Zonguldak. Although Bolu's government forbids Armenians from migrating elsewhere, they managed to come to Zonguldak through Turkish muleteers. Presently, although Armenians are not subject to harsh treatment in Bolu, the presence of the massacrers has had a horrific effect on the unfortunate people. Suffice it to say that Armenians have been left with nothing to provoke harsh treatment: no house, no household goods, no money, and no honor [left intact].

The Red Cross of Zonguldak helps them with its means by paying the travel expenses of the entirely poor. That journey takes three to four days by horse.

A group of four Armenian families—thirty-six people—left Bolu to travel to Zonguldak. They were arrested by Devrek's gendarmes eight hours away from Zonguldak and were taken to Devrek, where

տարած են դէպի երկրին ներսերը: Քանի մը ծանօթներ, որոնք վիրաւորուած են պատերազմի միջոցին, թշնամիին ձեռք չիյնալու համար թոյնով վերջ տուած են իրենց կեանքին: Հոկտեմբեր 14 եւ 15ին թշնամին ամէն կողմ անխնայ գտած մարդիկը ջարդած է: Վերջապէս այս անտանելի կացութեան առջեւ մաս մը ժողովուրդ՝ 400ի չափ, լեռ կ'ելլեն քաղաքը լքելով իր բաղդին: Հրամատար Ճէպէճի եւ թաղական բժիշկ Տիրան Թերզեան թոյնով վերջ կուտան իրենց կեանքին, իսկ Արամ Կայծակ եւ իր ընկերները պաշարման գիծը ճեղքելով կը հասնին մինչեւ Թլան, որ Սիսէն 3 ժամ հիւսիս է:

Լուրը Ատանա երբ կը հասնի, ժողովուրդը գերագրգռուած կը հաւաքուին հակառակ պաշարման վիճակին եւ կը յարձակին Առաջնորդին վրան եւ զայն կը վիրաւորեն: Առաջնորդը կը փոխադրուի ֆրանսական զինուորական հիւանդանոց: Ժողովուրդը կը յարձակի Ազգային Միութեան անդամներուն վրայ, կը գոցեն դուռները, բանալին կ'առնեն եւ կ'երթան եկեղեցին կը փակեն: Ամէն կողմ սեւ շղարշներ կը զետեղուին: Բազմութիւնը հետզհետէ կը ստուարանայ հակառակ կառավարական պահակներուն. կուսակցական ակումբներու շէնքեր ամէն կողմ սեւ պատած է: Սուգը աննախընթաց է եւ խոշոր. չյնուեցաւ ոչ մի զանգակի ղօղանջ եւ չկատարուեցաւ Կիրակիի եկեղեցական ո՛չ մի հանդիսութիւն եւ արարողութիւն: Բոլոր հաստատութիւնք եւ շուկան գոց են, կարծես թէ ընդհանուր սուգը կ'ողբան:

Իսկ Երկուշաբթի օր նոր ժամանող փախստականներու ներկայութիւնը Ատանան կը դնէ աւելի գերագրգիռ եւ խռովեալ վիճակի մը մէջ: Առտուն ժամը 8ին կը խռնուին ատոնք եկեղեցին եւ կը սկսին քաշել զանգակները: Մեծ բազմութիւն մը կը սկսի կուտակուիլ բակին մէջ եւ դուրսը: Ցուցարարները կ'ելլեն դուրս եւ կ'երթան Տամատեանին բնակարանը, որպէսզի կառավարութեան երթայ այս վիճակը պարզել եւ դարման մը պահանջելու համար Թլան ապաստանողներուն համար: Տամատեան կը հասնի կառքով, ժողովուրդը պաղարիւն կը հրաւիրէ, յիշեցնելով պաշարման վիճակը: Սակայն ժողովուրդը կը պնդէ իր խօսքին վրայ: Կրօնապետները եւ Տամատեան կ'որոշեն կրկին պատուիրակութիւն մը ղրկել կառավարչատուն, վասնզի նախորդ պատուիրակութեան ստացած պատասխանը անգոհացուցիչ էր եւ անբաւական:

Նոր պատուիրակութիւնը կը կատարէ նոր դիմում, սակայն դժբաղդաբար ֆրանսական կառավարութեան եւ հայ ազգին շահուն տեսակէտով անյարմար կը դատուի օգնական հայ ուժեր ղրկել. միայն կը խոստանան օդանաւ մը ղրկել Թլան եւ քննել դիրքերը, որուն վերադարձէն վերջ կրկին ղրկել ուրիշներ, եւ իրաւ ալ օդանաւը ճամբայ կը հանուի:

Ժողովուրդը դարձեալ կ'ապրի յուզման ժամեր, կը տիրէ իրարանցում եւ լաց ամէն կողմ:

- Վերջին պահուն Ատանայէն եկած մասնաւոր նամակէ մը կ'իմանանք որ 450 փախստականներ հասած են ապահով մինչեւ Ճիհան, որ ապահով վայր է, եւ ատկից շոգեկառքով պիտի փոխադրուին Ատանա:

Զօնկուլտաք (Թաղական Խորհուրդէն) – 1 Նոյեմբեր

14 Օգոստոս 1920ին Պոլսի հայոց վրայ տեղի ունեցող ջարդի մասին ստոյգ տեղեկութիւն մը չէր տրուած ցարդ, սակայն հիմա կարելի եղաւ ստոյգ եւ մանրամասն տեղեկութիւն քաղել այն վերապրող հայ կիներէն, որոնք Զօնկուլտաք ժամանեցին: Պոլսի կառավարութիւնը թէեւ կ'արգիլէ հայոց ուրիշ տեղ գաղթել եւ սակայն անոնք կը յաջողին թուրք ջորեպաններու միջոցաւ Զօնկուլտաք գալ. առ այժմ թէեւ Պոլսյի մէջ հայոց հանդէպ խստութիւն մը ցոյց չի տրուիր, բայց ջարդարարներու ներկայութիւնը սարսափ ազդած է խեղճերուն վրայ. թող թէ արդէն խստութիւն բանեցնելու բան մը չէ մնացած հայոց քով՝ ո՛չ տուն, ո՛չ կարասի, ո՛չ դրամ եւ ոչ ալ պատիւ մնացած է:

Զօնկուլտաքի Կարմիր Խաչը իր միջոցներով օգնութեան կը հասնի անոնց՝ բոլորովին աղքատներուն ճամբու ծախքը վճարելով: Այդ ճամբան 3-4 օր կը տեւէ ձիով:

Չորս ընտանիքէ եւ 36 անձէ բաղկացած խումբ մը հայեր՝ որոնք Զօնկուլտաք գալու համար ճամբայ ելած են Պոլսյէն, քաղաքէս 8 ժամ հեռու Տէվրէկի ժանտարմաներէն ձերբակալուելով կը

about thirty local Armenian families remain unable to migrate to Zonguldak. The government prohibits the people of Bolu also from migrating to Zonguldak. Only eight people from Bolu managed to escape at night and come to Zonguldak. Twenty-[eight] people remain in Devrek with the thirty local Armenian families.

As for the situation in Zonguldak, two and a half months ago, the government banned Armenians' travel to İstanbul. Despite all the appeals, obtaining permission, at least for merchants, has been impossible. French military functionaries informally were providing facilitation to Armenians on their way to İstanbul. Fifteen days ago, the protection the French rendered to about fifty Armenian migrants from Zonguldak and Bolu to facilitate their entry to a steamer dearly affected the Turkish government; wherefore, the Turkish government asked the French commander not to send Armenians to İstanbul and, as a result, they are no longer providing any facilitation to Armenians. Concerning the merchants and shopkeepers who went to İstanbul under the protection of the French, they have not returned yet, fearing that they might be punished by the Turkish government. There are already many rumors to this effect.

• On October 18, Hripsimé, the five-year-old daughter of Taniel from Malkara, a resident of this city, disappeared in front of their house. After an eight-day search, both by governmental and private means, she was found in the house of forest official Mehmet Bey, a Turkish resident in this city. The girl was handed over to her parents. Despite the parents' complaint, no legal action was taken against Mehmet Bey.

• The following list presents the state of Armenians before and after the Bolu massacre, according to the latest information.

	Armenian house	*Armenian person*	*Greek person*	*Armenian church*	*Armenian school*	*Armenian national building*
Before the event	*134*	*511*	*55*	*2*	*2*	*2 cafés and a tavern*
Damaged during the incident	*117*	*82*	*12*	*2*	*2*	*1 café*
Balance	*17*	*429*	*43*	*0*	*0*	*1 tavern*

Of 82 Armenian martyrs, 57 are men, and 25 are women and girls. The 12 martyrs of the Greeks are all male. Of the 429 survivors, 160 migrated [first] to Zonguldak, [then] from Zonguldak to İstanbul and Devrek. There are currently 269 people, old and young, left in Bolu, and there are hardly 10 adult men among them; the rest are women and children.

İzmit (from the primate)—November 20

It is said that the Hellenic government will withdraw from Akmeşe and definitely from İzmit also, and the English will not replace them to protect Adapazarı. Of course, the situation of Adapazarı, Akmeşe, and İzmit will turn dreadful.

It is even suspected that İstanbul will also be endangered in this way.

İzmit (from the primate)—November 23

Our local Circassian district governor, İbrahim Hakkı, suddenly left for Adapazarı on Thursday to define an administrative structure on the spot, to put an end to the structure that has been created by local means.

տարուին Տէվրէկ, ուր արդէն 30 տունի չափ տեղացի հայեր մնացած եւ չեն կրցած Զօնկուլտաք գաղթել: Կառավարութիւնը պօլուցիներն ալ կ'արգիլէ Զօնկուլտաք գաղթելէ. միայն 8 պօլուցիք կը յաջողին գիշերանց փախուստ տալ եւ Զօնկուլտաք գալ. իսկ 2[8] հոգին ցարդ կը մնան ի Տէվրէկ, տեղացի 30 տնուոր հայերու հետ:

Գալով Զօնկուլտաքի կացութեան, 2½ ամիս առաջ կառավարութիւնը արգիլած է հայոց Պոլիս երթալը: Հակառակ ամէն դիմումի, գէթ վաճառականներու համար արտօնութիւն ձեռք ձգել կարելի չեղաւ: Ֆրանսական զինուորական պաշտօնեաներ անպաշտօն կերպով ամէն դիւրութիւն կ'ընծայէին հայոց Պոլիս երթալու միջոցին: Ասկէ 15 օր առաջ 50ի չափ զօնկուլտաքցի եւ պօլուցի գաղթական հայերու շոգենաւ մտցնելու համար ֆրանսացւոց ընծայած պաշտպանութիւնը ծանր ազդած է թուրք կառավարութեան վրայ, ըստ որում թրքական կառավարութիւնը կը դիմէ ֆրանսացի հրամատարին, որպէսզի հայերը Պոլիս չղրկեն, որուն հետեւանքով անոնք ալ այլ եւս ոեւէ դիւրութիւն մը չեն ընծայեր: Իսկ այն վաճառականները եւ խանութպանները, որոնք ֆրանսացւոց պաշտպանութեամբ Պոլիս մեկնած էին, ցարդ դարձած չեն, վախնալով թէ մի գուցէ թուրք կառավարութեան կողմէ պատժոյ կ'ենթարկուին. արդէն այս մասին զրոյցներ ալ անպակաս են:

- Հոկտեմբեր 18ին քաղաքիս բնակիչներէն մալկարացի Դանիէլի հինգ տարեկան աղջիկը՝ Հռիփսիմէն, իրենց տունին առջեւէն անյայտացաւ: Թէ՛ կառավարական եւ թէ՛ անհատական 8 օրուան փնտռտուքէն վերջ կարելի եղաւ գտնել քաղաքիս թուրք բնակիչներէն անտառաց պաշտօնեայ Մէհմէտ պէյի տունէն. աղջիկը ծնողաց յանձնուեցաւ, իսկ Մէհմէտ պէյի դէմ ոեւէ օրինական հետապնդում տեղի չունեցաւ, հակառակ ծնողաց բողոքին:

- Յետագայ ցուցակը Պօլուի ջարդէն առաջ եւ յետոյ հայոց վիճակը կը ներկայացնէ, ըստ ամենավերջին տեղեկութեանց:

	հայ տուն	*հայ անձ*	*յոյն անձ*	*հայ եկեղեցի*	*հայ վարժարան*	*հայ ազգային շէնք*
Դէպքէն առաջ	*134*	*511*	*55*	*2*	*2*	*2 սրճարան եւ զինետուն*
Դէպքին փճացած	*117*	*82*	*12*	*2*	*2*	*1 սրճարան*
Մնացորդ	*17*	*429*	*43*	*0*	*0*	*1 զինետուն*

82 հայ նահատակներէն 57 հոգին այր եւ 25 հոգին կին եւ աղջիկ են. յոյն 12 նահատակները ամբողջովին այր են. ողջ մնացողներէ 429 հոգիէն 160 հոգին Զօնկուլտաք՝ Զօնկուլտաքէն Պոլիս եւ Տէվրէկ գաղթած են. այժմ Պօլուի մէջ կը մնայ 269 անձ մեծ, պզտիկ եւ ատոնց մէջ հազիւ կարելի է գտնել չափահաս 10 էրիկ մարդ. մնացածները՝ կին եւ երեխայ:

Նիկոմիդիա (Առաջնորդէն) – 20 Նոյեմբեր

Կ'ըսուի թէ հելլէն իշխանութիւնը պիտի քաշուի Արմաշէն եւ անպատճառ Նիկոմիդիայէն ալ եւ անգլիացիք ալ իրենն տեղը չպիտի բռն[են] եւ Ատաբազարը պաշտպան[են]: Անշուշտ Ատաբազարի, Արմաշի եւ Նիկոմիդիոյ վիճակը երկիւղալի պիտի դառնայ:

Նոյնիսկ կասկած կայ թէ այս կերպով Կ. Պոլիս եւս պիտի վտանգուի:

Նիկոմիդիա (Առաջնորդէն) – 23 Նոյեմբեր

Տեղւոյս չէրքէզ միւթէսարրիֆ Իպրահիմ Հազզը Հինգշաբթի օրը յանկարծ Ատաբազար մեկնեցաւ, տեղւոյն մէջ վարչական կազմակերպութիւն մը սահմանելու, որպէսզի տեղական միջոցներով եղած կազմակերպութիւնը դադրի:

• A Turkish delegation came from Adapazarı and sent a memorandum to all official bodies, such as the Armenian primate, the Greek metropolitan, the British ambassador, the military inspector Captain Perring, and others.

Mersin (National Union)—December 1, 1920

On November 29, some migrants previously sent to İzmir and İstanbul returned here. However, it is unfortunate to say that the French authorities detained twenty-three of them as soon as they got off the boat, allegedly for having been disarmed in the village of Akarca. According to an order given, they will remain in prison until further arrangement.

Gemlik (from the Keramet Neighborhood Council)—November 13

The fire in Keramet village by Milli gangs precisely one and a half months ago (September 30) is already known. Now, the most recent events arrived to perfect the misery of the unfortunate people of the village. The terrified people who survived the fire, encouraged by the Greek soldiers' settlement in Keramet, returned to the village. There, they huddled in forty houses that had not been burned, hoping to benefit from the olive harvest, which is the only means of livelihood and presents an unprecedented abundance this year; more than a million okkas with the least count.

Unfortunately, this time new Milli forces, along with the participation of numerous gangs gathered from the surrounding Turkish villages and especially armed with cannons, again attacked the village (on October 23) where the Greek soldiers were stationed. After a tenacious and fierce twenty-seven-hour battle, the Millis left their positions and retreated. Regardless, however, the Greek army also abandoned the village and the positions and fortifications it had set on the front. A day later, the army retreated eight or ten kilometers.

The defenseless people, once again, followed the Greek army, reluctantly and desperately, embarking again on the path of deportation. They are literally naked and hungry, as the Greek military authorities have terminated their bread allowance, which lasted only a few days.

But the gravest development of all is the abandonment of the olive harvest. An appeal was made to the Greek commander of Orhangazi to this effect, asking that they keep the soldiers in Keramet as before [so the people could harvest the crop]. Unfortunately, the answer received indicated that he had withdrawn them in accordance with an order from above.

İzmit (from the primate)—December 28[100]

The Millis besieged the village of Kartsi with three to four hundred people on December 22. They looted and killed six people—four men and two women—and left. Two days later (on December 24), the Hellenic Army entered Kartsi and, after staying overnight, returned to Yalova. On December 26, when the Millis learned of the departure of the Hellenic army, they returned to Kartsi and set it completely ablaze.

Five or six days before the siege of the village, the Hellenic soldiers guarding the area around Yalova were fired upon, and five or six of them were wounded.

It has been reported that the Millis looted and set fire also to the villages of Şakşak, Çukur, and Kılıç.

Now the people of the villages of Yalakdere, Avcıköy [Merdigöz], Kartsi, Kılıç, Şakşak, and Çukur remain hungry, thirsty, naked, helpless, deprived of everything, and with no help.

- Ատաբազարէն թուրք պատուիրակութիւն մը եկաւ, որ յիշատակագիր մը յղեց բոլոր պաշտօնական մարմիններուն, ինչպէս հայոց Առաջնորդին, յունաց Առաջնորդին, անգլիացի դեսպանին, զինուորական քննիչ Քէփիթըն Փէրրի[ն]կի եւայլն:

Մերսին (Ազգային Միութենէն) – 1 Դեկտեմբեր 1920

Նոյեմբեր 29ին՝ ասկէ առաջ Իզմիր եւ Պոլիս ղրկուած զաղթականներէն մաս մը հոս վերադարձաւ, սակայն ցաւալի է ըսել որ ֆրանսական իշխանութիւնք ասոնցմէ 23 հոգի իբր Ախարճա գիւղի մէջ զինաթափուածներ՝ բանտարկեց, անմիջապէս որ նաւէն ելան: Տրուած հրամանի մը համաձայն, ասոնք ցնոր տնօրինութիւն բանտ պիտի մնան:

Կէմլէյիկ (Քէրէմէթի Թաղական Խորհուրդէն) – 13 Նոյեմբեր

Ճիշդ մէկուկէս ամիս առաջ (30 Սեպտեմբեր) Միլլի հրոսախումբերու կողմանէ Քէրամէթ գիւղի հրդեհուիլը ծանօթ է արդէն: Այժմ նորագոյն դէպքեր կուգան կատարեալ ընել գիւղին դժբաղդ ժողովուրդին թշուառութիւնը: Հրդեհէն մազապուր փրկուած սարսափահար ժողովուրդը յոյն զինուորներու Քէրէմէթ հաստատուելէն սրտապնդուելով վերադարձած էր գիւղ՝ ուր հրդեհէ զերծ մնացած քառասունի չափ տուներու մէջ խճողուած կը յուսայինք կարենալ օգտագործել ձիթապտուղի բերքը, որ միակ միջոցը կը կազմէր մեր ապրուստին եւ որ այս տարի կը ներկայացնէ աննախընթաց առատութիւն մը, նուազագոյն հաշուով կէս միլիոն օխայէ աւելի:

Դժբաղդաբար այս անգամ Միլլի նոր ուժեր շրջակայ թուրք գիւղերէ հաւաքուած ստուար հրոսախումբերու մասնակցութեամբ եւ մանաւանդ թնդանօթներով զինուած կրկին յարձակեցան գիւղին վրայ (23 Հոկտեմբերին) ուր դիրք բռնած էր յոյն զինուորը: 27 ժամ տեւող յամառ եւ կատաղի կռիւէ մը վերջ թէեւ Միլլիները լքեցին իրենց դիրքերը ու նահանջեցին, սակայն յոյն բանակն ալ օր մը վերջ լքեց գիւղն ու իր յարդարած ճակատի դիրքերը ու շէնքերը եւ քաշուեցաւ 8–10 քիլօմէթր դէպի ետ:

Անպաշտպան ժողովուրդը յոյն բանակին ետեւէն կրկին անգամ ըլլալով ակամայ ու ճարահատ նորէն ձեռք առաւ տարագրութեան ուղին, բառին բովանդակ նշանակութեամբ մերկ ու անօթի՝ քանի որ յոյն զինուորական իշխանութիւններ դադրեցուցած են իրենց հացի նպաստը, որ քանի մը օր միայն տեւեց:

Սակայն ասոնցմէ շատ ծանր է ձիթապտուղի բերքին լքուիլը: Ասոր համար դիմում կատարուած է Օրխան Ղազիի յոյն հրամանատարութեան մօտ, խնդրելով որ ըստ առաջնոյն Քէրէմէթ պահ[է] զինուորները, սակայն դժբաղդաբար պատասխան առնուած է թէ վերէն եկած հրամանի մը համաձայն ետ քաշած է զանոնք:

Նիկոմիդիա (Առաջնորդէն) – 28 Դեկտեմբեր

Միլլիճիները 3–400 հոգիներով կը պաշարեն Քարցի գիւղն Դեկտեմբեր 22ին: Կը թալանեն եւ վեց հոգի, 4 այր եւ 2 կին կը սպանենն ու կ'երթան: Հելլէն զինուորները երկու օր յետոյ (Դեկտեմբեր 24ին) Քարցի կը մտնեն եւ գիշեր մը մնալէ յետոյ կը դառնան կրկին Եալովա: Դեկտեմբեր 26ին Միլլիճիները իմանալով հելլէն զինուորներու մեկնումը, կրկին կուգան Քարցի եւ ամբողջ կրակի կուտան:

Գիւղը պաշարելէն 5–6 օր առաջ Եալովայի շուրջ իբր պահակ սպասող հելլէն զինուորներուն վրայ կրակ կ'ընեն եւ 5–6 զինուոր կը վիրաւորեն:

Լուր կայ թէ Միլլիճիները Շագ-Շագ, Չուգուր եւ Գըլըճ գիւղերն ալ թալլած եւ կրակի տուած են:

Այժմ Եալովա կը մնան Եալագ-Տէրէ, Մերտիկէօզ, Քարցի, Գըլըճ, Շագշագ, Չուգուր գիւղերու ժողովուրդը անօթի, ծարաւ, մերկ, բոպիկ, եւ ամէն բանէ զուրկ, առանց ոեւէ օգնութեան:

Sugören [Çengiler] (from the Neighborhood Council)—January 1, 1921

Early this morning, a horrific attack took place on the village of Sugören by the Millis from the peaks of the northern mountains, as well as the vicinities of Ortaköy and Büyük-Yeniköy.

Thanks to the brave resistance of the Greek soldiers of Sugören, after three hours of firing, the Millis withdrew to the Armenian and Turkish villages of Yalova.

Barely surviving migrants from the Armenian villages of Yalova—Şakşak, Kartsi, Kılıç, and Çukur—are gathered now in Sugören.

Despite the panic in Sugören, there has been no emigration due to the resistance of the Greek soldiers. The people of Ortaköy and Büyük-Yeniköy were barely able to take their children and flee naked to the village of Pazarköy, where there are numerous Greek soldiers.

All the people of this region live in terror. About thirty-five hundred people are obliged to wander here and there because the Millis control some of the villages (such as Keramet, Ortaköy, and Büyük-Yeniköy).

Bursa (from the locum tenens)—January 16, 1921[101]

While there had been an expectation that the Armenians would return home with the Hellenic advance, unfortunately, [the advance] has had the opposite effect: the population of the places they entered and left again has been forced to give in to the Kemalist horror and merely try to save themselves. Thus, the Armenians of Bilecik also were added to them [the earlier migrants]. Schools and homes were provided to them, and bread began to be served in response to an appeal from the locum tenens.

Nobody from the villages around Bilecik was able to survive or travel to Bursa with the people of Bilecik. Only five hundred of the three to four thousand migrants arrived here.

Yalova (from Hovhannes Der Garabedian's private letter)—January 17, 1921102

The Kemalists attacked the fortifications on the hill south of Yalova at five o'clock in the evening of December 31, but the Hellenic forces repelled them. A bomb thrown by the Kemalists wounded five Greek soldiers. On January 2, the Kemalists attacked the villages of Kılıç and Çukur and thoroughly looted both. The inhabitants of these villages had already taken refuge in Yalova, that is, on the second day of the attack on Yalova. On January 5, the Kemalists burned the village of Kartsi.

The goal of the Kemalists, then, was to capture Yalova on December 31. Perhaps the Turks living here and in the surrounding areas were going to take part in that capture, but since they failed thanks to the resistance of the Hellenic forces, they took their ferocious revenge on the unfortunate Armenian villages. A few days after the burning of Kartsi, they attacked the fortifications of Sugören [Çengiler] and Büyük-Yeniköy but were repelled with the same failure.

The following Armenians were martyred during those attacks.

Çukur village: Hagop Zadigian, gunned down
Hovan Ghougasian, gunned down
Kılıç village: Hovagim Tavitian, shot
Mardig Donigian, hanged in Karamürsel [Karamursal]
Mariam Hovhannesian, shot
Şakşak village: Haroutyun Ateshian, hanged in Karamürsel
Kartsi: Varteres Kazmerian (village headman), slaughtered, eyes removed, nose and ears cut off
Baghdasar Davouljian, executed by shooting
Giragos Kapigian, slaughtered
Makrouhi Dedoyan, executed by shooting
Filor Ashemian, executed by shooting

Չէնկիլէր (Թաղական Խորհուրդէն) – 1 Յունվար 1921

Այս առաւօտ կանուխ Չէնկիլէր գիւղին հիւսիսային սարերու գագաթներէն, ինչպէս նաեւ Օրթաքէօյի եւ Մեծ-Նոր-Գիւղի շրջականերէն Միլլիներու կողմէ սոսկալի յարձակում մը գործուեցաւ:

Չէնկիլէրի յունական զինուորներու քաջ դիմադրութեան շնորհիւ, երեք ժամուան հրացանաձգութենէ վերջ, Միլլիճիները քաշուեցան Եալովայի հայ եւ թուրք գիւղերը:

Ներկայիս Չէնկիլէրի մէջ համախմբուած են Եալովայի Շագշագ, Քարցի, Գըլըճ եւ Չուգուր հայ գիւղերէ գաղթականներ, որոնք մազապուր ազատած են իրենց կեանքը:

Չէնկիլէրի մէջ թէեւ խուճապ առաջ եկած է, սակայն գաղթ չէ եղած շնորհիւ յոյն զինուորներու դիմադրութեան: Իսկ օրթաքէօյցիք եւ մեծ-նոր-գիւղցիք հազիւ իրենց զաւակները առած բոկոտն ու մերկ փախած են մինչեւ Բազար գիւղ, ուր բաւական թիւով յոյն զինուոր կայ:

Այս շրջանի բոլոր ժողովուրդը կը գտնուի սարսափի տակ եւ գիւղերէն մէկ մասը Միլլիճիներու ձեռքը ըլլալով (ինչպէս Քէրէմէթ, Օրթաքէօյ եւ Մեծ-Նոր-Գիւղ) իրենք պարտաւորուած են թափառիլ աստ անդ, մօտաւորապէս 3500 հոգի:

Պրուսա (Առաջնորդական Տեղապահէն) – 16 Յունվար 1921

Մինչ կը սպասուէր որ հելլէնական յառաջխաղացմամբ հայերը իրենց օճախը դառնային՝ դժբաղդաբար հակառակ արդիւնք տուաւ, այնպէս որ իրենց մտած եւ դարձեալ լքած տեղերու բնակչութիւնն ալ ստիպուեցաւ Քէմալական սարսափին տեղի տալով իրենց անձը միայն ազատելու ջանալ, որով առաջիններու վրայ աւելցան Պիլէճիկի հայ[եր]ն ալ, որոնց դպրոցներ եւ տուներ յատկացուեցան եւ Առաջնորդական Տեղապահին դիմումին վրայ սկսաւ հաց տրուիլ:

Պիլէճիկի շրջակայ գիւղերէն ոչ ոք չէ կրցած ազատիլ եւ չեն կրցած պիլէճիկցիներու հետ միասին հոս գալ: 3–4000 գաղթականներէն միայն 500ի չափ եկած են:

Եալովա (Յովհաննէս Տէր Կարապետեանի մասնաւոր նամակէն) – 17 Յունվար 1921

Քէմալականք 31 Դեկտեմբերին գիշեր ատեն ժամը 5ին յարձակեցան Եալովայի հարաւային կողմը բլուրին վրայ գտնուած ամրութեանց վրայ, սակայն հելլէն զօրքերու կողմէն ետ մղուեցան: Քէմալականներու կողմէ նետուած պոմպայէն 5 յոյն զինուոր վիրաւորուեցաւ: Յունվար 2ին Քէմալականք յարձակեցան Գըլըճ եւ Չուգուր գիւղերուն վրայ եւ բոլորովին կողոպտեցին: Այս գիւղերու բնակիչները արդէն կանխաւ Եալովա ապաստանած էին, այսինքն Եալովայի վրայ եղած յարձակումին երկրորդ օրը: Յունվար 5ին Քէմալականք Քարցի գիւղը այրեցին:

Ուրեմն Քէմալականներու նպատակն էր Դեկտեմբեր 31ին Եալովան գրաւել եւ թերեւս այդ գրաւման պիտի մասնակցէին տեղացի եւ շրջակայ թուրքեր, բայց որովհետեւ շնորհիւ հելլէն զօրքերու դիմադրութեան չյաջողեցան, ուստի իրենց վայրագ վրէժը առին խեղճ հայ գիւղերէն: Քարցին այրելէ վերջ մի քանի օր յետոյ յարձակեցան Չէնկիլէրի եւ Մեծ-Նոր-Գիւղի ամրութեանց վրայ եւ միեւնոյն անյաջողութեամբ ետ մղուեցան:

Այդ յարձակումներու շրջանին նահատակուեցան հետեւեալ հայերը.

Չուգուր գիւղ. Յակոբ Զատիկեան	հրացանի բռնուած
Յովան Ղուկասեան	հրացանի բռնուած
Գըլըճ գիւղ. Յովակիմ Դաւիթեան	զարնուած
Մարտիկ Տօնիկեան	կախուած Գարամուսալի մէջ
Մարիամ Յովհաննէսեան	զարնուած
Շագ-Շագ գիւղ. Յարութիւն Աթէշեան	կախուած Գարամուսալի մէջ
Քարցի. Վարդերես Գազմերեան (մուխտար)	մորթուած, աչքերը հանուած, քիթն ու ականջները կտրուած
Պաղտասար Տավուլճեան	գնդակահար
Կիրակոս Գաբիկեան	մորթուած

Altogether eight men and three women.

Kartsi is wholly burned; only eight or nine houses are left, and they are half-destroyed. The inhabitants of those four villages are primarily scattered in Yalova and Sugören. Some have migrated to Büyükada and İstanbul. After looting those three villages, the Millis completely dismantled the windows, doors, and decks [of the homes]. Fewer Millis have been seen around there since the Greek army advanced on Eskişehir; therefore, for several days now, some armed, young Armenians from Elmalık have been going there to collect at least the olives left on the trees. . . . Turks, whose dark past is well known to everyone and who took refuge in İstanbul from Yalova and its environs, continue to complain to the representatives of the Great Powers, alleging that Armenians and Greeks are attacking their villages, robbing them and so on. I think these are false accusations. . . . When the Armenians were deported, local Turks divided all their belongings among themselves; now that surviving Armenians have returned, identified their animals and goods and chattels, and are demanding their return, the Turks are reluctant to return what rightfully belongs to Armenians. There are no Turkish or mixed courts to restore the rights to their owners. Many await the future, but some individuals cannot wait hungry, and it is said that some have forcibly taken back their rights. By magnifying these one or two cases, the Turks want to defame the Christians and perhaps the Greek government, with whom we Christians are very satisfied and grateful.

Recently, an English captain, returning from an exploratory tour around Yenisölöz, called me at night, and he, too, insinuated that Christians had also begun to rob the Muslims. I protested against that slander, which had undoubtedly been voiced by the Turks, and said that the Armenians were just demanding what their right is, but the Turks, who have become accustomed to living off the fruits of the sweat of Christians for centuries, now find it very difficult to return the blanket or the cow that belongs to a naked Armenian to him. . . . We are terrified that the Greek army may withdraw. . . . I ask you to kindly send news immediately in the event of any disadvantageous change because the Turks are very sorry that they did not completely annihilate the Christians five years ago, and this time they openly say that they will put even suckling infants to the sword.

Keskin (from Reverend Father Kevork Sarajian)—December 16 [1920]

About one hundred Armenians from Bilecik arrived in Keskin in poor condition. They need money and clothes to pass the winter.

İzmit (from the primate)—February 21 [1921]

The Millis had already occupied the Armenian villages of Avcıköy [Merdigöz] and Yalakdere. Those of their residents who had managed to escape were sheltered in Yalova, Sugören [Çengiler], Darıca, and Büyük-Yeniköy. Only 80 were left in Avcıköy and 120 in Yalakdere. The Millis had assured them that they would not be harmed, but on February 11, they filled them into the churches, robbed them from head to toe, and beat them, saying: "Let your Greek and English defenders free you!" They rebuked [them], tortured them, and then moved them naked and barefoot toward İznik to take them to Ankara. The fate of those 200 Armenians is unknown.

Five or six of them barely managed to escape, but only one arrived in İzmit via Bahçecik. She is a thirty-year-old woman, Ghevondié, the wife of Artin Arslanian (of Avcıköy), with her three children:

Մաքրուհի Տէտոյեան գնդակահար
Փիլօր Աշեմեան գնդակահար

Ընդամէնը 8 այր եւ 3 կին մարդ:

Քարցի բոլորովին այրուած է, միայն կը մնան 8–9 տուներ, անոնք ալ կիսաւեր: Այդ չորս գիւղերու բնակիչները մեծ մասամբ Եալովայի եւ Չէնկիլէրի մէջ ցրուած են. իսկ մաս մըն ալ գաղթած են Մեծ-Կզզի եւ Պոլիս: Միլլիները այդ երեք գիւղերը կողոպտելէն վերջ՝ պատուհանները, դուռները եւ տախտակամածները բոլորովին քարուքանդ ըրած են: Յունական բանակին դէպի Էսկիշէհիր յառաջխաղացումէն ի վեր այդ կողմերը շատ Միլլիները չեն երեւիր, ուստի մի քանի օրէ ի վեր հայերէն ոմանք էյմալըկցիներէն երիտասարդներ զինեալ կ'երթան գոնէ ծառերուն վրայ մնացած ձիթապտուղները ժողովելու համար: ... Եալովայէն եւ շրջականերէն Պոլիս ապաստանող թիւրքեր, որոնց տխուր անցեալը ամենուն ալ ծանօթ է, հոն շարունակ, ինչպէս կը լսենք, մեծ պետութեանց ներկայացուցիչներուն բողոքներ կուտան, որպէս թէ հայեր եւ յոյներ իրենց գիւղերուն վրայ կը յարձակին, կը կողոպտեն եւայլն: Կը կարծեմ թէ սուտ զրպարտութիւններ են ատոնք: ... Երբ հայերը տարագրուեցան, անոնց բոլոր ունեցածները տեղացի թուրքեր իրենց մէջ բաժնեցին, հիմա վերապրող հայեր վերադառնալով եւ ճանչնալով իրենց անասունները եւ կահ կարասիները՝ ետ կը պահանջեն, թուրքերուն շատ դժուար կուգայ հայերուն արդար իրաւունքները ետ տալը: Թրքական կամ խառն դատարաններ չկան որ այդ իրաւունքները իրենց տէրերուն վերադարձնեն: Շատեր կան, որոնք կը սպասեն ապագային, բայց կը զտնուին անհատներ, որոնք մերկ եւ անօթի՝ չեն կարող համբերել եւ կ'ըսուի թէ մի քանիներ ալ բռնի ետ առած են իրենց իրաւունքը: Թուրքերը այդ մէկ երկու դէպքերը մեծցնելով կ'ուզեն անուանարկել քրիստոնեաները եւ թերեւս յունական իշխանութիւնը, որմէ մենք քրիստոնեաներս չափազանց գոհ եւ շնորհակալ ենք:

Անցեալները անգլիացի հարիւրապետ մը Սէօյէօզի կողմերէն քննական պտոյտէն վերադառնալով գիշեր ատեն զիս քովը կանչած էր, այն ալ կերպով մը յայտնեց որպէս թէ քրիստոնեաներն ալ տաճիկներ կողոպտել սկսած են: Բողոքեցի այդ զրպարտութեան դէմ, որ անշուշտ թուրքերու կողմանէ եղած էր եւ յայտնեցի որ հայերը իրենց արդար իրաւունքն է որ կը պահանջեն, սակայն թուրքերը որ երկար դարեր վարժուած են քրիստոնէից քրտանց արդիւնքով ապրիլ՝ այժմ իրենց շատ դժուար կուգայ մերկ հայուն վերմակը կամ կովը իրեն վերադարձնելը: ... Շատ կը վախնանք որ մի՛ գուցէ յունական բանակը ետ կը քաշուի: ... Կը խնդրեմ որ եթէ ռեւէ աննպաստ փոփոխութիւն մը ըլլայ՝ անմիջապէս լուր մը ղրկել բարեհաճիք, որովհետեւ թուրքերը շատ կ'ափսոսան թէ ինչու հինգ տարի առաջ բոլորովին բնաջինջ չեն ըրած քրիստոնէութիւնը եւ այս անգամ յայտնապէս կ'ըսեն, որ կաթնկեր մանուկներն անգամ սրէ պիտի անցնեն:

Քէսկին (Գէորգ Վարդապետ Սարաճեանէ) – 16 Դեկտեմբեր [1920]

Պիլէճիկէն 100ի մօտ հայեր Քէսկին գացած են խեղճ վիճակի մէջ: Ձմեռը կարենալ անցնելու համար դրամ եւ հագուստ կը պահանջեն:

Նիկոմիդիա (Առաջնորդէն) – 21 Փետրուար [1921]

Միլլիճիներն արդէն զրաւած էին Մերտիկէօզ եւ Եալագտէրէ հայ գիւղերը: Անոնց բնակիչներէն անոնք որ կրցած էին փախչիլ, ապաստանած էին Եալովա, Չէնկիլէր, Տարճա եւ Մեծ-Նոր-Գիւղ եւ միայն 80 հոգի մնացած էին Մերտիկէօզ եւ 120 հոգի Եալագտէրէ: Միլլիճիները ասոնց ապահոված էին թէ իրենց ռեւէ վնաս չպիտի հասցնեն, սակայն Փետրուար 11ին զանոնք եկեղեցիները կը լեցնեն եւ յոտից ցգլուխ կը կողոպտեն եւ ձեր յոյն եւ անգլիացի պաշտպանները թող զձեզ ազատեն ըսելով կը ծեծեն, կը նախատեն, կը խոշտանգեն եւ ապա մերկ ու բոպիկ կը տեղափոխեն դէպի Իզնիկի կողմերը՝ Էնկիւրիւ տանելու համար: Չի զիտցուիր թէ այդ 200ի մօտ հայերը ի՞նչ եղած են:

Ասոնցմէ 5–6 հոգի հազիւ կրցած են փախչիլ, սակայն միայն մէկը ցարդ Նիկոմիդիա եկած է Պարտիզակի ճամբով: Այս է կին մը՝ Արթին Արսլանեանի (մերտիկէօզցի) կինը՝ Ղեւոնտիէ (30

ten-year-old Hovhannes, seven-year-old Mgrdich, and nine-month-old daughter.

This woman was saved thanks to Artin Aydunyan of Avcıköy, who led her secretly to the Laz village of Hamidiye, where they stayed for five days hidden in a Laz's house. Artin Aydunyan left thence alone to come to İzmit, but he has not arrived yet, and it is unknown what happened to him.

• The profit tax, property tax, and the tax on incoming goods, goods at hand, and octroi threaten to ruin lives. Almost the whole market is desperate.

İzmit (from the primate)—March 4 [1921]

This morning, the Millis mercilessly slaughtered the inhabitants of the Greek seaside village of Zonca. Then they set on fire its six to seven hundred houses. The smoke of the fire was visible until evening.

• Six Armenians and one Greek from Şile were beaten and imprisoned there [in Zonca] for twenty-eight days. Recently, they were brought to İzmit and imprisoned here. They were released upon the intervention of the primate. One of them died as a result of the beating.

Zonguldak (from the Neighborhood Council)—March 2[103]

The Kemalist government of Anadolu [Anatolia] makes every effort to prevent communication with the outside world to conceal its actions.

This caution alone is enough to explain the critical moments that the Armenian remnants scattered in Anadolu are going through. Despite the absence of traffic and communication with the inner provinces, the random news that reaches us does not promise a good situation. Life in this city and the surrounding towns is burdensome to the point of calling it intolerable. No Christian has the right to go anywhere more than an hour away without a credential. Traveling to Devrek, Çaycuma, and other cities that are six, nine, or twelve hours away is strictly prohibited. Those who went to İstanbul six or seven months ago and are coming back to this city are being sent back without landing. The threats of massacre and robbery by individuals seem to be widespread expressions: a Turk upset about anything readily threatens, "You raised your heads again."

As if all these were not enough, on February 12, those born in 1894, 1895, and 1896 were enlisted, and military service of the Christians resumed. Those present were immediately taken to Bolu as soldiers, and the government locked the shops of the fugitives. The keys are still in the hands of the government, and some of the fugitives' close relatives have been detained. As for those who had gone to İstanbul or another occupied city before the draft, a close relative was detained immediately for each, to deliver the person sought after within forty days; otherwise, [the relative] would be released on bail, provided he himself is enlisted.

• Until four months ago, we enjoyed the protection of the military authorities in this city, at least in small matters. Particularly, they rendered all kinds of facilitation to travel to İstanbul, even under the auspices of the French gendarmerie, and they defended those returning from İstanbul when they were interrogated, with the Turkish government going easy on the matter. However, after the departure of Captain Zrgan, the head of Zonguldak's Information Bureau and the Passport Bureau, no facilitation has been provided to Armenians under his successor, Captain Boisson, and no Armenian has been able to travel to İstanbul in the last four months.

We were in this predicament when, on the opening day of the London Conference on February 21, we naívely perceived mitigation in the situation once we saw the severity of military and other issues eased and heard that the keys to the locked shops of [absent] deserters were being handed over to the parents [of the absentees].

տարեկան), հետը ունենալով իր երեք զաւակները՝ Յովհաննէս 10 տարեկան, Մկրտիչ 7 տարեկան եւ 9ամսեայ աղջիկը:

Այս կինը փրկուած է շնորհիւ մերտիկէօզցի Արթին Այտընեանի, որ զինքը առաջնորդած է գաղտնի Համիտիյէ լազ գիւղն ուր 5 օր մնացած են լազի մը տունը ծածկուած: Հոնկէ Արթին Այտընեան կը մեկնի առանձին Նիկոմիդիա գալու համար, սակայն մինչեւ հիմա չէ եկած եւ յայտնի չէ թէ ինչ եղած է:

- Թէմէթթիւի, կալուածական տուրքի եւ գալիք ապրանքի եւ պատրաստ ապրանքի օգթուրայի տուրքը կը սպառնայ կեանքը քայքայել: Ամբողջ շուկան գրեթէ յուսահատած է:

Նիկոմիդիա (Առաջնորդէն) – 4 Մարտ [1921]

Ա[յ]ս առաւօտ յունաց Չօնճա գիւղն, 6–7 հարիւր տուն եւ ծովեզերեայ, Միլլիճիները կրակի կուտան, բնակիչները անխնայ ջարդելէն վերջը: Հրդեհին մուխը մինչեւ իրիկուն կ'երեւար:

- Շիլէէն վեց հայ ու մէկ յոյն բռնած ծեծած եւ 28 օր հոն բանտ դրած էին: Վերջերս Նիկոմիդիա բերած եւ հոս բանտարկած են: Առաջնորդին միջամտութեամբ ազատ կ'արձակուին: Ասոնցմէ մէկը ծեծի հետեւանօք կը մեռնի:

Չօնկուլտաք (Թաղական Խորհուրդէն) – 2 Մարտ

Անատոլուի Քէմալական կառավարութիւնը ամէն ջանք կը թափէ որպէսզի արտաքին աշխարհի հետ յարաբերութիւն չկատարուի եւ իր արարքները չծանուցուին աշխարհի:

Միայն այս զգուշաւորութիւնը բաւական է բացատրելու թէ Անատոլուի մէջ ցրուած հայութեան բեկորները ինչ ճգնաժամային վայրկեաններ կ'անցնեն: Որքան որ ներքին գաւառներու հետ յարաբերութիւն եւ երթեւեկ գոյութիւն չունի, բայց պատահական լուրեր լաւ վիճակ մը չեն խոստանար. իսկ քաղաքիս եւ շրջակայ քաղաքներու մէջ կեանքը անտանելի ըսելու աստիճան ծանր է: Եւ ոչ մէկ քրիստոնեայ առանց վէսիքայի ժամուան մը հեռաւորութեամբ ուեւէ տեղ երթալու իրաւունք չունի: 6–9–12 ժամ հեռաւորութեամբ Տէվրէկ, Չայ-Ճումաա եւ այլ քաղաքներ երթալը բացարձակապէս արգիլուած է: 6–7 ամիս առաջ Պոլիս գացողներ, որոնք կը վերադառնան քաղաքս, առանց ցամաք հանելու ետ կը վերադարձուին եւ անհատներու կողմէ ջարդի ու կողոպուտի սպառնալիք կարծես թէ շատ սովորական խօսք մը եղած ըլլան, ուեւէ բանէ դառնացած թուրք մը անմիջապէս պատրաստ է «նորէն գլուխ վերցուցիք»ի սպառնալիքը ընելու:

Բոլոր ասոնք իբր թէ անբաւական եղած ըլլային, Փետրուար 12ին 312–13–14ի ծնունդները զէնքի տակ առնուեցան եւ քրիստոնեաներու զինուորագրութիւնը վերստին սկսաւ: Անոնք որ ներկայ էին իբր զինուոր անմիջապէս ճամբայ հանուեցան դէպի Պոլու, իսկ փախչողներուն խանութները կառավարութեան կողմէ արգելքի տակ առնուեցան: Բանալիները ցարդ կառավարութեան քով կը գտնուին եւ իրենց մօտաւոր ազգականներէն ոմանք բանտարկուեցան: Իսկ անոնք որ զօրակոչէն առաջ Պոլիս կամ ուրիշ գրաւեալ քաղաք մը գացած են, այդպիսիներուն մօտաւոր ազգականներէն մին անմիջապէս կը բանտարկուի, մինչեւ 40 օր փնտռուած անձը յանձնելու՝ իսկ հակառակ պարագային՝ ինք անձամբ զինուոր ըլլալու պայմանով երաշխաւորութեամբ ազատ կ'արձակուի:

- Ասկէ մինչեւ չորս ամիս առաջ քաղաքս գտնուող զինուորական իշխանութեան պաշտպանութիւնը կը վայելէինք զէթ մանր մունր խնդիրներու մէջ, ի մասնաւորի Պոլիս երթալ գալու համար ամէն դիւրութիւն կ'ընծայէին նոյն իսկ ֆրանսական ժանտարմըրըյի հովանաւորութեամբ եւ Պոլիսէն վերադարձողները երբ հարցաքննութեան ենթարկուէին, զանոնք կը պաշտպանէին եւ թուրք կառավարութիւնը խնդիրը կարճ կը կապէր: Սակայն Չոնկուլտաքի տեղեկատու դիւանի եւ վէսիքայի պիւրօյի պետ քաքիճէն Չրկանին հեռանալէն յետոյ՝ անոր յաջորդ քաքիճէն Պուազօնի օրով այլեւս ոչ մէկ դիւրութիւն տրուած է հայոց եւ վերջին չորս ամիսներուն մէջ ոչ մէկ հայ կրցած է Պոլիս գալ:

However, an incident today flipped our optimism upside down again.

Mourad Panosian, a merchant who had settled in the city for thirty years, and Garabed Agha Aduyamanlian, also a merchant who had settled in the city for fifteen years, went to İstanbul six or seven months ago and returned fifteen days ago. Because they traveled to İstanbul without a pass, they were immediately placed on a steamboat to be sent [back] to İstanbul under watch.

The only local Greek priest serving the city for eight or nine months was sent away with them. The reason for the expulsion of the Greek priest is entirely unknown.

Aleppo (from Karekin Jiyerjian)—February 25[104]

On January 29, 1921, upon a ciphered order issued by the deputy minister of the interior of the Ankara government, an Armenian merchant living in Harput for eighteen months was taken under police watch as a harmful element via Malatya-Adıyaman [Hısnımansur] to Nizip. Passing thence to Aleppo, he reported the following.

The Armenians in the whole prefecture of Harput had been in good condition until the end of January because Mustafa Kemal gave strict orders that it be so.

Harput and its villages, the city of Malatya, Arapkir, Kemaliye [Egin], and Akpazar [Çarsancak] with their villages have thirty thousand Armenians altogether: women, boys, girls, and adult men. They are engaged in crafts, trade, and various activities. They live pretty satisfactorily. In the last year and a half, eight or ten Armenians have been killed, and in the same period, four to five hundred Turks have killed each other because of personal adversity. It is true, though, that Armenians are constantly in fear because rumors deliberately arrive daily to irritate the Turks. For example, they spread rumors that the Armenians on the Gaziantep [Ayntab] front had helped the French, that the Armenian Republic had attacked Turkey, that anti-Turkish articles had been printed in the Armenian newspapers of İstanbul, and that the massacrers are being brought to court upon Armenians' request.

These reports have created a threatening atmosphere; therefore, the Armenians under the rule of Mustafa Kemal always remain under the threat of massacre.

The primate of Harput, Bishop Kyud, cultivates excellent relations with the government to appease the Turks. On the occasion of the holidays, he exchanges telegrams with Mustafa Kemal Pasha and with Nihat Pasha, prefect of Diyarbakır and commander of the Jazira front.

On the occasion of the war, Armenians also began to be recruited. Addressing Nihat Pasha, the primate tried to exempt the Armenians. Nihat Pasha responded politely and stated that he could not make an exception. An order from Ankara only excluded acolytes, so the primate ordained acolytes for the town and village churches (forty-four people in and around Harput). Until the end of January, the military authorities did not have a problem with this.

Traffic has been banned for a year. The primate worked hard [to have it lifted], but he could not succeed. He even cabled Mustafa Kemal Pasha in Ankara, asking only women to [be permitted to] go to America to join their children, brothers, or husbands, but to no avail.

Mustafa Kemal cabled the prefect of Harput, asking him to politely explain to the Armenian primate that the road could not be opened now.

The [Armenian] Political Assembly, together with the primate, administers the national estates and a few ownerless estates, which the prelacy has taken ownership of and the government has turned a blind eye to. Monaster[ies] and other lands are also used more or less. In Malatya, Arapkir, and Ke-

Այս դժբաղդ կացութեան մէջ էինք, երբ Փետրուար 21ին Լօնտօնի Խորհրդաժողովին բացման օրը, կացութեան մէջ պզտիկ մեղմացում մը տեսնելու միամտութիւնը ունեցանք, զինուորական եւ ուրիշ խնդիրներու խստութիւնները մեղմացած տեսնելով եւ զինուորական փախստականներու արգելքի տակ առնուած խանութներուն բանալիները իրենց ծնողաց յանձնելը լսելով:

Սակայն այսօր տեղի ունեցած դէպք մը մեր լաւատեսութիւնները դարձեալ վերիվայր շրջեց:

30 տարիներէ ի վեր քաղաքս հաստատուած վաճառական Մուրատ Փանոսեան եւ 15 տարիէ ի վեր քաղաքս հաստատուած Կարապետ աղա Ատըեամանլեան, երկուքն ալ վաճառական, 6–7 ամիս առաջ Պոլիս մեկնած եւ 15 օր առաջ վերադարձած էին. առանց վէսիքայի Պոլիս երթալնուն համար անմիջապէս ընդ հսկողութեամբ շոգենաւ դրուեցան Պոլիս ղրկուելու համար:

Իրենց հետ նաեւ ճամբուեցաւ տեղւոյս միակ յոյն քահանան, որ 8–9 ամիսէ ի վեր քաղաքս կը պաշտօնավարէր: Յոյն քահանային վտարուելուն պատճառը բոլորովին անյայտ է:

Հալէպ (Գարեգին Ճիլէրճեանէ) – 25 Փետրուար

1921 Յունվար 29ին Էնկիւրիւի կառավարութեան ներքին գործոց նախարարի փոխանորդին քաշած մէկ ծածկագիր հրամանին վրայ 18 ամիսներէ ի վեր Խարբերդ հաստատուած հայ վաճառական մը իբր վնասակար ոստիկանական հսկողութեան տակ Մալաթիա-Հիւսնի Մանսուրի ճամբով Նիզիպ կը տարուի եւ հոնկէ Հալէպ կ'անցնի, ուրկէ կը տեղեկագրէ հետեւեալները:

Խարբերդի ամբողջ կուսակալութեան մէջ հայերը մինչեւ Յունվարի վերջը լաւ վիճակ ունին, որովհետեւ Մուսթաֆա Քէմալ խիստ հրամաններ տուած է:

Խարբերդ եւ իր գիւղերը, Մալաթիա քաղաքը, Արաբկիր, Ակն, Չարսանճագ իրենց գիւղերով ընդամէնը ունին 30,000 հայ, կին, տղայ, աղջիկ եւ չափահաս մարդիկ: Ասոնք կը զբաղին արհեստով, առեւտուրով եւ զանազան աշխատութիւններով: Կ'ապրին բաւական գոհացուցիչ: Վերջին մէկուկէս տարուան միջոցին սպաննուած են 8–10 հայեր, իսկ նոյն միջոցին անձնական հակառակութեան բերմամբ թուրքերը իրար սպաննած են 4–500 անձ: Միայն ճիշտ է որ հայերը միշտ երկիւղի մէջ կ'ապրին, վասնզի ամէն օր կը հասնին թուրքերը գրգռող տեղեկութիւններ, որոնք դիտմամբ կը տարածայնուին: Այսպէս կը տարածայնեն թէ Այնթապի ճակատին վրայ հայերը ֆրանսացւոց օգնած են, Հայկական Հանրապետութիւնը Թուրքիոյ վրայ յարձակած է, թէ Կ. Պոլսոյ հայ լրագիրներուն մէջ թրքաց դէմ յօդուածներ կան, թէ ջարդարարները դատարան կը յանձնուին հայոց պահանջումով:

Այս լուրերը սպառնալից մթնոլորտ մը ստեղծած են, այնպէս որ Մուսթաֆա Քէմալի իշխանութեան տակ գտնուող հայերը միշտ ջարդի սպառնալիքի տակ են:

Խարբերդի Առաջնորդը՝ Գիւտ Եպիսկոպոս, կառավարութեան հետ խիստ լաւ յարաբերութիւններ կը մշակէ թուրքերը մեղմացնելու համար: Պայրամներու առթիւ Մուսթաֆա Քէմալ փաշայի եւ Տիարպէքիրի կուսակալ եւ Ճէզրա Ճէպ[ի]էսի հրամատար Նիհատ փաշայի հետ հեռագիրներ կը փոխանակէ:

Պատերազմի առթիւ հայերէն ալ զինուոր առնուիլ սկսաւ: Նիհատ փաշայի դիմելով Առաջնորդը աշխատեցաւ հայերը ազատել: Նիհատ փաշա քաղաքավար կերպով պատասխանելով կը յայտնէ թէ բացառութիւն չի կրնար ըլլալ: Էնկիւրիւէն եկած հրաման մը միայն դպիրներու բացառութիւն կ'ընէր, ուստի Առաջնորդը քաղաքին եւ գիւղերու եկեղեցիներուն վրայ ձեռնադրեց դպիրներ (44 անձ միայն Խարբերդ եւ շրջակայքը): Մինչեւ Յունվարի վերջը զինուորական իշխանութիւնները այս բանի համար դժուարութիւն չէին հաներ:

Երթեւեկը տարիէ մը ի վեր արգիլուած է: Առաջնորդը շատ աշխատեցաւ բայց չկրցաւ յաջողիլ: Նոյնիսկ Էնկիւրիւ Մուսթաֆա Քէմալ փաշայի հեռագրեց եւ միայն կանանց Ամերիկա իրենց զաւակներու եւ եղբայրներու եւ ամուսիններու քով երթալու հրաման խնդրեց, բայց չյաջողեցաւ:

Մուսթաֆա Քէմալ Խարբերդի կուսակալին հեռագրած էր որ հայոց Առաջնորդին քաղաքավարի լեզուով մը հասկցուցէք թէ հիմա ճամբան բանալ կարելի չէր:

maliye [Egin], too, thanks to the ingenuity of some Armenians, estates that had collapsed have been rebuilt and producing quite significant rent.

The people's financial situation would be much better if the people of Harput received help from their relatives in America. Previously, about one hundred thousand liras arrived in a peculiar way and after suffering a loss of almost thirty to forty percent. It has virtually stopped for six or seven months now. Recently, the Ottoman Bank began to take bills of exchange from these unfortunate people for America and elsewhere on the condition that when the bills are paid there, the bank will pay in Harput. The sum of these bills must be two hundred thousand dollars by now, and once it is paid, it will alleviate [the people's] misery quite noticeably. A couple of Turks and Christians also followed the Armenians' lead on that condition.

There are about forty-five hundred to five thousand orphans, women, and girls in the American orphanage in Harput. The dispensation is good, but not the administration. The Turks have occupied the two large German buildings where they [the orphans] were sheltered. The Turks turned these buildings into a school and explicitly say that if the Red Cross or the Relief serve humanitarian purposes, they must also care for Muslim orphans. From the governor-general to the last person, this is their constant theme.

We have several hundred orphans in the orphanages of Malatya, Arapgir, and Kemaliye.

There are four hundred fifty to five hundred orphans in the Harput National Orphanage. The monthly expense is four or five hundred liras, in addition to the local rent and clothing. This money has been coming through the Americans lately. In the winter, they provided clothes, for which they have not yet demanded the money. When the money sent rises to six hundred [liras], the orphans and newcomers can be admitted.

There are still many orphans, women, and girls in the villages with the Turks. Due to the monetary shortage, working to free them is impossible.

There are quite a considerable number of Armenians in Silvan, and the situation is comforting. The local governor is Mazhar Bey, a man of goodwill, and the military commander-in-chief is Nihat Pasha, who has strict orders. At the end of January, a communiqué was issued stating that anyone who maltreats non-Muslims would be punished severely and so on.

There are also a few hundred Armenian families in Hısnımansur; they are comfortable. There are [Armenians] also in villages, just as in a village in Rumkale, where two families have fled Gaziantep and are being sheltered by Kurds. There are two thousand Armenians in Birecik. The local lieutenant governor is a young man named Kemal Bey, an Armenologist. These Armenians are free to move between villages, and because of this, artisans benefit. There, too, the Armenians are being protected by the lieutenant governor. He severely punished several bandits who robbed a local priest.

İzmit (from the primate)—April 8 [1921]

Yesterday, the Millis burned the Greek villages of Karatepe near Arslanbey and Bahçecik (near Ilıca). This morning, the Armenian Döngöl was said to be burning. The smoke was indeed visible. The Ovacık fire can also be seen from İzmit.

Residents of the Greek village of Gündoğdu [Mihaliç] near İzmit have taken refuge in the city. There is a fear in İzmit that Christian neighborhoods will also be set on fire.

Sugören [Çengiler] (from the Neighborhood Council)—April 8 [1921]

Traffic on the Yalova-Orhangazi highway of the occupied region, which has been the only way to İstanbul for Armenian and Greek travelers, ceased as of April 3. On the same day, Vartan Mgrian, Dikran

Քաղաքական Ժողովը Առաջնորդին հետ կը մատակարարէ ազգային կալուածները, քիչ մըն ալ անտէր կալուածները, որոնց տէր կանգնած է Առաջնորդարանը եւ կառավարութիւնը աչք գոցած է: Վանքի եւ այլ հողեր ալ քիչ շատ կ'օգտագործուին: Նոյնպէս Մալաթիոյ, Արաբկիրի եւ Ակնայ մէջ կարգ մը ազգայիններու ճարպիկութեան շնորհիւ փլած կալուածները վերաշինուած են եւ բաւական կարեւոր վարձք մը կը բերեն:

Ժողովրդեան նիւթական վիճակը շատ աւելի պիտի բարւոքի եթէ խարբերդցիք կարենան իրենց Ամերիկա գտնուող ազգականներէն օգնութիւն ստանալ: Ասկէ առաջ 100 հազար լիրայի չափ եկած էր շատ անկանոն եղանակով եւ գրեթէ 30/40% կորուստով: Հիմա 6–7 ամիս է որ գրեթէ բոլորովին դադրած է: Վերջերս օսմանեան պանքան սկսաւ այս խեղճերէն փոխ գիր առնել Ամերիկայի եւ ուրիշ տեղերու վրայ այն պայմանով որ երբ հոն վճարուի, ինքն ալ Խարբերդի մէջ վճարէ: Ցարդ այս քաշուած փոխ գիրերուն համագումարը 200 հազար տոլար մը ըլլալու է, եւ եթէ անգամ մը վճարուի՝ բաւական խեղճութեան առաջքը առնուած կ'ըլլայ: Հայոց օրինակին հետեւելով, մէկ-երկու թուրք եւ քրիստոնեայ ալ առնել սկսան այդ պայմանով:

Խարբերդի ամերիկեան որբանոցին մէջ կան 4500–5000ի մօտ որբեր, կիներ եւ աղջիկներ: Մատակարարութիւնը լաւ է, սակայն ոչ վարչութիւնը: Թուրքերը գրաւած են գերմաններու երկու ահագին շէնքերը որոնց մէջ կը պատսպարուէին: Թուրքերը այդ շէնքերը դպրոց ըրին եւ բացարձակ կ'ըսեն թէ եթէ Կարմիր Խաչը կամ Րըլիֆը մարդասիրութեան համար է, թող իսլամ որբերուն ալ նայի: Վալիէն սկսեալ ամէնէն պզտիկը յանկերգը այս է:

Մալաթիայի, Արաբկիրի, Ակնայ որբանոցին մէջ քանի մը հարիւր որբեր ունինք:

Խարբերդի ազգային որբանոցին մէջ 450/500 որբ կայ եւ 4/5 հարիւր լիրա ամսական ծախք, բացի տեղի վարձքէն եւ վրայ գլուխէն: Այս դրամը վերջերս կուգայ ամերիկացիներուն ձեռամբ: Ձմեռը անոնք տուին հագուստ, որուն դրամը դեռ չեն պահանջած: Երբ ղրկուած դրամը 600ի բարձրանայ, թէ՛ որբերը եւ թէ՛ նոր գալիք որբերը կրնան առնուիլ:

Դեռ գիւղերը բաւական որբեր, կիներ, աղջիկներ կան թուրքերու քով: Դրամական անձկութեան պատճառով կարելի չ'ըլլար զանոնք ազատելու աշխատիլ:

Տիգրանակերտ բաւական թուով հայ կայ եւ վիճակնին մխիթարական է: Այն տեղի վալին է Մազհար պէյ, որ բարեացակամ է եւ զինուորական ընդհանուր հրամատարն է Նիհատ փաշա, [որ] խիստ հրամաններ ունի: Յունուարի վերջը յայտագիր մը կը հանեն թէ ամէն անոնք որոնք ոչ-իսլամներու հետ գէշ վարուին, խիստ պատիժներ պիտի կրեն եւայլն:

Հիւսնի Մանսուրի մէջ ալ կան քանի մը հարիւր հայեր, որոնք հանգիստ են: Գիւղերու մէջ ալ կան, ինչպէս Րում-Գալէ մէկ գիւղին մէջ կան երկու տուն որ Այնթապի շրջանակներէն փախած են եւ կը պատսպարուին քիւրտերու կողմէ: Պիրէճիկի մէջ կան 2000 հայեր: Տեղւոյն քայմաքամն է հայազգեաց Քեմալ պէյ անուն երիտասարդ մը: Ասոնք գիւղերը երթեւեկելու ազատ են եւ ասոր համար արհեստաւորները կ'օգտուին: Հոն ալ հայերը կը պաշտպանուին գայմագամէն, որ տեղւոյն քահանան կողոպտող քանի մը աւազակները խստիւ պատժած է:

Նիկոմիդիա (Առաջնորդէն) – 8 Ապրիլ [1921]

Երէկ Միլլիճիք այրեցին յունաց Գարայ Թէփէ գիւղն Արսլանպէկի մօտ եւ Պարտիզակի (Ըլըճայի մօտ) յունաբնակ Եէնի-Գիւղն: Այս առտու ալ հայոց Տէօնկէօյը ըսուեցաւ թէ կ'այրի. արդարեւ մուխն կ'երեւէր: Նոյնպէս Նիկոմիդիայէն կը տեսնուի Օվաճըգի հրկիզուիլը:

Նիկոմիդիոյ մերձակայ յունաբնակ Միսալիճ գիւղի բնակիչները քաղաք ապաստանած են: Նիկոմիդիոյ մէջ երկիւղ կայ որ քրիստոնեայ թաղերն ալ հրդեհի տրուին:

Չէնկիլէր (Թաղական Խորհուրդէն) – 8 Ապրիլ [1921]

Գրաւուած շրջանին Եալովա եւ Օրհան Կազի խճուղին, որ հայ եւ յոյն ճամբորդներուն Պոլսոյ միակ միջոցն էր, 3 Ապրիլէն սկսեալ երթեւեկը կը դադրի: Նոյն օրը Չէնկիլէր գիւղէն Վարդան

Dimoyan, Garabed Keremetsi, and Arakel Moutafian from the village of Sugören, somebody from Büyük-Yeniköy, and two Armenian teens (both of whom were traveling from Orhangazi to Yalova) were abducted by twenty-five çetes near the Sol-Maz spring of Esadiye and Soğucak village and taken in an unknown direction. About a quarter of an hour after the incident, when a Greek detachment was moving around, a signal was given to the bandits via a whistle and a gunshot from the Circassian village of Soğucak's elevation, indicating the approach of the troops. The bandits had planned to detain all the travelers on the same day; however, they failed because of the troop's arrival.

On Monday, April 4, the incident was reported to the Greek command of Orhangazi. The commander sent news to Yalova over the phone. Troops were sent to pursue the carrying out of due investigation in Yolova's Soğucak and the surrounding Laz villages.

At the same time, the armed Armenian youth of Sugören were allowed by the Greek commander of Orhangazi to launch an investigation in search of traces of the captured Armenian and Greek teens. Twenty of our young men arrived in the Circassian village of Soğucak at half past one in the afternoon. Suspicious Circassian villagers were terrified. When they [young Armenians] arrived at the scene, they found the goods piled on horses unloaded and buried in the bushes. The horses and the [detained] teens had been taken away.

After a long search, they found two [Circassian] teens from Soğucak under the bushes, one seventeen-year-old and the other fourteen. The testimony the teens gave confirms that on the same day, together with the [Armenian and Greek] teens, they, too, had been picked up on the road and taken to the nearby Turkish village of Gacık, where they promised to confess what had happened.

Here is the testimony of the Circassians who were trapped yesterday at half past four. It was taken at the Armenian coffeehouse of Sugören.

"We were coming from the mill. Four people from Reşadiye, together with Sergeant Hüseyin and fifteen people from Kurtköy [Delipazarı], took Armenians with them (five of them were tied up, and two of them were free). We came across them, and they took us with them. At night, we all arrived at Gacik's judge in Yalova. There they checked us and released us. Those seven people were dispatched to the district governor of Kapaklı with a letter."

When asked, "Who brought you here?" they responded: "The Millis brought us up here."

After the end of this preliminary investigation, the two Circassians were sent to Orhangazi. They testified in the same way there. The two teens are now in prison.

On Tuesday, the local priest, Father Hovsep, and the village headman, Mr. Garabed Pakosian, went with several armed men to the sheikh in Reşadiye and reported the incident. The sheikh promised to take the necessary steps to free the abducted teens. According to the Circassian teens' testimony, the abductees are alive in the center of the second-order administrative division of Kapaklı. (This administrative division is one of the villages of Karamürsel [Karamursal] and represents Karamürsel.)

All the young Turkish men of the villages of the occupied region have taken advantage of the open positions in the areas occupied by the Greek army to flee by way of the mountains and join the Milli forces of Karamürsel. The road has been entirely open in front of the Millis since the burning of Elmalı.

Մկրեան, Տիգրան Տիմոյեան, Կարապէտ Քէրէմէթցի, Առաքել Մութաֆեան, մեծ-նոր-գիւղացի ոմն եւ երկու հայ տղաքներ (այս երկուքն Օրխան Կազիէն Եալովա գացողներ) Էսատիյէ եւ Սօվուճագ գիւղին Սօլ-Մագ աղբիւրին քով 25 չէթէներու կողմէ կ'առեւանգուին եւ կը տարուին անծանօթ ուղղութեամբ: Դէպքը պատահելէն քառորդ ժամ վերջ երբ յունական զօրքերը միւֆրէզէ կը շրջին, Սօվուճագի չէրքէզ գիւղին բարձունքէն սուլիչի եւ հրացանի մէկ հարուածով նշան կը տրուի յիշեալ աւազակներուն թէ զօրք կուգայ: Աւազակները կ'ուզէին նոյն օրուան բոլոր ճամբորդները վար դնել, չեն կրցած յաջողիլ զօրքին հասնելուն վրայ:

Երկուշաբթի 4 Ապրիլ[ին] այդ դէպքը կը տեղեկագրուի Օրխան Կազիի յոյն հրամանատարու-թեան. յիշեալը հեռաձայնով լուր կուտայ Եալովա: Եալովայի Սօվուճագ եւ իր շուրջը գտնուած լազ գիւղերը պէտք եղած քննութիւնը կատարելու համար զօրքեր կը ղրկուին հետապնդելու:

Միեւնոյն ժամուն Օրխան Կազիի յոյն հրամանատարէն թոյլտուութիւն կը տրուի մեր Չէնկիլէրի հայ զինեալ երիտասարդներուն որպէսզի բռնուած հայ եւ յոյն տղաքներու հետքը փնտռելու համար քննութիւն կատարեն: Մեր տղաքներէն 20 հոգի օր ցերեկ ժամը մէկուկէսին (ը.ե.) կը հասնին Սօվուճագ չէրքէզ գիւղը: Կասկածելի չէրքէզ գիւղացիներ սարսափի կը մատնուին. դէպքին վայրը հասնելով կը գտնեն ձիերու բեռցուած ապրանքներն որոնք ձիերէն վար առնուած մացառներու մէջ թաղած էին, իսկ ձիերն ու տղաքները առած ու տարած:

Երկար խուզարկութիւններէ յետոյ մացառներու տակ պահուըտած կը գտնեն սօվուճագցի երկու տղաքներ՝ մէկը 17 տարեկան եւ միւսը 14: Տղոց տուած վկայութենէն կը հաստատուի որ նոյն օրը տղաքներու հետ մէկտեղ իրենք ալ ճամբէն առնուելով միասին տարած են մինչեւ մօտակայ Ղաճիկ թուրք գիւղը, ուր խոստացած են պատահածը ճշդութեամբ խոստովանիլ:

Ահա երէկ ժամը 4½ին այդ ծուղակն ինկած չէրքէզներուն վկայութիւնը, որ առնուած է Չէնկիլէրի ազգային սրճարանին մէջ:

«Պիզ տէյիրմէնտէն կէլիօր իտիք Րէշատիէտէն տէօրթ քիշի Հիւսէին չավուշտա պէրապէր. տէլի Բազարտան օն պէշ քիշի էրմէնիլէրի պէրապէր (պունլարտան պէշի պաղլը վէ իքիսի սէրպէսթ կէօթիւրիօլար իտի) պիզ տախի րասթ կէլտիք պիզի տա պէրապէր կէօթիւրտիլէր. կէճէ հէփիմիզ Եալըվանըն Ղաճիզ Գատիէսինէ վարտըգ. Օրատա թահգիգ իթթիլէր վէ պիզի սալը վերտիլէր. Օ եէտի քիշիի Գափազըը Գայմագամըըղա սէվգ իթթիլէր»:[15]

Երբ կը հարցուի իրենց թէ «ձեզ ով բերաւ հոս», կը պատասխանեն «պիզի պուրայա գատար Միլլիլէր թէսլիմ իթթիլէր»:[16]

Սոյն նախնական քննութենէն վերջ երկու չէրքէզներ[ը] կը ղրկուին Օրխան Կազի. հոն ալ նոյն ձեւով կը վկայեն. այդ երկու տղաքներն այժմ բանտարկուած են:

Երեքշաբթի օր քանի մը զինեալ անձերու հետ տեղւոյն քահանան՝ Տ. Յովսէփ եւ գիւղապետ պ. Կարապետ Բագոսեան Րէշատիէ Շէյխին կը ներկայանան եւ կը հաղորդեն պատահածը: Շէյխը յանձն կ'առնէ առեւանգուած տղաքներու ազատման համար պէտք եղածը ընել: Ըստ չէրքէզ տղոց վկայութեան, առեւանգուածները կը գտնուին Գափազըը գայմագամութեան կեդրոնը ողջ: (Այս գայմագամըըգը Գարամուսալի գիւղերէն է եւ կը ներկայացնէ Գարամուսալը):

Գրաւեալ շրջանակի գիւղերու բոլոր թուրք երիտասարդութիւնը օգտուելով յունական բանակին կողմէ գրաւուած վայրերու բաց ձգած դիրքերէն կը փախչին ու լեռի ճամբով կ'ընկերանան Գարամուսալի Միլլի ուժերուն: Էլմալը կրակուելէն ի վեր Միլլիի ճամբան բոլորովին բաց է:

Merzifon (a special report by the National Union presented identically)—22 September [1919]
The Milli Movement and Its Consequences[105]

The famous announcement of severance: A statement dated September 6, signed by the Milli Congress of Sivas, was released to the public. This delay showed that Merzifon's government had decided to join the Millis a little late, considering the unique situation in the city.

The summary of the declaration is as follows: "Because the Allied powers did not respect the terms of the armistice and the integrity of the Ottoman Empire is in danger, since the cabinet of Ferid Pasha, in addition to showing inability from the day of its formation, has taken a dictatorial course and continues to pursue its policy of destroying the country, we, members of the Milli Congress, who have come from all over the country, pledge first of all allegiance to the sultan, but demand the departure of Ferid Pasha's cabinet and the holding of parliamentarian elections. Therefore, henceforth, we have severed all ties with the cabinet and assumed all governmental responsibilities provisionally." It was added [in the declaration] that the articles of the particular decisions of the Congress had been sent directly to the sultan.

We were curious to learn the content of those articles. According to a reliable source, Article 3 guarantees the life, honor, and property of Anatolian Christians, while Article 11 states: "If the Allied powers move to occupy a portion of our land, whether for themselves or the creation of other small governments, we will consider the local Christians to be the motive and we will treat them accordingly."

Turkish people received the declaration with great enthusiasm, mentioning Mustafa Kemal and the sultan as saviors.

Migration movement: When the content of the declaration and Article 11 began to circulate among our people, it left a disconcerting impression. Consequently, the bustling local trade came to a standstill, commitments were abandoned, orders were withdrawn, and each family set its move to a port city or İstanbul as its purpose. Many families left the city for Samsun last week. They are waiting, watching the political events of the day.

Captain Salter and Samsun's district governor: Affected by this mass exodus, the captain and the district governor arrived here last week. They invited us separately to their presence and demanded an explanation. Our National Body stated that when our people hear such shocking news, mainly after they have survived terrible disasters in one way or another, they will undoubtedly be affected and are affected, and that they especially fear that they [the Millis] will close Samsun's road soon, and so on.

Captain Salter particularly stressed that the congressional government of Sivas guarantees the lives, honor, and property of Christians in these parts; that Samsun's district governor is second to its leader, Mustafa Kemal; that the final settlement of the Armenian Issue has been postponed for a year; that the Republic of Armenia has reasons for fear; that when going to Amasya with the district governor, he will make an announcement there, too, about security and so on. The district governor Bey also spoke along the same lines and insisted that we persuade the people and deter them from migrating.

These assurances were identically explained from church pulpits, but a new reality turned their impact upside down.

The withdrawal of the British soldiers: The new event was this. Captain Salter informed [us] that they will withdraw from Samsun, and since this order had come long ago, it has nothing to do with the current political situation in the country, that Samsun's troops will remain in place for a while, and so on. A few days ago, the soldiers withdrew with their ammunition and supplies. The Allied representative, Mr. Geisel, is leaving for America on vacation, and his term has ended. An English captain remains here with a controller.

Մարզուան (Ազգային Միութենէն մասնաւոր տեղեկագիր նոյնութեամբ ներկայացուած) – 22 Սեպտեմբեր [1919]

«Միլլի» Շարժումը ու անոր հետեւանքները

Խզումի նշանաւոր յայտարարութիւնը. Սեպտեմբեր 6 թուակիր, Սվազի Միլլի Գօնկրէ ստորագրութեամբ յայտարարութիւն մը 12 թիւ՝ ի տես հասարակութեան տրուեցաւ. այս ուշացումը կը ցուցնէր թէ Մարզուանի կառավարութիւնը Միլլիյէին միանալու որոշումը քիչ մը ուշ տուաւ, նկատելով քաղքին բացառիկ կացութիւնը:

Յայտարարութեան ամփոփումը հետեւեալն է. «Որովհետեւ զինադադարի պայմանները համաձայնական պետութիւններու կողմէն չեն յարգուիր ու Օսմանեան Կայսրութեան ամբողջութիւնը վտանգի տակ է, որովհետեւ Ֆէրիտ փաշայի դահլիճը իր կազմութեան օրէն իսկ անկարողութիւն ցոյց տալէ զատ, այսօր տիրդադորական ընթացք մըն ալ ձեռք առած՝ երկիրը քայքայելու իր քաղաքականութիւնը կը շարունակէ, մենք՝ Սվազի մէջ գումարուող Միլլի Գօնկրէի անդամներս, որ երկրին ամէն կողմերէն եկած ենք, ամէն բանէ առաջ Վեհափառ Սուլթանին հաւատարմութիւն կ'ուխտենք, սակայն կը պահանջենք որ Ֆէրիտ փաշայի դահլիճը քաշուի եւ երեսփոխանական ընտրութիւններու ձեռնարկուի. հետեւաբար այսօրուընէ իսկ ամէն յարաբերութիւն խզած ենք դահլիճին հետ, եւ առժամապէս ստանձնած ենք կառավարական ամէն պատասխանատուութիւն»: Ասոր վրայ կ'աւելցուէր թէ Գօնկրէին մասնաւոր որոշումներու յօդուածաշարքը ուղղակի Սուլթանին ղրկուած է:

Հետաքրքիր եղանք հասկնալու այդ յօդուածներուն պարունակութիւնը: Հաւաստի աղբիւրէ մը տեղեկացուցին թէ 3րդ յօդուածով կ'երաշխաւորուի Անատօլիյի քրիստոնէից կեանքը, պատիւը եւ ստացուածքը, իսկ 11րդ յօդուածին մէջ կ'ըսուի թէ «Համաձայնական տէրութիւնները՝ եթէ զինու զօրութեամբ, մեր հողէն եթէ մաս մը իրենց հաշուոյն թէ ուրիշ փոքր կառավարութիւններու կազմութեան համար, գրաւելու քայլը առնեն, տեղական քրիստոնեաները ատոր դրդապատճառը պիտի նկատենք ու ըստ այնմ պիտի վարուինք իրենց հետր»:

Յայտարարութիւնը թուրք ժողովուրդէն մեծ խանդավառութեամբ ընդունուեցաւ, Մուստաֆա Քէմալի անունը Սուլթանի անուան հետ իբրեւ փրկիչներ կը յիշուէին:

Արտագաղթի շարժումը. Երբ մեր ժողովրդական խաւերուն մէջ սկսան շրջան ընել յայտարարութեան եւ 11րդ յօդուածի պարունակութիւնքը, չափազանց գէշ տպաւորութիւն առաջ եկաւ, որուն հետեւանքով տեղական շատ բանուկ առուտուրը մէկէն կանգ առաւ, յանձնառութիւններ լքուեցան, յանձնարարութիւններ ետ առնուեցան եւ ամէն ընտանիք ինքզինքը նաւահանգիստ քաղաք մը կամ Պոլիս ձգելու առաջադրութիւններ ընել սկսաւ: Բաւական ընտանիքներ անցեալ շաբթուայ ընթացքին հեռացան քաղաքէն դէպի Սամսոն: Առ այժմ հոն կը սպասեն, դիտելով օրուան քաղաքականութեան իրադարձութիւնները:

Գաբիլթէն Սօլթէր եւ Սամսոնի միլթէսարրըֆը. Ազդուած այս զանգուածային գաղթէն, յիշեալները անցեալ շաբթուան ընթացքին հոս հասնելով՝ առանձինն մեզի իրենց ներկայութեան հրաւիրեցին եւ բացատրութիւններ պահանջեցին: Ազգային Մարմինս յայտնեց թէ մեր ժողովուրդը մանաւանդ ահաւոր աղէտներէ այս կամ այն միջոցներով ազատուելէ յետոյ, երբ այս կարգի ցնցող լուրեր լսէ՝ ի հարկէ պիտի ազդուէր եւ ազդուած ալ է. եւ մանաւանդ կը վախնայ որ շատ չանցած Սամսոնի ճամբան ալ գոցեն եւայլն:

Գաբ. Սօլթըր մանաւորապէս ծանրացաւ թէ այս կողմերու քրիստոնեաներուն կեանքը, պատիւը եւ ստացուածքը երաշխաւորուած է Սվազի գօնկրէական կառավարութենէն, թէ անոր պետին՝ Մուստաֆա Քէմալի երկրորդն է Սամսոնի միլթէսարրըֆը եւ Սամսոնի միացումն ալ երաշխիք մ'է ճամբուն բաց մնալուն, թէ հայկական խնդիրին վերջնական լուծումը տարի մը յետաձգուած է, թէ վախու պատճառներ Հայաստանի Հանրապետութիւնը ունի, թէ Միլթէսարրըֆին հետ Ամասիա ալ երթալով՝ հոն ալ ազդարարութիւն պիտի ընէ ապահովութեան մասին եւայլն: Միլթէսարրըֆ պէյն ալ միեւնոյն իմաստով խօսեցաւ եւ պնդեց որ ժողովուրդը համոզենք ու ետ կեցնենք գաղթելէ:

This sudden departure of theirs, coupled with the stream of fear caused by the declaration [mentioned above], made the issue of persuading the people even more difficult, if not impossible. No one gives value to the words of the district governor. As for Salter's assurances, rumors are circulating about him that he is a sold-out man and does not have a good past. Consequently, the idea of migrating has become stronger than ever. Even artisan women with modest financial means are preparing to leave the city with their family members.

The youth: Gathered around a purely developmental goal, the youth were engaged in commendable efforts to raise the level of national education. Rumors began circulating that they would be recruited as Ottomans for the "militia." As a result, some of them left the city, and the rest are determined to leave. Among them are the teachers of the Armenian school. Thus, a good educational endeavor that had hardly begun collapsed, and the schools that had opened were already closed. Three to four hundred children roam the streets today.

Local Lieutenant Governor Rumi Bey: Considering the closure of the schools as an unbecoming sign that encourages mass migration, yesterday, Sunday, our lieutenant governor visited the church and urged the people, from the pulpit, to desist from the idea of migrating. By inviting the National Body separately, he wanted to persuade us to reopen the schools. We put the facts out bare naked: almost no teacher remains, and our hopes for tuition have come to nothing, as even somewhat well-to-do families are preparing to leave. How can we manage the budget? The lieutenant governor personally insisted on the urgent orders he had received from the district governor and swore that there is nothing for us to fear, that this crazy run is as harmful to the government as it is to the Armenian people, and so on. After scrutinizing the current events, we also confirmed that there is no danger for the Christians of these parts for the time being, as the Armenian issue has not reached the phase of taking conquering steps. But who is responsible for tomorrow, and what are the firm guarantees that the current policy will continue unchanged tomorrow?

In particular, the lieutenant governor stated in a private meeting that ninety-five percent of the Turks in this country are Ittihadist and that five percent are the Ittilafist minority. The Ittilafists lack activists and have internal dissensions. They are unable to govern the country. This revelation is enough to confirm the opinion that in the event of a parliamentary election, the Ittihadists will win a large majority. More than words, many facts prove it: the entire eastern and central parts of the provinces have joined the [Milli] movement, and there are numerous Ittihadists among civil and military functionaries. The lieutenant governor also assures us that they have a large amount of money and have decided to use Agricultural Bank's money for that purpose.

Perhaps the current movement is a political demonstration or an unarmed opposition organized to influence the decisions of the Peace Conference. Perhaps the war is about Armenia simply. Nevertheless, the people's will to leave everything and take refuge in one of the coastal cities has grown indestructible today. We leave the task of counteracting this unorganized and aimless stream or administering a different effective means to Your Holiness.

September 22, [1]919, Merzifon

on behalf of the National Body

Secretary	for the Chairman
Tateos H. Zhamgochian	K. K. Donigian

Այս հաւաստիացումները նոյնութեամբ պարզուեցան եկեղեցիներու բեմերէն. սակայն նոր իրողութիւն մը վեր ի վայր շրջեց ասոր ալ ազդեցութիւնը:

Անգղիական զինուորներուն յետս կոչումը. Նոր եղելութիւնը աս էր: Գաբ. Սօլտըր իմացուց թէ անոնք պիտի քաշուին Սամսոն ու ասոր հրամանը շատոնց եկած ըլլալուն՝ բնաւ ոեւէ կապ չունի երկրին ներկայ քաղաքական կացութեան հետ, թէ Սամսոնի զինուորները առ այժմ պիտի մնան տեղին վրայ եւայլն: Զինուորները քանի մ'օր առաջ քաշուեցան իրենց ռազմամթերքով եւ պաշարեղէններով: Համաձայնական ներկայացուցիչ Մր. Կէզըլ արձակուրդով Ամերիկա կը մեկնի ու իր ալ պաշտօնը վերջացած է. հոս կը մնայ անգղիացի հարիւրապետ մը զօնթրօլէօռի մը հետ:

Անոնց այս անակնկալ մեկնումը՝ միացած յայտարարութեան առաջացուցած մտավախութեան հոսանքին, այլեւս եթէ ոչ անկարելի, գէթ շատ դժուար դարձուց ժողովուրդը համոզելու խնդիրը: Միւթէսարըֆին խոստումներուն արժէք ընծայող չկայ: Գալով Սօլտըրին հաւաստիացումներուն, անոր անձին շուրջն ալ շշուկներ կը պտըտին թէ ծախուած մարդ է եւ լաւ անցեալ մը չունի: Հետեւաբար գաղթելու գաղափարը աւելի քան երբեք զօրացած է եւ նիւթական համեստուկ միջոցներ ունեցող արհեստաւոր կիներ իսկ ընտանեկան պարագաներով կը պատրաստուին քաղաքը ձգելու:

Երիտասարդութիւնը. Միացած զուտ զարգացողական նպատակի մը շուրջը, երիտասարդութիւնը գովելի ճիգեր կ'ընէր բարձրացնելու համար ազգային կրթական մակարդակը: Շշուկներ շրջան ընել սկսան թէ «միլիսի» համար իբրեւ օսմանցիներ անոնցմէ ալ զօրահաւաքում պիտի ըլլայ, որուն հետեւանքով անոնցմէ մաս մը հեռացաւ քաղաքէն եւ մնացածներն ալ հաստատ մտադրեր են հեռանալ: Անոնց մէջ է նաեւ ազգային վարժարաններու ուսուցչութիւնը: Այսպէս, կրթական լաւագոյն գործ մը, հազիւ թէ սկսած, փլուզումի կ'ենթարկուի եւ դպրոցները, որոնց բացումը կատարուեր էր, արդէն իսկ գոցուեցան: 3/400 տղաք այսօր փողոցները կը թափառին:

Տեղւոյս Գայմաքամը Բումի պէյ. Վարժարաններու փակումը զանգուածային գաղթը քաջալերող գէշ նշան մը նկատելով՝ երէկ, Կիւրակէ, եկեղեցի այցելեց մեր գայմաքամը ու բեմէն յորդորեց ժողովուրդը որ ետ կենան գաղթելու գաղափարէն: Ազգային Մարմինս ալ առանձին հրաւիրելով կ'ուզէ համոզել որ վերաբանանք դպրոցները: Իրողութիւնները մերկապարանոց մէջտեղ դրինք: Ուսուցիչ գրեթէ մնացած չէ, տարեթոշակի մասին մեր յոյսերը կ'անէանան, քանի որ գէշ աղէկ նիւթական կարողութեան տէր ընտանիքներ իսկ մեկնելու պատրաստութիւններու մէջ են, ուրեմն ի՞նչպէս հոգալ պիւտճէն: Ինքը՝ գայմաքամը, միւթէսարըֆէն ստացած ստիպողական հրամաններուն վրայ կը պնդէ ու կ'երդնու թէ ոչինչ կայ մեզի համար վախու, թէ այս խելայեղ վազքը որքան կառավարութեան համար վնասակար, նոյնքան եւ աւելի եւս հայ ժողովուրդին համար փճացումի միջոց մըն է եւայլն: Ներկայ իրադարձութիւնները ուշի ուշով քննելով՝ մենք ալ կը հաստատենք թէ առ այժմ վտանգ չկայ այս կողմերու քրիստոնէից համար, քանի որ նուաճողական քայլեր առնելու վիճակին հասած չէ հայկական հարցը. սակայն ո՞վ է վաղուան պատասխանատուն եւ ի՞նչ հաստատուն երաշխիքներ կան թէ ներկայ քաղաքականութիւնը վաղն ալ անփոփոխ պիտի շարունակուի:

Գայմազամը մանաւանդ մասնաւոր տեսակցութեան մը մէջ յայտարարեց թէ այս երկրի թըրքութեան %95 մասը իթթիհատական է, թէ %5 իթիլաֆական փոքրամասնութիւն մը, որոնց մէջ գործիչի սով եւ տարակարծութիւն կայ, կարող չէ կառավարելու երկիրը: Այս յայտնութիւնը բաւական է որոշապէս հաստատելու այն կարծիքը թէ՝ երեսփոխանական ընտրութիւններու պարագային, իթթիհատականները ստուար մեծամասնութիւն պիտի շահին: Խօսքէն շատ աւելի իրողութիւններն ալ կ'ապացուցանեն. գաւառներու ամբողջ արեւելեան եւ կեդրոնական մասը միացած է շարժումին եւ զայն ղեկավարող քաղաքային ու զինուորական պաշտօնէութեան մէջ ստուարաթիւ է Իթթիհատականութիւնը: Գայմաքամը կը հաւաստէ նոյնպէս թէ բաւական խոշոր քանակութեամբ դրամ ալ ունին եւ Զրաաթ Պանքի դրամներն ալ այդ նպատակին գործածելու որոշում կայացուցած է:

Կարելի է թէ Խաղաղութեան Համաժողովի որոշումներուն վրայ ազդելու մտօք սարքուած քաղաքական ցոյց մը, անզէն ընդդիմութիւն մ'եղած ըլլայ ներկայ շարժումը: Կարելի է կռիւը

Հայաստանի շուրջ դառնայ պարզապէս: Միայն թէ այսօր անխորտակելի դարձած է ժողովուրդին ամէն ինչ լքել ծովեզերեայ քաղաքները ապաստանելու կամքը: Անկազմակերպ ու աննպատակ այս հոսանքին հակազդելու կամ տարբեր ազդու միջոց մը տնօրինելու հոգը ձեր Սրբազնութեան կը թողունք:

22 Սեպտեմբեր [1]919. Մարզուան

ի դիմաց Ազգային Մարմնոյն

Ատենադպիր — վ[սան] ատենապետի

Թադէոս Յ. Ժամկոչեան — Ք.Ք. Տօնիկեան

[Insecurity Notebook Number 15]
April–October 1921

Gemlik (from the Neighborhood Council of Sugören [Çengiler])—April 13

On April 9, at four o'clock daytime, Milli bandits attacked Sugören. The people resisted strongly and managed to escape with only two losses, Hadji Nemzar and Gyoulli Arabajian, and one wounded, M. Hovsep Vichenian's little daughter Donig.

The Millis fired hundreds of thousands of bullets at the people who got to Orhangazi terrified and thence went to Gemlik. The people of Sugören remain unprotected in the open air in Gemlik, without a single blanket, because they could not take anything with them at the time of their panicky departure. They number three thousand people.

[The people of] Ortaköy and Büyük-Yeniköy also suffered no casualties and have taken refuge in Gemlik like the people of Sugören.

The people of Büyük-Yeniköy have engaged in self-defense. According to recent news, Sugören has been completely burned. The church, the school, the national institutions, and a few other houses have also been burned down by the people of Reşadiye. Sugören is wholly reduced to ashes. Three helpless old women were left in flames.

Afyonkarahisar (from the vicar general)—April 2

On March 27, Sunday morning, the brave Greek soldiers captured Afyonkarahisar without incident.

There is no loss of life, except that during the reign of the Millis, seven months ago, about five hundred young Armenians between the ages of twenty and forty were deported to the town of Şereflikoçhisar [Koçhisar] near Konya. Now it has become impossible to communicate with them, so we do not know what their situation will be. We fear they will be endangered.

İzmit (from the primate)—April 11

It is said that a few days ago, the Greek military authorities brought from Sapanca to İzmit twenty to thirty armed Millis dressed in urban uniforms and tied up.

There is a rumor in İzmit that the Sapanca market and Türk Dağı have been set on fire by the Greeks.

It is also said that while [the Greek soldiers] were bringing the arrested and bound Millis from Sapanca to İzmit, they met an old Turk on his way to İzmit who was dressed in old and dirty rags. The Greek military authorities suspected him, so they searched the old Turk and found three bombs and some letters and papers ordering the burning of Christian houses in the city of İzmit. This old man was also arrested and brought to İzmit.

• It is heard that when six to seven houses were burning in Ovacık, Keratepe, Yeniköy, and Döngöl, forty to fifty people in one of the Turkish districts of İzmit convened and decided to set ablaze the Christian market and houses of İzmit. On this occasion, they wrote a letter to the Turks of Çepni telling them that when they notice İzmit burning, they should rush to İzmit for plunder and massacre and capture the city. As a result of unveiling this plot, Greek authorities arrested the Turkish suspects and set fire to the Turkish village of Çepni.

• Yesterday, news came from Avcıköy [Merdigöz] and Yalakdere that both of these Armenian villages have been set on fire.

• On April 7, the Greek military authorities in Bahçecik learned that the Millis were trying to besiege Bahçecik to loot, destroy, and burn the village, [and] slaughter the locals and the Greek migrants

[Անապահովութեան Տետր Թիւ 15]
1921 Ապրիլ – Յուլիս

Կէմլէյիկ (Չէնկիլէրի Թաղական Խորհուրդէն) – 13 Ապրիլ

Ապրիլ 9ին ցորեկի ժամը 4ին միլլի աւազակներ Չէնկիլէրի վրայ յարձակեցան: Ժողովուրդը զօրաւոր ընդդիմութիւն ըրաւ եւ կրցաւ ազատիլ երկու կորուստ տալով՝ մին Հաճի Նէմզար եւ միւսը Կիւլլի Արապաճեան եւ մէկ վիրաւոր՝ Մ. Յովսէփ Վիչէնեանի փոքր աղջիկը Տօնիկ:

Միլլիներու կողմէ հարիւր հազարներով կապար նետուեցաւ ժողովուրդին վրայ, որ լեղապատառ Օրխան Գազի հասաւ եւ անկէ ալ Կէմլէյիկ: Չէնկիլէրցիք Կէմլէյիկի մէջ կը մնան անպատսպար բացօթեայ, առանց ծածկոց մը իսկ ունենալու, վասնզի իրենց խուճապային մեկնումի պահուն բան մը չեն կրցած առնել: Ժողովուրդին թիւն է 3000:

Օրթաքէօյ, Մեծ-Նոր-Գիւղ եւս ոեւէ կորուստ չունին անձի եւ չէնկիլերցւոց պէս ապաստանած են Կէմլէյիկ:

Մեծ-նոր-գիւղցիք ինքնապաշտպանութեան դիմած են: Նոր լուրերու համաձայն, Չէնկիլէր ամբողջապէս այրած է: Եկեղեցի, դպրոց, ազգային հաստատութիւնները եւ մնացած քանի մը տուներն ալ զատ զատ րէշատիյէցիներու կողմէ կը վառուին: Չէնկիլէր բոլորովին մոխիրի վերածուած է: Երեք անկար ծեր կիներ բոցերու մէջ մնացած են:

Աֆիոն Գարահիսար (Առաջնորդական Փոխանորդէն) – 2 Ապրիլ

Մարտ 27 Կիրակի օր առտուն յունական քաջարի զինուորներու կողմէ Աֆիոն-Գարա-Հիսար առանց ոեւէ միջադէպի գրաւուեցաւ:

Կեանք[ի] կորուստ չկայ, միայն միլլի տիրապետութեան շրջանին, ասկէ եօթը ամիս առաջ, 500ի չափ 20էն 40 տարեկան հայ երիտասարդներ Գոնիայի մօտ Գօչ-Հիսար ըսուած գիւղաքաղաքը աքսորուած են: Հիմա անոնց հետ հաղորդակցիլ անկարելի դարձած ըլլալով, չենք գիտեր թէ ի՞նչ պիտի ըլլայ իրենց վիճակը: Կը վախնանք որ անոնք վտանգի ենթարկուին:

Նիկոմիդիա (Առաջնորդէն) – 11 Ապրիլ

Կ'ըսուի թէ Սապանճայէն 20–30 քաղաքային տարազով զինեալ միլլիճիներ կապուած քանի մը օր առաջ Նիկոմի[դ]իա կը բերեն հելլէն զինուորական իշխանութիւնները:

Նիկոմիդիոյ մէջ զրոյց կը շրջի թէ Սապանճայի շուկան եւ Թուրք Տաղը կրակի տրուած է հելլէններու կողմէ:

Նոյնպէս կ'ըսուի թէ Սապանճայէն ձերբակալուած եւ կապուած միլլիճիները Նիկոմիդիա բերուած ատեն ճամբան դէպի Նիկոմիդիա եկող ծերուկ թուրքի մը կը հանդիպին հին ու աղտոտ լաթերով: Հելլէն զինուորական իշխանութիւնները կը կասկածին եւ այդ ծեր թուրքին վրան կը խուզարկեն եւ [կը] գտնեն վրան երեք պօնպայ ու կարգ մը նամակներ եւ թուղթեր, որով հրահանգ կը տրուէր Նիկոմիդիա քաղաքին քրիստոնէից տուները այրելու: Այս ծերն ալ ձերբակալելով Նիկոմիդիա կը բերուի:

- Կը լսուի որ Օվաճըգ, Գարայ-Թեփէ, Եէնի գիւղն ու Տէօնկէօյի 6–7 տուները այրած օրերուն մէջ Նիկոմիդիոյ թուրք թաղերէն մէկուն մէջ 40–50 հոգիներ ժողով կ'ընեն, Նիկոմիդիա քրիստոնէից շուկան եւ տուները կրակի տալ [որոշելով]: Այս առթիւ գիր կը գրեն Չէփնիի թուրքերուն որ երբ Նիկոմիդիոյ հրկիզուիլը նշմարեն, Նիկոմիդիա խուժեն թալանի եւ ջարդի համար եւ քաղաքն գրաւեն: Այս դաւն երեւան ելած ըլլալով, հելլէն իշխանութիւնք ձերբակալած են թուրք կասկածելիները եւ Չէփնի թուրք գիւղն ալ կրակի տուած են:

- Երէկ Մէրտիկէօզէն եւ Եալազտէրէ[է]ն լուր հասաւ թէ այս երկու հայ գիւղերն ալ կրակի տրուած է:

- Ապրիլ 7ին Պարտիզակի հելլէն զինուորական իշխանութիւնները կը տեղեկանան որ

who have taken refuge there. A captain invited those with weapons to defend the village. About twenty-five to thirty Armenians and more Greeks are defending Bahçecik. Boatman Nshan was killed in this defense.

• The crowd of migrants gathered in İzmit is huddled in the church. There are neither houses nor means of sheltering and feeding them.

Bursa (from the vicar general)—April 14

Atrocities have been committed by Kemalists in areas liberated by the Greeks last time.

No damage has been done in the villages of the Gemlik area. However, more than one hundred youngsters native of Yenisölöz, who accompanied the Greeks during their advance, have not returned. It is said that they have been taken prisoner by the Kemalists.

Because the Armenians of Yenişehir and Marmaracık were relocated in advance, there have been no further losses in these areas. The 225 people who were unable to escape from Yenice and Cerrah remained there. Four of them, men and women, were killed, and 52 men were driven to the interior during the last attack. The rest, old women and children, have arrived in Bursa in extreme distress. The churches in these two villages have been looted, desecrated, and destroyed. Most of the houses also have been demolished.

Many of the ninety-four people from Bilecik and forty-four people from Göldağı—men aged eighteen to seventeen—have been exiled to Eskişehir, Ankara, and Beypazarı, while some have been taken somewhere unknown. It is not known whether they have been deported or killed. No information has been received from other nearby villages. The property and vessels of the church in Bilecik are looted, and the church is destroyed. During their escape, the Kemalists set the whole city on fire and burned it; only thirty to forty houses were rescued from the fire, thanks to Greek soldiers, who tried to extinguish the fire as soon as they set foot in Bilecik, but the [the rest of the] city had already entirely burned to ashes. The Christians—elderly, women, and children—have been saved by the direct occupation of the Greeks and have come here on foot in a very miserable condition. No one was able to bring anything with them due to the lack of transport carts. Fourteen hundred Armenians saved from Bilecik and vicinities managed to come to Bursa.

• Today, news reached Bursa that the Millis have attacked Sugören [Çengiler] and [Büyük-]Yeniköy. Sugören is completely burned, but the villagers of Büyük-Yeniköy are resisting.

• As of April 14, by the decision of the Greek Command, the allowance for bread to the migrants has been halted, and everyone is given two hundred drams of flour per day. The prelacy has been asked to submit a list of unemployed and supportless people. They make up 2,887 people.

Bursa (from the vicar general)—April 16

Witnesses from Pazarköy testified that Sugören [Çengiler] had been torched and Büyük-Yeniköy was under attack.

Sugören [Çengiler] (from the Neighborhood Council)—March 22

The district of Orhangazi has been occupied by the Greek army for about six and a half months. Many changes have taken place during this time. Yalova, Karamürsel, and İznik have also been captured. During all these conquests, the Armenians of the region and the Greek people partly, feeling liberated, resumed their peaceful work.

First, the massacre, looting, and arson of Kızderbent and Fulacık were carried out, and the sur-

միլլիճիները Պարտիզակը կողոպտելու, ջարդելու եւ այրելու համար գիւղին շուրջը պաշարելու ձեռնարկ կ'ընեն, գտնուած պարտիզակցիներն ու հոն ապաստանող յոյն գաղթականները կոտորելու համար: Հարիւրապետ մը զէնք ունեցողները կը հրաւիրէ գիւղն պաշտպանելու ու 25–30ի չափ հայ եւ աւելի թուով յոյներ Պարտիզակը կը պաշտպանեն: Այս պաշտպանութեան մէջ զոհուած է Նշան նաւավար:

– Նիկոմիդիա խռնուած գաղթականներու բազմութիւնը եկեղեցին լեցուած են: Ո՛չ տուն կայ, ո՛չ ալ զանոնք պատսպարելու եւ կերակրելու միջոցներ:

Պրուսա (Առաջնորդական Տեղապահէն) – 14 Ապրիլ

Հելլէններու կողմէ վերջին անգամ ազատագրուած վայրերու մէջ քէմալիստներու կողմէ տեղի ունեցած են վայրագութիւններ:

Կէմլէյիկի շրջանի գիւղերէն ոեւէ վնաս չկայ. միայն թէ Սէօլէօզի երիտասարդութիւնը՝ 100է աւելի, հելլէններու յառաջխաղացման միջոցին միասին գացած, անգամ մըն ալ ետ չեն վերադարձած: Կ'ըսուի թէ գերի ինկած են քէմալիստներու ձեռքը:

Եէնիշէհիրի եւ Մարմարճըգի հայերը նախապէս փոխադրուած ըլլալուն՝ այդ կողմերէն աւելի կորուստ չկայ: Եէնիճէ եւ Ճէրրահ փախչելու անկարողները՝ 225 հոգի, մնացած են, որոնցմէ 4 հոգի այր եւ կին մեռցուցած են, իսկ այր մարդիկը՝ 52 հոգի, վերջին յարձակման ատեն ներսերը քշած են: Մնացեալները՝ ծեր կիներ եւ մանուկներ, վերջին ծայր թշուառութեան մէջ Պրուսա եկած են: Այս երկու գիւղերուն եկեղեցիները թէ՛ կողոպտուած, թէ՛ պղծուած եւ թէ՛ քանդուած են: Տուներն ալ մեծ մասամբ քանդուած են:

Պիլէճիկէն՝ 94, Կէօլպազէն՝ 44 հոգի, այր մարդիկներ 18–70 տարու, Էսկիշէհիր, Էնկիւրիւ եւ Պէյ Բազար աքսորուած, մէկ մասն ալ յայտնի չէ թէ որ կողմ տարած են. աքսորա՞ծ, թէ՞ սպաննուած, յայտնի չէ: Շրջակայ միւս գիւղերէն որոշ տեղեկութիւններ չկան: Պիլէճիկի եկեղեցւոյ գոյքերը եւ անօթները յափշտակած եւ եկեղեցին քանդած են: Փախուստի միջոցին քէմալիստները ամբողջ քաղաքը կրակի տուած եւ այրած են, միմիայն եզերքներէն 30–40 տուն կրցած է ազատուիլ հրդեհէն, այն ալ շնորհիւ հելլէն զինուորներու, որոնք հազիւ Պիլէճիկ ոտք դրած, աշխատած են մարել հրդեհը, եւ սակայն քաղաքը արդէն ամբողջութեամբ հրոյ ճարակ եղած է: Քրիստոնեայ ժողովուրդը՝ ծեր, կին, տղայ, կրցած են ազատուիլ հելլէններու անմիջական գրաւումով եւ հետիոտն հոս եկած են շատ թշուառ վիճակի մէջ, այնպէս որ փոխադրութեան կառքերու չգոյութենէն ոչ ոք չէ կրցած իր հետ բան մը բերել: Այդ կողմէն ազատուող հայերէն 1400 հոգիի մօտ կրցած է Պրուսա գալ:

- Այսօր լուր հասաւ Պրուսա թէ միլլիճիք յարձակած են Չէնկիլէրի եւ [Մեծ]-Նոր-Գիւղի վրայ: Չէնկիլէր ամբողջովին այրած է, իսկ մեծ-նոր-գիւղացիք կը դիմադրեն:

- Ապրիլ 14էն սկսեալ հելլէն հրամատարութեան որոշումով գաղթականներու հացը դադրած է եւ մարդ գլուխ 200 տրամ օրական ալիւր կը տրուի: Առաջնորդարանէն պահանջուած է անգործներու եւ աննեցուկներու ցուցակը ներկայացնել: Ասոնց թիւը 2887 անձ է:

Պրուսա (Առաջնորդական Տեղապահէն) – 16 Ապրիլ

Բազար գիւղէն հասնող ականատեսներ կը վկայեն թէ Չէնկիլէր հրդեհ[ու]ած եւ Մեծ-Նոր-Գիւղի վրայ յարձակում եղած է:

Չէնկիլէր (Թաղական խորհուրդէն) – 22 Մարտ

Մօտ 6½ ամիս է Օրխան Ղազի գաւառը յոյն բանակին կողմէ գրաւուած է: Այս ժամանակամիջոցին մէջ շատ մը փոփոխական անցուդարձեր կատարուած [են]: Եալովա, Գարամուսալ, Նիկիա եւս գրաւման ներքեւ առնուեցան: Բոլոր այս գրաւումներու ժամանակ շրջանիս հայութիւնը եւ յոյն ժողովուրդը մասամբ ինքզինքը ազատուած զգալով իր խաղաղ աշխատանքը ձեռք առաւ:

Նախ Գըզտէրպէնտ[ի] եւ Փլաճըգի ջարդն ու թալանը, հրդեհները կատարուած են, որոնցմէ

vivors came to settle in the Armenian-populated villages of Sugören, Büyük-Yeniköy, and Keramet.

Eventually, the need to change military positions became significant, and the army that had been settled in Keramet moved its position to Çiftlik, below Büyük-Yeniköy, and, similarly, to Sugören to fortify its hills. During this time, the Armenian village of Keramet was also set on fire, and many Armenians perished.

A group of bandits from the village of Fevziye in Karamürsel, led by the Milli Davut Çavuş, attacked the village of Kartsi in Yalova. Some of its people had fled beforehand and taken refuge in Sugören, but many remained in the village upon the insistence of several locals. All those who remained were slaughtered by Davut and his men, which the Greek military authorities confirmed through a local investigation.

A few days after the burning and massacre of the village of Kartsi, the abovementioned bandit leader Davut and his men attacked the nearby Greek village of Elmalı. The people fled in a hurry to Sugören by way of the mountains and to Yalova through the plains. The elderly and the feeble remained in place. About eighty houses were set on fire from the north side of the village.

On March 15, an advance was made [by the Millis] on all of these fronts being protected by the Greek forces. The [Greek] troops defending Çiftlik, located in front of Orhangazi, Sugören, and Büyük-Yeniköy, retreated south of Lake İznik. Seeing that the army was withdrawing with all its equipment, in less than half an hour, the Turks brought out all their weapons stored in Orhangazi. So to have all the Turks of these occupied areas rise, the Turkish çetes sent special couriers to the Turkish villages of Reşadiye, Cihan, Esadiye, and Yalova, announcing that the army of infidels had been withdrawn. With the closure of all Orhangazi's shops and coffeehouses, all patriotic Turks were armed and ready to act in unison. The Greek flag was taken down from the government building to hang the Ottoman flag. Upon witnessing these events in horror, the Armenian and Greek refugees fleeing the villages of Orhangazi, who had taken refuge under the protection of the Greek soldiers, tried to escape to Gemlik.

Before this, the Turkish gendarmes had been giving all kinds of assurances to the occupying authority, saying they had no weapons. Behold, all things kept hidden have been uncovered. Let us not forget to say that at this moment, the Millis were already working on completing what had been left incomplete in the village of Elmalı: after [they previously burned] 80 houses, they burned 520 more houses.

Sheikh Şerafeddin, a well-known figure in the village of Reşadiye, sent his translator, Ziya Effendi, especially to Orhangazi to congratulate the Turkish administration and lieutenant governor, and some officials convened a meeting with the notables to prepare for the realization of their plans. All of this was confirmed in the presence of the Greek migrants in Orhangazi and the artisans native to the village of Sugören who were there. A soldier of a returning Greek detachment took down the Ottoman flag hoisted on the government building, took away the weapons carried by a group of gendarmes and local Turks, and interrogated and severely punished them.

The Greek army recaptured Orhangazi on March 17. The Turkish gendarmes were photographed, and their weapons were confiscated. The lieutenant governor, the gendarmes, and some others were arrested. Thereupon, after acting like wolves a few hours before, the Turkish population behaved like sheep.

The complaints are too many. The Turks have no answer because their whole secret has been revealed. All the houses were searched, and bullets were found in large quantities. A woman apprehended from a house was carrying numerous bullets on her. She is under surveillance. When [the Millis] were transporting the weapons by carts, eyewitnesses went and told the Greek command that the lives of the Armenian and Greek people would be in danger if the Greek army did not arrive in an hour.

մազապուր ազատուածներ, եկած հաստատուած են Չէնկիլէր եւ Մեծ-Նոր-Գիւղ եւ Քէրէմէթ հայաբնակ գիւղերը:

Ի վերջոյ ռազմական դիրքերու փոփոխման պէտքը զգալի ըլլալով, Քէրէմէթի զօրքը իր դիրքը փոխադրեց Մեծ-Նոր-Գիւղի ներքեւ գտնուող Չիֆթլիկը, նմանապէս Չէնկիլէր եւ անոր բլուրները ամրացուց: Այս ժամանակամիջոցին եւս հրդեհի տրուեցաւ Քէրէմէթ հայ գիւղը, որուն հետ նմանապէս զոհ գացին շատ մը հայեր:

Միլլի աւազակապետ Գարամուսալի Ֆէյզիէ գիւղէն Տաւուտ Չաւուշ անունով իր խումբով կը յարձակի Եալովայի Քարձի գիւղին վրայ, որուն ժողովուրդը մասամբ եւ օր առաջ փախած ու Չէնկիլէր ապաստանած էր, իսկ շատեր տեղւոյն քանի մը անձանց ստիպումով չէին հեռացած գիւղէն: Այդ մնացողները բոլորն ալ Տավուտի եւ իր մարդոց կողմէն ջարդուեցան, ինչ որ տեղական քննութեամբ հաստատեցին հելլէն զինուորական իշխանութիւնները:

Քարձի գիւղի հրկիզումէն ու ջարդէն քանի մը օր վերջ յիշեալ աւազակապետ Տավուտ եւ իր մարդիկը յարձակեցան մօտակայ Էլմալը յոյն գիւղը: Ժողովուրդը ահուդողով փախուստ տուաւ լերան ճամբով Չէնկիլէր ու դաշտի ճամբով Եալովա: Ծերեր ու անկարներ մնացին տեղւոյն մէջ: Գիւղին հիւսիսի կողմէն կրակի տրուեցաւ 80ի չափ տուն:

Մարտ 15ի օրը յոյն զօրաց բոլոր այս պաշտպանուած ճակատներուն վրայ յառաջխաղացման ցոյց մը տեղի ունեցաւ: Կէմլէյիկ, Օրխան Ղազի, Չէնկիլէր եւ Մեծ-Նոր-Գիւղի առջեւ գտնուող Չիֆթլիկը պաշտպանող զօրքը դէպի Նիկիոյ լճին հարաւային կողմը քաշուեցաւ: Թուրքերը տեսնելով որ զօրքը իր բոլոր կազմուածքներովը կը քաշուի, կէս ժամ չանցած Օրխան Ղազիի մէջ բոլոր պահուած զէնքերը մէջտեղ կը բերեն: Թուրք չէթէութիւնը գրաւուած այս վայրերուն բոլոր թրքութիւնը ոտքի հանելու համար մասնաւոր սուրհանդակներ ղրկուած են Րէշատիյէ, Ճիհան, Էսատիյէ ու Եալովայի թուրք գիւղերը աւետելու համար թէ կեավուրին զօրքը քաշուած է: Օրխան Ղազիի բոլոր խանութներն ու սրճարանները գոցուելով ամէն հայրենասէր թուրք իր զէնքին գլուխը կը գտնուի միահամուռ գործելու կազմ ու պատրաստ: Կառավարական շէնքին վրայի յունական դրօշը վար առնուելով տեղը Օսմանեան դրօշը կը կախուի: Օրխան Ղազիի մէջ գիւղերէն փախչող հայ եւ յոյն գաղթականութիւնը, որ յոյն զինուորին պաշտպանութեան տակ ապաստանած էր, այս ամենուն ականատես ըլլալով սարսափի մատնուած Կէմլէյիկ փախչիլ կը փորձեն:

Թուրք ժանտարմաներ զէնք մը իսկ չունինք ըսելով ասկէ առաջ գրաւող իշխանութեան ամէն տեսակ հաւաստիքներ կուտային: Ահա ամէն գաղտնիք մէջտեղ ելած է: Հոս չմոռնանք ըսելու որ այս պահուն արդէն Միլլին գործի սկսած էր Էլմալը գիւղին պակասը լրացնելու. 80 տունէն վերջ բոլոր կը վառեն 520 տուն եւս:

Րէշատիյէ գիւղին հանրածանօթ Շէխ Շէրէֆէտտին մասնաւորապէս իր թարգման Զիյա էֆէնտին կը ղրկէ Օրխան Ղազի շնորհաւորելու թուրք վարչութիւնը եւ գայմագամը, եւ կարգ մը պաշտօնեաներ էշրաֆներուն հետ ժողով գումարելով, կը պատրաստուին իրենց ծրագիրները գլուխ հանելու: Այս ամէնը Օրխան Ղազի գտնուող յոյն գաղթականներու եւ Չէնկիլէր գիւղացի հոդ գտնուող էսնաֆներու ներկայութեամբը հաստատուած է, եւ նոյնիսկ վերադարձող յոյն ջոկատի մը զինուորը ինքը անձամբ վար առած է Օսմանեան դրօշը, որ պարզուած էր պաշտօնատան վրայ եւ կարգ մը ժանտարմներու եւ տեղացի թուրքերու կրած զէնքերը առած ու նոյն միջոցին հարցաքննած ու սաստիկ պատիժ տուած է:

Օրխան Ղազի յոյն բանակէն վերագրաւուած է Մարտ 17ին: Թուրք ժանտարմաներու լուսանկարները քաշուած են եւ ձեռքերնին գտնուած զէնքերը առնուած [են]: Գայմագամը, ժանտարմաները եւ կարգ մը անձեր ձերբակալուած են: Ասոր վրայ քանի մը ժամ առաջ գայլ դարձող թուրք բնակչութիւնը գառնուկներ եղած են:

Բողոքներու թիւը մեծ է: Թուրքերը պատասխան չեն կրնար տալ, վասնզի ամբողջ գաղտնիքը պարզուած էր: Բոլոր տուները կը խուզարկուին եւ մեծաքանակ փամփուշտ կը գտնուի: Տունէ մը կին մը բռնուած է [որ իր] վրայ շատ մը փամփուշտներ կը կրէր. հսկողութեան տակ առնուած է:

Now the Greek soldiers have come to take hold of their positions.

This is the third time the people, as involuntary exiles, are abandoning their homes and places to escape just to save their lives. The current military authority is not openly assuring the absence of dangers and is not announcing even its departure in advance. Therefore, people are always fleeing in panic.

Gemlik (from Priest Hovsep Keosseyan of Sugören [Çengiler])—April 10

On Saturday, April 9, the Millis set Sugören on fire. On Friday, April 8, the surrounding Turkish çetes attacked the village from the northern heights of the village. The villagers strongly resisted. The shooting lasted two hours. The women and children moved two thousand meters from the village toward Orhangazi under the barrage of bullets. Two women (Noyemzar and Gyuliané) were killed, and a ten-year-old boy was wounded in the arm before they were out of the reach of the bullets.

As for the old men left behind in the village, they were left in flames.

The people did not even have time to take a blanket; now they roam the streets naked and barefoot. The lack of housing is also noticeable. Some are in Orhangazi, and some are in Gemlik.

Nobody is left in Sugören, Büyük-Yeniköy, and Ortaköy. The Millis have captured the hills surrounding the villages.

There has been no loss of life other than those reported above.

The villagers applied to the Greek command for bread, but no arrangement has yet been made.

Gemlik (from the headman of Büyük-Yeniköy)—April 11

On the day of the attack on Sugören [Çengiler], the Millis also attacked Büyük-Yeniköy, but thanks to the resistance, they were unable to enter. However, the people, seeing the success of the Millis in Sugören, panicked and migrated to Gemlik, where they remain in the corners of inns, naked and hungry. If this situation continues for a while, hunger and disease will completely eradicate the people.

Here, the few youths of the village are heroically resisting the salient superiority of the enemy and preventing the Millis from entering and destroying the village for five days. The Millis attack eight or ten times daily. All the Turkish and Circassian forces of the area occupied by the Greeks joined forces under the leadership of the men of Sheikh Şerafeddin of Reşadiye.

The Greek soldiers, who are only an hour away, are not providing help to the young Armenian fighters. Especially desperate because of the running out of bullets, the young fighters are considering abandoning their position. In that case, Büyük-Yeniköy will also be burned and the villagers will become a burden on the nation.

İzmir (from the primate)—April 21

Most of the Armenians of Afyonkarahisar migrated to Uşak the last time and thence, gradually, to Alaşehir and Manisa.

There are now 200 migrants in Manisa, 258 in Alaşehir, and the rest are in Uşak, about whom certain information has not yet been received.

Կառքերով զէնքը այլուր փոխադրած ատեն ականատեսներ գալով յոյն հրամանատարութեան հաղորդած են թէ հայ եւ յոյն ժողովուրդին կեանքը վտանգի տակ կը գտնուէր եթէ ժամ մը եւս չհասնէր յոյն բանակը: Այժմ յոյն զինուորը եկած հաստատուած է իր դիրքերուն վրայ:

Երրորդ անգամ ըլլալով ժողովուրդը այսպէս տարագիր ակամայ կը լքէ իւր տունն ու տեղը, միայն իր կեանքը փրկելու համար փախուստ կուտայ: Արդի զինուորական իշխանութիւնը բացէ ի բաց հաւաստիք չի տար թէ ռեւէ վտանգ չկայ եւ նոյնիսկ իր մեկնումը կանխաւ չի հաղորդեր: Այսպէսով ժողովուրդը միշտ խուճապի մատնուած փախուստ կուտայ:

Կէմլէյիկ (Յովսէփ Քահանայ Քէօսէեան Չէնկիլէրի քահանայէն) – 10 Ապրիլ

Ապրիլ 9 շաբաթ օր Չէնկիլէր Միլլի աւազակներու կողմէ հրդեհի տրուեցաւ:

8 Ապրիլ ուրբաթ օր շրջակայ թուրք չէթէներ գիւղին վրայ յարձակում գործեցին գիւղին հիւսիսային բարձունքէն: Գիւղացիք ուժգին կերպով կը դիմադրեն: Երկու ժամ հրացանաձգութիւն տեղի կ'ունենայ: Գիւղը գտնուող կիներ, մանուկներ, գնդակի տեղատարափին տակ գիւղէն 2000 մէթր կը հեռանան դէպի Օրխան Ղազի: Մինչեւ արձակուած հրացաններու հասողութենէն դուրս ելլալը երկու կին (Նոյեմզար եւ Կիւլեանէ) կը զոհուին, իսկ 10 տարեկան տղեկ մը կը վիրաւորուի ձեռքէն:

Գալով գիւղը ձգուած քանի մը ծերերու, անոնք բոցերու մէջ մնացած են:

Ժողովուրդը ծածկոց մը իսկ առնելու միջոց չունեցաւ. այժմ մերկ բոկոտն փողոցները կը դեգերին: Բնակարանի չգոյութիւնն ալ զգալի է: Մաս մը Օրխան Ղազի, մաս մըն ալ Կէմլէյիկ են:

Չէնկիլէր, Մեծ-Նոր-Գիւղ, Օրթագիւղ մարդ մնացած չէ: Միլլիները գիւղերուն շրջակայ բլուրները բռնած են:

Վերոգրեալ անձերէն զատ անձի կորուստ չկայ:

Գիւղացիք դիմում ըրած են հելլէն հրամատարութեան գէթ հաց ստանալու համար, սակայն դեռ ռեւէ կարգադրութիւն չէ եղած:

Կէմլէյիկ (Մեծ-Նոր-Գիւղի գիւղապետէն) – 11 Ապրիլ

Չէնկիլէրի վրայ յարձակուած օրը Միլլիները յարձակեցան նաեւ Մեծ-Նոր-Գիւղի վրայ, սակայն շնորհիւ ցոյց տրուած ընդդիմութեան, Միլլիճիները չյաջողեցան ներս մտնել, սակայն ժողովուրդը Չէնկիլէրի մէջ Միլլիճիներու ունեցած յաջողութիւնը տեսնելով ահաբեկ խուճապի մատնուեցաւ եւ Կէմլէյիկ գաղթեց, ուր կը մնայ ժողովուրդը խաներու անկիւնը, մերկ ու անօթի: Եթէ այս վիճակը ժամանակ մը եւս յարատեւէ, անօթութիւնը եւ հիւանդութիւնը ժողովուրդը բոլորովին բնաջինջ պիտի ընէ:

Աղին փոքր թիւով գիւղին երիտասարդութիւնը հինգ օրէ ի վեր թշնամիին աչքառու գերազանցութեան դէմ հերոսաբար կը դիմադրէ եւ չի թողուր որ Միլլիճիք գիւղ մտնեն եւ աւերեն: Ամէն օր ութը կամ տասը անգամ յարձակում կ'ըլլայ Միլլիճիներու կողմէ: Այս ոյժերուն հետ միացած են յունական գրաւման շրջանակի բոլոր թուրք եւ չէրքէզ ոյժերը՝ պարագլուխ ունենալով Րէշատիյէի շէյխ Շէրէֆէտտինին մարդիկը:

Յոյն զինուորը, որ հազիւ մէկ ժամ հեռու է, ռեւէ օգնութիւն չ'ընծայեր կռուող հայ երիտասարդներուն, որոնք յուսահատ՝ մանաւանդ փամփուշտի սպառումէն, իր[ենց] դիրքը լքանել կը մտած[են]: Այն պարագային Մեծ-Նոր-Գիւղն ալ պիտի այրեն եւ գիւղացիք պիտի բեռ ըլլան ազգին վրայ:

Իզմիր (Առաջնորդէն) – 21 Ապրիլ

Աֆիոն-Գարա-Հիսարի հայութեան կարեւոր մասը վերջին անգամ գաղթած է դէպի Ուշաք, ուրկէ հետզհետէ գաղթած են Ալաշէհիր եւ Մանիսա:

Մանիսայի մէջ այժմ կա[ն] 200 գաղթականներ, Ալաշէհիրի մէջ՝ 258, իսկ մնացեալները կը գտնուին Ուշաք, որոնց մասին դեռ որոշ տեղեկութիւն չէ ստացուած:

Supposedly, about two thousand people are still in Afyonkarahisar besides the migrants.

Aleppo (from Hovsep Boyajian)—March 24

The French authorities have provided fifteen hundred Ottoman liras cash as assistance to Armenian orphanages and are providing employment to able-bodied refugees, while the American Red Cross and, to a lesser extent, the Armenian General Benevolent Union are aiding vulnerable refugees. The fifteen hundred Ottoman liras provided by the French are being paid by the French Immigration Directorate.

Bursa (from the vicar general)—April 7

Recently, six hundred Armenian refugees from Bilecik arrived in the most miserable condition. They barely escaped and fled. Immediately a list of them was presented to General Papoulas, who ordered bread to be given to them.

İzmit (from the primate)—May 4[106]

A young Russian-Armenian man was killed in a Turkish house in a Turkish village near Akmeşe. An Armenian Catholic man detained in the same house was beheaded likewise.

The owner of the house where these crimes were committed has eleven to thirteen Turkish residents. He also killed his father and mother to keep the crimes concealed.

• Earlier, six people from İzmit, at the suggestion of a Turk, went twice to the Tatar village and brought cigarettes. For the third time, ten days ago, when they went, they did not return with their seventeen horses. A notable Muslim associated with the proposing Turk has been jailed, but we do not know if it will be possible to punish him.

The six missing people are:

1. Taniel Gevrejian from Arslanbey, 48 years old, married
2. Bedros Bedimian from Bahçecik, 65 years old, married, and with three grandchildren
3. Arshag M. Bedrosian from Arslanbey, 52 years old, married
4. Antranig Yesayan from Arslanbey, 35 years old, married, and with three children
5. Parounag M. Hagopian from Kurtbelen, 25, married, has a mother, two brothers, and a sister
6. Garabed Ajemian from Bahçecik, 25-year-old, has a sister and two nephews

• Armenag Chikinian from Bahçecik went to the Turkish village of Ayvalı to work as usual. He lodged at the house of a Turk named Süleyman and bought chickens, eggs, four hundred ears of corn, and a lamb. Leaving a portion of the corn in the village, he departed the village on a Saturday ten or thirteen days ago. His brother Aram went to look for him. He was told that his brother left two days before his arrival, promising to return at Easter. İlyas, the ranger of Ayvalı, explicitly made this statement.

It is suspected that the villagers took revenge when he [Aram] crossed Uzunbey, as he was robbed in the village before, but the Greek government had managed to recover the booty from them.

• On April 29, Onnig Kr[ikor] Chaferian of Bahçecik and a native of Bahçecik from the village of Çakır set out from Bahçecik to the village of Kumlar to grind wheat. They, too, are missing.

• More than one hundred Millis passing through Avcıköy [Merdigöz] and Yalakdere robbed the church and took the residents out of the villages, beating them. We do not know whether they left them alive or slaughtered them.

• The diocese of İzmit was composed of forty-five towns and villages. Today, only İzmit is left. Its one thousand houses are almost entirely burned; one hundred or one hundred fifty houses barely remain along with Adapazarı and Bahçecik. They, too, are in danger.

Կը կարծուի թէ գաղթականներէն դուրս 2000ի չափ ալ դեռ կը գտնուին Աֆիոն-Գարա-Հիսար:

Հալէպ (Յովսէփ Պօյաճեանէ) – 24 Մարտ

Ֆրանսական իշխանութիւնները 1500 օսմանեան լիրա հնչուն նպաստ յատկացուցած [են] հայ որբանոցներուն եւ կարող գաղթականներուն ալ գործ կը հայթայթ[են], իսկ տկար գաղթականներուն կ'օգնէ Ամերիկեան Կարմիր Խաչը, մաս մըն ալ Հայ Բարեգործական [Ընդհանուր] Միութիւնը: Ֆրանսացիներուն յատկացուցած 1500 օսմանեան լիրան կը վճարէ ֆրանսական ներգաղթի տնօրէնութիւնը:

Պրուսա (Առաջնորդական Տեղապահէն) – 7 Ապրիլ

Այս օրերս Պիլէճիկի կողմերէն 600 հոգի փախստական հայեր եկան ամենաթշուառ վիճակի մէջ, որոնք հազիւ հազ իրենց հոգիները ազատած եւ փախած են: Անմիջապէս ասոնց ցուցակը ներկայ[աց]ուած է հաց տրուելու համար եւ Զօրավար Բաքուլաս հրամայեց այս հացը տալ:

Նիկոմիդիա (Առաջնորդէն) – 4 Մայիս

Արմաշի մօտ թուրք գիւղի մը մէջ ռուսահայ երիտասարդ մը թուրքի մը տան մէջ սպաննած են: Հայ-հոռոմ մըն ալ, որ նոյն տունը բռնի վար դրուած էր, նոյնպէս գլխատուած է:

Տան տէրը, որուն տան մէջ կատարուած է այս ոճիրը, ունի 11էն 13 թուրք բնակիչներ: Կը սպաննէ նաեւ իր հայրը եւ մայրը, որպէսզի ոճիրները հրապարակ չելլեն:

- Ասկէ առաջ վեց անձեր Նիկոմիդիայէն, թուրքի մը առաջարկով, թաթար գիւղը գացած էին եւ երկու անգամ ծխախոտ բերած էին: Երրորդ անգամուն, ասկէ 10 օր առաջ, երբ կ'երթան, այլեւս չեն դառնար իրենց 17 ձիերով: Առաջարկող թուրքին հետ կապ ունեցող իսլամ երեւելի մը բանտարկուած է, սակայն չենք գիտեր թէ կարելի պիտի ըլլա՞յ պատժել:

Անհետացած վեց անձերն են.

1. Դանիէլ Կէվրէճեան արսլանպէկցի, 48 տարեկան, ամուսնացած
2. Պետրոս Պետիմեան պարտիզակցի, 65 տարեկան, ամուսնացած եւ երեք թոռան տէր
3. Արշակ Մ. Պետրոսեան արսլանպէկցի, 52 տարեկան, ամուսնացած
4. Անդրանիկ Եսայեան արսլանպէկցի, 35 տարեկան, ամուսնացած եւ երեք զաւակ
5. Բարունակ Մ. Յակոբեան գուրտպէլէնցի, 25 տարեկան, ամուսնացած, մայր ունի, երկու եղբայր, քոյր մը
6. Կարապետ Աճէմեան պարտիզակցի, 25 տարեկան, քոյր ունի եւ երկու քեռորդի

- Պարտիզակցի Արմենակ Չիքինեան Այվալը թուրք գիւղը կ'երթայ ըստ սովորութեան աշխատելու: Սուլէյման անուն թուրքի մը տունը կ'իջնէ, հաւ, հաւկիթ, 400 հատ եգիպտացորեն եւ գառնուկ մը կը գնէ: Եգիպտացորենէն մաս մը գիւղը ձգելով, շաբաթ օրը 10–13 օր առաջ գիւղէն կը մեկնի: Եղբայրը՝ Արամ, փնտռելու կ'երթայ: 2 օր առաջ գալէն մեկնեցաւ կ'ըսեն, Չատկին նորէն դառնալու խոստումով: Այս յայտարարութիւնը կ'ընէ մասնաւորապէս Այվալը գիւղի գօրուճի Իլիաս:

Կասկած կայ որ Ուզուն Պէյէն անցնելու ատեն այդ գիւղացիք վրէժ լուծած ըլլան, քանի որ ուրիշ անգամ այդ գիւղին մէջ կողոպտուած էր, բայց հեյլէն կառավարութիւնը գողօնը ետ առած էր իրենցմէ:

- Պարտիզակէն Օննիկ Գր. Չափերեան եւ Չաքար գիւղէն պարտիզակցի մը, 29 Ապրիլին Պարտիզակէն ճամբայ կ'ելլեն դէպի Գումլարի աղօրիքն՝ ցորենը ալիւր ընելու համար: Ասոնք ալ անհետացած են:

- Մէրտիկէօզէն ու Եալազտէրէէն անցնող 100էն աւելի Միլիճիները եկեղեցին կողոպտեր ու ծեծելով գիւղերէն դուրս տար[եր են] տեղւոյն բնակիչները եւ չենք գիտեր թէ ո՞ւր թողուցին, [թէ՞] սպաննեցին զանոնք:

İstanbul—May 8
The Turkish police arrested several Armenians, upon the testimony of some Turks, on charges of arson and robbery in İstanbul. They were residents of Yalova and the vicinities, and now they live in İstanbul.

The names of those arrested so far are:
from Çakır, villager Bedros Nigoghosian, 38-year-old
Khoren Misakian, 30-year-old
Yervant Berberian, 28-year-old
from Sugören [Çengiler], Panig Koumlarian, 22-year-old
Khashman Oghlanian
from Avcıköy [Merdigöz], Aghasi D. Ghevontian, 26-year-old
from Yelakdere, Toros Janverian, 40-year-old
from Kılıç, villager Sarkis Markarian, 30-year-old
from Muratça, Senekerim Hayrabedian, 28-year-old
from Keramet, Krikor Nalbandian

İstanbul (from the National Assistance)—May 9
On Thursday, several Turkish police officers entered the Hasköy deportees' station and arrested two deportees—Apraham Papazian and Bedros Ghazarian. The reason for their arrest was the testimony of someone who had come to the station to visit and had fired a round of bullets with his pistol, for which he was severely reprimanded. This person went to the Turkish police station and accused those sheltered in the station as çetes. The arrest was made because of this.

Mersin (from Zeytun Patriotic Union)—May 3
According to information received from Süleymanlı [Zeytun], the lives of the twenty-five hundred Armenians in Süleymanlı are in danger.

On April 12, the government of Maraş severed its relations with Süleymanlı and presented three proposals: a) evacuation of the barracks where the people of Süleymanlı were living after the deportation because the entire city was burned in 1915; b) hand over weapons; c) departure of the people to the interior of the country.

All three proposals were rejected for having the nature of annihilation. Therefore, the Kemalists marched on Süleymanlı with two cannons. The first collision took place in Kılavuz gorge, near the Ceyhan bridge. The Kemalists did not succeed in crossing the bridge, but no one believes that this situation can continue. Likely the Kemalists will try to attack with greater force, and the Armenians will not be able to resist.

The people of Süleymanlı possess barely two to three months' supplies. Some Armenian refugees from Saimbeyli [Hacın] have also taken refuge there. Süleymanlı will be destroyed if it receives no external aid.[107]

Dörtyol (from Zeytun Patriotic Union, Dörtyol)—May 3, 1921
According to reports, twenty-five thousand Kemalist troops are ready to march on Süleymanlı [Zey-

- Ամբողջ Նկիմոիդիոյ առաջնորդութիւնը ունէր 45 քաղաք եւ գիւղ, այսօր միայն Նիկոմիդիա մնացած է, որուն 1000 տուները գրեթէ ամբողջ այրած [են]: 100 կամ 150 տուն հազիւ կը մնայ, [ինչպէս նա]եւ Ատաբազար[ն] ու Պարտիզակը: Ասոնք ալ վտանգի տակ են:

Կ. Պոլիս – 8 Մայիս

Թուրք ոստիկանութիւնը կարգ մը թուրքերու ցուցմունքին վրայ ձերբակալած է Կ. Պոլսոյ մէջ հրձիգութեան եւ աւազակութեան նման ամբաստանութիւններով կարգ մը հայեր, որոնք Եալովայի եւ շրջականներու բնակիչներէն են եւ հիմա Կ. Պոլիս կը գտնուին:

Մինչեւ հիմա ձերբակալուածներուն անուններն են՝

Չաքար գիւղացի Պետրոս Նիկողոսեան 38 տարեկան

Խորէն Միսաքեան 30 տարեկան

Երուանդ Պէրպէրեան 28 տարեկան

Չէնկիլէրցի Բանիկ Գումլարեան 22 տարեկան

Խաչման Օղլանեան

Մէրտէկէօզցի Աղասի Տ. Ղեւոնդեան 26 տարեկան

Եալաքտէրէցի Թորոս Ճանվէրեան 40 տարեկան

Գըլըճ գիւղացի Սարգիս Մարգարեան 30 տարեկան

Մուրատ Չայցի Սեներքերիմ Հայրապետեան 28 տարեկան

Քէրէմէթցի Գրիգոր Նալբանտեան

Կ. Պոլիս (Ազգային Խնամատարութենէն) – 9 Մայիս

Հինգշաբթի օր Խասգիւղի տարագրեալներու կայանը մէկ քանի թուրք ոստիկաններ մտնելով կը ձերբակալեն երկու տարագիրներ՝ Աբրահամ Փափազեան եւ Պետրոս Ղազարեան անուն: Ասոնց ձերբակալութեան պատճառ եղած է մէկու մը ցուցմունքին վրայ, որ կայանը եկած էր այցելութեան եւ ձեռք մը ատրճանակ պարպած էր եւ ասոր համար խիստ կերպով յանդիմանուած էր: Այս անձը գացած է թուրք ոստիկանատուն եւ ամբաստանած է կայանի պատասխանատուները իբր չէթէ: Ասոր վրայ է որ կատարուած է այս ձերբակալութիւնը:

Մերսին (Զէյթունի Հայրենակցական Միութենէն) – 3 Մայիս

Զէյթունէն ստացուած տեղեկութեանց համաձայն Զէյթունի 2500 հայոց կեանքը վտանգի տակ է:

Մարաշի կառավարութիւնը Ապրիլ 12ին խզեց իր յարաբերութիւնները Զէյթունի հետ եւ ներկայացուց երեք առաջարկ՝ Ա. պարպում զօրանոցին ուր կը բնակին տարագրութենէն վերջ զէյթունցիք, վասնզի քաղաքը 1915ին ամբողջ այրած է: Բ. յանձնում զէնքերու. Գ. հեռացում ժողովուրդին դէպի երկրին ներսերը:

Բնաջնջումի բնոյթ կրող երեք առաջարկներն ալ մերժուած են: Ասոր վրայ քէմալականները երկու թնդանօթով քալած են Զէյթունի վրայ: Առաջին բախումը տեղի ունեցած է Գուլավուզի կիրճին մէջ, Ճիհունի կամուրջին քով: Քէմալականք չեն յաջողած անցնիլ կամուրջը, սակայն ոչ մէկ հաւատք կայ թէ այս վիճակը կրնայ շարունակուիլ: Հաւանական է որ քէմալականք աւելի մեծ ոյժերով յարձակում փորձեն եւ հայերը չկարենան դիմադրել:

Զէյթունցիք հազիւ 2–3 ամսուան պաշար ունին: Մաս մը փախստական հաճընցի հայեր ալ ապաստանած են հոդ: Եթէ արտաքին օգնութիւն չըլլայ, Զէյթուն պիտի բնաջնջուի:[17]

Տէօրթ-Եօլ (Զէյթունի Հայրենակցական Միութենէն, Չորք Մարզուան) – 3 Մայիս 1921

Առնուած տեղեկութեանց համաձայն, քէմալական 25,000 զինուորներ կազմ եւ պատրաստ են

tun]. Extermination is inevitable.[108]

Çanakkale [Dardanelles] (from Priest Tionis Drezian)—May 21, 1921
For quite some time now, bands of çetes have been raiding the area around Çanakkale. Recently, especially robberies and killings have become commonplace, and the organization of these bandits has grown to such an extent that it has become extremely dangerous for this city, mainly since Muslim villagers have been completely armed and are boasting and initiating threats.

İstanbul (from the Patriarchate)—June 4[109]
Three days ago, the people of Yalova were arrested again. Onnig Hagopian, a villager from Büyük-Yeniköy, was arrested on June 2. One person was arrested on June 3 while buying cherries from Yemiş İskelesi, and on the testimony of several Lazes, "this one also went to Yalova." Also, on June 3, in Mahmut Pazar, a native of Sugören [Çengiler] and a native of Büyük-Yeniköy were arrested when selling olives.

On June 1, Misak Ademian, a twenty-eight-year-old man from Büyük-Yeniköy, who had not been to Yalova for ten years, was arrested.

Bursa (from the primate)—June 4[110]
Fifteen young people from Göldağı (Bilecik) fled to come to Bursa. Five of them are thought to have been lost on the way and killed. The other ten arrived in Bursa three or four days ago. As eyewitnesses, they reported that of the villages of Bilecik, Göldağı had 320, Türkmen 400, Muratça 1,000, Hisarcık [Asarcık] sixty, Yayla 300, and Çalkara 1,000 people, respectively. Some were killed by the Millis. All the others were exiled. It is not known where they were taken.

The young men providing this testimony are 1. Hampartsoum Hovhannesian, 2. Siragan Torosian, 3. Krikor Seropian, 4. Hovsep Sarkisian, 5. Boghos Mardirosian, 6. Kevork Serovpian, 7. Krikor Sahagian, 8. Dzeroun M. Hagaopian, 9. Toros Boghosian, 10. Krikor Shabanian.

They were taken to Beypazarı from Göldağı, but escaping from there by way of mountain roads and hungry and thirsty, they reached the Greek lines, where they indicated their Armenianness and were let in.

İzmit (from the primate)—June 8
Traffic from İzmit to Adapazarı is banned because it is said that Turkish hocas and their adherents, who were meeting at the house of Mgrdich Jurgayan in Adapazarı, are being arrested.

• A rumor circulated in İzmit a few days ago that the headman of Akmeşe village Hagop Effendi and another Akmeşe resident went to negotiate with a Milli Turk named Hatip Muğla and that both did not return. Because of this, the people of Akmeşe took fright and fled to Adapazarı.

• A Turk from Akmeşe allegedly said to an Armenian acquaintance in İzmit that the village of İnaz had been set on fire. The intention to burn EskiMecidiye [Khaskal] and Akmeşe has also been mentioned.

• Migrants are in great distress due to unemployment and lack of livelihood.

դէպի Զէյթուն արշաւելու համար: Բնաջնջումը անխուսափելի է:[18]

Տարտանէլ (Դիոնիս Քահանայ Տրեզեանէ) – 21 Մայիս 1921

Բաւական ատենէ ի վեր չէթէական խումբեր Տարտանէլի շրջակայքը ապապատակութիւններ կ'ընէին, վերջերս մանաւանդ գողութիւնք եւ սպանութիւնք սովորական դարձան եւ այդ աւազակախումբերու կազմակերպութիւնը մեծ ծաւալ ստացաւ, այնպէս որ քաղաքիս համար իսկ վտանգաւոր ըլլալու աստիճանին հասաւ, մանաւանդ թէ խլամ գիւղերը բոլորովին զինուեցան եւ յոխորտանքն ու սպառնալիքը ծայր տուին:

Կ. Պոլիս (Պատրիարքարանէն) – 4 Յունիս

Երեք օրէ ի վեր դարձեալ եալովացիներ ձերբակալուիլ սկսած են: Ձերբակալուած է Օննիկ Յակոբեան մեծ-նոր-գիւղացի Յունիս 2ին: Յունիս 3ին ձերբակալուած է մէկը Եէմիշ Իսկէլէսի կեռաս առնելու գացած ատեն եւ քանի մը լազերու ցուցմունքին վրայ թէ «աս ալ Եալովա գացած է»: Նոյնպէս Յունիս 3ին Մահմուտ Փազարի մէջ մէկ չէնկիլէոցի եւ մէկ մեծ-նոր-գիւղացի կը ձերբակալուին ձիթապտուղ ծախած միջոցին:

Յունիս 1ին ձերբակալուած է Միսաք Ատեմեան մեծ-նոր-գիւղացի 28 տարեկան երիտասարդը, որ 10 տարիէ ի վեր Եալովա չէ գացած:

Պրուսա (Առաջնորդէն) – 4 Յունիս

Կէօլտաղցի (Պիլէճիկ) 15 երիտասարդներ խոյս կուտան իրենց տեղէն Պրուսա գալու համար: Ասոնցմէ 5-ը ճամբան կորսուած եւ սպաննուած կը կարծուին: Միւս 10-ը 3–4 օր առաջ Պրուսա կը հասնին եւ իբր ականատես վկաներ կը պատմեն թէ՝ Պիլէճիկի գիւղերէն Կէօլ Տաղ ունէր 320 հոգի, Թիւրքմէն՝ 400, Մուրատչայ՝ 1000, Ասարլըգ՝ 60, Եայլա՝ 300, Չալկարա՝ 1000 հոգի, որոնցմէ մաս մը Միլլիճիներու կողմէ սպաննուած եւ միւսները ամէնքն ալ աքսորուած են: Չի գիտցուիր թէ ո՞ւր տարած են:

Այս վկայութիւնը տուող երիտասարդներն են. 1. Համբարձում Յովհաննէսեան, 2. Սիրական Թորոսեան, 3. Գրիգոր Սերոբեան, 4. Յովսէփ Սարգիսեան, 5. Պօղոս Մարտիրոսեան, 6. Գէորգ Սերովբեան, 7. Գրիգոր Սահակեան, 8. Ծերուն Մ. Յակոբեան, 9. Թորոս Պօղոսեան, 10. Գրիգոր Շապանեան:

Ասոնք մինչեւ Պէյ Պազար տարուած են Կէօլտաղէն, սակայն անկէ փախելով, լեռնային ճամբաներով եւ անօթի ծարաւ հասած են հելլէնական գիծերը, ուր իրենց հայ ըլլալնին հասկցնելով ներս առնուած են:

Նիկոմիդիա (Առաջնորդէն) – 8 Յունիս

Նիկոմիդիայէն Ատաբազար երթեւեկը արգիլուած է, վասնզի կ'ըսուի թէ Ատա-Բազար Ծըր-կայեան Մկրտիչի տուն[ը] ժողով ընող թուրք հօճաներ ու անոնց համախոհներ կը ձերբակալուին:

- Չրոյց կը շրջի Նիկոմիդիոյ մէջ թէ քանի մը օրեր առաջ, Արմաշի գիւղապետ Յակոբ էֆէնտի եւ ուրիշ արմաշցի մը Հատըպ Մըլա ըսուած Միլլիճի թուրքի մը հետ բանակցութիւն մը ընելու գացած են եւ երկուքն ալ վերադարձած չեն եւ ասոր վրայ արմաշցիք վախցած եւ Ատաբազար փախած են:

- Թուրք մը, Արմաշի կողմերէն, Նիկոմիդիոյ մէջ, իր ծանօթ հայու մը իբր թէ ըսած է թէ Ինազ գիւղն կրակի տրուած է: Խասկալն ու Արմաշն ալ այրելու մտադրութիւնը կ'ըսուի:

- Գաղթականները մեծ նեղութեան մէջ են ապրուստի չգոյութեան եւ անգործութեան պատճառով:

Aleppo (from a personal letter from Israkoulian)—May 12

We have not had communication with Adana by land for a year. The çetes have destroyed the railway. Communication takes place by the sea. After the Maraş massacre, getting in touch with the eight to ten thousand Armenians that survived there was impossible. Through information we gather from travelers, we hear that the Armenians there are not in a desirable condition, having been subjected to a difficult situation of slavery. Süleymanlı [Zeytun] is under siege. Gaziantep [Ayntab] mounted a heroic resistance alongside the French forces, and it is free today. Although the French forces decided recently to evacuate the city, it was not implemented. Now, the French authorities are balancing the deficit in the local government budget again. On the holiday of Joan of Arc, a French flag was displayed on the government building by particular order. Hoisting the Turkish flag without the French flag is prohibited. After the news of the evacuation, these are considered promising signs.

• Mardin and Urfa, where there are many Armenian migrants, have been completely severed from us. We receive no news from them in any way. It has been heard from Muslim travelers that the Armenians there are very much oppressed by the Kemalists. They live a life of slavery, just like in Maraş. And from the more interior regions—Diyarbakır, Harput, and Malatya—we have no news at all; not even muleteers arrive.

As for Syria's situation, the cities are calm, but the roads are entirely perilous. The İskenderun-Aleppo road has been open for a month or two, but it is unsafe. The Beirut line was safe, but it has also come under significant attack by çetes recently. The country is completely disturbed.

We have refugees numbering twenty to twenty-five thousand and more in the Syrian region, but not in a desirable situation. Today, about two thousand male and female refugees are unemployed in Aleppo. Life is getting more complex day by day due to the prevailing costliness. One liter of flour (two and a half okkas) is one and a half silver mecidiyes. [Costliness with] a similar proportion applies to meat, oil, etc.

Gaziantep's situation, which I wrote about, applies to the whole region of Cilicia. If the French forces withdraw, something that has been decided but not yet implemented, the one hundred fifty thousand Armenians on the ground will be subjected to a very precarious situation.

More than one hundred people have been killed and two hundred fifty injured during the recent internal clashes in Jaffa.

When the country is in this state, a fair is being inaugurated in Beirut, which is surprising because when it is not possible to travel, what use is there of a fair?

İzmit (from vicar general Reverend Father Anania)—June 25

An urgent telegram addressed to the Patriarchate:

"Ten thousand people have been forced to evacuate immediately by order of the local military authorities. At least six transport vessels must come here if the slaughter of the entire population is undesired. Help!"

İstanbul—June 28

Acting upon the request for help by telegram, the National Assistance sent a steamboat to İzmit to transport the last remains of the Armenians there to Tekirdağ.

According to the information received, no Armenians are left in İzmit, except for the Armenian orphans in the American orphanage, who remain under American protection. Fearing the city's capture by the Millis—when it was decided to evacuate the Christian population, and a panicky escape began, anarchy reigned—and some misdoing occurred, such as murders, robberies, and arsons.

Հալէպ (անհատական նամակ Իսրագուլեանէ) – 12 Մայիս

Տարիէ մը ի վեր է որ ցամաքի ճամբով Ատանայի հետ յարաբերութիւն չունինք: Երկաթուղին չէթէներու կողմէ քանդուած է: Հաղորդակցութիւնները կը կատարուին ծովու ճամբով: Մարաշի ջարդէն յետոյ տեղւոյն վրայ վերապրող 8–10000 հայութեան հետ բնաւ կարելի չեղաւ յարաբերութեան մտնել: Ճամբորդներէ մեր քաղած տեղեկութիւններէն կը լսենք թէ հոն ցանկալի վիճակի մէջ չեն հայերը, ենթարկուած ըլլալով ստրկական ծանր կացութեան մը: Զէյթուն պաշարուած է: Այնթապ հերոսական դիմադրութիւն ըրաւ ֆրանսական ոյժերու կողքին եւ այսօր ազատ է. թէեւ վերջերս այս քաղաքը պարպելու որոշում տրուեցաւ ֆրանսական ոյժերու կողմէ եւ սակայն չգործադրուեցաւ, եւ այժմ ֆրանսական իշխանութիւնները տեղւոյն կառավարութեան պիւտճէի բացը կը գոցեն դարձեալ եւ Ժան տ՛Արքի տօնին օրը կառավարութեան շէնքին վրայ ֆրանսական դրօշակ պարզուած է յատուկ հրամանով եւ արգիլուած է առանց ֆրանսական դրօշակի թրքականը պարզել: Պարպումի լուրէն յետոյ ասոնք նպաստաւոր նշաններ կը համարուին:

- Մարտին եւ Ուրֆա, ուր ստուար թուով հայ գաղթականներ կան, մեզմէ անջատուած են բոլորովին եւ որեւէ կերպով լուր չենք կրնար առնուլ անոնցմէ: Իսլամ ճամբորդներէ կը լսուի թէ շատ կը նեղուին հոն հայերը քէմալականներու ձեռքին տակ, Մարաշի նման ստրկական կեանք մը ապրելով. իսկ աւելի խորերէն՝ Տիարպէքիրէն, Խարբերդէն, Մալաթիայէն բնաւ լուր չունինք, թուրք ջորեպաններ անգամ չեն գար:

Գալով Սուրիոյ կացութեան, քաղաքները հանգիստ են, բայց ճամբաները բոլորովին վտանգաւոր: Իսկէնտէրուն-Հալէպ ճամբան բաց է թէեւ մէկ երկու ամիսէ ի վեր, սակայն ապահով չէ: Ապահով էր Պէյրութի գիծը, այն ալ վերջերս կարեւոր յարձակումներ կրեց չէթէներու կողմէ: Երկիրը ամբողջութեամբ վրդովուած է:

Սուրիոյ շրջանին մէջ 20–25 հազարի չափ եւ աւելի գաղթականութիւն մը ունինք, բայց ոչ ցանկալի վիճակի մէջ: Հալէպի մէջ այսօր մօտ 2000ի չափ երկսեռ գաղթականներ անգործ են: Կեանքը օր աւուր կը դժուարանայ տիրող սղութեան պատճառով: Մէկ լիտր ալիւրը (2½ օխա) մէկուկէս արծաթ մէճիտ է, նոյն համեմատութեամբ նաեւ միս, իւղ, եւայլն:

Ինչ որ գրեցի Այնթապի մասին, նոյն վիճակն ունի նաեւ ամբողջ կիլիկեան շրջանը: Եթէ ֆրանսական ոյժերը քաշուին, բան մը որ վճռուած է բայց չէ գործադրուած ցարդ, շատ փափուկ կացութեան պիտի ենթարկուի տեղւոյն վրայ գտնուող 150000ի չափ հայութիւնը:

Եաֆայի մէջ վերջերս տեղի ունեցող ներքին կռիւներու ընթացքին 100ի չափ սպաննուածներ եւ 250ի չափ վիրաւորներ կան:

Երկրին այս դրութեան մէջ գտնուած պահուն Պէյրութի մէջ տօնավաճառ կը բացուի, ինչ որ զարմանք կը գրաւէ, վասնզի երբ ճամբորդել կարելի չէ, ի՛նչ օգուտ ունի տօնավաճառը:

Նիկոմիդիա (Առաջնորդական Փոխանորդ Տ. Անանիա Վարդապետէն) – 25 Յունիս

Ստիպողակ[ան] հեռագիր, ուղղուած պատրիարքարան.

«Տասը հազար ժողովուրդ տեղական զինուորական իշխանութեան հրամանով ստիպուած է վայրկեան առաջ փոխադրուիլ: Առնուազն վեց փոխադրանաւ անհրաժեշտ է որ հոս գայ, եթէ չ՛ուզուիր որ ամբողջ ժողովուրդը ջարդուի: Օգնութիւն»:

Կ. Պոլիս – 28 Յունիս

Հեռագրով եղած օգնութեան խնդրանքին վրայ Ազգ. Խնամատարութիւնը շոգենաւ մը ղրկելով Նիկոմիդիա, հոն գտնուած հայերուն վերջին մնացորդները փոխադրեց Ռոտոսթօ:

Առնուած տեղեկութիւններու համաձայն, Նիկոմիդիոյ մէջ հայերէն ոչ ոք մնացած է, բացի Ամերիկեան Որբանոց գտնուող հայ որբերէն, որոնք մնացած են ամերիկեան պաշտպանութեան տակ: Միլլիներու կողմէ քաղաքը գրաւելու երկիւղին տակ երբ քրիստոնեայ բնակչութիւնը պարպելու որոշում կը տրուի եւ խուճապային փախուստը կը սկսի, այս ժամանակամիջոցին մէջ անիշխա-

The migrants, whom the Greek government relocated, are said to have been taken to Lemnos and the other archipelago islands, as well as to Tekirdağ.

The Patriarchate has not heard from those taken to the islands.

Some of those who left the city with their personal means have arrived in İstanbul. The Turkish police have arrested some for allegedly having robbed the Turkish population.

Tekirdağ (from locum tenens Father Khoren Jamjian)—June 24

Today, two steamships of Armenian and Greek refugees arrived in Tekirdağ. The Armenians number about 650 people displaced from the villages of Bahçecik and the surrounding villages.

In addition to immediately providing bread, cheese, olives, and other necessities to the migrants, the Greek government also allocated barracks near the city for their comfort. The Armenian prelacy also formed a commission to undertake their care.

The refugees say that two thousand or more refugees also will come tomorrow or the next day.

The comers are the people of Bahçecik. There has been no information from İzmit yet.

The Greek government is working hard to accommodate them. The governor-general of Thrace is also expected here tomorrow. A final arrangement will be made under his auspices.

Tekirdağ (telegram from the vicar general)—June 25

Thousands of refugees are arriving. There is a great need for money and clothes.

Tekirdağ (telegram from the vicar general and Dr. Sdepanian)—June 26

Three thousand refugees have arrived. Thousands more are expected. Make appeals! Send a commission and especially money and all that is needed!

Aleppo (from the Armenian National Union)—May 27

The Armenians arriving from Urfa have presented the local economic and political situation in a very bitter way. Almost two months ago, with great difficulty, we were able to send them 240 Ottoman liras cash, but in the face of the prevalent misery and need, the sum was insignificant. It is understood from a secret letter that the situation in Urfa is very grave. "The military issue is like a fever attack, and living has become impossible." The poor will starve to death. The cost of a tümen of wheat (sixteen to eighteen okkas) was nine mecidiyes; it fell to four and a half mecidiyes. The people are perplexed. The 240 liras melted like water. The military authority seizes the wheat; the soldiers are hungry; the military and the municipality are fighting: one for its soldiers and the other for the people. It is impossible for Armenians to buy wheat in the market; trade is at a complete halt; the artisans are unemployed; the carpet factory was seized, but the equipment was transferred to the main church, where it is being installed. The ability to endure exists no more. The Armenians are strained in an iron ring. Surveillance has been tightened to the extreme; [even] a bird cannot fly.

The refugees arriving after this letter present the situation even more deteriorated. Notable individuals have been arrested and others are being sought.

There are seven thousand Armenians in Urfa generally living in a state of misery and there are no means to help them.

About ten thousand Armenian male and female survivors of various ages are gathered in Aleppo;

նութիւնը կը տիրէ եւ տեղի կ'ունենա[ն] կարգ մը անտեղութիւններ, ինչպէս՝ սպանութիւններ, կողոպուտ եւ հրձիգութիւն:

Գաղթականներէն անոնք որ յոյն կառավարութեան կողմէ փոխադրուած են, կ'ըսուի թէ տարուած են Լէմնոս եւ Արշիպեղագոսի միւս կղզիները, ինչպէս նաեւ Ռօտոսթօ:

Կղզիները տարուածներէն մինչեւ հիմա լուր չունի պատրիարքարանը:

Իսկ իրենց անձնական միջոցներովը քաղաքէն մեկնողներէն ոմանք Կ. Պոլիս եկած են: Ասոնց-մէ մէկ մասը թուրք ոստիկանութեան կողմէ ձերբակալուած են իբր կողոպտիչ թուրք բնակչութեան:

Ռօտոսթօ (Առաջնորդական Փոխանորդ Խորէն Քահանայ Ճամճեանէ) – 24 Յունիս

Այսօր երկու շոգենաւ հայ եւ յոյն գաղթականներ հասան Ռօտոսթօ: Հայոց թիւը մօտաւորապէս 650 է ու Պարտիզակի եւ շրջակայ գիւղերէն տեղահան են:

Տեղւոյս հելլէն կառավարութիւնը անմիջապէս եկող գաղթականներու հաց, պանիր, ձիթապտուղ [տայէ] եւ այլ պէտքերը հոգալէ զատ, անոնց հանգստութեան համար ալ քաղաքին մօտ գտնուող զօրանոցները յատկացուց: Հայոց առաջնորդարանն ալ յանձնաժողով մը կազմեց անոնց հոգատարութիւնը ստանձնելու համար:

Եկող գաղթականները կ'ըսեն թէ վաղը կամ միւս օր 2000 գաղթականներ եւս պիտի գան:

Յարդ եկողները պարտիզակցիներ են եւ Նիկոմիդիայէն դեռ որոշ տեղեկութիւն չկայ:

Հելլէն կառավարութիւնը լուրջ ջանքեր կը թափէ անոնց տեղաւորման համար: Վաղը հոս կը սպասուի նաեւ Թրակիոյ ընդհանուր կառավարիչը, որուն հովանաւորութեան տակ պիտի ըլլան վերջնական կարգադրութիւններ:

Ռօտոսթօ (հեռագիր Առաջնորդական Փոխանորդէն) – 25 Յունիս

Հազարաւոր գաղթականներ կը հասնին: Մեծ անհրաժեշտութիւն կայ դրամի եւ հագուստի:

Ռօտոսթօ (հեռագիր Առաջնորդական Փոխանորդէն եւ Տոք. Ստեփանեանէ) – 26 Յունիս

Երեք հազար գաղթականներ հասած են: Հազարաւորներ դեռ կը սպասուին: Դիմումներ ըրէք: Ղրկեցէք յանձնաժողով եւ մանաւանդ դրամ եւ ամէն ինչ որ պէտք է:

Հալէպ (Հայ Ազգային Միութենէն) – 27 Մայիս

Ուրֆայէն հասնող հայերը տեղւոյն տնտեսական թէ քաղաքական կացութիւնը շատ դառն կերպով կը ներկայացնեն: Թուականէս զրեթէ երկու ամիս առաջ մեծ դժուարութեամբ կարելի եղաւ իրենց հասցնել 240 օսմանեան լիրա հնչուն, սակայն տիրող թշուառութեան եւ կարօտութեան առջեւ շատ աննշան արժէք ունեցած է ան: Ստացուած գաղտնի նամակէ մը կը հասկցուի որ Ուրֆայի մէջ կացութիւնը շատ ծանր է: «Զինուորական հարցը ջերմի նոպայի մը կը նմանի, իսկ ապրուստը անկարելի դարձած է». աղքատները անօթութենէ պիտի մեռնին. թիմէն մը ցորենը (16–18 օխա) 9 մէճիտ էր 4½ մէճիտի ինկաւ. շուարած մնացած են: 240 ոսկին ջուրի պէս հալեցաւ: Զինուորական իշխանութիւնը կը գրաւէ ցորենները. զինուորները անօթի են. զինուորականութիւն եւ *պէշէտիէ* կը գօտեմարտին՝ մին իր զինուորներուն եւ միւսը ժողովրդին համար: Շուկան հայերուն համար անկարելի է ցորեն գնել. առեւտուրը բոլորովին կեցած է. արհեստաւորն անգործ է. գորգի գործարանը գրաւած են, սակայն գործիները փոխադրուած են մայր եկեղեցին, ուր կը զետեղուին: Ա՛լ համբերելու կարողութիւնը չէ մնա[ցա]ծ: Երկաթէ օղակի մը մէջ պրկուած են հայերը: Հսկողութիւնը վերջին ծայր խստացած է. թռչունն չի կրնար թռչիլ:

Այս նամակէն յետոյ հասնող փախստականները աւելի գէշ կը ներկայացնեն կացութիւնը: Ձերբակալուած են աչքի զարնող անհատներ եւ կը փնտռուին ուրիշներ:

Ուրֆայի հայոց թիւն է 7000, որոնք առհասարակ կը գտնուին դժնդակ կացութեան մէջ եւ իրենց օգնելու միջոցներ կը պակսին:

most of them have sheltered here from nearby cities. Money used to arrive from abroad, but now it has stopped, and it is difficult to obtain money locally; therefore, we will not be able to help Urfa.

According to reports received from Maraş on May 18, there are currently nine thousand Armenians in Maraş. The poor are being cared for by the American Near East Relief. The Turks are raising obstacles against the Relief. Armenians always go to the market accompanied by Turks. Thanks to the Milli movement's conversion into the regular military, the Armenians have been able to live so far; otherwise, they would have perished entirely. More than seventy men gradually disappeared at the hands of the Turks after the events in Maraş. The church buildings are partially renovated. The closed schools reopened, provided that teaching Armenian and foreign languages is banned. Turkish will be spoken and read both in the church and schools. The orphanages are in the hands of the Americans. More than three thousand male and female orphans are sheltered.

Twenty- to forty-year-old Armenians are enlisted and work for the army. Poverty has reached extreme levels in Maraş as well.

• Süleymanlı [Zeytun] was in communication with Maraş until three months ago. Contacts were cut when [the Turks] demanded their weapons. Still the people of Süleymanlı travel a distance of ten hours to provide themselves with supplies; regardless, the future is uncertain.

Bursa (from the vicar general)—July 1

These days, many migrants from Bahçecik, İzmit, and Adapazarı and its villages have come to Gemlik.

• Bighados Tekmezian, a forty- to forty-five-year-old coachman from Yenice, and Niko, a Greek coachman, frequent travelers from Bursa to Mustafakemalpaşa [Kirmasti], were robbed by the çetes the previous day. They then killed Niko by beheading him and wounded Bighados in the throat. Bighados, too, died after living twelve hours. The Greek government is pursuing the perpetrators.

Yalova (from Hovhannes Der Garabedian, headman of Kılıç village; Vagharshag Haroutyunian; and headman of Şağlak, Haroutyun Vanlian)—July 1

Today, the Greek commander announced that all Christians must leave Yalova in four days. The people, already financially exhausted, are stunned by this surprising development. They are thinking about where to go and how to live. They hesitate to come to İstanbul for fear of being arrested. So they plan to go to Tekirdağ, where they can at least farm and make a living.

There are five hundred Armenians in Yalova. One steamer will be enough to transport them to Tekirdağ.

Yalova (from Hovhannes Der Garabedian)—July 2

All the people are weeping. The sufferings of exile and the apparent danger have demoralized them. They are waiting for help.

Samsun (a telegram from Armenag Bardizmanian)—July 1

Priest Hovhannes is here with four hundred migrants from Adapazarı, Almalı, Akmeşe, Arslanbey, and EskiMecidiye [Khaskal]. The local government is doing its best to take care of them.

Հալէպի մէջ համախմբուած են 10000ի մօտ զանազան տարիքի երկսեռ հայ վերապրողներ, մեծ մասամբ շրջակայ քաղաքներէ տեղս ապաստանած: Ցարդ արտասահմանէն դրամ կը հասնէր, այժմ դադրած է, իսկ տեղւոյն վրայ դրամ ճարել դժուար է. հետեւաբար Ուրֆայի համար օգնութիւն չպիտի կարենանք ընել:

Մարաշէն ալ Մայիս 18ին առնուած լուրերու համաձայն, Մարաշի մէջ կան ցարդ 9000ի չափ հայեր, որոնցմէ աղքատները կը հոգացուին Ամերիկեան Նպաստամատոյցին կողմէ: Ռըլիֆի դէմ թուրքերը դժուարութիւն կը հանեն: Հայերը շուկայ կ'իջնեն միշտ թուրքերու ընկերակցութեամբ: Ազգայնական շարժման կանոնաւոր զինուորական ձեւ ստանալուն շնորհիւ հայերը կրցած են ապրիլ ցարդ. այլապէս բոլորովին պիտի ոչնչանային: Մարաշի դէպքերէն յետոյ հետզհետէ աւելի քան 70 այրեր անհետացած են թուրքերու կողմէ: Եկեղեցապատկան շէնքերը մասամբ վերանորոգուած են. դպրոցները փակուած եւ վերաբացուած են հայերէնի եւ օտար լեզուներու դասաւանդութիւնը արգիլուելու պայմանով: Պիտի խօսուի եւ կարդացուի թուրքերէն թէ՛ եկեղեցւոյ եւ թէ՛ դպրոցներու մէջ: Որբանոցները ամերիկացիներու ձեռքին տակ են. կը պատսպարուին 3000է աւելի որբեր եւ որբուհիներ:

Հայերը 20-էն 40 տարեկան զինուորագրուած են եւ իբրեւ գործաւոր կ'աշխատին բանակին համար: Մարաշի մէջ եւս աղքատութիւնը ծայրայեղ աստիճանի հասած է:

- Զէյթուն մինչեւ 3 ամիս առաջ յարաբերութեան մէջ է եղեր Մարաշի հետ: Երբ իրենց զէնքերը կ'ուզուին, յարաբերութիւնները կը խզուին, սակայն զէյթունցիք մինչեւ 10 ժամ հեռաւորութեան վրայ կ'երթեւեկեն եւ իրենց պաշար կը հայթայթեն. ապագան սակայն անորոշ է:

Պրուսա (Առաջնորդական Փոխանորդէն) – 1 Յուլիս

Այս օրերս բաւական թուով պարտիզակցի, իզմիթցի եւ ատաբազարցի ու գիւղերէ գաղթականներ Կէմլէյիկ եկած են:

- Պրուսայէն Քերմասթը գործով յաճախ երթեւեկող էէնիճէցի 40–45 տարեկան կառապան Պիղատոս Թէքմէզեան եւ յոյն կառապան Նիքօ անցեալ օր չէթէները կը կողոպտեն, յետոյ Նիքոյի գլուխը կտրելով կը սպաննեն եւ Պիղատոսը կոկորդէն կը վիրաւորեն: Պիղատոս եւս 12 ժամ միայն ապրելէ յետոյ մեռաւ: Հելլէն կառավարութիւնը ոճրագործները կը հետապնդէ:

Եալովա (Յովհաննէս Տէր Կարապետեան, Գըլըճ գիւղի մխթար՝ Վաղարշակ Յարութիւնեան, Շաղլախու մխթար՝ Յարութիւն Վանլըեան) – 1 Յուլիս

Այսօր հելլէն հրամանատարը ծանոյց որ չորս օրէն բոլոր քրիստոնեաները Եալովայէն պէտք է հեռանան: Ժողովուրդը արդէն նիւթապէս բոլորովին հիւծած, այս անակնկալէն շուարած՝ կը խորհի թէ ո՞ւր պիտի երթայ եւ ի՞նչպէս պիտի ապրի: Պոլիս գալու կը վարանին՝ վախնալով որ պիտի ձերբակալուին: Ուստի կը մտածեն Ռօտոսթօ երթալ, ուր գոնէ երկրագործութեամբ կրնան զբաղիլ եւ օրապահիկ հանել:

Եալովայի հայ բնակիչները 500 հոգի են եւ շոգենաւ մը բաւական է զանոնք Ռօտոսթօ փոխադրելու համար:

Եալովա (Յովհաննէս Տէր Կարապետեանէ) – 2 Յուլիս

Բոլոր ժողովուրդը լացուկոծի մէջ է. տարագրութեան տառապանքները, ակներեւ վտանգը ամէնքն ալ բարոյալքած [են]: Օգնութեան կը սպասեն:

Սամսոն (հեռագիր Արմենակ Պարտիզմանեանէ [*sic*]) – 1 Յուլիս

Տ. Յովհաննէս Քահանան կը գտնուի հոս 400 գաղթականներու հետ, որոնք Ատաբազարէն, Ալմալուէն, Արմաշէն, Ասլանպէյէն, Հասկալէն են: Տեղական կառավարութիւնը կարելին կ'ընէ անոնց հոգատարութեան համար:

İzmir (from the primate)—July 5

Refugees from Afyonkarahisar in İzmir reported that the Kemalists recently extorted six hundred liras each from young Armenians in Konya and Afyonkarahisar in exchange for [exemption from] military service and that all forty- to fifty-year-old males were later deported in unknown directions. On June 2, the Armenians and Greeks (men only) of all the cities of Anadolu [Anatolia] were deported by the arrangement and guidance of the upper Kemalist authorities, which means that the women, girls, and children are being left with the Turks.

Travelers arriving gradually confirm this information and describe the state of Christians living in the interior in gloomy colors.

Adana (from the primate)—June 18

A man named Khachig—son of Garabed, a native of Urfa settled in Konya—who managed to escape to Adana by pretending to be a Turk, relates that all Christian Armenian and Greek males living in Konya were recently deported by the Kemalist government as exiles toward Bitlis and Erzurum and that having already been completely robbed of their possessions on the way, they were subjected to pangs of death.

The person who narrates this incident managed to escape when he was six hours away from Sivas, thus defying his death, but the heartbreaking explanations he gives about the dreadful situation of the exiles indicate that the places of exile will be the graves of Armenian survivors [from their earlier deportation].

Gaziantep [Ayntab] (from the National Union)—June 9[111]

On February 7, 1921, after a long period of self-defense [by Armenians], when the city finally surrendered to the French, the Armenians thought that their unspeakable torments, which they had witnessed under the Turkish yoke, had ended.

The Armenians of Gaziantep thought that given their invaluable service to the French army during the 1920–21 war, which many French have recognized orally and in writing, had [gained] them the right to enjoy the high control of the noble French nation within its city administration and that, therefore, the sad memories of the past would disappear forever. And yet, on March 12, the Franco-Kemal Accord evaporated our rights and expectations, both so natural. The Milli atrocities—to which people were subjected, especially at the end of last year—began to rise like a hurricane before them. Moral despair set in and the people hurriedly began to migrate to other places. The animation in the city and efforts of vitality stopped immediately. The people have been idle for three months, waiting eagerly for the situation to become clear. True, there are signs that the previous policy is about to change, but the security of the vicinities and even the nearby villages and the economic situation caused by the siege of the Aleppo-Gaziantep road over the last month have brought forth an extreme economic crisis.

The people have barely been able to work for six months, after their return from migration, and today they are on the verge of spending the last dime of their savings. The National Union has barely a month and a half of food to help the poor, who number more than two thousand, to which more than two hundred are being added weekly. Those who used to help others are now forced to beg for help from others. This reality tremendously discourages Armenians.

At the end of a victorious war, economic misery will overcome these brave people, who have been able to maintain their national dignity high and make it shine in the eyes of strangers.

Of course, the people who showed so much military and administrative ability cannot be allowed

Զմիւռնիա (Առաջնորդէն) – 5 Յուլիս

Իզմիր գտնուող աֆիոն-գարահիսարցի գաղթականները կը հաղորդեն թէ վերջերս Գոնիայի եւ Աֆիոն Գարահիսարի մէջ քէմալականները հայ երիտասարդներէն գանձած են 600ական ոսկի իբր փրկանք զինուորական ծառայութեան փոխարէն, եւ յետոյ 40–50 տարեկան բոլոր էրիկ մարդիկը անծանօթ ուղղութեամբ աքսորած են: Իսկ Յունիս 2ին քէմալական վերին մարմիններու կարգադրութեամբ եւ ղեկավարութեամբ Անատոլուի բոլոր քաղաքներու հայերը եւ յոյները (միայն տղամարդիկը) տեղահան ըրած են, որով կը հետեւցուի թէ կիները, աղջիկները եւ մանուկները մնացած են թուրքերուն մօտ:

Հետզհետէ եկող ճամբորդները կը հաստատեն այս տեղեկութիւնները եւ տխուր գոյներով կը նկարագրեն քրիստոնէից վիճակը ներքին գաւառներու մէջ:

Ատանա (Առաջնորդական Տեղապահէն) – 18 Յունիս

Գոնիա հաստատուած բնիկ ուրֆացի Կարապետի որդի Խաչիկ անուն անձ մը, որ ինքզինքն թուրք ձեւացնելով կրցած է խոյս տալ եւ մեծ դժուարութիւններով հասնիլ Ատանա, կը պատմէ թէ Գոնիա բնակող հայ եւ յոյն բոլոր քրիստոնեայ այր մարդիկը քէմալական կառավարութեան կողմէ անխտիր վերջերս ճամբայ հանուած են որպէս աքսորական, ղրկուելու համար Պիթլիսի եւ Էրզրու-մի կողմերը եւ որոնք ճամբան՝ արդէն բոլորովին կողոպտուած իրենց ունեցածէն, ենթարկուած են մահուան գալարումներու:

Այս դէպքը պատմող անձը ինքը մինչեւ վեց ժամ Սեբաստիա մօտենալէն յետոյ, մահը աչք առնելով յաջողած է փախուստի ճամբան բռնել եւ սակայն աքսորականներու ենթարկուած դժնդակ կացութեան մասին տուած սրտակեղեք բացատրութիւններէն կը հասկցուի թէ աքսորավայր որոշուած տեղերը այդ վերապրող հայոց գերեզմանը պիտի ըլլա[ն]:

Այնթապ (Ազգային Միութենէն) – 9 Յունիս

1921 Փետրուար 7ին հայոց երկարատեւ ինքնապաշտպանութենէն յետոյ երբ քաղաքը վերջնականապէս անձնատուր եղաւ ֆրանսացւոց, հայերը կարծեցին թէ վերջ գտած է[ին] իրենց անլուր չարչարանքները, որոնց ականատես եղած էին թուրք լուծի տակ:

Այնթապի հայ[ութիւն]ը կը կարծէ[ր] որ 1920–21ի կռիւներուն ֆրանսական բանակին մատու-ցած իր անգնահատելի ծառայութեամբը, զոր քանիցս ֆրանսացիք եւս խոստովանեցան բերանացի եւ գրաւոր, այլեւս իրաւունք ունէր վայելելու ֆրանսական ազնիւ ազգին վերին հսկողութիւնը իր քաղքին վարչութեանը մէջ, որով մի անգամ ընդ միշտ պիտի անհետանային անցեալի տխուր յուշերը: Եւ սակայն Մարտ 12ին ֆրանքօ-քէմալական համաձայնութիւնը յօդս ցնդեց մեր այնքան բնական իրաւունքները եւ ակնկալութիւնները ու ուրականի մը պէս սկսան ցցուիլ ժողովրդեան առջեւ միլլիական խժդժութիւնները, որոնց ենթակայ պիտի ըլլար նամանաւանդ վերջին տարուան անցուդարձերէն վերջ: Բարոյական յուսալքում մը սկսաւ ու ժողովուրդը սկսաւ հայրենքով գաղթել ուրիշ վայրեր: Քաղաքին մէջ սկսած եռուզեռը ու կենդանութեան ճիգերը վայրկենապէս դադրեցան եւ այսօր երեք ամիսէ ի վեր ժողովուրդը անգործ կը սպասէ կացութեան պարզուելուն սրտատրոփ: Իրաւ է թէ նշաններ կան որ նախկին քաղաքականութիւնը փոխուելու վրայ է եւ սակայն շրջականերու եւ նոյնիսկ մօտակայ գիւղերու ապահովութիւնը ու վերջին ամսուան միջոցին Հալէպ-Այնթապ ճամբուն գոցուելովը առաջ եկած պաշարման վիճակը տնտեսական վերջին ծայր տագնապ մը առաջ բերին:

Գաղթականութենէն դարձէն ի վեր ժողովուրդը հազիւ կրցաւ վեց ամիս աշխատիլ ու այսօր այլեւս իր խնայողութեան վերջին լուման է որ ծախսելու վրայ է: Ազգային Միութիւնը հազիւ մէկուկէս ամսուան պարէն ունի օժանդակելու աղքատներուն, որոնց թիւը երկու հազարէն աւելի է ու ամէն շաբաթ երկու հարիւր հոգիէն աւելի կը բարդուի վրան: Անոնք որ նախապէս ուրիշներուն կ՚օգնէին, այսօր ստիպուած են իրենք օգնութիւն մուրալու ուրիշներէ ու այս պատկերը շատ կը

to come to nothing and perish. The people are in the most harsh financial situation. Even if the normal situation is suddenly restored, these people will need much financial support.

Beylerbeyi (from the principal of the Workshop-School)—July 14

These days, we are witnessing a series of ominous events in our neck of the wood.

An hour after midnight on July 7, a colossal shooting guided by the sound of a trumpet started from the Turkish street of Beylerbeyi. The principal jumped out of bed and went down to the yard. This almost ten-minute-long intense gunfire gradually ceased. The following morning, Beylerbeyi's police commissioner hurriedly crossed to Kuzguncuk several times. The principal, who is familiar with the commissioner, asked about the reason for his busy schedule. He recounted that robbers arrived in Beylerbeyi at night to steal sheep and that the landlord fired at them, and the people, thinking there was "something else," fired guns, and a scoundrel sounded the trumpet.

All these movements are not obscure. There is regular conscription here, and for that purpose, right across from the police school, a training station was opened where the [Milli] organization is very active in preparing for D-Day. Suspicious people in Laz uniforms walk around all day long. Turkish cavalrymen, often armed with Russian rifles, make mysterious movements every three minutes toward Kuzguncuk. This goes on for hours. Today, at three o'clock, three or four people stopped in front of the Workshop-Orphanage and said: "Behold . . . this is a good place for fishing," and so on. The [Milli] organization already has this place under its control. They know full well that there is a weapons warehouse here. There is a blatant provocation against this Armenian institution, and they do not even sell goods to it.

Bursa (from the locum tenens)—July 20[112]

One of the refugees coming to Bursa, Kocho Papa Tanashoghlu, a villager from Yalova's Kadıköy, testified that the farm in Yalova belonging to [the Armenian Patriarchate of] Jerusalem was set on fire by the Millis. All the Armenian villages in the Yalova region were also set on fire.

Tekirdağ (from the primate of İzmit)—July 19[113]

The escapees from İzmit are housed in five different buildings in Tekirdağ.

Thus:

1. 322 households—1,272 people—are sheltered in the St. Takvor church
2. 231 households—964 people—are sheltered in the Holy Cross church
3. 261 households—780 people—are sheltered in the coastal barracks
4. 117 households—384 people—are sheltered in the upper barracks
5. 13 households—34 people—are sheltered in the Jewish school

Total: 944 [households and] 3434 [people]:

Their situation is very bitter, and they are in great need of help.

փատեցնէ հայերը:

Ցաղթական կռիւէ մը վերջ տնտեսական թշուառութիւնը պիտի յաղթահարէ այս կտրիճ ժողովուրդը, որ կրցաւ այնքան բարձր պահել ազգային արժանապատուութիւնը ու զայն փայլեցնել յաչս օտարին:

Անշուշտ պիտի թոյլ չտրուի որ թէ՛ զինուորական եւ թէ՛ վարչական այսքան կարողութիւն ցուցնող ժողովուրդը փճանայ եւ կորսուի: Նիւթական ամենադառն կացութեան մատնուած է ժողովուրդը եւ եթէ յանկարծ բնականոն վիճակն ալ հաստատուի, այս ժողովուրդը կը կարօտի նիւթական մեծ աջակցութեան:

Պէյլէրպէյ (Արհեստանոց-Կրթարանի տնօրէնէն) – 14 Յուլիս

Այս օրերս մեր կողմերը տեղի ունեցա[ծ] կարգ մը չարագուշակ իրադարձութիւններու ականատես կ’ըլլանք:

Յուլիս 7ին, կէս գիշերը մէկ ժամ անցած, յանկարծ ահռելի հրացանաձգութիւն մը սկսաւ Պէյլէրպէյի թուրք փողոցին կողմէն, որ կը ղեկավարուէր շեփորի ձայնով: Տնօրէնը անկողնէն կը ցատկէ եւ բակը կ’իջնայ: Մօտաւորապէս 10 րոպէ տեւող այս բուռն հրացանաձգութիւնը հետզհետէ կը դադրի: Հետեւեալ առտուն Պէյլէրպէյի ոստիկանական քօմիսէրը քանիցս հեւ ի հեւ անցաւ Գուզկունճուգ: Տնօրէնը, որ ծանօթ է քօմիսէրին, կը հարցնէ իր զբաղեալ վիճակին պատճառը: Ցիշեալը կը պատմէ թէ ինչպէս գիշերը ոչխար գողնալու համար աւազակներ եկած էին Պէյլէրպէյ եւ թէ տանտէրը անոնց վրայ կրակ ըրած էր եւ թէ ժողովուրդն ալ «ուրիշ բան» կարծելով զէնք պարպած էր եւ թէ «հէրկէլէին» մէկն ալ *պօռազան* զարկած էր:

Այս բոլոր շարժումները անծանօթ չեն: Հոս կանոնաւոր զինուորագրութիւն կ’ըլլայ եւ այդ նպատակով *ժանտարմայ մէքթէպի*ին ճիշդ դիմացը *խուման եուրտու* մը բացուեցաւ, ուր «Թէշքիլաթը» մեծ գործունէութիւն ցոյց կուտայ որոշեալ օրուան պատրաստ ըլլալու համար: Լազի տարազներով կասկածելի մարդիկ օրն ի բուն կը շրջին: Թուրք հեծելազօրքեր, շատ անգամ ռուսական հրացանով զինուած, խորհրդաւոր շարժումներով իւրաքանչիւր երեք վայրկեանը հատ մը կ’անցնի ժամերով դէպի Գուզկունճուգ: Այսօր ժամը 3ին 3–4 հոգի Արհեստանոց-Որբանոցին դրան առջեւ կանգ առին եւ «իշթէ պուրասը ... էյի պալըք թուլթուլուր»[19] եւայլն ըսին: *Թէշքիլաթ*ը արդէն տեղս տիրապետած է եւ լաւ գիտէ թէ հոս կը գտնուի զէնքի մթերանոց: Ցայտնի գրգռութիւն կայ հայկական այս հաստատութեան դէմ եւ նոյնիսկ ապրանք չեն ծախեր անոր:

Պրուսա (Առաջնորդական Տեղապահէն) – 20 Յուլիս

Պրուսա եկող գաղթականներէն Եալովայի գատը-գիւղացի Գոչօ Բաբա Թանաշօղլու անձը կը վկայէ թէ Եալովայի երուսաղէմապատկան ագարակը միլլիճիներու կողմէ հրկիզուած է: Նոյնպէս կրակի տրուած են Եալովայի շրջանը գտնուող ամբողջ հայ գիւղերը:

Ռօտոսթօ (Նիկոմիդիոյ Առաջնորդէն) – 19 Յուլիս

Նիկոմի[դի]ոյ փախստականները Ռօտոսթօյի մէջ հիւրընկալուած են հինգ տարբեր շէնքերու մէջ:

Այսպէս՝

1. Ս. Թագւոր եկեղեցին պատսպարուած են	322 տնուոր	1272 անձ
2. Ս. Խաչ եկեղեցին պատսպարուած են	231 տնուոր	964 անձ
3. Ծովեզերեայ զօրանոց պատսպարուած են	261 տնուոր	780 անձ
4. Վերի զօրանոց պատսպարուած են	117 տնուոր	384 անձ
5. Հրէից վարժարան պատսպարուած են	13 տնուոր	34 անձ
Գումար	944	3434

Ասոնց վիճակը շատ դառն է եւ օգնութեան մեծապէս կարօտ:

[Insecurity Notebook Number 16]
July–September 1921

Adana (from catholicosal vicar Bishop Yeghishé)—July 12

We learned from the trusted information that reached Adana two days ago that of the people of Süleymanlı [Zeytun], those who are healthy and able to carry arms, facing the risk of starvation to death, chose to exit the city on June 24, leaving behind only 270 people—elderly, feeble, and children. After sporadic clashes, they reached Andırın to come thence to Osmaniye. However, about one hundred kilometers to this side of Andırın and away from Osmaniye, they were surrounded by troops that outnumbered them. They remained in a defensive position, unable to advance farther. Although the French authorities in Adana were asked to facilitate their entry into Cilicia, no action has been taken yet. The people of Süleymanlı remain abandoned to their fate. We hear that the 270 vulnerable people left in Süleymanlı have been transported to Maraş by the Turks.

There are no other details yet.

Adana (from Catholicos Sahag)—July 14[114]

Subsequent letters received from Osmaniye shed light on the recent calamity in Süleymanlı [Zeytun].

On July 8, Demircizade Abdullah, a resident of Kesmeburun, arrived in Osmaniye and recounted what he had heard from credible people. At the beginning of July, sixty families from the village Cevdetiye [Araplı] went to summer houses in Göksun [Kokison]. Near Gökkale, between Geben and Andırın, they were caught in a fight with two hundred bandit-like men. Several villagers were killed and robbed. The government of Andırın was notified, and two battalions were sent to the scene from the borders of Kozan [Sis].

The soldiers pulled the folks of Cevdetiye aside and started a regular war. The so-assumed bandits immediately separated into four groups: one in Gökkale, the second in a large cave, and the third and fourth in different positions. Then they continued the battle. The reporter thinks that the bandits are from Süleymanlı, there are also women, and seemingly everyone is not armed. The [so-assumed bandits] tried several times to reach Osmaniye but failed.

On July 10, it was written from Osmaniye: "Yesterday, Köse Osman Effendi, a native of Osmaniye, arrived. He had fled to Maraş during the çetes' war and had been there until [his arrival here]. He related [the following]. Three times soldiers were sent to Maraş from Süleymanlı to disarm them. Finally, the people of Süleymanlı asked for ten days to urge people to hand over their weapons. On the third day, June 24–[2]5, it was heard that 400 armed men had retreated to the mountains. When the soldiers became aware of this reality, they went down to the city and took the 270 people they found there—the elderly, women, minors, and the sick—to Maraş. Allegedly they handed them over to the Americans. From Maraş, Hovsep Khurlakian and three other people were sent to Kayseri. This story is corroborated by another Turk who arrived recently.

July 11. Tonight, fifteen-year-old Kevork Anabadian from Süleymanlı arrived in Osmaniye. He related: We have been under siege for two years. Neither have the Turks crossed to our side, nor did we cross to their side. Those crossing the borders on either side were killed. We waited a long time for help, but nobody reached out.

Finally, twenty-five days ago (probably on June 15), two thousand Turkish soldiers attacked us with artillery and machine guns. After five days of fierce fighting, we were forced to retreat to the mountain; the elderly, children, women, and the sick remained there [in Süleymanlı]. When we climbed up the mountain, we saw that we were surrounded by enemies, and we started fighting and

[Անապահովութեան Տետր Թիւ 16]
1921 Յուլիս – Սեպտեմբեր

Ատանա (Կաթողիկոսական Փոխանորդ Եղիշէ Եպիսկոպոսէն) – 12 Յուլիս

Երկու օր առաջ Ատանա հասած ստոյգ տեղեկութիւններէն կ'իմանանք թէ Զէյթունցիներէն քաջառողջ եւ զէնք բռնելու կարող անձեր սովամահ ըլլալու վտանգի առջեւ Յունիս 24ին,- ծեր, անկար եւ մանուկներ, ընդամէնը 270 հոգի, Զէյթունի մէջ ձգելով,- նախընտրած են դուրս ելնել քաղաքէն եւ տեղ տեղ ընդհարումներ ունենալէ յետոյ հասած են մինչեւ Անտրընի մօտերը, անկից գալու համար Օսմանիյէ: Սակայն Անտրընէն աւդին եւ Օսմանիէէն մօտաւորապէս հարիւր (100) քիլոմէթր հեռու տեղ մը, զինուորական թիւով գերազանց ոյժերէ պաշարուած ըլլալով, չեն կրցած աւելի յառաջանալ եւ մնացած են պաշտպանողական դիրքի վրայ: Թէեւ անոնց Կիլիկիա մուտքը դիւրացնելու համար Ատանայի ֆրանսական իշխանութեանց մօտ դիմում կատարուած է, սակայն դեռ ձեռնարկ մը չէ եղած եւ զէյթունցիք լքուած կը մնան իրենց բաղդին: Զէյթունի մէջ մնացող 270 անկարները կը լսենք թէ թուրքերու կողմէ փոխադրուած են Մարաշ:

Առ այժմ ուրիշ մանրամասնութիւնք չկան:

Ատանա (Սահակ Կաթողիկոսէն) – 14 Յուլիս

Օսմանիյէէն առնուած յաջորդական նամակները կը լուսաբանեն Զէյթունի վերջին եղեռնը:

Յուլիս 8ին Օսմանիյէ կը հասնի քէսմէ-պուրունցի Տէմիրճի Զատէ Ապտուլլահ եւ արժանահաւատ անձերէ լաւծները կը պատմէ: Յուլիսի սկիզբը Արապլու 60 տնուոր գիւղացիք ամարանոց կ'ելլեն Կոկիսոնի կողմը: Կապանի եւ Անտրինի միջեւ Կէօք-Գալէի մօտերը 200ի չափ հրոսակի նման մարդոց հետ կռուի կը բռնուին: Մի քանի գիւղացիներ կը սպաննուին եւ կը կողոպտուին: Անտրինի կառավարութեան տեղեկութիւն կուտան եւ Գոզանի սահմաններէն երկու թապուր զինուոր կը ղրկուի դէպքին վայրը:

Զինուորները արապլուիցիք մէկ կողմ առնելով՝ կանոնաւոր պատերազմի կը սկսին: Հրոսակ կարծուածները անմիջապէս չորս խումբի կը բաժնուին՝ մին Կէօք Գալէի մէջ, երկրորդը՝ մօտաւոր մեծ այրի մը մէջ, երրորդ եւ չորրորդը տարբեր դիրքերէ պատերազմը կը շարունակեն: Լրաբերը կը կարծէ թէ հրոսակները զէյթունցիներ են, կիներ ալ կան, ու որպէս թէ ամէնքն զէնք չունին: Քանիցս փորձած են դէպի Օսմանիյէ քաշուիլ բայց չեն յաջողած:

Յուլիս 10ին կը գրեն Օսմանիյէէն.- Երէկ տեղս ժամանեց բնիկ օսմանիյէցի Ք[է]օսէ Օսման էֆէնտի, որ չէթէական կռուին Մարաշ փախած էր եւ մինչեւ հիմա հոն կը գտնուէր ու կը պատմէ: Զէյթունի վրայ Մարաշէն երեք անգամ զինուոր ղրկուեցաւ զինաթափ ընելու: Վերջապէս զէյթունցիք տասն օր պայմանաժամ կը խնդրեն, որ իրենց մարդիկը յորդորեն զէնքերը յանձնելու: Երրորդ օրը, Յունիս 24–[2]5, լսուեցաւ որ 400 հոգի զինուած լեռ քաշուած են: Զինուորները երբ կը լսեն եղելութիւնը, քաղաք կ'իջնեն եւ այն տեղ գտնուած 270 հոգի՝ ծեր, կին, անչափահասներ եւ հիւանդներ, Մարաշ կը տանին եւ իբր թէ ամերիկացւոց կը յանձնեն: Մարաշէն Յովսէփ Խ[ը]րլագեան, ուրիշ երեք անձերու հետ դէպի Կեսարիա ճամբայ կը հանուի: Այս պատմութիւնը կը հաստատէ ուրիշ նորեկ թուրք մը:

Յուլիս 11.- Այս գիշեր Օսմանիյէ կը ժամանէ զէյթունցի 15ամեայ Գէորգ Անապատեան: Կը պատմէ.- Երկու տարիներէ ի վեր պաշարուած վիճակ մը ունէինք: Ո՛չ թուրքերը մեր կողմը եւ ո՛չ մենք անոնց կողմը կ'անցնէինք: Երկու կողմէն սահմանազանցները կը սպաննուէին: Շատ սպասեցինք օգնութեան, բայց ոչ մէկ կողմէն ձեռք մը չերկարեցաւ:

Վերջապէս, 25 օր առաջ (Յունիս 15 թերեւս) երկու հազար (2000) թուրք զինուոր եկան մեր վրայ հրետանիներով եւ գնդացիրներով: Հինգ օր սաստիկ պատերազմելէն ետքը ստիպուեցանք լեռը քաշուիլ, ծեր, երեխայ, կիներ եւ հիւանդներ հոն մնացին: Երբ լեռը ելանք, տեսանք որ թշնամիներէ պաշարուած ենք, սկսանք օրերով թէ՛ կռուիլ, թէ՛ քալել: Խմբապետները մեզի երեք խումբի

walking for days. The group leaders divided us into three groups, and we went in different directions. This division happened [in a place] between Geben and Andırın. Our group walked toward the Ceyhan River; I do not know where the other groups were headed. Aram Chavush led the other two groups. We were besieged while crossing the Ceyhan River. After a fierce four-hour battle, our group leader, Sergeant Manoug, ran out of ammunition and, unwilling to fall into Turkish hands, jumped into the water. Some followed his example, as I did. I managed to swim across the river and hide in the bushes because it was daytime. Some of us escaped, while others were captured by the Turks and taken captive. The other two groups are fighting in the mountains. The roads are closed everywhere; enemies abound in the mountains, canyons, and under every bush. All villages have been told that the roads are closed. It is as if the Turks are hunting lions. The unfortunate people of Süleymanlı did not intend to fight. They intended to withdraw to the French zone while defending themselves to be saved. Mr. Florent, the French governor of Osmaniye, made the teenager speak in his presence and listened to this story in detail.

July 12. Two of Kevork's friends, Toros Merchinian and Hayg Juddurian, arrived. It has been heard that six other people have arrived in Mamure. The other groups allegedly are sheltered in the Namud fortress, not too far from Toprakkale, and are under heavy siege.

From the day this information was received, oral and written pleas were made to [the French authorities] to send a plane to encourage the unfortunate people. The answer to these pleas was that it is strictly forbidden to cross certain borders, and the dispatch of troops is against the [Franco-Turkish] agreement. It has been requested that the guards receive readily any survivors from fire and water when they approach the border and be kind about clothing, feeding, and accommodating them. The proper order has been given; it has been said.

• The city of Süleymanlı had ten to twelve thousand inhabitants before the war. After the deportation, barely fifteen hundred people were gathered from Süleymanlı, Fırnız, and Çamlıbel [Alabaş]. Behold, these fragments are being persecuted severely to their detriment.

Adana (from the Armenian National Council of Cilicia)—July 16, 1921

When the people of Süleymanlı [Zeytun] tried to hand over their weapons and evacuate the barracks—the only place of residence for their families—the Kemalists, this time, brought in regular troops to attack the city using a cannon. After days of fierce fighting, all 500–600 armed and able-bodied men rushed out, breaking the siege, leaving 270 minors, elderly, and feeble people in the barracks. Those left behind were allegedly transported later to Maraş by the Kemalist authority.

As for those who escaped [the siege], they intended to reach the French occupation zone by all means. After four days of walking, they reached Andırın by night, only to be suddenly besieged by local çetes and regular soldiers and pressed to divide into three groups after a desperate battle. The first of them, made up of thirty people, without knowing the whereabouts of the other two, reached the banks of the Ceyhan River, where the group was caught in a fight. Only three people escaped and reached Osmaniye. The rest were massacred or drowned by jumping into the river. According to the latest news, one of the two large groups crossed the Ceyhan River and arrived near Ekbez. They can be considered partially saved by approaching the French occupation zone. The other allegedly is still beyond the Ceyhan River. It does not inspire hope since the group is extremely exhausted and surrounded by çetes from four sides.

բաժնեցին եւ մէկ մէկ կողմէ սկսանք քալել: Այս բաժանումը Կապանի եւ Անտրինի մէջտեղը եղած է: Մեր խումբը քալեց դէպի Ճիհան գետը, միւս խումբերը չգիտեմ ո՛ր կողմ քալեցին: Անոնց խմբապետն էր Արամ Չաւուշը: Մենք Ճիհան գետը անցնելու պահուն պաշարուեցանք, չորս ժամ կատաղի կռուէ մը ետքը մեր խմբապետը՝ Մանուկ Չաւուշ, փամփուշտները սպառած ըլլալուն եւ չուզելով թուրքաց ձեռքը ի[յ]նալ, ջուրը նետուեցաւ: Ոմանք անոր օրինակին հետեւեցան, ինչպէս եւ ես, եւ յաջողեցայ լողալով գետն անցնիլ, եւ որովհետեւ ցերեկ էր, մացառներու մէջ պահուըտեցայ: Մեզմէ մնացեալներէն ոմանք փախան եւ ոմանք բռնուեցան թուրքերէն եւ կապանօք տարուեցան: Միւս երկու խումբերը կը կռուին լեռներուն մէջ: Ամէն կողմ ճամբաները փակուած են, լեռ ու ձոր, եւ ամէն մացառի տակ թշնամիները լեցուն [են] եւ ամէն գիւղ լուր տրուած է որ ճամբաները փակած են: Կարծես առիւծներ կ'որսան: Ապաբաղդ զէյթունցիները նպատակ ունեցած չեն կռուելու, այլ ինքնապաշտպանութեամբ ֆրանսական գօտին քաշուիլ եւ ազատիլ: Օսմանիյէի ֆրանսական կառավարիչ պարոն Ֆլորան իր ներկայութեան տղուն խօսեցնել տուած է եւ այս պատմութիւնը մանրամասնօրէն լսած:

Յուլիս 12.- Գէորգի ընկերներէն երկու հոգի կը հասնին՝ Թորոս Մերչինեան եւ Հայկ Ճըտտրեան: Կը լսուի որ վեց հոգի ալ Մամուրէ հասած են: Միւս խումբերը իբրեւ թէ Թօփրագ-Գալէէն քիչ հեռու, Նամուտ բերդին մէջ ապաստանած եւ սաստիկ պաշարման տակ են:

Այս տեղեկութիւնները հասած օրէն, թէ՛ բերանացի եւ թէ՛ գրաւոր դիմումներ եղան, որպէսզի սաւառնակ մը ղրկուի ի քաջալերութիւն անբաղդներուն: Պատասխանուեցաւ թէ խստիւ արգիլուած է որոշեալ սահմաններէն անցնիլ, իսկ զօրքի առաքումը համաձայնութեան դէմ է: Խնդրուեցաւ, եթէ կրակէ ու ջուրէ ազատուողները սահմանին մօտենան, պահակները առանց դժուարութեանց ընդունին եւ զգեստի, ուտեստի եւ տեղաւորման մասին բարեհաճ գտնուին: Հարկ եղած հրամանը տրուած է, կ'ըսուի:

- Զէյթուն քաղաքը պատերազմէն առաջ 10–12 հազար բնակիչ ունէր. տարագրութենէ դարձին հազիւ 1500 հոգի համախմբուեցան Զէյթունէն, Ֆռնուզէն ու Ալապաշէն: Ահա այս բեկորներն են որ սաստկապէս կը հետապնդուին բնաջնջելու համար:

Ատանա (Կիլիկեան Հայ Ազգային Խորհուրդէն) – 16 Յուլիս 1921

Երբ զէյթունցիք կը փորձեն իրենց զէնքերը յանձնել եւ զօրանոցը՝ միակ բնակավայրը իրենց ընտանիքներուն՝ պարպել, քէմալականք այս անգամ կանոնաւոր զօրք կը բերեն թնդանօթով միասին յարձակելու համար քաղաքին վրայ: Այսպէս օրեր տեւող կատաղի կռիւէ մը յետոյ, բոլոր զէնք բռնողները եւ քալելու կարողութիւն ունեցողները, թուով 5–600 հոգի, պաշարման գիծը ճեղքելով դուրս կը խուժեն, զօրանոցին մէջ ձգելով պզտիկ տղաքներ, ծերեր եւ անկարներ, թուով 270 հոգի, որոնք իբր թէ վերջէն Մարաշ փոխադրուած են քէմալական իշխանութեան կողմէ:

Գալով դուրս ելլողներուն, որոնք ամէն պարագայի տակ ֆրանսական գրաւման գօտիին հասնիլ մտադրած էին, չորս օր քալելէ յետոյ գիշերանց կը հասնին Անտէրուն, բայց յանկարծ կը պաշարուին տեղւոյն չէթէներու ինչպէս նաեւ կանոնաւոր զինուորներու կողմէ եւ յուսահատական կռիւէ մը յետոյ կը ստիպուին բաժնուելու երեք խումբերու, որոնցմէ առաջինը 30 հոգիէ բաղկացեալ, առանց լուր ունենալու միւս երկուքէն, կը հասնի մինչեւ Ճիհան գետին եզերքը, ուր կռիւի կը բռնուի, այնպէս որ երեք հոգի միայն ազատուելով կը հասնին Օսմանիյէ, իսկ մնացածները կը ջարդուին եւ կը խեղդուին գետը նետուելով: Ամենավերջին լուրերուն նայելով, երկու մեծ խումբերէն մին Ճիհան գետը անցնելով հասած է Էկպէզի կողմերը եւ մասամբ ազատուած կրնան համարուիլ ֆրանսական գրաւման գօտիին մօտեցած ըլլալով, իսկ միւսը կը գտնուի եղեր տակաւին Ճիհան գետէն անդին, եւ վերջին ծայր յոգնած եւ պարտասած, չորս կողմէն չէթէներով պաշարուած ըլլալով, շատ յոյս չի ներշնչեր:

Adana (from Bishop Yeghishé Garoyan, Catholicosal Vicar)—July 18

A particular private official dispatched from Adana to Osmaniye relayed the following information about the most recent events in Süleymanlı [Zeytun], which he had received from three natives of Süleymanlı who escaped from Süleymanlı and arrived in Osmaniye.

"After the evacuation of Maraş by the French forces, we were almost wholly besieged. Sporadic minor incidents had always occurred. We suffered great hardship concerning food, and there was no salt at all. In the spring, the people were fed on grass. If grains were found by chance, they were distributed equally to everybody. Food was communal; one person's belonging was everybody's belonging by order of the National Union.

"On June 17, 1921, a gendarme arrived in Süleymanlı, announcing a Turkish delegation consisting of seven people—an army commander, two regimental commanders, a major and a captain from the military staff, a district governor, and the lieutenant governor of Çardak. They were waiting two hours away in Mimarsinan [Hırlavuk/Cırlavuk] and asking for a delegation with whom to negotiate.

"Messrs. Setrag Marganian, Haroutyun Kasabian, and Asadour Gyulvanian of the National Union were sent. The Turkish delegation told them: "The government of Ankara has decided to end your problem. You have formed an *Armenia* here with a separate government, you are in relations with the French, you get strength from them, and you are more hostile to us than the French. To remain unharmed, we suggest handing over your weapons, evacuating the barracks, and surrendering. If you accept the current conditions, fine; otherwise, the greatest force is ready for you, and we will strike unsparingly."

"Our delegates came on June 18, together with the Turkish captain, and informed the people of the Turks' conditions. The people, aware of the Turkish deception, refused to accept the terms but, to gain time, offered to send delegates to Maraş to negotiate with broader authority. Vartavar Baljian, Haroutyun Kasabian, and Asadour [Gyoulvanian] left for Maraş with the Turkish delegation. On June 22, our delegates returned from Maraş. The first thing they said was this: "Boys, be prepared, the enemy has already arrived with great force, and the danger is terrible." The Turks had brought with them from Maraş a young man from the Khurlakian family, allegedly sent by Mr. Lymen, to receive the surrendering people. We were given five hours to surrender, during which we thought of handing over the children, women, the weak, and the willing, so the rest of us could go up the mountain. Six hundred people were sent to the Turks' side to surrender, but half were immediately turned back. The Turks objected that they had left behind family members who, too, should surrender with them. As soon as the returnees reached us, we were fired at from all directions, and war broke out fiercely. We had 120 Mauser-Martins, as well as other ordinary rifles. We fought a fierce battle for four days. About three hundred bombs fell on us every day, damaging the barracks.

"On June 27, the fifth day of the war, realizing it was no longer possible to resist, we decided to leave the women and retreat to the mountains. However, upon the insistence of the women, we were obliged to set those able to walk on the road, and at three o'clock in the morning (according to the Turks), we set out as two wings, taking some of the women with us. We crossed through the siege chain in two places. On June 29, at four o'clock in the afternoon, we assembled behind Avcılar [Avakal, Avak-Gal] on Mount Kalaycık, five hours [away] from Süleymanlı. We noticed from there that enemy bombs were still exploding over those who had remained in the barracks. We saw from the same place that soldiers were pursuing us. We left a group of 20 people there to keep the pursuing force busy. On the 29th of June, crossing the Yayla-Abalı of Fırnız, we descended the same night in front of Akgümüş [Bunduk], together with 72 women and about 350 men. On the night of June 30, we set out and were attacked in front of Geben, where we lost two women and a priest. We buried the women but could not find the [corpse of the] priest because of the darkness.

Ատանա (Կաթողիկոսական Փոխանորդ Տ. Եղիշէ Եպիսկոպոս Կարօեանէ) – 18 Յուլիս

Ատանայէն Օսմանիյէ ղրկուած յատուկ մասնաւոր պաշտօնեայ մը Զէյթունէն ազատելով Օսմանիյէ հասնող երեք զէյթունցիներէն ստացած հետեւեալ տեղեկութիւնները կը հաղորդէ Զէյթունի վերջին անցքերուն վրայ:

«Ֆրանսական ուժերու կողմէ Մարաշի պարպումէն յետոյ գրեթէ բոլորովին պաշարուած վիճակի մէջ մնացինք: Հոս ու հոն շարունակ մանր մունր դէպքեր անպակաս կ'ըլլային. ուտելիքի մասին մեծ դժուարութիւն կը քաշէինք, իսկ աղ երբեք չկար: Այս գարնան ժողովուրդը խոտով կը կերակրուէր եւ եթէ ունէ կերպով կարելի ըլլար հացահատիկ գտնել, անխտիր բոլոր ժողովուրդին կը բաժնուէր հաւասար կերպով. ուտելիքը համայնական էր եւ մէկուն ունեցածը ամենուն կը պատկանէր Ազգային Միութեան կարգադրութեամբ:

1921 Յունիս 17ին ժանտարմա մը եկաւ Զէյթուն, յայտնելով որ թուրք պատուիրակութիւն մը՝ բաղկացած [եօթը հոգիէ],- Օրտու զօմանտանիէ մը, երկու Ալայ զօմանտանիէ, Էրքեանը հարպի հազարապետէ մը եւ հարիւրապետէ մը, միւթէսարըֆէ մը եւ Չարտաքի գայմագամէն,- երկու ժամ հեռաւորութեան վրայ Խըրլավուխը կը սպասեն եւ պատուիրակութիւն մը կ'ուզեն բանակցութեան համար:

Ազգային Միութեան անդամներէն պ.պ. Սեդրակ Մարկանեան, Յարութիւն Գասապեան եւ Ասատուր Կիւլվանեանը ղրկուեցան, որոնց կ'ըսուի.- «Էնգարէի կառավարութեան կողմէ վերջ տրուիլը որոշուած է ձեր խնդիրին. դուք այստեղ *Հայաստան* կազմեր էք առանձին կառավարութեամբ, ֆրանսացիներուն հետ յարաբերութեան մէջ էք, անոնցմէ ոյժ կը ստանաք եւ ֆրանսացիներէն աւելի թշնամի էք մեզ: Որպէսզի անվնաս մնաք, կ'առաջարկենք զէնքերը յանձնել, զօրանոցը պարպել, դուրս ելնելով անձնատուր ըլլալ: Եթէ կ'ընդունիք ներկայ պայմանները՝ լաւ, հակառակ պարագային ամենամեծ ուժը պատրաստ է ձեզ համար եւ պիտի զարնենք անխնայ:

18 Յունիսին մեր պատուիրակները եկան միասին բերելով հարիւրապետը եւ ժողովուրդին յայտնեցին պայմանները. ժողովուրդը՝ տեղեակ թրքական խաբեբայութեան, մերժեց ընդունիլ պայմանները եւ միայն որպէսզի օր շահուի, առաջարկեց պատուիրակներ ղրկել Մարաշ, աւելի լայն իրաւասութեամբ բանակցելու համար եւ թուրք պատուիրակութեան հետ Մարաշ մեկնեցան Վարդավառ Պալճեան, Յարութիւն Գասապեան եւ Ասատուր [Կիւլվանեան]: 22 Յունիսին մեր պատուիրակները վերադարձան Մարաշէն եւ իրենց առաջին խօսքը եղաւ. «Տղա՛ք, պատրաստ եղէք, թշնամին մեծ ուժով հասած է արդէն եւ վտանգը ահաւոր է»: Թուրքերը Մարաշէն բերեր էին նաեւ միասին Խըրլագեաններէն երիտասարդ տղայ մը, որպէս թէ ղրկուած ըլլար Մր. *Լայմրնի* կողմէ, անձնատուր եղածները յանձն առնելու համար: 5 ժամ պայմանաժամ տրուեցաւ մեզ անձնատուր ըլլալու համար, որոյ ընթացքին մտածուեցաւ մանուկները, կիները, տկարները եւ փափաքողները յանձնել եւ մնացածներս լեռ բարձրանանք: 600 հոգի ղրկուեցան թրքաց կողմ[ը] անձնատուր ըլլալու համար. սակայն անմիջապէս յետոյ գացածներէն կէսը ետ վերադարձուեցան այն առարկութեամբ թէ իրենց պարագաները ունին եւ պէտք է անոնք ալ միասին անձնատուր ըլլան: Հազիւ թէ ետ վերադարձուածները մեր քով հասան եւ ահա ամէն կողմէ կրակ բացուեցաւ եւ պատերազմը սկսաւ կատաղի կերպով: Մենք ունէինք 120 Մաուզէր-Մարթէն, նոյնքան ալ ուրիշ հասարակ հրացաններ: 4 օր կատաղի պատերազմ մղեցինք: Օրական մօտ 300 ռումբ կ'իյնար մեր վրայ՝ տակնուվրայ ընելով զօրանոցը:

Յունիս 27, պատերազմի հինգերորդ օրը, նկատելով որ այլեւս անկարելի է դիմադրել, որոշեցինք կիները ձգել եւ լեռ քաշուիլ. սակայն կիներուն ստիպման վրայ պարտաւորուեցանք ոտքը բռնողը ճամբայ հանել եւ գիշերուան ժամը երեքին (ըստ թրքաց) կիներէն ալ մաս մը միասին առնելով երկու թեւով ճամբայ ելանք: Երկու տեղ պաշարման շղթան կտրելով անցանք: 29 Յունիսին ցորեկուան ժամը 4ին (ը.թ.) միատեղ ամփոփուեցանք Աւագալի ետեւը, Գալաճըգի լեռը, 5 ժամ [հեռու] Զէյթունէն: Հոնկից նկատեցինք թէ զօրանոցը մնացողներուն վրայ թշնամի ռումբեր կը պայթին դեռ: Նոյն տեղէն տեսանք թէ մեր ետեւէն զինուորներ հետապնդման ելած են: 20 հոգինոց

"Walking by the night of July 1, we reached the castle of Azgıt near Andırın early in the morning. Its plain was covered with tents, whence a terrible attack was launched at us by the regular soldiers and the tribe. We left some of us there to continue the fight. We set the women out on the road, and at the end of a few hours, we reunited entirely on the plain of Yenigün [Mehirli] in front of Andırın. On July 2, a terrible shooting took place at us by night. We were forced to retreat to the mountain and spread out. Shortly after, only thirty-two of us were together with nine guns. We wandered around in search of the others, but in vain . . . Beyond that, we do not know where the others ended up.

"July 3: We did not know where we were. We started walking. We were attacked again; we fought for six hours and seized three rifles. We lost only one person.

"On July 4–5–6, we passed through unknown places, fought with the tribes living in tents, and lost three more people in the battles, we could not find food anywhere, and the forces pursuing us were ever-present. On July 7, we suddenly found the Ceyhan River before us. We positioned ourselves against the enemy at once and crossed fifteen people to the other side of the river. Antranig Chakrian, Manoug Kavakian, and Sergeant Nazaret's youngest son, Margos, were injured. Garabed Demirjian jumped into the river with all his bullets and weapons and drowned with the others. On July 8–12, without weapons, naked and barefoot, we managed to reach Osmaniye in secret."

The following was also reported to the Catholicos of Cilicia on July 15 from Osmaniye.

"Yesterday, we gathered the following information from a Turk arriving in Osmaniye. "The Turks blocked the road, preventing a large group of people from Süleymanlı from crossing to this side of Düziçi [Haruniye]. Sergeant Aram sent news, saying: 'Villagers, we have nothing against you. Let us cross the road; otherwise, we will fight to the last drop of blood.'

"The Turks did not listen and continued their fight. The people of Süleymanlı continued to fight in the village of Ayvalık, across from Kızılağaç, which is on the other side of Haçbel."

Likewise, yesterday afternoon, a man named Kızılbaş Nebi from the village of Kabaklar in İslahiye arrived here. He said: "A group of 120 people from Süleymanlı passed through the village of Bilenler [Şerikanlı] and went to Hassa." (The village of Bilenler [Şerikanlı] is half an hour away from Meidan Akbis [Meydan Ekbez] (in the mountains) and two hours away from İslahiye.)

İstanbul (gathered from natives of Merzifon)—13 August[115]

The Armenians who returned to Merzifon after deportation, along with those who were there after they had converted to Islam, count two thousand people. At the time of the deportation, the Turkish government had demolished some houses. The Armenian quarter, which was separate, had turned into small islands on one side of the city. From the letters being received from Samsun these days, it is understood that a fire broke out in the Armenian quarter on July 25–26. The whole neighborhood was looted, and the men under sixty were massacred. The women and children are scattered, and some have been taken to Turkish houses, as is understood from the news.

Bursa (from the locum tenens)—August 15[116]

Mr. Zhamgochian, a refugee from Eskişehir to Bursa, wrote down the following events, which he wit-

խումբ մը թողուցինք հոն հետապնդող ուժը զբաղեցնելու համար: Յունիս 29ին Փըրնուզի Եայլայ-Ապալուի վրայէն անցնելով նոյն օրը գիշերն իջանք Պունտուքի առջեւ, միասին ունենալով 72 կին եւ մօտ 350 այր: 30 Յունիսին գիշերը ճամբայ ելանք եւ Կապանի առջեւ ուժեղ յարձակումի մը ենթարկուեցանք, ուր կորսնցուցինք երկու կին եւ քահանայ մը: Կիները թաղեցինք, բայց քահանան չկրցինք գտնել մութին պատճառաւ:

Յուլիս 1ին գիշերը քալելով առտուն կանուխ հասանք Անտըրընի մօտ Ազըրտ բերդը, որուն տափարակը ծածկուած էր վրաններով, ուսկից սոսկալի յարձակում մը եղաւ մեր վրայ կանոնաւոր զինուորներու եւ աշիրէթի կողմէ: Մերիններէն մէկ մասը թողինք որ կռիւը շարունակէ: Մենք կիները ճամբայ հանեցինք եւ քանի մը ժամ վերջը դարձեալ ամբողջութեամբ միացանք դարձեալ Անտըրէնի առջեւը Մըհէրլիի տափարակը: Յուլիս 2ին այս տեղ գիշերանց սոսկալի կրակ բացուեցաւ մեր վրայ: Ստիպուեցանք դէպի լեռը քաշուիլ եւ տարածուիլ: Քիչ վերջը 32 հոգի միայն միատեղ կը գտնուէինք 9 հրացանով: Գտնուած տեղերնիս աջին անդին դարձանք միւսները գտնելու համար, բայց ի զուր... Ասկէ անդին չենք գիտեր թէ միւսները ուր մնացին այլեւս:

Յուլիս 3. չգիտէինք թէ ուր կը գտնուէինք: Սկսանք քալել: Դարձեալ յարձակում կրեցինք, ուր 6 ժամ կռիւ մղեցինք, 3 հրացան գրաւեցինք: Մեր կորուստը եղաւ միայն մէկ մարդ:

Յուլիս 4–5–6ին անծանօթ վայրերէ անցանք, վրանաքնակ աշիրէթներու հետ կռիւ ունեցանք, կռիւներու մէջ 3 հոգի եւս կորուսինք. որեւէ տեղ կերակուր չկրցինք ճարել եւ մեզ հետապնդող ուժեր անպակաս եղան միշտ: Յուլիս 7ին Ճիհանի գետը գտանք յանկարծակի մեր առջեւ. անմիջապէս դիրք բռնելով թշնամիին դէմ, 15 հոգի անցուցինք գետին միւս կողմը: Անդրանիկ Չագըրեանը, Մանուկ Գավազեանը, Նազարէթ Չավուշի պզտիկ տղան՝ Մարկոսը, վիրաւորուեցան: Կարապետ Տէմիրճեանը ամբողջ փամփուշտները եւ զէնքը վրան՝ գետը նետուեցաւ եւ միւսներուն հետ խեղդուեցաւ: Յուլիս 8–12 առանց զէնքի, մերկ ու բոպիկ, գաղտնաբար կրցանք հասնիլ Օսմանիյէ»:

Նաեւ Յուլիս 15 թուականով Օսմանիյէէն տեղեկագրուած է Կիլիկիոյ Կաթողիկոսին հետեւեալը:

«Երէկ Օսմանիյէ ժամանող թուրքէ մը հետեւեալ տեղեկութիւնները քաղեցինք.- «Զէյթունցինե-րու մեծ խումբ մը Հարունիէէն աջի կողմը անցած ատեն թուրքերը իրենց ճամբան կապեցին: Արամ Չավուշը լուր ղրկեց. «Գիւղացինե՛ր, մենք ձեզի հետ բան մը չունինք. ճամբայ տուէք որ անցնինք երթանք, հակառակ պարագային մինչեւ արեան վերջին կաթիլը կը կռուինք»:

Թուրքերը մտիկ չեն ըներ եւ կը շարունակեն իրենց կռիւը: Զէյթունցիք [կը կռուէին] Այվալըգ գիւղէն Գըզըլ Աղաճի դիմացը, որ Խաչպէշի միւս կողմը կը գտնուի:

Դարձեալ երէկ կէսօրէն վերջ տեղս հասաւ Իսլահիյէի Գապազլար գիւղէն Գըզըլպաշ Նէպի անուն մարդ մը: Ան կ'ըսէ. «Զէյթունցիներու 120 հոգինոց խումբ մը Շէրի Գանլը գիւղէն անցնելով գացին Խասսա»: (Շէրի Գանլը գիւղը Մէյտան Էքպէզէն կէս ժամ [հեռու] (լեռներու մէջ) իսկ Իսլա-հիյէէն 2 ժամ հեռու է:)

Կ. Պոլիս (Մարզուանցիներէ քաղուած) – 13 Օգոստոս

Մարզուանի տարագրութենէն յետոյ հոն դարձած եւ իսլամանալով հոն մնացած հայոց թիւը 2000 հոգիի չափ էր: Տարագրութեան ատեն թուրք կառավարութիւնը տուներէն մէկ մասը քակել տուած էր: Հայոց թաղը, որ առանձին էր, քաղաքին մէկ կողմը ինքնին կզզեակներու վերածուած էր: Այս օրերս Սամսոնէն առնուած նամակներէն կը հասկցուի թէ 25–26 Յուլիս օրերուն հայոց թաղին մէջ կրակ ձգուած է. ամբողջ թաղը կողոպտուած եւ այր մարդիկը մինչեւ 60 տարեկանները ջարդուած են: Կիները եւ մանուկները աջին անդին ցրուած եւ ոմանք թրքաց տուները առնուած են, ինչպէս առնուած լուրերէն կը հասկցուի:

Պրուսա (Առաջնորդական Տեղապահէն) – 15 Օգոստոս

Էսկի Շէհիրէն Պրուսա եկող գաղթական պ. Ժամկոչեան գրի առած է հետեւեալ անցքերը,

nessed after the departure of the British troops.

"When Eskişehir's English soldiers retreated to İstanbul, the people remained free for almost two months. Then, at the first opportunity, five thousand liras were demanded from the Armenians. The members of the Neighborhood Council allocated sums to the people according to their ability to pay. For the second time, almost a month after paying the first amount, another five thousand liras were demanded. The people paid again under the threat that nonpayers would be handed over to the Kemalists. The church had twenty-five hundred liras ready, which, I think, had been spent for Father Ghazaros Hovhannisian, the local priest. Arrests began in the fourth month. About twenty people were arrested for acting against the Turkish government during the control of the Allied troops. In late July, sixty-five wealthy people—locals and outsiders—were arrested overnight in Eskişehir and sent to Haymana after spending eight days in prison. They stayed there for four or five months. The second arrest took place on September 14, 1920, on Saturday, from nine o'clock in the evening until one o'clock past midnight. One hundred five people were arrested. At two o'clock, they were ordered to prepare, and after registering their names in the Central Command building, they were taken to the train station under the watch of fifty-five guards. They were unable to make any preparations for this sudden departure. In this unprepared condition, they were sent on foot to Sarıköy. They were given one loaf of bread a day. Later, in Beypazarı, they started to repair an inn ruined centuries ago, on the condition that they be given some bread. The people were not allowed to work with artisans to do a job. In this way, 280 people from Bilecik, Küplü, and the surrounding area joined us at the Sarıköy station.

"Other overnight arrests were made after this date. The detainees were sent to Ayaş or other places. [After that,] a few days later, the tailors and shoemakers were separated as volunteer soldiers and sent some to Eskişehir and the rest to Ankara. About 800 people were taken to Beypazarı, 650–700 to Ayaş, 200 to Sivrihisar, and more than 2,000 to Haymana. About 500 shoemakers and tailors are in Ankara from various cities. The military command provided their food. In October, they discontinued the volunteers of National Defense and turned them into simple soldiers. During this time, the non-natives found in Ankara and remote areas were exiled with the promise that they would be sent to their cities [of origin]. This method lasted two months. Then they started sending the people they found to Sivas in their nightclothes. On June 1, 1921, while in exile, I fled to Eskişehir, where I managed to hide until the Greek occupation. During this time, I learned that after our departure to Beyşehir, family members of people who were wanted were taken to the guardhouse and beaten until they confessed the whereabouts of the person sought. Thus, 30–40 women were arrested and released after imprisonment for several days.

"After the armistice, there were barely three hundred local and outsider Armenian families. There were only six hundred people among them between the ages of fifteen and sixty. Only one hundred of them were saved from this exile with the help of the railway administration, while about fifty people either hid in the places where they had been taken or did not leave the city. The rest traveled all the way to Harput. On March 22, when the Greeks attacked İnönü from Bilecik, [the people of] Çalkara and the surrounding Armenian villages, barely thirty families, fled to Eskişehir. When the Greek armies retreated, the Millis deported the remaining people of Çalkara to Ankara. Their destination thence is unknown. The arrests did not end. In April, about thirty Armenians and Greeks were expelled from the company's [*sic*] employees. After several days in prison, they were sent to the fortification battalion of eight hundred to one thousand Greek and Armenian youth. This army [battalion] operated in Karaçay and Sabuncupınar. Before the attack on the Greek army, it was transported to the sides of Güvemli [Mahmudiye] or Çifteler. The newspapers were printing assurances that it was impossible for the Greek army to enter Eskişehir, the key to Anadolu [Anatolia]. They were publishing provocative

որոնց ականատես եղած է անգլիացի զինուորներու մեկնումէն յետոյ:

«Երբ Էսկի Շէհիրի անգլիական զինուորները դէպի Կ. Պոլիս քաշուեցան, գրեթէ երկու ամիս ազատ մնաց ժողովուրդը: Յետոյ առաջին առիթով 5000 ոսկի պահանջուեցաւ հայ ազգէն: Թաղական Խորհուրդի անդամները ժողովուրդին իրեն կարողութեան համեմատ բաժնեցին: Երկրորդ անգամ, առաջին դրամը վճարելէ գրեթէ ամիս մը վերջը, 5000 ոսկի եւս պահանջուեցաւ: Նորէն ժողովուրդը վճարեց՝ չվճարողները քէմալականներու յանձնելու սպառնալիքին տակ: Եկեղեցին ունէր 2500 ոսկի պատրաստ դրամ, որ տեղւոյն քահանային՝ Տ. Ղազարոս Յովհաննէսեանի համար ծախսուած է կարծեմ: Չորրորդ ամիսին սկսան ձերբակալումներ: Համաձայնական զինուորներու տիրապետութեան տակ թուրք կառավարութեան դէմ գործողները, գրեթէ 20 հոգի, ձերբակալուեցան: Յուլիսի վերջերը Էսկի-Շէհիրի մէջ տեղացի կամ դրսեցի հարուստներէն 65 անձեր գիշերանց ձերբակալեցին, 8 օր մը բանտարկելէ վերջ ուղարկեցին դէպի Հայմանա: 4–5 ամիս հոն մնացին: Երկրորդ ձերբակալումը եղաւ 14 Սեպտեմբեր 1920ին, շաբաթ գիշեր ժամը 9էն մինչեւ ժամը 1: Ձերբակալուեցան 105 անձեր: Ժամը 2ին պատրաստուելու հրաման տուին եւ *մերքէզ գումանտանլըղը*ի շէնքին մէջ անոնց անունները արձանագրելէ յետոյ զանոնք 55 պահակներու հսկողութեամբ առաջնորդեցին շոգեկառքի կայարանը: Այս յանկարծական մեկնումին համար ոչ մէկ պատրաստութիւն կրցած էին տեսնել: Այս անպատրաստ վիճակին մէջ անոնք ղրկուեցան ոտքով Սարըքէօյ: Անոնց կը տրուէր օրական մէկ մէկ հաց: Յետոյ Պէյ Բազարի մէջ դարեր առաջ աւերակ դարձած խան մը նորոգել տալ սկսան միայն հաց մը տալու պայմանաւ: Ժողովուրդը չձգեցին որ գործով մը զբաղելու համար արհեստաւորներու քով աշխատի: Այս միջոցին թէեւ մեզի հետ մէկտեղ Սարըքէօյի կայարանը միացան 280 անձեր Պիլէճիկի, Քիւփրիի [Քիւփլի] եւ շրջականներու բնակիչներէն:

Այս թուականէն յետոյ կատարուեցան ուրիշ գիշերային ձերբակալութիւններ: Ձերբակալուածները կը ղրկուէին դէպի Այաշ եւ կամ ուրիշ վայրեր: Քանի մը օր վերջը դերձակները եւ կօշկակարները իբր կամաւոր զինուոր կը զատեն եւ մէկ մասը Էսկի Շէհիր, իսկ մնացեալները դէպի Էնկիւրիւ կը ղրկեն: Մօտ 800 անձ Պէյ բազար, 650–700 անձ՝ Այաշ, 200՝ Սիվրիհիսար, 2000էն աւելի Հայմանա կը տարուին: Իսկ 500ի մօտ կօշկակար եւ դերձակ կը գտնուին Անգարա: Ասոնք զանազան քաղաքներէն են: Ասոնց սնունդը կ՚ապահովէր զինուորական հրամանատարութիւնը: Հոկտեմբերի մէջ *Միւտաֆաայի Միլլիյէ*ի կամաւորները դադրեցուցին եւ պարզ զինուորականի վերածուեցան: Այս միջոցին Էնկիւրիւ եւ հեռուները գտնուող օտարները իրենց քաղաքը ղրկուելու խոստումով կ՚աքսորէին: Այս մեթոտը տեւեց երկու ամիս: Յետոյ սկսան աչքի առաջ գտնուող մարդիկը իրենց գիշերնոցներով ղրկել դէպի Սըվազ: 1921 Յունիս 1ին ես որ աքսորեալներու մէջ էի, փախայ դէպի Էսկի Շէհիր եւ յաջողեցայ պահուիլ մինչեւ հելլէնական գրաւում: Այս միջոցին տեղեկացայ թէ մեր Պէյշէհիր երթալէն յետոյ փնտռուած մարդիկ եթէ ձեռք չձգեն անոր ընտանիքը պահականոց տանելով կը ծեծեն որպէս[զի] փնտռուած անձին ուր գտնուիլը խոստովանի: Այսպէս 30–40 կիներ ձերբակալուած եւ քանի մը օր բանտարկուած մնալէ յետոյ արձակուած են:

Չինադաղարէն յետոյ տեղացի եւ օտար հազիւ 300 տնուոր հայութիւն մը կար: Անոնց մէջ գտնուող 15էն վեր եւ 60էն վար ընդամէնը 600 հոգի էր: Ասոնցմէ այս աքսորէն միայն 100 հոգիի չափ երկաթուղիի տնօրէնութեան օգնութեամբ ազատեցան: 50 հոգիի մօտ ալ տարուած տեղերնին կամ քաղաքէն դուրս չելլելով պահուեցան: Մնացեալները մինչեւ Խարբերդ գացած են: Մարտ 22ին երբ հելլէնները յարձակեցան Պիլէճիկի կողմէն Ին-Էօնիւի վրայ, Չալկարա եւ շրջակայ հայ գիւղերը փախուստ տուին Էսկիշէհիր, հազիւ 30 տունուոր: Երբ հելլէն բանակները ետ քաշուեցան, [միլլիները] մնացեալ չալկարացիները աքսորեցին Էնկիւրիւ, ուրկէ ո՞ւր երթալնին անյայտ է: Ձերբակալութիւնները չդադրեցան: Ապրիլի մէջ ընկերութեան պաշտօնեաներէն հայ եւ յոյն 30ի չափ մարդիկ հանեցին, քանի մը օր բանտարկելէ յետոյ յոյն եւ հայ երիտասարդներէ 800–1000 հոգիէ կազմուած *խըթի[հ]զամ թապուրի*ն ղրկեցին: Այս բանակը Քարա-չայի եւ Սապօնճի Բունարի մէջ կ՚աշխատէր: Հելլէնական բանակին յարձակումէն առաջ դէպի Մահմուտիէի կամ Չիֆթէլերի կողմերը փոխադրեցին: Լրագիրները կ՚ապահովէին որ անկարելի էր որ հելլէն բանակը Էսկիշէհիր՝ Անատոլուի

articles titled "Greek Evildoers." In recent days, they were even writing that the Greek army was killing ten times more children belonging to [Muslim] families in the areas of war compared with the number of soldiers they lost, and the papers were calling for retaliation for these acts of violence. This triggered [the Millis] to come up with the idea of deporting local Christian families, but when they convened a meeting, the local Turks prevented it, even though provocative publications with the same title continued daily.

"Almost every day [the Millis] stormed homes and sent the people caught to Haymana and beyond. In October of last year, they made the church and the schools evacuate. They gathered the church vessels and placed them in a ditch under the church, and then they turned the church into a prison and the school into an industrial tailor shop. We have had neither a church nor a school for a whole year. Christians have been treated very harshly. There were almost no [Armenian] shopkeepers left in the square. When the Greek invasion finally began on July 14, [the Millis] were in the midst of throwing elaborate banquets celebrating the capture of İzmit and Adapazarı and boasting, but [with the Greek invasion,] suddenly a whisper and a commotion began in the city that lasted for almost a day. A large number of people were running to the station with their families. On the second and third days, [people] were running haphazardly. Forty-six trains [full of Millis and adherers] fled from Eskişehir to Ankara within three days. The trains transported the entire war cache of ammunition and about ten thousand families to Ankara. The wagons were so full that there was no room to move. The roofs of the wagons also were piled with [people]. After the families from İzmir, Bursa, and other cities staying in Eskişehir had left, the locals also left. The management of the station left with the last group. The station manager and Dr. Hagop forced their way onto a wagon and left. Before leaving, [the Millis] told many people that they were leaving [but] that their trap had been set and that they would return on the third day to take the Greek army captive. One of the Kemalists' closest friends, lawyer Takettin Bey, took with him a man named Hacı Sadık on horseback to extend an invitation to the Greek commander. Greek, Armenian, and Catholic priests and prominent Turks brought the commander to the city together. Two days later, the war broke out in a place called Kanlıpınar, and after a fierce nine-hour battle, the Kemalists were brutally defeated. These nine hours were terrible hours for the Christians in the city. They were ready to escape.

"During the war, people heard of Takettin's flight on horseback and his arrest while fleeing. He was going to the Kemalists to provide information. His whereabouts is unknown at this time. The next day the city was peaceful, and many captives were being brought [to Eskişehir].

"Kemalist volunteers killed eight Armenians three hours away from Eskişehir in Hasırcı [Hasırca]. Eight to ten Armenians were also hanged.

"A few days ago, it was reported that the driver Chadujian had snitched a thirty-eight-wagon train full of ammunition from Eskişehir and had reached the Greek army near the bridge. However, he was wounded in three places during this escape. The Greeks rewarded his service with medals."

Bursa (from the locum tenens)—August 21[117]

On August 15, the locum tenens of Armenians of Bursa, Reverend Father Sarkis, set out at dawn and after passing by the dens of the Millis at the foot of Uludağ [Mount Olympus], he arrived in İnegöl, where, shortly after, also came the sacristan Mr. Hampartsoum of Yenice. He had miraculously escaped Millis' gunfire and reached İnegöl. The commander of İnegöl provided the locum tenens with some strong horses and soldiers to roam around İnegöl. Churches, schools, houses, and fields had all been ruined and [looked like] dens of owls, bats, and beasts. The devastation is indescribable. No building has a door or a window. The streets are covered with grass and broken glass. The buildings are in ruins.

բանալին մտնէր: «Հելլէն չարագործներ» վերնագրով գրգռիչ հրատարակութիւններ կ'ընէին: Վերջին օրերը նոյնիսկ կը գրէին թէ հելլէն բանակը պատերազմէ կորսնցուցած զինուորներու թուին տասնապատիկը կը սպաննէ պատերազմի վայրերը գտնուող ընտանիքներու տղաքներէն եւ յորդոր կը կարդային այս վայրագութիւնները փոխարինելու: Ասոր վրայ գաղափար յղացան տեղացի քրիստոնեայ ընտանիքներն ալ աքսորելու, բայց երբ ժողով գումարեցին` տեղացի թուրքերը չթողուցին, թէեւ ամէն օր նոյն վերնագրով գրգռիչ հրատարակութիւնները կը շարունակուէին:

Գրեթէ ամէն օր տուները կը կոխէին եւ ձեռք անցուածը կը ղրկէին Հայմանա, անկէ ալ աւելի հեռուները: Անցեալ տարի Հոկտեմբերին եկեղեցին եւ դպրոցները պարպել տուին: Եկեղեցիին անօթները եկեղեցիին տակ գտնուած գետնափորը տեղաւորել տալով եկեղեցին բանտի եւ դպրոցը *Սէնայի Թէրզիհանէ*ի վերածած էին: Տարի մը ամբողջ ո՛չ եկեղեցի եւ ո՛չ ալ դպրոց ունէինք: Շատ խժդժութեամբ կը վարուէին քրիստոնեաներու հետ: Հրապարակի վրայ, գրեթէ խանութպան չէր մնացած: Երբ վերջին անգամ Յուլիս 14ին հելլէն յարձակումը սկսաւ, մէկ կողմէն Նիկոմիդիոյ եւ Ատափազարի գրաւումներուն համար մեծ խնջոյքներ կ'ընէին, կը պարծենային, յանկարծ քաղաքին մէջ շշուկ մը եւ իրարանցում մը սկսաւ որ գրեթէ օր մը տեւեց: Ահագին թուով մարդիկ իրենց ընտանիքներով կը վազէին կայարան: Բ. եւ Գ. Օրերը իրենց կօշիկները ձեռք առած կը վազէին: Երեք օրուան միջոցին 46 կառախումբեր Էսկի-Շէհիրէն Անգարա փախան` բոլոր պատերազմի ռազմանիւթերը եւ 10000ի մօտ ընտանիք փոխադրելով Էնկիւրիւ: Վակօնները այնքան լեցուն էին որ շարժելու տեղ չկար: Վակօններուն վրաներն ալ լեցուած էին: Իզմիրէն, Պրուսայէն եւ ուրիշ քաղաքներէ Էսկիշէհիր մնացող ընտանիքները մեկնելէ յետոյ տեղացիք ալ մեկնեցան: Վերջին կառախումբով կայարանի տնօրէնութիւնը կը մեկնէր: Կայարանապետը եւ Տոք. Յակոբը բռնի կառախումբ կ'առնեն եւ կը փա[խչ]ին: Մեկնելէ առաջ շատերու կ'ըսեն թէ մենք կ'երթանք, [թ]ակարդնիս պատրաստ է, երրորդ օրը նորէն հոս պիտի ըլլանք եւ հելլէն բանակը գերի պիտի բռնենք: Քէմալականներու ամէնէն սրտակից ընկերներէն փաստաբան Դագէթտին պէյ իրեն հետ առնելով Հաճի Սատըգ կոչուած մէկը, ձիով կ'երթան հրաւիրել հելլէն հրամատարը: Յոյն, հայ եւ կաթոլիկ քահանաներ եւ թուրք երեւելիները միասին կը բերեն հրամատարը քաղաք: Երկու օր յետոյ սկսաւ պատերազմը Քանլը Բունար ըսուած վայրէն եւ 9 ժամուան բուռն ընդհարումէ մը յետոյ քէմալականները չարաչար պարտուեցան: Այս 9 ժամուան միջոցը քաղաքին քրիստոնեաներուն համար սոսկալի ժամեր եղան. կազմ եւ պատրաստ էին խոյս տալու:

Պատերազմի միջոցին լսուեցաւ Դագէթտինի ձիով փախչիլը [եւ] փախած ատեն ձերբակալուիլը: Անիկա Քէմալականներու կ'երթար լուր տանելու: Հիմա յայտնի չէ թէ ուր կը գտնուի: Յաջորդ օրը քաղաքը խաղաղած էր եւ բազմաթիւ գերիներ կը բերուէին:

Քէմալական կամաւորներ սպաննած են 8 հայեր Էսկիշէհիրէն 3 ժամ հեռու ի Հասըրճա: 8–10 հայեր ալ կախուած են:

Քանի մը օր առաջ լսուած է որ մեքենավար Չատըճեան 38 վակոն ռազմանիւթով կառախումբ մը փախուցած է Էսկիշէհիրէն եւ հասած է կամուրջին քով հելլէնական զօրաբանակին: Այս փախուստի միջոցին երեք տեղէ վիրաւորուած է: Իր ծառայութիւնը վարձատրած են հելլէնները շքանշաններով:»

Պրուսա (Առաջնորդական Տեղապահէն) – 21 Օգոստոս

Օգոստոս 15ին Պրուսայի հայոց Առաջնորդական Տեղապահ Տ. Սարգիս Վարդապետ արշալոյսին ճամբայ կ'ելլէ եւ Ողիմպոսի ստորոտը` Միլլիճիներու որջերը քերելով կը հասնի Իյնէկէօլ, ուր քիչ յետոյ կը հասնի Եէնիճէի լուսարար պ. Համբարձում, որ հրաշքով Միլլիճիներու կրակէն ազատած էր եւ հասած Իյնէկէօլ: Իյնէկէօլի հրամատարը քանի մը հժկու ձիեր եւ զինուորներ տրամադրելի կ'ընէ Իյնէկէօլի շրջանակին մէջ շրջելու համար: Եկեղեցիները, դպրոցները, տուները, արտերը ամէն ինչ աւերակ, բուերու, ջղջիկներու եւ գազաններու որջեր եղած են, եւ աւերն աննկարագրելի է: Չկայ շէնք մը որ դուռ ու պատուհան ունենայ: Փողոցները խոտերով ծածկուած, շէնքերը

The Millis who fired at Yenice's sacristan, Mr. Hampartsoum, have been arrested and punished. The Greek authorities summoned the headmen and mullahs and warned them that they would be held accountable and punished for any incident.

Greek officers told the Armenian spiritual leader that all Christian men over the age of twelve had been uprooted from Uşak, Afyonkarahisar, Ketanya, Eskişehir, and Aksakal and taken to Beypazarı, Harput, Yozgat, and Sivas. The same has been confirmed by a few escapees arriving in Bursa who managed to avoid deportation.

Afyonkarahisar (from the Neighborhood Council)—August 19

On September 25, 1920, 540 young people, ages twenty through forty, from the Armenian population of Afyonkarahisar were deported to a place called Şereflikoçhisar [Koçhisar], located between Konya and Ankara. Until [recently], they were in deplorable condition. Now it is not known where or in what condition they are.

On March 25, 1921, Afyonkarahisar was captured by the Greek army. The city's population had barely breathed a sigh of relief when the city was evacuated for military reasons. Due to the winter snow, blizzard, and heavy rains, the Christian population was not able to escape with the Greek army, so it became a toy in the hands of barbaric Kemalists again. The Armenian people suffered persecution and various tortures. Finally, they were deported again, this time all those between the ages of fourteen to seventy or seventy-five. Thus, more than four hundred Armenians and Greeks were rounded up and sent on foot to Sivas, Harput, and Malatya. The condition of the exiles, who were unprepared [as they were] arrested from the market and the hideouts of houses, is very distressing. There were among them those who set out with five to ten kuruş banknotes [only]. On July 13, 1921, when war was raging around this city, the mob of local Turks, women included, armed with axes, sickles, and all kinds of tools, approached and besieged the Armenian neighborhoods. A crier announced: "O children of Muhammad and believers of the Qur'an, prepare to crush the Christians, especially the Armenian infidels!" Hearing this terrifying announcement, about twenty fifteen- to twenty-year-old Armenian teenagers left their hideouts and ran to escape, but they were immediately caught and killed. Half an hour later, the Greek army captured the city and saved the lives of the remaining Christians.

On the same day, after calm in the city was restored, the corpses of four of the twenty murdered young men were found in the sewers in an unrecognizable condition. Their hands and feet had been mutilated, their eyes carved out, and their skins stripped from their bodies. The bodies of the other young men are still being searched for, but they have not been found.

There are now about one thousand Armenians in Afyonkarahisar, ninety of whom are deaf, mute, and blind men; the rest are women and children. There is no priest to comfort them spiritually or to give moral advice to the widows.

Samsun (from a private letter)—August 8[118]

There has been a horrible massacre in Samsun again. On July 20–21, Osman Ağa (nicknamed Topal Osman of Giresun) tried to deport Samsun's Greeks with his followers, but he could not do so. He wanted to burn [them] with a second attempt, but again he failed because of the opposition of the [city's Turkish] people and the help of foreign powers. He left Samsun upon this defeat and began to burn Greek women, girls, and children in their homes in Beşpınar [Çakal]. The men had already been long gone. Not satiated with Beşpınar, he did the same in Kavak. An eighty-six-year-old Greek was

փլատակ եւ ապակիներու բեկորներով լի են փողոցները:

Ենիճէի լուսարար պ. Համբարձումի վրայ կրակ ընող Միլիճիները ձերբակալուած եւ պատժուած են: Հելլէն իշխանութիւնը մխթարները եւ մօլաները կանչելով պատուէր տուած է որ ոեւէ դէպքի համար իրենք պատասխանատու պիտի բռնուին եւ պատժուին:

Հելլէն սպաներ հայոց Առաջնորդին պատմած են թէ Ուշագի, Աֆիոն-Գարահիսարի, Քէթանիայի, Էսկիշէհիրի, Աք-Սազալի եւայլն բոլոր քրիստոնեայ այր մարդիկը 12 տարեկանէ վեր հանած եւ տարած են Պէյ-Բազար, Խարբերդ, Եօզկաթ, Սըվազ: Նոյնը կը հաւաստեն Պրուսա հասնող սակաւաթիւ փախստականներ, որոնք կրցած են զերծ մնալ տեղահանութենէն:

Աֆիոն Գարահիսար (Թաղական Խորհուրդէն) – 19 Օգոստոս

1920 Սեպտեմբեր 25ին Աֆիոն Գարահիսարի հայ բնակչութեան 20–40 տարեկան երիտասարդներէ 540 հոգի աքսորուած էր Գոչհիսար կոչուած վայրը, որ կը գտնուի Գոնիայի եւ Էնկիւրիւի միջեւ: Մինչեւ հիմա հոն կը գտնուէին յետին աստիճան թշուառ վիճակի մէջ, սակայն այժմ յայտնի չէ թէ ո՞ւր եւ ի՞նչ վիճակի մէջ կը գտնուին:

1921 Մարտ 25ին Աֆ[իոն] Գարահիսար գրաւուեցաւ հելլէն բանակին կողմէ, բայց շաբաթ մը հազիւ քաղաքին բնակչութիւնը հանգիստ շունչ մը առած էր, ռազմական պատճառներով քաղաքը պարպուեցաւ: Ձմրան ձիւն ու բուքին ու սաստիկ անձրեւներու պատճառով քրիստոնեայ բնակչութիւնը չկրցաւ հելլէն բանակին հետ խոյս տալ եւ կրկին խաղալիկ դարձաւ բարբարոս քէմալիստներու ձեռքը: Հալածանքներ եւ զանազան տանջանքներ կրեց հայ ժողովուրդը: Վերջապէս կրկին տարագրուեցան, այս անգամ 14 տարեկանէն մինչեւ 70–75 տարեկան ծերունիները: Այսպէս՝ հայ եւ յոյն 400է աւելի անձեր ժողովուեցան եւ հետիոտն ղրկուեցան դէպի Սըվազ-Խարբերդ ու Մալաթիա: Արդէն անպատրաստ, շուկայէն ու տուներու թագստոցներէն բռնուած աքսորեալներու վիճակը շատ խղճալի էր: Նոյնիսկ կա[յին] իրենց մէջ 5–10 դրշ. թղթադրամով ճամբայ ելլողներ: 1921 Յուլիս 13ին երբ պատերազմը քաղաքիս շրջակայքը կը մղուէր, տեղացի թուրքեր, ինչպէս նաեւ թուրք կիներ, իբր խուժան, զինուած կացիններով, մանգաղներով եւ ամէն տեսակ հատու գործիքներով, հայոց թաղերուն մօտենալով եւ պաշարելով, մունետիկ կանչել տուին ըսելով. «Պատրաստուեցէ՛ք ով Մուհամմէտի զաւակներ ու Գուրանի հաւատացեալներ ջարդելու քրիստոնեայ, մանաւանդ հայ կեավուրները»: Այս ահարկու ձայնը լսող 15–20 տարեկան հայ պատանիներ ձգելով իրենց թագստոցը 20 հոգիի չափ դուրս կը վազեն փախչելու նպատակաւ, իսկոյն կը բռնուին եւ կը սպաննուին: Կէս ժամ վերջը յոյն բանակը գրաւելով քաղաքը, մնացեալ քրիստոնեաներու կեանքը կը փրկուի:

Նոյն օրը քաղաքին մէջ անդորրութիւնը հաստատուելէն վերջ 20 սպաննեալ երիտասարդներէն 4ին դիակները գտնուեցան կոյուղիներու մէջէն յօշոտուած, ձեռքերնին, ոտքերնին կտրուած, աչքերնին փորուած եւ մորթերնին քերթուած, անճանաչելի վիճակի մէջ: Դեռ կը փնտռուին մնացեալներուն դիակները, սակայն չեն գտնուած:

Այժմ Աֆիոն-Գարահիսարի մէջ կը գտնուին 1000ի մօտ հայեր, որոնց 90-ը կը բաղկանայ խուլ համր, կաղ ու կոյր էրիկ մարդոցմէ, իսկ մնացեալները կին ու պզտիկներ: Քահանայ չկայ որպէսզի հոգեւորապէս մխիթարէ եւ անայր կիներու բարոյական խրատներ տայ:

Սամսոն (մասնաւոր նամակէ) – 8 Օգոստոս

Մարզուան նորէն ջարդ եղած է սոսկալիօրէն: Յուլիս 20–21ին Օսման աղան (Կիրասոնի Թօփալ Օսման մականուանեալ) իր արբանեակներով միասին ուզեց Սամսոնի յոյները հանել, բայց չկրցաւ: Երկրորդ անգամ ուզեց այրել, նորէն ժողովուրդին ընդդիմութենէն եւ օտար պետութիւններու օգնութենէն նորէն չկրցաւ: Այս պարտութեան վրայ Սամսոնէն մեկնելով, Չախալէն սկսաւ յոյներու կիներ, աղջիկներ ու պզտիկներ տուներու մէջ այրել: Արդէն էրիկ մարդիկ շատոնց գացած էին: Չախալէն ալ չգոհանալով, Խավախ ալ նոյնը կ'ընէ: Հոն մէկ հատ 86 տարեկան յոյն մը կ'ա-

the only survivor there, at the plea of Bekir Pasha's wife. Third, [Osman] himself went to Havza. An hour before his entry, he sent the çetes to the city, and they surrounded it. Upon his arrival, he had all the Armenians and Greeks gathered together. However, before assembling them, he arranged for the escape of Bayram Effendi's clerk, Hagop, and his family. After all the men were gathered, he had them killed by the river. On the same day, they took eighteen brides and bridesmaids, abducting them after spending the night with them. The next day, they put them in a house during broad daylight and burned them completely. Over these two days, the forty-four villages around Havza were wholly burned down along with their inhabitants. Exceptions were Osmanoğlu and another village. The people in those villages were prepared before these events and had gone to the government of Havza saying, "Dispatch us." They had gone to Hünkar, but it is unknown what happened to them. The prices of goods brought from the villages during this massacre are unprecedented. Imagine a cow sold for fifty to one hundred kuruş. In short, the Havza massacre ended with this kind of destruction, and he [Osman] continued to Merzifon. On the day he entered Merzifon, he demanded money from all Armenians and Greeks, especially setting amounts beyond their means. The trembling and awe-stricken people gave it. Immediately after collecting [the money], [Osman arranged for] the [non-Muslim] people to be gathered, but not the Armenians.

At the time, Kabalci Yuvan was not present in Merzifon, so they [the çetes] went to his house, which was behind Tyuleg's house, and they [the residents of the house] resisted with weapons. Angry, the çetes set the house on fire. Meanwhile, [fires] started from other places as well. In short, they set fire to the city from all sides. During the fire, the people and the remaining Armenians came out [of their homes] to save their property. When they did, they were killed. The massacre was carried on until evening and for four days. Kabalci Yuvan killed his son and family with his own hands so he did not have to hand them over [to the çetes]. The day we received this news, the people of Merzifon had sent a cable [to all residents], but only Tyuleg and Vosganian received the news, along with Yezegielian. There has been no news from others. But in the end, we were left in despair; there was no additional information yet. The number of houses burned in Merzifon is between 1,800 to 2,000, from Yokuşbaşı to the college. You already know how many people were in the city (around 1,300). Now barely 200–250 of them are left, all women. There are hardly two or three men. It is not known who the remaining people are. There has only been news from the family of Hagop Effendi Aslanian, that is, from his family in Merzifon, the Yezegielians, and the Tyulegians. There has been no news from any other family.

The Turkish people, leading the çetes, pointed out the houses of Armenians. During the massacre, as [the çetes] struck and killed, they exclaimed: "How [dare you] turn into Armenians after you had become Turks?" This is the content of a cable that came under the name Zaroug: "I am naked, I have no food; send me money!" It was sent to Tyuleg and Elbig. The survivors are Vahan [son] of Apel, Merzifon's teacher Samson, and two or three men. Simon's murder is actual; the two elders of the Keremetian family were put to death atop each other. In short, an unbelievable and indescribable massacre has occurred in Merzifon, unseen since the beginning of the world.

Brides, women, and girls were abducted in the streets and taken away. For example, the wife and children of Vahan [son] of Apel were slaughtered, imagine, before that [*sic*]. Those who wanted to save their property during the Merzifon fire were caught and thrown into the fire. The death of Tyouleg's sisters happened in this way: when the house of Kabalci Yuvan was set on fire, they were inside and could not escape because the house was surrounded. The two sisters hugged each other and were burned in the house.

Gyonji's mother has allegedly lost her sanity, Gyonji himself died, and his son ran away. In short, we are left with fatigued minds.

զատի, այն ալ Պէքիր Փաշայի կնոջը աղաչանքովը: Գ. Խավզա կ'երթայ ինքը: Հոն մտնելէն մէկ ժամ առաջ չէթէները կը ղրկէ քաղաքը, ամբողջ կը շրջապատեն, իր գալուն քաղաքին մէջ գտնուող հայ եւ յոյները ամբողջ ժողովել կու տայ, միայն դեռ մարդիկը չժողված, Պայրամ էֆէնտիի Յակոբ անուն գրագիրը ընտանիքովը կը փախցնէ, ժողվել տալէ վերջ մարդիկը գետին մօտերը սպաննել կու տայ: Նոյն օրը 18 հատ հարս եւ աղջիկներ կ'առնեն գիշերը իրենց քով մնալէն վերջ կ'առեւանգեն եւ յաջորդ ցորեկին՝ տունի մը մէջ դնելով կ'այրեն ամբողջովին: Այս երկու օրուան մէջը Խավզայի շուրջ գտնուած 44 հատ գիւղերը ամբողջովին այրուած են իրենց բնակիչներով միասին: Միայն Օսման Օղլու եւ մէկ հատ ալ ուրիշ գիւղ մը այս դէպքերէն առաջ պատրաստուեր եւ Խավզայի կառավարութիւնը եկած «Մեզի *սէվգ* ըրէք» ըսելով Հիւնքեար գացած են, բայց անոնց ալ ինչ ըլլալը յայտնի չէ: Այս ջարդի միջոցին գիւղերէ բերուած ապրանքներու աժանութիւնը բնաւ մէկ տեղ տեսնուած չէ: Երեւակայեցէք մէկ հատ կովը 50–100 ղրշ.ի կը ծախուի: Վերջապէս Խավզայի ջարդը այս տեսակ աւերներ ընելով կը լմննայ, կ'անցնի Մարզուան: Մարզուան մտած օրը ամբողջ հայ եւ յոյն ժողովուրդէն դրամ կը պահանջէ, յատուկէն իրենց կարողութենէն վեր եղած գումարներով: Ժողովուրդը դողալով, վախնալով կը բերեն կու տան: Ժողովելէն անմիջապէս վերջը ժողովուրդ ժողովել կու տան, բայց ոչ հայերը:

Այս միջոցին Մարզուան Ղապալճի Իւվանը չի գտնուիր, անոր տունը կ'երթան, որ Թիւլէկին տունի[ն] ետեւն է եղեր, զէնքով կը սկսին դիմադրել: Չէթէները, ասոր վրայ, բարկանալով, տունը կրակի կու տան: Նոյն միջոցին ուրիշ տեղերէ ալ կը սկսի: Վերջապէս քաղաքին չորս կողմէն կրակ կու տան: Կրակին ժամանակ ժողովուրդը, մնացող հայերը իրենց գոյքերը ազատելու համար դուրս կ'ելլեն սակայն կը սպաննուին եւ այսպէս ջարդը կը կատարուի մինչեւ երեկոյ եւ չորս օր: Ղապալճի Եուվանը իր զաւակը եւ ընտանիքը չյանձնելու համար ինքը իր ձեռքով սպաննած է: Մենք այս լուրը առած օրերնիս, Մարզուանցիք ամբողջ հեռագիր տուած են, բայց հազիւ Թիւլէկը եւ Ոսկանեանը լուր կրցած են առնել եւ մէկ մըն ալ Եզեկիէլեանը. միւսներ[էն] դեռ ոչ մէկ լուր ելած է: Բայց վերջապէս յուսահատ մնացեր ենք. դեռ ոչ մէկ տեղեկութիւն կայ: Մարզուանի այրած տուներուն քանակութիւնը՝ 1800էն 2000 տուն, Եօքուշպաշըէն մինչեւ գօլէճը. քաղաքին մէջ գտնուած ժողովուրդին գումարը արդէն ձեզի ծանօթ էր (1300ի մօտ): Բայց հիմա անոնցմէ մնացած են հազիւ 200–250 հոգի, որոնք կիներ են. հազիւ երկու երեք հոգի այր մարդիկ կան: Դեռ մնացող ժողովուրդին ո՞վ եւ որո՞նք ըլլալը յայտնի չեն. միայն Ասլանեան Յակոբ էֆէնտիի ընտանիքէ[ն], այսինքն Մարզուանի տունէն, Եզեկիէլեաններէն եւ Թիւլէկեաններէն լուր կայ. ուրիշ ոչ մէկ տունէ լուր կայ:

Ջարդի ժամանակ թուրք ժողովուրդը չէթէներու առջեւ ինկած հայերու տուները ցոյց տուած են: Սպանութեան ժամանակին *Նա՛սըլ, թուրք օլըրքտան սօնրա, էրմէնի օլուրսընըզ*,[20] ըսելով զարկած սպաննած են: Հեռագրին մէկ հատին,- որ Ջարուկ անունով եկած է,- պարունակութիւնը այս է[21],- «Մերկ եմ, ուտելիք չունիմ, դրամ ղրկեցէք» ըսելով, Թիւլէկին եւ Էլպիկին եկած է: Ողջ մնացողներն ասոնք են՝ Աբէլին Վահանը, Մարզուանցի ուսուցիչը, որ Սամսոնն էր. երկու երեք հատ ալ այր մարդիկ: Սիմոնին սպանութիւնը իրաւ է, Քէրէմեթեաններու երկու ծերերը վրայ վրայի դնելով մեռցուցած են: Վերջապէս անհաւատալի եւ աննկարագրելի եւ աշխարհի սկիզբէն մինչեւ այսօր չտեսնուած ջարդ մ'եղած է Մարզուանի մէջ:

Փողոցներու մէջ առեւանգ[ու]ած հարսեր, կիներ, աղջիկներ իրենց հետ առնել տանիլ: Օրինակ, Աբէլի Վահանին կինը եւ զաւակները մորթուած են, երեւակայեցէք, անկէ առաջ: Մարզուանի հրդեհի ատեն գոյքերնին ազատել ուզողները բռնած կրակը նետած են: Թիւլէկին քոյրերուն մեռնիլը այսպէս եղած է: Երբ որ Ղապալճի Եուվանին տունը այրեցին, անոնք մէջն են եղեր, չեն կրցեր փախ[չ]իլ, որովհետեւ տունը ամբողջ շրջապատուած է եղեր: Երկու քոյր իրարու փաթթուելով, տունին մէջ այրած են:

Կէօնճիի մայրը խեւցած, Կէօնճին ինքը մեռած եւ տղան ալ փախած է եղեր: Վերջապէս ա՛լ խելքերնիս միտքերնիս յոգնած մնացեր ենք:

Adana (from the National Council)—September 20

It has been reported earlier that the Armenians leaving Süleymanlı [Zeytun] were caught in a fight with the Turks near Andırın and were forced to divide into different groups. One of the groups arrived in Ceyhan on foot, but they failed to cross the river and were almost completely wiped out by the çetes. Only three members of that group escaped to Osmaniye. These had no news about the other groups, but gradually the people of Süleymanlı who reached Adana enlightened us about them. After suffering heavy losses—especially women—and noticing that it was absolutely impossible to cross into the French occupation zone, these groups returned to Süleymanlı, always waiting for the right opportunity to set out again. Indeed, after gathering themselves and supplementing the necessary supplies and ammunition, they set out to descend to Osmaniye. The group comprised 153 people. They fought with the enemy for days and finally reached Şekeroba, three hours away from Kozdere [İntilli]. They entered a marsh filled with reeds, fighting with Turkish çetes in wait. The latter set fire to the reeds but failed to achieve anything. The people of Süleymanlı managed to escape by night. They headed to Kilis this time, having given up the aim of descending to Osmaniye.

When they were near Kilis, unfortunately, ten fell victim to a trap set by the çetes. The incident happened as follows.

When the Turkish çetes in the vicinity of Kilis noticed this armed group and realized that they were Armenians, band leaders native of Urfa who knew Armenian began to shout: "Come to us, we are Armenians, we are French guards, we can save you!" The people of Süleymanlı, thinking that çetes could not exist in those parts because of the proximity to the French zone, sent ten people—four women and six men—to the Armenian-speaking guards. At first, the Turks exchanged flattering words with them not to arouse suspicion, but when they began the search, the other vanguards of Süleymanlı Armenians, seeing this, became suspicious and immediately took up arms. The clash began, but the ten people had already been killed. The clash intensified gradually. A group of 108 people from Süleymanlı, who were waiting a short distance away, heard the gunfire, came forward, and joined the fight. At this time, the people of Süleymanlı sent some of their party to Kilis to brief the local authorities. The messengers reached their destination safe and sound. Upon learning the details of the incident, the French authorities sent forces, dispersed the çetes, and transported the 108 Armenians from Süleymanlı to the city, including the corpses of those murdered. The Armenians and the French authorities gave the survivors special compassionate treatment. The French government in Kilis reported the incident to the local General, and the latter relayed it to the Catholicos of Cilicia.

Although there is no exact information about the other [groups] and the number of survivors, former teacher N. Zeytountsian, who had been in a group separated from the others during the Şekeroba fight, provided the following numbers as an eyewitness after he arrived in Adana.

According to him, 1,050 people returned to Süleymanlı. About 500 were transferred to Maraş after being handed over to the Kemalists before the start of this war, and 320 cut through the siege line and took refuge on the mountain. That left 270 people in the barracks. They were also transferred to Maraş. The number of people transported to Maraş reached 770, although those arriving from Maraş mention only 600 people. On the other hand, during the retreat, the group of 320 people was reduced to 153, but not all of the unaccounted for were killed because 40 people in this group took shelter in Adana, Osmaniye, and Dörtyol, and 108 people took refuge in Kilis. Therefore, according to these explanations, if the people transported to Maraş are also alive, the victims should not exceed 105. There are 24 people from Süleymanlı in Adana: 3 women and 21 men.

• Apart from the people of Süleymanlı, there is a large community in Adana whose situation is gradually becoming unbearable. Subsidies have ended from all sides. The French authorities, even the [American Near East] Relief, provide minimal assistance to only a few. More than five thousand

Ատանա (Ազգային Խորհուրդէն) – 20 Սեպտեմբեր

Անկէ առաջ իմացուած էր թէ Զէյթունէն մեկնող հայերը Անտէրունի մօտ թուրքերու հետ կռիւի բռնուելով ստիպուած էին զանազան խումբերու բաժնուիլ: Ասոնցմէ մէկը մինչեւ Ճիհան եկած էր ոտքով, գետը չէր կրցած անցնիլ եւ գրեթէ ամբողջովին փճացած էր չէթէներու կողմէ: Այդ խումբէն երեք հոգի միայն ազատուելով հասած էին Օսմանիյէ: Ասոնք միւս խումբերէն լուր չունէին, բայց հետզհետէ Ատանա հասնող զէյթունցիներ մեզ լուսաբանած էին ատոնց մասին: Այդ խումբերը բաւական կորուստ տալէ յետոյ,- մանաւանդ կիները,- եւ նշմարելով որ բացարձակապէս անկարելի է ֆրանսական գրաւման գօտին անցնիլ, Զէյթուն կը վերադառնան, բայց միշտ յարմար առիթը կը սպասեն դարձեալ ճամբայ ելլելու համար: Արդարեւ, իրենք զիրենք ժողվելէ եւ պէտք եղած պաշարն ու ռազմանիւթը ամբողջացնելէ վերջ, ճամբայ կ'ելլեն ասոնք Օսմանիէ իջնելու նպատակով: Խումբը կը բաղկանար 153 հոգիէ: Ասոնք օրերով կը կռուին թշնամիին հետ եւ վերջապէս կը հասնին Ինթըլլիէն երեք ժամ հեռու Շէքէր-Օպայի առջեւ: Հոն եղեգնուտը կը մտնեն, բնականաբար կռուելով շրջակաները սպասող թուրք չէթէներու հետ: Այս վերջինները եղեգնուտը կրակի կուտան, բայց բան մը չեն կրնար ընել: Զէյթունցիները գիշերանց կը յաջողին դուրս ելլել եւ կ'ուղղուին այս անգամ դէպի Քիլիս, Օսմանիյէ իջնելու նպատակէն հրաժարելով:

Երբ Քիլիսի մօտերը կը հասնին, դժբախտաբար իրենց մէջէն 10 հոգի չէթէներու լարած մէկ թակարդին զոհ կ'երթան: Դէպքը տեղի կ'ունենայ հետեւեալ կերպով:

Քիլիսի շրջակաները գտնուող թուրք չէթէներ երբ այս զինուած խումբը կը նշմարեն եւ կը հասկնան թէ հայեր են, իրենց մէջէն ուրփացի հայերէն գիտցող խմբապետներ կը սկսին պոռալ. «Դէպի մեզ եկէք, մենք հայեր ենք, ֆրանսական պահակներ ենք, ձեզի կրնանք ազատել»: Զէյթունցիները մտածելով թէ այդ կողմերը ֆրանսական գօտիին շատ մօտ ըլլալով չէթէներ չէին կրնար գոյութիւն ունենալ, հայերէն խօսող պահակներուն քով կը ղրկեն 10 հոգի, չորսը կին եւ վեցը այր: Ասոնց հետ առաջին անգամ թուրքերը փաղաքշական խօսքեր կը փոխանակեն կասկած չտալու համար, բայց երբ խուզարկութեան կը սկսին, զէյթունցի միւս յառաջապահները այս բանը տեսնելով կը կասկածին ու անմիջապէս զէնքի կը փաթթուին: Ընդհարումը կը սկսի, բայց 10 հոգին արդէն սպաննուած էին: Ընդհարումը երթալով կը սաստկանայ, այնպէս որ քիչ մը հեռու սպասող զէյթունցիներու 108 հոգինոց խումբը հրացանի ձայներ լսելով դէպի առաջ կուգայ եւ կը մասնակցի կռուին: Այդ միջոցին զէյթունցիները իրենց մէջէն մի քանի հոգի կը ղրկեն Քիլիս տեղւոյն իշխանութեանց լուր տալու համար: Սուրհանդակները կը հասնին ողջ եւ առողջ եւ ֆրանսական իշխանութիւնը, դէպքին մանրամասնութիւնները իմանալէ վերջ, ուժ կը ղրկէ, չէթէները կը ցրուէ եւ 108 զէյթունցիները կը փոխադրէ քաղաք, սպաննուածներուն դիակներն ալ միասին, ուր անոնք թէ՛ հայերուն եւ թէ՛ ֆրանսական իշխանութեան կողմէ մասնաւոր գուրգուրանքի ու խնամքներու առարկայ կ'ըլլան: Քիլիսի ֆրանսական կառավարութիւնը տեղեկագրած է այս եղելութիւնը տեղւոյն զօրավարին եւ այս վերջինն ալ զանոնք հաղորդած Կիլիկ[իոյ] Կաթողիկոսին:

Թէեւ միւսներուն եւ ողջ մնացողներուն թիւին մասին ստոյգ տեղեկութիւն մը չկայ, բայց Շէքէր-Օպայի կռուին միջոցին խումբէն բաժնուելով մինչեւ Ատանա եկող երբեմնի ուսուցիչ պ. Ն. Զէյթունցեան կուտայ հետեւեալ թիւերը, իբր ականատես:

Անոր տեղեկութեանց համաձայն, Զէյթուն վերադարձած են 1050 հոգի, որոնցմէ շուրջ 500-ը տակաւին կռիւը չսկսած քէմալականներու յանձնուելով Մարաշ փոխադրուած են, իսկ 320-ը պաշարման գիծը ճեղքելով լեռը ապաստանած, զօրանոցի մէջ ձգելով 270 հոգի, որոնք նոյնպէս Մարաշ փոխադրուած են, ինչպէս կը լսուի: Մարաշ փոխադրուողներու թիւը կը հասնի 770ի, թէեւ Մարաշէն եկողները 600 հոգի կ'ըսեն միայն: Միւս կողմէ նախանցի ժամանակ 320 հոգինոց խումբին թիւը կ'իջնէ 153ի, բայց պակսողներուն ամէնն ալ սպաննուած չէին, որովհետեւ սոյն խումբին պատկանող 40 հոգի Ատանա, Օսմանիյէ եւ Տէօրթ-Եօլ կրցած են ապաստանիլ, իսկ 108 հոգի ալ Քիլիս: Հետեւաբար, այս բացատրութեանց համաձայն, եթէ Մարաշ փոխադրուողներն ալ ողջ են, զոհերուն թիւը 105-ը չ'անցնիր: Ատանայի մէջ գտնուող զէյթունցիները 24 հոգի են. 3 կին, 21 էրիկմարդ:

people—homeless, without food, and covered with rags—beg for help. The local people are in a state of economic depression; their condition is almost no different from the migrants. Some mothers are abandoning their children to be able to live. The national authorities do not have the means to satisfy the boundless need, at least partly. The Turkish population of the city, who left, is returning in groups and forcing the refugees settled in their apartments to evacuate them. This issue has been brought to the attention of the local authorities, but it is very difficult, if not impossible, to make an arrangement satisfying both sides.

Aleppo (from vicar general Father Haroutyun Yesayan)—September 27

We gather the following information from Miss McIntyre (of American [Near East] Relief) who recently arrived from Maraş. Maraş has ten thousand Armenians, of whom eight thousand were previously cared for by American [Near East] Relief. It now takes care of four thousand and intends to reduce it to twenty-five hundred. The local Armenians enlist in the army; that is, they are kept in the city with two loaves of bread a day and are paid one mecidiye as a reward once every fifteen days; therefore, their families are in terrible misery. One thousand drams of bread is worth one mecidiye. Money is essential both for the Armenians [to stay in Maraş] and as ransom to provide them with a bit of rest. Two to four hundred liras can ensure that local Armenians stay there; otherwise, they face the fear of deportation. In the past, the military authorities treated the Armenians quite kindly, but now, with the withdrawal of the military, the Armenians are facing great hardship from the city authorities. Especially, District Governor Rafet Bey treats Armenians with unparalleled severity. Only money can alleviate the Armenians' suffering. Most of the houses have been demolished, and there is a terrible shortage of apartments.

The American [Near East] Relief shelters twelve hundred orphans in the orphanage. Vicar general Reverend Father Khachadour and the Armenian Catholic prelate Bishop Avedis Arpiarian are active [within the community] in their capacity.

Hovsep Khurlakian and his two friends were taken to Kayseri for trial. It had been heard that they were pronounced innocent. As many as twenty Armenians have been jailed again on charges of communicating with Aleppo.

• The American [Near East] Relief initiated the opening of the Central School, but they were forced to postpone it due to a lack of budget. Nevertheless, it will continue [its efforts] if Armenians contribute at least part of the money to help with the budget.

• Six hundred twenty-four people from Süleymanlı [Zeytun] were brought to Maraş from Süleymanlı. Then they were deported to Besni, Adıyaman [Hısnımansur], and Malatya, but this deportation is very sad and heartbreaking: they were traveling on foot, and they had left most of their belongings in Maraş. About forty sick and weak people were left there temporarily.

In addition to these statements, the unmarried woman reporting these events repeated several times, emphatically, that only money for ransom can provide some relief from deportation to the Armenians of Maraş, especially while Lieutenant Governor Rafet Bey is in office.

• Twenty-four of the 114 Süleymanlı residents brought here from Kilis last Saturday were sent to Dörtyol by the [Armenian General] Benevolent [Union] yesterday. Regarding the rest, arrangements are being made by the Benevolent [Union], the National Union, and local means. The Armenian General Benevolent Union's attendance to this effect is particularly commendable.

- Չէյթունցիներէն զատ Ատանայի մէջ կայ խոշոր գաղութ մը, որոյ վիճակը հետզհետէ անտանելի կը դառնայ: Ամէն կողմէ նպաստները դադրած են. ֆրանսական իշխանութիւնք անգամ նաեւ Րըլիֆ[ը] շատ սահմանափակ օգնութիւններ միայն կ'ընձեռեն ան ալ շատ քիչերու. աւելի քան 5000 ժողովուրդ անբնակ, անսնունդ, ցնցոտիներու մէջ ասկից անկից ճար ճարակ կը մուրան: Տեղացի ժողովուրդը տնտեսական տագնապի մատնուած, ան ալ գաղթականներէն տարբեր վիճակ մը չունի գրեթէ: Մայրեր կան որ զաւակնին կը նետեն կարենալ ապրելու համար: Ազգային իշխանութիւնք միջոցներ չունին անսահման կարօտութեան գոնէ մասամբ հասնելու համար: Քաղաքին թուրք բնակչութիւնը, որ հեռացած էր, խումբ խումբ կը վերադառնայ եւ կը ստիպէ որ իր բնակարանին մէջ տեղաւորուած գաղթականները պարպեն զայն: Տեղական իշխանութեանց ուշադրութեան յանձնուած է այս պարագան, բայց երկու կողմն ալ գոհացնող կարգադրութիւն մը ըլլալ եթէ ոչ անհնարին, գէթ շատ դժուար է:

Հալէպ (Առաջնորդական Փոխանորդ Յար[ութիւն] Քահանայ Եսայեանէ) – 27 Սեպտեմբեր

Մարաշէն նոր եկող Օր. Մէքընթայրէ (Ամերիկեան Ռըլիֆէն) կը քաղենք հետեւեալ տեղեկութիւնները: Մարաշ ունի 10000 հայութիւն, որուն նախապէս 6000ը Ամերիկեան Րըլիֆը կը հոգար: Այժմ 4000ը կը հոգայ եւ մտադրած է 2500ի իջեցնել: Տեղւոյն հայերը կը զինուորագրուին տեղւոյն վրայ, այսինքն քաղաքին մէջ կը պահեն օրական երկուական հացով եւ 15 օրը մէկ անգամ մէյ մէկ մէճիտ տալով որպէս վարձ, որով սոսկալի թշուառութեան մատնուած է անոնց ընտանիքը: Հացի 1000 տրամը մէկ մէճիտ կ'արժէ: Դրամի ծայր աստիճան պէտք կայ թէ՛ հայութեան համար եւ թէ՛ անոնց հանգիստը քիչ մը ապահովելու համար որպէս փրկանք տալու համար: 200–400 ոսկիով կարելի է ապահովել տեղւոյն հայոց հոն մնալը, հակառակ պարագային տարագրուելու երկիւղին տակ կը գտնուին: Նախապէս զինուորական իշխանութիւնը բաւական բարեացակամութեամբ կը վարուէր հայոց հետ, սակայն այժմ զինուորականութիւնը քաշուած [ըլլալով,] քաղաքա[յին] իշխանութեան կողմէն սոսկալի կը նեղուին: Մանաւանդ միւթէսարրըֆ Րաֆէթ պէյ անօրինակ խստութեամբ կը վարուի հայոց հետ: Դրամով միայն կարելի է թեթեւցնել հայոց տառապանքը: Տուները մեծ մասամբ քանդուած ըլլալով, բնակարանի սոսկալի նեղութիւն կայ:

Որբանոցին մէջ 1200 որբ կը պատսպարուի Ամերիկեան Րըլիֆի կողմէ: Առաջնորդական Փոխանորդ Տ. Խաչատուր Վարդապետ եւ հայ կաթողիկէ Առաջնորդ Տ. Աւետիս Եպիսկոպոս Արփիարեան իրենց պաշտօնին գլուխն են:

Յովսէփ Խըրլագեան եւ երկու ընկերները Կեսարիա դատուելու տարուած էին: Կը լսուի թէ ատոնք անպարտ արձակուած են: 20-ի չափ հայեր նորէն բանտարկուած են Հալէպի հետ հաղորդակցութեան ամբաստանութեամբ:

- Ամերիկեան Րըլիֆը Կեդրոնական Վարժարանը բանալ ձեռնարկած է, բայց պիւտճէի անբաւականութեան պատճառով ստիպուած են յետաձգելու: Այսու հանդերձ պիտի շարունակէ եթէ հայերը գէթ մաս մը դրամով կարենան մասնակցիլ պիւտճէին օգնելու:

- Չէյթունէն Մարաշ բերուած 624 զէյթունցիներ տարագրուած են դէպի Պէհիսնի, Ադըեաման, Մալաթիա, բայց այս տարագրումը իր տեսակին մէջ շատ տխուր եւ սրտաճմլիկ [է]: Հետիոտն իւրաքանչիւր տարագրեալ իր իրեղէններէն մեծ մասը Մարաշ թողած, միմիայն 40ի չափ հիւանդներ եւ տկարներ թողուած են տեղւոյն վրայ առժամաբար:

Տեղեկատու օրիորդը այս յայտարարութիւններուն իբր շեշտեալ յաւելուած քանիցս կրկնեց թէ փրկանքի համար դրամն է որ Մարաշու հայութիւնը պիտի քիչ մը ապահովէ տարագրութենէն, մանաւանդ ներկայ միւթէսարրըֆ Րաֆէթ պէյի օրով:

- Շաբաթ մ'առաջ Քիլիսէն հոս բերուած 114 զէյթունցիներէն 24ը երէկ Բարեգործականի միջոցաւ Տէօրթ-Եօլ ղրկուեցան: Մնացեալներուն մասին Բարեգործականի, Ազգային Միութեան եւ տեղական միջոցներով կարգադրութիւնք կ'ըլլան: Մանաւանդ Հ.Բ.Ը. Միութեան առ այս հոգածութիւնը գովելի է:

[Insecurity Notebook Number 17]
September–December 1921

Kütahya (from vicar general Father Sahag Vartabedian)—September 12, 1921[119]

The misfortune that has befallen the Armenian population of Kütahya over the past year has been significant.

It was in the last week of last August 1920 that groups of bandits arrived in Kütahya, accompanied by one of Kemal's most prominent crime perpetrators, İsmail Hakkı, who began his days of doom by hanging and shooting dead whomever he considered guilty. He made the Armenian and Greek coachmen disappear together with their carts and horses, but only after making them labor for days in transportation. He killed two prominent Greek men near a nearby village, having them torn into pieces alive. His bandits killed about a dozen Greek and several Armenian Kütahya natives. Apart from these [murders], people have also been killed around the city. They remain unknown.

İsmail Hakkı, the despot, under the pretext of recruiting soldiers from the Armenians and Greeks, demanded a Mauser rifle for each soldier and two hundred soldiers from the Armenians. Through supplication and pleading, he accepted 124 Mausers from our people. To pay for them, many Armenians were forced to sell all their possessions, even their beds, because the cost of a Mauser is two hundred Ottoman liras. Therefore, the 350 Armenian families of Kütahya Armenians were obliged to pay the enormous amount of thirty thousand liras. İsmail Hakkı's satellites would take, on the one hand, these rifles and, on the other hand, their price and deliver them to him because the rifles sold already belonged to the government.

This was not enough: a few weeks later, he again demanded money from Christians who were thought to be wealthy. In particular, the names of twenty-three Armenians were written down, from each of whom was required two, three, or four thousand liras for a total of seventy-five thousand liras. The Armenians no longer had money to pay. They had given everything they possessed. He threatened to hang those who did not pay. He did whatever he wanted without any accountability; what he did was only a crime. Finding money was harder than dying; nevertheless, many wanted to sell their homes, but there were no buyers. Barely two thousand liras had been paid when this tyrant was recalled.

Immediately, high-ranking military commanders arrived, each surpassing the other in tyrannizing the Christians. On the night of September 9, 1920, they forced themselves into homes and began to take all the men, from seventeen- or eighteen-year-olds to the elderly, into custody and then deport them. The same cruelty marked the days that followed: they deported the feeble elderly, the lame, the blind, the disabled, the paralyzed, and the sick. These were driven all the way to Eskişehir on foot. Once there, although a physician examined the people and then sent them back to Kütahya the same week [considering they were unfit to continue the journey], along with the vicar general Father Sahag Vartabedian, Kütahya's military authorities detained them all and two days later exiled them again to Eskişehir. Then [they were driven] to Sivrihisar, Haymana, and Beypazarı, and six months later to Ankara, Kayseri, Sivas, Harput, and on to Diyarbakır where many remain until now. There has been no news from them for two months. Some died of misery and starvation, and others had their legs or arms amputated.

The elderly and the sick were ordered to be sent back to where they had come from, so they were sent to Eskişehir after their trial in Sivrihisar. They were detained there and not sent to Kütahya. Apart from that, houses were searched once in a while, and again the people were exiled to faraway places. The older people tried in Haymana and Beypazarı were not sent anymore. If they had been sent, more than one hundred people would have been saved today.

[Անապահովութեան Տետր Թիւ 17]
1921 Սեպտեմբեր – Դեկտեմբեր

Քէօթահիա (Առաջնորդական Փոխանորդ Սահակ Քահանայ Վար[դա]պետեանէ) – 12 Սեպտեմբեր 1921

Վերջին մէկ տարուան ընթացքին մէջ Քէօթահիոյ հայ բնակչութեան վրայ հասած դժբաղդութիւնները նշանաւոր եղած են:

Անցեալ 1920 Օգոստոսի վերջին շաբթուան մէջ էր որ Քէօթահիա կը հասնէին հրոսակներու խումբեր, որոնց հետ էր նաեւ Քէմալի եղեռնագործութեամբ հռչակաւոր մէկ գործիչը՝ Իսմայիլ Հազզը, որ իր արհաւիրքի օրերը սկսաւ կախաղան հանելով եւ հրացանի բռնելով ով որ մեղապարտ կը համարէր: Անհետացուց հայ եւ յոյն կառապանները իրենց կառքերովը ու ձիերովը միատեղ, փոխադրութեան համար զանոնք օրերով աշխատցնելէ յետոյ: Սպաննել տուաւ մօտաւոր գիւղի մը քով տեղւոյս յոյն երեւելիներէն երկու անձ, ողջ ողջ յօշոտել տալէ յետոյ զանոնք: Իր հրոսակները սպաննեցին քէօթահիացի մօտ տասներկու յոյներ եւ քանի մը հայեր: Ասոնցմէ դուրս քաղաքին շրջակայքն ալ սպաննուածներ կան, որոնք անծանօթ կը մնան:

Իսմայիլ Հազզը բռնաւորն՝ հայերէն եւ յոյներէն զինուոր առնելու պատրուակով՝ մէյմէկ մավզէր հրացան պահանջեց ամէն մէկ զինուորի համար: Մեր ժողովուրդէն ուզած 200 զինուորը աղաչելով պաղատելով, ոտք իյնալով 124 Մավզէրի իջեցուցին, զոր վճարելու համար շատ մը հայեր իրենց բոլոր ունեցածը, մինչեւ իսկ անկողինները ծախել հարկադրուեցան, վասնզի Մավզէր մը 200 լիրա օսմանեանի կ'առնուէր, այնպէս որ Քէօթահիայի 350 տուն հայերը 30,000 ոսկիի ահագին գումար մը վճարելու պարտաւորուեցան: Իսմայիլ Հազզըի արբանեակները մէկ կողմէն սոյն հրացանները, միւս կողմէն անոնց փոխարժէքը կը տանէին կը յանձնէին իրեն, վասնզի ծախուած հրացանները կառավարութեան կը պատկանէին արդէն:

Այս բաւական չէր եղած, քանի մը շաբաթ ետքը քրիստոնէից հարուստ կարծուածներէն դարձեալ ստակ պահանջեց, ի մասնաւորի մեր ազգէն 23 հոգիի անուն գրուած էր, որոնցմէ իւրաքանչիւրէն երկու, երեք, չորս հազար ոսկիի հաշուով 75,000 ոսկիի գումար մը պահանջեց, մինչդեռ հայերը այլեւս ստակ մը չունէին վճարելու, բոլոր ունեցածնին տուեր էին, չվճարողներուն կախա[ղ]ան սպառնաց, ուզածը կ'ընէր առանց ոչ մի պատասխանատուութեան եւ ինչ որ կ'ընէր ոճիր էր միայն: Ստակ գտնելը քան զմահ աւելի ծանր էր, սակայն շատերը իրենց տուները վաճառել կ'ուզէին, գնող չկար: Հազիւ 2000 ոսկիի չափ գումար մը եւս վճարուած էր երբ այս բռնաւորը ետ կանչուեցաւ:

Իսկոյն եկան զինուորական բարձրաստիճան հրամանատարներ, որոնք քրիստոնէից վրայ բռնանալու մէջ զիրար կը գերազանցէին: Ասոնք 1920 Սեպտ. 9ին գիշերը բռնի տուները մտան եւ սկսան բանտ տանիլ 17–18 տարեկան պատանիներէն մինչեւ ծերունիներ բոլոր այր մարդիկները եւ յետոյ աքսորել: Հետեւեալ օրերն եւս նշանաւոր եղան նոյն անգթութիւններով, աքսոր կը ղրկուէ[ին] անկար ծերունիներ ալ, նաեւ կաղեր, կոյրեր, անդամալոյծներ, կաթուածահարներ եւ հիւանդներ, որոնք մինչեւ Էսկիշէհիր հետիոտն քշուեցան եւ թէպէտ հոն բժիշկներէ քննուելով նոյն շաբթուան մէջ իսկ ետ ղրկուեցան ի Քէօթահիա, Առաջնորդական Տեղապահ Տ. Սահակ Քահանայ Վարդապետեան ալ միասին, սակայն Քէօթահիայի զինուորական իշխանութիւնը ամէնն ալ բանտարկեց եւ երկու օր յետոյ ամէնքը միասին նորէն աքսորուեցան Էսկիշէհիր, ուսկից Սիվրի-Հիսար, Հայմանա եւ Պէյ Բազար եւ վեց ամիս յետոյ ալ Էնկիւրիւ, Կեսարիա, Սրվազ, Խարբերդ եւ մինչեւ Տիարպէքիր, ուր շատեր կը մնան մինչեւ հիմա եւ երկու ամիս է որ ոչ մէկ լուր չկայ անոնցմէ: Եղան անոնց մէջ թշուառութենէ եւ անօթութենէ մեռնողներ, ոտքերնին կամ թեւերնին կտրուողներ[22]:

Աքսորեալներուն տարիքոտներն ու հիւանդները իրենց տեղերը ղրկուելու համար հրաման տրուած էր, Սիվրի Հիսարի մէջ ասոնք դատելով Էսկիշէհիր ղրկած էին: Հոն վար դրուեցան եւ չղրկուեցան Քէօթահիա: Ասկէ զատ տուները ատեն ատեն խուզարկուելով սկսան նորէն աքսորել հեռուները, իսկ Համանայի եւ Պէյ Բազարի մէջ ղրկուելու համար դատուած տարիքաւորները

The houses in Kütahya and Eskişehir were constantly raided. Fugitives or people hiding were sought; those found were taken to prison, severely beaten, and exiled. They would catch Armenian boys and hit them, forcing them to inform which houses have hidden people. They would ravage Armenian or Greek shops. They would enter and confiscate the goods and demand money or raki from the homes. The çetes would force the Armenian boys to bring raki, while the police would apprehend those who brought raki, beat them, and imprison them, saying nothing to the çetes who had ordered the raki.

Night or day, officers would force themselves into Armenian houses, live there, and oblige the householders to find beds, furniture, utensils, and food for them. Unfortunate mothers would be pressed to cook their food and do their laundry. Nevertheless, on the one hand, to save their children, and on the other hand, to send money to their exiled husbands, they would open the shops to not die of starvation. Many left their homes, handing their homes and belongings over to the çetes not to live with them because the çetes would threaten and demand that young women and girls be present in their homes to sit with them and get up with them. Many rejected this [situation], leaving their homes and everything to them [the çetes].

Some military commanders demanded food, fuel, laundry soap, coffee, tea, milk, sugar, and so on from the houses they entered, despite their high monthly salaries. Armenian families risked death if they were unable to comply with their demands. On October 17, upon the protest of the women remaining in Kütahya [regarding the lack of clergy], one Armenian, one Greek, and one Catholic priest were returned to Kütahya. It must be noted that the çetes did not enter Turkish houses ever, nor did they demand anything from them, only from Armenians and Greeks.

On their carts, they loaded carpets, chattels, tables, and benches from Armenian homes, and whatever else they found as luxurious furniture and took them away. Night and day, they summoned the Armenian priest and headman and demanded whatever they needed, threatening to hang them.

For a whole year, Kütahya, Eskişehir, Tavşanlı, and Afyonkarahisar endured innumerable sufferings.

During searches, shelves, cupboards, chests, and all other suspicious places were smashed with an ax, chimneys and wells were searched, and the grounds of houses were dug up. They reduced many houses to ruin during Easter week as they tried to find bombs.

On July 17, 1921, after a year of suffering, the Greek army entered the city without leaving time [to the Milli commanders] for looting or plunder. They had set fire in four hidden places to burn down Christian homes, but fortunately, it was prevented. The night they left, they stormed the Armenian houses and took six or seven Armenians with them.

Now the city is calm, and the Armenians have only one concern: what happened to their 320 exiles scattered from Ankara to Diyarbakır.

İstanbul (from Father Pascal Zouliquian, Jesuit)—October 7[120]

Fifteen days ago, he left Sivas and came to İstanbul, thanks to the Franco-Kemal agreement being signed.

In Sivas, the Kemalists have seized the Armenian cathedral (which has been turned into a prison), the Holy Savior church, the monastery of St. Nshan, the Aramian school, the prelacy, the printing house, the Armenian Protestant chapel, the Greek church, the Jesuit school, and the school and the house of the nuns. The Kemalists also carried away the copper vessels of the churches weighing 2,500 okkas.

The orphans sheltered in the prelacy have been transferred to the American college.

չղրկեցին այլեւս: Եթէ ասոնք ղրկուէին, այսօր 100 հոգի աւելի փրկուած պիտի ըլլար:

Քէօթահիա եւ Էսկիշէհիր միշտ տուները կը կոխուէին. փախչողները կամ պահուըտողները կը փնտռուէին, գտածնին բանտ կը տանէին եւ սաստիկ ծեծերով կը խոշտանգէին եւ ապա կ'աքսորէ-ին: Հայ տղաքը կը բռնէին եւ ծեծի տակ կը ստիպէին իմացնել իրենց թէ որու տան մէջ պահուըտող կայ, հայ կամ յոյն խանութները կը բռնաբարէին, կը մտնէին անոնց ապրանքը կը գրաւէին, տուներէ ստակ կամ օղի կը պահանջէին, չէթէները կը ստիպէին հայ տղաքը օղի բերել, իսկ բերողները բօլիս-ներ[ը] բռնելով կը ծեծէին ու կը բանտարկէին, բայց օղի բերել տուող չէթէներուն բան չէին ըսեր:

Գիշեր ցորեկ սպաները հայ տուները կը լեցուէին բռնի մտնելով, հոն կը բնակէին եւ կը ստիպէին տնեցիները իրենց անկողին, կահ կարասի եւ ուտելիք գտնել: Խեղճ մայրերը անոնց կերակուրը եփել, լուացքն ընել կը հարկադրուէին. այսու հանդերձ մէկ կողմէն իրենց զաւակները ապրեցնելու համար, միւս կողմէն իրենց աքսորեալ ամուսիններուն ստակ ղրկելու համար խանութ կը բանային, որպէսզի անօթութենէ չմեռնին անոնք: Շատեր իրենց տուներէն դուրս ելան չէթէներու յանձնելով իրենց տունն ու ունեցածը, որպէսզի անոնց հետ չբնակին, որովհետեւ սպառնալիքներով կը պահանջէին մանկամարդ կիներ ու աղջիկներ գտնուելու են տուներու մէջ իրենց հետ մէկտեղ նստիլ ելլելու համար: Խիստ շատեր մերժեցին զայն եւ հեռացան իրենց տուներէն ամէն ինչ անոնց թողլով:

Զինուորական հրամանատարներ գտնուեցան որոնք իրենց առած բարձր ամսականներուն հակառակ մտած տուներէն կը պահանջէին ուտելիք, վառելիք, լուացքի օճառ, սուրճ, թէյ, կաթ, շաքար եւն.: Հայ ընտանիքներ անոնց ուզածն ընելու անկարելիութեան հետ մահուան վտանգին առջեւ կը գտնուէին: Հոկտեմբեր 17ին Քէօթահիա մնացող կանանց բողոքին վրայ մէկ հայ եւ մէկ յոյն եւ մէկ կաթոլիկ քահանայ կը դարձուին կրկին Քէօթահիա: Դիտելի է որ չէթէները բնաւ թուրք տուներ չմտան եւ անոնցմէ ոչինչ չպահանջեցին. այլ միայն հայերէն եւ յոյներէն:

Շատ հայ տուներու գորգերն ու գոյքերը, սեղաններն ու նստարանները եւ ինչ որ գտան շքեղ կահկարասի իրենց կառքերուն վրայ բեռնաւորելով առին տարին: Գիշեր ցորեկ հայ քահանան եւ հայ մուխթարը կանչելով կը պահանջէին ինչ որ պէտք էր, իրենց կախաղանի սպառնալիք ընելով:

Ամբողջ տարի մը Քէօթահիա, Էսկիշէհիր, Թավշանլու եւ Աֆ[իոն] Գարահիսար անթիւ տառապանքի ենթարկուեցան:

Խուզարկութեանց միջոցին դարաններ ու պահարաններ, սնտուկներ եւ որեւէ կասկածելի երեւցած տեղեր կացինով խորտակուեցան, ծխնելյոզներ եւ ջրհորներ փնտռուեցան, գետնափոր տեղեր գտնելու համար տուներու գետինները փորեցին եւ պո[մ]պա գտնելու համար Չատկի շաբաթը շատ մը տուներ քար ու քանդ ըրին:

1921 Յուլիս 17ին մէկ տարուան տառապանքէ յետոյ առանց աւարառութեան եւ թալանի ժամանակ ձգելու հելլէն բանակը մտաւ քաղաք: Քրիստոնեայ տուները այրելու համար գաղտնի տեղեր կրակ տուած էին, ինչպէս չորս տեղ գտնուեցաւ, սակայն բարեբաղդաբար առաջքն առնուե-ցաւ: Իսկ իրենց մեկնած գիշերը կոխեցին հայոց տուները եւ 6–7 հայերը առին եւ միասին տարին:

Հիմա քաղաքը հանդարտ է եւ հայերը միակ մէկ մտատանջութիւն ունին, որ է թէ ինչ եղած են Էնկիւրիւէ մինչեւ Տիարպէքիր ցրուած իրենց 320 աքսորեալները:

Կ. Պոլիս (P. Pascal Zouliquian, Jesuith) – 7 Հոկտեմբեր

15 օր առաջ Սեբաստիայէն ճամբայ ելած է եւ Կ. Պոլիս եկած է շնորհիւ այն հանգամանքին որ ֆրանքօ-Քէմալ համաձայնութիւնը կնքուած է:

Սեբաստիոյ մէջ քէմալականաց կողմէ գրաւած են հայոց մայր եկեղեցին (որ բանտի վե-րածուած է), Ս. Փրկիչ եկեղեցին, Ս. Նշան վանքը, Արամեան վարժարանը, առաջնորդարանը, տպարանը, հայ բողոքականաց ժողովարանը, յունաց եկեղեցին, ժիզուիթներու դպրոցը, մայրա-պետներու դպրոցը եւ տուներ: Քէմալականները նաեւ առած են եկեղեցիներու սեփական 2500 օխայ պղնձեղէնները:

Որբերը՝ որոնք առաջնորդարան կը պատսպարուէին, փոխադրուած են Ամերիկեան Գօլէճը:

There is great misery in Sivas because a loaf of bread costs fifteen silver kuruş, and again the Armenians are being drafted. Three hundred of them have been taken as soldiers. Also, as many as fifty tall orphans have been drafted, judged only by their appearances.

Most of the soldiers taken from Sivas were driven to Pasinler [Hasankale]; a small number remained in Sivas. All enlisted Armenians are being used in the labor battalions and are given almost no rest. They stay in the open air without shelter.

The instigator of all the atrocities committed in the Sivas prefecture is [the] commander of the Third Army, Major Nurettin Bey, who stays in Amasya. The *Istiklal* [Independence] Court—which terrified this city by hanging sixty-one Greeks and thirteen Armenians, and gradually others regularly—is also located there. The *Istiklal* Court was later transferred to Tokat, where about ten Armenians and many others were hanged.

Because it was rumored that this court would come to Sivas, the city was thrown into a state of panic. On the way, he [Father Pascal] met the court that was going to Sivas. This horror was not unjustified because death sentences are issued mercilessly [by the court]. To give an idea, the passenger [Father Pascal] said that he had personally read in *İrâde-i Milliye* a three-column list of names of those hanged.

The governor of Sivas is Haydar Bey.

On the road, he [Father Pascal] witnessed scenes of deportation. At the place called Çengel Han, he encountered about two hundred Armenian and Greek men detained in the inn. A little later, he came across four thousand people with their families, all Greeks, who had been taken from Samsun to Tokat. He came [also] across many people in groups of twenty-five to thirty, who were being driven toward the interior by two soldiers per group. The deportees had almost all been robbed and taken away in chains. Armenians were forbidden to approach them; only Turks could come near and trade with them. A glass of water was sold to them for ten kuruş and a loaf of bread for twenty-five to thirty kuruş, although bread sells for eight kuruş elsewhere.

On the day he left Sivas, about fifteen hundred Greek women had arrived, only four hundred of whom were left there, and the rest were taken farther.

Aleppo (extracted from a private letter)—September 27

"Fifteen days ago, deportation decrees were prepared for seventy wretched Armenian families in Maraş. Deporting them individually or as a family has been the subject of consultation among the Turks. It is said that this has been implemented so far. You already know that they started incrementally like this and then they deported all of them at once. This time, however, they will unconditionally [separate and] slaughter the men after distancing [the deportees] for a few hours, just as they slaughtered in Besni the men of the six hundred people deported from Süleymanlı [Zeytun] to Maraş, [as] one or two of them, who escaped and came to Aleppo, relayed it. They [the Turks] will kill them also in the same way. You know the purpose of writing this: to report to whom this may concern, make every sacrifice, and find a way to delay the deportation. Those who are already there are in such a miserable condition that they want to die daily. The government has also occupied the building of Catholic nuns. The four to five hundred people there have been left in the churchyard, in the open air, and all of them will freeze from the winter cold. God help them."

Aleppo (from the vicar general)—October 14[121]

Today, a man named Garabed Jordian, a native of Eskişehir, arrived in Aleppo from Harput. He had been deported from his homeland by the Kemalist government on May 28, 1921. This person says that the Armenian and Greek male populations of Eskişehir and Kütahya were deported on August 10,

Սեբաստիոյ մէջ թշուառութիւնը մեծ է, վասնզի հացին օխան 15 ղրշ. արծաթ է եւ դարձեալ հայերը զինուորագրուած են: Առնուած զինուորներուն թիւն է 300 հոգի: 50-ի չափ ալ արտաքին կազմը խոշոր որբեր,- միայն երեսէն դատելով,- զինուորագրուած են:

Սեբաստիայէն առնուած զինուորները մեծ մասամբ տարուած են Հասան Գալէ, իսկ փոքր մաս մը կը մնայ Սեբաստիա: Բոլոր զինուորագրեալ հայերը *ամէլէ թապուրի*ի մէջ կը գործածուին եւ գրեթէ բնաւ հանգիստ չունին: Կը մնան բացօդեայ եւ առանց պատսպարանի:

Սեբաստիոյ կուսակալութեան մէջ գործադրուած բոլոր վայրագութեանց թելադիրն է հազարապետ Նուրէտտին պէյ, Գ. բանակին հրամատարը, որ Ամասիա կը գտնուի: Հոն է նաեւ *Իսթիգլալ*ի դատարանը, որ սարսափի մատնեց այս քաղաքը, մէկ անգամէն կախաղան բարձրացնելով 61 յոյն եւ 13 հայ, եւ հետզհետէ ուրիշներ պարբերաբար: *Իսթիգլալ*ի դատարանը յետոյ փոխադրուած է Թօգաթ, ուր կախաղան հանուած են 10-ի չափ հայեր եւ մնացածը յոյն բազմաթիւ անձեր:

Որովհետեւ լուր ելած էր թէ այս դատարանը Սվազ պիտի գար, քաղաքը ամբողջ սարսափի մէջ էր: Ճամբան արդէն ինքը հանդիպած էր այդ դատարանին որ Սվազ կ'երթար: Այս սարսափը անտեղի չէր, զի մահավճիռները անխնայ կը տրուին: Գաղափար մը տալու համար ուղեւորը ըսաւ թէ ինքն անձամբ «Իտարէի [*sic*] Միլլիյէ»-ի մէջ կարդացած էր երեք սիւնակ կախուողներու անունները:

Սեբաստիոյ կուսակալն է Հայտար պէյ:

Ճամբան ականատես եղած է տարագրութեան տեսարաններու: Չէնկէլ Խան ըսուած տեղը պատահած է 200-ի չափ հայ եւ յոյն էրիկ մարդոց, որոնք խանին մէջ բանտարկուած էին: Քիչ վերը պատահած է 4000 անձի ընտանիքներով, ամենքն ալ յոյն, որոնք Սամսոնէն Թօգաթ կը տարուէին եւ պատահած է բազմաթիւ խումբերու 25–30ական անձերու, որոնք երկուական զինուորով կը տարուէին դէպի ներս: Տարագրեալներն ամէնքն ալ գրեթէ կողոպտուած էին եւ շղթայի տակ կը տարուէին: Հայերուն արգիլուած էր անոնց մօտենալ. միայն թուրքերը կրնան մօտենալ եւ անոնց հետ առեւտուր ընել: Գաւաթ մը ջուրը 10 ղրշ.ի կը ծախուի անոնց եւ հացը՝ 25–30 ղուրուշի, հակառակ անոր որ ղուրսը 8 ղուրուշի կը ծախուի:

Իր Սվազէն ճամբայ ելած օրը հոն հասած էին 1500-ի չափ յոյն կիներ, որոնցմէ միայն 400-ը այնտեղ ձգուած է եւ մնացեալները աւելի առաջ տարուած են:

Հալէպ (մասնաւոր նամակէ մը քաղուած) – 27 Սեպտեմբեր

«Թուականէս 15 օր առաջ Մարաշ գտնուող թշուառ հայերէն 70 ընտանիքին տարագրման հրամանագիրները պատրաստուած եւ ասոնք անհատաբար կամ ընտանեօք տարագրելու խնդիրը խորհրդակցութեան առարկայ [եղած] է թրքաց մէջ: Կ'ըսուի թէ ասիկա մինչեւ հիմա գործադրուած է: Գիտէք արդէն որ առաջ այսպէս կամաց կամաց սկսան եւ յետոյ ամէնը մէկէն տարագրեցին: Սակայն այս անգամ անպատճառ այրերը քանի մը ժամ հեռացնելէ յետոյ պիտի ջարդեն, ինչպէս որ Մարաշէն տարագրուած 600 զէյթունցիներուն այրերը Պէհէսնիի մէջ կոտորեցին, որոնցմէ ազատած եւ Հալէպ եկած մէկ երկու հոգի պատմեցին: Ատոնք ալ այդ կերպով պիտի մեռցնեն: Այս բանը գրելուս նպատակը գիտէք, հոն պատկանեալ տեղերուն իմաց տալով, ամէն զոհողութիւն ընել եւ տարագրութիւնը յետաձգելու ճար մը գտնել: Արդէն հոն գտնուողները այնպիսի թշուառ վիճակի մէջ են [որ] ամէն օր մեռնիլ կը փափաքին: Կաթոլիկ մայրապետներու շէնքն ալ կառավարութեան կողմէ գրաւուած ըլլալով, հոն գտնուող 4–500 հոգին այդ եկեղեցւոյ բակը, բացօդեայ մնացած են եւ ձմրան ցուրտէն ամէնքն ալ պիտի սառին: Աստուած անոնց օգնէ»:

Հալէպ (Առաջնորդական Փոխանորդէն) – 14 Հոկտեմբեր

Խարբերդէն այսօր Հալէպ ժամանեց բնիկ Էսկիշէհիրցի Կարապետ Ծօրտեան անուն անձ մը, որ տարագրուած է եղեր իր հայրենիքէն քեմալական կառավարութեան կողմէ [1]921 Մայիս 28ին: Այս անձը կը պատմէ թէ Էսկիշէհիրի եւ Քէօթահիայի հայ եւ յոյն արու բնակչութիւնը տեղահան

1920, and dispersed around Sivrihisar, Beypazarı, and Haymana. [The Armenians of] Konya and its environs, as well as those who had avoided previous deportations, were exiled in May this year. He was in a group of 380 people first taken to Kayseri, where the whole group was imprisoned in a stable for twenty-four hours without any reason given. The next day, they were assembled in the courtyard of the government house. They were not even allowed to buy water. When Armenian women in Kayseri tried to distribute bread, the guards beat them and forbade them to do so. There are no Armenian men left in Kayseri.

The group reached Sivas in great distress; several sick people and those unable to walk died on the road without care. In Sivas, the government allowed everyone to roam freely in the city. The primate, Reverend Sarkis Ajemian, has been active and energetic and has shown a warm attitude toward the deportees. When the government suddenly gathered and sent everyone to Malatya nine or ten days later, the primate distributed two liras in banknotes and bread to each of them. Near Malatya, after being detained for ten days in the St. Gregory the Illuminator Monastery, they went to Harput without entering the city, where after staying at the Sürsürü [Sursuri] Monastery for a few days, fifty to one hundred people were scattered in Turkish and Kurdish villages. Most were allowed to stay in Elazığ [Mezre]. The American [Near East] Relief provides some assistance to those who appeal to them and the disabled. Those who have acquaintances in İstanbul and the United States can get in touch with them and receive money by telegram. In Harput, Bishop Kyud tries to do his best. There are a few Armenian shop owners, while most of [the exiles] are women making a living by digging soil for the Kurds and Turks. Thirty-three orphanages are administered by the [Near East] Relief, each containing one hundred to one hundred fifty orphans. Armenians have done their best to help the exiles.

No killings or robberies happened during the deportation, but the sick and those unable to walk remained on the road and died. Not only has the government not provided bread, but it has also banned the Turkish people from selling bread in many places. The guards charged large sums of money for rent and transportation and sold the bread at three or four times the price in many places. *There is not a single Armenian village left* in all of Anadolu [Anatolia], and Armenian women in the cities live the life of slaves.

Garabed Jordian fled with an Arab on September 18. On the way, he was robbed of even his clothes. By way of Çermik and Siverek, he came to Manbij, then to Bab, where the local French authorities sent him here by car. To facilitate the escape of others, his Arab companion forced him to produce a document stating that he had reached Aleppo. Escaping is extremely dangerous, and the chances of survival are very thin.

İstanbul (from Cilicia's refugees)—November 16[122]

In the Cilicia region, despair is almost universal after the Franco-Kemal agreement. The migration has already begun, but there are not enough steamboats. All the people rushed to the offices to get passes. Armenian schools were closed on November 3–4. On November 5, the French announced their decision to evacuate Cilicia in Tarsus and Mersin.

Some of the migrating Armenians are going to İskenderun in the French zone, while the more prosperous head to Cyprus, where each person is required to pay twenty British pounds as a guarantee.

The general mood of the Armenians in the western part of Cilicia is to migrate before the Turks arrived. Only means of transportation are lacking. For this, they are already preparing and have put out their belongings for sale, but the Turks have boycotted and will not buy anything sold by Armenians.

Some of the first groups of refugees leaving Cilicia have arrived in Cyprus. Some wanted to go to

եղած է 1920 Օգոստոս 10ին եւ տարտղնուած է Սիվրի-Հիսարի, Պէյ-Բազարի, Հայմանայի կողմերը: Իսկ Գոնիա եւ շրջակաները, ինչպէս նաեւ նախկին տեղահանութենէն խուսափողները աքսորուած են այս տարուան Մայիսին: Ինքը կը գտնուէր 380 հոգինոց խումբի մը մէջ, որ տարուած է նախ Կեսարիա, ուր ամբողջ խումբը ախոռի մը մէջ 24 ժամ առանց ոեւէ պատճառի դուրս հանուելու բանտարկուած է. յաջորդ օրը բոլորը միասին կառավար[չ]ատան բակին մէջ հաւաքուած են. արգիլուած է անոնց նոյնիսկ ջուր առնելը եւ երբ Կեսարիոյ մէջ գտնուող հայ կիները ուզած են հաց բաժնել, պահակները ծեծելով արգիլած են: Կեսարիոյ մէջ հայ այր մարդ չկայ եղեր:

Մեծ նեղութիւններու մէջ խումբը հասած է Սեբաստիա, քանի մը հիւանդ ու քալելու անկարողներ ճամբան մեռած են անխնամ: Սեբաստիոյ մէջ կառավարութիւնը արտօնած է բոլորին ազատ պտտիլ քաղաքին մէջ: Առաջնորդ Տ. Սարգիս Վարդապետ Աճէմեանը եռանդուն ու կորովի գործունէութիւն մը եւ տաք վերաբերում ցոյց տուած է տարագիրներուն եւ երբ 9-10 օր վերջ կառավարութիւնը յանկարծակի բոլորը մէկ հաւաքած ու ղրկած է Մալաթիա, Առաջնորդը ամէն մէկուն երկերկու լիրա թղթադրամ եւ հաց բաշխած է: Մալաթիոյ մօտ Ս. Գրիգոր Լուսաւորիչ վանքին մէջ 10 օր բանտարկուելէ վերջ, առանց քաղաք մտնելու գացած են Խարբերդ, ուր Սուրսուրի վանքը քանի մը օր կենալէ վերջ 50ական 100ական տարտղնուած են թուրք եւ քիւրտ գիւղերու մէջ: Մեծ մասին արտօնած են մնալ Մեզրէ: Ամերիկեան Ռըլիֆը իրենցմէ դիմողներուն եւ անկարողներուն որոշ չափով օգնութիւն կ'ընէ: Պոլսոյ եւ Ամերիկայի մէջ ծանօթ ունեցողները կրնան յարաբերիլ եւ դրամ ստանալ հեռագրով: Խարբերդի մէջ Գիւտ Եպիսկոպոս կ'աշխատի իր կարելին ընել: Կան քանի մը հայեր, որոնք խանութ ունին, իսկ մեծ մասը կիներ են, քիւրտին եւ թուրքին մօտ հող փորելով ապրող: Ռըլիֆի կողմէ մատակարարուող 33 որբանոցներ կան իւրաքանչիւրը 100-150 որբ պարունակող: Հայերը իրենց կարելի օգնութիւնը ըրած են աքսորուածներուն:

Տարագրութեան ընթացքին սպանութիւն եւ կողոպուտ չէ կատարուած, բայց հիւանդներն ու քալելու անկարողներ մնացած են ճամբան ու մեռած: Կառավարութիւնը ոչ միայն հաց չէ տուած, այլ թուրք ժողովուրդին ալ արգիլած է շատ տեղեր հաց ծախելը: Պահակները իբր օթեւանի եւ փոխադրութեան վարձք մեծ գումարներ գանձած են եւ շատ տեղեր հացը եռապատիկ, քառապատիկ գնով ծախած: Ամբողջ Անատոլուի մէջ *ոչ մէկ հայ գիւղ մնացած է*, քաղաքներու մէջ գտնուող հայ կիներն ալ գերիի կեանքը կ'ապրին:

Կարապետ Ծօրտեան Սեպտեմբեր 18ին փախած է արաբի մը հետ: Ճամբան զինքը կողոպտած են նոյնիսկ իր հագուստներէն: Ջերմեկի եւ Սէվէրէկի ճամբով եկած է Պումպուճ, յետոյ՝ Պապ, ուր տեղւոյն ֆրանսական իշխանութիւնները օթօմօպիլով[23] հոս ուղարկած են: Իրեն ընկերացող արաբը բռնութեամբ իր Հալէպ հասած ըլլալը հաստատող թուղթ մըն ալ առած է իրմէ, ուրիշներ ալ փախցնելու դիւրութիւն ունենալու համար: Փախուստը չափազանց վտանգաւոր եւ ազատելու հաւանականութիւնը շատ քիչ է:

Կ. Պոլիս (Կիլիկիոյ գաղթականներէն) – 16 Նոյեմբեր

Կիլիկիոյ շրջանին մէջ ֆրանքօ-Քէմալ համաձայնութեան յայտնուելէն յետոյ գրեթէ յուսահատութիւնը ընդհանուր է: Արդէն գաղթը սկսած է, սակայն շոգենաւ չկայ բաւականաչափ: Բոլոր ժողովուրդը անցագիր առնելու համար խուժած է պաշտօնատանց վրայ: Հայ վարժարանները Նոյեմբեր 3–4ին փակուած են: Ֆրանսացիք Նոյեմբեր 5ին Տարսոնի եւ 6ին Մերսինի մէջ հաղորդեցին Կիլիկիան պարպելու որոշումը:

Գաղթող հայերէն մէկ մասը կ'երթայ Իսկէնտէրուն ֆրանսական գօտին, եւ աւելի բարեկեցիկները Կիպրոս, ուր ամէն մէկ անձէ կը պահանջուի 20 անգլիական ոսկի, իբր երաշխաւորութիւն:

Կիլիկիոյ արեւմտեան բաժինին մէջ գտնուող հայոց ընդհանուր տրամադրութիւնն է գաղթել թուրքերու գալէն առաջ. միայն փոխադրութեան միջոցներն են որ կը պակսին: Ասոր համար արդէն կը պատրաստուին եւ իրենց ունեցածը ծախու հանած են, մինչ թուրքերը պօյքօթ ըրած են եւ հայոց ծախածները չեն առներ:

İzmir, but the Greek authorities did not allow them to enter, so they traveled to İstanbul.

The Armenians in the eastern part of Cilicia, that is, in Osmaniye, Ceyhan, and Dörtyol, show no haste to migrate because it is easy for them to cross to the French area. They can cross any time they want.

There is a rumor in Adana that the Turks have compiled a list of two thousand people and will kill them in any way at the first opportunity.

On November 4, a Turkish commission was to arrive to take control of the country's administration, but it was later said that the commission's arrival was postponed to November 20.

The French captives in Pozantı have been released and sent to Marseilles via Cilicia.

These captives have unreservedly related abominable facts that could be considered the primary evidence of Turkish barbarism. The Turks raped French soldiers, and the wife of an officer, who had the misfortune of falling into the hands of Turks along with her husband, was raped by Turkish soldiers with the knowledge and command of Turkish commanders.

Naturally, the Armenians neither could nor would trust a mass fed by this mentality and despicable passions.

That is why the despair [of Armenians] is total, and the impression that the Allies have exposed them to Turkish atrocities is common.

Gaziantep [Ayntab] (from Priest Nerses Tavoukjian)—November 4, 1921[123]

The Turkish nationalist movement had started here two years before the arrival of the French, and after the arrival of the French, the organization gained momentum. Our situation worsened in the early days of January 1920; a boycott and threat of death began against the Armenians. For three months, we lived under the shadow of death. We were confined to our homes and experienced casualties from time to time. However, always obeying the instructions of the French authorities, we were always patient, paying a very high price economically, morally, and for life. On April 1, 1920, the Turks, fifteen thousand people strong, attacked the Armenians, intending to exterminate them. The Armenians defended themselves and survived a seventy-day-long critical war. The French accepted promises from the Turks and then handed the Armenians over to their enemies. The cease-fire was more challenging for the Armenians than in the days of the war. It lasted two and a half months, and the Turkish-French fighting resumed. The Armenians were left between flame and sword for seven and a half months. Finally, on February 8, 1921, the Turks surrendered, and since the French had officially declared on August 11, [1920,] their mandate [over Cilicia] according to the Treaty of Sèvres, the Armenians took a breath, and we hoped that the Armenians of Gaziantep had been saved. At the beginning of March, the barricades were torn down in the city, and a new administration began to be formed, [but] barely had the Armenians engaged in earning their living when on March 21, the French announced that they would leave Gaziantep and Kilis to the Turks and withdraw their troops. The Armenians of Gaziantep were very upset by this news. Panic broke out. We made appeals in every direction, but months passed before we heard that the Grand [National] Assembly of Ankara had not accepted the agreement [offered by the Allies] and the Franco-Turkish pact previously agreed to in London had been breached. The Armenians began to calm down again and engage in work. After August, in September, life and movement began to surface more or less in the city. At the beginning of October, new whispers and rumors began. Finally, the Kemalist officers arriving in the city to exchange prisoners

Կիլիկիայէն մեկնող գաղթականներու առաջին խումբերէն մէկ մասը Կիպրոս անցած է, իսկ մէկ մասը Իզմիր ելլալ ուզած է, սակայն յունական իշխանութիւնները չեն առած ներս, որով ստիպուած Կ. Պոլիս եկած են:

Կիլիկիոյ արեւելեան մասին հայերը, այսինքն՝ Օսմանիյէ, Ճիհան, Տէօրթեօլ, գաղթելու անապարանք ցոյց չեն տար, վասնզի ֆրանսական շրջանակ անցնելու դիւրութիւններ ունին եւ ուզած ատեննին կրնան անցնիլ:

Ատանայի մէջ զրոյց կը շրջի թէ 2000 հոգիներու ցանկ մը կազմած են թուրքերը եւ առաջին առթիւ զանոնք պիտի սպաննեն որեւէ եղանակով մը:

Նոյեմբեր 4ին թուրք յանձնախումբ մը պիտի գար երկրին վարչութիւնը ձեռք առնելու համար, սակայն յետոյ ըսուեցաւ թէ 20 Նոյեմբերին յետաձգուեցաւ:

Պօզանթի գտնուող ֆրանսացի գերիները արձակուած են եւ արդէն Կիլիկիայէն անցնելով Մարսիլիա ղրկուած են:

Այս գերիները անվերապահ պատմած [են] զազրելի իրողութիւններ, որոնք թրքական բարբարոսութեան գլխաւոր ապացոյցները կրնան համարուիլ: Ֆրանսացի զինուորներ թուրքերու կողմէ բռնաբարուած են եւ սպայի մը կինը, որ իր ամուսնոյն հետ թրքաց ձեռքը գերի իյնալու դժբաղդութիւնը ունեցած էր, թուրք հրամանատարներու գիտութեամբ եւ հրամանով լլկուած է թուրք զինուորներու կողմէ:

Այս մտայնութեամբ եւ այսքան ստորին կիրքերով սնած զանգուածի մը վրայ բնական է թէ հայերը չէին կրնար վստահիլ եւ չեն վստահիր:

Ասոր համար է որ յուսահատութիւնը ընդհանուր է եւ Համաձայնութեան կողմէ թրքական վայրագութեանց մատնուած ըլլալու տպաւորութիւնը հասարակաց:

Այնթապ (Տ. Ներսէս Քահանայ Թավուգճեանէ) – 4 Նոյեմբեր 1921

Երկու տարի առաջ ֆրանսացիք դեռ հոս չեկած թուրք ազգայնական շարժումը հոս սկսած էր եւ ֆրանսացւոց գալէն յետոյ կազմակերպութեան թափը աւելցաւ եւ 1920 Յունվարի սկիզբի օրերը մեր կացութիւնը ծանրացաւ, *պօյքօթ*, մահուան սպառնալիք սկսաւ հայոց դէմ: Եւ երեք ամիս շարունակ տուներու մէջ քաշուած մահուան ստուերի տակ ապրեցան[ք] մերթ ընդ մերթ զոհեր տալով. բայց միշտ ֆրանսական իշխանութեան հրահանգներուն անսալով միշտ համբերեցին[ք] տնտեսական, բարոյական եւ կեանքի շատ սուղ գինով: 1920 Ապրիլ 1ին թուրքերը 15,000 հոգիով հայոց վրայ յարձակեցան հայերը բնաջնջելու մտքով: Հայերը ինքնապաշտպանութեան դիմեցին եւ 70 օրուան ճգնաժամային կռիւէն ողջ առողջ դուրս ելան: Ֆրանսացիք թուրքերէն խոստումներ առնելով հայերը յանձնեցին իրենց թշնամիներուն: 2½ ամիս տեւեց զինադադարը, որ հայոց համար կռիւի օրերէն աւելի ծանր էր. եւ թրքօ-ֆրանսական կռիւը դարձեալ սկսաւ: 7½ ամիս հուրի եւ սուրի մէջ մնացին հայերը եւ վերջապէս 1921 Փետրուար 8ին թուրքերը անձնատուր եղան եւ ֆրանսացիք Օգոստոս 11էն սկսեալ, ըստ Սէվրի Դաշնագրին, իրենց *մանտաթէ*ութիւնը պաշտօնապէս յայտարարած ըլլալով, շունչ մը առին հայերը եւ յուսացինք որ այլ եւս Այնթապի հայութեան կեանքը ազատուած է: Մարտ ամսուան սկիզբը պատնէշները քակուեցան քաղաքին մէջ, նոր վարչութիւն կազմուիլ սկսաւ, հազիւ հայերը իրենց օրապահիկը ճարելու համար գործի ձեռնարկեցին, ու ահա Մարտ 21ին ֆրանսացիք յայտարարեցին թէ Այնթապ եւ Քիլիս թուրքերուն պիտի թողուն եւ իրենց զինուորները պիտի քաշեն: Այնթապի հայութիւնը այս լուրին վրայ խռովեցաւ շատ, խուճապ սկսաւ, ամէն կողմ դիմումներ ըրինք, ամիսներ անցան եւ լսեցինք թէ Էնգարէի Մեծ Ժողովը համաձայնութիւնը չէ ընդունած եւ Լօնտօնի ֆրանքօ-թուրք դաշնագրութիւնը խզուած է: Հայերը դարձեալ սկսան հանդարտիլ եւ գործի ձեռնարկել Օգոստոսէն ետքը: Սեպտեմբերի մէջ քիչ ու շատ կեանք եւ շարժում յառաջ գալ սկսաւ քաղաքին մէջ: Հոկտեմբերի սկիզբը նոր շշուկներ եւ զրոյցներ սկսան եւ վերջապէս գերիներու փոխանակութեան համար քաղաքս ժամանող քէմալական սպաներ յայտարարեցին թէ Հոկտեմբեր 19/20ի գիշերը Ֆրանքօ-թուրք համաձայնութիւնը կնքուեցաւ

announced that on the night of October 19–20, the Franco-Turkish agreement had been signed in Ankara and that since Gaziantep had been designated to the Turks, the Kemalists would come soon and take over the city. This news once again shocked the Armenians and, this time, the Francophile Turks. When they turned to the French authorities for an explanation, they were told: "Although we do not have an official dispatch yet, it is very likely that we will evacuate this city, but you have nothing to fear from the Kemalists, because in our conditions there are articles that protect your life and property, and we are sure that the Kemalists will not infringe on their promises because they are our friends," and so on. The news was spread on October 23–24, and although no dispatch has been given to the French so far, there is a persistent rumor among the Turks that the agreement is a fait accompli and will be implemented soon. The French do not refute it. There have been various rumors about the terms of the agreement, but no one knows the terms for sure. The Armenians are waiting for an official announcement without losing their cool. But this time, the Armenians are in a more unfavorable situation than in March. First, because at that time, the agreement was accepted only by one party; this time, however, both sides have accepted it, so implementation is inevitable. Second, the first time it was spring, and summer was arriving; however, this time, autumn is about to end, and winter [has almost] come. Therefore, if the Armenians are forced to migrate, their situation will be terrible because Armenians and Francophile Turks think of fleeing the city as a way out for freedom. Despair is common. If the French evacuated the city, staying there would mean annihilation to Armenians because certain Kemalists were already saying how they would treat them. The Armenians say that no matter what the conditions, no matter how firm the promise of the Turks is or who the guarantor Great Power is, we cannot trust them because even in the presence of the French armies we know how they treated us and how they kept their promises.

When Gaziantep's vicar general, Priest Nerses Tavoukjian, was in Aleppo last April, he saw Colonel Abadie, who was on his way out from Gaziantep on March 7 and who had been in Gaziantep during the Armenian-Turkish war and witnessed the surrender of the Turks. He [Father Nerses] asked him: "If the French evacuate Gaziantep, what should the Armenians do? What do you recommend?" The colonel answered immediately: "Armenians must leave with the French."

"But in the agreement, the Turks guaranteed the security of the Armenians under certain conditions," I said. The colonel answered angrily: "The Turks do not recognize any promise, etc. They have promised and broken their promises many times in my presence. To believe in their word and promise, a human should be a different creature." Behold the testimony of a French authority and eyewitness, and this is the opinion of all the French officers [stationed] in Gaziantep last year. Therefore, the guarantees are deceptive, and one cannot believe them. And this [assessment] is based on three facts, as follows. At the beginning of 1920, in January, the Turks started threatening the Armenians. The incidents were reported daily to the French colonel Flye-Sainte-Marie. He instructed us not to engage in any provocative acts. The Armenians tolerated it. However, unable to find an excuse, on Saturday, January 31, during a fight between a French soldier from Tunisia and a Turk, [the Kemalists] attacked the Armenians in the market. They killed a young Armenian man and wounded seven Armenians. Again, the Armenians remained silent and, upon the colonel's instructions, convened a joint meeting with Turkish dignitaries at which they promised to inform the Turkish government of any deprivation, harmful act, and so on experienced by any Armenian and not to communicate with the French. The next day, on Sunday, February 1, a gendarme fought with a Turk in the market. There was a riot, Armenians were attacked, and two Armenians were wounded. The Armenians informed the government, and [the latter] attributed it to a mistake. In the same month, they began slaughtering Armenians spotted on the Kilis-Gaziantep road. They tore into pieces two Americans, along with their driver and another companion, on the road. They slew four Armenians on the village road an hour

Էնգարէյի մէջ եւ Այնթապ թուրքերուն մնացած ըլլալով, մօտերս քէմալականք պիտի գան եւ քաղաքը պիտի գրաւեն: Այս լուրը անգամ մըն ալ շանթահարեց հայերը եւ այս անգամ՝ *ֆրանքօֆիլ* եղած թուրքերն ալ: Երբ ֆրանսական իշխանութեան կը դիմեն լուսաբանութիւն առնելու, պատասխան կը ստանան. «Թէեւ մեզի տակաւին պաշտօնական հաղորդագրութիւն չկայ, բայց շատ հաւանական է որ մենք այս քաղաքը պիտի պարպենք, սակայն դուք քէմալիսթներէ վախնալու տեղի չունիք, որովհետեւ մեր պայմաններուն մէջ անանկ յօդուածներ կան որ ձեր կեանքն ու ինչքը կ'ապահովեն եւ մենք վստահ ենք որ քէմալականք մեզի բարեկամ ըլլալով իրենց խոստումները չպիտի դրժեն եւլն.» ըսին: Հոկտեմբեր 23–24 էր այս լուրին տարածուիլը եւ թէեւ մինչեւ այսօր ֆրանսացւոց հաղորդագրութիւն մը չեղաւ, բայց թուրքերուն մէջ յամառ զրոյց կը շրջի թէ համաձայնութիւնը կատարուած լմնցած իրողութիւն մըն է եւ մօտ օրէն պիտի իրագործուի. ֆրանսացիք ասոր հակառակ բան մը չեն ըսեր: Համաձայնութեան պայմաններու մասին այլեւայլ զրոյցներ կան, բայց ո՛րը ստոյգ է ոչ ոք չի գիտեր: Հայ ժողովուրդը առ այժմ առանց իր պաղարիւնութիւնը կորսնցնելու պաշտօնական յայտարարութեան կը սպասէ: Բայց այս անգամ Մարտ ամիսէն աւելի աննպաստ կացութեան մէջ են հայերը: Նախ անոր համար որ այն ատեն համաձայնութիւնը մէկ կողմէն միայն ընդունուած էր. իսկ այս անգամ երկու կողմն ալ ընդունած են, հետեւաբար գործադրութիւնը անխուսափելի է: Երկրորդ, այն ատեն գարուն էր եւ ամառ կու գար, այս անգամ աշուն[ը] լմննալու վրայ է եւ ձմեռ հասաւ: Հետեւաբար, եթէ գաղթելու հարկադրուին հայերը, շատ զէշ վիճակի պիտի ենթարկուին: Որովհետեւ թէ՛ հայեր եւ թէ՛ ֆրանսասէր թուրքեր՝ ազատութեան համար իբր ելք, քաղաքէն փախչիլ ելլելը կը խորհին: Յուսահատութիւնը ընդհանուր է: Եթէ ֆրանսացիք պարպեն քաղաքը, հայոց հոն մնալը փճացումի մատնուիլ կը նշանակէ, որովհետեւ այժմէն իսկ, քէմալականներէն ոմանք կ'ըսեն թէ ինչպէս պիտի վարուին իրենց հետ: Հայերը կ'ըսեն թէ ինչեր ալ ըլլան պայմանները, որչափ ալ ամուր խօսք տուած ըլլան թուրքերը եւ մեծազօր պետութիւններէն որոնք ալ ըլլան երաշխաւորները, մենք չենք կրնար վստահիլ, որովհետեւ նոյնիսկ ֆրանսական բանակներու ներկայութեան գիտենք թէ ինչպէս վերաբերուեցան մեզի հետ եւ ինչպէս պահեցին իրենց խոստումները:

Այնթապի Առաջնորդական Փոխանորդ Տ. Ներսէս Քահանայ Թավուգճեան երբ անցեալ Ապրիլ ամսուան մէջ Հալէպ էր, Այնթապէն Մարտ 7ին մեկնող Գնդապետ Ապատին,- որ հայ-թուրք կռիւի միջոցին եւ ֆրանքօ-թուրք կռիւին տեւողութեան Այնթապ կը գտնուէր եւ թուրքերուն անձնատուր ըլլալը տեսած էր,- կը տեսնէ հոն եւ կը հարցնէ անոր. «Ֆրանսացիք եթէ պարպեն Այնթապը, հայերը ի՞նչ պէտք է ընեն, դուք ի՞նչ կը յանձնարարէք»: Գնդապետը անմիջապէս կը պատասխանէ եւ կ'ըսէ. «Հայերը ֆրանսացւոց հետ պէտք է որ ելլեն»:

– «Հապա համաձայնութեան մէջ թուրքերը կարգ մը պայմաններով երաշխաւորած են հայոց ապահովութիւնը», ըսի: Գնդապետը զայրոյթով կը պատասխանէ. «Թուրքերը խոստում եւայլն չեն գիտեր. քանիցս իմ առջեւս խոստացան եւ դրժեցին. անոնց խօսքին եւ խոստումին հաւատալու համար տարբեր արարած մը ըլլալու է մարդ»: Ահա ֆրանսացի հեղինակաւոր եւ ականատես անձի մը վկայութիւնը եւ ասիկա անցեալ տարի Այնթապ գտնուող ֆրանսացի սպաներուն բոլորին ալ կարծիքն է: Հետեւաբար երաշխաւորութիւնները խաբուսիկ են եւ անոնց հաւատալ կարելի չէ: Եւ ասիկա երեք փաստերու վրայ հիմնուած է: Այսպէս, 1920ի սկիզբը, Յունվարին թուրքերը սկսան սպաննալ հայոց: Ամէն օր կը տեղեկագրուէր դէպքերը ֆրանսացի Գնդապետ Ֆլի Սէնթ Մարիի, որ հրահանգ կու տար գրգռիչ որեւէ արարքի մէջ չգտնուիլ: Հայերը կը հանդուրժէին: Սակայն թուրքերը պատրուակ մը չկրնալով գտնել, Յունվար 31 շաբաթ օր մը, թունուզցի ֆրանսական զինուորի մը թուրքի մը հետ կռիւին միջոցին, շուկայ գտնուող հայերուն վրայ յարձակեցան, հայ երիտասարդ մը մեռցուցին եւ եօթը հայ վիրաւորեցին: Դարձեալ հայերը լռեցին եւ գնդապետին հրահանգին վրայ թուրք երեւելիներու հետ խառն ժողով մը կազմեցին եւ կառավարութեան մէջ խոստացան ռեւէ հայուն հանդէպ եղած զրկանքն, վնասակար արարքը եւայլն ուղղակի թուրք կառավարութեան լուր տալ եւ ֆրանսացիներու հետ յարաբերութիւն չընել: Հետեւեալ օրը,

from the city. They killed eleven Armenians from Sason in the waterways around the city. The Armenians did not raise their voices against any of these events. All this happened in the presence of the French. Finally, on April 1, the Turks came upon us with fifteen thousand armed men. The French encamped in a college right next to our neighborhood and defended the Armenians. All these happened before the fight.

After the London Agreement, as the French were assuring the Armenians by saying that the Kemalists were not like the Ittihadists and that they would keep their promise, they were [also] assuring the Armenians by saying that they had taken guarantees to secure our lives, the Turks maintained the same position. No Armenian was able to travel on the Kilis-Gaziantep road. An Armenian could only go to a village around Gaziantep, an hour away. This year's harvest was reaped, and no Armenian was allowed to receive the proceeds of his estate. In the early days of the harvest, the Kemalists had announced that the proceeds of the Armenian estates would be confiscated, and so it was.

In addition, on Monday, May 2, 1921, an eight-year-old Armenian girl was abducted in Gaziantep. No one has looked for her to date. On Tuesday, April 19, two Armenian coachmen were kidnapped on the road to Kilis. On Sunday, May 15, coachmen were looted, and the Turks among them were released, while five young Armenians, two of whom were the last remnants of families that had perished during deportation, were abducted and torn into pieces. On May 18, coachmen were attacked on the road to Kilis. The bandits returned when they did not find any Armenians among the travelers during their search. On Friday, July 8, an Armenian policeman was wounded, and two Armenian policemen were abducted and killed in the village Kapçağız [Kabcuğaz] on the road to Kilis. On Saturday, July 16, on the road to Kilis, the Kemalist marauders attacked a caravan of coachmen in a place called Kartal. This time the people left their goods on the road and resorted to Gaziantep. The material damage was estimated at twenty to thirty thousand Ottoman liras. A day or two later, several Turks went to the scene and brought their goods; the goods of the Armenians vanished, which was a loss of several thousand liras. On Friday, July 22, half an hour from the city, a brave young man named Hovhannes Deyirmenjian was killed in the Kadı Değirmenı mill. Because that place was just twenty minutes away from the French camp, the young man considered it safe. On Monday, October 24, when the Kemalist officers were in Gaziantep to exchange prisoners and speak of the Franco-Turkish agreement and friendship, in a place called Kartal on the Kilis-Gaziantep road, where local gendarmes were guarding, Turkish marauders attacked them and killed a police officer. On Sunday, October 30, marauders attacked Armenian coachmen near a village called Almalı (on the Gaziantep-Kilis road) between the guardhouses of local gendarmes and French forces. They looted the goods, took ten fine horses, and tried to kidnap the Armenians, but fortunately, fearing the force that arrived from Zeytinli [Ulumasere], the Armenians escaped, and the Armenian coachmen were able to return unharmed.

Behold, all these events have happened most recently and before the eyes of the French authorities. When these things happen while French troops are on the road and in the city, and an agreement has been reached between the French and the Kemalists, how can the Armenians trust the security [promised] on paper?

Փետրուար 1 կիրակի շուկայի մէջ ժանտարմա մը թուրքի մը հետ կռիւի բռնուեցաւ, խառնակութիւն եղաւ, հայոց վրայ յարձակեցան եւ երկու հայ վիրաւորեցին: Կառավարութեան իմաց տուին հայերը ու սխալմունքի վերագրեց: Նոյն ամսուն մէջ Քիլիս-Այնթապ ճամբուն վրայ տեսնուած հայերը ջարդուիլ սկսան: Երկու ամերիկացի իրենց *շօֆէօր*ով եւ ուրիշ ընկերով ճամբու վրայ յօշոտեցին: Չորս հայերը քաղաքէն մէկ ժամ հեռու գիւղի ճամբուն վրայ մորթեցին. քաղաքին շուրջը ջրուղիներու[24] մէջ 11 սասունցի հայեր սպաննեցին, ոչ մէկուն համար ձայն չբարձրացուցին հայերը: Բայց այս բոլորը ֆրանսացւոց ներկայութեան եղան: Վերջապէս Ապրիլ 1ին 15,000 հոգիով սպառազինուած մեր վրայ եկան թուրքեր եւ ֆրանսացիք մեր թաղերուն անմիջապէս կից *զօլէժ*ի մէջ բանակած ըլլալով, հայերը ինքզինքնին պաշտպանեցին: Այս բոլորը կռիւէն առաջ:

Լոնտոնի համաձայնութենէն ետքը, երբ ֆրանսացիք կ'ապահովէին հայերը ըսելով թէ քէմալականք Իթթիհատին մարդոց պէս չեն եւ իրենց խոստումը կը կատարեն եւ կ'ապահովցնէին հայերը ըսելով թէ իրենք մեր կեանքը ապահովելու երաշխաւորութիւններ առած են, թուրքերը մնացին նոյն դիրքի վրայ: Քիլիս-Այնթապ ճամբու վրայ ոչ մէկ հայ չկրցաւ ճամբորդել: Այնթապի շուրջը նոյնիսկ մէկ ժամ հեռու գիւղ մը հայ մը չի կրնար երթալ: Այս տարուան հունձքը քաղուեցաւ եւ ոչ մէկ հայ իր կալուածին հասոյթը չկրցաւ առնել, եւ քէմալականք հունձքի սկիզբի օրերն իսկ յայտարարեցին թէ հայուն կալուածի հասոյթը չպիտի տրուի եւ պիտի գրաւուի ու այնպէս ալ եղաւ:

Առնցմէ զատ 1921 Մայիս 2 երկուշաբթի օրը Այնթապի մէջ 8 տարեկան հայ աղջիկ մը առեւանգուեցաւ եւ մինչեւ այսօր ոչ ոք փնտռեց: Ապրիլ 19 երեքշաբթի երկու հայ կառապաններ Քիլիսի ճամբուն վրայ առեւանգուեցան: Մայիս 15 կիրակի կառապաններ կողոպտեցին եւ անոնց մէջէն թուրքեր ազատ արձակուեցան եւ 5 հայ երիտասարդներ, որոնց երկուքը տարագրութեան միջոցին փճացած ընտանիքներու վերջմնացութիւններն էին, առեւանգուեցան եւ յօշոտուեցան: Մայիս 18, Քիլիսի ճամբուն վրայ կառապաններու վրայ յարձակեցան եւ յետ խուզարկութեան մէջերնին հայ չգտնելով վերադարձան ասպատակները: Յուլիս 8 ուրբաթ Քիլիսի ճամբուն վրայ *Գապճուղըպ* [Գապճուղըզ] անուն գիւղի մէջ մէկ հայ ոստիկան վիրաւորուեցաւ եւ երկու հայ ոստիկան առեւանգուելով սպաննուեցաւ: Յուլիս 16 շաբաթ օրը Քիլիսի ճամբուն վրայ Քէրթիլ կոչուած տեղը քէմալական ասպատակներ կառապաններու կարաւանի վրայ յարձակեցան: Այս անգամ մարդիկը իրենց ապրանքները ճամբու վրայ թողլով հասան Այնթապ. նիւթական վնասը 20–30 հազար լիրա օսմանեան ոսկեղրամ հաշուեցին: Բայց 1–2 օր յետոյ մի քանի թուրքեր դէպքին վայրը երթալով իրենց ապրանքները բերին եւ հայերունը կորսուեցաւ, որ քանի մը հազար լիրա վնաս մըն էր: Յուլիս 22 ուրբաթ քաղաքէն կէս ժամ հեռու *Գաւր տէյիրմէնի* անուն ջրաղացքին մէջ Յովհաննէս Տէյիրմէնճեան անուն քաջ երիտասարդը սպաննեցին, դէպքին վայրը ֆրանսական բանակատեղիէն 20 վայրկեան հազիւ հեռաւորութիւն ունենալուն, երիտասարդը ապահով նկատած էր այն տեղը: Գերիները փոխանակելու համար քէմալական սպաներուն Այնթապ գտնուած օրը, յորում ֆրանքօ-թուրք համաձայնութեան՝ բարեկամութեան վրայ կը ճառէին թուրք սպաներ, Հոկտեմբեր 24 երկուշաբթի օրը Քիլիս-Այնթապ ճամբուն վրայ Քէրթէլ կոչուած տեղը, ուր տեղական ժանտարմաներ պահակ կեցած էին, անոնց վրայ թուրք ասպատակներ յարձակեցան եւ ոստիկան սպայ մը սպաննեցին: Հոկտեմբեր 30 կիրակի օրը տեղական ժանտարմաներու եւ ֆրանսական զինուորներու պահականոցներու միջեւ Ալմալը կոչուած գիւղին մօտ (Այնթապ-Քիլիս ճամբուն վրայ) ասպատակներ յարձակեցան հայ կառապաններու վրայ, ապրանքներ կողոպտեցին, 10 ընտրեալ ձիեր առին եւ ուզեցին հայերը առեւանգել, բայց բարեբաղդաբար Ուլումնասէրյէն հասած ոյժէն վախնալով փախած եւ հայ կառապաններ ողջ առողջ կրցան դառնալ:

Ահա այս բոլոր դէպքերը կատարուած են շատ նոր ժամանակի եւ ֆրանսական իշխանութեան աչքին առջեւ: Երբ ֆրանսական զինուորական խումբեր ճամբու վրայ եւ քաղաքին մէջ եղած պահուն եւ քէմալականներու հետ ֆրանսացիներու միջեւ համաձայնութիւն կնքուելէ յետոյ պատահին այս դէպքերը, ա[յ]լեւս հայերը ինչպէ՞ս կրնան վստահիլ թուղթի վրայ եղած ապահովութեանց:

Aleppo (from Priest Haroutyun Yesayan, locum tenens)—November 12[124]

With its serious nature, the Franco-Turkish agreement has particularly shocked the Armenians of Gaziantep [Ayntab] and Kilis since last week. Last week, Gaziantep's French commander officially notified us of the decision that the French forces would leave shortly and stated that the protection of the material and moral rights of the minorities would be fully ensured, but the indignation and anxiety of the people are impossible to calm. These days, Kemalists are expected in Gaziantep and Kilis, and the Turks are preparing to go forward with a delegation to greet them in a grand procession and lead them to the city. The vicar general of Gaziantep, Priest Nerses, has been here for four days. Accompanied by him and His Eminence Archbishop Okosdinos [Sayeghian], we presented ourselves to General de Lamothe two days ago. Father Nerses asked the General to provide the necessary assistance to transfer the Armenians of the two cities to different parts of Syria by the French military authorities because it is impossible for the Armenians to live as Turkish subjects. The Armenians, particularly after the immense toll of destruction, had returned to rebuild their ruined nests, simply harboring the great hope that they would find security under the victorious French flag. However, now that those hopes are dashed, they are finding it impossible to breathe under a Turkish regime; therefore, they prefer to deliver their possessions to the French representative, leave their hometowns, and die in deserts and villages where the terror of the Turkish yoke does not threaten them. The general weighed in on the seriousness of the spirit of the agreement and tried to persuade Priest Nerses that all the rights of Christians, especially Armenians, are protected and seriously guaranteed according to the provisions of some articles of the Treaty of Sèvres. Upon the refutations of Priest Nerses, the general allowed the Armenian clergyman to appeal to Paris while at the same time stating that he could not provide any financial and moral support for the relocation of the people.

The people's horror defies description. There are 8,000 Armenians in Gaziantep and 5,100 in Kilis. Naturally, more or less those whose conditions allow will be able to migrate, but most of them, defying all danger and suffering, will leave the city on foot, carrying their little ones, but again, the more significant number of the wretched will remain.

There are 12,000 refugees in Aleppo, apart from 6,500 Armenians who were already considered local before the Great War. There are also 6,700 Catholic Armenians and 450 Protestant Armenians. A total of 25,650 people enjoy all facilities thanks to the local government and high French patronage. The Arabs treat the Armenians very well.

- Yesterday, on the third anniversary of the armistice, the local government sent an official letter announcing the need to offer thanksgiving prayers in all churches and mosques on the occasion of the Franco-Turkish agreement.
- Local Turks presented a letter of gratitude to the general.

Adana (from Catholicos Sahag)—November 22[125]

During the last ten to fifteen days, more than forty thousand Armenians have left. No Armenian shopkeeper remains. The world is amazed at this voluntary migration. It is thought that there is an unimaginable organization behind the migration; meanwhile, there was plenty of exhortation and advice to deter them from throwing themselves voluntarily into death. Nevertheless, the people preferred to die hungry and unsheltered, even drown in the sea, than to remain and be prey to revenge.

Barely two thousand people are left—lame, blind, widowed, and elderly women. If financial means can be found, their transfer also is an obligation because when the people of Kozan [Sis] were relocated,

Հալէպ (Առաջնորդական Տեղապահ Յարութիւն Քահանայ Եսայեան) – 12 Նոյեմբեր

Ֆրանքօ-թուրք համաձայնութիւնը իր լուրջ հանգամանքով շաբաթէ ի վեր, մանաւանդ շանթահարած է Այնթապու եւ Քիլիսի հայութիւնը: Անցեալ շաբաթ Այնթապի ֆրանսական հրամանատարը պաշտօնապէս ազդարարած ըլլալով ֆրանսական ոյժերու ի մօտոյ մեկնելու որոշումը, փոքրամասնութեան[ց] նիւթական եւ բարոյական իրաւանց պաշտպանութեան բոլորովին ապահովուած ըլլալն ալ յայտնած է. սակայն ժողովրդեան վրդովանքն ու յուզումը եւ ո՛չ մի բանով հանդարտեցնել կարելի չի նկատուիր: Այս օրեր քեմալականք կը սպասուին Այնթապ ու Քիլիս եւ թուրքերու կողմանէ պատրաստութիւն կը տեսնուի պատզամաւորութեամբ ընդ առաջ երթալ շքեղ թափօրով ողջագուրուելու եւ քաղաք առաջնորդելու զայնս: Չորս օրէ ի վեր հոս կը գտնուի Այնթապու Առաջնորդական Փոխանորդ Տ. Ներսէս Քահանան, որուն ընկերակցութեամբ եւ Գերապայծառ Տ. Օգոստինոս Արքեպիսկոպոսի հետ երկու օր առաջ Զօրավար Տըլամօթին ներկայացանք, ուր Տ. Ներսէս Քահանան խնդրեց Զօրավարէն որպէսզի այդ երկու քաղաքներու հայութեան Սուրիոյ զանազան կողմեր փոխադրուելուն հարկ եղած օժանդակութիւնը շնորհուի ֆրանսական զինուորական իշխանութեանց կողմանէ, քանի որ անկարելի է յետ այսու հայոց որպէս թրքահպատակ ապրիլը, եւ մանաւանդ հայեր իրենց այսքան քայքայումէն վերջ միմիայն ֆրանսական յաղթապանծ դրօշակին տակ ապահովութիւն գտնալու մեծ հաւատքով դարձած էին իրենց աւերեալ բոյներնին վերաշինելու. այժմ որ այդ յոյսերը կը ցնդին, անկարելի կը նկատեն թրքական րէժիմի մը տակ շնչել, ուստի կը նախընտրեն իրենց անշարժ ստացուածները ֆրանսական ներկայացուցչին յանձնելով դուրս ելնել իրենց ծննդավայր քաղաքներէն եւ մեռնիլ այն անապատ եւ գիւղերու մէջ, ուր թրքական լուծի արհաւիրքը չսպառնայ: Զօրավարը ծանրացաւ համաձայնագրոյն ոգիին լրջութեան [վրայ] եւ ջանաց համոզել Տ. Ներսէս Քահանան թէ քրիստոնէից, մանաւանդ հայերու բոլոր իրաւանց պաշտպանութիւնը լրջօրէն ապահովուած է ըստ Սէվրի Դաշնագրոյն որոշ յօդուածներու տրամադրութեանց: Տ. Ներսէս Քահանային ժխտումներուն վրայ Զօրավարը արտօնեց հայ եկեղեցականները դիմել Բարիզ, միեւնոյն ժամանակ յայտնեց թէ ինք չի կրնար ոեւէ նիւթական [եւ] բարոյական օժանդակութիւն [ընծայել] այդ ժողովրդեան փոխադրութեան համար:

Ժողովուրդին սարսափը կարելի չէ նկարագրել. 8000 հայութիւն կայ Այնթապի մէջ, 5100 ալ Քիլիսի մէջ: Բնական է որ քիչ ու շատ վիճակը ներողներն են որ պիտի կրնան գաղթել. իսկ մեծ մասն ալ ամէն վտանգ ու տառապանք աչք առնելով հետիոտն իր փոքրիկները շալկելով քաղաքէն պիտի ելնէ, եւ դարձեալ պիտի մնայ թշուառներու մեծագոյն մասը:

Հալէպի մէջ կայ 12,000 գաղթականութիւն, 6500 արդէն Ընդհանուր Պատերազմէն առաջ որպէս տեղացի համարուած հայերէն զատ: 6700 ալ հայ կաթոլիկ, 450 հայ բողոքական, համագումար 25650. շնորհիւ տեղական կառավարութեան եւ շնորհիւ ֆրանսական բարձր հովանաւորութեան ամէն դիւրութիւն կը վայելեն: Արաբները շատ լաւ կը վարուին հայոց հետ:

- Երէկ Չինադաղարի Գ. տարեդարձ[ին] տեղական կառավարութեան կողմանէ պաշտօնագրով ազդարարուեցաւ բոլոր եկեղեցիներու եւ ճամիներու մէջ ֆր[անքօ]-թուրք համաձայնութեան առթիւ գոհաբանական աղօթքներ մատուցանելու պէտքը:

- Տեղացի թուրքեր Զօրավարին ներկայացուցին շնորհակալութեան թուղթ մը:

Ատանա (Սահակ Կաթողիկոսէն) – 22 Նոյեմբեր

Վերջին 10–15 օրուան ընթացքին 40000էն աւելի հայեր մեկնեցան. հայ խանութպան չմնաց: Այս ինքնայօժար գաղթին համար աշխարհ կը զարմանայ: Կը կարծուի որ աներեւակայելի կազմակերպութիւն մը կայ գաղթի գլուխը անցած, մինչդեռ յորդորներ եւ խրատներ անպակաս եղան, որպէսզի կամաւորապէս մահուան գիրկը չնետուին, սակայն լաւագոյն համարեցին անօթի եւ անպատսպար, նոյնիսկ ծովին երեսը մեռնիլ, քան մնալ ու վրիժառութեան զոհ երթալ:

Հազիւ 2000 հոգի մնաց, կաղ, կոյր, այրի եւ պառաւ: Եթէ միջոց ըլլայ նիւթական, անոնք ալ փոխադրել պարտաւորութիւն է զի Սիսը երբ տեղափոխուեցաւ, մնացած 5–6 ծերունիները նոյն

the five or six elderly who remained were torn into pieces the same day and then burned with petroleum.

The clergy, at the urging of the French, went twice beyond the siege line to deliver exhortations and advice to the people to stop the migration, but the people will not stay, and the ships are transporting them to Cyprus for free. But who will give the bread? If camps are to be set up by the [Near East] Relief or the British government, half of these people will perhaps live.

On November 22 (today), the spiritual representatives went to negotiate or to exhort. The organizer was Colonel Sarrou, the companion of Mr. Franklin-Bouillon, who managed to reach an agreement with the government of Ankara. The Armenians have no remark about this because the interests of France allegedly demand it to be so. Nobody says anything about migration. All the Christians indiscriminately, even the Turks and the Arabs, migrated. Likely Colonel Sarrou, perhaps [also] Mr. [Franklin-]Bouillon, will blame the migration on the spiritual representatives, who have been simply helpless to prevent it. Colonel Sarrou even threatened the Protestant minister to have him deliver those who organized the migration to the military court.

Fortunately, granting passes has not been prohibited; otherwise, there could have been some tragic incidents. Now nobody is hurt. Adana's stations are empty, but [people] are crowded in an open field in Mersin.

Franklin-Bouillon, chairman of the handover committee, is expected today. The Armenians and their representatives do not have any problems to present because problems do not exist. There are only a handful of prisoners and orphans, as well as the population of Dörtyol, who, realizing that the Syrian road is closed before them, are going through a severe crisis.

The Catholicos, through the mediation of General Dufieux, wrote a letter to General Gouraud, asking for the admittance of the Armenians of Dörtyol to Syria. If denied, a collision is inevitable, and the end may be something like that experienced in Saimbeyli [Hacın]. Before the deportation, Dörtyol had successfully resisted the Turkish mob twice, but then it was strong in number and material organization; now it does not have the same capacity; therefore, it will be impossible to resist for long.

Kilis and Gaziantep [Ayntab] started migrating. There are fifteen thousand people in these places. Where will they be placed, and what will they live on?

Dörtyol (from Reverend Father Paren, catholicosal vicar of Dörtyol)—November 26[126]

The Armenians of Cilicia have migrated almost wholly. Only the Armenians of Dörtyol and vicinities, numbering eight to ten thousand, along with the fragments of various Armenian-populated provinces who had taken refuge here since the armistice, remained. They were relying on the advantage that they had the facility to cross over to İskenderun and could resist, thanks to their favorable geographical position. But then, realizing that resistance was no longer possible, they decided to migrate. They appealed to the immigration branch in İskenderun to provide two steamships to make it possible for the people of Dörtyol to migrate.

For this purpose, they appealed to the French commander Mr. Dumont, who, without objection, issued a collective visa to leave.

If the people of Dörtyol are not accepted in İskenderun, they will probably go to Cyprus.

İskenderun (from Priest Nerses Tavoukjian, catholicosal vicar of Gaziantep [Ayntab])—December 3[127]

On November 4, when the French officially announced that Gaziantep would be evacuated and handed over to the Kemalists, the next day, panic broke out among the Armenians. People of some means

օրն իսկ յօշոտեցին եւ կազով այրեցին:

Երկու անգամ եղաւ որ հոգեւոր ներկայացուցիչները ֆրանսացւոց յորդորմամբ կ'երթան զրաւման գօտիէն անդին [որ] յորդորներ ու խրատներ ընեն ժողովուրդին գաղթը կասեցնելու համար, բայց ժողովուրդը չմնաց եւ նաւեր ձրի կը փոխադրեն ի Կիպրոս: Սակայն հացը ո՞վ պիտի տայ. եթէ քէմփեր պիտի կազմուին Րըլիֆի կամ անգլիական կառավարութեան կողմէն, կը հաւատամ թէ կիսով հաւանականօրէն պիտի ապրի այս ժողովուրդը:

Նոյեմբեր 22 (այսօր) հոգեւոր ներկայացուցիչները գացին բանակցելու համար, կամ խրատ ընելու: Կազմակերպիչն էր Գօլօնէլ Սառօն, Մ. Ֆրանքլին Պույօնի ընկերը, որ յաջողեցաւ Էնկիւրի կառավարութեան հետ համաձայնութիւնը կնքել: Այս մասին ոեւէ դիտողութիւն չունին հայերը, քանի որ Ֆրանսայի շահը այդ կը պահանջէ եղեր: Բայց ոչ ոք դիտողութիւն չունի տեղի ունեցած գաղթին համար. անխտիր բոլոր քրիստոնեայք, նոյնիսկ թուրքեր եւ արաբներ գաղթեցին, որուն համար զօլօնէլ Սառօ, թերեւս պարոն Պույօն պիտի մեղադրեն հոգեւոր ներկայացուցիչները, որոնք անճրկած են պարզապէս առաջքն առնելու: Նոյնիսկ Գնդապետ Սառօն բողոքականաց պատուելի-ին սպառնացած է պատերազմական ատեանի յանձնել զանոնք որ գաղթը կազմակերպած են:

Բարեբաղդաբար անցագիր տալը չարգիլուեցաւ, եթէ ոչ ցաւառիթ դէպքեր կրնային պատահիլ: Հիմա ոչ ոքի քիթ չարիւնեցաւ: Ատանայի կայարանները դատարկուած են, բայց Մերսին բաց դաշտի մէջ խճողուած են:

Այսօր կը սպասուի Ֆրանքլին Պույօն, որ յանձնման յանձնաժողովի նախագահն է: Հայերը եւ իրենց ներկայացուցիչները մատուցանելիք ոեւէ խնդիր չունին, վասնզի չկան: Միայն կան կարգ մը բանտարկեալներ, որբեր եւ Տէօրթ-Եօլի բնակչութիւնը, որ իր առջեւ փակուած տեսնելով Սուրիոյ ճամբան, ծանր ճգնաժամ մը կ'անցնէ:

Կաթողիկոսը ժէնէրալ Տիւֆիոյի միջնորդութեամբ հեռագրած է Զօրավար Կուրոյին որպէսզի տէօրթ-եօլցիք Սուրիա ընդունուին: Եթէ այս շնորհ չըլլայ, բաղխումը անխուսափելի է եւ վախճանը թերեւս Հաճընի նման բան մը ըլլայ: Տարագրութենէն առաջ երկիցս Տէօրթ-Եօլ չափուած է թուրք խուժանին հետ, բայց այն ատեն թիւով եւ նիւթական կազմակերպութեամբ ուժեղ էր, հիմա նոյն վիճակը չունի, որով կարելի չէ որ կարենայ երկար դիմադրել:

Քիլիս եւ Այնթապ սկսած են գաղթել: Հոն տեղերը կան 15,000 հոգի. ո՞ւր պիտի զետեղուին եւ ինչո՞վ պիտի ապրին:

Տէօրթ-Եօլ (Փառէն Վարդապետ, Կաթողիկոսական Փոխանորդ Տէօրթ-Եօլի) – 26 Նոյեմբեր

Կիլիկիոյ հայութիւնը գրեթէ ամբողջովին գաղթած, միայն Տէօրթ-Եօլ շրջանակին հայութիւնը, որ 8–10 հազար կը հաշուուի, հայաբնակ զանազան գաւառներու բեկորներով մէկտեղ,- որոնք զինադադարէն ի վեր հոս ապաստանած էին,- կը մնար յոյս դնելով սա առաւելութեան վրայ թէ Իսկէնտէրունն անցնելու դիւրութիւն ունէր եւ աշխարհագրականապէս նպաստաւորուած ըլլալով կրնար դիմադրել: Սակայն յետոյ նկատելով թէ այլեւս կարելիութիւն չկար դիմադրութեան, կ'որոշէ գաղթել եւ կը դիմէ Իսկէնտէրունի գաղթականական մասնախումբին, որ 2 շոգենաւեր տրամադրէ որպէսզի տէօրթ-եօլցիք ալ մեկնին:

Այս նպատակով կը դիմեն ֆրանսացի հրամատար M. Dumont-ի, որ առանց ոեւէ առարկու-թեան հաւաքական անցա-արտօնագիր տուաւ մեկնելու համար:

Տէօրթ-եօլցիք եթէ Իսկէնտէրուն չընդունուին, հաւանօրէն պիտի երթան Կիպրոս:

Իսկէնտէրուն (Ներսէս Քահանայ Թավուգճեանէ, Կաթողիկոսական Փոխանորդ Այնթապու) – 3 Դեկտեմբեր

Նոյեմբեր 4ին երբ ֆրանսացիք պաշտօնապէս յայտարարեցին թէ Այնթապը պիտի պարպուի եւ քէմալիսթներու պիտի յանձնուի՝ հետեւեալը օրը իսկ խուճապը սկսաւ հայոց մէջ: Եւ քիչ շատ

began to flee. The majority procrastinated, figuring they had two months to settle their affairs. However, when people started to leave in large numbers, the French, with the consent of the local government, banned the migration and refused to issue visas as of November 14. In this way, seven to eight thousand people remained confined to Gaziantep. The Catholicos asked, through a petition and a telegram, for free passage and facilitation to have the people spread in Syria. A petition has been formally submitted to local functionaries and General de Lamothe in Aleppo, and a telegram [has been sent] to the central government in Paris, but to no avail.

It was dangerous for the Armenians of Gaziantep, especially the youth, to stay in the city because local Turks are outraged enemies against all Armenians, especially the youngsters. The new government will undoubtedly want to disarm the youngsters who do not want to be disarmed. Consequently, a new war would have started with the end being destruction, or the youth would have become prey to revenge after being disarmed.

Therefore, the only way to salvation for the Armenians of Gaziantep and Kilis was moving to Syria or, at least, eliminating the barriers against departers.

The French made many promises to the Armenians, but the most important among them was their always saying: "If one day we leave this country, we will take the Armenians with us," and it was with this assurance that Armenians remained in Gaziantep; otherwise, they would have withdrawn by now. For two years, the officers in Gaziantep, whether ranking high or low, became convinced that the Armenians could not live with the Turks after their departure. Even those who formally told us, "Do not be afraid, we have obtained assurances," and so on, during unofficial discussions, would say, "Our best advice for you is to leave this city after we leave." When Colonel Abadie, who witnessed the Armenian-Turkish and Franco-Turkish battles in Gaziantep for ten months and saw everything—the fighting and the cease-fire—was asked in Aleppo, after he had left Gaziantep, about his advice, he answered: "The only way out for Armenians is to get out of Gaziantep. I consider insane the person who believes in the assurance and promise given by a Turk. They do not know what a word, a promise, or honor is."

After Gaziantep's surrender, the district governor of this city, Celal Kadri Bey, said several times: "If you are deceived by promises and assurances this time as well, you will make a terrible mistake, and you will perish because I know well the mindset and plan of the Kemalists." And before the Franco-Turkish agreement was signed, the local Turks, who were sympathetic to the Kemalists, would already always say: "The French will leave soon, you will be in our hands again, [and] there are people among you who will be hanged in the square."

The ordinary people would openly say in the Armenians' faces: "We will build our mosques and minarets, which have been destroyed by bombardment, with Armenian heads," and a thousand more threats like that. . . .

կարողութեան տէր անձերը սկսան փախչիլ: Մեծամասնութիւնը նկատելով որ երկու ամիս միջոց կայ, իրենց գործերը կարգադրելու նպատակով տնտնացին: Սակայն երբ մեծաքանակ թուով ելլել սկսան, ֆրանսացիք տեղական կառավարութեան համաձայնութեամբ արգիլեցին գաղթը եւ Նոյեմբեր 14էն սկսեալ անցագիր չտուին: Եւ այս կերպով 7–8 հազար հոգի Այնթապի մէջ փակուած մնացին: Կաթողիկոսական Փոխանորդը ազատ անցք եւ Սուրիոյ մէջ տարածուելու համար դիւրութիւններ խնդրեց խնդրագրով եւ հեռագրով: Պաշտօնապէս խնդրագիր տրուած է տեղական պաշտօնէութեան ինչպէս նաեւ Հալէպ Ժէնէրալ տը Լամօթին եւ հեռագիր Բարիզ կեդրոնական կառավարութեան. սակայն ոեւէ օգուտ չունեցաւ:

Այնթապի հայութեան, մանաւանդ երիտասարդութեան քաղաքին մէջ մնալը վտանգաւոր էր, որովհետեւ տեղացի թուրքերը բոլոր հայութեան դէմ մանաւանդ երիտասարդներու դէմ կատղած թշնամիներ են: Նոր կառավարութիւնը անշուշտ պիտի ուզէ զինաթափ ընել երիտասարդները, որոնք երբեք չեն ուզեր զինաթափ ըլլալ: Հետեւաբար կա՛մ նոր կռիւ պիտի սկսէր, որուն վախճանը փճացում էր, կա՛մ զինաթափ ըլլալէ յետոյ վրիժառութեան զոհուիլ:

Հետեւաբար Այնթապ-Քիլիսի հայութեան փրկութեան միակ ելքն Սուրիա անցնիլ էր, կամ գէթ մեկնողներու դէմ արգելք ըլլալու չէր:

Ֆրանսացիք հայոց շատ մը խոստումներ տուած են, բայց անոնց մէջ ամէնէն կարեւորը միշտ կ'ըսէին թէ «եթէ երբեք օր մը մենք ելլենք այս երկրէն, հայերն ալ կ'առնենք եւ միասին կը տանինք» եւ այս վստահութեան վրայ էր որ Այնթապի մէջ հայեր մնացին, եթէ ոչ մինչեւ հիմա քաշուած կ'ըլլային: Երկու տարիէ ի վեր Այնթապ գտնուող սպաներ մեծ ու պզտիկ ամէնն ալ համոզուած էին թէ իրենց մեկնումէն ետքը հայերը թուրքերուն հետ չեն կրնար ապրիլ: Նոյնիսկ անոնք որոնք պաշտօնապէս մեզի «մի վախնաք, ապահովութիւն առած ենք եւայլն» կ'ըսէին, երբ ոչ-պաշտօնապէս խօսք ըլլար «մեր մեկնելէն ետքը ձեզի համար մեր լաւագոյն խրատն է այս քաղաքէն ելլել» կ'ըսէին: Քօլօնէլ Ապատի, որ տասը ամիս շարունակ ականատես եղաւ Այնթապի մէջ հայ-թուրք եւ ֆրանքօ-թուրք կռիւներուն, եւ կռիւ եւ զինադադար ամէնն ալ տեսաւ, իր Այնթապէն մեկնելէն յետոյ երբ Հալէպի մէջ իրեն խորհուրդ կը հարցուի, կը պատասխանէ. «Հայոց համար փրկութեան միակ ելքն է Այնթապէն ելլել: Խենթ կը համարեմ այն մարդը որ թուրքին տուած վստահութեան եւ խօսքին կը հաւատայ. անոնք խօսք, խոստում, պատիւ ի՛նչ է չեն գիտեր»:

Այնթապ անձնատուր ըլլալէն յետոյ քաղաքիս միւթէսարրֆը՝ Ճէլալ Գատրի պէյ, քանիցս ըսած է. «Եթէ այս անգամ ալ խաբուիք խոստումներէն եւ վստահութիւններէն, չարաչար կը սխալիք եւ կը փճանաք, որովհետեւ ես լաւ գիտեմ քէմալիսթներու մտայնութիւնն ու ծրագիրը» կ'ըսէր: Եւ արդէն տակաւին ֆրանքօ-թուրք համաձայնութիւնը չկնքուած, տեղացի թուրքեր, որոնք համակիր էին քէմալիսթներու, միշտ կ'ըսէին թէ «մօտ օրէն ֆրանսացիք պիտի երթան, դուք դարձեալ մեր ձեռքը պիտի մնաք, ձեր մէջ կան մարդիկ որոնք պիտի կախուին հրապարակին վրայ»:

Հասարակ ժողովուրդը հայոց երեսն ի վեր բացէիբաց կ'ըսէին. «Մեր ռմբակոծումէ քանդուած մզկիթներն ու մինարէները հայոց գլուխներով պիտի շինենք», եւ ասոր նման հազար տեսակ սպառնալիքներ: ...

[Insecurity Notebook Number 18]
[November 1921–March 1922]

. . . We Armenians know by experience that what is said in the upper circles is not realized, and what is said in the lower class becomes a reality. Consequently, the lives of the Armenians of Gaziantep [Ayntab] are certainly in danger. Therefore, these people, considering migration as the slightest of two evils, have voluntarily decided to undertake the exposure to terrible losses and migrate, but they [French] do not allow it; they forbid it.

The Armenians of Gaziantep ask by what law their freedom is being violated by those who had taken assurances for their safety. When they are violating their freedom now, how can Armenians believe in other promises they make?

İskenderun (from Sahag II, Catholicos of Cilicia)—November 29 [1921]

From the day the rumors of the Franco-Turkish agreement broke, spontaneously envisioning the coming catastrophes, the people initiated preparations for migration, and many even set out. When the agreement details were made public, it was clearly understood that the essential elements guaranteeing the security of life of Armenians and Christians, in general, were lacking. Everyone became tainted with the lone idea of migration, from the wealthy to the extremely poor and from the young to the near-the-grave-old.

Staying or migrating, either option, smelled and promised death; no one could commit to saying: "Do not migrate, ruthless death awaits you," nor could anyone say: "Migrate, for there is a life of paradise before you." Therefore, with the knowledge and approval of the French government, we invited the representatives of Adana, Tarsus, Mersin, Ceyhan, Osmaniye, and Dörtyol to a provincial meeting. After a long debate and consultation during several sessions, it was concluded that we could not suggest that the people stay, nor could we encourage the idea of migration, given the lack of means needed for migration and the adverse consequences of leaving the homeland. Despite the official assurances of some French functionaries, the people actualized the idea of migration on a large scale, heeding the suggestions of members of the Jesuit mission and even good-natured Muslims that the assurances given by the French were not to be trusted. Armenians, Greeks, Assyrians, Chaldeans, Arabs, and Turkish anti-[Kemalists] ventured en masse on the rocky and thorny road of foreignness. In a very short time, the city was vacated. Lamps were extinguished, along with the smoke of hearths.

The Kemalists probably were caught by surprise; therefore, they wrote from Pozantı and tried to contain and stop the migration, and through their public figures, they expressed their desire to meet with Armenian national representatives. The public figures or mediators were Effendis Süleyman Vahit, Gergerlizade Ali, Mücteba, and a fourth, Mustafa. They presented a letter to the spiritual leaders, signed by Suphi Pasha of Adana and the former mayor of Adana, Deblanzade Muhammed Effendi, indicating a wish to meet on Turkish soil in Dikili or Derebek. The French authorities encouraged and facilitated this visit by providing three cars for the trip.

The envoys, His Eminence Catholicosal Vicar Bishop Yeghishé, His Grace Bishop Haroutyun Keklikian, Reverend Haroutyunian, Sdepan Effendi Bzdigian from the Armenian notables, and the effendis Karayaghub Oglu Bodasaki and Shurki Oglu Aslan from the Greek notables, led by the abovementioned Turkish mediators, left early in the morning of November 15 for Dikili to wait for the travelers from Pozantı, but [in Dikili] the Turkish companions asked them to continue their journey to Gelincik. They arrived there and waited. The travelers from Pozantı arrived, and after polite greetings, Suphi Pasha said in his opening remarks that he represented no official capacity on the part of the government but was there as a compatriot triggered by compatriotic obligations. They wanted to convene this

[Անապահովութեան Տետր Թիւ 18]
[1921 Նոյեմբեր – 1922 Մարտ]

... Հայեր[ս] փորձառութեամբ գիտենք որ ինչ որ բարձր շրջանակներու մէջ կը խօսուի չ'իրագործուիր, իսկ ինչ որ ստորին դասակարգին մէջ կը խօսուի այն է որ կ'իրականանայ: Հետեւաբար Այնթապի հայութեան կեանքը վտանգի մէջ է ստոյգ կերպով: Հետեւաբար այս ժողովուրդը երկու չարեաց փոքրագոյնը նկատելով գաղթելը, զարհուրելի վնասներու ենթարկուիլը կամաւ յանձն առնելով որոշած է գաղթել, բայց չեն թողուր, կ'արգիլեն:

Այնթապի հայերը կը հարցնեն թէ ո՞ր օրէնքով կը բռնաբարեն իրենց ազատութիւնը, անոնք որ ապահովութիւններ առած էին իրենց համար: Հիմակու[ը]նէ երբ կը բռնաբարեն իրենց ազատութիւնը, ի՞նչպէս հաւատալ միւս խոստումներուն:

Իսկէնտէրուն (Տէր Սահակ Բ. Կաթողիկոսէն Կիլիկիոյ) – 29 Նոյեմբեր [1921][25]

Ֆրանքօ-թուրք համաձայնութեան շշուկները սկսած օրէն ժողովուրդը ինքնաբերաբար գալիք աղէտները աչքի առաջ բերելով՝ արտագաղթի պատրաստութեան ձեռնարկեց, նոյնիսկ շատերը ճամբայ ելան: Երբ համաձայնութեան մանրամասնութիւնը հրապարակ[ու]եցաւ եւ որոշ կերպով հասկցուեցաւ որ հայերու եւ ընդհանուր քրիստոնէից կեանքի ապահովութիւնը երաշխաւորող էական տարրեր կը պակսին, հարուստէն յետին աղքատը, երիտասարդէն գերեզմանամերձ ծերունին, արտագաղթի միակ գաղափարով վարակուեցան:

Մնալ եւ գաղթել երկուքն ալ մահաբոյր եւ մահառիթ էին, ոչ ոք պարտաւորութիւն կրնար առնել ըսելու. «Մի՛ գաղթէք, անողորմ մահը կը սպասէ [ձ]եզ» եւ ոչ ըսել. «Գաղթեցէ՛ք, որովհետեւ դրախտային կեանք մը կայ ձեր առջեւ»: Ուստի ֆրանսական կառավարութեան գիտութեամբ եւ հաւանութեամբ նահանգային ժողովի հրաւիրեցինք Ատանայի, Տարսոնի, Մերսինի, Ճիհանի, Օսմանիյէի եւ Տէօրթ-Եօլի ներկայացուցիչները: Մի քանի նիստերու մէջ երկար վիճաբանութեամբ եւ խորհրդակցութեամբ այն եզրակացութեան եկան թէ չենք կարող յանձնարարել ժողովուրդին մնալու, իսկ մենք գաղթելու միջոցներու պակասութիւնը եւ հայրենիքը լքելու տխուր հետեւանքները ի նկատի ունենալով, գաղթի գաղափարը չքաջալերեցինք: Ժողովուրդը՝ հակառակ ֆրանսական պաշտօնական հաւաստիքներուն ֆրանսացի ոմանց պաշտօնէից, [անսալով] Ցիուսեան միսիոնի անդամներուն եւ նոյնիսկ բարեմիտ մահմետականաց թելադրութեան՝ թէ մի հաւատաք տրուած հաւաստիքներուն, գաղթի գաղափարը իրականացուց եւ մեծ ծաւալ տուաւ: Հայ, յոյն, ասորի, քէլտանի, արապ եւ թուրք հակա[քեմալական]ներ խուռներամ ափ առին տարաշխարհիկութեան քարքարուտ ու փշալից ճանապարհը եւ շատ կարճ ժամանակի մէջ քաղաքը դատարկուեցաւ, ճրագները մարեցան եւ օճախներու մուխը մարեցաւ:

Քեմալականք թերեւս չէին սպասեր այս անակնկալին, ուստի Պոզանթիէն գրեցին ու փորձեցին առաջքն առնել եւ կասեցնել արտագաղթը եւ իրենց գործիչներուն միջոցաւ փափաք յայտնեցին տեսակցութիւն մ'ունենալ Ազգային ներկայացուցիչներու հետ: Գործիչները կամ միջնորդներն էին Սիւլէյման Վահիտ, Կէրկէրլի զատէ Ալի, Միւճթէպա եւ չորրորդ մը՝ Մուսթաֆա էֆենտիներ, որոնք նամակ մը կը ներկայացնեն հոգեւոր պետերուն, ստորագրեալ Ատանացի Սուպհի փաշայէն եւ Ատանայի նախորդ թաղապետութեան նախագահ Տըպլան զատէ Մուհամմէտ էֆէնտիէ, որոնք փափաք կը յայտնէին տեսնուիլ ի Տիքիլի կամ ի Տէրէպէք թրքական հողի վրայ: Ֆրանսական իշխանութիւնք ալ այս տեսակցութիւնը քաջալերեցին եւ դիւրութիւններ հայթայթեցին, երթեւեկի համար երեք օթօմօպիլ տրամադրելով:

Բանագնացները՝ Կաթողիկոսական Փոխանորդ Գերաշնորհ Եղիշէ Եպիսկոպոս, Գերապայծառ Քեբլիկեան Յարութիւն Եպիսկոպոս, Պատուելի Յարութիւնեան, հայ երեւելիներէն՝ Պզտիկեան Ստեփան էֆէնտի եւ յոյն երեւելիներէն Գարաեաղուպ օղլու Պօտոսաքի, Շիւրքի օղլու Ասլան էֆենտիներ, վերոյիշեալ թուրք միջնորդներու առաջնորդութեամբ Նոյեմբեր 15ի առաւօտուն

meeting to prevent, if possible, the migration of Christians, particularly Armenians, which would be doubly harmful to both the country and the migrants. [He said:] "The next government, to the extent of being just and exemplary, will apply the law equally to Muslims and Christians." Eşref Bey and Deblanzade spoke along the same line.

The spiritual leaders noted that there was nothing satisfactory about Christians in the signed agreement and that their compatriotic words would not be a sufficient guarantee for the return of those who had migrated or those who plan to migrate. The Armenians departed, saying that they would endeavor nevertheless.

The stream of migration is moving forward with new impetus. A few days after the first negotiations, on November 22, to satisfy the wishes of Hamit Bey—internal affairs adviser to the nationalist government who had been appointed extraordinary governor of Adana province—the military Muhittin Pasha, and especially Colonel Sarrou, the French authorities invited the first delegation, for the second time, to have a second meeting in Menije, where Franklin-Bouillon's arrival was expected by train. But before Bouillon's arrival, Hamit Bey took the opportunity to discuss the Armenian-Turkish relationship. He clarified the issue of mutual distrust and gave assurances of the Ankara government's justice and goodwill toward its Christian subjects, chiefly Armenians.

At four o'clock, Mr. Franklin-Bouillon arrived with his followers, as did Armenian and other national representatives from Mersin and Tarsus. Chaired by Mr. [Franklin-]Bouillon, with the participation of Hamit Bey and the newly appointed consul general Mr. Laporte, a consultative or advisory meeting was convened, repeating the commonplace words and exhortations of security and assurance to stop the migration of the people and bring back the departed. Objections of the representatives were heard: "Often the promises of the Turkish government have remained unheard [in the Interior] and unfulfilled. On the contrary, they have borne bloody fruits."

The next day, on the evening of November 23, the same assurances by the same personalities were repeated to religious representatives gathered in the residence of Franklin-Bouillon by special invitation, but the people, not persuaded by the arguments presented, en masse crowded the road of exodus with steam cars, cars, and carriages, including many on foot. With this heavy passage, barely two thousand people remained in the city, some of them officials and the rest [primarily] disabled men and women. The schools were closed because neither students nor teachers were left; church services ceased because no officiants remained. I considered my stay in this painful and deplorable situation unwise and pointless, especially considering the possibility of my deprivation from any contact, especially since the situation of Gaziantep [Ayntab] and Kilis was much more worrying. On November 21, I delivered to General Dufieux a telegram addressed to General Gouraud, asking him for:

1. the release of Armenian prisoners,
2. the relocation of Armenian orphans, [and]
3. the departure of the people of Dörtyol to İskenderun and thence their gradual dispersion to places of their choice. I also asked for permission to cross into Aleppo personally. The general promised to transmit my telegram immediately to the high commission conveying my intention to leave, adding on his part what was needed.

On November 23, General Dufieux wrote an autographed letter stating that the rendition for full facilitation of my departure with my followers on the 25th had been ordered, and, at the same time, secondly, he announced his departure and informed me that he would come to say farewell. This kind and favorable announcement obligated us to prepare [for departure] and move our property to the station.

On November 24, late evening, the new French consul general visited on behalf of Mr. [Franklin-]Buillon. A long meeting took place with the following summary: "The next government will be

կանուխ կը մեկնին ի Տիքիլի Պօզանթիէն գալիքներուն սպասելու, բայց թուրք ուղեկիցները կը խնդրեն շարունակել ճանապարհը մինչեւ ի Կէլէնչիկ, ուր հասնելով կը սպասեն. կու գան Պօզանթիէն եկողները եւ քաղաքավարական տեսակցութիւններէ ետքը, Սուպհի փաշա խօսք բանալով կ'ըսէ որ կառավարութեան կողմէ ոեւէ պաշտօնական հանգամանք չունի, այլ իբրեւ հայրենակից հայրենակցական պարտաւորութիւններէ թելադրեալ փափաքած են այս տեսակցութեան, որպէսզի եթէ կարելի ըլլայ քրիստոնէից, ի մասնաւորի հայոց, արտագաղթի առաջքն առնել, որ կրկնապէս վնասակար է թէ՛ երկրին եւ թէ՛ գաղթողներուն: Գալիք կառավարութիւնը արդարասէր եւ օրինակելի ըլլալու աստիճան, օրէնքը պիտի գործադրուի հաւասարապէս իսլամին եւ քրիստոնեային համար. միեւնոյն կերպով կ'արտայայտուին Էշրէֆ պէյ եւ Տրպլան զատէ:

Հոգեւոր պետերը դիտել կու տան որ ստորագրուած համաձայնագրին մէջ քրիստոնէից մասին զոհացուցիչ բան չկայ, իսկ իրենց հայրենակցական խօսքերն ալ բաւական երաշխիքներ չեն կրնար ըլլալ գաղթողները կամ գաղթելիքները յետ վերադարձնելու, այսուհանդերձ կ'աշխատինք ըսելով կը բաժնուին իրարմէ:

Գաղթականութեան հոսանքը նոր թափով յառաջ կ'երթայ եւ առաջին բանակցութենէն քանի մ'օր յետոյ, Նոյեմբեր 22ին ազգայնական կառավարութեան ներքին գործոց խորհրդական Համիտ պէյ, որ Ատանայի նահանգին արտասովոր վարիչ կարգուած է ու զինուորական Մուհետտին փաշայի, մանաւանդ գօլօնէլ Սառօյի փափաքին գոհացում տրուելու համար ֆրանսական իշխանութիւնը երկրորդ անգամ հրաւիրեց առաջին պատուիրակութիւնը որ Մէնիճէ երկրորդ տեսակցութիւն մը ունենայ, ուր ճեպընթացով ժամը 4ին Պ. Ֆրանքլին Պույ[ե]օն պիտի գայ: Բայց յառաջ քան Պույօնի ժամանումը, Համիտ պէյ պատեհութիւն կ'ունենայ հայ եւ թուրք յարաբերութիւնը շօշափել եւ փոխադարձ անվստահութեան խնդիրը լուսաբանել եւ իր կողմէ հաւաստիքներ տալ Էնգարայի կառավարութեան արդարասիրութեան եւ բարեացակամութեան հանդէպ հպատակ քրիստոնէից, առաւելապէս հայերու:

Ժամը 4ին՝ Պ. Ֆրանքլին Պույեօն կը հասնի իր հետեւորդներով, ինչպէս եւ Մերսինի եւ Տարսոնի հայ եւ այլ ազգաց ներկայացուցիչներ: Նախագահութեամբ Պ. Պույօնի, մասնակցութեամբ Համիտ պէյի եւ ֆրանսացի նորընտիր ժէնէրալ գոնսիլ[26] Պ. Լափօռթի, խորհրդակցական կամ խրատալուր ժողով մը կը կազմուի, կը կրկնուին ապահովութեան եւ երաշխաւորութեան չոր ու ցամաք խօսքերն ու յորդորները ժողովուրդի արտագաղթը կասեցնելու եւ մեկնողները վերադարձնելու համար: Կը լսուին ներկայացուցիչներու առարկութիւնները թէ՝ «յաճախ թուրք կառավարութեան խոստումներն անլսելի մնացած են եւ անգործադրելի, նաեւ ընդհակառակն արիւնալի պտուղներ տուած են»:

Հետեւեալ օրը, Նոյեմբեր 23ի երեկոյին, մասնաւոր հրաւիրագրով Ֆրանգլին Պույեօնի տունը հաւաքուած հոգեւոր ներկայացուցիչներուն նոյն հաւաստիքները կը կրկնուին միեւնոյն անձնաւորութեանց կողմանէ, սակայն ժողովուրդը չկրնալով համոզուիլ այդ տուիքներուն, գունդագունդ գաղթի ճանապարհը կը լեցունէ շոգեկառքով, օթօմօպիլով, կառքով եւ շատեր հետիոտն: Այս յորդահոս գնացքով քաղաքին մէջ հազիւ 2000 հոգի մնաց, մաս մը պաշտօնեայ եւ մնացեալները երկու սեռէ անկարներ: Դպրոցները փակուեցան, որովհետեւ ո՛չ ուսանող եւ ո՛չ ուսուցիչ մնացին, դադրեցան պաշտամունք, որովհետեւ պաշտօնակատարներ չմնացին, իրաց այս ցաւագին եւ տխրառիթ կացութեան մէջ մեր մնալն ալ անխորհուրդ եւ աննպատակ համարելով, մանաւանդ հաւանական սեպելով որ ամէն յարաբերութենէ պիտի զրկուիմ, իսկ Այնթապի եւ Քիլիսի կացութիւնը շատ աւելի մտահոգիչ էր, ուստի Նոյեմբեր 21ին Ժէնէրալ Տիւֆիէօի առ Ժէնէրալ Կուրօ ուղղեալ հեռագիր մը յանձնեցի[27], որով կը խնդրէի

1. Հայ բանտարկեալց ազատ թողուիլը,

2. Հայ որբերու տեղափոխութիւնը,

3. Տէօրթեօլցիներու ճանապարհի դրուիլը դէպի Իսկէնտէրուն, ուրկէ հետզհետէ ուզած տեղերնին ցրուին անոնք, խնդրեցի նաեւ արտօնել որ մենք անձամբ Հալէպ անցնինք: Ժէնէրալը

just. The rights of minorities will be protected with the exact provisions that Poland has adopted for the governance of its subjects of foreign origins and those professing other religions. The nationalist government will implement the agreement it signed for the first time with a civilized nation precisely to protect its interests and honor before the civilized world; therefore, the migrant people must be saved from misery, and work needs to be done for their return to protect their rights against the risk of losses. Your intention to leave will surmount the complete loss of people's trust in the French and Turkish governments.

I consider it superfluous to repeat my answers one by one: "They destroyed my seat, Kozan [Sis]; I am a guest in Adana; I will go to Syria, the French zone where I have as many people as there were in Adana. We believed in the French love of justice, and gathered, upon the abetment of Mr. Georges-Picot, high commissioner for Syria and Armenia, the migrant people from the deserts of Syria and Mesopotamia in Cilicia. Once we see that the new government loves justice, as you assure, we will gather them again." Laporte argued: "If no Christian people are left, how will the Turks prove their humanitarian spirit?" "The Turks have a sizeable Christian population in Anadolu [Anatolia], too; let them show their love of justice to them. Unfortunately, the information we receive confirms the opposite." Laporte was unable to offer a specific answer to our remark; he simply repeated that the interests of the Turks demand that they do not commit massacres; that this could be a last attempt to save their homeland; that our departure can also be considered an insult to France, which left five thousand of its sons here. The answer to this simple and vile expression was: "Christians cannot subject their lives and existence to experiment with the Turks' love of justice." And because he praised Hamit Bey's honesty, my answer was: "I know Hamit Bey as upright and kind. So long as he was the governor of Diyarbakır, there were no deportations or massacres there, but a nation cannot consider its existence secured [thus] because the government can oust Hamit Bey and send someone else as his replacement who will literally carry out the government's secret plans, as it happened to Hamit Bey in Diyarbakır, where someone else succeeded him and acted the opposite of his predecessor's goodwill entirely. We appreciate France's sacrifices in favor of the Armenians; we always feel pain and respect for the French forces who fell in Cilicia. They counted our sons in their ranks. But we cannot forget the thirty thousand Armenian martyrs who were sacrificed for the glory of France from the armistice to this day."

Mr. Laporte left half sad and half desperate, and on the morning of November 25, we left unhindered by train. At six o'clock in the evening, we arrived safely in İskenderun, where the representatives of the French and local governments and grieving Armenians welcomed us. Although I did not doubt that my trip could be banned, the news received day by day doubled my pain.

The gates of Syria, Palestine, Smyrna, and even Cyprus are completely closed before the Armenian migration. Travelers to Cyprus get their visas approved if they have first- or second-class tickets. Tens of thousands [Armenian migrants] have been left stranded in the cold and rainy weather in Mersin; one-fourth of [the Armenians of] Dörtyol have moved to İskenderun and wallow in the mud like frogs; ten thousand people from Dörtyol and Amanos wait every day for death or savior vessels. But time is running out, and the hyena government is expected [to take charge] today or tomorrow. The lion restrained in a cage will be forced to destroy the cage and throw itself into the claws of death. The people are willing to abandon the paradise of orange groves and leave without return.

Migration from Gaziantep and Kilis is said to be forbidden; if that is true, then some of the people of Gaziantep who left have been turned back halfway or are not allowed to continue their journey. This situation has no name or description. The people of Gaziantep fought for months in favor of the French. Several times they honorably reconciled at the request of the Turks and again, pressured by the French, they became enemies and fought against the enemies. Behold, these unique people have been left to their black destiny with the Franco-Turkish agreement and are being sacrificed to ruthless and blood-

խոստացաւ հեռագիրս անմիջապէս փոխանցել, պէտք եղածը իր կողմանէ աւելցնելով եւ մեկնումի մտադրութիւնը բարձր քոմիսէրութեան հաղորդել:

Նոյեմբեր 23ին Ժէնէրալ Տիւֆիօ ինքնագիր նամակով մը կը հաղորդէր որ մեր հետեւորդներով 25ին մեկնելու ամէն դիւրութիւն հրամայուած է եւ միեւնոյն ատեն՝ երկրորդ՝ իր մեկնումը ծանուցանելով «մնաք բարեաւ» ըսելու գալը կ'իմացնէր: Այս բարեսիրական եւ բարեյաջող զեկոյցին վրայ պարտաւորուեցանք պատրաստուիլ եւ գոյքերը կայարան փոխադրել:[28]

Նոյեմբեր 24ին, երեկոյին ուշ ատեն նորեկ ֆրանսական ընդհանուր հիւպատոսը այցելութեան եկաւ յանուն Պ. Պույեօնի, երկար տեսակցութիւն տեղի ունեցաւ, որուն ամփոփումն է «Գալիք կառավարութիւնը արդարասէր պիտի ըլլայ, փոքրամասնութեանց իրաւունքները պիտի պաշտպանուին, այն տրամադրութիւններով, զոր Լեհաստան ընդունած է իր օտարացեղ եւ օտարակրօն հպատակները կառավարելու համար:

Ազգայնական կառավարութիւնը քաղաքակիրթ ազգի մը հետ առաջին անգամ կնքած համաձայնագիրը ճշդիւ պիտի գործադրէ, իր շահը եւ պատիւը պաշտպանելու համար առաջի քաղաքակիրթ աշխարհի, ուստի պէտք է գաղթող ժողովուրդը թշուառութենէ ազատելու եւ իր իրաւունքները կորուստի մատնուելու վտանգէն զերծ պահելու համար աշխատիլ վերադարձնել, իսկ ձեր մեկնելու մտադրութիւնը բոլորովին կորսնցնել պիտի ըլլայ ժողովուրդին վստահութիւնը առ ֆրանսական եւ թրքական կառավարութիւնը:

Պատասխաններս մի առ մի կրկնել աւելորդ կը սեպեմ, «Իմ աթոռս՝ Սիս քար ու քանդ ըրին, Ատանայի մէջ հիւր եմ, պիտի մեկնիմ ի Սուրիա, ֆրանսական գօտին, ուր այնքան ժողովուրդ ունիմ որքան կային Ատանայի մէջ. մենք հաւատալով Ֆրանսայի արդարասիրութեան Սուրիոյ եւ Հայաստանի Բարձր Քոմիսէր Պրն. Ժօրժ Բիքօյի թելադրութեամբ Սուրիոյ եւ Միջագետքի անապատնեբէն ժողովեցինք գաղթող ժողովուրդը ի Կիլիկիա, երբ տեսնուի որ ձեր տուած հաւաստիքներուն համաձայն գալիք կառավարութիւնը արդարասէր ըլլայ, նորէն կը ժողովենք», որուն Լափօըթ առարկեց. «Եթէ քրիստոնեայ ժողովուրդ չմնայ, թուրքերը ի՞նչպէս պիտի ապացուցանեն իրենց մարդասիրական ոգին»: «Թուրքերը ունին նաեւ Անատօլուի մէջ բաւական քրիստոնեայ բնակչութիւն մը, թող իրենց արդարասիրութիւնը անոնց մասին ցոյց տան. դժբաղդաբար մեր առած տեղեկութիւնները հակառակը կը հաստատեն»: Լափօըթ դրական պատասխան մը չկրցաւ տալ մեր այս դիտողութեան, միայն կը կրկնէր թէ թուրքերու շահը կը պահանջէ որ ջարդ չընեն, այս վերջին փորձ մը կրնար ըլլալ իրենց հայրենիքը փրկելու համար, ձեր մեկնիլը նաեւ ապերախտութիւն մը կրնայ համարուիլ Ֆրանսայի դէմ, որ իր զաւակներէն 5000 հոգի թողուց հոս: Այս պարզ ու նուաստ արտայայտութեան պատասխանս եղաւ «Քրիստոնեաները չեն կարող իրենց կեանքը եւ գոյութիւնը թուրքի արդարասիրութեան փորձին ենթարկելու», եւ որովհետեւ Համիտ պէյի ուղղամտութիւնը գովեց, պատասխանս եղաւ. «Ես կը ճանաչեմ Համիտ [պէյը, որ ուղղամիտ] եւ բարեսէր է. որչափ որ Տիարպէքիրի վալի էր, տարագրութիւն եւ ջարդ տեղի չունեցաւ հոն, սակայն ազգ մը իր գոյութիւնը անցընելու վրայ չի կրնար ապահով համարիլ, որովհետեւ կառավարութիւնը կրնայ պաշտօնազրկել Համիտ պէյը եւ ուրիշ մը ղրկել տեղը, որ կառավարութեան գաղտնի ծրագիրները տառապէս կը գործադրէ, ինչպէս պատահեցաւ Համիտ պէյին Տիարպէքիր, ուր ուրիշ մը յաջորդեց իրեն եւ բոլորովին հակառակը ի գործ դրաւ իր նախորդի բարեացակամութեան: Մենք Ֆրանսայի ի նպաստ հայոց ըրած զոհողութիւնները կը գնահատենք, միշտ կը ցաւինք եւ կը յարգենք Կիլիկիոյ մէջ ինկող ֆրանսական զօրաց[29], որոնց մէջ կային եւ մեր զաւակներէն, բայց չենք կարող անյիշատակ թողուլ այն 30000 հայ նահատակները՝ որոնք զինադադարէն մինչեւ այսօր Ֆրանսայի փառքին համար զոհուեցան»:

Պրն. Լափօըթ կէս վշտացած եւ կէս յուսահատ մեկնեցաւ եւ մենք Նոյեմբեր 25ին առաւօտեան շոգեկառքով անարգել մեկնեցանք եւ երեկոյեան ժամը 6ին ողջամբ հասանք Ալէքսանդրէթ, ուր ֆրանսական եւ տեղական կառավարութեան ներկայացուցիչներ եւ վշտահար ազգայիններ բարի գալուստի դիմաւորութեամբ ընդունեցին մեզ: Թէեւ ուղեւորութիւննիս արգիլող ոեւէ կասկածէ

thirsty deaths. Behold, this is the hellish state of Cilicia!

My request, as well as the cry of agony of Cilicia, is to save this critical fragment of Armenians at all costs; first moving it somewhere, to a fox den or a bird's nest, and then to feed the needy for a while until the good God prepares a paradise of salvation with a new creation. If we, the people of Cilicia, will die, let us die in far, very far places, so the enemy will fail to make us hate our adorable Cilicia with our blood and bones.

I do not believe that the appeals will be helpful, yet let us appeal, knock on the doors of compassion and humanity hard enough to shatter them, then the petrified doors will perhaps open. Perhaps the world's pharaohs will relent, come to conscience, and save an ancient people who are falling victim to their devilish or diplomatic plots from imminent death.

If the Lord allows us to succeed, today we will leave for the Damascene Tripoli, to go thence to Aleppo. May this journey bring me closer to the grave!

Dörtyol (from Reverend Father Paren)—December 4 [1921][128]

On December 3, the French deputy commander-in-chief (since the commander Mr. Dumont was summoned to Adana by a telegram) called the Armenian spiritual representative to inform him that "the commander, at night, with his telegram from Adana, sends special greetings and announces the good news that he will return tomorrow to Dörtyol with good news."

Indeed, the same evening, the commander arrived and repeated the following hopeful and encouraging words to the Armenian spiritual representative: "The Turkish regime will never enter Dörtyol, and we will not withdraw, indefinitely, from this place, which I have high hopes will be annexed to Syria soon. TThe French diplomatic representative has taken great interest in your request and is studying it. In the near future, it will be resolved in a way advantageous for you and us, so let the people be calm and let them stop the migration. The system of a passport will be canceled effective tomorrow, and everyone will be free to go to Syria and come here thence."

The commander responded affirmatively to the Armenian spiritual representative's question about whether it is permissible to write to the homeless and miserable people crowded in İskenderun, telling them to return there [Dörtyol].

And when he was asked about his view regarding the condition of the part of Armenians who re-

ձերծ, սակայն օր ըստ օրէ առնուած լուրերը ցաւերնիս կրկնապատկեցին:

Սուրիոյ, Պաղեստինի, Զմիւռնիոյ, նոյնիսկ Կիպրոսի դռները փակուած են բոլորովին հայ գաղթին հանդէպ. Կիպրոս գնացողներէն առաջին եւ Բ. կարգի *պիլէթ* ունեցողներուն *փաս*երը *վիզէ* կ'ըլլուին: Մերսին տասնեակ հազարներով ցուրտ եւ անձրեւային եղանակին բացօդեայ մնացած են, Տէօրթեօլէն ¼ տեղափոխուած են Ալէքսանդրէթ եւ գորտերու նման ցեխերու մէջ կը քաշքշուին, տասն հազար ալ տէօրթ-եօլցի եւ ամանոսցի օրէ օր մահուան կամ ազատարար նաւերու կը սպասեն. բայց ժամանակը կը համառօտուի եւ բորենական կառավարութիւնը այսօր կամ վաղը կը սպասուի: Գառազեղի մէջ զսպուած առիւծը պիտի պարտաւորուի խորտակել գառազեղը եւ նետուիլ մահուան ճիրաններուն մէջ: Յօժար են թողուլ նարնջենեաց դրախտը եւ անդառնալի կերպով մեկնիլ:

Այնթապի եւ Քիլիսի գաղթը արգիլուած է կ'ըսուի, եթէ ստոյգ է՝ նոյնիսկ մաս մը մեկնող այնթապցիներ կէս ճանապարհէն ետ դարձուած են կամ արգիլուած են իրենց ճանապարհէն. այս կացութիւնը ո՛չ անուն եւ ո՛չ նկարագիր ունի. ի նպաստ ֆրանսացւոց ամիսներով կռուեցան այնթապցիք, քանիցս թուրքաց խնդրանքին վրայ պատուաւորապէս հաշտուեցան ու դարձեալ ֆրանսացւոց ստիպմամբ թշնամացան եւ կռուեցան թշնամիներուն հետ. ահա այս աննման ժողովուրդը ֆրանքօ-թուրք համաձայնութեամբ կը թողուի իր սեւ ճակատագրին եւ կը նուիրուի անողորմ եւ արիւնախում Մողոքին: Ահա այս է ցանկալի Կիլիկիային դժոխային վիճակը:

Խնդիրս, ինչպէս նաեւ բովանդակ Կիլիկիոյ օրհասական աղաղակն է ազատել ամէն գնով հայութեան այս կարեւոր բեկորը, նախ տեղ մը, աղուէսներու որջ մը կամ թռչնական բոյն մը տեղափոխել, ապա ժամանակ մը հաց տալ կարօտներուն մինչեւ Բարին Աստուած նոր ստեղծագործութեամբ փրկութեան դրախտ մը պատրաստէ: Եթէ պիտի մեռնինք մենք կիլիկեցիքս՝ հեռու, շատ հեռու տեղեր մեռնինք, որպէսզի թշնամին չյաջողի մեր արիւնով եւ մեր ոսկորներով ատելի դարձնել մեզ մեր պաշտելի Կիլիկիան:

Չեմ հաւատար թէ դիմումները օգուտ ունենան, այսուհանդերձ դիմենք, գթութեան ու մարդասիրութեան դռները բաղխենք՝ խորտակելու չափ ուժգնօրէն, թերեւս բացուին քարացած դռները, թերեւս աշխարհի փարաւոնները մեղմանան, խղճի զան եւ իրենց դիւական կամ դիւանագիտական դաւերուն զոհ եղող հնամենի ժողովուրդ մը փրկեն[30] վերահաս մահուանէ:

Եթէ Տէրը յաջողէ, այսօր Դամասկեան Տրիպոլիս կը մեկնինք, անկից Հալէպ երթալու համար. իղձ՛ւ այս ճամբորդութիւնս մօտեցնէր գերեզմանին:

Տէօրթեօլ (Փառէն Վարդապետէն) – 4 Դեկտեմբեր [1921]

Դեկտեմբեր 3ին ֆրանսական հրամանատարին փոխանորդը (հրամատար Մ. Տիւմօն հեռագրով կոչուած ըլլալով Ատանա) հայոց հոգեւոր ներկայացուցիչը կոչելով հաղորդեց թէ «հրամատարը, գիշերը, Ատանայէն քաշած իր հեռագրով, մասնաւոր բարեւներ ունի եւ կ'աւետէ թէ բարի լուրով կը վերադառնայ վաղը ի Տէօրթ-Եօլ»:

Արդարեւ նոյն իրիկունը հասաւ հրամատարը եւ դարձեալ հայ հոգեւոր ներկայացուցիչին ըսաւ հետեւեալ յուսատու եւ սրտապնդիչ խօսքերը: «Թուրք րէժիմը երբեք չպիտի մտնէ Տէօրթ-Եօլ, եւ մենք չպիտի քաշուինք, անորոշ ժամանակաւ, այս տեղէն՝ որ յոյս մեծ ունիմ, պիտի կցուի ի մօտոյ Սիւրիոյ: Մեծ շահագրգռութեամբ եւ կարեւորութեամբ ձեռք առած է եւ կ'ուսումնասիրէ ֆրանսացի դիւանագիտական ներկայացուցիչը ձեր խնդիրքը եւ մօտ օրէն ան կը լուծուի ձեզ եւ մեզ նպաստաւոր կերպով, հետեւաբար թող հանգիստ ըլլայ ժողովուրդը եւ դադրեցնէ գաղթը: Վաղուընէ սկսեալ ջնջուած է բասբօրի դրութիւնը եւ ամէն մարդ ազատ է Սուրիա երթալու եւ անկէ հոս գալու»:

Հայ հոգեւոր ներկայացուցիչին այն հարցումին թէ կ'արտօնուի՞ գրել Իսկէնտէրուն խճողուած, անտուն ու թշուառ մնացած ժողովուրդը հոն դառնալու, հրամատարը հաստատական պատասխան կուտայ:

Իսկ երբ հարցում եղաւ թէ ինչպէս զտած է Ատանա մնացած մաս մը հայերուն եւ Մերսինի

main in Adana and the ten to fifteen thousand Armenians who are waiting for the steamer on the shores of Mersin—of whom we have heard are very desperate and miserable, and many are thinking of returning to Adana under duress and reluctantly—the commander answered: "Their situation can certainly be described as very miserable, and we are thinking of moving them here when the border issue is finally resolved soon, which I have high hopes for."

This conversation encouraged the people of Dörtyol.

Dörtyol (from Reverend Father Paren)—December 10 [1921][129]

Special buildings were set up on May 4–5 for the Commission of Border Examination and Determination, which consists of three Frenchmen and nine Turks, with a twenty-four-strong cavalry patrol. The French members arrived and were waiting for the arrival of the Turkish members from Adana, but because the Turks were late, the French colonel went to Adana to invite them here; however, they have not yet arrived.

The Kemalists, having heard in Adana that Franklin-Buillon was planning to expand the border upon the request of the Armenians of Dörtyol and not tolerating at all that after the departure of Armenians of the Adana region from their homeland, the Armenians of Dörtyol may succeed in making such a critical enterprise, they tried to abort it. To do so, as of the first day of December, the Kemalists are sending their men to the Turkish villages around here and indoctrinating them and having them sign petitions in which they are expressing their wish to enter under the Kemalist government.

It was as a result of this that Franklin-Buillon traveled to Ankara to obtain the consent of the Grand National Assembly and its leader on the border issue, but he was late, barely returning to Adana a day or two ago, it has been reported. Nevertheless, the arrival of the Turkish members of the border commission is delayed. On the other hand, the Kemalist regime has re-established itself as far as Osmaniye and Erzin. It removed all the officials (even Turks) who served during the French rule and entrusted the positions, from chamberlain to sweeper, to trusted people from their organization. Here, however, the Kemalists never stepped foot in Çaylı, Papaz, Taba, and a few other Turkish villages and Dörtyol itself, and everything goes on as before. Even yesterday, fifty to sixty French cavalry and about three hundred infantrymen arrived and settled in the local garrison with their vehicles and equipment.

Dörtyol (from Reverend Father Paren)—14 December [1921][130]

French colonel Petla, one of the functionaries of Cilicia's evacuation, arrived here yesterday with a French colonel in charge of the border commission, [along with] the French consul general in Adana and his deputy. They invited the representatives of the people of Dörtyol, the Armenian primate, and local French and Turkish personnel to the government building and made an announcement and exhortations this way: "Before coming from Paris with this position, I saw Noradoungian and Chobanian, who assured me that the natives of Cilicia would be satisfied with the Franco-Turkish agreement and that non-Cilician refugee Armenians might want to migrate. But when I came to Adana, I saw regretfully that ninety out of one hundred people had already left. When I went to invite the ten to twenty thousand people waiting in Mersin to Adana, they told me that they had been deceived by the propaganda of committees from within and from outside, and particularly by the clergy's threats of ex-communication; but since we have already come here, leaving our homes and places behind, we can no longer return. Therefore, knowing this bitter and real confession, also knowing that the Armenian migrants from Cilicia are not accepted by any power and have been abandoned and that France again is hosting them on the Syrian coast, also knowing full well that there is no expectation from British,

ծովափը շոգենաւի սպասող 10–15,000 հայերու վիճակը, որոնց համար կը լսենք թէ շատ յուսահատ են եւ թշուառ եւ շատեր կը մտածեն Ատանա դառնալ, առ հարկի եւ յակամայս, հրամատարը կը պատասխանէ թէ «ստուգիւ շատ թշուառ կը նկարագրեն անոնց վիճակը եւ մենք կը մտածենք զանոնք հոս փոխադրել՝ երբ ի մօտոյ լուծուի վերջնականապէս սահմանի խնդիրը, որուն շատ մեծ յոյս ունիմ»:

Այս խօսակցութիւնը կ'ոգեւորէ տէօրթ-եօլցիքը:

Տէօրթեօլ (Փառէն Վարդապետէն) – 10 Դեկտեմբեր [1921]

Սահմանի քննիչ եւ ճշդող խառն յանձնաժողովին համար, որուն կ'անդամակցին 3 ֆրանսացի եւ 9 թուրք, 24 հեծեալ զինուորներու պահակախումբով մը, յատուկ շէնքեր պատրաստած էին ամսոյս 4–5ին եւ ֆրանսական անդամները եկած էին եւ կը սպասէին Ատանայէն գալիք թուրք անդամներուն, սակայն անոնք ուշանալնուն համար ֆրանսացի զնդապետը գնաց Ատանա զանոնք հոս հրաւիրելու համար, սակայն դեռ չեկան անոնք:

Ատանայի մէջ, Քէմալականք իմացած ըլլալով որ Տէօրթ-Եօլի հայերուն դիմումին վրայ Ֆրանքլին Պիյեօն կը ծրագրէ սահմանի ընդլայնում եւ չհանդուրժելով երբեք որ Ատանայի շրջանին ամբողջ հայութիւնը ազգովին իրենց երկիրը լքելէ զաղթելէ վերջ Տէօրթ-Եօլի հայութիւնը յաջողի այսպիսի կարեւոր ձեռնարկ մը ընել, կը ջանան վիժեցնել զայն եւ ասոր համար Դեկտեմբերի առաջին օրէն սկսեալ Քէմալականք իրենց մարդիկը կը ղրկեն այս կողմի թուրք գիւղերը եւ բռրբականտ կ'ընեն եւ հանրագրութիւններ ստորագրել կուտան, որոնցմով փափաք կը յայտնեն Քէմալական կառավարութեան տակ մտնելու:

Եւ ասոր վրայ էր որ Ֆրանքլին Պիյեօն, որ Էնկիւրիւ գացած էր սահմանի խնդրոյն նկատմամբ Ազգային Մեծ Ժողովին եւ անոր պետին հաւանութիւնը ձեռք բերելու համար եւ կ'ուշանար, հազիւ 1–2 օր առաջ Ատանա վերադարձած է, կ'ըսուի. բայց եւ այնպէս դեռ կ'ուշանայ սահմանի քոմիսիոնի թուրք անդամներուն հոս գալը: Մինչդեռ միւս կողմէ երբ Քէմալական ռէժիմը եկած եւ վերահաստատուած է արդէն մինչեւ Օսմանիյէ եւ Երզըն, ֆրանսական իշխանութեան օրով պաշտօնավարող բոլոր պաշտօնեաները հեռացնելով (նոյնիսկ թուրքերը) եւ սենեկեան աւելածուները իրենց օճախէն վստահելի անձերու յանձնելով, աղին Չայլը, Փափաս, Թապայի, այլ քանի մը գիւղեր (թուրք) եւ նոյնինքն Տէօրթ-Եօլի մէջ մուտք չեն գործած բնաւ Քէմալիստները եւ ամէն բան կ'ընթանայ ըստ առաջնոյն եւ նոյնիսկ երէկ 50–60 հեծեալ եւ 300ի մօտ հետեւակ ֆրանսական զօրքեր իրենց կառքերովը եւ կազմերովն եկան հաստատուեցան տեղւոյս զօրանոցին մէջ:

Տէօրթեօլ (Փառէն Վարդապետէն) – 14 Դեկտեմբեր [1921]

Երէկ հոս եկաւ Կիլիկիոյ պարպումի պաշտօնեաներէն ֆրանսացի քօլօնէլ Բէթլան՝ իր հետը ունենալով սահմանագիծ քոմիսիոնի պետ ֆրանսացի քօլօնէլ մը, Ատանայի ֆրանսական ընդհանուր հիւպատոսը եւ ասոր փոխանորդը, եւ կառավարական շէնքը հրաւիրելով Տէօրթ-Եօլի ժողովուրդի ներկայացուցիչները եւ հայոց Առաջնորդը եւ տեղւոյն ֆրանսացի եւ թուրք պաշտօնէութիւնը, յայտարարութիւն մը եւ յորդորներ ըրաւ սա կերպով: «Ես, դեռ Բարիզէն չեկած այս պաշտօնով, տեսնուած էի Նորատունկեանի եւ Չօպանեանի հետ, որոնք հաւաստեր էին ինձ թէ բնիկ կիլիկեցիները զոհ պիտի մնան ֆրանքօ-թուրք համաձայնագրէն եւ ոչ-կիլիկեցի գաղթական հայերը թերեւս հեռանալ ուզեն: Բայց Ատանա գալուս, ցաւով տեսայ որ ժողովուրդին 100ին 90-ը արդէն մեկնած է, որուն Մերսինի մէջ սպասող 10–20 հազարը երբ գացի Ատանա հրաւիրելու, ինծի յայտնեցին թէ մենք խաբուեցանք ներսէն եւ դուրսէն եղած քոմիթէներու բրօբականտներէն եւ մասնաւորաբար հոգեւորականներու *աֆարօզ*ի սպառնալիքներէն, բայց քանի որ մէյ մը մեր տունը տեղը թողած հոս եկեր ենք, այլեւս չենք կրնար վերադառնալ: Հետեւաբար գիտնալով այս դառն ու իրական խոստովանութիւնը, գիտնալով նաեւ որ կիլիկեան հայ գաղթականները չեն ընդունուիր ոչ մէկ տէրութեան կողմէ եւ լքուած են եւ դարձեալ Ֆրանսան է որ կը հիւրընկալէ զանոնք

Greek or American policies for Armenians whose dream of forming a little Armenia has vanished, as the recent past has shown, knowing all these well, I hope for the people of Dörtyol to employ their experience and farsightedness not to depart their lush and wonderful homeland but rather remain loyal to the regime to come, which has demonstrated practically—and we have tangibly seen from December onward—that it is just, it keeps its promises, and is kind to its subjects, especially toward the rights of minorities, and above all toward the Armenians. At the same time, I must say that there is no longer a question of expanding or correcting the border, and the ensuing rumor that the Kemalists have recently demanded that we leave the rural district of Hassa to them is only a misunderstanding. Therefore, I would like to understand how many Armenians there are in Dörtyol, how many are locals, how many have migrated from the villages around Amanos, and what the people think about whether to migrate or stay. The refugees can go to İskenderun immediately, and we have already decided to give them a special place in one corner of Syria." Incidentally, it was replied that there are about thirty thousand refugees from the villages of Amanos here; that is, from Hasanbeyli, Bahçe, Düziçi, Lataşli, Süleymanlı [Zeytun], Dönüklü [Fındıcak], and other places. As for Armenians of Dörtyol, only an equal number of them is left since more than half of them have already migrated to İskenderun.

When the colonel asked who would be able to answer on behalf of the people, the Armenian primate stated that he was reserving his answer and delegating the talking to the representatives of the people, who said: "We have been sheltering in Cilicia for three years, relying only on the patronage of the French knightly government, its solemn promises, and its goodwill. However, now that France is withdrawing and our last hope of being annexed to Syria is also fading, we are left with no choice but to migrate immediately to İskenderun and to wait there for steamers or our destiny, no matter how unfortunate and deadly it may be."

The colonel asked: "Will no people be remaining, at least enough to guard your homes and gardens or allow for the formation of a commission to oversee your property, trade, utilization, and maintenance?"

The answer was: "We, as a nation, after exposing ourselves and our souls to misery and death, do not care about material things. We leave them all to the regime to come, which we hope, as you do, will be fair and conscientious and will not destroy or waste them. Although the bitter experience and instance were given to us in 1915–16 when our millions of buildings and precious and sacred property were registered properly and entrusted to commissions, there is nothing left now."

The colonel then said that he was convinced that the Armenians had decided to migrate as a whole. He urged them not to cause panic and to leave gradually and in an orderly manner for İskenderun, as there was still time until January 3, when the French would leave. He also assured me that French passports would be valid until April 4.

The people replied that they would leave by the end of December, in any case, peacefully and in an orderly manner.

Thus, the last hope was over, and migration was decided upon when Mr. Cambola, one of the civil officers of Dörtyol, unexpectedly called the Armenian spiritual representative and spoke to him as follows:

"Yesterday, Colonel Petla deeply regretted that he had spoken so harshly and even made allusions to the clergy. That is why you may not have spoken, and perhaps you have something to say," [so] he commended that I frankly relay to him what I have to say.

The Armenian primate responded: "If I learn why you are interested in the handful people of Dörtyol, its buildings and properties, and the number of remaining young men, after giving the whole of Cilicia to the Kemalists, despite [French] commitments and solemn promises, and after all the Armenians of Cilicia were exposed to migration and misery; and if I learn that you are not making a new

սուրիական ծովեզերքներ, եւ քաջ գիտնալով որ անգլիական, յունական եւ ամերիկեան քաղաքականութենէն ոեւէ ակնկալիք մը չկայ հայերուն համար, որոնց *պզտիկ Հայաստան* մը կազմելու երազն ալ յօդս ցնդած է, ինչպէս ցոյց տուաւ մերձաւոր անցեալը, այս ամէնը քաջ գիտնալով կը յուսամ որ տէօրթ-եօլցիք փորձառու եւ հեռատես կը գտնուին իրենց այս կանաչագեղ եւ սքանչելի հայրենիքէն չհեռանալ եւ կը մնան գալիք ռէժիմին հնազանդելով, որ Դեկտեմբերէն աղին գործնականապէս ալ ցոյց տուած է եւ մենք շօշափած ու տեսած ենք թէ արդար, խոստ[մ]նապահ եւ բարեացակամ է դէպի իր հպատակները, մանաւորաբար դէպի փոքրամասնութեանց իրաւունքները եւ մանաւանդ դէպի հայերը: Միեւնոյն ատեն պէտք է ըսեմ թէ սահմանի սրբագրութեան եւ ընդլայնումի խնդիրն ալ գոյութիւն չունի եւ միայն թիւրիմացութիւն մըն է սա պարագայէն ծնունդ առած [տարածայնութիւնը] թէ վերջերս Քէմալիստները մեզմէ պահանջած ըլլալով *Խասսա* գաւառակը իրենց թողուլ Տէօրթ-Եօլի շրջանակը, բայց այս մեր հակառաջարկը ընդունուած չըլլալով խնդիրը փակուած է: Հետեւաբար ես կ'ուզէի հասկնալ թէ Տէօրթ-Եօլի հայութիւնը ո՞րքան է, ո՞րքանը տեղացի եւ ո՞րքանը Ամանոսի շրջակայ գիւղերէն գաղթած է եւ թէ ի՞նչ կը խորհի ժողովուրդը – կ'ուզէ՞ գաղթել թէ մնալ: Նաեւ գաղթականները անմիջապէս կարող են մեկնիլ դէպի Իսկէնտէրուն եւ անոնց համար մենք արդէն մասնաւոր տեղ մը տալ որոշած ենք Սուրիոյ մէկ անկիւնը»: Անցողակի պատասխանուեցաւ թէ 30000ի մօտ Ամանոսի գիւղերէն, այսինքն Հասան Պէյլիէն, Պահճէէն, Խառնըէն, Լաթաշըլըէն, Չէյթունէն, Ֆընտըճագէն եւայլն գաղթականներ կան հոս, իսկ տէօրթ-եօլցիներէն մնացած են նոյնքան հայեր միայն, ըստ որում տէօրթ-եօլցիներուն կէսէն աւելին գաղթած է արդէն Իսկէնտէրուն:

Եւ երբ հարցում ուղղեց քօլօնէլը թէ ո՞վ ի վիճակի է պատասխանելու յանուն ժողովուրդին, հայոց Առաջնորդը յայտարարեց թէ իր պատասխանը կը վերապահէ եւ խօսքը կուտայ ժողովուրդի ներկայացուցիչներուն, որոնք ըսին. «Մենք երեք տարիէ ի վեր Կիլիկիա ապաստանած ենք վստահելով միայն Ֆրանսայի ասպետական կառավարութեան հովանաւորութեան, հանդիսաւոր խոստումներուն եւ բարեացակամ վերաբերումին, իսկ հիմա որ Ֆրանսան կը քաշուի եւ մեր վերջին յոյսն ալ (Սուրիոյ կցուելու մասին) կը մարի, մեզի ուրիշ բան չի մնար եթէ ոչ անմիջապէս գաղթել Իսկէնտէրուն եւ հոն սպասել շոգենաւերուն կամ մեր բաղդին, որքան ալ դժբաղդ ու մահաբեր ըլլայ ան»:

Գնդապետը հարցուց թէ «Արդեօք բնաւ ժողովուրդ չի՞ մնար, գէթ այնքան մը որ հսկէ ձեր տուներուն եւ պարտէզներուն եւ կարելի ըլլայ քօմիսիոն մը կազմել անոնցմէ՝ հսկելու համար ձեր կալուածներուն, առուծախին, շահագործումին եւ պահպանումի մասին»:

Պատասխանուեցաւ թէ «Մենք ազգովին եւ մեր անձն ու հոգիներն թշուառութեան եւ մահուան մատնելէ վերջ՝ կարեւորութիւն չենք տար նիւթական բաներուն եւ անոնց ամէնքը կը թողունք գալիք ռէժիմին որ կը յուսանք ձեզի հետ, թէ արդար եւ բարեխիղճ կը գտնուի եւ չի փճացներ կամ կորսնցներ զանոնք: Թէպէտեւ դառն փորձն ու օրինակն տրուած է մեզի 1915–16 շրջանին երբ մեր միլիոնաւոր շէնքերն եւ թանկագին ու նուիրական գոյքերը կանոնաւոր կերպով արձանագրուած եւ քօմիսիոններու յանձնուած են, այլ սակայն հիմա ոչ մէկ բան մնացած է:

Քօլօնէլը ասոր վրայ յայտնեց թէ ինքն համոզում գոյացուցած է թէ հայերը ազգովին գաղթել որոշած են, եւ յորդորեց որ մաս-մաս եւ կանոնաւոր մեկնին Իսկէնտէրուն, խուճապի տեղի չտան, քանի որ դեռ ժամանակ կայ մինչեւ Յունվար 3 որ ատեն իրենք պիտի մեկնին: Նոյնպէս հաւաստեց թէ ֆրանսական անցագիրները զօրութիւն պիտի ունենան մինչեւ Ապրիլ 4:

Ժողովուրդը պատասխանեց թէ իրենք ամէն պարագայի մինչեւ Դեկտեմբերի վերջ մեկնած կ'ըլլան խաղաղ եւ կանոնաւոր կերպով:

Այսպէս վերջին յոյսն ալ վերջացած էր եւ որոշուած էր գաղթը երբ անակնկալ կերպով Տէօրթ-Եօլի քաղաքային պաշտօնատարներէն Մ. Գամպօլա իր քովը կը կանչէ հայոց հոգեւոր ներկայացուցիչը եւ սապէս կը խօսի.

«Երէկ Մ. Գօլօնէլ Փէթլան չափազանց ցաւ զգացած է որ խիստ ոճով մը արտայայտուած է եւ նոյնիսկ հոգեւոր պետերուն վերագրում եւ ակնարկութիւն ըրած է եւ ասոր համար թերեւս դուք

commitment in favor of the Kemalists, but rather that you are truly working out a knightly and benevolent plan; and, finally, if I learn that at last, the French have understood that the Armenians and French have mutual interests in Cilicia, the things I have to say may be advantageous to both the French and the Armenians at the same time. But if I am not sure about this, I consider talking about it useless."

Mr. Cambola, without giving decisive assurance, said that it is only for the benefit and good of the Armenians that they are interested and want to be helpful. Therefore, the Armenian spiritual representative wished to take leave without prolonging the conversation.

At that time, Mr. Cambola made the following proposal on behalf of Mr. Petla: "Won't the Armenians of Dörtyol want to stay here and obey the Kemalists if an Armenian lieutenant governor is installed in Dörtyol, and an Armenian gendarmerie with an Armenian leader is appointed?"

With the people's mood in mind, the Armenian spiritual representative responded negatively, arguing that Turkish promises are of no value and that an Armenian lieutenant governor can be ousted overnight and the Armenian gendarmerie dispersed.

Mr. Cambola inquired lengthily about the migration of the Armenians of Dörtyol, especially with their intention to resist. The Armenian clergyman stated that he cannot say anything decisive.

* That same evening, the military commander of Dörtyol, who had been ill and not present at Mr. Petla's statements, called upon the Armenian spiritual leader and repeated Mr. Cambola's offers to him, adding to it only the presence of a French consul or a commander as a control.

The answer was again negative, given that the presence of a consul nowhere in Turkey has prevented massacres, lootings, and atrocities.

Beirut (from Zakaria Bzdigian)—5 January [1922]

All the Armenians of Adana, Tarsus, Dörtyol, and Osmaniye Province [Cebelibereket] migrated. The number of Armenians left in Adana can hardly be set at fifty to sixty, in Mersin, eighteen to twenty, while not a single Armenian remains in Dörtyol and Osmaniye Province.

Moving on to the Armenians of Gaziantep [Ayntab] and Kilis, the migration continues with the means available. Gaziantep is almost empty of its prosperous element; there are about five thousand Armenians left in the city who do not have the financial means to migrate. The French government has not provided funds during this period; therefore, they may not be able to migrate soon, although they are not willing to stay at all.

Addressing the issue of the transportation of the Armenians in Mersin, a French steamship company transported them to Syria for money, not for free, it has been said. Each passenger paid 855 kuruş to travel from Mersin to Beirut. The steamships were extremely crowded.

After arriving in Syria, the migrants are abandoned. The French government is not willing to care for the migrants' livelihood. They do not even offer a discounted train fare for those going to Damascus. They set off only a few special trains after collecting payment from the travelers according to the tariff

չէք արտայայտուած եւ զուցէ ըսելիքներ ունէիք», յանձնարարեց որ այժմ հաղորդեմ իրեն ըսելիքներս համարձակօրէն:

Հայոց Առաջնորդը կը պատասխանէ թէ «Եթէ գիտնամ որ ամբողջ Կիլիկիան Քէմալիստներուն տալէն վերջ, հակառակ յանձնառութիւններու եւ հանդիսաւոր խոստումներու, եւ Կիլիկիոյ ամբողջ հայերը գաղթի եւ թշուառութեան մատնուելէն վերջը, ինչո՞ւ կը հետաքրքրուիք Տէօրթ-Եօլի ափ մը ժողովուրդովը եւ անոր շէնքերով ու կալուածներով եւ որբա՛ն մարդ՝ երիտասարդ մնալովը, եւ եթէ գիտնամ թէ՝ Քէմալիստներու ի նպաստ նոր յանձնառութիւն մը չէք ստանձներ, այլ իրօ՛ք ապետական եւ բարեացակամ ծրագիր մը կը մշակէք, եթէ գիտնամ վերջապէս թէ թող ըլլայ վերջին պահուն ֆրանսացիք ըմբռնած են թէ Կիլիկիոյ մէջ հայոց եւ ֆրանսացւոց շահերը համաձայն են իրարու, ունիմ ըսելիքներ, թերեւս ֆրանսացւոց եւ հայոց միեւնոյն ատեն նպաստաւոր: Սակայն եթէ վստահ չըլլամ այս մասին, աւելորդ կը համարեմ խօսիլ»:

Մ. Գամպօլա վճռական հաւաստիքը առանց տալու կ'ըսէ թէ միայն հայերուն օգուտին եւ բարւոյն համար է որ կը հետաքրքրուին եւ կ'ուզեն օգտակար ըլլալ, հետեւաբար հայ հոգեւոր ներկայացուցիչը առանց երկարելու խօսակցութիւնը հրաժեշտ առնել կ'ուզէ:

Մ. Գամպօլա այն ատեն Մ. Փէթլային կողմէ հետեւեալ առաջարկը կը դնէ. «Տէօրթ-Եօլի հայերը չե՞ն ուզեր արդեօք հոս մնալ եւ հնազանդիլ Քէմալիստներուն եթէ հայ գայմագամ մը կարգուի Տէօրթ Եօլի մէջ, հայ ժանտարմըրի եւ անոնց հայ պետ մը նշանակուի»:

Ժողովուրդին տրամադրութիւնը նկատի ունենալով հայոց հոգեւոր ներկայացուցիչը կը պատասխանէ ժխտական կերպով, պատճառաբանելով թէ թրքական խոստումները ոչ մէկ արժէք կը ներկայացնեն եւ հայ գայմագամ մը մէկ օրէն միւսը կրնայ պաշտօնանկ ըլլալ եւ հայ ժանտարմըրին ցրուիլ:

Մ. Գամպօլա եւս երկարօրէն կը հետաքրքրուի Տէօրթ-Եօլի հայոց գաղթով, մանաւանդ անոնց դիմադրելու մտադրութեամբ: Հայ եկեղեցականը կը յայտնէ թէ ինքը չի կրնար վճռական բան մը ըսել:

* Նոյն իրիկունը Տէօրթ-Եօլի զինուորական հրամատարը՝ որ հիւանդ էր եւ Մ. Բէթլայի յայտարարութեանց ներկայ չէր եղած, կը կոչէ իր քովը հայոց հոգեւոր պետը եւ անոր կը կրկնէ Մ. Գամպօլայի կողմէ իրեն եղած առաջարկները, աւելցնելով միայն ֆրանսական հիւպատոսի մը կամ հրամատարի մը ներկայութիւնը իբր քօնթրօլ:

Պատասխանը դարձեալ ժխտական կ'ըլլայ, նկատի առնելով թէ Թուրքիոյ մէջ ոչ մէկ տեղ հիւպատոսի մը ներկայութիւնը արգելք եղած է ջարդերու, թալաններու եւ խժդժութեանց:

Պէյրութ (Զաքարիա Պզտիկեանէ) – 5 Յունվար [1922]

Ատանայի, Տարսոնի, Տէօրթ-Եօլի եւ Ճէպէլի Պէրէքէթի ամբողջ հայութիւնը գաղթեց: Ատանա մնացող հայերու թիւ[ը] 50–60 հոգի հազիւ պէտք է հաշուել, Մերսին՝ 18–20 հոգի, մինչդեռ Տէօրթ-Եօլ եւ Ճէպէլի Պէրէքէթ մէկ հատ հայ չէ մնացած:

Գալով Այնթապի եւ Քիլիսի հայութեան՝ արտագաղթը կը շարունակէ կարելի եղած միջոցներով: Այնթապը պարպուած է գրեթէ իր բարեկեցիկ տարրէն, քաղաք կը մնան 5000ի չափ հայութիւն, որոնք նիւթական միջոց չունին գաղթելու համար: Ֆրանսական կառավարութիւնն ալ միջոցներ չէ տրամադրած այդ շրջանին, որով չեն կրցած շուտով գաղթել, թէեւ երբեք յօժարութեամբ մնալու տրամադիր չեն:

Գալով Մերսին զտնուած հայերու փոխադրութեան խնդրին, ֆրանսական շոգենաւային ընկերութիւն մը զանոնք Սուրիա փոխադրեց, դրամով եւ ոչ թէ ձրի, ինչպէս կ'ըսուի: Իւրաքանչիւր ճամբորդ Մերսինէն Պէյրութի համար վճարեց 855 դրշ.: Ծոցենաւերն ալ արտակարգ խճողուած էին:

Սուրիա հասնելէ յետոյ գաղթականները կը լքուին իրենց վիճակին: Ֆրանսական կառավարութիւնը տրամադիր չէ գաղթականներու ապրուստը հոգալու: Նոյնիսկ Դամասկոս գացողներու շոգեկառքի վարձքի զեղչ մը չեն ըներ: Միայն քանի մը մասնաւոր կառախումբեր ճամբայ հանեցին

while transporting property free of charge, considering that the travelers were paying the price for third-class wagons and being crammed in them with their belongings.

No organization accommodates the migrants. The number of Armenian migrants arriving in Syria is estimated to be thirteen to fourteen thousand people. Refugees from Gaziantep and Kilis are not included in this number.

As for orphans, the Mersin orphans of the Armenian General Benevolent Union were transferred here and from here to the village of Ashkut near the Zmmar Monastery in Lebanon. The Dörtyol orphans, too, are expected today or tomorrow and will be transported here. The orphans of the Armenian General Benevolent Union number about seven hundred. The females will be housed in a school building in the village of Ashkhut, and the males in the seminary of the Zmmar Monastery. The Zmmar congregation welcomed the orphans with great enthusiasm and caress.

* The French government established a commission in Adana four or five months ago to assess the damages caused during the French occupation following the armistice. This commission functioned until the recent Franco-Turkish agreement and hardly considered a small portion of the applications made by the applicants.

* Travelers to Beirut provided the following information about the current situation in Adana. When the Kemalist government came to Adana, it showed a feeble and lax spirit because it had no money or organization. Adana's situation is very deplorable. Even the clothes of the Kemalist troops and the gendarmes have been provided by the French so that they may enter Cilicia brilliantly, but the people already know all this. Only eight to nine hundred gendarmes and one battalion of soldiers were brought to Adana. All the officials have been changed, even the doorkeepers and the janitors, so there is dissatisfaction among the officials deprived of their positions. It is even assumed that an anti-Kemalist movement will start in Adana and its environs.

Adana's economic situation has been turned upside down completely; there are no artisans, no merchants. The city is full of Kurdish and Turkish muhacirs who beg in the streets all day. The situation cannot continue like this. This is also the opinion of Abdurrahman Bey, the deputy prefect of Adana, who is now in Beirut, a refugee fleeing Kemalists' revenge.

The district governor of Gaziantep is also in Beirut and speaks very ill about the Kemalists.

İstanbul (Mrs. Shoghagat's oral information)—January 9 [1922][131]

A woman came to İstanbul recently from Anadolu [Anatolia]. She had been in the town of Çarsancak near Harput and related that there are no Armenians in Çarsancak. The houses have been destroyed, and nobody is left in the villages. She saw three orphanages in Harput. There are very few men in Harput. She did not see Armenians in Arapgir while passing through, except for a few women who remained with the Turks. Divriği and Kemaliye [Egin] are in almost the same situation; there are very few Armenians. There are five or six orphanages in Sivas, [where] children have been gathered from everywhere. There are very few Armenians in the city with families. The older Armenian boys of the orphanages have been drafted and are working to build a road in Samsun. There are almost no Armenians in Trabzon either. The primate of Trabzon, Reverend Father Karekin, was there, but she could not see him. There is also a priest. The primate of Sivas and two priests and the primate of Harput, Bishop Kyud, are in office. Recently, Armenians have been enlisted as soldiers.

On the way from Sivas to Çiçekliyurt [Çakal Han], they passed treading over bones, skulls, and corpses.

սակագինին համաձայն վճարում առնելով ճամբորդներէն եւ գոյքերու փոխադրութիւնը ձրի կատարեցին, նկատելով որ ճամբորդները Գ. կարգով գին կը վճարէին եւ fourgon-ներու մէջ կը թխմուէին իրենց գոյքերով միասին:

Գաղթականները տեղաւորելու համար ոեւէ կազմակերպութիւն գոյութիւն չունի: Սուրիա հասնող հայ գաղթականներու թիւը մօտաւորապէս 13–14 հազար հոգի ըլլալու է: Այնթապի եւ Քիլիսի շրջանին գաղթականները այս թիւին մէջ չեն:

Գալով որբերու, Բարեգործականի Մերսին[ի] որբերը փոխադրուեցան հոս եւ հոսկէ ալ Լիբանան Զմմար վանքին մօտ Աշխուտ անուն գիւղ մը: Տէօրթ-Եօլի որբերն ալ կը սպասուին այսօր կամ վաղը եւ պիտի փոխադրուին հոս: Բարեգործականի որբերը մօտաւորապէս 700 են, որոնց իգական սեռը պիտի տեղաւորուի Աշխուտ գիւղը դպրոցի համար շինուած շէնք մը եւ մանչերն ալ Զմմարի վանքի ընծայարանը: Զմմարի Միաբանութիւնը որբերը ընդունեց մեծ խանդավառութեամբ եւ զգուանօք:

* Ֆրանսական կառավարութիւնը Ատանայի մէջ գօմիսիօն մը հաստատած էր ասկէ 4–5 ամիս առաջ, զինադադարէն յետոյ ֆրանսական զրաւման միջոցին եղած վնասները գնահատելու համար: Այս յանձնաժողովը կը գործէր մինչեւ վերջին ֆրանքօ-թուրք համաձայնութիւնը եւ հազիւ կրցաւ նկատի առնել դիմում կատարողներու դիմումներուն մէկ փոքր մասը:

* Ատանայի ներկայ կացութեան մասին Պէյրութ հասած ճամբորդներ տուած են սա տեղեկութիւնները: Քէմալական կառավարութիւնը երբ Ատանա եկաւ, շատ տկար եւ թոյլ ոգի մը ցոյց տուաւ, զի դրամ չունի, կազմակերպութիւն չունի: Ատանայի կացութիւնը շատ տխուր է: Քէմալական զօրքերու եւ ժանտարմաներու հագուստներն իսկ ֆրանսացիները տուած են, որպէսզի փայլուն կերպով Կիլիկիա մտնեն, բայց ժողովուրդը այս բոլորը գիտէ արդէն: 8–900 ժանտարմա եւ մէկ վաշտ (թապուր) զինուոր միայն բերած են Ատանա: Բոլոր պաշտօնեաները փոխուած են, նոյնիսկ բարապանները ու դռնապանները, այնպէս որ դժգոհութիւն երեւան եկած է այն պաշտօնեաներուն մէջ, որոնք իրենց պաշտօններէն զրկուած են: Կ'ենթադրուի նոյնիսկ թէ հակաքէմալական շարժում մը պիտի սկսի Ատանա եւ շրջակաները:

Ատանայի տնտեսական վիճակը տակնուվրայ եղած է բոլորովին, ո՛չ արհեստաւոր կայ, ո՛չ վաճառական. քաղաքը լեցուեր է քիւրտ եւ թուրք գաղթականներով, որոնք մինչեւ իրիկուն կը մուրան փողոցներուն մէջ: Այս կացութիւնը չի կրնար շարունակել այսպէս: Այս է գաղափարը նաեւ Ատանայի կուսակալի փոխանորդ Ապտուրրահման պէյի, որը հիմա Պէյրութ կը գտնուի, փախստական՝ Քէմալականաց վրէժխնդրութենէն խոյս տալով:

Այնթապի միւթէսարրըֆն ալ Պէյրութ է եւ շատ գէշ կը խօսի Քէմալականաց մասին:

Կ. Պոլիս (Տիկին Շողակաթի բերանացի տեղեկութիւնները) – 9 Յունվար [1922]

Անատոլուէն վերջերս Կ. Պոլիս եկած է տիկին մը, որ կը գտնուէր Խարբերդի մօտ Չարսանճագ քաղաքը, եւ կը պատմէ թէ Չարսանճագի մէջ հայ չկայ. տուները քանդուած են, գիւղերն ալ մարդ չէ մնացած: Խարբերդ երեք որբանոց տեսած է. Խարբերդի մէջ շատ քիչ էրիկ մարդ կայ: Արաբկիրի մէջ ինքն հայեր չէ տեսած իր անցած ատեն, բացի քանի մը կիներէ, որոնք թուրքերու մօտ կը մնան: Տիվրիկ եւ Ակն ալ գրեթէ նոյն վիճակը ունին եւ շատ քիչ թուով հայեր կան: Սեբաստիա 5–6 որբանոց կայ, ամէն տեղէ տղաքներ հաւաքուած են: Տունով քաղաքին մէջ հայ շատ քիչ կը գտնուի: Որբանոցներու մէջ գտնուած հայ հասակաւոր տղաքը զինուորագրուած են եւ Սամսոն ճամբայ շինելու կ'աշխատցուին: Տրապիզոնի մէջ ալ հայերը գրեթէ չկան: Տրապիզոնի Առաջնորդ Տէր Գարեգին Վարդապետը հոն է, բայց չէ կրցած տեսնել: Քահանայ մըն ալ կայ: Սեբաստիոյ Առաջնորդը եւ երկու քահանաներ եւ Խարբերդի Առաջնորդ Գիւտ Եպիսկոպոսը պաշտօնի վրայ են: Վերջին ատեններս հայ էրիկ մարդիկը դարձեալ զինուոր առնուած են:

Սեբաստիայէն Չաքալ Խան ճամբու վրայ անցած են ոսկորներու, գանկերու եւ դիակներու վրայէն:

The Greek people of Samsun and its villages have been displaced, and some of them were killed by Turks on the spot. In Kavak, they saw about two thousand young Greeks being taken to Amasya to be killed on the riverbank. There were twelve Greek priests with their beards and hair plucked. Wounded people were being transported half-dead in twenty-eight carriages. The lady inquired and learned that they had wanted to escape.

Samsun also has an orphanage, but the older boys have been enlisted as soldiers. Shops and houses have been looted everywhere. Just like the Armenians, the Greeks have been massacred and deported.

İstanbul (reported by His Eminence the Patriarch)—13 February [1922][132]

According to information received from Adapazarı, the Millis started a massacre when they entered the city. The number of massacred Armenians is estimated at 268, if not more.

On the second day, Kadir Çavuş, a gang leader residing in the Söğütlü neighborhood, gathered the Armenians who survived the massacre and abducted, from among them, Hadji Hripsimé Setragian, a thirty- to thirty-five-year-old woman, and Nvart Koundourajian, a seventeen-year-old girl.

On the third day, they took Arshavir Antreasian and Raphael Keohlanian from among them into the street and killed them.

After looting the rest of the miserable people, they locked them up in a building in the Turkish neighborhood and a month later settled them in a school. Now they work to earn their living. There are only 170 [Armenian] people in Adapazarı now.

The only aged local priest, Father Mikayel, survives sheltered in a Turk's house with his family.

Larnaca (from the Chairman of the Migration Commission)—12 February [1922][133]

According to information received from Adana, the commissions of "Abandoned Properties" are again very active. A house [ordinarily] rented for one hundred liras cash suffices to be a Christian property, gets rented for eighty to two hundred lira banknotes, while people occupy tiny houses without rent. Nobody argues about goods and chattels. Under the new law, sixty percent of all income-generating real estate belongs to the government, and fifty percent of imported goods must be left to the government as a subsidy. Seventeen- to forty-five-year-old Muslims and Jews are enlisted in the army. Where are the Gourauds, Bouillons, and Briands who claimed that Cilicia had become a paradise?

According to a recent letter from Mersin, the government is allegedly preparing a program for publication. This program would capture the assets of Armenians who do not return to Mersin within three months. The writer says, "Whereas those [Armenians] who come today are not being let in."

A migrant escapee from Maraş traveling here from İskenderun described the situation of the Armenians of Maraş as terrible. The tribulations had been so severe that living there had been impossible. A Turk agreed to save an Armenian by facilitating his escape in exchange for twenty-five liras, but while taking him out of the city, [another] Turk took the Armenian to a wedding, and there he said: "The bride needs a sacrifice." They laid him on the ground before the audience and slaughtered him.

According to information provided by incoming travelers, the Kemalist government declined to recognize passports issued by the French in Cilicia for [travel to] Syria. Allegedly, it thoroughly considers all [those who live in Asiatic Turkey] as Ottoman subjects.

Bandırma (from the primate)—March 12 [1922]

Four Turkish bands are operating in the Erdek and Edincik districts of Bandırma, [led by] a) Çakırcalı Mustafa, b) Osman Bey of Edincik, c) Bacak Hasan (from Edincik), and d) Recep Çavuş of Erdek.

Սամսոնի եւ գիւղերու յոյն ժողովուրդը տեղահան եղած են, մէկ մասն ալ թուրքերը տեղւոյն [վրայ] սպաննած են: Գավազ կը տեսնան 2000ի մօտ յոյն երիտասարդներ, որոնք Ամասիա կը տարուէին, զետեզը սպաննելու համար: 12 հատ յոյն քահանաներ կային մօրուքնին եւ մազերնին փեթթուած: 28 կառք վիրաւոր անձեր կիսամեռ կը տ[ա]նէին: Տիկինը հետաքրքրուած է եւ իմացած է որ փախչիլ ուզողներն են եղեր անոնք:

Սամսոն ալ որբանոց կայ, բայց մեծ տղաքը զինուոր առնուած են: Ամէն տեղ խանութները, տուները կողոպտուած են: Ճիշդ հայերու նման յոյներն ալ ջարդուած եւ տարագրուած են:

Կ. Պոլիս (Սրբազան Պատրիարքէն հաղորդուած) – 13 Փետրուար [1922]

Ատաբազարէն ստացուած տեղեկութեանց համաձայն, Միլիճիները քաղաք մտած ատեն կոտորածի սկսած են: Կոտորուած հայոց թիւը 268 հոգի ըլլալ կը հաշուուի, եթէ աւելի չէ:

Երկրորդ օրը՝ Սէօյիւտլի թաղը բնակող Գատիր Չավուշ, որ չէթէպաշի է, կոտորածէ փախած հայերը կը ժողվէ մէկտեղ եւ անոնցմէ Հաճի Հռիփսիմէ Սեդրաքեան 30–35 տարեկան կինը եւ Նուարդ Գունտուրաճեան 17 տարեկան աղջիկը կ'առեւանգեն եւ ցարդ երեւան չեն ելներ:

Երրորդ օրը անոնցմէ Արշաւիր Անդրէասեան եւ Ռափայէլ Քէօհլանեանը տանելով փողոցին մէջ սպաննած են:

Մնացեալ թշուառները կողոպտելէ յետոյ թուրքաց թաղին մէջ շէնքի մը մէջ կը բանտարկուին եւ ամիս մը յետոյ կը բնակեցուին վարժարանին մէջ: Այժմ իրենց աշխատանքով կ'ապրին: Ատաբազարի մէջ այժմ կայ միայն 170 հոգի:

Տեղւոյն միակ ծերունի քահանան՝ Տէր Միքայէլ, թուրքի մը տուն ապաստանելով իր ընտանիքով ողջ կը մնայ:

Լարնաքա (Գաղթականաց Յանձնաժողովի ատենապետէն) – 12 Փետրուար [1922]

Ատանայէն առնուած տեղեկութիւններու համաձայն, «Էմվալը Մէթրուքէ»ի յանձնաժողովները վերստին մեծ գործունէութեան մէջ են եղեր: 100 ինչուն ոսկի վարձք բերող տուն մը, բաւ է որ քրիստոնեայի ապրանք ըլլայ, 80–200 ոսկի թըթաղրամի վարձու կը տրուի, իսկ փոքր տուները առանց վարձքի կը գրաւուին. ապրանքի եւ գոյքերու խօսքը իսկ չ'ըլլար եղեր: Նոր օրէնքի համեմատ բոլոր հասութաբեր կալուածներու 60%ը կառավարութեան կը վերաբերի, նոյնպէս դուրսէն եկող ապրանքներու 50%ը նպաստի ձեւով կառավարութեան պէտք է ձգուի եղեր: 17–45 տարեկան իսլամ եւ հրեաները զօրք եղած են: Կիլիկիա դրախտի մը վերածուած ըլլալը պնդող Կուրօ, Պոյեօն, Պրիանները ո՞ւր են արդեօք:

Մերսինէն առնուած վերջին նամակի մը համաձայն, կառավարութիւնը հրատարակելու համար յայտագիր մը կը պատրաստէ եղեր. այս յայտագիրը մինչեւ երեք ամիս Մերսին չվերադարձող հայոց ինչքերը պիտի գրաւէ եղեր. գրողը կ'ըսէ թէ «մինչեւ այսօր եկողները չեն ընդունուիր»:

Իսկէնտէրունէն հոս եկող մարաշցի փախչող գաղթական մը Մարաշի հայերուն վիճակը շատ ահաւոր կը նկարագրէ. նեղութիւնները այն աստիճան ծանր եղած են, որ ապրիլը անկարելի եղած է: Թուրքին մէկը հայ մը ազատելով փախցունելու համար 25 ոսկիի կը համաձայնի եւ քաղաքէն դուրս հանելու միջոցին թուրք մը իր հարսնիքը տարած է եւ հոն «հարսին զոհ մը պէտք է» ըսելով հարսնիքի հասարակութեան աչքին առջեւ պառկեցնելով մորթած են:

Եկող ճամբորդներու տուած տեղեկութեանց համաձայն, Կիլիկիոյ մէջ ֆրանսացիներուն կողմէ Սուրիոյ համար տրուած անցագիրները Քէմալիսթ կառավարութիւնը չէ ճանչցած եւ ամբողջ ասիացիները իբր օսմանեան հպատակ կը ճանչնայ եղեր ամբողջապէս:

Պանտրմա (Առաջնորդէն) – 12 Մարտ [1922]

Պանտրմայի Էրտէքի եւ Էտինճիկի շրջանին մէջ կը գործեն չորս թուրք հրոսախումբեր, Ա.ը Չաքրճալը Մուսթաֆայի, Բ.ը էտինճիկցի Օսման պէյի, Գ.ը Պաճար Հասանի (էտինճիկցի), և Դ.ը

On the night of March 7, the Hellenic Army clashed with the first of these gangs, killing their leader, Çakırcalı Mustafa, and two followers. Upon the death of Çakırcalı Mustafa, the other three gangs joined together and decided to take revenge by planning to kill innocent and unarmed Armenian and Greek workers.

Consequently, on the morning of March 8, the united çete bands of Osman Bey, Bacak Hasan, and Recep Çavuş descended from the Turkish village of Çalışkanlar [Memun], located half an hour away from Bandırma toward the village of Aşağıyapıcı [Yapıcı] and the road to Erdek, to the north of Edincik, near the isthmus of Kapıdağ. They cut off the roads of Erdek and Ermeniköy, besieged the olive groves, separated one by one the Christians from among the workers going to cultivate the gardens, and after gathering them at the place called Kuruçeşme on the highway, shot them all dead.

Here are the names of the victims:

1. Bedros Petroyan	50 years old
2. Apraham Kasbarian	45 "
3. Vahram Vartevanian	35 "
4. Hagop Keoylouyan	21 "
5. Ardashes Menevsheyan	20 "
6. Garabed Torkomian	19 "
7. Haroutyun Zenopian	35 "
8. Levon Zenopian	30 "
9. Isgender Pilibosian	21 from Ermeniköy
10. Yanko	from Aşağıyapıcı [Yapıcı] village
11. Yorgi	from Aşağıyapıcı village

From this group of victims, the following four Armenians from Edincik remained alive by pretending to be dead and then returned to their homes.

1. Onnig Kazanjian	21-year-old, seriously injured
2. Sarkis Vosganian	28-year-old, slightly injured
3. Apraham Keoyluyan	40-year-old, slightly injured
4. Haroutyun Manikian	32-year-old, almost unhurt

One of them, Onnig Kazanjian, was sent by train to the local Hellenic hospital in Balıkesir for treatment. The others are being treated here.

The victims mentioned above were shot dead except for the martyred brothers Haroutyun and Levon Zenopian, who were stabbed to death and cruelly tortured. Levon had three wounds on his head, one on his right rib, [and] one on his right arm, and the fingers of his left hand had been amputated. [Haroutyun had one wound on his neck, three on his head, one on his cheek, one on his left rib, and one on his right hip.

It has been confirmed that Turkish thugs have rounded up these working, poor nationals under the guidance of local Tatar workers and upon their indications.

The primate performed the funeral for the victims, and their bodies were buried in the church's yard in Bandırma.

The terrified Christian people have begun to migrate to Bandırma, although the Hellenic local military authorities have taken the matter of dealing with the issue into their hands and are engaged in implementing the immediate necessary measures.

There is hope that the çetes could be conquered.][134]

էրտէքցի Րէճէպ Չավուշի գլխաւորութեամբ:

Սոյն հրոսախումբերէն առաջինին հետ Մարտ 7ին գիշերը հէլլէն զինուորները ընդհարում ունենալով՝ կը սպաննեն իրենց պարագլուխը՝ Չաքրճալը Մուսթաֆան իր երկու հետեւորդ հրոսակներով: Չաքրճալը Մուսթաֆայի սպանութեան վրայ միւս երեք հրոսախումբերը միանալով՝ կ’որոշեն վրէժ լուծել, անմեղ եւ անզէն գործաւոր հայեր եւ յոյներ սպաննել առաջադրելով:

Ըստ այսմ, Մարտ 8ի առտուն Օսման պէյի, Պաճաք Հասանի եւ Րէճէպ Չավուշի չէթէական միացեալ խումբերը Պանտրմայէն կէս ժամ հեռու Մամուն թրքաբնակ գիւղին վրայէն դէպի Եափըճը գիւղի եւ Էրտէքի ճամբուն վրայ իջնելով՝ Էտինճիկի հիւսիսային կողմը, Գաբու Տաղըի պարանոցին մօտիկ, Էրտէքի եւ Հայ գիւղի ճամբաները կտրելով՝ պաշարած են շրջակայ ձիթաստանները եւ պարտէզներու մշակութեան գացող գործաւորներու մէջէն քրիստոնեաները մէկիկ մէկիկ զատելով՝ խճուղիին վրայ Գուրու Չէշմէ կոչուած տեղը խմբելէ վերջ՝ բոլորը հրացանազարկ ըրած են:

Ահաւասիկ զոհերուն անունները.

1° Պետրոս Բէթրօեան 50 տարեկան
2° Աբրահամ Գասպարեան 45 “
3° Վահրամ Վարդէվանեան 35 “
4° Յակոբ Քէօյլիւեան 21 “
5° Արտաշէս Մէնէվշէեան 20 “
6° Կարապետ Թորգոմեան 19 “
7° Յարութիւն Չենոբեան 35 “
8° Լեւոն Չենոբեան 30 “
9° Իսկէնտէր Փիլիպոսեան 21 Հայ գիւղացի
10° Եանգօ Եափըճը գիւղ[ա]ցի
11° Եօրկի “ “

Սոյն զոհերու խումբին մէջէն ճարպիկութեամբ մեռեալ ձեւանալով ողջ մնացած եւ յետոյ տուներնին վերադարձած են հետեւեալ չորս Էտինճիկցի ազգայինները.

1° Օննիկ Գազանճեան 21 տարեկան ծանր վիրաւոր
2° Սարգիս Ոսկանեան 28 “ թեթեւ վիրաւոր
3° Աբրահամ Քէօյլիւեան 40 “ թեթեւ վիրաւոր
4° Յարութիւն Մանիքեան 32 “ գրեթէ անվնաս

Ասոնցմէ Օննիկ Գազանճեան շոգեկառքով Պալըքէսիր տեղւոյն հելլէնական հիւանդանոցը ղրկուած է դարմանումի համար եւ միւսները հոս կը դարմանուին:

Վերոյիշեալ զոհերը հրացանազարկ եղած են բացի Յարութիւն եւ Լեւոն Չենոբեան եղբայրնեպէն, որոնք դաշոյնի հարուածներով եւ չարաչար խոշտանգումներով նահատակուած են: Լեւոն[ի] վէրքերը՝ գլխուն վրայ երեք տեղ, աջ կողին վրայ մէկ, աջ թեւին վրայ մէկ, ձախ ձեռքին մատները կտրուած, իսկ *[Յարութիւնին վէրքերը՝ ծոծրակէն մէկ, գլուխէն երեք, այտէն մէկ, ձախ կողէն մէկ եւ աջ կող[մ]ի ազդրէն մէկ:*

Սոյն գործաւոր եւ աղքատիկ ազգայինները տեղացի թաթար գործաւորներու առաջնորդութեամբ եւ ցուցմունքներուն վրայ թուրք հրոսակներու կողմէ հաւաքուած ըլլալը հաստատուած է:

Զոհերուն յուղարկաւորութիւնը կատարուեցաւ Առաջնորդին նախագահութեամբ եւ թաղուեցան Պանտրմայի եկեղեցւոյ բակը:

Քրիստոնեայ ժողովուրդը ահ ու սարսափի մատնուած՝ դէպի Պանտրմա գաղթելու ձեռնարկած է, թէեւ հելլէն տեղական զինուորական իշխանութիւնը հարցին հետապնդութիւնը ձեռք առած եւ անմիջական անհրաժեշտ միջոցներու կիրարկումին սկսած է:

Յոյս կայ որ չէթէները նուաճուին:][31]

[Insecurity Notebook Number 19]
April 1922–October 1922

İskenderun (from Reverend Father Paren Melkonian)—April 12 [1922]

The Cilician refugees have been left in unhealthy conditions; their unemployed and miserable condition grows worse daily. There have been appeals to move them to the mountains around İskenderun, but the local authorities refused to help. On the contrary, there is an effort to disperse them to different parts of Syria.

The number of migrants is increasing daily due to those liberated and escapees from Maraş, Gaziantep [Ayntab], and even distant Armenia.

To date, five to six hundred people have come from Maraş and Gaziantep, and [their number] will surpass one thousand.

The Kemalists have announced in Gaziantep that from now on, passes will not be issued for traveling, except to those who go to Aleppo and on the condition that they do not return.

Besides the migrants traveling to Aleppo with this permission, there are also escapees as follows: On April 1, escaping from the threat of death of the Kurds and Turks of Kırıkhan and Kilis area, Vahan (sixteen-year-old) and the two brothers Bedros (twelve-year-old) and Krikor Chilingirian of Urfa arrived in İskenderun.

On April 7, arrived here six young men who fled from Kayseri's Kemalist orphanage to Adana and then were sent here through the efforts of V[ahan] Portoukalian, plus Garabed Ohan Dzarougian, Antranig Sarkis Haji Kevorkian, [and] Hovhannes Krikor Sahagian of Kayseri's Buröy village, Mihran YeKeshishian of Çakmak (Kayseri), Yeghia Avedis Lachinian of Develi, Drtad Haroutioun Kalpakian of Uzunlı: all of them between the ages of seventeen and twenty.

Similarly, the thirteen-year-old son of Noubar Garabed Nalbandian of Bolu was saved from Konia and sent to İstanbul.

Also arrived here yesterday two young men from Gaziantep and Nevşehir, aged twenty to twenty-five; they reported escaping from Mosul and other Kurdish areas to go to Aleppo and thence come here.

• The number of Kemalist propagandists is gradually increasing. They are provoking the Muslim Turkmen elements in the vicinities. On March 12–13, Bekir-Sami Bey, too, came to İskenderun and, after consulting with locals, left for Europe via the Aleppo-Beirut route.

• On May 26–27, Mr. Robert de Caix, the political representative of the French central authority, came here from Beirut accompanied by Dr. B[aghdasar] Melkonian, the representative of the Armenian National Delegation. Mr. Robert de Caix dealt with the situation of the Armenian migrants, toured the refugee camps, and offered to relocate the twenty-five hundred to three thousand migrants from Amanos settled in the Armenian Village to an unpopulated arable area near Hassa. The people of Amanos responded that they do not want to go anywhere other than their native villages and preferre to stay here, wanting only to be given jobs or compensation so that they could decide where to go collectively.

This mentality is present among almost all migrants, which makes the intention of the French government to disperse the migrants impossible.

Only partially and in small groups, the migrants are traveling to Tirebolu [Tripoli], Beirut, Lebanon, İzmir, and İstanbul.

In some places in Syria, the indigenous people oppose the settlement of Armenian migrants.

[Անապահովութեան Տետր Թիւ 19]
1922 Ապրիլ – 1922 Հոկտեմբեր

Իսկէնտէրուն (Փառէն Վարդապետ Մելքոնեանէ) – 12 Ապրիլ [1922]

Կիլիկեան գաղթականները հակառողջապահիկ պայմաններու մէջ մնացած եւ անգործ ու թշուառ վիճակը օրէ օր կը ծանրանայ: Դիմումներ եղան զանոնք Իսկէնտէրունի շուրջը լեռնաստանները փոխադրելու, սակայն տեղական իշխանութիւնք չեն օգներ: Ընդհակառակ, ջանք մը կայ զանոնք ցրուելու Սուրիոյ զանազան կողմերը:

Օրէ օր գաղթականներու թիւը կ'աւելնայ Մարաշէն եւ Այնթապէն եւ նոյնիսկ հեռաւոր Հայաստանէն ազատագրուողներով եւ փախողներով:

Մինչեւ ցարդ Մարաշէն եւ Այնթապէն 5–6 հարիւր հոգի եկան եւ 1000[ը] պիտի անցնի:

Քէմալիստները Այնթապի մէջ յայտարարած են թէ ասկէ վերջ երթեւեկի անցագիր չպիտի տրուի, այլ՝ միայն չվերադառնալու պայմանով Հալէպ գացողներուն պիտի տրուի:

Այս արտօնութեամբ եկող գաղթականներէն զատ փախուստով եկողներ ալ կան. Այսպէս՝ Ապրիլ 1ին Իսկէնտէրուն հասան եդեսացի Վահան (16 տարեկան) եւ Պետրոս (12 տարեկան) [ու] Գրիգոր Չիլինկիրեան երկու եղբայրները, Գըրըգ Խան եւ Քիլիսի շրջանի քիւրտ-թուրքերէն՝ մահուան սպառնալիքէն փախչելով:

Ապրիլ 7ին [հոս հասան] Կեսարիոյ քէմալական որբանոցէն փախչելով Ատանա ապաստանող եւ անկէ Վ[ահան] Փորթուգալեանի ջանքերով հոս ղրկուած վեց երիտասարդները, ինչպէս նաեւ Կեսարիոյ Պուրհան գիւղէն Կարապետ Օհան Ծառուկեան, Անդրանիկ Սարգիս Հաճի Գրիգորեան, Յովհաննէս Գրիգոր Սահակեան, չազմագցի (Կեսարիա) Միհրան Եսայի Քէշիշեան, էվէրէկցի Եղիա Աւետիս Լաջինեան, ուզունլուցի Տրդատ Յարութիւն Գալփագեան, ամէնքն ալ 17–20 տարեկան արհեստաւորներ:

Նոյնպէս Գոնիայէն ազատուած է պոլսեցի Նուպար Կարապետ Նալպանտեան 13 տարեկան տղան, որ Կ. Պոլիս ղրկուած է:

Երէկ հոս հասան նաեւ այնթապցի եւ նէվշէհիրցի երկու երիտասարդներ 20–25 տարեկան, որոնք կը յայտնէին թէ Մուսուլի եւ այլ քիւրտ շրջանակներէ փախչելով հասած են Հալէպ եւ անկէ հոս եկած:

- Քէմալական փրոփականտիստներու թիւը հետզհետէ կը բազմանայ: Ասոնք կը գրգռեն շրջակայ թիւրքմէն խլամ տարրերը: Մարտ 12–13ին Իսկէնտէրուն եկաւ նաեւ Պէքիր-Սամի պէյ եւ խորհրդակցելէ յետոյ տեղացիներու հետ՝ Հալէպ-Պէյրութի գիծով մեկնեցաւ Եւրոպա:

- Մայիս 26–27ին հոս եկաւ Պէյրութէն ֆրանսական կեդրոնական իշխանութեան քաղաքական ներկայացուցիչ Մ. Բօպէռ տը Քէօ: Իրեն կ'ընկերանայ Ազգային Պատուիրակութեան ներկայացուցիչ Տք. Պ[աղտասար] Մելքոնեան: Մ. Բօպէռ տը Քէօ զբաղեցաւ հայ գաղթականաց վիճակով եւ շրջեցաւ գաղթականաց քէմփերը եւ Հայկական Գիւղին մէջ հաստատուած 2500–3000 ամանոսցի գաղթականներուն առաջարկած է Խասայի մօտ պարապ եւ մշակելի շրջանը փոխադրել: Ամանոսցի[ք] պատասխանած են թէ իրենց հայրենի գիւղերէն զատ ուրիշ տեղ երթալ չեն ուզեր եւ կը նախընտրեն մնալ հոս, միայն կը փափաքին որ իրենց գործ տրուի, եթէ ոչ իրենց հատուցում ըլլայ՝ որ իրենք որոշեն թէ ուր պիտի երթան ազգովին:

Այս մտայնութիւնը գրեթէ բոլոր գաղթականներու մէջ կայ, որով ֆրանսական կառավարութեան գաղթականները ցրուելու մտադրութիւնը անկարելիութեան կը մատնուի:

Միայն մասնակի եւ պզտիկ խումբերով դէպի Թիրէպօլու [Թրիփոլի], Պէյրութ, Լիբանան եւ Իզմիր եւ Պոլիս գաղթողներ կան:

Սուրիոյ մէջ տեղ տեղ բնիկ տեղացի ժողովուրդը հայ գաղթականներու տեղաւորման կը հակառակի:

Aleppo (from Priest Sahag Der-Bedrosian of Maraş and Reverend Apraham Haroutyunian, minister of Maraş)—March 21

Besides [those staying in] the orphanages, there are about six thousand Armenians in Maraş. So far, approximately twenty-five hundred have left Maraş using their means and in despair.

Since the French abandoned Maraş, the decimated people have been living with the horror of massacre and deportation. Especially in the last year, the conscription of Armenians has made the remaining Armenians more impoverished. The people of Maraş have not yet found the courage to collect the bones of their relatives martyred during the massacre from wells, canyons, and polluted places to bury them in the cemetery. The people do not even dare to transport the newly dead to the cemetery without [the accompaniment of] gendarmes. When Armenians dare to take to the streets and markets, they are subjected to intolerable insults and affronts. Armenians outside the city have been dispossessed of their properties. It is absolutely impossible to go to the orchard, the garden, or the field because of insecurity. Against insignificant and nominal fees, the Turks have taken ownership of these properties, while the taxes for them continue to be diligently collected from the Armenians, even though they do not benefit [from them] at all. It is impossible to go out of town to work or to leave the house after dark. The houses of Armenians are being demolished continuously by a ruthless mob. Even the foundation stones are being sold.

The Armenians have withdrawn from the market and trade and are confined to their houses. Only a few Armenians operate under the protection of Turks or as partners with them.

The government seized the property of those who, risking their lives, fled Maraş after the departure of the French. These people are considered rebels who joined the enemy forces.

With the impossibility for Armenians to work, with their property and possessions looted, and with their homes and fields destroyed, Armenians think about migrating, especially since the American [Near East] Relief's providential subsidy on which they were living has ceased now.

The Turks mock the Armenians who think about migrating. Indeed, the iron circle [around them] is gradually closing, and the people of Maraş are ready to leave even at the expense of their economic destruction, but they have no money [for departure].

Gaziantep [Ayntab] (from Priest Karekin Bogharian)—April 4

After the announcement of the Franco-Turkish agreement of Ankara, migration from Gaziantep began and continues to this day. Numerous groups left daily in November and December and, after that, periodically, in smaller numbers. Migration had already started in 1920, from the period of the war and the siege. Initially, the migrating groups were mainly made up of orphans and expatriates. Later, the groups gradually came to include city dwellers, the wealthy, the merchants, the youth, and the intellectuals. There are now about four thousand Armenians, including a group of orphans protected by the Near East Relief, who will soon leave for Lebanon, where they will be cared for in orphanages. Most of those who remain here are orphans and widows who have been living on relief until now, and now that the Relief has stopped the subsidies, what will their situation be? If the rest of the people are not migrating, it is because the agonies of migration cause them no less fright.

The biggest misfortune is that now the Turks are hampering the Armenians' ability to work. It is preached to them constantly that "Turks should trade with Turks, should give their money to their compatriots, should not buy foreign goods, especially textiles; rather, they should produce them themselves and support their artisans." Although these are arrows directed at Europe, they harm the Armenians. Although the Armenian shopkeepers and traders can be counted on one hand and very few artisans remain, the Turks still raise difficulties. Thus, there is no domestic or foreign trade, and

Հալէպ (մարաշցի Տ. Սահակ Քահանայ Տէր-Պետրոսեանէ եւ Մարաշի հովիւ Պատուելի Աբրահամ Յարութիւնեանէ) – 21 Մարտ

Բացի որբանոցներէն, Մարաշի մէջ 6000ի մօտ հայեր կան եւ ցարդ մօտաւորապէս 2500 անձեր անհատապէս յուսահատ լքած ու մեկնած են Մարաշէն:

Ֆրանսացւոց Մարաշը լքելէն ի վեր ցարդ ջարդուփշուր տառապալից ժողովուրդը ջարդի ու տարագրութեան սարսափին մէջ կ'ապրի. մանաւանդ վերջին տարին հայերու զինաթափութեան պարագան աւելի խեղճութեան մատնած է մնացորդ հայութիւնը: Ցարդ համարձակութիւն չեն ունեցած մարաշցիք ջարդին նահատակուած իրենց ազգակիցներուն ոսկորները հորերէն, ձորերէն ու աղտոտ վայրերէն հաւաքելով գերեզմանատունը թաղելու: Նոյնիսկ նոր մեռեալները առանց ժանտարմայի գերեզմանատուն փոխադրելու քաջութիւնը չունի ժողովուրդը: Հայերը փողոցներու եւ շուկաներու մէջ եթէ համարձակին ելնել, անհանդուրժելի նախատինքներու եւ անարգանքներու կ'ենթարկուին: Քաղաքէն դուրս հայերը իրենց կալուածին տէրը չեն: Բացարձակ անկարելի է այգի, պարտէզ, արտ երթալ անապահովութեան պատճառով: Չնչին եւ անուանական վարձքի փոխարէն թուրքեր տէր եղած են անոնց, մինչ անոնց տուրքերը եռանդով կը գանձուին հայերէն, հակառակ անոր որ ոչ մէկ օգուտ կը քաղեն: Քաղաքէն դուրս աշխատելու երթալ եւ մութնալէն վերջ տուներէն դուրս ելլալ անկարելի է: Շարունակ հայոց տուները կը քանդուին անխիղճ խուժանին կողմէ եւ հիմերու քարերն իսկ կը ծախուին:

Հայերը շուկայէ եւ առեւտուրէ քաշուած տունը փակուած են եւ միայն քանի [մը] հայեր թուրքի պաշտպանութեամբ կամ ընկերակցութեամբ կը գործեն:

Ֆրանսացիներու մեկնումէն յետոյ իրենց կեանքը վտանգելով Մարաշէն խոյս տուող անձերու կալուածները կառավարութիւնը գրաւած է՝ զանոնք իբր թշնամի ոյժերու հետ միացող ապստամբներ նկատելով:

Հայոց աշխատութիւնը անկարելի, գոյքերը եւ ստացուածքը յափշտակուած եւ տունը եւ արտերը փչացուած ըլլալով, անոնք կը մտածեն գաղթել, մանաւանդ որ ամերիկեան Reliefի նախախնամական նպաստն ալ, որով կ'ապրէին, հիմա դադրած է:

Թուրքերը կը ծաղրեն հայերը որ գաղթելու վրայ կը խորհին: Իրապէս երկաթեայ շրջանակը հետզհետէ կը նեղնայ եւ մարաշցին նիւթապէս փճացումին զինովը պատրաստ է մեկնելու, սակայն դրամ չունի:

Այնթապ (Տ. Գարեգին Քահանայ Պօղարեանէ) – 4 Ապրիլ

Ֆրանքօ-թուրք Անկորայի համաձայնութիւնը հրապարակուելէն յետոյ Այնթապէն արտագաղթը սկսաւ եւ ցարդ կը շարունակէ՝ Նոյեմբեր Դեկտեմբերին գրեթէ ամէն օր եւ բազմաթիւ խումբերով, իսկ անկէ յետոյ պարբերաբար եւ փոքրաթիւ կերպով: Արդէն 1920ին պատերազմի եւ պաշարման շրջանէն սկսած էր արտագաղթը՝ մասնաւորաբար որբանոցներէ եւ պանդուխտներէ կազմուած խումբերով, հետզհետէ քաղաքացիներ, հարուստներ, առեւտրականք, երիտասարդներ եւ մտաւորականներ մեկնեցան: Հիմա 4000ի մօտ հայ[եր] կան, որոնց մէկ խումբն ալ Նիյր Իսթ Րըլիֆէ պաշտպանուած որբեր՝ մօտերս պիտի մեկնին Լիբանան, հոն որբանոցներու մէջ խնամուելու: Հոս մնացողներու մեծագոյն մասը որբեւայրի եւ կարօտներ են, որոնք նպաստով կ'ապրէին մինչեւ հիմա եւ հիմա որ Րըլիֆը նպաստը դադրեցուցած է, ի՛նչ պիտի ըլլայ անոնց վիճակը: Ժողովուրդի մնացեալ մասը եթէ չի գաղթեր, պատճառը այն է, որ գաղթականութեան թշուառութիւններն ալ ոչ նուազ իրեն սարսափ կը պատճառ[են]:

Դժբաղդութեան մեծագոյնը այն է որ հիմա թուրքերը հայոց աշխատութեան դէմ խոչընդոտ կը հանեն: Շարունակ անոնց կը քարոզուի թէ «թուրքը թուրքին հետ առուտուր պէտք է ընէ, իր դրամը արենակիցներու պէտք է տայ, օտար ապրանք, մանաւանդ գործուածները պէտք չէ գնէ, այլ՝ ինք պէտք է շինէ եւ իր արհեստաւորները քաջալերէ»: Ասոնք թէեւ Եւրոպայի դէմ նետուած նետեր են, սակայն հայուն կը վնասեն: Թէեւ հայ խանութպան եւ առեւտրական մատով կը համրուին եւ

textile making and carpetmaking, the primary source of Armenian livelihood, are expiring.

The national estates are either occupied or demolished and empty; therefore, the schools have no income and remain closed, and as many as one thousand boys and girls wander in the streets.

The confiscated properties of individuals are no longer returned, and the court does not consider complaints in this regard.

There is traffic on the Gaziantep-Kilis-Aleppo road, and no incidents have occurred so far.

Çanakkale [Dardanelles] (from Archpriest Tionis Drezian)—June 19

They report from Ezine. "Recently, due to the increase in banditry incidents, the Greek authorities have arranged for the relocation of the Armenian gypsies of Kızılköy and Balıklı to Ezine, and they have provided houses for everyone to live in. Being harvest time, last Friday evening, three gypsies—the Hadji Hagop [murdered later], his brother, and his cousin, both named Garabed—went to Kızılköy together with their Turkish headman friend of the same Kızılköy village, falling into a trap he had set for them. Early the following day (doubtlessly based on secret information given overnight), known bandit leaders Aziz and Karakadir entered the village with their joint group, caught the three Armenians, and drove them to the woods near the village. At that moment, coincidentally, the Greek mail detachment happened to pass by. A clash ensued between the two sides, and taking advantage of the commotion, the two Garabeds managed to escape, one slightly injured, the other unharmed. Hadji Hagop, however, due to his age (sixty-five years old), failed to take advantage of the opportunity, remained in the hands of the beasts, and was brutally killed. His body was brought to Ezine and solemnly buried. The slain Hadji Hagop had allegedly been the most famous and richest man in the village.

• Fifteen days ago, a British military detachment and the same çetes clashed near Ezine. At that time, two dead and three wounded British soldiers were brought to the city. Today, too, a slain British soldier was brought and buried. It is said to be the body of a soldier lost during the previous conflict.

Tekirdağ (from the National Central Guardianship of Thrace)—October 11

One hundred ninety-seven Armenian escapees have come from Biga to Dedeağaç, all women and children, except for four or five men.

They described Biga's massacre as follows:

"On August 12, 1922, when the Greek forces withdrew from the city, the British troops of Karabiga captured the city. After staying three days, they obtained assurance from the Turks that they would not touch the Christians. Leaving a British gendarmerie commander under their control, they retreated to Karabiga. After they had left, the Turks sent word to the villages to prepare themselves and come down to the city with their weapons. The word of the aghas was carried out. The Turkish mob entered the city, and the locals, as protectors of Christians, stood before the mob and persuaded them, saying, "We will raise money for you; spare them." They took thirty thousand liras from Armenians and Greeks and assured them they would not be touched. In the evening of the same day, they began to gather all the young people and imprison them. The next day, they set them free, [but] a few hours later, they stormed the houses, collected the young men, and put them to the sword. Quite a few young people hid for a few days. A crier invited all Christians to surrender to the government. When the young men came out of hiding and went to the government with their families, the Turks came, took the men,

արհեստաւորք շատ քիչ են, սակայն դարձեալ միշտ դժուարութիւն կը հանեն: Այսպէս ներքին առեւտուր չկայ, արտաքին առեւտուր ալ չկայ, մանուսագործութիւնը եւ գորգագործութիւնը,- որոնք գլխաւոր աղբիւրն էին հայոց,- օրհասականի վրայ են:

Ազգային կալուածները կա՛մ գրաւուած, կա՛մ քանդուած եւ պարապ են, որով դպրոցները հասոյթ չունին եւ փակ կը մնան, և 1000ի չափ երկսեռ տղաք փողոցները կը թափառին:

Անհատներու բռնագրաւուած կալուածները ա՛լ չեն դարձուիր եւ դատարանը այդ մասին եղած բողոքները նկատի չ'առներ:

Այնթապ-Քիլիս-Հալէպ ճամբուն վրայ երթեւեկ կը կատարուի եւ առ այժմ դէպքեր չեն պատահիր:

Տարտանէլ (Դիոնիս Աւագ Քահանայ Տրէզեանէ) – 19 Յունիս

Էզինէէն կը տեղեկագրեն: «Վերջերս աւազակային դէպքերու աւելնալուն պատճառով, հելլէն իշխանութեանց կարգադրութեամբ Գըզըլքէօյի եւ Պալըքլըի հայ բօշաները Էզինէ բերուելով, բնակութեան համար տուներ յատկացուած էին ամէնուն: Հունձքի ժամանակ ըլլալով, անցեալ ուրբաթ երեկոյին բօշաներէն երեք հոգի՝ սպանեալ հաճի Յակոբ, իր եղբայրը եւ քեռորդին՝ երկուքն ալ Կարապետ, իրենց գիւղացի բարեկամին՝ Գըզըլքէօյի թուրք մըխթարին լարած մէկ թակարդով, Գըզըլքէօյ կ'երթան, մըխթարն ալ միասին: Յաջորդ առտու կանուխ (անշուշտ գիշերը տրուած գաղտնի լրատուութեան վրայ), ծանօթ չէթէապետներ Ազիզ եւ Գարագատիր իրենց միացեալ խումբով գիւղը կը կոխեն եւ յիշեալ երեք հայերը բռնելով կը քշեն կը տանին գիւղին մօտակայ անտառներուն կողմը: Այդ պահուն զուգադիպօրէն այն կողմերէն անցնող հելլէն զինուորական փոսթա-ջոկատին հանդիպումով, երկուստեք ընդհարումէն յառաջ եկած խառնաշփոթութեան վրայ, երկու Կարապետները կը յաջողին խոյս տալ, մէկը՝ թեթեւապէս վիրաւոր, միւսը՝ անվնաս, իսկ հաճի Յակոբ տարեց (65 տարեկան) ըլլալուն համար չի կրնար առիթէն օգտուիլ, կը մնայ ճիւաղներուն ձեռքը եւ խուժդուժօրէն կը սպաննուի: Մարմինը Էզինէ բերուելով, մեծ հանդէսով կը թաղուի: Սպանեալ հաճի Յակոբ գիւղին ամենէն նշանաւորն ու հարուստն է եղեր:

- Ասկէ 15 օր առաջ անգլիական զինուորական ջոկատ մը եւ նոյն չէթէները Էզինէի մօտ ընդհարում մը ունեցած էին: Այն ատեն քաղաքս բերած էին 2 անգլիացի զինուոր մեռեալ եւ 3 անգլիացի զինուոր վիրաւոր: Այսօր ալ անգլիացի սպանեալ զինուոր մը բերին եւ թաղեցին: Կ'ըսուի թէ նախորդ ընդհարումի ատեն կորսուած զինուորի մը մարմինն է:

Ռօտոսթօ (Ազգային Կեդրոնական Խնամատարութենէն Թրակիոյ) – 11 Հոկտեմբեր

Պիղայէն փախստական եկած են Տէտէ Աղաճ 197 հայեր, բոլորն ալ կին ու երախայ, բացի 4–5 այրէ:

Ասոնք կը նկարագրեն Պիղայի ջարդը հետեւեալ կերպով.

«1922 Օգոստոս 12ին երբ քաղաքին յունական ույժերը հեռացան, Գարա-Պիղայի անգլիական զինուորները գրաւեցին քաղաքը: Երեք օր մնալէ վերջ, թուրքերէն ստորագրութիւն առին թէ քրիստոնեաներուն չպիտի դպչին: Անգլիական ժանտարմրիի հրամատար մը ձգելով իրենց քոնթ-րոլին տակ Գարա-Պիղա քաշուեցան: Անոնց մեկնումէն վերջ թուրքերը գիւղերը լուր կը ղրկեն որ պատրաստ զոնուին ու զէնքերնին առնելով քաղաք իջնեն: Աղաներուն խօսքը կը գործադրուի, ամբողջ թուրք խուժանը քաղաք կը մտնէ ու տեղացիները իբր քրիստոնեաներու պաշտպան խուժանին առջեւ կ'անցնին ու կը համոզեն ըսելով թէ ձեզի համար դրամ կը հաւաքենք, իրենց խնայեցէք: Հայերէն ու յոյներէն 30 հազար ոսկի կ'առնեն եւ ստորագրութիւն կուտան որ կեանքի չպիտի դպին: Նոյն օրը իրիկուան դէմ կը սկսին ամբողջ երիտասարդները ժողվել ու բանտարկել: Հետեւեալ օրը [ազատ] կը ձգեն, քանի մը ժամ վերջը տուները կը խուժեն եւ երիտասարդները հաւաքելով սուրէ կ'անցնեն: Բաւականաչափ երիտասարդներ քանի մը օր կը պահուին: Մունե-տիկը հրաւէր կը կարդայ որ ամբողջ քրիստոնեաները կառավարութեան յանձնուին: Պահուած

and killed them behind the government building. They shot a young man named Hmayag in front of the government [building]. The next day, they gathered all the girls from the houses, abducted a few of them, and returned them after an hour. There was a twelve-year-old girl, too, among them. They cut open the belly of Shahbazian Krikor Agha's pregnant daughter and threw the baby found in her womb from one bayonet to another. They tortured to death coffeemaker Kapriel Hekimian. The military commander took Annig Mardirosian forcibly as his wife. The Turkish lieutenant took Maria, the maid of Dr. Beylerian's house, and the surviving women stayed in the mountains hungry for fifteen days. After the Turkish soldiers committed all kinds of savagery, they left the women on the outskirts of Karabiga. Hearing the outcry and vociferation, the British naval commander sent soldiers to bring the women to Karabiga under their watch. He put them on a steamer and transported them to Dedeağaç. The Kemalists took twenty-seven Armenians captive, including Priest Nerses.

երիտասարդները ընտանիքներով միասին երբ կառավարութեան կ'երթան, թուրքերը կուզան երիտասարդները կ'առնեն ու կառավարական շէնքին ետեւը կը սպաննեն: Հմայեակ անուն երիտասարդ մը կառավարութեան [շէնքին] առջեւ կը զարնեն: Հետեւեալ օրը, տուները ինչքան աղջիկ որ կայ կը հաւաքեն, անոնց մէջէն քանի մը հատը կ'առեւանգեն եւ ժամ մը վերջ կը դարձնեն: Անոնց մէջ էր նաեւ 12 տարեկան պզտիկ աղջիկ մը: Ծաhպազեան Գրիգոր աղային աղջիկը, որ յղի էր, փորը կը ճեղքեն ու մօրը արգանդին մէջ գտնուող երախան սուինէ սուին կը նետեն: Սրճեփ Գաբրիէլ Հէքիմեանը տանջանքներու տակ կը մեռցնեն: Աննիկ Մարտիրոսեանը զինուորական հրամատարը բռնի կնութեան կ'առնէ: Տքթ. Պէյլէրեանի տան սպասուհին՝ Մարիան, թուրք տեղակալը կ'առնէ ու ողջ մնացած կիները 15 օր անօթի լեռները կը մնան: Թուրք զինուորը ամէն վայրագութիւն ընելէ վերջ, Գարա-Պիղայի դուրսերը կը ձգեն: Անգլիական ծովային հրամատարը գոռում գոչումը լսելով, զինուոր կը ղրկէ ու իրենց հսկողութեան տակ Գարա-Պիղա բերելով, շոգենաւ կը նստեցնեն ու Տէոէ-Աղաճ կը փոխադրեն: Քէմալականները 27 հայեր գերի կը տանին, որոնց մէջ կը գտնուի նաեւ Տ. Ներսէս Քահանան:

Notes

1 The Armenian-Greek Section's (AGS, herefater) 11th meeting, May 16, 1919.
2 AGS 12th meeting, May 20, 1919.
3 A unit of weight. Each dram is equal to 3.207 grams (0.1131 ounces).
4 AGS 12th meeting, May 20, 1919.
5 AGS 16th meeting, June 18, 1919.
6 Ibid.
7 Ibid.
8 Ibid.
9 AGS 15th meeting, June 11, 2019.
10 The name Garabed Sayeyan is written in the source, but erased with pencil, perhaps to keep it out from any report submitted to foreign representatives.
11 This name also is erased with a pencil, most likely for the same concern as above.
12 AGS 18th meeting, July 9, 1919.
13 This name also is erased with a pencil, most likely for the same concern as above.
14 AGS 20th meeting, August 6, 1919.
15 AGS 19th meting, July 23, 1919.
16 AGS 20th meeting, August 6, 1919.
17 AGS 21st meeting, August 20, 1919.
18 Ibid.
19 Ibid.
20 AGS 24th meeting, October 1, 2019.
21 Ibid.
22 Ibid.
23 1 okka = 1283 grams.
24 AGS 25th meeting, October 15, 1919.
25 Ibid.
26 AGS 26th meeting, October 26, 1919.
27 Ibid.
28 Ibid.
29 AGS 27th meeting, November 12, 1919.
30 Ibid.
31 Ibid.
32 Ibid.

Ծանօթագրութիւններ

[1] Բնագրին մէջ բառէն առաջ փակագծի մէջ արձանագրուած է Անդրանիկ Մայրեան անունը, որ, սակայն, ջնջուած է մատիտով, թերեւս բարձր յանձնակատարներուն ներկայացուելիք տեղեկագրերէն դուրս ձգելու կանխահոգութեամբ:

[2] Այս անունը եւս մատիտով ջնջուած է բնագրին մէջ, թերեւս բարձր յանձնակատարներուն ներկայացուելիք տեղեկագրերէն դուրս ձգելու նոյն կանխահոգութեամբ:

[3] Այս անունը եւս մատիտով ջնջուած է բնագրին մէջ, թերեւս բարձր յանձնակատարներուն ներկայացուելիք տեղեկագրերէն դուրս ձգելու նոյն կանխահոգութեամբ:

[4] Ոստիկան զօրաց հրամանատար Նուրի էֆէնտի երաշխաւորագնի մը դիմաց ազատ արձակած է հրոսախումբը Մէնթէշէլի Ռիզայի՝ hայոց ջարդի կազմակերպիչին: Հայ բնակչութիւնը ներկայիս կը գտնուի լեռներուն մէջ: Ինչպէս անցեալին՝ կիներու վաճառքը կը շարունակուի:

[5] Այս բառէն ետք ջնջած են բնագրին մէջ հաւանաբար անուշադրութեամբ արձանագրուած *կատարել տալ* բառակապակցութիւնը:

[6] Բնագրին մէջ՝ ... կազմակերպելու դիմադրութիւն համար:

[7] “Ո՛վ կեավուրներ, ձեր նկատմամբ դիրքս պիտի փոխեմ այլեւս: Արդէն մեր ծանրութիւնը օտարները առած են: Ձեզ ոչնչացնելով ես դարձեալ պիտի չդատուիմ»:

[8] Բնագրին մէջ՝ կուսակալը:

[9] Բնագրին մէջ՝ *մէջ*:

[10] Կասկած չկայ թէ այս գիրն ուղարկուած է հարկադրանքի ներքեւ, որովհետեւ այլ նամակներու մէջ Մարաշի հայոց կացութիւնը կը նկարագրուի մռայլ գոյներով (ինչպէս, օրինակ, Հալէպէն ուղարկուած 9 եւ 24 Յունիս 1920 թուակիրները, էջ 297 եւ 303): Հարկադրանքի մասին Ամերիկեան Կարմիր Խաչի պաշտօնեաներուն վկայութեան կը հանդիպինք Ուրֆայի hայոց կացութեան կապակցութեամբ՝ Հալէպէն առաքուած 30 Յունիս 1920 թուակիր նամակին մէջ (էջ 317):

[11] Պաշտօնական հերքում.- Անատոլուի մէջ հայերու վերստին կոտորածի ենթարկուելու վերաբերեալ վերջին ժամանակներուն կարգ մը լուրեր կը շրջին եւ այս լուրերը հայկական թերթերու միջոցով «Ժուռնալ տ’Օրիան» թերթը հրապարակած ու կրկնած է:
Մարաշի շրջակայքը թուրքերու եւ հայերու միջեւ դէպքեր պատահած են եւ առանց պատճառի խլամ բնակչութեան կեանքին վնասելու եւ պատիւը բռնաբարելու հայոց պատճառ եղած կռիւէն դուրս, Անատոլուի ոչ մէկ վայրը յարձակում եղած է: Այս լուրերը, երբ խնդրոյ առարկայ է Օսմանեան պետութեան ճակատագիրը, թէ՛ Եւրոպայի հանրային կարծիքի մօտ, թէ՛ Խաղաղութեան վեհաժողովի առջեւ բարձրաշուք կառավարութեան ի վնաս հոսանք մը յառաջացնելու յետին մտադրութեամբ կատարուիլը կը յայտարարուի:

[12] Բնագրին հարազատ մնալու համար պահպանած ենք Սիսի կրկնեալ նշումը: Նկատի առնելով, սակայն, յաջորդ տողերը, տրամաբանական պիտի ըլլայ երկրորդ Սիս-ը փոխարինել Մերսին-ով:

[13] Մերսինի ընկերվարական ներկայացուցիչ եւ ազգային ուժերու հրամանատար:

[14] Պանտրմայի գրաքննութեան կողմէ քննուած:

[15] Մենք ջաղացքէն կու գայինք: Ռեշատիյէէն չորս անձեր Հիւսէյին չավուշին հետ եւ Տէլի Պազարէն

33 Ibid.

34 A belt in which the wearer would hide gold coins or other valuables.

35 AGS 28th meeting, November 26, 1919.

36 Ibid.

37 Ibid.

38 AGS 29th meeting, December 10, 1919.

39 Ibid.

40 In the AGS 29th meeting minutes, the date is mentioned as November 5 mistakenly.

41 AGS 29th meeting, December 10, 1919.

42 Ibid.

43 Ibid.

44 Ottoman weight measurement equal to 1.2829 kilograms.

45 AGS 31st meeting, January 28, 1920.

46 Ibid.

47 Ibid.

48 AGS 33rd meeting, February 25, 1919.

49 Ibid.

50 AGS 34th meeting, March 10, 1920.

51 Ibid.

52 The text, undoubtedly, is written under coercion. It contradicts many accounts depicting the critical conditions of the Armenians in Maraş (e.g. the two telegrams from Maraş on February 12, 1920 [p. 172] and the reports from Aleppo on June 9 and June 24, 1920 [pp. 298 and 302, respectively]). Such coercion is reported by the American Red Cross staff concerning Urfa (see the letter dated June 30, 1920, p. 316).

53 AGS 34th meeting, March 10, 1920.

54 Ibid.

55 An allusion to the massacre of Armenians in Aleppo perpetrated on February 18, 1919. According to Aram Andonian, an eyewitness, the killings and lootings lasted five hours before it was contained, thanks to British troops' intervention in the city. Nevertheless, it cost the Armenians about four hundred lives, nearly three thousand injured, and financial losses ("Hale'bi Ch'arty" [The Massacre of Aleppo], *Veradzno'wnt*, Paris, April 1919, pp. 123–124). Attempts against Armenians on the same day in various localities in Cilicia and the apprehension of Ittihadist perpetrators in Aleppo led to the conclusion that the chain of events was planned and implemented upon the instigation of Ittihadists.

56 AGS 35th meeting, March 31, 1920.

57 Ibid.

58 Sis (Kozan) in the original text by mistake.

59 AGS 35th meeting, March 31, 1920.

60 Ibid.

61 Ibid.

62 AGS 36th meeting, April 21, 2020.

63 Ibid.

64 Ibid.

տասնհինգ անձեր իրենց հետ առած էին հայերը (անոնցմէ հինգը կապուած եւ երկուքը ազատ). իրենց դիմաց ելլելով, մեզ ալ իրենց հետ տարին: Գիշերը, բոլորս հասանք Եալովա, Ղանիքի դատաւորին մօտ: Հոն մեզ հարցաքննեցին եւ ազատ արձակեցին: Այդ եօթը անձերը պաշտօնագրով մը ուղարկեցին Գափաքլը գաւառակի կառավարիչին

16 Միլլիները մեզ բերին մինչեւ հոս:

17 Մատիտով աւելցուած՝ «Լուրը հերքուած ըլլալով չէ տրուած»:

18 Մատիտով աւելցուած՝ «Լուրը հերքուած ըլլալով չէ տրուած»:

19 Ահաւասիկ... ձուկ որսալու լաւ տեղ է ասիկա:

20 Ինչպէ՞ս թուրք դառնալէ յետոյ հայ կը դառնաք:

21 Բնագրին մէջ՝ *Հեռագրին մէկ հատին պարունակութիւնը այս է որ Զարուկ անունով եկած է*:

22 Ջնջուած տողեր.- Անգթութիւնները սոսկալի դարձան անցեալ տարուան Նոյեմ. 9էն վերջը: Այդ թուականին էր որ ասկից Պրուսա փախչող Համբարձում...

23 Բնագրին մէջ՝ *օթօմիպոյ*:

24 Բնագրին մէջ՝ ջրաղացքներու

25 Նոյնը հրատարակած է Սանդրո Բեհբուդեան (*Վաւերագրեր Հայ Եկեղեցու Պատմութեան, Գիրք Դ, Սահակ Բ Խապայեան Կաթողիկոս Կիլիկիոյ 1891–1940 Թ.Թ.* [Երեւան, 1997], 340–344): Նամակին օրինակը հրատարակուած է նաեւ այլուր՝ Փարիզի Նուպարեան Մատենադարանին մէջ պահպանուած բնագրին օգտագործումով (Պօյաճեան, 404–410), որ կը թուի թէ աւելի հարազատ կրնայ ըլլայ բնօրինակին, քան՝ այստեղ ներկայացուած վերարտադրութիւնը, որ արտագրման պահուն կրնար վրիպումներ ունենալ:

26 Բնագրին մէջ՝ դատարկ միջոց, բառն անընթեռնելի ըլլալուն: Բեհբուդեանի մօտ՝ *զոնսիւլ* (հիմա՛ հիւպատոս):

27 Բնագրին մէջ՝ *յանձնելու*:

28 Բնագրին մէջ՝ *կայքերը* կայարան փոխադրել, Բեհբուդեանի մօտ՝ *կայքերը կացարան* փոխադրել:

29 Նախադասութիւնը շարահիւսականօրէն թերի ըլլալով հանդերձ պահպանած ենք նոյնութեամբ:

30 Բնագրին մէջ, որոշապէս սխալմամբ՝ *ներքին*:

31 Ճեղագրեալ հատուածը կը բացակայի տետրէն: Զայն ամբողջացուցած ենք բնագիր նամակէն:

[65] AGS 37th meeting, May 5, 1920.
[66] Ibid.
[67] Ibid.
[68] AGS 38th meeting, May 19, 1920.
[69] Ibid.
[70] AGS 39th meeting, June 2, 1920.
[71] Ibid.
[72] Ibid.
[73] Ibid.
[74] AGS 40th meeting, June 16, 1920.
[75] bid.
[76] Ibid.
[77] AGS 41st meeting, June 30, 1920.
[78] Ibid.
[79] Ibid.
[80] AGS 42nd meeting, July 14, 1920.
[81] Ibid.
[82] AGS 43rd meeting, July 28, 1920.
[83] Reference to the reign of Sultan Abdülhamid II (1878–1909).
[84] AGS 43rd meeting, July 28, 1920.
[85] Ibid.
[86] AGS 44th meeting, August 18, 1920.
[87] Ibid.
[88] Ibid.
[89] AGS 45th meeting, September 1, 1920.
[90] Ibid.
[91] AGS 46th meeting, September 15, 1920.
[92] AGS 47th meeting, September 29, 1920. The date of the report is mentioned as September 16.
[93] Ibid.
[94] AGS 48th meeting, October 3, 1920. The date of the report is mentioned as September 28.
[95] Ibid.
[96] Ibid.
[97] AGS 49th meeting, November 10, 1920.
[98] AGS 50th meeting, November 24, 1920. The date of the report is mentioned as October 31.
[99] Ibid.
[100] AGS 53rd meeting, January 5, 1921.
[101] AGS 55th meeting, February 2, 1921.
[102] Ibid.
[103] AGS 59th meeting, March 31, 1921.
[104] Ibid.
[105] Deviating from the pattern, the original document is inserted in the notebook.

[illegible] - 1919 [illegible] - [illegible]
1500 [illegible]
[illegible], 6-7 [illegible]
[illegible] 5000 [illegible]
512 [illegible]

[illegible] - 1919 [illegible] 17 - [illegible]
500 [illegible]
[illegible] 1919 [illegible] 31 [illegible] 600 [illegible]

[illegible] - 1919 [illegible] 17 - [illegible]
[illegible] 200 [illegible]

[illegible] - 1919 [illegible] 15 - [illegible] 5000 [illegible]
[illegible] 50 [illegible]
[illegible] 200 [illegible]
200 [illegible]

[illegible] - 1919 [illegible]/16 [illegible] - [illegible]
[illegible] 146 - [illegible]
[illegible] 23 [illegible]
[illegible] 250,000 [illegible]

The first page of the first notebook.

[106] AGS 62nd meeting, May 11, 1921.

[107] A note added in pencil states: "The news was not delivered [to the AGS], as it was refuted."

[108] A note added in pencil states: "The news was not delivered [to the AGS], as it was refuted."

[109] AGS 64th meeting, June 8, 1921.

[110] AGS 65th meeting, June 22, 1921. The date of the report is mentioned as June 17.

[111] AGS 67th meeting, July 20, 1921. The date of the report is presented as June 7.

[112] AGS 68th meeting, August 3, 2021.

[113] Ibid.

[114] AGS 68th meeting, August 3, 1921. The date of the report is mentioned as July 12.

[115] AGS 69th meeting, August 17, 1921.

[116] AGS 70th meeting, August 31, 2021.

[117] Ibid.

[118] Ibid.

[119] AGS 74th meeting, October 26, 1921.

[120] AGS 75th meeting, November 9, 1921.

[121] AGS 74th meeting, October 26, 1921.

[122] AGS 76th meeting, November 23, 1921.

[123] AGS 77th meeting, December 7, 1921.

[124] Ibid.

[125] AGS 78th meeting, December 21, 1921.

[126] Ibid.

[127] Ibid.

[128] AGS 80th meeting, January 18, 1922. The date of the report is mentioned as December 3.

[129] Ibid.

[130] Ibid.

[131] AGS 81st meeting, February 1, 1922.

[132] AGS 81nd meeting, February 15, 1922.

[133] AGS 83rd meeting, March 1, 1922.

[134] The text in italics is missing from the notebook. It is completed from the original letter.

CHEMIN DE FER OTTOMAN
D'ANATOLIE

№ DU REGISTRE

Station H. Pacha Mois de Juin 1921

De Serindje

Soc. An. de Pap. et d'Imp. S. G. 1920. Mod. 65.

SERVICE № — *déposé le* * 25. VI. 1921 *à* 15 *h* 55 *m.* — *arrivé le* 192 *à* *h* *m.* — *expédié le* 192 *à* *h* *m.* — L'EMPLOYÉ

* Le signataire est prié de remplir cette rubrique.

urgent

TÉLÉGRAMME

CHEMIN DE FER OTTOMAN D'ANATOLIE

CHEMIN DE FER OTTOMAN
D'ANATOLIE

S. G. 1920. Mod. 65.

Reçu de la station de

Télégramme, service N°

, le 192 *à* *heures* *minutes.*

Copy of the original telegram Reverend Father Anania sent on June 25, 1921, to the Armenian Patriarchate and Archbishop Sdeppanos, primate of İzmit. It reads: "Ten thousand Armenian people have been forced to evacuate immediately by order of the local military authorities. At least six (6) transport vessels need to come here if the slaughter of the entire population is undesired. Help!" See *p. 424.*

Appendices
Յաւելուածներ

Appendix I

Minutes of meeting between Armenian Greek Section
and Colonel Villiers.

28th February 1919.

Present:-

Brigadier General Deedes
Commander Heathcote Smith
Major Foster
Mr. Hole
Colonel Villiers
Mr. Tchakirian.

Brigadier General Deedes explained that the provisions of Clause Four of the Armistice were read to extend to the recovery of orphans and islamised persons.

Commander Heathcote Smith outlined the previous procedure. The original scheme was that in each of the police districts there should be an Armenian with powers to conduct the Turkish Police to houses in which there was a suspected case and to seize the child. In practice this scheme was limited to an Armenian complaining to the Central Turkish Police and asking for assistence. This now hardly works at all.

Coloner Villiers explained that the area under his supervision was divided into six districts each under an allied officer and that in future in any suspected case the course for the Armenian to adopt would be to go to the head office in the district concerned and inform the Allied Officer in charge to

/whom is attached

-2-

whom is attached a Turkish Commissaire.

The Allied officer, the Turkish officer and the Armenian would then take the necessary measures to deal with the case.

I In case of dispute the child will be lodged in a "neutral" house. If any difficulty is met with from Moslem women, the actual search could be carried out by an Armenian women under Allied Police control.

Brigadier General Deedes asked what would be done in the case of refusal to surrender the child.

Commander Heathcote Smith said that that question was dealt with by the proposed scheme of the neutral house free of access to the disputants. The American Relief Mission is willing to provide the funds and the house will be ready in a few days. The Turkish police accepted this scheme.

Colonel Villiers observed that in conversation with him, Halil Bey had assured him of his willingness to co-operate in recovering Armenian children and would welcome the presence of an allied member on the Committee already dealing with the matter.

On the question of punishment for refusal to give up orphans, Colonel Villiers observed that such refusal could be taken as a refusal to obey the order of the Allied Military Authorities, and would render a person liable to three months' imprisonment and £200 fine.

DECISION. To request General Officer Commanding-in-Chief to instruct Police Commission to elaborate a fresh scheme to be presented by High Commissioner to Turkish Government.

666

Appendix II

that it was so.

Continuing, Dr. Tavitian declared that the situation at Diarbekir was distinctly strained; the Armenians were commencing to emigrate from there.

The Kurds in the Malatia District had revolted against the Nationalists; up to the present they had not mal-treated the Christians.

Dr. Theotokas said that they had not received much information from the Interior; the situation was unchanged, or slightly worse.

Bands had carried off 20 people from some of the villages near Adalia, and the Nationalists had imposed a levy of money and clothing on the town. The Christians were leaving Nigdé. A number of incidents were reported from the Machka Kaza of the Trebizond Vilayet.

Disturbances in the near neighbourhood of Constantinople continued to be numerous. Security was bad near Chilé and along the South Coast of the Sea of Marmora. Gendarmes, ostensibly in pursuit of a Greek brigand, named Kirmanis, had entered the church of the Monastery at Perama and had sacked it.

Disturbances were also numerous in the Rodosto and Chatalja Districts.

The recruiting of Christians was continuing in the villages near Guemlek.

Colonel Graves stated that a list of murders, etc. which had taken place close to Constantinople since the beginning of September was being compiled, with a view to representations being made to the Turkish Government.

2. R E L I E F

Dr. Theotokas said that at Eregli (Rodosto) families of refugees who had returned from Greece since the Armistice were being threatened with re-expulsion.

Appendix III

PATRIARCAT ARMENIEN
CONSTANTINOPLE

Samsoun- May 27 - Fifty Armenians deported from Samsoun, Tcharshamba, Bafara, Tokat etc. have arrived at Samsoun from Sokhoun in a very poor and miserable condition - There is no means to feed them. The houses of most of them are ruined and the Turks are hastening to demolish the houses of the newly returning, by night. The timber and tiles of such houses are carried off in open daylight even in a city like Samsoun.

In the vicinities of Samsoun, 400 out of the 500 Armenian houses are pulled down.

At Tcharshamba, the number of Armenians, both those that have remained there and those that have been deported but have now returned, amounts to a thousand. There are also 400-500 orphans detained in Turkish houses.

Complaints are made against Rahmi Bey the Chairman of the Emigrants Commission at Samsoun. He is charged as attempting to appropriate to himself part of the traveling expenses to be paid to emigrants. He has even proposed to pay only half of the fixed amount.

The 600-700 orphans, and the islamized young ladies of a considerable number, found in the diocese of Samsoun have not yet been gathered on account of the lack of means to take care of them.

Malatea - May 28- Great preparations for resistance are going on. The Kurdish chieftains of Arabkir, Maden, Petourig and other sandjaks and Kazas are united with the Turks and grow very active. They declare that since they are to die anyway it is better for them to die as bravely as possible.

More than 400 orphans and widows who have been gathered are thrust into great misery and need immediate relief.

The orphans that are found in the kazas and villages are not being handed over but made to labour gratis, by the Turks

Sivas- May 27- ~~by the Turks~~. Meeting on the occasion of the occupation of Smyrna. Fiery speeches and orations. Threat to declare djihad The threatening telegram of the Grand Vezier sent to the Council of Foura has strongly excited the Turks and rendered them more unmanageable.

Appendix IV

Greco-Armenian Agreement

MEMORANDUM

of the

Œcumenical Patriarchate

and of the

Armenian Patriarchate of Constantinople

for

The Peace Conference

The Greek and Armenian Nations, living for many years common life in the same towns and villages, thrown into daily contact and forming communities which merge into one another, feel that their destinies run in parallel lines and that they will be able to develop fully only if they keep in close union.

They have a common purpose: to obtain their liberty and an identical program: to establish security, civilization and prosperity in the Near East. During their long martyrdom, they have been able to appreciate one another and they are happy to state, that they cherish, for one another, a sincere friendship and absolute confidence.

It is for this reason, that they submit a joint appeal for justice.

The conduct of the Turks has not varied, from the time of their establishment in Anatolia and Europe, to this day. Their military and theocratic government has always employed the most odious and brutal methods, in the service of a most intolerant fanaticism. No reforms whatever, neither the Tanzimat, nor the constitution, have been able to alter this fundamental characteristic of the Ottoman Government.

Thus, there is a very clear line of division; on the one hand the Turks as the invader; on the other, the Christian, hated as a Giaour and oppressed in the quality as a rayah.

Even to-day, the Turk considers himself an absolute master, with full rights, to dispense life and death to the conquered peoples, and it is his sole interest that releases or arrests the forces of destruction.

Our history embodies the bloodiest and most frightful martyrdom recorded in history.

Insult, rapine, violation, forced conversions, murder, assassination and massacre have been the only method which the Government has employed in its dealings with us ininterruptedly [*sic*], during five centuries.

There is not a single spot in the whole Turkey, in Constantinople as well as in the smallest village, in which robbery and rapine are not, even to-day, officially recognized, from St. Sophia where the crescent has not yet been replaced, to the huts of the Armenian and Greek peasants, occupied now by the Turks, who come into their possession after expelling or massacring the proprietor.

It is inadmissible, that a crime should be absolved, or that robbery should constitute a right to ownership, on the ground, that it was committed a long time ago; moreover the drama which has been enacted in the Near East, in recent years has surpassed in horror the blackest pages of the Turkish annals themselves.

If our nations had enjoyed liberty, they would have numbered dozens of millions. To-day, they are reduced in Turkey to 2.500.000 Greeks and 1.500.000 Armenians.

It is only as a consequence of the most heinous crimes, that a Musulman majority exists in this or that locality and to recognize such a majority would be to excuse, to sanction and to encourage the measures of extermination which the Turks have employed against us.

We have always inhabited this country. We have irrigated its soil with our sweat and blood. Never has battlefield claimed more dead, for we have been massacred for five centuries without interruption.

But despite everything, we remain the only progressive and productive elements in the country. The Turk has been and remains to this day a terrible parasite living on our flesh. He has produced no work of civilisation [*sic*], he has built not a single city. He has everywhere sown death and ruin.

We demand, that we no longer be compelled to live under a Turkish Government, and we declare that we shall never submit to such a government, under whatever control it might be placed.

We ask for restoration of our national domain. If all the Greek and Armenian populations cannot be included within the limits of our respective States, it is an ardent desire that these populations should live under a Greek or an Armenian Government, according to the necessities of the case.

We ask for a great Armenia, with a free and broad access to the Black sea and to the Mediterranean, and we Greeks declare that we would be happy to see Cilicia integrally incorporated into the other six vilayets of Armenia and permitted to develop freely.

We ask for the restoration to Greece of all that she has been forcibly despoiled and which therefore rightfully belongs to her, and we Armenians, declare it to be our wish that Thrace, Constantinople, the vilayets of Aidin and or Broussa, and the Sandjaks of Ismidt (Nikomedia) and of Bigha should be integrally incorporated into Greece.

Our two countries, having thus realized their unity will become two most powerful factors of peace, progress, and civilization in the Orient.

The fulfilment of our demands will constitute a noble act of justice and reparation, and we are confident that it will serve not only the interests of our respective nations but the interests of humanity at large.

Constantinople, February 11/24, 1919.

Glossary, Tables, and Indices
Բառացանկ, Աղիւսակներ եւ Ցանկեր

Trilingual Glossary - Եռալեզու Բառացանկ

Source word	*Turkish*	*Armenian*	*English*
capitaine	kaptan, yüzbaşı	հարիւրապետ	captain
colonel	miralay	գնդապետ	colonel
controle	kontrol	հակակշիռ, հսկողութիւն	control
convoi	konvoy	կառախումբ	convoy
fourgon	furgon	բեռնակառք	fourgon
passport	pasaport	անցագիր	passport
père	rahib	հայր (եկեղեցական)	father (religious)
soeur	rahibe	քոյր (եկեղեցական)	sister (religious)
ալայ	alay	գունդ	regiment
ալայ գօմանտանի	alay komutanı	գունդի հրամանատար	regiment commander
ամելէ թապուրի	amele taburi	աշխատանքային ջոկատ	labor battalion
աշիրաթ (աշիրէթ)	aşiret	ցեղախումբ	tribe, clan
ատլիյէ	adliye	արդարադատութիւն/ դատարան	justice, court
աֆարօզ	aforoz	բանադրանք	anathema, ex-communication
բասբօռ	pasaport	անցագիր	passport
բէթրոլ	petrol	քարիւղ	petroleum
բոլիս (բօլիս, փօլիս)	polis	ոստիկան/ոստիկանութիւն	policeman, police
բոլիս միւտիրի	polis müdürü	ոստիկանապետ	chief of police
բրաթիք	pratik	գործնական	practical
բրոբականթիսթ/ բրոպականտիստ/ բրօբկանտիստ/ բռօբականթիսթ	propagandacı	քարոզիչ	propagandist
բրօբականտ/ բրօպականտ	propaganda	քարոզչութիւն	propaganda
բօսթ/բօսթա/բօստա	posta	թղթատար	mail, postal service, mail carrier
բօսթախանէ	postahane	նամակատուն	post office
գազա	kaza	ենթագաւառ	subdistrict
գազէսի միւթէսարրֆ	kazasi mutasarrıf	գաւառակի կառավարիչ	subdistrict governor
գազինօ	gazino, kumarhane	զբօսատուն, խաղատուն	casino
գաիմ հէօճէթի	kaim hüccet	վաւերական կալուածագիր	valid title
գայմագամ	kaymakam	տեղակալ	lieutenant or acting governor
գարագօլ	karakol	պահակակէտ/ ոստիկանատուն	sentry post որ police station
գէբթըն	kaptan, yüzbaşı	հարիւրապետ	captain
գըշլա	kışla	զօրանոց	barracks

գլիւպ (քլիւպ)	klüp	ակումբ	club
գոմանտան	kumandan	հրամանատար, պետ	commander
գոմիսէր	komiser	յանձնակատար/ ոստիկանապետ	commissioner/ police commissioner
գոմիսէր մուավինի	komiser muavini	ոստիկանապետի օգնական	aide to police commissioner
գոմիսիոն/քոմիսիոն	komisyon	յանձնաժողով	commission
գուվվէի միլլիէ	kuvay-i milliye	Միլլի Ուժեր	National Forces
գուրպան պայրամ	kurban bayramı	ողջակիզաց տօն	sacrificial feast
գօլ օրտու/քօլ օրտու	kolordu	զօրաբանակ	army corps
գօնթրօլըր/ քօնթրօլէօռ	kontrolör	վերահսկիչ	controller
գօնվուա	konvoy	կառախումբ	convoy
գօրուճը	korucu	պահակ	ranger
եազմաճը	yazmacı	ծաղկեայ կտաւ հիւսող (հայոց ուղղուած արհամարհանք)	hand-painted kerchief maker (derogatory reference to Armenians)
եավէր	yaver	օգնական	aide, adjutant
եիւզ պաշի	yüzbaşı	հարիւրապետ	captain
եպարքոս	veziriazam	Մեծ Վեզիր, վարչապետ	Grand Vizier
զապիթ	zabit	սպայ	officer
էզան	ezan	աղօթքի հրաւէր	azan (call for prayer)
էթֆայիէ	itfaiye	հրշէջ կայան	fire station
էմլագ քեաթիպի	emlak katibi	անշարժ գոյքի քարտուղար	real estate clerk
էմլաքը մէթրուքէ	emlak metruke	լքեալ կալուածներ	abandoned estates
էմվալը էմիրիյէ	emval-i emiriye	պետական գոյքեր	state property
էմվալը մէթրուքէ	emval-i metruke	լքեալ գոյքեր	abandoned properties
էյթամ	eytam	որբեր	orphans
էնթրիկ	entrika	մեքենայութիւն	intrigue, plot
էնճիւմէն	encümen	ժողով, խորհուրդ	assembly, council
էշրաֆ	eşraf	երեւելիներ	notables
էսնաֆ	esnaf	արհեստաւորներ	artisans, tradesmen
էտարէ/իտարէ	idare	վարչութիւն, տնօրէնութիւն	administration, management
էրքեան հարպ/ էրքեանը հարպ	erkanıharp	սպայակոյտ	staff
էֆէ	efe	չէթէյապետ	gang leader
թագավիտ պին պաշը	tekaüt binbaşı	պաշտօնաթող հազարապետ	retired major
թագըմ գօմանտանութիւն	takım komutanlığı	ջոկատապետութիւն	squad commandership
թագրիր	takrir	տեղեկագիր, զեկուցագիր	report, statement
թահսիլտար	tahsildar	հարկահաւաք	tax collector
թահրիրաթ	tahrirat	պաշտօնական հաղորդակցութիւններ	official communications
թահրիրաթ միւտիր	tahrirat müdür	պաշտօնական հաղորդա-կցութիւններու տնօրէն	director of official communications
թանք	tank	հրասայլ	tank
թաշքիլաթ/թէշքիլաթ	teşkilat	կազմակերպութիւն	organization
թապէլա	tabela	ցուցանակ	signboard

թապուր	tabur	գումարտակ	battalion
թասհիհի սին	tashih-i sin	տարիքի ճշդում	age correction
թափու	tapu	կալուածագիր	title deed
թափու մէմուրու	tapu memuru	կալուածագրային գրասենեակի քարտուղար	deed officer
թէալի քոմիթէ	teali komite	զարգացման կամ առաջընթացի յանձնաժողով	progress or advancement committee
թէգահիւտ/թէքաուտ	tekaüt	պաշտօնաթողութիւն	retirement
թէզքէրէ	tezkere	արտօնութիւն, արտօնագիր	permit, license
թէզքէրէի օսմանիէ	tezkere-i Osmaniye	Օսմանեան անձնաթուղթ	Ottoman ID
թէլէկրաֆճի	telegrafcı	հեռագրիչ	telegraphist
թէլէֆօն	telefon	հեռաձայն	telephone
թէմէթթիւ	temettü	շահ	profit
թէսլիմ	teslim	անձնատուր (ըլլալ)	surrender
թէքքալիֆը մէճպուրէ	tekalif-i mecbure	պարտադիր տուրք	mandatory tax
թիւթիւն	tütün	ծխախոտ	tobacco
թորփիլանավ/ թորփիտօ/թօրբէթօ	torpido botu	ականանաւ	torpedo boat
թռէն	tren	գնացք	train
թօփալ	topal	կաղ	lame
թօփճը	topçu	թնդանօթաձիգ, զնդացրորդ	gunner
ժանտարմա	jandarma	ոստիկան	gendarme
ժանտարմա զօմանտանը	jandarma komutanı	ոստիկան զօրաց պետ	commander of gendarmerie
ժանտարմայ մէքթէպի	jandarma mektebi	ոստիկանական դպրոց	police school
ժանտարմըրի	jandarma	ոստիկան զօրք	gendarmerie
ժէնէրալ	komutan	զօրավար	general
իմթիզաճ	imtizaç	միաբանութիւն	concord, reconcilliation
իմթիզաճ զօմիսիօն	imtizaç komisyon	միաբանական յանձնաժողով	accord committee
ինզըպաթ զօմանտան	inzibat komutanı	ռազմական ոստիկանութեան պետ	provost marshal
իսթի[հ]քամ թապուրի	istihkam taburu	ամրաշինութեան ջոկատ	fortification battalion
իսթիգլալ	istiklal	անկախութիւն	independence
իսթիհքամ	istihkam	պատուար, ամրութիւն	bulwark
իտատի	idadi	բարձրագոյն վարժարան	high school
իտարէ/էտարէ	idare	վարչութիւն, տնօրէնութիւն	administration, management
իտարէի էօրֆիէ	örfi idare	պատերազմական դրութիւն	martial law
իտարէի միլլիյէ	idare-i milliye	Միլլի վարչութիւն	Milli adminstration
իտման եուրտու	idman yurdu	մարզման կայան	training station
իրատէ	irade	կամք, կայսերական հրամանագիր	will, imperial decree
իւլէմա	ulema	իսլամագէտներ	ulema (Muslim scholars)
խաթեր	hatır	սիրոյն	sake
խալիֆա	halife	Խալիֆ/Մուհամմէտի յաջորդ	caliph
խային	hain	դաւաճան	traitor

խան	han	իջեւանատուն	inn
խթամէ (եղած)	mühür	կնքուած	sealed
կեավուր	gavur	անհաւատ	infidel
հաճի	hacı	մահտեսի	pilgrim
հանըմ	hanım	տիկին	dame
հաքիմ	hakim	դատաւոր	judge
հէյէթ	heyet	պատուիրակութիւն, մարմին, խորհուրդ	delegation, body, committee, board
հէյէթի ատիլէ գոմիսիոնը	heyet-i adile komisyonu	արդարութեան յանձնաժողով	Committee of justice
հէվալէ	havale	փոխանցում	transfer
հէրկէլէ	hergele	ստահակ	rascal
հիյէթը մէրքէզիյէ/ հիյյէթը մէրքէզիյէ	heyet merkezi	կեդրոնական յանձնաժողով	central committee
ղատը	kadı	իսլամ դատաւոր	Muslim judge
ղրուշ	kuruş	դահեկան, ղուրուշ	kurus, monetary unit equal to one hundredth lira
ճամի	cami	մզկիթ	mosque
ճարիյէ	cariye	աղախին	handmaiden
ճէզա	ceza	պատիժ, տուգանք	penalty, punishment
ճէմիէթի իսլամիէ/ ճէմիյէթը իսլամիյէ	cemiyet Islamiye	Իսլամական Միութիւն	Muslim Union
ճէպհէ	cephe	ռազմաճակատ	front
ճիհատ	cihad	սրբազան պատերազմ	jihad (holy war)
մազպաթա	mazbata	արձանագրութիւն	record
մաժէօր	binbaşı	հազարապետ	major
մալ	mal	ունեցուածք	property
մալ-միւտիրի	mal müdürü	շրջանի մը գանձարանային գործարքներու տնօրէն	fiscal director (of a district)
մախտում	mahdum	որդի	son
մանէթ	manet	ռուսական դրամ	Russian monetary unit
մանիֆաթուրա	manifatura	կտորեղէն	drapery
մանիֆաթուրաճի	manifaturacı	կտորավաճառ	draper
մանուսա	manusa	Մանիսա արտադրուած բամպակեայ գործուածք	cotton textile produced in Manisa
մանտաթէռ	mandaci	հոգատար	mandatery
մառթին	Martin tüfeği	հրացանի տեսակ	Martin rifle
մասաճի	masacı	սեղանագործ	table maker
Մավզէր	mavzer	հրացանի տեսակ	Mauser rifle
մավունա	mavuna	բեռնանաւ, լաստանաւ	barge
մարգա	marka	մակնիշ	brand
մեդրապօլիտ/ մեթրոպոլիտ/ մետրոպոլիտ	piskopos	Արեւելեան Ուղղափառ Եկեղեցւոյ թեմակալ	metropolitan
մեթրայէօզ/ միթրաեօզ/ միթրալեօզ/			

միթրալյէօզ	mitralyöz	գնդացիր	machine gun
մէրքէզ	merkez	կեդրոնի	
գոմանտանլըղ	kumandanlık	հրամանատարութիւն	center commandership
մէճլիս իտարէ/ մէճլիս իտարէի	meclis idare-i	վարչական կամ տնօրէն ժողով	administrative council
մէմուր	memur	պաշտօնեայ	official
մէպուս	mebus	երեսփոխան, ներկայացուցիչ, պատուիրակ	deputy, representative
մէպուսարան	mebuslar meclisi	խորհրդարան	parliament
մէրքէզ մէմուրի	merkez memuru	կեդրոնատեղիի վերակացու	headquarters' intendant
մէքթէպ	mektep	դպրոց	school
մէքթուպճի	mektupçu	նամակագիր	letter writer
մըխթար/մխթար/ մուխթար	muhtar	թաղապետ, գիւղապետ, տեղական իշխանաւոր	headman, local authority
միթինկ	miting	հաւաք	rally
միթրան	matrân/mıtrân	արքեպիսկոպոս	metropolitan
միլլէթ	millet	ազգ	nation
միլլիյէ	milliye	միլլի, ազգայնական	Milli, nationalist
միսիոն	misyon	առաքելութիւն	mission
միսիօնար	misyoner	քարոզիչ	missionary
միւզէ	müze	թանգարան	museum
միւթէսարըֆ/ մութասարըֆ	mutasarrıf	գաւառապետ	district (sancak) governor
միւնթէխիպը սանի	müntehib-i sani	երկրորդ քուէարկող	second voter
միւսթանթիք	müstantik	հարցաքննիչ դատաւոր	inquisitor judge, coroner
միւտաֆաայի միլլիյէ	müdafaa-i milliye	ազգային պաշտպանութիւն	national defence
միւտիր	müdür	տնօրէն, վերատեսուչ, վարիչ	director, intendant, administrator
միւրէթթէպիյէ եւ թէէտիպիյէ	mürettibiye ve tedibiye	կարգապահութիւն եւ կրթութիւն	discipline and education
միւֆէթթիշ	müfettiş	քննիչ	inspector
միւֆթի	müftü	իսլամ իրաւագէտ	mufti (a jurist who interprets Muslim religious law)
միւֆրէզէ	müfreze	անջատ ջոկատներ	detached units
մուավին	muavin	օգնական	aide, assistant, adjutant
մութասարըֆութիւն	mutasarrıflık	գաւառ	district (sancak)
մուհաճիր	muhacir	գաղթական (մահմետական)	refugee (Muslim)
մուհաճիր գոմիսիոն	muhacir komisyon	գաղթականաց յանձնաժողով	refugee commission
մուհասըպէճի	Muhasebeci	համարակալ, հաշուապահ	accountant
մուհաֆազաի միլլիյէ	muhafaza-i milli	ազգային պահպանութիւն	national safeguard
մուտտայի ումումի	müddeiumumi	ընդհանուր դատախազ	attorney general
մուրախաս	murahhas	լիազօր պատուիրակ	plenipotentiary envoy
մօթօր	motor	շարժիչով նաւակ	motorboat
մօթէօր	motor	ինքնաշարժ	automobile
մօլա	molla	օրէնսուսոյց, մզկիթի գլխաւոր կրօնական դէմք	mullah
նահիյէ	nahiye	վիճակ	canton, commune
նամէհրամ	namahrem	ոչ-ազգական	unrelated (person)

նաֆաա քեաթպ	nafaka katip	ապրելամիջոցի, նպաստից գրագիր	alimony clerk
նիքեահ/նիքիահ	nikah	ամուսնական պայմանագիր	marriage contract
նուֆուզ մէմուրի/ նֆուս մէմուրի	nüfus memuru	քաղաքացիական վիճակի գրասենեակի պաշտօնեայ	registrar of civil status
նուֆուզ միւտիրի	nüfus müdürü	քաղաքացիական վիճակի գրասենեակի տնօրէն	registrar of civil status
շէհիտ	şehit	նահատակ	martyr
շէյխ	şeyh	իսլամ կրօնաւոր, ցեղապետ	sheikh
շէյխ-իւլ-իսլամ	şeyhülislam	իսլամ գերագոյն կրօնապետ	shaykh al-Islam
շէրի	şeri	իսլամական կրօնական օրէնք	sharia (the code of law derived from the Koran and teachings
շէրհ	şerh	բացատրութիւն, մեկնաբանութիւն	explanation, comment
շէֆ	şef	ղեկավար, պետ	chief
շիւպէ րէիզի	şube	բաժնի/մասնաճիւղի պետ	branch or section chief
շօսէ	şose	խճուղի	causeway
շօֆէօռ/շօֆէօր/ շօֆֆէր	şoför	վարորդ	driver
ումումի	umumi	հանրային	public
չավուշ	çavuş	քսանապետ	sergeant
չէթէ /չէթա	çete	հրոսախումբ	gang, band
չէթէ րէյիսի	çete reisi	չէթէյապետ, հրոսակապետ	gang leader
չէթէպաշի	çete başı	չէթէյապետ, հրոսակապետ	gang leader
չէրքէզ/չէրքէս	çerkez	չէրքէզ	Circassian
չինի	çini	ճենապակի, յախճապակի	faience
չիֆթլիկ/չիֆլիկ	çiftlik	ագարակ	farm, ranch
չուխա	çuha	ասուի	drapery
պագալ/պագգալ	bakkal	նպարավաճառ	grocer
պաթանիէ	battaniye	ծածկոց	blanket
պայրամ	bayram	իսլամական տօն	Muslim festival, holiday
պանքա	banka	դրամատուն	bank
պաշը պօզուք	başıbozuk	վտանգաւոր չափով անկառավարելի անձ, անկանոն զինուոր	dangerously undisciplined person, irregular (troops)
պաշի	baş	ղեկավար, առաջնորդ	head, leader
պէզազ	bezzaz	ասուեվաճառ	draper
պէզկեաթէն	kapalı pazar yeri	գոց շուկայ	covered market
պէլէտիյէ	belediye	քաղաքապետարան	municipality
պէլէտիյէ րէյիս	belediye reisi	քաղաքապետ	mayor
պէյաննամէ	beyanname	յայտարարութիւն	proclamation, declaration
պէքճի	bekçi	պահակ	watchman
պէօլիւկ	bölük	վաշտ	company
պէօլիւք զօմանտանի	bölük komutanı	վաշտի հրամանատար	company commander
պիլէթ	bilet	տոմս	ticket
պինպաշը	binbaşı	հազարապետ	major
պոլշէվիկ	bolşevik	մեծամասնական	bolshevik

պօլշէվիքութիւն	bolşeviklik	մեծամասնականութիւն	bolshevism
պօղազ	boğaz	կիրճ	gorge
պօմպա/պօնպա	bomba	ռումբ	bomb
պօյքօթ/պօյքօթաժ	boykot	խեցեվճիռ	boycott
պօռազան	borazan	փող, շեփոր	bugle
պօստան	bostan	պարտէզ, բանջարանոց	garden, vegetable patch
պօրսա	borsa	արժետոմսերու շուկայ	stock market
ռէժիմ/րէժիմ	rejim	վարչակարգ	regime, system of government
սանճազ/սանճաք	sancak	գաւառ	district
սանճագը շէրիֆ	sancak-ı şerif	Սրբազան Պատերազմի պարագային պարզուող Մուհամմէտի սրբազան դրօշը	the holy standard of the Prophet
սապըգ	sabık	նախկին	former
սէյահաթ վարագասի	seyahat varakası	շրջագայութեան արտօնագիր	travel document
սէյեար վարագասի	seyyar varakası	ճամբորդական արտօնագիր	travel document
սէնայի թէրզիհանէ	sanayi terzihane	արդիւնաբերական դերձակատուն	industrial tailor shop
սէվապ	sevap	բարեգործութիւն	good deed
սէվք	sevk	ուղարկում	dispatch
սէր (քօմիսէր)	ser (komiser)	գլխաւոր (ոստիկանապետ)	chief commissioner
սէֆէրպէրլիք	seferberlik	զօրահաւաք	mobilization
սթասիօն	stasyon	կայարան	station
սիսթէմաթիք	sistematik	պարբերական, հետեւողական	systematic
սիվիլ	sivil	քաղաքացի	civil, in civilian clothes, secular
սօփա	sopa	բիր, գաւազան	cudgle, cane
վալի	vali	նահանգապետ, կուսակալ	governor general
վակոն	vagon	երկաթուղիի կառք	wagon
վէսիգա/վէսիքա	vesika	հաստատագիր	voucher, certificate, credential
վէքիլ	vekil	փոխանորդ	proxi, substitute, lieutenant
վիզէ	vize	մուտքի թոյլատրութիւն	visa
վիլայէթ	vilayet	նահանգ	province
տէբօ/տէփօ	depo	շտեմարան, մթերանոց	depot, storehouse
տէրօր	terör	ահաբեկչութիւն	terror
տէֆթէրհանէ	defterhane	կալուածագրային գրասենեակ	land registry and cadastre office
տէֆթէրտար/տէֆտէրտար	defterdar	նահանգային գանձապետ	provincial treasurer
տըմտըմ	dumdum kurşunu	թիրախը հարուածելով ընդարձակուող փամփուշտ	dumdum bullet
տիկտատորութիւն	diktatörlük	բռնատիրութիւն	dictatorship
տիկտատօր/թիկտատօր	diktatör	բռնատէր	dictator
տինամիթ/տինամիտ	dinamit	ուժանակ	dynamite
տինը իսլամի	islam dini	իսլամական կրօնք	Islamic religion
տիվանը հարպի տայիմ	Divanı Harp-i daim	ռազմական մնայուն ատեան	permanent court martial
տույունը ումումիյէ մէմուրու	Düyun-u Umumiye memuru	հանրային պարտուց պաշտօնեայ	public debt official

տրամ	dram	ծանրութեան չափ՝ 3.207 կ.	weight unit equal to 3.207 g.
տրէթնօթ	drednot	թնդանօթակիր նաւ	dreadnought
րաբորթ	rapor	տեղեկագիր, զեկուցագիր	report, statement
Րամազան	Ramazan	պահոց ամիս	the ninth month of fasting
Րէժի	Régie (tütün şirketi)	ծխախոտի տեսչութիւն	tobacco management
րէիս (րէյիս)	reis	պետ	chief, head
րըֆերանտօմ	referandum	հանրավճիռ	referendum
րուպլի	ruble	ռուսական դրամական միաւոր	ruble (Russian monetary unit)
փազարճի	pazarcı	շուկայի մէջ վաճառող, կրպակատէր	seller in the market, stallholder
փաս	pasaport	անցագիր	passport
քեաթիպ	katip	գրագիր	clerk
քեաֆիր	kafir	անհաւատ	infidel
քեհեա (քէհեա)	kahya	պահապան, վերակացու	steward, custodian
քէիւլէկ	külek	դոյլ	bucket
քէմբ (քէմփ)	kamp	բանակատեղ, վրանաքաղաք, գաղթականներու կայան	camp
քրիթիք	kritik	վճռական, ճգնաժամային	cricital
քօմէտի	komedi	կատակերգութիւն	comedy
քօմիթէ	komite	յանձնաժողով	committee
քօմիթէճի	komitacı	գաղտնի ընկերութեան անդամ, յեղափոխական	member of a secret society, revolutionary
քօնթրօլ	kontrol	վերահսկողութիւն	control
քօնկրէ	kongre	համաժողով	congress
քօքարտ	kokart	գլխարկանիշ	cockade
օթէլ	otel	պանդոկ	hotel
օթոմոպիլ	otomobil	ինքնաշարժ	automobile
օխա	okka	ծանրութեան չափ, 1.2829 ք.	oka (weight unit = 1.2829 kg.)
օղլու	oğul	որդի	son
օրման մէմուրի	orman memuru	անտառապահ	forester, woodsman
օրտու զօմանտանի	ordu komutanı	բանակի հրամանատար, զօրավար	army commander, general
ֆալախա	falaka	առասանակ, բարակ չուան, առատուկ	bastinado
ֆապրիքաթօռ	fabrikatör	արտադրիչ	manufacturer
ֆէթվա	fetva	կրօնական վճիռ	fatwa (an edict by Muslim religious authority)
ֆէլլահ	fellah	մշակ, շինական	agricultural laborer
ֆէրման	ferman	հրովարտակ	edict
ֆրանքօֆիլ	fransız hayranı	ֆրանսասէր	francophile
ֆրգա	fırka	դասակ	platoon
ֆրգա զօմանտանի	fırka komutanı	դասակի հրամանատար	platoon commander
ֆրէր	frer	եղբայր (ի Քրիստոս)	friar

Անձնանուններու Ցանկ

Տեղանուններու Ցանկ

Index of Personal Names

Index of Geographical Names

Comparative Table of Toponyms

Toponyms with square brackets indicate old Turkish names, while asterisks denote localities we have yet to be able to associate with certainty with their modern Turkish names.

	District, province or country	*As mentioned in the source materials*	*Transliteration*
Abana*	Giresun	Ապանայ	Abanah'
Adabelan*		Ատապելան	Adabelan
Adalı	Balıkesir	Ատալի	Adali
Adana	Adana	Ատանա	Adana
Adapazarı	Sakarya	Ատաբազար, Ատա-բազար, Ատապազար, Ատափազար, Ատըբազար	Adapazar, Ada-pazar, Adabazar, Adap'azar, Adypazar
Adıyaman [Hısnımansur]	Adıyaman	Ատըեաման, Ատիեաման, Հիւսնի Մանսուր	Adyeaman, Adieaman, Hiwsni Manso'wr
Adjara	Georgia	Աջարա	Ach'ara
Afyon/Afyonkarahisar	Afyonkarahisar	Աֆիոն Գարահիսար	Afio'n Karahisar
Ağin	Elazığ	Ակն	Agn
Ahairpazar*	Mersin	Ահայիրբազար	Ahah'irpazar
Ahallı	Samsun	Ախալլը	Axally
Akarca	Mersin	Ախարճա	Axarja
Akbez	Hatay	Էկպէզ, Էքպէզ	E'gbe'z, E'qbe'z
Akbulgur [Yeritsu]	Ağrı	Երիցու	Erico'w
Akçaabat	Trabzon	Բլաթանա	Plat'ana
Akçakiraz [Perçenç]	Elazığ	Փէրչէնճ	P'e'rche'nj
Akçakoca [Akçaşehir]	Düzce	Ագճէ-Շէհիր	Akje'-She'hir
Akçalıuşağı	Adana	Աղջալ-Ուշաղի	Aghch'al-O'wshaghi
Akdağmadeni	Yozgat	Ագտաղ-Մատէն, Աքտաղ-Մատէն	Akdagh-Made'n, Aqdagh-Made'n
Akdam	Adana	Աղտամ	Aghdam
Akdamar [Ağtamar]	Van	Աղթամար	Aght'amar

Akgümüş [Bunduk]	Kahramanmaraş	Պունտուք	Bo'wndo'wq
Akhisar	Sakarya	Ագհիսար, Ագ-Հիսար, Աքհիսար	Akhisar, Ak-Hisar, Aqhisar
Akın	Kayseri	Ագ-Ին	Ak-In
Akmeşe [Armaş]	Kocaeli	Արմաշ	Armash
Akpazar [Çarsancak]	Tunceli	Չարսանճագ	Charsanjak
Akpınar [Mahmat]	Ordu	Մահմատ	Mahmad
Aksaray	Aksaray	Ագսէրայ, Ագ-Սէրայ	Akse'rah', Ak-Se'rah'
Akşehir	Konya	Ագ-Շէհիր	Ak-She'hir
Aksıkalı	Balıkesir	Աք-Սագալ	Aq-Sakal
Aktaş	Bolu	Ագ Թաշ	Ak T'ash
Alablı	Düzce	Ալապլը	Alably
Alaca	Çorum	Ալաճա	Alaja
Alagöz	Kayseri	Ալակէօզ	Alage'oz
Alandağı	Samsun	Ալանտաղ	Alandagh
Alandüzü	Sakarya	Ալան Տիւզ	Alan Diwz
Alaşehir	Manisa	Ալաշէհիր	Alashe'hir
Alata	Mersin	Ալաթթա	Alat't'a
Alemdağı	İstanbul	Ալէմտաղի, Ալէմ Տաղի	Ale'mdaghi, Ale'm Daghi
Aleppo	Syria	Հալէպ	Hale'b
Alifuatpaşa	Sakarya	Geyvé Station	
Alınca	Eskişehir	Ալընճա	Alynja
Alipınar [Alipunar]	Diyarbakır	Ալի Փունար	Ali P'o'wnar
Almalı	Sakarya	Ալմալը, Ալմալու	Almaly, Almalo'w
Amanos	Osmaniye	Ամանոս	Amano's
Amasya	Amasya	Ամասիա	Amasia
Amik [Amuq]	Hatay	Ամուգ	Amo'wk
Anadolu [Anatolia]		Անատոլու, Անատօլի, Անատօլու	Anado'lo'w, Anadoli, Anadolo'w
Andırın	Kahramanmaraş	Անտէրուն, Անտըրէն, Անտըրըն, Անտրըն, Անտրին,	Ande'ro'wn, Andyre'n, Andyryn, Andryn, Andrin
Ankara	Ankara	Անգարա, Անկորա, Էնգարա, Էնգարէ, Էնկիւրի, Էնկիւրիւ	Ankara, Ango'ra, E'nkara, E'nkare', E'ngiwri, E'ngiwriw

Ankara and Eskişehir provinces (Galatia)		Գաղատիա	Kaghadia
Antakya	Hatay	Անտիոք	Andio'q
Antalya [Adalya]	Antalya	Ատալիա	Adalia
Apçağa [Abuçeğ]	Erzincan	Ապուչէխ	Abo'wche'x
Aragez*	Kocaeli	Արակէզ	Arage'z
Arapkir	Malatya	Արաբկիր, Արապկիր	Arapgir, Arabgir
Arifiye	Sakarya	Արիֆիյէ	Arifih'e'
Arkarası	Mersin	Արքարաշ	Arqarash
Armatoka*		Արմաթօքա	Armat'o'qa
Arslanbey	Kocaeli	Ասլանպէյ, Ասլանպէկ, Արսլանպէկ	Aslanbe'h', Aslanbe'g, Arslanbe'g
Arslanköy [Efrenk]	Mersin	Էֆրէնկ	E'fre'ng
Aşağıköy	Balıkesir	Աշաղը Քէօյ	Ashaghy Qe'oh'
Aşağıyapıcı [Yapıcı]	Balıkesir	Եափըճը	Eap'yjy
Ashkut	Lebanon	Աշխուտ	Ashxo'wd
Asmalı	Balıkesir	Ազմալը	Azmaly
Atina [Pazar]	Rize	Աթինա	At'ina
Atma	Erzincan	Աթմա	At'ma
Avcıköy [Merdigöz]	Kocaeli	Մերտիկէօզ, Մէրտիկէօզ, Մէրտէկէօզ	Merdige'oz, Me'rdige'oz, Me'rde'ge'oz
Avcılar [Avakal]	Kahramanmaraş	Աւագալ	Awakal
Ayaş	Ankara	Այաշ	Ah'ash
Aydıncık [Kilindire]	Mersin	Քելինտիր	Qelindir
Ayıcık*	Adana	Այէճըգ	Ah'e'jyk
Ayvalı	Eskişehir	Այվալը	Ah'valy
Ayvalık	Adana	Այվալըգ	Ah'valyk
Azadlı	İstanbul	Ազատլը	Azadly
Azgıt*	Kahramanmaraş	Ազղըտ	Azghyd
Bab	Syria	Պապ	Bab
Babaeski	Kırklareli	Պապա Էսկի	Baba E'sgi
Babayağmur	Kayseri	Պապա-Եաղմուր	Baba-Eaghmo'wr
Bafra	Samsun	Պաֆրա, Պաւրա	Bafra, Bawra
Bağarası [Feke, Vahga]	Adana	Վահկա, Ֆէքէ, Ֆէքքէ	Vahga, Fe'qe', Fe'qqe'

Baghdad	Iraq	Պաղտատ	Baghdad
Bağlar [Aykesdan]	Van	Այգեստան	Ah'kesdan
Bağlarbaşı	İstanbul	Պաղլար Պաշի	Baghlar Bashi
Bahçe	Osmaniye	Պահջէ, Պահճէ, Պաղճէ, Պաղչէ, Պաղջէ	Bahch'e', Bahje', Baghje', Baghche', Baghch'e'
Bahçecik	Kocaeli	Պարտիզակ	Bardizag
Balat	İstanbul	Պալաթ	Balat'
Balıkesir	Balıkesir	Պալըքեսիր, Պալըքէսէր, Պալըքէսիր	Balyqesir, Balyqe'se'r, Balyqe'sir
Balıklı	Çanakkale	Պալըքլը	Balyqly
Banaz	Uşak	Պանազ	Banaz
Bandırma	Balıkesir	Պանտըրմա, Պանտրմա	Bandyrma, Bandrma
Bartın	Bartın	Պարթըն	Bart'yn
Başak [Zidikan]	Şırnak	Զիտկան	Zidgan
Başiskele	Kocaeli	Պաշ Իսկէլէ	Bash Isge'le'
Başlamış	Hatay	Պաշլամըշլը	Bashlamyshly
Batumi	Georgia	Պաթում	Bat'o'wm
Bayat	Afyonkarahisar	Պայաթ	Bah'at'
Bayburt	Bayburt	Պայպուրտ	Bah'bo'wrd
Bayındır [Kokarca]	Bursa	Գօզարճայ	Kokarjah'
Beirut	Lebanon	Պէյրութ	Be'h'ro'wt'
Belen	Hatay	Պէյլան	Be'h'lan
Belpınar	Gaziantep	Պէլ Բունար	Be'l Po'wnar
Bergama [Pergamon]	İzmir	Պէրկամոն	Be'rgamo'n
Beşgöz	Gaziantep	Պէշ-Կէօզ	Be'sh-Ge'oz
Beşik Tepe	Amasya	Պէշիք Թէփէ	Be'shiq T'e'p'e'
Beşköprü	Sakarya	Պէշ Քէօփրիւ	Be'sh Qe'op'riw
Besni	Adıyaman	Պէհէսնի, Պէհիսնի	Be'he'sni, Be'hisni
Beşpınar [Çakal]	Samsun	Չախալ	Chaxal
Beyce [Adranos]	Bursa	Ատրանօզ	Adranoz
Beykoz	İstanbul	Պէյքօզ	Be'h'qoz
Beylerbeyi	İstanbul	Պէյլէրպէյ	Be'h'le'rbe'h'
Beymelek	Antalya	Պէյէմէլէկ	Be'h'e'me'le'g
Beyoba	Balıkesir	Պէյ Օպա, Պէյ-Օպա	Be'h' Oba, Be'h'-Oba

Beyoğlu [Pera]	İstanbul	Բերա	Pera
Beypazarı	Ankara	Պէյ-Բազար, Պէյ Բազար, Պէյ Պազար	Be'h'-Pazar, Be'h' Pazar, Be'h' Bazar
Beyşehir	Konya	Պէյշէհիր	Be'h'she'hir
Bezirhane	Kayseri	Պէզիր Խան	Be'zir Xan
Bıçkıcılar	Düzce	Պըչկըճըլար	Bychgyjylar
Biga	Çanakkale	Պիղա	Bigha
Bilari	Tokat	Պիլէրի	Bile'ri
Bıldırcınlık*		Պըլտըրճընկ	Byldyrjynlk
Bilecik	Bilecik	Պիլէճիկ, Պիլէճիք	Bile'jig, Bile'jiq
Bilenler [Şerikanlı]	Gaziantep	Շէրի Գանլը	She'ri Kanly
Birecik	Şanlıurfa	Պիրէճիկ	Bire'jig
Bitlis	Bitlis	Պիթլիս	Bit'lis
Boğaz	Amasya	Պօղազ	Boghaz
Boğazlıyan	Yozgat	Պօղազլեան, Պօղազլըեան	Boghazlean, Boghazlyean
Bolu	Bolu	Պոլու, Պօլու	Bo'lo'w, Bolo'w
Bor	Niğde	Պօր	Bor
Bostancık	İstanbul	Պօսթանճըգ	Bost'anjyk
Boyalıca	Bursa	Պօեալըճա, Պօխալըճա, Պոքալըճա	Boealyja, Boxalyja, Bo'qalyja
Bozkır	Konya	Պոզկըր, Պօզկըր	Bo'zgyr, Bozgyr
Boztepe	Trabzon	Պոզթէքէ	Bo'zt'e'pe'
Bsher*		Պշէր	Bshe'r
Bünyan Hamit	Kayseri	Պիւնեան-Համիտ	Biwnean-Hamid
Burcun	Bursa	Պուրճու[ն]	Bo'wrjo'w[n]
Burdur	Burdur	Պուտուր, Պուրտուր	Bo'wdo'wr, Bo'wrdo'wr
Burhaniye	Balıkesir	Պիւրհանիյէ, Պուրհանիյէ	Biwrhanih'e', Bo'wrhanih'e'
Burhanköy	Kayseri	Պիւրհան, Պուրհան	Biwrhan, Bo'wrhan
Burhanlı*	Kırıkkale	Պուրհանլը	Bo'wrhanly
Bursa	Bursa	Պրուսա	Bro'wsa
Büyük Derbent	Sakarya	Մեծ Տէվրէտ	Medz De'vre'd
Büyükada	İstanbul	Մեծ-Կղզի	Medz-Gghzi
Büyük-Yeniköy	Sakarya	Մեծ Նոր Գիւղ, Մեծ-Նոր-Գիւղ	Medz No'r Kiwgh, Medz-No'r-Kiwgh

Cağıt*		Ճաղըտ	Jaghyd
Çahna*	Kocaeli	Չախնայ	Chaxnah'
Çakır	Yalova	Չագար, Չաքար	Chakar, Chaqar
Çakırlı	Yalova	Չագըրլը, Չագրլը, Չաքըրլը, Չաքրլը	Chakyrly, Chakrly, Chaqyrly, Chaqrly
Çakmak	Kayseri, Yozgat	Չագմագ, Չագմաք, Չաքմաք	Chakmak, Chakmaq, Chaqmaq
Çalışkanlar [Memun]	Balıkesir	Մամուն	Mamo'wn
Çalkara	Eskişehir	Չալկարա	Chalgara
Çamalan	Mersin	Չամ Ալան	Cham Alan
Camidüzü [Kilisedüzü, Zhamavayr]	Kocaeli	Ժամավայր, Քիլիսէ Տիւզիւ	Zhamavah'r, Qilise' Diwziw
Çamlıbel [Alabaş]	Kahramanmaraş	Ալապաշ	Alabash
Çamlıca	İstanbul	Չամլըճա	Chamlyja
Çanakkale [Dardanelles]	Çanakkale	Տարտանէլ	Dardane'l
Çardak	Osmaniye	Չարտաք	Chardaq
Çardak Deresi	Karaman	Չարտակ Տէրէսի	Chardag De're'si
Çardaklı	Hatay	Չարտագլօ	Chardaklo
Çarşamba	Samsun	Չարշամպա	Charshamba
Çatalca	İstanbul	Չաթալճա	Chat'alja
Çataloluk	Kayseri	Չաթալ Օլուգ	Chat'al Olo'wk
Çatköy	Yozgat	Չաթ	Chat'
Çay Boğazı	Sakarya	Չայ Պօղազը	Chah' Boghazy
Çaycuma	Zonguldak	Չայ Ճումա'ա, Չայ-Ճումա, Չայ-Ճումաա	Chah' Jo'wma'a, Chah'-Jo'wma, Chah'-Jo'wmaa
Çaylı	Hatay	Չայլը	Chah'ly
Cebelibereket	Osmaniye	Ճէպէլի Պէրէքէթ	Je'be'li Be're'qe't'
Ceceli (also Tecili*)	Kahramanmaraş	Ճէճէլի, Ճէճէլլի, Թէճիլի	Je'je'li, Je'je'lli, T'e'jili
Çengel Han	Ankara	Չէնկէլ Խան	Che'nge'l Xan
Çengelkayı [Çengel]	Amasya	Չէնկէլ	Che'nge'l
Çengeller	Bilecik	Չէնկէլլէր	Che'nge'lle'r
Çepni	Sakarya	Չէփնի	Che'p'ni
Çermik	Diyarbakır	Ջերմեկ	Ch'ermeg
Cerrah	Bursa	Ճերահ, Ճերրահ, Ճէրահ, Ճէրրահ	Jerah, Jerrah, Je'rah, Je'rrah

Cevdetiye [Araplı]	Osmaniye	Արապլու	Arablo'w
Cevizlik	Trabzon	Ճէվիզլիկ	Je'vizlig
Ceyhan	Adana	Ճիհան, Ճիհուն	Jihan, Jiho'wn
Çğala*	Samsun	Չղալա	Ch'ghala
Çıbaklı	Kocaeli	Չպուգլու	Chbo'wklo'w
Çiçekli [Frengülüs]	Mersin	Ֆրանկիւլիւս	Frangiwliws
Çiçekliyurt [Çakal Han]	Sivas	Չաքալ Խան	Chaqal Xan
Çifliki Hümayun	Adana	Չիֆլիգը Հիւմայուն	Chifliky Hiwmah'o'wn
Çiftehan	Niğde	Չիֆթէ Խան	Chift'e' Xan
Çifteler	Eskişehir	Չիֆթէլեր	Chift'e'ler
Çiftlik	Sakarya	Չիֆթլիկ	Chift'lig
Cığızlar*		Ճըղըզլար	Jyghyzlar
Cihan	Bursa	Ճիհան	Jihan
Çiller	Bolu	Չիլէ	Chile'
Çimenli [Lazana]	Trabzon	Լազանա	Lazana
Çınardere	Sakarya	Չընար Տէրէ	Chynar De're'
Çınlık*	Mersin	Ճինլիք	Jinliq
Cıtrak*	Adana	Ճթրագ	Jt'rak
Çokradan	Yozgat	Չոգրատան, Չորգատան, Չորխատան	Cho'kradan, Cho'rkadan, Cho'rxadan
Çorlu	Tekirdağ	Չորլու, Չօրլու	Cho'rlo'w, Chorlo'w
Çorum	Çorum	Չորում	Cho'ro'wm
Çuferdan* [Çokradan, possibly]	Yozgat	Չուֆէրտան	Cho'wfe'rdan
Çuhahane*	Sakarya	Չուխախանէ	Cho'wxaxane'
Çukur	Sakarya	Չուգուր	Cho'wko'wr
Dagestan	Dagestan	Տաղեսթան	Daghest'an
Dağınıksu*	Kocaeli	Տաղընըք Սու	Daghynyq So'w
Dağkonak [Nerekh]	Şırnak	Նէրէկ	Ne're'g
Dağköy	Kocaeli	Տաղ-Գիւղ	Dagh-Kiwgh
Damascus	Syria	Շամ	Sham
Darıca	Kocaeli	Տարճա	Darja
Darıyeri	Düzce	Տարը Եէրի	Dary Ee'ri
Dedeağaç	Tekirdağ	Տէտէ Աղաճ	De'de' Aghaj

Değirmençay [Erçel]	Mersin	Էրչէլ	E’rche’l
Dendil*	Kahramanmaraş	Տէնտիլ	De’ndil
Denizçalı	Yalova	Տէնիզ-Չալը	De’niz-Chaly
Denizli	Elazığ	Տենիզլի	Denizli
Derbent [Pambucak]	Bursa	Բամբուճագ, Փամ[պ]ուճագ Տէրվէնթ	Pampo’wjak, P’am[b]o’wjak De’rve’nt’
Derebek*	Şanlıurfa	Տէրէպէք	De’re’be’q
Dereköy	Kahramanmaraş	Տէրէքէօյ	De’re’qe’oh’
Derinçay [Kotanı]	Ordu	Քօթան	Qot’an
Derince	Kocaeli	Տէրինճէ	De’rinje’
Der-Zor	Syria	Տէր-Զօր	De’r-Zor
Develi [Everek]	Kayseri	Էվերէկ, Էվէրէկ	E’vere’g, E’ve’re’g
Devrek	Zonguldak	Տէվրէկ, Տէվրէք, Տէօվրէկ, Տէօվրէք	De’vre’g, De’vre’q, De’ovre’g, De’ovre’q
Dikili	Şanlıurfa	Տիքիլի	Diqili
Dikili [Karakilise]	Erzurum	Գարաքիլիսա, Գարաքիլիսէ	Karaqilisa, Karaqilise’
Divriği	Sivas	Տիվրիկ	Divrig
Diyarbakır	Diyarbakır	Տիարպէքիր	Diarbe’qir
Doğanbeyli [Rumlu]	Adana	Ռում, Ռումլու, Րումլու	R’o’wm, R’o’wmlo’w, Ro’wmlo’w
Doğubayazıt	Ağrı	Պայազիտ	Bah’azid
Döl Tepesi*	Yozgat	Տէօլ Թէփէսի	De’ol T’e’p’e’si
Döngöl*	Sakarya	Տէօնկէօլ, Տէօնկէլ	De’onge’ol, De’onge’l
Dönüklü [Fındıcak]	Kahramanmaraş	Ֆընտըճագ, Ֆնտճագ	Fyndyjak, Fndjak
Dorak	Mersin	Տօրագ	Dorak
Dörtyol	Hatay	Չօք-Մարզուան, Տէօրթ-Եօլ, Տէօրթեօլ, Տէօրդ-Եօլ	Choq-Marzo’wan, De’ort’- Eol, De’ort’eol, De’ort-Eol
Drezhan*		Տրէժան	Dre’zhan
Düzce	Düzce	Տիւզճէ	Diwzje’
Düziçi [Haruniye]	Osmaniye	Խառնը, Խառնի, Հարունիյէ, Հարունիէ	Xar’ny, Xar’ni, Haro’wnih’e’, Haro’wnie’
Eşme	Sakarya	Էշմէ	E’shme’
Edincik	Balıkesir	Էտինճիգ, Էտինճիկ	E’dinjik, E’dinjig
Edirne	Edirne	Էտիրնէ	E’dirne’
Efkere	Kayseri	Էֆքէրէ	E’fqe’re’

Eğil	Diyarbakır	Ակիլ	Agil
Eğlence	Yozgat	Էյլէնճէ	E'h'le'nje'
Eğriağaç	Adana	Էյրի Աղաճ	E'h'ri Aghaj
Eğribük	Malatya	Էյրի-Պիւք	E'h'ri-Biwq
Ekbez*	Adana	Էքպէզ	E'qbe'z
Elazığ [Mamuretülaziz]	Elazığ	Մ[ամուրէթ] իւլ Ազիզ	M[amo'wre't'] iwl Aziz
Elazığ [Mezre]	Elazığ	Մեզրէ	Mezre'
Elbistan	Kahramanmaraş	Էլպիսթան	E'lbist'an
Eleşkirt	Ağrı	Ալաշկերտ	Alashgerd
Elmalı	Sakarya and Antalya	Էլմալը, Էլմալի	E'lmaly, E'lmali
Elmalık	Sakarya	Էլմալըկ	E'lmalyg
Emirdağ [Aziziye]	Afyonkarahisar	Ազիզիյէ	Azizih'e'
Epçeler	Sakarya	Էպճէլէր	E'bje'le'r
Erdek	Balıkesir	Էրտէկ, Էրտէք	E'rde'g, E'rde'q
Ereğli	Zonguldak	Երէյլի, Էրէյլի, Էրէկլէ, Էրէկլի	Ere'h'li, E're'h'li, E're'gle', E're'gli
Erenköy [Kâhtin]	Gaziantep	Գահտին	Kahdin
Ermeniköy	Sakarya	Հայ Գիւղ, Հայ-Գիւղ, Հայոց գիւղ	Hah' Kiwgh, Hah'-Kiwgh, Hah'o'c kiwgh
Erzin	Hatay	Երզըն, Էրզին	Erzyn, E'rzin
Erzincan	Erzincan	Երզնկա	Erznga
Erzurum (also Karin)	Erzurum	Էրզրում, Կարին	E'rzro'wm, Garin
Esadiye	Yalova	Էսատիյէ	E'sadih'e'
Esentepe [Mayer]	Trabzon	Մայեր	Mah'er
Eskicamiikebir [Develi]	Kayseri	Տէվէլու, Տէվէլլու	De've'lo'w, De've'llo'w
Eskikarahisar	Konya	Գարահիսար	Karahisar
EskiMecidiye [Khaskal]	Kocaeli	Խասկալ, Հասկալ	Xasgal, Hasgal
Eskişehir	Eskişehir	Էսկիշէհիր, Էսկի Շէհիր	E'sgishe'hir, E'sgi She'hir
Eyüp	İstanbul	Էյուպ	E'h'o'wb
Ezine	Çanakkale	Էզինէ	E'zine'
Fahralı	Yozgat	Ֆազրալը, Ֆախրա, Ֆախրալը, Ֆակրալը	Fakraly, Faxra, Faxraly, Fagraly
Felahiye [Rumdiğin]	Kayseri	Րումթիքէն, Րումտիկին, Րումտիքէն	Ro'wmt'iqe'n, Ro'wmdigin, Ro'wmdiqe'n
Feneke	Konya	Ֆէնէքէ	Fe'ne'qe'

Fenese	Kayseri	Ֆէնէսէ	Fe'ne'se'
Ferizli	Kocaeli	Ֆէրիզլի	Fe'rizli
Fevziye	Kocaeli	Ֆէյզիէ	Fe'h'zie'
Fındıklı	Sakarya	Ֆընտըգլը	Fyndykly
Fındıkpınarı	Mersin	Ֆընտըգ Բունար	Fyndyk Po'wnar
Fırakdın	Kayseri	Ֆըրագտըն	Fyrakdyn
Fırnız	Kahramanmaraş	Ֆըրնուզ, Ֆուրնուզ, Ֆռնուզ, Ֆրնուզ	Fyrno'wz, Fo'wrno'wz, Fr'no'wz, Frno'wz
Fulacık	Yalova	Ֆուլաճըգ, Ֆլաճըգ, Ֆուլաճըխ, Ֆօլաճըգ	Fo'wlajyk, Flajyk, Fo'wlajyx, Folajyk
Gacık	Yalova	Ղաճիկ	Ghajig
Ğarzan Kolind* [Yanarsu, possibly]		Ղարզան Գօլընտ	Gharzan Kolynd
Gaz	Sakarya	Ղազ	Ghaz
Gaziantep [Ayntab]	Gaziantep	Այնթապ	Ah'nt'ab
Geben	Kahramanmaraş	Կապան	Gaban
Gebze	Kocaeli	Կէյպզէ	Ge'h'bze'
Geke*	Kocaeli	Կէքէ	Ge'qe'
Gelibolu	Çanakkale	Կէլիպօլի	Ge'liboli
Gelincik	Şanlıurfa	Կէլէնչիկ	Ge'le'nchig
Gelingüllü	Yozgat	Կէլին Կիւլիւ	Ge'lin Giwliw
Gemerek	Sivas	Կէմէրէկ	Ge'me're'g
Gemlik	Bursa	Կէմլեյէկ, Կէմլէյիկ	Ge'mleh'e'g, Ge'mle'h'ig
Geyve	Sakarya	Կէյվէ	Ge'h've'
Giniden*	Yozgat	Կինիտէն	Ginide'n
Giresun	Giresun	Կիրասօն	Giraso'n
Godushla*		Կոտուշլա	Go'do'wshla
Gökçeler	Bilecik	Կէօքճէլէր, Կէօքչէլէր	Ge'oqje'le'r, Ge'oqche'le'r
Gökçeler [Gerdan]	Adana	Կերտան	Gerdan
Gökçeyol [Tlan]	Adana	Թլան	T'lan
Gökkale	Mersin	Կէօք Գալէ, Կէօք-Գալէ	Ge'oq Kale', Ge'oq-Kale'
Göksun [Kokison]	Kahramanmaraş	Կէօքսուն, Կոկիսոն	Ge'oqso'wn, Go'giso'n
Göldağı	Bilecik and Sinop	Կէօլ Տաղ, Կէօլտաղ	Ge'ol Dagh, Ge'oldagh
Gölyaka [Arapgazi]	Bursa	Արապղազի	Arabghazi

Gömedi	Kayseri	Կէօմէտի	Ge'ome'di
Gönen	Balıkesir	Կէօնէն	Ge'one'n
Gözlü	Mersin	Կէօզլիւ	Ge'ozliw
Gümüşçeşme [Narver]	Erzincan	Նարվեր	Narver
Gümüşgün [Ehneş]	Gaziantep	Էհնէշ	E'hne'sh
Gümüşhane	Gümüşhane	Կիւմիւշխանէ	Giwmiwshxane'
Gündoğdu [Mihaliç]	Kocaeli	Միխալիճ	Mxalij
Güneyköy	Afyonkarahisar	Կիւնէյքէօյ	Giwne'h'qe'oh'
Güngörmüş [Pütürge]	Adiyaman	Բեթիւրկէ, Բեդուրկէ, Բէյթուրկէ, Բիթիւրկէ	Pet'iwrge', Peto'wrge', Pe't'o'wrge', Pit'iwrge'
Gürçam [Fatsa]	Ordu	Ֆաթսա	Fat'sa
Gürçam [Fatsa]	Samsun	Ֆաթսա	Fat'sa
Gürle	Bursa	Կիւռլէ, Կիւրլէ	Giwr'le', Giwrle'
Güvemli [Mahmudiye]	Eskişehir	Մահմուտիէ	Mahmo'wdie'
Güvençli* [possibly Güveçli]	Yozgat	Կէօվէնչլի	Ge'ove'nchli
Habibli*	Hatay	Հապիպլի	Habibli
Haçbel*	Adana	Խաչպէլ	Xachbe'l
Halashana	Ankara	Խալասխանէ	Xalasxane'
Halfeti	Şanlıurfa	Խալֆէթի, Խէլէֆէթէ, Խէլֆէթէ, Խէլֆէթի	Xalfe't'i, Xe'le'fe't'e', Xe'lfe't'e', Xe'lfe't'i
Halkırı*	Mersin	Հալկըրը	Halgyry
Hama	Syria	Համա	Hama
Hamidiye	Yozgat	Համիտիյէ	Hamidih'e'
Hamidiye (Devrek)	Zonguldak	Համիտիյէ	Hamidih'e'
Hamidiye [Gazelli]	Kocaeli	Ղազէլլէր	Ghaze'lle'r
Harput	Elazığ	Խարբերդ	Xarpert
Hasanbeyli	Osmaniye	Հասան Պէյլի, Հասանպէյլի, Հասան-Պէյլի	Hasan Be'h'li, Hasanbe'h'li, Hasan-Be'h'li
Hasırcı [Hasırca]	Samsun	Հասըրճա	Hasyrja
Hasköy	İstanbul	Խասգիւղ	Xaskiwgh
Hassa	Hatay	Խասա, Խասսա	Xasa, Xassa
Havdi	Sakarya	Հաւտի	Hawdi
Haverdia*		Հավըրտիա	Havyrdia
Havza	Samsun	Խավզա, Խաւզա, Հավզա	Xavza, Xawza, Havza

Haymana	Kütahya	Հայմանա	Hah'mana
Hazan-Dere*	Sakarya	Խազան Տէրէ	Xazan De're'
Hazar [Gölcük, Dzovk]	Elazığ	Ծովք	Dzo'vq
Hazro	Diyarbakır	Հազրօ	Hazro
Hekimhan	Malatya	Հաքիմ խան	Haqim xan
Hendek	Sakarya	Խանտէկ, Խէնտէկ, Հէնտէք	Xande'g, Xe'nde'g, He'nde'q
Hınıs	Erzurum	Խնուս	Xno'ws
Hisar	Zonguldak	Հիսար	Hisar
Hisarcık [Asarcık]	Bilecik	Ասարճըգ	Asarjyk
Homs	Syria	Հոմս	Ho'ms
Hordum*	Adana	Հօրտում	Hordo'wm
Hozagara*		Հոզակարա	Ho'zagara
Hünkârçiftliği	Kocaeli	Հիւնքեար	Hiwnqear
İcadiye	Kocaeli	Իճատիյէ	Ijadih'e'
İflabiye*	Kocaeli	Իֆլապիյէ	Iflabih'e'
İğdeli	Yozgat	Իյտէ	Ih'de'
Iğdır	Iğdır	Իգտիր	Ikdir
İğne-Pazar	Sivas	Իյնէ-Բազար	Ih'ne'-Pazar
Ihdade*		Իհտատէ	Ihdade'
Ilıca	Bolu	Ըլըճա	Ylyja
İnaz*	Kocaeli	Ինազ	Inaz
İncesu	Kayseri	Ինճէսու	Inje'so'w
İncirli	Adana, Sakarya, Yozgat	Ինճիրլի	Injirli
İnebolu	Kastamonu	Ինէպօլու	Ine'bolo'w
İnegöl	Bursa	Իյնէկէօլ, Ինէկէօլ	Ih'ne'ge'ol, Ine'ge'ol
İnönü	Eskişehir	Ին-Էօնիւ	In-E'oniw
İnsiz Ada*		Ինսիզ Ատա	Insiz Ada
Işıklı [Şeyxli]	Hatay	Շէյխլի	She'h'xli
İskenderun	Hatay	Ալէքսանտրէթ, Ալէքսանդրէթ, Իսկէնտէրուն	Ale'qsandre't', Ale'qsantre't', Isge'nde'ro'wn
İslahiye	Gaziantep	Իսլահիէ, Իսլահիյէ	Islahie', Islahih'e'
Isparta	Isparta	Սպարտա	Sbarda
İstiklal [Papazköy]	Sakarya	Փափազ	P'ap'az

İzmir [Smyrna]	İzmir	Զմիւռնիա, Իզմիր	Zmiwr'nia, Izmir
İzmit [Nicomedia]	Kocaeli	Իզմիթ, Իզմիտ, Նիկոմիդիա	Izmit', Izmid, Nigo'mitia
İznik [Nicaea]	Bursa	Իզնիք, Իզնիկ, Նիկիա	Izniq, Iznig, Nigia
İzollu	Adıyaman	Իզօլա	Izola
Jaffa	Palestine	Եափա	Eafa
Jarablus	Syria	Ճարապլուս	Jarablo'ws
Jazira	Syria	Ճէզրա	Je'zra
Kabaklar	Gaziantep	Գապազլար	Kabaklar
Kadıköy	İstanbul, Yalova	Գատըգիւղ, Գատը-Գիւղ	Kadykiwgh, Kady-Kiwgh
Kadirli [Kars Pazarı]	Osmaniye	Կարս-Բազար, Կարս-Պազար	Gars-Pazar, Gars-Bazar
Kâhta	Adıyaman	Քեախթէ, Քեաղթէ	Qeaxt'e', Qeaght'e'
Kalaycık	Kahramanmaraş	Գալաճըգ	Kalajyk
Kale [Camustil]	Kahramanmaraş	Ճամըսդըլ, Ճամըսթալ, Ճամըսթըլ	Jamystyl, Jamyst'al, Jamyst'yl
Kamışlı	Gaziantep	Գամըշլը, Գամըշլի, Գամըշլօ	Kamyshly, Kamyshli, Kamyshlo
Kandıra	Kocaeli	Գանտըրա, Գանտրա	Kandyra, Kandra
Kangal	Sivas	Գանկալ	Kangal
Kanlıpınar	Eskişehir	Քանլը Բունար	Qanly Po'wnar
Kantar	Sakarya	Գանթար, Գանթարի	Kant'ar, Kant'ari
Kapaklı	Yalova	Գափազլը	Kap'akly
Kapçağız [Kabcuğaz]	Gaziantep	Գապճուղըպ [Գապճուղըզ]	Kabjo'wghyb [Kabjo'wghyz]
Kapıdağ	Balıkesir	Գաբու Տաղը	Kapo'w Daghy
Karaağaç	Edirne	Գարաաղաճ, Գարա Աղաճ, Գարաղաճ	Karaaghaj, Kara Aghaj, Karaghaj
Karabiga	Çanakkale	Գարա-Պիղա	Kara-Bigha
Karaburun	Mersin	Գարապուրուն	Karabo'wro'wn
Karacabey [Mihaliç]	Bursa	Գարաճապէյ, Գարաճա Պէյ, Գարաճա-պէյ, Միխալըճ, Մըխալըճ	Karajabe'h', Karaja Be'h', Karaja-be'h', Mixalyj, Myxalyj
Karaçay	Sakarya	Գարայ-Չայ, Քարա-չայ	Karah'-Chah', Qara-chah'
Karadere	Sakarya	Գարատէրէ	Karade're'
Karahacılı	Yozgat	Գարահաճըլու	Karahajylo'w
Karahalil	Kayseri	Գարա-Հալիլ	Kara-Halil
Karaköy	Kayseri	Գարաքէօյ	Karaqe'oh'

Karalık	Yozgat	Գարալըզ	Karalyk
Karaman	Karaman	Գարաման	Karaman
Karamürsel [Karamursal]	Kocaeli	Գարամուսալ, Գարայ-Մուրսալ	Karamo'wsal, Karah'-Mo'wrsal
Karapınar	Şanlıurfa	Գարաբունար	Karapo'wnar
Karasar	Tunceli	Գարասար	Karasar
Karasi	Balıkesir	Գարասի	Karasi
Karataş	Adana	Գարաթաշ, Գարա-Թաշ, Քարաթաշ	Karat'ash, Kara-T'ash, Qarat'ash
Karatepe	Kocaeli	Գարայ Թեփէ, Գարայ-Թէփէ	Karah' T'ep'e', Karah'-T'e'p'e'
Karay*	Kocaeli	Գարայ	Karah'
Karay Yavuz*	Kocaeli	Խարայ Եավուզ	Xarah' Eavo'wz
Kargılı	Mersin	Գարղըլը	Karghyly
Karpuz*	Kocaeli	Գարփուզ	Karp'o'wz
Karsak	Bursa	Գարսազ, Գարսաք	Karsak, Karsaq
Kartal	Gaziantep	Գարթալ, Քէրթիլ, Քէրթէլ	Kart'al, Qe'rt'il, Qe'rt'e'l
Kartsi*	Kocaeli	Քարծի, Քարցի	Qartzi, Qarci
Kasaba	Ankara	Գասապա	Kasaba
Kasımlar	Bilecik	Գասըմլար	Kasymlar
Kastamonu	Kastamonu	Գասթէմունի	Kast'e'mo'wni
Katırız*		Գաթըրըզ	Kat'yryz
Kavak	Samsun	Գավազ, Գավաք, Խավախ	Kavak, Kavaq, Xavax
Kavsaran	Mersin	Գավսարան	Kavsaran
Kayabey	Ağrı	Գայաբէկ	Kah'ape'g
Kaylançık*	Sakarya	Խայլանճըխ	Xah'lanjyx
Kayserci*	Elazığ	Քայսերճի	Qah'serji
Kayseri	Kayseri	Կեսարիա	Gesaria
Kazandere	Kocaeli	Գազան Տէրէ, Խազան Տէրէ	Kazan De're', Xazan De're'
Kazazan*		Գազազան	Kazazan
Kazıklı	Gaziantep	Գազըզլը	Kazykly
Keban	Elazığ	Կէպէն	Ge'be'n
Kefne İskele*	Kocaeli	Կէֆնէ Իսկէլէ	Ge'fne' Isge'le'
Keltepe	Kocaeli	Քէլ Թէփէ	Qe'l T'e'p'e'
Kemah	Erzincan	Քէմախ	Qe'max

Kemaliye [Egin]	Erzincan	Ակն	Agn
Kemerhisar [Kilisehisar]	Niğde	Քիլիսահիսար	Qilisahisar
Kepe*	Kocaeli	Կէփէ	Ge'p'e'
Keramet	Bursa	Քէրամէթ, Քէրէմէթ	Qe'rame't', Qe're'me't'
Keşan	Edirne	Քէշան	Qe'shan
Keşap	Ordu	Քէշապ	Qe'shab
Kesben	Malatya	Կէսպան	Ge'sban
Keskin [Denek Madeni]	Kırıkkale	Քէսկին, Տէնէկ-Մատէն, Տէնէք Մատեն, Տէնէք-Մատէն	Qe'sgin, De'ne'g-Made'n, De'ne'q Maden, De'ne'q-Made'n
Keskin-Madeni	Kırıkkale	Քէսկին Մատէն	Qe'sgin Made'n
Kesmeburun	Osmaniye	Քէսմէ-Պուրուն	Qe'sme'-Bo'wro'wn
Kessab	Syria	Քեսապ, Քէսապ	Qesab, Qe'sab
Kestanepınar	Samsun	Քէսթէնէ-Բունար	Qe'st'e'ne'-Po'wnar
Ketanya	Kütahya	Քէթանիա	Qe't'ania
Ketenciler	Kocaeli	Քէթէնճիլէր	Qe't'e'njile'r
Khoy	Iran	Խոյ	Xo'h'
Kiğı	Bingöl	Քղի	Qghi
Kılavuz	Gaziantep	Գուլավուզ	Ko'wlavo'wz
Kılıç	Yalova	Գըլըճ, Գըլճ	Kylyj, Kylj
Kilimli	Zonguldak	Քէլիմլի	Qe'limli
Kilis	Kilis	Քիլիս	Qilis
Kıncılar	Sakarya	Գընճըլար, Գնճըլար	Kynjylar, Knjylar
Kırıkhan	Hatay	Գըրըգ Խան	Kyryk Xan
Kırıt	Mersin	Կիրիտ	Girid
Kırklareli [Kırkkilise]	Edirne	Գըրքիլէսէ, Գըրք Քիլիսէ	Kyrqile'se', Kyrq Qilise'
Kırkpınar [Hretan]	Diyarbakır	Հըրէտան	Hyre'dan
Kırobası [Mara]	Mersin	Մարա	Mara
Kırşehir	Kırşehir	Գըրշէհիր, Գըր-Շէհիր	Kyrshe'hir, Kyr-She'hir
Kişifli	Kahramanmaraş	Գիշիֆլի, Քիշիֆլի	Kishifli, Qishifli
Kısıklı	İstanbul	Խըսխըլը	Xysxyly
Kıyak*	Edirne	Գըեաք	Kyeaq
Kızderbent	Kocaeli	Գըզ Տէրվէնտ, Գըզ Տէվրէնտ, Գըզտէվրէնտ, Գըզտէրպէնտ, Գըզ-Տէրպէնտ	Kyz De'rve'nd, Kyz De'vre'nd, Kyzde'vre'nd, Kyzde'rbe'nd, Kyz-De'rbe'nd

Kızılağaç	Adana	Գըզըլ Աղաճ	Kyzyl Aghaj
Kızılköy	Çanakkale	Գըզըլքէօյ	Kyzylqe'oh'
Kızın Elinde*	Sakarya	Կիզին Ելանտի	Gizin Elandi
Kızlan*		Գըզլան	Kyzlan
Kokaksu	Zonguldak	Քօքաք Սու	Qoqaq So'w
Konuklar [Ürnac]	Yozgat	Իւրնէճ, Իւրնէչ	Iwrne'j, Iwrne'ch
Konya	Konya	Գոնիա	Ko'nia
Köprü	Sakarya	Կամուրջ	Gamo'wrch'
Kozan [Sis]	Adana	Գոզան, Սիս	Ko'zan, Sis
Kozdere [İntilli]	Gaziantep	Ինթէլլի	Int'e'lli
Küçük Manzer*	Adana	Քիւչիւք Մանզըր	Qiwchiwq Manzyr
Kumkuyu	Yozgat	Գու[մ]գույու	Ko'w[m]ko'wh'o'w
Kumlar	Kocaeli	Գումլար, Ղումլար	Ko'wmlar, Gho'wmlar
Kündi-Beg*		Քիւնտի-Պէկ	Qiwndi-Be'g
Küp*	Sakarya	Քիւփ	Qiwp'
Küplü	Bilecik	Քիւբլիւ, Քիւփլի, Քիւփլիւ, Քիւփրի	Qiwpliw, Qiwp'li, Qiwp'liw, Qiwp'ri
Kürkçü	Yozgat	Քիւրքճի	Qiwrqji
Kurt Dağı		Քիւրտ Տաղ	Qiwrd Dagh
Kurtbelen	Sakarya	Գուրտպէլէն	Ko'wrdbe'le'n
Kurtköy [Delipazarı]	Yalova	Տէլի Բազար	De'li Pazar
Kurttepe	Adana	Գուրտ Թէփէ	Ko'wrd T'e'p'e'
Kuruçeşme	Balıkesir	Գուրու Չէշմէ	Ko'wro'w Che'shme'
Kütahya	Kütahya	Քէօթահիա	Qe'ot'ahia
Kuyluş	Kastamonu	Գույլուճ	Ko'wh'lo'wj
Kuzguncuk	İstanbul	Գուզկունճուգ	Ko'wzgo'wnjo'wk
Langa	İstanbul	Լանկա	Langa
Larnaca	Cyprus	Լարնաքա	Larnaqa
Lataşli*		Լաթաշլը	Lat'ashly
Lemnos	Greece	Լեմնոս	Lemno's
Lice	Giresun	Լիճէ	Lije'
Lüleburgaz	Kırklareli	Լիւլէ-Պուկազ	Liwle'-Bo'wgaz
Lycaonia	Lycaonia	Լիկաօնիա	Ligaonia
Maden	Elazığ	Մատէն	Made'n

Malatya	Malatya	Մալաթիա	Malat'ia
Malkara	Tekirdağ	Մալկարա	Malgara
Mamure*	Osmaniye	Մամուրէ	Mamo'wre'
Manbij	Syria	Պումպուճ	Bo'wmbo'wj
Manisa	Manisa	Մանիսա	Manisa
Manyas	Balıkesir	Մանիաս	Manias
Maraş	Kahramanmaraş	Մարաշ	Marash
Mardin	Mardin	Մարտին, Մերտին	Mardin, Merdin
Marmaracık	Bursa	Մարմարճըզ, Մարմաճըզ, Մարմաճուխ	Marmarjyk, Marmajyk, Marmajo'wx
Marseilles	France	Մարսիլիա	Marsilia
Mecidiye [Khach]	Kocaeli	Մէճիտիյէ, Խաչ, Խաչ-Գիւղ	Me'jidih'e', Xach, Xach-Kiwgh
Meidan Akbis [Meydan Ekbez]	Syria	Մէյտան Էքպէզ	Me'h'dan E'qbe'z
Menije*		Մէնիճէ	Me'nije'
Menteşe	Yozgat	Մէնթէշէ	Me'nt'e'she'
Mercin	Adana	Մերճին	Merjin
Mersin	Mersin	Մերսին	Mersin
Merzifon	Amasya	Մարզուան, Մարսուան	Marzo'wan, Marso'wan
Mesudiye	Ordu	Մեսուտիյէ	Meso'wdih'e'
Mimarsinan [Hırlavuk, Cırlavuk]	Kayseri	Խըրլավուխ	Xyrlavo'wx
Mira*	Sakarya	Միրա	Mira
Misis	Adana	Միսիս	Misis
Mollasüleyman	Ağrı	Մօլլասլէման	Mollasle'man
Moshkestan		Մշքսթան	Mshqst'an
Mosul	Iraq	Մուսուլ	Mo'wso'wl
Muratça	Bilecik	Մուրատ Չայ, Մուրատչայ	Mo'wrad Chah', Mo'wradchah'
Muş	Muş	Մուշ	Mo'wsh
Musa Dağı	Hatay	Ճէպէլ-Մուսա	Je'be'l-Mo'wsa
Mustafakemalpaşa [Kirmasti]	Bursa	Քերմասթի, Քերմասթը, Քըրմաստը	Qermast'i, Qermast'y, Qyrmasdy
Mut	Mersin	Մութ	Mo'wt'

Nallıhan	Ankara	Նալլը Խան, Նալլու Խան	Nally Xan, Nallo'w Xan
Namert Köprü*	Sakarya	Նամերտ, Նամէրտ Քէօփրիւ	Namerd, Name'rd Qe'op'riw
Namud*		Նամուտ	Namo'wd
Nevşehir	Nevşehir	Նէվշէհիր	Ne'vshe'hir
Niğde	Niğde	Նիյտէ, Նիկտէ	Nih'de', Nigde'
Niksar	Trabzon	Նիքսար	Niqsar
Nizip	Gaziantep	Նիզիպ	Nizib
Oba Altı*	Balıkesir	Օպա Ալթը	Oba Alt'y
Oltu	Erzurum	Օլթի	Olt'i
Olukbaşı [Alakilise]	Mersin	Աղաքիլիսէ	Aghaqilise'
Ömerli	Yozgat	Օմարլը	Omarly
Ordu	Ordu	Օրտու	Ordo'w
Orduzu	Malatya	Օրտուզ	Ordo'wz
Orhaneli [Adranos]	Bursa	Աթրանոս	At'rano's
Orhangazi [Pazarköy]	Bursa	Օրխան Կազի, Օրխան Գազի Օրխան Ղազի, Օրխանը Խազի, Օրխանը Ղազի, Օրխանխազի, Պազար	Orxan Gazi, Orxan Kazi, , Orxan Ghazi, Orxany Xazi, Orxany Ghazi, Orxanxazi, Bazar
Ormuzdere*	Bursa	Որմուզտէրէ	O'rmo'wzde're'
Ortaköy	Sakarya	Միջազիւղ, Օրթազիւղ, Օրթաքէօյ	Mich'akiwgh, Ort'akiwgh, Ort'aqe'oh'
Osmaneli [Lefke]	Bilecik	Լէֆքէ	Le'fqe'
Osmaniye	Osmaniye	Օսմանիէ, Օսմանիյէ	Osmanie', Osmanih'e'
Osmanoğlu	Amasya	Օսման Օղլու	Osman Oghlo'w
Ovacık	Sakarya	Օվաճըգ	Ovajyk
Ovacık [Ova]	Tunceli	Օվա	Ova
Özerli	Hatay	Էօզէրլի	E'oze'rli
Özsoğuksu [Soğuksu]	Hatay	Սովուգ-Սու	So'vo'wk-So'w
Palu	Elazığ	Բալու	Palo'w
Papaz	Hatay	Փափազ, Փափաս	P'ap'az, P'ap'as
Paşaköy	Yalova	Փաշաքէօյ	P'ashaqe'oh'
Pasinler [Hasankale]	Erzurum	Հասան Գալէ, Հասանգալէ, Հասանքալէ	Hasan Kale', Hasankale', Hasanqale'
Pazarköy	Sakarya	Բազար, Փազար	Pazar, P'azar
Pirahmet	Manisa	Փիր-Ահմէտ	P'ir-Ahme'd

Pozantı	Adana	Բիւզանթի, Պոզանթի, Պօզանթը, Պօզանթի	Piwzant'i, Bo'zant'i, Bozant'y, Bozant'i
Prud*	Elazığ	Բրուտ	Pro'wd
Qatma	Syria	Գաթմա	Kat'ma
Rajo	Syria	Ռաճօ	R'ajo
Reşadiye	Yalova	Րէշատիյէ, Րէշատիէ	Re'shadih'e', Re'shadie'
Revend*	Sakarya	Րէվէնտ	Re've'nd
Rize	Rize	Րիզէ	Rize'
Rumeli	Rumeli	Ռումելի, Ռումէլի	R'o'wmeli, R'o'wme'li
Rumkale	Gaziantep	Րում-Գալէ	Ro'wm-Kale'
Şabgahan*	Elazığ	Շապկահան	Shabgahan
Sabuncupınar	Kütahya	Սապօնճի Բունար	Sabonji Po'wnar
Şağlak*	Yalova	Շաղլախ	Shaghlax
Sağlık	Yozgat	Սաղլը-Գիւղ	Saghly-Kiwgh
Şahinler	Bilecik	Շահինլար	Shahinlar
Şahinyurdu [Benli]	Bursa	Պէնլի	Be'nli
Saimbeyli [Hacın]	Adana	Հաճըն	Hajyn
Sakarya	Sakarya	Սաքարիա	Saqaria
Şakşak*	Kocaeli	Շագշագ, Շագ-Շագ	Shakshak, Shak-Shak
Salkım [Khıyam]	Gaziantep	Խըյամ	Xyh'am
Salmanlı	Sakarya	Սալմանլը	Salmanly
Sam	Gaziantep	Սամ	Sam
Samandağı [Suedia]	Hatay	Սուետիա	So'wedia
Samsat	Adıyaman	Սամսատ, Սմսաթ	Samsad, Smsat'
Samsun	Samsun	Սամսոն	Samso'n
Şanlı [Şana]	Trabzon	Շանա	Shana
Sapanca	Sakarya	Սապանճա	Sabanja
Saraçlı	Sakarya	Սարաճլը	Sarajly
Saraçlıüstü	Sakarya	Սարաճլը Իւսթիւ, Սարաճլը Իւստիւ, Սարաճլը-Իւստիւ	Sarajly Iwst'iw, Sarajly Iwsdiw, Sarajly-Iwsdiw
Saray	Yozgat	Սէրայ	Se'rah'
Sarıdoğan	Sakarya	Սարը Տօղան	Sary Doghan
Sarıkaya [Terzili]	Yozgat	Թէրզիլի	T'e'rzili
Sarıköy	Sakarya	Սարըքէօյ	Saryqe'oh'

Şarköy	Adana	Շար	Shar
Sarmanlı	Sakarya	Սարմանլը	Sarmanly
Sason	Batman	Սասուն	Saso’wn
Satı	Kayseri	Սադու	Sato’w
Saylakkaya [Cibin]	Şanlıurfa	Ճիպին	Jibin
Sazlı	Sakarya	Սազլը	Sazly
Şebinkarahisar	Giresun	Շապին-Գարահիսար	Shabin-Karahisar
Şekeroba	Kahramanmaraş	Շէքէր-Օպա	She’qe’r-Oba
Sekili [Orul]	Gaziantep	Օրուլ	Oro’wl
Selamsız	İstanbul	Սէլամսըզ	Se’lamsyz
Selimiye [Ayvalıca]	Bursa	Այվալճայ	Ah’valjah’
Şereflikoçhisar [Koçhisar]	Afyonkarahisar	Գոչհիսար, Գօչ-Հիսար	Ko’chhisar, Koch-Hisar
Şerid Mumlu*	Kırıkkale	Շէրիտ Մումլը	She’rid Mo’wmly
Serindere	Sakarya	Սէրին Տէրէ	Se’rin De’re’
Şevketiye [Saçmalı]	Kocaeli	Շէֆքէթիյէ, Սաչմալը	She’fqe’t’ih’e’, Sachmaly
Seydi Dere*	Kocaeli	Սէյտի Տէրէ	Se’h’di De’re’
Şeyh Hasan	Malatya	Շէյխ Հասան	She’h’x Hasan
Seyhan	Adana	Սիհուն	Siho’wn
Şeyhmurat	Adana	Շէյխ Մուրատ, Շէյխ Մուրատլը	She’h’x Mo’wrad, She’h’x Mo’wradly
Sham [Damascus]	Syria	Շամ	Sham
Şile	İstanbul	Շիլէ	Shile’
Silifke	Mersin	Սելեւկիա, Սելեֆքէ, Սէլէֆքէ	Selewgia, Selefqe’, Se’le’fqe’
Silivri	İstanbul	Սիլիվրի	Silivri
Silvan [Dikranagerd]	Diyarbakır	Սըլիվան, Սլիվան, Տիգրանակերտ	Sylivan, Slivan
Sındırkı*	Balıkesir	Սընտըրկը	Syndyrgy
Sinop	Sinop	Սինոպ, Սինօպ	Sino’b, Sinob
Sirkeci	İstanbul	Սիրքէճի	Sirqe’ji
	Sivas	Սեբաստիա, Սըվազ, Սվազ	Sepasdia, Syvaz, Svaz
Siverek	Şanlıurfa	Սեւերէկ, Սէվէրէկ	Sewere’g, Se’ve’re’g
Sivrihisar	Eskişehir	Սիվրիհիսար, Սիվրի-Հիսար	Sivrihisar, Sivri-Hisar
Soğucak*	Yalova	Սովուճագ, Սօվուճագ	So’vo’wjak, Sovo’wjak

Soğuk Oğlu	Yozgat	Սօղուք Օղլու	Sogho'wq Oghlo'w
Söğüt	Eskişehir	Սէօյիւտ	Se'oh'iwd
Sokhumi	Abkhazia	Սօխում	Soxo'wm
Söl	Bursa	Սէօլ	Se'ol
Solsar	Kocaeli	Սօլսար	Solsar
Subaşı	Bolu	Սուպաշը	So'wbashy
Sugören [Çengiler]	Yalova	Չէնկիլէր	Che'ngile'r
Şükyan	Samsun	Շիւկեանի	Shiwgeani
Süleymanlı [Zeytun]	Kahramanmaraş	Զէյթուն	Ze'h't'o'wn
Sultanahmet	İstanbul	Սուլթան Ահմէտ	So'wlt'an Ahme'd
Sultançiftliği	İstanbul	Սուլթան Չիֆլիկ, Սուլթան Չիֆլիք	So'wlt'an Chiflig, So'wlt'an Chifliq
Sungurlu	Çorum	Սունկուրլու	So'wngo'wrlo'w
Sürmene	Trabzon	Սիւրմէնէ	Siwrme'ne'
Sürsürü [Sursuri]	Elazığ	Սուրսուր	So'wrso'wr
Suruç	Şanlıurfa	Սուրուճ	So'wro'wj
Suşehri [Endires]	Sivas	Էնտէրիս, Սու-Շէհիր	E'nde'ris, So'w-She'hir
Susurluk	Balıkesir	Սուսըզըրլըգ, Սուսուրլըգ	So'wsyzyrlyk, So'wso'wrlyk
Taba*	Hatay	Թապայի	T'abah'i
Tal Afar	Iraq	Թալաֆար	T'alafar
Talas	Kayseri	Թալաս	T'alas
Tamlık*	Kocaeli	Թամլըգ	T'amlyk
Tapan-Oğlu*	Adana	Թափան-Օղլու	T'ap'an-Oghlo'w
Taraklı	Sakarya	Թարագլը	T'arakly
Tarsus	Mersin	Թարսուս, Տարսոն	T'arso'ws, Darso'n
Taş Ocak	Yozgat	Թաշ Օճաղի	T'ash Ojaghi
Tavşanlı	Kütahya	Թավշանլու, Թաւշանլը	T'avshanlo'w, T'awshanly
Tbilisi	Georgia	Թիֆլիս	T'iflis
Tecili	Kahramanmaraş	Թէճիլի	T'e'jili
Tekirdağ	Tekirdağ	Ռոտոսթօ, Ռօտոսթօ, Ռօտօսդօ	R'o'do'st'o, R'odo'st'o, R'odosto
Telcık	Bursa	Թէլճուգ	T'e'ljo'wk
Tellikaya	Diyarbakır	Թէլլի Գայա	T'e'lli Kah'a
Temlik*	Kocaeli	Թըմլըգ	T'ymlyk

Tere	Bursa	Թէրէ	T’e’re’
Tezeren [Amad]	Ağrı	Ամատ	Amad
Thessaloniki	Greece	Սելանիկ, Սէլանիկ	Selanig, Se’lanig
Tirepoli [Tripoli]	Lebanon	Թիրէպօլու [Թրիփոլի]	T’ire’bolo’w [T’rip’o’li]
Tokat	Tokat	Թոզաթ, Թօզաթ, Թօզատ	T’o’kat’, T’okat’, T’okad
Tomarza	Kayseri	Թոմարզա, Թօմարզա	T’o’marza, T’omarza
Topçam [Gebeme]	Ordu	Կէպէմէ	Ge’be’me’
Toprakkale	Erzurum	Թօփրագ Գալէ, Թօփրագգալէ, Թօփրագ-Գալէ	T’op’rak Kale’, T’op’rakkale’, T’op’rak-Kale’
Toros Dağlari [Taurus]		Տաւրոս	Dawro’s
Tortum	Erzurum	Թորթում	T’o’rt’o’wm
Toybelen [Gemürgap]	Erzincan	Կամրկապ	Gamrgab [Gamargab]
Trabzon	Trabzon	Տրապիզոն	Drabizo’n
Tufanbeyli [Mağara]	Adana	Մաղարա	Maghara
Tumlu	Adana	Թումլու	T’o’wmlo’w
Tumlu Kale	Adana	Թումլու Գալա	T’o’wmlo’w Kala
Tunceli [Dersim]	Tunceli [Dersim]	Տերսիմ	Dersim
Türk Dağı*	Sakarya	Թուրք Տաղը	T’o’wrq Daghy
Türkmen	Bilecik	Թիւրքմէն	T’iwrqme’n
Türkoğlu [Eloğlu]	Kahramanmaraş	Ել-օղլու, Էլ Օղլու	El-oghlo’w, E’l Oghlo’w
Tüsı*	Sakarya	Թիւսիէ	T’iwsie’
Tuzaklı	Bilecik	Դուզագլը	To’wzakly
Üçhanlar	Samsun	Իւչ-Խանլար	Iwch-Xanlar
Üçoymak [Khoshian]	Ağrı	Խօշեան	Xoshean
Uludağ [Olympus]	Bursa	Ողիմպոս	O’ghimbo’s
Ulukışla	Niğde	Ուլու-Գըշլա	O’wlo’w-Kyshla
Ümit*	Samsun	Իւմիտ	Iwmid
Üngüt	Kahramanmaraş	Իւնկիւտ	Iwngiwd
Üreğil	Adana	Իւրէյլի	Iwre’h’li
Urfa	Şanlıurfa	Եդեսիա, Ուրֆա	Etesia, O’wrfa
Uşak	Uşak	Ուշագ, Ուշաք	O’wshak, O’wshaq
Üsküdar	İstanbul	Իւսկիւտար, Սկիւտար	Iwsgiwdar, Sgiwdar
Üst Bez*	Yalova	Վերի Պէզ	Veri Be’z
Uygur	Amasya	Ույկուր	O’wh’go’wr